All Music Guide to

THE Blues

The Experts' Guide to the Best Blues Recordings

Edited by
**Michael Erlewine
Vladimir Bogdanov
Chris Woodstra
Cub Koda**

●AMG All Music Guide Series

Miller Freeman Books
San Francisco

Published in 1996 by Miller Freeman Books, 600 Harrison Street, San Francisco, CA 94107
Publishers of GPI Books, *Guitar Player, Bass Player,* and *Keyboard* magazines
A member of the United Newspapers Group

un Miller Freeman

Distributed to the book trade in the U.S. and Canada by
    Publishers Group West, P.O. Box 8843, Emeryville, CA 94662
Distributed to the music trade in the U.S. and Canada by
    Hal Leonard Publishing, P.O. Box 13819, Milwaukee, WI 53213

ISBN 0-87930-424-3
Library of Congress Catalog Card Number 96-77864
Cover Design: Nita Ybarra
Production Editor: Dorothy Cox
Production: Carolyn Keating, Karen Hager, Wendy Davis, Jan Hughes, and Adolfo Cabral

Printed in the United States of America
96 97 98 99 00 9 8 7 6 5 4 3 2 1

CONTENTS

ALL MUSIC GUIDE DATABASE

The *All Music Guide* is more than this book. It is an ongoing database project, the largest collection of substantive album ratings and reviews ever assembled. In fact, the 2,600+ albums listed in this book represent a rather small subset (albeit an important one) of a very much larger collection of over 300,000 albums and reviews. The All Music Guide is also available in the following formats:

Books:
All Music Guide (Miller Freeman Books, 3rd Edition Fall 1996)
All Music Guide to Rock (Miller Freeman Books, 1995)
All Music Guide to Jazz, 2nd Edition (Miller Freeman Books, Summer 1996)
All Music Guide to World Music (Miller Freeman Books, available 1997)
All Music Guide to Country Music (Miller Freeman Books, available 1997)
VideoHound & *All-Movie Guide Stargazer* (Visible Ink, 1995)

Electronic Formats:
All Music Guide CD-ROM (Corel, release date to be announced)
All-Movie Guide CD-ROM (Corel)
MusicRoms (music and data) for Blues, Jazz, R&B, Latin, etc. (Selectware/Compton's)
All Music Guide (hard disk version) (Great Bear Technology)
World Beat CD-ROM (Medio)

In Store Kiosks:
Musicland's Soundsite
Phonolog's the Source
Sam Goody's

Online:
Internet AMG sites:
ALLMUSIC.COM
ALLMOVIE.COM
THENEWAGE.COM

Other Internet Sites:
Compact Disc Connection (BBS 408-730-9015)
CDNow! (CDNOW.COM)
Entertainment Connection (ECONNECTION, BBS 914-426-2285)
Music Boulevard (www.MusicBlvd.com)
CDUniverse (www.CDUNIVERSE.COM)

Billboard Online
Dimple Records
Reason Ware
The Microsoft Network: New Age Forum: New Age Music

We welcome your feedback. Perhaps we have left out some of your favorite albums, and/or included ones that you don't consider essential. Let us know about it. We welcome criticism, suggestions, additions, and/or deletions. The All Music Guide is a continuing project. Perhaps you are an expert on the complete output of a particular artist or group and would like to participate in future editions of the book and/or our larger computer database. We would be glad to hear from you. Call or write:

ALL MUSIC GUIDE
315 Marion Avenue
Big Rapids, MI 49307

616-796-3437
FAX 616-796-3060
A division of Matrix Software

FOREWORD

Blues is root music, always radical—the root or essence of other musics. Many music genres claim they have blues roots—rock, jazz, and rhythm & blues. Blues is pure food for fusion and many musics ground themselves in feelings through their bluesy elements. And yet blues still is fresh—untouched. That is because blues is a singularity rather than itself a fusion with something else. It is indivisible—recursive. The root of blues is the human experience and psyche itself.

We own a great debt to black Americans for delivering this great treasure to the world in the form we have it now, but blues is not a matter of color or form. Its root is the human experience itself—for all times and in all cultures. All people feel the blues in one way or another. You can hear the blues crying from many a proud country tune. And it is all through mountain and folk music. Gospel is its spiritual twin. If you have the ear, you can even hear it in the great classical composers—Bach's oboe lines or Mozart's bass lines. And classical music of the Renaissance period is nothing but blues! Eastern music, with its half and quarter tones, has mastered this form a long time ago. Blues has always been an integral part of us. But most of all you can hear the blues in the music described in this book, the sincere gift of the African American tradition to the world.

I would like to thank the entire All Music Guide staff for working so hard on getting this to you. In particular, editors Chris Woodstra, Stephen Thomas Erlewine, and Richie Unterberger did it the old-fashioned way—working 'til the wee hours of the morning to make sure that we got everyone we could into the number of pages we were allowed. And a very special thanks to our blues editor Cub Koda, who not only watched over the project like a mother hen but also (toward the end of the project) volunteered to work on site for many weeks with our staff to get it just right. We hope you enjoy this book.

—Michael Erlewine
Executive Editor
All Music Guide

CONTRIBUTORS

All Music Guide to the Blues

Acknowledgments:
Special thanks to: Cary Wolfson of *Blues Access*, Bill Dahl, Richie Unterberger,
Carl Bierling, and the staff of Holland Compact Disc.

Editors
Michael Erlewine
Vladimir Bogdanov
Chris Woodstra
Cub Koda
Stephen Thomas Erlewine
Richie Unterberger

AMG Production Staff
Jonathan Ball
Sherry Batchelder
Nancy Beilfuss
Sandra Brennan
John Bush
Julie Clark
Mark Donkers
Brandy Ellison
Elizabeth Erlewine
Sarah Erlewine
Mary Anne Henry
Steve Huey
Debbie Kirby
Luda Lobenko
Sara Sytsma

Matrix Staff
Kyle Alexander
Irene Baldwin
Richard Batchelder
Susan Brownlee
Stephanie Clement
Walt Crocket
Teresa Swift-Eckert
Iotis Erlewine
Margaret Erlewine

Phillip Erlewine
Stephen Erlewine
Kevin Fowler
Jeff Jawer,
Rock Jensen,
Mary King
Madeline Koperski
Forest Ray
Robert Walker

Contributors
George Bedard
Myles Boisen
Rob Bowman
Sandra Brennan
John Bush
Bil Carpenter
James Chrispell
Rick Clark
Bill Dahl
Hank Davis
Scott Dirks
Bruce Eder
Michael Erleiwne
Daniel Erlewine
Stephen Thomas Erlewine
John Floyd
Dan Forte
Niles J. Frantz
Robert Gordon
Bob Gottlieb
Jeff Hannusch
Dan Heilman
Bob Hinkle
Larry Hoffman
Steve Huey

Mark A. Humphrey
Steve James
David Jehnzen
Cub Koda
Kip Lornell
Decibel Dennis MacDonald
David L. Mayers
John Mcdonough
Richard Meyer
David A. Milberg
Dan Morgenstern
Michael G. Nastos
Jim O'Neal
Jas Obrecht
Thom Owens
Richard Pack
Roch Parisien
Barry Lee Pearson
Bob Porter
Jim Powers
Bruce Boyd Raeburn
John Storm Roberts
William Ruhlmann
Bob Rusch
Richard Skelly
Sara Sytsma
David Szatmary
Jeff Tamarkin
Cary Wolfson
Jan Mark Wolkin
Chris Woodstra
Jim Worbois
Ron Wynn
Scott Yanow

Michael Erlewine

All Music Guide editor Michael Erlewine helped form the Prime Movers Blues Band in Ann Arbor, Michigan in 1965. He was the lead singer and played amplified harmonica in this pace-setting band (the first of its kind). The original band included a number of now well-known musicians including Iggy Pop (drums), "Blue" Gene Tyranny (piano; now a well-known avant-garde classical composer); Jack Dawson (bass; became bass player for Siefal-Schwall Blues Band); and Michael's brother Dan Erlewine (lead guitar; now monthly columnist for *Guitar Player* magazine). Michael has extensively interviewed blues performers, both in video and audio, and, along with his band, helped to shape the first few Ann Arbor Blues festivals. Today Michael is a systems programmer and director of Matrix Software. Aside from the company's work in music and film data, Matrix is the largest center for astrological programming and research in North America. Michael has been a practicing astrologer for more than 30 years and has an international reputation in that field.

Michael is also very active in Tibetan Buddhism and serves as the director of the Heart Center Karma Thegsum Choling, one of the main centers in North America for the translation, transcription, and publication of psychological texts and teachings of the Karma Kagyu Lineage of Tibetan Buddhism. Michael has been married for 23 years, and he and his wife Margaret live in Big Rapids, Michigan. They have four children.

Vladimir Bogdanov

Russian mathematician and programmer Vladimir Bogdanov has been involved in the design and development of *All Music Guide* databases since 1991. Having experience in many different fields such as nuclear physics, psychology, social studies and ancient chronology he now applies his knowledge to the construction of unique music reference tools utilizing the latest computer technologies. His personal interest lies in applying artificial intelligence and other mathematical methods to areas with complex semantic structures, like music, film, literature. Vladimir's ultimate goal is to provide people with the means to find what they need, even if they don't know what they are looking for.

Chris Woodstra

Chris Woodstra has had a lifelong obsession with music and is an avid record collector. He has worked many years in music retail, he was a DJ, hosting programs in every genre of music, and has been a contributing editor for several local arts and entertainment magazines. Working as an editor for the *All Music Guide* database has given him the opportunity to combine his technical skills, a B.S. in Physics and Mathematics, and his love of music for the first time in his life. Being a perfectionist by nature, Chris makes sure that that any information that goes into the database has been carefully researched and verified.

Cub Koda

Cub Koda is a musician and a journalist with a long and varied career. As a musician, Koda achieved his greatest chart success as a member of the '70s rock 'n' roll band Brownsville Station, who had a number three hit in 1973 with his song, "Smokin' In the Boy's Room." After the breakup of Brownsville in 1979, Cub began a wildly eclectic solo career, during which he played with Hound Dog Taylor's band, the Houserockers, performing a number of concerts and releasing several acclaimed albums during the '80s and '90s. In the late '70s, Koda began writing a monthly music column called "The Vinyl Junkie" for Goldmine, now published in *DISCoveries* magazine. The column established Cub as a lively, knowledgeable music journalist and by the early '90s, he was contributing liner notes to reissues for a variety of labels. In 1996, Koda won the *Living Blues* Magazine's critics poll award for Best Reissue Liner Notes for 1995, based on his work for AVI Records' Excello series.

Stephen Thomas Erlewine

Stephen Thomas Erlewine studied English at the University of Michigan and was the arts editor of the school's newspaper, *The Michigan Daily*. In addition to editing the *All Music Guide*, Erlewine is a freelance writer and musician.

Richie Unterberger

Richie Unterberger is a writer and editor who lives in San Francisco. He was the editor of the travel and music sections of *The Millenium Whole Earth Catalog* (Harper Collins, 1994). Between 1985 and 1991, he was the editor of *Option* magazine, the national publication devoted to coverage of all types alternative and independently produced music. In his professional work, he is dedicated to enhancing the appreciation of the arts, culture, and history in as educational, entertaining, and affordable a fashion as possible, in both multimedia technologies and more traditional print mediums. Since watching *A Hard Day's Night* at the age of four, his favorite group has been the Beatles.

BLUES STYLES

CLASSIC FEMALE BLUES

The earliest recorded form of the blues. This genre features female vocalists singing material with close connections to pop music of the period (mid-'20s to early '30s) and primarily jazz backings. Main proponents: Mamie Smith, Bessie Smith, Ma Rainey, Lucille Bogan, and Victoria Spivey.

DELTA BLUES

Also known as Mississippi blues, this is the earliest guitar-dominated music to make it onto record. Consisting of performers working primarily in a solo, self-accompanied context, it also embraces the now-familiar string-band/small-combo format, both precursors to the modern-day blues band. Main proponents: Charlie Patton, Robert Johnson, and Son House.

COUNTRY-BLUES

A term that delineates the depth and breadth of the first flowering of guitar-driven blues, embracing all regional styles and variations (Piedmont, Atlanta, early Chicago, ragtime, folk, songster, etc.). Primarily acoustic guitarists, some country-blues performers later switched to electric guitars without changing their style. Major proponents: Henry Thomas, Skip James, Barbecue Bob, Leadbelly, Mississippi John Hurt, Lonnie Johnson, Blind Blake, and Tommy Johnson.

MEMPHIS BLUES

A strain of country-blues all its own, the Memphis style gives us the rise of two distinct forms, the jug band (humorous, jug-style blues played on homemade instruments) and the beginnings of assigning parts to guitarists for solo (lead) and rhythm, a tradition that is now part-and-parcel of all modern-day blues bands. The later, post-WWII electric version of this genre featured explosive guitar work, thunderous drumming, and declamatory vocals. Main proponents: Cannon's Jug Stompers, Furry Lewis, Memphis Minnie, and the early recordings of B.B. King and Howlin' Wolf.

TEXAS BLUES

A subgenre earmarked by a more relaxed, swinging feel than other styles of blues. The earlier, acoustic version embraced both songster and country-blues traditions, while the post-war electric style featured jazzy, single-string soloing over predominantly horn-driven backing. Main proponents: Blind Lemon Jefferson, Lightnin' Hopkins, Clarence "Gatemouth" Brown, and T-Bone Walker.

CHICAGO BLUES

Delta blues fully amplified and put into a small-band context. Later permutations of the style took their cue from the lead guitar work of B.B. King and T-Bone Walker. Main proponents: Muddy Waters, Howlin' Wolf, Little Walter, Big Walter Horton, Jimmy Rogers, Elmore James, Jimmy Reed, Otis Rush, Magic Sam, and Buddy Guy.

JUMP BLUES

Uptempo, jazz-tinged blues, usually featuring a vocalist in front of a large, horn-driven orchestra with less reliance on guitar work than other styles. Main proponents: Amos Milburn, Johnny Otis, Roy Brown, Wynonie Harris, and Big Joe Turner.

NEW ORLEANS BLUES

Primarily (but not exclusively) piano- and horn-driven, this genre strain is enlivened by Caribbean rhythms, party atmosphere, and the "second-line" strut of the Dixieland music so indigenous to the area. Main proponents: Professor Longhair, Guitar Slim, and Snooks Eaglin.

WEST COAST BLUES

More piano-based and jazz-influenced than anything else, the West Coast style (California in particular) also embraces post-war Texas guitar expatriates and jump-blues practitioners. Main proponents: Charles Brown, Pee Wee Crayton, Lowell Fulson, and Percy Mayfield.

PIANO BLUES

A genre that runs through the entire history of the music itself, this embraces everything from ragtime, barrelhouse, boogie-woogie, and smooth West Coast jazz stylings to the hard-rocking rhythms of Chicago blues. Main proponents: Big Maceo Merriweather, Leroy Carr, Sunnyland Slim, Roosevelt Sykes, Albert Ammons, and Otis Spann.

LOUISIANA BLUES

A looser, more laidback and percussive version of the Jimmy Reed side of the Chicago style. Production techniques on most of the recordings utilize massive amounts of echo, giving the performances a "doomy" sound and feel. Main proponents: Slim Harpo, Lightnin' Slim, and Lazy Lester.

R&B/SOUL BLUES

A more modern form, this fuses elements of Black popular music (the rhythm and blues strain of the '50s and the Southern soul style of the mid-'60s) to a wholly urban blues amalgam of its own.

MODERN ACOUSTIC BLUES

Newer artists reviving the older, more country-derived styles of blues. Main proponents: John Hammond, Rory Block, John Cephas, Taj Mahal, and the earlier recordings of Bonnie Raitt.

MODERN ELECTRIC BLUES

An eclectic mixture, this genre replicates older styles of urban blues while simultaneously recasting them in contemporary fashion. Main proponents: Stevie Ray Vaughan, the Fabulous Thunderbirds, Robert Cray, and Roomful of Blues.

BRITISH BLUES

More than a mere geographical distinction, the British style pays strict adherence to replicating American blues genres, with an admiration for its originators bordering on reverence. Main proponents: Alexis Korner, John Mayall, and the early recordings of Fleetwood Mac and the Rolling Stones.

— Cub Koda

HOW TO USE THIS BOOK

ARTIST NAME   (Alternate name in parentheses).

VITAL STATISTICS   For indivdual performers, date and place of birth and death, if known.

INSTRUMENT(S) / STYLE   Major instruments for each performer, followed by one or more styles of music associated with each performer or group.

BIOGRAPHY   A quick view of the artist's life and musical career. For major performers, proportionately longer biographies are provided.

ALBUM REVIEWS   These are the albums selected by our editors and contributors.

KEY TO SYMBOLS   ● ☆ ★

☆ ESSENTIAL RECORDINGS   Albums marked with a star should be part of any good collection of the genre. Often, these are also a good first purchase (filled star). By hearing these albums, you can get a good overview of the entire genre. These are must-hear and must-have recordings. You can't go wrong with them.

●★ FIRST PURCHASE   Albums marked with either a filled circle or a filled star should be your first purchase. This is where to begin to find out if you like this particular artist. These albums are representative of the best this artist has to offer. If you don't like these picks, chances are this artist is not for you. In the case of an artist who has a number of distinct periods, you will find an essential pick marked for each period. Albums are listed chronologically when possible.

ALBUM RATINGS: ✦ TO ✦✦✦✦✦   In addition to the stars and circles used to distinguish exceptional noteworthy albums, as explained above, all albums are rated on a scale from one to five diamonds.

ALBUM TITLE   The name of the album is listed in bold as it appears on the original when possible. Very long titles have been abbreviated, or repeated in full as part of the comment, where needed.

DATE   The year of an album's first release, if known.

RECORD LABEL   Record labels indicate the current (or most recent) release of this recording. Label numbers are not included because they change frequently.

REVIEWERS   The name of each review's author are given at the end of the review. "AMG" indicates a review written by the *All Music Guide* staff.

Juke Boy Bonner

b. Mar. 22, 1932, Bellville, TX, **d.** Jun. 29, 1978, Houston, TX
Guitar, Harmonica, Vocals / Electric Texas Blues

One-man bands weren't any too common on the postwar blues scene. Joe Hill Louis and Dr. Ross come to mind as greats who plied their trade all by their lonesome—and so did Juke Boy Bonner, a Texan whose talent never really earned him much in the way of tangible reward.

Born into impoverished circumstances in the Lone Star State during the Depression, Weldon Bonner took up the guitar in his teens. He caught a break in 1947 in Houston, winning a talent contest that led to a spot on a local radio outlet. He journeyed to Oakland in 1956, cutting his debut single for Bob Geddins' Irma imprint ("Rock with Me Baby"/"Well Baby") with Lafayette "Thing" Thomas supplying the lead guitar. Goldband Records boss Eddie Shuler was next to take a chance in 1960; Bonner recorded for him in Lake Charles, LA, with Katie Webster on piano, but once again, nothing happened career-wise.

Troubled by stomach problems during the '60s, Bonner utilized his hospital downtime to write poems that he later turned into songs. He cut his best work during the late '60s for Arhoolie Records, accompanying himself on both guitar and racked harmonica as he weaved extremely personal tales of his rough life in Houston. A few European tours ensued, but they didn't really lead to much. Toward the end of his life, he toiled in a chicken processing plant to make ends meet. Bonner died of cirrhosis of the liver in 1978. —*Bill Dahl*

Going Back to the Country / 1968 / Arhoolie ✦✦✦✦✦

● **Life Gave Me a Dirty Deal** / 1969 / Arhoolie ✦✦✦✦✦
Likely the most consistent and affecting collection you'll encounter by this singular Texas bluesman, whose strikingly personal approach was stunningly captured by Arhoolie's Chris Strachwitz during the late '60s in Houston. Twenty-three utter originals include "Stay Off Lyons Avenue," "Struggle Here in Houston," "I Got My Passport," and the title track. Bonner sang movingly of his painfully impoverished existence for Arhoolie, and the results still resound triumphantly today. —*Bill Dahl*

One Man Trio / 1979 / Flyright ✦✦✦✦✦

☆ **The Struggle** / 1981 / Arhoolie ✦✦✦✦✦
Recorded in extreme stereo, with drums on one channel and Bonner's guitar on the other, this is Juke Boy Bonner's most cohesive album. Great songwriting and performances throughout. —*Cub Koda*

Juke Boy Bonner, 1960-1967 / 1991 / Flyright ✦✦✦
There's a Lightnin' Hopkins-meets-Jimmy Reed sound on these delightfully funky guitar/harp-accompanied blues by this Houstonian, whose ironic lyrics are half the fun. —*Jas Obrecht*

Things Ain't Right / Sequel ✦✦
This set is somewhat disappointing compared to the Arhoolie sides. —*Bill Dahl*

INTRODUCTION

*"I live across the street from a juke box, baby–
All night long it plays the blues."*

I was recently talking to a friend of mine and was telling them about the project you now hold in your hands, the blues entry into the *All Music Guide* series of reference books. As I was explaining to him about the avalanche of information to be checked and cross-checked, the myriad essays highlighting the music's history, the thousands of albums and compilations to be listened to and the blues maps to show how all the different styles came together and who influenced who, my buddy put his index finger up to his pursed lips, like he always does when I'm yammering on and on and he wants me to shut up. Then he smiled and said, "So, is this another blues revival we're going through?" I smiled back and thought to myself, blues *explosion* is more like it.

The blues is big business these days, bigger than ever and if you don't believe me, just turn on your TV set or radio; the sound and style is seemingly everywhere. The blues–in all its myriad strains–has become party music for the millennium. Just look at the short list of irrefutable facts in the last decade of the 20th century: A chain franchise of blues clubs with weekly syndicated TV broadcasts emanating from them? Howlin' Wolf and Muddy Waters' faces emblazoned on the front of t-shirts that you can order out of catalogs? A blues chart in *Billboard* magazine? The Pillsbury Dough Boy selling blueberry muffins on TV with a honking blues riff in the background? Robert Johnson guitar picks and polishing cloths with a facsimile of his autograph on one and his picture on the other?

Instructional videos for aspiring guitarists and harmonica blowers by the carload? John Lee Hooker doing Pepsi commercials? Do you think *any* of this could have happened–or even have been conceivable–30 years ago? No way. The days of the blues as a growth industry have definitely arrived. If you've come to this guide from a rock'n'roll background, we certainly have no intentions of making you feel stupid or ashamed of it, quite the contrary. To be honest, that's where most of us came in. As a matter of fact, one of the really cool things about the blues is its inclusionary nature; there's room for everybody. You don't have to be a walking blues encyclopedia to hear and get its basic message. That rock'n'roll comes straight from the blues is one of the few facts about its history that you can get a room full of critics, musicians or fans to agree on. Now whether you define the moment of its mass acceptance as Elvis cutting loose in the Sun studios or Eric Clapton recycling Robert Johnson for the first time, and whether or not you believe that they (and myriad others) took the music somewhere the originators couldn't have imagined, is usually where the arguments start up.

But the blues are far more than just your standard 'seminal' genre influence, like comparing Louis Armstrong's recordings from the '20s to some contemporary, horn-tooting be-bopper and saying, "*This* is where it came from!" The music is now so interwoven into the fabric of rock and popular music, we take something like hearing the music of Muddy Waters in a TV commercial or a bunch of child actors attempting to sing the blues while extolling the virtues of Kraft Macaroni and Cheese–a couple of notions that would have been unthinkable just a few years back–as nothing out of the ordinary. As rock and country music become more manufactured and fragmented, the blues as a popular music force becomes stronger and stronger. This still surprises some folks, who–while changing channels on their remote control–watch John Lee Hooker picking up Grammy awards while singing duets with Bonnie Raitt, listen to slide guitar and harmonica wailings in beer commercials, gaze at B.B. King and Buddy Guy duking it out on the Tonight Show while ZZ Top does the endless boogie on MTV, then usually say something profound along the lines of, "Wow, the blues are really gettin' popular!" These poor, misguided people react as if the music just pitched a tent in their back yard, moving in while they were asleep. But to quote Lord Chesterfield, "An honest mistake is to be pitied, not ridiculed."

Because the blues has *always* been here. Part of its resiliency stems from it being such a bedrock musical form. The other part of the equation is the fact that blues can run the emotional roller coaster from sounding sad and lonesome one minute to the rockinest party you've ever been to the next, and every place in between. It'll definitely go thru surges of popularity, but it originally found its way onto records (big, clunky 10 inch ones that went around the turntable at 78 RPM and broke in half if you sat on them) because it *was* popular music. It sounded good, it sounded different. It was like hearing the same song over and over again, but all with their own distinct flavor. The familiarity of its basic structure–and how *far* you could go with it–made it sound as comfortable as the music felt. But no matter how familiar the form was, it was always developing, going different places. And like all evolving American art forms infused by commerce (in this case, the recording industry), the blues kept on changing, splintering off into new permutations, reinventing itself to keep pace with the modern world. Of course, like any other self-respecting branch of indigenous American music, it's a genre filled with absolutely great songs. Most of these numbers have stood the test the time, becoming part and parcel of everyone's set list, from the legendary greats that spawned them to the local bar band playing down the street. Now a great song can always come back and find a new audience, sometimes without changing a single note and other times just dressing it up in contemporary clothes, not unlike an audio Mary Kay makeover. If you think this theory doesn't really hold water, then how else do you explain David Lee Roth having a hit with Louis Prima material? (A man who made so many records for so many different labels, by the way, that he could easily qualify for his *own* All Music Guide.) Most of the music's originators didn't live long enough to reap the big paycheck from all this, but it is all of one piece, a taut connecting thread that links it all together. Elmore James may not have lived long enough to jam on M-TV with Eric Clapton and the Rolling Stones, but it all comes from *somewhere*, and Henri Cartier Bresson, famous art photographer from the '40s and '50s, perhaps said it best; "There are no new ideas in the world, only new ways of doing them." That's pretty good, but maybe President Harry S. Truman said it even better; "The only thing new is the history you don't know." And *that*, dear reader, is where this book comes in.

What you are now holding in your hands is a very real collection of American musical history, something that leaps boundaries between blues and its bastard child, rock'n'roll with stops along the way between jazz, jump, New Orleans zydeco and sweet soul music. If you're an old hardliner, who's done more than your fair share of excavating into the dark past of American roots music, most of these artists and their work will be as plain as the nose on your face. If you're coming to this guide with an interest in the blues that outweighs your knowledge of its history (which roughly parallels the history of recorded music), you're fully expected to keep smacking the

side of your head and exclaiming, "So *that's* where that came from!" while you wade through it all, using our handy little maps to tie it all together. We'll do our best to turn you on to the good stuff. Then it's up to you to decide which ones *you* want to add to your collection.

But in the final analysis, it really doesn't matter who you are or what you know or don't know, because the blues are for *everybody*, from old hippies who were there when Howlin' Wolf and Son House had their first encounters playing to a sea of White faces to young affluent yuppies to whom Howlin' Wolf is just a Black face on a postage stamp. This volume does not purport to be the 'ultimate' blues book and considering the raft of other books currently out there (a long way down the research highway from 30 years ago when Robert Johnson was more a fictional romantic vision than a set of cold facts with a couple of photographs to go along with it), the notion of there even *being* such an animal is at best subjective. As a famous bluesman once told me backstage at a genre mixed pop festival back in the '70s, "You can't be the best, you just try to be a good 'un" and that's what we have honestly strived for here. A lot of sweat, hard work and a steady diet of warmed over coffee and even colder pizza have gone into these pages. And a lot of love for the music and the people that make it, too. There's no didactic axe to grind out of any of the writers contributing to this book; if there was, their revisionist historical opinions would be promptly filed by the editors into the round file cabinet next to their respective desks, if you get my drift. We've tried to keep the bios and essays unclouded by romantic projection while still being infused with verve, wit and style and we certainly make no apologies for our various contributors' unabashed passion for certain artists. After all, this *is* a music of and about passion and when the blues hits you hard, it's easy to get swept up in that passion, too.

While the book definitely tips its hat to the music's pioneers and originators–the true giants of the blues in a very spiritual sense–we also haven't tried to make too many distinctions about what is and isn't the blues. Long before the Blue Brothers were doing their own brand of minstrel show for folks who thought Lightnin' Slim was a weight loss program, the old critical saw of 'can white men sing the blues?' had been raging at full throttle. We don't make those kind of decisions here, that's somebody else's book. We don't care what color somebody's skin is, their point of ethnic origin or their economic strata. If they can sing and play the blues and sound good doing it, you're going to be reading about it here. While perhaps not quite adopting a 'let it all in and let 'em sort it out later' attitude, we've tried to illustrate the depth and wide breadth of the music, while giving current artists of substantive worth their moment in the sun as well. Just don't expect to find a listing for the *101 Strings Play The Blues* album anywhere between these covers, ok?

What we *have* done is try to assemble the definitive picks on every artist and compilation listed. Walking into any new disc emporium these days can be a fairly daunting task. Most well stocked stores have a decent sized blues section. But there's a hundred Lightnin' Hopkins CDs here; which ones are the *good* ones? Which one do I buy first? That's where we come in; if it's good, we want to steer you straight to it. Also along the way, you'll see the occasional buyer beware alert review listed as well. If it's a stinkburger, no sense in you getting stuck with it. We also realize that not everybody has the financial outlay to go purchasing multi-disc box sets just because that's the definitive statement on a particular artist or genre. So wherever possible we've listed single disc best of's as well. If you're coming to an artist for the very first time, that 12 song mid line priced compilation just might be the perfect one to start with. And if your old favorite moth eaten vinyl album that you've had since

Kennedy was President isn't listed here, don't despair. Now that record companies have figured out a way to sell us back our own record collections, eventually *everything* will get reissued on compact disc sooner or later.

So in putting this book to bed, we here at the All Music Guide are struck with the inescapable conclusion that the blues continue to roll on, its history continuing to be rewritten at every turn. While sadly most of the originators are gone (and wouldn't it be nice to watch that Robert Johnson video that never got made right about now?), their achievements have outlasted the vagaries of fads and fashion and will undoubtedly continue to do so into the next century. This is a music of great substance. We've done our best to steer you to the best of it, while giving it a sense of place and time. So please enjoy this book and don't let anybody tell you different; until time travel is perfected and we can all go back and watch Charlie Patton and Son House jamming in a Mississippi juke joint, *these* are the good old days for the music. Just listen to these blues.   *—Cub Koda*

A

Johnny Ace (John Alexander)

b. Jun. 9, 1929, Memphis, TN, **d.** Dec. 25, 1954
Vocals, Piano / R&B

The senseless death of young pianist Johnny Ace while indulging in a round of Russian roulette backstage at Houston's City Auditorium on Christmas Day of 1954 tends to overshadow his relatively brief but illustrious recording career on Duke Records. That's a pity, for Ace's gentle, plaintive vocal balladry deserves reverence on its own merit, not because of the scandalous fallout resulting from his tragic demise.

John Marshall Alexander was a member in good standing of the Beale Streeters, a loosely knit crew of Memphis youngbloods that variously included B.B. King, Bobby Bland, and Earl Forest. Signing with local deejay David Mattis' fledgling Duke logo in 1952, the rechristened Ace hit the top of the R&B charts his very first time out with the mellow ballad "My Song." From then on, Ace could do no musical wrong, racking up hit after hit for Duke in the same smooth, urbane style. "Cross My Heart," "The Clock," "Saving My Love for You," "Please Forgive Me," and "Never Let Me Go" all dented the uppermost reaches of the charts. And then, with one fatal gunshot, all that talent was lost forever (weepy tribute records quickly emerged by Frankie Ervin, Johnny Fuller, Varetta Dillard, and the Five Wings).

Ace scored his biggest hit of all posthumously. His haunting "Pledging My Love" (cut with the Johnny Otis orchestra in support) remained atop *Billboard's* R&B lists for ten weeks in early 1955. One further hit, "Anymore," exhausted Duke's stockpile of Ace masters, so they tried to clone the late pianist's success by recruiting Johnny's younger brother (St. Clair Alexander) to record as Buddy Ace. When that didn't work out, Duke boss Don Robey took singer Jimmy Lee Land, renamed him Buddy Ace, and recorded him all the way into the late '60s. *—Bill Dahl*

● **Memorial Album** / 1955 / MCA ✦✦✦✦

It's downright bizarre that Ace's catalog hasn't enjoyed a fresh reissue in 40 years. This 12-song CD is the exact same package that Don Robey rushed out following the pianist's death, with all the velvety hits ("Pledging My Love," "My Song," "The Clock," "Never Let Me Go") and a mere two blistering rockers, "How Can You Be So Mean" and "Don't You Know." A more thorough examination of Ace's discography is definitely in order! *—Bill Dahl*

The Aces

Group

Common wisdom says that Muddy Waters was the man responsible for turbo charging the Delta blues and creating what we now call Chicago Blues. Muddy's importance is inestimable, but to lay all the credit at his feet is to ignore the contributions of those who quite literally used Muddy's music as a jumping off point, and blazed historical trails of their own. Of all the great musicians who passed through Muddy's bands, perhaps the most important of all was harmonica player and singer Little Walter Jacobs. Little Walter left Muddy's band at the age of 22, already a seasoned veteran of the road and the recording studio. He quickly recruited his own superb band, and came very close to eclipsing his former boss' success during the heyday of Chicago Blues in the 1950s, with two number 1 hits among his ten appearances on the nationwide *Billboard* R&B charts; Muddy himself had twelve songs reach the *Billboard* charts but never scored a number 1 hit. Much of Little Walter's success can be attributed to the fact that

he was doing something new, different, and thoroughly urban; where Muddy's appeal lay heavily with southern emigres longing for familiar sounds, Walter's swinging, modern, jazz-inflected style found favor with a younger generation of city blues fans not so closely tied to the "down-home" sounds of the south.

But Little Walter couldn't have done it alone—he needed accompanists who shared his desire to push the edge of the blues envelope, so he recruited his band from among the most accomplished and forward-thinking blues musicians available in Chicago. His first recording and touring band in 1952 was a band that he'd sometimes sat in with while still with Muddy—The Aces, featuring brothers David and Louis Myers on guitars. The Myers brothers were born in Byhalia, MS, and had learned the rudiments of guitar from their father before the family relocated to Chicago in the early 1940s while both brothers were still in their early teens. There their musical tastes were formed by equal doses of the big band swing that was popular at the time, pop ballads they heard on the radio, and the blues that was being played all around their south side neighborhood. By the late '40s they had assumed the roles they'd play for much of their musical careers: older brother Dave providing bass lines and chords into which Louis wove his tastefully jazzy blues riffing. Their rock-solid musical foundation provided the perfect base for the veteran bluesman they soon found themselves backing, but their musical precociousness drove them to eventually form The Aces, which incorporated some of the more modern and sophisticated influences that had raised eyebrows with the older blues crowd. The Aces were rounded out by schooled jazz drummer Fred Below, a Chicago native for whom the rough southern blues rhythms were almost completely foreign; after his first gig with the group he was so musically disoriented that he decided to quit the band, but was persuaded to stick it out and adapt his jazz techniques to the blues, ultimately becoming the most in-demand blues drummer in Chicago (in addition to putting the beat to many of rock and roll pioneer Chuck Berry's early hits). Little Walter approached his harmonica like a jazz saxophone player, and The Aces provided the propulsive backing of a swinging big band. It would have been nearly impossible at the time to find three musicians who were better suited to providing the solid foundation for Walter's musical innovations than The Aces, who had the musical and dynamic range, swing sensibilities, and melding of individual strengths that made them the standard by which all of Little Walter's later ensembles—and most harp-led blues bands since—have been measured.

Unfortunately this band was not to last; The Aces had been establishing their own name around town, but when their first records with Little Walter were released by the Chess Records subsidiary Checker as by "Little Walter and His Night Caps" or "…and His Jukes" (to capitalize on the popularity of his first hit "Juke," recorded during a session while he was still with Muddy), there was dissension in the ranks. The first to leave was Louis, who was replaced by Robert Jr. Lockwood in 1954. Almost 40 years old at the time, Lockwood's roots were in the Delta; as Robert Johnson's stepson, he had a firm handle on the deepest of blues, but had been studying jazz guitarists since at least the 1930s, and had been recording since before WWII. He proved to be an adept foil for Walter's harp excursions, and many of Walter's jazziest adventures were supported and driven by Lockwood's sophisticated guitar riffing.

Dave Myers was the next to leave, joining his brother Louis in 1955 in a reformed Aces that featured Junior Wells (who had played with the band pre-Walter) and later Otis Rush. Dave was replaced by 19-year-old guitar prodigy Luther Tucker, who had been hanging around the band and occasionally sitting in with them, as well as with other local blues acts. Although Tucker's role was initially the same as Dave's—thumping out bass lines on his guitar and providing chordal fills behind Lockwood—he soon distinguished himself as one of the flashiest of the new breed of guitarists in Chicago. When given the chance to take the lead, Tucker's fleet-fingered bursts of nervous energy helped push Little Walter's music in new and exciting directions. The first wave of rock and roll was cresting, aggressively played electric guitar was moving to the forefront of popular music, and Luther Tucker was among the blues guitarists at the leading edge.

It was around this time that Fred Below vacated the drum seat, although as was the custom at Chess/Checker Records, he continued to be brought in for recording sessions for the next several years. Replacing him on the road for a time was his old drum school classmate Odie Payne Jr., who had been playing and recording in Chicago since the late '40s with the likes of Tampa Red, Memphis Minnie, Memphis Slim and Elmore James, and who later worked as the house drummer at Cobra Records, playing behind Buddy Guy, Magic Sam, Otis Rush and others. Payne's slightly more orthodox but still distinctly jazzy style was by all accounts ideally suited to Walter's music, although there's no documentation of him ever appearing on any of Walter's records.

After a short time with a still young and rambunctious Little Walter and the even younger Luther Tucker, Lockwood was began to tire of the grind, and he left Walter's band, although he continued to appear on records with him (and also notably with Sonny Boy Williamson) until the late '50s. In 1956 Jimmie Lee Robinson joined Little Walter's band, pushing Luther Tucker into the lead role that Lockwood had vacated. Robinson was another Chicago native, who had grown up around the blues-rich Maxwell Street Market area, and knew Walter from his escapades there during his earliest years in Chicago. Robinson's formative years included musical apprenticeship on Maxwell Street, followed by formal music lessons for a time, and then time spent with guitarists Freddie King, Elmore James, Eddie Taylor and others in the early '50s. His guitar style had similarities to Tucker's, and eventually their roles carrying the top and bottom of the music melded to the point where they would trade back and forth even during songs. Unfortunately there are only a few examples of Jimmie Lee's years with Walter on record, due to the record label's insistence on not tampering with the successful studio formula that had been established by the Tucker/Lockwood/Below ensemble (usually augmented by Willie Dixon on string bass).

By the end of the 1950s, Little Walter's hit-making days were behind him, and his bands soon became a revolving door through which a number of local musicians passed. In 1959 guitarist Freddie Robinson joined the band for a time (replacing Jimmie Lee Robinson, a move that has caused much confusion among discographers over the years), during which he sometimes played electric bass. Odie Payne left the band after a short time to be replaced by the solid if less musically adventurous George Hunter. During sessions over the next few years the drum throne (on sessions, at least) was also occupied by Billy Stepney, session ace Al Duncan, and even the return of Fred Below for a 1960 session. But blues tastes were changing, and Little Walter's great ensembles of the past had all scattered and moved on to other pursuits with varying degrees of success. —Scott Dirks

Arthur Adams

Vocals, Guitar / Electric Memphis Blues
As house bandleader at B.B. King's Los Angeles blues club, Arthur Adams cranks out searing blues for the well-heeled tourists who tread the length of Universal Studios' glitzy City Walk. But the great majority of his transient clientele can't begin to imagine the depth and variety of the guitarist's career.

The shaven-headed Tennessee native began playing guitar in the mid-'50s, taking early inspiration from the man whose name adorns the club that now employs him (Howard Carol, axeman for gospel's Dixie Hummingbirds, also was a principal influence). He studied music at Tennessee State University, playing briefly with the school's resident jazz and blues aggregation.

Touring as a member of singer Gene Allison's band, Adams found himself stranded in Dallas, where he dazzled the locals with his fancy fretwork. Relocating to L.A. in 1964, he began to do session work for jazz great Quincy Jones and cut singles for the Bihari brothers' Kent label and Hugh Masekela's Motown-

distributed Chisa imprint. His late-'60s R&B sides for the latter were co-produced by Stewart Levine and featured support from most of the Crusaders. Adams' 1970 debut LP for Blue Thumb, *It's Private Tonight*, was co-produced by Bonnie Raitt and Tommy Lipuma. More recently, Adams wrote two songs for King's *There Is Always One More Time* album. —Bill Dahl

It's Private Tonight / 1972 / Blue Thumb ◆◆◆
● **Home Brew** / 1975 / Fantasy ◆◆◆◆◆
Midnight Serenade / 1977 / Fantasy ◆◆◆
I Love Love Love My Lady / 1979 / A&M ◆◆

Johnny Adams

b. Jan. 5, 1932, New Orleans, LA
Vocals / Soul Blues
Renowned around his Crescent City homebase as "the Tan Canary" for his extraordinary set of soulfully soaring pipes, veteran R&B vocalist Johnny Adams has tackled an exceptionally wide variety of material for Rounder in recent years—elegantly rendered tribute albums to legendary songwriters Doc Pomus and Percy Mayfield preceded forays into mellow, jazzier pastures. But then, Adams was never particularly into the parade-beat grooves that traditionally define the New Orleans R&B sound, preferring to deliver sophisticated soul ballads draped in strings.

Adams sang gospel professionally before crossing over to the secular world in 1959. Songwriter Dorothy LaBostrie—the woman responsible for cleaning up the bawdy lyrics of Little Richard's "Tutti Frutti" enough for worldwide consumption—convinced her neighbor Adams to sing her tasty ballad "I Won't Cry." The track, produced by a teenaged Mac Rebennack, was released on Joe Ruffino's Ric logo, and Adams was on his way. He waxed some outstanding follow-ups for Ric, notably "A Losing Battle" (the Rebennack-penned gem proved Adams' first national R&B hit in 1962) and "Life Is a Struggle."

After a prolonged dry spell, Adams resurfaced in 1968 with an impassioned R&B revival of Jimmy Heap's country standard "Release Me" for Shelby Singleton's SSS imprint that blossomed into a national hit. Even more arresting was Adams' magnificent 1969 country-soul classic "Reconsider Me," his lone leap into the R&B Top Ten; in it, he swoops effortlessly up to a death-defying falsetto range to drive his anguished message home with fervor.

Despite several worthy SSS follow-ups ("I Can't Be All Bad" was another sizable seller), Adams never traversed those lofty commercial heights again (particularly disappointing was a short stay at Atlantic). But he's found a new extended recording life at Rounder—his 1984 set, *From the Heart*, proved to the world that this Tan Canary can still chirp like a champ. —Bill Dahl

Heart & Soul / 1969 / SSS ◆◆◆◆◆
This country-soul collection, containing all his hits from 1962-1968, was produced by Shelby Singleton. —Richard Pack

Stand by Me / 1976 / Chelsea ◆◆
This is a relaxed, live-in-the-studio recording of standards. —Richard Pack

After All the Good Is Gone / 1978 / Ariola ◆◆
From the Heart / 1984 / Rounder ◆◆◆◆
First-class production by Scott Billington, a delicious Crescent City combo led by longtime cohort Walter "Wolfman" Washington on guitar and Red Tyler on tenor sax, and Adams' perennially luxurious pipes tab this as one of his finest contemporary outings. Nice song selection: the pens of Tony Joe White, Percy Mayfield, Sam Cooke, and Doc Pomus were all tapped. Johnny unfurls his "mouth trombone"—an uncanny vocal 'bone imitation—on Mayfield's "We Don't See Eye to Eye." —Bill Dahl

A Tan Nightingale / 1984 / Charly ◆◆◆
After Dark / 1986 / Rounder ◆◆◆◆◆
When Adams signed with Rounder in the mid-'80s, few outside the R&B/soul and blues world were aware of his skills or eclectic range. *After Dark* was Adams' second Rounder session. It includes amazing covers of Doc Pomus' "I Don't Know You" and "Give A Broken Heart A Break," John Hiatt's "Lovers Will" and the Dan Penn/Chips Moman soul classic "Do Right Woman—Do Right Man." This is one of the first records on which Adams'

wondrous voice, with its extensive range at the top and bottom, is both well-produced and effectively mastered and recorded. — *Ron Wynn*

● **Reconsider Me** / 1987 / Charly ✦✦✦✦✦
This 22-song British compilation is the only place to find a decent cross-section of Adams' SSS sides, including his two biggest hits, the stately "Release Me" and the truly stunning "Reconsider Me." Not all of Adams' late-'60s waxings were ballads; "South Side of Soul Street" is a sizzling upbeat workout. But it's as a balladeer that Adams has always excelled; some of his finest soul senders are to be found right here. —*Bill Dahl*

Room with a View of the Blues / 1988 / Rounder ✦✦✦✦
Although calling Johnny Adams a blues singer is far too confining, he's certainly among the finest to perform in that idiom. He's equally brilliant at slow or uptempo numbers, can effectively convey irony, heartache or triumph, and is a masterful storyteller. These ten blues numbers cover every emotional base, allowing Adams a chance to show his proficiency. With great support from an instrumental corps that includes guitarists Walter "Wolfman" Washington and Duke Robillard, keyboardist Dr. John, and saxophonists Red Tyler and Foots Samuel, plus Ernie Gautreau on valve trombone, Adams didn't just cut a blues album, he made unforgettable blues statements. —*Ron Wynn*

Christmas in New Orleans / 1988 / Ace ✦✦
This is a disappointing effort from "The Tan Canary," who is in fine voice but weighed down with poor arrangements. Adams also stays in control too much, rarely letting that tenor voice take flight. —*Decibel Dennis MacDonald*

Walking on a Tightrope / 1989 / Rounder ✦✦✦✦
Whenever Johnny Adams does a repertory album, it's as much his own showcase as a forum for the spotlighted composer. Even Percy Mayfield's lyrically brilliant works don't stop Adams from displaying his special magic; his treatments on the session's ten tunes range from excellent to magnificent. Adams is gripping on "My Heart Is Hangin' Heavy," nicely bemused on "The Lover and the Married Woman" and convincing on the title track and "Danger Zone." Although he's done numerous Rounder vehicles, Adams hasn't yet turned in a dud. —*Ron Wynn*

Johnny Adams Sings Doc Pomus: The Real Me / 1991 / Rounder ✦✦✦✦✦
Having paid elegant tribute to Percy Mayfield on his previous album, Adams this time thrillingly croons the songbook of the great Doc Pomus, who wrote several fresh compositions for the project that nestle snugly alongside chestnuts such as "Still in Love" and "There Is Always One More Time." Red Tyler and Mac Rebennack are on board the session, along with eminently tasty guitarist Duke Robillard. —*Bill Dahl*

● **I Won't Cry** / 1991 / Rounder ✦✦✦✦✦
Even on his earliest singles, Adams already had developed a velvety crooning style seemingly at odds with his raucous hometown. This 14-track collection of Adams' 1959-63 work for Ric Records contains some stunning stuff, most of it in the big-voiced ballad mode (with an occasional nod to Ray Charles). "I Won't Cry," "A Losing Battle," and "Lonely Drifter" capture Adams' tender, mellifluous delivery beautifully. —*Bill Dahl*

Good Morning Heartache / 1993 / Rounder ✦✦✦
Adams could sing the phone book and make it sound sweet, so his personalized rendition of the title track and several more jazz standards on this collection shouldn't come as too much of a surprise. Nevertheless, it's a long way from "Reconsider Me," and perhaps a bit too jazzy for some R&B fans. —*Bill Dahl*

The Verdict / 1995 / Rounder ✦✦✦✦
Fans of Adams' R&B dusties may well not find everything on this jazz-based collection to their taste, but Adams' vocal ease within the jazz idiom is undeniable. Noteworthy sidemen include Harry Connick, Jr., and Houston Person. —*Bill Dahl*

Ray Agee

b. Apr. 10, 1930, Dixon Mills, Alabama, **d.** 1990
Vocals, Guitar / Electric California Blues
Known primarily for his tough 1963 remake of the blues standard "Tin Pan Alley" (featuring the moaning lead guitar of Johnny Heartsman) for the tiny Sahara logo, vocalist Ray Agee recorded for a myriad of labels both large and small during the 1950s and '60s without much in the way of national recognition

outside his Los Angeles homebase. That's a pity—he was a fine, versatile blues singer whose work deserves a wider audience (not to mention CD reissue).

The Alabama native was stricken with polio at age four, leaving Agee with a permanent handicap. After moving to L.A. with his family, he apprenticed with his brothers in a gospel quartet before striking out in the R&B field with a 1952 single for Eddie Mesner's Aladdin Records (backed by saxist Maxwell Davis' band). From there, his discography assumes daunting proportions; he appeared on far too many logos to list here (Elko, Spark, Ebb, and Cash among them).

James Agee slowly slipped away from the music business in the early '70s. Reportedly, he died around 1990. —*Bill Dahl*

● **Tin Pan Alley** / 1982 / Diving Duck ✦✦✦✦✦
This obscure Dutch LP is the only collection of Agee's vintage singles you're likely to encounter until someone decides to do some serious cross-licensing. Yes, the doom-laden "Tin Pan Alley" is aboard, along with the distinctive "You Hit Me Where It Hurts" and "The Gamble." —*Bill Dahl*

Dave Alexander

b. Mar. 10, 1938, Shreveport, LA
Piano / Electric West Coast Blues
Pianist and drummer Dave Alexander is both an effective vocalist and outstanding instrumentalist, who's best known for many festival and club appearances, and his Arhoolie albums. Also known as Omar Hakim Khayyam, Alexander's an articulate writer and advocate for the blues and African-American music. He's written several articles for *Living Blues*. A self-taught pianist, Alexander's played with LC Robinson, Big Mama Thornton, Jimmy McCracklin, and Lafayette Thomas. —*Ron Wynn*

● **The Rattler / Dirt on the Ground** / Arhoolie ✦✦✦✦✦
The compact disc *The Rattler / Dirt on the Ground* contains one of Dave Alexander's '70s albums and one of his more recent efforts. The compilation offers a good portrait of Alexander's eclectic, entertaining blues. —*Thom Owens*

Luther Allison

b. Aug. 17, 1939, Widener, AR
Guitar, Harmonica, Vocals / R&B, Modern Electric Blues, Chicago Blues
An American-born guitarist, singer and songwriter who's lived in France since 1980, Luther Allison has been the man to book at blues festivals in the mid-'90s. Allison's comeback into the mainstream was ushered in by a recording contract with an American record company, Chicago-based Alligator Records. Allison began working with Alligator in 1994, and since then, it seems his career has been on a steady upward climb.

Born August 17, 1939, in Widener, AR, Allison was the 14th of 15 children, the son of cotton farmers. His parents moved to Chicago when he was in his early teens, but he had a solid awareness of blues before he left Arkansas, as he played organ in the church and learned to sing gospel in Widener as well. Allison recalled that his earliest awareness of blues came via the family radio in Arkansas, which his dad would play at night. Allison recalls listening to both the Grand Ole Opry and B.B. King on the King Biscuit Show on Memphis' WDIA. Although he was a talented baseball player and had begun to learn the shoemaking trade in Chicago after high school, it wasn't long before Allison began to focus more of his attention on playing blues guitar. Allison had been hanging out in blues clubs all through high school, and with his brother's encouragement, he honed his string bending skills and powerful, soul-filled vocal technique.

It was while living with his family on Chicago's West Side that he had his first awareness of wanting to become a full-time bluesman, and he played bass behind guitarist Jimmy Dawkins, whom Allison grew up with. Also in Allison's neighborhood were established blues greats like Freddie King, Magic Sam and Otis Rush. He distinctly remembers everyone talking about Buddy Guy when he came to town from his native Louisiana. After the Allison household moved to the South Side, they lived a few blocks away from Muddy Waters, and Allison and Waters' son Charles became friends. When he was 18 years old, his brother showed him basic chords and notes on the guitar, and the super bright Allison made rapid progress after that. Allison went on to "blues college" by sitting in with some of the most legendary names in blues in Chicago's local venues: Muddy Waters, Elmore James and Howlin' Wolf among them.

His first chance to record came with Bob Koester's then-tiny Delmark Record label, and his first album, *Love Me Mama*, was released in 1969. But like anyone else with a record out on a small label, it was up to him to go out and promote it, and he did, putting in stellar, show-stopping performances at the Ann Arbor Blues festivals in 1969, 1970 and 1971. After that, people began to pay attention to Luther Allison, and in 1972 he signed with Motown Records. Meanwhile, a growing group of rock 'n' roll fans began showing up at Allison's shows, because his style seemed so reminiscent of Jimi Hendrix, and his live shows clocked in at just under four hours!

Although his Motown albums got him to places he'd never been before, like Japan and new venues in Europe, the recordings didn't sell well. He does have the distinction of being one of a few blues musicians to record for Motown. Allison stayed busy in Europe through the rest of the 1970s and 1980s, and recorded *Love Me Papa* for the French Black and Blue label in 1977. He followed with a number of live recordings from Paris, and eventually settled outside of Paris, since France and Germany were such major markets for him. At home in the U.S., Allison continued to perform sporadically, when knowledgeable blues festival organizers or blues societies would book him. Allison has been based near Paris since 1984, and in a recent interview, he seemed hopeful that he would eventually move back to the States, if the climate for blues continued to improve, as it has since the mid-'80s emergence of Stevie Ray Vaughan.

As accomplished a guitarist as he is, Allison will be the first to tell you he doesn't consider himself a straightahead Chicago blues musician. He learned the blues long before he got to Chicago. What Allison does so successfully is take his base of Chicago blues and add touches of rock, soul, reggae, funk and jazz. He feels that as an artist, it's part of his responsibility to keep the music evolving. As he said in a 1995 interview for *Goldmine*, "I can play the old blues. I've done that trip....I mean look at [Clarence] "Gatemouth" Brown. He can do country, he can do blues, he can do jazz, he can do all of these things." Allison's two most recent albums for the Alligator label, *Soul Fixin' Man* and *Blue Streak*, are arguably two of his strongest. His talents as a songwriter are fully developed, and he's well recorded and well produced, often with horns backing his band. Another album to look for is a 1992 reissue on Evidence, *Love Me Papa*. In 1996, Motown reissued some of the three albums worth of material he recorded for that label (between 1972 and 1976) on compact disc.

Now in his mid-50s, Allison continues to delight club and festival audiences around the world with his lengthy, sweat-drenched, high energy shows, complete with dazzling guitar playing and inspired, soulful vocals. —*Richard Skelly*

Love Me Mama / 1969 / Delmark ✦✦✦
Although it has its moments—particularly on the title track—Luther Allison's debut album, *Love Me Papa*, is on the whole uneven, featuring more mediocre tracks than killer cuts. Nevertheless, it offers intriguing glimpses of the style he would later develop. —*Thom Owens*

Luther's Blues / 1973 / Gordy ✦✦✦✦✦
Luther's Blues is where Luther Allison began to come into his own, developing a fluid, gutsy style full of soulful string bending. There are still a few weak spots, but the album remains an effective slice of contemporary Chicago blues. —*Thom Owens*

Night Life / 1976 / Gordy ✦
On *Night Life*, Luther Allison tried to make a soul crossover album but the slick production fails to provide a suitable bed for his bluesy guitars and vocals. Occasionally, he spits out a good solo, but only the most devoted listeners will be able to dig them out, since they're buried beneath a glossy varnish. —*Thom Owens*

● **Love Me Papa** / Dec. 13, 1977 / Evidence ✦✦✦✦✦
Luther Allison is the blues' proverbial little boy with the curl; when he's good, he's great. When he's bad, he's awful. Allison is on throughout most of the nine tracks (three bonus cuts) on this 1977 date recently reissued by Evidence on CD, playing with the ferocity, direction, and inventiveness that is often missing from his more uneven efforts. His covers of Little Walter Jacobs' "Last Night" and "Blues With A Feeling" are not reverential or respect-

ful but are launching pads for high-octane, barreling riffs, snappy phrases, and exciting solos. His vocals are not always that keen, but Allison at least stretches them out and adds verbal embellishments, yells, and shouts of encouragement. —*Ron Wynn*

Gonna Be a Live One in Here Tonight / 1979 / Rumble ✦✦
Gonna Be a Live One in Here Tonight is a solid, no-frills documentation of a late-'70s club show from Luther Allison. Though it's not an exceptional performance, it certainly isn't a disappointing one and dedicated fans will find it worth their time. —*Thom Owens*

Power Wire Blues / 1979 / Charly ✦
Power Wire Blues is a collection of outtakes from his uneven *Rumble* album. Since the best takes of these sessions were pretty weak, these lesser tracks have even less to distinguish—much less recommend—them. It's one to be avoided. —*Thom Owens*

Serious / 1987 / Blind Pig ✦✦✦✦✦
Serious marks the beginning of Luther Allison's late-'80s/early-'90s hot streak. The more streamlined, rock-oriented approach actually is a benefit, since it gives Allison a shot of energy that makes his guitar simply burn all the way through the record. —*Thom Owens*

Soul Fixin' Man / 1994 / Alligator ✦✦✦✦✦
This new venture, recorded in Memphis, is Allison's finest session since his days at Delmark. He blends blues, soul/R&B and even occasional funk, and his guitar playing is alternately flashy and refined, sometimes explosive, sometimes carefully measured. His vocals are powerful, convincing and earnest on all 12 selections. Luther Allison finally gives American blues fans the definitive portrait they wanted. —*Ron Wynn*

Blue Streak / Oct. 1995 / Alligator ✦✦✦✦
Luther Allison's run of winning contemporary blues albums continues with *Blue Streak*, a typically enjoyable set of hot guitar playing and impassioned singing, hampered only slightly by occasionally perfunctory songwriting. —*Thom Owens*

The Motown Years 1972-1976 / Feb. 1996 / Motown ✦✦✦
Allison's reign as Motown's only bluesman saw the guitarist offer competently executed, but basically unmemorable, blues with some soul and rock influences. This 17-track compilation includes selections from all three of the LPs he issued on the label (drawing most heavily from his second, *Luther's Blues*), and adds a previously unreleased live cut from the 1972 Ann Arbor Blues Festival. Pop influences can be heard in the occasional wah-wah guitar and brass-conscious production; Berry Gordy even co-wrote one of the tracks ("Someday Pretty Baby"), and Randy Brecker arranged the horns on Allison's final Motown full-length. —*Richie Unterberger*

Hand Me Down My Moonshine / Inakustik ✦✦✦
Hand Me Down My Moonshine is a refreshing all-acoustic session from Allison that demonstrates a previously hidden side of his talent. Though there are some hard-rocking stomps, his playing reveals new grace and subtlety, making it a necessary purchase for all diehard fans. —*Thom Owens*

Mose Allison

b. Nov. 11, 1927, Tippo, MS
Piano, Vocals / Jazz Blues
Not unlike his namesake, Luther Allison, pianist Mose Allison has suffered from the "categorization problem," given his equally brilliant career. Although his boogie woogie and bebop-laden piano style is innovative and fresh sounding when it comes to blues and jazz, it is as a songwriter that Allison really shines. Allison's songs have been recorded by The Who ("Young Man Blues"), Leon Russell ("I'm Smashed"), and Bonnie Raitt ("Everybody's Cryin' Mercy"). Other admirers include Tom Waits, John Mayall, Georgie Fame, the Rolling Stones and Van Morrison. But because he's always played both blues and jazz, and not one to the exclusion of the other, his career has suffered. As he himself admits, he has a "category" problem that lingers to this day. "There's a lot of places I don't work because they're confused about what I do," he explained in a 1990 interview in *Goldmine* magazine. Despite the lingering confusion, Allison remains one of the finest songwriters in 20th century blues.

Born in Tippo, MS, on November 11, 1927, Allison's first exposure to blues on record was through Louis Jordan recordings, including "Outskirts of Town" and "Pinetop Blues." Allison credits Jordan as being a major influence on him, and also credits

Nat "King" Cole, Louis Armstrong and Fats Waller. He started out on trumpet but later switched to piano. In his youth, he had easy access, via the radio, to the music of Pete Johnson, Albert Ammons and Meade Lux Lewis. Allison also credits the songwriter Percy Mayfield, "The Poet Laureate of the Blues," as being a major inspiration on his songwriting.

After a stint in college and the Army, Allison's first professional gig was in Lake Charles, LA, in 1950. He returned to college to finish up at Louisiana State University in Baton Rouge, where he studied English and Philosophy, a far cry from his initial path as a chemical engineering major.

Allison began his recording career with the Prestige label in 1956, shortly after he moved to New York City. He recorded an album with Al Cohn and Bobby Brookmeyer, and then in 1957 got his own record contract. A big break was the opportunity to play with Cohn and Zoot Sims shortly after his arrival in New York, but he later became more well known after playing with saxophonist Stan Getz. After leaving Prestige Records, where he recorded now classic albums like *Back Country Suite* (1957), *Young Man Mose* (1958), and *Seventh Son* (1958-59), he moved to Columbia for two years before meeting up with Neshui Ertegun of Atlantic Records. He recalled that he signed his contract with Atlantic after about ten minutes in Neshui's office. Allison spent a big part of his recording career at Atlantic Records, where he became most friendly with Ertegun. After the company saw substantial growth and Allison was no longer working directly with him, he became discouraged and left. Allison has also recorded for Columbia (before he began his long relationship with Atlantic), and the Epic and Prestige labels.

Allison's discography is a lengthy one, and there are gems to be found on all of his albums, many of which can be found in vinyl shops. His output since 1957 has averaged at least one album a year until 1976, when he finished up at Atlantic with the classic *Your Mind Is on Vacation.* There was a gap of six years before he recorded again, this time for Elektra's Musician subsidiary in 1982, when he recorded *Middle Class White Boy.* Since 1987, he's been with Blue Note/Capitol. His debut for that label was *Ever Since the World Ended.* Allison has recorded some of the most creative material of his career with the Bluenote subsidiary of Capitol Records, including *My Backyard* (1992) and *The Earth Wants You* (1994), both produced by Ben Sidran. Also in 1994, Rhino Records released a boxed set, *Allison Wonderland. —Richard Skelly*

Mose Allison / Mar. 7, 1957–Nov. 8, 1957 / Prestige ✦✦✦
Reissue of two fine Allison albums, *Back Country Suite* (1957) and *Local Color* (1957). —*Michael Erlewine*

Back Country Suite / Mar. 7, 1957 / Prestige ✦✦✦
A wonderful date mixing his country blue warblings, dynamic piano playing, and cabaret-from-the-backwoods styles. —*Ron Wynn*

Mose Allison Plays for Lovers / Mar. 7, 1957–Feb. 13, 1959 / Prestige ✦✦✦
Selections from five albums from 1957 to 1959. —*Michael Erlewine*

The Seventh Son / Mar. 7, 1957–Mar. 19, 1957 / Prestige ✦✦✦✦
This is a compilation of cuts from Allison's albums from 1957 to 1959: *Back Country Suite, Local Color, Young Man Mose, Ramblin' with Mose, Creek Bank* and *Autumn Song.* —*AMG*

Local Color / Nov. 8, 1957 / Prestige ✦✦✦
Another fine date. This one's more strictly jazz style. —*Ron Wynn*

● **Greatest Hits** / Nov. 8, 1957–Feb. 13, 1959 / Prestige ✦✦✦✦
Basic, no-frills anthology of 13 of his better late-'50s Prestige sides, all of which feature his vocals. It has most of his most famous songs, particularly to listeners from a rock background, including his versions of "The Seventh Son," "Eyesight to the Blind" (covered by The Who on *Tommy,* though Sonny Boy Williamson did it before Allison), "Parchman Farm" (done by John Mayall), and "Young Man's Blues" (also covered by The Who). Were it not for the significant omission of "I'm Not Talking" (retooled by The Yardbirds), this would qualify as the basic collection for most listeners, although more thorough retrospectives are available (particularly Rhino's *Anthology*). *Greatest Hits* does include liner notes by Pete Townshend, originally penned for a 1972 collection. —*Richie Unterberger*

Ol' Devil Mose / 1958 / Prestige ✦✦✦
This was actually a two-album set combining songs from the

Allison releases *Rambling with Mose* and *Autumn Song.* They are trio dates, and feature prime Allison vocals, excellent solos, and great interaction between the pianist, bassist Addison Farmer, and drummer Ronnie Free. —*Ron Wynn*

Creek Bank / Jan. 24, 1958+Aug. 15, 1958 / Prestige ✦✦✦✦✦
When Mose Allison recorded his six early albums for Prestige, he was best-known as a bop-based pianist who occasionally sang. This single CD (which reissues in full *Young Man Mose* and *Creek Bank*) has 15 instrumentals including a rare appearance by Allison on trumpet ("Stroll"), but it is his five typically ironic vocals that are most memorable, particularly Allison's classic "The Seventh Son" and "If You Live." His piano playing, even with the Bud Powell influence, was beginning to become original and he successfully performs both revived swing songs and moody originals. —*Scott Yanow*

Autumn Song / Feb. 13, 1959 / Prestige ✦✦✦
Fine trio outing with the witty, always engaging Mose Allison in good vocal form and also adding sparkling piano accompaniment and solos. He's backed by Addison Farmer (Art's brother) on bass and Ronnie Free on drums. This set includes an early version of the signature song "Eyesight To The Blind." —*Ron Wynn*

I Don't Worry About a Thing / Mar. 15, 1962 / Rhino ✦✦✦✦✦
Mose Allison was already 34 and had recorded nine records as a leader before cutting his debut for Atlantic (which has been reissued on CD by Rhino), but this was his breakthrough date. One of jazz's greatest lyricists, at the time, Allison was making the transition from being a pianist who occasionally sang to becoming a vocalist who also played his own unusual brand of piano. In addition to the original versions of "Your Mind Is on Vacation," "I Don't Worry About a Thing (Because I Know Nothing Will Turn out Right)" and "It Didn't Turn out That Way," he sings bluish versions of two standards ("Meet Me at No Special Place" and "The Song Is Ended") and plays five instrumentals with his trio. There are only 33-1/2 minutes of music on this straight reissue of the original LP, but the set is one of Mose Allison's most significant recordings. —*Scott Yanow*

Mose Alive! / Oct. 22, 1965–Oct. 31, 1965 / Edsel ✦✦✦
Flashy piano and funny, inventive vocals. —*Ron Wynn*

☆ **Western Man** / Feb. 2, 1971–Mar. 4, 1971 / Atlantic ✦✦✦✦✦
A first-rate set. —*Ron Wynn*

Mose in Your Ear / Apr. 25, 1972–Apr. 26, 1972 / Atlantic ✦✦✦
Super on both ends: singing and playing. —*Ron Wynn*

Middle Class White Boy / Feb. 2, 1982 / Elcktra ✦✦✦✦✦
This Elektra LP finds the unique Mose Allison well-featured in a sextet also including Joe Farrell on tenor and flute and guitarist Phil Upchurch. Allison's unusual mixture of bop, country-blues and his own eccentric personality have long given him a distinctive sound on piano but it is his ironic vocals and superb lyric-writing abilities that make him a major figure. In addition to such originals as "How Does It Feel? (To Be Good Looking)," "I Don't Want Much" and "I'm Nobody Today," Allison brings new life to such standards as "When My Dreamboat Comes Home," "I'm Just a Lucky So-and-So" and "The Tennessee Waltz." —*Scott Yanow*

Lesson in Living / Jul. 21, 1982 / Elektra ✦✦✦
Lou Donaldson (as) brings a welcome blues and soul-jazz flavor to an already impressive cast and musical menu. —*Ron Wynn*

Ever Since the World Ended / May 11, 1987–Jun. 2, 1987 / Blue Note ✦✦✦
A wonderful update of his sound, with dauntless work by Mose. With Arthur Blythe (as), and Kenny Burrell (g). —*Ron Wynn*

My Backyard / Dec. 5, 1989–Dec. 7, 1989 / Blue Note ✦✦✦
A 1990 set. Good vocals, but the music's not as inspired. —*Ron Wynn*

Earth Wants You / Sep. 8, 1993–Sep. 9, 1993 / Blue Note ✦✦✦✦✦
Mose Allison, one of the top lyricists of the '90s, shows throughout this entertaining CD that his powers as a pianist and singer are also very much intact. The album introduces new classics in "Certified Senior Citizen," "This Ain't Me" and "Who's in, Who's Out." His voice is still in prime form and his piano playing remains unique. It is true that the guests on the set (guitarist John Scofield, altoist Joe Lovano, Bob Malach on tenor and trum-

peter Randy Brecker) are not necessary but Allison's performance makes this an excellent showcase for his music. —*Scott Yanow*

★ **Allison Wonderland: Anthology** / 1994 / Rhino ✦✦✦✦✦
Only Dave Frishberg and possibly Mark Murphy can rival Mose Allison when it comes to creative use of irony in lyric writing, and neither compares as an instrumentalist. He's a fine bop pianist able to play challenging instrumentals and eclectic enough to integrate country blues and gospel elements into his style. Allison's unique mix of down-home and uptown styles has made him a standout since the '50s. He's one of the few jazz musicians on Atlantic's roster ideally suited for Rhino's two-disc anthology format. Allison recorded so many different kinds of songs and was always as much, if not more, of a singles than an album artist. In addition, Rhino thankfully sequenced the selected songs—which span over 40 years, from 1957 to 1989, and include all of his best-known songs—chronologically. Allison does reflective duo and trio pieces, moves into uptempo combo numbers with a jump beat, then returns to the intimate small group sound. His delivery, timing, pacing, and ability to highlight key lyrics are all superb. The set includes such classics as "Back Country Blues," "Parchman Farm," "Western Man," and "Ever Since the World Ended," plus definitive covers of of Willie Dixon's "The Seventh Son" and Sonny Boy Williamson II's "Eyesight to the Blind." It's an essential introduction to Allison's catalog. —*Ron Wynn*

High Jinks!: Mose Allison Trilogy / 1994 / Columbia/Legacy ✦✦✦✦✦
Trilogy compiles the three original albums Mose Allison cut for Columbia and Epic Records during the early '60s (*Transfiguration of Hiram Brown, I Love the Life I Live, V-8 Ford Blues*), adding all the unreleased tracks and alternate takes from the sessions that comprised the three albums. In other words, it's the complete Mose Allison on Columbia. Although this material is not as well-known as the Prestige albums that preceded it or the Atlantic albums that followed, that doesn't mean it's not as good—in fact the best moments on these discs rival anything he's every recorded. —*Thom Owens*

Kip Anderson

b. 1930s, Anderson, SC
Vocals / Soul Blues
Without benefit of anything resembling a chart hit, Kip Anderson has amassed an impressive Southern soul legacy over the last three-plus decades. And how many other R&B artists were named after Rudyard Kipling, anyway?

Anderson still lives in the same rural region of South Carolina where he grew up. The singer learned his way around his folks' upright piano as a youth, composing his first tune in 1959. Anderson later bounced from label to label, cutting "I Will Cry" for producer Bobby Robinson in 1963, "That's When the Crying Begins" for ABC-Paramount the following year, and several gems for Checker in 1965-66 (including one of his best-known numbers, "A Knife & a Fork," in Muscle Shoals under the supervision of Rick Hall and Gene "Daddy G" Barge). By 1969, Anderson was inked to Nashville-based Excello, where he waxed the impassioned deep soul gem "I Went Off and Cried."

Anderson's hearty vocal talents have popped up most recently on Ichiban Records. He's cut two albums for the Atlanta firm and contributed the jolliest track of all, "Gonna Have a Merry Christmas," to the label's 1994 anthology *Ichiban Blues at Christmas Volume Three*. —*Bill Dahl*

● **A Dog Don't Wear No Shoes** / 1992 / Ichiban ✦✦✦✦✦
A Dog Don't Wear No Shoes is an energetic latter-day record from Kip Anderson that proves that the vocalist has lost very little of his power or charisma over the years. All of the music is in the deep soul tradition and he doesn't alter the formula much at all, but with a vocalist as gritty and impassioned as Anderson, that doesn't matter. —*Thom Owens*

A Knife & a Fork / 1993 / Ichiban ✦✦✦
A Knife & a Fork is nearly a carbon copy of its predecessor, *A Dog Don't Wear No Shoes*, but that's not necessarily a bad thing. Though the material is slightly weaker than the previous album, Kip Anderson makes the weakest songs somewhat convincing with his wonderful voice. —*Thom Owens*

Little Willie Anderson

b. May 21, 1920, d. Jun. 20, 1991
Vocals, Harmonica / Chicago Blues
Some folks called Chicago harpist Little Willie Anderson "Little Walter Jr.," so faithfully did Anderson's style follow that of the legendary harp wizard. But Anderson was already quite familiar with the rudiments of the harmonica before he ever hit the Windy City, having heard Sonny Boy Williamson, Robert Nighthawk, and Robert Jr. Lockwood around West Memphis.

Anderson came to Chicago in 1939, eventually turning pro as a sideman with Johnny Young. Anderson served as Walter's valet, chauffeur, and pal during the latter's heyday, but his slavish imitations probably doomed any recording possibilities for Anderson—until 1979, that is, when Blues on Blues label boss Bob Corritore escorted him into a Chicago studio and emerged with what amounts to Anderson's entire recorded legacy. —*Bill Dahl*

● **Swinging the Blues** / Jun. 1981 / Blues Over Blues ✦✦✦✦
Blues on Blues has been defunct for quite some time, but Earwig recently restored Anderson's only album to digital print. It's a loose, informal affair, Anderson's raw vocals and swinging harp backed by an all-star crew: guitarists Robert Jr. Lockwood, Sammy Lawhorn, and Jimmie Lee Robinson; bassist Willie Black, and drummer Fred Below. Anderson only revived one Walter standard, having brought a sheaf of his own intermittently derivative material to the session (although he does take a stab at bluesifying Lester Young's jazz classic "Lester Leaps In"). —*Bill Dahl*

Pink Anderson

b. Feb. 12, 1900, Spartanburg, SC, d. Oct. 12, 1974
Vocals, Guitar / Acoustic Blues
A good-natured finger-picking guitarist, Anderson played for about 30 years as part of a medicine show. He did make a couple of sides for Columbia in the late '20s with Simmie Dooley, but otherwise didn't record until a 1950 session, the results of which were issued on a Riverside LP that also included tracks by Gary Davis. Anderson went on to make some albums on his own after the blues revival commenced in the early '60s, establishing him as a minor but worthy exponent of the Piedmont school, versed in blues, ragtime, and folk songs. Anderson also became an unusual footnote in rock history when Syd Barrett, a young man in Cambridge, England, combined Pink's first name with the first name of another obscure bluesman (Floyd Council) to name his rock group, Pink Floyd, in the mid-'60s. —*Richie Unterberger*

Ballad & Folksinger, Vol. 3 / 1961 / Prestige/Bluesville ✦✦✦✦✦
As the title implies, this is more weighted toward folk and ballad material, along the lines of "John Henry" and "The Wreck of the Old 97," than straight traditional blues. Whether you prefer this or the *Carolina Blues Man* CD may thus depend on what your favorite sorts of genres are, though to this reviewer the performances on *Ballad & Folksinger* are more interesting and engaging. —*Richie Unterberger*

● **Carolina Blues Man, Vol. 1** / 1962 / Bluesville ✦✦✦✦✦
Anderson runs through both blues and folk standards on this relaxed and engaging, if somewhat slight, session. The CD reissue adds the track "Try Some of That," previously available on Bluesville's *Bawdy Blues* compilation. —*Richie Unterberger*

The Animals

Group / British Blues, Rock & Roll
One of the most important bands originating from England's R&B scene during the early '60s, The Animals were second only to The Rolling Stones in influence among R&B-based bands in the first wave of the British Invasion. The Animals had their origins in a Newcastle-based group called The Kansas City Five, whose membership included pianist Alan Price, drummer John Steel, and vocalist Eric Burdon. Price exited to join The Kontours in 1962, while Burdon went off to London. The Kontours, whose membership included Bryan "Chas" Chandler, eventually were transmuted into the Alan Price R&B Combo, with John Steel joining on drums. Burdon's return to Newcastle in early 1963 heralded his return to the lineup. The final member of the combo, guitarist Hilton Valentine, joined just in time for the recording of a self-produced EP under the band's new name, The

Animals. That record alerted Graham Bond to The Animals; he was likely responsible for pointing impresario Giorgio Gomelsky to the group.

Gomelsky booked the band into his Crawdaddy Club in London, and they were subsequently signed by Mickie Most, an independent producer who secured a contract with EMI's Columbia imprint. A studio session in February 1964 yielded their Columbia debut single, "Baby Let Me Take You Home" (adapted from "Baby Let Me Follow You Down"), which rose to number 21 on the British charts. For years, it has been rumored incorrectly that The Animals got their next single, "House of the Rising Sun," from Bob Dylan's first album, but more recently it has been revealed that, like "Baby Let Me Take You Home," the song came to them courtesy of Josh White. In any event, the song—given a new guitar riff by Valentine and a soulful organ accompaniment devised by Price—shot to the top of the U.K. and U.S. charts early that summer. This success led to a follow-up session that summer, yielding their first long-playing record, The Animals. Their third single, "I'm Crying," rose to number eight on the British charts. The group compiled an enviable record of Top Ten successes, including "Don't Let Me Be Misunderstood," and "We've Gotta Get Out of This Place," along with a second album, Animal Tracks.

In May of 1965, immediately after recording "We've Gotta Get Out of This Place," Alan Price left the band, citing fear of flying as the reason; subsequent biographies of the band have indicated that the reasons were less psychological. When "House of the Rising Sun" was recorded, using what was essentially a group arrangement, the management persuaded the band to put one person's name down as arranger. Price came up the lucky one, supposedly with the intention that the money from the arranger credit would be divided later on. The money was never divided, however, and as soon as it began rolling in, Price suddenly developed his fear of flying and exited the band. Others cite the increasing contentiousness between Burdon and Price over leadership of the group as the latter's reason for leaving the band. In any case, a replacement was recruited in the guise of Dave Rowberry.

In the meantime, the group was growing increasingly unhappy with the material they were being given to record by manager Mickie Most. Not only were the majority of these songs much too commercial for their taste, but they represented a false image of the band, even if many were successful. "It's My Life," a number seven British hit and a similar smash in America, caused The Animals to terminate their association with Most and with EMI Records. They moved over to Decca/London Records and came up with a more forceful, powerful sound on their first album for the new label, Animalisms. The lineup shifts continued, however—Steel exited in 1966, after recording Animalisms, and he was replaced by Barry Jenkins, formerly of The Nashville Teens. Chandler left in mid-1966 after recording "Don't Bring Me Down" and Valentine remained until the end of 1966, but essentially "Don't Bring Me Down" marked the end of the original Animals.

Burdon reformed the group under the aegis of Eric Burdon and the New Animals, with Jenkins on drums, John Weider on guitar and violin, Danny McCulloch on bass, and Vic Briggs on guitar. He remained officially a solo act for a time, releasing a collection of material called Eric Is Here in 1967. As soon as the contract with English Decca was up, Burdon signed with MGM for worldwide distribution, and the new lineup made their debut in mid-1967. Eric Burdon and the New Animals embraced psychedelia to the hilt amid The Summer of Love. By the end of 1968, Briggs and McCulloch were gone, to be replaced by Burdon's old friend keyboard player/vocalist Zoot Money and his longtime stablemate guitarist Andy Summers, while Weider switched to bass. Finally, in 1969, Burdon pulled the plug on what was left of the Animals. He hooked up with a Los Angeles-based group called War, and started a subsequent solo career that continues to this day.

The original Animals reunited in 1976 for a superb album called Before We Were So Rudely Interrupted, which picked up where Animalisms had left off a decade earlier, and which was well-received critically but failed to capture the public's attention. In 1983, a longer lasting reunion came about between all the original members, augmented with Zoot Money on keyboards. The resulting album, Ark, consisting of entirely new material, was well received by critics and charted surprisingly high, and a

world tour followed. By the end of the year and the heavy touring schedule, however, it was clear that this reunion was not going to be a lasting event. The quintet split up again, having finally let the other shoe drop on their careers and history, and walked away with some financial rewards, along with memories of two generations of rock fans cheering their every note. — Bruce Eder

The Animals [US] / 1964 / MGM ◆◆◆
Early blues-oriented material rounded out by a few more commercial tracks—this album is stronger than the British version, as it includes commercial tracks off their singles. —Bruce Eder

Animals [UK] / 1964 / Columbia ◆◆
The group's British debut long-player in England is a somewhat dry collection of blues and R&B covers, showing the group still trying to gain some confidence within the studio. Note: All material from this album appears on EMI's Complete Animals double-CD set. —Bruce Eder

In the Beginning / 1965 / Sundazed ◆◆◆
Recorded in December of 1963 at a live concert, this CD captures The Animals at their rawest and most animated on record, ripping ferociously through a bunch of standards (by Chuck Berry, James B. Oden et al.), playing the crowd and making snide comments about their London rivals The Rolling Stones, all with Sonny Boy Williamson II hanging somewhere around the stage. Sundazed has actually taped the original master to this oft-bootlegged piece of rock/blues history. —Bruce Eder

Animal Tracks [UK] / 1965 / Columbia ◆◆◆◆◆
The band's second British album displays far more energy and dexterity than its predecessor. Originals such as "For Miss Caulker" are paired up with excellent covers like "Bright Lights Big City," "I Ain't Got You," and "Roadrunner," along with Ray Charles' "Hallelujah I Love Her So" and "I Believe to My Soul." Note: All tracks appearing on this album are available on EMI's Complete Animals double CD. —Bruce Eder

Animalization / 1966 / PolyGram ◆◆◆◆◆
The best of the group's early albums, mostly sophisticated blues-based rock which, for the first time on a long-player, managed to capture the spontaneity of their live sound while also allowing them a chance to really stretch out in the studio. Around this time in the band's history, however, the albums get confusing—Animalization, released in September of 1966 by MGM in America, was simply the British Animalisms with three tracks missing, and four other songs ("Don't Bring Me Down," "Cheating," "Inside Looking Out," and "See See Rider") added. But MGM's Animalism, released two months later, consisted of tracks recorded in America during the original group's final U.S. tour that never saw the light of day in England. —Bruce Eder

Animalism [US] / 1966 / MGM ◆◆◆
The last gasp of the original Animals, albeit with Barry Jenkins on the drums in place of John Steel and Dave Rowberry on the ivories in lieu of Alan Price. A superb collection of rock numbers, as advanced from the band's early classics as The Stones' Aftermath repertory was from "It's All Over Now." Loud, intense, well-focused, hard-rocking blues. —Bruce Eder

Animalisms / 1966 / Decca ◆◆◆◆◆
Very similar in line-up to the American Animalization, this is probably the group's best non-compilation album, with a finely developed R&B sound throughout and excellent playing, all yielding an incomparable collection of good, solid, bluesy, ballsy rock numbers, highlighted by "Gin House Blues" and "Don't Bring Me Down." —Bruce Eder

The Animals with Sonny Boy Williamson / 1988 / Charly ◆◆
Another repackaging of the group's early live recording with American blues great Sonny Boy Williamson, in moderately good sound—the group's set sounds better on Sundazed's In the Beginning. —Bruce Eder

★ **The Best of the Animals** / 1988 / ABKCO ◆◆◆◆◆
The original Animals' American hits, including "House of the Rising Sun," "Don't Let Me Be Misunderstood," "It's My Life," and "We Gotta Get Out of This Place," in a compilation originally released in 1965. The lineup of songs is strong but the sound is indifferent—the British Complete Animals covers the same territory and a lot more to much greater effect, at only twice the cost with three times the music and infinitely superior sound and notes. —Bruce Eder

Inside Looking Out: The 1965-1966 Sessions / 1990 / Sequel
✦✦✦✦✦

Together with the double-CD *The Complete Animals*, *Inside Looking Out* forms a complete retrospective of the great British Invasion band. This 22-song compilation features all of the essential recordings cut by the group in 1965 and 1966 after they broke with their original producer Mickie Most, and before Eric Burdon dissolved the core of the original lineup to pursue solo stardom with an Animals group featuring entirely different musicians. These tracks were perhaps more soul-oriented than their previous recordings, but the group still burns on the hits "Inside Looking Out" and "Don't Bring Me Down." Despite the absence of original keyboardist Alan Price, the group continued to showcase Burdon's passionate vocals and a burning, vibrant organ (by Price's replacement Dave Rowberry) on both renowned and obscure R&B tunes, with an occasional original thrown in. Besides the entirety of their final British LP "Animalisms" (from 1966) and the above-mentioned singles, the CD includes the hits "Help Me Girl" and "See See Rider" (credited to "Eric Burdon and the Animals," these were possibly Burdon solo records). The four tracks from their first release, an independently released 1963 EP featuring primitive R&B standards, are small but noteworthy bonus cuts that close this collection. —*Richie Unterberger*

★ **The Complete Animals** / Jul. 1990 / EMI ✦✦✦✦
The title is a bit of a misnomer; this double CD does include the complete sessions that The Animals recorded with producer Mickie Most in 1964 and 1965. The 40 songs capture the band at their peak, including most of their best and biggest hits: "House Of The Rising Sun," "Don't Let Me Be Misunderstood," "Bring It On Home To Me," "We Gotta Get Out Of This Place," "I'm Crying," "It's My Life," and "Boom Boom." Most of the rest of the tunes don't match the excellence of these smashes, though they're solid. The great majority of them are covers of vintage R&B/rock tunes by Chuck Berry, Fats Domino, and the like, which aren't quite as durable as reinterpretations from the same era by The Stones and Yardbirds. When they hit the mark, though, The Animals produced some great album tracks that have been mostly forgotten by time, such as "I'm Mad Again" (originally by John Lee Hooker), "Worried Life Blues," and "Bury My Body." After leaving Most, the group would maintain their peak for another year or so (this period is represented on the fine import collection *Inside Looking Out*) despite the departure of one of rock's all-time finest organists, Alan Price. This compilation has everything that Price recorded with the group, including four previously unreleased cuts and the non-LP Eric Burdon original on the B-side of "It's My Life," "I'm Gonna Change The World." —*Richie Unterberger*

Billy Boy Arnold

b. Sep. 16, 1935, Chicago, IL
Vocals, Harmonica / Electric Chicago Blues
Talk about a comeback! After too many years away from the studio, Chicago harpist Billy Boy Arnold has returned to action in a big way with two fine albums for Alligator: 1993's *Back Where I Belong* and 1995's *Eldorado Cadillac*. Retaining his youthful demeanor despite more than four decades of blues experience, Arnold's wailing harp and sturdy vocals remain in top-flight shape following the lengthy recording layoff.

Born in Chicago rather than in Mississippi (as many of his musical forefathers were), young Billy Boy gravitated right to the source in 1948. He summoned up the courage to knock on the front door of his idol, harmonica great John Lee "Sonny Boy" Williamson, who resided nearby. Sonny Boy kindly gave the lad a couple of harp lessons, but their relationship was quickly severed when Williamson was tragically murdered. Still in his teens, Arnold cut his debut 78 for the extremely obscure Cool logo in 1952. "Hello Stranger" went nowhere but gave him his nickname when its label unexpectedly read "Billy Boy Arnold."

Arnold made an auspicious connection when he joined forces with Bo Diddley and played on the shave-and-a-haircut-beat specialist's two-sided 1955 debut smash "Bo Diddley"/"I'm a Man" for Checker. That led, in a roundabout way, to Billy Boy's signing with rival Vee-Jay Records (the harpist mistakenly believed Leonard Chess didn't like him). Arnold's "I Wish You Would," utilizing that familiar Bo Diddley beat, sold well and inspired a later famous cover by the Yardbirds. That renowned British blues-rock group also took a liking to another Arnold classic on Vee-Jay, "I Ain't Got You." Other Vee-Jay standouts by Arnold included "Prisoner's Plea" and "Rockinitis," but by 1958, his tenure at the label was over.

Other than a Samuel Charters-produced *More Blues on the South Side*, Arnold's profile diminished over the years in his hometown (though European audiences enjoyed him regularly). Fortunately, that's changed: *Back Where I Belong* restored this Chicago harp master to prominence, and *Eldorado Cadillac* drove him into the winner's circle a second time. —*Bill Dahl*

More Blues on the South Side / 1964 / Prestige ✦✦✦✦
Over half a decade away from the studio didn't hinder Arnold one bit on this 1963 session. His still-youthful vocals, strong harp, and imaginative songs are very effectively spotlighted, backed by a mean little Chicago combo anchored by guitarist Mighty Joe Young and pianist Lafayette Leake. The CD reissue adds a previously unreleased, "Playing with the Blues." —*Bill Dahl*

Blow the Back Off It / 1975 / Red Lightnin' ✦✦✦
Bootleg vinyl collection of the harpist's Vee-Jay stuff suffering from truly rotten sound quality. Its only saving grace is the appearance of Arnold's ultra-rare 1953 debut 78, "Hello Stranger," but its aural reproduction is worst of all (you can barely discern the music from the scratches and noise). —*Bill Dahl*

● **I Wish You Would** / 1980 / Charly ✦✦✦✦✦
The harpist's indispensable dozen 1955-1957 waxings for Vee-Jay, including the classic "I Wish You Would" and its blues-soaked flip "I Was Fooled" (stinging guitar by Jody Williams), the often-covered (but never bettered, except maybe by Jimmy Reed) "I Ain't Got You," and the vicious "Don't Stay Out All Night" and "You've Got Me Wrong." Also included are a pair of rarities Arnold cut for Chess as Diddley's sideman; "Sweet on You Baby" and "You Got to Love Me" feature big bad Bo on guitar and the ever-dynamic Jerome Green shakin' the maracas. —*Bill Dahl*

Crying and Pleading / 1980 / Charly ✦✦✦✦✦
This vinyl collection of Arnold's complete Vee-Jay output is mid-'50s Chicago blues at its best. Includes "I Wish You Would," "I Was Fooled," "Rockinitis" and the original "I Ain't Got You," later covered by The Yardbirds. (Import) —*Cub Koda*

Ten Million Dollars / 1984 / Evidence ✦✦
Recording opportunities were scarce for Arnold stateside in 1984. But over in France, Black & Blue welcomed the harpist into their studios to cut this set, backed by guitarist Jimmy Johnson's professional outfit. Only a handful of originals here; the set is predominated by hoary standards such as "My Babe," "Just a Little Bit," "Last Night," and "I Done Got Over It" (but at least they're played with a bit more panache than usual). —*Bill Dahl*

Back Where I Belong / 1993 / Alligator ✦✦✦✦
Indeed he is. Recorded in Los Angeles with a crew of young acolytes offering spot-on backing (guitarists Zach Zunis and Rick Holmstrom acquit themselves well), Arnold eases back into harness with a remake of "I Wish You Would" before exposing some fine new originals (the chunk Chuck Berry-styled rocker "Move on Down the Road" is a stomping standout) and an homage to his old mentor Sonny Boy (a romping "Shake the Boogie"). —*Bill Dahl*

Going to Chicago / 1995 / Testament ✦✦✦
Uneven but intriguing 1966 collection, most of it previously unreleased. The first half-dozen sides are the best, full of ringing West Side-styled guitar licks by Mighty Joe Young and Jody Williams and Arnold's insinuating vocals (he rocks "Baby Jane" with a Chuck Berry-inspired fury). An odd drumless trio backs Arnold on the next seven selections, which get a little sloppy at times but retain period interest nonetheless. —*Bill Dahl*

Eldorado Cadillac / 1995 / Alligator ✦✦✦✦
This time around, Arnold recorded in his hometown with another gang of well-seasoned players behind him (guitar duties were ably handled by ex-Muddy Waters bandsman Bob Margolin and James Wheeler), retaining the same high standards set by his previous offering. Seven originals are joined by solid covers of Roosevelt Sykes' downbeat "Sunny Road" and Ray Charles' streetwise "It Should Have Been Me." —*Bill Dahl*

Kokomo Arnold (James "Kokomo" Arnold)

b. Feb. 15, 1901, Lovejoys Station, GA, d. Nov. 8, 1968, Chicago, IL
Guitar, Vocals / Acoustic Blues
A popular recording artist of the '30s, James "Kokomo" Arnold

was a left-handed bottleneck guitarist who usually recorded solo, occasionally with piano accompaniment. His first Chicago session (Decca, 1934) produced the widely covered "Milk Cow Blues" and "Old Original Kokomo Blues" (the model for Robert Johnson's "Sweet Home Chicago"), as well as the first appearance on record of the classic "I believe I'll dust my broom" line (in "Sagefield Woman Blues"). Critic Hugues Panassi wrote, "Arnold is one of the greatest blues singers ever recorded." Arnold continued to play for a few years in Chicago after his last session (1938) but later took a job in a steel mill, disillusioned with the music business. Interviewed by two Frenchmen in 1959, Arnold said, "I'm finished with music and that mad way of life." —*Jim O'Neal*

Complete Recorded Works, Vols. 1-4 / 1991 / Document ✦✦✦
The four-volume set *Complete Recorded Works* contains all the material slide guitarist Kokomo Arnold recorded during the '30s. Arnold was one of the most distinctive and influential blues singers of the decade, but his most essential material is compiled on Yazoo's single-disc *Bottleneck Guitar of the 30's.* That leaves this multi-disc set—which is available in four separate volumes— as the province of historians and completists. For those listeners, *Complete Recorded Works* is invaluable, featuring a wealth of rare, unreleased material, including several alternate takes. However, casual fans—and listeners that have only a curiosity about solo acoustic blues—will find that Yazoo's compilation is preferable. —*Thom Owens*

Kokomo Arnold/Peetie Wheatstraw / Blues Classics ✦✦✦✦✦
Eight tracks each by Kokomo Arnold and Peetie Wheatstraw. Includes "Milk Cow Blues." —*Michael Erlewine*

★ **Bottleneck Guitar of the 30's** / Yazoo ✦✦✦✦✦
Bottleneck Guitar of the 30's collects all of Kokomo Arnold's classic tracks from the '30s, including the classic "Milk Cow Blues." It's an essential item for a blues library—within these sides lay the groundwork for the Delta and Chicago blues to come, from Robert Johnson to Elmore James. —*Thom Owens*

B

Etta Baker

b. 1913, Caldwell County, NC
Banjo, Fiddle, Guitar, Piano, Vocals / Acoustic Country Blues
Etta Baker's first recordings appeared on a 1956 set called *Instrumental Music of the Southern Appalachians*, but only in recent years has her beautiful finger-picked acoustic blues been presented onstage and once again on record. Her traditional instrumental performances draw on old folk tunes such as "John Henry" and "Lost John" as well as on early blues, breakdowns, rags, and spirituals. *Blues & Rhythm*'s Robert Tilling noted that most of her present-day repertoire is so timeless it "could have been recorded 80 years ago." —*Jim O'Neal*

One-Dime Blues / 1991 / Rounder ✦✦✦✦✦
Guitarist/vocalist Etta Baker hadn't made any recordings or even been in a studio since 1956 before making the 20 numbers comprising this CD. But judging from the arresting vocals, prickly accompaniment and commanding presence she displays on each song, it seems as if she had been cutting tracks daily. Baker moves from sassy and combative blues tunes like "Never Let Your Deal Go Down" and "But On The Other Hand Baby" to chilling numbers like "Police Dog Blues," novelty tunes, double-entendre cuts, folk pieces, and even country-flavored material. Singing and playing in vintage Piedmont style with a two- and three-finger technique, Etta Baker offers timeless, memorable performances. —*Ron Wynn*

LaVern Baker

b. Nov. 11, 1929, Chicago, IL
Vocals / R&B
LaVern Baker was one of the sexiest divas gracing the mid-'50s rock 'n' roll circuit, boasting a brashly seductive vocal delivery tailor-made for belting the catchy novelties "Tweedlee Dee," "Bop-Ting-A-Ling," and "Tra La La" for Atlantic Records during rock's first wave of prominence.

Born Delores Williams, she was singing at the Club DeLisa on Chicago's South side at age 17, decked out in raggedy attire and billed as "Little Miss Sharecropper" (the same handle that she made her recording debut under for RCA Victor with Eddie "Sugarman" Penigar's band in 1949). She changed her name briefly to Bea Baker when recording for Okeh in 1951 with Maurice King's Wolverines, then settled on the first name of LaVern when she joined Todd Rhodes' band as featured vocalist in 1952 (she fronted Rhodes' aggregation on the impassioned ballad "Trying" for Cincinnati's King Records).

LaVern signed with Atlantic as a solo in 1953, debuting with the incendiary "Soul on Fire." The coy, Latin-tempoed "Tweedlee Dee" was a smash in 1955 on both the R&B and pop charts, although her impact on the latter was blunted when squeaky-clean Georgia Gibbs covered it for Mercury. An infuriated Baker filed suit over the whitewashing, but she lost. By that time, though, her star had ascended: Baker's "Bop-Ting-A-Ling," "Play It Fair," "Still," and the rocking "Jim Dandy" all vaulted into the R&B Top Ten over the next couple of years.

Baker's statuesque figure and charismatic persona made her a natural for TV and movies. She co-starred on the historic R&B revue segment on Ed Sullivan's TV program in November of 1955 and did memorable numbers in Alan Freed's rock movies *Rock, Rock, Rock* and *Mr. Rock & Roll.* Her Atlantic records remained popular throughout the decade—she hit big in 1958

with the ballad "I Cried a Tear," adopted a pseudo-sanctified bellow for the rousing Leiber & Stoller-penned gospel sendup "Saved" in 1960, and cut a Bessie Smith tribute album before leaving Atlantic in 1964. A brief stop at Brunswick Records (where she did a sassy duet with Jackie Wilson, "Think Twice") preceded a late-'60s jaunt to entertain the troops in Vietnam. She became seriously ill after the trip and was hospitalized, eventually settling far out of the limelight in the Philippines. She remained there for 22 years, running an NCO club on Subic Bay for the U.S. government.

Finally, in 1988, Baker returned stateside to star at Atlantic's 40th anniversary bash at New York's Madison Square Garden. That led to a soundtrack appearance in the film *Dick Tracy*, a starring role in the Broadway musical *Black & Blue* (replacing her ex-Atlantic labelmate Ruth Brown), a nice comeback disc for DRG (*Woke up This Mornin'*), and a memorable appearance at the Chicago Blues Festival. Unfortunately, illness has reportedly curtailed her musical pursuits of late. —*Bill Dahl*

LaVern Baker / 1957 / Atlantic ✦✦✦✦✦
Includes her hits "Tweedlee Dee" and "Jim Dandy." Some formulaic material (like "Tra-La-La," an obvious attempt at recapturing "Tweedlee Dee") is included, but there's some good stuff too. —*George Bedard*

Sings Bessie Smith / Jan. 27, 1958 / Atlantic ✦✦✦✦✦
This is an album that should not have worked. LaVern Baker (a fine R&B singer) is joined by all-stars from mainstream jazz (including trumpeter Buck Clayton, trombonist Vic Dickenson, tenor saxophonist Paul Quinichette and pianist Nat Pierce) for 12 songs associated with the great '20s blues singer Bessie Smith. Despite the potentially conflicting styles, this project is quite successful and often exciting. The arrangements by Phil Moore, Nat Pierce and Ernie Wilkins do not attempt to recreate the original recordings, Baker sings in her own style (rather than trying to emulate Bessie Smith) and the hot solos work well with her vocals. —*Scott Yanow*

Blues Ballads / 1959 / Atlantic ✦✦✦
Before she became a successful rock and roll vocalist, LaVern Baker did straight jazz and gutbucket blues, and that's what she's singing here. These tunes didn't have any crossover appeal, but they're gritty, unpolished, and sung with the intensity and energy that made Baker's later material so memorable. —*Ron Wynn*

Precious Memories / 1959 / Atlantic ✦✦✦
LaVern Baker sings gospel with passion, exuberance, and reverence on this '59 session. She is backed by a small combo with the Alex Bradford singers and sounds more magnificent and moving than at any time she had done jazz, blues or R&B. This one is very hard to find and has not as of yet been reissued on CD. —*Ron Wynn*

Saved / 1961 / Atlantic ✦✦✦
Early '60s jazz and blues material by LaVern Baker. She returned in the '60s to the songs she had cut prior to her rock and roll success. There is an interesting crew of guest stars on these sessions, among them Phil Spector on guitar, Sticks Evans on bass drums, and Taft Jordan on trumpet. Baker had a hit with a single from some earlier sessions, "You're the Boss with Jimmy Ricks." This song was issued on a single, but there's no listing for any album. —*Ron Wynn*

The Best of LaVern Baker / 1963 / JCI ✦
Simply awful budget ripoff with horrendous sound. Get the Atlantic! —*Ron Wynn*

Her Greatest Hits / 1971 / Atlantic ✦✦✦
This 14-track compilation album of songs LaVern Baker recorded for Atlantic Records between 1953 and 1962 was the most
thorough best-of in her catalog from the time of its release until
the appearance of *Soul on Fire* in 1991. That is not to say that it
was consistently available—it went out of print in the 1970s—or
that it constitutes a complete portrait of Baker's work for the
label. Of her 19 pop hits on Atlantic, only seven are included; of
her 20 Atlantic R&B hits, only eight are here. The album does
include some of her biggest hits—"Tweedlee Dee," "Jim Dandy,"
"I Cried A Tear," "Saved," "See See Rider"—but it must be considered a bare minimum, especially now in light of the far more
complete *Soul on Fire*. —*William Ruhlmann*

● **Soul on Fire: The Best of LaVern Baker** / 1991 / Rhino ✦✦✦✦✦
The cream of this vivacious 1950s R&B belter's Atlantic catalog
comprises this 20-track hits collection. Includes Baker's bouncy
"Tweedlee Dee," the storming rockers "Jim Dandy" and "Bop-Ting-
A-Ling," the pseudo-gospel raveup "Saved," and Baker's torchy
blues ballads "Soul on Fire" and "I Cried a Tear." She imparts "See
See Rider" with a lighthearted reading that contrasts starkly with
Chuck Willis' Atlantic smash of a few years before. —*Bill Dahl*

LaVern Baker Live in Hollywood '91 / 1992 / Rhino ✦✦✦
LaVern Baker Live in Hollywood '91 shows Baker can still belt out
a song, nearly 40 years after her hit-making heyday. She's returned
to the jazz and jazzy blues sound of her youth. —*Ron Wynn*

Woke up This Mornin' / Apr. 1992 / DRG ✦✦✦
Credible comeback effort that spotlights Baker's still-seductive
pipes on a program of mostly familiar standards—everything from
the straightahead blues "Rock Me Baby" to the Stax-era "Knock on
Wood" and "I Can't Turn You Loose" to the Bee Gees' "To Love
Somebody" and Carole King's sappy "You've Got a Friend." Supple
backing by a cadre of New York session aces—guitarist Cornell
Dupree, drummer Bernard Purdie, keyboardist Paul Griffin, bassist
Chuck Rainey—adds the proper grooves for each. —*Bill Dahl*

Blues Side of Rock 'n' Roll / 1993 / Star Club ✦✦✦✦✦
This import may be of slightly dubious origins (sounds like
everything was dubbed from vinyl, though sound quality is quite
acceptable), but it delves a lot deeper into LaVern Baker's
Atlantic discography (26 cuts) than Atlantic's own CD: "Tra La La,"
"Voodoo Voodoo," "Hey Memphis" (Baker's sequel to Elvis' "Little Sister"), and a
hellacious version of "He's a Real Gone Guy" sporting a vicious
King Curtis sax break. —*Bill Dahl*

Long John Baldry

b. Jan. 12, 1941, London, England
Harmonica, Vocals / Electric British Blues
Like Cliff Richard, Chris Farlowe, Slade, Blur, and eel pie, Long
John Baldry is one of those peculiarly British phenomenons that
doggedly resists American translation. As a historical figure, he
has undeniable importance. When he began singing as a teenag-
er in the 1950s, he was one of the first British vocalists to per-
form folk and blues music. In the early '60s, he sang in the band
of British blues godfather Alexis Korner, Blues Incorporated,
which also served as a starting point for future rock stars Mick
Jagger, Jack Bruce, and others. As a member of Blues
Incorporated, he contributed to the first British blues album,
R&B at the Marquee (1962). He then joined the Cyril Davies
R&B All Stars, taking over the group (renamed Long John
Baldry and His Hoochie Coochie Men after Davies' death in
early 1964. This band featured Rod Stewart as a second vocalist,
and also employed Geoff Bradford (who had been in an embryonic version of the Rolling Stones) on guitar.
In the mid-'60s, he helped form Steampacket, a proto-super-
group that also featured Stewart, Julie Driscoll, and Brian Auger.
When Steampacket broke up, he fronted Bluesology, the band
that gave keyboardist Reg Dwight—soon to become Elton John—
his first prestigious gig. He was a well-liked figure on the
London club circuit, and in fact the Beatles took him on as a
guest on one of their 1964 British TV specials, at a time when
the Fab Four could have been no bigger, and Baldry was virtually unknown.
All of these famous associations, alas, don't change the hard
fact that Baldry wasn't much of a singer. His dry-as-dust, charm-
less croak approximated what Manfred Mann's Paul Jones
(whom Baldry resembled slightly physically) may have sounded

like while recovering from a tonsillectomy. His greatest commercial success came not with blues, but unbearably gloppy
orchestrated pop ballads that echoed Engelbert Humperdinck.
The 1967 single "Let the Heartaches Begin" reached number one
in Britain, and Baldry had several other small British hits in the
late '60s, the biggest of which was "Mexico" (1968). (None of
these made an impression in the U.S.)
The commercial success of his ballads led Baldry to forsake
the blues on record for a few years. Cruel as it may be to say, it
wasn't much of a loss to the blues world; Baldry's early blues
recordings don't hold a candle even to second-tier acts like
Graham Bond, let alone the Stones or the Bluesbreakers. He
returned to blues and rock in 1971 on *It Ain't Easy*, for which
Rod Stewart and Elton John shared the production duties. The
album contained a tiny American chart item, "Don't Try to Lay
No Boogie-Woogie on the King of Rock'n'Roll," and Stewart and
John split the production once again on the 1972 follow-up,
Everything Stops for Tea. Baldry never caught on as an international figure, though, and by 1980 had become a Canadian citizen. If he was heard at all after that, it was usually via commercial voiceovers, or as the voice of Captain Robotnick in children's
cartoons. —*Richie Unterberger*

● **Long John's Blues** / 1964 / Ascot ✦✦
Stacked up against other British blues/R&B albums of the
time, this is a distinctly lower-echelon effort, much stiffer and
more routine than the recordings of The Stones, John Mayall,
Graham Bond, Duffy Power, and others. What made early
British efforts in this style exciting was the sense of risk-tak-
ing, even recklessness. Baldry and the Hoochie Coochie Men
are totally lacking in that department, displaying a by-the-
numbers approach in arrangements (particularly in the trad
piano rolls) and material selection, which consists almost
entirely of overdone standards like "My Babe," "Got My Mojo
Working," and "Goin' Down Slow." Stacked up against Baldry's
own work, though, this qualifies as his most "essential" effort,
if only because it is for his contributions to the British blues
scene that he is most remembered. This is the most accurate
reflection of his work in that field, and Baldry is in better voice
here than he is on much of his later '60s work. The album is
still mediocre or worse, although it does feature Geoff
Bradford (who played in a very early precursor to The Rolling
Stones) on guitar. The BGO CD reissue combines *Long John's
Blues* and the 1966 LP *Looking at Long John* on one disc. —
Richie Unterberger

Baldry's Out! / 1979 / EMI ✦✦✦
On Stage Tonight—Baldry's Out! nicely rectifies a 30-year oversight—the gentleman had never previously released a live
recording. Captured in Germany, the disc blends the strongest
tracks from Baldry's *It Still Ain't Easy* comeback album with
updated past greats. And it just wouldn't be Baldry (especially
live) without the ferocious backing of longtime soulmate Kathi
McDonald. While Baldry's blues can sometimes be a tad too
"polite," *On Stage Tonight* captures that unique smoky growl in
top form. —*Roch Parisien*

● **Long John's Blues / Looking at Long John** / 1995 / BGO
✦✦✦✦✦
Long John Baldry's first two albums are combined on this single
disc compilation. —*AMG*

Marcia Ball

b. Mar. 20, 1949, Orange, TX
Piano, Vocals / Modern Electric Texas Blues
Pianist, singer and songwriter Marcia Ball is a living example of
how east Texas blues meets southwest Louisiana swamp rock.
Ball was born March 20, 1949, in Orange, TX, but grew up
across the border in Vinton, LA. That town is squarely in the
heart of "the Texas triangle," an area that includes portions of
both states and that has produced some of our country's greatest blues talents: Janis Joplin, Johnny and Edgar Winter, Queen
Ida Guillory, Lonnie Brooks, Zachary Richard, Clifton Chenier
and Kenny Neal, to name a few. Ball's earliest awareness of blues
came over the radio, where she heard people like Irma Thomas,
Professor Longhair and Etta James, all of whom she now credits
as influences. She began playing piano at age five, learning from
her grandmother and aunt and also taking formal lessons from
a teacher.
Ball entered Louisiana State University in the late '60s as an

English major. In college, she played in a psychedelic rock 'n' roll band, Gum. In 1970, Ball and her first husband were headed west in their car to San Francisco, but the car needed repairs in Austin, where they had stopped off to visit one of their former bandmates. After hearing, seeing and tasting some of the music, sights and food in Austin, the two decided to stay there. Ball has been based in Austin since then.

Her piano style, which mixes equal parts boogie woogie with zydeco and Louisiana swamp rock, is best exemplified on her series of excellent recordings for the Rounder label. They include *Soulful Dress* (1984), *Hot Tamale Baby* (1986), *Gatorhythms* (1989) and *Blue House* (1994). Also worthy of checking out is her collaboration with Angela Strehli and Lou Ann Barton on the Antone's label, *Dreams Come True* (1990). Ball, like her peer Angela Strehli, is an educated business woman, fully aware of all the realities of the record business. Ball never records until she feels she's got a batch of top-notch, quality songs. Most of the songs on her albums are her own creations, so songwriting is a big part of her job description.

Although Ball is a splendid piano player and a more than adequate vocalist, "the songwriting process is the most fulfilling part of the whole deal for me," she said in a 1994 interview, "so I always keep my ears and eyes open for things I might hear or see....I like my songs to go back to blues in some fashion." As much a student of the music as she is a player, some of Ball's albums include covers of material by O.V. Wright, Dr. John, Joe Ely, Clifton Chenier and Shirley and Lee.

Ball, who's established herself as an important player in the club scenes in both New Orleans and Austin, continues to work at festivals and clubs throughout the U.S., Canada and Europe. —*Richard Skelly*

Soulful Dress / 1984 / Rounder ✦✦✦
Marcia Ball got things started in a celebratory fashion on her debut Rounder release, doing the title track in a taunting, challenging manner aided by flashy guitar riffs from Stevie Ray Vaughan. From there, she artfully displayed other sides of her personality, from dismayed to defiant and assured. Her rendition of "Soul on Fire" was heartfelt, but didn't approach the majestic quality of LaVern Baker's original. She did much better on "I Don't Want No Man," striking the air of disdain and dissatisfaction that Bobby "Blue" Bland immortalized on "I Don't Want No Woman"; guitarist Kenny Ray even got the Wayne Bennett licks down perfectly. —*Ron Wynn*

Hot Tamale Baby / 1986 / Rounder ✦✦✦✦✦
Marcia Ball solidified the favorable impression made with her debut Rounder effort with this rousing second outing. She dedicated it to the late King of Zydeco, Clifton Chenier, and was backed by a fine band of veteran pros that included saxophonist Alvin Tyler. Ball ripped through Booker T. Jones' soul gem "Never Like This Before" and Chenier's title composition, while also demonstrating her own facility with R&B on "That's Enough Of That Stuff" and "Love's Spell." She came close, but didn't quite hit the mark on O.V. Wright's "I'm Gonna Forget About You," turning in a more than acceptable rendition that still didn't approach the original. But other than that one misstep, which she compensated for with a charged version of "I Don't Know," Marcia Ball proved that her debut was no fluke. —*Ron Wynn*

● **Gator Rhythms** / 1989 / Rounder ✦✦✦✦✦
Marcia Ball explored R&B and honky-tonk country on this album, keeping her blues chops in order while expanding her repertoire. She included a pair of tunes by country vocalist Lee Roy Parnell, "What's A Girl To Do" and "Red Hot," doing both in a feisty, attacking fashion. She also was challenging and upbeat on Dr. John's "How You Carry On" and "Find Another Fool." Her third Rounder album was her most entertaining and dynamic, as Ball became less of an interpreter and more of an individualist. —*Ron Wynn*

Dreams Come True / 1990 / Antone's ✦✦✦
Dreams Come True is an all-star session by vocalists Marcia Ball, Lou Ann Barton and Angela Strehli. The three women sing with a band led by Dr. John and the session features guest appearances by such luminaries as David "Fathead" Newman and Jimmie Vaughan. The music is straight out of the Texas school of roadhouse R&B and blues boogie, but it's delivered with a gritty, heartfelt edge, particularly on the part of the three vocalists. *Dreams Come True* may follow formula, but it's followed

with style and affection, which makes it a very enjoyable listen. —*Thom Owens*

Blue House / 1994 / Rounder ✦✦✦

Barbecue Bob (Robert Hicks)

b. Sep. 11, 1902, Walnut Grove, GA, **d.** Oct. 21, 1931, Lithonia, GA
Guitar, Vocals / Acoustic Country Blues
Barbecue Bob may be a familiar name to some blues fans today because at least two young White musicians have adopted the name, but back in the '20s the original Barbecue Bob (Robert Hicks) was a big name on the Black "race-records" scene. Recording for Columbia from 1927 to 1930, Hicks was the most popular of the Atlanta blues guitarists of his time, and Columbia's best-selling bluesman. But Barbecue Bob died of pneumonia at the age of 29, and some of his contemporaries like Blind Willie McTell are much better known to modern-day audiences. Most of Bob's recordings were solo outings featuring rhythmic 12-string bottleneck-guitar work and original lyrical themes. In historian Stephen Calt's opinion, "For sheer musical verve and punch, Hicks easily rivals Charley Patton." —*Jim O'Neal*

Brownskin Gal / 1978 / Agram ✦✦✦
A boxed import set with a variety of blues, hokum, and comedy routines. Includes an 80-page bio and transcription book. Unfortunately, this compilation is marred by weak sound quality. —*Barry Lee Pearson*

● **Chocolate to the Bone** / Yazoo ✦✦✦✦✦
Fourteen selections from popular '20s Atlanta 12-string slide artist Robert Hicks, aka Barbecue Bob. A fine American collection, with good sound quality. —*Barry Lee Pearson*

Complete Recorded Works, Vols. 1-3 / Document ✦✦✦
Over the course of three CDs, Document Records compiled every note Barbecue Bob recorded in the late '20s. The first volume covers everything he cut between March 25, 1927 and April 13, 1928; the second, April 21, 1928 to November 3, 1929; the third November 6, 1929 to December 8, 1930. In between the first song on the set—which has been issued as individual volumes—and the last song, there is some incredible country blues; there was a reason why he was among the most popular bluesmen of his time. Although there is too much music here for any one but dedicated country blues fans to be able to digest and the sound quality isn't terrific (which isn't surprising, considering that the series had to be mastered from 78s), Document's *Complete Recorded Works in Chronological Order* is an excellent historical document that happens to contain music that still sounds fresh and vital decades after it was recorded. —*Thom Owens*

John Henry Barbee

b. Nov. 14, 1905, Henning, TN, **d.** Nov. 3, 1964, Chicago, IL
Guitar, Vocals / Acoustic Country Blues
A strong storyteller and good guitarist, John Henry Barbee learned music playing in various homes throughout Henning, TN as a youth. He worked for a short time with John Lee Williamson (Sonny Boy Williamson I) in 1934, then began playing with Sunnyland Slim. They made appearances across the Mississippi Delta. Barbee later moved to Chicago, where he recorded for Vocalion in 1938. He played with Moody Jones' group on Maxwell Street in the '40s, but then left the music business for several years. Barbee recorded for Spivey and Storyville in the mid-'60s, and toured Europe as part of the American Folk Blues Festival. A portion of the tour's concert in Hamburg, Germany, was issued by Fontana. Barbee was involved in an auto accident in 1964, and suffered a heart attack while in jail waiting for the case to come to court. —*Ron Wynn*

● **Blues Masters, Vol. 3: I Ain't Gonna Pick No More Cotton** / Storyville ✦✦✦✦✦

Barkin' Bill

Vocals / Electric Chicago Blues
Blessed with a lush, deeply burnished baritone that's seemingly the antithesis of the rough-hewn Chicago blues sound, Barkin' Bill Smith finally broke through in 1994 with his own debut album for Delmark. Influenced by the likes of Joe Williams (Count Basie's smooth crooner, not the gruff nine-string gui-

tarist), Brook Benton, and Jimmy Witherspoon, the natty dresser grew up in Mississippi and stopped off to sing in East St. Louis and Detroit before settling in the Windy City.

Slide guitarist Homesick James anointed Bill with his enduring stage handle in 1958 when the two shared a stage. After scuffling for decades on the South and West sides, Smith finally hooked up with young guitarist Dave Specter & the Bluebirds and made his recorded debut on the band's 1991 Delmark release, *Bluebird Blues*. After leaving Specter's employ, Smith's own album bow *Gotcha!* emerged three years later. —*Bill Dahl*

● **Gotcha!** / 1994 / Delmark ◆◆◆◆
The veteran vocalist wraps his suave, bottomless pipes around a well-chosen cross-section of covers, from Duke Henderson's jump blues "Get Your Kicks" and Johnny "Guitar" Watson's "I Love to Love You" to tougher straightforward blues originally cut by Freddy King, Guitar Slim, Jimmy Rogers, and Little Walter. A cadre of local session pros provides fine support, especially guitarist Steve Freund (who receives a couple of instrumental showcases). —*Bill Dahl*

Roosevelt "Booba" Barnes

b. Sep. 25, 1936, Longwood, MS, d. Apr. 2, 1996
Guitar, Vocals / Electric Delta Blues
Booba Barnes and his Playboys band rocked the hardest of all the juke-joint combos in the Mississippi delta during the '80s, and after the release of his debut album (*The Heartbroken Man*, 1990), "Booba" took his act and his band north to Chicago, following the trail of his idols Howlin' Wolf and Little Milton. In a *Guitar Player* review, Jas Obrecht called Barnes "a wonderfully idiosyncratic guitar player and an extraordinary vocalist by any standard."

Roosevelt Booba Barnes began playing music professionally in 1960, playing guitar in a Mississippi band named the Swinging Gold Coasters. Four years later, he moved to Chicago, where he performed in blues clubs whenever he could get work. Barnes returned to his home state of Mississippi in 1971, where he began playing bars and clubs around Greenville.

Barnes continued to play the juke joints of Mississippi for the next decade. In 1985, he opened his own joint, the Playboy Club. With Barnes and his backing band, the Playboys, acting as the house band, the bar became one of the most popular in the Delta. Soon, the band was popular enough to have a record contract with Rooster Blues. Their first album, *The Heartbroken Man*, was released in 1990. After its release, Barnes and the Playboys toured the U.S. and Europe. They continued to tour, as well as occasionally record, throughout the '90s. —*Jim O'Neal & Stephen Thomas Erlewine*

● **The Heartbroken Man** / 1990 / Rooster Blues ◆◆◆◆◆
Featured is a no-frills recording of hair-raising modern Delta blues. —*Jas Obrecht*

Lou Ann Barton

b. Feb. 17, 1954, Fort Worth, TX
Vocals / Modern Electric Texas Blues
Although she doesn't tour nearly as much as she probably could, Austin-based vocalist Lou Ann Barton is one of the finest purveyors of raw, unadulterated roadhouse blues from the female gender that you'll ever hear. Like Delbert McClinton, she can belt out a lyric so that she can be heard over a two-guitar band with horns. Born February 17, 1954, in Fort Worth, she's a veteran of thousands of dance hall and club shows all over Texas. Barton moved to Austin in the 1970s and later performed with the Fabulous Thunderbirds and Stevie Ray Vaughan and Double Trouble.

Although she has a few great recordings out, notably *Old Enough* (1982, Asylum Records), produced by Jerry Wexler and Glenn Frey, Barton has to be seen live to be fully appreciated. She belts out her lyrics in a twangy voice so full of Texas that you can smell the barbecue sauce. She swaggers confidently about the stage, casually tossing her cigarette to the floor as the band kicks in on its first number. The grace, poise and confidence she projects on stage is part of a long tradition for women blues singers. The blues world still needs more good female blues singers like Barton, to help to broaden the appeal of the music to diverse audiences and to further its evolution.

Barton has several other excellent albums out on the Austin-based Antone's Records, *Read My Lips* (1989) and her coopera-

tive effort with fellow Texas blues women Marcia Ball and Angela Strehli, *Dreams Come True* (1990). *Old Enough* was reissued on compact disc in 1992 on the Antone's label. The only criticism one could level at Barton—and it may be unfair because of business complications—is that she hasn't recorded much. Here's hoping that this premier interpreter of Texas roadhouse blues will be well recorded through the rest of the 1990s. —*Richard Skelly*

● **Old Enough** / 1982 / Antone's ◆◆◆◆◆
Lou Ann Barton arrived fully formed with her debut album, *Old Enough*. It was clear from the outset that she was a magnificent singer, full of bold, gritty sensuality. Though there are a few hints of gloss on the album, Barton tears through any pretense and delivers a scorching first album. —*Thom Owens*

Forbidden Tones / 1986 / Spindletop ◆◆◆

Read My Lips / 1989 / Antone's ◆◆◆◆◆
Barton's lascivious delivery of roadhouse R&B chestnuts by Hank Ballard, Slim Harpo, and others is hotter than four-alarm chili on a Texas summer night. Members from The Fabulous Thunderbirds, Stevie Ray Vaughan's band, and other Austin heavy-hitters ensure that songs like "Sexy Ways," "Shake Your Hips," "You Can Have My Husband," "Sugar Coated Love," and "Rocket in My Pocket" have the right amount of grease. —*Rick Clark*

Dreams Come True / 1991 / Antone's ◆◆◆
Dreams Come True is an all-star session by vocalists Marcia Ball, Lou Ann Barton and Angela Strehli. The three women sing with a band led by Dr. John and the session features guest appearances by such luminaries as David "Fathead" Newman and Jimmie Vaughan. The music is straight out of the Texas school of roadhouse R&B and blues boogie but it's delivered with a gritty, heartfelt edge, particularly on the part of the three vocalists. *Dreams Come True* may follow formula, but it's followed with style and affection, which makes it a very enjoyable listen. —*Thom Owens*

Carey Bell

b. Nov. 14, 1936, Macon, MS
Harmonica, Vocals, Electric Bass, Drums, Guitar / Electric Chicago Blues
His place on the honor roll of Chicago blues harpists long ago assured, Carey Bell has truly come into his own during the last few years as a bandleader with terrific discs for Alligator and Blind Pig. He learned his distinctive harmonica riffs from the Windy City's very best (both Walters—Little *and* Big—as well as Sonny Boy Williamson II), adding his own signature effects for good measure (an other-worldly moan immediately identifies many of his more memorable harp rides).

Born Carey Bell Harrington in the blues-fertile state of Mississippi, he was already playing the harp when he was eight and working professionally with his godfather, pianist Lovie Lee, at 13. The older and more experienced Lee brought Carey with him to Chicago in search of steady musical opportunities in 1956. Gigs frequently proved scarce, and Carey eventually took up electric bass, playing behind Robert Nighthawk, Johnny Young, and his mentor Big Walter Horton. Finally, in 1969, Bell made his debut album (on harp) for Delmark, and he was on his way.

Bell served invaluable early-'70s stints in the bands of Muddy Waters and Willie Dixon, touring extensively and recording with both legends. Alligator Records has been responsible for much of Bell's best recorded work as a leader, beginning with a joint venture with Horton back in 1972. Four cuts by Bell on the first batch of Alligator's *Living Chicago Blues* anthologies in 1978 preceded his participation in the 1990 harmonica summit meeting *Harp Attack!*, which brought him into the studio with fellow greats James Cotton, Junior Wells, and Billy Branch. His recent solo set for Alligator, *Deep Down*, rates as his finest album to date. Bell has sired a passel of blues-playing progeny; best-known of the brood is mercurial guitarist Lurrie Bell. —*Bill Dahl*

Carey Bell's Blues Harp / 1969 / Delmark ◆◆◆
It's a mite ragged around the edges, but Bell's 1969 debut session certainly sports the proper ambience—and no wonder, with guitarists Eddie Taylor and Jimmy Dawkins and pianist Pinetop Perkins on hand to help out. No less than four Little Walter cov-

ers and two more from Muddy Waters' songbook dot the set, but many of the best moments occur on the original numbers. Delmark's CD reissue includes three previously unissued items. —*Bill Dahl*

Heartaches and Pain / 1977 / Delmark ✦✦✦
Legendary producer Ralph Bass supervised this quickie session back in 1977, but it failed to see the light of day domestically until Delmark rescued it from oblivion. They did the blues world a favor: it's a worthwhile session, Bell storming through a mostly original setlist (the omnipresent Little Walter cover this time is "Everything's Gonna Be Alright"). Aron Burton and Sam Lay comprise the rhythm section, and son Lurrie contributes lead guitar. —*Bill Dahl*

Son of a Gun / 1984 / Rooster Blues ✦✦✦
The raucous pairing of this harpist and his guitarist son Lurrie creates some sparks. —*Bill Dahl*

Harp Attack! / 1990 / Alligator ✦✦✦✦
Four of Chicago's preeminent blues harpists—Bell, James Cotton, Junior Wells, and relative newcomer Billy Branch—gathered in a downtown studio to wax this historic summit meeting. Bell's vocal showcases include two originals, "Hit Man" and "Second Hand Man," and a Muddy Waters cover, "My Eyes Keep Me in Trouble." —*Bill Dahl*

Mellow Down Easy / 1991 / Blind Pig ✦✦✦✦
The harpist hooked up with a young Maryland-based band called Tough Luck for this disc, certainly one of his better outings. The traditional mindset of the combo pushed Bell back to his roots, whether on the originals "Just like You" and the Horton homage "Big Walter Strut" or revivals of Muddy Waters' "Short Dress Woman" and "Walking Thru the Park" and the classic Little Walter title cut. —*Bill Dahl*

● **Deep Down** / 1995 / Alligator ✦✦✦✦✦
More than a quarter century after he cut his debut album, Bell recently made his finest disc to date. Boasting superior material and musicianship (guitarists Carl Weathersby and Lurrie Bell and pianist Lucky Peterson are all stellar) and a goosed-up energy level that frequently reaches incendiary heights, the disc captures Bell outdoing himself vocally on the ribald "Let Me Stir in Your Pot" and a suitably loose "When I Get Drunk" and instrumentally on the torrid "Jawbreaker." For a closer, Bell settled on the atmospheric Horton classic "Easy"; he does it full justice. —*Bill Dahl*

Last Night / 1995 / One Way ✦✦✦
Nothing flashy or outrageous here, just a meat-and-potatoes session produced by Al Smith that satisfyingly showcases Bell's charms. Once again, there are hearty tributes to Little Walter ("Last Night") and Muddy Waters ("She's 19 Years Old"), but there's some original stuff too, backed by a combo that boasted a daunting collective experience level: Taylor and Perkins return, along with bassist David Myers and drummer Willie "Big Eyes" Smith. —*Bill Dahl*

Lurrie Bell

Guitar, Vocals / Modern Electric Blues
Lurrie Bell was born to play the blues. His famous father, harpist Carey Bell, had him working out on guitar as a wee lad. By 1977, he was recording with his dad and playing behind a variety of established stars, tabbed by many observers as the time as a sure star on the rise. But personal problems took their toll on his great potential; Bell's recorded output and live performances have been inconsistent over the last decade or so.

Among the highlights of Lurrie's discography: three tracks in tandem with harpist Billy Branch under the Sons of Blues banner (Lurrie was a founding member of the still-thriving band) from Alligator's first batch of 1978 *Living Chicago Blues* anthologies and a 1984 collaboration with his old man for Rooster Blues, *Son of a Gun* (the latter remains unavailable on CD). Then there's his recent set for Delmark, *Mercurial Son*, as bizarre a contemporary blues album as you're likely to encounter. —*Bill Dahl*

● **Son of a Gun** / 1984 / Rooster Blues ✦✦✦✦
Lurrie and his dear old dad democratically split the vocals and most of the solo space on this LP to generally winning effect. Nothing overly polished or endlessly rehearsed; just solid mainstream Chicago blues. —*Bill Dahl*

Everybody Wants to Win / 1989 / JSP ✦✦✦
Mercurial Son / Oct. 3, 1995 / Delmark ✦✦
Don't blame Lurrie for the overbearingly weird vibe of this album. Producer/drummer Steve Cushing supplied much of the material, which is delivered by Bell so incomprehensibly that the printed lyrics inside the booklet are the only way to decipher them (once you read up on the misogynistic "Your Daddy Done Tripped the Trigger" and the bizarre "Blues in the Year One-D-One," you'll wish you hadn't). Big Time Sarah was recruited to belt "Your Wild Thing Ain't Wild Enough," one of the dirtiest and most childish diatribes ever recorded in the name of blues. Bell's guitar work, however, remains sharp, and when he sings something of his own—"Lurrie's Cool Groove," or "Tell Me About Your Love"—the magic temporarily returns. —*Bill Dahl*

Fred Below

b. Sep. 6, 1926, Chicago, IL, **d.** 1988
Drums
Fred Below was born in Chicago on September 16, 1926. Below played drums in high school and went on to study percussion at the Roy C. Knapp School of Percussion. Primarily a jazz drummer at the time, he played bebop and joined the Army as part of the 427th Army band. After the service, he returned to Chicago in 1951 to find that blues gigs were what was happening. Jazz was in a lull.

Then Muddy Waters drummer Elgin Evans introduced Below to a group called the Three Aces—Junior Wells (vocals, harp), Louis Myers (guitar), and Dave Myers (bass)—who needed a drummer. As a jazz drummer, Below did not know blues drumming and it was a rough fit at first. The next big event came when Little Walter (on the sudden success of his instrumental "Juke") quit the Muddy Waters band and was replaced by Junior Wells. Little Walter then joined the Three Aces, which he had been itching to do because Muddy Waters did not play in the uptempo style that Walter was into. Little Walter and the Four Aces (later renamed the Jukes) were a perfect fit and this four-piece electric blues combo became the hottest band in Chicago.

It is hard to estimate the effect of this band on the Chicago music scene, and a large part of this success is due to the refined and elegant drumming of Below. He plays on almost all of Walter's greatest hits. He was in total demand for recording sessions. Everyone wanted him, and he recorded for Muddy Waters, Willie Dixon, Chuck Berry, Otis Rush, Elmore James, Junior Wells, Buddy Guy, Dinah Washington, John Brim, the Platters, the Moonglows, the Drifters, Bo Diddley, John Lee Hooker, Howlin' Wolf, and many more. Fred Below and the Aces pretty much created the standard for the blues shuffle beat. Below also was known for his use of the ride cymbal, the wood block, tom-tom fills, and many other embellishments. Just check out his drum solo on Little Walters' classic tune "Off the Wall." —*Michael Erlewine*

Duster Bennett (Anthony Bennett)

b. England, **d.** Mar. 25, 1976
Guitar, Harmonica, Drums, Vocals / Electric British Blues
Duster Bennett was a British blues singer and harmonica player. He signed to Mike Vernon's Blue Horizon label in 1967 and was backed on his debut album, *Smiling Like I'm Happy* (1968), by members of Fleetwood Mac. He was a session harmonica player and a member of John Mayall's Bluesbreakers. He was killed in a car accident in 1976. —*William Ruhlmann*

● **Smiling Like I'm Happy** / 1968 / Blue Horizon ✦✦✦✦✦
One of the unsung heroes of British blues, this one-man band was a fine harmonica player and singer, a decent guitarist, and a soulful enough singer to make one overlook his distinctly *un*bluesy high voice. The opening "Worried Mind"—just Duster on harp, guitar, voice, high-hat and kick drum—is a marvelously sloppy shuffle romp that holds its own with the Fabulous Thunderbirds' work ten years hence. On other tracks Bennett is backed by three-fourths of the original Fleetwood Mac, who provide simple, effective support without stealing any limelight; solos are kept to a minimum. Originals "My Lucky Day" (with chromatic harmonica) and "Jumping at Shadows" (which Mac would later cover) are absolutely outstanding, and Duster does justice to Magic Sam's "My Love Is Your Love." —*Dan Forte*

Out in the Blue / 1995 / Indigo ✦✦✦✦
Odds and ends, mostly from 1966-68, with a few tracks from 1975 and 1976, the year Bennett was killed in a car wreck. Two

tracks feature fine lead guitar by Duster's longtime friend (and original Yardbird) Top Topham—home tapes worthy of inclusion if only for Top's amazing and expressive vibrato. Five tracks feature Peter Green, including a demo of his "Trying So Hard to Forget" that's especially moody and the fascinating snippet "Two Harps" instrumental duet (unaccompanied harmonicas, as the title implies), showing the similarity in the pair's harp styles. The final cut, "Everyday," from 1976, sets one of Bennett's finest vocal performances against a string backdrop. What a contrast to the one-man band shouting "Worried Mind"—and it works. —*Dan Forte*

Tab Benoit

b. Nov. 17, 1967, Los Angeles, CA
Guitar, Vocals / Electric Louisiana Blues
Guitarist, singer and songwriter Tab Benoit makes his home south of New Orleans in Houma, LA. Born November 17, 1967, he's one of a handful of bright rising stars on the modern blues scene. For most of the 1990s, he's been working each of his records the old fashioned way, by playing anywhere and everywhere he and his band can play. Unlike so many others before him, Benoit understands that blues is not a medium in favor with 50,000 watt commercial rock radio stations, so as a consequence, he's worked each of his releases with as many shows as he can possibly play. Since the release of his first album for Justice, Benoit has taken his brand of Cajun-influenced blues all over the U.S., Canada and Europe. *Nice and Warm*, his debut album for Houston-based Justice Records, prompted some critics to say he's reminiscent, at times, of three blues guitar gods: Albert King, Albert Collins and Jimi Hendrix.

Although the hardworking, modest guitarist scoffs at those comparisons, and doesn't think he sounds like them (and does not try to sound like them), Benoit doesn't appear to be one who's easily led into playing rock 'n' roll in favor of his downhome blend of swamp blues and east Texas guitar-driven blues. Talk to Tab at one of his shows, and he'll tell you about his desire to "stay the course," and not water down his blues by playing items that could be interpreted as "alternative" rock. Despite the screaming guitar licks he coaxes from his Telecaster and his powerful songwriting and singing abilities, Benoit's laidback, down-to-earth personality off stage is the exact opposite of his live shows.

Benoit has three releases, all for Justice Records. They include *Nice & Warm* (1992), *What I Live For* (1994) and *Standing on The Bank* (1995). All three have sent shock waves through the blues community: How can a guy who's so young be so powerful? And since each of Benoit's records has surpassed the 50,000 mark (impressive numbers for an independent record label), he's well on his way to a career that could rival the kind of popularity that the late Stevie Ray Vaughan enjoyed in the late '80s. —*Richard Skelly*

● **Nice & Warm** / 1992 / Justice ✦✦✦✦✦
Tab Benoit's debut album *Nice & Warm* is a startlingly fresh debut. The guitarist has a gutsy, fuel-injected style that adds real spice to his swampy blues. Benoit draws equally from the Louisiana and Texas traditions and *Nice & Warm* proves it; not only does he carry on the tradition, he offers a fresh take on it as well. —*Thom Owens*

What I Live For / 1994 / Justice ✦✦✦
What I Live For is a white-hot sophomore effort by Tab Benoit, showcasing a more assured and confident guitarist. Although he hasn't changed his basic musical approach—it's all hard-driving Southern blues—his sound is fuller and more direct this time around, proving that his debut was no fluke. —*Thom Owens*

Standing on the Bank / 1995 / Justice ✦✦✦
On his third album, Tab Benoit stripped his sound to its bare essentials by recording live, directly to a two-track. Naturally, the process gives *Standing on the Bank* a startling immediacy, as the guitarist shreds a number of originals to pieces with his piercing solos. —*Thom Owens*

Buster Benton

b. Jul. 19, 1932, Texarkana, AR
Guitar
Despite the amputation of parts of both his legs during the course of his career, Chicago guitarist Buster Benton never gave up playing his music—an infectious hybrid of blues and soul that he dubbed at one point "disco blues" (an unfortunate appellation in retrospect, but useful in describing its danceability). In the late

'70s, when blues was at low ebb, Benton's waxings for Ronn Records were a breath of fresh air.

Inspired by the music of Sam Cooke and B.B. King, the gospel-bred Benton began playing the blues during the mid-'50s while living in Toledo, OH. By 1959, he was leading his own band in Chicago. During the '60s, he cut a series of soul-slanted singles for local concerns (Melloway, Alteen, Sonic, Twinight) before hooking up with the great Willie Dixon in 1971.

Benton was a member of Dixon's Blues All-Stars for a while, and Dixon is credited as songwriter of Benton's best-known song, the agonized slow blues "Spider in My Stew." Its release on Stan Lewis' Shreveport-based Jewel Records gave Benton a taste of fame; its follow-up, "Money Is the Name of the Game," solidified his reputation. A 1979 LP for Jewel's Ronn subsidiary (logically titled *Spider in My Stew*) stands as one of the most engaging Chicago blues LPs of its era, its contemporary grooves abetting Benton's tasty guitar work and soulful vocals.

Benton cut three albums later on for Ichiban, but compared to his Ronn output, they were disappointing. On the Chicago circuit, Benton's extreme courage in the face of physical adversity will long be cited. He was on kidney dialysis for the last few years of his life as a result of diabetes, and a portion of his right leg was amputated in 1993 due to poor circulation (he had already lost part of the other a decade earlier). Still, he continued to play his brand of uplifting blues until the end. —*Bill Dahl*

● **Spider in My Stew** / 1978 / Ronn ✦✦✦✦✦
Without a doubt, this album, originally released on Ronn in 1979, stands as the best place to begin an in-depth examination of Benton's legacy. "Spider in My Stew," obviously, is here, along with the wonderful Cooke-influenced R&B outing "Lonesome for a Dime," an irresistibly funky "Sweet 94" (Ron Scott's gurgly electric saxophone gives this cut and several others a unique feel), a driving "Funny About My Money," and the mournful minor-key blues "Sorry." Ronn has beefed the CD program up still further with three additions: the doomy, Bobby Bland-styled "Money Is the Name of the Game," a shuffling "Dangerous Woman," and Benton's happy-go-lucky cover of David Dee's "Going Fishin'." —*Bill Dahl*

Buster Benton Is the Feeling / 1980 / Ronn ✦✦✦
The guitarist's 1981 follow-up didn't pack quite the same knock-out punch as its predecessor, but it's a decidedly solid encore effort nonetheless, with tight backup from a talented unit (harpist Carey Bell, pianist Lafayette Leake, rhythm guitarist Jimmy Johnson, and saxist Scott). —*Bill Dahl*

Blues at the Top / Nov. 22, 1983–May 2, 1985 / Evidence ✦✦✦✦
A compilation of the two albums Benton made for the French Black & Blue label in 1983 and 1985, this 15-song collection rates with his best. Two separate bands are involved, and the sound changes with them: backed by harpist Billy Branch's Sons of Blues, Benton exercises his R&B-laced chops, while the older hands behind him on "Honey Bee," "The Hawk Is Coming," and "Hole in My Head" (guitarist Johnny Littlejohn, pianist Leake, drummer Odie Payne) assure that the grooves stay more in the mainstream. —*Bill Dahl*

I Like to Hear My Guitar Sing / Ichiban ✦✦
Ironically, Benton's axe doesn't have much room to sing on this disappointing outing. —*Bill Dahl*

Why Me / Ichiban ✦✦
The pleading title track is a worthy addition to the Benton canon, but this album isn't nearly as consistent as the guitarist's superior Ronn output. —*Bill Dahl*

Big Maybelle (Mabel Louise Smith)

b. May 1, 1924, Jackson, TN, d. Jan. 23, 1972, Cleveland, OH
Vocals / Electric Jump Blues
Her mountainous stature matching the sheer soulful power of her massive vocal talent, Big Maybelle was one of the premier R&B chanteuses of the 1950s. Her deep, gravelly voice was as singular as her recorded output for Okeh and Savoy, which ranged from down-in-the-alley blues to pop-slanted ballads. In 1967, she even covered ? & the Mysterians' "96 Tears" (it was her final chart appearance). Alleged drug addiction leveled the mighty belter at the premature age of 47, but Maybelle packed a lot of living into her shortened lifespan.

Born Mabel Louise Smith, the singer strolled off with top honors at a Memphis amateur contest at the precocious age of eight.

Gospel music was an important element in Maybelle's intense vocal style, but the church wasn't big enough to hold her talent. In 1936, she hooked up with Memphis bandleader Dave Clark; a few years later, Maybelle toured with the International Sweethearts of Rhythm. She debuted on wax with pianist Christine Chatman's combo on Decca in 1944 before signing with Cincinnati's King Records in 1947 for three singles of her own backed by trumpeter Hot Lips Page's band.

Producer Fred Mendelsohn discovered Smith in the Queen City, rechristened her Big Maybelle, and signed her to Columbia's Okeh R&B subsidiary in 1952. Her first Okeh platter, the unusual "Gabbin' Blues" (written by tunesmith Rosemarie McCoy and arranger Leroy Kirkland) swiftly hit, climbing to the upper reaches of the R&B charts. "Way Back Home" and "My Country Man" made it a 1953 hat trick for Maybelle and Okeh. In 1955, she cut a rendition of "Whole Lot of Shakin' Goin' On" a full two years before Louisiana piano pumper Jerry Lee Lewis got his hands and feet on it. Mendelsohn soon brought her over to Herman Lubinsky's Savoy diskery, where her tender rendition of the pop chestnut "Candy" proved another solid R&B hit in 1956. Maybelle rocked harder than ever at Savoy, her "Ring Dang Dilly," "That's a Pretty Good Love," and "Tell Me Who" benefitting from blistering backing by New York's top sessioneers. Her last Savoy date in 1959 reflected the changing trends in R&B; Howard Biggs's stately arrangements encompassed four violins. Director Bert Stern immortalized her vivid blues-belting image in his documentary *Jazz on a Summer's Day*, filmed in color at the 1958 Newport Jazz Festival.

Maybelle persevered throughout the '60s, recording for Brunswick, Scepter (her "Yesterday's Kisses" found her coping admirably with the uptown soul sound), Chess, Rojac (source of "96 Tears"), and other labels. But the good years were long gone when she slipped into a diabetic coma and passed away in a Cleveland hospital in 1972. —*Bill Dahl*

Blues, Candy and Big Maybelle / 1958 / Savoy ✦✦✦
Sixteen tracks of late '50s R&B from the Savoy label. Mickey Baker appears on guitar. —*Bill Dahl*

Saga of the Good Life and Hard Times / 1969 / Rojac ✦✦✦
A mix of soul and blues from her last sessions is sung with despair. —*Richard Pack*

The Okeh Sessions / 1983 / Charly ✦✦✦✦✦
A mix of R&B and blues on 22 tracks recorded from 1952-1955. Included are Sam "The Man" Taylor (ts) and Mickey Baker (g). —*Richard Pack*

● **The Complete Okeh Sessions 1952–'55** / 1994 / Epic/Legacy ✦✦✦✦✦
Maybelle's entire Okeh output—26 tracks—including her three R&B chart items, "Whole Lotta Shakin' Goin' On," and the risque slow blues "I'm Getting 'Long Alright." "Gabbin' Blues," her 1952 Okeh debut smash, is a humorous dialog between Maybelle and gossiping rival Rosemarie McCoy, the tune's co-writer. Maybelle was no mere copyist; her sandpapery vocals stood in sharp contrast to the many interchangeable thrushes then populating the R&B world. Great support from New York session wizards such as tenor saxist Sam "The Man" Taylor and guitarist Mickey Baker throughout. —*Bill Dahl*

Candy / 1994 / Savoy Jazz ✦✦✦✦✦
The belter moved over to Newark, NJ-based Savoy midway through the decade and continued to prosper: "Candy," "Ramblin' Blues," and the intense "Blues Early, Early" rate with her finest cuts. "Ring Dang Dilly" and "Tell Me Who" rock with the seemingly effortless swing peculiar to New York's R&B scene at the time, thanks to the presence of saxists Warren Lucky and Jerome Richardson and guitarists Baker and Kenny Burrell, among others. —*Bill Dahl*

Big Shoulders

Group / Jazz Blues
Utilizing an unusually vast array of influences, Big Shoulders has cut a pair of albums for Rounder that are difficult to categorize, encompassing rock, blues, jazz, and ethnic origins. Vocalist/keyboardist Ken Saydak and harpist Ron Sorin are veterans of the Chicago blues circuit. Other band members are guitarist Larry Clyman, bassist Gary Krolak, and drummer Lenny Marsh. —*Bill Dahl*

● **Big Shoulders** / Jan. 1990 / Rounder ✦✦✦✦✦
This eclectic, blues-influenced Chicago quintet's impressive

debut features keyboardist Ken Saydak's gravelly vocals. —*Bill Dahl*

Nickel History / Jul. 8, 1991 / Rounder ✦✦✦
More ambitious genre-mixing—everything from polkas to Percy Mayfield. —*Bill Dahl*

The Big Three Trio

Group / Acoustic Chicago Blues
For the legendary Willie Dixon, the Big Three Trio was an important launching pad for a fantastic career. Pianist Leonard "Baby Doo" Caston and guitarist Bernardo Dennis (replaced after a year by Ollie Crawford) joined upright bassist Dixon to form the popular trio in 1946. Caston was just out of the service (where he'd played on USO tours during World War II); Dixon had been a conscientious objector. Dixon had previously worked with Caston in the Five Breezes and with Dennis in the Four Jumps of Jive.

Sharing vocal (they specialized in three-part harmonies) and writing duties democratically, the trio signed with Jim Bulleit's Bullet imprint in 1946 for a solitary session before making a giant jump in stature to Columbia Records in 1947. Their polished, pop-oriented presentation resulted in one national hit, "You Sure Look Good to Me," in 1948, and a slew of other releases that stretched into 1952 (toward the end, they were shuttled over to the less prestigious Okeh subsidiary).

Incidentally, Dixon dusted off two songs the trio waxed for Okeh, "Violent Love" and "My Love Will Never Die," and handed them to Otis Rush a few years later when the burly bassist was working as a producer at Eli Toscano's Cobra Records. Rush's tortured "My Love Will Never Die" was a postwar masterpiece; the corny "Violent Love" may be the worst thing the southpaw guitarist ever committed to tape.

Caston split at the end of 1952, effectively breaking up the trio. But Dixon's destiny was at Chess Records, where he was already making inroads as a session bassist and songwriter. Pretty soon, he'd be recognized as one of the most prolific and invaluable figures on the Windy City scene. —*Bill Dahl*

I Feel Like Steppin' Out / 1986 / Dr. Horse ✦✦✦
I Feel Like Steppin' Out compliments the Columbia release *The Big Three Trio*, gathering most of the material that was left off that disc and only duplicating "Signifying Monkey." The Big Three played the blues very loosely, adding bits of jazz and pop to their sound—unlike most blues groups of their time, they all sang in unison. Though this compilation isn't quite as strong as the Columbia disc, it's worthwhile for dedicated fans. —*Thom Owens*

● **The Big Three Trio** / 1990 / Columbia ✦✦✦✦✦
The only domestic compilation celebrating this trio's accomplishments is a 21-track affair containing Dixon's "dozens" diatribe "Signifying Monkey," the catchy "Tell That Woman" (later covered by Peter, Paul & Mary as "Big Boat Up the River"), several crackling instrumentals ("Big 3 Boogie," "Hard Notch Boogie Beat") that show what fine musicianship this triumvirate purveyed. Points off, though, for not including their only legit hit, "You Sure Look Good to Me." —*Bill Dahl*

Big Time Sarah

b. 1953, Coldwater, MS
Vocals / Electric Chicago Blues
A rousing vocalist and dynamic entertainer, "Big Time" Sarah Streeter's among the more enterprising contemporary blues performers. She moved to Chicago from Coldwater, MS, as a child, and sang in South Side gospel choirs before debuting as a blues vocalist on stage at Morgan's Lounge at 14. She later worked with Buddy Guy and Junior Wells, Johnny Bernard and Sunnyland Slim. A single on Slim's Airways label helped launch her solo career. Streeter's been a featured performer at many North Side clubs since the late '70s, and appeared at several blues festivals. She formed The Big Time Express in 1989, and Delmark issued her most recent recording, *Lay It on 'em Girls*, in 1993. —*Ron Wynn*

● **Lay It on 'em Girls** / 1993 / Delmark ✦✦✦✦✦
"Big Time" Sarah Streeter has the power, struttin' tone and booming voice ideal for stomping, sassy numbers. This CD spotlights the band Streeter formed in 1989, The BTS Express. Streeter's songs explore the familiar battle between the sexes,

with Streeter sometimes angry, sometimes confused and often confrontational in the "classic" blues style. She covers three numbers by Willie Dixon, as well as material from Bill Withers, George Gershwin and Leonard Feather, and displays both a vibrant style and more versatility than might be expected. —*Ron Wynn*

Big Twist & the Mellow Fellows

Group / Electric Chicago Blues
Larry "Big Twist" Nolan heartily epitomized the image "300 pounds of heavenly joy." Based in Chicago, the huge singer and his trusty R&B band, the Mellow Fellows, were one of the hottest draws on the midwestern college circuit during the 1980s, with a slickly polished sound modeled on the soul-slanted approach of Bobby Bland, Little Milton and Tyrone Davis.

Twist started out singing and playing drums in rough-and-tumble country bars in downstate Illinois during the late '50s and early '60s (chicken wire-enclosed stages were a necessity on this raucous scene). Young saxist Terry Ogolini jammed often with the big man at a joint called Junior's in a Prairie State burg called Colp. Ogolini and guitarist Pete Special spearheaded the nucleus of the first edition of the Mellow Fellows in the college town of Carbondale during the early '70s, with Twist doubling on drums. After taking southern Illinois by storm, the unit relocated en masse to Chicago in 1978.

Their eponymous 1980 debut album for Flying Fish accurately captured the group's slick sound, while the 1982 follow-up, *One Track Mind*, attempted to be somewhat more contemporary without losing the band's blues/R&B base. A move to Alligator in 1983 elicited an album co-produced by Gene "Daddy G" Barge, whose sax solos previously enlivened R&B classics by Chuck Willis, Gary (U.S.) Bonds, Little Milton and countless more. The group's final album with Twist up front was the *Live from Chicago!—Bigger Than Life!!*

Numerous personnel changes over the years failed to scuttle the band, and neither did the death of Twist in 1990 from diabetes and kidney failure. Martin Allbritton, an old singing buddy of Twist's from downstate who had previously gigged around Chicago as front man for Larry & the Ladykillers, had already been deputizing for the ailing Twist, so it fell to Allbritton to assume the role full time. Barge shared the singing duties at selected gigs and on the band's 1990 album *Street Party*.

Special left the organization not long after that, taking the name Mellow Fellows with him when he hit the door. That's when the remaining members adopted the handle of the Chicago Rhythm & Blues Kings. With Ogolini and longtime trumpeter Don Tenuto comprising a red-hot horn section, they're still a popular, dance-friendly fixture around the Chicago scene. —*Bill Dahl*

Big Twist & The Mellow Fellows / Jun. 1981 / Flying Fish ✦✦✦✦
The upbeat rhythms and charismatic persona of Big Twist always afforded this group an accessibility greater than that of most hardcore Chicago blues acts. This debut set followed the same formula, mixing time-tested favorites such as Tyrone Davis' "Turn Back the Hands of Time" with the inevitable crowd-pleaser "The Sweet Sound of Rhythm & Blues." —*Bill Dahl*

One Track Mind / 1982 / Flying Fish ✦✦✦
A slicker affair than their first album, highlighted by a revival of Albert King's "Cold Women" and the rousing "Living It Up." —*Bill Dahl*

● **Playing for Keeps** / 1983 / Alligator ✦✦✦✦
Twist's adopted theme song, the Willie Dixon-penned "300 Pounds of Heavenly Joy," hails from this goodtime collection, co-produced by tenor-sax legend Gene "Daddy G" Barge. —*Bill Dahl*

Live from Chicago! Bigger Than Life! / 1987 / Alligator ✦✦✦✦
Recorded live in 1987 at Biddy Mulligan's, a longtime Chicago blues institution that fell on hard times not too long thereafter, this disc showcases the Mellow Fellows' strengths in front of a rabidly devoted crowd. "300 Pounds of Heavenly Joy," "Turning Point," and the playful "Too Much Barbeque" rate among the highlights, as Twist's onstage charisma makes the show go. —*Bill Dahl*

Big Wheeler

Harmonica, Vocals / Electric Chicago Blues
He's been part of the Chicago circuit for four decades, but

Golden "Big" Wheeler waited until 1993 to release his debut album on Delmark. As befits such a veteran, Wheeler's sturdy harmonica style is a throwback to the 1950s and his idol, Little Walter.

Wheeler was first turned onto the harp while driving a cab by one of his regular fares, Buster Brown. Brown's shot at "Fannie Mae"-fired stardom was still a few decades down the line, but Wheeler's was even further off. He left Georgia in 1941, eventually settling in Chicago, where he met Little Walter. The two became friends, Walter acting as something of a mentor. Wheeler began fronting his own combo in 1956 but never really sustained a musical career (he worked as a mechanic to pay the bills).

In 1993, Delmark unleashed the harpist's debut disc, *Big Wheeler's Bone Orchard*, which found him backed by a young local outfit, the Ice Cream Men. Wheeler's brother, guitarist James Wheeler, is also a longtime denizen of the Windy City scene; he's currently a mainstay of Mississippi Heat after spending an extended stint behind Otis Rush. —*Bill Dahl*

● **Big Wheeler's Bone Orchard** / 1993 / Delmark ✦✦✦✦✦
The veteran Chicago harpist's long-overdue debut album is quite credible, but you can't help but think he's got a far more satisfying set within him yet. Dreary backing by the overly cautious Ice Cream Men is the prime reason the set only occasionally soars— with a less derivative combo, Wheeler could come up with something special before he's through. —*Bill Dahl*

Elvin Bishop

b. Oct. 21, 1942, Glendale, CA
Guitar, Vocals / Contemporary Electric Blues
Elvin Bishop was born in Glendale, CA, on October 21, 1942. He grew up on a farm in Iowa with no electricity and no running water. His family moved to Oklahoma when he was ten. Raised in an all-White community, he had no exposure to Blacks or their music except through the radio, where he would listen to sounds from far away Mexico and blues stations in Shreveport, LA; in particular, the piercing sound of Jimmy Reed's harmonica got his attention. Bishop says it was like a crossword puzzle that he had to figure out. What is this music? Who makes it? Where and how do Black people live? What is this music all about? He put the pieces together.

But it was not until he won a National Merit Scholarship to the University of Chicago in 1959 that he found the real answers to his questions. Suddenly, there he was right in the heart of the Chicago blues scene. Live. It was a dream come true. "The first thing I did when I got there was to make friends with the black guys working in the cafeteria. They took me to all the clubs. I sunk myself totally in the blues life as quick as I could," says Bishop.

After two years of college, he just dropped out and was into music full time. Howlin' Wolf guitarist Smokey Smothers befriended Bishop and taught him the basics of blues guitar. In the early '60s he met and teamed up with Paul Butterfield to become the core of the Butterfield Blues Band. Although only playing guitar for a few years, he practiced day and night on the blues music that he loved. He and Butterfield played together in just about every place possible—campuses, houses, parks, and clubs. They began to become well known in 1963 when they took a job at Big John's on Chicago's North Side and the Paul Butterfield Blues Band was born. Bishop helped to create and played on the first several Butterfield albums. (The Pigboy Crabshaw is Bishop's countrified persona referred to in the title of the third Butterfield album.)

When he left the Butterfield band after the *In My Own Dream* album (1968), Bishop relocated to and settled in the San Francisco area, where he appeared often at the Fillmore with artists like Eric Clapton, B. B. King and Jimi Hendrix. He recorded for Epic (four albums) and later signed with Capricorn in 1974. His recording of "Traveling Shoes" (from the album *Let It Flow*) hit the charts, but he scored big with the lovely tune "Fooled Around and Fell in Love" (from his album *Struttin' My Stuff*) in 1976. He was (and is) famous for having fun on stage (putting on a great show) and letting the good times roll. Over the next few years the Elvin Bishop Group dissolved. He released his album *Best Of* in 1979, and was not heard from much until he signed with Alligator in 1988.

Bishop then released *Big Fun* (1988) and *Don't Let the*

Bossman Get You Down (1991), which were well received. He also participated in Alligator's 1992 20th Anniversary cross-country tour. His latest release is *Ace in the Hole* (1995). Over the years, Bishop has graced the albums of many great bluesmen including Clifton Chenier and John Lee Hooker. He toured with B.B. King in 1995. Bishop is known for his sense of humor, his unique style of slide guitar, and fusion of blues, gospel, R&B, and country flavors. He lives with his wife and family in the San Francisco area, is a prodigious gardener, and continues to play dates in the U.S. and abroad. —*Michael Erlewine*

The Elvin Bishop Group / Oct. 1969 / Fillmore ✦✦

Feel It! / Oct. 1970 / Fillmore ✦✦✦

Rock My Soul / Sep. 1972 / Epic ✦✦✦

Let It Flow / May 1974 / Capricorn ✦✦✦✦✦
For his fourth album, Elvin Bishop organized a new backup group and switched to Capricorn Records. Capricorn was known as the standard bearer of the Southern rock movement—the Allman Brothers Band, The Marshall Tucker Band, etc.—and Bishop was able to emphasize the country/blues aspects of his persona and his music in the move from Marin County, CA, to Macon, GA. The guest artists included the Allmans' Dickey Betts, Marshall Tucker's Toy Caldwell, Charlie Daniels, and Sly Stone, and Bishop turned in one of his best sets of songs, including "Travelin' Shoes" (with its Allmans-like twin lead guitar work), which became his first charting single, just as the album was his first to make the Top 100 LPs. —*William Ruhlmann*

Juke Joint Jump / Apr. 1975 / Capricorn ✦✦✦
Elvin Bishop's Macon takeover continued on his second Capricorn album, which had a slightly less country feel than *Let It Flow* but continued to be dominated by twin guitar playing (courtesy of Bishop and Johnny "V" Vernazza) and honky tonk piano playing (from Phil Aaberg). The song quality wasn't quite as consistent this time, but "Sure Feels Good" became Bishop's second singles chart entry. —*William Ruhlmann*

The Best of Elvin Bishop: Crabshaw Rising / Sep. 1975 / Epic ✦✦✦
This ten-track compilation selects from the albums *The Elvin Bishop Group, Feel It!,* and *Rock My Soul,* effectively summarizing this phase in Bishop's career. Long out of print, it was superseded in 1994 by the 18-track CD *The Best of Elvin Bishop: Tulsa Shuffle,* which contained nine of its selections. Then, oddly enough, it was reissued in 1996! (Originally released in September 1975 on Epic Records, *The Best of Elvin Bishop: Crabshaw Rising* was reissued on April 16, 1996, on Epic/Legacy.) —*William Ruhlmann*

Struttin' My Stuff / Dec. 1975 / Capricorn ✦✦✦
Features the hit single "Fooled Around and Fell in Love," sung by Mickey Thomas. —*William Ruhlmann*

Hometown Boy Makes Good! / Oct. 1976 / Capricorn ✦✦
Elvin Bishop broke the bank with the success of "Fooled Around and Fell in Love" in the spring of 1976, so when he returned with this album in the fall, he turned up on the cover holding bags of money. The question, of course, was whether the hit would turn out to be a breakthrough or a fluke. The nearest thing to a follow-up to "Fooled Around" was "Spend Some Time," a ballad on which Mickey Thomas again sang soulfully. But it barely scraped into the charts, and the rest was typical Bishop good-time boogie (along with trendy tastes of disco and reggae), the relatively thin songwriting reflecting a rushed recording schedule—this was Bishop's fourth new album in just over two-and-a-half years. —*William Ruhlmann*

Raisin' Hell / Jul. 1977 / Capricorn ✦✦

Hog Heaven / 1978 / Capricorn ✦✦✦
Capricorn Records, having switched distribution from Warner Brothers to Phondisc, was on its way out by the time it released this, its sixth Elvin Bishop album, which may help explain why, only two years after he was in the Top Ten with "Fooled Around and Fell in Love," he didn't even reach the charts with this album. It's also true that lead singer Mickey Thomas had decamped to join Jefferson Starship, leaving Bishop to reestablish his country blues boy persona. But Maria Muldaur had signed on (she sings lead on "True Love"), and with two years between studio albums, Bishop had found the time to write some good vehicles for his guitar work and Southern rock back-up band. —*William Ruhlmann*

Big Fun / 1988 / Alligator ✦✦✦
In the ten years between the release of *Hog Heaven* and this comeback record, Elvin Bishop was represented in record stores by a *Best Of* on Capricorn and an album released only in Germany (*Is You Is Or Is You Ain't My Baby?* on Line Records). Then he signed with Bruce Iglauer's independent blues label Alligator and made this record, which, naturally, emphasizes his more blues-oriented guitar playing, although without sacrificing his country boy identity. Dr. John tickles some of the ivories, and harmonica player Norton Buffalo (of Commander Cody and His Lost Planet Airmen) also guests. —*William Ruhlmann*

Don't Let the Bossman Get You Down! / 1991 / Alligator ✦✦✦✦✦
On *Don't Let the Bossman Get You Down,* Bishop projects a good-natured, humorous persona in the extended spoken-word sections of his songs, but still finds time to play a lot of tasty blues guitar. —*William Ruhlmann*

● **Sure Feels Good: The Best of Elvin Bishop** / 1992 / PolyGram ✦✦✦✦✦
A fine collection of the blues-rock guitarist's best moments, which covers more material than the earlier compilation, *Best of Elvin Bishop/Crabshaw Rising.* —*Stephen Thomas Erlewine*

Best of Elvin Bishop: Tulsa Shuffle / May 10, 1994 / Epic/Legacy ✦✦✦✦✦
In his first manifestation as a band leader (1969–1972), Elvin Bishop lived in Marin County, CA, and performed under the auspices of promoter Bill Graham. Not surprisingly, the three albums he cut in that period fit into the soul-blues-rock style of post-psychedelic San Francisco, even to the point of featuring an extended instrumental, "Hogbottom," on which Bishop takes Carlos Santana's place fronting the Santana percussion section. This 18-track compilation selects from the albums *The Elvin Bishop Group, Feel It!,* and *Rock My Soul,* effectively summarizing this phase in Bishop's career. The only thing wrong with it is that it would be easy to make the mistake of thinking that it covers all of his solo career rather than only the first four years, especially because there have now been four different albums released with the title *The Best of Elvin Bishop.* —*William Ruhlmann*

Ace in the Hole / 1995 / Alligator ✦✦✦
On Elvin Bishop's third Alligator release, *Ace in the Hole,* his guitar playing remains as fiery as ever, but the overall quality of the songwriting has slipped somewhat, making it his least-consistent effort on the label. —*Thom Owens*

Billy Bizor

b. 1917, Centerville, TX, **d.** Apr. 4, 1969, Houston, TX
Harmonica, Vocals / Texas Blues
Billy Bizor, a little-known associate of Lightnin' Hopkins, left only a brief recorded legacy (some as a sideman with Hopkins), but within his few recordings are some of the deepest blues grooves ever to rumble out of a studio. Few modern Texas-blues recordings can compare with the 1968-69 sides Bizor did in Houston for producer Roy Ames. His blues were distinguished by highly emotional singing, gut-level intensity, and spare, hypnotic rhythms. —*Jim O'Neal*

Blowing My Blues Away / Collectables ✦✦✦✦✦
Blowing My Blues Away was recorded in 1968 and 1969, at the height of the blues revival. Billy Bizor wasn't very well known before the blues revival and that's part of the reason why his style didn't change very much from the '30s and '40s—his blues is still deeply indebted to the stripped-down sounds of Lightnin' Hopkins, who happens to be Bizor's cousin. All of the material on *Blowing My Blues Away* was previously unreleased, so it's designed for hardcore blues collectors, but for those listeners that are interested, this is an entertaining curiosity. —*Thom Owens*

Black Ace

b. Dec. 21, 1907, Hughes Springs, TX, **d.** Nov. 7, 1972, Fort Worth, TX
Guitar, Vocals / Acoustic Texas Blues
A solid guitarist and vocalist, Babe Turner, aka Black Ace, built his own guitar as a child, then taught himself to play. He was also in a gospel choir in Hughes Springs, TX. Turner honed his skills playing at community functions during the '20s, then

worked with Smokey Hogg at dances in Greenville, TX in the '30s. Hogg and Buddy Woods were frequent partners for Turner, who made several solo tours in the '30s and '40s. He appeared in the 1941 film *The Blood Of Jesus* and 1962 movie *The Blues*. Turner had a show on Fort Worth radio station KFJZ from 1936–1941. He recorded for Decca in 1937. After a stint in the Army during the early '40s, Turner's jobs were mostly non-musical, except for his film stints. He did make a 1960 LP for Arhoolie. Turner took his nickname from the 1937 recording "Black Ace." —*Ron Wynn*

● **I'm the Boss Card in Your Hand, 1937-60** / Arhoolie ✦✦✦✦✦
This compilation contains his original 1960 Arhoolie album in its entirety, unissued material from that session, and the added bonus of six sides from his 1937 recording debut for Decca. Rustic and heartfelt, with a large dollop of good humor thrown in for good measure (check out "Your Leg's Too Little"), the no-frills production makes for riveting, personal performances throughout. —*Cub Koda*

Otis Blackwell

b. 1931, Brooklyn, NY
Songwriter, Piano / Urban Blues
Few 1950s rock 'n' roll tunesmiths were as prolifically talented as Otis Blackwell. His immortal compositions include Little Willie John's "Fever," Elvis Presley's "Don't Be Cruel" and "All Shook Up," Jerry Lee Lewis' "Great Balls of Fire" and "Breathless," and Jimmy Jones' "Handy Man" (just for starters).

Though he often collaborated with various partners on the thriving '50s New York R&B scene (Winfield Scott, Eddie Cooley and Jack Hammer, to name three), Blackwell's songwriting style is as identifiable as that of Willie Dixon or Jerry Leiber and Mike Stoller. He helped formulate the musical vocabulary of rock 'n' roll when the genre was barely breathing on its own.

Befitting a true innovator, Blackwell's early influences were a tad out of the ordinary. As a lad growing up in Brooklyn, he dug the Westerns that his favorite nearby cinema screened. At that point, Tex Ritter was Otis' main man. Smooth blues singers Chuck Willis and Larry Darnell also made an impression. By 1952, Blackwell parlayed a victory at an Apollo Theater talent show into a recording deal with veteran producer Joe Davis for RCA, switching to Davis' own Jay-Dee label the next year. He was fairly prolific at Jay-Dee, enjoying success with the throbbing "Daddy Rollin' Stone" (later covered by the Who). From 1955 on, though, Blackwell concentrated primarily on songwriting (Atlantic, Date, Cub, and MGM later issued scattered Blackwell singles).

"Fever," co-written by Cooley, was Blackwell's first winner (he used the pen name of John Davenport, since he was still contractually obligated to Jay-Dee). Blackwell never met Elvis in person, but his material traveled a direct pipeline to the rock icon; "Return to Sender," "One Broken Heart for Sale," and "Easy Question" also came from his pen. Dee Clark ("Just Keep It Up" and "Hey Little Girl"), Thurston Harris, Wade Flemons, Clyde McPhatter, Brook Benton, Ben E. King, the Drifters, Bobby Darin, Ral Donner, Gene Vincent, and plenty more of rock's primordial royalty benefitted from Blackwell's compositional largesse before the British Invasion forever altered the Brill Building scene.

In 1977, Blackwell returned to recording with a Herb Abramson-produced set for Inner City comprised of his own renditions of the songs that made him famous. A 1991 stroke paralyzed the legendary songscribe, but his influence remains so enduring that it inspired *Brace Yourself!*, an all-star 1994 tribute album that included contributions by Dave Edmunds, Joe Ely, Deborah Harry, Chrissie Hynde, Kris Kristofferson, Graham Parker, and bluesman Joe Louis Walker. —*Bill Dahl*

All Shook Up / 1995 / Shanachie ✦✦
If only Blackwell had access to the above band when he recorded his own songbook for producer Herb Abramson in October of 1976. Instead, a graceless rock group named Grande Union, apparently Blackwell's band of choice at the time, was used, and the results are disappointing. "Back Trail," one of the few new compositions Blackwell brought to the party, was redone in superior fashion by Chicago bluesman Lonnie Brooks on his 1983 Alligator LP *Hot Shot*. Shanachie has added a handful of rare vintage Blackwell demos at the end of the CD that outshine

anything from the original *Inner City* album; especially valuable is Blackwell's original treatment of "One Broken Heart for Sale" (Presley's phrasing, as usual, faithfully mirrored Blackwell's). —*Bill Dahl*

● **Otis Blackwell 1953-55** / Flyright ✦✦✦✦
The British Flyright logo has neatly compiled all 17 known titles that Blackwell cut for Jay-Dee, including "Daddy Rollin' Stone," the equally ominous "On That Power Line, and four sides with a killer New York combo featuring tenor sax wailer Sam "The Man" Taylor and guitarist Mickey Baker. —*Bill Dahl*

Scrapper Blackwell (Francis Blackwell)

b. Feb. 21, 1903, Syracuse, NC, **d.** Oct. 27, 1962, Indianapolis, IN
Guitar, Vocals / Acoustic Chicago Blues
Scrapper Blackwell was best known for his work with pianist Leroy Carr during the early and mid-'30s, but he also recorded many solo sides between 1928 and 1935. A distinctive stylist whose work was closer to jazz than blues, Blackwell was an exceptional player with a technique, built around single-note picking, that anticipated the electric blues of the 1940s and 1950s. He abandoned music for more than 20 years after Carr's death in 1935, but re-emerged at the end of the 1950s and began his career anew, before his life was taken in an apparent robbery attempt.

Francis Hillman "Scrapper" Blackwell was of part-Cherokee Indian descent, one of 16 children born to Payton and Elizabeth Blackwell in Syracuse, NC. His father played the fiddle, and Blackwell himself was a self-taught guitarist, having started out by building his own instrument out of cigar boxes, wood, and wire. He also took up the piano, an instrument that he played professionally on occasion. By the time he was a teenager, Blackwell was working as a part-time musician, and traveled as far away as Chicago. By most accounts, as an adult Blackwell had a withdrawn personality, and could be difficult to work with, although he had an exceptionally good working relationship with Nashville-born pianist Leroy Carr, whom he met in Indianapolis in the mid-'20s. They made a natural team, for Carr's piano playing emphasized the bass, and liberated Blackwell to explore the treble strings of his instrument to the fullest.

Carr and Blackwell performed together throughout the midwest and parts of the south, including Louisville, St. Louis, Cincinnati, and Nashville, and were notably successful. With Blackwell's help, Carr became one of the top blues stars of the early '30s, and the two recorded well over 100 sides together between 1928 and 1935. They might've had major success going into the war years and beyond. It was not to be, however, as Carr's heavy drinking and a nephritis condition caused his death in Indianapolis on April 29, 1935.

Blackwell also recorded without Carr, both as a solo and also occasionally with other partners, including Georgia Tom Dorsey and an obscure singer named Black Bottom McPhail, and occasionally worked with blues bands such as Robinson's Knights of Rest. His biggest success and greatest effectiveness, however, lay in his work with Carr, and after the latter's death he continued working long enough to cut a tribute to his late partner. His withdrawn personality didn't lend itself to an extended solo career, and he gave up the music business before the end of the 1930s.

Blackwell's career might've ended there, preserved only in memory and a hundred or so sides recorded mostly with Carr. At the end of the 1950s, however, with the folk/blues revival gradually coming into full swing, he was rediscovered living in Indianapolis, and prevailed upon to resume playing and recording. This he did, for the Prestige/Bluesville label, with at least one album's worth of material that showed his singing and playing unmarred by age or other abuse. Blackwell appeared ready to resume his career without missing a beat, and almost certainly would've been a prime candidate for stardom before the burgeoning young White audience of college students and folk enthusiasts that embraced the likes of Furry Lewis, the Rev. Gary Davis, and Mississippi Fred McDowell. In 1962, however, soon after finishing his work on his first Prestige/Bluesville long-player (which, for reasons best understood by the label's current parent company, Fantasy Records, has never been re-released on CD), Blackwell was shot to death in a back alley in Indianapolis, the victim of a mugging. The crime was never solved.

Scrapper Blackwell was one of the most important guitar players of the 1920s and early '30s, with a clean, dazzlingly articulate style that anticipated the kind of prominent solo work that would emerge in Chicago as electric blues in the 1940s and 1950s, in the persons of Robert Nighthawk and the young Muddy Waters. His "string-snapping" solos transcend musical genres and defy the limitations of his period. Although Blackwell's recordings were done entirely on acoustic guitar, the playing on virtually every extant track is—and this is no joke—electrifying in its clarity and intensity. Along with Tampa Red (who also had some respect in jazz circles, and who was a more derivative figure, especially as a singer), Blackwell was one of a handful of pre-war blues guitarists whose work should be known by every kid who thinks it all started with Chuck Berry or even Muddy Waters.

Note: In addition to the albums credited to Scrapper Blackwell, his recordings can also be found on collections of Leroy Carr's work (virtually all of which feature Blackwell), including such releases as Magpie Records' *The Piano Blues: Leroy Carr 1930-35*, and one Carr/Blackwell duet, "Papa's on the Housetop," which is not on *The Virtuoso Guitar of Scrapper Blackwell*, but shows up on Yazoo's *Uptown Blues: Guitar Piano Duets* anthology. —*Bruce Eder*

★ **Virtuoso Guitar 1925-1934** / 1991 / Yazoo ♦♦♦♦♦
It's for recordings like this that a lot of blues guitar fans started listening to the music in the first place. The definitive Blackwell collection to date, featuring not only his best extant solo sides, but also his work in association with Leroy Carr, Black Bottom McPhail, and Tommy Bradley. The 14 songs here all have something to offer in the playing—and generally the singing as well—that will give the listener pause: a run, an arpeggio, a solo passage that makes you say, "Whoa, what was that?" The sound is surprisingly good, and one only wishes there were more than 14 songs here, although it's hard to imagine anything that could follow the last track, Leroy Carr's "Barrelhouse Woman No. 2." —*Bruce Eder*

Bobby "Blue" Bland

b. Jan. 27, 1930, Rosemont, TN
Vocals / Electric R&B
Bobby Bland earned his enduring blues superstar status the hard way: without a guitar, harmonica, or any other instrument to fall back upon. All Bland had to offer was his magnificent voice, a tremendously powerful instrument in his early heyday, injected with charisma and melisma to spare. Just ask his legion of female fans, who deem him a sex symbol to this day.

For all his promise, Bland's musical career ignited slowly. He was a founding member of the Beale Streeters, the fabled Memphis aggregation that also included B.B. King and Johnny Ace. Singles for Chess in 1951 (produced by Sam Phillips) and Modern the next year bombed, but that didn't stop local deejay David Mattis from cutting Bland on a couple of 1952 singles for his fledgling Duke logo.

Bland's tormented crying style was still pretty rough around the edges before he entered the Army in late 1952. But his progress upon his 1955 return was remarkable; with saxist Bill Harvey's band (featuring guitarist Roy Gaines and trumpeter Joe Scott) providing sizzling support, Bland's assured vocal on the swaggering "It's My Life Baby" sounds like the work of a new man. By now, Duke was headed by hard-boiled Houston entrepreneur Don Robey, who provided top-flight bands for his artists. Scott soon became Bland's mentor, patiently teaching him the intricacies of phrasing when singing sophisticated fare (by 1962, Bland was credibly crooning "Blue Moon," a long way from Beale Street).

Most of Bland's savage Texas blues sides during the mid-to-late '50s featured the slashing guitar of Clarence Hollimon, notably "I Smell Trouble," "I Don't Believe," "Don't Want No Woman," "You Got Me (Where You Want Me)," and the torrid "Loan a Helping Hand" and "Teach Me (How To Love You)." But the insistent guitar riffs guiding Bland's first national hit, 1957's driving "Farther up the Road," were contributed by Pat Hare, another vicious picker who would eventually die in prison after murdering his girlfriend and a cop. Later, Wayne Bennett took over on guitar, his elegant fretwork prominent on Bland's Duke waxings throughout much of the '60s.

The gospel underpinnings inherent to Bland's powerhouse

delivery were never more apparent than on the 1958 outing "Little Boy Blue," a vocal tour de force that wrings every ounce of emotion out of the grinding ballad. Scott steered his charge into smoother material as the decade turned—the seminal mixtures of blues, R&B and primordial soul "I Pity the Fool," the Brook Benton-penned "I'll Take Care of You," and "Two Steps from the Blues" were tremendously influential to a legion of up-and-coming southern soulsters.

Scott's blazing brass arrangements upped the excitement ante on Bland's frantic rockers "Turn on Your Love Light" in 1961 and "Yield Not to Temptation" the next year, but the vocalist was learning his lessons so well that he sounded just as conversant on soulful R&B rhumbas (1963's "Call on Me") and polished ballads ("That's the Way Love Is," "Share Your Love with Me") as with an after-hours blues revival of T-Bone Walker's "Stormy Monday Blues" that proved a most unlikely pop hit for him in 1962. With "Ain't Nothing You Can Do," "Ain't Doing Too Bad," and "Poverty," Bland rolled through the mid-'60s, his superstar status diminishing not a whit.

In 1973, Robey sold his labels to ABC Records, and Bland was part of the deal. Without Scott and his familiar surroundings to lean on, Bland's releases grew less consistent artistically, though *His California Album* in 1973 and *Dreamer* the next year boasted some nice moments (there was even an album's worth of country standards). The singer reteamed with his old pal B.B. King for a couple of mid-'70s albums that broke no new ground but further heightened Bland's profile, while his solo work for MCA teetered closer and closer to MOR (Bland has often expressed his admiration for ultra-mellow pop singer Perry Como).

Since the mid-'80s, Bland has recorded for Jackson, MS Malaco Records. His pipes undeniably reflect the ravages of time, and those phlegm-flecked "snorts" he habitually emits become annoying in large doses. But Bobby "Blue" Bland endures as a blues superstar of the loftiest order. —*Bill Dahl*

Blues Consolidated / May 1958 / Duke/MCA ♦♦♦♦♦
An album split between Bland and his Blues Consolidated touring partner Junior Parker, featuring great early-'50s sides by these two Houston-based performers. —*Cub Koda & Hank Davis*

☆ **Two Steps from the Blues** / 1962 / Duke/MCA ♦♦♦♦♦
Including classics like "Don't Cry No More," "I Pity The Fool," and "Little Boy Blue," this early-'60s set captures Bland at the point where his sound had just fully matured into a horn-punctuated blend of blues, gospel, and early soul. All 12 of the songs are included on MCA's *Duke Recordings* series, though, making this unnecessary if you're building a complete collection of Bland on CD. —*Richie Unterberger*

Call on Me / 1963 / MCA ♦♦♦♦♦
A near-perfect collection of early-'60s sides documents the man at his best. —*Hank Davis*

Ain't Nothing You Can Do / 1964 / MCA ♦♦♦
Fine soulful mid-'60s sides, including the title track, "Loneliness Hurts," and a cathartic reading of the soul classic "Blind Man." —*Cub Koda & Hank Davis*

Touch of the Blues / 1968 / Duke ♦♦♦♦♦
During his Duke tenure, Bobby "Blue" Bland's rich, creamy voice was at its stark, dramatic peak. Like his other label releases, even when he got overly sentimental or just plain corny material, or the songs were overarranged, Bland's smashing leads made everything work. —*Ron Wynn*

Barefoot Rock & You Got Me / Duke ♦♦♦
Half Junior Parker, half Bobby Bland, and all classic '50s R&B. —*Bill Dahl*

Here's the Man! / Duke ♦♦♦
The soulful vocals are backed by superb jazzy arrangements by Joe Scott. —*Hank Davis*

★ **The Best of Bobby Blue Bland** / 1972 / MCA ♦♦♦♦♦
Excellent compilation of the sides that made the legend. Includes "Call on Me," "Farther Up the Road," "I Pity the Fool," and "Turn on Your Love Light." —*Cub Koda*

His California Album / 1973 / MCA ♦♦♦
And his first for ABC-Dunhill in 1973 after more than two decades with Duke (Robey's still represented, though, under his songwriting alias of Deadric Malone on four cuts, including the album's biggest hit, "This Time I'm Gone for Good"). Producer

Steve Barri contemporized Bland by having him cover Leon Russell's "Help Me Make It Through the Day," Luther Ingram's "(If Loving You Is Wrong) I Don't Want to Be Right," and Gladys Knight & the Pips' "I've Got to Use My Imagination." —*Bill Dahl*

Dreamer / 1974 / MCA ✦✦✦
Barri's slightly antiseptic production style and Michael Omartian's arrangements weren't the equivalent of Joe Scott's immaculate collaborations with Bland, but this 1974 album's "Ain't No Love in the Heart of the City" and a meaty "I Wouldn't Treat a Dog (The Way You Treated Me)" were both huge hits. —*Bill Dahl*

Together for the First Time ... Live / 1974 / MCA ✦✦✦
Although the duo of Bobby Blue Bland and B.B. King was one of the most popular touring acts of the '70s and '80s, their first duet album—appropriately titled *Together for the First Time ... Live*—doesn't quite live up to expectations. Both musicians are in fine form, but rarely do any sparks fly. Occasionally, King turns out a good solo and Bland sings with passion, but usually the vibe of the record is too relaxed to be truly engaging. It's a pleasant record, just not the essential listening that it should have been. —*Thom Owens*

Together Again ... Live / 1976 / MCA ✦✦
This not-so-exciting second Bobby "Blue" Bland and B.B. King pairing was recorded in Los Angeles' Coconut Grove. There is more show business theatrics and less solid, soulful blues vocalizing than on their acclaimed debut, but there are still enough good moments to make it acceptable. —*Ron Wynn*

Members Only / 1985 / Malaco ✦✦✦
After some fairly soporific early-'80s releases for MCA, this album re-energized Bland's recording fortunes. The Larry Addison-penned title track caught on with blues-soul fans, making it to the middle reaches of the R&B charts as a single. —*Bill Dahl*

☆ **The Best of Bobby Blue Bland, Vol. 2** / MCA ✦✦✦✦✦
Features the classics "It's My Life Baby," "Queen for a Day," and "Two Steps from the Blues." —*Cub Koda*

The 3B Blues Boy—The Blues Years: 1952-59 / 1991 / Ace ✦✦✦
25-track compilation of bluesy material that Bland recorded for Duke between 1952 and 1959. Bland had previously released a few sides for Chess and Modern in the early '50s, but these sides represent the era in which he began to find his voice. It still catches him at a relatively early stage in his development, concentrating on jump blues-oriented material, sometimes with horn sections, showing the considerable influence of B.B. King. There's some sharp guitar on these sides (including some by Roy Gaines, who also played with Chuck Willis and Hound Dog Thornton), and the vocals are full and confident, if a bit overripe. But neophytes should begin with his early and mid-'60s sides, when his blend of blues and soul reached a much higher level of maturity. —*Richie Unterberger*

The Voice: Duke Recordings 1959-69 / 1991 / Ace ✦✦✦✦✦
A 26-track compilation of Duke sides from Bland's peak decade (1959-1969). MCA's two-volume *The Duke Recordings* covers this period in greater depth, and will be more readily available to most North American consumers. On its own terms, though, it's an excellent collection. Contains most of his biggest R&B hits ("Turn On Your Love Light," "Stormy Monday Blues," "Call On Me," "Ain't Nothing You Can Do"), as well as some cuts that did not make it onto *The Duke Recordings*. —*Richie Unterberger*

★ **I Pity the Fool/The Duke Recordings, Vol. 1** / 1992 / MCA ✦✦✦✦✦
Everything the young Bland waxed for Duke between 1952 and the 1960 date that produced "Cry, Cry, Cry" and the R&B-laced "Don't Cry No More." From 1955 on, this is uniformly seminal stuff, Bland's vocal confidence growing by the session and buttressed by the consistently innovative riffs and solos of guitarists Clarence Hollimon, Wayne Bennett (he's amazing on a torrid "You Did Me Wrong"), Roy Gaines, and Pat Hare. "Farther Up the Road," the exotic ballad "Hold Me Tenderly," "Little Boy Blue," and the title track are but few of the two-disc collection's many standouts. No blues fan should be minus this set! —*Bill Dahl*

Years of Tears / 1993 / Malaco ✦✦✦✦
Perhaps no artist has flourished at Malaco more than Bobby "Blue" Bland. Bland's animated, raw voice, though not as wide-ranging, still has a character and quality unmatched in blues, soul or vintage R&B. This CD is his finest for the label since *Members Only*. The opening number "Somewhere Between Right & Wrong" has a simmering track, Bland's mournful, explosive leads, tasty organ, tight drumming, and on-the-money lyrics from composers Johnny Barranco and Jackson. It sets the stage for nine additional country-tinged and bluesy soul tunes, including three from Frederick Knight, who also produced his compositions. It's not his Duke material, but it's close enough to satisfy. —*Ron Wynn*

☆ **Turn on Your Love Light/The Duke Recordings, Vol. 2** / 1994 / MCA ✦✦✦✦✦
Picking up right where the first volume left off and continuing into 1964, this two-disc compilation (50 tracks!) showcases one of Bland's most appealing periods at Duke. Joe Scott was experimenting boldly with his protege's repertoire, his brass-powered arrangements urging Bland to increased heights of incendiary energy on "Turn on Your Love Light" and "Yield Not to Temptation" (driven by future James Brown drummer Jabo Starks' funky traps) and advanced sophistication levels for the honey-smooth "Share Your Love with Me" and "That's the Way Love Is." Bennett's crackling blues licks invest "Stormy Monday Blues," "The Feeling Is Gone," and "Black Night" with T-Bone-derived tradition, while Bland handles Charlie Rich's "Who Will the Next Fool Be" with just the right amount of bluesy resignation. —*Bill Dahl*

Sad Street / Oct. 24, 1995 / Malaco ✦✦
Malaco's well-oiled, violin-enriched studio sound fits Bland's laid-back contemporary approach just fine these days (even if his voice admittedly ain't what it used to be). With top-flight songwriters George Jackson, Robert Johnson, and Sam Mosley contributing material to the project, the results are agreeable if less than earthshaking. Why Bland chose to cover Rod Stewart's "Tonight's the Night" remains a mystery, however. —*Bill Dahl*

Touch of the Blues/Spotlighting The Man / Mobile Fidelity ✦✦✦✦
Two of Bland's better albums for Duke coupled on one great-sounding CD. Both LPs were issued originally in 1969 but contained tracks from as far back as his 1967 Top Ten R&B hit "That Did It" and its immediate follow-up, "Touch of the Blues." Bland never turned his back on the style that brought him to prominence (he digs into Charles Brown's "Driftin' Blues" aggressively, Bennett providing luscious chording behind him), even if his stately reading of Joe Turner's "Chains of Love" is sweetened considerably by strings. On the other hand, the husky singer's unwise whack at Anthony Newley's Broadway showstopper "Who Can I Turn To" is about as far removed from blues tradition as is imaginable. —*Bill Dahl*

Blind Blake (Arthur Phelps)

b. 1890s, Jacksonville, FL, **d.** 1933, Florida
Guitar, Vocals / Acoustic Country Blues, Piedmont Blues
What happened to Blind Blake? His disappearance in 1932 from the Chicago blues scene, where he was undisputed king of the string and recorded 81 solo sides for Paramount, is one of the unresolved mysteries of early blues. Similarly mysterious is Blake's prodigious fingerstyle guitar technique, which has plank spankers to this day asking: "How the hell did he do that!?"

Like many early blues recording artists, Blake was regionally well-known, if not legendary, before he began making records. His peregrinations through the Southeast and Midwest were those of the itinerant songster; his repertoire included everything from blues to rags to music hall novelties. On Paramount records he broke out in 1926 with his debut release, a finger-buster called "West Coast Blues." Through the late '20s he performed and recorded with banjoists Papa Charlie Jackson and Gus Cannon, chanteuses Ma Rainey and Ida Cox, pianist Charlie Spand and a host of others as first-call guitar on Paramount's studio A-team. His best playing, however, was reserved for solo outings like "Diddie-Wah-Diddie" or "Police Dog Blues." On these he spun off guitar variations so dense they were dubbed "piano sounding" by his label. The hot licks framed lyrics often laced with suggestive double entendre. His hypermetabolic instrumentals were full of diffident spoken asides in an accent that gave credence to his supposed Southern seaboard origins.

Blake spent part of 1930 and 1931 touring with the vaudeville show "Happy-Go-Lucky" and returned to the Paramount studios in Grafton, WI, for his final session in 1932. His subsequent whereabouts, including rumors of his murder or death by mishap, have never been substantiated. It's commonly supposed that, as the Depression knocked the bottom out of the race record industry, Blake simply moved back to the South so beloved in his song lyrics, and died there soon after.

Blake's influence, especially in the folk/blues revival, was pervasive. His brilliant playing was touted by guitar godfathers like Josh White and Gary Davis; his songs covered by contemporary acousticians including Dave Van Ronk, Leon Redbone and Ry Cooder. On guitar, he's still the one to beat…probably always will be. As he says himself, "Here's somethin' gonna make you feel good!" —*Steve James*

★ **Ragtime Guitar's Foremost Fingerpicker** / 1984 / Yazoo ✦✦✦✦✦
Ragtime Guitar's Foremost Fingerpicker contains a total of 28 prime tracks from Blind Blake. Alternating between solo acoustic numbers and songs recorded with a string band, the set demonstrates how exceptionally gifted the guitarist was—he's playing arrangements and rhythms that several subsequent generations were never able to completely figure out. Blind Blake was one of the finest acoustic guitarists of the '20s and '30s and this is the definitive compilation. —*Thom Owens*

Complete Recorded Works, Vols. 1-4 / 1991 / Document ✦✦✦
Over the course of four discs—which are all sold individually— Document Records presents everything Blind Blake recorded in the late '20s and early '30s for Paramount Records. During that time, he was one of the most popular bluesmen in Chicago and these 80-plus sides show why. Blake had a unique guitar style that influenced a number of successive generations. For that reason alone, *Complete Recorded Works in Chronological Order* would be of interest, but the music itself is compelling and gripping. However, the length and comprehensiveness of the set makes it a collection that only musicologists and dedicated fans would find necessary. For more casual listeners, Yazoo's *Ragtime Guitar's Foremost Fingerpicker* is a better purchase, since it distills all of his classic tracks to one disc. —*Thom Owens*

Rory Block

b. New York, NY
Guitar, Vocals / Modern Acoustic Blues
Rory Block is one of the brightest stars among a galaxy of modern-day country-blues interpreters. Rory's superb renderings of classic songs by Robert Johnson, Tommy Johnson, Charley Patton, and others display her deep passion and instinct for historic preservation, but seldom are her covers mere mimics. With its body-pounds, potent bass-string snaps, and precision rhythms, her fierce acoustic-guitar attack recalls the great Willie Brown. Rory's originals are often as strong as her covers, a standout being the title track from *Mama's Blues*. Her urgent, soulful voice is in a class of its own. As Taj Mahal says, "She's very simply the best there is."

Born and raised in New York's Greenwich Village, Rory Block began playing music as child. When she was ten years old, she became infatuated with the Village's folk music scene and she began playing guitar, taking classical guitar lessons. While she was a teenager she heard the blues and fell in love with the music. She played and took lessons from bluesmen like Rev. Gary Davis, Mississippi John Hurt, and Son House. In her mid-teens, Block left New York for California with fellow blues guitarist Stefan Grossman. After she arrived in California, she played clubs and coffeehouses, but she soon stopped performing, choosing to raise a family instead.

In the mid-'70s, Rory returned to performing, landing a record contract with the independent label Blue Goose in 1975. That same year, the label released her debut album, *Rory Block (I'm In Love)*. After its release, she was signed by Chrysalis Records, which released *Intoxication So Bitter Sweet* and *You're the One* in 1977 and 1978, respectively. During the late '70s, her music was spiked with contemporary R&B and pop production techniques in an ill-fated attempt to reach a mass audience.

Block didn't come into her own until she signed with Rounder Records in 1981. Beginning with *High Heeled Blues*, her first album for the label, she returned to her roots—solo acoustic country blues. Featuring a mixture of standards and originals, *High Heeled Blues* received positive reviews from both blues-oriented and mainstream publications. The positive reviews

paved the way for popular success—throughout the '80s and '90s, Block was one of the most popular attractions on the blues circuit. Toward the beginning of the '90s, she expanded her sonic pallette somewhat, recording with other musicians and occasionally a full band. However, the bulk of her work remains straightforward, traditional Delta acoustic blues and she is one of the artists that brought the genre to a mass audience in the '80s. Rory Block remains a popular artist in the '90s, selling numerous albums and concert tickets. —*Jas Obrecht & Stephen Thomas Erlewine*

High Heeled Blues / 1982 / Rounder ✦✦✦✦✦
This was the most blues-oriented release of the three sessions Block issued in 1989 for Rounder; it was also the most concentrated and successful. There were none of the experimental or tentative qualities that sometimes marred the other two dates; Block was in command from the opening moments of her cover of "Walkin' Blues" to the final bars of "Uncloudy Day." Her voice had fire, soul and grit, and she never sounded maudlin or unconvincing, whether doing "Hilarity Rag" or "Devil Got My Man." Her playing was also dynamic and focused, and John Sebastian obviously made a good production partner, as Block got back on track after making records that contained some good cuts but weren't as consistent. —*Ron Wynn*

Blue Horizon / 1983 / Rounder ✦✦✦
Block bounced all over the musical lot on this session. She did vintage folk tunes such as "Frankie and Johnny" effectively and covered Rev. Gary Davis' "Feel Just Like Goin' On" and the spiritual "Swing Low" with vigor, but wasn't as compelling on "Catastrophe Rag" or the bittersweet/satiric "Just Like A Man." Block's voice and talents are versatile enough to handle multiple styles, but she remains first and foremost a fine interpreter of classic blues and gospel. When she opts for the singer/songwriter bit or folk/country mode, she's professional enough to bring it off, but lacks the flair or distinctiveness to make it sound anything except competent. —*Ron Wynn*

Rhinestones & Steel Strings / 1984 / Rounder ✦✦✦✦
Guitarist/vocalist Rory Block's mix of traditional blues covers, originals, satirical and folk/country material was featured on this album. Her versions of Robert Wilkins' "No Way For Me To Get Along" and Rev. Gary Davis' "Sit Down On The Banks" were among the high points, as well as Block's "Dr. Make It Right" and "I Might Find A Way." For the most part, the songs were nicely performed and varied between upbeat and somber themes. Block's vocals were frequently outstanding and never less than convincing, while her playing was strong and steady. —*Ron Wynn*

I've Got a Rock in My Sock / 1986 / Rounder ✦✦
Rory Block was combative, poignant, energetic and laid-back on this record. She did a good cover of Charlie Patton's "Moon's Going Down," which changed things considerably from the strident mood established on the opening selection "Send The Man Back Home." She handled the melancholy title track, was playful on "Lovin' Whiskey" and introspective on the final song "Highland Overture," a guitar/synthesizer duet that almost, but didn't quite plunge into the New Age/background music abyss. This seemed like an experimental/searching session for Block, who sometimes was enjoyable, but overall didn't fare as well as on most of her other releases. —*Ron Wynn*

House of Hearts / 1987 / Rounder ✦✦✦
A somber, morose mood permeated this album dedicated to Block's son, guitarist Thiele David Biehusen, who died in a car crash at age 20 and whose voice can be heard on the answering machine in the lengthy final cut "House of Hearts." There are also other equally gripping tunes, like "Farewell Young Man," "Heavenly Bird" and "Bonnie Boy." Block's voice was at its most mournful, and this is both a deeply moving work and a downer of an album. It's impossible not to be affected hearing Block's singing or these lyrics; anyone who's been through any remotely similar experience will feel the pain, and even those who haven't can't help but share in her sadness. —*Ron Wynn*

● **Best Blues & Originals** / 1988 / Rounder ✦✦✦✦✦
Best Blues & Originals collects the highlights from Rory Block's '80s albums for Rounder, saving a bunch of fine tracks from otherwise spotty releases. It's a nice overview and, consequently, a solid introduction to her catalog. —*Thom Owens*

Mama's Blues / 1991 / Rounder ✦✦✦
Although she competently covers many musical areas, vocal-

ist/guitarist Rory Block's best genre has always been traditional blues. She emphasizes that idiom here, doing strong, declarative versions of Robert Johnson's "Terraplane Blues," Tommy Johnson's "Bye Bye Blues" and "Big Road Blues" and her own originals "Ain't No Shame," "Got To Shine" and the title track. She concludes the session in what has become a regular album feature, the rousing gospel number "Sing Good News." —*Ron Wynn*

Ain't I a Woman / 1992 / Rounder ✦✦✦✦✦
Rory Block's 11th album marks both a personal and professional milestone. Now a thoroughly experienced singer, Block sounds much more confident and assured doing traditional blues tunes. Her performance on the title cut is both assertive and definitive, while she also displays her customary versatility, doing country and folk-flavored numbers such as "Silver Wings" and "Rolling Log" in addition to a stunning gospel number, "Walk In Jerusalem." Block's vocals and guitar work have blossomed, toughened and greatly improved over her career, and are in prime form here. —*Ron Wynn*

Angel of Mercy / Feb. 28, 1994 / Rounder ✦✦✦
Block moves completely away from the blues form on this release, doing original pieces that evoke the familiar themes of alienation, anguish, and romantic conflicts, but in a production climate geared more toward folk and singer/songwriter arrangements than 12-bar settings. She still plays excellent guitar solos and accompaniment, but her vocals are now powerful or mournful, questioning or declarative, and she's unconcerned with trying to capture the quality of someone else's compositions. The disc's final selection, the nine-minute-plus "A Father and Two Sons," reworks the biblical Prodigal son tale with a contemporary focus, featuring wonderful vocal interaction between Block and her son Jordan. This album showcases Rory Block's own sound and vision and deserves widespread praise and attention. —*Ron Wynn*

When a Woman Gets the Blues / 1995 / Rounder ✦✦✦

Tornado / Mar. 19, 1996 / Rounder ✦✦✦
After establishing her blues credentials with the traditional "Mississippi Bottom Blues," Rory Block turns to a set of original folk-rock songs on which she is joined by a band and such guests as David Lindley (who plays a guitar solo on "Pictures of You") and Mary-Chapin Carpenter (who sings harmony on "You Didn't Mind"). Block brings a blues simplicity and directness to her music and lyrics, which helps ease her transition from folk-blues interpreter to folk-rock singer/songwriter. —*William Ruhlmann*

The Early Tapes 1975-1976 / Alcazar ✦✦
On *The Early Tapes 1975-1976*, Rory Block is still trying to find a distinctive style. She samples from her idols—Robert Johnson, Charley Patton, and several others—adding slight blues and folk influences to her solo acoustic blues. However, she hasn't arrived at an original sound on any of these takes. Consequently, *Early Tapes* is of interest to historians and Rory Block completists, but few other listeners. —*Thom Owens*

Michael Bloomfield

b. Jul. 28, 1943, Chicago, IL, **d.** Feb. 15, 1981
Guitar / Electric Chicago Blues
Michael Bloomfield was born July 28, 1943, in Chicago, IL. An indifferent student and self-described social outcast, Bloomfield immersed himself in the multicultural music world that existed in Chicago in the 1950s.

He got his first guitar at age 13. Initially attracted to the roots-rock sound of Elvis Presley and Scotty Moore, Bloomfield soon discovered the electrified big-city blues music indigenous to Chicago. At the age of 14 the exuberant guitar *wunderkind* began to visit the blues clubs on Chicago's South Side with friend Roy Ruby in search of his new heroes: players such as Muddy Waters, Otis Spann, Howlin' Wolf, and Magic Sam. Not content with viewing the scene from the audience, Bloomfield was known to leap onto the stage, asking if he could sit in as he simultaneously plugged in his guitar and began playing riffs.

Bloomfield was quickly accepted on the South Side, as much for his ability as for the audiences' appreciation of the novelty of seeing a young White player in a part of town where few Whites were seen. Bloomfield soon discovered a group of like-minded outcasts. Young White players such as Paul Butterfield, Nick

Gravenites, Charlie Musselwhite, and Elvin Bishop were also establishing themselves as fans who could hold their own with established bluesmen, many of whom were old enough to be their fathers.

In addition to playing with the established stars of the day, Bloomfield began to search out older, forgotten bluesmen, playing and recording with Sleepy John Estes, Yank Rachell, Little Brother Montgomery and Big Joe Williams, among others. By this time he was managing a Chicago folk music club, the Fickle Pickle, and often hired older acoustic blues players for the Tuesday night blues sessions. Big Joe Williams memorialized those times in the song "Pick a Pickle" with the line "You know Mike Bloomfield...will always treat you right...come to the Pickle, every Tuesday night." Bloomfield's relationship with Big Joe Williams is documented in "Me and Big Joe," a moving short story detailing Bloomfield's adventures on the road with Williams.

Bloomfield's guitar work as a session player caught the ear of legendary CBS producer and talent scout John Hammond, Sr., who flew to Chicago and immediately signed him to a recording contract. However CBS was unsure of exactly how to promote their new artist, declining to release any of the tracks recorded by Bloomfield's band, which included harp player Charlie Musselwhite.

With a contract but not much else, Bloomfield returned to playing clubs around Chicago until he was approached by Paul Rothchild, the producer of the Paul Butterfield Blues Band albums. Bloomfield was recruited to play slide guitar and piano on early recordings (later released as *The Lost Elektra Sessions*) which were rejected for not fully capturing the sound of the band. Although more competitors than friends ("I knew Paul, was scared of him," remembered Mike), the addition of Bloomfield to the Butterfield Band provided Paul Butterfield with a musician of equal caliber—Paul and Michael inspired and challenged each other as they traded riffs and musical ideas, one establishing a pattern and the other following it, extending it, and handing it back.

In between recording sessions with the Butterfield Band, Bloomfield backed up Bob Dylan on the classic *Highway 61 Revisited* album, and appeared with him at the Newport Folk Festival in 1965 when Dylan stunned the purist "folk" crowd by playing electric rock 'n' roll. Declining an offer from Dylan to join his touring band, Bloomfield and the Butterfield Blues Band returned to the studio; with the addition of pianist Mark Naftalin they finally captured their live sound on vinyl.

The first two Butterfield Blues Band albums, the Dylan sessions, and the live appearances by the Butterfield Band firmly established Bloomfield as one of the most talented and influential guitar players in America. The second album featured the Bloomfield composition "East-West," which ushered in an era of long instrumental psychedelic improvisations.

Bloomfield left the Butterfield Blues Band in early 1967 ostensibly to give original guitarist Elvin Bishop, in Mike's words, "a little space." Undoubtedly he had also become uncomfortable with Paul Butterfield's position as bandleader and was anxious to lead his own band.

That band, The Electric Flag, included Bloomfield's old friends from Chicago, organist Barry Goldberg and singer/songwriter Nick Gravenites, as well as bass player Harvey Brooks and drummer Buddy Miles. The band was well received at its official debut at the Monterey Pop Festival but quickly fell apart due to drugs, egos, and poor management.

Bloomfield, weary of the road, suffering from insomnia, and uncomfortable in the role of guitar superstar, returned to San Francisco to score movies, produce other artists, and play studio sessions. One of those sessions was a day of jamming in the studio with keyboardist Al Kooper, who had previously worked with Bloomfield on the 1965 Dylan sessions.

Super Session, the resultant release, with Bloomfield on side one and guitarist Stephen Stills on side two, once again thrust Bloomfield into the spotlight. Kooper's production and the improvisational nature of the recording session captured the quintessential Bloomfield sound: the fast flurries of notes, the incredible string bending, the precise attack, and his masterful use of tension and release.

Although *Super Session* was the most successful recording of his career, Bloomfield considered it to be a "scam," more of an excuse to sell records than a pursuit of musical goals. After a follow-up live album, he "retired" to San Francisco and lowered his visibility.

In the '70s, Bloomfield played gigs in the San Francisco area and infrequently toured as Bloomfield and Friends, a group which usually included Mark Naftalin and Nick Gravenites. Bloomfield also occasionally helped out friends by lending his name to recording projects and business propositions, such as the ill-fated Electric Flag reunion in 1974 and the KGB album in 1976. In the mid-'70s Bloomfield recorded a number of albums with a more traditional blues focus for smaller record labels. He also recorded an instructional album of various blues styles for *Guitar Player* magazine.

By the late '70s, Bloomfield's continuing drug and health problems caused erratic behavior and missed gigs, alienating a number of his old associates. Bloomfield continued playing with other musicians, including Dave Shorey and Jonathan Cramer. In the summer of 1980, he toured Italy with classical guitarist Woody Harris and cellist Maggie Edmondson. On November 15, 1980, Bloomfield joined Bob Dylan on stage at the Warfield Theater in San Francisco and jammed on "Like a Rolling Stone," the song they had recorded together 15 years earlier.

Michael Bloomfield was found dead in his car of a drug overdose in San Francisco, CA, on February 15, 1981.

Nick Gravenites remembers Michael Bloomfield this way: "I thought he was a huge giant of a person. I think the totality of his character is the thing that impressed me most. People forget how charismatic he was. He had a certain charisma about him, people wanted to be around him, touch the hem of his garment, that sort of thing. I think it was the totality of his character I was impressed with, not only his musical ability but also his intellect, his sense of humor, his compassion, his generosity, all those things that make up a human being. And those are my fondest memories, of character.

"He was quite a forceful personality. He was quite a wit. And also had a very deep character—was very generous, very soulful. The effect that he had on me and people around him, people that knew him and loved his music and stuff was profound.

"Michael's friends, the ones that were closest to him, really loved the guy. And they did it for a lot of reasons. He helped them live their lives, made something out of their lives in many ways, very profoundly. I can still think in terms of those major, those big terms, when I think about Michael." —*Jan Mark Wolkin*

● **Super Session** / 1968 / Columbia ◆◆◆◆◆
Al Kooper was the mastermind behind this appropriately named album, one side of which features his "spontaneous" studio collaboration with Mike Bloomfield and the other a session with Stephen Stills. The recordings have an off-the-cuff energy that displays the inventiveness of the two guitarists to best advantage. The best-selling recording of Bloomfield's career, it inspired the follow-up *The Live Adventures of Mike Bloomfield and Al Kooper.* —*Jeff Tamarkin*

It's Not Killing Me / 1969 / Columbia ◆◆
Let's see. For his first solo album, take a brilliant young guitarist who can barely sing and put the emphasis on…his vocals. Well, somebody thought it was a good idea. Too bad they were wrong. There are just a few examples of that B.B. King-inflected guitar style among the rock and country-flavored throwaways. —*Cary Wolfson*

The Live Adventures of Mike Bloomfield and Al Kooper / 1969 / Columbia ◆◆
Recorded over three nights in 1968 at the Fillmore Auditorium in San Francisco, the follow-up to the acclaimed *Super Session* has its moments, but is mostly long on '60s noodly grooviness and lacking in focus and inspiration. It's notable (sort of) for Bloomfield's singing debut. —*Cary Wolfson*

Live at Bill Graham's Fillmore West / 1969 / Columbia ◆◆◆◆
This session from early 1969 featured Nick Gravenites, Mark Naftalin, John Kahn and Snooky Flowers (among others), with cameos from Taj Mahal and Jesse Ed Davis, but it's clear from the opening notes who the real star is. Over the years, Bloomfield's titanic solos on "Blues on a Westside" have dwarfed the rest of the album in my memory, but the truth is his playing just burns across every track. (More of Michael's great guitar work from these shows is on Nick Gravenites' *My Labors* on Columbia.) —*Cary Wolfson*

Triumvirate / 1973 / Columbia ◆◆◆
In 1973 someone at Columbia evidently decided to try and recoup some of the investment the label made in Bloomfield and John Hammond—they were thrown into a recording studio along with Dr. John, who had recently scored a hit with "Right Place, Wrong Time." It probably sounded like a good idea at the time, but the results were uninspired. Pass by this CD and pick up any one of their solo recordings instead. — *Jan Mark Wolkin*

Try It Before You Buy It / 1975 / One Way ◆◆
Try It Before You Buy It is one of Michael Bloomfield's neglected albums, and there's a reason why—although there's some very fine playing scattered throughout the album, the performances are uneven and unfocused. Furthermore, the album leans too close to a straight rock 'n' roll direction for blues purists. If you dig hard, there are some rewards on *Try It Before You Buy It*, but on the whole, it's one that should be left on the shelf. —*Thom Owens*

Mill Valley Session / 1976 / Polydor ◆◆◆

If You Love Those Blues, Play 'Em As You Please / 1977 / Guitar Player ◆◆◆

Analine / 1977 / Takoma ◆◆

Michael Bloomfield / 1978 / Takoma ◆◆◆

Between the Hard Place and the Ground / 1979 / Takoma ◆◆

Living in the Fast Lane / 1980 / AJK ◆◆◆
Michael Bloomfield was a pioneer in blues-rock, one of the performers who found a way to maintain his own sound while paying tribute to the blues greats that created the music he idolized. The ten tracks presented on *Living in the Fast Lane* weren't as vital as his earlier material, but were done with the same intensity and passion that marked all his numbers. They were backed on several cuts by Duke Tito And The Marin Country Playboys, while on "When I Get Home," The Singers of The Church of God In Christ joined lead vocalist Roger Troy for a rousing, spirit-filled performance that was the album's high point. —*Ron Wynn*

Cruisin' for a Bruisin' / 1981 / Takoma ◆◆◆

The Best of Michael Bloomfield / 1987 / Takoma ◆◆◆◆
While the title's accuracy is debatable, this CD contains 10 fine tracks drawn from three albums produced by Norman Dayron for Takoma between 1978 and 1980. Arrangements are spare (with one horn-powered exception) and Bloomfield's vocals are greatly improved over his early attempts. Run-time, as on all the Takoma releases, is short at 43:30. —*Cary Wolfson*

● **Don't Say That I Ain't Your Man** / 1994 / Sony ◆◆◆◆◆
Fifteen tracks covering the pioneering blues-rock guitarist's '60s work, which was by far his best and most influential. Bloomfield worked with a bunch of bands during the decade, and the compilation flits rather hurriedly from his contributions to The Paul Butterfield Blues Band and Electric Flag to his collaborations with Al Kooper and some late-'60s solo tracks (none of his groundbreaking mid-'60s work with Dylan is here). Collectors will be interested in the first five songs, which date from previously unreleased sessions produced by John Hammond in late 1964 and early 1965. Featuring Charlie Musselwhite on harmonica, this pre-Butterfield Blues Band outfit plays convincingly, but the material is standard-issue, and Bloomfield's vocals are thin and weak (they didn't improve much over time). As befits Bloomfield's considerable but erratic talent, this is an interesting but erratic compilation; seek out the first two Paul Butterfield albums for a more cohesive showcase of his skills. —*Richie Unterberger*

I'm With You Always / Demon ◆◆◆
This release, recorded at McCabe's Guitar Shop in Santa Monica, CA, in 1977, captures a superb live show, with Bloomfield in top form as he performs before an appreciative audience in an intimate setting. Michael's singing is spirited and his guitar playing is precise and inventive as he plays favorite songs from his repertoire. Highlights include solo acoustic performances of two songs written by Shelton Brooks in the early 1900s, a piano/guitar duet demonstrating the rapport he had with pianist Mark Naftalin, and hot performances by Bloomfield, Naftalin and a rhythm section of Buddy Helm on drums and Buell Neidlinger on bass. Bloomfield shows what he had been doing all those years out of the spotlight—refining his technique and researching the music he loved. —*Jan Mark Wolkin*

The Root of Blues / Laserlight ✦✦✦
A budget-label reissue of the instructional blues LP released by *Guitar Player* magazine in 1976, this CD includes most of the songs but omits Michael's spoken passages about each track. Bloomfield pays tribute to his influences and favorites: acoustic and electric, solo and with a band. Standout tracks include "Death in My Family," played in the style of Guitar Slim, "WDIA," a tribute to B.B. King, "City Girl," dedicated to T-Bone Walker, and an acoustic version of "Kansas City," played, in Bloomfield's words, "in a style I would call 'Travis Picking', after Merle Travis. It seems an anomaly to use a modern style for such an old song, but the method of syncopated contrapuntal fingerpicking is well suited to the song because the key of E has so many open strings." —*Jan Mark Wolkin*

Blues Boy Willie (Willie McFalls)

b. 1946, Memphis, TX
Harmonica, Vocals / Modern Electric Blues
Willie McFalls, a native Memphian from Texas, not Tennessee, took the chitlin circuit by surprise in 1990 when the comical blues dialog of "Be-Who?" put his second album on the *Billboard* charts and his act on the road. Blues Boy Willie came to Ichiban Records courtesy of his boyhood friend from Texas, bluesman-producer Gary B. B. Coleman. Willie's three albums to date all bear the typical Coleman touch—competent but predictable blues tracks with a small studio band. It has been the spunky spoken repartee between Willie and his wife Miss Lee on the novelty numbers that has earned Willie an unexpected niche on the Southern soul-blues scene. —*Jim O'Neal*

● **Strange Things Happening** / 1989 / Ichiban ✦✦✦✦✦
This blues/R&B vocalist has a very contemporary Southern sound. —*Niles J. Frantz*

Be Who? 2 / 1990 / Ichiban ✦✦✦

I Got the Blues / 1992 / Ichiban ✦✦✦

Don't Look Down / 1993 / Ichiban ✦✦

Juke Joint Blues / 1995 / Ichiban ✦✦✦✦

The Blues Project

Group / Modern Electric Blues
They've been called New York's first "underground" group, and in his autobiography, *Backstage Passes*, Al Kooper half-jokingly referred to his former band as the Jewish Beatles. Unfortunately, they didn't stay together long enough to realize such potential. After playing on a 1965 Elektra sampler title, *The Blues Project*, folk-blues guitarist/singer Danny Kalb used that name when he formed an electric band with Steve Katz (guitarist with Elektra's Even Dozen Jug Band), conservatory trained Andy Kulberg (on bass and flute), jazz-inflected drummer Roy Blumenfeld, and singer/harmonica player Tommy Flanders. Al Kooper—a Tin Pan Alley songwriter (Gary Lewis' "This Diamond Ring" and various Gene Pitney flipsides) who had played guitar with the Royal Teens and organ with Bob Dylan (on "Like a Rolling Stone")—sat in for the band's Columbia audition and joined up. (They eventually signed to Verve.) The band took a more eclectic approach to blues than, say, Butterfield, incorporating jazz, rock, folk, and classical. After their debut, recorded live at New York's Cafe Au-Go-Go, Flanders left to pursue a solo career that never took flight. Kooper wrote the band's only charted single, "No Time Like the Right Time," but left before their third LP was released (although he appears on it), forming the horn-laden Blood, Sweat & Tears, into which Katz quickly followed. After Kalb split (due to ill health) Kulberg and Blumenfeld added Don Kretmar (saxophone and bass), John Gregory (guitar and vocals) and violinist Richard Greene to record *Planned Obsolescence*, and then renamed the band Seatrain. After attempted regroupings with Kalb or Flanders, five of the original members (everyone but Flanders) reunited for a 1973 concert in Central Park. Their most recent reunion was for Kooper's live double-CD retrospective *Soul of a Man* (on Music Masters). —*Dan Forte*

Live at the Cafe Au-Go-Go / May 1966 / Verve/Forecast ✦✦✦
Although Tommy Flanders (who'd already left the band by the time this debut hit the streets) is credited as sole vocalist, four of the then-sextet's members sang; in fact, Danny Kalb handles as many leads as Flanders (four each), Steve Katz takes center stage on Donovan's "Catch the Wind," and Al Kooper is featured on "I Want to Be Your Driver." The band could be lowdown when

appropriate (Kalb's reading of "Jelly, Jelly"), high-energy (Muddy Waters' "Goin' Down Louisiana" sounds closer to Chuck Berry or Bo Diddley), and unabashedly eclectic (tossing in Donovan and Eric Anderson with no apologies). Kalb's moody take on "Alberta" is transcendent, and the uptempo arrangement of "Spoonful" is surprisingly effective. —*Dan Forte*

Projections / Nov. 1966 / Verve/Forecast ✦✦✦✦✦
Produced by Tom Wilson (Dylan, Zappa), the Blues Project's second effort was their finest hour. In less than a year the enthusiastic live band had matured into a seasoned studio ensemble. Steve Katz's features are lightweight folk but Al Kooper reworks two gospel themes ("Wake Me, Shake Me," "I Can't Keep from Crying") into ambitious blues-rock compositions, and Danny Kalb proves he's no mere folkie on extended versions of "Two Trains Running" and "Caress Me Baby." Bassist Andy Kulberg switches to flute and Kalb gets psychedelic on the jazzy "Flute Thing," penned by Kooper. —*Dan Forte*

Live at Town Hall / Sep. 1967 / Verve/Forecast ✦✦✦
Released just after Al Kooper left the band, one imagines that neither he nor the other members of the group were pleased with this LP. According to Kooper, it was a pastiche of studio outtakes and a few live performances, and only one of the songs was actually recorded at New York City's Town Hall. Anyway, this has a meandering, ten-minute "Flute Thing" and decent live versions of "Wake Me, Shake Me" and "I Can't Keep From Crying" which, despite a somewhat rawer feel, are not necessary supplements to the fine studio takes. "Where There's Smoke, There's Fire" and the great "No Time Like The Right Time" had already been released as singles; to hear them without canned applause, you only need to turn to Rhino's first-rate *Best Of The Blues Project* instead. That compilation also contains the other cut of note on this album, an outtake-sounding cover of Patrick Sky's "Love Will Endure." —*Richie Unterberger*

Reunion in Central Park / 1973 / MGM ✦✦✦
Considering that the original lineup had broken up six years earlier, this ranks as one of the most artistically successful reunions in blues or rock. If there were any ego problems, they don't show; typically Kalb and Kooper shine, but all five are playing as a team. Most important, the members seem to respect their own past—and recreate it with spontaneity and energy. —*Dan Forte*

● **The Best of The Blues Project** / 1989 / Rhino ✦✦✦✦✦
With the exception of a live version of "Flute Thing" from The Blues Project's 1973 reunion concert included only on the CD version, this compilation is culled entirely from the albums *Live at the Cafe Au-Go-Go, Projections,* and *The Blues Project Live At Town Hall,* all recorded and released in the period 1966-67. Just as those individual albums do, it confirms the acclaim accorded The Blues Project at the time. The group's sophistication and ability to create a hybrid of musical styles keeps the music from sounding dated. In fact, this music not only stands as among the best of its time, but it continues to appeal where much of the music made simultaneously fails to escape its era. (Not to be confused with *Best of The Blues Project*, Verve Forecast FTS 3077, released in 1969, which is an earlier compilation with a different selection of songs.) —*William Ruhlmann*

Projections from the Past / 1989 / Hablabel ✦✦✦
A double album of dubious legality, but fairly easy availability. This captures The Blues Project's best lineup—Kooper, Katz, Kalb, Kulberg, and Blumenfeld—live at the Matrix club in San Francisco on September 1, 1966. If there's any revelation to be had from these fair-quality tapes, it's that there's not much of a revelation at all. The group performs a lot of the stronger material from their first and second albums in versions very close to the records. They shine brightest on the more adventurous material with jazz and folk tangents, like "Steve's Song," "Flute Thing," "Catch The Wind," and "Cheryl's Going Home." Most of the rest is competent but not especially brilliant white-boy blues renditions of numbers like "Hoochie Coochie Man," "You Can't Catch Me," and "You Can't Judge A Book By The Cover"; the swaggering "Shake That Baby" is about the best of these. Essential only for serious collectors. Be warned that there are a few (not many) clumsy edits, and that the entire fourth side is simply tracks lifted from their *Live at Town Hall* LP. —*Richie Unterberger*

Lucille Bogan (Lucille Armstrong)

b. Apr. 1, 1897, Amory, MS, **d.** Aug. 10, 1948, Los Angeles, CA
Vocals / Classic Female Blues
The big-voiced Bogan made some important sides in the classic female blues tradition throughout the mid-'20s and early '30s. Singing with astonishing forthrightness about abusive men, prostitution, and predilections for both whiskey and sex, her recorded work is all solidly imbued with proto-feminist outlooks, all the more surprising given the time frame in which her best work exists. After scoring a "race" hit in 1927 with "Sweet Petunia," she changed her name (and her vocal style with it) to Bessie Jackson. Her best known tune, the salacious "Shave 'Em Dry," has shown up on numerous compilations of bawdy blues material and is always the track everyone plays first, as its x-rated lyrical content has cross-generational appeal. Unlike other women singers from the genre, she seldom strayed into pop-style music, remaining essentially a straightahead blues stylist with a rock solid sense of time and big old heart. —*Cub Koda*

Lucille Bogan (1923-1935) / 1989 / Story Of Blues ✦✦✦✦✦
A solid 18-track compilation of Lucille's best sides from her peak period. (Import) —*Cub Koda*

● **Lucille Bogan & Walter Roland, 1927-1935** / Yazoo ✦✦✦✦✦
Fourteen-track compilation split evenly down the middle between Bogan and her main piano accompanist, Roland, who also doubles on guitar on some tracks. The Bogan sides are a particular delight, featuring a version of "Barbecue Bess" that is nothing short of sublime. As all of these tracks are rescued off highly battered 78s, the fidelity is about what you would expect. But that's no reason to deter you from enjoying this timeless music. —*Cub Koda*

Deanna Bogart

Piano, Saxophone, Vocals / Contemporary Electric Blues
The amazing Ms. Bogart is a triple-threat entertainer; she's more than capable of pounding the piano with a barrelhouse ferocity that belies the cool jazz chords she fits into the music, blowing rough-hewn tenor sax (with an obviously stylistic debt to Eddie Shaw) or singing with a throaty passion. Her unique songwriting has consistently become more and more focused with each successive release. A regular fixture on the roots music and blues festival circuit, the copious amounts of energy she puts into her personal blues hybrid (both in the studio and in person) makes her obviously something very special. —*AMG*

● **Out to Get You** / May 1991 / Blind Pig ✦✦✦✦✦
Debut album by this delightful two-fisted boogie-woogie pianist, saxophonist, and songster. Highlights abound everywhere, but of particular note are her striking originals "Over Thirty" and "Morning Glory." —*Cub Koda*

Crossing Borders / 1992 / Flying Fish ✦✦✦
The follow-up album to Bogart's debut effort is chock-full of the kind of wonderful cross-breeding of styles this artist brings to her work. "Don't Know a Thing About Love" is a slice of low-down funk 'n' nasty while the kickoff track, "Tell Me," rocks as hard as anything on the album. Of course, Deanna's specialty—the piano boogie—is represented nicely by the tracks "Eclectic Boogie" and "Backstage Boogie." —*Cub Koda*

Zuzu Bollin

b. Sep. 5, 1922, **d.** Oct. 2, 1990
Guitar, Vocals / Electric Texas Blues
Two 78s in the early '50s and a 1989 rediscovery album don't add up to much of a recorded legacy. But Zuzu Bollin's contribution to the Texas blues legacy shouldn't be overlooked—his T-Bone Walker-influenced sound typified postwar Lone Star blues guitar.
Born A.D. Bollin, Zuzu listened to everyone from Blind Lemon Jefferson and Leroy Carr (on records) to Joe Turner and Count Basie. He picked up his nickname while in the band of Texan E.X. Brooks; seems he had a sweet tooth for a brand of ginger snap cookies called ZuZus! Bollin formed his own combo in 1949, featuring young saxist David "Fathead" Newman. After a stint with Percy Mayfield's band, Bollin resumed playing around Dallas. In late 1951, he made his recording debut for Bob Sutton's Torch logo. Newman and saxist Leroy Cooper, both future members of Ray Charles' band, played on Bollin's "Why Don't You Eat Where You Slept Last Night" and "Headlight

Blues." A Torch follow-up, "Stavin' Chain"/"Cry, Cry, Cry," found Bollin backed by Jimmy McCracklin's combo.
No more recording ensued after that, though Bollin toured with bandleaders Ernie Fields and Joe Morris before chucking the music biz in 1964 to go into a more stable profession: dry cleaning. Bollin's 1987 rediscovery was the Dallas Blues Society's doing: they engineered a series of gigs and eventually a fine 1989 album, *Texas Bluesman*, that beautifully showcased Bollin's approach. Their efforts were barely in time—Bollin died in 1990. —*Bill Dahl*

● **Texas Bluesman** / 1988 / Antone's ✦✦✦✦✦
Zuzu's principal contribution to Texas blues history is an immaculately realized collection that includes remakes of both sides of his debut 78 (the original version of "Why Don't You Eat Where You Slept Last Night" is available on *Vol. 3* of Rhino's *Blues Masters* series, "Texas Blues") and a uniformly tasty lineup of jump blues goodies. The sterling band includes guitarist Duke Robillard (who co-produced), drummer George Rains, and saxists David Newman and Kaz Kazanoff. —*Bill Dahl*

Son Bonds

b. Mar. 16, 1909, Brownsville, TN, **d.** Aug. 31, 1947, Dyersburg, TN
Guitar, Kazoo, Vocals / Acoustic Country Blues
An associate of Sleepy John Estes and Hammie Nixon, Bonds played very much in the same rural Brownsville style that the Estes-Nixon team popularized in the '20s and '30s. Curiously, either Estes or Nixon (but never both of them together) played on all of Bonds' recordings. The music to one of Bonds' songs, "Back and Side Blues" (1934), became a standard blues melody when John Lee "Sonny Boy" Williamson from nearby Jackson, TN, used it in his classic "Good Morning, (Little) School Girl" (1937). According to Nixon, Bonds was shot to death, while sitting on his front porch, by a nearsighted neighbor who mistook him for another man. —*Jim O'Neal*

Complete Recorded Works in Chronological Order / Wolf ✦✦✦✦✦
Blues from Brownsville (1934-1941), it features Hammie Nixon and Sleepy John Estes. —*Jas Obrecht*

Juke Boy Bonner

b. Mar. 22, 1932, Bellville, TX, **d.** Jun. 29, 1978, Houston, TX
Guitar, Harmonica, Vocals / Electric Texas Blues
One-man bands weren't any too common on the postwar blues scene. Joe Hill Louis and Dr. Ross come to mind as greats who plied their trade all by their lonesome—and so did Juke Boy Bonner, a Texan whose talent never really earned him much in the way of tangible reward.
Born into impoverished circumstances in the Lone Star State during the Depression, Weldon Bonner took up the guitar in his teens. He caught a break in 1947 in Houston, winning a talent contest that led to a spot on a local radio outlet. He journeyed to Oakland in 1956, cutting his debut single for Bob Geddins' Irma imprint ("Rock with Me Baby"/"Well Baby") with Lafayette "Thing" Thomas supplying the lead guitar. Goldband Records boss Eddie Shuler was next to take a chance in 1960; Bonner recorded for him in Lake Charles, LA, with Katie Webster on piano, but once again, nothing happened career-wise.
Troubled by stomach problems during the '60s, Bonner utilized his hospital downtime to write poems that he later turned into songs. He cut his best work during the late '60s for Arhoolie Records, accompanying himself on both guitar and racked harmonica as he weaved extremely personal tales of his rough life in Houston. A few European tours ensued, but they didn't really lead to much. Toward the end of his life, he toiled in a chicken processing plant to make ends meet. Bonner died of cirrhosis of the liver in 1978. —*Bill Dahl*

Going Back to the Country / 1968 / Arhoolie ✦✦✦✦✦
● **Life Gave Me a Dirty Deal** / 1969 / Arhoolie ✦✦✦✦✦
Likely the most consistent and affecting collection you'll encounter by this singular Texas bluesman, whose strikingly personal approach was stunningly captured by Arhoolie's Chris Strachwitz during the late '60s in Houston. Twenty-three utter originals include "Stay Off Lyons Avenue," "Struggle Here in Houston," "I Got My Passport," and the title track. Bonner sang movingly of his painfully impoverished existence for Arhoolie, and the results still resound triumphantly today. —*Bill Dahl*

One Man Trio / 1979 / Flyright ◆◆◆◆◆

☆ **The Struggle** / 1981 / Arhoolie ◆◆◆◆◆
Recorded in extreme stereo, with drums on one channel and Bonner's guitar on the other, this is Juke Boy Bonner's most cohesive album. Great songwriting and performances throughout. —*Cub Koda*

Juke Boy Bonner, 1960-1967 / 1991 / Flyright ◆◆◆
There's a Lightnin' Hopkins-meets-Jimmy Reed sound on these delightfully funky guitar/harp-accompanied blues by this Houstonian, whose ironic lyrics are half the fun. —*Jas Obrecht*

Things Ain't Right / Sequel ◆◆
This set is somewhat disappointing compared to the Arhoolie sides. —*Bill Dahl*

Boogie Woogie Red

b. Oct. 18, 1925, Rayville, LA, d. 1985
Piano, Vocals / Piano Blues
Though a Louisiana native, Vernon Harrison was associated with the Detroit blues sound as long as anyone. A Motor City resident since 1927, he began performing in the local clubs as a teenager. As a sideman he worked locally with Sonny Boy Williamson, Baby Boy Warren, and John Lee Hooker. Despite Red's renown for the blues and boogie-woogie style that earned him his nickname, he recorded only a few times as a featured artist, and aside from a bit of European touring in the '70s, he remained a local Detroit treasure, rarely appearing outside the area. —*Jim O'Neal*

● **Live at the Blind Pig** / 1974 / Blind Pig ◆◆◆◆
A crudely recorded but fun live album, it captures the somewhat demented 80-proof charm of this Detroit pianist. Recorded in the basement of the Blind Pig in Ann Arbor, MI, this album features guest appearances by John Nicholas, Fran Christina, and Bill Heid. —*George Bedard*

Red Hot / 1977 / Blind Pig ◆◆◆◆

Roy Book Binder

b. Oct. 5, 1941, New York, NY
Guitar / Modern Acoustic Blues
An often stirring folk/blues guitarist and vocalist, Roy Book Binder's been playing country blues since the mid-'60s, when he began recording for Blue Goose. Greatly influenced by Rev. Gary Davis and Pink Anderson, Book Binder played in East Coast coffeehouses in the early '60s, then began accompanying Rev. Davis on tours in the mid-'60s. He also played with Larry Johnson, Arthur "Big Boy" Crudup and Homesick James. Besides constant concerts and tours, Book Binder's made additional recordings for Blue Goose, as well as Adelphi and Rounder.

Book Binder began playing blues guitar while he was enlisted in the Navy. Following his discharge from the military, he enrolled in Rhode Island Junior College. After a brief spell there, he attended New York's New School for Social Research. Book Binder quit school in 1967, after he met the Rev. Gary Davis. Roy became Davis's chauffeur, during which time he took extensive lessons from the blind guitarist. Book Binder started his recording career slowly, cutting some singles for Kicking Mule and Blue Goose in 1968. In 1969, he toured England with Arthur "Big Boy" Crudup and Homesick James. The following year, he released his first album, *Travelin' Man*, on Adelphi. After the release of *Travelin' Man*, he began touring America extensively.

Book Binder began playing with fiddler Fats Kaplin in 1973, recording *Git Fiddle Shuffle* the same year. Roy and Fats were a duo for three years, playing numerous concerts and recording a second album, *Ragtime Millionaire* in 1976. Following the release of *Ragtime Millionaire*, the duo stopped performing together and Book Binder bought a motor home, which became his permanent residence. Live performances became his primary concern after the release of *Goin' Back to Tampa* in 1979. For nearly ten years, he toured the country in the motor home, driving himself from club to club, hitting numerous coffeehouses and festivals along the way.

Book Binder returned to recording in 1988, releasing *Bookaroo!* on Rounder Records. During the '80s, he recorded regularly—releasing an album every two to four years—in addition to his constant touring. —*Ron Wynn & Stephen Thomas Erlewine*

Goin' Back to Tampa / 1979 / Flying Fish ◆◆◆
Although Roy Book Binder doesn't put a new spin on acoustic Delta blues, he is passionate about the music and, as his debut *Goin' Back to Tampa* proves, he can replicate the sound of the genre exactly. *Goin' Back to Tampa* didn't exactly launch his recording career—it would take him a decade to release another album—but it captured the spirit of his music quite effectively. —*Thom Owens*

Bookeroo! / 1988 / Rounder ◆◆◆
The line between sincere appreciation and blind imitation is a thin one, and too often contemporary blues or country musicians cross it when covering classic songs. Roy Book Binder avoids the problem by refusing to become overwhelmed by idolatry, and instead enjoying himself while doing vintage material. That is evident on the 12 songs that comprise this session. While Book Binder's convivial vocals make his versions of Jesse Thomas' "Friend Like Me," Merle Haggard's "Nobody Knows I'm Hurtin'" or Jimmie Rodgers' "Waiting for a Train" appealing, his guitar solos and band interaction give the songs a vital, modern kick. —*Ron Wynn*

● **The Hillbilly Blues Cats** / 1992 / Rounder ◆◆◆◆◆
Roy Book Binder and his Hillbilly Blues Cats band expertly convey the urgency of vintage blues by performing them with a brash rockabilly attitude. They cover classic songs in a manner that's neither reverential nor disrespectful, putting their own spin on such numbers as Blind Willie McTell's "Statesboro Blues" or Happy Traum's "Mississippi John." Book Binder's vocals are joyous, exuberant and sometimes comical, while his trio provides stomping backgrounds and harmonies. Although Book Binder and the band can't improve upon the originals, they do nothing to detract from an appreciation of them. —*Ron Wynn*

Live Book...Don't Start Me Talkin'... / May 2, 1994 / Rounder ◆◆◆
*Live Book...Don't Start Me Talkin'...*captures Roy Book Binder in concert, playing a selection of standards and originals with conviction and energy. In fact, the record is frequently more compelling and exciting than his studio efforts, which tend to sound a bit too clean and studied. Here, he just plays the blues and the results are always engaging. —*Thom Owens*

James Booker (James Carroll Booker III)

b. Dec. 17, 1939, New Orleans, LA, d. Nov. 8, 1983
Piano / Acoustic New Orleans Blues
Certainly one of the most flamboyant New Orleans pianists in recent memory, James Carroll Booker III was a major influence on the local rhythm and blues scene in the '50s and '60s. Booker's training included classical instruction until age 12, by which time he had already begun to gain recognition as a blues and gospel organist on radio station WMRY every Sunday. By the time he was out of high school he had recorded on several occasions, including his own first release, "Doing the Hambone" in 1953. In 1960 he made the national charts with "Gonzo," an organ instrumental, and over the course of the next two decades played and recorded with artists as varied as Lloyd Price, Aretha Franklin, Ringo Starr, the Doobie Brothers, and B.B. King. In 1967 he was convicted of possession of heroin and served a one-year sentence at Angola Penitentiary (referred to as the "Ponderosa"), which took the momentum out of an otherwise promising career. The rediscovery of "roots" music by college students during the '70s (focusing primarily on "Fess"—Professor Longhair) provided the opportunity for a comeback by 1974, with numerous engagements at local clubs like Tipitina's, The Maple Leaf, and Snug Harbor. As with "Fess," Booker's performances at the New Orleans Jazz & Heritage Festivals took on the trappings of legendary "happenings," and he often spent his festival earnings to arrive in style, pulling up to the stage in a rented Rolls-Royce and attired in costumes befitting the "Piano Prince of New Orleans," complete with a cape. Such performances tended to be unpredictable: he might easily plant some Chopin into a blues tune or launch into a jeremiad on the CIA with all the fervor of a "Reverend Ike-meets-Moms Mabley" tag-team match.

Booker's left hand was simply phenomenal, often a problem for bass players who found themselves running for cover in an attempt to stay out of the way; with it he successfully amalgamated the jazz and R&B idioms of New Orleans, adding more than a touch of gospel thrown in for good measure. His playing was also highly improvisational, reinventing a progression (usually his own) so that a single piece would evolve into a medley of itself. In addition, he had a plaintive and searing vocal style which was equally comfortable with gospel, jazz standards, blues, or popular songs. Despite his personal eccentricities, Booker had the respect of New Orleans' best musicians, and elements of his influence are still very much apparent in the playing of pianists like Henry Butler and Harry Connick Jr. —*Bruce Boyd Raeburn*

Junco Partners / 1976 / Hannibal ✦✦✦✦✦
A superb effort from a premier New Orleans piano master who made far too few recordings. The rumbling licks, often astonishing technique, and variety of rhythms and styles that Booker fused were always matched by his energy and exuberance. These sessions have since been reissued on CD. —*Ron Wynn*

New Orleans Piano Wizard: Live! / Nov. 27, 1977 / Rounder ✦✦✦✦✦
Why so much of what pianist/vocalist James Booker recorded in the 1970s didn't surface until the '90s is a mystery, but that's secondary compared to the greatness routinely presented on this CD. It contains nine Booker selections which he performed at the 1977 Boogie Woogie and Ragtime Piano Contest held in Zurich. His relentless, driving style, ability to switch from a hard-hitting tune to a light, soft one without skipping a beat, and wild mix of sizzling keyboard licks and bemused, manic vocals is uniformly impressive. It's a bit short for a CD at 37 minutes, but it has so much flamboyant music and singing that it shouldn't be missed. —*Ron Wynn*

Resurrection of the Bayou Maharajah / 1977–1982 / Rounder ✦✦✦✦✦
Pianist/vocalist James Booker was a wondrous player and a rollicking, unpredictable performer. This collection of late-'70s and early-'80s tracks feature amazing chordal forays, splintering riffs, barrelhouse, boogie-woogie, and second-line-tinged R&B solos. Booker rambles, cajoles, exaggerates, mocks and soars while punctuating his wry singing with astonishing keyboard maneuvers. There is nothing here that isn't first-rate. While Booker's demise was a tragedy, this and other sessions that he left behind are the ultimate tribute to his greatness. —*Ron Wynn*

★ **Classified** / Oct. 18, 1982+Oct. 20, 1982 / Rounder ✦✦✦✦✦
While there has suddenly been a flood of CDs featuring masterful New Orleans keyboard wizard and vocalist James Booker, his best release arguably remains *Classified*. The 12-track set, recently issued on CD, is a landmark album, as Booker displayed every facet of his distinctive style. He did uptempo blues, quasi-classical, rock and R&B, making them all sound easy while performing frequently awesome keyboard feats. His "Professor Longhair Medley: Bald Head/Tipitina" pays homage to a legend while also demonstrating how much farther Booker's pianistic skills had developed. While his vocals sometimes aren't the equal of his brilliant playing, they're never less than effective and are sometimes almost frightening in their intensity. —*Ron Wynn*

Spiders on the Keys / 1993 / Rounder ✦✦✦
The eclectic New Orleans piano master was captured live in a local bar; there are plenty of surprises. —*Bill Dahl*

King of the New Orleans Keyboard / Junco Partner ✦✦✦✦✦
Spectacular date by a great New Orleans pianist whose personal difficulties prevented him from both long life and sustained career achievement. Booker was cited as an inspiration by everyone from Dr. John to Harry Connick, Jr., and played with array of performers, from Lloyd Price to Aretha Franklin, B.B. King, Ringo Starr, and the Doobie Brothers. He seamlessly fused a blues base, jazz touches, and R&B/gospel feeling, and this was among his best (and few) recordings. —*Ron Wynn*

Eddie Boyd (Edward Riley Boyd)

b. Nov. 25, 1914, Stovall, MS, **d.** Jul. 13, 1994
Piano, Vocals / Chicago Blues, Piano Blues
Few postwar blues standards have retained the universal appeal of Eddie Boyd's "Five Long Years." Cut in 1951, Boyd's masterpiece has attracted faithful covers by B.B. King, Muddy Waters, Jimmy Reed, Buddy Guy, and too many other bluesmen to recount here. But Boyd's discography is filled with evocative compositions, often full of after-hours ambience.

Like so many Chicago blues stalwarts, Boyd hailed from the fertile Mississippi Delta. The segregationist policies that had a

stranglehold on much of the South didn't appeal to the youngster, so he migrated up to Memphis (where he began to play the piano, influenced by Roosevelt Sykes and Leroy Carr). In 1941, Boyd settled in Chicago, falling in with the "Bluebird beat" crowd that recorded for producer Lester Melrose. He backed harp legend Sonny Boy Williamson on his 1945 classic "Elevator Woman," also accompanying Bluebird stars Tampa Red and Jazz Gillum on wax. Melrose produced Boyd's own 1947 recording debut for RCA as well; the pianist stayed with Victor through 1949.

Boyd reportedly paid for the date that produced "Five Long Years" himself, peddling the track to JOB Records (where the stolid blues topped the R&B charts during 1952). Powerful deejay Al Benson signed Boyd to a contract with his Parrot imprint and promptly sold the pact to Chess, inaugurating a stormy few years with Chicago's top blues outlet. There he waxed "24 Hours" and "Third Degree," both huge R&B hits in 1953, and a host of other Chicago blues gems. But Boyd and Leonard Chess were often at loggerheads, so it was on to Narvel "Cadillac Baby" Eatmon's Bea & Baby imprint in 1959 for eight solid sides with Robert Jr. Lockwood on guitar and a slew of lesser labels after that. A serious auto wreck in 1957 stalled his career for a spell.

Sick of the discrimination he perceived towards African-Americans in this country, Boyd became enamored of Europe during his tour with the 1965 American Folk Blues Festival, so he moved to Belgium. The recording opportunities long denied him in his native land were plentiful overseas; Boyd cut prolifically during the late '60s, including two LPs for producer Mike Vernon. In the early '70s, he settled in Helsinki, Finland, where he played often and lived comfortably until his death. —*Bill Dahl*

7936 South Rhodes / 1968 / Epic ✦✦✦
Recorded in London in January 1968 with three members of the early lineup of Fleetwood Mac (the one that played blues, not pop/rock): Peter Green (guitar), John McVie (bass), and Mick Fleetwood (drums). It's an adequate setting for Boyd's straight Chicago piano blues, going heavier on the slow-to-mid-tempo numbers than the high-spirited ones, though Green is a far more sympathetic accompanist than the rhythm section. —*Richie Unterberger*

● **Third Degree** / 1993 / Charly ✦✦✦✦✦
Amazingly, the only comprehensive overview of Boyd's 1951–1959 Chess stint available on CD. Both "Third Degree" and "24 Hours" are aboard this 20-track compilation, along with the lesser-known standouts "I Got the Blues," "Nothing but Trouble," and "Cool Kind Treatment." Boyd's sturdy, concise piano work and darkly introspective vocals were brilliantly captured on tape by Leonard Chess, even if the two weren't exactly the best of pals. —*Bill Dahl*

Five Long Years / EVI ✦✦✦✦
One of the first and best of Boyd's many overseas recordings, cut while he was in the midst of that auspicious 1965 American Folk Blues Festival tour of Europe. While the caravan was ensconced in London, young producer Mike Vernon spirited Boyd and a rhythm section (guitarist Buddy Guy, bassist Jimmie Lee Robinson, and drummer Fred Below) off to the studio, where Boyd ran through some of his classics ("I'm Comin' Home," "24 Hours," the title track) and a few less familiar items while alternating between piano and organ. —*Bill Dahl*

Rattin' and Running Around / Crown Prince ✦✦✦✦
Import vinyl containing a nice cross-section of Boyd's RCA and Chess efforts, including three sides from 1947 with Bill Casimir on tenor sax; the doomy Chess entries "The Nightmare Is Over," a rocking "Driftin'," and "Life Gets to Be a Burden," and the bouncy 1956 rhumba "Don't." —*Bill Dahl*

Ishmon Bracey

b. Jan. 9, 1901, Byram, MS, **d.** Feb. 12, 1970, Jackson, MS
Vocals, Guitar / Acoustic Delta Blues
One of the early giants of the Delta blues, Ishmon Bracey often worked with local Jackson, MS, legends like Tommy Johnson, Son Spand and Charlie McCoy. He cut a small handful of sides for the Paramount label in 1930, some of the most coveted discs in blues history. Bracey's best work is marked by a tremulous vibrato to his largely nasal voice and simple but effective guitar work. As a parenthetical note, when Bracey was trying to be coaxed out of retirement to record in the '60s, to get researchers

off his back he directed them to the whereabouts of another Delta legend—Skip James. —*Cub Koda*

Complete Recorded Works (1928–1929) / Document ✦✦✦✦✦
Bracey's complete recorded works (1928–1929) are presented in chronological order on this single disc, with the bonus of four tracks by the elusive Charley Taylor. Since Bracey only recorded a handful of sides, this compilation is far more accessible than most of Document's *Complete Recorded Works* discs. Furthermore, Bracey was one of the best Delta blues artists of the '20s and his work is consistently engaging. *Complete Recorded Works (1928–1929)* is the best compilation available on Bracey— not only does it work as a concise introduction, it has everything completists will need. —*Cub Koda & Stephen Thomas Erlewine*

Tiny Bradshaw

b. Sep. 23, 1905, Youngstown, OH, **d.** Nov. 26, 1958, Cincinnati, OH
Piano, Drums, Vocals / Electric Jump Blues
Myron "Tiny" Bradshaw was a principal member of the mighty jump blues roster that Cincinnati's King Records assembled during the late '40s, when the swinging horn-powered sound was at its floor-rattling height. Bradshaw's gregarious vocals belied his sophisticated background; he reportedly majored in psychology (not a bad sideline for a bandleader, actually) at Wilberforce University.

Bradshaw was already a grizzled veteran of the dance band wars when he signed on with King. He'd put in dues-paying time with the Mills Blue Rhythm Band (as had labelmate Lucky Millinder) before recruiting his own orchestra in 1933 (waxings for Decca followed the next year). He signed on at King in 1949 and hit big— the jiving, nearly out-of-control "Well, Oh Well" was a massive smash in 1950, followed by "I'm Going to Have Myself a Ball" and "Walkin' the Chalk Line" and a pair of scorching instrumentals: "Soft" (featuring Red Prysock's wailing tenor sax) and "Heavy Juice."

But Tiny's best-known offering didn't make the charts. His blistering 1951 platter "The Train Kept A-Rollin'" was dressed up in rockabilly attire by the Johnny Burnette Trio five years later (complete with Paul Burlison's groundbreaking distorted guitar solo) and revived again by the Yardbirds another decade or so down the line.

As for Tiny (whose band also spawned another R&B tenor sax titan, Sil Austin), he was gradually incapacitated by a series of strokes in the mid-'50s that curtailed his musical career. The times were changing, anyway; his last session for King in 1958 included a horrendous cover of the Royal Teens' "Short Shorts" that may well have hastened his demise.—*Bill Dahl*

Great Composer / 1959 / King ✦✦✦
Domestic CD collection that duplicates one of the popular jump blues bandleader's early albums from the King catalog. —*Bill Dahl*

● **Breaking Up the House** / Charly ✦✦✦✦✦
Sixteen of Tiny Bradshaw's biggest and hardest-swinging King label waxings from 1950–52, notably "The Train Kept A-Rollin'," "Well, Oh Well," "Two Dry Bones on the Pantry Shelf," "Walkin' the Chalk Line," and the jiving title item. Unfortunately, the torrid big band-styled instrumental arrangements that also defined Bradshaw's output are nowhere to be found on this collection. — *Bill Dahl*

Doyle Bramhall

b. 1949, Dallas, TX
Guitar, Vocals / Electric Texas Blues
Born in Dallas in 1949, this singer/songwriter/drummer grew up listening to Dallas radio (with heavy doses of Jimmy Reed, Ray Charles and Bobby Blue Bland on rock 'n' roll stations) and locals the Nightcaps, one of the country's first White electric blues bands. In high school he joined the Chessmen, which soon included a young Jimmie Vaughan on guitar; they opened in Dallas on Jimi Hendrix's first U.S. tour. Moving to Austin in 1970, he and Vaughan formed Texas Storm, which later shortened its name to Storm and occasionally included Jimmie's younger brother Stevie on bass. Doyle next formed the Nightcrawlers with Stevie (now on lead guitar), who later credited Bramhall as a primary vocal influence. During this time the two also co-wrote "Dirty Pool," which Vaughan included on his debut, *Texas Flood*. Doyle wrote or co-wrote seven more songs on subsequent

Stevie Ray albums, and collaborated on three for *Family Style* by the Vaughan Brothers (which also featured Bramhall on drums). While drumming with Marcia Ball and Mason Ruffner in the early '80s, Bramhall began stockpiling solo recordings, which eventually comprised his long-awaited debut on CD, featuring both Vaughans and Doyle's son, guitarist Doyle Bramhall II, formerly of the Arc Angels. Recently he began a collaboration that should prove interesting—with pop singer Jennifer Warnes. —*Dan Forte*

● **Bird Nest on the Ground** / 1994 / Antone's ✦✦✦✦✦
Dripping-with-soul vocals and solid Texas blues drumming attest to Bramhall's stature in the Lone Star State, but his songwriting sets him apart from the pack. This solo debut was recorded over a 12-year period, with a pre-Stevie Ray Vaughan rendition of Bramhall's "Change It" (with slide guitar from Robin Syler and *Beavis & Butthead* creator Mike Judge on bass) shining brightest. Both Stevie Ray and Jimmie Vaughan make cameos, and guitarist David Murray knifes through a surprisingly fresh take on Albert King's "The Hunter," while Syler (and Doyle) grease up Hooker's "In the Mood." Hopefully it won't be another 12 years for a follow-up. —*Dan Forte*

Billy Branch (William Earl Branch)

b. Oct. 3, 1951, Great Lakes, IL
Harmonica, Vocals / Modern Electric Blues, Chicago Blues
If blues harmonica has a long-term future on the Chicago circuit, Billy Branch will likely play a leading role in shaping its direction. Educator as well as musician, Branch has led the Sons of Blues, his skin-tight quartet, since the late '70s. Despite numerous personnel changes, the SOBs have never wavered in their dedication to pure, unadulterated Chicago blues.

Although he was born just north of the Windy City, Branch grew up in Los Angeles, only to return to Chicago in 1969 to attend the University of Illinois. Spurred on by the entrancing riffs of mouth organ masters Carey Bell, Big Walter Horton, and Junior Wells, Branch began to make a name for himself. He replaced Bell in Willie Dixon's Chicago Blues All-Stars, recording with the prolific legend and touring extensively.

The SOBs really were dominated by second-generation talent at the start—guitarist Lurrie Bell was Carey Bell's son, while bassist Freddie Dixon was the offspring of Willie Dixon. They contributed three tunes to Alligator's first batch of *Living Chicago Blues* anthologies in 1978. The SOBs waxed *Where's My Money?*, their Red Beans Records LP, in 1984; by then, personnel included guitarist Carlos Johnson, bassist J.W. Williams, and drummer Moses Rutues. Shortly after that album was completed, guitarist Carl Weathersby was installed as co-front man, where he remains (as does Rutues; bass is now handled by Nick Charles).

Other than co-headlining Alligator's 1990 summit meeting *Harp Attack!* with fellow harp masters Junior Wells, Carey Bell, and James Cotton, Branch largely busied himself with extensive sideman work (he's first-call session harpist around the Windy City) and teaching an innovative "Blues in the Schools" program until 1995, when Verve issued his *The Blues Keep Following Me Around*, an impressive showcase for his gravelly vocals and spellbinding harp.

A lot is expected of Billy Branch in the near future. He'll have to usher Chicago's proud blues harp tradition into the next century—a task he's eminently capable of pulling off. —*Bill Dahl*

Harp Attack! / 1990 / Alligator ✦✦✦✦
Four of the Windy City's undisputed harmonica masters in the same studio, trading solos and vocals with good-natured abandon. Billy's showcases are the apt original "New Kid on the Block" and a deft cover of Little Walter's "Who." —*Bill Dahl*

Mississippi Flashback / Jan. 1992 / GBW ✦✦✦

● **The Blues Keep Following Me Around** / 1995 / Verve ✦✦✦✦✦
Branch and Carl Weathersby ventured down to Maurice, LA, to cut this impressive disc with a home-grown rhythm section, only Branch's name appears on its front. Certainly the harpist is the star of the show, growling covers of dusties by Sonny Boy Williamson, Willie Dixon, and Howlin' Wolf. Nevertheless, guitarist Weathersby provides two of the set's highlights, passionately singing his own "Should Have Been Gone" and "Should Have Known Better." —*Bill Dahl*

Where's My Money? / 1995 / Evidence ✦✦✦
Slightly scattershot 1984 LP, originally released on the now-

defunct Red Beans logo, that hits more than it misses. At its best—the sardonic title track, a couple of vocals by veteran pianist Jimmy Walker, a stunning "Son of Juke" that spotlights Branch's harp wizardry—it's a fine introduction to the SOB's multi-faceted attack. —*Bill Dahl*

Billy Branch & Hubert Sumlin / Wolf ✦✦✦✦✦
This disc is a fine portrait of Chicago blues—past and present. Award-winning harpist Billy Branch and legendary giant of the famed Howlin' Wolf Band, Hubert Sumlin, here join hands with some of the finest contemporary musicians in the Windy City— among them: Willie Kent, John Primer, Johnny B. Moore, and Carl Weathersby. Sumlin offers two superb band tracks as well as five acoustic duets with guitarist John Primer. In addition, there are four Billy Branch numbers that recast the work of Jimmy Rogers, Jimmy Reed, and Little Walter without ever becoming slavish. The dual-guitar work of Johnny B. Moore and John Primer is exceptional. —*Larry Hoffman*

Jackie Brenston

Vocals, Saxophone / Electric Jump Blues
Determining the first actual rock 'n' roll record is a truly impossible task. But you can't go too far wrong citing Jackie Brenston's 1951 Chess waxing of "Rocket 88," a seminal piece of rock's fascinating history with all the prerequisite elements firmly in place: practically indecipherable lyrics about cars, booze, and chicks; Raymond Hill's booting tenor sax, and a churning, beat-heavy rhythmic bottom.

Sam Phillips, then a fledgling in the record business, produced "Rocket 88," Brenston's debut waxing, in Memphis. The singer/saxist was backed by Ike Turner's Kings of Rhythm, an aggregation that Brenston had joined the previous year. Turner played piano on the tune; Willie Kizart supplied dirty, distorted guitar. Billed as by Jackie Brenston & His Delta Cats, "Rocket 88" drove up to the top slot on the R&B charts and remained there for more than a month. But none of his Chess follow-ups sported the same high-octane performance, though "My Real Gone Rocket" was certainly a deserving candidate.

Brenston's slide from the spotlight was swift. After a few more Chess singles stiffed (including a duet with Edna McRaney, "Hi-Ho Baby"), Brenston reunited with Turner in 1955, holding down the baritone sax chair until 1962. He cut a series of terrific sides fronting Turner's Kings of Rhythm along the way: "Gonna Wait for My Chance" and "Much Later" for Federal in 1956, "You've Got to Lose" for Chicago's Cobra label in 1958 (also doing session work there with Otis Rush and Buddy Guy), and "You Ain't the One" for Sue in 1961. After a final single for Mel London's Mel-Lon imprint, Brenston was through—he worked as a truck driver and showed little interest in reliving his glory years. —*Bill Dahl*

● **Rocket 88** / 1991 / Charly ✦✦✦✦✦
If Brenston's "Rocket 88" was in actuality the very first rock 'n' roll record, as many experts claim, the rest of his brief Chess legacy adds up to quite a definitive rockin' statement. Among these 16 sides dating from 1951–53 are his amazing sequel "My Real Gone Rocket," which probably rocks even harder than "Rocket 88" as Ike Turner pounds the keys, "Tuckered Out," the evocative "Fat Meat Is Greasy" (one of several items only out in Japan before the advent of this British CD), and seven sides Brenston cut in Chicago without Sam Phillips to guide him, or Turner's Kings of Rhythm to back him up. Great stuff deserving of domestic release! —*Bill Dahl*

John Brim

b. Apr. 10, 1922, Hopkinsville, KY
Vocals, Guitar, Harmonica / Electric Chicago Blues
One of the last still-active links to the classic 1950s Chicago blues sound that once thrived at Chess Records (only one of Brim's several label associations during the 1950s), John Brim may be best-known for writing and cutting the original "Ice Cream Man" that David Lee Roth and Van Halen covered on their first album. That's a pity, for the seriously underrecorded Brim made some exceptionally hard-nosed waxings.

Brim picked up his early guitar licks from the 78s of Tampa Red and Big Bill Broonzy before venturing first to Indianapolis in 1941 and Chicago four years later. He met his wife Grace in 1947; fortuitously, she was a capable drummer who played on several of John's records. In fact, she was the vocalist on a 1950

single for Detroit-based Fortune Records that signaled the beginning of her hubby's discography.

John recorded for Random, JOB, Al Benson's Parrot label (the socially aware "Tough Times"), and Chess ("Rattlesnake," his answer to Big Mama Thornton's "Hound Dog," was pulled from the shelves by Chess for fear of a plagiarism suit). Cut in 1953, the suggestive "Ice Cream Man" had to wait until 1969 to enjoy a very belated release. Brim's last Chess single, "I Would Hate to See You Go," was waxed in 1956 with a stellar combo consisting of harpist Little Walter, guitarist Robert Jr. Lockwood, bassist Willie Dixon, and drummer Fred Below (clearly, Chess had high hopes for Brim, but to no avail).

After a hiatus of a few decades, Brim made a welcome return to studio action with a recent set for Tone-Cool Records, *The Ice Cream Man*. He still plays occasionally around Chicago. —*Bill Dahl*

● **Whose Muddy Shoes** / 1991 / MCA/Chess ✦✦✦✦✦
First unleashed back in 1969 on vinyl as part of the Chess Vintage Series, this hard-hitting disc couples six of Brim's meanest Parrot and Chess sides with nine Elmore James gems. Brim is at his toughest on the threatening "Be Careful" and "Lifetime Baby." —*Bill Dahl*

Ice Cream Man / 1994 / Tone Cool ✦✦✦
Brim's vocals don't quite possess the same snap, crackle, and pop that they did in the mid-'50s, but thanks to a savvy song selection and sympathetic backing by the likes of guitarist Bob Margolin and harpist Jerry Portnoy, Brim's comeback album is a generally successful project. —*Bill Dahl*

Hadda Brooks

Piano, Vocals / Piano Blues
In the mid-to-late '40s, Black popular music began to mutate from swing jazz and boogie-woogie into the sort of rhythm & blues that helped lay the foundation for rock 'n' roll. Singer and pianist Hadda Brooks was one of the many figures who were significant in aiding that transition, although she's largely forgotten today. While her torchsong delivery was rooted in the big-band era, her boogie-woogie piano looked forward to jump blues and R&B. Ironically, the same qualities that made her briefly successful—her elegant vocals and jazzy arrangements—left her ill-equipped to compete when harder-driving forms of rhythm & blues, and then early rock 'n' roll, began to dominate the marketplace in the early '50s.

Brooks got a recording deal through a chance meeting with jukebox operator Jules Bihari, who was looking to record some boogie-woogie. The Los Angeles-based Bihari, along with his brother Joe, would become major players in early R&B via their Modern label, which issued sides by B.B. King, John Lee Hooker, Etta James, Jesse Belvin, and other stars. Brooks actually preferred ballads to boogie-woogies, but worked up her style by listening to Pete Johnson, Albert Ammons, and Meade Lux Lewis records. Her first record, the pounding "Swingin' the Boogie," was a sizable regional hit in 1945. Joe Bihari would later tell author Arnold Shaw that the single was instrumental in establishing the Biharis in the record business.

Brooks' first records were instrumental, but by 1946 she was singing as well. She had a fair amount of success for Modern in the late '40s, reaching the R&B Top Ten with "Out of the Blue" and her most famous song, "That's My Desire" (which was covered for a big pop hit by Frankie Laine). Her success on record led to some roles in films, most notably in a scene from *In a Lonely Place*, which starred Humphrey Bogart.

Brooks briefly left Modern for an unsuccessful stint with major label London in 1950. After a similarly unrewarding return to Modern in the early '50s, and a brief stay at Okeh, she largely withdrew from recording onto the nightclub circuit. For most of the 1960s, in fact, she was based in Australia, where she hosted her own TV show. Her profile was boosted in the mid-'90s by her induction into the Rhythm & Blues Foundation Hall of Fame, and by the inclusion of her recording of "Anytime, Anyplace, Anywhere" in the film *The Crossing Guard*. A new album on Pointblank, *Time Was When*, was released in early 1996. —*Richie Unterberger*

● **That's My Desire** / 1994 / Virgin ✦✦✦✦✦
Twenty-five tracks from her prime, recorded for Modern in the 1940s and 1950s, including her hits "That's My Desire" and "Out of the Blue," as well as "Anytime, Anyplace, Anywhere." While

Brooks was an important figure of the L.A. 1940s R&B scene, latter-day listeners may find this rather tame. Vocally she owed much more to pop-jazz stylings than gritty R&B influences. Her most durable and influential performances were her instrumental ones at the piano bench, especially on the pounding "Swingin' the Boogie," which leads off this collection. —*Richie Unterberger*

Time Was When / Feb. 20, 1996 / Virgin ◆◆◆

Lonnie Brooks

b. Dec. 18, 1933, Dubuisson, LA
Guitar, Vocals / Modern Electric Blues
Having forged a unique Louisiana/Chicago blues synthesis unlike anyone else's on the competitive Windy City scene, charismatic guitarist Lonnie Brooks has long reigned as one of the town's top bluesmen. A masterful showman, the good-natured Brooks puts on a show equal to his recordings (and that's saying a lot, considering there's four decades of wax to choose from).

Born Lee Baker, Jr., in Louisiana, Lonnie took his time when choosing his vocation—he didn't play guitar seriously until he was in his early 20s and living in Port Arthur, TX. Rapidly assimilating the licks of B.B. King and Long John Hunter, he landed a gig with zydeco pioneer Clifton Chenier (not a bad way to break into the business) before inaugurating his own recording career in 1957 with the influential swamp-pop ballad "Family Rules" for Eddie Shuler's Lake Charles, LA-based Goldband Records. The young rock 'n' roller—then billed as Guitar Junior—enjoyed more regional success on Goldband with the rocking dance number "The Crawl" (much later covered by the Fabulous Thunderbirds). Mercury also issued two 45s by Guitar Junior.

When Sam Cooke offered the young rocker a chance to accompany him to Chicago, he gladly accepted. But two problems faced him once he arrived: there was another Guitar Junior in town (precipitating the birth of Lonnie Brooks), and the bayou blues that so enthralled Gulf Coast crowds didn't cut it up north. Scattered session work (he played on Jimmy Reed's Vee-Jay classic "Big Boss Man") and a series of R&B-oriented 45s for Midas, USA, Chirrup, and Chess ensued during the '60s, as Lonnie learned a new style of blues. The Guitar Junior sobriquet was dusted off briefly in 1969 for his Capitol album debut, *Broke an' Hungry*, but its lack of success buried the alias for good.

By the late '70s, Brooks was gaining a deserved reputation as an exceptionally dynamic Chicago bluesman with a fresh perspective. He cut four outstanding sides for Alligator's first batch of *Living Chicago Blues* anthologies in 1978 that quickly led to his own 'Gator debut LP, *Bayou Lightning*, the next year. Five more albums of his own for the firm and extensive touring have cemented Brooks' standing as a Chicago blues giant. Son Ronnie Baker Brooks is a chip off the proverbial block, playing rhythm guitar in his old man's band and duetting on "Like Father, Like Son" on Lonnie's last album, 1991's *Satisfaction Guaranteed.* —*Bill Dahl*

Broke an' Hungry / 1969 / Capitol ◆◆◆
A momentary 1969 return to the Guitar Junior monicker—for Capitol Records, no less—was produced by Eddie Shuler's son Wayne and focuses on Lonnie Brooks' enduring swamp blues roots (long after he'd jettisoned the style). Unavailable on CD (Crosscut reissued it on vinyl), the LP consists of interpretations of oldies first rendered by Guitar Slim, Lightnin' Slim, Elton Anderson, Larry Davis, Hop Wilson, and Professor Longhair (along with Brooks' own "The Train and the Horse"). —*Bill Dahl*

Sweet Home Chicago / Dec. 8, 1975 / Evidence ◆◆
The French Black & Blue label was savvy enough to spirit Brooks into a studio when he was touring the continent in 1975 as part of Chicago Blues Festival '75. As befits the jam-session ambience of the date (pianist Willie Mabon, harpist Mack Simmons, and two-thirds of the Aces are on hand), hoary standards predominate: "Crosscut Saw," "Things I Used to Do," "Mama Talk to Your Daughter," and the ubiquitous title track (which remains a signature song). The omnipresent "The Train and the Horse" returns as well. —*Bill Dahl*

Let's Talk It Over / 1977 / Delmark ◆◆◆
Of all the quickie dates produced by Ralph Bass in 1977 for a project that never came to real fruition, Lonnie Brooks' contribution to the series is likely the most satisfying—thanks to a tight band (his working unit at the time) and a sheaf of imaginative originals (notably "Crash Head on into Love," "Greasy

Man," and the title cut). An ingenious reworking of Lowell Fulson's "Reconsider Baby" doesn't hurt either. —*Bill Dahl*

● **Bayou Lightning** / 1979 / Alligator ◆◆◆◆◆
All the promise that Lonnie Brooks possessed was realized on this album, his finest and most consistent to date. The churning bayou groove of "Voodoo Daddy," a soul-steeped "Watch What You Got," a bone-chilling remake of Junior Parker's "In the Dark," rollicking covers of Tommy Tucker's "Alimony" and Brooks' own "Figure Head," and the swaggering originals "You Know What My Body Needs" and "Watchdog" are among the set's many incendiary highlights. —*Bill Dahl*

Turn on the Night / 1981 / Alligator ◆◆◆
Inconsistent in comparison to its illustrious predecessor, his encore Alligator offering still contains some goodies. Chief among them are the infectious originals "Eyeballin'" and "Don't Go to Sleep on Me," along with a delicious revival of Bobby "Blue" Bland's "I'll Take Care of You." —*Bill Dahl*

Hot Shot / 1983 / Alligator ◆◆◆◆
A return to rollicking good-time form, boasting the roaring "Don't Take Advantage of Me" and "I Want All My Money Back," relentless rocking revivals of Otis Blackwell's "Back Trail" and J.B. Lenoir's "One More Shot," and a faithful remake of Lonnie Brooks' own "Family Rules" from the Guitar Junior era. —*Bill Dahl*

The Crawl / 1984 / Charly ◆◆◆◆◆
Lonnie Brooks' pervasive 1950s bayou blues roots, laid bare and rocking hard. "Family Rules" was highly influential to the blossoming swamp-pop movement soon sweeping southern Louisiana; "The Crawl," "I Got It Made (When I Marry Shirley Mae)," "Roll, Roll, Roll," and "Knocks Me Out" (the latter one of his Mercury singles) drive with youthful abandon. The youngster's ears were wide-open—he even covered Harlan Howard's country ditty "Pick Me Up on Your Way Down," investing it with serious swamp angst. —*Bill Dahl*

Live at Pepper's 1968 / 1985 / Black Top ◆◆◆
Lonnie Brooks in his jukebox bluesman mode, playing the hits of the day for an appreciative crowd at one of Chicago's legendary blues joints. First issued on the European Black Magic label, the set captures his showmanship effectively as he attacks "You Don't Have to Go," "Sweet Little Angel," "Hide Away," and Johnnie Taylor's soul workout "Who's Making Love." Even in 1968, he was stockpiling originals—a rocking "Shakin' Little Mama" and a distinctive "The Train & the Horse" are all his. —*Bill Dahl*

Wound up Tight / 1986 / Alligator ◆◆◆
More energetic efforts with a decidedly rocked-up edge. Johnny Winter, long an ardent admirer of Brooks back to the Guitar Junior days, drops by with a passel of fiery guitar licks for the title track and "Got Lucky Last Night." —*Bill Dahl*

Live from Chicago / 1988 / Alligator ◆◆◆
Cut live at Chicago's B.L.U.E.S. Etcetera nightclub, the disc captures the high-energy excitement of Lonnie Brooks' live show. Many familiar titles from his Alligator catalog, along with a handful of never-before released tunes and a marathon "Hide Away" where Brooks pulls out all the guitaristic tricks at his command. —*Bill Dahl*

Satisfaction Guaranteed / 1991 / Alligator ◆◆
Only intermittently satisfying, contrary to its title: a little more subtlety would have benefitted drummer Kevin Mitchell, and some of the material is a bit lightweight. Nevertheless, there are some nice moments, especially on the tunes Brooks penned himself. "Like Father, like Son," the duet between Lonnie and son Ronnie, seems a mite contrived. —*Bill Dahl*

Big Bill Broonzy (William Lee Conley Broonzy)

b. Jun. 26, 1893, Scott, MS, d. Aug. 15, 1958, Chicago, IL
Guitar, Vocals, Mandolin, Violin / Acoustic Country Blues
In terms of his musical skill, the sheer size of his repertoire, the length and variety of his career and his influence on contemporaries and musicians who would follow, Big Bill Broonzy is among a select few of the most important figures in recorded blues history. Among his hundreds of titles are standards like "All by Myself" and "Key to the Highway." In this country he was instrumental in the growth of the Chicago Blues sound, and his travels abroad rank him as one of the leading blues ambassadors.

Literally born on the banks of the Mississippi, he was one of a family of 17 who learned to fiddle on a homemade instrument. Taught by his uncle, he was performing by age ten at social functions and in church. After brief stints on the pulpit and in the Army, he moved to Chicago where he switched his attention from violin to guitar, playing with elders like Papa Charlie Jackson. Broonzy began his recording career with Paramount in 1927. In the early '30s he waxed some brilliant blues and hokum and worked Chicago and the road with great players like pianist Black Bob, guitarist Bill Weldon and Memphis Minnie.

During the Depression years Big Bill Broonzy continued full steam ahead, doing some acrobatic label-hopping (Paramount to Bluebird to Columbia to Okeh!). In addition to solo efforts, he contributed his muscular guitar licks to recordings by Bumble Bee Slim, John Lee (Sonny Boy) Williamson and others who were forging a powerful new Chicago sound.

In 1938, Broonzy was at Carnegie Hall, (ostensibly filling in for the fallen Robert Johnson) for John Hammonds' revolutionary Spirituals to Swing Series. The following year he appeared with Benny Goodman and Louis Armstrong in George Seldes' film production *Swingin' the Dream*. After his initial brush with the East Coast cognoscenti, however, Broonzy spent a good part of the early '40s barnstorming the South with Lil Green's road show or kicking back in Chicago with Memphis Slim.

He continued alternating stints in Chicago and New York with coast-to-coast road work until 1951, when live performances and recording dates overseas earned him considerable notoriety in Europe and led to worldwide touring. Back in the States he recorded for Chess, Columbia and Folkways, working with a spectrum of artists from Blind John Davis to Pete Seeger. In 1955, *Big Bill Blues*, his life as told to Danish writer Yannick Bruynoghe, was published.

In 1957, after one more British tour, the pace began to catch up with Broonzy. He spent the last year of his life in and out of hospitals and succumbed to cancer in 1958. He survives though; not only in his music, but in the remembrances of people who knew him... from Muddy Waters to Studs Terkel. A gentle giant they say... tough enough to survive the blues world... but not so tough he wouldn't give a struggling young musician the shirt off his back. His music, of course, is absolutely basic to the blues experience. —*Steve James*

Big Bill Broonzy Sings Folk Songs / 1962 / Smithsonian/Folkways ✦✦✦✦✦
Big Bill Broonzy was a narrative genius; someone who could take lyrics, situations, and themes and make them resonate with pain, sadness, anger, or joy. This 11-song set takes a slightly different tack. It's a compilation with Broonzy doing his renditions of well-known (some obscure) folk songs. From the woeful laments of "Backwater Blues" and "Tell Me Who" to the assertive strains of "This Train" and "I Don't Want No Woman (To Try to Be My Boss)," Broonzy puts his own stamp on every number, even shopworn items like "John Henry" and "Bill Bailey." —*Ron Wynn*

Big Bill Broonzy & Washboard Sam / 1962 / MCA ✦✦✦
Although Chess didn't bother to anthologize these sides into album form until the early '60s, this marvelous collection actually dates from 1953. Broonzy and Sam are both in great form here, sharing the vocals throughout and recalling their earlier days as Bluebird label and session mates. The sound is fleshed out by the addition of guitarist Lee Cooper (who at times almost sounds a bit too modern for the genre being explored here, throwing in what can only be desribed as Chuck Berry licks) and Big Crawford on upright bass. —*Cub Koda*

Big Bill Broonzy Sings Folk Songs / 1962 / Smithsonian/Folkways ✦✦✦✦✦
Two different sessions provided the material for this collection of folk songs, spirituals, and blues standards. Half the disc is previously unreleased material from Broonzy's final Folkways recording session. The other half of the disc was recorded at a live broadcast with Pete Seeger for radio station WFMT Chicago in front of an audience of friends; Seeger joins Broonzy during "John Henry." Although his vocal range is not quite what it used to be, Bill sings with authority and vibrance, using the occasional strained notes for effect. His fluid guitar technique remains unhampered. Unlike many of his peers, Big Bill Broonzy was able to utilize the late-'50s folk boom as an opportunity to be recognized while he was still alive. This disc shows

Broonzy in his element as one of the classic blues masters. —*Jim Powers*

★ **The Young Big Bill Broonzy (1928-35)** / 1968 / Yazoo ✦✦✦✦✦
The young Bill Broonzy was as far removed from his later folk blues posturings as you could imagine. If you're only familiar with his later work, these early sides will come as quite a jolt. Big Bill whips off some fleet-fingered single note leads and his rhythmic drive is never less than spot on. Great stuff. —*Cub Koda*

☆ **Big Bill's Blues** / Portrait ✦✦✦✦✦
If you're going to sweat a Big Bill Broonzy collection down to only one disc, this is the one to keep in the collection. It's really his most representative work, spotlighting most of the best-known numbers from his extensive repertoire and the high-points are numerous (including a hilarious "When I've Been Drinkin'," in which he supposedly downs several shots on microphone during the take). —*Cub Koda*

☆ **Do That Guitar Rag (1928-1935)** / 1973 / Yazoo ✦✦✦✦
This a marvelous little companion piece to *Young Big Bill Broonzy (1928-35)* on Yazoo. Broonzy's ragtime guitar picking is textbook in its scope and his vocals are as warm as can be. Dubbed from old 78s, the ultra high quality of the music make any audiophile nitpicking a moot point indeed. Broonzy at his youngest and full of pep. —*Cub Koda*

★ **Good Time Tonight** / 1990 / Columbia/Legacy ✦✦✦✦✦
If you're following the 30-plus year career of Bill Broonzy and already have the two early compilations available on Yazoo, here's where you go next. These are basically ensemble works covering the time frame between 1930 to 1940 and Broonzy sounds very comfortable in the company of Blind John Davis and Joshua Altheimer. The 20 tracks compiled here (culled from various Vocalion, ARC and Columbia sessions) sound pretty great, benefitting mightily from modern sound restoration devices. —*Cub Koda*

☆ **Blues in the Mississippi Night** / 1990 / Rykodisc ✦✦✦✦✦
Writer, producer, and historian Alan Lomax managed something truly unique in 1946. He not only brought together pianist Memphis Slim, guitarist Big Bill Broonzy, and harmonica player Sonny Boy Williamson together for a concert, but managed to get them to talk frankly and specifically about their experiences in the segregated Deep South. At this time, few people outside the region really knew what was happening there, and even fewer who lived under the system ever discussed it openly. The anecdotes and incidents described are shocking and disgusting; they were even more shocking when aired in 1946. The complete version appears here in all its hard-hitting glory. —*Ron Wynn*

Complete Recorded Works in Chronological Order, Vols. 1-11 / 1991 / Document ✦✦✦
If having it *all* is your ultimate goal as a blues collector, this 11-CD set will certainly aid and abet in that pursuit. On this exhaustive collection from 1927-1942 you *will* find a plethora of great sides, including "C-C Rider," "Milkcow Blues," and his finest instrumental, "House Rent Stomp." Collecting up 15 years of recorded works and running them in strict chronological order is a most laudable effort, but this certainly is not the place to start in building up a great Big Bill Broonzy collection. For completists only. —*Cub Koda*

Andrew Brown

b. Feb. 25, 1937, Jackson, MS, d. Dec. 11, 1985
Guitar, Vocals / Electric Chicago Blues
Tragically underrecorded until late in his career, Chicago blues guitarist Andrew Brown still had time enough to wax a handful of great singles during the mid-'60s and two 1980s albums (unfortunately, both of them were only available as imports) that beautifully showcased his fluid, concise lead guitar and hearty vocals.

The Mississippi native moved to Chicago in 1946. With Earl Hooker teaching him a few key licks, Brown matured quickly; he was playing in south suburban clubs—his main circuit—by the early '50s. His 45s for USA (1962's "You Better Stop") and 4 Brothers (the mid-'60s sides "You Ought to Be Ashamed" and "Can't Let You Go") were well-done urban blues. But it wasn't until 1980, when Alligator issued three of his songs on its second batch of *Living Chicago Blues* anthologies, that Brown's name began to resonate outside the Windy City.

Producer Dick Shurman was responsible for Brown's only two albums: the Handy Award-winning *Big Brown's Chicago Blues* for Black Magic in 1982 and *On the Case* for Double Trouble three years later. But Brown was already suffering from lung cancer when the second LP emerged. He died a short time later. —*Bill Dahl*

● **Big Brown's Chicago Blues** / 1982 / Black Magic ✦✦✦✦✦
Quite an impressive full-length debut, even if American audiences were hard-pressed to locate a copy. Well-chosen covers—Joe Tex's "I Want To (Do Everything for You)," Betty Everett's "Your Love Is Important to Me," Bobby Rush's "Mary Jane"—mingle with six attractive originals. —*Bill Dahl*

On the Case / 1985 / Double Trouble ✦✦✦✦
Another classy contemporary blues album that frustratingly still awaits domestic CD reissue, just like its predecessor. Once again, the tasty guitarist exhibits intriguing taste in covers, reviving Donna Hightower's "Right Now," Little Milton's "Losing Hand," and the immortal Birdlegs & Pauline's "Spring." But the majority of the set consists of well-conceived originals. Jimmy Johnson is on board as rhythm guitarist. —*Bill Dahl*

Buster Brown

b. Aug. 15, 1911, Georgia, **d.** Jan. 31, 1976, Brooklyn, NY
Harmonica, Vocals / Electric Harmonica Blues
Whooping blues harpists nearing the age of 50 with number one R&B hits to their credit were predictably scarce in 1959. Nevertheless, that's the happy predicament Buster Brown found himself in when his infectious "Fannie Mae" paced the charts. Even more amazingly, the driving number made serious inroads on the pop airwaves as well.

The Georgian, whose harp style was clearly influenced by Sonny Terry, had never made a professional recording (there was a 1943 Library of Congress session that laid unissued at the time) before Fire Records boss Bobby Robinson brought the short, stockily built Brown into a New York studio in June of 1959 to wax "Fannie Mae."

Brown's reign as an unlikely star was short-lived. He managed minor follow-up hits on Fire with a rather ragged 1960 revival of Louis Jordan's "Is You Is or Is You Ain't My Baby" and his 1962 farewell bow, the effervescent rocker "Sugar Babe." A subsequent 1964 stop at Chicago's Checker Records produced a glistening update of the old blues "Crawlin' Kingsnake" that sank without a trace. —*Bill Dahl*

● **The New King of the Blues** / 1959 / Collectables ✦✦✦✦✦
Best of the Fire sessions, including #1 hit "Fannie Mae" and "Is You Is or Is You Ain't My Baby?" —*Barry Lee Pearson*

Raise a Ruckus Tonight / 1976 / DJM ✦✦✦✦✦
Twenty-one Fire Records masters by the whooping harmonica ace, including his classic "Fannie Mae" (in crystal-clear stereo), the irresistible "Sugar Babe," and a load of similar stompers that should have been hits but weren't—"Good News," "Doctor Brown," the previously unissued "No More," "Lost in a Dream." Brown occasionally made an unwise stab at something other than 12-bar fare; "Blueberry Hill," "St. Louis Blues," and the Moonglows' "Sincerely" definitely didn't suit Brown's raucous, untutored approach. —*Bill Dahl*

Charles Brown

b. Sep. 13, 1922, Texas City, TX
Piano, Vocals / Electric West Coast Blues
How many blues artists remain at the absolute top of their game after more than a half century of performing? One immediately leaps to mind: Charles Brown. His incredible piano skills and laidback vocal delivery remain every bit as mesmerizing today as they were way back in 1945, when his groundbreaking waxing of "Drifting Blues" with guitarist Johnny Moore's Three Blazers invented an entirely new blues genre for sophisticated postwar revelers—an ultra-mellow, jazz-inflected sound perfect for sipping a late-night libation in some hip after-hours joint. Brown's smooth trio format was tremendously influential to a host of high-profile disciples—Ray Charles, Amos Milburn, and Floyd Dixon, for starters.

Classically trained on the ivories, Brown earned a degree in chemistry before moving to Los Angeles in 1943. He soon hooked up with the Blazers (Moore and bassist Eddie Williams), who modeled themselves after Nat "King" Cole's trio but retained a bluesier tone within their ballad-heavy repertoire. With Brown installed as their vocalist and pianist, the Blazers' "Drifting Blues" for Philo Records remained on *Billboard*'s R&B charts for 23 weeks, peaking at number two. Follow-ups for Exclusive and Modern (including "Sunny Road," "So Long," "New Orleans Blues," and their immortal 1947 Yuletide classic "Merry Christmas Baby") kept the Blazers around the top of the R&B listings from 1946 through 1948, until Brown opted to go solo.

If anything, Brown was even more successful on his own. Signing with Eddie Mesner's Aladdin logo, he visited the R&B Top Ten no less than ten times from 1949 to 1952, retaining his mournful, sparsely arranged sound for the smashes "Get Yourself Another Fool," the chart-topping "Trouble Blues" and "Black Night," and "Hard Times." Despite a 1956 jaunt to New Orleans to record with the Cosimo's studio band, Brown's mellow approach failed to make the transition to rock's brasher rhythms, and he soon faded from national prominence (other than when his second holiday perennial, "Please Come Home for Christmas," hit in 1960 on the King label).

Occasionally recording without causing much of a stir during the '60s and '70s, Brown began to regroup by the mid-'80s. *One More for the Road*, a set cut in 1986 for the short-lived Blue Side logo, announced to anyone within earshot that Brown's talents hadn't diminished at all while he was gone (the set later reemerged on Alligator). Bonnie Raitt took an encouraging interest in Brown's comeback bid, bringing him on tour with her as her opening act (thus introducing the blues vet to a whole new generation or two of fans). His recording career took off too, with a series of albums for Bullseye Blues (the first entry, 1990s *All My Life*, is especially pleasing), and more recently, a disc for Verve.

Today touring extensively with a terrific combo in tow headed by guitarist Danny Caron, Charles Brown is finally receiving at least a portion of the recognition he's deserved for so long as a genuine rhythm and blues pioneer. But the suave, elegant Brown is by no means a relic, as anyone who's witnessed his thundering boogie piano style will gladly attest! —*Bill Dahl*

Sunny Land / 1979 / Route 66 ✦✦✦✦✦
This is a nice cross-section of the pianist's smooth early work for a variety of labels. —*Bill Dahl*

One More for the Road / 1986 / Alligator ✦✦✦
One of the first comeback salvos that the veteran pianist fired after suffering the slings and arrows of anonymity for much too long. Typically delectable in a subtle, understated manner, Brown eases through a very attractive program. —*Bill Dahl*

Driftin' Blues / 1990 / DCC ✦✦
Brown's balladeer leanings come heavily to the fore on these lushly arranged 1963 sides, originally produced by Bob Shad for issue on his Mainstream logo. He croons Steve Lawrence's "Go Away Little Girl," Ruby & the Romantics' "Our Day Will Come," and Henry Mancini's "Days of Wine and Roses" in his mellowest supper-club style—which simply doesn't match up to what came before. Charles plays organ on this album, contributing to the lounge-like ambience. —*Bill Dahl*

All My Life / 1990 / Bullseye Blues ✦✦✦✦✦
By far Brown's best contemporary effort (and the set that really got his recording career back in high gear). Cameos by Dr. John and Ruth Brown certainly didn't hurt the set's chances, but it's the eternally suave pianist and his excellent road band (especially guitarist Danny Caron and saxist Clifford Solomon) that make this such a delightful collection. —*Bill Dahl*

Someone to Love / 1992 / Bullseye Blues ✦✦✦
Bonnie Raitt, who played such an integral role in Brown's successful comeback, guests on two tracks on the pianist's Bullseye Blues encore, which isn't quite the tour de force that his previous outing was but is eminently solid nonetheless. Caron and Solomon once again shine in support of their leader. —*Bill Dahl*

★ **Driftin' Blues: The Best of Charles Brown** / 1992 / EMI America ✦✦✦✦✦
If your budget only allows the acquisition of a single CD of Brown's Aladdin material, let it be this one. It sports most of the truly important hits that inspired so many West Coasters—"Driftin' Blues," "Black Night," "Trouble Blues," and many others. —*Bill Dahl*

Just a Lucky So and So / 1993 / Bullseye Blues ✦✦
Charles Brown's casual, yet stunning phrasing, inventive voicings and piano accompaniment are wonderfully presented on this ten-song set. Ron Levy's production and the arrangements of Wardell Quezergue and Brown are tasteful, breezy and geared for his carefully constructed, teasing solos and rich, creamy leads. Such numbers as Brown's classic "Drifting Blues," as well as "Gloomy Sunday" and "I Won't Cry Anymore," convey despair and hurt, yet retain a certain appeal and charm. Brown keeps making fine records, sounding as convincing in the 1990s as he did at the start of his career. —*Ron Wynn*

☆ **The Complete Aladdin Recordings of Charles Brown** / 1994 / Mosaic ✦✦✦✦✦
Every single brilliant side—some 109 in all—that this elegant, tremendously influential pianist cut for the Mesner brothers' Philo and Aladdin imprints from 1945 to 1956 is housed in this lavishly produced five-disc boxed set. Mosaic's customary attention to detail is evident in the packaging and the sound; Brown's brilliance makes the entire box a delight, from his earliest sessions with the Three Blazers through his hitmaking run as a solo star during the late '40s and early '50s. The genesis of the entire West Coast "club blues" style resides in this box; its expense is well worth it. —*Bill Dahl*

Snuff Dippin' Mama / 1995 / Night Train ✦✦✦✦✦
Even with the above box, you won't own all of Brown's seminal work. In 1946, he and the Blazers landed at Exclusive Records, which is the era that this collection examines via 19 fine sides including the jivey "Juke Box Lil" and "C.O.D.," a mournful "Sunny Road," and the jazzy "B-Sharp You'll See." Guitarist Johnny Moore and bassist Eddie Williams were indeed sharp in smooth support. —*Bill Dahl*

The Boss of the Blues / Mainstream ✦✦
More 1963-64 Mainstream sides with some duplication—the first six tracks here also appear on the DCC compilation. Tracks seven through sixteen find Brown surrounded by strings as he smoothly intones "Pledging My Love," "Blueberry Hill," and "Cottage for Sale" (they didn't even let him sit down at the keyboard at all for these dates!). —*Bill Dahl*

Clarence "Gatemouth" Brown

b. Apr. 18, 1924, Vinton, LA
Guitar, Mandolin, Violin, Drums, Vocals, Bass / Texas Blues
Whatever you do, don't refer to multi-instrumentalist Clarence "Gatemouth" Brown as a bluesman, although his imprimatur on the development of Texas blues is enormous. You're liable to get him riled. If you must pigeonhole the legend, just call him an eclectic Texas musical master whose interests encompass virtually every roots genre imaginable.

Brown learned the value of versatility while growing up in Orange, TX. His dad was a locally popular musician who specialized in country, cajun, and bluegrass—but not blues. Later, Gate was entranced by the big bands of Count Basie, Lionel Hampton, and Duke Ellington (a torrid arrangement of "Take the 'A' Train" remains a centerpiece of Brown's repertoire). Tagged with the "Gatemouth" handle by a high school instructor who accused Brown of having a "voice like a gate," Brown has used it to his advantage throughout his illustrious career. (His guitar-wielding brother, James "Widemouth" Brown, recorded "Boogie Woogie Nighthawk" for Jax in 1951.)

In 1947, Gate's impromptu fill-in for an ailing T-Bone Walker at Houston entrepreneur Don Robey's Bronze Peacock nightclub convinced Robey to assume control of Brown's career. After two singles for Aladdin stiffed, Robey inaugurated his own Peacock label in 1949 to showcase Gate's blistering riffs, which proved influential to a legion of Houston string-benders (Albert Collins, Johnny Copeland, Johnny "Guitar" Watson, Cal Green, and many more have pledged allegiance to Brown's riffs). Peacock and its sister label Duke prospered through the '50s and '60s.

Gate stayed with Peacock through 1960. The R&B charts did not reflect Brown's importance (he hit only once nationwide with 1949's two-sided smash "Mary Is Fine"/"My Time Is Expensive"). But his blazing instrumentals ("Boogie Uproar," "Gate Walks to Board," 1954's seminal "Okie Dokie Stomp"), horn-enriched rockers ("She Walked Right In," "Rock My Blues Away"), and lowdown Lone Star blues ("Dirty Work at the Crossroads") are a major component of the rich Texas postwar blues legacy. Brown broke new ground often—even in the '50s, he insisted on sawing

his fiddle at live performances, although Robey wasn't interested in capturing Gate's violin talent until "Just Before Dawn" (his final Peacock platter in 1959).

The '60s weren't all that kind to Brown. His cover of Little Jimmy Dickens' country novelty "May the Bird of Paradise Fly Up Your Nose" for tiny Hermitage Records made a little noise in 1965 (and presaged things to come stylistically). But the decade was chiefly memorable for Brown's 1966 stint as house bandleader for *The!!!!Beat,* a groundbreaking syndicated R&B television program out of Dallas hosted by WLAC deejay Bill "Hoss" Allen.

When Gate began to rebuild his career in the '70s, he was determined to do things his way. Country, jazz, even calypso now played a prominent role in his concerts; he's as likely to launch into an oldtime fiddle hoedown as a swinging guitar blues. He turned up on *Hee Haw* with pickin' and grinnin' pal Roy Clark after they cut a sizzling 1979 duet album for MCA, *Makin' Music.* Acclaimed discs for Rounder, Alligator, and Verve over the last 15 years have proven that Gatemouth Brown is a steadfastly unclassifiable American original. —*Bill Dahl*

Cold Strange / 1973 / Black & Blue ✦✦✦
Swinging guitar and tasty vocals. —*Bill Dahl*

Just Got Lucky / Mar. 1973-Jul. 1, 1977 / Evidence ✦✦✦✦
More goodies from the same French 1973 dates (originally issued on Black & Blue). Lots of Jordan covers, along with Brown's own "Here Am I" and "Long Way Home," three Peacock remakes, and a sizzling revival of Bill Doggett's "Honey Boy." The last three titles date from a 1977 session, again cut in France, and are all Brown originals. —*Bill Dahl*

Sings Louis Jordan / 1974 / Black & Blue ✦✦✦
Enjoyable foray thru Jordan's songbook by a master guitarist. —*Bill Dahl*

Gate's on the Heat / 1975 / Barclay ✦✦
The worst Brown album currently on the shelves. Cut back in the '70s with a band that wouldn't know how to swing if it were permanently marooned on a playground (the rhythm guitarist is particularly abominable), this one's a must to avoid. —*Bill Dahl*

Black Jack / Dec. 1978 / Music Is Medicine ✦✦✦
It may not be the strongest LP in his catalog, but Gate's first domestic album offered more than a hint of things to come with its daring mixture of country, jazz, and blues numbers. —*Bill Dahl*

Makin' Music [Roy Clark] / 1979 / MCA ✦✦✦✦
Surround two of the most versatile guitar pickers on the planet in a studio with a cadre of world-class sidemen and what do you get? This irresistible duet album by Gate and Roy Clark, first out on MCA. Good vibes abound as the fun-loving pair blast out "Caldonia," "Take the 'A' Train," "The Drifter," "Justice Blues," and more, trading licks, vocals, and quips with a jam session-oriented looseness. —*Bill Dahl*

San Antonio Ballbuster / 1982 / Red Lightnin' ✦✦✦✦
Considering how sub-par the sound quality is on this disc (it's a CD reproduction of an old Red Lightnin' bootleg), it wouldn't rate a recommendation if the material therein were otherwise available. But many of these Peacock masters aren't obtainable anywhere else—the stunning 1953 instrumental "Boogie Uproar," storming rockers "Win with Me Baby," "You Got Money," and "Just Got Lucky," and the after-hours hit "I've Been Mistreated," for starters. So until something better comes along …—*Bill Dahl*

Alright Again! / 1982 / Rounder ✦✦✦✦✦
One of the most satisfying contemporary Brown discs of all for the discerning blues fan. Nothing but swinging, horn-abetted blues adorn this album, as Gate pays tribute to an influence and a protege by covering T-Bone Walker's "Strollin' with Bones" and Albert Collins' "Frosty." Brown jauntily revives Junior Parker's "I Feel Alright Again" and Percy Mayfield's "Give Me Time to Explain," while his own numbers—a funky "Dollar Got the Blues," the luxurious blues "Sometimes I Slip"—are truly brilliant. —*Bill Dahl*

One More Mile / 1983 / Rounder ✦✦✦
Considerably more varied than its predecessor, with nods toward the Louisiana swamp ("Sunrise Cajun Style," complete with pedal steel guitar), sentimental ballads (Cecil Gant's "I Wonder"), and jazz ("Big Yard"). Blues purists will perk up for revivals of

Junior Parker's "Stranded" and Roy Milton's "Information Blues."
—*Bill Dahl*

★ **The Original Peacock Recordings** / 1984 / Rounder ♦♦♦♦♦
Only 12 songs long, this collection remains the best place to
begin appreciating why so many young Texas blues guitarists
fell in love with Gatemouth Brown's style (until MCA decides to
compile the ultimate Brown package, anyway). Listen to the way
his blazing axe darts and weaves through trombonist Pluma
Davis' jazzy horn chart on 1954's "Okie Dokie Stomp," or the
stratospheric licks drenching "Dirty Work at the Crossroads."
Brown proves that a violin can adapt marvelously to the blues
(in the right hands, anyway) on "Just Before Dawn," and blows
a little atmospheric harp on "Gate's Salty Blues." —*Bill Dahl*

Real Life (Live) / 1986 / Rounder ♦♦♦
Live set cut in Fort Worth, TX, that presents an accurate depic-
tion of the breadth and scope of a Gatemouth Brown concert.
Switching between guitar and violin, Gate offers everything
from a reprise of "Okie Dokie Stomp" to a tender "Please Send
Me Someone to Love" from Percy Mayfield's songbook and per-
sonalized renditions of "St. Louis Blues" and "Frankie and
Johnny." —*Bill Dahl*

Pressure Cooker / 1987 / Alligator ♦♦♦♦
Before Gate was able to rebuild a following stateside, he frequently toured Europe. He recorded the contents of this inexorably swinging set in France in 1973 with all-star backing by
keyboardists Milt Buckner and Jay McShann, saxists Arnett
Cobb and Hal Singer, and others. Brown indulges his passion for
Louis Jordan by ripping through "Ain't That Just like a Woman"
and "Ain't Nobody Here but Us Chickens" and exhibits his
immaculate fretwork on the torrid title item. —*Bill Dahl*

Standing My Ground / 1989 / Alligator ♦♦♦♦
A delightfully eclectic program spotlighting nearly all of Gate's
musical leanings—blues, jazz, country, even a hearty taste of
"Louisiana Zydeco"—and a revealing glimpse of his multi-instru-
mental abilities: he plays guitar, violin, drums, and piano! There's
a tender remake of the Chuck Willis R&B ballad and a funk-
tinged update of "Got My Mojo Working," but everything else is
from Brown's own pen. —*Bill Dahl*

No Looking Back / 1992 / Alligator ♦♦♦
Easily one of the most varied sets of Gate's lengthy career—and
that's saying something! Country songwriting legend John D.
Loudermilk, a longtime Brown backer, wrote some pretty outrageous stuff for the set—the anti-drug diatribe "Dope," a cutesy
novelty about an "Alligator Eating Dog," and a MOR-styled ballad, "I Will Be Your Friend," that Gate croons with Michelle
Shocked (and a few of his fans undoubtedly *were* shocked by
that turn of events!). Several hard-swinging instrumentals and
the contemporary-slanted "Better off with the Blues" are closer
to traditional fare. —*Bill Dahl*

San Antonio Ballbuster / 1992 / Charly ♦♦♦
It's 1965, and Gate's guitar sound is different—not so brash and
trebly but smoother, with more of a jazz and occasional country
kick. Most of these sides were never issued after being acquired
by Chess. There are two takes of Little Jimmy Dickens' C&W
novelty hit "May the Bird of Paradise," both of 'em swinging
easy. Gate was in a Sonny Boy Williamson mood that day, reviving three of the harpist's oldies along with a few of his own and
the ominous blues "Long Way Home," which threatens mayhem
most charmingly. —*Bill Dahl*

Man / 1995 / Verve ♦♦♦
Brown made the big jump to major-label stature for this typically unclassifiable set, which feistily sweeps through zydeco
("Big Mammou"), country ("Up Jumped the Devil"), Louis Jordan
("Early in the Morning"), and even a little blues along its unpredictable course. Cajun accordionist Jo-El Sonnier receives several solos in a guest-starring role. —*Bill Dahl*

Long Way Home / 1996 / Verve ♦♦
One of the few lousy recordings of this determinedly eclectic
multi-instrumentalist's lengthy career. He's stuck going the
superstar cameo route a la John Lee Hooker (there's less Gate on
this disc than on any other Gate set), welcoming Eric Clapton
aboard for some amazingly generic guitar solos; vocally duetting
with frog-voiced Leon Russell and chirpy Maria Muldaur, and
backing John Loudermilk as he sings his own composition
"Tobacco Road" (where's Lou Rawls when you need him?). A
handful of acoustic numbers add depth, but there's not much

here at all that's likely to satisfy Gate's legion of blues fans. —
Bill Dahl

J.T. Brown

b. Apr. 2, 1918, Mississippi, **d.** Nov. 24, 1969
Saxophone, Vocals / Chicago Blues
His braying tenor sax tone earned J.T. Brown the dubious distinction of being told his horn sounded like a "nanny goat." That
didn't stop the likes of Elmore James from hiring Brown for
some of his most important sessions for Meteor and Modern,
though; Brown's style was truly distinctive.

Mississippi-born John T. Brown was a member of the Rabbit
Foot Minstrels down south before arriving in the Windy City. By
1945, Brown was recording behind pianist Roosevelt Sykes and
singer St. Louis Jimmy Oden, later backing Eddie Boyd and
Washboard Sam for RCA Victor. He debuted on wax as a bandleader in 1950 on the Harlem label, subsequently cutting sessions in 1951 and 1952 for Chicago's United logo as well as JOB.

Brown's sideman credentials included wailing riffs beside
slide guitarist Elmore James and pianist Little Johnny Jones for
the Bihari brothers' Meteor and Flair labels in 1952 and 1953.
Meteor issued a couple of singles under Brown's own name
(well, sort of) during the same time frame: "Round House
Boogie"/"Kickin' the Blues Around" was credited to the Bep
Brown Orchestra, while "Sax-ony Boogie" was listed as by
Saxman Brown and its flip, the vocal "Dumb Woman Blues," as
by J.T. (Big Boy) Brown! All four are available on Flair's four-disc
James box set, incidentally.

After a final 1956 date for United that laid unissued at the
time, Brown's studio activities were limited to sideman roles. In
January of 1969, he was part of Fleetwood Mac's *Blues Jam at
Chess* album, even singing a tune for the project, but he died
before the close of that year. —*Bill Dahl*

● **Rockin' with J T** / 1984 / Krazy Kat ♦♦♦♦♦
Chicago jump blues, wailing stuff from the late '40s and early
'50s. —*Bill Dahl*

Windy City Boogie / Pearl ♦♦♦♦♦
Inexplicably still unavailable on CD, this LP showcases Brown's
hearty vocals and "nanny goat horn" in a bandleading role. With
frequent cohort Little Brother Montgomery deftly tinkling the
ivories, Brown delivers "Blackjack Blues" and "When I Was a
Lad." Storming boogie instrumentals were an integral part of
Brown's repertoire; this set (spanning 1951–1956) boasts a host
of stellar houserockers. —*Bill Dahl*

Nappy Brown

b. Oct. 12, 1929, Charlotte, NC
Vocals / Electric Jump Blues
Nobody sounded much like Nappy Brown during the mid-'50s.
Exotically rolling his consonants with sing-song impugnity
(allegedly, Savoy Records boss Herman Lubinsky thought Brown
was singing in Yiddish), bellowing the blues with gospel-inspired
ferocity, Brown rode rock 'n' roll's first wave for a few glorious
years before his records stopped selling. But a dozen years ago
or thereabouts, Brown seemingly rose from the dead to stage a
comeback bid. Now he's ensconced once again as a venerable
blues veteran who'll stop at nothing (including rolling around
the stage in sexual simulation) to enthrall his audience.

Napoleon Brown's sanctified screams come naturally—he
grew up in Charlotte, NC, singing gospel as well as blues. He
was fronting a spiritual aggregation, the Heavenly Lights, who
were signed to the roster of Newark, NJ's Savoy Records when
Lubinsky convinced the leather-lunged shouter to cross the secular line in 1954. Voila! Nappy Brown the R&B singer was born.

Brown brought hellfire intensity to his blues-soaked Savoy
debut, "Is It True," but it was "Don't Be Angry" the next year that
caused his fortunes to skyrocket. The sizzling rocker sported
loads of Brown's unique vocal gimmicks and a hair-raising tenor
sax solo by Sam "The Man" Taylor, becoming his first national
smash. Those onboard New York session aces didn't hurt the
overall ambience of Brown's Savoy dates—Taylor's scorching
horn further enlivened "Open up That Door," while Budd
Johnson or Al Sears took over on other equally raucous efforts.
Novelty-tinged upbeat items such as "Little by Little" and
"Piddily Patter Patter" defined Nappy's output, but his throat-
busting turn on the 1957 blues "The Right Time" (borrowed by

Ray Charles in short order!) remains a highlight of Brown's early heyday.

After decades away from the limelight, Nappy resurfaced in 1984 with a very credible album for Landslide Records, *Tore Up*, with guitarist Tinsley Ellis' band, the Heartfixers. Since then, he's recorded a fine set for Black Top (*Something Gonna Jump Out the Bushes*) with Anson Funderburgh, Ronnie Earl, and Earl King sharing guitar duties, and some not-so-fine CDs for other labels. —*Bill Dahl*

That Man / 1985 / Swift ✦✦✦✦✦
That Man collects 17 songs Nappy Brown recorded for Savoy Records between 1954 and 1961, including "The Right Time," "Down in the Alley," and "Is It True." The compilation spotlights his lesser-known recordings, not his hits, but these songs are every bit as good as his more popular material from the same era. —*Thom Owens*

I Done Got Over / 1985 / Stockholm ✦✦
I Done Got Over features some good vocal performances from Nappy Brown, but this album—which essentially runs through his '50s hits, with a couple new tracks thrown in for good measure—is one of his lesser works. Brown is supported by the Roosters, a stiff Swedish band that can't get the music cooking. Consequently, Brown never puts forth much of an effort. The result is a disappointingly uninspired record. —*Thom Owens*

★ **Don't Be Angry!** / 1985 / Savoy ✦✦✦✦✦
Rolling his consonants like a crazed cantor, shouter Nappy Brown brought a gospel-imbued fervor to his rocking mid-'50s R&B that few of his peers could match. Backed by some of New York's finest sessioneers, Brown roars 16 of his best early Savoy sides on this essential purchase. "Don't Be Angry," "Just a Little Love," "Open Up That Door," and "Bye Bye Baby" rate with his hottest jump efforts, "I Cried like a Baby" and "It's Really You" are hair-raising blues, and "Little by Little" rides a bouncy, pop-accessible groove. Now where's volume two?? —*Bill Dahl*

Something Gonna Jump out the Bushes / 1988 / Black Top ✦✦✦✦
Ultra-solid support from guitarists Anson Funderburgh, Eugene Ross, Ronnie Earl, and Earl King and Black Top's superb house horn section make this Dallas-cut set Brown's best contemporary album to date. His lusty shouting style works well on covers of the Dominoes' "Have Mercy Baby," the "5" Royales' title track, a pair of Earl King-penned numbers, and Robert Ward's "Your Love Is Real." —*Bill Dahl*

Tore Up / 1989 / Alligator ✦✦✦
After too many years during which he was missing and presumed forever lost in action, Brown returned to prominence with this very credible album, cut with backing by guitarist Tinsley Ellis and the Heartfixers and originally issued on the tiny Landslide label. He reprises his salacious blues "Lemon Squeezin' Daddy" and rolls his R's like the good old days on dusties by Little Walter, the Midnighters, Howlin' Wolf, and even Bob Dylan and the Allmans. —*Bill Dahl*

Deep Sea Diver / 1989 / Meltone ✦✦
Deep Sea Diver is a competent, but not particularly inspiring, live album recorded in 1989. Occasionally, Nappy Brown turns in a fiery performance—particularly on "Things Have Changed" and the title track—but just as often, his singing is workmanlike. There's enough good moments to make the album worthwhile for fans, but it is not an essential purchase. —*Thom Owens*

Aw! Shucks / 1991 / Ichiban ✦✦
Aw! Shucks is one of Nappy Brown's most uninspired efforts. Out of the nine songs, only one was written by Brown; the remaining eight were written by various songwriters, including members of the Ichiban staff. None of the songs are engaging and they're made even worse by flat, uninspired performances. The musicians may be accomplished professionals, but they can't breathe life into any of these songs. —*Thom Owens*

Apples & Lemons / Ichiban ✦✦✦
Jump blues, shouting R&B, and gospel-edged soul from Nappy Brown, who made his finest material in the '50s and '60s, but has done some exuberant material during the '80s and '90s. While his voice doesn't have the swagger or ferocity it did in its heyday, it's still impressive enough to give this the residue of authenticity. —*Ron Wynn*

Roy Brown

b. Sep. 10, 1925, New Orleans, LA, **d.** May 25, 1981, San Fernando, CA
Piano, Vocals / Electric Jump Blues
When you draw up a short list of the R&B pioneers who exerted a primary influence on the development of rock 'n' roll, respectfully place singer Roy Brown's name near its very top. His seminal 1947 DeLuxe Records waxing of "Good Rockin' Tonight" was immediately ridden to the peak of the R&B charts by shouter Wynonie Harris and subsequently covered by Elvis Presley, Ricky Nelson, Jerry Lee Lewis, and many more early rock icons (even Pat Boone!). In addition, Brown's melismatically pleading, gospel-steeped delivery impacted the vocal styles of B.B. King, Bobby Bland, and Little Richard (among a plethora of important singers). Clearly, Roy Brown was an innovator—and from 1948-1951, an R&B star whose wild output directly presaged rock's rise.

Born in the Crescent City, Brown grew up all over the place: Eunice, LA (where he sang in church and worked in the sugar-cane fields), Houston, TX, and finally Los Angeles by age 17. Back then, Bing Crosby was Roy's favorite singer—but a nine-month stint at a Shreveport, LA, nightclub exposed him to the blues for the first time. He conjured up "Good Rockin' Tonight" while fronting a band in Galveston, TX. Ironically, Harris wanted no part of the song when Brown first tried to hand it to him. When pianist Cecil Gant heard Brown's knockout rendition of the tune in New Orleans, he had Roy sing it over the phone to a sleepy DeLuxe boss, Jules Braun, in the wee hours of the morning! Though Brown's original waxing (with Bob Ogden's band in support) was a solid hit, Harris' cover beat him out for top chart honors.

Roy didn't have to wait long to dominate the R&B lists himself. He scored 15 hits from mid-1948 to late 1951 for DeLuxe, ranging from the emotionally wracked crying blues "Hard Luck Blues" (his biggest seller of all in 1950) to the party-time rockers "Rockin' at Midnight," "Boogie at Midnight," "Miss Fanny Brown," and "Cadillac Baby." Strangely, his sales slumped badly from 1952 on, even though his frantic "Hurry Hurry Baby," "Ain't No Rockin' No More," "Black Diamond," and "Gal from Kokomo" for Cincinnati's King Records rate among his hottest houserockers.

Brown was unable to cash in on the rock 'n' roll idiom he helped to invent, though he briefly rejuvenated his commercial fortunes at Imperial Records in 1957. Working with New Orleans producer Dave Bartholomew, then riding high with Fats Domino, Brown returned to the charts with the original version of "Let the Four Winds Blow" (later a hit for Fats) and cut the sizzling sax-powered rockers "Diddy-Y-Diddy-O," "Saturday Night," and "Ain't Gonna Do It." Not everything was an artistic triumph; Brown's utterly lifeless cover of Buddy Knox's "Party Doll"—amazingly, a chart entry for Brown—may well be the worst thing he ever committed to wax (rivaled only by a puerile "School Bell Rock" cut during a momentary return to King in 1959).

After a long dry spell, Brown's acclaimed performance as part of Johnny Otis' troupe at the 1970 Monterey Jazz Festival and a 1973 LP for ABC-BluesWay began to rebuild his long-lost momentum. But it came too late—Brown died of a heart attack in 1981 at age 56, his role as a crucial link between postwar R&B and rock's initial rise still underappreciated by the masses. —*Bill Dahl*

☆ **Blues Deluxe** / 1991 / Charly ✦✦✦✦✦
More tracks (two dozen in all) from Brown's voluminous DeLuxe and King catalogs make this British import well worth searching around for. Hellacious jumps—"Cadillac Baby," "Good Rockin' Man"—and plenty of rarities distinguish this collection by one of the true pioneers of R&B. —*Bill Dahl*

Mighty Mighty Man! / 1993 / Ace ✦✦✦✦✦
Another British import that really delivers the rocking goods! This time zeroing in on Brown's 1953-59 King sides exclusively, the 22-cut CD shows that Brown actually picked up his tempos to meet rock's rise head on. The clever sequel "Ain't No Rocking No More," "Black Diamond," "Gal from Kokomo," and "Shake 'Em Up Baby" rate with his hottest rockers, with great support from a crew of Crescent City stalwarts. —*Bill Dahl*

★ **Good Rocking Tonight: The Best of Roy Brown** / 1994 / Rhino ✦✦✦✦✦
An unassailable 18-cut cross-section of the monstrously popular

and influential New Orleans jump blues shouter's sides for the DeLuxe, King, and Imperial labels that spans 1947–57 and takes in his seminal "Good Rocking Tonight" (where it all began!), "Rockin' at Midnight," "Boogie at Midnight," and "Love Don't Love Nobody," the almost unbearably tortured "Hard Luck Blues," and the unbelievably raunchy two-parter "Butcher Pete." Looking for the origins of rock? Here they are! —*Bill Dahl*

The Complete Imperial Recordings / Oct. 1995 / Capitol ◆◆◆
In the mid-'50s Brown, like many other early R&B pioneers, was a bit lost at sea amid the rock 'n' roll explosion. From 1956 to 1958, he recorded these 20 tracks for Imperial under the direction of legendary New Orleans R&B producer Dave Bartholomew. Brown and Bartholomew were attempting to update Brown's jump blues/R&B hybrid with a lot of Fats Domino-type Crescent City influence on these sides. The results weren't bad, but with Bartholomew co-writing most of the tunes and using local musicians like saxophonist Lee Allen, Brown sounded more like a journeyman New Orleans R&B singer than an innovative, bluesy forefather of rock 'n' roll. There were a couple of commercial successes; his cover of Buddy Knox's "Party Doll" made the R&B Top 20, and "Let the Four Winds Blow" actually made the pop Top 40, although Fats Domino would have much greater success with the same song when he covered it a few years later. Diluted by occasional pop and rock influences, as well as a substandard variation of "Good Rockin' Tonight," this compilation shouldn't be the first Brown on your shelf. But for those who want to go a little further, it's packaged very well, with thorough liner notes and seven previously unissued cuts. —*Richie Unterberger*

Ruth Brown

b. Jan. 30, 1928, Portsmouth, VA
Vocals / R&B
They called Atlantic Records "the house that Ruth built" during the 1950s, and they weren't referring to the Sultan of Swat. Ruth Brown's regal hitmaking reign from 1949 to the close of the '50s helped tremendously to establish the New York label's predominance in the R&B field. Later, the business all but forgot her—she was forced to toil as domestic help for a time—but she's back on top now, her status as a postwar R&B pioneer (and tireless advocate for the rights and royalties of her peers) recognized worldwide.

Young Ruth Weston was inspired initially by jazz chanteuses Sarah Vaughan, Billie Holiday, and Dinah Washington. She ran away from her Portsmouth home in 1945 to hit the road with trumpeter Jimmy Brown, whom she soon married. A month with bandleader Lucky Millinder's orchestra in 1947 ended abruptly in Washington, D.C., when she was canned for delivering a round of drinks to members of the band. Cab Calloway's sister Blanche gave Ruth a gig at her Crystal Caverns nightclub and assumed a managerial role in the young singer's life. Deejay Willis Conover dug Brown's act and recommended her to Ahmet Ertegun and Herb Abramson, bosses of a fledgling imprint named Atlantic.

Unfortunately, Brown's debut session for the label was delayed by a nine-month hospital stay caused by a serious auto accident en route to New York that badly injured her leg. When Ruth finally made it to her first date in May of 1949, she made up for lost time by waxing the torch ballad "So Long" (backed by guitarist Eddie Condon's band), which proved her first hit. Brown's seductive vocal delivery shone incandescently on her Atlantic smashes "Teardrops in My Eyes" (an R&B chart-topper for 11 weeks in 1950), "I'll Wait for You" and "I Know" in 1951, 1952's "5-10-15 Hours" (another number one rocker), the seminal "(Mama) He Treats Your Daughter Mean" in 1953, and a tender Chuck Willis-penned "Oh What a Dream" and the timely "Mambo Baby" the next year. Along the way, Frankie Laine tagged her "Miss Rhythm" during an engagement in Philly. Brown belted a series of her hits on the groundbreaking TV program *Showtime at the Apollo* in 1955, exhibiting delicious comic timing while trading sly one-liners with emcee Willie Bryant (ironically, ex-husband Jimmy Brown was a member of the show's house band!)

After an even two dozen R&B chart appearances for Atlantic that ended in 1960 with "Don't Deceive Me" (many of them featuring hell-raising tenor sax solos by then-hubby Willis "Gator" Jackson), Brown faded from view. After raising her two sons and

working a nine-to-five job, Brown began to rebuild her musical career in the mid-'70s. That comedic sense served Ruth well during a TV sitcom stint co-starring with McLean Stevenson in *Hello, Larry,* in a meaty role in director John Waters' 1985 sockhop satire film *Hairspray,* and during her 1989 Broadway starring turn in *Black and Blue* (which won her a Tony Award).

There have been more records for Fantasy in recent years (notably 1991's jumping *Fine and Mellow*), and a lengthy tenure as host of National Public Radio's *Harlem Hit Parade* and *BluesStage.* Brown's nine-year ordeal to recoup her share of royalties from all those Atlantic platters led to the formation of the non-profit Rhythm & Blues Foundation, an organization dedicated to helping others in the same frustrating situation.

Factor in all those time-consuming activities, and it's a wonder Ruth Brown has time to sing anymore. But she does (quite royally, too), her pipes mellowed but not frayed by the ensuing decades that have seen her rise to stardom not once, but twice. —*Bill Dahl*

Ruth Brown Sings Favorites / 1956 / Atlantic ◆◆◆
Ruth Brown had extensive gospel and jazz roots, which Atlantic honed to perfection, turning her into an R&B queen. These songs aren't quite the same, but they show her full stylistic range and also how powerful and strong her voice was in the '50s. —*Ron Wynn*

Ruth Brown / 1957 / Atlantic ◆◆◆
Ruth Brown at her stinging, assertive, bawdy best, doing the sizzling, innuendo-laden R&B that helped make Atlantic the nation's prime independent during the early days of rock 'n' roll. There's also plenty of equally fiery, hot musical accompaniment, with then-husband Willis Jackson sometimes featured on tenor sax. —*Ron Wynn*

Late Date with Ruth Brown / Jan. 27, 1959+Feb. 2, 1959 / Atlantic ◆◆◆
Good after-hours, smoky blues and R&B session featuring Ruth Brown in prime form. Nobody, male or female, sang with more spirit, sass, and vigor than Brown during the '50s, and this session reminded those who had forgotten that Brown could also hold her own with sophisticated material as well as sexy stuff. —*Ron Wynn*

Along Comes Ruth / 1962 / Philips ◆◆◆
Good, but not essential, early '60s session showing that both Ruth Brown and her brain trust were about to run dry. She still had the powerhouse vocals, but there are fewer inspiring songs, and by the end of side two, Brown is getting by on energy alone. —*Ron Wynn*

The Best of Ruth Brown / 1963 / Atlantic ◆◆◆
Another good anthology compiling Ruth Brown's major hits. This isn't as inclusive or comprehensive and is really geared toward fans with only chart items. It's a good buy for the cost-conscious, and even better for someone who wants a reasonable, but not exhaustive, Brown package. —*Ron Wynn*

Ruth Brown '65 / Dec. 1964 / Mainstream ◆◆◆
Underrated, nicely produced mid-'60s album putting Ruth Brown more in the blues and interpretative mode that she moved away from during the hit years. She can still belt out numbers, but also shows some wit and some flourishes that were sacrificed for impact when she was doing rock 'n' roll. —*Ron Wynn*

Sweet Baby of Mine (1949-1956) / 1987 / Route 66 ◆◆◆◆◆
Excellent collection covering blues and R&B songs Brown did prior to becoming a huge hit artist for Atlantic in the late '50s. These were R&B gems, but such artists as Patti Page and Georgia Gibbs were covering them for the White market and Brown was locked out until 1957. But she enjoyed 11 Top Ten R&B hits, which are contained on this anthology. —*Ron Wynn*

Have a Good Time / May 10, 1988–May 11, 1988 / Fantasy ◆◆◆
Nice recent material, with Brown showing she's still got some power. —*Ron Wynn*

★ **Miss Rhythm (Greatest Hits and More)** / 1989 / Rhino ◆◆◆◆◆
They used to refer to Atlantic Records in its early years as "the house that Ruth built," and the 40 tracks inhabiting these two discs offer unassailable insight as to why. As one of the premier R&B divas of the early '50s, Brown's seductive, earthy style found her belting the rockers (the R&B chart-toppers "Teardrops from My Eyes," "Mama He Treats Your Daughter Mean," "5-10-15

Hours") and caressing the ballads ("So Long," "Have a Good Time," "Oh What a Dream"), backed by some of New York's finest session players (including then-hubby Willis "Gator" Jackson on scorching tenor sax). Covers 1949–1960 and takes Brown from the beginnings of R&B to the heyday of rock ("Wild Wild Young Men" is positively frantic, while the Bobby Darin-penned "This Little Girl's Gone Rockin'" is lightweight yet utterly charming). Essential stuff! —*Bill Dahl*

Blues on Broadway / Jun. 12, 1989–Jun. 13, 1989 / Fantasy ✦✦✦✦✦
A great mix of show business panache with a bluesy undergirding. —*Ron Wynn*

Fine and Mellow / 1991 / Fantasy ✦✦✦
Nice contemporary effort with a strongly swinging R&B flavor running throughout. Ruth Brown goes back to the '40s (Louis Jordan's "Knock Me a Kiss," Dinah Washington's "Salty Papa Blues") and '50s (Brook Benton's "It's Just a Matter of Time," Jackie Wilson's "I'll Be Satisfied," the Lula Reed/Ray Charles dirge "Drown in My Own Tears") for much of the disc, paying loving tribute to her main lady Billie Holiday with the tasty title cut and delivering a pair of Duke Ellington numbers along the way. —*Bill Dahl*

Songs of My Life / 1993 / Fantasy ✦✦✦
Before Ruth Brown became an R&B and rock legend in the '50s, she was a jazz, blues, and gospel stylist. She shows that aspect of her talent on *The Songs of My Life*, a fine set produced by guitarist Rodney Jones, who also did the arrangements and conducted the backing band. While she displays her timing, interpretive skills, and still-impressive delivery and enunciation throughout, Brown also demonstrates on her rendition of Eric Clapton's "Tears In Heaven" that she retains an interest in and awareness of contemporary songs that fit her style. Ruth Brown proves that it's not the song or the lyric but the singer who makes a tune work. —*Ron Wynn*

Walter Brown

b. Aug. 1917, Dallas, TX, **d.** Jun. 1956, Lawton, OK
Vocals / Jazz Blues
Blues singer Walter Brown fronted the roaring Jay McShann Orchestra (which included young alto saxist Charlie Parker) in 1941, when the roaring Kansas City aggregation cut their classic "Confessin' the Blues" and "Hootie Blues" for Decca. The Dallas native remained with McShann from 1941 to 1945 before going solo (with less successful results). —*Bill Dahl*

● **Confessin' the Blues** / 1981 / Affinity ✦✦✦✦✦

Bob Brozman

b. Mar. 8, 1954, New York, NY
Guitar, Ukulele / Acoustic Country Blues
Multi-instrumentalist, historian and educator Bob Brozman was born in New York on March 8, 1954. His uncle, Barney Josephson, was a prominent clubowner who ran Cafe Society in Greenwich Village, one of the first places in New York, or anywhere, where Black and White musicians played on stage together.

Brozman studied music and ethnomusicology at Washington University in St. Louis. Brozman is not only a master of classic blues from the '20s and '30s, but also a competent performer of early jazz and ragtime. In the mid-'70s while still in college, he would make trips down south to find, interview and play with the older blues artists from the 1920s and '30s whom he admired.

Brozman recorded several fine albums in the early and mid-'80s for the Kicking Mule and Rounder labels, and though they may not have been reissued on compact disc, for students of early, vintage blues and for vintage guitar aficionados, they're well worth digging out of the vinyl shops. Brozman's albums include *Blue Hula Stomp* (1981) and *Snapping the Strings* (1983), both for the California-based Kicking Mule label. In 1985, he recorded *Hello Central, Give Me Dr. Jazz* for the Massachusetts-based Rounder label and followed up in 1988 with *Devil's Slide*. For die-hard blues fans who seek an album devoid of any of the other genres Brozman so easily interprets (like ragtime and calypso), the album to get is *Truckload of Blues*, a 1992 Rounder release. —*Richard Skelly*

Hello Central: Give Me Dr. Jazz / Sep. 1985 / Rounder ✦✦✦
Bob enlists George Winston and others to faithfully re-create the 78-rpm era, focusing on early-jazz standards, hokum and blues. —*Myles Boisen*

● **Devil's Slide** / 1988 / Rounder ✦✦✦✦✦
Blues, Hawaiian, calypso, hot jazz—slide-wizard Bob can do it all with startling authenticity and humor. This CD compilation has five cuts from his *Hello Central* album to boot. —*Myles Boisen*

A Truckload of Blues / 1992 / Rounder ✦✦✦✦✦
Guitarist Bob Brozman's long-awaited all-blues album covers similar territory as others who have turned in heartfelt treatments of traditional and Delta blues tunes. But the difference between Brozman and many of his predecessors is that he has fun doing these songs. He's wise enough to understand that there are only so many ways one can sing "Old Dog Blues" or "Kitchen Man," and that many of the great veterans really enjoyed what they sang. Brozman is also a technical marvel, particularly on bottleneck. But just as his vocals aren't simply replications, he doesn't merely whip out licks and display flash; there's thought in the soloing, creativity in the riffs and plenty of heart in the grooves. Brozman emerges with one of the better and more memorable repertory projects, one that seems more like his take on traditional blues rather than one more museum piece. —*Ron Wynn*

George "Mojo" Buford

b. Nov. 10, 1929, Hernando, MS
Harmonica / Electric Chicago Blues
When Muddy Waters deemed a harp player talented enough to follow Little Walter and James Cotton into his peerless combo, he must have been someone special. Mojo Buford spent several stints in the employ of the Chicago blues legend, and was his harpist of choice in the final edition of the Waters band.

George Buford left Mississippi for Memphis while still young, learning his early blues lessons there. He relocated to Chicago in 1952, eventually forming a band called the Savage Boys that mutated into the Muddy Waters Jr. Band (no, they weren't fronted by a Waters imitator; they subbed for their mighty sponsor at local clubs when he was on the road). Buford played with Muddy as early as 1959, but a 1962 uprooting to Minneapolis to front his own combo and cut a couple of solid but extremely obscure LPs for Vernon and Folk-Art removed him from the Windy City scene for a while. Buford returned to Muddy's combo in 1967 for a year, put in a longer stint with Waters during the early '70s, and came back for the last time after Jerry Portnoy exited with the rest of his mates to form the Legendary Blues Band.

Buford has recorded as a bandleader for Mr. Blues (later reissued on Rooster Blues) and the British JSP logo, never drifting far from his enduring Chicago blues roots. —*Bill Dahl*

Exciting Harmonica Sound of Mojo Buford / 1964 / BluesRecordSoc ✦✦✦
One of his best and earliest LPs. —*Bill Dahl*

● **Mojo Buford's Blues Summit** / 1981 / Rooster Blues ✦✦✦✦✦
Buford in the company of guitarists Little Smokey Smothers, Pee Wee Madison, Sammy Lawhorn, and Sonny Rogers, with a rhythm section pounding it out like crazy. —*Cub Koda*

State of the Blues Harp / 1989 / JSP ✦✦✦

Built For Comfort Blues Band

Group / Contemporary Electric Blues
Built for Comfort was a short-lived Syracuse, NY group featuring two brothers on guitar and harmonica/vocals. But the real stars were the rhythm section of Mark Tiffault on drums and Paul "Big Daddy" LaRonde on bass, the two most in-demand musicians in that area of the country. Adept in a number of styles, LaRonde and Tiffault are currently the rhythm section for the New Orleans-inspired group Lil Georgie & the Shuffling Hungarians. —*AMG*

Be Cool / 1992 / Blue Wave ✦✦✦
Local Syracuse blues quartet running through a typical set of Chicago standards. No new ground broken here, but the rhythm section of Paul LaRonde and drummer Mark Tiffault swings admirably. —*AMG*

Bumble Bee Slim (Amos Easton)

b. May 7, 1905, Brunswick, GA, **d.** 1968, Los Angeles, CA
Guitar, Vocals / Acoustic Country Blues
Popular and prolific, Bumble Bee Slim parlayed a familiar but rudimentary style into one of the earliest flowerings of the Chicago style. Much of what he performed he adapted from the

groundbreaking duo Leroy Carr and Scrapper Blackwell—Slim built on Carr's laconic, relaxed vocal style and Blackwell's guitar technique. During the mid-'30s, Bumble Bee Slim recorded a number of sides for a variety of labels, including Bluebird, Vocalion, and Decca, becoming one of the most-recorded bluesmen of the decade.

Born in Georgia, Bumble Bee Slim left his home when he was a teenager. He joined a circus and travelled throughout the South and the Midwest for much of his adolescence and early adulthood. Eventually, he made a home in Indianapolis, where he played local parties and dance halls.

Bumble Bee Slim moved to Chicago in the early '30s. After a few years in the city, he began a recording career; his first singles appeared on Bluebird. Slim wrote and recorded frequently during the mid-'30s, selling more records than most of his contemporaries. In addition to cutting his own sides, he played on records by Big Bill Broonzy and Cripple Clarence Lofton, among others.

Bumble Bee Slim moved back to Georgia in the late '30s. After a few years, he left the state once again, relocating to Los Angeles in the early '40s. During the '50s, Slim cut some West Coast blues for Specialty and Pacific Jazz, which failed to gain much interest. For the rest of his career, he kept a low profile, playing various Californian clubs. Bumble Bee Slim died in 1968. —*Cub Koda & Stephen Thomas Erlewine*

● **1931-1937** / Document ✦✦✦✦
A solid 18-track import compilation of all his best sides. —*Cub Koda*

Eddie "Guitar" Burns

b. Feb. 8, 1928, Belzoni, MS
Guitar, Vocals, Harmonica / Modern Electric Blues
Detroit boasted a vibrant blues scene during the postwar era, headed by John Lee Hooker and prominently featuring Eddie Burns, who hit the Motor City in 1948 and musically flourished there. While still in Mississippi, Burns picked up his early blues training from the 78s of Sonny Boy Williamson, Tommy McClennan, and Big Bill Broonzy. When he hit Detroit, Burns was exclusively a harp player. He cut "Notoriety Woman," his first single for Holiday in 1948, with partner John T. Smith on guitar. Burns added guitar to his personal arsenal the next year, cutting sessions with Hooker. Burns' own discography was slim but select—he cut singles for DeLuxe in 1952 ("Hello Miss Jessie Lee"), Checker in 1954 ("Biscuit Baking Mama"), JVB and Chess in 1957 ("Treat Me Like I Treat You"). In 1961, Burns waxed the slashing "Orange Driver" and several more R&B-slanted sides for Harvey Fuqua's Harvey Records.

More recently, Burns made a fine album for Blue Suit Records, *Detroit*, that showed his versatility on two instruments to good advantage. Incidentally, blues talent runs in the Burns family: brother Jimmy is a blues-soul performer based in Chicago, with his own impressive discography stretching back to the '60s. —*Bill Dahl*

Eddie Burns Blues Band / 1993 / Evidence ✦✦✦
Eddie Burns is not an especially attractive vocalist, but when you listen closely to his weary sighs, straining delivery, and anguished inflections, it's hard not to be swayed by his expressiveness. His playing is not loaded with catchy hooks, spinning lines, distorted fills, or other rock/blues devices, but is simple, tight, and nicely executed. Burns' band includes keyboardist Joe Hunter, bassist Frank Bryant, and drummer Bobby Smith, all of whom are also straightforward, no-frills types. These are lean, direct, unsophisticated tunes. Burns' music won't appeal to those seeking innovation or flair, but it is a good outing of conventional, often derivative blues material. —*Ron Wynn*

Detroit / May 1993 / Evidence ✦✦✦✦
Impressive contemporary outing that captures Burns' traditional leanings very effectively. Backed by a mean little combo that includes ex-Motown staff pianist Joe Hunter, Burns revives his classic "Orange Driver" and offers a few fresh compositions as well. Originally issued on Toledo, OH-based Blue Suit Records. —*Bill Dahl*

Eddie Burns / Blue Suit ✦✦✦✦✦
Eddie Burns features solid, contemporary backing against Burns' impassioned vocals. —*Cub Koda*

● **Treat Me Like I Treat You** / Moonshine ✦✦✦✦✦
With everything dubbed from vinyl onto vinyl, the sound quali-

ty on this LP won't be top-notch—but as it contains Burns' rough-edged 1948-1965 Detroit blues and boogies, it's the best cross-section of his early work compiled thus far. The guitarist/harpist's first few singles were marvelously raw affairs—"Treat Me like I Treat You" and "Biscuit Baking Mama" drip Hastings Street ambience—while Burns' 1961 sides for Harvey Fuqua's Harvey logo—"Messin' with My Bread," "Orange Driver"—are driving R&B. —*Bill Dahl*

R.L. Burnside

b. Nov. 23, 1926, Oxford, MS
Vocals, Guitar / Electric Delta Blues
North Mississippi guitarist R.L. Burnside is one of the paragons of state-of-the-art Delta juke joint blues. The guitarist, singer and songwriter was born November 23, 1926 in Oxford, MS, and makes his home in Holly Springs, in the hill country above the Delta. He's lived most of his life in the Mississippi hill country, which, unlike the Delta region, consists mainly of a lot of small farms. He learned his music from his neighbor, Fred McDowell, and the highly rhythmic style that Burnside plays is evident in McDowell's recording as well. Despite the otherworldly country-blues sounds put down by Burnside and his family band, known as the Sound Machine, his other influences are surprisingly contemporary: Muddy Waters, John Lee Hooker and Lightnin' Hopkins. But Burnside's music is pure country Delta juke joint blues, heavily rhythm-oriented and played with a slide.

It's only recently that he's been hitting full stride with his tours and his music, thanks to the efforts of Fat Possum Records. In recent years, the label has issued recordings made by a group of Burnside's peers, including Junior Kimbrough, Dave Thompson and others.

Up until the mid-'80s, Burnside was primarily a farmer and fisherman. After getting some attention in the late '60s via folklorists David Evans and George Mitchell (Mitchell recorded him for the Arhoolie label), he recorded for the Vogue, Swingmaster and Highwater record labels. Although he had done short tours, it wasn't until the late '80s that he was invited to perform at several European blues festivals. In 1992, he was featured alongside his friend Junior Kimbrough (who's Holly Spings juke joint Burnside lives next to), in a documentary film, *Deep Blues*. His debut recording, *Bad Luck City*, was recorded and released the following year on Fat Possum Records. Burnside has a second record out on the Oxford-based Fat Possum label, *Too Bad Jim* (1994). Since both records are distributed and marketed via Capricorn Records, they're easily located in record stores.

Both recordings showcase the raw, barebones electric guitar stylings of Burnside, and on both recordings he's accompanied by a small band, which includes his son, Dwayne, on bass and son-in-law, Calvin Jackson, on drums. Both recordings also adequately capture the feeling of what it must be like to be in Junior Kimbrough's juke joint, where both men have been playing this kind of raw, unadulterated blues for over 30 years. This is the kind of downhome, backporch blues played today as it has been for many decades. —*Richard Skelly*

● **Bad Luck City** / May 1991 / Fat Possum ✦✦✦✦✦
Welcome to Mississippi. This is the sound you would be likely to hear in any juke joint hosting the talents of the real-life Burnside family band. What you can't see on this disc is the picture of them grinning ear-to-ear as they play—or the sight of R.L.'s son Dwayne duck-walking while his dad smiles and nods to friends across the floor. His other son, Joseph, would likely be pounding out the solid bass line, while his son-in-law Calvin Jackson proudly presided over the drums. No, you can't see it but you can hear it if you listen closely. This set was recorded live at Syd's in Oxford, MS. As for the music, it's rough, real, and one-of-a-kind...the way blues should be. —*Larry Hoffman*

Too Bad Jim / 1993 / Fat Possum ✦✦✦✦✦
Too Bad Jim is cut from the same cloth as its predecessor, *Bad Luck City*. It features R.L. Burnside fronting a small juke joint combo, tearing through some greasy blues. However, *Too Bad Jim* is the better album, simply from a performance standpoint. Burnside sounds more relaxed and the band steps back from the spotlight slightly, letting the guitarist burn brightly on his own, showcasing his deep blues roots. —*Thom Owens*

Harold Burrage

b. Mar. 30, 1931, Chicago, IL, d. Nov. 26, 1966, Chicago, IL
Piano, Vocals / Electric R&B
Pianist Harold Burrage started out singing blues and R&B during the 1950s and ended up as a linchpin of the emerging Chicago soul sound of the '60s; he made recordings in both styles and more than a few idiomatic shades in between. Burrage mentored young soul singers Otis Clay and Tyrone Davis, but never had a chance to see them fully blossom; he died young in 1966.

Burrage debuted on wax in 1950 with a jumping "Hi-Yo Silver" for Decca with Horace Henderson's band in support. Singles for Aladdin and States preceded one of his most prolific studio periods with Eli Toscano's Cobra imprint. In 1956, Burrage cut the amusing "You Eat Too Much" for Cobra, backed by a solid combo featuring guitarist Wayne Bennett and bassist Willie Dixon. Jody Williams added stinging guitar to Burrage's 1957 Cobra offering "Messed Up," while "Stop for the Red Light," his third Cobra 45, was a novelty complete with auto wreck sound effects. "Betty Jean," his last Cobra single, is unabashed rock 'n' roll, with Otis Rush on guitar. Burrage also served as a session pianist for the firm, backing up Magic Sam and Charles Clark.

After a romping 1960 effort for Vee-Jay, "Crying for My Baby," Burrage revamped his vocal approach considerably when recording rather prolifically for One-derful's M-Pac! subsidiary during the early-to-mid-'60s. There he sang in a very credible soul style, enjoying his only national R&B hit in 1965 with the driving "Got to Find a Way" (later revived by one of Burrage's protégés, Otis Clay). —*Bill Dahl*

She Knocks Me Out! / 1981 / Flyright ++++
Only showcases one facet of the late piano-playing singer's multi-faceted discography, but it's one of the most fascinating—his 1956-1958 stay at Chicago's Cobra Records. Under Willie Dixon's supervision, Burrage recorded in a variety of styles—rockin' blues ("Satisfied," the amusing "You Eat Too Much"), novelty stuff ("Stop for the Red Light," complete with crashing sound effects reminiscent of Nervous Norvus), and straight-ahead rock 'n' roll ("Betty Jean"). —*Bill Dahl*

Aron Burton

b. Mississippi
Bass, Vocals / Electric Chicago Blues
Long recognized as a rock-solid bassist (and a master landscaper for the Chicago Park District), Aron Burton has begun to emphasize his vocal talents more prominently of late. His 1993 Earwig album *Past, Present and Future* showcased both of Burton's specialties, eastablishing him as bandleader instead of bandsman.

Burton left Mississippi for Chicago in 1955. He got his feet wet as a singer and bassist in the late '50s with Freddy King at Walton's Corner on the West side (King bought Aron his first bass). He got drafted in 1961, came out four years later, and got back into playing with various rock (notably Baby Huey & the Babysitters) and blues (Junior Wells, Fenton Robinson) groups.

Burton did sessions with Wild Child Butler, Jackie Ross, Carey Bell, and a 45 of his own for Eddy Clearwater's Cleartone label ("Garbage Man"), but it was his signing on as a charter member of Albert Collins' Icebreakers in 1978 (Aron's brother Larry was the band's rhythm guitarist) that catapulted him into the spotlight. He played on Collins' landmark Alligator LP *Ice Pickin'* and toured extensively with the Master of the Telecaster before getting restless and leaving the band.

Burton did sessions with Johnny Littlejohn, James Cotton, and Fenton Robinson before taking a three-year European hiatus in the late '80s. That's where he cut his debut LP, *Usual Dangerous Guy*, with Champion Jack Dupree guesting on piano. Since returning to Chicago, Burton has picked up where he left off—he's playing, singing, and leading his own band instead of backing others. —*Bill Dahl*

● **Past, Present, & Future** / 1994 / Earwig ++++
A compendium of tracks cut back in the 1980s (some with the late pianist Champion Jack Dupree) over in Europe (the "past" part of the title) and a few more recent sides waxed in his Chicago hometown, this collection effectively spotlights bassist Aron Burton's talents as a front man. —*Bill Dahl*

George "Wild Child" Butler

b. Oct. 1, 1936, Autaugaville, AL
Harmonica, Vocals, Guitar / Electric Chicago Blues
From all accounts, George Butler was indeed a "wild child." But he found time between the youthful shenanigans that inspired his mom to bestow his descriptive nickname to learn some harp basics at age 12. He was gigging professionally as a bandleader by the late '50s, but Butler's recording career didn't blossom until he moved to Chicago in 1966 and signed with Shreveport, LA-based Jewel Records (his sidemen on these sessions included bassist Willie Dixon and guitarist Jimmy Dawkins).

The harpist didn't have much luck in the recording wars—his 1969 Mercury album sank with little trace, while a 1976 LP for TK, *Funky Butt Lover*, did equally little for his fortunes (it was later reissued in slightly altered form on Rooster Blues as *Lickin' Gravy*). Around 1981, Butler moved up north to Ontario, Canada, and continued his career. A decade later, he cut the first of two albums for British producer Mike Vernon; *These Mean Old Blues* was an engaging set of original material cut in London. *Stranger*, the fruits of another English session, emerged in 1994. —*Bill Dahl*

Lickin' Gravy / 1977 / Rooster Blues +++
Before it finally saw the light of day, this 1976 album had to undergo some overdubbing touchups a full decade later that replaced certain guitar tracks with Pinetop Perkins' keyboards. Not the best way to make an album, but the results are nevertheless pretty decent, as Butler dishes up a set of his own material, a couple of Willie Dixon copyrights, and Lightnin' Slim's "Rooster Blues." —*Bill Dahl*

● **Open up Baby** / 1984 / Charly +++++
Solid collection of Butler's best sides for the Jewel label. (Import) —*Cub Koda*

Keep on Doing What You're Doing / Jan. 1991 / Mercury +++

These Mean Old Blues / 1992 / Bullseye Blues ++++
The combination of veteran southern blues harpist Wild Child Butler and a British band works surprisingly well on this solid collection produced by the eminently experienced Mike Vernon. Another major plus: everything here is an original composition, all the better to properly spotlight Butler's down-home vocal phrasing and meat-and-potatoes harmonica style. —*Bill Dahl*

Stranger / 1994 / Bullseye Blues ++++
Another set of impressive originals cut in England and produced by Mike Vernon with the same attention to traditional detail as their fine previous collaboration. Butler's understated approach reeks of an authenticity that grows harder to find with every passing year, whether on his own "Weak in the Knees" and "Face It Baby" or the Vernon-generated "High I.Q." and "I'm Not Guilty." —*Bill Dahl*

Paul Butterfield Blues Band

b. Dec. 17, 1942, Chicago, IL, d. May 4, 1987
Harmonica, Guitar, Vocals, Flute / Electric Chicago Blues
Butterfield grew up in Chicago's Hyde Park, and according to his brother Peter, "There was a lot of music around Hyde Park, a place unique in Chicago because it was an island in the Southside ghetto, and a bastion of liberal politics. When we grew up there was a crime problem—mostly due to scattered groups of Puerto Ricans and poor white trash—but no one made a connection to the black community as a source of crime. We grew up about half a block from something called the International Houses and you would see people from all over the world in the immediate area. "

Butterfield was culturally sophisticated. His father was a well-known attorney in the Hyde Park area, and his mother was an artist—a painter. Butterfield took music lessons (flute) from an early age and by the time he reached high school, was studying with the first-chair flautist of the Chicago Symphony. He was exposed to both classical music and jazz from an early age. Butterfield ran track in high school and was offered a running scholarship to Brown University, which he had to refuse after a serious knee injury. From that point onward, he turned toward the music scene around him. He began learning the guitar and harmonica.

He met singer Nick Gravenites and started hanging around outside of the Chicago blues clubs, listening. He and Gravenites began to play together at various campuses—Ann Arbor,

University of Wisconsin, and the University of Chicago. His parents sent him off to the University of Illinois, but he would put in a short academic week, return home early (but not check in) and instead play and hang out at the blues clubs. Soon, he was doing this six or seven days a week with no school at all. When this was discovered by his parents, he then dropped out of college and turned to music full time.

Butterfield practiced long hours by himself—just playing all the time. His brother Peter writes, "He listened to records, and he went places, but he also spent an awful lot of time, by himself, playing. He'd play outdoors. There's a place called The Point in Hyde Park, a promontory of land that sticks out into Lake Michigan, and I can remember him out there for hours playing. He was just playing all the time...It was a very solitary effort. It was all internal, like he had a particular sound he wanted to get and he just worked to get it."

In the meantime, Elvin Bishop had come from Oklahoma to the University of Illinois on a scholarship and had discovered the various blues venues for himself. Elvin remembers, "One day I was walking around the neighborhood and I saw a guy sitting on a porch drinking a quart of beer—white people that were interested in blues were very few and far between at that time. But this guy was singing some blues and singing it good. It was Butterfield. We gravitated together real quick and started playing parties around the neighborhood, you know, just acoustic. He was playing more guitar than harp when I first met him. But in about six months, he became serious about the harp. And he seemed to get about as good as he ever got in that six months. He was just a natural genius. And this was in 1960 or 1961."

Butterfield and Bishop began going down to the clubs, sitting in, and playing with all the great Black blues players—then in their prime. Players like Otis Rush, Magic Sam, Howlin' Wolf, Junior Wells, Little Walter, and especially Muddy Waters. They often were the only Whites there, but were soon accepted because of their sincerity, their sheer ability, and the protection of players like Muddy Waters, who befriended them.

An important event in the history of introducing blues to White America came in 1963 when Big John's, a club located on Chicago's White North Side, invited Butterfield to bring his band there and play on a regular basis. He said "sure," and Butterfield and Bishop set about putting such a band together. They pulled Jerome Arnold (bass) and Sam Lay (drums) from Howlin' Wolf's band (with whom they had worked for the past six years!), by offering them more money. Butterfield and Bishop (the core team), Arnold, and Lay were all about the same age, and these four became the Butterfield Blues Band. They had been around for a long time and knew the Chicago blues scene and its repertoire cold. This new racially mixed band opened at Big John's, was very successful, and made a first great step to opening up the blues scene to White America.

When the new group thought about making an album, they looked around for a lead guitarist. Michael Bloomfield, who was known to Butterfield from his appearances at Big John's, joined the band early in 1965. Bloomfield, somewhat cool at first to Butterfield's commanding manner, warmed to the group as Butterfield warmed to his guitar playing. It took a while for Bloomfield to fit in, but by the summer of that year, the band was cookin'. Mark Naftalin, another music student, joined the band as the first album was being recorded, in fact while they were actually in the studio creating that first album on Elektra. He sat in (playing the Hammond organ for the first time!), Butterfield liked the sound, and Naftalin recorded eight of the 11 tracks on the first album during that first session. After the session, Paul invited Naftalin to join the band and go on the road with them. These six, then, became the Paul Butterfield Blues Band.

The first two Butterfield Blues albums are essential from an historical perspective. While East-West, the second album, with its Eastern influence and extended solos set the tone for psychedelic rockers, it was that incredible first album that alerted the music scene to what was coming.

Although it has been perhaps over-emphasized in recent years, it is important to point out that the release of The Paul Butterfield Blues Band on Elektra in 1965 had a huge effect on the White music culture of the time. Used to hearing blues covered by groups like the Rolling Stones, that first album had an enormous impact on young (and primarily White) rock players. Here is no deferential imitation of Black music by Whites, but a

racially mixed hard-driving blues album that, in a word, rocked. It was a signal to White players to stop making respectful tributes to Black music, and just play it. In a flash the image of blues as old-time music was gone. Modern Chicago style urban blues was out of the closet and introduced to mainstream White audiences, who loved it. The Butterfield band appeared at the Newport Folk Festival late in 1965 to rave reviews.

Perhaps the next major event in the Butterfield band came when drummer Sam Lay became ill, late in 1965. Jazz drummer Billy Davenport was called in and soon became a permanent member of the group. Davenport was to become a key element in the development of the second Butterfield Blues Band album, East-West, and particularly in the development of the extended solo of the same name.

Fueled by Bloomfield's infatuation with Eastern music and Indian ragas at the time and aided by Davenport's jazz-driven sophistication on drums, there arose in the group a new music form that was to greatly affect rock music—the extended solo. There is little question that here is the root of psychedelic (acid) rock—a genuine fusion between East and West.

Those first two albums served as a wake-up call to an entire generation of White would-be blues musicians. Speaking as one who was on the scene, that first Butterfield album stopped us in our tracks and we were never the same afterward. It changed our lives.

The third album (released in 1967), The Butterfield Blues Band; The Resurrection of Pigboy Crabshaw is the last album that preserves any of the pure blues direction of the original group. By this time, Bloomfield had left to create his own group, The Electric Flag and, with the addition of a horn section (including a young David Sandborn), the band drifted more toward an R&B sound. Mark Naftalin left the group soon after this album and the Butterfield band took on other forms.

Aside from these first three albums, later Butterfield material somehow misses the mark. He never lost his ferocity or integrity, but the synergy of that first group was special. There has been some discussion in the literature about the personal transformation of Butterfield as his various bands developed. It is said that he went from being a self-centered bandleader (shouting orders to his crew à la Howlin' Wolf) to a more democratic style of leadership, providing his group with musical freedom (like Muddy Waters). For what it's worth, it is clear that the best music is in those first two (maybe three) albums. Subsequent albums, although also interesting, have not gotten as much attention then or now from reviewers.

When I knew Butterfield (during the first three albums), he was always intense, somewhat remote, and even, on occasion, downright unfriendly. Although not much interested in other people, he was a compelling musician and a great harp player. Bloomfield and Naftalin, also great players, were just the opposite—always interested in the other guy. They went out of their way to inquire about you, even if you were a nobody. Naftalin, well known around the San Francisco Bay Area, continues to this day to support blues projects and festivals (Marin County Blues Festival, etc.) in the San Francisco Bay area.

After Bloomfield and Naftalin left the group, Butterfield spun off on his own more and more. The next two albums, In My Own Dream (1968) and Keep on Moving (1969) moved still farther away from the blues roots until in 1972, Butterfield dissolved the group, forming the group Better Days. This new group recorded two albums, Paul Butterfield's Better Days and It All Comes Back. After that, Butterfield faded into the general rock scene, with an occasional appearance here and there, as in the documentary The Last Waltz (1976)—a farewell concert from The Band. The albums Put It in Your Ear (1976) and North South (1981) were attempts to make a comeback, but both failed. Paul Butterfield died of drug-related heart failure in 1987.

Even to this day, Butterfield remains one of the only White harmonica players to develop his own style (another is William Clarke), a style respected by Black players. Butterfield has no real imitators. Like most Chicago-style amplified harmonica players, Butterfield played the instrument like a horn—a trumpet. Although he sometimes used a chromatic harmonica, Butterfield mostly played the standard Hohner Marine Band in the standard cross position. Remember, he was left handed and held the harp in his left hand, but in the standard position with the low notes facing to the left. He tended to play single notes rather than bursts of chords. His harp playing is always intense, understated, concise, and serious—only Big Walter Horton has a better sense of note selection.

The effect of the Butterfield Blues Band on aspiring White blues musicians was enormous and the impact of the band on live audiences was stunning. Butterfield the performer was always intense, serious, and definitive—no doubt about this guy. Blues purists sometimes like to quibble about Butterfield's voice and singing style, but the moment he picked up a harmonica, that was it. He is one of the finest harp players (period).

Butterfield and the six members of the original Paul Butterfield Blues Band made a huge contribution to modern music, turning a whole generation of White music lovers onto the blues as something other than a quaint piece of music history. The musical repercussions of the second Butterfield album, *East-West*, continue to echo through the music scene even today!

[Thanks to *Blues Access* magazine for permission to use the quotes by Peter Butterfield and Elvin Bishop from the excellent article by Tom Ellis.] —*Michael Erlewine*

☆ **Paul Butterfield Blues Band** / 1965 / Elektra ✦✦✦✦✦
Butterfield's unique amplified harmonica style is already present on this classic first album—a wake-up call for a generation of young White players used to hearing blues filtered through covers by groups like the Rolling Stones or as a part of music history. Here was a racially mixed group of brilliant young players that rocked—an historic album. Great guitar from Michael Bloomfield and Elvin Bishop. With Mark Naftalin (organ), Jerome Arnold (bass), and Sam Lay (drums). —*Michael Erlewine*

★ **East-West** / 1966 / Elektra ✦✦✦✦✦
The second Butterfield album had an even greater effect on music history, paving the way for experimentation that is still being explored today. This came in the form of an extended blues-rock solo (some 13 minutes)—a real fusion of jazz and blues inspired by the Indian raga. This ground-breaking instrumental was the first of its kind and marks the root from which the acid rock tradition emerged. —*Jeff Tarmarkin and Michael Erlewine*

With John Mayall / 1967 / Decca ✦✦

The Resurrection of Pigboy Crabshaw / 1968 / Elektra ✦✦✦✦✦
In his third album, Butterfield adds a horn section and the direction of the group has started to veer away from straight Chicago-style blues toward a sound more influenced by R&B. By this time, Bloomfield has left the group and Elvin Bishop (aka Pigboy Crabshaw) takes over on lead guitar. A lot of great tunes here, like "Driftin' and Driftin'." —*Michael Erlewine*

An Offer You Can't Refuse / 1972 / Red Lightnin' ✦✦✦
An album released on the Red Lightnin' label in 1972 consisting of one side of Big Walter Horton and the other side with very early Paul Butterfield (1963). Contains six tracks with Butterfield, Smokey Smothers on guitar, Jerome Arnold on bass, and Sam Lay on drums. This was recorded at Big John's, the North side Chicago club where the Butterfield Band first played in 1963—some two years before the material on the first Paul Butterfield Blues Band album, which was released in 1965. The six tracks include two instrumentals, "Got My Mojo Working" and the Butterfield-authored tune "Loaded." Although this is very early Butterfield, the harp playing is excellent and already in his own unique style. The singing is a little rough and heavy sounding. Butterfield fans will want to find this rare vinyl for musical and historical reasons. —*Michael Erlewine*

The Original Lost Elektra Sessions / 1995 / Rhino ✦✦✦✦✦
All but one of these 19 tracks were recorded in December, 1964, as Butterfield's projected first LP; the results were scrapped and replaced by their official self-titled debut, cut a few months later. With both Bloomfield and Bishop already in tow, these sessions rank among the earliest blues-rock ever laid down. Extremely similar in feel to the first album, it's perhaps a bit rawer in production and performance, but not appreciably worse or different than what ended up on the actual debut LP. Dedicated primarily to electric Chicago blues standards, Butterfield fans will find this well worth acquiring, as most of the selections were never officially recorded by the first lineup (although different renditions of five tracks showed up on the first album and the *What's Shakin'* compilation). —*Richie Unterberger*

Strawberry Jam / 1995 / Winner ✦✦✦
These nine cuts are from various live performances of the Paul Butterfield Blues Band during their heyday in the middle-to-late '60s. This album was put together by Mark Naftalin, who played keyboards on those first few incredible Butterfield albums. Don't look for the clearest sound (it's adequate) because these are live tunes recorded at clubs, often with minimal equipment. It is the music that is in focus here—a window into that incredible band at a time when they were hot. Those of us who were on the scene at the time know that, although the original Butterfield albums are great, the band was a total knockout when heard live. Featuring Butterfield's harmonica, here are glimpses into that time and music. Most of the tunes have appeared elsewhere, but the extended instrumental "Strawberry Jam" (written by Naftalin) is unique to this album—worth hearing. It features great guitar by Elvin Bishop. —*Michael Erlewine*

East-West Live / Sep. 1996 / Winner ✦✦✦✦
The tune "East-West" from the second Butterfield Blues Band album of the same name made music history. It is arguably the first extended rock solo, a fusing of blues-rock with Eastern scales and tone. Here is the root of psychedelic acid rock. Now, thanks to Mark Naftalin (the original Butterfield keyboardist), we have three live recordings of "East-West" recorded in 1966-1967 that capture the origin and development of this classic tune. The first example (some 12 minutes) was taped prior to the edited studio version; the second (16 minutes) and third (28 minutes) were recorded after the album cut. There is some great music (and music history) here. —*Michael Erlewine*

C

Chris Cain Band

b. San Jose, CA

Guitar, Vocals / Modern Electric Blues

Chris Cain's crisp lead guitar and gravelly vocals have brought him national recognition. Influenced by B. B. and Albert King as well as various jazz players, Cain has cooked up a jumping sound on the Bay Area circuit.

A native of San Jose, CA, Cain began playing California blues clubs in the mid-'80s, most notably the JJ's Cafe and JJ's Lounge South Bay circuit. Soon, his following was large enough to earn him a contract with an independent record label, Blue Rock-It. Cain's debut album, *Late Night City Blues,* was released in 1987. By this time, his backing band featured lead tenor saxophonist Noel Catura, bassist Ron Torbensen, saxophonist Mark Whitney, and drummer Robert Higgins. The album received good reviews, which led to national bookings for Cain and his band, as well as several European dates. In 1988, Cain and his band received a handful of WC Handy Award nominations, including blues band of the year and guitarist of the year. Cain signed to Blind Pig in 1990, releasing his second album, *Cuttin' Loose,* the same year. The guitarist stayed at Blind Pig for the next few years, releasing *Can't Buy A Break* in 1993 and *Somwhere Along the Way* in 1995. Cain and his band remain a popular concert attraction in the '90s. *—Bill Dahl & Stephen Thomas Erlewine*

Late Night City Blues / 1987 / Blue Rock-It ✦✦✦

This debut album was rewarded with four Handy Award nominations. *—Bill Dahl*

● **Cuttin' Loose** / 1990 / Blind Pig ✦✦✦✦✦

This is a wonderful, big-voiced, contemporary West Coast bluesman and superb guitar player. There are several horns in the band, giving it a great, huge sound. Even better things will be coming. *—Niles J. Frantz*

Can't Buy a Break / 1992 / Blind Pig ✦✦✦✦✦

Can't Buy a Break is a slow-burning, laidback contemporary blues record that positively swings. Cain's licks are clean, warm and fluid—he's able to seamlessly bounce back and forth between R&B, funk, jazz, jump blues, and Chicago blues. Furthermore, he proves himself to be an adept saxophonist, keyboardist and vocalist, as well as songwriter. This album is a true tour-de-force. His backing band is tight and sympathetic, giving the impression that Cain is fronting a much larger band than he is. It's a refreshing, diverse, and relaxed record that shows there is more to contemporary blues than wailing blues-rock. *—Thom Owens*

Somewhere Along the Way / Nov. 1995 / Blind Pig ✦✦✦

Eddie C. Campbell

b. May 6, 1939, Duncan, MS

Guitar, Vocals / Modern Electric Blues

Happily, Eddie C. Campbell is currently back in Chicago after spending a decade entrenched in Europe. His shimmering West Side-styled guitar style and unusually introspective songwriting have been a breath of fresh air on the Windy City circuit, reuniting the veteran bluesman with fans he left behind in 1984.

Campbell left rural Mississippi for the bright lights of Chicago at age ten, sneaking a peek at Muddy Waters at the 1125 Club soon after he arrived and jamming with his idol when he was only 12. He fell in with some West Side youngbloods—Luther Allison, Magic Sam—and honed a guitar attack rooted deep in

the ringing style. Campbell paid his sideman dues on the bandstand with everyone from Howlin' Wolf and Little Walter to Little Johnny Taylor and Jimmy Reed. Koko Taylor recommended Eddie to Willie Dixon, who hired him as a Chicago Blues All-Star in 1976.

Campbell cut his own debut album, the rousing *King of the Jungle,* in 1977 for Steve Wisner's short-lived Mr. Blues label (now available on Rooster Blues, it includes the guitarist's lighthearted Yuletide perennial "Santa's Been Messin' with the Kid"). But he split the country for calmer European climates, recording a nice 1984 album with a Dutch group, *Let's Pick It!,* that first came out on Black Magic and now adorns the Evidence catalog.

When Eddie C. finally returned stateside for the birth of his son, he made up for lost time by gigging steadily around Chicago and making a comeback album for Blind Pig, *That's When I Know,* that contained some very distinctive originals. Hopefully, he'll stay put for a while. *—Bill Dahl*

● **King of the Jungle** / 1977 / Rooster Blues ✦✦✦✦✦

Flamboyant West Side-styled guitarist's debut album, first issued on the short-lived Mr. Blues label, remains his best, with his slashing guitar and lowdown vocals beautifully presented on covers of material by Magic Sam, Muddy Waters, Percy Mayfield, Willie Mabo, and his own Yuletide perennial "Santa's Messin' with the Kid." Great band, too: harpist Carey Bell, pianist Lafayette Leake, bassist Bob Stroger, and drummer Clifton James. *—Bill Dahl*

Let's Pick It / Oct. 1984 / Evidence ✦✦✦✦

Recorded while Eddie Campbell was on a European sojourn that lasted a decade or so, this disc, cut back in 1984 for Black Magic with an overseas combo, is a very convincing effort mixing Campbell's own "Cold and Hungry," "Dream," and "Messin' with My Pride" with songs by Albert King, Jimmy Reed, Jimmie Lee Robinson, and Magic Sam. *—Bill Dahl*

The Baddest Cat on the Block / 1985 / JSP ✦✦

This is not his best album. *—Bill Dahl*

Mind Trouble / 1988 / Double Trouble ✦✦✦

That's When I Know / 1994 / Blind Pig ✦✦✦✦

During that long decade away from home, Eddie C.'s skills as a unique blues songwriter certainly blossomed. His triumphant homecoming set contains some highly distinctive material—a homespun "Sister Taught Me Guitar," the incandescent title track, a forceful "Sleep," "Busted," and a decidedly mystical "Son of Sons." *—Bill Dahl*

John Campbell

b. Jan. 20, 1952, Shreveport, LA, **d.** Jun. 13, 1993

Guitar / Contemporary Electric Blues

Guitarist, singer and songwriter John Campbell had the potential of turning a whole new generation of people onto the blues in the 1990s, much the same way Stevie Ray Vaughan did in the 1980s. His vocals were so powerful and his guitar playing so fiery, you couldn't help but stop what you were doing and pay attention to what you were hearing. But unfortunately, because of frail health and a rough European tour, he suffered a heart attack while sleeping on June 13, 1993, at the age of 41.

Campbell was born in Shreveport, LA, on January 20, 1952, and grew up in Center, TX. Although he got his own guitar at age eight and began playing professionally when he was 13, he didn't get serious about playing blues for a living until he was involved in a near-fatal drag racing accident that broke several ribs, collapsed a lung and took his right eye. In his teens, Campbell opened for people like Clarence "Gatemouth" Brown, Albert Collins and Son Seals, but he later got sidetracked by drag racing, and it was while he was recuperating from his near-death drag racing accident that he re-learned guitar, developing his own distinctive, rhythm and slide-heavy style, based in some measure on the music of Lightnin' Hopkins.

In 1985, after playing a variety of clubs between east Texas and New Orleans, Campbell moved to New York. One night in New York, guitarist Ronnie Earl happened upon Campbell in a club, playing with Johnny Littlejohn. Earl was so impressed that he offered to produce an album by Campbell, and the result was *A Man and His Blues* (Crosscut 1019), a Germany-only release that has since been made available in the U.S. That album earned Campbell a W.C. Handy Award nomination in 1989, and not long after that, the rock 'n' roll world started to take notice of him. Although he never sent a tape to a record company in his life, after drawing ever-growing crowds to the downtown New York clubs where he played, executives at Elektra Records took notice of him and signed him to a contract. Both of his albums for Elektra, *One Believer* (1991) and *Howlin' Mercy* (1993) are brilliant, well-produced recordings, yet they only hint at Campbell's potential for greatness, had he lived longer. — *Richard Skelly*

One Believer / 1991 / Elektra ♦♦♦♦♦
A ten-tune program of mostly original compositions, it was co-written with Dennis Walker, who co-produced it. The Robert Cray Band rhythm section is on hand for half of this very impressive album. — *Bob Porter*

● **Howlin' Mercy** / 1993 / Elektra ♦♦♦♦♦
There are plenty of fine performers who do credible, down-and-dirty, swampy blues. John Campbell is the whole swamp. *Howlin' Mercy* is contemporary blues at its most powerful. On the whole, the album is anchored by a thundering rhythm section and Campbell's grinding, cement-mixer voice—a riveting instrument that expresses the torment of a life experience you really only want to know about second hand. — *Roch Parisien*

Canned Heat

Group / Modern Electric Blues
A hard-luck blues band of the '60s, Canned Heat was founded by blues historians and record collectors Al Wilson and Bob Hite. They seemed to be on the right track and played all the right festivals (including Monterey and Woodstock, making it very prominently into the documentaries about both) but somehow never found a lasting audience.

Certainly their hearts were in the right place. Their debut album—released shortly after their appearance at Monterey—was every bit as deep into the roots of the blues as any other combo of the time mining similar turf, with the exception of the original Paul Butterfield band. Hite was nicknamed "The Bear" and stalked the stage in the time-honored tradition of Howlin' Wolf and other large-proportioned bluesmen. Wilson was an extraordinary harmonica player, with a fat tone and great vibrato. His work on guitar, especially in open tunings (he played on Son House's rediscovery recordings of the mid-'60s, incidentally) gave the band a depth and texture that most other rhythm players could only aspire to. Henry Vestine—another dyed-in-the-wool record collector—was the West Coast's answer to Michael Bloomfield and capable of fretboard fireworks at a moment's notice. Their breakthrough moment occurred with the release of their second album, establishing them with hippie ballroom audiences as the "kings of the boogie." As a way of paying homage to the one who gave them the idea in the first place, they later collaborated on an album with John Lee Hooker that was one of the elder bluesman's most successful outings with a young White (or Black, for that matter) combo backing him up. After two big chart hits with "Goin' up the Country" and an explosive version of Wilbert Harrison's "Let's Work Together," Wilson died under mysterious (probably drug-related) circumstances in 1970, and Hite carried on with various reconstituted versions of the band until his death just before a show in 1981, from a heart seizure. — *Cub Koda & Bruce Eder*

● **The Best of Canned Heat** / 1972 / EMI America ♦♦♦♦♦
All of Canned Heat's best tracks and biggest hits ("Goin' Up the Country," "On the Road Again") are included on this single-disc collection. — *Stephen Thomas Erlewine*

Uncanned! the Best of Canned Heat / May 17, 1994 / EMI America ♦♦♦♦♦
Uncanned! The Best of Canned Heat is exactly what it claims to be—the definitive portrait of the blues-soaked hippie boogie band. Spreading 41 tracks (including numerous rarities, alternate takes, and Levi commercials) over two CDs, the set is perfect for the hardcore Canned Heat collector. For casual fans, the collection simply contains too much music; they would be better served by the single-disc collection, *The Best of Canned Heat*. — *Stephen Thomas Erlewine*

Gus Cannon

b. Sep. 12, 1885, Bed Banks, MS, **d.** Oct. 15, 1979, Memphis, TN
Banjo, Fiddle, Guitar, Jug, Kazoo, Piano / Acoustic Memphis Blues
A remarkable musician (he could play five-string banjo and jug simultaneously!), Gus Cannon bridged the gap between early blues and the minstrel and folk styles that preceded it. His band of the '20s and '30s, Cannon's Jug Stompers, represents the apogee of jug band style. Songs they recorded, notably the raggy "Walk Right In," were staples of the folk repertoire decades later, and Cannon himself continued to record and perform into the 1970s.

Self-taught on an instrument made from a frying pan and a raccoon skin, he learned early repertoire in the 1890s from older musicians, notably Mississippian Alec Lee. The early 1900s found him playing around Memphis with songster Jim Jackson and forming a partnership with Noah Lewis whose harmonica wizardry would be basic to the Jug Stompers' sound. In 1914, Cannon began work with a succession of medicine shows which would continue into the 1940s, and where he further developed his style and repertoire.

His recording career began with Paramount sessions in 1927. He continued to record into the '30s as a soloist and with his incredible trio. which included Noah Lewis along with guitarists Hosea Wood or Ashley Thompson. (Side projects included duets with Blind Blake and the first ever recordings of slide banjo!) Often obliged to find employment in other fields than music, Cannon continued to play anyway, mostly around Memphis. He resumed his stalled recording efforts in 1956 with sessions for Folkways. Subsequent sessions paired him with other Memphis survivors like Furry Lewis. Advancing age curtailed his activities in the '70s, but he still played the occasional cameo, sometimes from a wheelchair, until shortly before his death. — *Steve James*

Complete Recorded Works, Vol. 2 (1929-1930) / 1990 / Document ♦♦♦

Complete Recorded Works, Vol. 1 (1927-1928) / 1990 / Document ♦♦♦

Complete Recorded Works, Vols. 1-2 / Document ♦♦♦
All of the recordings Gus Cannon—both as a solo artist and with his band the Jug Stompers—made between 1927 and 1930 are collected on the two-volume set, *Complete Recorded Works* (each disc is sold separately). For historians and completists, this set is essential, but casual fans will find Yazoo's *Complete Works* more manageable. — *Thom Owens*

★ **Complete Works** / Yazoo ♦♦♦♦♦
Complete Works compiles all of the recordings Cannon's Jug Stompers made in the late '20s. Gus Cannon and the Jug Stompers were the definitive jug band and all of their classic tracks, including "Walk Right In," are featured on this essential single-disc collection. — *Thom Owens*

Chuck Carbo

Vocals / New Orleans R&B
The mellifluous vocal tones of Chuck Carbo were a principal ingredient in the success of the Spiders, the premier R&B vocal group around New Orleans during the 1950s. He's mounted a strong comeback bid of late as a smooth solo artist, cutting two albums for Rounder: *Drawers Trouble* in 1993 and 1996's *The Barber Blues*.

The gospel-steeped Carbo (whose actual first name is Hayward) and his brother Chick (real first name: Leonard) shared frontman duties for the Spiders, whose hits for Imperial included the two-sided smash "I Didn't Want to Do It"/"You're the One" and a ribald "I'm Slippin' In" in 1954 and "Witchcraft" (later covered by Elvis Presley) the next year. Imperial's main man in the Crescent City, Dave Bartholomew, produced the quintet's 1954–56 output, as well as writing many of their best numbers (notably a risqué "The Real Thing"). Carbo cut a few 45s under his own name for Imperial, Rex, and Ace after going solo; Chick waxed 45s of his own for Atlantic, Vee-Jay, and Instant.

Chuck Carbo never stopped performing entirely, although he made his living as a lumber truck driver when gigs got scarce. In 1989, he scored a local hit with his cover of Jeannie and Jimmy Cheatham's "Meet Me with Your Black Drawers On." It was reprised on *Drawers Trouble*, a comeback set reuniting Carbo with pianists Mac "Dr. John" Rebennack and Edward Frank. *The Barber's Blues* ensured Carbo's return to the spotlight with two more Cheatham copyrights and a second-line "Hey, Mardi Gras! (Here I Am)." —*Bill Dahl*

● **Drawers Trouble** / 1993 / Rounder ✦✦✦✦
Veteran New Orleans R&B singer Carbo proves he's a capable front man even without the presence of his '50s vocal group, the Spiders, on this infectious comeback set. With Crescent City vet Edward Frank handling piano and arranging duties, Carbo smoothly intones a mostly original lineup of songs (Jeannie & Jimmy Cheatham's lascivious lead "Meet Me with Your Black Drawers On" being one of the few exceptions). Dr. John contributes his considerable skills on keyboard and guitar to the project. —*Bill Dahl*

The Barber's Blues / 1996 / Rounder ✦✦✦
Ex-Spiders lead Carbo returns with a Rounder encore that eschews Dr. John but brings back Edward Frank as co-producer and pianist. Some of the selections are a little on the hackneyed side (a permanent moratorium on "Everyday I Have the Blues," please!), but Carbo's second line-based "Hey, Mardi Gras! (Here I Am)," the title item, and an easy-on-the-ears reprise of the Cheathams' "Don't Boogie with Your Black Drawers On" hit the spot. —*Bill Dahl*

Barbara Carr

Vocals / Electric R&B
Folks only familiar with her more recent work may be mildly surprised that alluring singer Barbara Carr recorded for Chess back in 1966. Carr's "Don't Knock Love" was a delicious slice of Chicago soul arranged by Phil Wright that got dusted off and released by Chess a second time in 1970 when she came back to the company and cut "Think About It Baby" (written, arranged, and produced by St. Louis saxist Oliver Sain).

After a lengthy fallow period, Carr returned with an infectious "Good Woman Go Bad" for (presumably) her own Bar-Car label. Carr also did a credible job on "Messin' with My Mind," a George Jackson number that both Otis Clay and Clarence Carter have also cut. Stan Lewis' Shreveport-based Paula Records recently issued an album of Carr material from this era that deftly mixes blues and soul genres. —*Bill Dahl*

● **Good Woman Go Bad** / Paula ✦✦✦✦✦

Leroy Carr

b. Mar. 27, 1905, Nashville, TN, d. Apr. 29, 1935, Indianapolis, IN
Piano, Vocals / Piano Blues
The term "urban blues" is usually applied to post-World War II blues-band music, but one of the forefathers of the genre in its pre-electric format was pianist Leroy Carr. Teamed with the exemplary guitarist Scrapper Blackwell in Indianapolis, Carr became one of the top blues stars of his day, composing and recording almost 200 sides during his short lifetime, including such classics as "How Long, How Long," "Prison Bound Blues," "When the Sun Goes Down," and "Blues Before Sunrise." His blues were expressive and evocative, recorded only with piano and guitar, yet as author Sam Charters has noted, Carr was "a city man" whose singing was never as rough or intense as the country bluesmen's; and as reissue producer Francis Smith put it, "He, perhaps more than any other single artist, was responsible for transforming the rural blues patterns of the '20s into the more city-oriented blues of the '30s."

Born in Nashville, Leroy Carr moved to Indianapolis as a child. While he was still in his teens, he taught himself how to play piano. Carr quit school in his mid-teens, heading out for a life on the road. For the next few years, he would play piano at various parties and dances in the Midwest and South. During this time, he held a number of odd jobs—he joined a circus, he

was in the Army for a while, and he was briefly a bootlegger. In addition to his string of jobs, he was married for a short time.

Carr wandered back toward Indianapolis, where he met guitarist Scrapper Blackwell in 1928. The duo began performing and shortly afterward they were recording for Vocalion, releasing "How Long How Long Blues" before the year was finished. The song was an instant, surprise hit. For the next seven years, Carr and Blackwell would record a number of classic songs for Vocalion, including "Midnight Hour Blues," "Blues Before Sunrise," "Hurry Down Sunshine," "Shady Lane Blues" and many others.

Throughout the early '30s, Carr was one of the most popular bluesmen in America. While his professional career was successful, his personal life was spinning out of control, as he sunk deeper and deeper into alcoholism. His addiction eventually cut his life short—he died in April 1935. Carr left behind an enormous blues catalog and his influence could be heard throughout successive generations of blues musicians, as evidenced by artists like T-Bone Walker, Otis Spann, and Champion Jack Dupree. —*Jim O'Neal & Stephen Thomas Erlewine*

★ **Blues Before Sunrise** / 1962 / Portrait ✦✦✦✦✦
Despite minimal sound quality, this reissue contains some prime Leroy Carr/Scrapper Blackwell material. They were arguably the greatest piano and guitar duo to emerge in the late '20s and early '30s. You can find these tracks on other import collections, but this was among the first reissues available on a domestic label. —*Ron Wynn*

Singin' the Blues / 1973 / Biograph ✦✦✦✦✦
This is late period Carr, superb material done in 1934. It's hard to believe, considering the depth of his piano playing and the vocal quality, that by the end of the next year, Carr's career would be finished. The sound quality is good enough to convey the range and might in Carr's piano fills and delivery. —*Ron Wynn*

☆ **Naptown Blues (1929–1934)** / 1988 / Yazoo ✦✦✦✦✦
A seminal piano/guitar duo, Leroy Carr was among the most influential early blues singer/pianists, and Scrapper Blackwell was a remarkably fluid guitarist. —*Mark A. Humphrey*

1930–1935 / Magpie ✦✦✦✦
It's an incomplete collection, but *1930–1935* collects the great majority of Leroy Carr and Scrapper Blackwell's duets from the early '30s and provides a good introduction to one of the seminal Chicago blues guitar and piano duos. —*Thom Owens*

Vols. 1-3 (1928–1932) / Document ✦✦✦
Over the course of three discs—which are all sold separately—Document has collected every song Leroy Carr cut in the late '20s and early '30s. For completists, the compilation is ideal, but there is too much music for casual fans of Carr or pre-war blues. There's important material here, but it is presented elsewhere on better, more manageable collections. —*Thom Owens*

Bo Carter (Armenter Chatmon)

b. Mar. 21, 1893, Bolton, MS, d. Sep. 21, 1964, Memphis, TN
Banjo, Bass, Clarinet, Guitar, Vocals / Acoustic Delta Blues
Bo Carter (Armenter "Bo" Chatmon) had an unequaled capacity for creating sexual metaphors in his songs, specializing in such ribald imagery as "Banana in Your Fruit Basket," "Pin in Your Cushion," and "Your Biscuits Are Big Enough for Me." One of the most popular bluesmen of the '30s, he recorded enough material for several reissue albums, and he was quite an original guitar picker, or else three of those albums wouldn't have been released by Yazoo. (Carter employed a number of different keys and tunings on his records, most of which were solo vocal and guitar performances.) Carter's facility extended beyond the risqué business to more serious blues themes, and he was also the first to record the standard "Corrine Corrina" (1928). Bo and his brothers Lonnie and Sam Chatmon also recorded as members of the Mississippi Sheiks with singer/guitarist Walter Vinson. —*Jim O'Neal*

● **Greatest Hits, 1930–1940** / Feb. 1970 / Yazoo ✦✦✦✦
With mostly solo selections by Carter, plus a couple of Mississippi Sheiks songs, it features very fine and distinctive country-blues guitar playing and singing. Most of the songs are of the double-entendre variety—a possible reason why he's not as well known as he deserves to be, since some blues researchers did not deem his material worthy. As with most

Yazoo releases, the liner notes include various guitar tunings and chord progressions for each song—fascinating for guitarists. — *George Bedard*

Banana in Your Fruit Basket / 1978 / Yazoo ✦✦✦✦
Some of Carter's best double-entendre material, including the salacious "I Got Ants in My Pants." — *Cub Koda*

Bo Carter, Vol. 5 (1938–1940) / 1991 / Document ✦✦✦
Bo Carter, Vol. 2 (1931–1934) / 1991 / Document ✦✦✦
Bo Carter, Vol. 3 (1934–1936) / 1991 / Document ✦✦✦
Bo Carter, Vol. 4 (1936–1938) / 1991 / Document ✦✦✦
Bo Carter (1931–1940) / Yazoo ✦✦✦
Bo Carter, Vol. 1 (1928–1931) / Document ✦✦✦
Bo Carter, Vols. 1-5 (1928–1940) / Document ✦✦✦
Document's five-disc series—sold individually, not as a package—cover everything Bo Carter recorded between 1928–1940. Although there is plenty of fine music on these discs, only a historian or a completist needs to listen to the entire series—any of Carter's single-disc collections give a better, more concise overview of his music. However, musicologists and die-hard fans will find each of the five worthwhile. — *Stephen Thomas Erlewine*

Goree Carter

b. 1930, Texas, d. Dec. 29, 1990
Guitar, Vocals / Electric Texas Blues
T-Bone Walker inspired a legion of young Texas blues guitarists during the years following World War II with his elegant electrified riffs and fat chords. Among his legion of disciples was Houston's Goree Carter, whose big break came when Solomon Kahal signed him to Houston's Freedom Records circa 1949.
Carter's best-known waxing, the torrid "Rock Awhile" (billed to Goree Carter & His Hepcats) emerged not long thereafter, its sizzling opening lick sounding quite a bit like primordial Chuck Berry. Freedom issued plenty of Carter platters over the next few years, and he later recorded for Imperial/Bayou, Sittin' in With, Coral, Jade, and Modern without denting the national charts. Eventually, he left music behind altogether. — *Bill Dahl*

● **Unsung Hero** / Collectables ✦✦✦✦✦
Houston guitarist Goree Carter's slashing late-'40s/early-'50s sides for Freedom display a strong T-Bone Walker influence, though his best-known effort, the storming "Rock Awhile," kicks a lot harder than Walker's elegant output. These 14 sides are fine examples of the horn-leavened Lone Star sound of the early '50s; while derivative, Carter was a very competent axe-handler. — *Bill Dahl*

Joe Carter

b. Nov. 6, 1927, Midland, GA
Vocals, Slide Guitar / Electric Chicago Blues
One of the truly great unsung heroes of the Chicago club scene of the 1950s, Joe Carter was a slide-playing twin disciple of Elmore James and Muddy Waters. Born in Georgia, Carter came under the early tutelage of local player Lee Willis, who showed the youngster various tunings and how to use a thumb pick. Arriving in Chicago by 1952, Joe made a beeline to the area's club scene to see his idols Muddy Waters and Elmore James. It was Muddy who lent Carter the money to purchase his first electric guitar. Shortly thereafter, Joe started up his first group with guitarist Smokey Smothers and Lester Davenport on harmonica, quickly establishing himself as a club favorite throughout Chicago. Sadly, Carter never recorded with this group—or any other configuration—during his heyday. A contract with Cobra Records was offered (with a young Freddie King being added in the studio to his regular group), but Joe declined as he felt the money would in no way equal what he was pulling down in club work. A true shame and a moment of blues history forever lost as Carter didn't end up being documented until he returned to active playing in the '70s, recording his lone album for the Barrelhouse label in 1976. The intervening years hadn't changed his approach one bit, still full of biting guitar and hoarse, shouted vocals over a bedrock simple foundation. The hoarseness of the vocals, unfortunately, were a portend of the future, as Carter retired from playing in the '80s after a bout with throat cancer. Joe Carter clearly worked in the mode of Elmore and Muddy—seldom contributing much in the way of original material—but

it was all delivered with a passion that was 100% genuine, easily making him an emblematic figure of '50s-style Chicago blues in its heyday. — *Cub Koda*

● **Mean & Evil Blues** / Jan. 1978 / Barrelhouse ✦✦✦✦✦
Joe Carter's lone recorded effort for the tiny Barrelhouse label remains to this day one of the great lost blues albums of the '70s, if not at the top of the list. On the surface, its content could not be more at odds with the standard blues album of that decade; a two guitars-drums-no bass combo running through a set of Chicago staples largely plucked from the repertoires of Muddy Waters and Elmore James, minus any modern embellishments, recorded in studio environs that could best be described as crude. But the intensity and emotional commitment radiates off of Carter like laser beams on every single track, making the starkness of this album all the more appealing. With a guitar tone from his massive Epiphone hollow body that cuts like a knife coupled with a voice that wavers between phlegmatic, stentorian and utterly agonized (the second verse of "Treat Me the Way You Do"), Carter creates a mood on these sides so loaded with ambience that the listener is immediately sucked in from beginning to end. As real as any Hound Dog Taylor Alligator album of the period minus the good-time slant, this is eerie, late-night, juke-joint music of the highest order. Currently MIA on compact disc (as of press time), its non-appearance is one of the great tragedies of the reissue field, considering the dearth of lesser albums from this period being re-released. Needless to say, its appearance in any form is a worthwhile addition to any blues collection. — *Cub Koda*

John Cephas and Phil Wiggins

Group / Modern Acoustic Blues
Piedmont blues specialists John Cephas (guitar) and Phil Wiggins (harmonica) are among a handful of blues musicians who've benefited from the renewed interest in acoustic music in recent years. Cephas has been praised by the *New York Times* and other important media as "one of the outstanding exponents of the Piedmont style guitar."
Both were born in Washington, D.C., though Wiggins is 25 years younger than his guitar-playing partner. Both sing well, and their albums are a mix of standard classic blues as well as their own originals. Along with John Jackson from Virginia, they are some of the names that come to mind when we think of Piedmont blues. The Piedmont region (a geological term referring to foothills) includes the hills between the Appalachian mountains and the Atlantic Coastal plain that runs from northern Virginia to Florida. Piedmont blues refers to a blues sub-genre that is characteristic of performers from Virginia, the Carolinas, Florida and Georgia. Piedmont blues performers include Peg Leg Howell, Pink Anderson, Jackson, Blind Blake and Willie Walker.
"Bowling Green" John Cephas is so nicknamed because though he was born in Washington (Sept. 4, 1930), he was raised in Bowling Green, VA. Cephas got his first exposure to blues from his aunt while growing up in Virginia. His aunt and her boyfriend both played guitar, and after his aunt showed him blues chords when he was eight or nine, he was off and running. Cephas' playing is influenced by the styles of Blind Boy Fuller and Rev. Gary Davis. "Harmonica Phil" Wiggins (b. May 8, 1954), a self-taught harmonica player, cites Sonny Terry, Little Walter, Hammie Nixon, Big Walter, Junior Wells and Sonny Boy Williamson (Rice Miller) as influences. He began playing while he was still in high school and by 1976 he was playing the Washington, D.C., Street Fair with gospel singer Flora Molton.
The pair met at a jam session at a friend's house in Washington in 1977, and both performed as regular members of Wilbert "Big Chief" Ellis' Barrelhouse Rockers for a time before Ellis died later that year and the group disbanded. Since becoming a professional touring duo in 1978, Cephas and Wiggins have performed on tours sponsored by the U.S. State Department, including tours of Europe, Africa, Asia, and South and Central America and the Soviet Union.
The duo's albums include several critically acclaimed releases for Marimac Recordings, Flying Fish Records and most recently, *Cool Down* for the Chicago-based Alligator Records. The pair's Flying Fish releases from the 1980s include *Dog Days of August*, *Guitar Man* and *Flip, Flop & Fly*. All are great examples of state-of-the-art, acoustic Piedmont blues. They remain a popular festi-

val act, and can be seen throughout the summer months at most U.S. blues festivals. —*Richard Skelly*

Sweet Bitter Blues / 1984 / L & R Music ◆◆◆
A fine German import featuring several compositions by blues poet Otis Williams. —*Barry Lee Pearson*

Let It Roll: Bowling Green / 1985 / Marimac ◆◆◆
Similar to *Dog Days of August*, but includes five other cuts. —*Barry Lee Pearson*

● **Dog Days of August** / 1986 / Flying Fish ◆◆◆◆◆
Handy Award-winning acoustic guitar and harmonica Piedmont blues. Includes ballads "John Henry," "Staggerlee," and ten original compositions. —*Barry Lee Pearson*

Guitar Man / 1987 / Flying Fish ◆◆◆◆
Their second Handy Award winner includes slide guitar, Piedmont finger-picking, and wonderful harmonica. —*Barry Lee Pearson*

Walking Blues / 1988 / Marimac ◆◆◆◆◆
A fine assortment of Piedmont blues, ragtime, and country. Includes "Walking Blues." —*Barry Lee Pearson*

Flip, Flop & Fly / 1992 / Flying Fish ◆◆◆

Ray Charles (Ray Charles Robinson)

b. Sep. 23, 1930, Albany, GA
Piano, Vocals / Jazz Blues, Acoustic R&B
Hyperbole aside, Ray Charles has earned his "genius" tag countless times over. As much as any one artist, the blind piano-playing visionary was responsible for inventing what we now term soul music by combining his gritty blues style with sanctified gospel grooves during the mid-'50s. Not everyone was won over immediately—blues stalwart Big Bill Broonzy went on record as stating the mixing of the genres was flat-out wrong. But it was Broonzy who was in serious error; Ray Charles' massive appeal has transcended stylistic boundaries ever since. More than four decades after he blasted to stardom on Atlantic Records with his groundbreaking R&B smashes "I've Got a Woman" and "Hallelujah I Love Her So," Brother Ray remains an American musical icon.

Born into abject poverty in rural Georgia, Ray Charles Robinson grew up in tiny Greenville, FL. He picked up his earliest boogie-woogie piano riffs from Wylie Pitman, proprietor of the Red Wing Cafe in Greenville. The Red Wing also housed a jukebox stocked with 78s by boogie masters Pete Johnson, Meade Lux Lewis, and Albert Ammons.

Tragedy struck twice when Charles was only five. First, his little brother drowned in a tub of water in the backyard. A few months later, Charles began to go blind. It took a couple of years for the child to completely lose his sight. He was sent to the State School for the Blind in St. Augustine, where he honed his pianistic talents and dug the styles of Art Tatum, Nat King Cole, Louis Jordan, and Charles Brown (the latter would exert an obvious influence on Charles' early 78s for Swing Time).

By the mid-'40s, Charles was gigging wherever he could around Florida. He joined forces with guitarist Gosady McGee in Tampa, but times were still tough—tough enough to necessitate a relocation to Seattle, WA, in 1948. McGee soon followed, and with bassist Milton Garred, they formed the McSon Trio and became a popular local attraction. He cut his first professional recordings with the trio for Jack Lauderdale's Down Beat Records in 1949: "Confession Blues" and "I Love You, I Love You." The spectres of Charles Brown and Nat Cole hung heavy in the air.

But Charles gradually developed his own rougher-edged style during his tenure at Down Beat/Swing Time, scoring hits in 1949 with the aforementioned "Confession Blues," in 1951 with "Baby Let Me Hold Your Hand," and the next year with a stomping "Kissa Me Baby" that signaled the emergence of the real, unexpurgated Ray Charles—gospel-soaked and brimming with soul.

Charles moved to Los Angeles in 1950, recording for Swing Time with a horn-driven band as well as in a trio format. He hit the road with his labelmate, guitarist Lowell Fulson, as opening act, band pianist, and arranger in 1950-1951. But that wouldn't last for long—Charles was rapidly becoming a star in his own right. He switched over to Atlantic Records in 1952, and magic swiftly commenced.

Charles' first Atlantic offerings, notably the Brown-like "Roll with My Baby" and a horn-blasting "Jumpin' in the Mornin'," didn't sound too different from the Swing Time stuff. But with the roaring "Mess Around" and its mournful blues flip "Funny (But I Still Love You)" in 1953, Charles transcended his influences permanently. Living at the time in New Orleans, Charles arranged and played piano on his pal Guitar Slim's 1954 R&B chart-topper "The Things That I Used to Do" for Specialty (and did a moving version of Slim's "Feelin' Sad" for Atlantic).

The mid-'50s were when it all came together for Brother Ray. He visited the R&B charts early and often on Atlantic: the catchy "It Should've Been Me" and a powerful blues, "Don't You Know," preceded the seminal "I've Got a Woman," his first number one R&B single (and one of many classic Charles-penned originals), in 1955. The blues/gospel synthesis was now complete, Charles' church-drenched 88s and melismatic screams powering hit after hit: "Come Back Baby," "A Fool for You," "This Little Girl of Mine" (covered successfully a few years later by the Everly Brothers), "Blackjack," the witty jump item "Greenbacks" (all in 1955 alone!), "Drown in My Own Tears," "Mary Ann," "Hallelujah I Love Her So," and "Lonely Avenue" (all 1956, with the last title marking the recorded debut of the Raelettes, Charles' longtime female backup singers), and 1957's "Ain't That Love" brought an undiluted, rousing sanctified spirit to the R&B world. It would never recover (thank God!). In 1956, Charles hired marvelous saxist David "Fathead" Newman, who would graduate to jazz stardom in his own right.

Atlantic didn't put limits on Charles' prodigious talents. Since the label boasted a strong commitment to jazz, it was only natural that Charles' leanings in that direction would be properly documented as well on the acclaimed LPs *The Great Ray Charles, Soul Brothers* and *Soul Meeting* (the latter pair with Milt Jackson). In 1959, he cut his landmark album, *The Genius of Ray Charles*, which boasted gorgeous arrangements for strings and brass as Charles crooned ballads light years away from his then-popular smash "What'd I Say," which grafted the call-and-response structure of the church onto an irresistibly sexy R&B groove laid down by Brother Ray on his electric Wurlitzer piano. The tune, like so many of Charles' hits, would be covered constantly forever after—Elvis, Jerry Lee, et al.

All good things must someday come to an end, and so it was with the seemingly made-in-heaven hookup between Charles and Atlantic. In 1960, Brother Ray moved over to ABC-Paramount Records, where he grew even more eclectic. That year, he hit with the R&B rocker "Sticks and Stones" and his immortal rendering of the graceful standard "Georgia on My Mind," which topped the pop lists.

That same year, he waxed a jazz-based big-band album, *Genius Plus Soul Equals Jazz*, for Impulse (ABC's jazz subsidiary) that contained a Latin-beat instrumental version of the Clovers' "One Mint Julep" (another R&B chart-topper). Songwriter/performer Percy Mayfield supplied Charles with his classic "Hit the Road Jack" the next year, a track featuring the Raelettes as prominently as the man himself. "Unchain My Heart" also paced the charts in 1961.

In 1962, Charles turned his attention to re-inventing Country & Western music in his own image (he had actually played with a hillbilly band back in Florida during his formative years). The groundbreaking result was *Modern Sounds in Country and Western Music*, which contained Charles' radically retooled reading of Don Gibson's plaintive "I Can't Stop Loving You." The single topped both the pop and R&B charts and sold a million copies. He worked the formula hard for a while, hitting with the follow-ups "You Don't Know Me," "You Are My Sunshine," "Take These Chains from My Heart," and the Harlan Howard-penned "Busted."

After that astonishing parade of hits, Brother Ray cooled off a bit during the mid-'60s (although his version of Buck Owens' "Crying Time" and the soul gem "Let's Go Get Stoned" were major hits in 1966). Whether crooning the Beatles' "Yesterday," a patriotic "America the Beautiful," or the Sesame Street kiddie favorite "It's Not Easy Being Green," Ray Charles has retained his beloved status ever since. He even starred (as himself) in a weepy 1964 movie, *Ballad in Blue*, and cut a hit title theme for another, 1967's *In the Heat of the Night*.

As his 1978 autobiography, *Brother Ray* (co-written with David Ritz), points out, it hasn't all been a breeze—Charles suffered several well-publicized bouts with heroin addiction during the '60s. But Ray Charles has always steadfastly done things his way, founding his own label, Tangerine Records, during the 1960s (his talent roster included Louis Jordan, Percy Mayfield, and the Raelettes), owning and operating his own recording studio, even allegedly driving an auto (with a little help from a friend on the latter, obviously!). Clearly, blindness hasn't stopped Ray Charles from enjoying an incredible career—one that thrives to this day. —*Bill Dahl*

The Great Ray Charles / 1956 / Atlantic ✦✦✦
A superb late '50s instrumental album showcasing the jazz side of Ray Charles. Quincy Jones provided the arrangements, and the Charles band included Fathead Newman and Hank Crawford. The CD version includes six marvelous bonus cuts, among them a remarkable cover of Fats Waller's "Ain't Misbehavin'." —*Ron Wynn*

Ray Charles at Newport / Oct. 1958 / Atlantic ✦✦✦✦✦
For his appearance at the Newport Jazz Festival on July 5, 1958, Charles pulled out all the stops, performing raucous versions of "The Right Time," "I Got A Woman," and "Talkin' 'Bout You." (This album was reissued in 1973 as a two-record set, packaged with *Ray Charles In Person* under the title *Ray Charles Live* [Atlantic].) —*William Ruhlmann*

What'd I Say / Sep. 1959 / Atlantic ✦✦✦
At a concert held at Herndon Stadium in Atlanta on May 28, 1959, Ray Charles turns in a blistering version of "What'd I Say" and takes on the big band era with versions of Tommy Dorsey's "Yes Indeed!" and Artie Shaw's "Frenesi," not to mention performances of "The Right Time" and "Tell the Truth." (This album was reissued in 1960 under the title *Ray Charles In Person* and again in 1973 as a part of a two-record set, packaged with *Ray Charles at Newport* under the title *Ray Charles Live* [Atlantic].) —*William Ruhlmann*

The Genius of Ray Charles / 1960 / Atlantic ✦✦✦✦✦
Half lushly orchestrated (by Ralph Burns) blues ballads that spotlight the sophisticated (dare we say tender?) side of the man, the other half big band-backed gems (including Charles' glorious remake of Louis Jordan's "Let the Good Times Roll" and the jauntiest version of "Alexander's Ragtime Band" you'll ever hear), this 1959 album marked his ascension to genuine Genius status and remains a benchmark of his lengthy career. —*Bill Dahl*

The Genius Sings the Blues / Oct. 1961 / Atlantic ✦✦✦✦
Down-home, anguished laments and moody ballads were turned into triumphs by Ray Charles. He sang these songs with the same conviction, passion, and energy that made his country and soul vocals so majestic. This has not as of yet turned up in the reissue bins, but is probably headed in that direction. —*Ron Wynn*

Ingredients in a Recipe for Soul / Jul. 1963 / DCC ✦✦✦✦
Ray Charles' 1963 ABC-Paramount album digitally verbatim, followed by four bonus tracks, notably the rare 1959 single "My Baby (I Love Her, Yes I Do)," an obscure Percy Mayfield goodie from 1964 ("Something's Wrong"), and Charles' 1960 version of Big Maceo's "Worried Life Blues." Charles tapped a host of disparate songwriters for this solid LP—everyone from Mel Tormé to Leroy Carr to Oscar Hammerstein—but the most memorable item is probably his irresistibly brassy remake of Harlan Howard's C&W classic "Busted." —*Bill Dahl*

Greatest Hits, Vol. 1 / 1988 / DCC ✦✦✦✦✦
The first of two DCC compilations to collect the best of Brother Ray's 1960s stint at ABC-Paramount Records, when he flew off in a dozen different stylistic directions. Included on this 20-track disc are Charles' immortal rendering of "Georgia on My Mind," the sinuously bluesy "Unchain My Heart," the Latin-beat instrumental "One Mint Julep," personalized remakes of the country standards "Born to Lose," "Your Cheating Heart," and "Crying Time," and his exultant rendition of the soulful "Let's Go Get Stoned." —*Bill Dahl*

Greatest Hits, Vol. 2 / 1988 / DCC ✦✦✦✦✦
More seminal performances from the '60s ABC catalog of the Genius (DCC split the classics evenly between the two discs, making both of them indispensable). His beloved "Hit the Road Jack" (one of several Percy Mayfield copyrights dotting Charles' repertoire), the daring country crossover "I Can't Stop Loving You," an electric-piano powered "Sticks and Stones," a wise "Them That Got," and a wonderfully mellow "At the Club" rank with the 20-song disc's standouts (though versions of the Beatles'

"Yesterday" and the corny "Look What They Done to My Song, Ma" end the set on a bummer note). —*Bill Dahl*

☆ **The Birth of Soul** / 1991 / Rhino ✦✦✦✦✦
The title isn't just hype—this absolutely essential three-disc box is where soul music first took shape and soared, courtesy of Ray Charles' church-soaked pipes and bedrock piano work. Brother Ray's formula for inventing the genre was disarmingly simple: he brought gospel intensity to the R&B world with his seminal "I Got a Woman," "Hallelujah I Love Her So," "Leave My Woman Alone," "You Be My Baby," and the primal 1959 call-and-response classic "What'd I Say." There's plenty of brilliant blues content within these 53 historic sides: Charles' mournful "Losing Hand," "Feelin' Sad," "Hard Times," and "Blackjack" ooze after-hours desperation. No blues collection should be without this boxed set, which comes with well-researched notes by Robert Palmer, a nicely illustrated accompanying booklet, and discographical info aplenty. —*Bill Dahl*

The Birth of a Legend / 1992 / Ebony ✦✦✦✦✦
Of all the countless compilations that have been stitched together of Ray Charles' early sides for Jack Lauderdale's Swing Time Records, this two-disc box is the only CD package that treats these enormously important works with the reverent respect that they deserve (meaning decent mono sound quality instead of murky electronic reprocessed stereo dubbed from vinyl, cogent liner notes, and full discographical annotation). This is where the Genius began, imitating Charles Brown at the very start (1949) and sounding like nobody but Brother Ray by 1952 (when he defected to Atlantic and hit the real bigtime). Features 41 tracks in all. —*Bill Dahl*

Blues & Jazz / 1994 / Rhino/Atlantic ✦✦✦✦✦
Another easy access point for Charles' seminal Atlantic catalog. This two-disc set is evenly split between his bluesiest sides on the first disc and a selection of his greatest jazz sides on disc two (gorgeously showcasing the sax work of David "Fathead" Newman on several pieces). Charles was a masterful blues purveyor; his "I Believe to My Soul" is simultaneously invested with heartbreak and humor, while the earlier "Sinner's Prayer," "The Sun's Gonna Shine Again," and the gospel-based "A Fool for You" emanate both hope and deep pain. —*Bill Dahl*

★ **Best of Atlantic** / 1994 / Rhino ✦✦✦✦✦
For fans who don't want to invest in the three-disc box set, this is a good single-disc collection of Charles' ground-breaking Atlantic singles. —*AMG*

The Early Years / 1994 / Tomato ✦✦✦
In the late '40s and early '50s, Charles recorded several dozen sides for the Swingtime/Downbeat label, 30 of which are presented here. As has been noted many times by critics, these usually found Charles in a Nat "King" Cole swing-blues groove that was much smoother than the gritty R&B/soul he'd record for Atlantic in the later '50s; the influence of urban blues balladeer Charles Brown is also evident. Some critical essays, in fact, may lead you to believe that this work is trivial, but while it's undeniably derivative, it's enjoyable on its own terms, and not without strong hints of the searing soulfulness that was to come. Some of the selections are delivered with such refined polish that it doesn't even sound like Charles. But on the more anguished and fast-tempoed cuts in particular, you can hear him starting to arrive at the phrasing and emotion that would flower in the mid-'50s. Unfortunately, like most Tomato reissues, the sound is substandard; even assuming that the master tapes can't be located, a better job was probably possible, and a couple of cuts even duplicate skips from the vinyl. Exact dates and songwriting credits are also missing, although Pete Welding's essay does at least discuss the material on the discs in some detail, unlike many of Tomato's liner notes. —*Richie Unterberger*

Sam Chatmon

b. Jan. 10, 1897, Bolton, MS, d. Feb. 2, 1983, Hollandale, MS
Guitar, Vocals / Acoustic Country Blues
A product of the prodigious Chatmon family that included not only Lonnie of the famous Mississippi Sheiks but also the prolific Bo Carter and several other blues-playing brothers, Sam Chatmon survived to be hailed as a modern-day blues guru when he began performing and recording again in the '60s. Sam continued brother Bo's tradition of sly double-entendre blues to entertain a new generation of aficionados, but he also showed a

more serious side on songs like the title track of the early Arhoolie anthology *I Have to Paint My Face.*

Chatmon began playing music as a child, occasionally with his family's string band, as well as the Mississippi Sheiks. Sam launched his own solo career in the early '30s. While he performed and recorded as a solo act, he would still record with the Mississippi Sheiks and with his brother Lonnie. Throughout the '30s, Sam travelled throughout the South, playing with a variety of minstrel and medicine shows. He stopped travelling in the early '40s, making himself a home in Hollandale, MS, where he worked on plantations.

For the next two decades, Sam Chatmon was essentially retired from music and only worked on the plantations. When the blues revival arrived in the late '50s, he managed to capitalize on the genre's resurgent popularity. In 1960, he signed a contract with Arhoolie and he recorded a number of songs for the label. Throughout the '60s and '70s, he recorded for a variety of labels, as well as playing clubs and blues and folk festivals across America. Chatmon was an active performer and recording artist until his death in 1983. *—Jim O'Neal & Stephen Thomas Erlewine*

● **Sam Chatmon's Advice** / 1979 / Rounder ♦♦♦♦♦
Outstanding blues and double-entendre delights. *—Ron Wynn*

Sam Chatmon & His Barbecue Boys / 1987 / Flying Fish ♦♦♦
An excellent set of trio recordings by this underrated performer. *—Ron Wynn*

Clifton Chenier

b. Jun. 25, 1925, Opelousas, LA, **d.** Dec. 12, 1987, Lafayette, LA
Accordion, Vocals / Cajun, Zydeco
Clifton Chenier was a master Louisiana musical chef of the highest order. On a good night with a crowd in high spirits, Chenier's musical gumbo had Cajun two-steps and waltzes sitting right next to slow blues or a scorching rendition of "Bon Ton Roulet," which was Clifton's version of Louis Jordan's "Let the Good Times Roll" sung in French. The musical hybrid that he helped to create—zydeco, or "zodico," its spelling variant and superior phonetic pronunciation—is as rich and as deep as the area from which it sprang. Chenier may not have invented the form—an accordion-driven, blues-inspired variant of Cajun music played for dancing—but he single-handedly helped give it shape and define the form as we know it today. In his own words, "What I did was to put a little rock 'n' roll into the zydeco to mix it up a bit. You see, people been playing zydeco for a long time, old style, like French music. But I was the first one to put the pep to it." Chenier had taken a backwoods art form, mixed it up with rock 'n' roll, country, R&B, and blues, put a heavier beat to it, and ended up bringing this spicy gumbo concoction to the world. Of course, it also helps that Clifton put this Creole hybrid over with personality to spare, singing and playing his squeeze box with a high energy approach that made the music damn near impossible to ignore. While the crown for the king of the blues sits uneasily on a number of heads, merely ask anyone in the South who was there during his reign and there's absolutely no doubt that Clifton *was* the King of Zydeco, and had the crown to prove it.

Chenier was born in 1925 near Opelousas, LA, to a sharecropping family who played music on the side. Early inspirations for him included his father, John Chenier, who played accordion and fiddle and his guitar-playing uncle, Maurice "Big" Chenier, as well as local player Izeb Laza, who gave him his first accordion. But the musician who really turned Clifton's head around came with his early exposure to the records of Amedee Ardoin, the first Black Creole musician to play the blues on an accordion.

Ardoin was the Charlie Patton of the music, king of the Louisiana dance music being dispensed as far back as 1928—then called French lala's—making the sounds on the front porch, loose, rough and informal. The accordion was usually accompanied by a triangle, a washboard, and a fiddle. It was homegrown music, based on the two steps and waltzes of Cajun music, and when Ardoin became the first to put blues licks to ancient French melodies, a livelier version of the form immediately existed. Once Clifton heard Ardoin's records, he was hooked; here was a dance music that was elastic enough in form to be able to change, update and expand its vocabulary. Yet at the same time that Chenier was learning Ardoin's lively versions of the old French-Cajun dance tunes, Chenier learned his very first

tune on the accordion, the Joe Liggins jump blues hit, "The Honeydripper."

By the age of 17, Chenier was already working weekend gigs in nearby Lake Charles, with his older brother Cleveland playing the rubboard. Their good-time party music was perfectly suited for the numerous "joys" (little dance halls, which were usually nothing more than a shack) that dotted the coastal region, and they worked a lot at their uncle "Big" Chenier's club. Soon the duo expanded and by the early '50s, Clifton had his first electric band together, the Hot Sizzling Band (aka the Hot Sizzlers), a perfect description of the sound that the seven-piece combo was laying down. With electric guitar, piano, tenor saxophone, bass and drums fleshing out the sound of the two Chenier brothers, this was clearly a long ways away from a triangle player tinging along with a squeeze box in the backyard. With a piece of the Louisiana club and outdoor frolic circuit clearly in his back pocket, how Clifton came to make records in 1954 out in California is still a matter of speculation. But the conventional wisdom is that Beaumont, TX, bluesman Clarence Garlow—who had been booking Chenier at his Bon Ton Drive In for three years in a row—put in the good word to Los Angeles record man J.R. Fullbright. Legend has it that when Garlow put the telephone up to Clifton's amplifier and J.R. heard the sound of the music, he told Clarence, "I'm coming to get him."

With Fullbright behind the controls, Chenier and his band cut seven sides at a Lake Charles radio station. The first single issued ("Louisiana Stomp") kicked up enough noise on J.R.'s Elko label that four more sides from the session were quickly issued on an Imperial subsidiary, Post.

By the following year, Fullbright had hooked Clifton up with Specialty Records in Hollywood; the 1955 sessions that he cut for the label is where his success story—and that of the music—truly begins. After quickly signing in April, a session in Los Angeles was immediately set up with Bumps Blackwell (who would later produce Little Richard) in charge. Legend has it that Blackwell pulled half of the band—which included Philip Walker and later, Cornelius "Lonesome Sundown" Green on guitar—off of the session to give greater focus to Chenier's accordion in the mix. A quick listen to the two sessions reveals that this appears to been have a track-by-track decision; some feature the full band and players drift in and out of the lineup on other tracks while most are just Clifton and the rhythm section vainly trying to keep up with him on boogie woogie instrumentals that jump time every chorus and a third. But Clifton's first Specialty single—"Ay-Te Te Fee" and "Boppin' the Rock," released a month after it was cut—became a left field R&B charter, moving enough copies to get him booked on package shows with the likes of Etta James and Jimmy Reed. But rock 'n' roll was also coming in strong and with Richard's "Tutti Frutti" outselling everyone else in the Specialty catalog *combined*, Chenier suddenly found himself without a recording contract. But he quickly signed for a short stint with Chess, resulting in two excellent singles and a couple of years later became a part of Crowley, LA, producer Jay Miller's stable, recording for his Zynn label between 1958 and 1960.

Meanwhile, Chenier stayed a hot road attraction, playing all through Texas and Louisiana, for dances, picnics, nightclubs and anyplace else that was ready to party down and hear the real thing on a Saturday night. It was after relocating to Houston's Frenchtown quarter in 1960 that his next (and longest) recording partnership came about. A young California-based folklorist and record label owner was in town, and after Lightnin' Hopkins hooked the two of them up, Chenier was quickly signed to Chris Strachwitz's fledgling Arhoolie label.

Not that everything was always an easy road to travel between the two men. Strachwitz wanted to keep the music as close as possible to the rubboard, drums and accordion format of the old-time French lala material, while Clifton wanted to rip through a set of the tunes that people danced to on a live gig. Though Chenier stayed with Strachwitz for several albums and singles into the '70s, he was also recording during the same period for Floyd Soileau's Bayou label, with both men later leasing material to labels like Bell and Blue Thumb. In addition to Arhoolie and Bayou, Clifton would also record for Crazy Cajun, Blue Star, GNP Crescendo, Jin, Caillier, Maison de Soul and his final stop, Alligator Records in 1982.

After the release of the Arhoolie albums, Europe came a-calling and in 1969 Chenier was bowling over crowds on the American Folk Blues Festival tour, staying overseas and adding extra play dates to his already crowded calendar. By the '70s, Clifton and his Red Hot Louisiana Band seemingly covered the globe, touring Stateside and abroad, bringing the sound of the bayou to places as far away from the hot sauce capital of New Iberia, LA, as anyone could have possibly imagined.

Unfortunately by the dawn of the following decade, Clifton was slowly becoming a very sick man. Diagnosed with diabetes and with a road schedule that was unrelenting, the ravages of the disease—failing kidneys that needed dialysis treatment every third day and a partially amputated foot—started to take their toll. In 1984 he played the White House and didn't bother to look back, but his health finally gave out on December 12, 1987. However, in the numerous recordings he left behind and especially in the modern day work of his many disciples, the music lives on. Bon Ton Roulet, indeed. —*Cub Koda*

Zodico Blues & Boogie / 1955 / Specialty ♦♦♦♦♦
Clifton Chenier's mid-'50s singles for Specialty were among his rawest and simplest; they were short ditties with rippling accordion and gritty vocals on top and driving rhythms and surging instrumental accompaniment underneath. That's the formula displayed on this 20-cut presentation of Chenier's early work, where he was often backed by guitarists Phillip Walker or Cornelius Green (Lonesome Sundown), with his brother Cleveland handling rubboard duties. This is Chenier in his stylistic infancy, building and nurturing what ultimately became a signature sound. —*Ron Wynn*

Louisiana Blues & Zydeco / 1965 / Arhoolie ♦♦♦
Featured is excellent small-combo zydeco. —*Jeff Hannusch*

Bayou Blues / 1970 / Specialty ♦♦♦♦♦
Bayou Blues compiles a selection of 12 tracks Clifton Chenier cut for Specialty Records in 1955, including the original versions of "Boppin' the Rock," "Eh, Petite Fille," "I'm On My Way" and "Zodico Stomp." It may not be a definitive retrospective, but it's an entertaining and necessary sampler of Chenier at the beginning of his career. —*Thom Owens*

Out West / 1974 / Arhoolie ♦♦♦♦♦
Special guests Elvin Bishop and Steve Miller joined Chenier for an excellent outing blending blues and rock influences with zydeco. Chenier's vocals were tough and convincing, while Bishop and Miller, along with saxophonist Jon Hart, were outstanding. —*Ron Wynn*

In New Orleans / 1979 / GNP ♦♦♦
In New Orleans was recorded in the late '70s with one of Clifton Chenier's classic bands, which featured his brother on washboard, saxophonist John Hart, and guitarist Paul Senegal, among others. The album is textbook Chenier—it rocks & rolls, wails and shouts. It may be a typical record for the king of zydeco, but that means it's very, very enjoyable. —*Thom Owens*

Bon Ton Roulet / May 1981 / Arhoolie ♦♦♦♦
Great rock'em-sock'em zydeco. —*Jeff Hannusch*

I'm Here! / May 1982 / Alligator ♦♦♦
Although not so good as his Arhoolie albums, this won Chenier a Grammy. —*Jeff Hannusch*

The King of Zydeco Live at Montreux / 1984 / Arhoolie ♦♦♦
This is a nice concert set. —*Mark A. Humphrey*

Live! / 1985 / Arhoolie ♦♦♦
The 19 selections on this disc were done in the early '80s, when Chenier was past his romping prime but still keeping the zydeco engine running. He has done them all before on other releases, but keeps them entertaining and enjoyable through sheer will and personality. —*Ron Wynn*

Sings the Blues / 1987 / Arhoolie ♦♦♦
Lots of great accordion and unique vocals come from the blues side of the bayou. —*Jeff Hannusch & Mark A. Humphrey*

Bogalusa Boogie / Jul. 1987 / Arhoolie ♦♦♦
Backed by a fuller band on this release, he sounds great. Here's the hottest of the red-hot Louisiana bands, and they're feelin' frisky. —*Jeff Hannusch & Mark A. Humphrey*

Live at St. Mark's / 1988 / Arhoolie ♦♦♦
Live at St. Mark's captures a rollicking concert performed in San Francisco. Chenier leads the band through a blend of zydeco and blues, singing with gusto and spice all along. Furthermore, he plays to the audience, telling jokes and stories, which give the album a special, intimate feel. With all the wonderful music and joy that *Live at St. Marks* radiates, there's little question that it is one of Chenier's finest live albums. —*Thom Owens*

☆ **60 Minutes with the King of Zydeco** / 1988 / Arhoolie ♦♦♦♦♦
Zydeco at its best, it compiles his greatest hits from the Arhoolie label. —*Jeff Hannusch*

★ **Zydeco Dynamite: The Clifton Chenier Anthology** / 1993 / Rhino ♦♦♦♦♦
Clifton Chenier was to zydeco what Elvis Presley was to rockabilly, only more so—the genre's founding father and tireless ambassador. Rhino has done an admirable job of collecting the accordionist's important work for this two-disc, 40-track set, harking back to a wonderfully chaotic "Louisiana Stomp" that he waxed in Lake Charles, LA, in 1954 for J.R. Fullbright's tiny Elko label. Whether you're in the market for one zydeco collection to summarize the entire genre or ready to delve deeply into the legacy of the idiom's pioneer, this is precisely where to begin. —*Bill Dahl*

The Chicago Blue Stars

Group / Electric Chicago Blues
This was in actuality Charlie Musselwhite's band circa 1969, but because of his Vanguard contract he could not sing or be pictured on the sextet's only LP—although his harp playing is credited. Boasting perhaps the greatest Chicago rhythm section ever (drummer Fred Below and bass monster Jack Myers), the group showcased steel guitarist Freddie Roulette, pianist Skip Rose, and Aces guitarist Louis Myers. —*Dan Forte*

Coming Home / Mar. 1970 / Blue Thumb ♦♦♦
Because Musselwhite's contract forbid him to sing and Roulette had yet to develop into a strong vocalist, Louis Myers bears most of the vocal weight, and Rose and Below make one rather weak attempt each. But instrumentally—two Roulette spotlights and Musselwhite's jazzy arrangement of the title track—back up their legendary status. As welcome as this "group" effort is, it's a shame the unit never recorded in the context it was formed—as Musselwhite's stellar backup band. —*Dan Forte*

Chicken Shack

Group / British Blues
This British blues-rock group is remembered mostly for their keyboard player, Christine Perfect, who would join Fleetwood Mac after marrying John McVie and changing her last name. Although they were one of the more pedestrian acts of the British blues boom, Chicken Shack were quite popular for a time in the late '60s, placing two albums in the British Top 20. The frontperson of Chicken was not Perfect/McVie, but guitarist Stan Webb, who would excite British audiences by entering the crowds at performances, courtesy of his 100-meter-long guitar lead. They were signed to Mike Vernon's Blue Horizon label, a British blues pillar that had its biggest success with early Fleetwood Mac.

Chicken Shack were actually not far behind Mac in popularity in the late '60s, purveying a more traditional brand of Chicago blues, heavily influenced by Freddie King. Although Webb took most of the songwriting and vocal duties, Christine Perfect also chipped in with occasional compositions and lead singing. In fact, she sang lead on their only British Top 20 single, "I'd Rather Go Blind" (1969). But around that time, she quit the music business to marry John McVie and become a housewife, although, as the world knows, that didn't last too long. Chicken Shack never recovered from Christine's loss, commercially or musically. Stan Webb kept Chicken Shack going, with a revolving door of other musicians, all the way into the 1980s, though he briefly disbanded the group to join Savoy Brown for a while in the mid-'70s. —*Richie Unterberger*

Forty Blue Fingers, Freshly Packed and Ready to Serve / 1968 / Epic ♦♦♦♦
If one can overlook Stan Webb's hyperventilating vocal excesses (which ain't easy), this is a promising debut, especially noteworthy for Webb's Freddie King-inspired guitar sting and Christine Perfect's understated vocals (only two, unfortunately, compared to Webb's six). Webb does justice to his mentor with two instrumentals, King's "San-Ho-Zay" and his own "Webbed Feet." and Perfect proves the ideal counterpart—one of the few pianists paying homage to King's longtime collaborator Sonny Thompson. Nice spare sound, typical of Mike Vernon's Blue Horizon label. —*Dan Forte*

O.K. Ken? / 1969 / BGO ✦✦
This was Chicken Shack's most popular album, making the British Top Ten. If you're looking for relics of the British Blues Boom, however, you'd be much better off with Ten Years After, to say nothing of legitimate artists such as Fleetwood Mac and John Mayall. British blues at its best could be exciting (if usually derivative), but it's difficult to fathom how this relentlessly plodding, monotonous effort met with such success. Stan Webb took most of the songwriting and vocal chores, emulating the slow-burning Chicago boogie with little skill or subtlety (though he wasn't a bad guitarist). Christine Perfect did write and sing a few songs, but these unfortunately found both her compositional and vocal chops at a most callow stage of development. To nail the coffin, most of the songs were preceded by excruciating comic dialog that made Cheech & Chong sound sophisticated in comparison. —*Richie Unterberger*

● **Collection** / 1988 / Castle ✦✦✦
Collection contains the cream of Chicken Shack's uneven albums and provides a perfect introduction to the British blues band. —*Thom Owens*

Eric Clapton (Eric Patrick Clapp)

b. Mar. 30, 1945, Ripley, England
Guitar, Vocals / British Blues, Rock & Roll
By the time Eric Clapton launched his solo career with the release of his self-titled debut album in August 1970, he was long established as one of the world's major rock stars due to his group affiliations—the Yardbirds, John Mayall's Bluesbreakers, Cream, and Blind Faith—affiliations that had demonstrated his claim to being the best rock guitarist of his generation. That it took Clapton so long to go out on his own, however, was evidence of a degree of reticence unusual for one of his stature. And his debut album, though it spawned the Top 40 hit "After Midnight," was typical of his self-effacing approach: it was, in effect, an album by the group he had lately been featured in, Delaney & Bonnie & Friends.

Not surprisingly, before his solo debut had even been released, Clapton had retreated from his solo stance, assembling from the D&B&F ranks the personnel for a group, Derek & the Dominos, with which he played for most of 1970. Clapton was largely inactive in 1971 and 1972, due to heroin addiction, but he performed a comeback concert at the Rainbow Theatre in London on January 13, 1973, resulting in the album *Eric Clapton's Rainbow Concert* (September 1973).

But Clapton did not launch a sustained solo career until July 1974, when he released *461 Ocean Boulevard,* which topped the charts and spawned the #1 single "I Shot the Sheriff."

The persona Clapton established over the next decade was less that of guitar hero than arena rock star with a weakness for ballads. The follow-ups to *461 Ocean Boulevard, There's One in Every Crowd* (April 1975), the live *E.C. Was Here* (August 1975), and *No Reason to Cry* (August 1976), were less successful. But *Slowhand* (November 1977), which featured both the powerful "Cocaine" (written by J.J. Cale, who had also written "After Midnight") and the hit singles "Lay Down Sally" and "Wonderful Tonight," was a million seller, and its follow-ups, *Backless* (November 1978), featuring the Top Ten hit "Promises," the live *Just One Night* (May 1980), and *Another Ticket* (April 1981), featuring the Top Ten hit "I Can't Stand It," were all big sellers.

Clapton's popularity waned somewhat in the first half of the '80s, as the albums *Money and Cigarettes* (February 1983), *Behind the Sun* (March 1985), and *August* (November 1986) indicated a certain career stasis. But he was buoyed up by the release of the boxed set retrospective *Crossroads* (April 1988), which seemed to remind his fans of how great he was. *Journeyman* (November 1989) was a return to form.

It would be his last new studio album for nearly five years, though in the interim he would suffer greatly and enjoy surprising triumph. On March 20, 1991, Clapton's four-year-old son was killed in a fall. While he mourned, he released a live album, *24 Nights* (October 1991), culled from his annual concert series at the Royal Albert Hall in London, and prepared a movie soundtrack, *Rush* (January 1992). The soundtrack featured a song written for his son, "Tears in Heaven," that became a massive hit single.

In March 1992, Clapton recorded a concert for *MTV Unplugged* that, when released on an album in August, became

his biggest selling record ever. Two years later, Clapton returned with a blues album, *From the Cradle.* —*William Ruhlmann*

Eric Clapton / Jul. 1970 / Polydor ✦✦✦✦
Eric Clapton's eponymous solo debut was recorded after he completed a tour with Delaney & Bonnie. Clapton used the core of the duo's backing band and co-wrote the majority of the songs with Delaney Bramlett—accordingly, *Eric Clapton* sounds more laidback and straightforward than any of the guitarist's previous recordings. There are still elements of blues and rock 'n' roll, but they're hidden beneath layers of gospel, R&B, country, and pop flourishes. And the pop element of the record is the strongest of the album's many elements—"Blues Power" isn't a blues song and only "Let It Rain," the album's closer, features extended solos. Throughout the album, Clapton turns out concise solos that de-emphasize his status as guitar god, even when they display astonishing musicality and technique. That is both a good and a bad thing—it's encouraging to hear him grow and become a more fully rounded musician, but too often the album needs the spark that some long guitar solos would have given it. In short, it needs a little more of Clapton's personality. —*Stephen Thomas Erlewine*

E.C. Was Here / Aug. 1975 / Polydor ✦✦✦
Since Eric Clapton and his longtime fans have always thought of him primarily as a bluesman, it is curious that this live album, which is devoted to extended guitar solos on blues standards like "Have You Ever Loved a Woman," "Rambling On My Mind," and "Further On Up the Road," didn't become a massive hit. Maybe it was that the once reclusive Clapton was now spitting out new albums every six months, but *E.C. Was Here* did not achieve the renown it deserved upon release, and Clapton, who had been reluctant to put out a straight blues album to begin with, didn't try anything similar again for almost 20 years, instead making sure to keep his records within a pop framework that usually diluted their effectiveness. In its CD reissue, with "Drifting Blues" extended out to its full 11 1/2 minutes, the album is even more impressive. —*William Ruhlmann*

Slowhand / Nov. 1977 / Polydor ✦✦✦✦
After the all-star *No Reason to Cry* failed to make much of an impact commerically, Eric Clapton returned to using his own band for *Slowhand.* The difference is substantial—where *No Reason to Cry* struggled hard to find the right tone, *Slowhand* opens with the relaxed, bluesy shuffle of J.J. Cale's "Cocaine" and sustains it throughout the course of the album. Alternating between straight blues ("Mean Old Frisco"), country ("Lay Down Sally"), mainstream rock ("Cocaine," "The Core") and pop ("Wonderful Tonight"), *Slowhand* doesn't sound schizophrenic because of the band's grasp of the material. This is laidback virtuosity—although Clapton and his band are never flashy, their playing is masterful and assured. That assurance and the album's eclectic material makes *Slowhand* rank with *461 Ocean Boulevard* as Eric Clapton's best album. —*Stephen Thomas Erlewine*

Just One Night / Apr. 1980 / Polydor ✦✦✦✦
Although Eric Clapton has released a bevy of live albums, none of them have ever quite captured the guitarist's raw energy and dazzling virtuosity. The double-live album *Just One Night* may have gotten closer to that elusive goal than most of its predecessors, but it is still lacking in many ways. The most notable difference between *Just One Night* and Clapton's other live albums is his backing band. Led by guitarist Albert Lee, the group is a collective of accomplished professionals that have managed to keep some grit in their playing. They help push Clapton along, forcing him to spit out crackling solos throughout the album. However, the performances aren't consistent on *Just One Night*—there are plenty of dynamic moments like "Double Trouble" and "Rambling On My Mind," but they are weighed down by pedestrian renditions of songs like "All Our Past Times." Nevertheless, more than any other Clapton live album, *Just One Night* suggests the guitarist's in-concert potential. It's just too bad that the recording didn't occur on a night when he *did* fulfill all of that potential. —*Stephen Thomas Erlewine*

Money and Cigarettes / Feb. 1983 / Reprise ✦✦✦✦
Recorded with some old friends—including Ry Cooder, Duck Dunn, and Albert Lee—*Money and Cigarettes* is one of Clapton's finest albums. Instead of being an empty exercise in studio professionalism, the record is an appealing, low-key effort featuring

some of the smoothest blues Clapton has ever played. —*Stephen Thomas Erlewine*

☆ **Crossroads** / Apr. 1988 / Polydor ✦✦✦✦✦
A four-disc box set spanning Eric Clapton's entire career—running from the Yardbirds to his '80s solo recordings—*Crossroads* not only revitalized Clapton's commerical standing, but it established the rock 'n' roll multi-disc box set retrospective as a commercially viable proposition. Bob Dylan's *Biograph* was successful two years before the release of *Crossroads*, but Clapton's set was a bonafide blockbuster. And it's easy to see why. *Crossroads* manages to sum up Clapton's career succinctly and thoroughly, touching upon all of his hits and adding a bevy of first-rate unreleased material (most notably selections from the scrapped second Derek & the Dominos album). Although not all of his greatest performances are included on the set—none of his work as a session musician or guest artist is included, for instance—every truly essential item he recorded is present on these four discs. No other Clapton album accurately explains why the guitarist was so influential, or demonstrates exactly what he accomplished. —*Stephen Thomas Erlewine*

24 Nights / Oct. 8, 1991 / Reprise ✦✦
Eric Clapton, who had not released a live album since 1980, had several good reasons to release one in the early '90s. For one thing, his spare backup band of keyboardist Greg Phillinganes, bassist Nathan East, and drummer Steve Ferrone, was his best live unit ever, and its powerful live versions of Cream classics like "White Room" and "Sunshine Of Your Love" deserved to be documented. For another, since 1987, Clapton had been playing an annual series of concerts at the Royal Albert Hall in London, putting together various special shows—blues nights, orchestral nights, etc. *24 Nights*, a double album, was culled from two years of such shows, 1990 and 1991, and it demonstrated the breadth of Clapton's work, from his hot regular band to assemblages of bluesmen like Buddy Guy and Robert Cray to examples of his soundtrack work with an orchestra led by Michael Kamen. The result was an album that came across as a lavishly constructed retrospective and a testament to Clapton's musical stature. But it made little impact upon release (though it quickly went gold), perhaps because events overcame it—three months later, Clapton's elegy for his baby son, "Tears In Heaven," was all over the radio, and a few months after that he was redefining himself on *MTV Unplugged*—a live show as austere as *24 Nights* was grand. Still, it would be hard to find a more thorough demonstration of Clapton's abilities than the one presented here. —*William Ruhlmann*

Unplugged / Aug. 18, 1992 / Reprise ✦✦✦✦✦
Clapton's *Unplugged* was responsible for making acoustic-based music, and unplugged albums in particular, a hot trend in the early '90s. Clapton's concert was not only one of the finest *Unplugged* episodes, but was also some of the finest music he had recorded in years. Instead of the slick productions that tainted his '80s albums, the music was straightforward and direct, alternating between his pop numbers and traditional blues songs. The result was some of the most genuine, heartfelt music the guitarist has ever committed to tape. And some of his most popular—the album sold over seven million copies in the U.S. and won several Grammies. —*Stephen Thomas Erlewine*

From the Cradle / Sep. 13, 1994 / Reprise ✦✦✦✦✦
For years, fans craved an all-blues album from Clapton; he waited until 1994 to deliver *From the Cradle*. The album manages to recreate the ambience of post-war electric blues, right down to the bottomless thump of the rhythm section. If it wasn't for Clapton's labored vocals, everything would be perfect. As long as he plays his guitar, he can't fail—his solos are white-hot and evocative, original and captivating. When he sings, Clapton loses that sense of originality, choosing to mimic the vocals of the original recordings. At times, his overemotive singing is painful; he doesn't have the strength to pull off Howlin' Wolf's growl or the confidence to replicate Muddy Waters' assured phrasing. Yet, whenever he plays, it's easier to forget his vocal shortcomings. Even with its faults, *From the Cradle* is one of Clapton's finest moments. —*Stephen Thomas Erlewine*

● **The Cream of Clapton** / Mar. 7, 1995 / Polydor ✦✦✦✦✦
Eric Clapton was contracted to Polydor Records from 1966 to 1981, first as a member of Cream, then Blind Faith, and later as a solo artist and as the leader of Derek & the Dominos. This 19-track, 79-minute disc surveys his career, presenting an excellent selection from the period, including the Cream hits "Sunshine Of Your Love," "White Room," and "Crossroads"; "Presence Of The Lord," Clapton's finest moment with Blind Faith; "Bell Bottom Blues" and "Layla" from Derek & the Dominos; and 11 songs from Clapton's solo work, among them the hits "I Shot The Sheriff," "Promises," and "I Can't Stand It." The selection is thus broader and better than that found on 1982's *Time Pieces* collection, and with excellent sound and liner notes by Clapton biographer Ray Coleman, *The Cream of Clapton* stands as the single-disc best-of to own for Clapton's greatest recordings. (Not to be confused with the popular 1987 Polydor [U.K.] compilation *The Cream of Eric Clapton*, which has since been retitled *The Best of Eric Clapton*.) —*William Ruhlmann*

Crossroads 2: Live in the '70s / Apr. 2, 1996 / Polydor/Chronicles ✦✦✦
Crossroads was a box set that appealed to both beginners and fanatics. *Crossroads 2: Live in the '70s* only appeals to fanatics. Spanning four discs and consisting almost entirely of live material (there are a handful of studio outtakes), this is music that will only enthrall completists and archivists. For those listeners, there is a wealth of fascinating, compelling performances here, as well as a fair share of mediocre, uninspired tracks. The key word for the entire album is detail—it is an album for studying the intricacies of Clapton's playing and how it evolved. For example, it's easy to hear the differences and progressions between the four versions of Robert Johnson's "Rambling On My Mind." And it is Clapton that evolves, not his supporting band—although they are proficient, they are hardly exciting. However, their static, professional support provides a nice bed to chart Slowhand's growth over the course of the decade, simply because he is *always* the focal point. *Crossroads 2* may only be for a collector, but for those collectors, it is a treasure, even if some of the tracks are fool's gold. —*Stephen Thomas Erlewine*

W.C. Clark Blues Review

b. Austin, TX
Guitar, Vocals / Modern Electric Blues, Texas Blues
A mainstay of the burgeoning Austin, TX, blues circuit, guitarist W.C. Clark began playing during the 1950s. He was a member of the Triple Threat Revue with a young Stevie Ray Vaughan and Lou Ann Barton, and co-wrote one of their best-known songs, "Cold Shot" (which appears on Clark's long-overdue 1994 national CD debut, *Heart of Gold*, for Black Top Records). —*Bill Dahl*

● **Heart of Gold** / May 2, 1994 / Black Top ✦✦✦✦✦
This Austin veteran puts together an excellent national debut CD. —*Bill Dahl*

William Clarke

b. Mar. 29, 1951, Inglewood, CA
Harmonica, Vocals / Modern Electric Blues
I have had the very good fortune to hear great Chicago harp (harmonica) players like Little Walter, Junior Wells, Big Walter Horton, and others playing live in the clubs of Chicago. Those days are gone and I had given up hope of ever hearing a new voice on amplified blues harp again in my lifetime. Then came William Clarke. Technically, Clarke is a master of both the cross and chromatic harps. He takes blues on the chromatic up to and well beyond where Little Walter left it years ago. But far more important than the technique is the music. Clarke plays straightahead blues that is music to the ears and it rocks.

William Clarke was born March 29, 1951, in Inglewood, CA, and became turned onto blues during the 1960s, oddly enough by hearing covers of blues tunes by groups like the Rolling Stones. Although he had played some guitar and drums, Clarke started playing the harmonica in 1967. He states that his main early influences were Big Walter Horton, James Cotton, Junior Wells, and Sonny Boy Williamson II. In mid-1968, Clarke began listening to jazz organists such as Jack McDuff, Jimmy McGriff, Shirley Scott, and Richard "Groove" Holmes. "This had a huge influence on my playing," says Clarke. "Along with jazz saxophonists Eddie Lockjaw Davis, Gene Ammons, Lyne Hope, and Willis Jackson, the combination of tenor-sax and absorbing the grooves of tenor-sax-led organ trios had an everlasting effect on my direction in music. For my style, I incorporated the hardcore attitude and tone of the classic Chicago harmonica players along with the swinging and highly rhythmic grooves of the organ trios and to this I add my style and ideas and you have the William Clarke sound."

By the middle of 1969, Clarke was spending a lot of time in the Los Angeles ghetto clubs—South-Central Los Angeles. There he met T-Bone Walker, Pee Wee Crayton, Shakey Jake Harris, Big Joe Turner, Ironing Board Sam, J.D. Nicholson, and George "Harmonica" Smith, who would later become his greatest influence on the chromatic harp. Clarke would go from one club until it closed at 2 AM, switch to an after-hours club from 2 AM to 6 AM, and then go to jam sessions that could last until 11 AM—and still hold down a day job! Clarke spent 20 years working as a machinist and family man before launching his blues career.

Then Clarke began to see and listen more to George "Harmonica" Smith—a veteran of the Muddy Waters band. Clarke says, "To me George was bigger than life. I was always afraid to start up a conversation with him, not because I thought he was mean, but because I thought of him like a god on the harmonica." Around 1977, they became friends and started performing together. They worked together until Smith passed away in 1983. Clarke was George Smith's protégé and he became the godfather to Clarke's son Willie. Clarke says, "George and me were very close friends and in a lot of ways he was like a father to me."

Clarke recorded a number of albums prior to releasing his first CD. They are *Hittin' Heavy* (Good Time, 1978), *Blues from Los Angeles* (1980), *Can't You Hear Me Calling* (Watch Dog, 1983), *Rockin' the Boat* (Riviera, 1985), and *Tip of the Top* (Satch, 1987—nominated for a Handy Award). He won the 1991 Handy Award for blues song of the year, "Must Be Jelly," and has also received six W.C. Handy Award nominations.

Clarke writes most of his own songs, and many of them are real ear catchers. He has a working-class background and songs like "Gambling for my Bread" and "Pawnshop Bound" are right on the money—just great tunes.

William Clarke (along with Big Walter Horton and Paul Butterfield) has an almost impeccable sense of which notes to play. There are a lot of players out there (White and Black) that basically play what's on the records of the great Chicago artists. Nothing wrong with this, but no news there either. Clarke is an original. Having heard him play live a number of times, I can testify that here is the real thing—an extension of the classic Chicago-style amplified harp tradition into the present. Just listen to those first two Alligator albums—it's all on the CDs.

Harmonica recording artist Charlie Musselwhite says that Clarke is his "favorite living harp player—no doubt about it." I am in total agreement with Musselwhite. While most great players are either dead or on the decline, Clarke is available and cookin' right now. He's been playing about 200 gigs a year. Check him out. —*Michael Erlewine*

Hittin' Heavy / 1978 / Good Times ✦✦

Blues from Los Angeles / 1980 / Hittin' Heavy ✦✦

Can't You Hear Me Calling / 1983 / Rivera ✦✦✦
Can't You Hear Me Calling only gives a glimmer of what's to come from this new genius of the blues, but it is enjoyable nonetheless. —*Cub Koda*

Tip of the Top / 1987 / Satch ✦✦✦
Tip of the Top is a loose tribute to William Clarke's mentor, George Harmonica Smith, who taught Clarke many of his tricks. Clarke plays a selection of tracks that were staples in Smith's catalog (including a version of "Hard Times," which features Smith himself), as well as newer songs written in the same style. But what really makes *Tip of the Top* notable is how William Clarke begins to develop his distinctive, idiosyncratic sound on the record. Unlike his debut *Can't You Hear Me Calling, Tip of the Top* explores some new sounds, which would come to fruition in his next few albums. —*Thom Owens*

Rockin' the Boat / 1988 / Rivera ✦✦✦✦
Recorded live in 1987, this features Clarke and his regular working band on a wide variety of material showcasing his formidable talents as a vocalist and harmonica man extraordinaire. —*Cub Koda*

★ **Blowin' Like Hell** / 1990 / Alligator ✦✦✦✦✦
The title says it all. William Clarke cooks on this one, his first CD. And these are new sounds. Songs like "Lollipop Mama," "Gambling for My Bread," and "Lonesome Bedroom Blues" (all

written by Clarke) are just great tunes. "Must Be Jelly" won Clarke a W.C. Handy Award for blues song of the year in 1991. I find myself humming them. Clarke's timing and music is right on the money. With the great Alex Schultz on lead guitar. There is no doubt that Clarke is one of the few modern bluesmen who are exploring and extending the amplified blues harp tradition without violating any of its principles. No one plays chromatic blues harp with this kind of passion and sheer conviction. Hear for yourself. —*Michael Erlewine*

☆ **Serious Intentions** / 1992 / Alligator ✦✦✦✦✦
His follow-up to *Blowin' Like Hell* burns with a ferocious intensity, particularly for his groundbreaking work on chromatic harp and his ability to cover all styles with remarkable elan. Again, he wrote most of the songs, and "Pawnshop Bound," "Trying to Stretch My Money," and "With a Tear in My Eye" are real songs. Instrumentals like "Chasin' the Gator" feature Clarke with Alex Schulz on lead guitar. —*Cub Koda and Michael Erlewine*

Groove Time / 1994 / Alligator ✦✦✦✦
Here is Clarke, hot again. This time he has added a horn section on some cuts for this recording. No problem. Alex Schultz is there on lead guitar to make sure that this album rocks. Clarke once again writes most of the songs—all 15 fat tracks. By this time, his Alligator albums have a style and feel (all his own) that one looks forward to. Plenty of high-impact amplified chromatic harmonica here of the push-the-band-hard variety that Clarke does so well plus some tasty acoustic thrown in, too. —*Michael Erlewine*

The Hard Way / 1996 / Alligator ✦✦✦✦✦
His fourth CD from Alligator is his jazziest and bluesiest recording to date. Clarke has written half of the compositions and put his own sound and style on those he did not write. Highlights include "The Boss" (inspired by saxophonist Willis Jackson), which is a fast jump that finds chromatic harp riffing along with a horn section—some interesting ideas. Other tracks are the Benny Moten song "Moten Swing," "My Mind Is Working Overtime," (a Latin-tinged tune written by Clarke), and "Letter from Home." —*Michael Erlewine*

Francis Clay

b. Nov. 16, 1923, Rock Island, IL
Drums
Drummer Francis Clay was born in Rock Island, IL, on November 16, 1923. Learning music from his family, Clay was playing some guitar and entering amateur contests at the age of five. But it was drums that fascinated him and he would create his own drum set from things around the house. He turned professional when he was 15 years old. In 1941 Clay formed his first band—Francis Clay and His Syncopated Rhythm—playing behind acts like Gypsy Rose Lee, in circuses, on riverboats, etc. This lasted until around 1944. He returned to his home in 1946 and ran a booking office, recording studio, and taught drums. Around 1947 Clay was playing with George "Harmonica" Smith in Chicago. In the early '50s he toured with jazz organist Jack McDuff.

In 1957, Clay took a fill-in job with Muddy Waters and, since he had only played jazz, had no idea how to play the blues. Muddy Waters taught him and in several days they had the thing together. Waters asked him to stay on and Clay was there for the next four years.

In 1962, Clay left Muddy Waters and formed a band with James Cotton, which lasted about a year. Clay then worked with Otis Rush, Buddy Guy, Bobby Fields, and others. In 1965, Clay rejoined Muddy Waters for a stint of almost two years.

In the late '60s, Clay worked and recorded with a number of artists including James Cotton, Muddy Waters, Lightnin' Hopkins, John Lee Hooker, Big Mama Thornton, Victoria Spivey, George "Harmonica" Smith, Shakey Jake Harris, Sunnyland Slim and others. Due to knee problems, Clay has not done much playing in recent years. Francis Clay has been called "the definitive Muddy Waters drummer." He resides in San Francisco. —*Michael Erlewine*

Willie Clayton

b. Mar. 29, 1955, Mississippi
Vocals / Chicago Blues
As long as he's been recording (since 1969), one might think that Willie Clayton is an old geezer. No way—he's barely past the age of 40 and is just hitting his commercial stride with a couple of recent blues-soul albums for Ace that have sold well to the

Southern market (where the two interrelated idioms have never been deemed mutually exclusive).

After his debut single for Duplex, "That's the Way Daddy Did," went nowhere, Clayton left Mississippi for Chicago in 1971. Like his older Windy City compatriots Otis Clay and Syl Johnson, the young singer ended up contracted to Hi Records in Memphis, where he worked with producer Willie Mitchell and the vaunted Hi rhythm section. Hi issued a series of fine Clayton efforts on its Pawn subsidiary, including "I Must Be Losin' You," "It's Time You Made Up Your Mind," and "Baby You're Ready," but none of them hit. Finally, in 1984, Clayton enjoyed a taste of soul success when his "Tell Me" (produced by General Crook) and "What a Way to Put It" for Compleat Records nudged on to the R&B charts.

Let's Get Together, Clayton's 1993 album for Johnny Vincent's Ace logo, was a smooth soul-blues hybrid dominated by originals but titled after Al Green's immortal hit. *Simply Beautiful,* his Ace follow-up, found Clayton mixing dusties by Rev. Al, Aretha Franklin, and Arthur Crudup with his own stuff. —*Bill Dahl*

Let's Get Together / 1993 / Ace ♦♦♦
Contemporary Southern deep soul with a strong taste of blues underlying. The clever "Three People (Sleeping in My Bed)" and "Back Street Love Affair," along with the self-penned "Feels like Love" and "Let Me Love You," are attractive showcases for Clayton's warm, assured vocal delivery. —*Bill Dahl*

Simply Beautiful / 1994 / Ace ♦♦♦
More of the same—Clayton's intimate confident vocals framed in terms midway between deep soul and contemporary blues. His own "Lose What You Got" and "Crazy for You" rate highly, along with Frank Johnson's "Love Stealing Ain't Worth Stealing" and the singer's delicate revival of Al Green's title cut. —*Bill Dahl*

No Getting Over Me / 1995 / Ichiban ♦♦♦♦♦
Worth the price of admission for Clayton's soulful remake of country crooner Ronnie Milsap's title track alone—but there's plenty more contemporary deep soul to be found on this exceptionally solid set. —*Bill Dahl*

Ace in the Hole / Feb. 13, 1996 / Ace ♦♦♦♦
The most consistent and satisfying of Clayton's contemporary output for Johnny Vincent's reactivated Ace imprint, thanks to top-flight soul-blues items like "Hurt by Love" and "My Baby's Cheating on Me," the Bob Jones-penned "Equal Opportunity" and "Bartender's Blues," and the singer's own "Happy." —*Bill Dahl*

Never Too Late / Mercury ♦♦♦♦
Underrated soul/R&B vocals. —*Ron Wynn*

Tell Me / Polydor ♦♦♦
Southern soul singer Willie Clayton shortened his first name and cut one late '80s album for Polydor. It was a well-produced and nicely sung date, but the songs, focus, and approach were so "deep" soul-oriented that it didn't get any attention from the urban contemporary types at major record companies. Nor did the company pick a single and push it. Clayton soon returned to the Kirstee label. —*Ron Wynn*

Feels Like Love / Ichiban ♦♦♦

Eddy Clearwater

b. Jan. 10, 1935, Macon, MS
Guitar, Vocals / Electric Chicago Blues
Once dismissed by purists as a Chuck Berry imitator (and an accurate one at that), tall, lean and lanky Chicago southpaw Eddy Clearwater is now recognized as a prime progenitor of West Side-style blues guitar. That's not to say he won't liven up a gig with a little duck-walking or a frat party rendition of "Shout"—after all, Clearwater brings a wide array of influences to the party. Gospel, country, '50s rock, and deep-down blues are all incorporated into his slashing guitar attack. But when he puts his mind to it, "The Chief" (a nickname accrued from his penchant for donning native American headdresses on stage) is one of the Windy City's finest *bluesmen.*

Eddy Harrington split Birmingham, AL, for Chicago in 1950, initially billing himself on the city's South and West sides as Guitar Eddy. His uncle, Rev. Houston H. Harrington, handed his nephew his initial recording opportunity—the good Reverend operated a small label, Atomic-H. Eddy made the most of it, laying down a shimmering minor-key instrumental, "A-Minor Cha

Cha" and the Berry-derived "Hillbilly Blues" (both on Delmark's *Chicago Ain't Nothin' but a Blues Band* anthology).

Drummer Jump Jackson invented Eddy's stage moniker as a takeoff on the name of Muddy Waters. As Clear Waters, he waxed another terrific Berry knockoff, "Cool Water," for Jackson's LaSalle label. By the time he journeyed to Cincinnati in 1961 to cut the glorious auto rocker "I Was Gone," a joyous "A Real Good Time," and the timely "Twist Like This" for Federal Records producer Sonny Thompson, he was officially Eddy Clearwater. Things were sparse for quite a while after that; Clearwater occasionally secured a live gig dishing out rock and country ditties when blues jobs dried up.

But Rooster Blues' 1980 release of *The Chief,* an extraordinarily strong album by any standards, announced to the world that Eddy Clearwater's ascendancy to Chicago blues stardom was officially underway. Two encores for Rooster Blues and a set for Blind Pig (1992's *Help Yourself*), along with consistently exciting live performances, have cemented Clearwater's reputation as a masterful blues showman whose principal goal is to provide his fans with a real good time. —*Bill Dahl*

● **The Chief** / 1980 / Rooster Blues ♦♦♦♦♦
This was the charismatic southpaw's debut album back in 1980, and remains his best to date. He rocks like Chuck Berry used to (but no longer can) on "I Wouldn't Lay My Guitar Down," tears up the West Side-based "Bad Dream" and "Blues for a Living," imparts a hard-driving Chi-town shuffle to "Find You a Job" and "I'm Tore Up," and gives "Lazy Woman" a decidedly un-lazy Latin tempo. One of the best Chicago blues LPs of the 1980s. —*Bill Dahl*

Two Times Nine / 1981 / New Rose ♦♦♦
Recorded originally for Clearwater's own Cleartone label and later leased to Ron Bartolucci's Baron imprint, these late-'70s sides were potent indicators of his maturing blues style. These weren't homemade sessions; all-star sidemen include drummer Casey Jones, guitarist Jimmy Johnson, and saxist Abb Locke. The title cut is a blistering Chuck Berry-styled rocker, "Came Up the Hard Way" displays a firm grasp of the West Side sound, and "A Little Bit of Blues, A Little Bit of Rock & Roll" utilizes a funky groove to foot-stomping advantage. —*Bill Dahl*

Flimdoozie / 1986 / Rooster Blues ♦♦♦
As yet unavailable on compact disc, Clearwater's encore LP for Rooster Blues wasn't quite the equal of its predecessor but registered as a solid enough outing nonetheless. The Chief coined a new term for the rollicking title track, engaged in some harrowing blues during a lengthy "Black Night" medley, and rocked the house with a '50s-styled "Do This Town Tonight." —*Bill Dahl*

Blues Hang Out / Dec. 3, 1989 / Evidence ♦♦♦
Eddy Clearwater has had a tough time shaking his "Chuck Berry imitator" label, and he includes Berry-tinged numbers at the halfway point and end of this nice, if thoroughly derivative, urban blues set recorded in 1989 for Black and Blue and recently reissued by Evidence on CD, with the familiar country boogie shuffle and tinkling licks. Clearwater could not do a set without the signature "Lay My Guitar Down," and this rendition is surging and enjoyable although inferior to the definitive one. Otherwise, it is a pile-driving and urgently performed date; Clearwater and Will Crosby swap slashing lines, crackling phrases, and answering fills. Clearwater's session contains several robust, entertaining passages, even if there is absolutely nothing you have not heard before. —*Ron Wynn*

Real Good Time: Live! / 1990 / Rooster Blues ♦♦♦♦♦
Eddy Clearwater delivers on the promise of this set's title on his best concert recording to date, recorded at a couple of Indiana nightspots. Those enduring (and endearing) Berry roots surface anew on a storming medley of "A Real Good Time" and "Cool Water," and there are more '50s-style rockers in "Hi-Yo Silver" and "Party at My House." But he exhibits a social conscience on the decided departure "Tear Down the Wall of Hate." —*Bill Dahl*

Help Yourself / 1992 / Blind Pig ♦♦♦
Clearwater wrote the lion's share of this well-produced collection, reaching back for material by Jimmy Reed, Otis Rush, and Willie Mabon to round it out. There's the usual infectious mix of shimmering West Side blues, hauling rockabilly, and even a touch of funk on "Little Bit of Blues." Guitarist Will Crosby shares lead chores with his boss, and Carey Bell (Eddy's cousin) handles the harp work. —*Bill Dahl*

Boogie My Blues Away / 1995 / Delmark ✦✦✦
Veteran producer Ralph Bass produced this collection back in
1977 for a blues LP series that never materialized; Delmark
finally brought it to domestic light recently. Solid, unpretentious
package that shows both Clearwater's West Side-styled southpaw
guitar sound and his Chuck Berry-oriented capacity for rocking
the house. —*Bill Dahl*

Mean Case of the Blues / 1996 / Cleartone ✦✦✦
Eddy's latest disc also marks the reactivation of his own record
label, Cleartone. The title item and an uncompromising "Hard
Way to Make an Easy Living" rate with the set's highlights, along
with a reprise of "Party at My House" and a feisty "Don't Take
My Blues." Eddy's current band provides supple support, aided
by harpist Billy Branch. —*Bill Dahl*

Chicago Blues Session, Vol. 23 / Wolf ✦✦
This OK live set isn't the equivalent of his later *Rooster Blues*
concert set, though. —*Bill Dahl*

Willie Cobbs

b. Jul. 15, 1932, Monroe, AR
Harmonica, Vocals / Modern Electric Blues
If for nothing else, the name of Willie Cobbs will always ring
immortal for the prominence of his composition "You Don't Love
Me," covered by everyone from Junior Wells to the Allman
Brothers. But Cobbs' own discography is dotted with other triumphs, including a 1994 album for Rooster Blues, *Down to
Earth*, that made it clear that Cobbs was alive, well, and committed to playing the blues.
    Cobbs decided the prospect of rice farming didn't appeal to
him enough to stick around his native Arkansas, so he migrated
to Chicago in 1947. He hung out with Little Walter and Eddie
Boyd while honing his harp chops on Maxwell Street. But Cobbs'
recording career didn't fully blossom until 1960, when his waxing of "You Don't Love Me" for Billy Lee Riley's Memphis-based
Mojo logo made him something of a regional star (one previous
45 for Joe Brown's Ruler imprint back in Chicago had stiffed
instantly). "You Don't Love Me" eventually was leased to Vee-
Jay—no doubt warming Cobbs' heart, since Vee-Jay boss Jimmy
Bracken had once turned down Cobbs' audition, explaining that
he sounded too much like Vee-Jay breadwinner Jimmy Reed.
    Throughout the '60s, '70s, and '80s, Cobbs recorded a slew of
obscure singles, often for his own labels (Riceland, Ricebelt,
C&F), and operated nightclubs in Arkansas and Mississippi
before cutting his long-overdue album for Rooster Blues (backed
by labelmates Johnny Rawls and L.C. Luckett). He's also managed to slip in a little cinematic action into his schedule, appearing in the films *Mississippi Masala* and *Memphis*. —*Bill Dahl*

Hey Little Girl / 1991 / Wilco ✦✦✦
Underrated blues and soul composer and vocalist Willie Cobbs
got rare time in the spotlight with this early-'90s release.
Although things were erratic in production and sound quality,
Cobbs' warm, soulful delivery made it consistently entertaining,
if not always satisfying. —*Ron Wynn*

● **Down to Earth** / 1994 / Rooster Blues ✦✦✦✦✦
The only CD widely available by the Arkansas harpist whose
chief claim to blues fame resides with his classic composition
"You Don't Love Me" (later revived by Junior Wells and the
Allman Brothers, among many others). With tasty backing by
labelmates Johnny Rawls and L.C. Luckett adding luster to
Cobbs' sturdy vocals and harp, the disc is a strong reminder that
blues is alive and well in its southern birthplace. And yes, there's
an accurate remake of his hit (segued with another of his gems,
"Hey Little Girl"). —*Bill Dahl*

Gary B.B. Coleman

b. 1947, Paris, TX
Bass, Guitar, Keyboards, Vocals / Modern Electric Blues
After a career as a local bluesman and blues promoter in Texas
and Oklahoma, Gary Coleman found his niche when he signed
over his first album, a self-produced outing originally issued on
his own label, to the fledgling Ichiban company out of Atlanta in
1986. Since that time, both Coleman and Ichiban have made
their marks in the blues field—not only has Coleman released
half a dozen of his own albums, he has also overseen production
of the bulk of Ichiban's hefty blues catalog, bringing to the studio a number of artists he'd booked or toured with in his previ-

ous career (Chick Willis, Buster Benton, and Blues Boy Willie,
among others). A singer/guitarist onstage, Coleman has often
taken on a multi-instrumentalist's role in the studio. His music
remains true to the blues and to The King legacy saluted in his
"B.B." moniker and in his acknowledged debt to fellow-Texan
Freddie King.
    Coleman began listening to the blues as a child and by the
time he was 15, he was working with Freddie King. Following
his association with King, Coleman supported Lightnin'
Hopkins and formed his own band, which played around Texas.
Gary also began booking blues musicians into clubs in Texas,
Oklahoma, and Colorado. He continued to play gigs and book
concerts for nearly two decades. In 1985, he formed Mr. B's
Records, his own independent label. Coleman released his
debut album *Nothin' But the Blues* the following year. The
album was popular and gained the attention of Ichiban Records,
which signed Coleman and re-released *Nothin' But the Blues* in
1987.
    If You Can Beat Me Rockin', Coleman's second album, was
released in 1988. That same year, he began producing albums
for a number of other artists, as well as writing songs for other
musicians and acting as an A&R scout for Ichiban. Between 1988
and 1992, he released six records and produced another 30,
including albums for Little Johnny Taylor and Buster Benton.
Coleman continued to be active in the mid-'90s, both as a performing and recording artist, as well as a producer. —*Jim O'Neal
& Stephen Thomas Erlewine*

Nothin' But the Blues / 1987 / Ichiban ✦✦✦✦✦
With a dark overall tone, this album is sad and introspective, and
one of his more consistent records. It includes two very good
slow blues, "Let Me Love You Baby" and "Shame on You." —*Niles
J. Frantz*

If You Can Beat Me Rockin'... / 1988 / Ichiban ✦✦✦✦✦
Coleman was influenced by Jimmy Reed, T-Bone Walker, B.B.
King, and Lightnin' Hopkins, along with Country & Western,
Cajun, and early rock 'n' roll. —*Niles J. Frantz*

● **The Best of Gary B. B. Coleman** / 1991 / Ichiban ✦✦✦✦✦
This is a good career overview, though it does expose a certain
lack of originality and diversity. —*Niles J. Frantz*

Romance Without Finance... / 1991 / Ichiban ✦✦✦
Romance Without Finance Is a Nuisance is a little funkier and
a little more naughty than other Coleman recordings. —*Niles J.
Frantz*

Jaybird Coleman

b. May 20, 1896, Gainsville, AL, d. Jan. 28, 1950, Tuskegee, AL
Guitar, Vocals, Harmonica, Jug / Acoustic Delta Blues
Jaybird Coleman was an early blues harmonica player. Although
he only recorded a handful of sides and his technique wasn't particularly groundbreaking, his music was strong and a good representation of the sound of country-blues harmonica in the early
'30s.
    Coleman was the son of sharecroppers. As a child, he taught
himself how to play harmonica. He would perform at parties,
both for his family and friends. Coleman served in the Army
during World War I. After his discharge, he moved to the
Birmingham, AL, area. While he lived in Birmingham, he would
perform on street corners and occasionally play with the
Birmingham Jug Band.
    Jaybird made his first recordings in 1927—the results were
released on Gennett, Silvertone, and Black Patti. For the next few
years, he simply played on street corners. Coleman cut his final
sessions in 1930, supported by the Birmingham Jug Band. These
recordings appeared on the Okeh record label.
    During the '30s and '40s, Coleman played on street corners
throughout Alabama. By the end of the '40s, he had disappeared
from the state's blues scene. In 1950, Jaybird Coleman died of
cancer. —*Stephen Thomas Erlewine*

● **1927–1930** / 1993 / Document ✦✦✦✦
Jaybird Coleman wasn't one of the most distinctive early country blues harmonica players, but he nevertheless made engaging, entertaining music. All of his recordings—which only
totalled 11 sides—are collected on Document's *1927–1930*. For
fans of the genre, there are some cuts of interest here, but the
music doesn't have enough weight to be of interest to anyone
but country blues fanatics. —*Thom Owens*

Albert Collins

b. Oct. 3, 1932, Leona, TX, **d.** Nov. 24, 1993, Las Vegas, NV
Guitar, Vocals / Electric Texas Blues

Albert Collins, "The Master of the Telecaster," "The Iceman," and "The Razor Blade" was robbed of his best years as a blues performer by a bout with liver cancer that ended with his premature death on November 24, 1993. He was just 61 years old. The highly influential, totally original Collins, like the late John Campbell, was on the cusp of a much wider worldwide following via his deal with Virgin Records' Pointblank subsidiary. However, unlike Campbell, Collins had performed for many more years, in obscurity, before finally finding a following in the mid-'80s.

Collins was born October 1, 1932, in Leona, TX. His family moved to Houston when he was seven. Growing up in the city's Third Ward area with the likes of Johnny "Guitar" Watson and Johnny "Clyde" Copeland, Collins started out taking keyboard lessons. His idol when he was a teen was Hammond B-3 organist Jimmy McGriff. But by the time he was 18 years old, he switched to guitar, and hung out and heard his heroes, Clarence "Gatemouth" Brown, John Lee Hooker, T-Bone Walker and Lightnin' Hopkins (his cousin) in Houston-area nightclubs. Collins began performing in these same clubs, going after his own style, characterized by his use of minor tunings and a capo, by the mid-'50s. It was also at this point that he began his "guitar walks" through the audience, which made him wildly popular with the younger White audiences he played for years later in the 1980s. He led a ten-piece band, the Rhythm Rockers, and cut his first single in 1958 for the Houston-based Kangaroo label, "The Freeze." The single was followed by a slew of other instrumental singles with catchy titles, including "Sno-Cone," "Icy Blue" and "Don't Lose Your Cool." All of these singles brought Collins a regional following. After recording "De-Frost" b/w "Albert's Alley" for Hall-Way Records of Beaumont, TX, he hit it big in 1962 with "Frosty," a million-selling single. Teenagers Janis Joplin and Johnny Winter, both raised in Beaumont, were in the studio when he recorded the song. According to Collins, Joplin correctly predicted that the single would become a hit. The tune quickly became part of his ongoing repertoire, and was still part of his live shows more than 30 years later, in the mid-'80s. Collins' percussive, ringing guitar style became his trademark, as he would use his right hand to pluck the strings. Blues-rock guitarist Jimi Hendrix cited Collins as an influence in any number of interviews he gave.

Through the rest of the 1960s, Collins continued to work day jobs while pursuing his music with short regional tours and on weekends. He recorded for other small Texas labels, including Great Scott, Brylen and TFC. In 1968, Bob "The Bear" Hite from the blues-rock group Canned Heat took an interest in the guitarist's music, traveling to Houston to hear him live. Hite took Collins to California, where he was immediately signed to Imperial Records. By later 1968 and 1969, the '60s blues revival was still going on, and Collins got wider exposure opening for groups like the Allman Brothers at the Fillmore West in San Francisco. Collins based his operations for many years in Los Angeles before moving to Las Vegas in the late '80s.

He recorded three albums for the Imperial label before jumping to Tumbleweed Records. There, several singles were produced by Joe Walsh, since the label was owned by Eagles' producer Bill Szymczyk. The label folded in 1973. Despite the fact that he didn't record much through the 1970s and into the early '80s, he had gotten sufficient airplay around the U.S. with his singles to be able to continue touring, and so he did, piloting his own bus from gig to gig until at least 1988, when he and his backing band were finally able to use a driver. Collins' big break came about in 1977, when he was signed to the Chicago-based Alligator Records, and he released his brilliant debut for the label in 1978, *Ice Pickin'.* Collins recorded six more albums for the label, culminating in 1986's *Cold Snap,* on which organist Jimmy McGriff performs. It was at Alligator Records that Collins began to realize that he could sing adequately, and working with his wife Gwynn, he co-wrote many of his classic songs, including items like "Mastercharge" and "Conversation with Collins."

His other albums for Alligator include *Live in Japan, Don't Lose Your Cool, Frozen Alive!* and *Frostbite.* An album he recorded with fellow guitarists Robert Cray and Johnny "Clyde" Copeland for Alligator in 1987, *Showdown!,* brought a Grammy

award for all three musicians. His *Cold Snap,* released in 1986, was nominated for a Grammy.

In 1989, Collins signed with the Pointblank subsidiary of major label Virgin Records, and his debut, *Iceman,* was released in 1991. The label released *Collins Mix* in 1993, posthumously. Other compact-disc reissues of his early recordings were produced by other record companies who saw Collins' newfound popularity on the festival and theater circuit, and they include *The Complete Imperial Recordings* on EMI Records (1991) and *Truckin' with Albert Collins* (1992), on MCA Records. Collins' sessionography is also quite extensive. The albums he performs on include David Bowie's *Labyrinth,* John Zorn's *Spillane,* Jack Bruce's *A Question of Time,* John Mayall's *Wake Up Call,* B.B. King's *Blues Summit,* Robert Cray's *Shame and a Sin,* and Branford Marsalis' *Super Models in Deep Conversation.*

Although he'd spent far too much time in the 1970s without recording, Collins could sense that the blues were coming back stronger in the mid-'80s, with interest in Stevie Ray Vaughan at an all-time high. Collins enjoyed some media celebrity in the last few years of his life, via concert appearances at Carnegie Hall, on *Late Night with David Letterman,* in the Touchstone film, *Adventures in Babysitting,* and in a classy Seagram's Wine Cooler commercial with Bruce Willis. The blues revival that Collins, Vaughan and the Fabulous Thunderbirds helped bring about in the mid-'80s has continued into the mid-'90s. But sadly, Collins has not been able to take part in the ongoing evolution of the music. *—Richard Skelly*

Truckin' with Albert Collins / 1969 / MCA ✦✦✦✦✦
Truckin' with Albert Collins is a 1969 Blue Thumb reissue of *The Cool Sound of Albert Collins,* which was originally released on TCF Hall Records in 1965. These are the earliest recordings that Collins made and already his trademark sound is in place—his leads are stinging, piercing and direct. The album features a set of blistering instrumentals (with the exception of the vocal "Dyin' Flu") that would eventually become his signature tunes, including "Frosty" and "Frostbite." Collins doesn't just stick to blues, he adds elements of surf, rock, jazz, and R&B. These songs may not have been hits at the time, but they helped establish his reputation as the Master of the Telecaster. *—Thom Owens*

★ **Ice Pickin'** / 1978 / Alligator ✦✦✦✦✦
Ice Pickin' is the album that brought Albert Collins directly back into the limelight, and for good reason, too. The record captures the wild, unrestrained side of his playing that had never quite been documented before. Though his singing doesn't quite have the fire or power of his playing, the album doesn't suffer at all because of that—he simply burns throughout the album. *Ice Pickin'* was his first release for Alligator Records and it set the pace for all the albums that followed. No matter how much he tried, Collins never completely regained the pure energy that made *Ice Pickin'* such a revelation. *—Thom Owens*

Frostbite / 1980 / Alligator ✦✦✦
Frostbite was the first indication that Albert Collins' Alligator albums were going to follow something of a formula. The album replicated all of the styles and sounds of *Ice Pickin',* but the music lacked the power of its predecessor. Nevertheless, there was a wealth of fine playing on the album, even if the quality of the songs themselves is uneven. *—Thom Owens*

Frozen Alive! / 1981 / Alligator ✦✦✦
Frozen Alive! demonstrates the exuberant power of Albert Collins in concert and contains enough first-rate solos to make it a worthwhile listen for fans of his icy style. *—Thom Owens*

Don't Lose Your Cool / 1983 / Alligator ✦✦✦
This fourth Alligator Records effort is consistently satisfying. —*Bill Dahl*

Live in Japan / 1984 / Alligator ✦✦✦
Compared to *Frozen Alive!, Live in Japan* is a little more drawn-out and funky, featuring extended jamming on several songs. That isn't necessarily a bad thing—Collins and his bandmates can work a groove pretty damn well. Of course, the main reason to listen to an Albert Collins album is to hear the man play. And play he does throughout *Live in Japan,* spitting out piercing leads with glee. On the whole, it's not quite as consistent as *Frozen Alive!,* but that's only by a slight margin. *—Thom Owens*

Cold Snap / 1986 / Alligator ✦✦✦
Cold Snap has a stronger R&B direction than Collins' previous Alligator releases, most notably in the presence of a slicker pro-

duction. That approach doesn't suit him particularly well—he's at his best when he's just playing the blues, not when he's trying to sing. Nevertheless, he turns out a number of gripping solos, and that is what prevents *Cold Snap* from being too much of a disappointment. —*Thom Owens*

Showdown / 1987 / Alligator ✦✦✦
A summit meeting between Texas guitar veterans Collins and Johnny Copeland and newcomer Robert Cray, the set is scorching all the way. —*Bill Dahl*

★ **The Complete Imperial Recordings** / 1991 / EMI ✦✦✦✦✦
Texan Albert Collins was in the very first rank of post-war blues guitarists. This two-CD set is a reissue of all 36 sides he cut for Imperial from 1968 to 1970—representing this artist's second major recording stint. Instrumentals comprise roughly three-fourths of the material. They frame his distinctive guitar-work with a tight ensemble of organ, bass, and drums, adding at times a piano and/or second guitar, punctuated by a horn section. About ten of these tunes are as great as anything Collins ever did. They are riddled with the biting, incisive, dramatic, and economical playing that made him a legend. There are also some outstanding vocals. Although this set is not without its clinkers, it is a solid package and a must for any Collins fan. —*Larry Hoffman*

Iceman / 1991 / Capitol ✦✦✦
Albert Collins doesn't change anything for his major label debut, *Iceman*. Like its predecessors, it is slick and professional, featuring a variety of shuffles, R&B tunes, and slow blues, all stamped with Collins' trademark icy wail. None of the songs or performances are particularly noteworthy, but *Iceman* is a solid set that delivers the goods for fans of his style. —*Thom Owens*

Collins Mix (The Best Of) / Oct. 5, 1993 / Point Blank ✦✦✦✦
This album provides fresh looks at 11 Collins classics, among them such epic numbers as "Don't Lose Your Cool," "Frosty," "Honey Hush" and "Tired Man." There are slow, wailing ballads with blistering solos, electrifying uptempo wailers with a great horn section answering Collins' phrases with their own bleats, and first-rate mastering and production. Guest stars include B.B. King, Branford Marsalis, Kim Wilson and Gary Moore, while Collins injects vitality into numbers he'd already made standards years ago. This set is a wonderful tribute to an incredible guitarist and musician. —*Ron Wynn*

Live 92/93 / Sep. 12, 1995 / Point Blank ✦✦✦
Compiling a number of performances recorded shortly before Albert Collins' death, *Live 92-93* offers definitive proof that the guitarist remained vital until his last days. — *Thom Owens*

Sam Collins

b. Aug. 11, 1887, Louisiana, **d.** Oct. 20, 1949, Chicago, IL
Guitar, Vocals / Acoustic Country Blues
One of the earliest generation of blues performers, Collins developed his style in South Mississippi (as opposed to the Delta). His recording debut single ("The Jail House Blues," 1927) predated those of legendary Mississippians such as Charley Patton and Tommy Johnson and was advertised as "Crying Sam Collins and his Git-Fiddle." Collins did not become a major name in blues—in fact his later records appeared under several different pseudonyms, most notably the name Jim Foster —but his rural bottleneck guitar pieces were among the first to be compiled on LP when the country-blues reissue era was just beginning. Sam Charters wrote in *The Bluesmen*: "Although Collins was not one of the stylistic innovators within the Mississippi blues idiom, he was enough part of it that, in blues like "Signifying Blues" and "Slow Mama Slow," he had some of the intensity of the Mississippi music at its most creative level." —*Jim O'Neal*

● **Jailhouse Blues** / 1990 / Yazoo ✦✦✦✦✦
One of the '20s most fascinating, eccentric obscurities, although a little Collins goes a long way. —*Mark A. Humphrey*

Complete Recorded Works (1927-1931) / Document ✦✦✦
Every track that Sam Collins recorded at the end of the '20s and early in the '30s is included on Document's *Complete Recorded Works (1927-1931)*. Although the comprehensiveness of the set is a little intimidating for casual listeners—they should stick with the better-sequenced *Jailhouse Blues*—historians will find the collection invaluable. —*Thom Owens*

Joanna Connor

b. Sep. 13, 1962, Brooklyn, NY
Guitar, Vocals / Modern Electric Blues
What sets Joanna Connor apart from the rest of the pack of guitar-playing female blues singers is her skill on the instrument. Even though Connor has become an accomplished singer over time, her first love was guitar playing, and it shows in her live shows and on her recordings.

Brooklyn-born, Massachusetts-raised Joanna Connor was drawn to the Chicago blues scene like a bee to a half-full soda can. Connor, a fiery guitarist raised in the 1970s—when rock 'n' roll was all over the mass media—just wanted to play blues. She was born August 13, 1962, in Brooklyn, NY, and raised by her mother in Worcester, MA. She benefitted from her mother's huge collection of blues and jazz recordings, and a young Connor was taken to see people like Taj Mahal, Bonnie Raitt, Ry Cooder and Buddy Guy in concert.

Connor got her first guitar at age seven. When she was 16, she began singing in Worcester-area bands, and when she was 22, she moved to Chicago. Soon after her arrival in 1984, she began sitting in with Chicago regulars like James Cotton, Junior Wells, Buddy Guy and A.C. Reed. She hooked up with Johnny Littlejohn's group for a short time before being asked by Dion Payton to join his 43rd Street Blues Band. She performed with Payton at the 1987 Chicago Blues Festival. Later that year, she was ready to put her own band together.

Her 1989 debut for the Blind Pig label, *Believe It!*, got her out of Chicago clubs and into clubs and festivals around the U.S., Canada and Europe. Her other albums include 1992's *Fight* for Blind Pig (the title track a Luther Allison tune), *Living on the Road* (1994) and *Rock and Roll Gypsy* (1995), the latter two for the Ruf Records label.

In the 1990s, Connor, still in her early 30s, has blossomed into a gifted blues songwriter. Her songwriting talents, strongly influenced by greats like Luther Allison, will insure that she stays in the blues spotlight for years to come. —*Richard Skelly*

● **Believe It!** / 1989 / Blind Pig ✦✦✦✦✦
On the surface, *Believe It!* is standard-issue bar-band blues-rock, but it is distinguished by Joanna Connor's passion for the music. Connor believes in the music so much, it can't help but appear in the grooves every once in a while. In particular, her guitar playing is noteworthy—it's tough, greasy, and powerful. *Believe It!* suffers from a lack of memorable songs—she's still trying to develop a distinctive songwriting voice—but Connor's strong performances carry the album through any weak moments. — *Thom Owens*

Fight / 1992 / Blind Pig ✦✦✦
To date, Joanna Connor's studio work has not lived up to the live-wire energy of her personal performances. *Fight* takes a major step toward setting this right. This stuff wails, especially Robert Johnson's "Walking Blues," which Connor reinvents courtesy of some stinging slidework. While Connor's lack of dependence on cover material rates bonus points, not all her songs are memorable—even if the guitar playing is. —*Roch Parisien*

Believe It! / Blind Pig ✦✦

Ry Cooder

b. Mar. 15, 1947, Los Angeles, CA
Guitar, Vocals / Modern Electric Blues, Modern Acoustic Blues
Whether serving as a session musician, solo artist, or soundtrack composer, Ry Cooder's chameleon-like fretted instrument virtuosity, songwriting, and choices of material encompass an incredibly eclectic range of North American musical styles, including rock 'n' roll, blues, reggae, Tex-Mex, Hawaiian, Dixieland jazz, country, folk, R&B, gospel, and vaudeville. The 17-year-old Cooder began his career in 1963 in a blues band with Jackie DeShannon and then formed the short-lived Rising Sons in 1965 with Taj Mahal and Spirit drummer Ed Cassidy. Cooder met producer Terry Melcher through the Rising Sons and was invited to perform at several sessions with Paul Revere and the Raiders. During his subsequent career as a session musician, Cooder's trademark slide guitar work graced the recordings of such artists as Captain Beefheart (*Safe as Milk*), Randy Newman, Little Feat, Van Dyke Parks, the Rolling Stones (*Let It Bleed, Sticky Fingers*), Taj Mahal, and Gordon Lightfoot. He also appeared on the soundtracks of *Candy* and *Performance*.

Cooder made his debut as a solo artist in 1970 with a self-titled album featuring songs by Leadbelly, Blind Willie Johnson, Sleepy John Estes, and Woody Guthrie. The follow-up, *Into the Purple Valley*, introduced longtime cohorts Jim Keltner on drums and Jim Dickinson on bass, and it and *Boomer's Story* largely repeated and refined the syncopated style and mood of the first. 1974 saw what is generally regarded as Cooder's best album, *Paradise & Lunch*, and its follow-up, *Chicken Skin Music*, showcased a potent blend of Tex-Mex, Hawaiian, gospel, and soul music and featured contributions from Flaco Jimenez and Gabby Pahuini. 1979's *Bop Till You Drop* was the first major-label album to be recorded digitally. In the early '80s, Cooder began to augment his solo output with soundtrack work on such films as *Blue Collar, The Long Riders* and *The Border*. He has gone on to compose music for *Southern Comfort, Goin' South, Paris, Texas, Streets of Fire, Bay, Blue City, Crossroads, Cocktail, Johnny Handsome, Steel Magnolias,* and *Geronimo*. 1995's *Music by Ry Cooder* compiled two discs' worth of highlights from Cooder's film work.

In 1992, Cooder joined Keltner, John Hiatt, and renowned British tunesmith Nick Lowe, all of whom had played on Hiatt's *Bring the Family*, to form Little Village, which toured and recorded one album. Cooder next turned his attention to world music, recording the album *A Meeting by the River* with Indian musician V.M. Bhatt. Cooder's next project, a duet album with renowned African guitarist Ali Farka Toure titled *Talking Timbuktu*, won the 1994 Grammy for Best World Music Recording. —*Steve Huey*

Ry Cooder / 1970 / Reprise ✦✦✦
His debut serves as a neat prototype, with its Sleepy John Estes and Woody Guthrie covers. It also introduces a most talented musician in its leader. But it's still a prototype; the best was yet to come. —*Jeff Tamarkin*

Into the Purple Valley / Jan. 1971 / Reprise ✦✦✦✦✦
As there are no credits for other musicians on this album, and because of Ry Cooder's reputation for honesty in music, I will assume that he plays all the instruments, including the ones with no strings. He is known as a virtuoso on almost every stringed instrument and on this CD he demonstrates this ability on a wide variety of instruments. The main focus of the music here is on the era of the Dust Bowl, and what was happening in America at the time, socially and musically. There is one song by Woody Guthrie, one by Leadbelly, and some from a variety of other people all showing Ry's encyclopedic knowledge of the music of this time combined with an instinctive feel for the songs. Phenomenal is the descriptive word to describe his playing, whether it is on guitar, Hawaiian "slack key" guitar, mandolin or some more arcane instrument he has found. This is a must for those who love instrumental virtuosity, authentic reworkings of an era, or just plain good music. —*Bob Gottlieb*

Boomer's Story / Feb. 1972 / Reprise ✦✦✦✦✦
Largely laidback and bluesy, this album features a number of paeans to an America long lost. —*Jeff Tamarkin*

Jazz / 1978 / Reprise ✦✦✦
A tribute to Dixieland, with a stopover at the blues hotel. Joseph Byrd's arrangements on tunes by Bix Beiderbecke, Joseph Spence, et al., are inspired. —*Jeff Tamarkin*

Music by Ry Cooder / 1995 / Warner Brothers ✦✦✦✦✦
Since he's a limited vocalist with erratic songwriting skills, one could justifiably argue that the soundtrack medium is the best vehicle for Cooder's talents, allowing him to construct eclectic, chiefly instrumental pieces drawing upon all sorts of roots music and ethnic flavors (often, but not always, employing his excellent blues and slide guitar). This two-CD, 34-song compilation gathers excerpts from 11 of the soundtracks he worked on between 1980 and 1993 (three of the cuts, from the 1981 film *Southern Comfort*, are previously unreleased). As few listeners (even Cooder fans) are dedicated enough to go to the trouble of finding all of his individual soundtracks, this is a good distillation of many of his more notable contributions in this idiom, although it inevitably leaves out some fine moments. Still, it's well-programmed and evocative, often conjuring visions of ghostly landscapes and funky border towns. —*Richie Unterberger*

Johnny Copeland

b. Mar. 27, 1937, Haynesville, LA
Guitar, Vocals / Electric Texas Blues
Considering the amount of time he's spent steadily rolling from gig to gig, Houston-native Johnny "Clyde" Copeland's rise to prominence in the blues world in recent years isn't all that surprising. In the last few years, he's earned some well-deserved breaks: a contract with the PolyGram/Verve label has put his 1990s recordings into the hands of thousands of blues lovers around the world. It's not that Copeland's talent has changed all that much since he recorded for Rounder Records in the 1980s; it's just that major companies are again beginning to see the potential of great, hardworking blues musicians like Copeland. Unfortunately, Copeland has been forced to slow down in 1995-96 by heart-related complications, but as of this writing, Copeland had received a left ventricular assist device (L-VAD) for his heart and was continuing to perform shows within a two-hour drive of his home in northern New Jersey.

Johnny Copeland was born March 27, 1937, in Haynesville, LA, about 15 miles south of Magnolia, AR (formerly Texarkana, a hotbed of blues activity in the 1920s and '30s). The son of sharecroppers, his father died when he was very young, but Copeland was given his father's guitar. His first gig was with his friend Joe "Guitar" Hughes. Soon after, Hughes "took sick" for a week and the young Copeland discovered he could be a front man and deliver vocals as well as anyone else around Houston at that time.

His music, by his own reasoning, falls somewhere between the funky R&B of New Orleans and the swing and jump blues of Kansas City. After his family (sans his father) moved to Houston, Copeland was exposed, as a teen, to musicians from both cities. While he was becoming interested in music, he also pursued boxing, mostly as an avocation, and it is from his days as a boxer that he got his nickname "Clyde."

After recording numerous regional singles, beginning with "Rock 'n' Roll Lily" in 1958, and touring around the "Texas triangle" of Louisiana, Texas and Arkansas, he relocated to New York City in 1974, at the height of the disco boom. It seems moving to New York City was the best career move Copeland ever made, for he had easy access to clubs in Washington, D.C., New York, Philadelphia, New Jersey, and Boston, all of which still had a place for blues musicians like him. Meanwhile, back in Houston, the club scene was hurting, owing partly to the oil-related recession of the mid-'70s. Copeland took a day job at a Brew 'n' Burger restaurant in New York and played his blues at night, finding receptive audiences at clubs in Harlem and Greenwich Village.

Copeland has recorded seven albums for Rounder Records, beginning in 1981 and including *Copeland Special, Make My Home Where I Hang My Hat, Texas Twister, Bringing It All Back Home, When the Rain Starts a Fallin', Ain't Nothing but a Party* (live, nominated for a Grammy) and *Boom Boom*, and he won a Grammy award in 1986 for his efforts on an Alligator album, *Showdown!*, with Robert Cray and the late Albert Collins.

Although Copeland has a booming, shouting voice and is a powerful guitarist and live performer, what most people don't realize is just how clever a songwriter he is. His more recent releases for the PolyGram/Verve/Gitanes label, including *Flyin' High* (1993) and *Catch Up with the Blues*, provide ample evidence of this on "Life's Rainbow (Nature Song)" (from the latter album) and "Circumstances" (from the former album).

Because Copeland was only six months old when his parents split up and he only saw his father a few times before he passed away, Copeland never realized he had inherited a congenital heart defect from his father. He discovered this in the midst of another typically hectic tour in late 1994, when he had to go into the hospital in Colorado. Although he's been in and out of the hospital many times since then for costly heart surgeries, fundraising efforts for Copeland continue out of a New York City club, Manny's Car Wash. As of this writing, Copeland awaits a heart transplant at Columbia Presbyterian Medical Center in New York City. Since Copeland is more visible than most patients in need of a heart transplant, he's been put to good use to publicize the L-VAD, a recent innovation for patients suffering from congenital heart defects. In 1995, Copeland appeared on CNN and ABC-TV's *Good Morning America*, wearing his L-VAD.

Despite his health problems, Copeland's always spirited performances have not diminished all that much. His outlook on life remains positive and filled with a sense of wonder. With his recent heart troubles, Copeland has become a living symbol of the perseverance and determination that are the basis of so many great blues lyrics.

In a recent radio interview, Copeland said that doctors at the hospital told him a normal (i.e., less fit) person of his age and weight would have been dead from the kinds of heart troubles he's suffered. When told that normal people don't drive in a van for 15 hours, sleep for two hours and then fly off to Germany to do more shows there, he laughed. "I did all that crazy stuff... and if I get the chance, I'm gonna do it all over again." —*Richard Skelly*

● **Copeland Special** / 1977 / Rounder ✦✦✦✦✦
This immaculate collection put the veteran Houston axeman among the blues elite; it features searing guitar and soulful vocals. —*Bill Dahl*

Make My Home Where I Hang My Hat / 1982 / Rounder ✦✦✦
This second Rounder Records album has its share of incendiary moments. —*Bill Dahl*

Texas Twister / 1983 / Rounder ✦✦✦✦✦
Johnny Copeland's tenure on Rounder Records was mostly productive. He made several albums that ranged from decent to very good, increased his audience and name recognition and got better recording facilities and company support than at most times in his career. The 15 numbers on this anthology cover four Rounder sessions, and include competent renditions of familiar numbers. But what makes things special are the final three selections; these were part of Copeland's superb and unjustly underrated *Bringing It Back Home* album, recorded in Africa, which matched Texas shuffle licks with swaying, riveting African rhythms. —*Ron Wynn*

I'll Be Around / 1984 / Mr. R&B ✦✦✦✦
Exceptional collection of Copeland's primordial work. —*Bill Dahl*

Showdown! / 1985 / Alligator ✦✦✦✦✦
A summit meeting between Texas guitar veterans Albert Collins and Johnny Copeland and newcomer Robert Cray, the set is scorching all the way. —*Bill Dahl*

Down on Bending Knee / 1985 / Mr. R&B ✦✦✦✦✦
This second volume of his early sides is equally impressive. —*Bill Dahl*

Bringin' It All Back Home / 1986 / Rounder ✦✦✦✦
Imaginative hybrid of blues and African idioms. —*Bill Dahl*

Ain't Nothing But a Party [Live] / 1988 / Rounder ✦✦✦
Texas guitarist and vocalist Johnny Copeland didn't turn in a formula job on these six tunes recorded live at the 1987 Juneteenth festival. Indeed, the concert setting seems to put some juice in Copeland's singing; his voice isn't raspy or detached, and he actually seems exuberant about doing the umpteenth version of "Big Time" and "Baby, Please Don't Go." His band, especially saxophonist Bert McGowan, also seem to get new life from the crowd reaction and dig in behind Copeland with renewed vigor. Even Copeland's shuffle licks and patterns, which can become awfully predictable, were executed with some sharp twists and surprising turns. —*Ron Wynn*

Collection, Vol. 1 / 1988 / Collectables ✦✦✦
These early 1960-1968 Houston sides are obscure but satisfying. —*Bill Dahl*

When the Rain Starts Fallin' / 1988 / Rounder ✦✦✦
More highlights from his Rounder Records material. —*Bill Dahl*

Boom Boom / 1990 / Rounder ✦✦
Sometimes Copeland's Texas shuffle blues just don't have any bite. He came perilously close on this set to having to depend on gimmicks and experience. Copeland couldn't find any way to refresh material like "Beat the Boom Boom Baby" and "Pie In The Sky," although he tried hard with shouts, cries and moans. He was more successful on "Nobody But You," "I Was Born All Over" and "Blues Ain't Nothin'," where his soul and gospel roots helped inject some life into the lyrics. His band tried to help matters, but really couldn't elevate the proceedings. If you're only a warm to casual fan, this wasn't one of Copeland's greatest. —*Ron Wynn*

Flyin' High / Sep. 1992 / Verve ✦✦
Johnny Copeland's patented "Texas twister" style isn't as flamboyant or forceful on this ten-cut CD as on past occasions (at least instrumentally), but his vocals are in fairly good shape. Copeland is at his best on tunes where the emphasis is on style rather than lyric meaning and elaboration. He seems ill at ease on other tunes, notably the cover of "Jambalaya," where he never

gets comfortable with the bayou beat and plows on through, concluding the number competently, but never offering anything distinctive. The album doesn't cook or boil like Copeland's regional singles, or even his best Alligator material. Instead, it simmers, but winds up just slightly missing the mark. —*Ron Wynn*

Further Up the Road / 1993 / AIM ✦✦✦
This live Australian import is a no-frills Texas guitar feast. —*Bill Dahl*

Catch Up with the Blues / 1994 / PolyGram ✦✦✦

Jungle Swing / May 1996 / Verve ✦✦
Johnny Copeland's eclectic nature is on display on *Jungle Swing*, an ambitious collaboration with jazz pianist Randy Weston. Weston brings a selection of African rhythms and melodic textures to the table, which are incorporated subtly into the rhythmic underpinnings of each song. In no sense is *Jungle Swing* a worldbeat experiment—it's just a small, affectionate tribute. Even so, the African flourishes don't dominate the sound of the record. Like always, Copeland takes center stage with his clean, precise licks. At this point in his career, he knows exactly what to play and the guitarist never overplays throughout the course of the disc. There are a few weak moments on the disc, but the sheer strength of Copeland's musicianship—and his willingness to stretch out ever so slightly—make it worth the time for any of his fans. —*Thom Owens*

Collection, Vol. 2 / Collectables ✦✦✦
This is an intriguing selection of his early efforts. —*Bill Dahl*

James Cotton

b. Jul. 1, 1935, Tunica, MS
Harmonica, Vocals, Drums, Guitar / Electric Chicago Blues
At his high-energy 1970s peak as a bandleader, James Cotton was a bouncing, sweaty, whirling dervish of a bluesman, roaring his vocals and all but sucking the reeds right out of his defenseless little harmonicas with his prodigious lungpower. Due to throat problems, Cotton's vocals are no longer what they used to be, but he remains a masterful instrumentalist.

Cotton had some gargantuan shoes to fill when he stepped into Little Walter's slot as Muddy Waters' harp ace in 1954, but for the next dozen years, the young Mississippian filled the integral role beside Chicago's blues king with power and precision. Of course, Cotton prepared for such a career move for a long time, having learned how to wail on harp from none other than Sonny Boy Williamson himself.

Cotton was only a child when he first heard Williamson's fabled radio broadcasts for *King Biscuit Time* over KFFA out of Helena, AR. So sure was Cotton of his future that he ended up moving into Williamson's home at age nine, soaking up the intricacies of blues harpdom from one of its reigning masters. Six years later, Cotton was ready to unleash a sound of his own.

Gigging with area notables Joe Willie Wilkins and Willie Nix, Cotton built a sterling reputation around West Memphis, following in his mentor's footsteps by landing his own radio show in 1952 over KWEM. Sam Phillips, whose Sun label was still a fledgling operation, invited Cotton to record for him, and two singles commenced: "Straighten Up Baby" in 1953 and "Cotton Crop Blues" the next year. Legend has it Cotton played drums instead of harp on the first platter.

When Waters rolled through Memphis minus his latest harpist (Junior Wells), Cotton hired on with the legend and came to Chicago. Unfortunately, Chess Records insisted on using Little Walter on the great majority of Waters' waxings until 1958, when Cotton blew behind Waters on "She's Nineteen Years Old" and "Close to You." At Cotton's instigation, Waters had added an Ann Cole tune called "Got My Mojo Working" to his repertoire. Walter played on Muddy Waters' first studio crack at it, but that's Cotton wailing on the definitive 1960 reading (cut live at the Newport Jazz Festival).

By 1966, Cotton was primed to make it on his own. Waxings for Vanguard, Prestige, and Loma preceded his official full-length album debut for Verve Records in 1967. His own unit then included fleet-fingered guitarist Luther Tucker and hard-hitting drummer Sam Lay. Throwing a touch of soul into his eponymous debut set, Cotton ventured into the burgeoning blues-rock field as he remained with Verve through the end of the decade. In 1974, Cotton signed with Buddah and released *100% Cotton*, one of his most relentless LPs, with Matt "Guitar"

Murphy sizzlingly backing him up. A decade later, Alligator issued another standout Cotton LP, *High Compression,* that was split evenly between traditional-style Chicago blues and funkier, horn-driven material. *Harp Attack!,* a 1990 summit meeting on Alligator, paired Cotton with three exalted peers: Wells, Carey Bell, and comparative newcomer Billy Branch. Antone's Records was responsible for a pair of gems: a live 1988 set reuniting the harpist with Murphy and Tucker and a stellar 1991 studio project, *Mighty Long Time.*

Cotton still commands a huge following, even though serious throat problems (he sometimes sounds as though he's been gargling Drano) have tragically robbed him of his once-ferocious roar. That malady ruined parts of his last Grammy-nominated album for Verve, *Living the Blues;* only when he stuck to playing harp was the customary Cotton energy still evident. *—Bill Dahl*

Chicago/ the Blues/ Today!, Vol. 2 / 1964 / Vanguard ◆◆◆◆◆
Classic compilation, also starring Otis Rush and Homesick James. *—Bill Dahl*

Live & on the Move / 1966 / One Way ◆◆◆
Originally released on two vinyl platters in 1976 by Buddah, this set was digitally unleashed anew by the British Sequel label. It faithfully captures the boogie-burning capabilities of the mid-'70s Cotton outfit, fired by its leader's incendiary harp wizardry and Murphy's scintillating licks. *—Bill Dahl*

The James Cotton Blues Band / 1967 / Verve ◆◆◆
Upbeat, soul-influenced mid-'60s work by Cotton's initial solo aggregation. *—Bill Dahl*

Cut You Loose! / 1967 / Vanguard ◆◆◆
One of Cotton's earlier solo efforts. *—Bill Dahl*

100% Cotton / Mar. 1974 / One Way ◆◆◆◆
The ebullient, roly-poly Chicago harp wizard was at his zenith in 1974, when this cooking album was issued on Buddah. Matt "Guitar" Murphy matched Cotton note for zealous note back then, leading to fireworks aplenty on the non-stop "Boogie Thing," a driving "How Long Can a Fool Go Wrong," and the fastest "Rocket 88" you'll ever take a spin in. *—Bill Dahl*

High Energy / 1975 / One Way ◆◆
Shipping Cotton off to New Orleans during the mid-'70s to work with producer Allen Toussaint wasn't a good idea at all. The end result can for the most part be described as disco blues with a Crescent City funk tinge, without much to recommend it on any level. *—Bill Dahl*

● **High Compression** / 1984 / Alligator ◆◆◆◆◆
This is the best contemporary Cotton album gracing the shelves today, thanks to its ingenious formatting: half the set places Cotton in a traditional setting beside guitarist Magic Slim and pianist Pinetop Perkins, and a solid rhythm section; the other half pairs him with a contemporary combo featuring guitarist Michael Coleman's swift licks and a three-piece horn section. Both combinations click on all burners. Includes scorching theme song, "Superharp." *—Bill Dahl*

Live from Chicago Mr. Superharp Himself / 1986 / Alligator ◆◆
Thoroughly disappointing live collection taped at a Chicago nightspot called Biddy Mulligan's. Band is sloppy (especially horn section), and the harpist himself sounds uninspired. *—Bill Dahl*

Take Me Back / 1988 / Blind Pig ◆◆◆
Another back-to-the-roots campaign for the powerhouse harmonica ace, powered by guitarists Sammy Lawhorn and John Primer and piano patriarch Pinetop Perkins. Cotton attacks nothing but covers, largely of the Chicago subspecies: Little Walter's "My Babe," Jimmy Reed's "Take Out Some Insurance" and "Honest I Do," Muddy Waters' "Clouds in My Heart." Hardly indispensable, but heartfelt. *—Bill Dahl*

Live at Antone's / 1988 / Antone's ◆◆◆◆
Reuniting Cotton with his former guitarists Matt Murphy and Luther Tucker, pianist Pinetop Perkins, and Muddy Waters' ex-rhythm section (bassist Calvin Jones and drummer Willie Smith) looks like a great idea on paper, and it worked equally well in the flesh, when this set was cut live at Antone's Night Club in Austin, TX. *—Bill Dahl*

Harp Attack! / 1990 / Alligator ◆◆◆◆
Four Chicago harmonica greats, one eminently solid album.

Teamed with Junior Wells, Billy Branch, and Carey Bell, Cotton sings Willie Love's Delta classic "Little Car Blues" and Charles Brown's "Black Night" and plays along with his cohorts on most of the rest of the set. *—Bill Dahl*

Mighty Long Time / 1991 / Antone's ◆◆◆◆
Although the titles are all familiar (most of them a little too much so), Cotton and his all-star cohorts (guitarists Jimmie Vaughan, Matt Murphy, Luther Tucker, Hubert Sumlin, and Wayne Bennett, the omnipresent Perkins on keys) pull the whole thing off beautifully. Cotton's cover of Wolf's "Moanin' at Midnight" is remarkably eerie in its own right, and he romps through Muddy Waters' "Blow Wind Blow" and "Sugar Sweet" with joyous alacrity. *—Bill Dahl*

3 Harp Boogie / 1994 / Tomato ◆◆
The music on this set is actually all right, It gets a low rating because of its odd patchwork assembly. Five of the tracks come from a 1963 acoustic session recorded at an apartment on the South Side, featuring Elvin Bishop on guitar, Cotton on vocals and harmonica, Paul Butterfield on harmonica, and Billy Boy Arnold on harmonica (hence the title *3 Harp Boogie*). The other four selections are taken from his 1967 Verve album *James Cotton Blues Band,* available in its entirety on the *Best of the Verve Years* compilation. That means you probably only want this for the rarer acoustic cuts, which are good, but short value for a CD purchase, unless you're a very big Cotton fan. *—Richie Unterberger*

Living the Blues / 1994 / Verve ◆◆
All the guest stars in the world (Joe Louis Walker, Dr. John, Lucky Peterson, Larry McCray) can't mask the simple fact that Cotton's voice was thoroughly shot when he made this disc (apparently the Grammy nominating committee gratuitously overlooked this). The instrumentals, obviously, aren't affected by this malady; they're typically rousing. But whenever Cotton opens his mouth, he sounds as though he's been gargling Drano. *—Bill Dahl*

● **Best of the Verve Years** / 1995 / Verve ◆◆◆◆
Taken from the high-energy harpist's first three albums for Verve following his split from Muddy Waters (including the entirety of his fine eponymous 1967 debut), this 20-track anthology is a fine spot to begin any serious Cotton collection. In those days, Cotton was into soul as well as blues—witness his raucous versions of "Knock on Wood" and "Turn on Your Lovelight," backed by a large horn complement. Compiler Dick Shurman has chosen judiciously from his uneven pair of Verve follow-ups, making for a very consistent compilation. *—Bill Dahl*

Robert Covington

b. Dec. 13, 1941, Yazoo City, MS, d. Jan. 17, 1996, Chicago, IL
Drums, Vocals
Robert Covington, born in Yazoo City, MS, on December 13, 1941, grew up taking music and voice lessons. Active as a teenager in the drum and bugle corps, Covington played in a number of bands, including Little Melvin and the Downbeats. About to go to college (what became Alcorn State University in Lorman, MS), he chose instead to join Big Joe Turner's group when that player passed through town looking for a drummer. Turner's stage presence and vocal technique became a major inspiration and mentor for him, and they toured the South all that summer and fall.

In 1962, Covington had some small success with the Lee Covington Review and his single, "I Know." His group had a horn section, female backup signers, and backed groups like Ernie K-Doe and Ted Taylor.

Covington moved to Chicago in 1965 and played with Little Walter, Buddy Guy, Fenton Robinson, Buddy Guy, Junior Wells, and Lonnie "Guitar Junior" Brooks. He sat in with Sunnyland Slim at the Flying Fox and they began to work together on a regular basis. In 1983 he became a full-time member of the Sunnyland Slim Band. As Slim's frequency of performing declined (in his later years), Covington fronted his own band and established his own reputation. He was a hot act at Kingston Mines in Chicago, where he served as the swing singer; he even headlined one night a week. Covington's smooth delivery and big-band style voice has earned him the nickname, "golden voice." Robert Covington died on January 17, 1996, in Chicago. *—Michael Erlewine*

Blues in the Night: The Golden Voice of Robert Covington / Evidence ✦✦✦✦✦
Covington wrote six of the nine songs on this album (formerly released in 1988 on Red Beans). His strong reassuring voice is in good form, in particular on "Trust in Me." With Carl Weathersby on guitar. —*Michael Erlewine*

Ida Cox

b. Feb. 25, 1896, Toccoa, GA, **d.** Nov. 10, 1967, Knoxville, TN
Vocals / Classic Female Blues
One of the finest classic blues singers of the 1920s, Ida Cox was singing in theaters by the time she was 14. She recorded regularly during 1923-29 (her "Wild Woman Don't Have the Blues" and "Death Letter Blues" are her best-known songs). Although she was off record during much of the 1930s, Cox was able to continue working and in 1939 she sang at Cafe Society, appeared at John Hammond's "Spirituals to Swing" concert and made some new records. Ida Cox toured with shows until a 1944 stroke pushed her into retirement; she came back for an impressive final recording in 1961.

Cox left her hometown of Toccoa, GA, as a teenager, travelling the South in vaudeville and tent shows, performing both as a singer and a comedienne. In the early '20s, she performed with Jelly Roll Morton, but she had severed her ties with the pianist by the time she signed her first record contract with Paramount in 1923. Cox stayed with Paramount for six years, recording 78 songs, which usually featured accompaniment by Love Austin and trumpeter Tommy Ladnier. During that time, she also cut tracks for a variety of labels, including Silvertone, using several different pseudonyms, including Velma Bradley, Kate Lewis, and Julia Powers.

During the '30s, Cox didn't record often, but she continued to perform frequently, highlighted by an appearance at John Hammond's 1939 Spirituals to Swing concert at Carnegie Hall. The concert increased her visibility, particularly in jazz circles—following the concert, she recorded with a number of jazz artists, including Charlie Christian, Lionel Hampton, Fletcher Henderson, and Hot Lips Page. She toured with a number of different shows in the early '40s until she suffered a stroke in 1944. Cox was retired for most of the '50s, but she was coaxed out of retirement in 1961 to record a final session with Coleman Hawkins. In 1967, Ida Cox died of cancer. —*Scott Yanow & Stephen Thomas Erlewine*

Ida Cox / Jan. 27, 1954 / Riverside ✦✦✦

★ **Blues for Rampart Street** / 1961 / Riverside ✦✦✦✦✦
With Coleman Hawkins. This is latter-period Cox, with jazz all-stars. Some of her best tunes. —*Michael G. Nastos*

Wild Women Don't Have the Blues / 1961 / Rosetta ✦✦✦✦✦
Ida Cox's *Wild Women Don't Have the Blues* was recorded at the end of her career. Surprisingly, Cox's voice hadn't faded away—she could belt out a song with nearly as much power as she did in her early career. In fact, *Wild Women Don't Have the Blues* ranks as one of her finest albums. Not only is Cox in fine voice, the support Coleman Hawkins and his small group lends is strong and sympathetic, making this album one to treasure. —*Thom Owens*

The Moanin' Groanin' Blues / Jul. 1961 / Riverside ✦✦✦✦✦

Harry Crafton

b. Philadelphia, PA
Guitar, Vocals / Jump Blues
Not much is known about this Philadelphia-based guitarist and blues shouter. He produced some tasty jump blues and R&B in the early '50s for the Philly-based Gotham label with his band, The Jivetones (later, The Craft Tone). Later he recorded for various labels with The Nite Riders Orchestra, featuring blues pianist Harry Van Walls. Evidently influenced by guitarists T-Bone Walker and Tiny Grimes and vocalists Eddie "Cleanhead" Vinson and Jimmy Witherspoon. —*Niles J. Frantz*

Harry Crafton / 1987 / Collectables ✦✦

Robert Cray

b. Aug. 1, 1953, Columbus, GA
Guitar, Vocals / Modern Electric Blues
Tin-eared critics have frequently damned him as a yuppie blues wanna-be whose slickly soulful offerings bear scant resemblance

to the real downhome item. In reality, Robert Cray is one of a precious few young (at this stage, that translates to under 50 years of age) blues artists with the talent and vision to successfully usher the idiom into the 21st century without resorting either to slavish imitation or simply playing rock while passing it off as blues. Just as importantly, his immensely popular records helped immeasurably to jump-start the contemporary blues boom that still holds sway to this day.

Blessed with a soulful voice that sometimes recalls '60s great O.V. Wright and a concise lead guitar approach that never wastes notes, Cray's rise to international fame was indeed a heart-warming one. For a guy whose 1980 debut album for Tomato, *Who's Been Talkin'*, proved an instantaneous cutout, his ascendancy was amazingly swift—in 1986 his breakthrough *Strong Persuader* album for Mercury (containing "Smoking Gun") won him a Grammy and shot his asking price for a night's work skyward.

An Army brat who grew up all over the country before his folks settled in Tacoma, WA, in 1968, Cray listened intently to soul and rock before becoming immersed in the blues (in particular, the icy Telecaster of Albert Collins, who played at Cray's high school graduation!). Cray formed his first band with long-time bassist Richard Cousins in 1974. They soon hooked up with Collins as his backup unit before breaking out on their own.

The cinematic set caught a brief glimpse of Cray (even if they weren't aware of it) when he anonymously played the bassist of the frat party band Otis Day & the Knights in *National Lampoon's Animal House*. Cray's Tomato set, also featuring the harp of Curtis Salgado, was an excellent beginning, but it was the guitarist's 1983 set for HighTone, *Bad Influence*, that really showed just how full of talent Cray was.

Another HighTone set, *False Accusations*, preceded the emergence of the Grammy-winning 1985 guitar summit meeting album *Showdown!* for Alligator, which found the relative newcomer more than holding his own alongside Collins and Texan Johnny Copeland. *Strong Persuader* made it two Grammys in two years and made Cray a familiar face even on video-driven MTV.

Unlike too many of his peers, Cray continues to experiment within his two preceding genres, blues and soul. Sets such as *Midnight Stroll*, *I Was Warned* and *Shame + a Sin* for Mercury show that the "bluenatics" (as he amusedly labels his purist detractors) have nothing to fear and plenty to anticipate from this innovative, laudably accessible guitarist. —*Bill Dahl*

Who's Been Talkin' / 1980 / Atlantic ✦✦✦✦
The Pacific Northwest-based blues savior's first album in 1980 boded well for his immediate future. Unfurling a sterling vocal delivery equally conversant with blues and soul, Cray offers fine remakes of the Willie Dixon-penned title tune, O.V. Wright's deep soul romp "I'm Gonna Forget About You," and Freddy King's "The Welfare (Turns Its Back on You)," along with his own "Nice as a Fool Can Be" and "That's What I'll Do." —*Bill Dahl*

☆ **Bad Influence** / 1983 / HighTone ✦✦✦✦✦
One of Cray's best albums ever, and the one that etched him into the consciousness of blues aficionados prior to his mainstream explosion. Produced beautifully by Bruce Bromberg and Dennis Walker, the set sports some gorgeous originals ("Phone Booth," "Bad Influence," "So Many Women, So Little Time") and two well-chosen covers, Johnny "Guitar" Watson's "Don't Touch Me" and Eddie Floyd's Stax-era "Got to Make a Comeback." Few albums portend greatness the way this one did. —*Bill Dahl*

False Accusations / 1985 / HighTone ✦✦✦✦
If its predecessor hadn't been so powerful, this collection might have been a little more striking in its own right. As it is, a solid if not overwhelming album sporting the memorable "Playin' in the Dirt" and "I've Slipped Her Mind." —*Bill Dahl*

Showdown! / 1985 / Alligator ✦✦✦✦✦
Cray found himself in some pretty intimidating company for this Grammy-winning blues guitar summit meeting, but he wasn't deterred, holding his own alongside his idol Albert Collins and Texas great Johnny Copeland. Cray's delivery of Muddy Waters' rhumba-rocking "She's into Something" was one of the set's many highlights. —*Bill Dahl*

★ **Strong Persuader** / 1986 / Mercury ✦✦✦✦✦
The set that made Cray a pop star, despite its enduring blues base. Cray's smoldering stance on "Smoking Gun" and "Right

Next Door" rendered him the first sex symbol to emerge from the blues field in decades, but it was his innovative expansion of the genre itself that makes this album a genuine 1980s classic. "Nothing but a Woman" boasts an irresistible groove pushed by the Memphis Horns and some metaphorically inspired lyrics, while "I Wonder" and "Guess I Showed Her" sizzle with sensuality. —*Bill Dahl*

Don't Be Afraid of the Dark / 1988 / Mercury ✦✦✦
A follow-up to *Strong Persuader*, this suffers from weak songs, but is worthwhile for fans. —*John Floyd*

Too Many Cooks / 1990 / Tomato ✦✦✦✦
Too Many Cooks is a reissue of Robert Cray's first album, *Who's Been Talking.* —*AMG*

Midnight Stroll / Jun. 1990 / Mercury ✦✦✦
Cray went into a more soul-slanted direction for this solid collection, coarsening his vocal cords for "The Forecast (Calls for Pain)" and the rest of the set. —*Bill Dahl*

I Was Warned / Apr. 1992 / Mercury ✦✦✦
Heavy on Southern-soul influence, Cray has the voice to pull it off. —*Bill Dahl*

Shame + a Sin / Oct. 5, 1993 / Mercury ✦✦✦✦
This time, Cray veered back toward the blues (most convincingly, too), even covering Albert King's "You're Gonna Need Me" and bemoaning paying taxes on the humorous "1040 Blues." Unlike his previous efforts, Cray produced this one himself. Also, long-time bassist Richard Cousins was history, replaced by Karl Sevareid. —*Bill Dahl*

Some Rainy Morning / 1995 / Mercury ✦✦✦✦
Typically well-produced and well-played outing—mostly originals, with smoldering covers of Syl Johnson's "Steppin' Out" and Wilson Pickett's "Jealous Love" for good measure. Cray's crisp, concise guitar work and subtly soulful vocals remain honed to a sharp edge. —*Bill Dahl*

Pee Wee Crayton

b. Dec. 18, 1914, Rockdale, TX, d. Jun. 25, 1985, Los Angeles, CA
Guitar, Vocals / Electric West Coast Blues
Although he was certainly inexorably influenced by the pioneering electric guitar conception of T-Bone Walker (what axe-handler wasn't during the immediate postwar era?), Pee Wee Crayton brought enough daring innovation to his playing to avoid being labeled as a mere T-Bone imitator. Crayton's recorded output for Modern, Imperial, and Vee-Jay contains plenty of dazzling, marvelously imaginative guitar work, especially on stunning instrumentals such as "Texas Hop," "Pee Wee's Boogie," and "Poppa Stoppa," all far more aggressive performances than Walker usually indulged in.

Like Walker, Connie Crayton was a transplanted Texan. He relocated to Los Angeles in 1935, later moving north to the Bay Area. He signed with the Bihari brothers' L.A.-based Modern label in 1948, quickly hitting paydirt with the lowdown instrumental "Blues After Hours" (a kissin' cousin to Erskine Hawkins' anthem "After Hours"), which topped the R&B charts in late 1948. The steaming "Texas Hop" trailed it up the lists shortly thereafter, followed the next year by "I Love You So." But Crayton's brief hitmaking reign was over, through no fault of his own.

After recording prolifically at Modern to no further commercial avail, Crayton moved on to Aladdin, and in 1954, on to Imperial. Under Dave Bartholomew's savvy production, Crayton made some of his best waxings in New Orleans—"Every Dog Has His Day," "You Know Yeah," and "Runnin' Wild" found Crayton's guitar turned up to the boiling point over the fat cushion of saxes characterizing the Crescent City sound.

From there, Crayton tried to regain his momentum at Vee-Jay in Chicago; 1957's "I Found My Peace of Mind," a Ray Charles-tinged gem, should have done the trick, but no dice. After one-off 45s for Jamie, Guyden, and Smash during the early '60s, Crayton largely faded from view until Vanguard unleashed his LP, *Things I Used to Do*, in 1971. After that, Pee Wee Crayton's profile was raised somewhat—he toured and made a few more albums prior to his passing in 1985. —*Bill Dahl*

☆ **Pee Wee Crayton** / 1959 / Crown ✦✦✦✦✦
An ancient but indispensable collection of his Modern label output, it includes the instrumentals "Texas Hop" and "Blues After Hours." —*Bill Dahl*

The Things I Used to Do / 1970 / Vanguard ✦✦✦✦
Solid later album by the California guitar legend. —*Bill Dahl*

Peace of Mind / 1982 / Charly ✦✦✦✦✦
Mid-'50s Vee-Jay rockers. —*Bill Dahl*

Rocking Down on Central Avenue / 1982 / Ace ✦✦✦✦
Nice vinyl selection of Crayton's Modern output, split between mellow vocals and blistering instrumentals. —*Bill Dahl*

● **Blues After Hours** / 1993 / P-Vine ✦✦✦✦✦
Regrettably, this is the only compact disc available of Crayton's brilliant early sides for Modern—and it's expensive, make no mistake. But it's worth it (until Pointblank sees fit to anoint us with a domestic collection, anyway)—its 19 sides include the essential instrumentals "Blues After Hours" and "Texas Hop," along with a variety of fine vocal efforts by this California blues guitar mainstay of the late '40s and early '50s. —*Bill Dahl*

● **The Complete Aladdin and Imperial Recordings** / 1996 / Capitol ✦✦✦✦✦
Crayton was fading fast commercially by the time he cut these sides in the 1950s, though his vocal and instrumental skills, particularly his stinging guitar, were undimmed. Aside from two 1951 tracks cut for Aladdin in 1951, this 20-song compilation is devoted to his mid-'50s hitch with Imperial. The label had him record in New Orleans with Dave Bartholomew and other local musicians, giving many of these sides a hybrid jump blues/New Orleans R&B feel (Imperial would use the same approach with Roy Brown around this time). It's not his very best work, but even at its slightest this is pleasant. It's most effective, however, when the Crescent City touches are muted in favor of slicing straightahead blues riffing, as on the instrumental "Blues Before Dawn." Another obscure cut, "Do Unto Others," is nothing less than a revelation, boasting a light-years-ahead-of-its-time opening riff that sounds almost identical—we kid you not—to the blast of notes that opens the Beatles' "Revolution," cut nearly 15 years later. —*Richie Unterberger*

Arthur "Big Boy" Crudup

b. Aug. 24, 1905, Forest, MS, d. Mar. 28, 1974, Nassawadox, VA
Guitar, Vocals / Electric Delta Blues
Arthur Crudup may well have been Elvis Presley's favorite bluesman. The swivel-hipped rock god recorded no less than three of Big Boy's Victor classics during his seminal rockabilly heyday—"That's All Right Mama" (Elvis' Sun debut in 1954), "So Glad You're Mine," and "My Baby Left Me." Often lost in all the hubbub surrounding Presley's classic covers are Crudup's own contributions to the blues lexicon. He didn't sound much like anyone else, and that makes him an innovator, albeit a rather rudimentary guitarist (he didn't even pick up the instrument until he was 30 years old).

Around 1940, Crudup migrated to Chicago from Mississippi. Times were tough at first—he was playing for spare change on the streets and living in a packing crate underneath an elevated train track when powerful RCA/Bluebird producer Lester Melrose dropped a few coins in Crudup's hat. Melrose hired Crudup to play a party that 1941 night at Tampa Red's house attended by the cream of Melrose's stable—Big Bill Broonzy, Lonnie Johnson, Lil Green. A decidedly tough crowd to impress—but Crudup overcame his nervousness with flying colors. By September of 1941, he was himself an RCA artist.

Crudup pierced the uppermost reaches of the R&B lists during the mid-'40s with "Rock Me Mama," "Who's Been Foolin' You," "Keep Your Arms Around Me," "So Glad You're Mine," and "Ethel Mae." He cut the original "That's All Right" in 1946 backed by his usual rhythm section of bassist Ransom Knowling and drummer Judge Riley, but it wasn't a national hit at the time. Crudup remained a loyal and prolific employee of Victor until 1954, when a lack of tangible rewards for his efforts soured Crudup on Nipper (he had already cut singles in 1952 for Trumpet disguised as Elmer James and for Checker as Percy Lee Crudup).

In 1961, Crudup surfaced after a long layoff with an album for Bobby Robinson's Harlem-based Fire label dominated by remakes of his Bluebird hits. Another lengthy hiatus preceded Delmark boss Bob Koester's following the tip of Big Joe Williams to track down the elusive legend (Crudup had drifted into contract farm labor work in the interim). Happily, the guitarist's sound hadn't been dimmed by Father Time: his late-'60s work for Delmark rang true as he was reunited with Knowling (Willie Dixon also handled bass duties on some of his sides). Finally, Crudup began to make some decent money, playing various blues and folk festivals for appreciative crowds for a few years prior to his 1974 death. —*Bill Dahl*

That's Allright Mama / 1961 / Relic ♦♦♦
After a long studio hiatus, Crudup reentered the studio in 1961 at the behest of producer Bobby Robinson of Fire/Fury Records. The results of their brief liaison show that Crudup hadn't altered his approach one whit during the layoff—these remakes of his RCA classics sound amazingly similar to the originals. There are a few unfamiliar titles aboard this 18-song collection to make it all the more worthwhile. —*Bill Dahl*

Look on Yonder's Wall / 1969 / Delmark ♦♦♦
This late-60s Delmark session represents the third stage of his career history. —*Barry Lee Pearson*

★ **That's Allright Mama** / 1991 / RCA ♦♦♦♦♦
This may not have been where rock 'n' roll all started, but it's very likely where Elvis Presley's knowledge of blues began: 22 tracks dating from 1941 to 1954 by the guitarist whose "That's All Right" proved Presley's ticket to Sun Records stardom. Crudup was fairly limited on guitar—his accompaniment is rudimentary at best—but his songs were uncommonly sturdy (Elvis also covered "So Glad You're Mine" and "My Baby Left Me," both here in their original incarnations) and his vocals strong. —*Bill Dahl*

Meets the Master Blues Bassists / 1994 / ♦♦♦
Delmark boss Bob Koester brought Crudup back from obscurity one more time during the late '60s, and by golly, he still sounded pretty much the same. The recordings comprising this disc date from 1968-69 and team the veteran guitarist with two upright bassists of legendary status: Willie Dixon and Crudup's longtime cohort Ransom Knowling. A few remakes are aboard, but plenty of new material as well. —*Bill Dahl*

D

Larry Dale

b. 1923, Texas
Guitar / Electric Blues
A New York session guitarist who's backed some of the city's top artists, Larry Dale also made a handful of fine singles as a singer during the 1950s and early '60s.

Taking initial inspiration on his guitar from B.B. King during the early '50s, Dale made some solid sides as a leader for Groove in 1954 (including "You Better Heed My Warning" with "Please Tell Me") with a band that included another local guitar great, Mickey Baker, and pianist Champion Jack Dupree. Dale was a frequent studio cohort of the rollicking pianist, playing his axe on all four of Dupree's 1956-58 sessions for RCA's Groove and Vik subsidiaries and, under his legal handle of Ennis Lowery, on the definitive Dupree LP, 1958's *Blues from the Gutter,* for Atlantic. Dale also recorded with saxist Paul Williams during the mid-'50s for Jax, providing the vocal on "Shame Shame Shame."

Dale worked the New York club circuit during the '50s with pianist Bob Gaddy, who had a fairly successful single for Old Town in 1955, "Operator." From 1956 to 1958, Dale played with bandleader Cootie Williams before rejoining Gaddy. At last report, the two still played together.

Dale made most of his best sides as a leader when the decade turned. For Glover Records, he waxed the storming party blues "Let the Doorbell Ring" and an equally potent "Big Muddy" in 1960, then revived Stick McGhee's "Drinkin' Wine-Spo-Dee-O-Dee" in 1962 on Atlantic. Alas, none of those worthy sides made much of a splash. —*Bill Dahl*

Billy Davenport

b. Apr. 23, 1931, Chicago, IL
Drums
Drummer Billy Davenport was born April 23, 1931, in Chicago. His parents were sharecroppers from rural Alabama that migrated to Chicago in 1928. He began learning drums at the age of six, after finding an old pair of drumsticks in an alley behind the Twin Door Lounge on the South side of Chicago. A natural musician, his parents soon recognized his gift and encouraged him. He started out playing on tin cans after seeing a movie about Gene Krupa. He also admired Sid Catlett. He took drum lessons while in the Boy Scouts and went on to play jazz in high school, in the R.O.T.C., in swing bands, and various venues in the Chicago area. In 1949, he studied music for one year at Midwestern School of Music in Chicago. He played with Bob Hadley, Leo Parker, Slam Steward, Neal Anderson, Tampa Red, Sonny Stitt, and others. He got to hear everyone live—Billie Holiday, Charlie Parker, Billy Eckstine, Gene Ammons—all the greats. His drum influences included Art Blakey, Louis Bellson, and Max Roach.

From 1951 to 1955, Davenport was in the U.S. Navy, in the Mechanic Drum and Bugle Corps. In the middle 1950s, the jazz scene was on the decline and Davenport turned to blues gigs to pay the rent. In the late '50s, he played with Billy Boy Armond, Dusty Brown, and Freddy King. In 1960 he played with the Ernie Fields Orchestra and joined Otis Rush in 1961, working with him for about a year. He also worked with harp player Little Mack Simmons, Syl Johnson, Junior Wells, Mighty Joe Young, James Cotton, Muddy Waters, and Howlin' Wolf.

He met Paul Butterfield at Pepper's Lounge in 1964 and sat in with them at their gig at Big Johns on Chicago's North side.

When Butterfield's drummer Sam Lay became ill late in 1965, Butterfield called on Davenport to join the group and tour with them. Davenport's jazz background brought a different quality to the Butterfield group. It was at this time that Bloomfield was absorbing Eastern scales and with the more sophisticated drumming of Davenport, they began to work on a tune they called "The Raga." This resulted in the tune "East/West," the extended tune that was to have such an impact on rock music history. Much of this success was due to Davenport's ability to add color and tone to the composition, something not generally found in straightahead blues drummers.

Davenport retired from music in 1968 due to illness, but was playing again from 1972-1974 with Jimmy Dawkins, Willie Dixon, and Buster Benton. He again retired from 1974 to 1981, after which he joined the Pete Baron Jazztet, with whom he still works. Davenport describes his own drumming as a combination of his two idols: the two bass drums of Louis Bellson and the unique drum roll of Art Blakey. —*Michael Erlewine*

Charles "Cow Cow" Davenport
(Charles Edwards Davenport)

b. Apr. 23, 1894, Anniston, AL, **d.** Dec. 3, 1955, Cleveland, OH
Piano, Organ / Piano Blues
Charles "Cow Cow" Davenport is one of those seldom remembered names in the annals of early blues history. But a little investigation will unearth the salient fact that he played an important part in developing one of the most enduring strains of the music; yes, "Cow Cow" Davenport was one hell of a boogie-woogie piano player. Davenport worked on numerous vaudeville tours on the TOBA circuit in the 20s and early 30s, usually in the company of vocalist Dora Carr. While he's principally noted as the composer of his signature tune, "The Cow Cow Boogie," which would be revived by jazz band vocalist Ella Mae Morse during the boogie woogie craze of the early 40s, he also claimed to have written Louis Armstrong's "I'll Be Glad When You're Dead, You Rascal You," selling the tune outright and receiving no royalties or composer credits. He recorded for a variety of labels from 1929 to 1946, eventually settling in Cleveland, Ohio, where he died in 1955 of hardening of the arteries. —*Cub Koda*

● **Alabama Strut** / 1979 / Magpie ♦♦♦♦♦
Mostly solo instrumental, this is Davenport at his best. —*Cub Koda*

Charles "Cow Cow" Davenport 1926-1938 / Best of Blues ♦♦♦♦♦
The material ranges from magnificent Cow Cow Davenport solo tunes to good and not-so-good duets with a host of performers. Ivy Smith and Dora Carr are the artists with whom Davenport works best. Since these were dubbed from 78s, don't expect pristine sound. —*Ron Wynn*

Lester Davenport

b. Jan. 16, 1932
Harmonica, Vocals / Electric Chicago Blues
Until 1992, Lester Davenport's chief claims to blues fame were the 1955 Bo Diddley Chess session he played harp on (it produced "Pretty Thing" and "Bring It to Jerome") and a lengthy, much more recent stint holding down the harmonica slot with the multi-generational Gary, IN band, the Kinsey Report. That instantly changed with the issue of Davenport's own album for

64

Earwig, *When the Blues Hit You*; now this Chicago blues veteran has something on the shelves to call his very own.

Davenport hit Chicago in 1945 at age 14. He quickly soaked up the sights and sounds of the local blues scene, checking out Arthur "Big Boy" Spires, Snooky Pryor, and Homesick James, who invited the youngster to jam sessions and tutored him on the intricacies of the idiom. Gigs with Spires and James preceded his brief hookup with Bo Diddley (which included a booking behind Diddley at New York's famous Apollo Theater). Davenport led his own band while holding down a day job as a paint sprayer during the 1960s, remaining active on the West side prior to joining forces with the Kinseys during the 1980s.

Now, about that "Mad Dog" handle: it seems that Davenport liked to prowl the stage while playing a few notes on every instrument on the bandstand during his younger days. The schtick earned him the name; his tenacious playing did the rest. —*Bill Dahl*

● **When the Blues Hit You** / Aug. 1991 / Earwig ✦✦✦✦✦
Although he'd been on the Chicago scene since the 1950s, backing Bo Diddley on some of his earliest Chess recordings, this was harpist "Mad Dog" Lester Davenport's long-overdue debut album. And a fine one it was, too, filled with mainstream Windy City blues immersed in the '50s tradition. His band for the project included pianist Sunnyland Slim and guitarist John Primer. —*Bill Dahl*

Cyril Davies

b. 1932, England, **d.** Jan. 7, 1964, England
Harmonica, Vocals / British Blues
Although he's barely remembered at all at the end of the 20th century, Cyril Davies was one of the most important and influential musicians in England during the late '50s and early '60s— and, with his partner, Alexis Korner, he was one of the earliest British musicians to play a major role in the history and development of the blues as a popular medium.

Davies' first musical love was American jazz, which he started playing professionally in the early '50s. His original instruments were the banjo and guitar, and he played in various jazz outfits before meeting up with Alexis Korner in the early '50s, when they were both members of Chris Barber's jazz band. By that time, Davies had discovered American blues and had taken up the harmonica, which was to be his primary instrument for the rest of his life.

Davies and Korner discovered that they were both on the same wavelength, and formed a partnership, Korner on the guitar and Davies on blues harp. By 1955, they'd left Barber's band to try playing as a duo, and organized the London Blues and Barrelhouse Club, playing the blues one night each week in London. At that time, the crowds they attracted were small, though dedicated, and it wasn't quite a living, although they did manage to make a limited edition 10-inch album. By early 1956, they were back with Barber backing his singer/wife Ottilie Patterson in a blues-style set each night.

Then, in 1958, the blues caught fire in England in the wake of Muddy Waters' electrifying first concert tour of Great Britain. He changed the whole image of American blues in England. Now hundreds, and even thousands of teenagers began listening to American blues, and many of them began seeking out Korner and Davies. They were back on their own in 1958, and this time they were amplified. By 1962, they'd established themselves in London with a band called Blues Incorporated, and had a permanent spot on the bill each week at the Marquee Club, and recorded an album for England's Decca Records.

Davies was one of the least likely candidates for stardom. A balding, gnome-like figure, he looked more like the business manager for a jazz band than a featured soloist. But he played harmonica better than almost anyone in England at the time— he was no Sonny Boy Williamson or Little Walter, but he was as close as anyone from Buckinghamshire or anywhere else on the Sceptered Isle. His playing was soulful, and he was equally adept in a support role or stepping up to carry a number. He was also a very credible singer, with more authenticity than many younger rivals—"Someday Baby" is one of the best, and most convincing British covers of an American blues standard from the era.

Davies was a direct inspiration for numerous young blues enthusiasts, including Brian Jones and Mick Jagger, both of

whom regularly attended and even sat in with Blues Incorporated at their performances. Additionally, he had a passionate feel for the music. Davies was especially devoted to the stripped-down electric blues coming out of labels like Chess and Cobra in Chicago, and he saw (or heard) American blues as a high-energy medium.

Korner's vision of the blues, however, was more oriented toward jazz. By the time Blues Incorporated's first album, *R&B from the Marquee*, was released, Davies had quit the band over Korner's decision to add horns to the group. Blues Incorporated continued under Korner's leadership, working in a more big-band type idiom, but never again captured the attention of the public or press as the original group had. By 1963, bands like the Rolling Stones and the Animals, made up of one-time admirers of Korner and Davies, were beginning to elicit crowds and record sales beyond anything their mentors had ever dreamt of.

Davies saw what was happening and decided to compete with the new, younger bands on their own terms. He hired the Savages, the backup band for Screaming Lord Sutch, a British eccentric who might have been a parody of Screamin' Jay Hawkins—Carlo Little on drums, Cliff Barton on bass, and Nicky Hopkins on the piano could rock as hard as anyone in England. Davies added a Black vocal trio, the Velvettes, and threw in Long John Baldry to share the vocal chores with him, and the Cyril Davies Rhythm and Blues All-Stars were born.

Davies proved adept at picking songs for them as well, recording a very hard, soulful rendition of "Not Fade Away" before the Rolling Stones' cover was a hit. A handful of singles followed, for Pye and other labels, and the group flirted briefly with the pop charts during 1963.

Davies never lived to see the group succeed. He collapsed late in the year, was hospitalized with what proved to be an advanced state of leukemia, and died in early January of 1964, not yet 32 years old. His passing was mourned throughout England jazz and blues communities, and even then people on the scene knew that it would never be quite the same. Baldry kept the band going as the Hoochie Coochie Men, playing gigs and also doing session work behind the likes of Eric Clapton, Jeff Beck, and Jimmy Page.

Cyril Davies never lived long enough to see his one-time protégés the Rolling Stones begin their climb to success. But his influence can be heard indirectly on any early track by the band featuring Brian Jones' or Mick Jagger's harmonica, from "Not Fade Away" onward. It's difficult to imagine Brian Jones, in particular, ever taking up the harmonica as seriously as he did, when he did—and he may have been a better harpist than he was a guitarist—without Davies' influence and presence, amid the records of Sonny Boy Williamson, Little Walter, et al. —*Bruce Eder*

The Legendary Cyril Davies / 1957 / Folklore ✦✦✦
Early acoustic sides by Davies and Korner, reissued in 1970 on the Folklore label. The two hadn't found their way yet, and while the playing is raw and interesting, the work is a little too unfinished to be truly representative of either artist. The Marquee Club album is more representative. —*Bruce Eder*

● **R&B from the Marquee** / 1962 / Decca ✦✦✦✦
The most important of Blues Incorporated's albums, this record features Davies throughout, and is his one reasonably representative album. He may be the best thing here; his blues harp is the most accomplished and authentic sounding instrument, and his vocals are quite convincing and natural as well. —*Bruce Eder*

Dealing with the Devil: Immediate Blues, Vol. 2 / 1992 / CBS ✦✦✦✦
A multi-artist compilation that includes Davies' and the All-Stars' cover of "Someday Baby." The rest ain't bad, either. —*Bruce Eder*

Stroll On / 1992 / Sony ✦✦✦✦
Another compilation, this time featuring "Not Fade Away" and worthwhile on that basis alone. —*Bruce Eder*

Debbie Davies

b. Aug. 22, 1952, Los Angeles, CA
Guitar, Vocals / Modern Electric Blues
Like Joanna Connor and Sue Foley, Debbie Davies' first love was playing guitar. Writing good songs and developing her vocal chops came about later for this Los Angeles native now living in Connecticut. Born August 22, 1952, to musician parents in Los Angeles, Davies cut her teeth in the San Francisco Bay Area,

playing blues and rock 'n' roll for a time in college. Back in Los Angeles in 1986, she joined Maggie Mayall and the Cadillacs, an all-female R&B band led by John Mayall's wife before joining Albert Collins' Icebreakers in the late '80s. Collins used Davies to open his shows, and as part of Collins' band for three years, she got to travel throughout the U.S., Europe and Canada, playing dueling guitars nightly with Collins.

In 1991, Davies became lead guitarist for Fingers Taylor and the Ladyfingers Revue, a band made up of many of the nation's best female musicans. This group opened for Jimmy Buffett's "Outpost Tour."

Davies takes most of her inspiration from two blues guitar masters she's payed the most attention to, her late boss Albert Collins and Eric Clapton. A talented songwriter, vocalist, and most importantly, ensemble guitar player, Davies has been leading her own band since September, 1991. She has two excellent albums for the San Francisco-based Blind Pig label, *Picture This* and *Loose Tonight*. —*Richard Skelly*

● **Picture This** / 1993 / Blind Pig ✦✦✦✦✦
Debbie Davies played with Albert Collins and that experience carries her through her debut album, *Picture This*. All the way through the album, she plays and sings with a barely restrained energy, spitting out burning leads and positively wailing her vocals. The album is a mixture of solid originals and classic covers, including a version of "I Wonder Why" that features a cameo from Collins. On the whole, *Picture This* is an exciting debut. —*Thom Owens*

Loose Tonight / 1994 / Blind Pig ✦✦✦
Davies' second album, *Loose Tonight*, contains the same high-octane blues, R&B and rock 'n' roll as her first, only delivered with a slightly rougher edge. The roughness kick-starts the record into high gear, which means *Loose Tonight* delivers just as many thrills as *Picture This*. —*Thom Owens*

Blind John Davis

b. Dec. 7, 1913, Hattiesburg, MS, **d.** Oct. 12, 1985, Chicago, IL
Piano, Vocals / Piano Blues
Versatility was integral to the musical mindset of John Davis. Although he was world-renowned as a blues pianist, he was proud of his innate ability to play ragtime, a little jazz, even a schmaltzy Tin Pan Alley ditty or two. And he did it all for more than half a century.

Born in Mississippi, Davis was in reality a Chicagoan, having moved there before the age of three. He lost his eyesight after stepping on a nail when he was nine, but that didn't stop him from learning the piano as a teen. That way, he could pick up a few bucks by playing in his father's "sporting houses."

Davis held down the enviable position of house pianist for prolific record producer Lester Melrose from 1937 to 1942, rolling the ivories behind the illustrious likes of Sonny Boy Williamson, Tampa Red, and Memphis Minnie for Bluebird, Columbia, Decca, and any other firm with which the powerful Melrose was connected. After World War II, the blind pianist assembled his own trio, recording for MGM in 1949-51. He traveled to Europe with Broonzy in 1952 in what may well have been the first overseas jaunt for any American blues artist.

The pianist remained musically active after that, but seldom recorded domestically, saving most of his studio energy for his European tours (a jaunty, typically eclectic 1985 album for Chicago's Red Beans label being a notable exception). Davis' suave, genteel approach didn't jibe with the rough-edged Chicago blues of the 1950s, but his sophistication was timeless. —*Bill Dahl*

Alive "Live" and Well / 1976 / Chrischaa ✦✦✦

● **Stompin' on a Saturday Night** / 1978 / Alligator ✦✦✦✦✦
Solid blues piano. Excellent phrasing and rhythms. —*Ron Wynn*

You Better Cut That Out / 1985 / Red Beans ✦✦✦
His final session, with hot piano licks and failing vocals. —*Ron Wynn*

Rev. Gary Davis

b. Apr. 30, 1896, Laurens, SC, **d.** May 5, 1972, Hammonton, NJ
Guitar, Vocals / Acoustic Country Blues, Gospel, Piedmont Blues
In his prime of life, which is to say the late '20s, the Reverend Gary Davis was one of the two most renowned practitioners of the East Coast school of ragtime guitar. Thirty-five years later,

despite two decades spent playing on the streets of Harlem, he was still one of the giants in his field, playing before thousands of people at a time, and he was an inspiration to dozens of modern guitarist/singers including Bob Dylan, Taj Mahal, and Donovan, and Jorma Kaukonen, David Bromberg, and Ry Cooder, who studied with Davis.

Davis was partially blind at birth, and lost what little sight he had before he was an adult. He was self-taught on the guitar, beginning at age six, and by the time he was in his 20s he had one of the most advanced guitar techniques of anyone in blues—his only peers among ragtime-based players were Blind Arthur Blake, Blind Lemon Jefferson, and Blind Willie Johnson. Davis himself was a major influence on Blind Boy Fuller.

Davis' influences included gospel, marches, ragtime, jazz, and minstrel hokum, and he integrated them into a style that was his own. In 1911, when Davis was still a teenager, the family moved to Greenville, SC, and he fell under the influence of such local guitar virtuosi as Willie Walker, Sam Brooks and Baby Brooks. Davis moved to Durham in the mid-'20s, by which time he was a full-time street musician, and celebrated not only for the diversity of styles that his playing embraced, but also for his skills with the guitar, which were already virtually unmatched in the blues field.

Davis went into the recording studio for the first time in the '30s with the backing of a local businessman. Davis cut a mixture of blues and spirituals for the American Record Company label, but there was never an equitable agreement about payment for the recordings, and following these sessions, it was 19 years before he entered the studio again. During that period, he went through many changes. Like many other street buskers, Davis always interspersed gospel songs amid his blues and ragtime numbers, to make it harder for the police to interrupt him. He began taking the gospel material more seriously, and in 1937 he became an ordained minister. After that, he usually refused to perform any blues.

Davis moved to New York in the early '40s and began preaching and playing on streetcorners in Harlem. He recorded again at the end of the 1940s, with a pair of gospel songs, but it wasn't until the mid-'50s that a real following for his work began developing anew. His music, all of it now of a spiritual nature, began showing up on labels such as Stinson, Folkways, and Riverside, where he recorded seven songs in early 1956. Davis was "rediscovered" by the folk revival movement, and after some initial reticence, he agreed to perform as part of the budding folk music revival, appearing at the Newport Folk Festival, where his raspy-voiced sung sermons, most notably his transcendent "Samson and Delilah (If I Had My Way)"— a song most closely associated with Blind Willie Johnson—and "Twelve Gates to the City," were highlights of the proceedings for several years. He recorded a live album for the Vanguard label at one such concert, as well as appearing on several Newport live anthology collections. He was also the subject of two television documentaries, one in 1967 and one in 1970.

Davis became one of the most popular players on the folk revival and blues revival scenes, playing before large and enthusiastic audiences—most of the songs that he performed were spirituals, but they weren't that far removed from the blues that he'd recorded in the 1930s, and his guitar technique was intact. Davis' skills as a player, on the jumbo Gibson acoustic models that he favored, were undiminished, and he was a startling figure to hear, picking and strumming complicated rhythms and countermelodies. Davis became a teacher during this period, and his students included some very prominent White guitar players, including David Bromberg and the Jefferson Airplane's Jorma Kaukonen (who later recorded Davis' "I'll Be Alright" on his acclaimed solo album *Quah!*).

The Reverend Gary Davis left behind a fairly large body of modern (i.e., post-World War II) recordings, well into the 1960s, taking the revival of his career in his stride as a way of carrying the message of the gospel to a new generation. He even recorded anew some of his blues and ragtime standards in the studio, for the benefit of his students. —*Bruce Eder*

Pure Religion & Bad Company / 1957 / Smithsonian/Folkways ✦✦✦✦✦
Moses Asch became the first producer to record Davis in a full-length album release, showcasing his dazzling guitar style more fully than ever before. —*Bruce Eder*

At Newport / 1959 / Vanguard ✦✦✦✦
One of the finest single-artist albums to come out of Newport,

not quite in the league of Muddy Waters' performance but a superb introduction to the range of his repertoire, from ragtime and novelty tunes to gospel numbers. —*Bruce Eder*

☆ **1935–1949** / 1960 / Yazoo ✦✦✦✦✦
Davis' first recordings, encompassing his short-lived 1930s studio career and a pair of sides from after the war. The 1930s material is the real article, showing Davis in his prime as a singer and player. —*Bruce Eder*

Say No to the Devil / 1961 / Bluesville ✦✦✦✦
Say No to the Devil is Rev. Gary Davis' third Bluesville album. Davis was in fine form throughout the session, playing some startlingly intricate 12-string guitar licks, blowing some rootsy harp, and singing with conviction. Between the songs, Davis tells some rambling stories, which are just as gripping and fascinating as the music itself. —*Thom Owens*

Gospel, Blues & Street Songs / Jul. 1961 / Riverside ✦✦✦✦✦
Eight of Davis' best-known gospel songs, cut in 1956 in New York, and among the most glowing sides of his career. Paired up with seven tracks cut by Pink Anderson for Riverside in 1950. —*Bruce Eder*

From Blues to Gospel / Mar. 1971 / Biograph ✦✦✦
This particular set was recorded one year before Davis' death, when he was 76 years old. Producer Arnold Caplin has combined two LPs to create this package and believes these to be the artist's very last recordings. Although the master picker pulls off some prodigious playing here—on both the six- and 12-string guitars—he is no match for his own earlier work recorded between 1935–60. Listeners already familiar with the younger Davis' playing will feel great affection and gratitude for these last recordings. —*Larry Hoffman*

Blues & Ragtime / 1993 / Shanachie ✦✦✦✦✦
The Rev. Gary Davis forsook his gospel calling for a little while between 1962 and 1966 to set down formal studio versions of many of his most important blues and ragtime repertoire. Some of the material here runs over ten minutes, as Davis lays out his best playing and singing voice. The booklet includes a fairly detailed biography as well as musical annotation. —*Bruce Eder*

Rev. Blind Gary Davis: Complete Works (1935–1949) / 1994 / Document ✦✦✦✦✦
The multi-volume series *Rev. Blind Gary Davis: Complete Works (1935–1949)* presents every track the guitarist recorded druing the late '30s and '40s. Although there is a staggering amount of brilliant music here, it is presented in a way that only makes it of interest to historians and completists. Most of the best material here is available on more concise collections and the majority of blues fans will find those albums, particularly Yazoo's *Complete Early Recordings*, preferable to this massive series. —*Thom Owens*

★ **Complete Early Recordings** / 1994 / Yazoo ✦✦✦✦
Complete Early Recordings collects the highlights of Rev. Gary Davis' work from the late '30s, presented in an intelligent and wisely-sequenced fashion. This is country blues at its purest and finest, and a necessary addition to nearly any blues collection. —*Thom Owens*

New Blues & Gospel / ✦✦✦
As the title suggests, *New Blues & Gospel* is equally divided between blues and gospel recordings. Recorded in 1971, Gary Davis was past his prime when these tracks were cut, but he still manages to invest the songs with grit and passion. It's a minor entry in his catalog, but completists will find the album of interest. —*Thom Owens*

At "Al Matthes" / ✦✦✦
At "Al Matthes" is taken from a collection of private acetates from 1966 and the sound suffers somewhat, but not the performances. Rev. Gary Davis runs through a selection of blues and rags—his performances are divided equally between instrumentals and vocals. Davis is relaxed and engaging, making this a small rough gem in his catalog. —*Thom Owens*

Guy Davis

b. May 12, 1952
Guitar, Vocals / Modern Acoustic Blues
Guy Davis is one of the most talked-about arrivals on the acoustic blues scene in recent years. Although he's been quietly honing his craft in the bars and coffeehouses around his Bronx,

NY home for the last ten years, this talented playwright, director, actor, scriptwriter, songwriter, singer and guitarist has only recently gained national attention through his acclaimed debut for the Minneapolis-based Red House label, *Stomp Down Rider*.

The son of famous African-American thespians and playwrights Ossie Davis and Ruby Dee, Davis was born May 12, 1952. He's written and performed in blues-oriented plays (*In Bed with the Blues: The Adventures of Fishy Waters*) and has also used his musical talents in plays written by his mother, Ruby Dee.

Along with Keb Mo, Cephas & Wiggins and a handful of other mostly acoustic practitioners of the art form, Davis has been making inroads at festivals and clubs across the U.S. and Canada since the 1995 release of his debut. Although he won a 1993 W.C. Handy "Keeping the Blues Alive" Award for theater, it is likely that he'll be a winner in future years based on the strength of his albums. Several critics have listed Davis' *Stomp Down Rider* as one of the Top Ten blues albums of 1995.

Davis' live shows are naturally compelling because he incorporates many of the same theatrical devices (i.e., comedy, storytelling) that he learned as the child of acting parents. Before blues music chose him, Davis worked in several soap operas and in different theatrical productions around his native New York City. —*Richard Skelly*

Stomp Down Rider / Oct. 17, 1995 / Red House ✦✦✦✦
Guy Davis' debut is a surprisingly fresh collection of acoustic blues, entirely comprised of original material. Davis already sounds like a seasoned pro, delivering crisp, intelligent and passionate songs that suggest he's only beginning to achieve his potential. —*Thom Owens*

James Davis

b. Nov. 10, 1938, Prichard, AL, d. Jan. 24, 1992, St. Paul, MN
Vocals / Modern Electric Blues
James Davis went out the way entertainers often dream of. While performing at the Blues Saloon in St. Paul, MN, he suffered a fatal heart attack in mid-set and died onstage. The tragic event ended a comeback bid that warmed the heart of blues aficionados; Davis' whereabouts were so unknown prior to his triumphant reemergence that he was rumored to be dead.

His melismatic vocal delivery betraying strong gospel roots, Davis secured his first pro gig in 1957 as opening act for Guitar Slim. The flamboyant guitarist was responsible for tagging Davis with his "Thunderbird" moniker. Davis lost a drinking contest to his boss that sent him to the hospital; the singer's libation of choice that fateful day was Thunderbird wine (which Davis swore off for life).

Davis signed on with Don Robey's Houston-based Duke Records in 1961. Robey utilized his new discovery as a demo singer for Bobby Bland when Davis wasn't cutting his own singles. Two of Davis' Duke offerings, the tortured blues "Blue Monday" and "Your Turn to Cry," rank with finest blues 45s of the early '60s but did little for Davis at the time. He left Duke in 1966, opening for Joe Tex and O.V. Wright on the road before settling down.

After just about giving up entirely on show biz, Davis was tracked down in Houma, LA, by Black Top Records boss Hammond Scott and two cohorts. A 1989 album called *Check Out Time* was the happy result; sidemen on the date included two former cohorts, bassist Lloyd Lambert (Guitar Slim's bandleader) and guitarist Clarence Hollimon. The resultant acclaim catapulted Davis back into the limelight for the last years of his life. —*Bill Dahl*

Check Out Time / 1989 / Black Top ✦✦✦✦
Thought by many to be deceased, singer James Davis returned from musical invisibility to make this sparkling comeback set for Black Top. His hearty pipes sounding anything but over-the-hill, Davis roared a combination of his own fine tunes and remakes of songs first done by Bobby Bland, James Carr, and Wynonie Harris in front of a terrific combo (guitarists Anson Funderburgh and Clarence Hollimon, saxist Grady Gaines). A revival of his own slow blues "Your Turn to Cry" recalled Davis' early-'60s glory days. —*Bill Dahl*

Larry Davis

b. Dec. 4, 1936, Kansas City, MO, d. 1994
Guitar, Vocals / Electric Texas Blues
Anyone who associates "Texas Flood" only with Stevie Ray

Vaughan has never auditioned Larry Davis' version. Davis debuted on vinyl in 1958 with the song, his superlative Duke Records original remaining definitive to this day despite Vaughan's impassioned revival many years down the road.

Davis grew up in Little Rock, AR, giving up the drums to play bass. Forging an intermittent partnership with guitarist Fenton Robinson during the mid-'50s, the pair signed with Don Robey's Duke label on the recommendation of Bobby Bland. Three Davis 45s resulted, including "Texas Flood" and "Angels in Houston," before Robey cut Davis loose. From there, Davis was forced to make the most of limited opportunities in the studio. He lived in St. Louis for a spell and took up the guitar under Albert King's tutelage while playing bass in King's band.

A handful of singles for Virgo and Kent, and a serious 1972 motorcycle accident that temporarily paralyzed Davis' left side, preceded an impressive 1982 album for Rooster Blues, *Funny Stuff*, produced by Gateway City mainstay Oliver Sain. But follow-up options remained hard to come by; few blues fans could find a copy of the guitarist's 1987 Pulsar LP *I Ain't Beggin' Nobody*.

Finally, in 1992, Ron Levy's Bullseye Blues logo issued a first-class Davis set, *Sooner or Later*, that skillfully showcased his rich, booming vocals and concise, Albert King-influenced guitar. Unfortunately, it came later rather than sooner—Davis died of cancer in the spring of 1994. —*Bill Dahl*

Funny Stuff / Jun. 1983 / Rooster Blues ✦✦✦✦
Larry Davis didn't record that often, but when he did, he certainly made it count. That's the case with this fine St. Louis recording, not available yet on CD but well worth searching for at your favorite used vinyl emporium. Produced by Oliver Sain (who handled all sax work) and featuring Billy Gayles on drums and pianist Johnnie Johnson, the set is a ringing endorsement of Davis' slashing, tremolo-enriched guitar and booming vocals. —*Bill Dahl*

I Ain't Beggin' Nobody / 1985 / Evidence ✦✦✦✦✦
Only bad luck and the follies of the record industry have prevented Larry Davis from being the well-known blues star he should be. Davis never received either sustained label support or concentrated marketing and thus is only a footnote when he should be a full chapter. His playing is energetic and varied, while his vocals are animated, soulful, and expressive. He recorded the nine tracks on this '85 date (newly reissued on CD by Evidence) with longtime blues and soul producer and instrumentalist Oliver Sain at the controls, and Davis demonstrated his convincing appeal on Sain's title track, as well as the defiant "I'm A Rolling Stone" (another Sain original), Davis' own anguished "Giving Up On Love," and "Please Don't Go," a Chuck Willis composition. —*Ron Wynn*

● **Sooner or Later** / 1992 / Bullseye Blues ✦✦✦✦✦
Unless someone has the ultimate Larry Davis album still awaiting release somewhere, the late guitarist's final album looks to be his best. Sumptuously produced by organist/Bullseye Blues boss Ron Levy with the Memphis Horns providing punchy interjections, Davis roars a finely conceived concoction of covers and his own material ("Goin' Out West," "Little Rock") that represent contemporary blues at its finest. —*Bill Dahl*

Little Sammy Davis

b. Mississippi
Harmonica, Vocals / Electric Harmonica Blues
No, he never hung out with the Rat Pack on the martini-stained Vegas strip, and it's highly doubtful that he honors requests for "The Candy Man." This Little Sammy Davis is a veteran harp blower with a discography dating back to 1952 and a fine debut album on Delmark, *I Ain't Lyin'.* Where's he been all these years? Poughkeepsie, NY, of course!

Davis learned his way around a harmonica at age eight. He eventually left Mississippi for Florida, where he worked in the orange groves and met guitarist Earl Hooker. Davis cut four sides in 1952 for Henry Stone's Rockin' label in Miami as Little Sam Davis (with Hooker providing classy accompaniment) that comprised the bulk of his discography until recently. He visited Chicago in 1953, hanging out with harp genius Little Walter, Jimmy Reed, and Muddy Waters. But Davis rambled on, eventually settling in Poughkeepsie.

Other than a 45 for Pete Lowry's Trix logo, things were pretty quiet for Davis until a few years back, when he joined forces with guitarist Fred Scribner and got back into playing. Now, he's a favorite guest of popular New York morning radio personality Don Imus, he has his own band and an album on the shelves, and with any luck at all, nobody will mistake him for another diminutively proportioned entertainer by the same name. —*Bill Dahl*

I Ain't Lyin' / Oct. 3, 1995 / Delmark ✦✦✦✦✦
From out of nowhere came Little Sam Davis with this sterling set, making it clear that at least a few blues harpists of post-war vintage are still roaming around out there, just waiting to be rediscovered. Backed by a sharp rhythm section, Davis shows that he's been keeping his ear to the ground over the decades. His harp mastery and enthusiastic vocals are equally arresting. —*Bill Dahl*

Maxwell Davis

b. Kansas
Songwriter, Saxophone / Electric West Coast Blues
As a prolific all-purpose producer/songwriter/sideman, tenor saxman Maxwell Davis filled some of the same pivotal roles on the 1950s Los Angeles R&B scene that Willie Dixon handled so skillfully in Chicago. Davis arranged and produced a myriad of West Coast sessions for Modern, Aladdin, and other postwar R&B indies from the late '40s on, lending his husky sax to scads of waxings.

Davis left Kansas for L.A. in 1937, working in Fletcher Henderson's orchestra before being bitten by the R&B bug. Modern/ Kent probably kept him employed the steadiest throughout the '50s and '60s; he worked with Pee Wee Crayton, Etta James, Johnny "Guitar" Watson, Lowell Fulson, Z.Z. Hill, and plenty of others on the Bihari brothers' star-studded roster. Over at Aladdin, he worked closely with Amos Milburn and Peppermint Harris, among others. Davis didn't have much luck recording as a bandleader, although his instrumentals "Look Sharp–Be Sharp" (an R&B adaptation of the Gillette march) for Aladdin and "Tempo Rock"/"Cool Diggin'" on RPM packed a wallop. —*Bill Dahl*

● **Father of West Coast R & B** / Ace ✦✦✦✦✦

Jimmy Dawkins

b. Oct. 24, 1936, Tchula, MS
Guitar, Vocals / Modern Electric Blues, Chicago Blues
Chicago guitarist Jimmy Dawkins would just as soon leave his longtime nickname "Fast Fingers" behind. It was always something of a stylistic misnomer anyway; Dawkins' West Side-styled guitar slashes and surges, but seldom burns with incendiary speed. Dawkins' blues are generally of the brooding, introspective variety—he doesn't engage in flashy pyrotechnics or outrageous showmanship.

It took a long time for Dawkins to progress from West Side fixture to nationally known recording artist. He rode a Greyhound bus out of Mississippi in 1955, dressed warm to ward off the Windy City's infamous chill factor. Only trouble was, he arrived on a sweltering July day! Harpist Billy Boy Arnold offered the newcomer encouragement, and he eventually carved out a niche on the competitive West Side scene (his peers included Magic Sam and Luther Allison).

Sam introduced Dawkins to Delmark Records boss Bob Koester. *Fast Fingers*, Dawkins' 1969 debut LP for Delmark—still his best album to date—was a taut, uncompromising piece of work that won the Grand Prix du Disque de Jazz from the Hot Club of France in 1971 as the year's top album. Andrew "Big Voice" Odom shared the singing and Otis Rush the second guitar duties on Dawkins' 1971 encore *All for Business.* But after his Delmark LP *Blisterstring*, Dawkins' subsequent recordings lacked intensity until 1992's oddly titled *Kant Sheck Dees Bluze* for Chicago's Earwig Records. Since then, Dawkins has waxed a pair of discs for Ichiban and continues to tour extensively. —*Bill Dahl*

● **Fast Fingers** / 1969 / Delmark ✦✦✦✦✦
Still his toughest and most satisfying album to date, and still not available on CD. Dawkins burst onto the blues scene with this album at the dawn of the '70s, his slashing, angular guitar lines and reserved vocal style beautifully captured throughout the set. —*Bill Dahl*

Tribute to Orange / Nov. 30, 1971–Nov. 2, 1974 / Black & Blue
◆◆◆
Jimmy Dawkins' infrequent albums are always a joy, and that was the case when he made his first sojourn to Europe in 1970 and recorded LPs for Black & Blue, Vogue, and Excello in France and England. This disc features eight numbers pairing Dawkins and the great Gatemouth Brown and another four matching him with equally sensational Otis Rush. The Brown/Dawkins tandem duel, match, and challenge each other as Dawkins' sometimes enigmatic, sometimes bemused and often compelling vocals set the stage for their instrumental encounters. The same holds true on the Rush/Dawkins cuts. While Rush provides searing licks and twisting solos, Dawkins' singing sets the tone with its urgent inflections and weary, resigned quality. —*Ron Wynn*

All for Business / 1973 / Delmark ◆◆◆
This time around, Dawkins handed the the majority of the vocal duties to Andrew "Big Voice" Odom and concentrated on his guitar (actually, he had some potent help in that department, too: Otis Rush was on second guitar). A generally solid but not overly enthralling set, with two bonus cuts and an alternate take of "Moon Man" added to the CD version. —*Bill Dahl*

Blisterstring / Jun. 1977 / Delmark ◆◆◆
Not as impressive as either of his previous outings for Delmark, but still a great deal better than some of what would follow over the course of the next few years. —*Bill Dahl*

Hot Wire 81 / Mar. 1981 / Evidence ◆◆
Actually, more like tepid—Dawkins wasn't exactly tearing up the strings on this low-key set, which positively pales in comparison to his previous Delmark releases. —*Bill Dahl*

Kant Sheck Dees Bluze / Jun. 1991 / Earwig ◆◆◆◆
Incredibly weird title (many of the songs sport equally bizarre spellings), but a major step back in the right direction for the guitarist, whose dirty, distorted tone won't thrill the purists. —*Bill Dahl*

Blues & Pain / 1994 / Wild Dog ◆◆◆
Dawkins is back on the right track, making solid if less than earthshaking recordings that at least hint at why he once was billed "Fast Fingers." —*Bill Dahl*

B Phur Real / 1995 / Wild Dog/Ichiban ◆◆◆
Here we go again with the off-the-wall spellings...more listenable modern work from the Chicago guitarist, who's found his groove again after quite a few years of less than enthralling releases. —*Bill Dahl*

Paul deLay

b. Jan. 31, 1952, Portland, OR
Harmonica / Modern Electric Blues
Paul deLay was born in Portland, OR, on January 31, 1952, but grew up in Milwaukie, OR—a suburb of Portland. He grew up listening to classical, jazz (big band), Dixieland, barrelhouse piano, and barbershop quartets. He came to blues through rock and the various blues covers of British artists. When he discovered Chess records and the original blues recordings, he had found his vocation.
DeLay joined the band Brown Sugar in 1970, and the band played a combination of blues, soul, and R&B. They stayed together for about ten years working the local bar scene, dances, and coffeehouses. In 1979, deLay formed his own four-piece Chicago-style blues band. This became the Paul deLay Band. DeLay took Paul Butterfield as his model early on but says of his playing, "I guess, more or less, what I've ended up sounding like is a combination between Big Walter, George Smith, Sonny Boy II, and Toots Thielemans."
In 1990, deLay was arrested on cocaine-related charges and spent three years in federal prison. In the early '90s, the band released two CDs *The Other One*, and *Paulzilla*, both now available on one CD from Evidence. Almost all the songs on these CDs were written by deLay.
While deLay was serving time, his band teamed up with singer Linda Hornbuckle, calling themselves the "No Delay Band" and waited for Paul to return. Upon Paul's release, they reformed as the "Paul deLay Band" and are releasing their first post-prison album, *Ocean of Tears*, in September of 1996. The main (long standing) members of the deLay band include Peter Dammann (lead guitar), Louis Pain (keyboards), and Dan

Fincher (sax). Dammann was raised in Chicago and traces his musical roots to the blues scene there.
DeLay has an excellent voice—an apologist-style singer in the manner of Bobby Bland and Junior Parker. As a harp player, he is superb. Not just another White guy playing the records of other bluesmen, deLay is expert on both the standard Marine Band Hohner and the chromatic. He (along with William Clarke) has taken the blues chromatic to new heights. DeLay has received a number of awards, including a Handy Award nomination, and appeared at many blues and jazz festivals.
DeLay's music shows R&B, jazz, and gospel influence, but still hangs more or less in the blues groove. He has written some excellent songs in the apologetic style of singers like Bobby "Blue" Bland. He claims, "I'm really a frustrated Dixieland saxophone player." —*Michael Erlewine*

Teasin' / 1982 / Criminal ◆◆
The deLay band's first recording gave birth to Criminal Records. —*Michael Erlewine*

American Voodoo / 1984 / Criminal ◆◆◆
The standout album from the early material, this second deLay album reached #2 on the Italian blues charts. Worth seeking out. —*Michael Erlewine*

The Blue One / 1985 / Criminal ◆◆
Six tunes with the earlier band, including "Something's Got a Hold on Me." —*Michael Erlewine*

Burnin' / 1988 / Criminal ◆◆◆◆◆
Reached #20 on the *Living Blues* chart. This album was the debut of guitarist Peter Dammann. Includes hornwork by ex-Mayall sax player Chris Mercer. —*Michael Erlewine*

The Other One / 1990 / Criminal ◆◆◆
All 11 songs written by deLay plus plenty of fine harp playing. With Peter Dammann on guitar and Louis Pain on keyboards. —*Michael Erlewine*

The Best of Paul deLay: You're Fired / 1990 / Red Lightnin' ◆◆◆◆
A collection of deLay material released by the British label Red Lightnin' in May of 1990. —*Michael Erlewine*

Paulzilla / 1992 / Criminal ◆◆◆◆◆
Declared the album of the year by the Cascades Blues Association, this was completed just days before deLay's three-year visit to the pen. DeLay wrote most of the songs and there is plenty of first-rate chromatic harp playing here. With Peter Dammann on guitar and Louis Pain on keyboards. —*Michael Erlewine*

• **Take It From The Turnaround** / 1996 / Evidence ◆◆◆◆◆
Combining the best of two albums (1991's *Just This One* and 1992's *Paulzilla*) on one CD, *Take It from the Turnaround* heralds the arrival of a harp player who's been a certified blues legend in his native region of Portland, OR. DeLay blows with authenticity and a full command of his instrument and way more than a hint of reckless abandon. Traditional blues, even by modern bar-band standards, this ain't, but the high creative level of deLay's songwriting on numbers like "Second Hand Smoke," "Merry Way" and the heartfelt "Just This One" heralds the arrival of a new way of looking at things and bodes well for future recordings. As a parenthetical note, the liner notes that accompany this release are superlative, telling deLay's story in a way that's both horrifying and inspiring. The man has lived a life in the blues and not only lived to tell the tale, but has triumphed over the worst elements a road musician has to suffer through. —*Cub Koda*

Ocean of Tears / Sep. 1996 / Evidence ◆◆◆◆
Due to be released in September 1996, this features deLay after he was released from prison with his original band doing ten tunes, all written by deLay either by himself or as coauthor. Features the title cut "Ocean of Tears," "What Went Wrong" and a duet with Linda Hornbuckle, "Maybe Our Luck Will Change." —*Michael Erlewine*

Derek & the Dominos

Group / British Blues, Rock & Roll
Derek & The Dominos was a group formed by guitarist/singer Eric Clapton (born Eric Patrick Clapp, Mar. 30, 1945, Ripley, Surrey, England) with other former members of Delaney & Bonnie & Friends, in the spring of 1970. The rest of the lineup

was Bobby Whitlock (b. 1948, Memphis, TN) (keyboards, vocals), Carl Radle (b. 1942, Oklahoma City, OK,–d. May 30, 1980) (bass), and Jim Gordon (b. 1945, Los Angeles) (drums). The group debuted at the Lyceum Ballroom in London on June 14 and undertook a summer tour of England. From late August to early October, they recorded the celebrated double album *Layla and Other Assorted Love Songs* (November 1970) with guitarist Duane Allman sitting in. They then returned to touring in England and the U.S., playing their final date on December 6.

The *Layla* album was successful in the U.S., where "Bell Bottom Blues" and the title song charted as singles in abbreviated versions, but it did not chart in the U.K. The Dominos reconvened to record a second album in May 1971, but split up without completing it. Clapton then retired from the music business, nursing a heroin addiction.

In his absence, and in the wake of Allman's death in a motorcycle accident on October 29, 1971, The Dominos and *Layla* gained in stature. Rereleased as a single at its full, seven-minute length in connection with the compilation album *History of Eric Clapton* (Atco 803) (March 1972), "Layla" hit the Top Ten in the U.S. and the U.K. in the summer of 1972. It would return to the U.K. Top Ten in 1982. A live album, *Derek and the Dominos in Concert* (January 1973), taken from the 1970 U.S. tour, was also a strong seller.

Time has only added to the renown for the group, which is now rated among Eric Clapton's most outstanding achievements. The 1988 Eric Clapton boxed set retrospective *Crossroads* featured material from the abortive second album sessions. *The Layla Sessions* was a 1991 boxed set expanding that album across three CDs/cassettes. And *Live at the Fillmore* (1994) offered an expanded version of the *In Concert* album. —*William Ruhlmann*

★ **Layla and Other Assorted Love Songs** / Nov. 1970 / Polydor ✦✦✦✦✦
Quite simply, this is Eric Clapton's finest moment, full of gutsy, impassioned playing and tortured vocals. None of the love songs are simple, and the band rocks away their blues in a series of long jams that are never boring. —*Stephen Thomas Erlewine*

Derek & The Dominos in Concert / Jan. 1973 / Polydor ✦✦✦✦✦
While it isn't nearly as intense as *Layla*, *Derek & The Dominos In Concert* offers some fine playing by Clapton and his band and easily ranks among his best live albums. —*Stephen Thomas Erlewine*

The Layla Sessions / Sep. 1990 / Polydor ✦✦✦
Featuring two discs of outtakes and jams, the three-CD box *The Layla Sessions* manages to detract from the original by surrounding it with endless, dull instrumentals. Then again, all the unreleased material proves what a well-constructed album *Layla* is. —*Stephen Thomas Erlewine*

Live at the Fillmore / Feb. 22, 1994 / Polydor ✦✦✦
In his liner notes, Anthony DeCurtis calls *Live at the Fillmore* "a digitally remixed and remastered version of the 1973 Derek & The Dominos double album *In Concert*, with five previously unreleased performances and two tracks that have only appeared on the four-CD Clapton retrospective, *Crossroads*." But this does not adequately describe the album. *Live at the Fillmore* is not exactly an expanded version of *In Concert*; it is a different album culled from the same concerts that were taped to compile the earlier album. *Live at the Fillmore* contains six of the nine recordings originally released on *In Concert*, and three of its five previously unreleased performances are different recordings of songs also featured on *In Concert*—"Why Does Love Got To Be So Sad?," "Tell The Truth," and "Let It Rain." The other two, "Nobody Knows You When You're Down And Out" and "Little Wing," have not been heard before in any concert version. Even when the same recordings are used on *Live at the Fillmore* as on *In Concert*, they have, as noted, been remixed and, as not noted, re-edited. In either form, Derek & The Dominos' October 1970 stand at the Fillmore East, a part of the group's only U.S. tour, finds them a looser aggregation than they seemed to be in the studio making their only album, *Layla And Other Assorted Love Songs*. A trio backing Eric Clapton, the Dominos leave the guitarist considerable room to solo on extended numbers, five of which run over ten minutes each. Clapton doesn't show consistent invention, but his playing is always directed, and he plays more blues than you can hear on any other Clapton live recording. —*William Ruhlmann*

Bo Diddley (Ellas Otha Bates McDaniel)

b. Dec. 30, 1928, McComb, MS
Guitar, Violin, Vocals / R&B, Rock & Roll
He only had a few hits in the 1950s and early '60s but, as Bo Diddley sang, "You Can't Judge a Book by its Cover." You can't judge an artist by his chart success, either, and Diddley produced greater and more influential music than all but a handful of the best early rockers. The Bo Diddley beat—bomp, ba-bomp-bomp, bomp-bomp—is one of rock 'n' roll's bedrock rhythms, showing up in the work of Buddy Holly, the Rolling Stones, and even pop-garage knockoffs like the Strangeloves' 1965 hit "I Want Candy." Diddley's hypnotic rhythmic attack and declamatory, boasting vocals stretched back as far as Africa for their roots, and looked as far into the future as rap. His trademark otherworldly vibrating, fuzzy guitar style did much to expand the instrument's power and range. But even more important, Bo's bounce was fun and irresistibly rocking, with a wisecracking, jiving tone that epitomized rock 'n' roll at its most humorously outlandish and freewheeling.

Before taking up blues and R&B, Diddley had actually studied classical violin, but shifted gears after hearing John Lee Hooker. In the early '50s, he began playing with his longtime partner, maraca player Jerome Green, to get what Bo called "that freight train sound." Billy Boy Arnold, a fine blues harmonica player and singer in his own right, was also playing with Diddley when the guitarist got a deal with Chess in the mid-1950s (after being turned down by rival Chicago label Vee-Jay).

His very first single, "Bo Diddley"/"I'm A Man" (1955), was a double-sided monster. The A-side was soaked with futuristic waves of tremolo guitar, set to an ageless nursery rhyme; the flip was a bump-and-grind, harmonica-driven shuffle, based around a devastating blues riff. But the result was not exactly blues, or even straight R&B, but a new kind of guitar-based rock 'n' roll, soaked in the blues and R&B, but owing allegiance to neither.

Diddley was never a top seller on the order of his Chess rival Chuck Berry, but over the next half-dozen or so years, he produced a catalog of classics that rival Berry's in quality. "You Don't Love Me," "Diddley Daddy," "Pretty Thing," "Diddy Wah Diddy," "Who Do You Love?," "Mona," "Road Runner," "You Can't Judge a Book by its Cover"—all are stone-cold standards of early, riff-driven rock 'n' roll at its funkiest. Oddly enough, his only Top 20 pop hit was an atypical, absurd back-and-forth rap between him and Jerome, "Say Man," that came about almost by accident as the pair were fooling around in the studio.

As a live performer, Diddley was galvanizing, using his trademark square guitars and distorted amplification to produce new sounds that anticipated the innovations of '60s guitarists like Jimi Hendrix. In Great Britain, he was revered as a giant on the order of Chuck Berry and Muddy Waters. The Rolling Stones in particular borrowed a lot from Bo's rhythms and attitude in their early days, although they only officially covered a couple of his tunes, "Mona" and "I'm Alright." Other British R&B groups like the Yardbirds, Animals, and Pretty Things also covered Diddley standards in their early days. Buddy Holly covered "Bo Diddley" and used a modified Bo Diddley beat on "Not Fade Away"; when the Stones gave the song the full-on Bo treatment (complete with shaking maracas), the result was their first big British hit.

The British Invasion helped increase public awareness of Diddley's importance, and ever since then he's been a popular live act. Sadly, though, his career as a recording artist—in commercial and artistic terms—was over by the time the Beatles and Stones hit America. He recorded with ongoing and declining frequency, but after 1963, he never wrote or recorded any original material on par with his early classics. Whether he'd spent his muse, or just felt he could coast on his laurels, is hard to say. But he remains a vital part of the collective rock 'n' roll consciousness, occasionally reaching wider visibility via a 1979 tour with the Clash, a cameo role in the film *Trading Places*, a late '80s tour with Ronnie Wood, and a 1989 television commercial for sports shoes with star athlete Bo Jackson. —*Richie Unterberger*

Bo Diddley Is a Gunslinger / 1963 / MCA/Chess ✦✦✦✦
Not only does it sport one of the most striking album covers of its era (Diddley decked out in cowboy finery, about to get the drop on some unfortunate varmint with one of his fiercest guitars lying at his feet), this 1960 album contains some fine music. The title track continues the legend of you-know-who, while "Ride on Josephine" and "Cadillac" rock like hell (and Ed

Sullivan must have been glad to see that Diddley finally learned "Sixteen Tons"). Two bonus cuts, "Working Man" and "Do What I Say," make this one a must. —*Bill Dahl*

Bo Diddley's Beach Party / 1963 / Checker ✦✦✦✦
A blistering live album. Currently out of print but well worth any search. —*Cub Koda*

☆ **Bo Diddley/Go Bo Diddley** / 1986 / MCA/Chess ✦✦✦✦✦
There are precious few weak tracks on this combination of Bo Diddley's first two late-'50s albums for Chess/Checker, which boasts a plethora of classics ("Bo Diddley," "I'm a Man," "Before You Accuse Me," "Crackin' Up," "Little Girl," even his electric violin workout "The Clock Struck Twelve"). The only drawback: someone failed to notice that "Dearest Darling" was on both LPs, so...it's on here twice! —*Bill Dahl*

In the Spotlight / 1987 / MCA/Chess ✦✦✦✦✦
Another excellent original Checker album from 1960 that features some of Diddley's better work (including the soaring smash "Road Runner"), transferred verbatim to CD (no bonus items this time). He was in an amazingly prolific groove during this timeframe, churning out album after album, and they're all worth collecting. —*Bill Dahl*

★ **The Chess Box** / 1990 / MCA/Chess ✦✦✦✦✦
Not every single track you'll ever want or need by the legendary shave-and-a-haircut rhythm R&B/rock pioneer, but a great place to begin. Two discs (45 songs) in a great big box with a nice accompanying booklet contain the groundbreaking introduction "Bo Diddley" (never again would he be referred to as Ellas McDaniel), its swaggering flipside "I'm a Man," the killer follow-ups "Diddley Daddy," "I'm Looking for a Woman," "Who Do You Love?," and "Hey Bo Diddley;" signifying street-corner humor ("Say Man"), piledriving rockers ("Road Runner," "She's Alright," "You Can't Judge a Book by its Cover"), and numerous stunning examples of his daringly innovative guitar style. —*Bill Dahl*

Rare & Well Done / Sep. 10, 1991 / MCA/Chess ✦✦✦✦
Sixteen extreme rarities from the deepest recesses of the Chess vaults that date from 1955-1968. The grinding "She's Fine, She's Mine" and snarling "I'm Bad" are comparatively well-known, at least to collectors; far more obscure are the previously unissued "Heart-O-Matic Love," "Cookie-Headed Diddley," and "Moon Baby." —*Bill Dahl*

Two Great Guitars / 1992 / MCA/Chess ✦✦
Diddley shared this 1964 Chess album with his labelmate Chuck Berry. They duel it out on a pair of incredibly lengthy instrumentals (brilliantly titled "Chuck's Beat" and "Bo's Beat") that get tiresome long before they run their full course. Better (and briefer) are two numbers where they don't cross paths—Diddley's rendering of "When the Saints Go Marching In" and Berry's amazing country breakdown "Liverpool Drive." A couple of bonus Bo Diddley sides ("Stay Sharp" and "Stinkey") also make this digital re-incarnation worth acquiring. —*Bill Dahl*

Bo's Blues / 1993 / Ace ✦✦✦✦
22 of Bo Diddley's best blues-oriented sides from the Chess catalog, including some rare stuff—the rip-roaring 1959 outing "Run Diddley Daddy," a jive-loaded "Cops and Robbers" from 1956 that features maraca-shaker Jerome Green more than Diddley, and a surging "Down Home Special." If you think that everything Bo Diddley ever made has that same shave-and-a-haircut beat, this collection will set you straight! —*Bill Dahl*

Bo Diddley is a Lover...Plus / 1994 / See For Miles ✦✦✦
Very welcome digital British import reissue of Bo's 1961 Checker album, bolstered by a handful of bonus tracks (including his rendering of Willie Dixon's "My Babe"). On second guitar for many of these sides is Peggy Jones, one of Diddley's prize pupils. Some of the better-known titles include "Not Guilty," "Hong Kong, Mississippi," and the bragadocious title cut. —*Bill Dahl*

Let Me Pass Plus / 1994 / See For Miles ✦✦✦
Another British import version of a vintage Checker album, with a few highly desirable bonus cuts at the end to further recommend it. Most of the CD mirrors Diddley's 1965 *500% More Man* LP (the title track obviously being a sequel to his "I'm a Man"), but the extra items include the amusing "Mama, Keep Your Big Mouth Shut" and a danceable "We're Gonna Get Married." —*Bill Dahl*

A Man Amongst Men / May 21, 1996 / Code Blue ✦✦
Bo Diddley's major-label '90s comeback effort *A Man Amongst*

Men is overflowing with guest stars, but it rarely gels into something distinctive. The presence of such heavyweights as Keith Richards, Ron Wood, and Jimmie Vaughan actually weighs down the set, preventing Diddley from digging deep into the grooves. The band never quite rocks hard enough and no one tears off an inspired solo—*A Man Amongst Men* is pleasant, but it never approachs compelling listening. —*Stephen Thomas Erlewine*

Floyd Dixon

b. Feb. 8, 1929, Marshall, TX
Piano, Vocals / R&B, Electric West Coast Blues
Floyd Dixon was an unabashed admirer of Charles Brown's mellow "club blues" sound, but he added a more energetic, aggressive jump blues edge to his sound during the early '50s—a formula that made the L.A.-based pianist an R&B star.

A Texas emigre like so many of his postwar California contemporaries, Dixon hit the City of Angels at age 13. Influenced by Louis Jordan and Amos Milburn along with Brown, Dixon was swept up in the late '40s R&B boom, recording for Supreme in 1947 and signing with Modern Records in 1949. He nudged into the R&B Top Ten with "Dallas Blues" and just missed similar lofty stature with "Mississippi Blues" later in 1949. After cutting prolifically for Modern, he switched over to Eddie Mesner's Aladdin logo and hit in 1950 with "Sad Journey Blues" (also issued on Peacock), "Telephone Blues" the next year (backed by Johnny Moore's Three Blazers, the same crew that catapulted Charles Brown to stardom), and the mournful "Call Operator 210" in 1952.

But there was a playfully ribald side to Dixon, too. The double-entendre "Red Cherries," a storming "Wine, Wine, Wine," and the two-sided 1951 live waxing "Too Much Jelly Roll" (penned by a young Jerry Leiber and Mike Stoller) and "Baby, Let's Go Down to the Woods" showcased his more raucous leanings. The hits ceased, but Dixon's West Coast R&B odyssey continued with dates for Specialty in 1953, Atlantic's Cat subsidiary in 1954 (where he waxed the rollicking "Hey Bartender," likely his best-known tune thanks to covers by Koko Taylor and the execrable Blues Brothers), Ebb (where he challenged Little Richard's galvanic energy levels on the torrid "Oooh Little Girl" in 1957), and Checker.

The self-proclaimed "Mr. Magnificent" is still at it today. His career should enjoy a renaissance, thanks to an upcoming release on Alligator Records. —*Bill Dahl*

Opportunity Blues / 1976 / Route 66 ✦✦✦
Vinyl-only examination of the pianist's early sides for several West Coast R&B indies that spans 1948-1961. Dixon's ballad style was quite reminiscent of Charles Brown's but his jump blues leanings—here typified by "Wine, Wine, Wine" and "Real Lovin' Mama"—were all his own. —*Bill Dahl*

Houston Jump / 1979 / Route 66 ✦✦✦
Another cross-section of Dixon's 1947-1960 output that hasn't made the jump to the digital age as of yet. Surveys a wide array of labels, including a 1954 date for Atlantic's short-lived Cat subsidiary that produced "Roll Baby Roll" and "Is It True." —*Bill Dahl*

● **His Complete Aladdin Recordings** / 1996 / Capitol ✦✦✦✦
It's a matter of opinion as to whether Dixon's Aladdin output was his peak; many would give his Specialty sides (available on the *Marshall Texas Is My Home* compilation) the nod. Still, his late-'40s and early-'50s work for the label included some of his most popular and best tracks, such as "Wine, Wine, Wine," "Call Operator 210," "Tired, Broke and Busted," "Let's Dance," "Telephone Blues," and "Too Much Jelly Roll" (the last of which was one of Leiber-Stoller's first recorded compositions). This two-CD, 48-track compilation is geared more toward the completist collector than the average fan, especially with the inclusion of five Sonny Parker sides (which Dixon now says he didn't play on, despite some reports to the contrary) and about ten songs that feature Mari Jones on vocals. The best stuff is jump blues at its best, though, with good guitar work by Johnny and Oscar Moore (the latter of whom had played with Nat King Cole), Dixon's fine piano playing, and witty, knowing vocals and lyrics. —*Richie Unterberger*

Marshall Texas Is My Home / Specialty ✦✦✦✦✦
Dixon landed at Art Rupe's Specialty label in 1953, his music jumping harder than ever. These 22 tracks rate with his best; many featuring the wailing tenor sax of Carlos Bermudez in lusty support of the pianist. By 1957, when he momentarily paused at Ebb Records, Dixon could do a pretty fair breathless imitation of

Little Richard, as the scorching "Oooh Little Girl" definitively proves. Also includes Dixon's best-known number, the often-covered rocker "Hey Bartender" (first out on Atlantic's Cat subsidiary in 1954). —*Bill Dahl*

Willie Dixon

b. Jul. 1, 1915, Vickburg, MS, **d.** Jan. 29, 1992, Burbank, CA
Bass, Guitar, Vocals / Electric Chicago Blues, Acoustic Chicago Blues

Willie Dixon's life and work was virtually an embodiment of the progress of the blues, from an accidental creation of the descendants of freed slaves to a recognized and vital part of America's musical heritage. That Dixon was one of the first professional blues songwriters to benefit in a serious, material way—and that he had to fight to do it—from his work also made him an important symbol of the injustice that still informs the music industry, even at the end of this century. A producer, songwriter, bassist and singer, he helped Muddy Waters, Howlin' Wolf, Little Walter and others find their most commercially successful voices.

He got an early start on the road toward being a songwriter, with help from his mother Daisy, who would habitually try to rhyme everything she said. Young Dixon learned this very quickly, and by the time he was in grade school he was writing poems that his classmates loved. His earliest remembered musical reference was pianist Little Brother Montgomery, whose band was pulled by a truck through town once with Dixon following behind. By the time he was a teenager, Dixon was writing songs and selling copies to the local bands. He also studied music with a local carpenter, Theo Phelps, who taught him about harmony singing. With his bass voice, Dixon later joined a group organized by Phelps, the Union Jubilee Singers, who appeared on local radio. Dixon eventually made his way to Chicago, where he won the Illinois State Golden Gloves Heavyweight Championship, and for a short time worked as a sparring partner to Joe Louis.

He might have been a successful boxer, but he turned to music instead, thanks to Leonard "Baby Doo" Caston, a guitarist who had seen Dixon at the gym where he worked out and occasionally sang with him. The two formed a duo playing on street-corners, and later Dixon took up the bass as an instrument. They later formed a group, the Five Breezes, who recorded for the Bluebird label. The group's success was halted, however, when Dixon refused induction into the armed forces as a conscientious objector.

Dixon was eventually freed after a year, and formed another group, the Four Jumps of Jive. In 1945, however, Dixon was back working with Caston in a group called the Big Three Trio, with guitarist Bernardo Dennis (later replaced by Ollie Crawford).

During this period, Dixon would occasionally appear as a bassist at late-night jam sessions featuring members of the growing blues community, including Muddy Waters. Later on when the Chess brothers—who owned a club where Dixon occasionally played—began a new record label, Aristocrat (later Chess), they hired him, initially as a bassist on a 1948 session for Robert Nighthawk. The Chess brothers liked Dixon's playing, and his skills as a songwriter and arranger, and during the next two years he was working regularly for the Chess brothers. He got to record some of his own material, but Dixon was seldom featured as an artist—apart from his bass work—at any of these sessions.

Dixon's real recognition as a songwriter began with Muddy Waters' recording of "Hoochie Coochie Man." The success of that single, "Evil" by Howlin' Wolf, and "My Babe" by Little Walter saw Dixon established as Chess' most reliable tunesmith, and the Chess brothers continually pushed Dixon's songs on their artists. As Dixon later pointed out, he was also faced with the problem of using psychology to get various Chess stars to record his songs. By convincing Waters, Wolf, or Walter that he was actually considering giving a particular song to one of the others, he could get the one it was really intended for to give it his best shot in the studio. In addition to writing songs, Dixon continued as bassist and recording manager of many of the Chess label's recording sessions, including those by Lowell Fulson, Bo Diddley (whose "Pretty Thing" and "You Can't Judge a Book" were Dixon songs) and Otis Rush. Dixon's remuneration for all of this work, including the songwriting, was minimal—he was barely able to support his rapidly growing family on the $100 a week that the Chess brothers were letting him have, and a short

stint with the rival Cobra label at the end of the 1950s didn't help him much.

During the mid-'60s, Chess gradually phased out Dixon's bass work in favor of the electric bass, thus reducing his presence at many of the sessions. At the same time, a European concert promoter named Horst Lippmann had begun a series of shows called the American Folk-Blues Festival, for which he would bring some of the top blues players in America over to tour the continent.

Dixon ended up organizing the musical side of these shows for the first decade or more, recording on his own as well and earning a good deal more money than he was seeing from his work for Chess. At the same time, he began to see a growing interest in his songwriting from the British rock bands that he saw while in London—his music was getting covered regularly, and when he visited England, he even found himself cajoled into presenting his newest songs to their managements. Dixon was unaccustomed to being in so much demand, and was pleased to see his songs getting covered by the likes of the Rolling Stones, the Yardbirds, the Animals, Fleetwood Mac, and many others.

Back at Chess, Howlin' Wolf and Muddy Waters continued to perform Dixon's songs, as did newer artists such as Koko Taylor, who had her own hit with "Wang Dang Doodle," a song originally performed by Howlin' Wolf. Gradually, however, after the mid-'60s, Dixon saw his relationship with Chess Records come to a halt. Partly this was a result of time—the passing of artists such as Little Walter and Sonny Boy Williamson was part of the problem, and the death of Leonard Chess and the sale of the company called a halt to Dixon's involvement.

By the end of the 1960s, Dixon was eager to try his hand as a performer again, a career that had been interrupted when he'd gone to work for Chess as a producer. He recorded an album of his best-known songs, *I Am the Blues*, for Columbia Records, and organized a touring band, the Chicago Blues All-Stars, to play concerts in Europe. Suddenly, in his 50s, he began making a major name for himself on stage for the first time in his career. At around this same time, Dixon began to have grave doubts about the nature of the songwriting contract that he had with Chess' publishing arm, Arc Music. He was seeing precious little money from songwriting, despite the recording of hit versions of such Dixon songs as "Spoonful" by the Cream. He had never seen as much money as he was entitled to as a songwriter, but during the 1970s he began to understand just *how much* money he'd been deprived of, by design or just plain negligence on the part of the publisher doing its job on his behalf.

Arc Music sued Led Zeppelin for copyright infringement over "Bring It on Home" on *Led Zeppelin II*, saying that it was Dixon's song (and also that "The Lemon Song" was Howlin' Wolf's "Killing Floor"), and won a settlement that Dixon never saw any part of until his manager did an audit of Arc's accounts. Dixon and Muddy Waters would later file suit against Arc Music to recover royalties and the ownership of their copyrights. Additionally, many years later Dixon brought suit against Led Zeppelin for copyright infringement over "Whole Lotta Love" and its resemblance to Dixon's "You Need Love." Both cases resulted in out-of-court settlements that were generous to the songwriter.

The 1980s saw Dixon as the last survivor of the Chess blues stable and he began working with various organizations to help secure song copyrights on behalf of blues songwriters who, like himself, had been deprived of revenue during previous decades. In 1988, Dixon became the first producer/songwriter to be honored with a boxed-set collection, when MCA Records released *Willie Dixon: The Chess Box*, which included several rare Dixon sides as well as the most famous recordings of his songs by Chess' stars. The following year, Dixon published *I Am the Blues* (Da Capo Press), his autobiography, written in association with Don Snowden.

Dixon continued performing, and was also called in as a producer on movie soundtracks such as *Gingerale Afternoon*, and *La Bamba*, producing the work of his old stablemate Bo Diddley. By that time, Dixon was regarded as something of an elder statesman, composer, and spokesperson of American blues. In 1989, he appeared with Koko Taylor as a performer at the inaugural ball for President George Bush.

Dixon suffered from increasingly poor health, and lost a leg to diabetes, which didn't slow him down very much. He died peacefully in his sleep early in 1992. —*Bruce Eder*

Willie's Blues / 1959 / Bluesville ✦✦✦
This is a tasty, understated 1959 session with singer/pianist Memphis Slim and bassist/singer/songwriter Willie Dixon. — *Mark A. Humphrey*

I Am the Blues / 1970 / Mobile Fidelity ✦✦✦
The material is superb, consisting of some of Dixon's best-known songs of the 1960s, and the production is smoothly professional, but none of the performances here are likely to make you forget the hits by Howlin' Wolf, Muddy Waters et al. Reissued on CD by Mobile Fidelity and more recently by Sony Music—unfortunately, none of the unreleased tracks from the session seem to have survived. — *Bruce Eder*

★ **The Chess Box** / 1989 / MCA/Chess ✦✦✦✦✦
There are a few holes in this collection, but not many. As it is, the material is virtually a best-of-Chess collection, featuring some of the best tracks in the respective outputs of Muddy Waters, Howlin' Wolf, Little Walter, Sonny Boy Williamson, Bo Diddley, Lowell Folsom, Koko Taylor et al. — *Bruce Eder*

The Original Wang Dang Doodle / 1995 / MCA/Chess ✦✦✦✦
This is a good collection of hard-to-find and previously unreleased Dixon sides, although there are several Chess tracks that were left off that would have made it much more valuable. The title track is especially worthwhile, as is "Tail Dragger," but it is also easy to see from this collection why Dixon was never quite a star in his own right as a performer—he has a good voice, but not a very memorable or powerful one, compared with Muddy Waters, Howlin' Wolf et al. — *Bruce Eder*

Lefty Dizz (Walter Williams)

b. 1937, Arkansas, d. Sep. 7, 1993
Guitar, Vocals / Electric Chicago Blues
In a town like Chicago, where the competition in blues clubs was tough and keen (and still is on a hot night), certain musicians quickly learned that sometimes red hot playing and singing didn't always get the job done by themselves. You had to entertain, put on a show, because there was *always* someone looking to take your gig away from you. Only those willing to protect their bandstand—and their livelihood in the long run—by peppering their presentation with a small to large dollop of showmanship were smart enough to hang in for the long run, keeping both their hometown audience and their turf intact. Although blues revisionist history always seems to overlook this, the show that T-Bone Walker, Guitar Slim, Howlin' Wolf, Muddy Waters, Little Walter, Buddy Guy and others did in front of a Black audience was wilder and far more audacious than the one a more reserved White audience *ever* got to see. For wild-ass showmen in blues history, though, one would certainly have to go a far piece to beat Walter Williams, known to blues fans in Chicago and Europe as Lefty Dizz.

A regular fixture of the Chicago scene from the mid-'60s into the early '90s, Lefty was quite a sight back in those days; fronting his band, Shock Treatment, playing and singing with an unbridled enthusiasm while simultaneously putting on a show that would have oldtimers guffawing in appreciation while scaring White patrons out of their wits. As an entertainer, he was simply nothing less than a modern day Guitar Slim informed with the outrage of a Hendrix, pulling out every trick in the book to win over an audience, whether he was protecting his home turf bandstand or stealing the show while sitting in somewhere else. It was nothing for him to play a slow blues, bring the band down, and start walking through the crowd dragging his beat up Stratocaster behind him like a sack of potatoes, playing it with one hand the entire time. Or take on some young Turk axeman gunning for his scalp (and gig) by kicking off Freddie King's "Hideaway" at an impossibly fast tempo, calling for break after break while infusing all of them with so many eye-popping gags that the young Turk in question was merely reduced to becoming another member of the audience. As a bluesman, he was nothing less than deep and 100% for real. Nobody messed with Lefty Dizz.

Born in Arkansas in 1937, Dizz (the nickname was bestowed on him by Hound Dog Taylor and the HouseRockers, appropriating it from drummer Ted Harvey, who used the name when he was "playing jazz in the alley") started playing guitar at age 19 after a four-year hitch in the Air Force. Entirely self-taught, he played a standard right-handed model flipped upside down, without reversing the strings. His sound was raw and distorted,

and his style owed more to the older bluesmen than to the hipper West Side players like Otis Rush and Buddy Guy working in the B.B. King mode. By the time he came to Chicago, he had honed his craft well enough to become a member of Junior Wells' band in 1964, recording and touring Africa, Europe and Southeast Asia with him until the late '60s. At various times during the '60s and early '70s, he'd also moonlight as a guitarist with Chicago stalwarts J.B. Lenoir and Hound Dog Taylor, while sitting in everywhere and playing with seemingly everyone. While being well known around town as a "head cutter," Lefty Dizz was always welcome on anyone's bandstand. His personality, while seemingly carefree and humourous, masked a deep, highly intelligent individual who had also earned a degree in economics from Southern Illlinois University.

He kept soldiering on in the blues trenches through the '90s when he was diagnosed with cancer of the esophagus. While chemotherapy helped, Lefty went back to work far too soon and far too hard to stay on top of his game for much longer. The unflappable Dizz, who could seemingly make the best out of any given situation without complaint and had friends in the blues community by the truckload, finally passed away on September 7, 1993. And with his passing, the blues lost perhaps its most flamboyant showman. — *Cub Koda*

Lefty Dizz with Big Moose Walker / Black & Blue ✦✦
It has been argued by more than one blues critic that for all his performing acumen, Lefty Dizz never recorded an album that captured even a smidgeon of his live intensity. This poorly produced album, recorded for the French Black and Blue imprint, would certainly support that claim. While the performances are workmanlike enough, Dizz's guitar sound (apparently routed direct to the board, bypassing his amp) gives new meaning to the words flabby and lifeless. Out of print for the time being and perhaps deservedly so. — *Cub Koda*

● **Somebody Stole My Christmas** / Isabel ✦✦✦✦
Dizz fares much better on this sophomore outing. Featuring a nice take on the title cut and fairly solid playing from all parties concerned, this certainly falls short of the fervor he could produce live but is still the best of the bunch. — *Cub Koda*

Ain't It Nice to Be Loved / JSP ✦✦
Dizz recorded his final outing at Sotosound studios in Evanston, IL, surrounded with a collection of players who knew his style. Therefore, that this effort falls so short of the mark is all the more puzzling. If anyone truly needed a producer, Dizz was the man. The arrangements meander, the mix (such as it is) buries Lefty's guitar and evidently nobody bothered to tune up before or during the session. JSP has never been much noted for quality releases on either audio or artistic levels, but this is just plain embarrassing. — *Cub Koda*

Dr. John (Mac Rebennack)

b. Nov. 21, 1940
Piano, Vocals / R&B, Rock & Roll, Pop/Rock, New Orleans R&B
Although he didn't become widely known until the 1970s, Dr. John had been active in the music industry since the late '50s, when the teenager was still known as Mac Rebennack. A formidable boogie and blues pianist with a lovable growl of a voice, his most enduring achievements have fused New Orleans R&B, rock, and Mardi Gras craziness to come up with his own brand of "voodoo" music. He's also quite accomplished and enjoyable when sticking to purely traditional forms of blues and R&B. On record, he veers between the two approaches, making for an inconsistent and frequently frustrating legacy that often makes the listener feel as if the Night Tripper (as he's nicknamed himself) has been underachieving.

In the late '50s, Rebennack gained prominence in the New Orleans R&B scene as a session keyboardist and guitarist, contributing to records by Professor Longhair, Frankie Ford, and Joe Tex. He also did some overlooked singles of his own, and by the 1960s had expanded into production and arranging. After a gun accident damaged his hand in the early '60s, he gave up the guitar to concentrate on keyboards exclusively. Skirting trouble with the law and drugs, he left the increasingly unwelcome environs of New Orleans in the mid-'60s for Los Angeles, where he found session work with the help of fellow New Orleans expatriate Harold Battiste.

Rebennack renamed himself Dr. John the Night Tripper when he recorded his first album, *Gris-Gris*. According to legend, this was hurriedly cut with leftover studio time from a Sonny & Cher session, but it never sounded hastily conceived. In fact, its mix of New Orleans R&B with voodoo sounds and a tinge of psychedelia was downright enthralling, and may have resulted in his greatest album. He began building an underground following with both his music and his eccentric stage presence, which found him conducting ceremonial-type events in full Mardi Gras costume.

Dr. John was nothing if not eclectic, and his next few albums were granted mixed critical receptions because of their unevenness and occasional excess. They certainly had their share of admirable moments, though, and Eric Clapton and Mick Jagger helped out on *The Sun Moon and Herbs* in 1971. The following year's *Gumbo,* produced by Jerry Wexler, proved Dr. John was a master of traditional New Orleans R&B styles, in the mold of one of his heroes, Professor Longhair. In 1973, he got his sole big hit, "In the Right Place," which was produced by Allen Toussaint, with backing by the Meters. In the same year, he also recorded with Mike Bloomfield and John Hammond, Jr. for the *Triumvirate* album.

The rest of the decade, unfortunately, was pretty much a waste musically. Dr. John could always count on returning to traditional styles for a good critical reception, and he did so constantly in the 1980s. There were solo piano albums, sessions with Chris Barber and Jimmy Witherspoon, and *In a Sentimental Mood* (1989), a record of pop standards. These didn't sell all that well, though. A more important problem was that he's capable of much more than recastings of old styles and material. In fact, by this time he was usually bringing in the bacon not through his own music, but via vocals for numerous commercial jingles.

It's continued pretty much in the same vein throughout the 1990s: New Orleans supersessions for the *Bluesiana* albums, another outing with Chris Barber, an album of New Orleans standards, and *another* album of pop standards. 1994's *Television* did at least offer some original material. However, at this point it seems like he will usually rely upon cover versions for the bulk of his recorded work, though his interpretive skills will always ensure that these are more interesting than most such efforts. His autobiography, *Under a Hoodoo Moon,* was published by St. Martin's Press in 1994. —*Richie Unterberger*

Gris Gris / 1968 / Repertoire ◆◆◆◆◆
The most exploratory and psychedelic outing of Dr. John's career, a one-of-a-kind fusion of New Orleans Mardi Gras R&B and voodoo mysticism. Great rasping, bluesy vocals, soulful backup singers, and eerie melodies on flute, sax, and clarinet, as well as odd Middle Eastern-like chanting and mandolin runs. It's got the setting of a strange religious ritual, but the mood is far more joyous than solemn. —*Richie Unterberger*

Babylon / 1969 / Atco ◆◆◆
Dr. John's ambition remained undiminished on his second solo album, *Babylon,* released shortly after the groundbreaking voodoo-psychedelia-New Orleans R&B fusion of his debut, *Gris-Gris.* The results, however, were not nearly as consistent or impressive. Coolly received by critics, the album nonetheless is deserving of attention, though it pales a bit in comparison with *Gris-Gris.* The production is sparser and more reliant on female backup vocals than his debut. Dr. John remains intent on fusing voodoo and R&B, but the mood is oddly bleak and despairing, in comparison with the wild Mardi Gras-gone-amok tone of his first LP. The hushed, damned atmosphere and afterhours R&B sound a bit like Van Morrison on a bummer trip at times, as peculiar as that might seem. "The Patriotic Flag-Waiver" (sic), in keeping with the mood of the late '60s, damns social ills and hypocrisy of all sorts. An FM underground radio favorite at the time, its ambitious structure remains admirable, though its musical imperfections haven't worn well. To a degree, you could say the same about the album as a whole. But it has enough of an eerie fascination to merit investigation. —*Richie Unterberger*

Dr. John's Gumbo / Apr. 1972 / Atco ◆◆◆◆◆
Gumbo bridged the gap between post-hippie rock and early rock 'n' roll, blues and R&B, offering a selection of classic New Orleans R&B, including "Tipitina" and "Junko Partner," updated with a gritty, funky beat. There are not as many psychedelic flourishes as there were on his first two albums, but the ones that are present enhance his sweeping vision of American roots

music. And that sly fusion of styles makes *Gumbo* one of Dr. John's finest albums. —*Stephen Thomas Erlewine*

Tango Palace / 1979 / Horizon ◆◆
Dr. John's second and final album for the Horizon jazz subsidiary of A&M Records finds him working with producers Tommy LiPuma and Hugh McCracken on a rollicking set that emphasizes his New Orleans roots while attempting to update his sound with '70s effects such as deep, plucked bass notes and occasional disco rhythms. The album leads off with "Keep That Music Simple," a somewhat caustic admonishment to musicians and the music business whose message is disregarded elsewhere on the record, as LiPuma and McCracken seek to cover all stylistic bases from funk to fusion to second line. Dr. John emerges from the production intact, but he is not quite as swampy as when heard at his best. —*William Ruhlmann*

Brightest Smile in Town / 1983 / Clean Cuts ◆◆◆
Doctor John's second solo piano album finds him combining country, blues, and New Orleans standards with originals, half of them instrumentals and half of them containing vocals that sound like they were recorded off the piano microphone. This is not a high-tech recording, by any means, but in its unadorned way it captures the flavor of Doctor John as directly as any record he's made. —*William Ruhlmann*

In a Sentimental Mood / Apr. 1989 / Warner Brothers ◆◆◆
On Dr. John's first major-label effort and first vocal studio album in ten years, he performs a set of pop standards including Cole Porter's "Love For Sale" and Johnny Mercer's "Accentuate The Positive." After starting out with a wild stage act and unusual costumes, Dr. John has evolved into a vocal stylist and piano virtuoso, which makes the idea of doing this sort of material appealing. And he does it well, turning out a leisurely duet with Rickie Lee Jones on "Makin' Whoopee" that won a Grammy (Best Jazz Vocal Performance, Duo or Group) and giving sad feeling to "My Buddy." Maybe he has changed since the *Gris-Gris* days, but even a mellowed Dr. John is a tasty one. —*William Ruhlmann*

Bluesiana II / 1991 / Windham Hill ◆◆◆
Previously, Windham Hill Records released *Bluesiana Triangle,* a jazz trio album by drummer Art Blakey, pianist Dr. John, and reed man David "Fathead" Newman. Blakey passed away in 1990, but in the spring of 1991, Dr. John and Newman organized this second Bluesiana session, featuring trombonist Ray Anderson, drummer Will Calhoun, bassists Essiet Okon Essiet and Jay Leonhart (on different tracks), and percussionist Joe Bonadio. The resulting music again justifies the name, blues played in a funky Louisiana style with plenty of room for extended jazzy soloing. Though much of the material was written by Dr. John and he does sing occasionally, this is not a conventional Dr. John vocal album. It does contain some excellent playing, however. —*William Ruhlmann*

Goin' Back to New Orleans / Jun. 23, 1992 / Warner Brothers ◆◆◆
Having cut an album of standards on his first Warner Brothers album, *In A Sentimental Mood* (1989), Dr. John turned for its followup to a collection of *New Orleans* standards. On an album he described in the liner notes as "a little history of New Orleans music," Dr. John returned to his hometown and set up shop at local Ultrasonic Studios, inviting in such local musicians as Pete Fountain, Al Hirt, and the Neville Brothers and addressing the music and styles of such local legends as Jelly Roll Morton, Huey "Piano" Smith, Fats Domino, James Booker, and Professor Longhair. The geography may have been circumscribed, but the stylistic range was extensive, from jazz and blues to folk and rock. And it was all played with festive conviction—Dr. John is the perfect archivist for the music, being one of its primary popularizers, yet he had never addressed it quite as directly as he did here. —*William Ruhlmann*

Anthology / 1993 / Rhino ◆◆◆◆◆
Over his 35 years of recording, Mac "Dr. John" Rebennack has worn many hats, from '50s greasy rock 'n' roller to psychedelic '70s weirdo to keeper of the New Orleans music flame. All of these modes, plus more, are excellently served up on this two-disc anthology. From the early New Orleans sides featuring Rebennack's blistering guitar work ("Storm Warning" and "Morgus The Magnificent") to the fabled '70s sides as The Night Tripper to his present day status as repository of the Crescent

City's noble musical tradition, this is the one you want to have for the collection. —*Cub Koda*

Television / Mar. 29, 1994 / GRP ✦✦
Dr. John's debut for GRP doesn't deviate from any release he's made for several other labels. It's still his chunky, humorous take on New Orleans funk; these are his songs, visions and performances, and there's none of the elevator material or laid-back, detached fare that's a customary GRP byproduct. Such songs as "Witchy Red," "Spaceship Relationship" and the title selection are a delicate mix of seemingly outrageous but actually quite sharp commentary and excellent musical performances from Dr. John on keyboards, Hugh McCracken on guitar, and several other veterans, among them the great Red Tyler on tenor sax. While not quite as fiery as his classic sessions for Atlantic, if anyone can bring the funk to a company that's famous for avoiding it, it's Dr. John. —*Ron Wynn*

● **The Very Best Of Dr. John** / 1995 / Rhino ✦✦✦✦✦
The Very Best of Dr. John compiles the best moments from the comprehensive double-disc *Anthology,* making it a more effective, and cheaper, introduction for casual fans. —*Stephen Thomas Erlewine*

Afterglow / Feb. 7, 1995–Feb. 9, 1995 / Blue Thumb ✦✦✦
Producer and GRP Records president Tommy LiPuma, a longtime associate of Dr. John's, revived his old Blue Thumb label as an imprint of GRP/MCA with this album, which served as something of a sequel to the last Dr. John/Tommy LiPuma collaboration, *In A Sentimental Mood.* On that earlier album, the two had covered pop standards. Here, they again turned to evergreens by the likes of Irving Berlin and Duke Ellington. But if *Sentimental Mood* was stylistically linked to the '20s and '30s, *Afterglow* was more a recreation of the late '40s and early '50s, with its big-band arrangements and the inclusion of jump blues numbers like Louis Jordan's "I Know What I've Got." Such songs allowed Dr. John plenty of room to play his trademark New Orleans piano solos, and, in the second half of the record, some of the Doctor's own compositions were snuck in among the classics without disturbing the mood. Of course, the dominant sound remained Dr. John's gravel-and-honey voice, an even more appropriate instrument for these bluesier standards than it was for the *Sentimental* ones. —*William Ruhlmann*

Doctor Ross

b. Oct. 21, 1925, Tunica, MS
Guitar, Harmonica, Vocals / Acoustic Country Blues
A triple-threat guitarist, harp blower, and vocalist, Dr. Ross decided to fire his sidemen more than thirty years ago and carry on as a one-man band, a tradition that also includes Joe Hill Louis, Daddy Stovepipe, and Jesse Fuller. Ross' music does not depend on novelty effect, yet it has a distinctly recognizable sound, in part because he learned to play his own way and essentially plays everything backwards. His guitar is tuned to open *G* (like John Lee Hooker and other Delta artists), but Ross plays it left-handed and upside-down. He also plays harmonica in a rack, but it is turned around with the low notes to the right. As an instrumentalist, Ross has perfected the interplay between guitar and harmonica. Unlike other Delta artists who tune in *G,* Ross doesn't use slide, preferring a series of banjo-like strummed riffs, a percussive approach reminiscent of Atlanta twelve-string guitarist Barbecue Bob. A strong vocalist and excellent songwriter, Ross gained early experience playing Delta jukes and eventually landed radio shows in Clarksdale and Memphis, where he also recorded for Sam Phillips' Sun label.

At the peak of Ross' career, he quit Sun, concerned that his royalties were being used to promote Elvis Presley's recordings. Relocating in Michigan, he recorded for his own label and for several Detroit labels, while working for General Motors. Returning to music as a recording artist, he recently worked the festival circuit. To the present day, Ross' music retains the spirit of his live radio and juke-joint work. I feel the sides he recorded with a band for Sun produced his best material, including classics like "Chicago Breakdown" and "Boogie Disease." As Dr. Ross put it in an interview ten years ago, "I'm kind of like the little boy from the West; I'm different from the rest." Different, yes, but very good. —*Barry Lee Pearson*

● **Boogie Disease** / 1954 / Arhoolie ✦✦✦✦✦
This one will make your teeth rattle. A veteran of the early '50s Sun Studio in Memphis, Ross became known as the "one-man band," a routine gleaned from his mentor Joe Hill Louis. He

plays both fine harp (of the Sonny Boy Williamson I mold) and exciting rhythm guitar characterized by churning, mesmerizing rhythms spiced by treble fills. These 22 infectious tracks are the good doctor's first recordings, and they present him with rhythm section—a style that pre-dates his "one-man" days. —*Larry Hoffman*

Call the Doctor / Jun. 1965 / Testament ✦✦✦✦
If you're looking for one-man blues, this is one of the better efforts in that vein available. Ross is in fine form and strong voice on his first full-length album, sometimes pulling out as many stops as his limbs allow for all-out stompers, at other times just accompanying himself on harmonica. The tracks are largely adaptations of well-worn material like "Good Morning, Little Schoolgirl," "32-20," and "Going to the River"; the opening blast of "Cat Squirrel" is especially good. The one-man band approach gets a bit wearing over the course of 17 songs, though, unless you're a sucker for the style. The CD reissue adds the previously unissued bonus track "Jivin' Blues." —*Richie Unterberger*

I'd Rather Be an Old Woman's Baby / 1971 / Fortune ✦✦✦
A wild, chaotic session, featuring the title cut, "Good Things Come to My Remind," and the original version of "Cat Squirrel." —*Cub Koda*

Dr. Ross: His First Recording / 1972 / Arhoolie ✦✦✦✦✦
His best material, originally recorded for the Sun label in the 50s. Outstanding Delta blues in the unique Dr. Ross guitar-and-harmonica style. —*Barry Lee Pearson*

Fats Domino

b. Feb. 28, 1928, New Orleans, LA
Vocals, Piano / Rock & Roll, New Orleans R&B
The most popular exponent of the classic New Orleans R&B sound, Fats Domino also sold more records than any other Black rock 'n' roll star of the 1950s. His relaxed, lolling boogie-woogie piano style and easygoing, warm vocals anchored a long series of national hits from the mid-'50s to the early '60s. Through it all, his basic approach rarely changed. He may not have been one of early rock's most charismatic, innovative, or threatening figures, but he was certainly one of its most consistent.

Domino's first single, "The Fat Man" (1949), is one of the dozens of tracks that have been consistently singled out as a candidate for the first rock 'n' roll record. As far as Fats was concerned, he was just playing what he'd already been doing in New Orleans for years, and would continue to play and sing in pretty much the same fashion even after his music was dubbed "rock 'n' roll."

The record made number two on the R&B charts, and sold a million copies. Just as important, it established a vital partnership between Fats and Imperial A&R man Dave Bartholomew. Bartholomew, himself a trumpeter, would produce Domino's big hits, co-writing many of them with Fats. He would also usually employ New Orleans session greats like Alvin Tyler on sax and Earl Palmer on drums—musicians who were vital in establishing New Orleans R&B as a distinct entity, playing on many other local recordings as well (including hits made in New Orleans by Georgia native Little Richard).

Domino didn't cross over into the pop charts in a big way until 1955, when "Ain't That a Shame" made the Top Ten. Pat Boone's cover of the song stole some of Fats' thunder, going all the way to number one (Boone was also bowdlerizing Little Richard's early singles for hits during this time). Domino's long-range prospects weren't damaged, however; between 1955 and 1963, he racked up an astonishing 35 Top 40 singles. "Blueberry Hill" (1956) was probably his best (and best-remembered) single; "Walking to New Orleans," "Whole Lotta Loving," "I'm Walking," "Blue Monday," and "I'm in Love Again" were also huge successes.

After Fats left Imperial for ABC-Paramount in 1963, he would only enter the Top 40 one more time. The surprise was not that Fats fell out of fashion, but that he'd maintained his popularity so long while the essentials of his style remained unchanged. This was during an era, remember, when most of rock's biggest stars had their careers derailed by death or scandal, or were made to soften up their sound for mainstream consumption. Although an active performer in the ensuing decades, his career as an important artist was essentially over in the mid-'60s. He did stir up a bit of attention in 1968 when he covered the

Beatles' "Lady Madonna" single, which had been an obvious homage to Fats' style. —*Richie Unterberger*

★ **My Blue Heaven: Best of Fats Domino** / Jul. 30, 1990 / EMI America ✦✦✦✦✦
For the budget-minded fan, this 20-track single disc compilation of Fats Domino's Imperial smashes will serve nicely. Not much of his early pre-rock stuff—"The Fat Man" and "Please Don't Leave Me" are all that's here—but there's plenty of his hit-laden output from 1955 on—"Ain't It a Shame," "Blue Monday," "I'm in Love Again," "Blueberry Hill," "I'm Ready," etc. One small but substantial difference between this set and the larger packages is that it uses non-sped-up masters of his mid-'50s material (some of his hits from this era were mastered slightly faster than true pitch). Even if they're not historically correct, these versions actually sound better! —*Bill Dahl*

☆ **They Call Me the Fat Man . . . : The Legendary Imperial Recordings** / 1991 / EMI America ✦✦✦✦✦
If you can't quite finance the Bear Family box, this four-disc compilation is the next best thing. An even 100 of the best Imperial sides, including a great many from 1958 on that turn up in crystal-clear stereo (as they also do on the Bear Family package). All the hits are aboard, along with a nice cross-section of the important non-hits. The saxes (usually including Herb Hardesty and sometimes Lee Allen) roar with typical Crescent City power, Fats rolls the ivories, and magic happens—over and over again! Another nice booklet with plenty of photos (but a less detailed discography without sideman credits). —*Bill Dahl*

☆ **Fats Domino: Out Of New Orleans** / 1993 / Bear Family ✦✦✦✦✦
An amazing piece of work—a massive eight-disc boxed set that contains every one of Fats Domino's 1949-1962 Imperial waxings. That's a tremendous load of one artist, but the legacy of Domino and his partner Dave Bartholomew is so consistently innovative and infectious that it never grows tiresome for a second. From the clarion call of "The Fat Man," Domino's 1949 debut, to the storming "Dance with Mr. Domino" in 1962, he typified everything charming about Crescent City R&B, his Creole patois and boogie-based piano a non-threatening vehicle for the rise of rock 'n' roll. A thick, photo-filled book accompanies the disc, and there's an exhaustive discography that makes sense of Domino's many visits to Cosimo Matassa's studios. If you care about Fats Domino, this is the package to purchase! —*Bill Dahl*

Thomas A. Dorsey

b. Jul. 1, 1899, Atlanta, GA, d. Jan. 23, 1993
Piano, Vocals, Guitar / Acoustic Chicago Blues, Gospel
One of the key figures in the development of modern gospel music, composer Thomas Andrew Dorsey helped bring the blues to contemporary gospel music. It was he who coined the term "gospel songs" in the 1920s; prior to that they were called evangelistic songs. Dorsey was a versatile composer whose songs ranged from sentimental syrup to rollicking hard-gospel. Though he composed many gospel standards, his biggest mainstream song is "Precious Lord," which has been recorded by artists ranging from the Heavenly Gospel Singers to Red Foley to Elvis Presley. Other well-known Dorsey works include his adaptation of an old spiritual "We Shall Walk Through the Valley in Peace," "I'm Gonna Live the Life I Sing About in My Song," and "Singing in My Soul."

A native of Atlanta, GA, Thomas Dorsey was the son of a Southern Baptist preacher. Though greatly influenced by Dr. Watts' hymns, Dorsey also listened to early jazz and blues music. A child prodigy, Dorsey taught himself to play a number of instruments. He got his start playing blues and ragtime piano. As a young man, Dorsey billed himself as "Georgia Tom," and began writing many notorious, witty and double entrendre-filled blues songs and accompanying blues legend Ma Rainey in Chicago. Though performing secular music, Dorsey was still interested in religious music and particularly the blues-tinged songs of composer C.A. Tindley, another father of modern gospel.

In 1926, during Dorsey's recovery from a lingering illness, his son suddenly died of acute appendicitis. The irony that he, who had been sick for six months, had survived his child, who only suffered a few hours, cut deeply. In the midst of his despair, Dorsey claims to have been visited by a heavenly messenger who directed the composer to write "If You See My Savior, Tell

Him That You Saw Me." He sent out five hundred copies of the song to various churches, but it did not become a hit until 1930 when it was sung at the Jubilee Session of National Baptist Convention in Chicago. Impressed by the song, the convention directors Lucie Campbell and E.W. Isacc suggested he sell his music.

Dorsey wrote most prolifically during the Depression. Many of the songs were designed to raise the battered spirits of those hardest hit and during this time a new sub-genre was created, "gospel blues." In addition to writing songs, Dorsey also created and led gospel choirs. A mutual friend introduced him to young shouter Sallie Martin and he invited her to join his group at the Ebenezer Baptist Church in February, 1932. She eventually became his main soloist and business partner. She helped him understand the huge untapped market for gospel sheet music, and between 1932 and 1940, they toured across the country setting up choirs to demonstrate his music during his "Evening with Dorsey" performances. Together Dorsey and Martin founded the first Gospel Singers Convention. Martin ended their partnership in 1940, but he continued hosting those performances through 1944. From 1939 through 1944, he toured with Mahalia Jackson. Dorsey retired from traveling and composing in the 1960s, but remained the director of the Convention for many years afterward. He died at the age of 92. —*Sandra Brennan*

★ **Precious Lord** / 1994 / Columbia/Legacy ✦✦✦✦✦
Precious Lord collects 18 of Georgia Thomas Dorsey's greatest songs, offering a terrific introduction to one of the greatest gospel country blues singers of the '30s. —*Thom Owens*

Come on Mama Do That Dance 1931–1940 / Yazoo ✦✦✦✦✦
Hard to believe that America's greatest writer of gospel songs could come up with this solid collection of risque blues tunes in his earlier, "sinful" days. Believe it. —*Cub Koda*

Complete Recorded Works, Vol. 2 (1930–1934) / Document ✦✦✦✦✦

Complete Recorded Works, Vol. 1 (1928–1930) / Document ✦✦✦✦✦

Complete Recorded Works, Vols. 1–2 / Document ✦✦✦
The two-volume *Complete Recorded Works* contains all of the recordings Georgia Thomas Dorsey recorded between 1928 and 1934, including his inspirational and secular material. Most listeners will be better served with *Precious Lord* and *Come On Mama Do That Dance*, which separate his gospel recordings from his racy blues records. Historians and completists, however, will find this series a necessary purchase. —*Thom Owens*

K.C. Douglas

b. Nov. 21, 1913, Sharon, MS, d. Oct. 18, 1975, Berkeley, CA
Guitar, Vocals / Electric Country Blues, West Coast Blues
K.C. Douglas was a Mississippi bluesman who transplanted himself and his music, not to Chicago, but to the San Francisco Bay Area in 1945. He became one of the rare Californians with such a down-home rural style, as many of his recordings were remakes of old blues he knew from Mississippi. (His first album, an obscure item on the Cook label, was entitled *K.C. Douglas, a Dead Beat Guitar and the Mississippi Blues*.) His re-creations of Tommy Johnson's blues were of particular interest to fans of pre-war blues, but his own compositions attracted attention as well (K.C.'s music was introduced to rock listeners when his "Mercury Boogie" was redone by The Steve Miller Band.) —*Jim O'Neal*

● **K.C.'s Blues** / 1961 / Bluesville ✦✦✦✦✦
Traditional Mississippi Delta blues, this is a 1990 CD reissue of 1961 recordings. —*Niles J. Frantz*

Driftin' Slim (Elmon Mickle)

b. Feb. 24, 1919, d. Sep. 15, 1977
Harmonica, Guitar, Drums, Vocals / Electric Blues
Elmon "Driftin' Slim" Mickle was a harmonica player from Keo, AR, a stone's throw away from Little Rock. He got his early harmonica training when he saw John Lee "Sonny Boy" Williamson and Yank Rachell perform and approached Sonny Boy to teach him the rudiments of the instrument. By the mid-'40s, he was playing the local juke joint circuit with Sonny Boy Williamson II and King Biscuit Boy drummer Peck Curtis while doing radio stints with stations KDRK and KGHI. In 1951, he had formed his first band with locals Baby Face Turner and Junior Brooks and recorded his first sides for the Modern label. By 1957, he had

moved to Los Angeles, refurbishing his act as a one-man band, adding drums and guitar to his neck rack harmonica work. He recorded sporadically, issuing singles on his own and other labels through the early '60s. In the flush of the "folk-music boom" of the mid-'60s, Slim was rediscovered and recorded for a number of collectors' labels. By the turn of the decade, ill health had forced him to retire from music and when he passed away in 1977, a chapter of American music—that of the one-man band—had virtually died with him. —*Cub Koda*

● **Driftin' Slim and His Blues Band** / Dec. 1969 / Milestone ✦✦✦✦✦
Slim's only full album (his earlier recordings show up on several compilations) is one of the great "rediscovery" albums of the genre. Five of the 15 tracks here are with a full band, but the real treasure trove is the remaining solo performances. These range from full-stops-out one-man-band numbers ("I'm Hunting Somebody" is a true classic) to unaccompanied harmonica pieces ("Mama Blues," "Jonah") to autobiographical recitations like "A Dip of Snuff and a Narrow Escape" that are utterly charming in their simplicity. As of press time, this album was still unavailable on compact disc, but it is still well worth seeking out as it's a true gem with loads of folkish charm. —*Cub Koda*

Chris Duarte

Guitar, Vocals / Modern Electric Blues
Austin-based guitarist, songwriter and singer Chris Duarte is such a promising young upstart in the world of modern blues that he's already being compared with the late Stevie Ray Vaughan. It's heady stuff for the 32-year-old musician, who plays a rhythmic style of Texas blues-rock that is at times reminiscent of Vaughan's sound, and at other times reminiscent of Johnny Winter. The truth is, Duarte has his own sound that draws on elements of jazz, blues and rock 'n' roll. Although he is humbled by the comparisons with the late Vaughan, the San Antonio-raised musician began playing out in clubs there when he was 15 years old.

After Duarte moved to Austin when he was 16, he began taking his guitar playing much more seriously, and at that time, Vaughan was still around playing in Austin-area clubs. Duarte was one of those lucky few thousand who got to see Vaughan at the Continental Club before the late guitarist got his first break with David Bowie. After a short stint in an Austin jazz band, Duarte joined Bobby Mack and Night Train, and began getting heavily into blues at that point. He traveled all over Texas with that band before a big break came his way in 1994, when New York-based Silvertone Records released his critically praised debut album, *Texas Sugar Strat Magik.*

Duarte would be the first to tell you his sound is not straight-ahead blues; the influences he cites as most important to him include people like saxophonist John Coltrane and jazz guitarist John McLaughlin. Locally, he cites people like Austin-based musicians Denny Freeman and Derek O' Brien as having an impact on his playing. "Our live shows are usually eclectic," he said a few months after the release of his Silvertone debut, "it's not always straightahead blues, but it's got integrity, it's got soul." —*Richard Skelly*

● **Texas Sugar Strat Magik** / 1994 / Silvertone ✦✦✦✦
Guitarist Chris Duarte's *Texas Sugar Strat Magik* is an impressive debut album, showcasing his fiery, Stevie Ray Vaughan-derived blues-rock. As a songwriter, Duarte is still developing—he fails to come up with anything memorable, although he does contribute several competent, unexceptional genre pieces—but as an instrumentalist, he's first-rate, spitting out solos with a blistering intensity or laying back with gentle, lyrical phrases. And that's what makes *Texas Sugar Strat Magik* a successful record—it's simply a great guitar album, full of exceptional playing. —*Stephen Thomas Erlewine*

Champion Jack Dupree

b. Jul. 4, 1910, New Orleans, LA, d. Jan. 21, 1992, Hanover, Germany
Guitar, Piano, Drums, Vocals / Piano Blues
A formidable contender in the ring before he shifted his focus to pounding the piano instead, Champion Jack Dupree often injected his lyrics with a rowdy sense of downhome humor. But there was nothing lighthearted about his rock-solid way with a boo-

gie; when he shouted "Shake Baby Shake," the entire room had no choice but to acquiesce.

Dupree was notoriously vague about his beginnings, claiming in some interviews that his parents died in a fire set by the Ku Klux Klan, at other times saying that the blaze was accidental. Whatever the circumstances of the tragic conflagration, Dupree grew up in New Orleans' Colored Waifs' Home for Boys (Louis Armstrong also spent his formative years there). Learning his trade from barrelhouse 88s ace Willie "Drive 'em Down" Hall, Dupree left the Crescent City in 1930 for Chicago and then Detroit. By 1935, he was boxing professionally in Indianapolis, battling in an estimated 107 bouts.

In 1940, Dupree made his recording debut for Lester Melrose and Okeh Records. Dupree's 1940-41 output for the Columbia subsidiary exhibited a strong New Orleans tinge despite the Chicago surroundings; his driving "Junker's Blues" was later cleaned up as Fats Domino's 1949 debut, "The Fat Man." After a stretch in the Navy during World War II (he was a Japanese POW for two years), Dupree decided tickling the 88s beat pugilism any old day. He spent most of his time in New York and quickly became a prolific recording artist, cutting for Continental, Joe Davis, Alert, Apollo, and Red Robin (where he cut a blasting "Shim Sham Shimmy" in 1953), often in the company of Brownie McGhee. Contracts meant little—Dupree masqueraded as Brother Blues on Abbey, Lightnin' Jr. on Empire, and the truly imaginative Meat Head Johnson for Gotham and Apex.

King Records corralled Dupree in 1953 and held onto him through 1955 (the year he enjoyed his only R&B chart hit, the relaxed "Walking the Blues"). Dupree's King output rates with his very best—the romping "Mail Order Woman," "Let the Doorbell Ring," and "Big Leg Emma's" contrasting with the rural "Me and My Mule" (Dupree's vocal on the latter emphasizing a harelip speech impediment for politically incorrect pseudo-comic effect).

After a year on RCA's Groove and Vik subsidiaries, Dupree made a masterpiece LP for Atlantic. 1958's *Blues from the Gutter* is a magnificent testament to Dupree's barrelhouse background, boasting marvelous readings of "Stack-O-Lee," "Junker's Blues," and "Frankie & Johnny" beside the risque "Nasty Boogie."

Dupree was one of the first bluesmen to leave his native country for a less racially polarized European existence in 1959. He lived in a variety of countries overseas, continuing to record prolifically for Storyville, British Decca (with John Mayall and Eric Clapton lending a hand at a 1966 date), and many other firms.

Perhaps sensing his own mortality, Dupree returned to New Orleans in 1990 for his first visit in 36 years. While there, he played the Jazz & Heritage Festival and laid down a zesty album for Bullseye Blues, *Back Home in New Orleans.* Two more albums of new material were captured by the company the year prior to the pianist's death in January of 1992. Jack Dupree was a champ to the very end. —*Bill Dahl*

★ **Blues from the Gutter** / 1958 / Atlantic ✦✦✦✦✦
The 1958 masterwork album of Dupree's long and prolific career. Cut in New York (in stereo!) with a blasting band that included saxist Pete Brown and guitarist Larry Dale, the Jerry Wexler-produced Atlantic collection provides eloquent testimony to Dupree's eternal place in the New Orleans blues and barrelhouse firmament. There's some decidedly down-in-the-alley subject matter—"Can't Kick The Habit," "T.B. Blues," a revival of "Junker's Blues"—along with the stomping "Nasty Boogie" and treatments of the ancient themes "Stack-O-Lee" and "Frankie & Johnny." —*Bill Dahl*

Sings the Blues / 1961 / King ✦✦✦✦
A domestic no-frills collection of Champion Jack Dupree's aforementioned King label material, albeit containing fewer tracks and little in the way of annotation—but you can't argue with the wonderful music therein! —*Bill Dahl*

Blues at Montreux / 1973 / Atlantic ✦✦✦
Rough around the edges, this set, caught live (and lively) at the 1971 Montreux Jazz Festival, teams Texas-born sax great King Curtis with the irrepressible Dupree. Curtis' young band copes reasonably well with Dupree's unpredictable sense of time, and despite their age differences, everyone has a good time. Only three months later, Curtis would tragically be stabbed to death on his New York doorstep. —*Bill Dahl*

Blues for Everybody / 1990 / Charly ✦✦✦✦✦
Although Dupree seldom paused at any one label for very long,

the piano pounder did hang around at Cincinnati-based King Records from 1951 to 1955—long enough to wax the 20 sides comprising this set and a few more that regrettably aren't aboard. By this time, Dupree was a seasoned R&B artist, storming through "Let the Doorbell Ring" and "Mail Order Woman" and emphasizing his speech impediment on "Harelip Blues" (one of those not-for-the-politically correct numbers). Most of these tracks were done in New York; sidemen include guitarist Mickey Baker and saxist Willis Jackson. —*Bill Dahl*

Back Home in New Orleans / 1990 / Bullseye Blues ✦✦✦✦
By far the best of Dupree's three albums for Bullseye Blues, this collection was cut during the pianist's first trip home to the Crescent City in 36 long years. With his longtime accompanist Kenn Lending on guitar, Dupree sounds happy to be back in his old stomping grounds throughout the atmospheric set. —*Bill Dahl*

Forever & Ever / 1991 / Bullseye Blues ✦✦✦
Dupree's Bullseye Blues encore partly misses the mark compared to his previous effort—the material isn't quite as strong as before. —*Bill Dahl*

New Orleans Barrelhouse Boogie (The Complete Champion Jack Dupree) / 1993 / Columbia/Legacy ✦✦✦✦✦
The barrelhouse boogie piano specialist's earliest sides for Okeh, dating from 1940–1941 and in a few cases sporting some groundbreaking electric guitar runs by Jesse Ellery. Dupree rocks the house like it's a decade later on two takes of "Cabbage Greens" and "Dupree Shake Dance," while his drug-oriented "Junker's Blues" was later cleaned up a bit by a newcomer named Fats Domino for his debut hit 78 "The Fat Man." —*Bill Dahl*

One Last Time / 1993 / Bullseye Blues ✦✦✦
Dupree's last album for the label, slightly more consistent than his last but not the equivalent of his first. —*Bill Dahl*

E

Snooks Eaglin

b. Jan. 21, 1936, New Orleans, LA
Guitar, Vocals / Acoustic New Orleans Blues, Electric New Orleans Blues

When they refer to consistently amazing guitarist Snooks Eaglin as a human jukebox in his New Orleans hometown, they're not dissing him in the slightest. The blind Eaglin is a beloved figure in the Crescent City, not only for his gritty, Ray Charles-inspired vocal delivery and imaginative approach to the guitar, but for the storehouse of oldies that he's liable to pull out on stage at any second (often confounding his bemused band in the process).

Born Ford Eaglin, Jr. and blind since very early childhood due to glaucoma and a brain tumor, the lad (named after radio character Baby Snooks, who shared his mischievous ways) picked up the guitar at age six and commenced to mastering every style imaginable. Gospel, blues, jazz—young Snooks Eaglin could play it all. He spent time with a Crescent City band, the Flamingoes, whose members also included pianist Allen Toussaint, played around town as Little Ray Charles, and recorded for Chess as accompanist to Sugar Boy Crawford before going it alone on the streets of the French Quarter.

His earliest recordings in 1958 for Folkways presented Eaglin as a solo acoustic folk-blues artist with an extremely eclectic repertoire. His dazzling finger-picking was nothing short of astonishing, but Eaglin really wanted to be making R&B with a band. Imperial Records producer Dave Bartholomew granted him the opportunity in 1960, and the results were sensational. Eaglin's fluid, twisting lead guitar on the utterly infectious "Yours Truly" (a Bartholomew composition first waxed by Pee Wee Crayton) and its sequel "Cover Girl" was unique on the New Orleans R&B front, while his brokenhearted cries on "Don't Slam That Door" and "That Certain Door" were positively mesmerizing. Eaglin stuck with Imperial through 1963, when the firm closed up shop in New Orleans, without ever gaining national exposure.

A dry period followed for the guitarist, but he came back first as accompanist to Professor Longhair (who was in the midst of a rather remarkable comeback bid himself) and then on his own. Eaglin has reasserted his brilliance in recent years with a series of magnificent albums for hometown Black Top Records (notably his last two, *Teasin' You* and *Soul's Edge*). *—Bill Dahl*

Country Boy Down in New Orleans / 1958 / Arhoolie ✦✦✦✦
Country Boy Down in New Orleans collects 23 tracks Snooks Eaglin recorded in the '50s. During this time, he was a street musician, playing with just one guitar or as a one-man band. On these tracks, he is accompanied by a couple of washboard players and a harpist. As expected, the sound is stripped-down, but it is exciting. Eaglin's early repertoire included a broad variety of blues, folk, and gospel songs and all of these genres are covered thoroughly on this delightful single disc. It may not be the ripping electric blues of his best-known records, but it is just as enjoyable. *—Thom Owens*

That's All Right / 1961 / Prestige ✦✦✦
Recorded during the time in which Eaglin was doubling as a blues/folk singer and a commercial R&B artist (for Imperial). He addresses the acoustic folk and blues side of his repertoire, performing everything solo on six and 12-string guitars. Time will probably judge these not to be as interesting as his full-band New Orleans R&B recordings. But this is warm, good-natured acoustic blues, with interpretations of traditional tunes, early blues by Robert Johnson, and then-recent R&B hits by Ray Charles, Arthur Crudup, and Amos Milburn. *—Richie Unterberger*

Down Yonder / 1978 / GNP ✦✦✦✦
Sam Charters produced this marvelously funky collection of oldies rendered Eaglin-style with an all-star Crescent City combo: pianist Ellis Marsalis, saxist Clarence Ford, and the French brothers as rhythm section. Eaglin's revisit of "Yours Truly" floats over a rhythmic bed so supremely second-line funky that it's astonishing, while he personalizes the New Orleans classics "Oh Red," "Down Yonder," and "Let the Four Winds Blow" as only Snooks Eaglin can. *—Bill Dahl*

Baby, You Can Get Your Gun / 1987 / Black Top ✦✦✦✦✦
The first of the masterful guitarist's amazing series of albums for Black Top is an earthly delight; his utterly unpredictable guitar weaves and darts through supple rhythms provided by New Orleans vets Smokey Johnson on drums and Erving Charles, Jr. on bass (David Lastie is on sax). Few artists boast Eaglin's "human jukebox" capabilities; his amazingly vast knowledge of eclectic numbers takes in the Four Blazes' "Mary Jo," Tommy Ridgley's "Lavinia," and the Ventures' version of "Perfidia." *—Bill Dahl*

Out of Nowhere / 1988 / Black Top ✦✦✦✦
Another wonderful lineup of Eaglinized oldies ranging from standbys by Tommy Ridgley, Benny Spellman, and Smiley Lewis to the always unexpected (Nappy Brown's "Wella Wella Baby-La," the Isleys' "It's Your Thing," the Falcons' "You're So Fine"). Guitarist Anson Funderburgh's band is used for backup on half the set; a combo sporting saxist Grady Gaines on most of the rest (Eaglin goes it alone on "Kiss of Fire"). *—Bill Dahl*

New Orleans 1960–61 / 1988 / Sundown ✦✦✦✦✦
Great R&B sides for Imperial with full band. *—Bill Dahl*

☆ **Teasin' You** / 1992 / Black Top ✦✦✦✦✦
The best of Eaglin's terrific series of Black Top efforts so far—song selection is absolutely unassailable (lots of savage New Orleans covers, from Lloyd Price and Professor Longhair to Willie Tee and Earl King), the band simmers and sizzles with spicy second-line fire (bassist George Porter, Jr. and drummer Herman Ernest III are a formidable pair indeed), and Eaglin's churchy, commanding vocals and blistering guitar work are nothing short of mind-boggling throughout the entire disc. *—Bill Dahl*

Soul's Edge / 1995 / Black Top ✦✦✦✦✦
Give this New Orleans master enough studio time, and he'll redo the entire history of post-war R&B his own way. Here he lays his mind to Joe Simon's powerhouse soul ballad "Nine Pound Steel," the Midnighters' "Let's Go, Let's Go, Let's Go," even Bill Haley & the Comets' "Skinny Minnie" and the Five Keys' loopy "Ling Ting Tong," giving each the same singular treatment that he's always brought to his recordings. Porter and Ernest return to lay down their immaculate grooves, and Fred Kemp blows sturdy sax on Eaglin's parade-beat "I Went to the Mardi Gras." *—Bill Dahl*

● **Complete Imperial Recordings** / Oct. 24, 1995 / Capitol ✦✦✦✦✦
These days, Eaglin is apt to be classified as a blues singer with considerable New Orleans R&B influences. This collection of his early-'60s recordings for the Imperial label would be much more appropriately categorized as exactly the opposite Produced by Dave Bartholomew (who also wrote over half of the material), the thrust of these recordings is most definitely in the classic-'50s/early-'60s New Orleans R&B mold, though Eaglin's vocal delivery may be bluesier than some other practitioners of the

sound. It doesn't suffer for this in the least; it's solid stuff betraying the influence of Guitar Slim and Ray Charles (though Eaglin's style is sometimes compared to the latter, it isn't extremely similar, with sparer arrangements and a distinct creole vocal slur). This compiles 26 tracks (seven previously unreleased) that he cut between 1960 and 1963, none of which were hits, perhaps because the commercial peak of classic New Orleans R&B had already passed. But it's well worth looking into if you like records from the same period by the likes of Bartholomew, Lee Dorsey, and the early Nevilles. —*Richie Unterberger*

Ronnie Earl & the Broadcasters

b. Mar. 10, 1953, New York, NY
Guitar / Modern Electric Blues
Guitarist Ronnie Earl (b. Ronald Horvath) was born March 10, 1953, in New York City, but later moved to Boston. In 1975, while attending a Muddy Waters concert, he was so moved by what he heard that he decided to learn the guitar and dedicate himself to mastering the blues tradition. He was soon playing in clubs in and around the Boston area as well as backing various blues artists on tour. He claims that his main influences were T-Bone Walker, B.B. King, Magic Sam, and Robert Jr. Lockwood. In 1980, he replaced Duke Robillard in Roomful of Blues and worked with that band for eight years, helping to take the band to national acclaim.

In the 1980s, he recorded three solo albums with his band the Broadcasters that were very well received: *Smokin'* (Black Top, 1987), *They Call Me Mr. Earl* (Black Top, 1984), and *I Like It When It Rains* (Antone, 1990). Earl left Roomful of Blues in 1988 and continues to perform and record. His intense guitar style, somewhat in the style of T-Bone Walker, has made him one of the most respected young players in the business—much in demand as a backup musician for recording dates. —*Michael Erlewine*

Soul Searchin' / 1976 / Black Top ♦♦
They Call Me Earl / Sep. 1986 / Black Top ♦♦♦
Smokin' / 1987 / Black Top ♦♦♦
I Like It When it Rains / 1988 / Antone's ♦♦♦♦♦
Deep Blues / Black Top ♦♦♦
Peace of Mind / Nov. 1990 / Black Top ♦♦♦♦♦
Peace of Mind features some nice, swinging stuff. —*Bill Dahl*
Surrounded by Love / May 1991 / Black Top ♦♦♦
Ronnie Earl recorded *Surrounded by Love* with a new version of the Broadcasters. The most notable factor of the new lineup is the reappearance of Sugar Ray Norcia, the finest vocalist/harpist Earl ever recorded with. The band sounds tight and energetic, especially on the three tracks they cut with Robert Jr. Lockwood. Parts of the album are a little slow, but the album is very entertaining, even with its minor flaws. —*Thom Owens*
Still River / 1994 / Audioquest ♦♦
Language of the Soul / 1994 / Bullseye Blues ♦♦♦
Blues and Forgiveness / 1995 / Bullseye Blues ♦♦♦
Blues Guitar Virtuosso Live In Europe / 1995 / Bullseye Blues ♦♦
● **Test of Time** / Black Top ♦♦♦♦♦
Test of Time collects the highlights from Ronnie Earl's six Black Top albums. The 18-song compilation showcases one of the finest blues guitarists of the '80s, picking nearly all of his finest material, which happen to include duets with Robert Jr. Lockwood and Hubert Sumlin. The album is an excellent introduction to Earl, as well as his most consistently entertaining release. —*Thom Owens*

David Honeyboy Edwards

b. Jun. 28, 1915, Shaw, MS
Guitar, Vocals, Harmonica / Acoustic & Electric Delta Blues
Living links to the immortal Robert Johnson are few. There's Robert Jr. Lockwood, of course—and David "Honeyboy" Edwards. Until relatively recently, Edwards was an underappreciated figure, but no longer—his slashing, Delta-drenched guitar and gruff vocals are as authentic as it gets.

Edwards had it tough growing up in Mississippi, but his blues prowess (his childhood pals included Tommy McClennan and

Robert Petway) impressed Big Joe Williams enough to take him under his wing. Rambling around the south, Honeyboy experienced the great Charlie Patton and played often with Robert Johnson. Musicologist Alan Lomax came to Clarksdale, MS, in 1942 and captured Edwards for Library of Congress-sponsored posterity.

Commercial prospects for the guitarist were scant, however—a 1951 78 for Artist Record Co., "Build a Cave" (as Mr. Honey), and four 1953 sides for Chess that were unissued until "Drop Down Mama" turned up 17 years later on an anthology constituted the bulk of his early recorded legacy, although Edwards was in Chicago from the mid-'50s on.

The guitarist met young harpist/blues aficionado Michael Frank in 1972. Four years later, they formed the Honeyboy Edwards Blues Band to break into Chicago's then-fledgling North side club scene; they also worked as a duo (and continue to do so on occasion). When Frank inaugurated his Earwig label, he enlisted Honeyboy and his longtime pals Sunnyland Slim, Big Walter Horton, Floyd Jones, and Kansas City Red to cut a rather informal album, *Old Friends*, as his second release in 1979. In 1992, Earwig assembled *Delta Bluesman*, a stunning combination of unexpurgated Library of Congress masters and recent performances that show Honeyboy Edwards has lost none of his blues fire.—*Bill Dahl*

White Windows / Sep. 1988 / Evidence ♦♦♦♦♦
David "Honeyboy" Edwards is one of the last surviving Delta blues warriors and is among the originators of a musical style as evocative and vibrant as any this nation has ever experienced. Edwards' voice, with its ironic, colorful, weary tonal qualities and cutting, keen delivery are contrasted by a crisp, slicing guitar approach. Edwards does not rely on slickness, inventiveness, or niceties; his riffs, lines, phrases, and licks are as aggressive and fiery as his vocals. He showed what real traditional blues singing was all about when he recorded for Blue Suit in 1988. Evidence has reissued that 13-song session in splendid digital glory, as Edwards' triumphant, resounding voice rings through each number. —*Ron Wynn*
● **Delta Bluesman** / 1992 / Earwig ♦♦♦♦♦
Contains the most important recordings of the slide guitarist's incredibly lengthy career, which is still going strong: his 1942 Library of Congress sides for musicologist Alan Lomax. Robert Johnson's former running partner was a formidable solo Delta bluesman in his own right; "Water Coast Blues" and "Wind Howlin' Blues" are startling in their fiery intensity. But Honeyboy remains a vital blues figure—the set is rounded out by recent waxings (some with a Chicago combo) that celebrate the ongoing contributions of this living link with Delta tradition. —*Bill Dahl*

Willie Egan

b. Louisiana
Piano / Piano Blues
Known by true aficionados for the handful of great boogie rockers that he cut for the L.A.-based Mambo and Vita imprints during the mid-'50s, pianist Willie Egan should have enjoyed a considerably larger share of fame than he did.

Born on the bayou outside of Shreveport, Egan was lucky to escape his rustic existence for Los Angeles at the age of nine. Piano swiftly became his passion, as he listened to and learned from the recordings of Amos Milburn, Hadda Brooks, and Camille Howard. A 1954 single for John R. Fullbright's Elko label preceded a series of 1955-56 gems for Larry Mead's Mambo and Vita labels, notably "Wow Wow," "What a Shame," "Come On," "She's Gone Away, But," and "Wear Your Black Dress." Egan's surname was frequently misspelled on these platters as Eggins or Egans. After a stint as one of Marvin Phillips' duet partners (billed as Marvin & Johnny), Egan largely hung it up (a 1983 European tour got him back in the studio for one album). —*Bill Dahl*

● **Come on** / Relic ♦♦♦♦♦
The R&B boogie pianist waxed some rip-roaring rockers for the tiny Los Angeles-based Vita and Mambo logos during the mid-'50s. Fourteen of his best are collected here for a long-overdue airing. This guy deserved a lot more respect than he got, judging from the jumping Louisiana-tinged "Wow Wow," "Come On," and "She's Gone Away, But...". Also aboard: 11 more obscure goodies from the same labels' vaults, notably four tracks by

Harmonica Slim (including "Drop Anchor") and Big Boy Groves' lament "You Can't Beat the Horses." —*Bill Dahl*

Robert "Mojo" Elem

b. Itta Bena, MS
Bass, Vocals, Guitar / Electric Chicago Blues

When talking about deep bluesmen who are also great entertainers, the conversation will eventually get around to the coolest bassman/singer/showman the Windy City has in its blues arsenal, Big Mojo Elem. As a singer, he possesses a relatively high-pitched voice that alternately drips with honey and malice. As a bassist, his unique approach to the instrument makes him virtually one of a kind. Unlike most bass players, Elem seldom plays standard walking bass patterns, instead using a single-note groove that lends to any band he's a part of a decidedly juke-joint groove. And as a showman, he possesses an energy that makes other performers half his age look like they're sitting down. Born in Itta Bena, MS, Elem grew up in fertile blues territory. Originally a guitarist, he soaked up licks and ideas by observing masters like Robert Nighthawk and a young Ike Turner first-hand. By his 20th birthday he had arrived in Chicago and was almost immediately pressed into professional service playing rhythm guitar behind Arthur "Big Boy" Spires and harmonica man Lester Davenport. By 1956 Elem had switched over to the newly arrived (in Chicago) electric bass, simply to stand out from the pack of guitar players searching the clubs looking for work. He formed a band with harp player Earl Payton and signed on a young Freddie King as their lead guitarist, playing on King's very first single for the El-Bee label in late 1956. After Freddie's success made him the bandleader, Big Mojo stayed with King off and on for the next eight years. The '50s and '60s also found him doing club work—mostly on the West side—with Magic Sam, Junior Wells, Shakey Jake Harris, Jimmy Dawkins and Luther Allison, with a short stint in Otis Rush's band as well. Aside from a stray anthology cut and a now out-of-print album for a tiny European label, Elem's career has not been documented in much depth, but he remains one of the liveliest players on the scene. —*Cub Koda*

Mojo Boogie / 1995 / St. George ✦✦✦✦✦
Blessed with a sweet growl of a voice and grinding out a single-note groove heavier than any ZZ Top record you've got, this thing romps like nobody's business, and is the perfect showcase for Elem's hard driving, bare-bones honest singing and bass-pumping talents. Studebaker John Grimaldi plays nice lead, even nicer slide and blows fine amplified harp when needed, while Twist Turner's no-frills drumming slots with Mojo's bass hunch. A balance between old favorites and original material, most of it co-written with producer George Paulus. —*Cub Koda*

Big Chief Ellis

b. Nov. 10, 1914, Birmingham, AL **d.** Dec. 20, 1977, Birmingham, AL
Piano, Vocals / Piano Blues

Prickly insights and sensitive accompaniment were the stock-in-trade of pianist and vocalist Wilbert Thirkield "Big Chief" Ellis. A self-taught player, Ellis performed at house parties and dances during the '20s, then left his native Alabama. He traveled extensively for several years, working mostly in non-musical jobs. After a three-year Army stint from 1939 to 1942, Ellis settled in New York. He accompanied many blues musicians during their visits to the New York area. He started recording for Lenox in 1945, and also did sessions for Sittin' In and Capitol in the '40s and '50s, playing with Sonny Terry and Brownie McGhee for Capitol. Though Ellis reduced his performance schedule after moving from New York to Washington D.C., his career got a final boost in the early '70s. He recorded for Trix and appeared at several folk and blues festivals until his death in 1977. —*Ron Wynn*

● **Big Chief Ellis Featuring Tarheel Slim** / Jun. 1977 / Trix ✦✦✦✦✦
Some rare late-period blues from two very underrated New York musicians. Big Chief Ellis and Tarheel Slim weren't the greatest technical singers, but each was a fine interpreter, and that makes this late-'70s session quite instructive. —*Ron Wynn*

Tinsley Ellis & The Heartfixers

b. Atlanta, GA
Guitar, Vocals / Modern Electric Blues

Guitarist/vocalist Tinsley Ellis knew he was fated to be a bluesman at age 14 when he was sitting in the front row of a B.B.

King concert in Miami Beach and the King of the Blues broke a string. After replacing it, he tossed it right to Ellis, who took it as a sign and has kept it ever since. Born in Atlanta, GA, Ellis was raised in South Florida and got his first guitar around age seven. Primary influences for Ellis include Elmore James, B.B. King, Freddie King, and Gatemouth Brown. While attending Emory University in Atlanta, Ellis worked in a few local bands, including the Alley Cats along with Preston Hubbard, who became a bassist for the Fabulous Thunderbirds. In the early '80s, Ellis and harpman Bob Nelson founded the Heartfixers, a rather eclectic club band that played blues, rockabilly, R&B, and early rock. They became popular on the Southeast club circuit and by 1986 had recorded four albums. Early on, Ellis was compared to Johnny Winter and Stevie Ray Vaughan, but though he had a healthy following in his region, his name was largely unknown to the mainstream. He left the Heartfixers in 1987 and began recording as a solo artist. Though recorded for Landslide, his debut, *Georgia Blue*, was distributed by Alligator Records the following year to good response. A fiery guitarist and talented songwriter, Tinsley plays a unique blend of Memphis R&B, Southwest blues, and urban funk. He prefers the raw, live sound to the studio-slick sound affected by many modern artists. When he records, it is with a minimum of technical wizardry and this gives his work the feeling of listening to a live performance. Subsequent albums, all for Alligator, include *Trouble Time* (1992) and *Storm Warning* (1994). A tireless live performer, Tinsley and his eponymous band tour constantly and log over 200 performances per year. —*Sandra Brennan*

Live at the Moon Shadow / 1983 / Landslide ✦✦✦
Atlanta blues/rockers Tinsley Ellis & The Heartfixers hit in concert with vocalist Chicago Bob Nelson. —*Michael G. Nastos*

Cool on It / Jan. 91, 1986 / Alligator ✦✦✦✦
High-energy roadhouse-rock and blues-rock with The Heartfixers. —*Niles J. Frantz*

Georgia Blue / 1989 / Alligator ✦✦
This is filled with hot, blistering guitar, mediocre songs, and flat vocals. For fans of blues guitar, there's plenty to hear—the licks and solos burn with a wild, uncontrolled fury. Others might find the album a little tedious, but not without virtue. —*Thom Owens*

● **Fanning of the Flames** / 1989 / Alligator ✦✦✦✦✦
Fanning of the Flames is an erratic but impressive set from Tinsley Ellis. While his basic sound is indebted to Stevie Ray Vaughan, the guitarist borrows from every other major blues artist. Furthermore, he has a tendency to overplay his licks, giving the album a feeling of unfocused fury. However, that sound can be overwhelming—his technique is impressive, even if he doesn't know when to reign it in. As a consequence, *Fanning of the Flames* is of interest only to guitar fans, not general listeners, but for guitar fans, there's plenty of music to treasure here. —*Thom Owens*

Trouble Time / 1992 / Alligator ✦✦
Storm Warning / 1994 / Alligator ✦✦✦

John Ellison

b. West Virginia
Vocals / R&B

The sky-high level of soulful intensity John Ellison brought to his lead vocals with the Soul Brothers Six came straight from the church. No surprise there, since he grew up in a religious household. But the way Ellison harnessed that sanctified passion on the group's secular sides was anything but common.

Leaving the coal mines of West Virginia for a more musically opportune Rochester, NY, at age 18, Ellison sang soul and styled hair before hooking up with four brothers named Armstrong (Sam, Charles, Harry, and Moses) and bassist Vonell Benjamin. The Soul Brothers Six were a completely self-contained unit—they played their own instruments in addition to singing. Their first 45s on Fine (1965's "Move Girl") and Lyndell ("Don't Neglect Your Baby" the following year) veritably dripped gospel-soaked inspiration but went nowhere.

The sextet decided to relocate to Philadelphia. On the way there, Ellison wrote the magnificent "Some Kind of Wonderful," the song that put the group on the map. Atlantic Records issued the irresistible soul workout in 1967, and it slipped onto the pop charts (becoming their only hit). Deserving encores on Atlantic didn't recapture the 45's success, and the original lineup broke up in 1969. Ellison assembled another band by the same name and soldiered on at Phil L.A. of Soul Records during 1972-73. Meanwhile, Grand Funk Railroad's graceless cover of "Some Kind of Wonderful" proved a gigantic pop smash in 1974.

The John Ellison story might have ended there (he's mostly been ensconced in Canada since then). But not too long ago, After Hours Records bosses Marty Duda and Gregory Townson happened upon the long-lost legend sitting in at a Rochester gin-mill with bluesman Joe Beard. The upshot was a 1993 solo Ellison disc, *Welcome Back*, that reintroduced the singer to the American market. Two tracks, including a remade "Some Kind of Wonderful," even reunited the singer with the Armstrong brothers. Pretty wonderful, eh? —*Bill Dahl*

Welcome Back / 1993 / After Hours/Ichiban ✦✦✦
John Ellison was once a member of The Soul Brothers Six, a fine group that didn't score many hits, but made one unforgettable number, the anthemic "Some Kind Of Wonderful." Ellison's gritty, crisp voice doesn't sound any softer or less soulful in the 1990s than it did in the 1960s. This includes a good, if not quite transcendent, remake of "Some Kind Of Wonderful," and also contains some heartfelt ballads, a quasi-country number in "You Ain't Ready" and a couple of decent mid-tempo and dance-flavored tunes. The production, sensibility and mood are vintage 1960s, which will limit its appeal and possibilities. But it's good to hear John Ellison again, even if his disc is more a nod to the past than a beacon to the future. —*Ron Wynn*

● **The Very Best of John Ellison and The Soul Brothers Six** / 1995 / Forevermore ✦✦✦✦
Well, not quite all their best: this gospel-rooted R&B group enjoyed one real hit in 1967 for Atlantic, the glorious "Some Kind of Wonderful." Alas, a recent remake of the tune, albeit a nice one, graces this 20-track collection. The best stuff is the chronologically earliest—a previously unissued 1966 outing "(You're Gonna) Be by Yourself" and obscure mid-'60s 45s "Move Girl" and "Don't Neglect Your Baby" that soar to the heavens with rich sanctified harmonies. Ten 1972-73 Soul Brothers Six items for Phil L.A. of Soul are also aboard, as are five items from Ellison's recent comeback disc for After Hours. —*Bill Dahl*

Billy "The Kid" Emerson

b. Jan. 22, 1938, Florida
Piano, Vocals / Electric Memphis Blues
Slashing blues, infectious R&B, formulaic rock 'n' roll, moving gospel—keyboardist Billy "The Kid" Emerson played all those interrelated styles during a lengthy career that began in Florida and later transported him up to Memphis and Chicago.

Emerson had already learned his way around a piano when he entered the Navy in 1943. After the war, he began playing around Tarpon Springs, attending Florida A&M during the late '40s and early '50s. He picked up his nickname while playing a joint in St. Petersburg; the club owner dressed the band up in cowboy duds that begged comparison with a certain murderous outlaw.

A 1952-53 stint in the Air Force found Emerson stationed in Greenville, MS. That's where he met young bandleader Ike Turner, who whipped Emerson into shape as an entertainer while he sang with Turner's Kings of Rhythm. Turner also got Emerson through the door at Sun Records in 1954, playing guitar on the Kid's debut waxing "No Teasing Around."

Emerson's songwriting skills made him a valuable commodity around Sun—but more as a source for other performers' material later on. His bluesy 1955 outing "When It Rains It Pours" elicited a cover from Elvis a few years later at RCA, while Emerson's "Red Hot" (a takeoff on an old cheerleaders' chant from Emerson's school days) became a savage rockabilly anthem revived by Billy Lee Riley for Sun and Bob Luman on Imperial.

After his "Little Healthy Thing" failed to sell, Emerson exited Sun to sign with Chicago's Vee-Jay Records in late 1955. Despite first-rate offerings such as the jumping "Every Woman I Know (Crazy 'Bout Automobiles)" and a sophisticated "Don't Start Me to Lying," national recognition eluded Emerson at Vee-Jay too.

It was on to Chess in 1958, recording "Holy Mackerel Baby" and the unusual novelty "Woodchuck" (a remake of an earlier Sun single) during his year or so there. 45s for Mad, USA, M-Pac! (where he waxed the dance workout "The Whip"), and Constellation preceded the formation of Emerson's own logo, Tarpon, in 1966. In addition to Emerson's own stuff, Tarpon issued Denise LaSalle's debut single.

A prolific writer, Emerson penned songs for Junior Wells, Willie Mabon, Wynonie Harris, and Buddy Guy during the early '60s, often in conjunction with Willie Dixon. When recording opportunities slowed, Emerson played jazzy R&B in lounges and supper clubs (guitarist Lacy Gibson was a member of his trio for a while). Emerson took Europe by surprise with a dynamic segment on the American Blues Legends 1979 tour. More recently, he's rumored to have reverted to playing gospel in Florida. —*Bill Dahl*

● **Little Healthy Thing** / 1980 / Charly ✦✦✦✦✦
Since no CD reissues are easily accessible by this important Florida-born R&B pianist, this vinyl compendium of his 1954-55 Sun catalog will have to suffice for now. Emerson's jumping proto-rock style at Sun supplied notable rockabillies with killer material—"Red Hot," as first cut by Emerson, was later done full justice by Billy Lee Riley, while Elvis found the hip-grinding "When It Rains It Pours" to his liking. Emerson's bluesy "No Teasing Around" (with Ike Turner on guitar), the upbeat "Something for Nothing," and the title cut are among the many highlights of this enjoyable LP. —*Bill Dahl*

Crazy 'bout Automobiles / 1982 / Charly ✦✦✦✦
Another vinyl-only collection, this one a ten-incher with only ten songs, covering Emerson's 1955-57 stay at Chicago's Vee-Jay label. Emerson bonded well with Vee-Jay's house bands, especially on the romping "Every Woman I Know (Crazy 'Bout Automobiles)" and a sophisticated "Don't Start Me to Lying." As with his Sun stuff, the big-voiced Emerson was a captivating performer. —*Bill Dahl*

Sleepy John Estes (John Adams Estes)

b. Jan. 25, 1899, Ripley, TN, d. Jun. 5, 1977, Brownsville, TN
Guitar, Vocals / Acoustic Country Blues
Big Bill Broonzy called John Estes' style of singing "crying" the blues because of its overt emotional quality. Actually, his vocal style harks back to his tenure as a work-gang leader for a railroad maintenance crew, where his vocal improvisations and keen, cutting voice set the pace for work activities. Nicknamed "Sleepy" John Estes, supposedly because of his ability to sleep standing up, he teamed with mandolinist Yank Rachell and harmonica player Hammie Nixon to play the houseparty circuit in and around Brownsville in the early '20s. Forty years later, the same team reunited to record for Delmark and play the festival circuit. Never an outstanding guitarist, Estes relied on his expressive voice to carry his music, and the recordings he made from 1929 on have enormous appeal and remain remarkably accessible today.

Despite the fact that he worked to mixed Black and White audiences in string band, jug band, or medicine show formats, his music retains a distinct ethnicity and has a particularly plaintive sound. Astonishingly, he recorded during six decades for Victor, Decca, Bluebird, Ora Nelle, Sun, Delmark, and others. Over the course of his career, his music remained simple yet powerful, and despite his sojourns to Memphis or Chicago he retained a traditional down-home sound. Some of his songs are deeply personal statements about his community and life, such as "Lawyer Clark" or "Floating Bridge." Other compositions have universal appeal ("Drop Down Mama" or "Someday Baby") and went on to become mainstays in the repertoires of countless musicians. One of the true masters of his idiom, he lived in poverty, yet was somehow capable of turning his experiences and the conditions of his life into compelling art. —*Barry Lee Pearson*

The Legend of Sleepy John Estes / 1962 / Delmark ✦✦✦✦
The best of his Delmark rediscovery recordings. —*Barry Lee Pearson*

1929-1940 / 1967 / Smithsonian/Folkways ✦✦✦✦✦
Sleepy John Estes' finest period vocally was the prewar era. This LP includes several expressive and delightful numbers in which Estes' narrative skills are especially strong. He was never a great guitarist, but the accompaniment works here because it's sparse and limited. —*Ron Wynn*

Jazz Heritage—Down South Blues (1935-1940) / MCA ✦✦✦
Part of an '80s MCA budget blues series, this album includes "Drop Down Mama" and "Someday Baby." With Hammie Nixon on harmonica. —*Barry Lee Pearson*

★ **Sleepy John Estes 1929–1940: I Ain't Gonna Be Worried No More** / 1992 / Yazoo ✦✦✦✦✦

I Ain't Gonna Be Worried No More compiles 23 songs Sleepy John Estes recorded between 1929 and 1941, capturing the bluesman at the height of his creative powers. Unlike many Delta bluesmen of his era, Estes worked with a full jug band, which gave his music a greater variety of textures. His music swings, with a loose, relaxed feel that isn't heard on many Delta blues records. Furthermore, his songs are inventive, featuring pseudo-autobiographical lyrics loaded with evocative imagery. Nearly all of his best material is included on *I Ain't Gonna Be*

Worried No More, making it as close to a definitive retrospective of Estes' music as possible. *— Thom Owens*

Complete Works, Vols. 1–2 / Document ✦✦✦

Document's two-volume collection of Sleepy John Estes' recordings contains everything the bluesman cut between 1929 and 1941, presented in chronological order. Although there is plenty of fine music on the collection, the presentation is overwhelming for anyone but completists and historians. If you're neither, stick with Yazoo's single-disc collection, *I Ain't Gonna Be Worried No More. — Thom Owens*

F

The Fabulous Thunderbirds

Group / Electric Texas Blues

With their fusion of blues, rock 'n' roll, and R&B, the Fabulous Thunderbirds helped popularize roadhouse Texas blues with a mass audience in the '80s and, in the process, helped kick-start a blues revival during the mid-'80s. During their heyday in the early '80s, they were the most popular attraction on the blues bar circuit, which eventually led to a breakthrough to the pop audience in 1986 with their fifth album, *Tuff Enuff*. The mass success didn't last too long, and founding member Jimmie Vaughan left in 1990, but the Fabulous Thunderbirds remained one of the most popular blues concert acts in America during the '90s.

Guitarist Jimmie Vaughan formed the Fabulous Thunderbirds with vocalist/harpist Kim Wilson in 1974; in addition to Vaughan and Wilson, the band's original lineup included bassist Keith Ferguson and drummer Mike Buck. Initially, the group also featured vocalist Lou Ann Barton, but she left the band shortly after its formation. Within a few years, the Thunderbirds became the house band for the Austin club Antone's, where they would play regular sets and support touring blues musicians. By the end of the decade, they had built a strong fan base, which led to a record contract with the local Takoma Records.

In 1979, the Fabulous Thunderbirds released their eponymous debut on Takoma. The record was successful enough to attract the attention of major labels and Chrysalis signed the band the following year. *What's the Word*, the group's second album, was released in 1980 and it was followed in 1981 by *Butt Rockin'*. By the time the Thunderbirds recorded their 1982 album *T-Bird Rhythm*, drummer Mike Buck was replaced by Fran Christina, a former member of Roomful of Blues.

Although the Fabulous Thunderbirds had become favorites of fellow musicians—they opened shows for both the Rolling Stones and Eric Clapton—and had been critically well-received, their records didn't sell particularly well. Chrysalis dropped the band following the release of *T Bird Rhythm*, leaving them without a record contract for four years. While they were in limbo, they continued to play concerts across the country. During this time, bassist Keith Ferguson left the band and was replaced by Preston Hubbard, another former member of Roomful of Blues. In 1985, they finally landed another record contract, signing with Epic/Associated.

After the deal with Epic/Associated was complete, the T-Birds entered a London studio and recorded their fifth album with producer Dave Edmunds. The resulting album, *Tuff Enuff*, was released in the spring of 1986 and, unexpectedly, became a major crossover success. The title track was released as a single and its accompanying video received heavy play on MTV, which helped the song reach the American Top Ten. The success of the single sent the album to number 13 on the charts; *Tuff Enuff* would eventually receive a platinum record. "Wrap It Up," a cover of an old Sam & Dave song, was the album's second single and became a Top Ten album rock track. Later in 1986, the T-Birds won the W.C. Handy Award for best blues band.

The Fabulous Thunderbirds' followup to *Tuff Enuff, Hot Number*, arrived in the summer of 1987. Initially, the album did fairly well—peaking at number 49 on the charts and spawning the Top Ten album rock hit "Stand Back"—but it quickly fell off the charts. Furthermore, its slick, radio-ready sound alienated their hardcore following of blues fans. "Powerful Stuff," a single from the soundtrack of the Tom Cruise film *Cocktail*, became a

number three album rock hit in the summer of 1988. It was included on the following year's *Powerful Stuff* album, which proved to be a major commercial disappointment—it only spent seven weeks on the charts.

After the two poorly-received followups to *Tuff Enuff*, Jimmie Vaughan left the band to play in a duo with his brother, Stevie Ray Vaughan; following Stevie Ray's death in the summer of 1990, Jimmie pursued a full-time solo career. The Fabulous Thunderbirds replaced Vaughan with two guitarists, Duke Robillard and Kid Bangham. The first album from the new line-up, *Walk That Walk, Talk That Talk*, appeared in 1991. Following the release of *Walk That Walk, Talk That Talk*, Epic/Associated dropped the Fabulous Thunderbirds from their roster.

During the early '90s, the Fabulous Thunderbirds were in limbo, as Kim Wilson recorded a pair of solo albums—*Tigerman* (1993) and *That's Life* (1994). Wilson re-assembled the band in late 1994 and they recorded their ninth album, *Roll of the Dice*, which was released on Private Music in 1995. Following its release, the band returned to actively touring the United States. *—Stephen Thomas Erlewine*

Fabulous Thunderbirds / 1979 / Chrysalis ✦✦✦✦✦
Their debut album, with the original lineup of Wilson, Vaughn, Buck, and Ferguson stompin' through a roadhouse set of covers and genre-worthy originals. One of the few White blues albums that works. *—Cub Koda*

What's the Word / 1980 / Chrysalis ✦✦✦✦✦
Second album, equally powerful. Some of their best, including the off-kilter "Los Fabulosos Thunderbirds" and "Running Shoes." *—Cub Koda*

Butt Rockin' / 1981 / Chrysalis ✦✦✦

T Bird Rhythm / 1982 / Chrysalis ✦✦✦

Tuff Enuff / 1986 / Epic ✦✦✦
Their breakthrough success. The title track and soul covers point the band in a new, more mainstream direction. *—Cub Koda*

Hot Number / 1987 / Epic ✦✦

Powerful Stuff / 1989 / Epic ✦✦
Like the previous *Hot Number, Powerful Stuff* is a weak collection of watered-down blues-rock that makes too many concessions to the commerical constraints of AOR radio stations. Occasionally, the band works up some energy, or Jimmie Vaughan or Kim Wilson turn out a good solo, but for the most part, *Powerful Stuff* is bland, faceless mainstream rock 'n' roll. *—Thom Owens*

The Essential / 1991 / Chrysalis ✦✦✦✦✦
Nice compilation of the early Chrysalis albums on one CD. *—Cub Koda*

Walk That Walk, Talk That Talk / Dec. 1991 / Epic ✦✦✦
The first album the Fabulous Thunderbirds recorded without Jimmie Vaughan. It takes two guitarists–two good guitarists, by the way–to fill his place and even with Duke Robillard and Kid Bangham on board, there is something missing. Though the T-birds have returned to straight-ahead blues-rock, abandoning the overly commercial production of their previous three albums, they don't sound as distinctive as they did with Vaughan. Kim Wilson blows some good harp, Robillard throws out a few stellar solos and Bangham can almost keep up with him, but on the whole, the album is a disappointment. *—Thom Owens*

● **Hot Stuff: The Greatest Hits** / 1992 / Epic ✦✦✦✦✦
The best tracks from The Fabulous Thunderbirds' more rock-oriented years at CBS Associated Records are collected in this single-disc compilation/ —*Stephen Thomas Erlewine*

Wrap It Up / 1993 / Sony Special Products ✦✦✦
Wrap It Up is an enjoyable budget-priced collection of hits and album tracks from the Fabulous Thunderbirds' Epic era, including the title track, which is a cover of Sam & Dave's hit. It's a fine sampler, but not a definitive collection by any stretch of the imagination —*Stephen Thomas Erlewine*

Roll of the Dice / 1995 / Private Music ✦✦✦
The Fabulous T-Birds' second album without Jimmie Vaughan is an improvement over *Walk That Walk, Talk That Talk,* featuring a tighter, more focused band and hotter playing. Nevertheless, the band takes a couple of missteps, particularly with a limp version of "Zip-A-Dee-Doo-Dah." –*Stephen Thomas Erlewine*

H-Bomb Ferguson (Robert Ferguson)

b. 1929
Piano, Blues / Electric Jump Blues
His extroverted antics and multi-colored fright wig might invite the instant dismissal of Cincinnati-based singer Robert "H-Bomb" Ferguson as some sort of comic lightweight. In reality, he's one of the last survivors of the jump blues era whose once-slavish Wynonie Harris imitations have mellowed into a highly distinctive vocal delivery of his own.

Ferguson's dad, a minister, paid for piano lessons for his son, demanding he stick to sacred melodies on the 88s. Fat chance— by age 19, Bobby Ferguson was on the road with Joe Liggins & the Honeydrippers. When they hit New York, Ferguson branched off on his own. Comedian Nipsey Russell, then emcee at Harlem's Baby Grand Club, got the singer a gig at the nightspot. Back then, Ferguson was billed as "The Cobra Kid."

Singles for Derby, Atlas, and Prestige preceded a 1951-52 hookup with Savoy Records that produced some of Ferguson's best waxings. Most of them were obvious Harris knockoffs, but eminently swinging ones with top-flight backing (blasting saxists Purvis Henson and Count Hastings were aboard the dates). Drummer Jack "The Bear" Parker, who played on the Savoy dates, allegedly bestowed the singer with his explosive monicker. Other accounts credit Savoy producer Lee Magid with coining H-Bomb's handle; either way, his dynamite vocals fulfilled the billing.

Ferguson eventually made Cincinnati his home, recording for Finch, Big Bang, ARC, and the far more prestigious Federal in 1960. H-Bomb terminated his touring schedule in the early '70s. When he returned from premature retirement, his unique wig-wearing schtick (inspired by Rick James' coiffure) was in full bloom. Backed by his fine young band, the Medicine Men, Ferguson waxed his long-overdue debut album, *Wiggin' Out,* for Chicago's Earwig logo in 1993. It showed him to be as wild as ever (witness the gloriously sleazy "Meatloaf"), a talented pianist to boot, and more his own man than ever before. —*Bill Dahl*

Life Is Hard / Nov. 1987 / Savoy ✦✦✦✦
The atomic one in his early-'50s jump blues mode, when he made a living as an unabashed Wynonie Harris clone (and a damned good one at that). Swinging New York bands and Ferguson's hearty vocals make the similarities entirely forgivable. Hopefully, this LP will be available digitally before too long. —*Bill Dahl*

● **Wiggin' Out** / Feb. 1993 / Earwig ✦✦✦✦✦
Somewhere over the last 40 years or so, this purple wig-wearing R&B pioneer dropped his slavish Wynonie Harris imitations and became his own man, learning how to play piano to boot. His long-overdue debut album joyously recalls the heyday of jump blues via salacious rockers like "Meatloaf" and "Shake Your Apple Tree." Ferguson's young band, the Medicine Men, do a fine job of laying down exciting grooves behind the singer. —*Bill Dahl*

Fleetwood Mac/Peter Green

Group / British Blues
To most people watching VH-1, Fleetwood Mac is that group of bell-bottomed, sunny Californians fronted by the chirpy vocal talents of Stevie Nicks, whose pop hits dominated the airwaves and sales charts for over a decade, making them the '70s version

of Hootie & the Blowfish. *That* story is writ large in the annals of rock history books. But in the beginning—though you'd never know it by listening to any of their greatest hits—the original Fleetwood Mac was one hell of a blues band. Fueled by a driving rhythm section (Mick Fleetwood on drums and John McVie on bass), sporting two lead guitar players (single string wizard Peter Green and slideman Jeremy Spencer)—and eventually three (Danny Kirwan)—and a show that spiraled from dazzling originals, full-throttle Chicago blues to outrageous sendups of '50s rock 'n' roll, the original Fleetwood Mac was one hell of a band, period.

Their British blues credentials couldn't come any higher up on the food chain; the nucleus of the group met while playing as members of John Mayall's Bluesbreakers, with Peter Green having the unenviable task of replacing Eric Clapton. The young guitarist, whom everyone affectionately called "Greenie," quickly established himself on the next release (*A Hard Road*) and Mayall showed his appreciation by donating some free studio time to the guitarist as a birthday present in 1967. Greenie grabbed Fleetwood and McVie for the rhythm section and went in and cut three songs that day: "It Hurts Me Too" by Elmore James, "Double Trouble" by Otis Rush and an untitled instrumental he had composed. When pressed by the engineer for a title, Green leaned over the recording console and scrawled "Fleetwood Mac" across the tape box. Of such events, legends are born and bands are named.

Greenie and Fleetwood left Mayall at about the same time, but McVie didn't want to give up the steady paycheck that working in the Bluesbreakers provided him with and Bob Brunning "replaced" him until McVie could be coaxed into the new band, odd behavior considering that it was partially named after him to begin with. Green, who loathed all kinds of guitar hero worship, felt that the trio format was too limited and also wanted someone in the band to take part of the singing and performing load off his shoulders. Enter the diminutive Jeremy Spencer, and Greenie had found exactly what he wanted and needed for the new combo to take flight. Spencer played a hollow-body guitar almost as big as he was and had the slashing slide wailings of his hero, Elmore James, down cold. Blues history revisionists like to downplay Spencer's credentials, but what he was accomplishing was something more on the level of recreated art than merely copying his record collection and strangling his Midlands voice to sound like James. With Spencer aboard to provide the boogie, Green felt that the band was ready and on August of 1967, they played their debut gig in front of 30,000 people at the prestigious Windsor Jazz and Blues Festival, blasting out a red-hot 30-minute set in front of John Mayall's Bluesbreakers. Fleetwood Mac made a strong enough impression that Sunday to quickly become the talk of English blues circles, especially when John McVie left Mayall three weeks later to join them permanently.

They cut their first album, basically a re-creation of their live show, in only three days. With Green's moody, introspective takes on the B.B. King style juxtaposed against Spencer's Elmore James slide boogie, the mixture proved irresistible to 1968 British audiences and the debut stayed on the pop charts for 17 weeks. Their instant success caused them to not really change their music so much (at first), but to definitely start monkeying around with its presentation in a live format. Tired of the pious-faced, staid British blues band facade that seemed to have begun with Blues Incorporated and handed down to each new band that wanted to be considered *authentic,* Fleetwood Mac—this time led by the mischievous Jeremy Spencer—began to rebel. Suddenly the band was like some high-voltage, drunken vaudeville English music-hall show gone terribly awry that played stone solid blues while condoms filled with milk dangled off the tuning pegs of their guitars. Reportedly in love with '50s rock 'n' roll music while being simultaneously disgusted with its then-current-day revivalists, the band would leave the stage, grease their hair up into pompadours and with Spencer as a drunk Elvis front man goading them on, Britain's most respected new blues band mutated into a '50s lunatic factory called Earl Vince and the Valiants. It was exactly these kind of drunken hijinks that got them banned from the prestigious Marquee Club in London, but make no mistake about it, it *was* a regular fixture in the original band's stage presentation, both in the U.K. and on original tours in the U.S. as well.

They began to get further away from the blues format with

each successive release; the first single attempt, Green's "Black Magic Woman," flopped in the U.K. but became a hit for Santana, a band that had opened for them in the U.S. Green grew restless; he wanted a bigger sound and was displeased at Spencer's limitations, both as a performer and as a non-contributing songwriter. Enter guitarist Danny Kirwan, who grew up enthralled with Peter Green the way Greenie was with Eric Clapton. Late in 1968, the band caught its first taste of global chart success with the release of Green's instrumental, "The Albatross." But they hadn't forgotten their blues roots and in January of 1969 assembled in the Chess studios with some of the city's blues greats, including Big Walter Horton, Otis Spann, J.T. Brown, and Willie Dixon for a marathon blues recording session. The band was getting bigger and bigger everyday; in Europe they were outselling the Beatles and the Rolling Stones and were on the verge of their American breakthrough on the ballroom and festival circuit.

But this success didn't make Peter Green very happy at all. Psychedelic drugs and cult religion made him want to play all future gigs for nothing, effectively giving all the band's money away, his departure to eventually become a grave digger signaled the beginning of the end for the original group. With Kirwan and Spencer attempting to front the band in Greenie's absence, the strain proved to be too much for little Jeremy Spencer. In February of 1971, on the eve of a West Coast tour, Spencer left his Hollywood hotel room to go for a walk, never to return. A few days later, he was found—his head shaved bald—in a locked and guarded warehouse run by the religious cult, the Children of God. With a six-week tour ahead of them and half their act gone, the band coaxed Peter Green back into the fold to finish out the remaining dates. When it was over, he left again, never to return, effectively ending the days of Fleetwood Mac, kings of British blues-rock. The rest, as they say, is rock 'n' roll. —Cub Koda

Peter Green's Fleetwood Mac / Feb. 1968 / Blue Horizon [UK] ✦✦✦✦✦
Fleetwood Mac's debut LP was a highlight of the late '60s British blues boom. Green's inspired playing, the capable (if erratic) songwriting, and the panache of the band as a whole placed them leagues above the overcrowded field. Elmore James is a big influence on this set, particularly on the tunes fronted by Jeremy Spencer ("Shake Your Moneymaker," "Got to Move"). Spencer's bluster, however, was outshone by the budding singing and songwriting skills of Green. The guitarist balanced humor and vulnerability on cuts like "Looking for Somebody" and "Long Grey Mare," and with "If I Loved Another Woman," he offered a glimpse of the Latin-blues fusion that he would perfect with "Black Magic Woman." The album was an unexpected smash in the U.K., reaching number 4 on the British charts. —Richie Unterberger

English Rose / Jan. 1969 / Epic ✦✦✦✦✦
Under the direction of Peter Green, Fleetwood Mac is heard as a British blues group, although its most notable performances are on Green's original tunes "Black Magic Woman" and "Albatross," both British hits. —William Ruhlmann

Pious Bird of Good Omen [Comp] / Aug. 1969 / Blue Horizon ✦✦✦✦✦
This is a compilation of Fleetwood Mac's early period, 1967–1968, featuring both sides of its debut single, "I Believe My Time Ain't Long"/"Rambling Pony" and many blues covers, as well as the hits "Albatross" and "Black Magic Woman." —William Ruhlmann

Then Play On / Oct. 1969 / Reprise ✦✦✦
The most diverse and accomplished album by the Peter Green-led lineup. Features some wrenching, introspective originals that draw from both blues and progressive rock, highlighted by the British hit single "Oh Well." —Richie Unterberger

Kiln House / Sep. 1970 / Reprise ✦✦✦
Fleetwood Mac's first album after the departure of their nominal leader, Peter Green, finds the remaining members, Mick Fleetwood, John McVie, Jeremy Spencer, and Danny Kirwan (plus McVie's wife Christine) trying to maintain the band's guitar-heavy, blues-rock approach, with the burden falling on Spencer and Kirwan. They don't embarrass themselves, but none of this is of the caliber of Green's work. —William Ruhlmann

Black Magic Woman / 1971 / Epic ✦✦✦✦✦
No U.S. label has seen fit to provide a multi-disc retrospective of

the Peter Green-era Fleetwood Mac for the digital age. If you suspect that this richly warranted project will never come to fruition, you might want to hunt down this double LP of pre-Then Play On material. Originally issued in the early 1970s, it pairs Peter Green's Fleetwood Mac with English Rose, and is highlighted by the essential British hits "Albatross" and "Black Magic Woman." —Richie Unterberger

Greatest Hits [CBS] / 1971 / CBS ✦✦✦✦✦
Unissued in the United States, this is a well-chosen, concise 12-song best-of covering the Peter Green era. Besides "Black Magic Woman," "Albatross," and "Man of the World," it includes the hard-to-find (in the States, anyway) British hit singles "Man of the World" and "The Green Manalishi." —Richie Unterberger

Fleetwood Mac in Chicago / 1975 / Sire ✦✦
A two-record set culled from sessions the Peter Green/Danny Kirwan/Mick Fleetwood/John McVie edition of the band held at Chess Studios in Chicago in January 1969 with such blues legends as Otis Spann and Willie Dixon. Despite their awe, the Brits hold their own on a set of standards. (Reissued on CD under the title In Chicago 1969 on April 26, 1994.) —William Ruhlmann

Original Fleetwood Mac / 1977 / Sire ✦✦
This collection of outtakes from the group's early days probably dates from 1967–68, and finds the band at their most reverently bluesy. Peter Green wrote most of the material on this set, which is quite similar to the band's first couple of albums in its purist British take on traditional electric blues forms. The material, however, isn't nearly as strong as the best early Fleetwood Mac; not that the band should be faulted for that, as this is an outtake collection, after all. A couple of the tunes featuring Jeremy Spencer are actually taken from an audition that Spencer's pre-Fleetwood Mac outfit, The Levi Set, recorded for the Blue Horizon label in England. The best track is the driving instrumental "Fleetwood Mac," and has been rumored to be an outtake from Green's days with John Mayall's Bluesbreakers. —Richie Unterberger

Jumping at Shadows / 1985 / Varrick ✦✦✦
Recorded live in Boston in 1969, this finds the Peter Green-era Mac at their best on seven lengthy but focused cuts. Includes versions of "Black Magic Woman" and "Oh Well," as well as a couple of straight blues covers and some Danny Kirwan material. —Richie Unterberger

Cerulean / 1985 / Shanghai ✦✦✦
From the same 1969 Boston gigs that produced Jumping At Shadows, this double album's appeal is more limited, with a heavier emphasis on straight blues boogie and eccentric fifties rock 'n' roll parodies that featured Jeremy Spencer. Highlights are the 16-minute version of the British hit "Green Manalishi" and the 24-minute version of "Rattlesnake Shake." —Richie Unterberger

Peter Green's Fleetwood Mac Live At The BBC / Oct. 1995 / Raw Power ✦✦✦
A substantial (and official) supplement to the band's recorded legacy with Peter Green, this double CD features 36 songs broadcast between 1967 and 1971, in mostly superlative sound (and the few numbers that aren't 100% clean are certainly of listenable fidelity). The title, though, isn't completely accurate; half a dozen tracks were recorded shortly after Green left the band, and since Green is still listed as part of the lineup for all but one of these in the liner notes, the record company either has the dates or personnel wrong. (Also, one track, "I Need Your Love So Bad," is not even listed on the sleeve.) Anyway, the music gives a good idea of the range of the band in their earliest, and by many accounts, best incarnation. It is not, however, all blues-rock by any means; quite a lot of this is given over to Jeremy Spencer-dominated parodies of '50s rock, and while these are entertaining in a modest fashion, the best moments, unsurprisingly, are when guitarists Danny Kirwan and (more particularly) Green play their own material. Some of Green's most well-known compositions from the era are here ("Man of the World," "Albatross," "Rattlesnake Shake," and "Oh Well"), and in the usual BBC tradition these have a sparer and rougher feel than the studio versions, though they don't either match or redefine them. Of most interest to early Mac fans will be the inclusion of several numbers that they never recorded in the studio (although some, like "Sandy Mary" and "Only You," did appear on live albums that weren't issued until the 1980s). "Preachin',"

"Preachin' Blues," and "Early Morning Come" are otherwise unavailable showcases for Spencer, Green, and Kirwan respectively that demonstrate their facility with no-nonsense, downhome blues when they got in a serious mood. While this isn't as essential a collection as *Then Play On* or the numerous best-of anthologies covering the Peter Green era, it presents more solid evidence of the band's skills in both blues-rock and surpisingly straight rock (a cover of Tim Hardin's "Hang on to a Dream" is the surprise find of the set), though some may find the detours into comedy and '50s rock irksome. —*Richie Unterberger*

Sue Foley Band

b. Mar. 29, 1968, Ottawa, Canada
Guitar / Modern Electric Blues
This highly touted vocalist/guitarist originally hails from Ottawa, Canada, although her homebase shifted to Austin, TX, when she signed with Antone's Records and cut her debut set, *Young Girl Blues*, in 1992 (an encore, *Without a Warning*, quickly followed). Foley's wicked lead guitar makes her a rarity among blueswomen.

When she was a child in Ottawa, Foley listened to rock 'n' roll and blues-rock groups like the Rolling Stones. Although these bands sowed the seeds of her affection for the blues, her love for the music didn't blossom until she saw James Cotton in concert when she was 15 years old. Cotton inspired Foley to pick up the electric guitar. During her late teens and early '20s, she jammed with local Ottawa bar bands—she didn't form her own group until she moved to Vancouver in the mid-'80s.

Foley sent a demo tape of herself to Antone's Records in 1990. Impressed, the label arranged an audition. Sue moved to Austin and soon signed a recording contract with Antone's. In 1992, her debut album, *Young Girl Blues*, was released. It was acclaimed by a number of blues publications. Two years later she released her second album, *Without a Warning*. It was followed by *Big City Blues* in 1995. —*Bill Dahl & Stephen Thomas Erlewine*

● Young Girl Blues / 1992 / Antone's ✦✦✦✦✦
Sue Foley's debut album is an impressive effort. Not only is Foley a wild, adventurous guitarist, she can write songs that don't merely rehash standard blue clichés. Her songs have a passion that is heightened by her array of gutsy guitar textures, which are rooted in blues tradition but never tied down to it. —*Thom Owens*

Without a Warning / 1994 / Antone's ✦✦✦
Big City Blues / 1995 / Antone's ✦✦✦✦

The Charles Ford Blues Band

Group / Electric West Coast Blues
After leaving Ukiah, CA, and moving south to San Francisco to form the Charles Ford Band (named for their father) in the late '60s with harmonica player Gary Smith, brothers Pat (drums) and Robben (guitar) were enlisted by Charlie Musselwhite and were pivotal members of one of the best groups the harpist ever led. Leaving Musselwhite after recording Arhoolie's *Takin' My Time*, they recruited bassist Stan Poplin and younger brother Mark, then age 17, on harmonica and played as the Real Charles Ford Band. Heavily influenced by the original Butterfield Blues Band and the Chess catalog, the quartet was famous for their live jazz explorations—often jamming for 30 minutes or more on a John Coltrane and George Benson tune—and hear-a-pin-drop dynamics (with Mark abandoning mike and amp to play acoustically into the room or Robben turning the volume all the way off on his fat-body Gibson L-5). Muddy Waters sat in with and praised the young band, and Chess Records even came courting, but the brothers split on New Year's Eve, 1971, recording their sole LP posthumously, as it were. Robben went on to major cult status via session work and sporadic solo releases, and after lengthy hiatuses Mark and Pat continue to gig around the Bay Area and Europe (Pat founding his own Blue Rock'it label). Twenty-five years after their dissolution, the band's influence in Northern California is still enormous, particularly among guitar players who continue to ape licks Robben forgot two decades ago. —*Dan Forte*

● The Charles Ford Band / 1972 / Arhoolie ✦✦✦✦✦
Recorded after the quartet had packed it in, their sole vinyl document inevitably left much to be desired for anyone who'd witnessed their through-the-roof club appearances. Still, the expressive opener, "Blue and Lonesome," manages to create a space of its own, avoiding comparisons with Little Walter's original. Middle brother Robben's expressive vocals defy his 20 years, and his Bloomfield-inspired guitar playing is even more authoritative. Meanwhile harmonica-playing Mark, only age 18, gives Butterfield a run for his money. A later CD reissue gives a glimpse at the band's jazz leaning with a live rendition of John Coltrane's "The Promise." —*Dan Forte*

A Reunion / 1982 / Blue Rock ✦✦✦
Ten years after disbanding the Ford brothers reunited at a Bay Area club for this live set. But despite some incredible soloing from Robben and Mark, the repertoire presents only blues standards; thus, what made this outfit different (its jazz chops) never saw the light of day. An exciting night, yes, but not one that holds up to repeated listenings. —*Dan Forte*

Here We Go! / 1990 / Crosscut ✦✦✦

The Ford Blues Band / Blue Rock-It ✦✦✦

Robben Ford

b. 1951, Ukiah, CA
Guitar / Blues, Fusion, Crossover
Robben Ford has had a diverse career. He taught himself guitar when he was 13 and considered his first influence to be Mike Bloomfield. At 18 he moved to San Francisco to form the Charles Ford Band (named after his father who was also a guitarist) and was soon hired to play with Charles Musselwhite for nine months. In 1971 the Charles Ford Blues Band was re-formed and recorded for Arhoolie in early 1972. Ford played with Jimmy Witherspoon (1972-73), the L.A. Express with Tom Scott (1974), George Harrison and Joni Mitchell. In 1977 he was a founding member of the Yellowjackets, which he stayed with until 1983, simultaneously having a solo career and working as a session guitarist. In 1986 Ford toured with Miles Davis and he had two separate periods (1985 and 1987) with Sadao Watanabe but he seemed to really find himself in 1992 when he returned to his roots, the blues. Robben Ford formed a new group, The Blue Line, and has since recorded a couple of blues-rock dates for Stretch that are among the finest of his career. —*Scott Yanow*

Robben Ford & The Blue Line / 1992 / Stretch ✦✦✦
An effective combination of fusion and mainstream players unite for a session that alternates between light, pleasant instrumentals and more challenging numbers. Ford's guitar solos try to balance things and sometimes get a bit bland, then loosen up whenever the songs are more involved. The lineup includes outstanding drummer Marvin Smith. —*Ron Wynn*

● Handful of Blues / Sep. 12, 1995 / Blue Thumb ✦✦✦✦
On *Handful of Blues*, Robben Ford strips his sound back to the basics, recording a set of blues with only a bassist and a drummer. The group runs through a handful of standards, including "Don't Let Me Be Misunderstood" and "I Just Want to Make Love to You," and a number of made-to-order originals. Throughout the album, the musicians play well, but Ford's voice is never commanding. However, this is a minor flaw, since his guitar speaks for itself. —*Stephen Thomas Erlewine*

Jesse Fortune

b. Hattiesburg, MS
Vocals / Electric Chicago Blues
Chicago vocalist Jesse Fortune's voice is as large as his discography is small. A mere handful of 45s headed by his 1963 classic "Too Many Cooks" and a 1993 album on Delmark constitute his entire catalog—but as an active artist on the Windy City circuit, he still has time to fatten it up.

Fortune grew up in Hattiesburg, MS, influenced by the pleading blues vocals of B.B. King. He arrived in Chicago in 1952 and started singing professionally with guitarist Little Monroe. He also worked with Otis Rush and Buddy Guy before the prodigious Willie Dixon officially discovered him. In April of 1963, Fortune waxed four sides for USA Records under Dixon's supervision, including the Dixon-penned minor-key rhumba "Too Many Cooks" (his sidemen at the session included Guy, Big Walter Horton on harp, and pianist Lafayette Leake). Robert Cray revived the tune for his 1980 debut album on Tomato, *Who's Been Talkin'.*

Dissatisfied with the monetary return on his date, Fortune shied away from recording (he made his living as a barber) until young guitarist Dave Specter began working the club circuit with the powerful singer. The upshot was *Fortune Tellin' Man*, the singer's debut disc for Delmark, with swinging support from Specter and his Bluebirds. —*Bill Dahl*

Fortune Tellin' Man / 1993 / Delmark ♦♦♦♦♦
Team one of the criminally overlooked blues vocalists inhabiting Chicago's West side with a tight young combo sporting a decidedly retro approach and you get this fine album, veteran singer Jesse Fortune's debut set. Guitarist Dave Specter & The Bluebirds admirably back the big-voiced Fortune as he recuts his Willie Dixon-penned USA label classic "Too Many Cooks," and shouts some lesser-known B.B. King gems and a few new items. Definitely a case of better late than never! —*Bill Dahl*

Leroy Foster

b. Feb. 1, 1923, Algoma, MS, **d.** May 26, 1958, Chicago, IL
Vocals, Drums, Guitar / Electric Chicago Blues
As a charter member of the Headhunters, the brash crew that also included Muddy Waters and Jimmy Rogers (so named because of their penchant for entering nightclubs featuring other musicians and blowing them off the stage with their superior musicianship), "Baby Face" Leroy Foster was on hand to help develop the postwar Chicago blues idiom. Unfortunately, he wasn't around long enough to enjoy the fruits of his labors.

The Mississippi native came to Chicago in 1945 in the star-crossed company of harpist Little Walter and pianist Johnny Jones. He worked with Sunnyland Slim and Sonny Boy Williamson before hooking up with the young and hungry Waters aggregation. Foster played drums on 1948 dates for Tempo-Tone that produced Floyd Jones' brooding "Hard Times," Little Walter's "Blue Baby," and a Sunnyland Slim-fronted "I Want My Baby."

He switched to rhythm guitar to accompany Waters on several of his 1948–49 Aristocrat 78s, notably "You're Gonna Miss Me (When I'm Dead and Gone)," "Mean Red Spider," and "Screamin' and Cryin'," as well as Johnny Jones' rolling "Big Town Playboy." Foster also recorded for Aristocrat as a front man: "Locked Out Boogie" and "Shady Grove Blues" were done at a 1948 date that produced six Muddy masters.

Waters got in some hot water with the Chess brothers when he moonlighted on Foster's rip-roaring eight-song session for Parkway in January of 1950. Though Foster's crashing drums are prominent throughout, Muddy's slashing slide and mournful moans are clearly heard on Foster's two-part "Rollin' and Tumblin'"—enough so that Waters was forced to wax his own version for Aristocrat to kill sales on Foster's rendition by his bosses.

Those Parkway masters had amazing resiliency–Foster's raunchy "Red Headed Woman" reemerged on Savoy in 1954 ("Boll Weevil" had turned up on Herald the previous year). Two singles for JOB–1950s "My Head Can't Rest Anymore"/"Take a Little Walk with Me" (with Muddy and Rogers in support, it was later released on Chess) and 1952's "Pet Rabbit"/"Louella" (with Sunnyland and guitarist Robert Jr. Lockwood lending a hand)–round out his slim vinyl legacy. Alcoholism brought Baby Face down early–he was only 35 when he died in 1958. —*Bill Dahl*

Carol Fran & Clarence Hollimon

b. Oct. 23, 1933, Lafayette, LA
Vocals / Electric Louisiana Blues
Just call Carol Fran and her husband Clarence Hollimon the new sweethearts of the blues. Not only are they a coosome twosome offstage, the pair share uncommon empathy onstage as well.

The couple first met in 1957 in New Orleans. Fran was a winsome Louisiana chanteuse with a Gulf Coast hit on Excello, "Emmitt Lee," to her credit; Hollimon was a fiery young guitar slinger who had backed Big Mama Thornton on the road before playing sizzling solos on many of Bobby "Blue" Bland's classic waxings for Duke. But love wasn't in the cards just then. In 1983, fate brought the pair back together at a Houston nightclub, and they've been a romantic item ever since. Two albums on Black Top, *Soul Sensation* in 1992 and *See There!* two years later, have cemented their musical bonds.

Fran toured with bandleader Joe Lutcher when she was a mere 15 years old in 1949. Famed producer J.D. Miller was behind the board when Carol Fran cut "Emmitt Lee" in Crowley, LA, in 1957. Her later waxings for Port and other diskeries tend-

ed toward the R&B side of the stylistic tracks. Fran's soulful 1965 reading of "Crying in the Chapel" was crushed by Elvis Presley's competing version. Meanwhile, Hollimon became a studio stalwart, playing on sides by Bland, Junior Parker, Joe Hinton, and a host of others.

Nothing substantial had been heard from Fran or Hollimon prior to their hooking up with Black Top only a few years ago. Lucky in music and in love, they are a versatile duo–she sings jazzy ballads as convincingly as swinging R&B, and Hollimon's fleet fingers are conversant with virtually any chord progression known to man. —*Bill Dahl*

Soul Sensation / 1992 / Black Top ♦♦♦♦
The new sweethearts of the blues' debut for Black Top is an uncommonly varied affair, the pair performing blues, jazz, and every stylistic stripe in between. Hollimon's red-hot licks are seldom short of amazing (his instrumental showcase "Gristle" is a stunner), and Fran's full-throated vocals shine on everything from a Gulf Coast-styled "My Happiness" and a reprise of Mitty Collier's emotionally charged "I Had a Talk with My Man" to the lounge-slanted "Anytime, Anyplace, Anywhere" and the rousing sanctified closer "This Little Light." —*Bill Dahl*

● **See There!** / 1994 / Black Top ♦♦♦♦♦
The duo's Black Top encore was a slightly more focused effort than their debut. They still exhibit considerable versatility on a highly infectious dance number, "Door Poppin'," the Louisiana-rooted "Daddy, Daddy, Daddy," and soulful remakes of Tyrone Davis' "Are You Serious" and Gladys Knight & the Pips' earthy "I Don't Want to Do Wrong," but there's a more satisfying context overall. The album was waxed in New Orleans and Texas with two entirely different bands, lending laudable variety to the selections. —*Bill Dahl*

Denny Freeman

b. Dallas, TX
Guitar / Modern Texas Blues
This Dallas native and Austin fixture was co-lead guitarist in the Cobras with Stevie Vaughan, before joining Angela Strehli (cutting two solo LPs during his stint with the songstress), contributing to *Big Guitars from Texas*, and recording with Lou Ann Barton. More original and out-on-a-limb than most textbook-blues players, he co-wrote "Baboom/Mama Said" on the Vaughan Brothers' *Family Style* and played guitar and piano on tour with Jimmie Vaughan following the latter's *Strange Pleasure*. —*Dan Forte*

Blues Cruise / 1986 / Amazing ♦♦♦♦♦
"Rockin' with B.B." and "Steelin' Berry's" not only reveal two of Freeman's major influences but do justice to Mr. King and Chuck Berry–the latter featuring a fine pedal steel guitar turn by Jimmie Vaughan. The melodic "Denny's Blues" is also a standout. Three lackluster vocal numbers (one each by Angela Strehli, Kim Wilson and Bill Carter) detract from the continuity (and level) of Freeman's instrumental set. —*Dan Forte*

Out of the Blue / 1987 / Amazing ♦♦♦♦♦
All instrumental this time, and a bit more varied, with gospel, jazz ("My Dominique"), exotica (Freeman's "Lost Incas" from the *Big Guitars from Texas* album), and even a nod to Billy Gibbons on "Z." Jimmie Vaughan cameos again, on steel and 6-string bass, along with the usual Austin crew (George Rains, Sarah Brown, Mel Brown, Derek O'Brien, Kaz Kazanoff, etc.). —*Dan Forte*

Denny Freeman and the Cobras / Cross Cut ♦♦♦
● **Blues Cruise / Out of the Blue** / Amazing ♦♦♦♦♦
Freeman's two LPs wedged onto one CD, with three tunes unfortunately hitting the editing room floor. Two vocals interrupt the all-instrumental proceedings, and somehow Jimmie Vaughan's steel work on "Louisiana Luau" (from *Blues Cruise*) got the axe. —*Dan Forte*

Frank Frost (Frank Otis Frost)

b. Apr. 15, 1936, Augusta, AR
Guitar, Harmonica, Vocals, Piano, Organ / Electric Delta Blues
The atmospheric juke-joint blues of Frank Frost remain steeped in unadulterated Delta funk. But his ongoing musical journey has taken him well outside his Mississippi homebase.

He moved to St. Louis in 1951, learning how to blow harp first from Little Willie Foster and then from the legendary Sonny Boy Williamson who took him on the road–as a guitar player–from

1956 to 1959. Drummer Sam Carr, a longtime Frost ally, was also part of the equation, having enticed Frost to front his combo in 1954 before hooking up with Sonny Boy.

Leaving Williamson's employ in 1959, Frost and Carr settled in Lula, MS. Guitarist Jack Johnson came aboard in 1962 after sitting in with the pair at the Savoy Theatre in Clarksdale. The three meshed perfectly—enough to interest Memphis producer Sam Phillips in a short-lived back-to-the-blues campaign that same year. *Hey Boss Man!*, issued on Sun's Phillips International subsidiary as by Frank Frost and the Nighthawks, was a wonderful collection of uncompromising Southern blues (albeit totally out of step with the marketplace at the time).

Elvis Presley's ex-guitarist Scotty Moore produced Frost's next sessions in Nashville in 1966 for Jewel Records. Augmented by session bassist Chip Young, the trio's tight downhome ensemble work was once again seamless. "My Back Scratcher," Frost's takeoff on Slim Harpo's "Baby Scratch My Back," even dented the R&B charts on Shreveport-based Jewel for three weeks.

Chicago blues fan Michael Frank sought out Frost in 1975. He located Frost, Johnson, and Carr playing inside Johnson's Clarksdale tavern, the Black Fox. Mesmerized by their sound, Frost soon formed his own record label, Earwig, to capture their raw, charismatic brand of blues. 1979's *Rockin' the Juke Joint Down*, billed as by the Jelly Roll Kings (after one of the standout songs on that said Phillips International LP), showcased the trio's multi-faceted approach—echoes of R&B, soul, even Johnny & the Hurricanes permeate their Delta-based attack.

In the years since, Frost has waxed his own Earwig album (1988's *Midnight Prowler*) and appeared on Atlantic's 1992 *Deep Blues* soundtrack—an acclaimed film that reinforced the fact that blues still thrives deep in its southern birthplace. —*Bill Dahl*

● **Hey Boss Man** / Phillips ◆◆◆◆◆
One of the last great blues recordings produced by the legendary Sam Phillips. Frost and his Mississippi cohorts Jack Johnson and Sam Carr played Southern juke-joint blues rough and ready in the classic mold, with plenty of dynamic interplay and nasty, lowdown grooves. —*Bill Dahl*

Frank Frost / 1973 / Paula ◆◆◆
More down-home eclectic blues from the harpist/keyboardist. *Bill Dahl*

Ride with Your Daddy Tonight / 1985 / Charly ◆◆◆◆◆
Frost's best sides for the Jewel label. Some of the most downhome '60s blues ever recorded. —*Cub Koda*

Midnight Prowler / 1989 / Earwig ◆◆◆
Frost is front-and-center with a program that's decidedly downhome. This is what modern Mississippi blues sounds like—tough, uncompromising, still rooted mainly in the 1950s with a few modern touches. —*Bill Dahl*

Jelly Roll Blues / 1991 / Paula ◆◆◆◆
Same band, different producer: this time it was Elvis Presley's legendary guitarist, Scotty Moore, behind the glass as Frost and his pals dished out the lowdown sounds during the mid-'60s for Stan Lewis' Jewel label. "My Back Scratcher" owes a stylistic debt to Slim Harpo but feels mighty good all the same. The 13-song disc reeks of steamy juke-joint ambience. —*Bill Dahl*

Deep Blues / 1992 / Appaloosa ◆◆◆
Harmonica wizard and veteran blues vocalist Frank Frost has plenty left in his harp and voice. His venerable, still vibrant sound fortifies this album, as Frost takes the spotlight with biting, rolling harmonica riffs, extended lines, wailing refrains and wise, often ironic and bittersweet vocals. This time he's backed by Freddie & The Screamers, a unit able to supply both hot uptempo support and low-down assistance. Maybe he did it better years ago, but Frank Frost hasn't slipped that far in the 1990s. —*Ron Wynn*

Rockin' the Juke Joint Down (as Jelly Roll Kings) / 1993 / Earwig ◆◆◆◆
Michael Frank inaugurated his Earwig imprint with this 1979 album reteaming Frost, Johnson, and Carr in all their glory. Frank was mesmerizied by the trio's almost telepathic musical interplay, a trait captured vividly by the album itself. This trio's repertoire was varied—the no-holds-barred "Slop Jar Blues" is offset by the bubbly instrumental "Sunshine Twist." Frost and Johnson share vocal duties. —*Bill Dahl*

Blind Boy Fuller

b. 1908, Wadesboro, NC, d. Feb. 13, 1941, Durham, NC
Guitar, Vocals / Acoustic Country Blues, Piedmont Blues
Unlike blues artists Big Bill or Memphis Minnie who recorded extensively over three or four decades, Blind Boy Fuller recorded his substantial body of work over a short, six-year span. Nevertheless, he was one of the most recorded artists of his time and by far the most popular and influential Piedmont blues player of all time. Fuller could play in multiple styles: slide, ragtime, pop, and blues were all enhanced by his National steel guitar. Fuller worked with some fine sidemen, including Davis, Sonny Terry, and washboard player Bull City Red. Initially discovered and promoted by Carolina entrepreneur H. B. Long, Fuller recorded for ARC and Decca. He also served as a conduit to recording sessions, steering fellow blues musicians to the studio.

In spite of Fuller's recorded output, most of his musical life was spent as a street musician and house party favorite, and he possessed the skills to reinterpret and cover the hits of other artists as well. In this sense, he was a synthesizer of styles, parallel in many ways to Robert Johnson, his contemporary who died three years earlier. Like Johnson, Fuller lived fast and died young in 1942, only 33 years old. Fuller was a fine, expressive vocalist and a masterful guitar player best remembered for his uptempo ragtime hits "Rag Mama Rag," "Trucking My Blues Away," and "Step It Up and Go." At the same time he was capable of deeper material, and his versions of "Lost Lover Blues" or "Mamie" are as deep as most Delta blues. Because of his popularity, he may have been overexposed on records, yet most of his songs remained close to tradition and much of his repertoire and style is kept alive by North Carolina and Virginia artists today. —*Barry Lee Pearson*

★ **Truckin' My Blues Away** / 1978 / Yazoo ◆◆◆◆◆
Piedmont blues at its best, with fine guitar work from this popular and influential bluesman. —*Barry Lee Pearson*

East Coast Piedmont Style / Aug. 1991 / Columbia/Legacy ◆◆◆◆◆
A very good 20-cut roots and blues collection with Sonny Terry, Gary Davis, and Bull City Red. —*Barry Lee Pearson*

Blind Boy Fuller, Vols. 1-4 / Document ◆◆◆
The finest collection ever of blues and ragtime. Fuller is here both solo and with Gary Davis, Sonny Terry, and Bull City Red. This is Piedmont blues at its best (1935-1940), a must for anyone interested in down-home blues. —*Barry Lee Pearson*

Jesse Fuller

b. Mar. 12, 1896, Jonesboro, GA, d. Jan. 29, 1976, Oakland, CA
Guitar, Harmonica, Kazoo, Fotdella, Vocals / Acoustic Country Blues, Acoustic West Coast Blues
Equipped with a bandful of instruments operated by various parts of his anatomy, Bay Area legend Jesse Fuller was a folk-music favorite in the '50s and '60s. His infectious rhythm and gentle charm graced old folk tunes, spirituals, and blues. One of his inventions was a homemade, foot-operated instrument called the "footdella" or "fotdella." Naturally, Fuller never needed accompanists to back his one-man show. His best-known songs include "San Francisco Bay Blues" and "Beat It on Down the Line" (the first one covered by Janis Joplin, the second by The Grateful Dead).

Born and raised in Georgia, Jesse Fuller began playing guitar when he was a child, although he didn't pursue the instrument seriously. In his early '20s, Fuller wandered around the South and West, eventually settling down in Los Angeles. While he was in southern California, he worked as a film extra, appearing in *The Thief of Bagdad, East of Suez, Hearts in Dixie*, and *End of the World*. After spending a few years in Los Angeles, Fuller moved to San Francisco. While he worked various odd jobs around the Bay Area, he played on street corners and parties.

Jesse's musical career didn't properly begin unitl the early '50s, when he decided to become a professional musician—he was 55 years old at the time. Performing as a one man band, he began to get spots on local television shows and nightclubs. However, Fuller's career didn't take off until 1954, when he wrote "San Francisco Bay Blues." The song helped him land a record contract with the independent Cavalier label, and in 1955, he recorded his first album, *Folk Blues: Working on the Railroad with Jesse Fuller.* The albums was a success and soon he was making records for a variety of labels, including Good Time Jazz and Prestige.

In the late '50s and early '60s, Jesse Fuller became one of the key figures of the blues revival, helping bring the music to a new, younger audience. Throughout the '60s and '70s, he toured America and Europe, appearing at numerous blues and folk festivals, as well as countless coffeehouse gigs across the U.S. Fuller continued performing and recording until his death in 1976. — *Jim O'Neal & Stephen Thomas Erlewine*

Jazz, Folk Songs, Spirituals & Blues / Apr. 1958 / Good Time Jazz ✦✦✦✦✦
Jesse Fuller was among the greatest one-man bands in blues history. The title of this 1958 date adequately described the session's musical width and depth; Fuller handled everything from old spirituals such as as "I'm Going To Meet My Loving Mother" to the rollicking "Memphis Boogie" and "Fingerbuster" and the concluding "Hesitation Blues." As sole performer, melodic, rhythmic and performing focus, Fuller's energy never wanes through the CD's 11 numbers. He nicely conveys the varying moods, themes and sentiments, knowing which lyrics to emphasize, when to intensify the pace and when to lower his voice and let the music make the point. — *Ron Wynn*

The Lone Cat Sings and Plays Jazz, Folk Songs, Spirituals and Blues / Aug. 1961 / Good Time Jazz ✦✦✦
This album features oldtime blues, ragtime, and string band songs, all performed by the one-man band Jesse Fuller. With his 12-string guitar, harmonica, kazoo, cymbals, and six-string bass (which he played with his foot), Fuller created a very unique sound that surprisingly didn't sound particularly jokey—instead, it sounded like it was part of a tradition. None of his best-known songs are included on *Lone Cat,* but there is an abundance of strange, wonderful music on the record. — *Thom Owens*

Favorites / 1965 / Prestige ✦✦✦
Jesse Fuller's *Favorites* is a highly enjoyable collection of the singer's favorite blues standards. Performing everything as a solo piece, he runs through classics like "Key to the Highway," "The Midnight Special," and "Brownskin Gal" with humor and warmth. It's a small, but entertaining, gem. — *Thom Owens*

Frisco Bound / 1968 / Arhoolie ✦✦✦✦
A one-man band with guitar, harmonica, kazoo, and "footdella" bass, these are some of his first recordings, circa 1955. Innocent echoes of turn-of-the-century rural America. — *Mark A. Humphrey*

● **San Francisco Bay Blues** / 1988 / Good Time Jazz ✦✦✦✦
Fuller's hit and more includes no misses. — *Mark A. Humphrey*

Johnny Fuller

b. Apr. 20, 1929, Edwards, MS, **d.** 1985
Guitar, Vocals, Organ, Piano / Electric West Coast Blues
Johnny Fuller was a West Coast bluesman who left behind a spate of 1950s recordings that jumped all kinds of genre fences with seemingly no trace of his Mississippi born roots. He was equally at home with low-down blues, gospel, R&B, and rock 'n' roll, all of it imbued with strong vocals and a driving guitar style. Although his Mississippi roots were never far below the surface of his best work, Johnny is usually categorized as a West Coast bluesman. Making the Bay Area his home throughout his career, Fuller turned in classic sides for Heritage, Aladdin, Specialty, Flair, Checker, and Hollywood; all but one of them West Coast-based concerns. His two biggest hits, "All Night Long" and the original version of "The Haunted House," improbably found him in the late '50s on rock 'n' roll package shows, touring with the likes of Paul Anka and Frankie Avalon! By and large retiring from the music scene in the '60s (with the exception of one excellent album in 1974), Fuller worked as a garage mechanic until his passing in 1985.—*Cub Koda*

Fool's Paradise / 1984 / Diving Duck ✦✦✦
Fuller's Blues / 1988 / Diving Duck ✦✦✦

Lowell Fulson

b. Mar. 31, 1921, Tulsa, OK
Guitar, Vocals / R&B, Electric West Coast Blues, Acoustic West Coast Blues
Lowell Fulson has recorded every shade of blues imaginable. Polished urban blues, rustic two-guitar duets with his younger brother Martin, funk-tinged grooves that pierced the mid-'60s

charts, even an unwise cover of the Beatles' "Why Don't We Do It in the Road"! Clearly, the veteran guitarist, who's been at it now for more than half a century, isn't afraid to experiment. Perhaps that's why his last couple of discs for Rounder are so vital and satisfying—and why he's been an innovator for so long.

Exposed to the western swing of Bob Wills as well as indigenous blues while growing up in Oklahoma, Fulson joined up with singer Texas Alexander for a few months in 1940, touring the Lone Star state with the veteran bluesman. Fulson was drafted in 1943. The Navy let him go in 1945; after a few months back in Oklahoma, he was off to Oakland, CA, where he made his first 78s for fledgling producer Bob Geddins. Soon enough, Fulson was fronting his own band and cutting a stack of platters for Big Town, Gilt Edge, Trilon, and Down Town (where he hit big in 1948 with "Three O'Clock Blues," later covered by B.B. King).

Swing Time records president Jack Lauderdale snapped up Fulson in 1948, and the hits really began to flow: the immortal "Every Day I Have the Blues" (an adaptation of Memphis Slim's "Nobody Loves Me"), "Blue Shadows," the two-sided holiday perennial "Lonesome Christmas," and a groovy mid-tempo instrumental "Low Society Blues" that really hammers home how tremendously important pianist Lloyd Glenn and alto saxist Earl Brown were to Fulson's maturing sound (all charted in 1950).

Fulson toured extensively from then on, his band stocked for a time with dazzling pianist Ray Charles (who later covered Lowell's "Sinner's Prayer" for Atlantic) and saxist Stanley Turrentine. After a one-off session in New Orleans in 1953 for Aladdin, Fulson inked a longterm pact with Chess in 1954. His first single for the firm was the classic "Reconsider Baby," cut in Dallas under Stan Lewis' supervision with a sax section that included David "Fathead" Newman on tenor and Leroy Cooper on baritone.

The relentless mid-tempo blues proved a massive hit and perennial cover item—even Elvis Presley cut it in 1960, right after he got out of the Army. But apart from "Loving You," the guitarist's subsequent Checker output failed to find widespread favor with the public. Baffling, since Fulson's crisp, concise guitar work and sturdy vocals were as effective as ever. Most of his Checker sessions were held in Chicago and L.A. (the latter his home from the turn of the '50s).

Fulson stayed with Checker into 1962, but a change of labels worked wonders when he jumped over to Los Angeles-based Kent Records. 1965's driving "Black Nights" became his first smash in a decade, and "Tramp," a loping funk-injected workout co-written by Fulson and Jimmy McCracklin, did even better, restoring the guitarist to R&B stardom, gaining plenty of pop spins, and inspiring a playful Stax cover by Otis Redding and Carla Thomas only a few months later that outsold Fulson's original.

A couple of lesser follow-up hits for Kent ensued before the guitarist was reunited with Stan Lewis at Jewel Records. That's where he took a crack at that Beatles number, though most of his outings for the firm were considerably closer to the blues bone. Fulson has never been absent for long on disc; 1992's *Hold On* and its 1995 follow-up *Them Update Blues*, both for Ron Levy's Bullseye Blues logo, are among his recent efforts, both solid.

Few bluesmen have managed to remain contemporary the way Lowell Fulson has for more than five decades. And fewer still will make such a massive contribution to the idiom. — *Bill Dahl*

Back Home Blues / 1959 / Night Train ✦✦✦
Back Home Blues collects several tracks Lowell Fulson cut early in his career for Swing Time, when he was performing jump blues. This is high-energy, enjoyable blues—even though Fulsom doesn't sound as comfortable with jump blues as he does with postwar Chicago and Southern blues, he is completely creditable on these performances. It's an essential purchase for Fulson fans that want to dig deep into his roots. — *Thom Owens*

Now / 1969 / United ✦✦✦
More funky blues with lots of covers. — *Bill Dahl*

In a Heavy Bag / 1970 / Jewel ✦✦
Too rock-oriented for comfort. — *Bill Dahl*

Lowell Fulson (Early Recordings) / 1975 / Arhoolie ✦✦✦
Mostly the country blues roots of the Oklahoma-born guitarist. The first ten tracks, duets with brother Martin on second guitar, are worlds apart from the swinging horn-powered R&B efforts

that Fulson is famous for. The last four numbers, though, revert to that attractive format—especially the scorching instrumental closer "Lowell Jumps One." —*Bill Dahl*

Man of Motion / 1981 / Charly ✦✦
Vinyl collection of Fulson's late-'60s stint at Shreveport's Jewel Records. In truth, not the guitarist's shining hour—some of this stuff is competent blues (some backed by the Muscle Shoals house band of the era), others abominable attempts at cracking the blues-rock market (his rendering of the Beatles' "Why Don't We Do It in the Road" stands as the worst thing Fulson ever committed to tape). —*Bill Dahl*

Everyday I Have the Blues / 1984 / Night Train ✦✦✦✦✦
The first of two extremely solid compilations of the guitarist's late-'40s/early-'50s output for Jack Lauderdale's Los Angeles-based Swing Time imprint. You'll need 'em both, since the essentials are spread across 'em about evenly—Fulson's smashes "Every Day," "Lonesome Christmas," and "Blue Shadows" regally inhabit this 20-cut disc. —*Bill Dahl*

One More Blues / Mar. 11, 1984 / Evidence ✦✦✦
Fulson hasn't been as prolific over the last couple of decades as during the 1950s, but when he does get a chance to enter a studio, he usually emerges with some impressive work. This 1984 album, first out on Black & Blue over in France, is no exception—the band is tight (Phillip Walker is rhythm guitarist), and Fulson came prepared with a sheaf of solid originals. —*Bill Dahl*

Blue Days Black Nights / 1986 / Ace ✦✦✦
This album collects 15 tracks Lowell Fulson recorded in the late '60s, including the classic "Tramp." During this era, he was playing Chicago blues and Southern soul, with the occasional flourish of laidback, Western blues. Although this material is first-rate, it is available on better collections, including Flair's two-fer of *Tramp* and *Soul*. —*Thom Owens*

San Francisco Blues / 1988 / Black Lion ✦✦✦✦✦
Guitarist and vocalist Lowell Fulson helped establish his reputation with a string of fine songs for the Swingtime label in the late '40s and early '50s. Fulson showed he could belt out hard-hitting blues, do sentimental ballads, double-entendre novelty pieces or irony-filled laments, and also play riveting solos. This '92 CD reissue collects 16 early Fulson numbers, all original compositions, and features Fulson leading a group with Lloyd Glenn, King Solomon or Rufus J. Russell on piano, Ralph Hamilton, Billy Hadnott or Floyd Montgomery on bass, and Bob Harvey or Asal Carson on drums. —*Ron Wynn*

It's a Good Day / 1988 / Rounder ✦✦✦
While no one was anticipating blues great Lowell Fulson to equal or even approach his masterful 1950s work on this session, he turned in a pleasantly competent date of both heartache numbers and more upbeat tunes. Fulson's leads were clear and nicely phrased, his guitar work tasty and clever. He interspersed some swamp-pop, Texas shuffle and urban blues riffs into his material, and on "Blues and My Guitar" displayed the fluidity and performance magic that made his classic sides unforgettable. —*Ron Wynn*

Tramp/Soul / 1991 / Flair ✦✦✦✦
The veteran guitarist's two best mid-'60s albums for Kent Records on one packed-to-the-gills CD. Fulson cannily made the leap into soul-slanted grooves while at Kent, scoring a major R&B smash with "Tramp." Also aboard is Fulson's classic "Black Nights;" "Talkin' Woman" (later revived most memorably by Albert Collins as "Honey Hush"), and a fine version of Smokey Hogg's enduring "Too Many Drivers." —*Bill Dahl*

Hold On / May 1992 / Bullseye Blues ✦✦✦✦
Nothing dated about this fine album, produced by organist Ron Levy—Fulson sounds at once both contemporary and timeless, slashing through a mostly original set with Jimmy McCracklin helping out on piano and the sax section including Bobby Forte and Edgar Synigal. —*Bill Dahl*

Reconsider Baby / 1993 / Charly ✦✦✦✦✦
A more in-depth assessment of Fulson's Chess years (20 titles), minus a few of the most important sides nestled on *Hung Down Head* but boasting a few others of nearly equal import: "Lonely Hours," "Rollin' Blues," "Don't Drive Me Baby," and especially the insane 1957 rocker "Rock This Morning," where Fulson does his best Little Richard imitation as Eddie Chamblee blows up a tenor sax hurricane. —*Bill Dahl*

Them Updated Blues / 1995 / Bullseye Blues ✦✦✦
A half century after he made his debut waxings, Fulson is still going strong—and not as some museum piece, either. Still a vital blues artist who refuses to rest on his massive laurels, Fulson's latest is a fine addition to his vast discography, comprised mostly of fresh originals and featuring his customary biting guitar and insinuating vocals. —*Bill Dahl*

Sinner's Prayer / 1995 / Night Train ✦✦✦✦✦
Twenty more Swing Time essentials, notably Lowell Fulson's original reading of the mournful "Sinner's Prayer" (soon revived by his one-time band pianist Ray Charles), the exultant instrumental "Low Society" (featuring Earl Brown's sturdy alto sax), and one of Fulson's wildest rockers, "Upstairs." —*Bill Dahl*

Lowell Fulson / MCA/Chess ✦✦✦
The rest of Fulson's 1955-62 Chess output is classic stuff. —*Bill Dahl*

★ **Hung Down Head** / MCA/Chess ✦✦✦✦✦
The most indispensable collection in Fulson's vast discography. He was hitting on all burners during the mid-'50s when he was with Chess, waxing the immortal "Reconsider Baby," swinging gems like "Check Yourself," "Do Me Right," and "Trouble, Trouble," and the supremely doomy "Tollin' Bells," here in many truncated false takes before he and the band finally gel. —*Bill Dahl*

Anson Funderburgh & the Rockets

b. Nov. 15, 1954, Dallas, TX
Guitar / Modern Electric Texas Blues
In recent years, Dallas-based guitarist Anson Funderburgh has taken his band the Rockets out of the clubs and onto the festival stages with his critically-acclaimed recordings for the BlackTop label out of New Orleans. With Jackson, MS-native Sam Myers delivering the vocals and harmonica treatments, this band mixes up a powerful gumbo of Texas jump blues and Delta blues that can't be found anywhere else. Funderburgh and his Rockets are a particularly hard-working band, performing across the U.S. and Europe nearly 300 nights a year.

Funderburgh was born November 15, 1954, and got hooked on the blues when he got his first guitar at age seven or eight. His first musical experiences happened in the clubs in Dallas. He developed his team approach to blues music while learning from the likes of Freddie King, Jimmy Reed and Albert Collins when these great bluesmen were passing through Dallas-area clubs, but Funderburgh had already taught himself guitar mostly from listening to classic blues records. He never had the chance to see Muddy Waters, but he did get to play with Lightnin' Hopkins in the late '70s. Funderburgh formed the Rockets in 1978, but didn't meet Sam Myers until 1982.

Funderburgh recorded with the Fabulous Thunderbirds on their *Butt Rockin'* album, and went solo in 1981, when the New Orleans-based BlackTop label released *Talk to You by Hand*, the label's first release. Funderburgh added Myers on harmonica and lead vocals in 1986. Myers had traveled for years on the chitlin circuit, where he accompanied people like Elmore James and Robert Junior Lockwood. Funderburgh admits that adding Myers on vocals and harmonica was a turning point for the Rockets, partly because of the image they project from the stage, a big towering Black man and three White guys backing him up.

Funderburgh and the Rockets have six releases for the BlackTop label in addition to the *Talk to You by Hand* album. They include *She Knocks Me Out*, *My Love Is Here to Stay*, *Sins*, *Rack'Em Up*, *Tell Me What I Want to Hear* and *Live at the Grand Emporium*. BlackTop has also issued an introductory album, *Thru the Years: A Retrospective*, that features Funderburgh's guitar work in a variety of musical conglomerations.

The endlessly creative Funderburgh is just coming into his prime by way of his songwriting talents, so his career deserves close watching in the coming years. The best is yet to come from this guitarist and bandleader. —*Richard Skelly*

Talk to You by Hand / 1984 / BlackTop ✦✦

She Knocks Me Out! / 1985 / BlackTop ✦✦

Knock You Out / 1985 / Spindrift ✦✦✦

My Love Is Here to Stay / 1986 / BlackTop ✦✦✦
This is the first record where Sam Myers (who had been performing with Robert Jr Lockwood, Myers' latest gig in a professional career that began in the mid-'50s) joined Funderburgh's

band. This successful coupling has here and since made some truly wonderful music. —*Niles J. Frantz*

Sins / 1987 / BlackTop ✦✦✦✦✦

Sins is a good fusion of Texas and Delta blues, alternating between rocking shuffles and laidback ballads. Funderburgh's playing is tasteful—he has an enticing sound, but he never falls into grandstanding—and Sam Myers' voice is rich and his harp playing intoxicating. Furthermore, the selection of material is first-rate, featuring sharp originals and well-chosen covers from the likes of Percy Mayfield and Elmore James. The result? One of Anson Funderburgh's best albums. —*Thom Owens*

Rack 'em Up / 1989 / BlackTop ✦✦✦

Rack 'Em Up is a straightforward blues album that demonstrates Anson Funderburgh's affection for the Texas shuffle. Nobody on the album, whether it's Funderburgh or the Kamikaze Horns, overplays their hand and it delivers the goods efficiently although without flair. —*Thom Owens*

Tell Me What I Want to Hear / 1991 / BlackTop ✦✦✦✦✦

First-rate, contemporary Texas shuffle and blues with tasteful, biting guitar comes from Funderburgh and great vocals and harp from Mississippian Sam Myers. This is their most varied and ambitious release to date (the band seems to get better with each album). The title track was used in the movie *China Moon.* "Rent Man Blues" is a humorous dialog between Myers and guest-vocalist Carol Fran. Myers also adds an "answer" song to the blues classic "Sloppy Drunk." —*Niles J. Frantz*

● **Thru the Years: a Retrospective (1981-1992)** / 1992 / BlackTop ✦✦✦✦✦

This album collects the highlights from Funderburgh's albums for BlackTop, drawing from all the different bands he fronted in that decade or so. The best tracks remain his cuts with Sam Myers or Darrell Nulisch, but the finest songs from his lesser bands are included, making *Thru the Years* an excellent way to get acquainted with the modern blues guitar hero. —*Thom Owens*

G

Bob Gaddy
b. 1924
Piano, Vocals / Electric East Coast Blues
Both as a session man and featured recording artist, pianist Bob Gaddy made his presence known on the New York blues scene during the 1950s. He's still part of that circuit today. Gaddy was drafted in 1943, and that's when he began to take the 88s seriously. He picked up a little performing experience in California clubs while stationed on the West Coast before arriving in New York in 1946. Gaddy gigged with Brownie McGhee and guitarist Larry Dale around town, McGhee often playing on Gaddy's waxings for Jackson (his 1952 debut, "Bicycle Boogie"), Jax, Dot, Harlem, and from 1955 on, Hy Weiss' Old Town label. There Gaddy stayed the longest, waxing the fine "I Love My Baby," "Paper Lady," "Rip and Run," and quite a few more into 1960. Sidemen on Gaddy's Old Town sessions included guitarists Joe Ruffin and Wild Jimmy Spruill and saxist Jimmy Wright.

Since then, Gaddy hasn't recorded anything of note for domestic consumption, but like his longtime cohort Larry Dale, he remains active around New York. *—Bill Dahl*

Grady Gaines & the Texas Upsetters
b. May 14, 1934
Saxophone / Electric Texas Blues
Some of the atomic energy that Little Richard emitted nightly during the mid-'50s must have spilled onto Grady Gaines. As the hardy tenor sax blaster with Richard's road band, the Upsetters, Gaines all but blew the reed out of his horn with his galvanic solos. He wails with the same unquenchable spirit today.

The perpetually ebullient Louis Jordan was Grady's main saxman while growing up in Houston (in particular, Gaines loved his "Caldonia"). Grady wasn't the only musician in the Gaines household—brother Roy was an excellent guitarist who supplied the stinging solo on Bobby Bland's 1955 Duke waxing "It's My Life Baby" before leaving to do his own thing.

Grady was working as a session saxist at Don Robey's Duke/Peacock Records (soloing like a man possessed on Big Walter Price's "Pack Fair and Square" and proudly populating the reed section on Gatemouth Brown's searing "Dirty Work at the Crossroads") prior to getting a fateful 1955 call from Little Richard to head up his newly formed band.

Gaines recorded with the piano-pounding rock icon only sparingly—that's his storming wail on "Keep a Knockin'" and "Ooh! My Soul"—but you wouldn't know it from watching Richard's show-stopping appearances in the films *Don't Knock the Rock, The Girl Can't Help It,* and *Mr. Rock and Roll.* In every flick, Gaines is seen on screen, horn-syncing Lee Allen's sax solos!

The Upsetters remained intact long after Richard flipped out and joined the ministry in 1957. They hit the road with Dee Clark (then a Richard clone himself), Little Willie John, Sam Cooke, James Brown, Jackie Wilson, and Joe Tex. The band recorded for Vee-Jay in 1958 behind Clark and with Upsetters vocalist/saxist Wilbert Smith, who went by the name of Lee Diamond and hailed from New Orleans. More sessions at Vee-Jay, Gee, Fire, and Little Star (where they briefly reunited with Richard) followed.

After the Upsetters broke up, Grady hit the road with a variety of R&B luminaries, including Millie Jackson and Curtis Mayfield, before retiring in 1980. Fortunately, he decided to strap his horn back on in 1985, playing in Houston until Black Top Records cajoled him into cutting Full Gain, a veritable Houston

blues motherlode, in 1988. Brother Roy Gaines, pianist Teddy Reynolds, guitarist Clarence Hollimon, and singer Joe Medwick were all involved in the project. Horn of Plenty followed on Black Top in 1992. Gaines and his entourage continue to blow up a Texas-sized storm wherever they touch down. *—Bill Dahl*

● **Full Gain** / 1988 / BlackTop ♦♦♦♦♦
A meeting of Houston-based all-stars that scorches from the first track to the last. Tenor saxman Grady Gaines is in charge of the proceedings, wailing on the instrumentals "There Is Something on Your Mind" and "Soul Twist," while pianist Teddy Reynolds, Gaines' guitar-wielding brother Roy Gaines, and Joe Medwick divvy up the vocals. Outstanding guitarist Clarence Hollimon is also on board. *—Bill Dahl*

Horn of Plenty / 1992 / BlackTop ♦♦♦
Gaines is surrounded by more vocal talent this time—Carol Fran, Teddy Reynolds, and Gaines' Texas Upsetters pals Big Robert Smith and Paul David Roberts. Hollimon and Anson Funderburgh are the guitar heroes, as Gaines whips up another Lone Star-size sax storm with his lusty tenor. *—Bill Dahl*

Rory Gallagher
b. Mar. 2, 1949, Ballyshannon, Ireland, **d.** Jun. 14, 1995
Guitar, Vocals / British Blues
For a career that was cut short by illness and a premature death, guitarist, singer and songwriter Rory Gallagher sure accomplished a lot in the blues music world. Although Gallagher didn't tour the U.S. nearly enough, spending most of his time in Europe, he was known for his no-holds-barred, kick-ass, marathon live shows at clubs and theaters around the United States.

Gallagher was born in Ballyshannon, County Donegal, Irish Republic on March 2, 1949. He passed away from complications owing to liver transplant surgery on June 14, 1995, at age 46. Shortly after his birth, his family moved to Cork City in the south, and at age nine, he became fascinated with American blues and folk singers he heard on the radio. An avid record collector, he had a wide range of influences including Leadbelly, Buddy Guy, Freddie King, Albert King, Muddy Waters and John Lee Hooker. Gallagher would always try to mix some simple country blues songs onto his recordings.

Gallagher began his recording career after moving to London, when he formed a trio called Taste. The group's self-titled debut album was released in 1969 in England and later picked up for U.S. distribution by Atco/Atlantic. Between 1969 and 1971, with producer Tony Colton behind the board, Gallagher recorded three albums with the group before they split up. Gallagher began performing under his own name in 1971, after recording his 1970 debut, *Rory Gallagher* for Polydor Records in the U.K. The album was picked up for U.S. distribution by Atlantic Records, and later that year he recorded *Deuce*, also released by Atlantic in the U.S.

His prolific output continued, as he followed up *Deuce* with *Live in Europe* (1972) and *Blueprint* and *Tattoo*, both in 1973. *Irish Tour 1974*, like *Live in Europe*, did a good job of capturing the excitement of his live shows on tape, and he followed that with *Calling Card* for Chrysalis in 1976, and *Photo Finish* and *Jinx* for the same label in 1978 and 1982. By this point Gallagher had made several world tours, and he took a few years rest from the road. He got back into recording and performing live again with the 1987 release (in the U.K.) of *Defender.* His last album,

Fresh Evidence, was released in 1991 on the Capo/I.R.S. label. Capo was his own record and publishing company that he set up in the hopes of eventually exposing other great blues talents.

Some of Gallagher's best work on record isn't under his own name, it's stuff he recorded with Muddy Waters on *The London Sessions* (Chess, 1972) and with Albert King on *Live* (RCA/Utopia). Gallagher made his last U.S. tours in 1985 and 1991, and he has admitted in interviews that he's always been a guitarist who feeds off the instant reaction and feedback a live audience can provide.

In a 1991 interview, he told this writer: "I try to sit down and write a Rory Gallagher song, which generally happens to be quite bluesy. I try to find different issues, different themes and different topics that haven't been covered before...I've done songs in all the different styles...train blues, drinking blues, economic blues. But I try to find a slightly different angle on all these things. The music can be very traditional, but you can sort of creep into the future with the lyrics."

For a good introduction to Gallagher's unparalleled prowess as a guitarist, singer and songwriter, pick up *Irish Tour 1974, Calling Card* or *Fresh Evidence*, all available on compact disc. —*Richard Skelly*

Rory Gallagher / 1971 / Atlantic ✦✦✦
Rory Gallagher's eponymous debut is an entertaining, but relatively undistinguished collection of blues-rock, highlighted by his flash slide guitar. —*Thom Owens*

Deuce / 1971 / Atlantic ✦✦
On *Deuce*, Rory Gallagher was just beginning to develop a distinctive style. He doesn't quite have all of the elements mastered yet—his concentration seems to slip on certain tracks, while other cuts aren't particularly strong songs—but it's fascinating to hear him forge something new out of his Chicago blues roots. —*Thom Owens*

Live in Europe/Stage Struck / 1972 / IRS ✦✦✦
The live album *Live in Europe/Stage Struck* captures Rory Gallagher at his finest, as he tears his way through many of his very best songs. Though the performance quality is a little uneven, there are gems scattered throughout the record, including smoking versions of "Messin' with the Kid" and "Laundromat." —*Thom Owens*

Tattoo / 1973 / Castle ✦✦✦
Rory Gallagher forges a distinctive style on *Tattoo*, one of his strongest albums. Working with a tight quartet, he's given a solid foundation for his terrific solos—it's especially exciting to hear him supported by a piano. All of the players deliver with conviction and studied passion, which makes the record an exciting listen. —*Thom Owens*

Irish Tour '74 / 1974 / IRS ✦✦✦✦✦
With *Irish Tour '74*, Rory Gallagher hit his high-water mark. Recorded live on his successful 1973 tour, Gallagher displays a remarkable empathy with his band, as they both churn out crunching riffs and fluid, soulful solos. Many of his best songs are included on the set and these far eclipse the studio versions. —*Thom Owens*

Calling Card / 1976 / IRS ✦✦✦✦✦
Following the excellent live set *Irish Tour '74*, Rory Gallagher delivered his best studio album, *Calling Card*. The record captures the dynamic interplay between the guitarist and his band—they burn with a roaring intensity. It also doesn't hurt that the songs are the best batch that Gallagher ever came up with for a record. The combination of top-notch performances and first-rate songs equals the hardest-edged and most rewarding studio set the guitarist ever cut. —*Thom Owens*

● **Edged in Blue** / 1992 / Edsel ✦✦✦✦✦
Edged in Blue is a solid, if not exactly definitive, retrospective of Rory Gallagher's career that offers a fine introduction to the blues star. —*Thom Owens*

The Bullfrog Interlude / 1992 / Castle ✦✦

Calling Hard (Pts. 1 & 2) / 1992 / Castle ✦✦

Blue Day for the Blues / Oct. 24, 1995 / IRS ✦✦✦

Cecil Gant

b. 1915, d. 1952
Vocals, Piano / Piano Blues
Pianist Cecil Gant seemingly materialized out of the wartime

mist to create one of the most enduring blues ballads of the 1940s. Gant was almost age 30 when he burst onto the scene in a most unusual way—he popped up in military uniform at a Los Angeles war bonds rally sponsored by the Treasury Department. Private Gant proceeded to electrify the assembled multitude with his piano prowess, leading to his imminent 1944 debut on Oakland's Gilt-Edge Records: the mellow pop-slanted ballad "I Wonder," which topped the R&B charts despite a wartime shellac shortage that hit tiny independent companies like Gilt-Edge particularly hard. Its flip, the considerably more animated "Cecil's Boogie," was a hit in its own right.

Pvt. Gant shot to the upper reaches of the R&B charts for Gilt-Edge like a guided missile with his "Grass Is Getting Greener Every Day" and "I'm Tired" in 1945, recording prolifically for the imprint before switching over to the Bullet label for the 1948 smash "Another Day—Another Dollar" and 1949's "I'm a Good Man but a Poor Man" (in between those two, Gant also hit with "Special Delivery" for Four Star). Urbane after-hours blues, refined ballads, torrid boogies—Gant ran the gamut during a tumultuous few years in the record business (he also turned up on King, Imperial, Dot, and Swing Time/Down Beat), but it didn't last. His "We're Gonna Rock" for Decca in 1950 (as Gunter Lee Carr) presaged the rise of rock 'n' roll later in the decade, but Gant wouldn't be around to view its ascendancy; the one-time "G.I. Sing-Sation" died in 1952 at the premature age of 37. —*Bill Dahl*

● **Rock Little Baby** / 1976 / Flyright ✦✦✦✦✦
British record collectors were hip to 1940s boogie and blues pianist Cecil Gant long before American aficionados were (not that there's much recognition of him here even now). Flyright assembled this vinyl slab of Gant goodies in loving tribute, with titles like "Screwy Boogie," "Owl Stew," and the stinging "Rock Little Baby" among the upbeat highlights. Gant's "I'm a Good Man but a Poor Man" has been adapted by many blues artists since the pianist waxed this one. —*Bill Dahl*

Cecil Boogie / 1976 / Flyright ✦✦✦✦✦
A second generous helping of boogies and blues by "the G.I. Sing-Sation," as Pvt. Gant was billed on his earliest mid-'40s sides for Gilt-Edge. His thundering boogie piano style on "We're Gonna Rock," "Nashville Jumps," and "Cecil Boogie" presaged the rise of rock 'n' roll. —*Bill Dahl*

I'm Still Singing the Blues Today / Oldie Blues ✦✦✦✦
Gant only recorded during the immediate postwar era, but he was remarkably prolific during those years. Here we have 20 more gems in the pianist's inimitable style—boogies, blues, ballads, even his personalized rendition of "Coming Round the Mountain!" —*Bill Dahl*

Larry Garner

Guitar, Vocals / Electric Louisiana Blues
Folks in Europe were hip to Larry Garner long before most blues fans in the states. The Baton Rouge guitarist had already toured extensively overseas, with two British albums to his credit, before Verve issued his stunning domestic debut, *You Need to Live a Little*, in 1995. Rooted in the swamp blues tradition indigenous to his Baton Rouge environs, Garner brings a laudable contemporary sensibility and witty composing skills to his craft.

Inspired by local swamp bluesmen Silas Hogan and Clarence Edwards, Larry Garner learned how to play guitar from his uncle and a couple of gospel-playing elders. After completing his military service in Korea, he returned to Baton Rouge and embarked on a part-time musical career (he worked at a Dow chemical plant for almost two decades until his recent retirement).

The British JSP label released Garner's first two albums: *Double Blues* and *Too Blues* (the latter an ironic slap at an unidentified tin-eared U.S. blues label boss who deemed Garner's demo tape "too blues"). With the emergence of *You Need to Live a Little*, where Garner delivers creative originals detailing the difficulty of keeping "Four Cars Running" and the universal pain of suffering through "Another Bad Day," Larry Garner is poised for 21st-century blues stardom. —*Bill Dahl*

● **You Need to Live a Little** / 1995 / Verve ✦✦✦✦✦
A witty, imaginative songwriter, crisply concise guitarist, and convincing singer, Baton Rouge Larry Garner is the proverbial triple threat—and a good bet to rise to blues stardom in the immediate future. His major-label debut is a wondrous collection filled with songs that don't embrace simple clichés ("Four

Cars Running," "Another Bad Day," and "Shak Bully" are anything but routine). "Miracles of Time" is almost pop-soul in its structure, while "Rats and Roaches in My Kitchen," Garner's lowdown tribute to swamp blues pioneer Silas Hogan, benefits from Sonny Landreth's burrowing slide guitar. —Bill Dahl

Clifford Gibson

b. Apr. 17, 1901, Louisville, KY, **d.** Dec. 21, 1963, St. Louis, MO
Guitar / Prewar Acoustic Blues
Though not a particularly great singer, Clifford "Grandpappy" Gibson was an excellent guitarist, among the finest pure players in country blues. Gibson moved from Kentucky to St. Louis in the '20s, where he lived the remainder of his life. He frequently played St. Louis clubs during the '20s and '30s, and began recording for QRS and Victor in 1929. Greatly influenced by Lonnie Johnson, Gibson also accompanied Jimmie Rodgers on a Victor single in 1931, then spent parts of the next three decades playing in the streets around St. Louis. Gibson resurfaced on recordings in 1960 with a Bobbin date, and worked another three years in St. Louis' Gaslight Square before his death in 1963. —Ron Wynn

● **Beat You Doing It** / 1972 / Yazoo ◆◆◆◆◆
Beat You Doing It contains all of the prime tracks Clifford Gibson recorded, offering an excellent, concise overview of the country blues guitarist. —Thom Owens

Complete Recorded Works in Chronological Order (1929-1931) / 1991 / Document ◆◆◆◆
Document's 23-track collection *Complete Recorded Works* presents everything Clifford Gibson recorded between 1929-1931. Since Gibson was a fine guitarist but not an exceptional vocalist, this is primarily of interest only to diehard country blues fans. Those casual fans that do want a taste of Gibson are better served by Yazoo's more concise collection, *Beat You Doing It*. —Thom Owens

Lacy Gibson

b. 1936, North Carolina
Guitar, Vocals / Electric Chicago Blues
Slowly returning to musical action following major surgery, guitarist Lacy Gibson has been an underappreciated figure on the Windy City circuit for decades.

Lacy and his family left North Carolina for Chicago in 1949. It didn't take long for Gibson to grow entranced by the local action—he learned from veterans Sunnyland Slim and Muddy Waters and picked up pointers from immaculate axemen Lefty Bates, Matt "Guitar" Murphy, and Wayne Bennett. Gibson made a name for himself as a session player in 1963, assuming rhythm guitar duties on sides by Willie Mabon for USA, Billy "The Kid" Emerson for M-Pac!, and Buddy Guy on Chess. Gibson made his vocal debut on the self-penned blues ballad "My Love Is Real" at Chess the same year, though it wasn't released at the time (when it belatedly emerged, it was mistakenly attributed to Guy).

A couple of bargain-basement 45s for the remarkably obscure Repeto logo (that's precisely where they were done—in Lacy Gibson's basement!) preceded Gibson's inconsistent album debut for then-brother-in-law Sun Ra's El Saturn label. Ralph Bass produced an album by Gibson in 1977, but the results weren't issued at the time (Delmark is currently releasing the set domestically).

A stint as Son Seals' rhythm axeman (he's on Seals' *Live and Burning* LP) provided an entree to Alligator Records, which included four fine sides by Gibson on its second batch of *Living Chicago Blues* anthologies in 1980. Best of all was a Dick Shurman-produced album for the Dutch Black Magic logo in 1982, *Switchy Titchy*, that brilliantly spotlighted Gibson's clean fretwork and hearty vocals. Now that he's regaining his health, it's about time for Lacy Gibson to enter the studio again. —Bill Dahl

Jazz Gillum (William McKinley Gillum)

b. Sep. 11, 1904, Indianola, MS, **d.** Mar. 29, 1966, Chicago, IL
Harmonica / Chicago Blues
Next to John Lee "Sonny Boy" Williamson, no harmonica player was as popular or as much in demand on recording sessions during the '30s as Jazz Gillum. His high, reedy sound meshed perfectly on dozens of hokum sides on the Bluebird label, both as a sideman and as a leader.

Born in Indianola, MS, (B.B. King's birthplace as well) in 1904, Gillum was evidently teaching himself how to play harmonica by the tender age of six. After running away from home in 1911

to live with relatives in Charleston, Mississippi, Jazz spent the next dozen or so years working a day job and spending his weekends playing for tips on local streetcorners. When he visited Chicago in 1923, he found the environment very much to his liking and put down roots there.

There he met guitarist Big Bill Broonzy and the two of them started working club dates around the city as a duo. By 1934, Gillum started popping up on recording dates for ARC and later Bluebird, RCA Victor's budget label. This association would prove to be a lasting one as Chicago producer Lester Melrose frequently called on Gillum as a sideman—as well as cutting sides on his own—as part of the 'Bluebird beat' hose band. His career seemed to screech to a halt when the label folded in the late '40s and aside from a Memphis Slim session in 1961, he seems to have been largely inactive throughout the '50s until his death from a gunshot wound as a result of an argument in 1966. —Cub Koda

● **Roll Dem Bones 1938-49** / Wolf ◆◆◆◆◆
Best selection of Gillum sides available. Not a bad one in this bunch. (Import) —Cub Koda

Lloyd Glenn

b. Nov. 21, 1909, San Antonio, TX, **d.** May 23, 1985, Los Angeles, CA
Piano / Piano Blues
As a integral behind-the-scenes fixture on the L.A. postwar blues scene, pianist/arranger/A&R man Lloyd Glenn had few equals. His rolling ivories anchored many of Lowell Fulson's best waxings for Swing Time and Checker, and he scored his own major hits on Swing Time with the imaginative instrumentals "Old Time Shuffle Blues" in 1950 and "Chica Boo" the next year.

Glenn was already an experienced musician when he left the Lone Star state for sunny California in 1942. His early sessions there included backing T-Bone Walker at the 1947 Capitol date that produced the guitarist's immortal "Call It Stormy Monday." Glenn recorded for the first time under his own name the same year for Imperial with his band, the Joymakers, which included guitarist Gene Phillips, saxist Marshall Royal, and singer Geraldine Carter.

Massively constructed guitarist Tiny Webb introduced Glenn to Swing Time owner Jack Lauderdale in 1949, inaugurating a five-year stint as A&R man at the firm for Glenn. After Swing Time's demise, the pianist moved to Aladdin Records, issuing more catchy instrumentals for Eddie Mesner's firm through 1959. There was also an isolated session for Imperial in 1962 that produced "Twistville" and "Young Date." The pianist remained active into the 1980s, often touring as Big Joe Turner's accompanist. —Bill Dahl

Piano Styling / 1957 / Score ◆◆◆◆
Glenn's tasty piano ticklings were to the fore on his 1950s sides for the Mesners' Aladdin logo. The dozen instrumentals on this LP (still not on CD) include remakes of "Chica-Boo" and "Old Time Shuffle" and the engaging workouts "Tiddleywinks," "Glenn's Glide," "Nite-Flite," "Footloose," and "Southbound Special." —Bill Dahl

Honky Tonk Train / 1983 / Night Train ◆◆◆◆
In addition to waxing his own bouncy instrumentals during his late-'40s/early-'50s stay at Swing Time Records (an unissued take of "Old Time Shuffle," one of his own hits, graces this disc), pianist Lloyd Glenn also arranged and played behind several of the firm's veteran vocalists—explaining the presence of exceptional blues outings by Joe Pullum and Jesse Thomas. —Bill Dahl

● **Chica Boo** / 1988 / Night Train ◆◆◆◆◆
Quite a bit of duplication between this 18-song collection and Night Train's previous disc, but since this one contains both of his hits—"Old Time Shuffle" and "Chica Boo"—it wins hands down. Pullum and Thomas are back as guest vocalists on these 1947-1952 waxings. This is lightly swinging West Coast blues with an elegant, understated edge, Glenn's tasty approach to the 88s always in the pocket. —Bill Dahl

Barry Goldberg

b. 1941, Chicago, IL
Piano, Organ / Electric Chicago Blues
Barry Goldberg was a regular fixture in the White blues firma-

ment of the middle '60s that seemed to stretch from Chicago to New York. A keyboardist (organ seemed to be his specialty), Barry was an in-demand session man—he appears with Michael Bloomfield on a Mitch Ryder album, for instance—along with Al Kooper and his blues playing contemporary from the original Butterfield band, Mark Naftalin. Goldberg was a member of Charlie Musselwhite's first band, contributing great piano and organ lines to the *Stand Back!* album (his work on "Cristo Redentor" is moody and introspective, with a strong jazz-inflected feel, while still retaining strong blues roots) and a handful of others throughout the decade. —*Cub Koda*

● **Two Jews Blues** / 1969 / One Way ✦✦✦✦
This is one of those late-'60s collaborations where I expected the world to explode when I put it on, and felt disappointed when it didn't. However, when you get past looking at players in the band, and listen to the music, there are a number of wonderful cuts. Enough of them for me to replace the vinyl with the CD. "Blues for Barry And..." is Bloomfield at his best with a solid band behind him cranking out this slow blues you wish wouldn't end. Barry Goldberg has always played a solid organ, whether with Harvey Mandel, Charlie Musselwhite, or out on his own. This is his chance to be the leader of an all-star lineup. My regrets are that it is only 35 minutes, and most importantly I would have liked to put all the guitar players together for a cut or two; they never get to play off one another. —*Bob Gottlieb*

Good Rockin' Charles (Charles Edwards)

b. Mar. 4, 1933, Pratts, AL
Harmonica / Electric Chicago Blues
Harpist Good Rockin' Charles is best known for a solo he didn't play. Suffering from a bad case of studio fright, Charles chickened out of playing on guitarist Jimmy Rogers' 1956 Chess waxing of "Walking by Myself"—leaving the door wide open for Big Walter Horton to blow a galvanic solo that rates among his very best. Charles' domestic solo discography consists of one nice album for Steve Wisner's short-lived Mr. Blues logo in 1975.

Inspired by both Sonny Boys and Little Walter, Charles Edwards began playing harp shortly after hitting Chicago in 1949. He played with a plethora of local luminaries—Johnny Young, Lee Jackson, Arthur Spires, Smokey Smothers—before joining Rogers' combo in 1955. Cobra Records also tried and failed to corral him for a session in 1957.

Bassist Hayes Ware was instrumental in finally convincing the elusive Good Rockin' into a studio for Mr. Blues, where he shook the walls with revivals of classics by both Sonny Boys, Rogers, and Jay McShann. Unfortunately, it would prove the extent of the mysterious harpist's recorded legacy. —*Bill Dahl*

Good Rockin' Charles / 1976 / Rooster Blues ✦✦✦✦✦
The elusive Chicago harpist's one and only full-length album, originally issued on Steve Wisner's short-lived Mr. Blues logo and later picked up by Rooster Blues (but not available on CD as yet). Cut in 1975, this set shows that Charles never left the 1950s stylistically—backed by a nails-tough combo, he pays tribute to both Sonny Boys and his ex-boss Jimmy Rogers while betraying more than a hint of Little Walter influence. —*Bill Dahl*

Blind Roosevelt Graves

b. Mississippi
Guitar, Vocals / Delta Blues
Blind Roosevelt Graves was a Mississippi guitarist and singer who mixed secular and sacred material and cut some entertaining, celebratory party tunes as well as reverential spirituals in the '20s and '30s. He played with pianists Will Ezell and Cooney Vaughn, and clarinetist Baby Jay. Graves was also a member of the Mississippi Jook Band, along with his brother—singer and tambourine player Uaroy Graves—and Vaughn.

Very few biographical details of Blind Roosevelt Graves' life are known. He and his brother Uaroy began playing juke joints in the Mississippi Delta in the early '20s. In 1929, the two brothers cut a number of sides for the Paramount and American Record Companies, which all appeared under Blind Roosevelt's name. They would continue to record until 1936. In the mid-'30s, the pair formed the Mississippi Jook Band with pianist Cooney Vaughn. The band recorded for the American Record Company in the mid- and late '30s.

After leaving behind a handful of recordings, Graves disap-

peared in the early '40s. It is not known where he settled, nor is his death date known. —*Ron Wynn & Stephen Thomas Erlewine*

● **Complete Recorded Works (1929-1936)** / Document ✦✦✦✦✦

Henry Gray

b. Jan. 19, 1925, Kenner, LA
Piano, Vocals / Electric Chicago Blues
Henry Gray was among the Chicago blues piano elite during the 1950s. Unlike most of his contemporaries there, he was from Louisiana rather than Mississippi—and since 1968, he's been living there once again, a stalwart on the swamp blues circuit.

Gray rolled into Chicago in 1946 after fighting for his country during World War II in the Philippines. The formidable Big Maceo was a primary influence on Gray's two-fisted playing. He procured steady gigs with Little Hudson's Red Devil Trio and guitarist Morris Pejoe before moving into extensive work as a session musician behind Jimmy Reed, Little Walter, Bo Diddley, Jimmy Rogers, Billy Boy Arnold, and Pejoe. In 1956, he joined the combo of the great Howlin' Wolf, digging in for a dozen-year run.

The pianist retreated to his homebase outside Baton Rouge after leaving Wolf's employ. In 1988, he returned to Chicago long enough to cut his debut domestic album, *Lucky Man*, for Blind Pig Records. Guitarist Steve Freund produced and played on the set, an alluring combination of Windy City blues and bayou boogie. —*Bill Dahl*

● **Lucky Man** / 1988 / Blind Pig ✦✦✦✦✦
Renowned as a piano-rippling sideman on the 1950s Chicago scene, Henry Gray returned to his native Louisiana in 1968 before anyone recorded him too prolifically as a leader. This album at least partially makes up for the oversight; backed by a solid Chicago combo, Gray alternates his own stuff with classics by Big Maceo, Little Walter, and Jimmy Reed, his ruminative voice and rumbling ivories prowess nicely spotlighted. —*Bill Dahl*

Cal Green

b. Jun. 22, 1937, Dayton, TX
Guitar / Modern Electric Blues
Few blues guitarists can boast the varied résumé of Texas native Cal Green. From blues to doo wop to jazz, Green has played 'em all—and done each idiom proud in the process.

Green's idol as a teenager was Lone Star wonder Clarence "Gatemouth" Brown. So pervasive was Gate's sway that Green and his ninth-grade pal Roy Gaines used to stage mock guitar battles imitating their idols (Gaines was a T-Bone Walker disciple) at various Houston bars. Cal didn't have to leave the house to find worthy competition; his older brother Clarence was also an accomplished picker who cut a load of killer instrumentals (notably 1962's "Red Light") for small Lone Star diskeries.

Cal Green played on RPM Records releases by Quinton Kimble and pianist Connie McBooker, but his main claim to fame is as the guitarist for Hank Ballard & the Midnighters, who roared through Houston in 1954 looking to replace their just-drafted axeman Arthur Porter, scooped up teenaged Green, and went on their way.

Green received plenty of solo space during his Midnighters stint. His ringing guitar provided a sturdy hook for the group's rocker "Don't Change Your Pretty Ways" and figured prominently on "Tore Up Over You" (later revived in blistering fashion by rockabilly giant Sleepy LaBeef) and "Open Up the Back Door." The Midnighters' label, Cincinnati-based Federal Records, thought enough of Green's slashing Texas licks to cut a couple of 45s of him in 1958: the double-sided instrumental "The Big Push"/"Green's Blues" and a pair of vocals, "I Can Hear My Baby Calling"/"The Search Is All Over."

A 1959 marijuana bust sent Green to a Texas slammer for 21 months, but he briefly rejoined the Midnighters in 1962. After that, jazz became Green's music of choice. He gigged with organist Brother Jack McDuff and then singer Lou Rawls, eventually settling in L.A.

An acclaimed but tough-to-find 1988 album for Double Trouble, *White Pearl*, showed conclusively that Cal Green still knows his way around the blues on guitar. —*Bill Dahl*

● **White Pearl** / 1988 / Double Trouble ✦✦✦✦✦

Clarence Green & the Rhythmaires

b. 1937, Houston, TX
Guitar, Vocals / Modern Texas Blues
Though not one of the best known of the modern Texas blues

guitarists, Clarence Green is regarded by his peers as one of the best. Green (not to be confused with the late Clarence "Candy" Green, a Texas blues pianist) did session work for Duke Records in the '60s with Junior Parker, Bobby Bland, and others, and performed with stars from Fats Domino to Johnny Nash. His own recordings have mostly been for small Houston labels. As Marcel Vos from Double Trouble Records wrote, "The Clarence Green of today plays a brand of Texas blues that is mixed with soul, jazz, and funk, not unlike the music of fellow Texans such as Roy Gaines, Cornell Dupree, and of course, his brother Cal Green." — *Jim O'Neal*

● **Green's Blues** / 1991 / Collectables ◆◆◆◆◆
A CD reissue of Texas blues, R&B, and pop, it's all very danceable and very enjoyable. The recordings are from 1958 to 1965. —*Niles J. Frantz*

Big John Greer

Saxophone / East Coast Blues
Never attaining the same glistening level of fame that fellow New York sax blasters Sam "The Man" Taylor and King Curtis enjoyed, Big John Greer nevertheless blew strong and sang long on a terrific series of waxings for RCA Victor and its Groove subsidiary from 1949 to 1955.

Greer was a childhood pal of future King Records producer Henry Glover. The pair attended high school together in Hot Springs and progressed to Alabama A&M College. Glover moved up quickly, playing trumpet and arranging for popular bandleader Lucky Millinder by 1948; when Millinder saxist Bull Moose Jackson split the group to promote his blossoming solo career, Glover called his pal Big John Greer to fill Moose's chair. Greer's first record date as a leader was for Bob Shad's fledgling Sittin' in With label, but the great majority of his discography lies in Victor's vaults.

Initially recording as a singer/saxist with Millinder's unit for RCA, Greer stayed put when Millinder defected to King in 1950. That worked out nicely for Greer, who blew scorching tenor sax behind King stars Wynonie Harris (on "Mr. Blues Is Coming to Town" and "Bloodshot Eyes") and Bull Moose Jackson (on the incredibly raunchy "Nosey Joe"). Greer enjoyed his biggest hit as a vocalist in 1952 with the tasty blues ballad "Got You On My Mind" for RCA. The Howard Biggs-Joe Thomas composition attracted covers over the years from a mighty disparate lot, notably the Big Three Trio, Cookie & the Cupcakes, and Jerry Lee Lewis.

Greer's RCA and (from 1954 on) Groove platters were of uncommonly high standards, even for the polished New York scene. But no more hits ensued ("Bottle It Up and Go" and "Come Back Maybellene" certainly deserved a wider audience) for the powerful saxist. Glover brought him over to King in 1955, but a year there didn't slow his slide. Booze was apparently taking its toll on Greer's employment prospects; by 1957, he was back in Hot Springs, through as anything but a local attraction. He died at age 48, forgotten by all but the most dedicated R&B fans. —*Bill Dahl*

● **Rockin' With Big John** / 1992 / Bear Family ◆◆◆◆◆
Three discs of an R&B saxist with only one legit R&B hit to his everlasting credit? Yep, and this 92-track examination of Greer's 1949-1955 stay at RCA Victor virtually never grows stale, either, thanks to the torrid jump blues tempos Greer often favored. "Got You on My Mind," the often-covered blues ballad that proved Greer's lone hit, is here, as are rocking renditions of "Bottle It Up and Go," "Come Back Maybelline," and "Clambake Boogie." Guest vocalists include the Du Droppers, Annisteen Allen, and Damita Jo. Typically exhaustive liner notes and discographical info in the Bear Family tradition. —*Bill Dahl*

Grey Ghost (Roosevelt Thomas Williams)

Piano / Texas Blues
Sparse and poorly recorded sessions are unfortunately the basis of Grey Ghost's (born Roosevelt Thomas Williams) fame. An exciting, if erratic, Texas barrelhouse pianist who's been active since the '20s, Grey Ghost has enjoyed a slight career boost in the '90s. Other than older fans who'd seen him playing around Austin and hardcore collectors, few people knew anything about The Ghost until the LP *Grey Ghost* surfaced on Catfish. A reissue of '65 field recordings, its horrendous recording quality obscured the often captivating rhythms and his spirited vocals.

But since its appearance, The Ghost has been featured at several festivals, and was heard on a "Bluestage" show for National Public Radio in '94. —*Ron Wynn*

● **Grey Ghost** / Oct. 30, 1992 / Spindletop ◆◆◆◆◆
Although he's been playing around Austin and throughout the Southwest and nation since the 1920s, even much of the blues hardcore was unaware of Grey Ghost. Despite some rambling sections and others where rhythmic organization isn't a strong point, there's plenty of vintage boogie and good-natured barrelhouse playing and singing on this set. He's not among the greatest in the genre, but certainly belongs in the group close to the top. —*Ron Wynn*

Guitar Shorty (David Kearney)

b. Sep. 8, 1939, Tampa, FL
Guitar, Vocals / West Coast Blues
When he's not turning somersaults, doing backwards flips, and standing on his head—all while playing, of course—Guitar Shorty is prone to cutting loose with savagely slashing licks on his instrument. Live, he's simply amazing—and after some lean years, his two recent albums for Black Top have proven that all that energy translates vividly onto tape.

At age 17, David Kearney was already gigging steadily in Tampa, FL. One night, he was perched on the bandstand when he learned that the mysterious "Guitar Shorty" advertised on the club's marquee was none other than he! His penchant for stage gymnastics was inspired by the flamboyant Guitar Slim, whose wild antics are legendary. In 1957, Shorty cut his debut single, "You Don't Treat Me Right," for Chicago's Cobra Records under Willie Dixon's astute direction. Three superb 45s in 1959 for tiny Pull Records in Los Angeles (notably "Hard Life") rounded out Shorty's discography for quite a while.

During the '60s, he married Jimi Hendrix's stepsister and lived in Seattle, where the rock guitar god caught Shorty's act (and presumably learned a thing or two about inciting a throng) whenever he came off the road. Shorty's career had its share of ups and downs—once he was reduced to competing on Chuck Barris' zany *The Gong Show*, where he copped first prize for delivering "They Call Me Guitar Shorty" while balanced on his noggin.

Los Angeles had long since reclaimed Shorty by the time things started to blossom anew with the 1991 album *My Way on the Highway* for the British JSP logo (with guitarist Otis Grand in support). From there, Black Top signed Shorty; 1993's dazzling *Topsy Turvy* and 1995's *Get Wise to Yourself* have been the head-over-heels results so far. —*Bill Dahl*

● **My Way on the Highway** / 1991 / JSP ◆◆◆◆
Until he joined forces with British guitarist Otis Grand's band and waxed this very credible comeback set, David "Guitar Shorty" Kearney's legacy was largely limited to a solitary single for Cobra and a handful of great but legendarily obscure followups for Los Angeles-based Pull Records during the late '50s. The acrobatic guitarist informed everyone he was alive and lively with this one, exhibiting his Guitar Slim roots on "Down Thru the Years" and slashing with a vengeance on "No Educated Woman" and the title cut (but shouldn't it have read "or the highway?"). —*Bill Dahl*

● **Topsy Turvy** / 1993 / Black Top ◆◆◆◆◆
More impressive than Shorty's British venture thanks to superior production values and a better handle on his past (there's a stellar remake of "Hard Life"), Topsy Turvy made it clear that Guitar Shorty was back to stay stateside. Black Top assembled a fine New Orleans combo for the majority of the album, as Shorty proved that his act translates beautifully to record minus the crowd-pleasing acrobatic antics. —*Bill Dahl*

● **Get Wise To Yourself** / 1995 / Black Top ◆◆◆◆
No sophomore jinx for this veteran L.A. blues guitar wildman. Other than the discordant pseudo-New Orleans number "A Fool Who Wants to Stay," this is non-stop red-hot blues axe with a funky Crescent City twist and a skin-tight horn section led by saxist Kaz Kazanoff. —*Bill Dahl*

Guitar Slim (Eddie Jones)

b. Dec. 10, 1926, Greenwood, MS, **d.** Feb. 7, 1959, New York, NY
Guitar, Vocals / Electric New Orleans Blues
No 1950s blues guitarist even came close to equalling the flam-

boyant Guitar Slim in the showmanship department. Armed with an estimated 350 feet of cord between his axe and his amp, Slim would confidently stride onstage wearing a garishly hued suit of red, blue, or green—with his hair usually dyed to match! It's rare to find a blues guitarist hailing from Texas or Louisiana who doesn't cite Slim as one of his principal influences; Buddy Guy, Earl King, Guitar Shorty, Albert Collins, Chick Willis, and plenty more have enthusiastically testified to Slim's enduring sway.

Born Eddie Jones in Mississippi, Slim didn't have long to make such an indelible impression. He turned up in New Orleans in 1950, influenced by the atomic guitar energy of Gatemouth Brown. But Slim's ringing, distorted guitar tone and gospel-enriched vocal style were his alone. He debuted on wax in 1951 with a mediocre session for Imperial that barely hinted at what would soon follow. A 1952 date for Bullet produced the impassioned "Feelin' Sad," later covered by Ray Charles (who would arrange and play piano on Slim's breakthrough hit the next year).

With the emergence of the stunning "The Things That I Used to Do" on Art Rupe's Specialty logo, Slim's star rocketed to blazing ascendancy nationwide. Combining a swampy ambience with a churchy arrangement, the New Orleans-cut track was a monster hit, pacing the R&B charts for an amazing 14 weeks in 1954. Strangely, although he waxed several stunning follow-ups for Specialty in the same tortured vein—"The Story of My Life," "Something to Remember You By," "Sufferin' Mind"—as well as the blistering rockers "Well I Done Got Over It," "Letter to My Girlfriend," and "Quicksand," Slim never charted again.

The guitar wizard switched over to Atlantic Records in 1956. Gradually, his waxings became tamer, though "It Hurts to Love Someone" and "If I Should Lose You" summoned up the old fire. But Slim's lifestyle was as wild as his guitar work. Excessive drinking and life in the fast lane took its inevitable toll over the years, and he died in 1959 at age 32. Only in recent years has his monumental influence on the blues lexicon begun to be fully recognized and appreciated.

Incidentally, one of his sons bills himself as Guitar Slim, Jr. around the New Orleans circuit, his repertoire heavily peppered with his dad's material. —Bill Dahl

The Things That I Used to Do / 1964 / Specialty ♦♦
Great stuff, but irreparably changed by organ and guitar overdubs in an ill-advised attempt to update the classic New Orleans sound. —Bill Dahl

Atco Sessions / Jul. 1988 / Atlantic ♦♦♦
Sometimes a bit subdued compared to his bone-chilling output for Specialty, these 1956–1958 sides for Atco still possess considerable charm, especially the tough "It Hurts to Love Someone" and "If I Should Lose You," which conjure up the same hellfire and brimstone intensity as Slim's earlier work. — Bill Dahl

★ **Sufferin' Mind** / 1991 / Specialty ♦♦♦♦♦
His guitar fraught with manic high-end distortion and his vocals fried over church-fired intensity, Eddie "Guitar Slim" Jones influenced a boatload of disciples while enjoying the rewards that came with his 1954 R&B chart-topper "The Things That I Used to Do." This 26-song survey of Slim's seminal 1953-1955 Specialty catalog rates with the best New Orleans blues ever cut—besides the often-imitated but never-duplicated smash, his "Story of My Life," "Sufferin' Mind," and "Something to Remember You By" are overwhelming in their ringing back-alley fury. Slim could rock, too: "Well I Done Got Over It," "Quicksand," "Certainly All," and the raucous introduction "Guitar Slim" drive with blistering power (saxist Joe Tillman was a worthy foil for the flamboyant guitarist in the solo department). —Bill Dahl

Guitar Slim, Jr. (Rodney Armstrong)

b. 1951, New Orleans, LA
Guitar, Vocals / Electric New Orleans Blues
Despite the fact that his first and only album to date earned a Grammy nomination, Guitar Slim, Jr. remains a somewhat shadowy figure to the blues public. The son of Eddie "Guitar Slim" Jones, his real name is Rodney Armstrong. According to New Orleans historian Jeff Hannusch's notes on Slim's 1988 album, he "has been a fixture on the Black New Orleans club circuit for the better part of 20 years... [but] doesn't get to play the posher

uptown clubs." His Orleans album featured mostly covers of his father's inspirational blues, which he was loathe to play earlier in life, but Slim is also known for his extensive soul repertoire. —Jim O'Neal

● **Story of My Life** / 1988 / Orleans ♦♦♦♦♦
Contemporary blues, blues-rock, and soul comes from the son of the late blues/R&B legend. With mostly credible covers of his father's tunes, it was a Grammy nominee. —Niles J. Frantz

Buddy Guy

b. Jul. 30, 1936, Lettsworth, LA
Guitar, Vocals / Electric Chicago Blues
He's Chicago's blues king today, ruling his domain just as his idol and mentor Muddy Waters did before him. Yet there was a time, and not all that long ago either, when Buddy Guy couldn't even negotiate a decent record deal. Times sure have changed for the better—Guy just racked up another Grammy for his last studio album, *Slippin' In* (his third in three tries for the Silvertone label). His latest disc, a sizzling live collection recorded with G.E. Smith's horn-powered Saturday Night Live Band at his own spacious Chicago venue, Buddy Guy's Legends, threatens to make it four for four. Eric Clapton unabashedly calls Buddy Guy his favorite blues axeman, and so do a great many adoring fans worldwide.

High-energy guitar histrionics and boundless onstage energy have always been Guy trademarks, along with a tortured vocal style that's nearly as distinctive as his incendiary rapid-fire fretwork. He's come a long way from his beginnings on the 1950s Baton Rouge blues scene—at his first gigs with bandleader "Big Poppa" John Tilley, the young guitarist had to chug a stomach-jolting concoction of Dr. Tichenor's antiseptic and wine to ward off an advanced case of stage fright. But by the time he joined harpist Raful Neal's band, Guy had conquered his nervousness.

Guy journeyed to Chicago in 1957, ready to take the town by storm. But times were tough initially, until he turned up the juice as a showman (much as another of his early idols, Guitar Slim, had back home). It didn't take long after that for the new kid in town to establish himself. He hung with the city's blues elite: Freddy King, Muddy Waters, Otis Rush, and Magic Sam, who introduced Buddy Guy to Cobra Records boss Eli Toscano. Two searing 1958 singles for Cobra's Artistic subsidiary were the result: "This Is the End" and "Try to Quit You Baby" exhibited more than a trace of B.B. King influence, while "You Sure Can't Do" was an unabashed homage to Guitar Slim. Willie Dixon produced the sides.

When Cobra folded, Guy wisely followed Rush over to Chess. With the issue of his first Chess single in 1960, Guy was no longer aurally indebted to anybody. "First Time I Met the Blues" and its follow-up, "Broken Hearted Blues," were fiery, tortured slow blues brilliantly showcasing Guy's whammy-bar-enriched guitar and shrieking, hellhound-on-his-trail vocals.

Although he's often complained that Leonard Chess wouldn't allow him to turn up his guitar loud enough, the claim doesn't wash: Guy's 1960-1967 Chess catalog remains his most satisfying body of work. A shuffling "Let Me Love You Baby," the impassioned downbeat items "Ten Years Ago," "Stone Crazy," "My Time After Awhile," and "Leave My Girl Alone," and a bouncy "No Lie" rate with the hottest blues waxings of the '60s. While at Chess, Guy worked long and hard as a session guitarist, getting his licks in on sides by Waters, Howlin' Wolf, Little Walter, Sonny Boy Williamson, and Koko Taylor (on her hit "Wang Dang Doodle").

Upon leaving Chess in 1967, Guy pacted with Vanguard. His first LP for the firm, *A Man and His Blues*, followed in the same immaculate vein as his Chess work and contained the rocking "Mary Had a Little Lamb," but *This is Buddy Guy* and *Hold That Plane!* proved somewhat less consistent. Guy and harpist Junior Wells had long palled around Chicago (Guy supplied the guitar work on Wells' seminal 1965 Delmark set *Hoodoo Man Blues*, initially billed as "Friendly Chap" because of his Chess contract); they recorded together for Blue Thumb in 1969 as *Buddy and the Juniors* (pianist Junior Mance being the other Junior) and Atlantic in 1970 (sessions co-produced by Eric Clapton and Tom Dowd) and 1972 for the solid album *Buddy Guy & Junior Wells Play the Blues*. Buddy and Junior toured together throughout the '70s, their playful repartee immortalized on *Drinkin' TNT 'n' Smokin' Dynamite*, a live set cut at the 1974 Montreux Jazz Festival.

Guy's reputation among rock guitar gods such as Eric Clapton, Jimi Hendrix, and Stevie Ray Vaughan was unsurpassed, but prior to his Grammy-winning 1991 Silvertone disc *Damn Right, I've Got the Blues*, he amazingly hadn't issued a domestic album in a decade. That's when the Buddy Guy bandwagon really picked up steam—he began selling out auditoriums and turning up on network television (David Letterman, Jay Leno, etc.). *Feels Like Rain*, his 1993 encore, was a huge letdown artistically, unless one enjoys the twisted concept of having one of the world's top bluesmen duet with country hat act Travis Tritt and hopelessly overwrought rock singer Paul Rodgers. By comparison, 1994's *Slippin' In*, produced by Eddie Kramer, was a major step back in the right direction, with no hideous duets and a preponderance of genuine blues excursions.

A Buddy Guy concert can sometimes be a frustrating experience. He'll be in the middle of something downright hair-raising, only to break it off abruptly in mid-song, or he'll ignore his own massive songbook in order to offer imitations of Clapton, Vaughan, and Hendrix. But Guy, whose club remains the most successful blues joint in Chicago (you'll likely find him sitting at the bar whenever he's in town), is without a doubt the Windy City's reigning blues artist—and he rules benevolently. —*Bill Dahl*

I Left My Blues in San Francisco / 1967 / MCA/Chess ♦♦♦♦♦
Featuring such classic Buddy Guy performances as "Buddy's Groove" and "She Suits Me to a Tee," *I Left My Blues in San Francisco* ranks as one of the guitarist's finest albums. All of this material is also available on the double-disc set, *The Complete Chess Recordings*. —*Thom Owens*

I Left My Blues in San Francisco / 1967 / MCA/Chess ♦♦♦
A late-'60s Chess LP that included several standout efforts from Guy's early catalog—"Leave My Girl Alone," "Every Girl I See," and the searing "Mother-In-Law Blues." —*Bill Dahl*

A Man and His Blues / 1968 / Vanguard ♦♦♦♦
The guitarist's first album away from Chess—and to be truthful, it sounds as though it could have been cut at 2120 S. Michigan, with Guy's deliciously understated guitar work and a tight combo anchored by three saxes and pianist Otis Spann laying down tough grooves on the vicious "Mary Had a Little Lamb," "I Can't Quit the Blues," and an exultant cover of Mercy Dee's "One Room Country Shack." —*Bill Dahl*

Buddy and the Juniors / 1970 / MCA ♦♦
Strange, off-the-cuff set originally issued on Blue Thumb pairing Buddy Guy and Junior Wells with jazz pianist Junior Mance and no rhythm section. Guy plays acoustic guitar, Wells amplified harp, and the hoary setlist includes "Hoochie Coochie Man," "Five Long Years," and "Rock Me Mama." —*Bill Dahl*

Buddy Guy & Junior Wells Play the Blues / 1972 / Rhino ♦♦♦
Considering the troubled background of this album (Eric Clapton, Ahmet Ertegun, and Tom Dowd only ended up with eight tracks at a series of 1970 sessions in Miami; two years later, the J. Geils Band was brought in to cut two additional songs to round out the long-delayed LP for 1972 release), the results were pretty impressive. Guy contributes dazzling lead axe to their revival of "T-Bone Shuffle;" Wells provides a sparkling remake of Sonny Boy's "My Baby She Left Me," and Guy is entirely credible in a grinding Otis Redding mode on the southern soul stomper "A Man of Many Words." —*Bill Dahl*

Hold That Plane / 1972 / Vanguard ♦♦
Lackluster set comprised of only seven lengthy workouts, including Guy's renditions of "I'm Ready," "Watermelon Man," and Sugar Pie DeSanto's "Hello San Francisco." Jazzman Junior Mance is pianist for the somewhat underwhelming album. —*Bill Dahl*

I Was Walkin' Through the Woods / 1974 / MCA/Chess ♦♦♦♦♦
Ten of the mercurial guitarist's best recordings ever for Chess, cut during his early-'60s peak. "First Time I Met the Blues" and "Broken Hearted Blues" are harrowing downbeat blues of enormous power, Guy's shrieks and tremolo-rich guitar bursts boasting an intensity level he's only achieved intermittently ever since. Even better, they're here in stereo—unlike virtually every other Chess collection to follow. —*Bill Dahl*

Live in Montreux / Jul. 9, 1977 / Evidence ♦♦♦
No blues tandem in recent memory has given more alternately brilliant and infuriating performances as the duo of Junior Wells

and Buddy Guy. They can inspire or anger, stimulate or disgust, amaze or bore. They were in a great groove during the selections recorded at this concert for Isabel. They have been recently reissued with two bonus cuts as part of Evidence's huge cache of blues material. Wells' often rambling, sometimes disjointed and unorganized vocals were not only focused on this occasion but delivered with verve, direction, and intensity. Guy stayed in the background, but when summoned, played with less flair and more power, dispensing with distortion and feedback gimmicks and providing neat fills, slashing lines, and meaty riffs. Fine Wells/Guy material that is close, if not completely equal to, their best. —*Ron Wynn*

Pleading the Blues / Oct. 1979 / Evidence ♦♦♦♦♦
Recorded on Halloween night in 1979, this pairs up Wells and Guy in a fashion that hasn't been heard since Hoodoo Man Blues, their first, and best collaboration. Solid backing by The Philip Guy band (Buddy's brother) makes this album a rare treat. —*Cub Koda*

Stone Crazy! / 1981 / Alligator ♦♦♦
Buddy Guy mostly indulges his histrionic side throughout this high-energy set, first issued in France and soon picked up for domestic consumption by Alligator. It's a particularly attractive proposition for rock-oriented fans, who will no doubt dig Guy's non-stop incendiary, no-holds-barred guitar attack and informal arrangements. Purists may want to look elsewhere. —*Bill Dahl*

Drinkin' TNT 'n' Smokin' Dynamite / 1982 / Blind Pig ♦♦♦
Cut at the 1974 Montreux Jazz Festival with Stones' bassist Bill Wyman anchoring the rhythm section, the set captures some of the ribald musical repartee that customarily distinguished the pairing of Buddy Guy and Junior Wells, though they certainly break no new ground as they roll through their signature songs. —*Bill Dahl*

Alone & Acoustic / 1991 / Alligator ♦♦♦
An admirable attempt to lower the humongous decibel levels that these Chicago blues titans usually record in by setting them up in an unplugged format. But the results are disarmingly lowkey; Guy needs electricity to support his rapid-fire fret barrage, which doesn't translate all that comfortably into an acoustic framework. —*Bill Dahl*

Damn Right, I've Got the Blues / 1991 / Silvertone ♦♦♦♦♦
Grammy-winning comeback set that brought Guy back to prominence after a long studio hiatus. Too many clichéd cover choices—"Five Long Years," "Mustang Sally," "Black Night," "There Is Something on Your Mind"—to earn unreserved recommendation, but Guy's frenetic guitar histrionics ably cut through the superstar-heavy proceedings (Eric Clapton, Jeff Beck, and Mark Knopfler all turn up) on the snarling title cut and a handful of others. —*Bill Dahl*

☆ **The Complete Chess Studio Sessions** / 1992 / MCA/Chess ♦♦♦♦♦
Here's everything that fleet-fingered Buddy Guy waxed for Chess from 1960 to 1966, including numerous unissued-at-the-time masters, offering the most in-depth peek at his formative years imaginable. Stone Chicago blues classics ("Ten Years Ago," "My Time After Awhile," "Let Me Love You Baby," "Stone Crazy"), rockin' oddities ("American Bandstand," "$100 Bill," "Slop Around"), even a cut that features guitarist Lacy Gibson's vocal rather than Guy's ("My Love Is Real")—some 47 sizzling songs in all. —*Bill Dahl*

● **The Very Best of Buddy Guy** / 1992 / Rhino ♦♦♦♦♦
Credible attempt to digitally summarize Guy's entire pre-Silvertone career on a single 18-song disc. Encompasses the guitarist's 1957 demo "The Way You Been Treating Me," two killer Cobras, four of his hottest Chess sides, a couple notable Vanguards, a pair of alluring Atlantics, and three tremendously unsubtle 1981 items from Guy's days with the British JSP label. —*Bill Dahl*

Feels Like Rain / 1993 / Jive/Novus ♦♦♦
The followup to the Grammy winner *Damn Right I've Got The Blues!*, this mines similar turf with similar results. Buddy turns in powerhouse renditions of James Brown's "I Go Crazy," Guitar Slim's "Sufferin' Mind," and Ray Charles' "Mary Ann," while the obligatory guest duets reach their high point with Bonnie Raitt's turn on John Hiatt's title cut. The synthesizer lushness of Marvin Gaye's "Trouble Man" may enrage true believers, but Guy pours his heart into it, making it a surprise highlight. —*Cub Koda*

Slippin' In / 1994 / Silvertone ✦✦✦✦✦
Now this is more like it: no sign of any superfluous duets, and far fewer hoary standards to contend with (only the Z.Z. Hill title track, in fact). Lots of high-energy guitar fireworks and vocal intensity from the perpetually eager-to-please blues superstar, as he drives through well-chosen numbers first rendered by Bobby Bland, Jimmy Reed, Charles Brown, and Fenton Robinson and Guy's own impassioned "Cities Need Help" and "Little Dab-A-Doo." —*Bill Dahl*

Southern Blues 1957-63 / 1994 / Paula ✦✦✦
Kind of a thrown-together hodgepodge, but still a worthwhile add to your CD collection. Guy's four indispensable 1958 sides for Cobra are here (along with alternates of "This Is the End" and the Guitar Slim-influenced "You Sure Can't Do"), while Guy provides crackling lead guitar on four 1963 outings by singer Jesse Fortune (notably the minor-key rhumba "Too Many Cooks").

Finally, there are two demos that Guy cut at a Baton Rouge radio station back in 1957—or they're supposed to be here, anyway: the crudely engaging "The Way You Been Treatin' Me" is definitely Buddy Guy, but "I Hope You Come Back Home" isn't (no guesses from this corner on exactly who it may be, either). —*Bill Dahl*

Live—The Real Deal / 1996 / Silvertone ✦✦✦✦
As close as Buddy Guy's ever likely to come to recapturing the long-lost Chess sound. Cut live at his popular Chicago nightspot, Buddy Guy's Legends, with guitarist G.E. Smith's horn-leavened Saturday Night Live Band and pianist Johnnie Johnson in lush support, Guy revisits his roots on sumptuous readings of "I've Got My Eyes on You," "Ain't That Lovin' You," "My Time After Awhile," and "First Time I Met the Blues." No outrageous rock-based solos or Cream/Hendrix/Stevie Ray homages; this is the Buddy Guy album that purists have salivated for the last quarter century or so. —*Bill Dahl*

H

John Hammond, Jr. (John Paul Hammond)

b. Nov. 13, 1942, New York, NY
Guitar, Harmonica, Vocals / Modern Acoustic Blues

With a career that now spans more than three decades, John Hammond is one of a handful of White blues musicians who was on the scene at the beginning of the first blues renaissance of the mid-'60s. That revival, brought on by renewed interest in folk music around the U.S., brought about career boosts for many of the great classic blues players, including Mississippi John Hurt, Rev. Gary Davis, and Skip James. Some critics have described Hammond as a White Robert Johnson, and Hammond does justice to classic blues by combining powerful guitar and harmonica playing with expressive vocals and a dignified stage presence. Within the first decade of his career as a performer, Hammond began crafting a niche for himself that is completely his own: the solo guitar man, harmonica slung in a rack around his neck, reinterpreting classic blues songs from the 1930s, '40s, and '50s. Yet, as several of his mid-'90s recordings for the Pointblank label demonstrate, he's also a capable bandleader who plays wonderful electric guitar. This guitar-playing and ensemble work can be heard on *Found True Love* and *Got Love If You Want It*, both for the Pointblank/Virgin label.

Born November 13, 1942, in New York City, the son of the famous Columbia Records talent scout, John Hammond, Sr., what most people don't know is that young Hammond didn't grow up with his father. His parents split when he was young, and he saw his father several times a year. He first began playing guitar while attending a private high school, and he was particularly fascinated with slide guitar technique. He saw his idol, Jimmy Reed, perform at New York's Apollo Theatre, and he's never been the same since.

After attending Antioch College in Ohio on a scholarship for a year, he left to pursue a career as a blues musician. By 1962, with the folk revival starting to heat up, Hammond had attracted a following in the coffeehouse circuit, performing in the tradition of the classic country blues singers he loved so much. By the time he was just 20 years old, he had been interviewed for the *New York Times* before one of his East Coast festival performances, and he was a certified national act.

When Hammond was living in the Village in 1966, a young Jimi Hendrix came through town, looking for work. Hammond offered to put a band together for the guitarist, and got the group work at the Cafe Au Go Go. By that point, the coffeehouses were falling out of favor and instead the bars and electric guitars were coming in with folk-rock. Hendrix was approached there by Chas Chandler, who took him to England to record. Hammond recalls telling the young Hendrix to take Chandler up on his offer. "The next time I saw him, about a year later, he was a big star in Europe," Hammond recalled in a 1990 interview. In the late '60s and early '70s, Hammond continued his work with electric blues ensembles, recording with people like Band guitarist Robbie Robertson (and other members of the Band when they were still known as Levon and the Hawks), Duane Allman, Dr. John, harmonica wiz Charlie Musselwhite, Michael Bloomfield and David Bromberg.

As with Dr. John and other blues musicians who've recorded more than two dozen albums, there are many great recordings that provide a good introduction to the man's body of work. His self-titled debut for the Vanguard label has now been reissued on compact disc by the company's new owners, the Welk Music

Group, and other good recordings to check out (on vinyl and/or compact disc) include *I Can Tell* (recorded with Bill Wyman from the Rolling Stones), *Southern Fried* (1968), *Sourcepoint* (1970, Columbia) and his most recent string of early- and mid-'90s albums for Pointblank/Virgin Records, *Got Love If You Want It*, *Trouble No More* (both produced by J.J. Cale), and *Found True Love*.

He didn't know it when he was 20, and he may not realize it now, but Hammond deserves special commendation for keeping many of the classic blues songs alive. When fans see Hammond perform them, as Dr. John has observed many times with his music and the music of others, the fans often want to go back further, and find out who did the original versions of the songs Hammond now plays.

Although he's a multi-dimensional artist, one thing Hammond has never professed to be is a songwriter. In the early years of his career, it was more important to him that he bring the art form to a wider audience by performing classic—in some cases forgotten—songs. Now, more than 30 years later, Hammond continues to do this, touring all over the U.S., Canada, and Europe from his base in northern New Jersey. Anything can happen at a John Hammond concert, and he selects tunes from his vast repertoire like buckets of water from a well.

Whether it's with a band or by himself, Hammond can do it all. Seeing him perform live, one still gets the sense that some of the best is still to come from this energetic bluesman. *—Richard Skelly*

Big City Blues / 1964 / Vanguard ++++
Hammond's second effort was one of the first electric White blues recordings, and one of the very first that could be said to be blues-rock. Covering a variety of Chess Records classics and electrifying some older tunes, the playing, featuring Hammond, Billy Butler, and James Spruill on electric guitar, is first-rate. But Hammond's vocals are overly mannered and overwrought, and although he would improve, these flaws would keep him from rising to the top rank of White bluesmen. *—Richie Unterberger*

Country Blues / 1964 / Vanguard ++++
Although Hammond had already recorded electric material, he went back to a solo acoustic format for his fourth album, accompanying himself on guitar and harmonica on faithful interpretations of standards by Robert Johnson, Blind Willie McTell, John Lee Hooker, Sleepy John Estes, Jimmy Reed, Willie Dixon, and Bo Diddley. If it sounds a bit unimaginative and routine today, one has to remember that the general listening audience was much less aware of these artists and songs in the mid-'60s. Hammond did a commendable job of rendering them here, with fine guitar work and vocals that were a considerable improvement over his earliest efforts. *—Richie Unterberger*

So Many Roads / 1965 / Vanguard +++++
One of young Hammond's better early albums. *—Bill Dahl*

Nobody But You / 1988 / Flying Fish +++
Hammond usually performs solo, but here he is backed by a five-piece band, including pianist Gene Taylor. It's good to hear him in this context. All the numbers are blues classics or standards written by John Lee Hooker, Muddy Waters, Arthur Crudup, Little Walter, and B.B. Fuller. *—Michael G. Nastos*

● **The Best of John Hammond** / 1989 / Vanguard +++++
The best early works of this folk-blues artist. Acoustic and essential. *—Michael G. Nastos*

Got Love If You Want It / 1992 / Charisma ✦✦✦
In many ways, *Got Love If You Want It* is standard-issue John Hammond, Jr. The album is filled with covers by great bluesmen like Son House and Slim Harpo, as well as rock & rollers like Chuck Berry. The difference is ability. Hammond is a professional and is able to pull off convincing performances of these warhorses. Backed by Little Charlie and the Nightcats—who have rarely sounded better, incidentally–Hammond tears through these songs with passion, which makes even the oldest songs sound rather fresh. *—Thom Owens*

John Hammond Live / Jan. 15, 1992 / Rounder ✦✦✦✦✦
A definitive live set featuring Hammond on guitar and harmonica. *—Michael G. Nastos*

Trouble No More / Jan. 25, 1994 / Point Blank ✦✦✦

Found True Love / Jan. 23, 1996 / Virgin ✦✦

W.C. Handy

b. Nov. 16, 1873, Muscle Shoals, AL, **d.** Mar. 28, 1958
Piano, Bandleader, Songwriter / Early American Blues
Often referred to as the "father of the blues," William Christopher Handy was born on November 16, 1873, in Muscle Shoals, AL. He studied music early on, starting with the cornet in a brass band, working with a vocal quartet, and eventually playing throughout the South in minstrel and tent shows. It was during his many travels that he began to notate the music he heard, including Delta blues. He would adapt these tunes and sounds to his own performance, in this way popularizing the music he heard, the blues in particular. He was the first to add flatted thirds and sevenths (so-called "blue notes") to published compositions.

He became music director of Mahara's Minstrels in 1896, a group that played rags, popular dance numbers, and even some light classical compositions. They toured the South in the late 1800s and early 1900s. He recorded in New York in 1917 with his Memphis Orchestra.

Handy was the first to compose and publish a tune with the word "blues" in it–"Memphis Blues" in 1912. He composed and published many classic blues tunes including "St. Louis Blues," "Beale Street Blues," "Ole Miss," and "Yellow Dog Blues." Handy's foray into writing and publishing blues songs inspired other writers, including Perry Bradford, the author of "Crazy Blues"– the first blues song ever recorded (1920).

Handy moved himself and his Memphis Orchestra to New York in 1917, started the Handy Record Company (a failure) in 1922, and recorded with his own band until 1923. Throughout the later 1920s and 1930s Handy, who had developed eye problems, was forced to work less. Still, he continued working with many orchestras. He was on recording sessions with Red Allen and Jelly Roll Morton. His autobiography *Father of the Blues* was written in 1938, the same year that he was given a tribute concert in Carnegie Hall. In his later years, Handy was not very active. He died on March 28, 1958. The movie *St. Louis Blues* was released in 1958, starring Nat King Cole. It is not considered to be very reflective of the facts of Handy's life. A legend in Memphis, Handy has a park named after him there containing a statue of himself. The W.C. Handy Award is the most prestigious honor currently awarded to blues artists. Handy, along with Duke Ellington, appears on a U.S. postage stamp.

Although no one person is the father of the blues, and Handy was not by temperament or cultivation what we might call a bluesman, W.C. Handy did much to popularize and publicize what had been until that time a very personal and local pheonomenon. Handy helped to broadcast the blues form to the world. *—Michael Erlewine*

Pat Hare

Guitar, Vocals / Electric Memphis Blues
If highly distorted guitar played with a ton of aggression and just-barely-suppressed violence is your idea of great blues, then Pat Hare's your man. Born with the improbable name of Auburn Hare (one of those biographical oddities that even the most fanciful blues historian couldn't make up in a million years), he worked the '50s Memphis circuit, establishing his rep as a top-notch player with a scorching tone only rivaled by Howlin' Wolf's guitarist, Willie Johnson. Our first recorded glimpse of him occurs when he showed up at Sam Phillips' Memphis Recording Service sometime in 1953 to play on James Cotton's debut session for the Sun label. His aggressive, biting guitar work on both

sides of that oft-anthologized single—"Cotton Crop Blues" and "Hold Me in Your Arms"–featured a guitar sound so overdriven that with the historical distance of several decades, it now sounds like a direct line to the coarse, distorted tones favored by modern rock players. But what is now easily attainable by 16-year-old kids on modern-day effects pedals just by stomping on a switch, Hare was accomplishing with his fingers and turning the volume knob on his Sears & Roebuck cereal-box-sized amp all the way to the right until the speaker was screaming.

After working with Cotton and many others around the Memphis area, Hare moved North to Chicago, and by the late '50s was a regular member of the Muddy Waters band, appearing on the legendary *Live at Newport, 1960* album. By all accounts Pat was a quiet, introspective man when sober, but once he started drinking the emotional tables turned in the opposite direction. After moving to Minneapolis in the '60s to work with fellow Waters bandmate Mojo Buford, Hare was convicted of murder after a domestic dispute, spending the rest of his life behind bars. In one of the great ironies of the blues, one of the tracks Pat Hare left behind in the Sun vaults was an original composition entitled, "I'm Gonna Murder My Baby." *—Cub Koda*

Mystery Train / 1990 / Rounder ✦✦✦✦✦
A fine set of Junior Parker's Sun recordings, including the cool original version of the title cut. It's great to compare with the hot Presley version. These classic uptown presentations also feature tracks by James Cotton and Pat Hare. *—Barry Lee Pearson*

James Harman

b. CA
Harmonica, Vocals / Modern Electric Blues
James Harman is a California-based blues singer, harmonica player, songwriter, and bandleader with an agenda that definitely distances him from the rest of the pack. A veteran of the blues roadhouse circuit, he has led various combinations of the James Harman Band over the years, most featuring top-notch talent (like guitarists Hollywood Fats and Kid Ramos) to match his own. With roots in the deepest of blues harmonica sources (Little Walter, Walter Horton, Sonny Boy Williamson), Harman scores consistently both live and on record. His most recent recorded efforts show a genuine flair for writing original material (always more important to Harman than just regurgitating his record collection), all of it laced with a generous dollop of wisecracking good humor. Always willing to stretch the boundaries and conceptions of what a good bar band should be capable of, Harman combines rich traditions and beatnik craziness for a blend that's mighty hard to resist.*—Cub Koda*

Those Dangerous Gentlemen / 1987 / Rhino ✦✦✦

Extra Napkins / 1988 / Rivera ✦✦

Live in '85, Vol. 1 / 1990 / Rivera ✦✦

● **Do Not Disturb** / 1991 / Black Top ✦✦✦✦✦
James Harman's *Do Not Disturb* is a first-rate blues album, one that captures all the different sides of postwar blues. At its core, *Do Not Disturb* is Chicago blues, but Harman touches on swing, jump, and Texas roadhouse blues, banging out gritty, greasy harp licks with intensity. His band is up to the challenge of keeping up with him—they tear through the uniformly excellent songs with abandon. *Do Not Disturb* establishes Harman as one of the most exciting blues tradtionalists of the '90s. *—Thom Owens*

Two Sides to Every Story / Jun. 1, 1993 / Black Top ✦✦✦✦

Cards on the Table / May 28, 1994 / Black Top ✦✦✦

Black & White / 1995 / Black Top ✦✦

The James Harman Band / Black Top ✦✦

Harmonica Slim (Travis L. Blaylock)

b. Dec. 21, 1934, Douglassville, TX
Harmonica, Vocals / Texas Blues
Over the history of the blues, there have been at least three different people plying their wares as Harmonica Slim, with one of them being far better known as Slim Harpo. But *this* Harmonica Slim was born Travis L. Blaylock down in Texas. He picked up the instrument around the age of 12 and was soon working as part of the Sunny South Gospel Singers gospel group, broadcasting over radio station KCMC in his hometown of Texarkana

from the mid-'40s on. By 1949, he moved to Los Angeles, ingratiating himself into the burgeoning blues community, working package shows with Lowell Fulson and the like. He first recorded as a sideman on a group of dates in the mid-'50s for West Coast labels like Aladdin, Spry, and Vita. After spending most of the '60s working dates with Percy Mayfield, Harmonica Fats, B.B. King, T-Bone Walker and others, Slim finally got to record a full album under his own name for the Bluestime label in 1969. — *Cub Koda*

● **Back Bottom Blues** / Oct. 1995 / Trix ✦✦✦✦

Slim Harpo (James Moore)

b. Jan. 11, 1924, Lobdell, LA, d. Jan. 31, 1970, Baton Rouge, LA
Guitar, Harmonica, Vocals / Electric Louisiana Blues
In the large stable of blues talent that Crowley, LA producer Jay Miller recorded for the Nashville-based Excello label, no one enjoyed more mainstream success than Slim Harpo. Just a shade behind Lightnin' Slim in local popularity, Harpo played both guitar and neck-rack harmonica in a more down-home approximation of Jimmy Reed, with a few discernible, and distinctive, differences. Slim's music was certainly more laid-back than Reed's, if such a notion was possible. But the rhythm was insistent and, overall, Harpo was more adaptable than Reed or most other bluesmen. His material not only made the national charts, but also proved to be quite adaptable for White artists on both sides of the Atlantic, including the Rolling Stones, Yardbirds, Kinks, Dave Edmunds with Love Sculpture, Van Morrison with Them, Sun rockabilly Warren Smith, Hank Williams, Jr. and the Fabulous Thunderbirds.

A people-pleasing club entertainer, he certainly wasn't above working rock & roll rhythms into his music, along with hard-stressed, country & western vocal inflections. Several of his best tunes were co-written with his wife Lovelle and show a fine hand for song construction, appearing to have arrived at the studio pretty well-formed. His harmonica playing was driving and straightforward, full of surprising melodicism, while his vocals were perhaps best described by writer Peter Guralnick as "if a Black country and western singer or a White rhythm and blues singer were attempting to impersonate a member of the opposite genre." This perhaps was Harpo's true genius, and what has allowed his music to have a wider currency. By the time his first single became a Southern jukebox favorite, his songs were adapted and played by White musicians left and right. Here was good-time Saturday night blues that could be sung by elements of the Caucasian persuasion with a straight face. Nothing resembling the emotional investment of a Howlin' Wolf or a Muddy Waters was required; it all came natural and easy, and its influence has stood the test of time.

He was born James Moore just outside of Baton Rouge, LA. After his parents died, he dropped out of school to work every juke joint, streetcorner, picnic and house rent party that came his way. By this time he had acquired the alias of Harmonica Slim, which he used until his first record was released. It was fellow bluesman Lightnin' Slim who first steered him to local record man J.D. Miller. The producer used him as accompanist to Hopkins on a half dozen sides before recording him on his own. When it came time to release his first single ("I'm a King Bee"), Miller informed him that there was another Harmonica Slim recording on the West Coast, and a new name was needed before the record could come out. Moore's wife took the slang word for harmonica, added an 'o' to the end of it, and a new stage name was the result, one that would stay with Slim Harpo the rest of his career.

Harpo's first record became a double-sided R&B hit, spawning numerous follow-ups on the "King Bee" theme, but even bigger was "Rainin' in My Heart," which made the *Billboard* Top 40 pop charts in the summer of 1961. It was another perfect distillation of Harpo's across-the-board appeal, and was immediately adapted by country, cajun, and rock & roll musicians; anybody could play it and sound good doing it. In the wake of the Rolling Stones covering "I'm a King Bee" on their first album, Slim had the biggest hit of his career in 1966 with "Baby, Scratch My Back." Harpo described it as "an attempt at rock & roll," and its appearance in *Billboard's* Top 20 pop charts prompted the dance-oriented follow-ups "Tip on In" and "Tee-Ni-Nee-Ni-Nu," both R&B charters. For the first time in his career, Harpo appeared in such far-flung locales as Los Angeles and New York

City. Flush with success, he contacted Lightnin' Slim, who was now residing outside of Detroit, MI. The two reunited and formed a band, touring together as a sort of blues mini-package to appreciative White rock audiences until the end of the decade. The new year beckoned with a tour of Europe (his first ever) all firmed up, and a recording session scheduled when he arrived in London. Unexplainably, Harpo—who had never been plagued with any ailments stronger than a common cold—suddenly succumbed to a heart attack on January 31, 1970. —*Cub Koda*

Rainin' in My Heart / 1961 / Excello ✦✦✦✦
The original 12-song Excello album with the addition of six extra tracks, all of which were originally issued as singles only. With the exception of "Dream Girl," "My Home Is A Prison" and "What A Dream," everything on here also appears on the AVI double disc collection. —*AMG*

Shake Your Hips / 1986 / Flyright ✦✦✦✦
The second installment in Ace's overview of Harpo's swamp blues career, spanning 1962-1966 and including all four of the harpist's rare 1962 sides for Imperial (cut during a brief rift with his producer J.D. Miller). More rarities and unissued gems, including a few tracks that exhibit slight soul tendencies (a genre that Harpo took to surprisingly well). —*Bill Dahl*

● **Scratch My Back: The Best of Slim Harpo** / 1989 / Rhino ✦✦✦✦
All the hits, including the original "I'm a King Bee," "Baby, Scratch My Back," "I Got Love If You Want It," "Shake Your Hips," "Rainin' in My Heart," "Tip on In," and "Strange Love." A best-of that really is, with top-flight sound as a bonus. —*Cub Koda*

I'm a King Bee / 1989 / Flyright ✦✦✦✦
Very generous 24-song collection emphasizing the laconic harpist's early (1957-1964) Excello output. The British import boasts the required "I'm a King Bee," "I Got Love If You Want It," and "Rainin' in My Heart," but also the more obscure and previously unissued (including Slim's take on John Lee Hooker's "Boogie Chillun"). —*Bill Dahl*

☆ **Hip Shakin': The Excello Collection** / 1995 / AVI-Excello ✦✦✦✦
A shapely two-disc retrospective, *Hip Shakin'* is the definitive Slim Harpo package. Collecting all of his hits ("I'm A King Bee," "Got Love If You Want It," "Baby, Scratch My Back") along with other defining moments from his stay with the label, this 44-track compilation also includes three live recordings from a 1961 fraternity dance. —*AMG*

The Scratch: Rare & Unissued / Feb. 1996 / AVI-Excello ✦✦✦✦
A 25-track single-disc comp loaded with previously unissued sides and alternate takes (the title track is an interesting variant of his hit, "Baby, Scratch My Back"), making it the perfect companion volume to the above. This also has the added bonus of more (and even wilder) live recordings from the infamous 1961 frat party dance in Alabama. Dodgy sound on the live sides, but performances too great to leave in the can either way. —*AMG*

Peppermint Harris (Harrison Nelson, Jr.)

b. Jul. 17, 1925, Texarkana, TX
Guitar, Vocals / Electric Jump Blues
The contemporary blues boom has resuscitated the career of many a veteran blues artist who's been silent for ages. Take guitarist Peppermint Harris, who in 1951 topped the R&B charts with his classic booze ode "I Got Loaded." Nobody expected a new Peppermint Harris CD in 1995, but Home Cooking producer Roy C. Ames coaxed one out of old Pep for Collectables nonetheless. *Texas on My Mind* may not be as enthralling as Harris' early '50s output, but it's nice to have him back in circulation.

By the time he was in his early 20s, Harrison Nelson, Jr. was lucky enough to have found a mentor and friend on the Houston blues front: Lightnin' Hopkins took an interest in the young man's musical development. When Harris was deemed ready, Lightnin' accompanied him to Houston's Gold Star Records. Nothing came of that jaunt, but Harris eventually recorded his debut 78 for the company in 1948 (as Peppermint Nelson).

Bob Shad's Sittin' in With label was the vehicle that supplied Harris' early work to the masses—especially his first major hit, "Raining in My Heart," in 1950. These weren't exactly formal sessions—legend has it one took place in a Houston bordello! Nor was Shad too cognizant of Pep's surname—when he couldn't recall it, he simply renamed our man Harris.

Harris moved over to Eddie Mesner's Aladdin Records in 1951, cutting far tighter sides for the firm in Los Angeles (often with the ubiquitous Maxwell Davis serving as bandleader and saxist). After "I Got Loaded" lit up the charts in 1951, Harris indulged in one booze ode after another: "Have Another Drink and Talk to Me," "Right Back On It," "Three Sheets in the Wind." But try as they might, the bottle let Harris down as a lyrical launching pad after that.

He drifted from Money and Cash to RCA's short-lived subsidiary "X" and Don Robey's Duke logo (where he allegedly penned "As the Years Go Passing By" for Fenton Robinson) after that, but it wasn't until a long-lasting association with Stan Lewis' Shreveport, LA-based Jewel Records commenced in 1965 that Harris landed for longer than a solitary single.

Later, Harris worked various day jobs around Houston, including one at a record pressing plant, before retiring to Sacramento, CA (until recently, anyway). —*Bill Dahl*

Peppermint Harris / 1962 / Time ♦♦♦
Nice early-'50s Texas R&B. —*Bill Dahl*

Sittin' in With / 1979 / Mainstream ♦♦♦♦
Fifteen well-chosen 1950–1951 masters from Bob Shad's Sittin' in With label by Houston bluesman Peppermint Harris, including his hit "Rainin' in My Heart." Rowdy little bands behind the powerful singer sometimes included Goree Carter on guitar. —*Bill Dahl*

● **I Got Loaded** / 1987 / Route 66 ♦♦♦♦♦
Harris hit his full stride after signing with Aladdin Records in 1951 and moving his recording base to Los Angeles. Under saxist Maxwell Davis' direction, Harris waxed his smash "I Got Loaded" and a few more potent rounds after that ("Three Sheets in the Wind," "Have Another Drink and Talk to Me"). Unfortunately not yet available on CD, these sides comprise Pep's chief claim to fame. —*Bill Dahl*

Texas On My Mind / Dec. 1995 / Collectables ♦♦♦
From the late '40s through the early '60s, Peppermint Harris recorded for a variety of labels to moderate success. Although he had a few records in the '70s, he was basically retired until 1995, when he recorded *Texas on My Mind* at the age of 72. Although the songs on the album are quite good (most of the numbers are originals), Harris' abilities have dwindled; with his limited voice and guitar skills, he simply doesn't have the power to captivate an audience. —*Thom Owens*

Being Black Twice / Collectables ♦♦♦
These are '60s and '70s sides from the Jewel label. A good vocalist with some unusual material. —*Hank Davis*

Shakey Jake Harris

b. Apr. 12, 1921, Earle, AR, **d.** Mar. 2, 1990, AR
Harmonica, Vocals / Chicago Blues
Jake Harris knew how to shake a pair of dice in order to roll a lucrative winner. He also realized early on that his nephew, guitarist Magic Sam, was a winner as a bluesman. Harris may have not been a technical wizard on his chosen instrument, but his vocals and harp style were proficient enough to result in a reasonably successful career (with Sam and without).

Born James Harris, the Arkansas native moved to Chicago at age seven. Admiring the style of Sonny Boy Williamson, Harris gradually learned the rudiments of the harp but didn't try his hand at entertaining professionally until 1955. Harris made his bow on vinyl in 1958 for the newly formed Artistic subsidiary of Eli Toscano's West Side-based Cobra Records. His only Artistic 45, "Call Me If You Need Me"/"Roll Your Moneymaker," was produced by Willie Dixon and featured Sam and Syl Johnson on guitars.

The uncompromising Chicago mainstream sound of that 45 contrasted starkly with Jake Harris' next studio project. In 1960, Prestige's Bluesville subsidiary paired him with a pair of jazzmen—guitarist Bill Jennings and organist Jack McDuff—for a full album, *Good Times* (the unlikely hybrid of styles working better than one might expect). The harpist encored later that year with *Mouth Harp Blues,* this time with a quartet including Chicagoan Jimmie Lee Robinson on guitar and a New York rhythm section (both of his Bluesville LPs were waxed in New Jersey).

Jake Harris and Magic Sam remained running partners for much of the 1960s. They shared bandstands at fabled West Side haunts such as Sylvio's—where he was captured on tape in 1966 singing "Sawed Off Shotgun" and "Dirty Work Goin' On" (now available on a Black Top disc by Sam)—and Big Bill Hill's Copacabana before Harris moved to Los Angeles in the late '60s. He recorded for World Pacific and briefly owned his own nightclub and record label before returning to Arkansas (where he died in 1990). —*Bill Dahl*

Good Times / 1961 / Bluesville ♦♦♦♦
Chicago harpist Shakey Jake Harris journeyed all the way to New Jersey to make his debut album in 1960. It was a huge stylistic departure for Harris—he was paired with jazz mainstays Brother Jack McDuff on simmering Hammond organ and bluestinged guitarist Bill Jennings. The trio located some succulent common ground even without a drummer, Harris keeping his mouth organ phrasing succinct and laying out when his more accomplished session mates catch fire. —*Bill Dahl*

● **Mouth Harp Blues** / 1962 / Bluesville ♦♦♦♦
When Harris returned to New Jersey later that same year to wax his Bluesville encore, he brought along fellow Chicagoan Jimmie Lee Robinson as his guitarist. A full rhythm section was used this time (New York cats all), but the overall approach was quite a bit closer to what he was used to hearing on Chicago's West side. —*Bill Dahl*

The Devil's Harmonica / 1972 / Polydor ♦♦♦♦

Wynonie Harris

b. Aug. 24, 1915, Omaha, NE, **d.** Jun. 14, 1969, Los Angeles, CA
Drums, Vocals / Electric Jump Blues
No blues shouter embodied the rollicking good times that he sang of quite like raucous shouter Wynonie Harris. "Mr. Blues," as he was not-so-humbly known, joyfully related risque tales of sex, booze, and endless parties in his trademark raspy voice over some of the jumpingest horn-powered combos of the postwar era.

Those wanton ways eventually caught up with Harris, but not before he scored a raft of R&B smashes from 1946 to 1952. Harris was already a seasoned dancer, drummer, and singer when he left Omaha for L.A. in 1940 (his main influences being Big Joe Turner and Jimmy Rushing). He found plenty of work singing and appearing as an emcee on Central Avenue, the bustling nightlife strip of the Black community there. Wynonie Harris' reputation was spreading fast—he was appearing in Chicago at the Rhumboogie Club in 1944 when bandleader Lucky Millinder hired him as his band's new singer. With Millinder's orchestra in brassy support, Harris made his debut on shellac by boisterously delivering "Who Threw the Whiskey in the Well" that same year for Decca. By the time it hit in mid-1945, Harris was long gone from Millinder's organization and back in L.A.

The shouter debuted on wax under his own name in July of 1945 at an L.A. date for Philo with backing from drummer Johnny Otis, saxist Teddy Edwards, and trumpeter Howard McGhee. A month later, he signed on with Apollo Records, an association that provided him with two huge hits in 1946: "Wynonie's Blues" (with saxist Illinois Jacquet's combo) and "Playful Baby." Harris' own waxings were squarely in the emerging jump blues style then sweeping the West Coast. After scattered dates for Hamp-Tone, Bullet, and Aladdin (where he dueled it out with his idol Big Joe on a two-sided "Battle of the Blues"), Harris joined the star-studded roster of Cincinnati's King Records in 1947. There his sales really soared.

Few records made a stronger seismic impact than Harris' 1948 chart-topper "Good Rockin' Tonight." Ironically, Harris shooed away its composer, Roy Brown, when he first tried to hand it to the singer; only when Brown's original version took off did Wynonie cover the romping number. With Hal "Cornbread" Singer on wailing tenor sax and a rocking, socking backbeat, the record provided an easily followed blueprint for the imminent rise of rock & roll a few years later (and gave Elvis Presley something to place on the A side of his second Sun single).

After that, Harris was rarely absent from the R&B charts for the next four years, his offerings growing more boldly suggestive all the time. "Grandma Plays the Numbers," "All She Wants to Do Is Rock," "I Want My Fanny Brown," "Sittin' on It All the Time," "I Like My Baby's Pudding," "Good Morning Judge,"

"Bloodshot Eyes" (a country tune that was first released on King by Hank Penny), and "Lovin' Machine" were only a portion of the ribald hits Harris scored into 1952 (13 in all)—and then his personal hit parade stopped dead. It certainly wasn't Harris' fault—his King output rocked as hard as ever under Henry Glover's supervision—but changing tastes among fickle consumers accelerated Wynonie Harris' sobering fall from favor.

Sides for Atco in 1956, King in 1957, and Roulette in 1960 only hinted at the raunchy glory of a short few years earlier. The touring slowed accordingly. In 1963, his chauffeur-driven Cadillacs and lavish New York home a distant memory, Harris moved back to L.A., scraping up low-paying local gigs whenever he could. Chess gave him a three-song session in 1964, but sat on the promising results. Throat cancer silenced him for good in 1969, ending the life of a bigger-than-life R&B pioneer whose ego matched his tremendous talent. —Bill Dahl

☆ **Good Rocking Tonight** / 1990 / Charly ◆◆◆◆◆
Equally splendid compilation of the raspy shouter's King label output from the British Charly logo. Contains 20 sides, including a few essentials that Rhino didn't bother with: a roaring "Rock Mr. Blues" that grants Harris vocal group backing; the lascivious rocker "I Want My Fanny Brown" and "Lollipop Mama," and a celebratory "Mr. Blues Is Coming to Town." Harris and King always used inexorably swinging bands—saxists include Red Prysock, David Van Dyke (who duel it out on the amazing "Quiet Whiskey"), Big John Greer, Hal Singer, and Tom Archia. —Bill Dahl

★ **Bloodshot Eyes: The Best of** / 1993 / King/Rhino ◆◆◆◆◆
Wynonie Harris was a hard-living, rousing R&B shouter who made some of the most sexually explicit songs in modern popular music history. Harris didn't leave much to the imagination, but he also possessed a booming voice with wonderful tone and range, and the comedic skill to execute these tunes without becoming raunchy. There are many hilarious cuts on this 18-track anthology, among them "I Like My Baby's Pudding," "Grandma Plays The Numbers" and "Good Morning Judge." Harris roars, struts, and wails over equally feverish arrangements, and earns a draw with Joe Turner on "Battle Of The Blues." These songs give a good portrait of a delightful, often spectacular vocalist who could be both provocative and compelling. —Ron Wynn

Women, Whiskey & Fish Tails / 1993 / Ace ◆◆◆◆
British compiler Ray Topping focuses on Harris' 1952-1957 King output on this 21-song collection, when he was undeniably on the downslide as far as making hits. But there was still plenty of wind in the shouter's sails, judging from "Greyhound," "Christina," "Shake That Thing" (an update of an ancient blues theme), "Git to Gittin' Baby," and "Mr. Dollar." Harris even supplied a savvy sequel to one of his immortal numbers with "Bad News Baby (There'll Be No Rockin' Tonite)." —Bill Dahl

Everybody Boogie! / 1996 / Delmark ◆◆◆◆
This is a marvelous collection of 1945 recordings made for Apollo Records with Harris' powerhouse vocals backed by jump blues bands led by jazz greats Illinois Jacquet, Oscar Pettiford and Jack McVea. No real honking and bar walking going on here; quite the opposite, as the Pettiford sides have bop lines creeping in throughout. But Harris seems oblivious to it all as tracks like "Time to Change Your Town," "Here Come the Blues," "Stuff You Gotta Watch," and "Somebody Changed the Lock on My Door" are on an equal par for sheer bravado and intensity with the best of his later work for King. A welcome compilation. —Cub Koda

Wilbert Harrison

b. Jan. 5, 1929, Charlotte, NC, **d.** Oct. 26, 1994
Vocals, Piano, Guitar, Drums / R&B
Perceived by casual oldies fans as a two-hit wonder (his 1959 chart-topper "Kansas City" and a heartwarming "Let's Work Together" a full decade later), Wilbert Harrison actually left behind a varied body of work that blended an intriguing melange of musical idioms into something quite distinctive.

Country and gospel strains filtered into Wilbert Harrison's consciousness as a youth in North Carolina. When he got out of the Navy in Miami around 1950, he began performing in a calypso-based style. Miami entrepreneur Henry Stone signed Harrison to his Rockin' logo in 1953; his debut single, "This Woman of Mine," utilized the very same melody as his later reading of "Kansas City" (the first rendition of the Jerry Leiber/Mike Stoller composition by pianist Little Willie Littlefield came out in 1952, doubtless making an impression).

Its flip, a country-tinged "Letter Edged in Black," exhibited Harrison's eclectic mindset.

After moving to Newark, NJ, Harrison wandered by the headquarters of Savoy Records one fortuitous day and was snapped up by producer Fred Mendelsohn. Harrison recorded several sessions for Savoy, beginning with a catchy cover of Terry Fell's country tune "Don't Drop It." Top New York sessioneers—arranger Leroy Kirkland, saxist Buddy Lucas and guitarists Mickey Baker and Kenny Burrell—backed Harrison on his 1954-56 Savoy output, but hits weren't forthcoming.

That changed instantly when Harrison waxed his driving "Kansas City" for Harlem entrepreneur Bobby Robinson in 1959. With a barbed-wire guitar solo by Wild Jimmy Spruill igniting Harrison's no-frills piano and clenched vocal, "Kansas City" paced both the R&B and pop charts soon after its issue on Fury Records (not bad for a $40 session). Only one minor problem: Harrison was still technically under contract to Savoy (though label head Herman Lubinsky had literally run him out of his office some years earlier!), leading to all sorts of legal wrangles that finally went Robinson's way. Momentum for any Fury follow-ups had been fatally blunted in the interim, despite fine attempts with "Cheatin' Baby," the sequel "Goodbye Kansas City," and the original "Let's Stick Together."

Harrison bounced from Neptune to Doc to Constellation to Port to Vest with little in the way of tangible rewards before unexpectedly making a comeback in 1969 with his infectious "Let's Work Together" for Juggy Murray's Sue imprint. The two-part single proved a popular cover item—Canned Heat revived it shortly thereafter, and Brian Ferry chimed in with his treatment later on. Alas, it was an isolated happenstance—apart from "My Heart Is Yours," a bottom-end chart entry on SSS International in 1971, no more hits were in Wilbert's future. But Harrison soldiered on, sometimes as a one-man band, for years to come. —Bill Dahl

Listen to My Song / 1954-1957 / Savoy ◆◆◆◆
Harrison's first label association of any endurance commenced when he signed with Herman Lubinsky's Savoy logo in 1954 for a two-year stretch. Top New York sessioneers like guitarists Mickey Baker and Kenny Burrell and saxists Buddy Lucas and Budd Johnson help out on these 16 Savoy tracks (still unavailable on CD). He liked that C&W; Terry Fell's "Don't Drop It" is a tremendously catchy hillbilly tune given an R&B flavor by the young singer. —Bill Dahl

Let's Work Together / 1969 / Sue ◆◆◆
Quickie album supervised by Juggy Murray to cash in on the unexpected success of Harrison's "Let's Work Together," but not a bad effort all the same. Harrison brings his unique vocal delivery to oldies such as "Blue Monday," "Stagger Lee," "Louie Louie," and "Stand by Me," imparting his own personal stamp to each. This LP deserves digital reissue somewhere down the line. —Bill Dahl

The Small Labels / 1986 / Krazy Kat ◆◆◆◆
Vinyl survey of Harrison's forays away from the famous indie diskeries, both before and after he hit with "Kansas City." Weirdly, his 1953 effort "This Woman of Mine" uses the same melody as "Kansas City," some six years prior to his hitting big with it. Harrison was liable to try anything to land a hit—he brands himself a "Calypso Man," tries a hillbilly tack on "Letter Edged in Black," and offers a salute to the 1964 "New York World's Fair"—all in that distinctive slurred voice of his. —Bill Dahl

● **Kansas City** / 1991 / Relic ◆◆◆◆◆
Finally, paydirt! Harrison smashed the charts in 1959 with his massive hit "Kansas City" for Bobby Robinson's Fury logo. Here we have 22 fine sides from the Fury hookup, some in stereo and many with Wild Jimmy Spruill on lead guitar. "Cheatin' Baby," "C.C. Rider," "1960," and the inevitable sequel "Goodbye Kansas City" are prime examples of Harrison's slightly off-kilter approach to his craft, while this infectious "Let's Stick Together" developed into the more worldly "Let's Work Together" toward the end of the decade. —Bill Dahl

Buddy Boy Hawkins

Guitar, Vocals / Acoustic Blues
Walter "Buddy Boy" Hawkins' background and origins are uncertain. He's been cited being born in four different states and at least three different times. What's truly clear is that he was a marvelous vocalist and relaxed, distinctive guitarist in the vintage country blues mode. He recorded for Paramount in the late

'20s; these are his finest tracks. Hawkins also did some dates with William Harris. —*Ron Wynn*

Buddy B Hawkins and His Buddies / Yazoo ✦✦✦✦✦
This is somewhat deceptive packaging, as Hawkins only has half of the selections and the "buddies" have the other half. But since the buddies include Texas Alexander, their contributions are worth close scrutiny. Hawkins' fine vocals and distinctive guitar are still dominant, though. —*Ron Wynn*

Roy Hawkins

Piano, Vocals / West Coast Blues
Not only was Roy Hawkins dogged by bad luck during his career (at the height of his popularity, the pianist lost the use of an arm in a car wreck), he couldn't even cash in after the fact. When B.B. King blasted up the charts in 1970 with Roy Hawkins' classic "The Thrill Is Gone," the tune was mistakenly credited to the wrong composers on early pressings.

Little is known of Hawkins' early days. Producer Bob Geddins discovered Hawkins playing in an Oakland, CA nightspot and supervised his first 78s for Cavatone and Downtown in 1948. Modern Records picked up the rights to several Downtown masters before signing Hawkins to a contract in 1949. Two major R&B hits resulted: 1950s "Why Do Things Happen to Me" and "The Thrill Is Gone" the following year. Hawkins recorded for the Bihari brothers' Modern and RPM imprints into 1954. After that, a handful of 45s for Rhythm and Kent were all that was heard of the Bay Area pianist on vinyl. He's rumored to have died in 1973. —*Bill Dahl*

Highway 59 / 1984 / Ace ✦✦✦✦
Early-'50s rarities from the vaults of the Bihari brothers' Modern label, with a good amount of unissued masters recommending this 16-song LP (no CD equivalent yet). Hawkins' cool California blues piano blends well with the tasty little combos Modern provided; of special interest are the title cut and "Would You," a pair of 1952 gems that feature T-Bone Walker's incomparable guitar work. —*Bill Dahl*

● **Why Do Everything Happen To Me** / Route 66 ✦✦✦✦
A cross-section of the West Coast pianist's best-known early-'50s output, including the often-covered title item. Hawkins has been an unjustly overlooked figure for far too long, and this material is no exception—it has yet to make it to CD. —*Bill Dahl*

Screamin' Jay Hawkins

b. Jul. 18, 1929, Cleveland, OH
Vocals / R&B
Screamin' Jay Hawkins was the most outrageous performer extant during rock's dawn. With a tendency to emerge from coffins onstage, a flaming skull named Henry his constant companion, Screamin' Jay was an insanely theatrical figure long before it was even remotely acceptable.

Hawkins' life story is almost as bizarre as his onstage shtick. Originally inspired by the booming baritone of Paul Robeson, Hawkins was unable to break through as an opera singer. His boxing prowess was every bit as lethal as his vocal cords; many of his most hilarious tales revolve around Jay beating the hell out of a musical rival!

Hawkins caught his first musical break in 1951 as pianist/valet to veteran jazz guitarist Tiny Grimes. He debuted on wax for Gotham the following year with "Why Did You Waste My Time," backed by Grimes and his Rockin' Highlanders (they donned kilts and tam o' shanters on stage). Singles for Timely ("Baptize Me in Wine") and Mercury's Wing subsidiary (1955's otherworldly "[She Put The] Wamee [On Me]," a harbinger of things to come) preceded Hawkins' immortal 1956 rendering of "I Put a Spell on You" for Columbia's Okeh imprint.

Hawkins originally envisioned the tune as a refined ballad. After he and his New York session aces (notably guitarist Mickey Baker and saxist Sam "The Man" Taylor) had imbibed to the point of no return, Hawkins screamed, grunted, and gurgled his way through the tune with utter drunken abandon. A resultant success despite the protests of uptight suits-in-power, "Spell" became Screamin' Jay's biggest seller ("Little Demon," its rocking flip, is a minor classic itself).

Hawkins cut several amazing 1957–58 follow-ups in the same crazed vein—"Hong Kong," a surreal "Yellow Coat," the Jerry Leiber/Mike Stoller-penned "Alligator Wine"—but none of them clicked the way "Spell" had. Deejay Alan Freed convinced

Screamin' Jay that popping out of a coffin might be a show-stopping gimmick by handing him a $300 bonus (long after Freed's demise, Screamin' Jay Hawkins is still benefitting from his crass brainstorm).

Hawkins' next truly inspired waxing came in 1969 when he was contracted to Phillips Records (where he made two albums). His gross "Constipation Blues" wouldn't garner much airplay, but remains an integral part of his legacy to this day.

The cinema has been a beneficiary of Screamin' Jay's larger-than-life persona in recent years. His featured roles in *Mystery Train* and *A Rage in Harlem* have made Hawkins a familiar visage to youngsters who've never even heard "I Put a Spell on You." Hawkins remains musically active, though his act doesn't seem all that bizarre anymore. —*Bill Dahl*

Live & Crazy / Jun. 1988 / Evidence ✦✦
While Screamin' Jay Hawkins can't really shout with the force or volume of the past and doesn't have the energy to keep a whole set moving briskly, he gets off enough good one-liners to make things a bit interesting. His band plays routine blues shuffles, workouts, R&B covers, and Hawkins originals such as "The Whammy," "Constipation Blues" and of course "I Put A Spell On You." While nearly an hour of this eventually becomes tedious, Hawkins' fans will still enjoy it, and others can satisfy themselves with the occasional nuggets. —*Ron Wynn*

● **Voodoo Jive: Best of Screamin' Jay Hawkins** / 1990 / Rhino ✦✦✦✦✦
Some maintain that Hawkins was a one-hit fluke and a one-dimensional performer with a limited singing voice and no other discernible skills. Others insist that Hawkins was a decent R&B and blues singer and an excellent entertainer and personality whose real talents were overshadowed by the success of "I Put A Spell On You." This anthology doesn't convincingly answer the argument, but it does collect 17 Hawkins singles from Okeh, Enrica and Phillips, including all of his major hits. The high (or low) point is perhaps 1969's "Constipation Blues." —*Ron Wynn*

Cow Fingers and Mosquito Pie / 1991 / Epic/Legacy ✦✦✦✦✦
Magically weird 19-song collection of the bizarre shouter's mid-'50s Okeh/Epic output, when he was at the height of his strange and terrifying vocal powers. In addition to the prerequisite "I Put a Spell on You" and the surreal rockers "Yellow Coat," "Hong Kong," "Alligator Wine," and "Little Demon," there's the amusing "There's Something Wrong with You," a previously unissued "You Ain't Foolin' Me," and a deranged takeoff on the cowboy ditty "Take Me Back to My Boots and Saddle" (and what Jay does to the formerly stately "I Love Paris" and "Orange Colored Sky" is truly indescribable!). —*Bill Dahl*

Ted Hawkins

b. 1936, Biloxi, MS, **d.** Jan. 1, 1995
Guitar, Vocals / Modern Acoustic Blues, Singer-Songwriter
Overseas, he was a genuine hero, performing to thousands. But on his L.A. home turf, sand-blown Venice Beach served as Ted Hawkins' makeshift stage. He'd deliver his magnificent melange of soul, blues, folk, gospel, and a touch of country all by his lonesome, with only an acoustic guitar for company. Passersby would pause to marvel at Hawkins' melismatic vocals, dropping a few coins or a greenback into his tip jar on the way by.

That was the way Ted Hawkins kept body and soul together until 1994, when DGC/Geffen Records issued *The Next Hundred Years*, his breakthrough album. Suddenly, Hawkins was poised on the brink of stardom. And then, just after Christmas that same year, ironically, he died of a stroke.

Ted Hawkins' existence was no day in the park. Born into abject poverty in Mississippi, an abused and illiterate child, Hawkins was sent to reform school when he was 12 years old. He encountered his first musical inspiration there from New Orleans pianist Professor Longhair, whose visit to the school moved the lad to perform in a talent show. But it wasn't enough to keep him out of trouble. At age 15, he stole a leather jacket and spent three years at Mississippi's infamous state penitentiary at Parchman Farm.

Roaming from Chicago to Philadelphia to Buffalo after his release, Hawkins left the frigid weather behind in 1966, purchasing a one-way ticket to L.A. Suddenly, music beckoned; he bought a guitar and set out to locate the ex-manager of Sam Cooke (one of his idols). No such luck, but he did manage to cut his debut 45, the soul-steeped "Baby"/"Whole Lot Of Women," for

Money Records. When he learned no royalties were forthcoming from its sales, Hawkins despaired of ever making a living at his music and took to playing on the streets.

Fortunately, producer Bruce Bromberg was interested in Hawkins' welfare, recording his delightfully original material in 1971 both with guitarist Phillip Walker's band ("Sweet Baby" was issued as a single on the Joliet label) and in a solo acoustic format (with Ted's wife Elizabeth occasionally adding harmonies). The producer lost touch with Hawkins for a while after recording him, Hawkins falling afoul of the law once again. In 1982, those tapes finally emerged on Rounder as *Watch Your Step,* and Hawkins began to receive some acclaim (*Rolling Stone* gave it a five-star review). Bromberg corralled him again for the 1986 encore album *Happy Hour,* which contained the touching "Cold & Bitter Tears."

At the behest of a British deejay, Hawkins moved to England in 1986 and was treated like a star for four years, performing in Great Britain, Ireland, France, even Japan. But when he came home, he was faced with the same old situation. Once again, he set up his tip jar on the beach, donned the black leather glove he wore on his fretting hand, and played for passersby—until DGC ever so briefly propelled him into the major leagues.

Ted Hawkins was a unique talent, unclassifiable and eminently soulful. For a year or so, he was even a star in his own country. —*Bill Dahl*

Watch Your Step / 1982 / Rounder ♦♦♦
Guitarist/vocalist Ted Hawkins was an instant sensation when this session was originally released in 1982. At a time when slick, heavily produced urban contemporary material was establishing its domination on the R&B scene, Hawkins' hard-edged, rough, cutting voice, plus his crisp acoustic guitar accompaniment and country blues roots, seemed both dated and extremely fresh. This 15-track CD includes four numbers with Hawkins backed by Phillip Walker and his band, and others ranging from the humorous "Who Got My Natural Comb?" to the poignant "If You Love Me" and two versions of the title track. He also teamed with his wife Elizabeth on "Don't Lose Your Cool" and "I Gave It All I Had" for moving duets. —*Ron Wynn*

Songs from Venice Beach / 1985 / Evidence ♦♦♦♦
Blending every form of roots music imaginable into his own singular soulful stew, the incomparable Ted Hawkins stuck mostly to R&B covers on this splendid 1985 solo outing—songs by Sam Cooke (his idol), Jerry Butler, Bobby Bland, the Temptations, and Garnet Mimms receive gorgeous readings by the acoustic guitarist. But even though he only contributed one original, the touching "Ladder of Success," to the set, Hawkins wasn't content to remain in one genre—his commanding revival of Webb Pierce's hillbilly weeper "There Stands the Glass" ranks with the disc's very best moments (of which there are many). —*Bill Dahl*

● **Happy Hour** / 1987 / Rounder ♦♦♦♦♦
Guitarist/vocalist Ted Hawkins' second Rounder record enhanced his reputation. *Happy Hour* features Hawkins' memorable compositions, plus a wonderful version of Curtis Mayfield's "Gypsy Woman." Hawkins' vocals were even more gritty and striking, as was his acoustic guitar backing and chording. He teamed with his wife Elizabeth on "Don't Make Me Explain It," "My Last Goodbye," and "California Song," and with guitarist Night Train Clemons on "Gypsy Woman" and "You Pushed My Head Away." Hawkins blended soul and urban blues stylings with country and rural blues inflections and rhythms, making another first-rate release. —*Ron Wynn*

The Next Hundred Years / 1994 / DGC ♦♦♦
The former L.A. street musician's major label breakthrough was in a great many ways a far weaker outing than what came before, largely due to a plodding band unwisely inserted behind Hawkins that tends to distract rather than enhance his impassioned vocals and rich acoustic guitar strumming. Mostly originals ("There Stands the Glass" returns, as does "Ladder of Success") that would have sounded so much better in an intimate solo context. —*Bill Dahl*

Clifford Hayes

Violin / Jazz Blues
A shadowy figure in jazz and blues history, Clifford Hayes was an okay violinist but more significant as a leader of recording sessions. He recorded with Sara Martin (1924) and often teamed up with banjoist Cal Smith in early jug bands including the Old Southern Jug Band, Clifford's Louisville Jug Band, the well-

known Dixieland Jug Blowers (1926-27) and Hayes' Louisville Stompers (1927-29). One of the Dixieland Jug Blowers' sessions featured the great clarinetist Johnny Dodds while pianist Earl Hines was a surprise star with the otherwise primitive Louisville Stompers (a jugless group with a frontline of Hayes' violin and Hense Grundy's trombone). Clifford Hayes' last recordings were in 1931 and all of his sessions (plus those of some other jug bands) are available on four RST CDs. —*Scott Yanow*

Clifford Hayes & The Louisville Jug Bands, Vol. 1 / Sep. 16, 1924–Dec. 10, 1926 / RST ♦♦♦♦
The first of four volumes from the Austrian RST label that reissue the complete output from several historic jug bands from Louisville features violinist Clifford Hayes in several contexts. In 1924 he led the first jug band on record, backing blues singer Sara Martin on some exuberant performances that overcame the primitive recording quality. In addition, this CD has Hayes leading The Old Southern Jug Band, Clifford's Louisville Jug Band, and The Dixieland Jug Blowers; all of the groups greatly benefit from the exciting playing of Earl McDonald on jug. The CD is rounded out by four selections from Whistler's Jug Band. Historic and generally enjoyable music, it's recommended to 1920s collectors. —*Scott Yanow*

● **Clifford Hayes & The Louisville Jug Bands, Vol. 2** / Dec. 10, 1926–Apr. 30, 1927 / RST ♦♦♦♦♦
The second of four CDs in a very valuable series from the Austrian RST label has 12 selections from The Dixieland Jug Blowers (a very spirited sextet with violinist Clifford Hayes, the colorful jug blowing of Earl McDonald and on six numbers, clarinetist Johnny Dodds as a guest), eight from Earl McDonald's Original Louisville Jug Band and four by Whistler's Jug Band (its leader Buford Threlked doubles on guitar and nose whistle). The monologue on the former group's "House Rent Rag" is quite memorable and still humorous. Of the four CDs, this is the most essential one because it finds these historic groups in their prime. —*Scott Yanow*

Clifford Hayes & The Louisville Jug Bands, Vol. 3 / Jun. 6, 1927–Feb. 6, 1929 / RST ♦♦♦♦♦
The third of four CDs from the Austrian RST label has the final ten selections from The Dixieland Jug Blowers along with 14 by Clifford Hayes' Louisville Stompers. Although the former no longer had the powerful jug playing of Earl McDonald, the mysterious H. Clifford was a good substitute and the three-horn septet (which features two guest vocalists) certainly had plenty of spirit. The Louisville Stompers is essentially a stripped-down jugless version of The Jug Blowers, a jazz-oriented quartet comprised of violinist Clifford Hayes, trombonist Hense Grundy, pianist Johnny Gatewood, and the impressive guitarist Cal Smith who makes "Blue Guitar Stomp" a classic. The final seven Stompers performances are a bit surprising, because the pianist is the great Earl Hines, who has a few short solos although mostly in a supporting role. All four of the CDs are easily recommended to collectors of the era. On the whole they contain the complete output of these unusual groups. —*Scott Yanow*

Dixieland Jug Blowers / Jun. 7, 1927–Jun. 1, 1928 / Yazoo ♦♦♦♦♦
Jug band material in the hokum and country blues variety. This one goes about as far to the margin as any jug band ever journeyed, thanks to Clifford Hayes' violin and Earl McDonald's jug. —*Ron Wynn*

Clifford Hayes & The Louisville Jug Bands, Vol. 4 / Feb. 6, 1929–Jun. 17, 1931 / RST ♦♦♦♦♦
The fourth and final CD in this brief but important series from the Austrian RST label features jug bands in a variety of roles. There are the three last performances by Clifford Hayes' Lousville Stompers (the two versions of "You're Ticklin' Me" have Earl Hines on piano while "You Gonna Need My Help" features the classic blues singer Sippie Wallace), the Kentucky Jazz Babies (a quartet with violinist Clifford Hayes and trumpeter Jimmy Strange) do a good job on two numbers and Phillips' Louisville Jug Band (an odd quartet with Hooks Tifford on C-melody sax and Charles "Cane" Adams playing what is called "walking cane flute") performs eight songs. In addition Whistler and His Jug Band play two primitive numbers while violinist Clifford Hayes backs the minstrel singer Kid Coley and reunites with the great jug player Earl McDonald behind the vocals of country pioneer Jimmie Rodgers, Ben Ferguson and John Harris.

An interesting set, to say the least, and all four CDs in this series are recommended to fans of the era. —*Scott Yanow*

Patrick Hazell

Piano, Drums, Harmonica, Vocals / Modern Electric Blues
Patrick Hazell is a White, one-man band (piano, neck rack harmonica, and drums) from Washington, IA. But skin color and point of origin hardly matters, as Hazell sounds like a complete throwback to the recordings of the late '40s and early '50s. His rhythmic drive is superlative while his sound and style is highly reminiscent of Memphis one-man-band star Joe Hill Louis. His raspy harp and vocals (sung into the same distorted microphone he plays through) are fortified with strong material, an unrelenting beat and sensational ambience as he ekes out a piece of blues turf that hasn't been occupied in a very long time. In the current White-boy blues community—where seemingly every streetcorner has five people on it with shades, pleated pants and beat-up Stratocasters in hand—Patrick Hazell stands out as something very unique and cool. —*Cub Koda*

● **Blues on the Run** / 1995 / Blue Rhythm ♦♦♦♦♦
Hazell's debut opus has all the marks of an album you'll find yourself still listening to ten years from now, both for its content and its sheer uniqueness. The title track is five minutes of nasty modal shouting and honking while the opener, "Here I Go Again," answers the question, "what would it have sounded like if Joe Hill Louis had cut a rock & roll record at Sun." Hazell sounds his best when interpreting his own material, but even his take on a time-worn favorite like "Wang Dang Doodle" is well worth the listen. That he manages to pull off his one-man-band turn without the use of overdubbing makes the performances on this album all the more amazing. —*Cub Koda*

Johnny Heartsman

b. Feb. 9, 1937, San Fernando, CA
Bass, Flute, Guitar, Keyboards, Vocals / Modern Electric Blues
Shaven-headed Johnny Heartsman does so many musical things so well that he's impossible to pigeonhole. His low-moaning lead guitar work greatly distinguished a myriad of Bay Area blues recordings during the '50s and '60s, and he still plays his axe with delicious dexterity and dynamics. But Heartsman is just as likely to cut loose on organ or blow a titillating solo on flute (perhaps the unlikeliest blues instrument imaginable). He possesses a mellow, richly burnished voice to boot.

Through one of his principal influences, guitarist Lafayette "Thing" Thomas, a teenaged Heartsman hooked up with Bay Area producer Bob Geddins. Heartsman played bass on Jimmy Wilson's 1953 rendition of "Tin Pan Alley," handling guitar or piano at other Geddins-supervised dates. He cut his own two-part instrumental, the "Honky Tonk"-inspired "Johnny's House Party," for Ray Dobard's Music City imprint and watched it become a national R&B hit in 1957.

The early '60s brought a lot more session work—Heartsman played on Tiny Powell's "My Time After Awhile" (soon covered by Buddy Guy) and Al King's remake of Lowell Fulson's "Reconsider Baby." By then, Heartsman's imaginative twiddling of the volume knob with his finger to produce an eerie moan had become his guitaristic trademark.

Stints in show bands, jazzy cocktail lounge gigs, and a stand as soul singer Joe Simon's trusty organist came prior to the inauguration of Heartsman's edifying back-to-the-blues campaign. In 1991, Dick Shurman produced Heartsman's most satisfying set to date for Alligator, *The Touch*. He remains as versatile as ever. —*Bill Dahl*

Sacramento / 1987 / Crosscut ♦♦♦

Music of My Heart / 1989 / Cat 'n Hat ♦♦♦
Solid LP that catches up with all of Heartsman's varied musical interests: blues, jazz, R&B, and all points in between. "Goose Grease" is a humorous Heartsman vocal outing, while powerful singer Frankie Lee guests on a remake of "My Time After Awhile" and harpist Curtis Salgado takes over behind the mike on "My First Mind." —*Bill Dahl*

● **The Touch** / 1991 / Alligator ♦♦♦♦♦
The Bay Area multi-instrumentalist assuredly put it all together on this sumptuous release, produced by Dick Shurman. It's a superlative showcase for Heartsman's deeply burnished vocals, moaning guitar, jazzy keyboard skills, and lilting flute work. —*Bill Dahl*

Jessie Mae Hemphill

b. 1934, MS
Guitar, Vocals / Acoustic Delta Blues
A Mississippi singer/guitarist, Jesse Mae Hemphill weaves strong Delta traditions into her idiosyncratic style. Hemphill comes from a musical background—reportedly, her grandfather was recorded in the fields by Alan Lomax in the '40s. Jesse Mae learned how to play guitar as a child by watching her relatives perform. Throughout the '60s and '70s, she sang with various Mississippi bar bands. In the early '80s, she decided to pursue a solo career.

Hemphill began playing solo dates, supporting herself only with an acoustic guitar and percussion. In 1981, she released her debut album, *She-Wolf*, on the European record label, Vogue. In 1987, her first American record, *Feelin' Good*, was released. In 1987 and 1988, she won the WC Handy Award for best traditional female blues artist. Hemphill abandoned a recording career after the late '80s, but she continued to perform into the '90s. —*Cub Koda & Stephen Thomas Erlewine*

She-Wolf / 1981 / Vogue/Blues Today ♦♦♦

● **Feelin' Good** / 1987 / High Water ♦♦♦♦♦
An excellent set from this idiosyncratic Delta blues artist. —*Cub Koda*

Duke Henderson

Vocals / West Coast Blues
For someone with as voluminous a discography as Los Angeles shouter Duke Henderson, one would think someone might possess concrete biographical information about the guy. No such luck.

Henderson got his start as a recording artist with Apollo Records, a New York firm that sent a rep to Los Angeles in 1945 with the intention of recording blues. Tenor saxist Jack McVea recommended Henderson, who ended up cutting three Apollo dates that year with backing from some of L.A.'s finest sessioneers: saxists Wild Bill Moore, Lucky Thompson, and McVea, guitarist Gene Phillips, bassists Shifty Henry and Charlie Mingus, and drummers Lee Young and Rabon Tarrant.

Swinging as they were, Henderson's Apollo platters failed to sell in sufficient quantities to extend his contract. Thus began a label-hopping odyssey from Globe to Down Beat/Swing Time to Specialty to Modern to Imperial and finally to Flair, where he exhibited a knowledge of then-current sexual trends with his "Hey Mr. Kinsey" (issued by Big Duke in 1953). Later, Henderson renounced his wicked blues-shouting past, sending the L.A. sanctified set as Brother Henderson, a minister and gospel deejay broadcasting for a time over XERB (the same powerful south-of-the-border frequency that Wolfman Jack dominated). —*Bill Dahl*

● **Get Your Kicks** / 1994 / Delmark ♦♦♦♦♦
Blues shouter Henderson was quite a popular jump blues shouter on the postwar L.A. scene. His 1945 output for Apollo, collected here, rates with his best; backed by top-drawer sidemen including saxists Lucky Thompson, Wild Bill Moore, and Jack McVea, and guitarist Gene Phillips, Henderson's pipes convey the proper party spirit on these 20 swinging sides. —*Bill Dahl*

Jimi Hendrix

b. Nov. 27, 1942, Seattle, WA, **d.** Sep. 18, 1970, London, England
Guitar / Rock & Roll, Blues Rock
Psychedelic Jimi Hendrix in a book on the blues? Damn right. Jimi Hendrix's place in the annals of blues history is assured and agreed upon by everyone except the handful of ultra-purists who believe the music went straight to hell the minute Muddy Waters decided to pick up that electric guitar. That Hendrix took that instrument—and the music—to places no one could have dreamt of is indisputable. He may have been a "rock star," but the parallels between his story and the legendary bluesmen that came before him are just too numerous and downright eerie to ignore; the years as a teenager being too inexperienced to be allowed to sit in with the older players (Robert Johnson before he got good), the years as a young gun sideman behind bigger name stars (Little Walter with Muddy Waters), and finally, a chance to go out on his own and start melding blues with other sources—in this case, a modern R&B songwriting of the Curtis Mayfield flavor, free form jazz a la Bird, Coltrane, and Sun Ra, all of it imbued

with lots of amplification and wedded to a heavier beat—to create an amalgam of his own that allowed a new strain of blues to begin (Muddy Waters goes electric and invents the modern day Chicago blues band). And don't forget the legends that reinforce the other parallels, either; the famous on-stage guitar battles with other fretboard hot shots (B.B. vs. Albert King, Freddie King vs. Magic Sam), the eye-popping tricks he could perform with the instrument that made him *the* showman of his time (Charlie Patton, T-Bone Walker, Guitar Slim), the competitive nature he exhibited onstage that drove him to outdo anyone else on the bill, even if he set his guitar on fire to do it (Howlin' Wolf), the otherworldly visions he brought to his art, and his passing at an early age from too much life in the fast lane, robbing the music world of a great resource (Robert Johnson and several other entries in this book). If all of this had happened in Chicago in 1954, they'd be selling plastic figurines of him through the merchandising end of the House of Blues and you'd being seeing his face adorning a United States postage stamp, pompadour haircut and all.

Of course it didn't happen that way at all; Hendrix's four year run of fame on an international level happened in the late '60s with the psychedelicized world of rock & roll as its backdrop instead of South Side Chicago. But if the conventional wisdom of blues as party music gives us the standardized caricature of a bunch of folks dancing their tails off to Charlie Patton while being good and drunk on moonshine whiskey, then step up the scenario a good 40 years and you have Jimi as maker of its mightiest dope music, playing to an audience of young Whites *and* Blacks—together in harmony and matching headbands—swaying in stoned ecstasy. Again, those parallels—even the ones that are stretching it—just keep piling up and keep getting harder to ignore. But one fact's irrefutable; Jimi Hendrix definitely belongs in this book, because in every form of musical experimentation he delved into, he always played the blues. Granted, "Purple Haze" doesn't sound much like B.B. King doing "Sweet Little Angel," but B.B. doing *that* number doesn't sound much like Robert Johnson doing "Hellhound On My Trail," either. Once again, the blues reinvents itself to keep pace with a changing world.

Jimi was born James Marshall Hendrix in Seattle, Washington in 1942 and was playing left handed guitar by the time he was 11. Anxious to plug into Seattle's burgeoning rock & roll scene, Jimi would bring his guitar and amp down to the Spanish Castle (alluded to in both "Spanish Castle Magic" and "Castles Made of Sand"), waiting for a chance to be called up onstage for a chance to sit in with anyone willing to give the teenager a chance. The chance seldom came.

After dropping out of high school, he joined the Army, serving in the 101st Airborne. One of his Division buddies was bass player Billy Cox, who would later play in Jimi's Band of Gypsys. According to Cox, Hendrix dug a wide range of music but especially blues (he loved Elmore James), always listening to records and soaking up influences like a sponge. Upon his discharge in 1961, Jimi became a fixture on the chitlin circuit, lending his guitar talents to various R&B road units, including Little Richard and the Isley Brothers. He recorded and toured with both acts in the mid-'60s, but found himself on a short leash creatively in each situation. When a similar tour with Curtis Knight and the Squires ended in New York City in 1965, he began to put down roots and get ideas.

He found the city to his liking, even if he was scuffling for work most of the time. Les Paul tells the story about the night he walked into a club and heard Jimi playing, vowing to come back later to hear more of this phenomenal unknown guitarist. After tending to his other business appointments, Les headed back to the club only to find that Hendrix had been fired for playing too loud. The next time he saw Jimi's face was on the cover of his debut album, *Are You Experienced?*. Hendrix drifted into the Greenwich Village scene and soon got a regular gig working behind John Hammond, Jr., who was putting his first band together in the wake of Paul Butterfield's success, whose band featured the red hot guitar picking of Michael Bloomfield. With both combos playing across the street from each other, Bloomfield decided to use his break time one night to check out this new guitarist that everyone was buzzing about. Hendrix *certainly* knew who Bloomfield was—then the hottest new guitar player in American music—and proceeded to systematically destroy his ego with a double whammy display of fretboard wiz-

ardry and showmanship that left the guitarist in a state of shock. As he later related in an interview, "every sound I ever heard him get on record later I heard that night, right in that room, and he was doing it all with nothing more than a Stratocaster, a Twin and extreme volume."

This much talent couldn't go unnoticed for very long and when Chas Chandler—bass player for the Animals, now easing into production and management—caught the act, he enticed Hendrix to drop everything and come to England. The guitarist acquiesced—legend has it because Chandler promised to introduce him to Eric Clapton—and by late 1966 had formed the Jimi Hendrix Experience, playing the hip London club circuit and putting English guitar heroes through the same kind of head-cutting shock therapy that Bloomfield had been through stateside. The hits in the U.K. charts that came the following year quickly made Hendrix the newest star in the British rock sweepstakes, while the release of his debut album spread the word that here was a guitarist doing a lot more than just recycling B.B. King licks through a big amplifier. His American breakthrough came with a legendary set at the Monterey Pop Festival in 1967 and, after wasting his time on an ill-conceived tour opening for the Monkees (some claim it was purposely set up to enhance his reputation as an underground act), he quickly became the king of the festival and ballroom circuit, spreading his musical message around the globe, as hot as the news to come. At the absolute top of his game, his influence extended back into the Black community to R&B singer-producers like Sly Stone and George Clinton looking for a piece of the action to White youngsters just picking up the guitar like Stevie Ray Vaughan.

Stories concerning his state of mind and future musical plans at the time of his accidental death in 1970 are as numerous and fanciful as the ones that proliferate about Robert Johnson. One of them has him turning his back on rock stardom and planning on becoming a serious bluesman. But whether it's truth or fanciful myth, those of us who've been mesmerized hearing him play "Red House," "Voodoo Chile," and "Little Wing" already know that no such career reassessments were ever necessary; Jimi Hendrix was *always* a serious bluesman. —*Cub Koda*

☆ **Are You Experienced?** / 1967 / Reprise ✦✦✦✦
From the dissonant fanfare of "Purple Haze" to the hypnotic closing cadence of the title track, the Jimi Hendrix Experience's audacious debut built upon the experimental hard rock groundwork of groups like The Yardbirds, focusing it through a ferociously interactive trio format. Hendrix fused spacey Dylan-influenced imagery with R&B derived song structures and chordal voicings to create an unique style. Tracks like "Fire," "Foxey Lady," "Manic Depression," the haunting "The Wind Cries Mary," and "May This Be Love" make this disc essential for any rock collection. —*Rick Clark*

☆ **Axis: Bold As Love** / 1967 / Reprise ✦✦✦✦✦
Continuing Hendrix's groundbreaking streak, this one matches his guitar pyrotechnics with a more refined collection of originals. The album features gorgeously unconventional ballads like "Little Wing," "Castles Made of Sand," "One Rainy Wish," and "Bold as Love," which shone alongside hyperspace rockers like "You Got Me Floatin'," "Up from the Skies," and the psychedelic hard jazz-rock free-for-all of "If 6 Was 9." —*Rick Clark*

☆ **Electric Ladyland** / Feb. 1968 / Reprise ✦✦✦✦✦
Hendrix's funky psychedelia reached a zenith on *Electric Ladyland*, one of the greatest albums of the rock era. His aggressively otherworldly production did as much for advancing the possibilities of recorded music as Phil Spector's "Wall of Sound" did in the early '60s. Hendrix's imaginatively fiery guitar work (and The Experience's brilliant interplay) here became the textbook source of inspiration for generations of musicians. Among *Electric Ladyland*'s many highlights are "Voodoo Child (Slight Return)," with its kamikaze lead-guitar work, the transcendentally dense "Burning of the Midnight Lamp," the searing remake of Dylan's "All along the Watchtower," and the beautifully spacey "1983...(A Merman I Should Turn to Be)." —*Rick Clark*

Band of Gypsys / 1970 / Capitol ✦✦✦✦
Hendrix, sans The Experience, hooked up with bassist Billy Cox and drummer Buddy Miles to record this hard electric funk outing live at the Fillmore East in New York on December 31, 1969. While the rhythm section may have lacked the chops for wild free-form excursions, they provided Hendrix with a no-nonsense

groove for his funkier R&B experiments. "Machine Gun," the album's highlight, features some of Hendrix's greatest playing. His dramatically violent soundscapes convey the horror of the war experience, with brilliantly controlled use of feedback and rapid-fire bursts of notes. —*Rick Clark*

The Cry of Love / 1971 / Reprise ✦✦✦✦✦
The posthumously released *The Cry of Love* revealed Hendrix turning toward a more subdued, less psychedelic style, with songs like "Night Bird Flying" and "Angel." Hendrix does deliver a few strong rockers with "Freedom," "Ezy Ryder," and "Astro Man." —*Rick Clark*

Plays Monterey / 1986 / Reprise ✦✦✦✦✦
Hendrix's show at the 1967 Monterey Pop Festival was the performance that broke him in the United States. While half of this was previously available as one side of an LP that also featured a side of live Otis Redding from the same event, this has his whole performance. Jimi and the Experience were in fine, lean, fiery form on this nine-song set, which showcased the most well-known tunes from the *Are You Experienced?* album and covers of "Killing Floor," "Like a Rolling Stone," "Rock Me Baby," and "Wild Thing." —*Richie Unterberger*

Live at Winterland / 1987 / Rykodisc ✦✦✦✦✦
Jimi Hendrix's sonic assaults and attacks hypnotized, frightened, and amazed audiences in the late '60s. His studio recordings helped him attain his reputation, but his live works validated it. That's the case on the 13 songs from a 1968 Winterland concert that made their way onto CD in 1987. Whether he was doing short, biting songs like "Fire" or stretching out for sprawling blues statements like "Red House" and "Killing Floor," Jimi Hendrix turned the guitar into a battering ram, forcing everyone to notice and making every solo and note a memorable one. —*Ron Wynn*

Radio One / 1989 / Rykodisc ✦✦✦✦✦
These late '60s songs done for British radio merely reaffirm the Jimi Hendrix Experience's greatness; Hendrix's soaring, crashing blues-based riffs and the ability of Noel Redding and Mitch Mitchell to stay out of Hendrix's way, support him minimally, and yet not be obliterated in the exchanges. These were the songs that helped generate word-of-mouth publicity for the Hendrix machine in the late '60s, and also demonstrated to any and all concerned that Jimi Hendrix was a guitar talent for the ages. —*Ron Wynn*

● **The Ultimate Experience** / Apr. 27, 1993 / MCA ✦✦✦✦✦
As a single-disc compilation, *The Ultimate Experience* is hard to beat. Drawing from all of the original Jimi Hendrix Experience albums, the 20-track collection hits all of the major highpoints—"Purple Haze," "All Along the Watchtower," "Little Wing," "Red House," "The Wind Cries Mary," "Highway Chile," "Angel"—and gives an accurate impression of why Hendrix was so revolutionary and influential. All three of Hendrix's completed studio albums are mandatory listening, but *The Ultimate Experience* is a terrific introduction to the guitarist. —*Thom Owens*

☆ **Jimi Hendrix: Blues** / 1994 / MCA ✦✦✦✦✦
While Hendrix remains most famous for his hard rock and psychedelic innovations, more than a third of his recordings were blues-oriented. This CD contains eleven blues originals and covers, eight of which were previously unreleased. Recorded between 1966 and 1970, they feature the master guitarist stretching the boundaries of electric blues in both live and studio settings. Besides several Hendrix blues-based originals, it includes covers of Albert King and Muddy Waters classics, as well as a 1967 acoustic version of his composition "Hear My Train A-Comin'." —*Richie Unterberger*

Jimi Hendrix: Woodstock / 1994 / MCA ✦✦✦
Hendrix's entire legendary set at Woodstock is featured on this set for the first time. Hardcore Hendrix fans may enjoy this good-sounding set, but it's a lot of endless jamming and general noodling for even the average fan to ingest. Besides his incendiary reading of "The Star Spangled Banner" and moments where the playing really comes together, better live Hendrix sets can be found elsewhere, like *Jimi Hendrix in the West*. —*Rick Clark*

Voodoo Soup / Apr. 1995 / MCA ✦✦✦
Voodoo Soup was supposed to be the outtake album that got it right. Instead, it was another in a line of botched attempts to

recreate Jimi Hendrix's unfinished final studio album. For most fans, the re-recorded drum tracks by the drummer of The Knack was the most unforgivable sin, yet the album is also poorly sequenced and lacks several important tracks. The sound is polished to a disturbingly bright sheen, while the cover art is garishly retro. —*Stephen Thomas Erlewine*

Clarence "Frogman" Henry

b. 1937
Piano, Trombone, Vocals / New Orleans R&B
He could sing like a girl, and he could sing like a frog. That latter trademark croak, utilized to the max on his 1956 debut smash "Ain't Got No Home," earned good-natured Clarence Henry his nickname and jump-started a rewarding career that endures to this day around the Crescent City.

Naturally, Fats Domino and Professor Longhair were young Clarence Henry's main influences while growing up in the Big Easy. He played piano and trombone with Bobby Mitchell & the Toppers from 1952 to 1955 before catching on with saxist Eddie Smith's band. Henry improvised the basic idea behind "Ain't Got No Home" on the bandstand one morning in the wee hours; when the crowd responded favorably, he honed it into something unique. Paul Gayten (New Orleans A&R man for Chess Records) concurred, hustling Henry into Cosimo Matassa's studio in September of 1956. Local deejay Poppa Stoppa laid the "Frogman" handle on the youngster when he spun the 45 (issued on the Chess subsidiary Argo), and it stuck.

Despite some fine follow-ups—"It Won't Be Long," "I'm in Love," the inevitable sequel "I Found a Home"—Frog sank back into the marsh sales-wise until 1960, when Allen Toussaint's updated arrangement melded beautifully with a country-tinged Bobby Charles composition called "(I Don't Know Why) But I Do." Henry's rendition of the tune proved a huge pop smash in early 1961, as did a Domino-tinged "You Always Hurt the One You Love" later that year.

Frogman continued to record a variety of New Orleans-styled old standards and catchy originals for Argo (Chess assembled a Henry album that boasted what may be the worst cover art in the history of rock & roll), even recording at one point with Nashville saxist Boots Randolph and pianist Floyd Cramer. But the hits dried up for good after 1961. Henry opened 18 concerts for the Beatles across the U.S. and Canada in 1964, but his main source of income came from the Bourbon Street strip, where he played for 19 years. You'll likely find him joyously reviving his classics at the New Orleans Jazz & Heritage Festival every year come spring—and his croak remains as deep and melodious as ever. —*Bill Dahl*

● **Ain't Got No Home: Best of Clarence "Frogman" Henry** / 1994 / MCA ✦✦✦✦✦
The New Orleans R&B singer with the joyous frog's croak in his voice is served well by this 18-song collection of his 1956-1964 output for the Chess subsidiary Argo Records. Begins with his definitive "Ain't Got No Home," follows with his vicious Crescent City rockers "Troubles, Troubles," "It Won't Be Long," and "I'm in Love," and visits his comeback hits "But I Do" and "You Always Hurt the One You Love." —*Bill Dahl*

But I Do / 1994 / Charly ✦✦✦✦✦
20 Argo waxings by the roly-poly pianist—much duplication with the easier-to-locate MCA disc as far as the hits go, though the inclusion of the sequel "I Found a Home" and the lesser-known rockers "Steady Date," "Oh Why," and "Live It Right" certainly make this one worth looking for. —*Bill Dahl*

Blind Joe Hill

Vocals, Guitar, Harmonica / Electric Chicago Blues
A good one-man band performer in the tradition of Joe Hill Louis and Dr. Ross, Blind Joe Hill accompanies his craggy vocals on guitar, bass, and drums. He's among the last in the tradition, and that adds some value to his recordings, despite a derivative playing style and erratic compositional skills. —*Ron Wynn*

Boogie in the Dark / Jan. 1978 / Barrelhouse ✦✦✦✦✦
Opinions vary regarding the quality of Blind Joe Hill's one-man band recordings. He certainly wasn't the greatest in the genre, but he was a creditable exponent. There's nothing especially exciting here, but it was done with sincerity and energy. —*Ron Wynn*

Z.Z. Hill (Arzell Hill)

b. Sep. 30, 1935, Naples, TX, **d.** Apr. 27, 1984, Dallas, TX
Vocals / Soul Blues

Texas-born singer Z.Z. Hill managed to resuscitate both his own semi-flagging career and the entire genre at large when he signed on at Jackson, MS's Malaco Records in 1980 and began growling his way through some of the most uncompromising blues to be unleashed on black radio stations in many a moon.

His impressive 1982 Malaco album *Down Home Blues* remained on *Billboard*'s soul album charts for nearly two years, an extraordinary run for such a blatantly bluesy LP. His songs "Down Home Blues" and "Somebody Else Is Steppin' In" have graduated into the ranks of legitimate blues standards (and there haven't been many of those come along over the last couple of decades).

Arzell Hill started out singing gospel with a quintet called the Spiritual Five, but the output of B.B. King, Bobby Bland, and especially Sam Cooke made a more indelible mark on his approach. He began gigging around Dallas, fashioning his distinctive initials after those of B.B. King. When his older brother Matt Hill (a budding record producer with his own label, M.H.) invited Z.Z. to go west to southern California, the young singer did.

His debut single on M.H., the gutsy shuffle "You Were Wrong" (recorded in an L.A. garage studio), showed up on *Billboard*'s pop chart for a week in 1964. With such a relatively successful showing his first time out, Hill's fine subsequent singles for the Bihari brothers' Kent logo should have been even bigger. But "I Need Someone (To Love Me)," "Happiness Is All I Need," and a raft of other deserving Kent 45s (many produced and arranged by Maxwell Davis) went nowhere commercially for the singer.

Excellent singles for Atlantic, Mankind, and Hill (another imprint operated by brother Matt, who served as Z.Z.'s producer for much of his career) preceded a 1972 hookup with United Artists that resulted in three albums and six R&B chart singles over the next couple of years. From there, Z.Z. moved on to Columbia, where his 1977 single "Love Is So Good When You're Stealing It" became his biggest-selling hit of all.

Hill's vocal grit was never more effective than on his blues-soaked Malaco output. From 1980 until 1984, when he died suddenly of a heart attack, Z.Z. bravely led a personal back-to-the-blues campaign that doubtless helped to fuel the current contemporary blues boom. It's a shame he couldn't stick around to see it blossom. *—Bill Dahl*

Lot of Soul / 1969 / Kent ✦✦✦

Brand New Z.Z. Hill / 1971 / Mankind ✦✦✦
This is a '70s Swamp Dogg-produced concept album. *—Richard Pack*

The Best Thing That's Happened to Me / 1972 / United Artists ✦✦✦

Keep on Loving You / 1975 / United Artists ✦✦✦
Soul material predominates here. *—Bill Dahl*

Let's Make a Deal / 1978 / Columbia ✦✦✦
One of the most commercial of Hill's albums, this disco-tinged release included the minor hits "This Time They Told the Truth" and "Love Is So Good When You're Stealing It." *—Richie Unterberger*

The Mark of Z.Z. Hill / 1979 / Columbia ✦✦✦
Hill's second and final Columbia LP was essentially a continuation of the first. On both, Hill sounds like a journeyman Southern soul singer embellished with period disco/mainstream R&B production, which neither added to the quality of the music nor made it unlistenable. *—Richie Unterberger*

Z.Z. Hill / 1981 / Malaco ✦✦✦✦
The initial step in Hill's amazing rebirth as a contemporary blues star, courtesy of Jackson, MS's Malaco Records and producers Tommy Couch and Wolf Stephenson. The vicious blues outings "Bump and Grind" and "Blue Monday" were the first salvos fired by Hill at the blues market, though much of the set—"Please Don't Make Me (Do Something Bad to You)," "I'm So Lonesome I Could Cry"—was solidly in the Southern soul vein. *—Bill Dahl*

The Rhythm & The Blues / 1982 / Malaco ✦✦✦✦
Led by Hill's second immediate standard—the Denise LaSalle-penned "Someone Else Is Steppin' In"—Hill's third Malaco album

was another consistent effort, if not quite the blockbuster that his previous effort was. Hill again dipped into the Little Johnny Taylor songbook for a humorous slow blues, "Open House at My House," while relying on talented songwriters George Jackson and Frank Johnson for most of his tailor-made material. *—Bill Dahl*

☆ **Down Home** / 1982 / Malaco ✦✦✦✦✦
One of the very few classic blues albums of the 1980s. Hill revitalized the genre among African-American listeners with his "Down Home Blues," which earned instant standard status. But the entire album is tremendously consistent, with the percolating R&B workouts "Givin' It Up for Your Love" and "Right Arm for Your Love" contrasting with an intimate "Cheatin' in the Next Room" and the straight-ahead blues "Everybody Knows About My Good Thing" and "When It Rains It Pours." *—Bill Dahl*

I'm a Blues Man / 1983 / Malaco ✦✦✦✦
Fueled by more impressive material from the pens of Jackson, Johnson, and LaSalle, Hill was in an amazing groove during the years prior to his untimely demise, and the crack Malaco house band was certainly up to the task. Just like the title track ably demonstrated, Z.Z. Hill had indeed rechristened himself as a blues man of the first order. *—Bill Dahl*

Bluesmaster / 1984 / Malaco ✦✦✦
Issued the year he died, *Bluesmaster* boasted more competent soul-blues hybrids by the man who reenergized the blues idiom with his trademark growl. LaSalle's "You're Ruining My Bad Reputation," "Friday Is My Day" (written by legendary Malaco promo man Dave Clark), and a nice reading of Paul Kelly's slinky "Personally" rate with the standouts. *—Bill Dahl*

★ **In Memorium (1935–1984)** / 1985 / Malaco ✦✦✦✦✦
Most of the highlights of Hill's glorious blues-singing stint at Malaco, although the individual albums possess more than their share of worthwhile moments that aren't here. But with hallowed titles like "Down Home Blues," "Someone Else Is Slippin' In," and "Everybody Knows About My Good Thing," this stunning collection neatly summarizes Hill's heartwarming rise to blues power. *—Bill Dahl*

A Man Needs a Woman / 1986 / Topline ✦✦

Whoever Is Thrilling You / 1986 / Stateside ✦✦✦

Greatest Hits / 1986 / Malaco ✦✦✦✦✦
Faultless bluesy soul from 1980-1984. *—Richard Pack*

● **Best of ZZ Hill** / 1987 / Malaco ✦✦✦✦✦

The Down Home Soul of Z.Z. Hill / 1992 / Kent ✦✦✦✦✦
Before Hill made his sensational 1980s comeback as a blues growler, he sang a slightly sweeter brand of West Coast soul during the mid-'60s at Kent. Under saxist Maxwell Davis' supervision, Hill waxed a series of magnificent R&B ballads—"Happiness Is All I Need," "I Need Someone (To Love Me)"—that should have hit but inexplicably didn't. Gathered on one 22-track import disc, they sound terrific in retrospect. *—Bill Dahl*

The Complete Hill Records Collection/United Artists Recordings 1972–1975 / 1996 / Capitol ✦✦✦✦
The gritty singer made three albums for United Artists (mostly under his brother Matt's supervision) from 1972 to 1975, and they were an idiomatically mixed bag. All three LPs are housed in their entirety on this two-disc set, its selections ranging from the deep soul sincerity of "I've Got to Get You Back" and "Your Love Makes Me Feel Good" and the country-soul hybrids "You're Killing Me (Slowly But Surely)" and "Country Love" to the funky Lamont Dozier-produced "I Created a Monster" and an Allen Toussaint-supervised "I Keep on Lovin' You." *—Bill Dahl*

Love Is So Good When You're Stealing It / 1996 / Ichiban Soul Classics ✦✦✦
Although Hill is often classified as a soul/blues crossover artist, his late-'70s albums for Columbia are more properly pigeonholed as soul/disco crossover efforts. This is an 18-track anthology of material from his *Let's Make a Deal* (1978) and *The Mark of Z.Z. Hill* (1979) LPs, including the minor hits "This Time They Told the Truth" and "Love Is So Good When You're Stealing It." Certainly Hill is in good voice, but you can't help wondering if this wouldn't have sounded much better with straightforward Southern soul production. And if you appreciate Hill as a soul or

soul/blues singer, there are far rootsier efforts to check out than this one. —*Richie Unterberger*

Faithful & True / Pair ✦✦✦

Silas Hogan

b. Sep. 15, 1911, **d.** Feb. 1994
Vocals, Guitar / Electric Louisiana Blues
In the collection of local Louisiana blues stars that made their mark on phonograph records bearing the Excello imprint under the aegis of Crowley producer Jay Miller, Silas Hogan was a local phenom who finally had a chance to record at a time when the commercial appeal of his sound was waning in the national marketplace. Hogan recorded for Excello from 1962 to early 1965, seeing the last of his single releases being issued late that year.

Sometime in the late '20s Silas learned the basics of the guitar from his two uncles, Robert and Frank Murphy, who later went on to influence the idiosyncratic style of Robert Pete Williams. Learning his trade by playing assorted house parties and picnics in the local vicinity, by the late '30s Hogan was working regularly with guitarist Willie B. Thomas and fiddler Butch Cage, making the local juke-joint circuit his new-found home. A move to the Baton Rouge area in the early '50s brought changes to his music. Armed with a Fender electric guitar and amp, Hogan formed his first electric combo—the Rhythm Ramblers—becoming one of the top draws on the Louisiana juke-joint circuit. In 1962, at the ripe old age of 51, Hogan was introduced by Slim Harpo to producer Jay Miller and his recording career finally began in earnest. The recordings he produced in the Crowley studio were solid, no-frills performances that mirrored the many variants of the "sound of the swamp." After a few singles, Hogan's recording career came to an abrupt halt when Miller clashed with the new owners in 1966, ending the flow of Crowley product on the label. No longer an Excello recording artist, Hogan disbanded his group, going back to his day job at the Exxon refinery near Baton Rogue. The chance to record came around again in the 1970s, with Hogan cutting sides for labels like Arhoolie and Blue Horizon while remaining active on the Southern blues festival circuit for pretty much the rest of the decade. With as little fanfare as his Excello singles were greeted in the marketplace, Silas Hogan quietly passed away in February of 1994, seven months shy of his 83rd birthday. —*AMG*

● **Trouble: The Best Of The Excello Masters** / 1995 / AVI-Excello ✦✦✦✦✦

This 26-track single-disc retrospective may not have every last alternate take extant on it, but you'll never need a better compilation mirroring Hogan's stay at the label. "Trouble At Home Blues," "I'm Gonna Quit You Pretty Baby" and "Here They Are Again" are just about as low down as Louisiana swamp blues gets and Jay Miller's studio sorcery is clearly on hand. —*AMG*

Smokey Hogg

b. Jan. 27, 1914, Westconnie, TX, **d.** May 1, 1960, McKinney, TX
Vocals, Guitar / Acoustic & Electric Texas Blues
Smokey Hogg was a rural bluesman navigating a postwar era infatuated by R&B, but he got along quite nicely nonetheless, scoring a pair of major R&B hits in 1948 and 1950 and cutting a thick catalog for a slew of labels (including Exclusive, Modern, Bullet, Macy's, Sittin' in With, Imperial, Mercury, Recorded in Hollywood, Specialty, Fidelity, Combo, Federal, and Showtime).

During the early '30s, Hogg, who was influenced by Big Bill Broonzy and Peetie Wheatstraw, worked with slide guitarist Black Ace at dances around Greenville, TX. Hogg first recorded for Decca in 1937, but it was an isolated occurrence—he didn't make it back into a studio for a decade. Once he hit his stride, though, Hogg didn't look back. Both his chart hits—1948's "Long Tall Mama" and 1950s "Little School Girl"—were issued on Modern, but his rough-hewn sound seldom changed a whole lot no matter what L.A. logo he was appearing on. Hogg's last few sides were cut in 1958 for Lee Rupe's Ebb label.

Smokey's cousin John Hogg also played the blues, recording for Mercury in 1951. —*Bill Dahl*

Dave Hole

b. , England
Guitar / Modern Electric Blues
Slide guitarist Dave Hole played 20 years in remote western Australian towns before making *Short Fuse Blues*, an album he financed, produced, and recorded with his band, Short Fuse, in

three days around 1990. He then hawked the album during club performances. On a whim he sent a copy to *Guitar Player* magazine in the U.S. The editor listened to it, liked it, wrote a praise-filled article hailing him as the newest guitar wizard and comparing him to such greats as Stevie Ray Vaughan and Albert King. He then helped Hole land a distribution deal with Alligator Records.

As a performer, Hole is noted for his energetic, high-volume rock & roll/blues music and unusual playing style. Though left-handed, Hole plays right-handed guitar and instead of fretting the usual way, developed a technique to compensate for a finger injury in which he places his fingers over the top of the neck. He also uses a pick for a slide and when playing normally utilizes finger picking.

Born in England, but raised from age four in Perth, Australia, Hole became interested in blues guitar around age six after hearing a schoolmate's Muddy Waters album. He received his first guitar at age 12, but became discouraged trying to learn it by himself (teachers were apparently in short supply in isolated Perth) and abandoned it until he was 16. This time he began picking up riffs and techniques from records. Primary influences include Eric Clapton, Jimi Hendrix, Robert Johnson, Elmore James, and Mississippi Fred McDowell. Hole became a professional in 1972 working with a band in London. Returning to Perth in 1974, he began his long stint touring the western Australian club circuit. The American debut of *Short Fuse Blues* earned Hole considerable praise and was well-received by the public. Though best-known in Australia, Hole, with the release of his second and third albums, *Working Overtime* (1993) and *Steel on Steel* (1995), both for Alligator, have garnered him a respectable following in the U.S. and Europe. —*Sandra Brennan*

Short Fuse Blues / 1992 / Alligator ✦✦✦
Dave Hole's American debut album is a stunning display of slide guitar pyrotechnics. Hole runs through a dizzying array of licks and solos, pulling out a variety of different tones and textures from his guitar. He can play it straight and greasy or spooky, tough and gritty or subtle and melodic—his technique is quite impressive. Although the songs themselves are occasionally weak, *Short Fuse Blues* is essentially a guitar record, so the songs don't matter as much as the playing. And the playing is superb throughout *Short Fuse Blues*. —*Thom Owens*

● **Working Overtime** / 1993 / Alligator ✦✦✦✦✦
Hole's second disc features nine original compositions and covers of Muddy Waters and Big Bill Broonzy, rendered in a vocal and guitar style somewhat similar to Johnny Winter's best blues work but with an edge of youthful vigor. "Biting slide guitar work" is an understatement. Hole can also play the thoughtful Roy Buchanan card on the likes of "Berwick Road." —*Roch Parisien*

Steel on Steel / 1995 / Alligator ✦✦✦
With his third album, *Steel on Steel*, Dave Hole turns in another set of ready-made originals and covers, all highlighted by his sizzling slide guitar work. —*Stephen Thomas Erlewine*

Billie Holiday (Eleanora Fagan)

b. Apr. 7, 1915, Baltimore, MD, **d.** Jul. 17, 1959, New York, NY
Vocals / Swing
Billie Holiday remains the most famous of all jazz singers. "Lady Day" (as she was named by Lester Young) had a small voice and did not scat, but her innovative behind-the-beat phrasing made her quite influential. The emotional intensity that she put into the words she sang (particularly in later years) was very memorable and sometimes almost scary; she often really did live the words she sang.

Her original name and birthplace have been wrong for years but are listed correctly above thanks to Donald Clarke's definitive Billie Holiday biography *Wishing on the Moon*. Holiday's early years are shrouded in legend and rumors due to her fanciful ghostwritten autobiography *Lady Sings the Blues* but it is fair to say that she did not have a stable life. Her father Clarence Holiday (who never did marry her mother) played guitar with Fletcher Henderson and abandoned his family early, while her mother was not a very good role model. Billie essentially grew up alone, feeling unloved and gaining a lifelong inferiority complex that led her to taking great risks with her personal life and become self-destructive.

Holiday's life becomes clearer after she was discovered by

John Hammond singing in Harlem clubs. He arranged for her to record a couple of titles with Benny Goodman in 1933 and, although those were not all that successful, it was the start of her career. Two years later she was teamed with a pickup band led by Teddy Wilson and the combination clicked. During 1935–42 she would make some of the finest recordings of her career, jazz-oriented performances in which she was joined by the who's who of swing. Holiday sought to combine Louis Armstrong's swing and Bessie Smith's sound; the result was her own fresh approach. In 1937 Lester Young and Buck Clayton began recording with Holiday and the interplay between the three of them was timeless.

Lady Day was with Count Basie's Orchestra during much of 1937 but, because they were signed to different labels, all that exists of the collaboration are three songs from a radio broadcast. She worked with Artie Shaw's Orchestra for a time in 1938 but the same problem existed (only one song was recorded) and she had to deal with racism, not only during a Southern tour but in New York too. She had better luck as a star attraction at Cafe Society in 1939. Holiday made history that year by recording the horribly picturesque "Strange Fruit," a strong anti-racism statement that became a permanent part of her repertoire. Her records of 1940–42 found her sidemen playing a much more supportive role than in the past, rarely sharing solo space with her.

Although the settings were less jazz-oriented than before (with occasional strings and even a background vocal group on a few numbers) Billie Holiday's voice was actually at its strongest during her period with Decca (1944–49). She had already introduced "Fine and Mellow" (1939) and "God Bless the Child" (1941) but it was while with Decca that she first recorded "Lover Man" (her biggest hit), "Don't Explain," "Good Morning Heartache" and her renditions of "Ain't Nobody's Business If I Do," "Them There Eyes" and "Crazy He Calls Me." Unfortunately it was just before this period that she became a heroin addict and she spent much of 1947 in jail. Due to the publicity she became a notorious celebrity and her audience greatly increased. Lady Day did get a chance to make one Hollywood movie (*New Orleans*) in 1946 and, although she was disgusted at the fact that she was stuck playing a maid, she did get to perform with her early idol Louis Armstrong.

Billie Holiday's story from 1950 on is a gradual downhill slide. Although her recordings for Norman Granz (which started in 1952) placed her once again with all-star jazz veterans (including Charlie Shavers, Buddy DeFranco, Harry "Sweets" Edison and Ben Webster), her voice was slipping fast. Her unhappy relationships distracted her, the heroin use and excessive drinking continued, and by 1956 she was way past her prime. Holiday had one final burst of glory in late 1957 when she sang "Fine and Mellow" on *The Sound of Jazz* telecast while joined by Lester Young (who stole the show with an emotional chorus), Ben Webster, Coleman Hawkins, Gerry Mulligan and Roy Eldridge, but the end was near. Holiday's 1958 album *Lady in Satin* found the 43-year-old singer sounding 73 (barely croaking out the words) and the following year she collapsed; in the sad final chapter of her life she was placed under arrest for heroin possession while on her deathbed!

Fortunately Billie Holiday's recordings have been better treated than she was during her life and virtually all of her studio sides are currently available on CD. —*Scott Yanow*

Billie Holiday: The Legacy Box 1933–1958 / Nov. 27, 1933–Feb. 19, 1958 / Columbia ◆◆◆
The logic behind this sampler is puzzling. Rather than reissue the very best of Billie Holiday's Columbia recordings on a three-CD box set or a package of her rare alternate takes, CBS tries it both ways by including 60 common selections already available in the *Quintessential* series along with 10 rarities that were either unissued or alternates. This otherwise attractive box (which includes a colorful booklet) will drive completists and veteran collectors crazy. The music (mostly from 1933–42 with three weaker performances from 1957–58) is often classic but duplicates more coherent reissues. —*Scott Yanow*

★ **The Quintessential Billie Holiday, Vol. 1 (1933–1935)** / Nov. 27, 1933–Dec. 3, 1935 / Columbia ◆◆◆◆◆
After years of reissuing her recordings in piecemeal fashion, Columbia finally got it right with this nine-CD *Quintessential* series. All of Lady Day's 1933–42 studio recordings (although

without the alternate takes) receive the treatment they deserve in this program. *Vol. 1* has Holiday's first two tentative performances from 1933 and along with her initial recordings with Teddy Wilson's all-star bands. Highpoints include "I Wished On the Moon," "What a Little Moonlight Can Do," "Miss Brown to You," and "Twenty-Four Hours a Day." —*Scott Yanow*

★ **The Quintessential Billie Holiday, Vol. 2 (1936)** / Jan. 30, 1936–Oct. 21, 1936 / Columbia ◆◆◆◆◆
The second of nine volumes in this essential series (all are highly recommended) continues the complete reissue of Billie Holiday's early recordings (although the alternate takes are bypassed). This set is highlighted by "I Cried for You" (which has a classic alto solo from Johnny Hodges), "Billie's Blues" (from Holiday's first session as a leader), "A Fine Romance," and "Easy to Love." Holiday's backup crew includes such greats as pianist Teddy Wilson, baritonist Harry Carney, trumpeters Jonah Jones and Bunny Berigan and clarinetist Artie Shaw. There's lots of great small-group swing. —*Scott Yanow*

★ **The Quintessential Billie Holiday, Vol. 3 (1936–1937)** / Oct. 28, 1936–Feb. 18, 1937 / Columbia ◆◆◆◆◆
The third of nine CDs that document all of Billie Holiday's studio recordings of 1933–42 for Columbia has classic versions of "Pennies from Heaven," "I Can't Give You Anything but Love" (on which she shows the influence of Louis Armstrong) and "My Last Affair," along with Lady Day's first meeting on record with tenor saxophonist Lester Young. Their initial encounter resulted in four songs including "This Year's Kisses" and "I Must Have That Man." All nine volumes in this admirable series (if only the alternate takes had been included!) are highly recommended. —*Scott Yanow*

☆ **The Quintessential Billie Holiday, Vol. 4 (1937)** / Mar. 31, 1937–Jun. 15, 1937 / Columbia ◆◆◆◆◆
The fourth of nine CDs in this essential series of Billie Holiday's studio recordings of 1933–42 features the great tenor Lester Young on eight of the 16 performances. Prez and Lady Day make a perfect match on "I'll Get By" (although altoist Johnny Hodges steals the honors on that song), "Mean to Me," "Easy Living," "Me Myself and I," and "A Sailboat in the Moonlight." Other strong selections without Young include "Moanin' Low," "Let's Call the Whole Thing Off," and "Where Is the Sun." It's highly recommended along with all of the other CDs in this perfectly done Billie Holiday reissue program. —*Scott Yanow*

★ **The Quintessential Billie Holiday, Vol. 5 (1937–1938)** / Jun. 15, 1937–Jan. 27, 1938 / Columbia ◆◆◆◆◆
The fifth of nine CDs in the complete reissue of Billie Holiday's early recordings (sans alternate takes), this great set has 18 selections, all but four featuring tenor saxophonist Lester Young and trumpeter Buck Clayton. Among the classics are "Getting Some Fun out of Life," "Trav'lin' All Alone," "He's Funny That Way," "My Man," "When You're Smiling" (on which Prez takes a perfect solo), "If Dreams Come True," and "Now They Call It Swing." All nine volumes in this series are highly recommended, but if one can only acquire a single entry, this is the one. —*Scott Yanow*

☆ **Quintessential Billie Holiday, Vol. 6 (1938)** / May 11, 1938–Nov. 9, 1938 / Columbia ◆◆◆◆◆
The sixth of nine CDs in this very worthy series traces Billie Holiday's recording career throughout much of 1938. Although not containing as many true classics as *Vol. 5*, most of these 18 selections are quite enjoyable, particularly "You Go to My Head," "Having Myself a Time," "The Very Thought of You" and "They Say." All of the sets in this reissue program are recommended, featuring Lady Day when she was youthful and still optimistic about life. —*Scott Yanow*

The Quintessential Billie Holiday, Vol. 7 (1938–1939) / Nov. 28, 1938–Jul. 5, 1939 / Columbia ◆◆◆◆◆
By 1939 when the bulk of these 17 selections were recorded, Billie Holiday was dominating her own recordings, allocating less space for her sidemen to solo. This was not really a bad thing since Lady Day's voice was getting stronger each year. On the seventh of nine CD volumes that reissue all of Holiday's 1933–42 Columbia recordings (other than the alternate takes which have been bypassed), Holiday sounds at her best on "More than You Know, Sugar" (featuring a superb Benny Carter alto solo), "Long Gone Blues" and "Some Other Spring." It's recommended along with all of the other entries in the *Quintessential* series. —*Scott Yanow*

Billie Holiday / Apr. 20, 1939–Apr. 8, 1944 / Commodore ✦✦✦✦✦
This CD includes all of Billie Holiday's Commodore recordings (the master takes but no alternates): four titles from 1939 (including the still haunting "Strange Fruit" and "Fine and Mellow") and the remainder dating from 1944 when Holiday's voice was at its peak. The latter sessions are highlighted by "I'll Get By," "Billie's Blues," "He's Funny That Way" and "I'm Yours." Pianist Eddie Heywood has many sparkling solos on the 1944 selections. This definitive single CD contains music essential for every jazz collection. —Scott Yanow

☆ **Quintessential Billie Holiday, Vol. 8 (1939–1940)** / Jul. 5, 1939–Sep. 12, 1940 / Columbia ✦✦✦✦✦
The eighth of nine volumes that feature all of the master takes from Billie Holiday's Columbia recordings of 1933–42 is one of the better sets although all nine CDs are recommended. Highpoints include "Them There Eyes," "Swing, Brother, Swing," "The Man I Love," "Ghost of Yesterday," "Body And Soul," "Falling in Love Again," and "I Hear Music." Among the variety of all-stars backing her, tenor saxophonist Lester Young makes his presence known on eight of the 18 numbers. —Scott Yanow

Quintessential Billie Holiday, Vol. 9 (1940–1942) / Oct. 15, 1940–Feb. 10, 1942 / Columbia ✦✦✦✦✦
The final volume in this nine-CD series contains all of Billie Holiday's recordings from her final 16 months with the label. Highlights include "St. Louis Blues," "Loveless Love," "Let's Do It," "All of Me" (arguably the greatest version ever of this veteran standard), "Am I Blue," "Gloomy Sunday" and "God Bless the Child." All 153 of Lady Day's Columbia recordings (even the occasional weak item) are well worth hearing and savoring. —Scott Yanow

Billie's Blues / Jun. 12, 1942–Jan. 5, 1954 / Blue Note ✦✦✦✦
Most of this excellent CD features one of Billie Holiday's finest concert recordings of the 1950s. Recorded in Europe before an admiring audience, this enjoyable set finds Lady Day performing seven of her standards with her trio and joining in for jam session versions of "Billie's Blues" and "Lover Come Back to Me" with an all-star group starring clarinetist Buddy DeFranco, vibraphonist Red Norvo and guitarist Jimmy Raney. These performances (which find Holiday in stronger voice than on her studio recordings of the period) have also been included in Verve's massive CD box set. This program concludes with Holiday's four rare sides for Aladdin in 1951 (between her Decca and Verve periods) which are highlighted by two blues and "Detour Ahead," and her 1942 studio recording of "Trav'lin' Light" with Paul Whiteman's Orchestra. —Scott Yanow

Fine and Mellow / Jan. 18, 1944–Apr. 15, 1959 / Collectables ✦✦✦
This CD contains 20 selections featuring Billie Holiday in a variety of live performances covering a 15-year period. Starting with two songs in 1944 in which she was backed by the Esquire All-Stars and continuing through TV appearances and club dates, one can hear the gradual aging and decline of Lady Day's voice which definitely took a turn for the worse between 1955–56. And yet oddly enough the last five numbers, which were performed April 15, 1959 (making them Holiday's final recordings), actually find her sounding stronger than she had in a few years, perhaps in a final gasp of energy. Of great historical value, this set has plenty of strong moments to justify its acquisition. —Scott Yanow

★ **The Complete Decca Recordings** / Oct. 4, 1944–Mar. 8, 1950 / Decca ✦✦✦✦✦
Billie Holiday is heard at her absolute best on this attractive two-CD set. During her period on Decca, Lady Day was accompanied by strings (for the first time), large studio orchestras and even background vocalists, so jazz solos from her sidemen are few. But her voice was at its strongest during the 1940s (even with her personal problems) and to hear all 50 of her Decca performances (including alternate takes and even some studio chatter) is a real joy. Among the highpoints of this essential set are her original versions of "Lover Man" (Holiday's biggest selling record), "Don't Explain," "Good Morning Heartache," "Tain't Nobody's Business If I Do," "Now or Never," "Crazy He Calls Me," and remakes of "Them There Eyes" and "God Bless the Child." —Scott Yanow

☆ **The Complete Billie Holiday on Verve 1945–1959** / Feb. 12, 1945–Mar. 1, 1959 / Verve ✦✦✦✦✦
This is a rather incredible collection, ten CDs enclosed in a tight black box that includes every one of the recordings that Verve owns of Billie Holiday, not only the many studio recordings of 1952–57 (which feature Lady Day joined by such jazz all-stars as trumpeters Charlie Shavers and Harry "Sweets" Edison, altoist Benny Carter and the tenors of Flip Phillips, Paul Quinichette and Ben Webster) but prime performances at Jazz at the Philharmonic concerts in 1945–47, an enjoyable European gig from 1954, her "comeback" Carnegie Hall concert of 1956, Holiday's rather sad final studio album from 1959 and even lengthy tapes from two informal rehearsals. It's a perfect purchase for the true Billie Holiday fanatic. —Scott Yanow

Lady Sings the Blues / 1954–1956 / Verve ✦✦✦
Immaculate 1954 and 1956 recordings with an all-star lineup and smashing Holiday cuts. One of her last great dates. —Ron Wynn

Lady in Satin / Feb. 18, 1958–Feb. 20, 1958 / Columbia ✦✦✦✦✦
This is the most controversial of all Billie Holiday records. Lady Day herself said that this session (which finds her accompanied by Ray Ellis' string orchestra) was her personal favorite and many listeners have found her emotional versions of such songs as "I'm a Fool to Want You," "You Don't Know What Love Is," "Glad to Be Unhappy" and particularly "You've Changed" to be quite touching. But Holiday's voice was essentially totally gone by 1958, and although not yet 43, she could have passed for 73. Ellis' muzaky arrangements do not help; most of this record is very difficult to listen to. Late in life, Billie Holiday expressed the pain of life so effectively that her croaking voice had become almost unbearable to hear. —Scott Yanow

The Holmes Brothers

Group / Modern Electric Blues
Rooted in gospel music as they are, the Holmes Brothers have become one of the favorite groups for festival organizers. The group's unique synthesis of gospel-inflected blues harmonies, accompanied by good drumming and rhythm-based guitar playing, gives them a down-home rural feeling that no other touring blues group can duplicate.

Brothers Sherman and Wendell Holmes, along with drummer Popsy Dixon (the falsetto voice), are the group's core members, although they occasionally tour with extra musicians. All three harmonize well together. The Holmes Brothers are so versatile, they're booked solid every summer at folk, blues, gospel and jazz festivals, as they play a style of music that is a gumbo of church tunes, blues and soul. Although people like Bo Diddley and especially Jimmy Reed were early influences on Wendell and Sherman, gospel music also played an important role in their respective upbringings.

Although they'd been performing in Harlem for years, the Holmes Brothers—originally from Christchurch, VA—have only recently become international blues touring stars. Thanks to a fair deal at Rounder Records, the group has released three recordings from that label, beginning with a 1989 release, *In the Spirit*. When this album made waves and got them off and running on the festival and club circuit around the U.S. and Europe, they followed it up two years later with *That's Where It's At* (1991) and then *Soul Street* (1993).

The group's career has been aided by the interest of people like Peter Gabriel, who recruited them for his WOMAD (world music) Festivals in England and who also recorded them in a gospel context on the album *Jubilation*, for his Real World subsidiary of Virgin Records in 1992. —Richard Skelly

In the Spirit / 1990 / Rounder ✦✦✦✦✦
The Holmes Brothers' voices are too potent, their harmonies too smashing, and their love of vintage sounds too immense for them to be content with producer-dominated, softer urban contemporary sounds. This set included some riveting gospel tunes like "None But The Righteous" and "Up Above My Head," plus a credible (if a little lengthy) version of "When Something Is Wrong With My Baby" and the tighter, hard-hitting tunes "Please Don't Hurt Me," "Ask Me No Questions," and "The Final Round." If straight-ahead, rousing shared leads and booming harmonies interest you, The Holmes Brothers do it the way they used to throughout the South in the '60s and '70s. —Ron Wynn

Where It's At / 1991 / Rounder ✦✦✦✦
The Holmes Brothers' second release contained 11 more wonderful tunes that easily moved from surging R&B to rousing
blues with an occasional venture into gospel or country. They
covered "Drown In My Own Tears" and "High Heel Sneakers"
and had the requisite qualities for each one down pat, as well as
"Never Let Me Go," "The Love You Save," and "I Saw The Light."
But their own numbers, like "I've Been A Loser" and the title
track, were even better, displaying a contemporary sensibility
and classic style and sound. —*Ron Wynn*

Jubilation / 1992 / Real World ✦✦✦
Jubilation is a revealing, wonderful collection of the Holmes
Brothers' distinctive soul. The brothers tie together a seemingly disconnected array of styles—everything from straightforward blues, R&B, and gospel to worldbeat and country—and
come up with a cohesive whole. Even when the group delves
into soukous or works with a Chinese flautist, it manages to
retain the pure qualities of American blues and R&B. —*Thom
Owens*

● **Soul Street** / 1993 / Rounder ✦✦✦✦✦
This album continued The Holmes Brothers' tradition of doing
tremendous covers ("You're Gonna Make Me Cry," "Down In
Virginia," and "Fannie Mae"), authentic originals ("I Won't Hurt
You Anymore," "Dashboard Bar") and adding gospel ("Walk In
The Light") and honky-tonk ("There Goes My Everything") into
their blend. There's little to criticize about The Holmes Brothers;
their sound, vocals, and harmonies aren't laid-back or restrained,
and everything they sing is done with exuberance and integrity.
It may not be commercially viable, but it's musically sound. —
Ron Wynn

Earl Hooker (Earl Zebedee Hooker)

b. Jan. 15, 1930, Clarksdale, MS, d. Apr. 21, 1970, Chicago, IL
Guitar, Vocals / Electric Chicago Blues
If there was a more immaculate slide guitarist residing in
Chicago during the 1950s and '60s than Earl Hooker, his name
has yet to surface. Boasting a fretboard touch so smooth and
clean that every note rang as clear and precise as a bell, Hooker
was an endlessly inventive axeman who would likely have been
a star had his modest vocal abilities matched his instrumental
prowess and had he not been dogged by tuberculosis (it killed
him at age 41).
Born in the Mississippi Delta, Hooker arrived in Chicago as a
child. There he was influenced by another slide wizard, veteran
Robert Nighthawk. But Hooker never remained still for long. He
ran away from home at age 13, journeying to Mississippi. After
another stint in Chicago, he rambled back to the Delta again,
playing with Ike Turner and Sonny Boy Williamson. Hooker
made his first recordings in 1952 and 1953 for Rockin', King, and
Sun. At the latter, he recorded some terrific sides with pianist
Pinetop Perkins (Sam Phillips inexplicably sat on Hooker's blazing rendition of "The Hucklebuck").
Back in Chicago again, Hooker's dazzling dexterity was intermittently showcased on singles for Argo, C.J., and Bea & Baby
during the mid-to-late '50s before he joined forces with producer Mel London (owner of the Chief and Age logos) in 1959. For
the next four years, he recorded both as sideman and leader for
the producer, backing Junior Wells, Lillian Offitt, Ricky Allen,
and A.C. Reed and cutting his own sizzling instrumentals ("Blue
Guitar," "Blues in D-Natural"). He also contributed pungent slide
work to Muddy Waters' Chess waxing "You Shook Me."
Opportunities to record grew sparse after Age folded; Hooker
made some tantalizing sides for Sauk City, Wisconsin's Cuca
Records from 1964 to 1968 (several featuring steel guitar virtuoso Freddie Roulette).
Hooker's amazing prowess (he even managed to make the
dreaded wah-wah pedal a viable blues tool) finally drew
increased attention during the late '60s. He cut LPs for Arhoolie,
ABC-BluesWay, and Blue Thumb that didn't equal what he'd
done at Age, but they did serve to introduce Hooker to an audience outside Chicago and wherever his frequent travels deposited him. But tuberculosis halted his wandering ways permanently in 1970. —*Bill Dahl*

Two Bugs and a Roach / 1966 / Arhoolie ✦✦✦✦✦
A nice representative sample from Chicago's unsung master of
the electric guitar, it includes the title track, "Anna Lee," and the
atmospheric instrumental, "Off the Hook." —*Bruce Lee Pearson*

Sweet Black Angel / 1970 / One Way ✦✦✦
Ike Turner co-produced this set with Blue Thumb Records boss
Bob Krasnow. It's a wide-ranging collection, as its oddly generic
song titles ("Country and Western," "Shuffle," "Funky Blues")
would eloquently indicate. —*Bill Dahl*

Leading Brand / 1978 / Red Lightnin' ✦✦✦✦✦
Hooker's best early-'60s instrumentals for Mel London, along
with a few sides that feature his guitar by Ricky Allen, Lillian
Offett, etc. Also featured are several equally memorable workouts by guitarist Jody Williams. —*Bill Dahl*

● **Blue Guitar** / 1981 / Paula/Flyright ✦✦✦✦✦
The slide guitar wizard's immaculate fretwork was never cap-
tured more imaginatively than during his early-'60s stay with
Mel London's Age/Chief labels. Twenty-one fascinating tracks
from that period include Hooker's savage instrumentals "Blue
Guitar," "Off the Hook," "The Leading Brand," "Blues in D
Natural," and "How Long Can This Go On," along with tracks by
A.C. Reed, Lillian Offitt, and Harold Tidwell that cast Hooker as
a standout sideman. —*Bill Dahl*

Play Your Guitar Mr Hooker / 1985 / Black Top ✦✦✦
1964–1967 output by the guitarist that was largely done for the
tiny Cuca logo of Sauk City, WI. The normally tight-lipped
Hooker proves that he could sing on this romping version of
"Swear to Tell the Truth," while A.C. Reed, Little Tommy, Frank
Clark, and Muddy Waters, Jr. help out behind the mike elsewhere. A pair of live cuts from 1968 find Hooker stretching out
in amazing fashion. —*Bill Dahl*

John Lee Hooker

b. Aug. 17, 1920, Clarksdale, MS
Guitar, Vocals / Electric Delta Blues, Acoustic Delta Blues
He's beloved worldwide as the king of the endless boogie, a genuine blues superstar whose droning, hypnotic one-chord grooves
are at once both ultra-primitive and timeless. But John Lee
Hooker has recorded in a great many more styles than that over
a career that stretches back more than half a century.
The Hook is a Mississippi native who became the top gent on
the Detroit blues circuit in the years following World War II. The
seeds for his eerily mournful guitar sound were planted by his
stepfather, Will Moore, while Hooker was in his teens. Hooker
had been singing spirituals before that, but the blues took hold
and wouldn't let go. Overnight visitors left their mark on
the youth, too—legends like Blind Lemon Jefferson, Charlie
Patton, and Blind Blake, who all knew Moore.
Hooker heard Memphis calling while he was still in his teens,
but he couldn't gain much of a foothold there. So he relocated to
Cincinnati for a seven-year stretch before making the big move
to the Motor City in 1943. Jobs were plentiful, but Hooker drifted away from day gigs in favor of playing his unique free-form
brand of blues. A burgeoning club scene along Hastings Street
didn't hurt his chances any.
In 1948, the aspiring bluesman hooked up with entrepreneur
Bernie Besman, who helped him hammer out his solo debut
sides, "Sally Mae" and its seminal flip, "Boogie Chillen." This was
blues as primitive as anything then on the market; Hooker's
dark, ruminative vocals were backed only by his own ringing,
heavily amplified guitar and insistently pounding foot. Their
efforts were quickly rewarded. Los Angeles-based Modern
Records issued the sides and "Boogie Chillen"—a colorful,
unique travelogue of Detroit's blues scene—made an improbable
jaunt to the very peak of the R&B charts.
Modern released several more major hits by the Boogie Man
after that: "Hobo Blues" and its raw-as-an-open wound flip,
"Hoogie Boogie"; "Crawling King Snake Blues" (all three 1949
smashes), and the unusual 1951 chart-topper "I'm in the Mood,"
where Hooker overdubbed his voice three times in a crude early
attempt at multi-tracking.
But Hooker never, ever let something as meaningless as a
contract stop him for making recordings for other labels. His
early catalog is stretched across a roadmap of diskeries so complex that it's nearly impossible to fully comprehend (a vast array
of recording aliases don't make things any easier).
Along with Modern, Hooker recorded for King (as the geo-
graphically challenged Texas Slim), Regent (as Delta John, a far
more accurate handle), Savoy (as the wonderfully surreal
Birmingham Sam and his Magic Guitar), Danceland (as the
downright delicious Little Pork Chops), Staff (as Johnny

Williams), Sensation (for whom he scored a national hit in 1950 with "Huckle Up, Baby"), Gotham, Regal, Swing Time, Federal, Gone (as John Lee Booker), Chess, Acorn (as the Boogie Man), Chance, DeLuxe (as Johnny Lee), JVB, Chart, and Specialty before finally settling down at Vee-Jay in 1955 under his own name. Hooker became the point man for the growing Detroit blues scene during this incredibly prolific period, recruiting guitarist Eddie Kirkland as his frequent duet partner while still recording for Modern.

Once tied in with Vee-Jay, the rough-and-tumble sound of Hooker's solo and duet waxings was adapted to a band format. Hooker had recorded with various combos along the way before, but never with sidemen as versatile and sympathetic as guitarist Eddie Taylor and harpist Jimmy Reed, who backed him at his initial Vee-Jay date that produced "Time Is Marching" and the superfluous sequel "Mambo Chillun."

Taylor stuck around for a 1956 session that elicited two genuine Hooker classics, "Baby Lee" and "Dimples," and he was still deftly anchoring the rhythm section (Hooker's sense of timing was his and his alone, demanding big-eared sidemen) when the Boogie Man finally made it back to the R&B charts in 1958 with "I Love You Honey."

Vee-Jay presented Hooker in quite an array of settings during the early '60s. His grinding, tough blues "No Shoes" proved a surprisingly sizable hit in 1960, while the storming "Boom Boom," his top seller for the firm in 1962 (it even cracked the pop airwaves), was an infectious R&B dance number benefiting from the reported presence of some of Motown's house musicians. But there were also acoustic outings aimed squarely at the blossoming folk-blues crowd, as well as some attempts at up-to-date R&B that featured highly intrusive female background vocals (allegedly by the Vandellas) and utterly unyielding structures that hemmed Hooker in unmercifully.

British blues bands such as the Animals and Yardbirds idolized Hooker during the early '60s; Eric Burdon's boys cut a credible 1964 cover of "Boom Boom" that outsold Hooker's original on the American pop charts. Hooker visited Europe in 1962 under the auspices of the first American Folk Blues Festival, leaving behind the popular waxings "Let's Make It" and "Shake It Baby" for foreign consumption.

Back home, Hooker cranked out gems for Vee-Jay through 1964 ("Big Legs, Tight Skirt," one of his last offerings on the logo, was also one of his best), before undergoing another extended round of label-hopping (except this time, he was waxing whole LPs instead of scattered 78s). Verve-Folkways, Impulse, Chess, and BluesWay all enticed him into recording for them in 1965–66 alone! His reputation among hip rock cognoscenti in the states and abroad was growing exponentially, especially after he teamed up with blues-rockers Canned Heat for the massively selling album *Hooker 'n' Heat* in 1970.

Eventually, though, the endless boogie formula grew incredibly stagnant. Much of Hooker's 1970s output found him laying back while plodding rock-rooted rhythm sections assumed much of the workload. A cameo in the 1980 movie *The Blues Brothers* was welcome, if far too short.

But Hooker wasn't through—not by a long shot. With the expert help of slide guitarist extraordinaire/producer Roy Rogers, the Hook waxed *The Healer*, an album that marked the first of his guest star-loaded albums (Carlos Santana, Bonnie Raitt, and Robert Cray were among the luminaries to cameo on the disc, which picked up a Grammy).

Major labels were just beginning to take notice of the growing demand for blues records, and Pointblank snapped Hooker up, releasing *Mr. Lucky* (this time teaming Hooker with everyone from Albert Collins and John Hammond to Van Morrison and Keith Richards). Once again, Hooker was resting on his laurels by allowing his guests to wrest much of the spotlight away from him on his own album, but by then, he'd earned it. Another Pointblank set, *Boom Boom*, soon followed.

Happily, Hooker is now enjoying the good life. He's in semiretirement, splitting his relaxation time between several houses he's acquired up and down the California coast. Baseball also takes up much of his interest during the summer months; he's an inveterate Dodger fan. When the right offer comes along, though, he takes it, as that amusing TV commercial for Pepsi indicates.

The King of the Boogie is also one of the last living links to the pre-war blues tradition. He's a true original. —*Bill Dahl*

Everybody's Blues / 1950–1954 / Specialty ✦✦✦
John Lee Hooker reissues abound, as might be expected of a singer and guitarist who's recorded hundreds of songs for countless labels since the late '40s. What makes the 20 tracks on *Everybody's Blues* different from the mountain of other Hooker material available is the fact that seven of them are newly issued, and most were done in the studio with Hooker wailing and accompanying himself on guitar minus any backing chorus or production armada. Even the cuts with a supporting combo are animated and loose, with the vocal trademarks that are now established Hooker clichés sounding fresh and genuine. —*Ron Wynn*

House of the Blues / 1960 / MCA/Chess ✦✦✦✦
Verbatim CD reissue of a 1959 Chess album that collected 1951-1954 efforts by the Hook. Some important titles here: an ominous "Leave My Wife Alone," the stark "Sugar Mama" and "Ramblin' by Myself," and with Eddie Kirkland on second guitar, "Louise" and "High Priced Woman." —*Bill Dahl*

I'm John Lee Hooker / 1960 / Vee-Jay ✦✦✦✦✦
Some of The Boogie Man's best stuff for Vee-Jay. —*Bill Dahl*

The Country Blues of John Lee Hooker / Jan. 1960 / Riverside ✦✦✦
Hooker was still churning out R&B-influenced electric blues with a rhythm section for Vee Jay when he recorded this, his first LP packaged for the folk/traditional blues market. He plays nothing but acoustic guitar, and seems to have selected a repertoire with old-school country blues in mind. It's unimpressive only within the context of Hooker's body of work; in comparison with other solo outings, the guitar sounds thin, and the approach restrained. —*Richie Unterberger*

☆ **John Lee Hooker Plays and Sings the Blues** / 1961 / MCA/Chess ✦✦✦✦✦
Recorded in 1951 and 1952, *Plays and Sings the Blues* features twelve songs by John Lee Hooker at his best, including "Baby Please Don't Go," "Bluebird," "Hey Baby," and "Worried Life Blues." —*Stephen Thomas Erlewine*

Plays & Sings the Blues / 1961 / MCA/Chess ✦✦✦✦
A 1961 Chess album restored to digital print by MCA that's filled with 1951-1952 gems from the Hook's heyday. Chess originally bought "Mad Man Blues" and "Hey Boogie" from the Gone label; the rest first came out on Chess during Hooker's frenzied early days of recording, when his platters turned up on nearly every R&B indie label existing at the time. —*Bill Dahl*

Dont Turn Me from Your Door / 1963 / Atlantic ✦✦✦
Don't Turn Me from Your Door comprises a set of 1953 sessions that were originally released in 1963 and later in 1972, under the title *Detroit Special*. Despite its twisted historical background, this is fine, first-rate Hooker. A few tracks feature the support of guitarist/vocalist Eddie Kirkland, a few others an unnamed bassist, but this is pretty much pure John Lee Hooker—just him and a guitar, running through a set of spare, haunting blues that include such tracks as "Blue Monday" and "Stuttering Blues." There are none of his best-known tracks on the album, but it's one of his most consistent original records. —*Thom Owens*

John Lee Hooker at Newport / 1964 / Vee-Jay ✦✦✦✦✦
Arguably his finest live date, this was John Lee Hooker minus the self-congratulatory mugging now an almost mandatory part of his sets. Instead, there's just lean, straight, defiant Hooker vocals and minimal, but effective backing. —*Ron Wynn*

Live at Cafe Au Go Go / 1966 / HMV ✦✦✦
A decent if somewhat low-key electric set, recorded in August of 1966. One of his better live bands, featuring support from Otis Spann and other members of Muddy Waters' group. The eight songs include Hooker standbys like "One Bourbon, One Scotch and One Beer" and "I'll Never Get Out of These Blues Alive." —*Richie Unterberger*

The Real Folk Blues / 1966 / MCA/Chess ✦✦✦
Although the great majority of the albums in Chess' *Real Folk Blues* series were vintage compilations, this disc was cut in 1966 with longtime cohort Eddie Burns on second guitar and an uncredited band behind him. Not exactly essential in Hooker's personal pantheon, but decent nonetheless. —*Bill Dahl*

Urban Blues / 1967 / MCA ✦✦✦
The Boogie Man's 1967 ABC-BluesWay album in its entirety, with three bonus numbers from a couple of years later added on

the end. Hooker's Chicago sidemen (including Eddie Taylor, Wayne Bennett, and Louis Myers) deftly handle Hooker's eccentricities on "Mr. Lucky," the harrowing "The Motor City Is Burning," and a sprightly remake of "Boom Boom." —*Bill Dahl*

Simply the Truth / 1969 / Bluesway ✦✦✦
Overseen by noted jazz producer Bob Thiele, this session had Hooker backed by some of his fullest arrangements to date, with noted session drummer Pretty Purdie and keyboards in addition to supplementary guitar and bass. The slightly modernized sound was ultimately neither here nor there, the center remaining Hooker's voice and lyrics. His words nodded toward contemporary concerns with "I Don't Wanna Go to Vietnam" and "Mini Skirts," but the songs were mostly consistent with his usual approaches. Another of his many characteristically solid efforts, although it's not one of his more interesting albums. —*Richie Unterberger*

That's Where It's At! / 1969 / Stax ✦✦✦
A characteristic solo outing with moody compositions and that doomy one-electric-guitar-and-stomping-foot ambience. One of his sparer and more menacing post-'50s outings, highlighted by "Two White Horses" and a seven-minute "Feel So Bad," which features extended verbal sparring with an unidentified male partner. —*Richie Unterberger*

Get Back Home / Nov. 30, 1969 / Evidence ✦✦✦✦✦
John Lee Hooker's greatness lies in his ability to perform the same songs the same way yet somehow sound different and memorable in the process. He operates at maximum efficiency in minimal surroundings with little production or assistance. That was the case on a 1969 session for Black and Blue; it was just Hooker and his guitar moaning, wailing, and narrating on 10 tracks which included familiar ditties "Boogie Chillen," "Love Affair," "Big Boss Lady," and "Cold Chills." Evidence has now not only reissued these 10 but has added another six bonus cuts, bringing the CD total to 16. If you have ever heard any Hooker, you will not be surprised or stunned by these renditions; you will simply enjoy hearing him rework them one more time, finding a new word, phrase, line, or riff to inject. —*Ron Wynn*

Hooker & Heat / 1971 / EMI America ✦✦✦
Probably no other White blues band took John Lee Hooker's boogie rhythms and made a career out of it as much as Canned Heat. It was certainly inevitable that the two forces would unite for a joint recording project and this double CD package (recorded in 1970 and originally a double album) is the delightful result. Canned Heat certainly knew what they were going after, as Hooker brandishes a mean guitar tone that hadn't surfaced since his early Detroit recordings. Surprisingly, Canned Heat hangs back a bit as over half the material are riveting solo recordings, with the full band only coming in as support on the second half. Compare this with most of his 70s recordings for Bluesway (now MCA) and you'll quickly realize that these sides contain some of his most cohesive work with a band, ever. —*Cub Koda*

Boogie Chillun / 1972 / Fantasy ✦✦✦
Recorded live in November 1962 in San Francisco, this dates from the period in which Hooker often presented himself as a sort of blues/folk singer for the coffeehouse crowd, toning down his volume and aggressiveness somewhat. There's something of a muted "unplugged" feel to these solo performances (though an electric guitar *is* used). It's not ineffective, though not among his best work; it's the kind of Hooker you might want to put on past midnight, just before going to sleep. Hooker's never been bashful about recycling songs, and "Boogie Chillun" appears here in one of its many versions, as does "Dimples" (retitled as "I Like to See You Walk"). He also tackles the rock/soul standard "Money," changing the title to "I Need Some Money," for which he also seemingly gets awarded the songwriting credit on the sleeve. —*Richie Unterberger*

Chess Masters / 1982 / MCA/Chess ✦✦✦✦
Although Hooker recorded for Chess in both the 1950s and '60s, much of what he did in the early '50s only found its way onto albums in the 1960s. This now out-of-print collection contains some prime singles, and if you can find it, grab it, since the Rhino collection, out of necessity, only spotlights nuggets from the array of labels that issued Hooker material. —*Ron Wynn*

Detroit Blues / 1987 / Flyright ✦✦✦
Interesting collection of old 78s that Hooker recorded under various pseudonyms (Johnny Williams, John Lee) in 1950. Along

with the original version of "House Rent Boogie" and five others that ended up on the Philadelphia Gotham label, we have the bonus of a half dozen tracks by Hooker sideman Eddie Burns and Detroit bluesman Baby Boy Warren's first single. The sound is rough in the extreme, but the music's great. —*Cub Koda*

40th Anniversary Album / 1989 / DCC ✦✦✦
Fourteen rarities from the seemingly bottomless 1948-1952 stash of Detroit producer Bernie Besman, joined by a 1961 stereo "Blues for Abraham Lincoln" that's painfully out-of-tune. Includes "Boogie Chillen" and an alternate version of "I'm in the Mood." —*Bill Dahl*

The Healer / 1989 / Chameleon ✦✦
The Healer was a major comeback for John Lee Hooker. Featuring a wide array of guest stars, including Bonnie Raitt, Keith Richards, Johnnie Johnson, and Los Lobos, *The Healer* captured widespread media attention because of all the superstar musicians involved in its production. Unfortunately, that long guest list is what makes the album a fairly unengaging listen. Certainly there are moments were it clicks, but that's usually when the music doesn't greatly expand on his stripped-down boogie. The other moments are professional, but not exciting. It's a pleasant listen, but never quite an engaging one. —*Thom Owens*

Boogie Awhile / 1990 / Krazy Kat ✦✦✦✦✦
This was originally issued as a 31-track, double LP full of Hooker's earliest and rarest sides, almost all of it taken from goodly hacked-up acetates and 78 pressings. The compact disc deletes 11 of the most chewed up and attempts to clean up the rest with varying results. But this is one time when audiophile concerns don't count for much because this is quite simply Hooker at his earliest, his rarest and his very best. —*Cub Koda*

Mr. Lucky / 1991 / Point Blank ✦✦✦
His tracks for Virgin's blues division, contains some entertaining material. It's not a classic, but its not half-bad either. — *Ron Wynn*

★ **The Ultimate Collection (1948–1990)** / 1991 / Rhino ✦✦✦✦✦
The single best place to begin appreciating the Boogie Man's incredible contributions to the blues lexicon, since it surveys a wide cross-section of labels and eras. Disc one contains "Boogie Chillen," "Sally Mae," "Huckle Up Baby," "I'm in the Mood," "Dimples," and "It Serves Me Right." The second spottier CD sports "Boom Boom," "One Bourbon, One Scotch, One Beer," a snarling "I'm Bad like Jesse James," and an utterly superfluous finale with Bonnie Raitt from a Showtime TV program. At only 31 songs, it could unequivocally be longer, but this anthology serves as a convenient spot for the neophyte to delve into Hookerology. —*Bill Dahl*

More Real Folk Blues: the Missing Album / Sep. 10, 1991 / MCA/Chess ✦✦✦
Produced by Ralph Bass in 1966 but not issued by Chess at the time, *More Real Folk Blues* was unearthed by MCA only a few years back. It's no masterpiece, but certainly deserved release in its day—backed by Burns and a Chicago rhythm section that copes as well as can be expected with Hooker's singular sense of timing, the Boogie Man answers Sir Mack Rice with his "Mustang Sally & Gto" and keeps things way lowdown on several other cuts. —*Bill Dahl*

Boom Boom / 1992 / Point Blank ✦✦
Another guest-heavy collection. —*Bill Dahl*

The Best of John Lee Hooker 1965–1974 / 1992 / MCA ✦✦✦
MCA's *The Best of John Lee Hooker* has a misleading title. All of the 16 selections are taken from his recordings for ABC, which were made at the end of the '60s and beginning of the '70s. During this time, his producers were experimenting with his sound, adding contemporary sonic touches like funk rhythms and wah-wah pedals. Needless to say, this sound didn't sit particularly well with Hooker's lean, haunting blues. However, these songs do take the best material from generally poor albums—anyone who wants to sample his ABC material should turn here first and they'll realize that they don't need to explore much further. —*Thom Owens*

Graveyard Blues [Specialty Reissue Series] / 1992 / Specialty ✦✦✦✦
At the beginning of his career, Hooker's sides were leased to several different labels. This 20-song anthology of material from the

late '40s and early '50s was originally released on the Sensation and Specialty labels; while the track listings indicate a timespan of 1948–50, the liner notes say that much of it was recorded in 1954. Doesn't anyone proofread these things? Anyway, this was mostly recorded solo, and boasts its characteristic spooky electric minimalist boogie sound. *The Legendary Modern Recordings*, covering the same era, is a better place to start for this kind of thing due to its stronger content. If you want more of the same, though, this (and Capitol's *Alternative Boogie*) is the next stop. —*Richie Unterberger*

On Vee-Jay 1955–1958 / 1993 / Vee-Jay ✦✦✦✦✦
Some of Hooker's finest recordings with a band were also some of his first recordings with a band. The unpredictable guitarist seemed to mesh well with guitarist Eddie Taylor, harpist Jimmy Reed, and the rest of the sidemen he was given on his 1955–58 Vee-Jay output. Includes the classic "Baby Lee" and "Dimples," along with 20 more that crackle with electricity. —*Bill Dahl*

1965 London Sessions / 1993 / Sequel ✦✦✦
Considering how these dates were done—first, Hooker was backed by a British band, Tony McPhee and the Groundhogs; later horns were overdubbed for American consumption—the results aren't too shabby at all. —*Bill Dahl*

★ **The Legendary Modern Recordings 1948–1954** / 1994 / Virgin ✦✦✦✦✦
As anyone who has collected John Lee Hooker albums over the years will tell you, this material has been around the block more times than a patrol car in a bad neighborhood. Chopped up, poorly edited and sometimes "rechanneled for electronic stereo" over the years, ending up on a pile of $1.98 bargain bin albums, it's utterly amazing to think that music this important could have been so poorly served. But while sub-standard Hooker albums glut the blues bins, it's great to have this fine sounding collection among them as it's a superlative compilation of his earliest and greatest sides. Recorded in Detroit between 1948 and 1954, Hooker's wordless moans, slashing guitar and doom-laden foot-stomping make for one potent mixture. All the hits are here ("Boogie Chillen," "Crawling Kingsnake," "I'm in the Mood," "Drifting from Door to Door," "Queen Bee," "Howlin' Wolf") , the ones that made Hooker a star in the Black community and a total anachronism in the face of the smooth supper-club sounds that were dominating the R&B charts at the time. These 24 tracks (all of them the "correct" takes, by the way) are the perfect introduction to his music and an indispensable part of any blues collection, getting our highest recommendation. —*Cub Koda*

☆ **The Early Years** / 1994 / Tomato ✦✦✦✦✦
Hooker's voluminous output for Vee-Jay Records is scattered across numerous compilations. This double CD contains 31 songs spanning the mid-'50s to the mid-'60s, and is probably the most extensive and satisfying retrospective of his Vee-Jay work (at least domestically). That's not to say it's perfectly assembled; Tomato, as usual, declines to include trimmings like songwriter credits, although Pete Welding's liner notes do (unlike most Tomato releases) provide dates and discuss the sessions in some detail. Hooker's Vee-Jay material was in most ways the most commercially-minded of his early efforts, often employing a rhythm section and R&B-influenced arrangements, and occasionally using horns. It's sometimes been said that this approach diluted Hooker's strengths, but one listen to this collection refutes that notion soundly. This is by and large prime Hooker, with some of his best (and best-selling) songs, like "Boom Boom," "Dimples," "I'm So Excited," and "One Bourbon, One Scotch, One Beer." Hooker may have sometimes sounded a bit ill at ease with a band, but he usually worked with backing musicians very well. Non-purists will find these tracks to be some of his most accessible and dynamic performances. —*Richie Unterberger*

Chill Out / 1995 / Point Blank ✦✦
Chill Out isn't the superstar blowout of John Lee Hooker's late-'80s albums, yet it retains that flavor. Featuring some extended soloing from Carlos Santana, *Chill Out* is filled with long blues workouts, all captured in pristine, state-of-the-art technology. Nothing on the disc captures the raw vitality of Hooker's prime material—it's all relaxed blues-rock jams. The clean, sterile production doesn't help the basically directionless music. Certainly nothing on *Chill Out* is outright bad; in fact, most of it is pleas-

ant, yet few of the songs on the album warrant repeated listens. —*Stephen Thomas Erlewine*

★ **Very Best Of** / Apr. 25, 1995 / Rhino ✦✦✦✦✦
The Very Best of John Lee Hooker provides a definitive introduction to the seminal bluesman, presenting over 15 classic tracks in their original hit versions. —*Stephen Thomas Erlewine*

Alternative Boogie: Early Studio Recordings 1948–1952 / Oct. 24, 1995 / Capitol ✦✦✦✦✦
A whopping three CDs, and 56 songs, from Hooker's early sessions that were unreleased at the time, although they were available for a while in the early 1970s on some United Artists LPs. Like his more widely-known material of the period, it mostly features Hooker unaccompanied, though he's aided by piano and second guitarists on a few tracks. Some of these are alternates of songs that were released in different versions, or embryonic renditions of compositions that evolved into somewhat different shapes. Especially interesting are early versions of his big hit "I'm in the Mood for Love." It's too much at once, and too unvarying in approach, for anyone but Hooker specialists. General fans are advised to stick with *The Legendary Modern Recordings*, which has 24 more renowned, and somewhat more accomplished, tracks from the same era. It's certainly a well-done package, though, containing a 38-page insert with detailed liner notes and session information. —*Richie Unterberger*

The Best of Hooker 'n Heat / 1996 / EMI ✦✦✦
These ten songs were originally released as part of a 1971 album (on Liberty 35002); this reissue, despite the lack of historical liner notes, isn't exactly short value, clocking in at 56 minutes. Canned Heat gets top billling, but really it's Hooker's show, as he sings all the tracks and takes all the songwriting credits for the material, which includes remakes of classics like "Dimples," "Boogie Chillen," "Burning Hell," and "Bottle Up and Go." With Hooker fronting a White blues-rock-boogie group, this doesn't offer the optimum circumstances to hear the man. But it's not bad either, Canned Heat playing with spirit and relative economy, although the 11-minute "Boogie Chillen" is excessive. —*Richie Unterberger*

Burning Hell / 1964 / Original Blues Classics ✦✦✦
In April 1959, Hooker recorded a couple of solo acoustic albums for Riverside that were his first efforts geared toward the folk/acoustic blues audience, rather than the commercial R&B one. One of these albums (*The Country Blues of John Lee Hooker*) was issued at the time; the other, *Burning Hell*, wasn't issued until 1964, and then only in England (in 1992, it finally came out in the U.S. on CD). This is very similar to *Country Blues*, mixing originals with covers of tunes by Muddy Waters, Howlin' Wolf, Lightnin' Hopkins, and Big Bill Broonzy. To my ears it has a slight edge—the singing and performances sound a little more committed. But anyone who likes one LP will like the other, though neither ranks among the best of Hooker's one-man recordings. —*Richie Unterberger*

Hook: 20 Years of Hits / Chameleon ✦✦✦
Yet another Vee-Jay compilation, with the expected ("Boom Boom," "No Shoes," "Dimples") and a handful of lesser-known numbers ("You Ain't No Big Thing," "Nightmare") among its 16 selections. —*Bill Dahl*

King of the Boogie / Drive Archive ✦✦
Budget-priced 14-song expedition through the Vee-Jay motherlode, with mediocre sound quality on some tunes. "Boom Boom" and "Big Legs, Tight Skirt" rock hard, while these remakes of "Boogie Chillen" and "Crawlin' Kingsnake" don't emit the same naked emotion as the originals, but aren't bad by any means. —*Bill Dahl*

Lightnin' Hopkins (Sam Hopkins)

b. Mar. 15, 1912, Centerville, TX, **d.** Jan. 30, 1982, Houston, TX
Organ, Guitar, Piano, Vocals / Electric Texas Blues, Acoustic Texas Blues

Sam Hopkins was a Texas country bluesman of the highest caliber whose career began in the 1920s and stretched all the way into the 1980s. Along the way, Hopkins watched the genre change remarkably, but he never appreciably altered his mournful Lone Star sound, which translated onto both acoustic and electric guitar. Hopkins's nimble dexterity made intricate boogie riffs seem easy, and his fascinating penchant for improvising lyrics to fit whatever situation might arise made him a beloved blues troubadour.

Hopkins' brothers John Henry and Joel were also talented bluesmen, but it was Sam who became a star. In 1920, he met the legendary Blind Lemon Jefferson at a social function, and even got a chance to play with him. Later, Hopkins served as Jefferson's guide. In his teens, Hopkins began working with another pre-war great, singer Texas Alexander, who was his cousin. A mid-'30s stretch in Houston's County Prison Farm for the young guitarist interrupted their partnership for a time, but when he was freed, Hopkins hooked back up with the older bluesman.

The pair was dishing out their lowdown brand of blues in Houston's Third Ward in 1946 when talent scout Lola Anne Cullum came across them. She had already engineered a pact with Los Angeles-based Aladdin Records for another of her charges, pianist Amos Milburn, and Cullum saw the same sort of opportunity within Hopkins' dusty country blues. Alexander wasn't part of the deal; instead, Cullum paired Hopkins with pianist Wilson "Thunder" Smith, sensibly rechristened the guitarist Lightnin', and presto! Hopkins was very soon an Aladdin recording artist.

"Katie May," cut on November 9, 1946, in L.A. with Smith lending a hand on the 88s, was Lightnin' Hopkins' first regional seller of note. He recorded prolifically for Aladdin in both L.A. and Houston into 1948, scoring a national R&B hit for the firm with his "Shotgun Blues." "Short Haired Woman," "Abilene," and "Big Mama Jump," among many Aladdin gems, were evocative Texas blues rooted in an earlier era.

A load of other labels recorded the wily Hopkins after that, both in a solo context and with a small rhythm section—Modern/RPM (his uncompromising "Tim Moore's Farm" was an R&B hit in 1949), Gold Star (where he hit with "T-Model Blues" that same year), Sittin' in With ("Give Me Central 209" and "Coffee Blues" were national chart entries in 1952) and its Jax subsidiary, the major labels Mercury and Decca, and in 1954, a remarkable batch of sides for Herald where Hopkins played blistering electric guitar on a series of blasting rockers ("Lightnin's Boogie," "Lightnin's Special," the amazing "Hopkins' Sky Hop") in front of drummer Ben Turner and bassist Donald Cooks (who must have had bleeding fingers, so torrid were some of the tempos).

But Hopkins' style was apparently too rustic and old-fashioned for the new generation of rock & roll enthusiasts (they should have checked out "Hopkins' Sky Hop"). He was back on the Houston scene by 1959, largely forgotten. Fortunately, folklorist Mack McCormick rediscovered the guitarist, who was dusted off and presented as a folk-blues artist—a role that Hopkins was born to play. Pioneering musicologist Sam Charters produced Hopkins in a solo context for Folkways Records that same year, cutting an entire LP in Hopkins' tiny apartment (on a borrowed guitar). The results helped introduced his music to an entirely new audience.

Lightnin' Hopkins went from gigging at back-alley gin joints to starring at collegiate coffeehouses, appearing on TV programs and touring Europe to boot. His once-flagging recording career went right through the roof, with albums for World Pacific, Vee-Jay, Bluesville, Bobby Robinson's Fire label (where he cut his classic "Mojo Hand" in 1960), Candid, Arhoolie, Prestige, Verve, and in 1965, the first of several LPs for Stan Lewis' Shreveport-based Jewel logo.

Hopkins generally demanded full payment before he'd deign to sit down and record, and seldom indulged a producer's desire for more than one take of any song. His singular sense of country time befuddled more than a few unseasoned musicians; from the 1960s on, his solo work is usually preferable to band-backed material.

Filmmaker Les Blank captured the Texas troubadour's informal lifestyle most vividly in his acclaimed 1967 documentary, *The Blues Accordin' to Lightnin' Hopkins.* As one of the last great country bluesmen, Hopkins was a fascinating figure who bridged the gap between rural and urban styles. —*Bill Dahl*

Blues Train / 1951 / Mainstream ✦✦✦✦
Classic sides from Hopkins' 1950-1951 stint with Bobby Shad's Sittin' in With logo. The disc's 15 selections include two of his biggest hits, "Hello Central" and "Coffee Blues." —*Bill Dahl*

Lightnin' Hopkins / 1959 / Smithsonian/Folkways ✦✦✦✦✦
Lightnin' Hopkins was a master storyteller, underrated guitarist,

and marvelous performer whose albums could be irritating, inspirational, or uneven, but were seldom predictable or tepid. This 1959 session, reissued without bonus cuts or alternate takes, has mostly short, crisply narrated anecdotes or songs with ironic resolutions sung in Hopkins' usual declarative, wry tone. His "Reminiscences of Blind Lemon" spins one of his wonderful yarns, while "See That My Grave Is Clean" and "Bad Luck and Trouble" pivot around his sparse guitar and emphatic, dry vocals. —*Ron Wynn*

How Many More Years I Got / 1962 / Fantasy ✦✦✦
Repackaging of three earlier albums, *Walkin' This Road by Myself, Lightnin' & Co.* and *Smokes like Lightnin'.* Lightnin' plays electric with small band support on these sides, which probably come the closest to what he sounded like in the juke joints around Houston in the early '60s. —*Cub Koda*

Lightnin' Hopkins / 1962 / Smithsonian/Folkways ✦✦✦✦✦
This is Hopkins' initial "rediscovery" recording, taped in a rented room in Houston in 1959. Hundreds of recordings would follow in the '60s and '70s, but none are more quietly personal than this, perhaps the quintessential Hopkins album. The sound is fine; the music is essential.—*Mark A. Humphrey, Rock & Roll Disc.*

Blue Lightnin' / 1965 / Jewel ✦✦✦
After a slew of albums aimed primarily at the folk-blues audience that resuscitated his flagging career during the early '60s, Hopkins attempted to regain his original fan base with these unpretentious 1965 sessions for Stan Lewis' Jewel logo. Pretty convincingly, too, with the two-part "Move on Out" and a down-in-the-alley "Back Door Friend" among the standouts. Elmore Nixon, another Houston mainstay, plays piano on several cuts. —*Bill Dahl*

The Herald Material 1954 / 1988 / Collectables ✦✦✦✦✦
Lightnin' Hopkins in a heavily amplified mode (especially for 1954) and tearing it up with some of the wildest licks of his long and storied career! It's hard to fathom a more torrid tempo than the one he employs for "Hopkins' Sky Hop," and "Flash Lightnin'," "Lightnin's Boogie," and "Lightnin' Stomp" aren't far behind. Alas, Hopkins' Herald waxings didn't sell particularly well though they're downright astonishing in retrospect. —*Bill Dahl*

The Herald Recordings, Vol. 2 / 1989 / Collectables ✦✦✦✦
Hopkins left a ton of tapes behind at New York-based Herald Records—enough to support this second volume of 1954 gems. —*Bill Dahl*

Gold Star Sessions, Vol. 1 / 1991 / Arhoolie ✦✦✦✦✦
The first of two discs devoted to Hopkins' extensive recording activities during the late '40s for Bill Quinn's Gold Star logo. —*Bill Dahl*

Gold Star Sessions, Vol. 2 / 1991 / Arhoolie ✦✦✦✦✦
More wonderfully sparse ruminations by the Texas blues troubadour for Quinn's Gold Star label. Hopkins was amazingly prolific during his first few years of recording, and nearly everything he did back then has great artistic merit. —*Bill Dahl*

☆ **The Complete Aladdin Recordings** / 1991 / Aladdin/EMI ✦✦✦✦✦
This is where it all began for the Houston troubadour: 43 solo sides, as evocative and stark as any he ever did, from 1946-1948. The first 13 sides find the guitarist in tandem with pianist Wilson "Thunder" Smith (who handles the vocals on a few tracks), but after that, old Lightnin' Hopkins went the solo route. "Katie May," "Short Haired Woman," "Abilene," "Shotgun"—all these and more rate with his seminal performances. —*Bill Dahl*

☆ **Complete Prestige/Bluesville Recordings** / 1991 / Bluesville ✦✦✦✦✦
This seven-disc boxed set of Hopkins' complete Prestige/Bluesville recordings includes Sam Charters' brilliant liner notes. —*Jas Obrecht*

Sittin' in With / 1992 / Mainstream ✦✦✦✦
The second installment of Sittin' in With masters, some with bassist Donald Cooks and drummer Connie Kroll providing rock-solid support (L.C. Williams takes over as vocalist for two cuts). Supple boogies and dusty rural blues, all woven expertly by the Texas guitarist. —*Bill Dahl*

It's a Sin to Be Rich / 1993 / Verve ✦✦
It's a sin that these sloppy, uninspired 1972 tapes ever saw the

light of day. Hopkins and his cohorts (including John Lee Hooker, who also should have known better) stumble and bumble their way through some of the most disposable performances the guitarist ever knocked off. —*Bill Dahl*

Houston Bound / 1993 / Relic ✦✦✦✦
Thirteen of the last sides he cut for his former R&B audience. Under Bobby Robinson's tutelage, Hopkins' 1960 Fire sides rank with his finest—especially his boogie-based "Mojo Hand," a title he subsequently remade early and often. —*Bill Dahl*

★ **Mojo Hand: The Anthology** / May 18, 1993 / Rhino ✦✦✦✦✦
As with its John Lee Hooker two-disc set, Rhino offers a very pleasant way to begin serious appreciation of Hopkins' humongous recorded legacy with this 41-track anthology. His Aladdin, Gold Star, RPM, Sittin' in With, and Mercury output are all liberally sampled on disc one, and there are a half dozen of those electrifying 1954 Herald sides that verged on rock & roll. Disc two is a less exciting affair, those 1960s folk-blues and later efforts usually paling in comparison to seminal early works. Still, for a cogent overview of the guitarist's daunting discography, this is the place to start. —*Bill Dahl*

Lightnin' Hopkins, 1946–1960 / Da Music ✦✦✦
21 songs from, as the title indicates, 1946 to 1960, mostly Lightnin' solo on guitar, although there are occasional additional instruments. This rather scattershot anthology isn't the best way to collect Hopkins. On the other hand, if you're not concerned with building a comprehensive discography, it's not a bad pickup, including an hour of decent music. —*Richie Unterberger*

Big Walter "Shakey" Horton

b. Apr. 6, 1917, Horn Lake, MS, d. Dec. 8, 1981, Chicago, IL
Harmonica, Vocals / Electric Chicago Blues
Big Walter "Shakey" Horton is one of the all-time great blues harp (harmonica) players. Along with Little Walter, Horton defined modern amplified Chicago-style harmonica. There is no harp player (and that includes Little Walter) with Horton's big tone and spacious sense of time. Horton (who is said to have been somewhat shy) was not a natural group leader and therefore has produced few solo albums. His best work is as a sideman; his backup harmonica and virtuoso harp solos have graced many great Chicago blues recordings—turning an otherwise good cut into a dynamite jam.

Walter is the master of the single note and his characteristic walking bass line (usually with a deep tone and selection of notes that is unsurpassed) is instantly recognizable. As an accompanist, he has few equals. His backup harp is always unobtrusive yet bright and fresh—enhancing whatever else is going on. Give Big Walter a chance to solo and you are in for some of the most tasteful lines Chicago-style harp has ever produced. He made a specialty of playing entire tunes (often in blues style) on the harmonica ("La Cucaracha," "Careless Love," "I Almost Lost My Mind," etc). This might sound trite, but give them a listen. You'll see.

As for harmonicas, he used Hohner's Marine Band. He was just as comfortable playing first position (A harp in the key of A) as with the more standard cross harp (D harp in the key of A). He did not do much with chromatic harmonicas. Although Big Walter could play in the style of other harp players (and was often asked to do so), he has no credible imitators. He is one of a kind.

Walter Horton was born in Horn Lake, MS (April 6, 1917), but his mother soon moved to Memphis where Walter taught himself how to play the harmonica at five years of age. He later learned more about his instrument by working with harp players Will Shade and Hammie Nixon.

In the late '20s, he performed and recorded with the Memphis Jug Band (1927) and generally worked the Southern dance and juke-joint circuit as well as Memphis street corners. Horton moved to Chicago in the late '40s, but was often to be found back in Memphis for recording dates with Sun and Modern/RPM labels. He claimed to be blowing amplified harp as early as 1940, which would make him the first. Johnny Shines recalls that Sonny Boy Williamson (Rice Miller) used to come to Walter for lessons. He also says that he used the name "Little Walter" before the Little Walter Jacobs did, but gave it up to Jacobs. Jacobs acknowledges that he "ran" with Big Walter in Memphis during the 1940s. Horton later called himself "Big

Walter" to distinguish himself. The term "Shakey" came from the way he moved his head while playing.

He recorded four sides in 1951 for the Modern/RPM label under the name "Mumbles," but was not fond of that moniker. It was not until 1953 that he really left Memphis and relocated to Chicago to work as a sideman with his friend Eddie Taylor. He soon joined the Muddy Waters band (replacing Junior Wells, who had been drafted into the military) and played with Muddy for about a year.

Over the next few years, Horton worked with Chicago blues artists such as Johnny Shines, Jimmy Rogers, and Otis Rush—both in the Chicago blues clubs and at record studios. He recorded with Chess, Cobra, and States throughout the 1950s. During the 1960s, Horton continued to work with Jimmy Rogers, Shines, Tampa Red, Big Mama Thornton, Robert Nighthawk, Johnny Young, and Howlin' Wolf. In the 1970s, Walter was active in the blues clubs, in recording studios, and also began to appear at blues and folk festivals—primarily with Willie Dixon's Blues All-Stars. He died in Chicago on Dec. 8, 1981, and was inducted into the Blues Foundation's Hall of Fame in 1982.

While his early acoustic recordings in Memphis (1951–1954) are excellent, it is the recordings from the late '50s and mid-'60s that are unrivaled. When Horton's music is discussed in print, often the reference is to his later albums on Blind Pig (*Can't Keep Lovin' You* and *Fine Cuts*) and Alligator (*Big Walter Horton with Carey Bell*). I don't want to take anything away from these albums, but this is not what has made Walter a legend. Here is what has:

The recording of "Easy" with guitarist Jimmy DeBerry (recorded by Sam Phillips of Sun Records in the early '50s) is a striking harp instrumental that remains unrivaled for sheer power. For a superb example of Big Walter playing behind Muddy Waters (and soloing), try the cut "Mad Love (I Want You to Love Me)" that was recorded in 1953. Walter also plays on the classic Jimmy Rogers tune "Walking by Myself," on the Otis Rush tune "I Can't Quit You Baby," and many others. Also hear great Walter on the Flyright album, *Johnny Shines & Robert Lockwood, Joe Hill Louis: The Be-Bop Boy* on Bear Family, *Memphis Harmonica 1951–1954* on Sun, and *The Blues Came Down from Memphis* on Charly. This last album contains the incredible instrumental, "Easy."

Walter's singing is seldom mentioned except in an apologetic way. This is something I have never understood. I love to hear Walter sing and his singing style has all the elements of his harp playing, in particular, sincerity and (above all) humor. Make a point to listen to some Big Walter songs like "Need My Baby," "Everybody's Fishin',"and "Have a Good Time." They are priceless. His original recording of "Hard Hearted Woman" on the album *Chicago Blues—the Early Fifties* (Blues Classics) never fails to raise the hair on the back of my neck. His hard-to-find first album for Chess, *The Soul of Blues Harmonica*, is also worth a listen, although not definitive.

But if you want to hear Walter at his best, pick up the Vanguard CD *Chicago/The Blues/Today!, Volume 3* and listen to the music Walter lays down. Both as backup harp and in solos, this is not only classic Big Walter, but Chicago blues at its finest—not to be missed. The music on this album is incredible—Horton's contrapuntal backup harp seems to float in the background, loping along, always stretching and opening up the time. And Horton's taste in notes and depth of tone is unparalleled in the history of amplified Chicago-style harmonica. As Willie Dixon says, "Big Walter is the best harmonica player I ever heard." I agree. He was the man. —*Michael Erlewine*

The Soul of Blues Harmonica / Jan. 13, 1964 / MCA/Chess ✦✦✦
Big Walter's first album and with an all star cast—Buddy Guy (guitar), Jack Myers (bass), Willie Dixon (vocals), and Willie Smith (drums). Although not definitive, this album is worth seeking out for Horton fans. It features Walter in a variety of musical styles, including a good rendition of "Hard Hearted Woman" and a wild version of "La Cucaracha." —*Michael Erlewine*

★ **Chicago/The Blues/Today!, Vol. 3** / 1967 / Vanguard ✦✦✦✦✦
One of the all-time great blues albums. Period. It features Big Walter with the Johnny Shines Blues Band, the Johnny Young South Side Blues Band, and Big Walter Horton's Blues Harp Band (with Charlie Musselwhite). The timing and sense of musi-

cal spaciousness is incredible. Walter's backup harp and harmonica solos mark a high point in his career. A must hear. — *Michael Erlewine*

Offer You Can't Refuse [1 Side] / 1972 / Red Lightnin' ✦✦✦
This album released on the Red Lightnin' label in 1972 consists of one side of Big Walter Horton and the other side with very early Paul Butterfield (1963) (See: Paul Butterfield). The Horton side consists of eight tracks of Horton with guitarist Robert Nighthawk (no bass or drums). Nighthawk is playing pure backup here, very little else. It is not clear when these were recorded. Perhaps not classic Walter, but any Big Walter is worth a listen. There are three instrumentals that make for good listening, including a version of "Easy" (not up to the original Walter recording). The instrumental "West Side Blues" has some interesting Walter harp licks that I have not heard elsewhere. The other five cuts are Walter singing. Of these, there is a great version of "Louise" and Walter singing "Tin Pan Alley" which never fails to raise the hair on the back of my neck. If you can find this album, it is good to have. —*Michael Erlewine*

Live at the El Mocambo / 1973 / Red Lightnin' ✦
Recorded at the El Mocambo Club in Toronto on July 25, 1973, this is not vintage Horton. —*Michael Erlewine*

Big Walter Horton with Carey Bell / Jan. 1973 / Alligator ✦✦✦✦
The teacher/pupil angle might be a bit unwieldy here—Bell was already a formidable harpist in his own right by 1972, when Horton made this album—but there's no denying that a stylistic bond existed between the two. A showcase for the often recalcitrant harp master, and only his second domestic set as a leader. —*Bill Dahl*

Fine Cuts / Apr. 1979 / Blind Pig ✦✦✦✦✦
This is perhaps the best of the later Horton material from the late '70s when he was working with John Nicholas. Horton reworks many of his earlier classics including "Everybody's Fishin'," "Need My Baby," and "La Cucaracha." Not as riveting as the originals, but any Big Walter is worth a listen. —*Michael Erlewine*

Little Boy Blue / 1980 / JSP ✦✦✦
A 1980 live recording in Boston. Working with a pickup band consisting of Ronnie Earl on guitar, Mudcat Ward on bass, and Ola Dixon on drums, Horton catches fire and quite simply blows his heart out. The album features some of Horton's best late-period playing. —*Cub Koda*

Harmonica Blues Kings / May 1987 / Pearl Flapper ✦✦✦✦✦
Six cuts (one side) of an album shared with Alfred Harris. This is very early amplified Walter, recorded in the fall of 1954 for the Black-owned United/States labels. On four of the cuts, Big Walter is playing backup harp and solos for singer Tommy Brown; the other two cuts represent Big Walter's first Chicago record under his own name. Includes the definitive recording of the classic Walter tune "Hard Hearted Woman." —*Michael Erlewine*

Mouth Harp Maestro / 1988 / Ace ✦✦✦✦✦
These 16 cuts are from the Sam Phillips recordings from the early '50s. Features Walter on acoustic harp. Contains many of the same cuts on the Kent/Crown album, but lacks the amplified songs given there. —*Michael Erlewine*

Can't Keep Lovin' You / 1989 / Blind Pig ✦✦✦
Probably from the mid-'70s, this is later Horton, with John Nicholas on guitar and Ron Levy on piano. The album features a variety of material, including a good version of "Hard Hearted Woman." Not vintage, but worth a listen. —*Michael Erlewine*

Memphis Recordings 1951 / 1991 / Kent ✦✦✦✦
These are the Modern/Cobra masters—17 cuts from the sessions Walter did with Sam Phillips in 1951, including several alternate takes. This is mostly great acoustic harp, but it does contain the songs "Have a Good Time," and "Need My Baby" with Walter playing amplified harp—and great songs and solos these are! Worth finding. —*Michael Erlewine*

Son House

b. Mar. 21, 1902, Riverton, MS, d. Oct. 19, 1988, Detroit, MI
Guitar, Vocals / Acoustic Delta Blues
Son House's place, not only in the history of Delta blues, but in the overall history of the music, is a very high one indeed. He was a major innovator of the Delta style, along with his playing partners Charlie Patton and Willie Brown. Few listening experiences in the blues are as intense as hearing one of Son House's original 1930s recordings for the Paramount label. Entombed in a hailstorm of surface noise and scratches, one can still be awe struck by the emotional fervor House puts into his singing and slide playing. Little wonder then, that the man became more than just an influence on some White English kid with a big amp; he was the main source of inspiration to both Muddy Waters and Robert Johnson, and it doesn't get much more pivotal than *that*. Even after his rediscovery in the mid-'60s, House was such a potent musical force that what would have been a normally genteel performance by any other bluesmen in a 'folk' setting, turned into a night in the nastiest juke joint you could imagine, scaring the daylights out of young White enthusiasts expecting something far more prosaic and comfortable. Not out of Son House, no sir. When the man hit the downbeat on his National steel bodied guitar and you saw his eyes disappear into the back of his head, you *knew* you were going to hear some blues. And when he wasn't shouting the blues, he was singing spirituals, a cappella. Right up to the end, no bluesman was torn between the sacred and the profane more than Son House.

He was born Eddie James House, Jr., on March 21, 1902, in Riverton, MS. By the age of 15, he was preaching the gospel in various Baptist churches as the family seemingly wandered from one plantation to the next. He didn't even bother picking up a guitar until he turned 25; to quote House, "I didn't like no guitar when I first heard it; oh gee, I couldn't stand a guy playin' a guitar. I didn't like *none* of it." But if his ambivalence to the instrument was obvious, even more obvious was the simple fact that Son hated plantation labor even more and had developed a taste for corn whiskey. After drunkenly launching into a blues at a house frolic in Lyon, MS, one night and picking up some coin for doing it, the die seemed to be cast; Son House may have been a preacher, but he was part of the blues world now.

If the romantic notion that the blues life is a life full of trouble, then Son found a barrel of it one night at another house frolic in Lyon. He shot a man dead that night and was immediately sentenced to imprisonment at Parchman Farm. He ended up only serving two years of his sentence, with his parents both lobbying hard for his release, claiming self defense. Upon his release—after a Clarksdale judge told him never to set foot in town again—he started a new life in the Delta as a full time man of the blues.

After hitchhiking and hoboing the rails, he made it down to Lula, MS, and ran into the most legendary character the blues had to offer at that point, the one and only Charlie Patton. The two men couldn't have been less similar in disposition, stature and in musical and performance outlook if they had purposely planned it that way. Patton was described as a funny, loud-mouthed little guy, who was a noisy, passionate showman, using every trick in the book to win over a crowd. The tall and skinny House was by nature a gloomy man, with a saturnine disposition who still felt extremely guilt-ridden about playing the blues and working in juke joints. Yet when he ripped into one, Son imbued it with so much raw feeling that the performance *became* the show itself, sans gimmicks. The two of them argued and bickered constantly, and the only thing these two men seemed to have in common was a penchant for imbibing whatever alcoholic potable came their way. Though House would later refer in interviews to Patton as a 'jerk' and other unprintables, it was Patton's success as a bluesman—both live and especially on record—that got Son's foot in the door as a recording artist. He followed Patton up to Grafton, WI, and recorded a handful of sides for the Paramount label. These records today (selling scant few copies in their time, and the few that did surviving a life of huge steel needles, even bigger scratches and generally lousy care) are some of the most highly prized collector's items of Delta blues recordings, much tougher to find than, say, a Robert Johnson or even a Charlie Patton 78. Paramount used a pressing compound for their 78 singles that was so noisy and inferior sounding, that should someone actually come across a clean copy of any of Son's original recordings, it's a pretty safe bet that the listener would still be greeted with a blizzard of surface noise once the needle made contact with the disc.

But audio concerns aside, the absolutely demonic performances House laid down on these three two-part 78s ("My Black Mama," "Preachin' the Blues, and "Dry Spell Blues," with an unreleased test acetate of "Walkin' Blues" showing up decades later) cut through the hisses and pops like a brick through a stained glass window.

It was those recordings that led Alan Lomax to his door in 1941 to record him for the Library of Congress. Lomax was cutting acetates on a "portable" recording machine weighing over 300 pounds. Son was still playing (actually at the peak of his powers, some would say), but had backed off of it a bit since Charlie Patton died in 1934. House did some tunes solo, as Lomax asked him to do, but also cut a session backed by a rocking little string band. As the band laid down long and loose (some tracks went on for over six minutes) versions of their favorite numbers, all that was missing was the guitars being plugged in and a drummer's back beat and you were getting a glimpse of the future of the music.

But just as House had gone a full decade without recording, this time after the Lomax recordings he just as quickly disappeared, moving to Rochester, NY. When folk blues researchers finally found him in 1964, he was cheerfully exclaiming that he hadn't touched a guitar in years. One of the researchers, a young guitarist named Alan Wilson (later of the blues-rock group Canned Heat, literally sat down and retaught Son House how to play like Son House. Once the old master was up to speed, the festival and coffeehouse circuit became his oyster. He recorded again, the recordings becoming an important introduction to his music and for some, a lot easier to take than those old Paramount 78s from a strict audio standpoint. In 1965, he played Carnegie Hall and four years later found himself the subject of an eponymously-titled film documentary, all of this another world removed from Clarksdale, MS, indeed. Everywhere he played, he was besieged by young fans, asking him about Robert Johnson, Charlie Patton, and others. For young White blues fans, these were merely exotic names from the past, heard only to them on old, highly prized recordings; for Son House they were flesh and blood contemporaries, not just some names on a record label. Hailed as the greatest living Delta singer still actively performing, nobody dared call themselves the king of the blues as long as Son House was around.

He fell into ill health by the early '70s; what was later diagnosed as both Alzheimer's and Parkinson's disease first affected his memory and his ability to recall songs onstage and later, his hands, which shook so bad he finally had to give up the guitar and eventually live performing altogether by 1976. He lived quietly in Detroit, MI, for another 12 years, passing away on October 19, 1988. His induction into the Blues Foundation's Hall of Fame in 1980 was no less than his due. Son House *was* the blues. —*Cub Koda*

Blues from the Mississippi Delta / Aug. 1964 / Smithsonian/ Folkways ◆◆◆◆◆

Legendary Son House: Father of the Folk Blues / 1965 / CBS ◆◆◆◆◆
Although not at his strongest during the "rediscovery" phase, Son House could still sing and play riveting country blues in the mid-'60s. This features him doing well-known and obscure material in nearly the same manner as when he was defining the genre during the 1930s. —*Ron Wynn*

☆ **Son House & the Great Delta Blues Singers** / 1990 / Document ◆◆◆◆◆
With stunning vocals, the complete 1930 session includes Willie Brown, Rube Lacy, and others. (Import) —*Jas Obrecht*

Delta Blues / 1991 / Biograph ◆◆◆◆◆
In 1941 and 1942, folklorist Alan Lomax recorded these sides on House on a pair of field trips with a bulky, 300-pound acetate cutting machine for the Library of Congress. House was in peak form and the sides Lomax recorded are absolutely revelatory. The 1941 session finds him in the company of a driving little string band combo with the legendary Willie Brown (the man mentioned in Robert Johnson's "Crossroads") on second guitar. The effect of hearing Son House in this context is fairly astounding. The 1942 batch are solo recordings and equally as riveting. While there's other versions of these sides available in import form, the sound on this Biograph features the best sound restoration. —*Cub Koda*

● **Father of the Delta Blues: The Complete 1965 Sessions** / 1992 / CBS ◆◆◆◆◆
After being rediscovered by the folk-blues community in the early '60s, Son House rose to the occasion and recorded this

magnificent set of performances. Allowed to stretch out past the shorter running time of the original 78s, House turns in wonderful, steaming performances of some of his best-known material. On some tracks, House is supplemented by folk-blues researcher/musician Alan Wilson, who would later become a member of the blues-rock group Canned Heat and here plays some nice second guitar and harmonica on several cuts. This two-disc set features alternate takes, some unissued material and some studio chatter from producer John Hammond, Sr. that ocassionally hints at the chaotic nature inherent to some of these '60s "rediscovery" sessions. While not as overpowering as his earlier work (what could be?), all of these sides are so power-packed with sheer emotional involvement from House, they're an indispensable part of his canonade. —*Cub Koda*

Masters of the Delta Blues: the Friends of Charlie Patton / 1994 / Yazoo ◆◆◆◆◆
If you've only heard Son House's 1965 rediscovery recordings for Columbia (or his excellent 1941–1942 Library of Congress sessions), boy, are you in for a shock. This various artists compilation collects House's original 1930 recordings for the Paramount label, some of the rarest and hardest-to-find 78s in blues history. Recorded in Grafton, WI, House sounds positively demonic on the six issued titles (all of them two-part numbers, each being a separate take, rather than a single performance spread over both sides of a single) and with the inclusion of a previously unissued test acetate of "Walking Blues," this is the most complete document of his first recording session that has survived on this important Delta bluesman. The original Paramount 78s were always considered of inferior pressing quality even back in the days when turntables were called victrolas and the hailstorm of surface noise on these sides seems by and large resistant to all forms of modern noise reduction devices employed here. But House's performances here cut through the crackles, pops and hisses like slicing up a cold stick of butter with a soldering iron. Absolutely indispensable. —*Cub Koda*

Delta Blues and Spirituals / Oct. 1995 / Capitol ◆◆◆◆◆

★ **Delta Blues** / Biograph ◆◆◆◆◆
All of the recordings Alan Lomax made of Son House in 1941 and 1942 are collected on this essential CD. —*Stephen Thomas Erlewine*

Bee Houston

b. Apr. 19, 1938, San Antonio, TX
Guitar, Vocals / Texas Blues
Guitarist/vocalist Edward Wilson "Bee" Houston's an exciting performer whose style blends elements of Texas shuffle blues and Southern gospel-tinged soul. Houston played in a high school drum and bugle corps as a youngster in San Antonio, and played in the backing bands of Little Willie John, Junior Parker, Bobby "Blue" Bland and others in the late '50s and early '60s. After a two-year Army stint, Houston moved to the West Coast. He toured and recorded frequently with Big Mama Thornton in the '60s, and also accompanied several visiting blues players during West Coast visits. Houston recorded for Arhoolie in the '60s and '70s, and also made several festival appearances and club dates. —*Ron Wynn*

Bee Houston: His Guitar & Band / 1981 / Arhoolie ◆◆◆
While not an instrumental giant, Bee Houston made many delightful and very explosive recordings. He seldom did covers, and this collection has several enjoyable originals. —*Ron Wynn*

Frank Hovington

b. Jan. 9, 1919, Reading, PA
Vocals, Guitar, Ukulele, Banjo / Country Blues
A tremendous country blues musician who was singing vividly and playing with flair well after the genre's heyday, Franklin "Frank" Hovington started on ukulele and banjo as a child. He teamed with Willliam Walker in the late '30s and '40s playing at house parties and dances in Frederica, PA. Hovington moved to Washington D.C. in the late '40s, and backed such groups as the Stewart Dixon's Golden Stars and Ernest Ewin's Jubilee Four. He also worked with Billy Stewart's band. Hovington moved to Delware in 1967, then was recorded by Flyright in 1975. His 1975 LP was a masterpiece, and alerted many in the blues community to his abilities. —*Ron Wynn*

Lonsome Road Blues / 1975 / Rounder ◆◆◆◆◆
By the time Frank Hovington got a chance to record, the

folk/blues boom had passed and there was almost no interest in country blues except among academics. But that didn't stop him from making a definitive album, which compared favorably to the genre's classics done in a different era. It's a textbook case of the right stuff at the wrong time. —*Ron Wynn*

Camille Howard

b. Mar. 29, 1914
Piano, Vocals / Jump Blues
Piano-tinkling chanteuses were quite the rage during the war years. But Camille Howard's two-fisted thundering boogie style, much like her Los Angeles contemporary, Hadda Brooks, was undoubtedly the equivalent of any 88s ace, male or female.

Howard was part of the great migration from Texas to the West Coast. She was installed as pianist with drummer Roy Milton & the Solid Senders sometime during World War II, playing on all their early hits for Art Rupe's Juke Box and Specialty labels (notably the groundbreaking "R.M. Blues" in 1945).

Sensing her potential following the success of Milton's 1947 hit "Thrill Me" (with Howard's vocal), Rupe began recording her as a featured artist at the end of the year. Legend has it that Howard's biggest hit, the roaring instrumental "X-Temporaneous Boogie," was improvised at the tail end of her first date as a leader (its flip, the torch ballad "You Don't Love Me," was a hit in its own right).

Howard's vocal abilities were pretty potent too. Her "Fiesta in Old Mexico" was a hit in 1949, while "Money Blues," credited to Camille Howard & Her Boyfriends, registered strong coin in 1951. Howard cranked out storming boogies and sultry ballads for Specialty through 1953, then jumped from Federal to Vee-Jay before landing in Los Angeles for good. Howard's strong religious ties put a stop to her secular music career long ago. —*Bill Dahl*

● Rock Me Daddy, Vol. 1 / 1993 / Specialty ◆◆◆◆◆
25-song reissue of her 1947-52 Specialty material, about half previously unreleased. Includes "You Don't Love Me" and "Money Blues," but not the chart items "Fiesta In Mexico" and "XTemporaneous Boogie." Perhaps too suave and refined for the R&B/rock era, as comfortable with jazzy ballads as boogies, Howard was nonetheless an important, and nowadays overlooked, star of the transitional era between jump blues and R&B. —*Richie Unterberger*

X-Temporaneous Boogie, Vol. 2 / 1996 / Specialty ◆◆◆◆◆
Twenty of these 25 sides, recorded for Specialty between 1947 and 1952, were previously unissued. But there's no difference in quality between these and the better-known ones presented on Volume one; the label's decision on what to release was based more on marketing strategies than the level of the performances. Divided between instrumentals and pop-influenced vocal numbers, Howard again proves herself the master of boogie and jump blues piano styles, sometimes slowing things down into a jazzier mode. In addition to the storehouse of vault material, this compilation also includes a couple of late-'40s Top Ten R&B hits, "Thrill Me" and "X-Temporaneous Boogie." —*Richie Unterberger*

Howlin' Wolf (Chester Arthur Burnett)

b. Jun. 10, 1910, West Point, MS, d. Jan. 10, 1978, Hines, IL
Guitar, Harmonica, Vocals / Electric Chicago Blues
In the history of the blues, there has never been anyone quite like the Howlin' Wolf. Six foot three and close to 300 pounds in his salad days, the Wolf was the primal force of the music spun out to its ultimate conclusion. A Robert Johnson may have possessed more lyrical insight, a Muddy Waters more dignity, and a B.B. King certainly more technical expertise, but no one could match him for the singular ability to rock the house down to the foundation while simultaneously scaring its patrons out of its wits.

He was born in West Point, Mississippi and named after the 21st President of the United States. His father was a farmer and Wolf took to it as well until his 18th birthday, when a chance meeting with Delta blues legend Charlie Patton changed his life forever. Though he never came close to learning the subtleties of Patton's complex guitar technique, two of the major components of Wolf's style (Patton's inimitable growl of a voice and his propensity for entertaining) were learned first-hand from the Delta blues master. The main source of Wolf's hard-driving, rhythmic style on harmonica came when Aleck "Rice" Miller

(Sonny Boy Williamson) married his half-sister Mary and taught him the rudiments of the instrument. He first started playing in the early '30s as a strict Patton imitator, while others recall him at decades' end rocking the juke joints with a neck-rack harmonica and one of the first electric guitars anyone had ever seen. After a four-year stretch in the Army, he settled down as a farmer and weekend player in West Memphis, AR, and it was here that Wolf's career in music began in earnest.

By 1948, he had established himself within the community as a radio personality. As a means of advertising his own local appearances, Wolf had a 15-minute radio show on KWEM in West Memphis, interspersing his down-home blues with farm reports and like-minded advertising that he sold himself. But a change in Wolf's sound that would alter everything that came after was soon in coming, because when listeners tuned in for Wolf's show, the sound was up-to-the-minute electric. Wolf had put his first band together, featuring the explosive guitar work of Willie Johnson, whose aggressive style not only perfectly suited Wolf's sound, but aurally extended and amplified the violence and nastiness of it as well. In any discussion of Wolf's early success–both live, over the airwaves and on record–the importance of Willie Johnson cannot be overestimated.

Wolf finally started recording in 1951, when he caught the ear of Sam Phillips, who first heard him on his morning radio show. The music Wolf made in the Memphis Recording Service studio was full of passion and zest and Phillips simultaneously leased the results to the Bihari brothers in Los Angeles and Leonard Chess in Chicago. Suddenly Howlin' Wolf had two hits at the same time on the R&B charts with two record companies claiming to have him exclusively under contract. Chess finally won him over and as Wolf would proudly relate years later, "I had a four-thousand dollar car and $3,900 in my pocket. I'm the oniliest one drove out of the South like a gentleman." It was the winter of 1953 and Chicago would be his new home.

When Wolf entered the Chess studios the next year, the violent aggression of the Memphis sides was being replaced with a Chicago backbeat and, with very little fanfare, a new member in the band. Hubert Sumlin proved himself to be the Wolf's longest-running musical associate. He first appears as a rhythm guitarist on a 1954 session, and within a few years' time his style had fully matured to take over the role of lead guitarist in the band by early 1958. In what can only be described as an "angular attack," Sumlin played almost no chords behind Wolf, sometimes soloing right through his vocals, featuring wild skitterings up and down the fingerboard and biting single notes. If Willie Johnson was Wolf's second voice in his early recording career, then Hubert Sumlin would pick up the gauntlet and run with it right to the end of the howler's life.

By 1956, Wolf was in the R&B charts again, racking up hits with "Evil" and "Smokestack Lightnin'." He remained a top attraction both on the Chicago circuit and on the road. His records, while seldom showing up on the national charts, were still selling in decent numbers down South. But by 1960, Wolf was teamed up with Chess staff writer Willie Dixon and for the next five years, he would record almost nothing but songs written by Dixon. The magic combination of Wolf's voice, Sumlin's guitar, and Dixon's tunes sold a lot of records and brought the 50-year-old bluesman roaring into the next decade with a considerable flourish. The mid-'60s saw him touring Europe regularly with "Smokestack Lightnin'" becoming a hit in England some eight years after its American release. Certainly any list of Wolf's greatest sides would have to include "I Ain't Superstitious," "The Red Rooster," "Shake for Me," "Back Door Man," "Spoonful," and "Wang Dang Doodle," Dixon compositions all. While almost all of them would eventually become Chicago blues standards, their greatest cache occurred when rock bands the world over started mining the Chess catalog for all it was worth. One of these bands was the Rolling Stones, whose cover of "The Red Rooster" became a number one record in England. At the height of the British Invasion, the Stones came to America in 1965 for an appearance on ABC-TV's rock music show, *Shindig.* Their main stipulation for appearing on the program was that Howlin' Wolf would be their special guest. With the Stones sitting worshipfully at his feet, the Wolf performed a storming version of "How Many More Years," being seen on his network TV debut by an audience of a few million. Wolf never forgot the respect the Stones paid him, and he spoke of them highly right up to his final days.

Dixon and Wolf parted company by 1964 and Wolf was back in the studio doing his own songs. One of the classics to emerge from this period was "Killing Floor," featuring a modern backbeat and a incredibly catchy guitar riff from Sumlin. Catchy enough for Led Zeppelin to appropriate it for one of their early albums, cheerfully crediting it to themselves in much the same manner as they had done with numerous other blues standards. By the end of the decade, Wolf's material was being recorded by artists including the Doors, the Electric Flag, the Blues Project, Cream, and Jeff Beck. The result of all these covers brought Wolf the belated acclaim of a young White audience. Chess' response to this was to bring him into the studio for a "psychedelic" album, truly the most dreadful of his career. His last big payday came when Chess sent him over to England in 1970 to capitalize on the then-current trend of *London Session* albums, recording with Eric Clapton on lead guitar and other British superstars. Wolf's health was not the best, but the session was miles above the earlier, ill-advised attempt to update Wolf's sound for a younger audience.

As the '70s moved on, the end of the trail started coming closer. By now Wolf was a very sick man; he had survived numerous heart attacks and was suffering kidney damage from an automobile accident that sent him flying through the car's windshield. His bandleader Eddie Shaw firmly rationed Wolf to a meager half-dozen songs per set. Ocassionally some of the old fire would come blazing forth from some untapped wellspring and his final live and studio recordings show that he could still tear the house apart when the spirit moved him. He entered the Veterans Administration Hospital in 1976 to be operated on, but passed away on January 10th of that year.

But his passing did not go unrecognized. A life-size statue of him was erected shortly after in a Chicago park. Eddie Shaw kept his memory and music alive by keeping his band, the Wolf Gang, together for several years afterward. A child-education center in Chicago was named in his honor and in 1980 he was elected to the Blues Foundation Hall of Fame. In 1991, he was inducted into the Rock and Roll Hall of Fame. A couple of years later, his face was on a United States postage stamp. Live performance footage of him exists in the CD-ROM computer format. Howlin' Wolf is now a permanent part of American history. —*Cub Koda*

The Real Folk Blues / 1963 / MCA/Chess ✦✦✦✦✦
This was originally released by Chess in 1966 to capitalize on the then-current folk music boom. The music, however—a collection of Wolf singles from 1956 to 1965—is full-blown electric featuring a nice sampling of Wolf originals with a smattering of Willie Dixon tunes. Some of the man's best middle-period work is aboard here; "Killing Floor," "Louise," the hair-raisingly somber "Natchez Burning," and Wolf's version of the old standard "Sitting on Top of the World," which would become his set closer in later years. The Mobile Fidelity version sounds as sonically sharp as anything you've ever heard on this artist and its heftier price tag is somewhat justified by the inclusion of two bonus cuts. But those on a budget who just want the music minus the high-minded audiophile concerns will be happy to note that this is also available as a Chess budget reissue. —*Cub Koda*

More Real Folk Blues / 1967 / MCA/Chess ✦✦✦✦
This companion volume to the *Real Folk Blues* album was issued in 1967 (after the Wolf had appeared on network television with the Rolling Stones, alluded to in the original liner notes) and couldn't be more dissimilar in content to the first one. Whereas the previous volume highlighted middle period Wolf, this one goes all the way back to his earliest Chess sessions, many of which sound like leftover Memphis sides. The chaotic opener, "Just My Kind," sets a familiar Wolf theme to a "Rollin' & Tumblin'" format played at breakneck speed and what the track lacks in fidelity is more than made up in sheer energy. For a classic example of Wolf's ensemble Chicago sound, it's pretty tough to beat "I Have a Little Girl" where the various members of his band seem to be all soloing simultaneously—not unlike a Dixieland band—right through Wolf's vocals. For downright scary, the demonic sounding "I'll Be Around" is an absolute must-hear. Wolf's harp solo on this slow blues is one of his best and the vocal that frames it sounds like the microphone is going to explode at any second. As soul singer Christine Ohlman commented upon hearing this track for the first time, "Boy, I'd sure hate to be the woman he's singing that one to." —*Cub Koda*

The London Howlin' Wolf Sessions / 1971 / MCA/Chess ✦✦
For the casual blues fan with a scant knowledge of the Wolf, this 1971 pairing, with Eric Clapton, Bill Wyman, and Charlie Watts from the Rolling Stones, Ringo Starr, and other British superstars, appears on the surface to be one hell of a super session. But those lofty notions are quickly dispelled once you slip this disc into the player and hit play. While it's nowhere near as awful as some blues purists make it out to be, the disparity of energy levels between the Wolf and his U.K. acolytes is not only palpable but downright depressing. Wolf was a very sick man at this juncture and Norman Dayron's non-production idea of just doing remakes of earlier Chess classics is wrongheaded in the extreme. The rehearsal snippet of Wolf trying to teach the band how to play Willie Dixon's "Little Red Rooster" shows just how far off the mark the whole concept of this rock superstar melange truly is. Even Eric Clapton, who usually welcomes *any* chance to play with one of his idols, has criticized this album repeatedly in interviews, which speaks volumes in and of itself. The rest of the leftover tracks are collected on the 1974 hodgepodge *London Revisited*, later repackaged for compact disc consumption as *Muddy & the Wolf*. Avoid both of these turkeys like the plague they are. —*Cub Koda*

Live & Cookin' at Alice's Revisited / 1972 / MCA/Chess ✦✦✦
A compact disc reissue of Wolf's 1972 live album with the addition of two stellar bonus cuts. The first one, "Big House," first showed up on a hodgepodge Wolf bootleg album from the '70s. Its non-appearance on the original abum is somewhat of a mystery since it's arguably one of the best performances here. Set at a medium tempo, Wolf stretches out comfortably for over seven minutes, singing certain verses he likes two or three times as the band locks in with deadly authority. Certainly any list of great Howlin' Wolf vocal performances would have to have to include this one. The second bonus track, "Mr. Airplane Man," is Wolf working his one-riff-fits-all voodoo for all it's worth. You can tell from note one of his vocal entrance that the pilot light of inspiration is fully lit and the ensuing performance is the Wolf at his howlin' best. Also of special note are the wild and wooly takes on "I Had a Dream," "I Didn't Know," and Muddy Waters' "Mean Mistreater." There are mistakes galore out of the band and some p.a. system feedback here and there, both of which only add to the charm of it all. A great document of Wolf toward the end, still capable of bringing the heat and rocking the house down to the last brick. —*Cub Koda*

London Revisited / 1974 / MCA/Chess ✦✦
Mediocre superstar collaboration. —*Bill Dahl*

Memphis Days . . . / 1989 / Bear Family ✦✦✦✦
These are Wolf's earliest and rarest sides recorded at the Sun studios, as raw and explosive as blues records come. Much of this was issued on various European albums during the '70s, always transferred off of muffled-sounding copy tapes. These 21 tracks (all but two of them off the master tapes) featuring the amp-on-11 guitar work of Willie Johnson and the cave man drumming of Willie Steele, are loose, somewhat chaotic with Wolf sounding utterly demonic. The real bonus on this volume is the first-time inclusion of both sides of the only known acetate of Wolf's first session at Sam Phillips' 706 Union Avenue studio from 1951. With only Johnson and Steele in support (no bass, no piano), these early versions of "How Many More Years" and "Baby Ride with Me (Riding in the Moonlight)" are Wolf at his most primitive. —*Cub Koda*

☆ **The Chess Box** / 1991 / MCA/Chess ✦✦✦✦✦
This three-CD box set currently rates as the best—and most digestible—overview of Wolf's career. Disc one starts with the Memphis sides that eventually brought him to the label, including hits like "How Many More Years," but also compiling unissued sides that had previously only been available on vinyl bootlegs of dubious origin and fidelity. The disc finishes with an excellent cross section of early Chicago sessions including classic Wolf tracks like "Evil," "Forty Four," "I'll Be Around," and "Who Will Be Next." Disc two picks it up from there guiding us from mid-to-late-'50s barnburners like "The Natchez Burnin'" and "I Better Go Now" to the bulk of the Willie Dixon classics. The final disc runs out the last of the Dixon sessions into mid-'60s classics like "Killing Floor," taking us to a nice selection of his final recordings. A really nice bonus on this box set is the inclusion on the first two discs of snippets from a 1968 Howlin' Wolf interview and two performances of Wolf playing solo

acoustic. If you've heard the sound of the Wolf, here's where you go to get a lot of it in one place. Definitely *not* the place to start (unless you have money to burn), but maybe just the perfect place to end up. —*Cub Koda*

☆ **Howlin' Wolf Rides Again** / 1993 / Flair-Virgin ✦✦✦✦✦
While both Bear Family sets deal with a largely unissued wealth of material, this collection is devoted in the main to all the Memphis recordings from 1951 and 1952 that saw the light of day on a number of Los Angeles-based labels owned by the Bihari brothers, being issued and reissued and reissued again on a plethora of $1.98 budget albums. Featuring recordings done in Sam Phillips' Memphis Recording Service and surreptitious sessions recorded by a young Ike Turner in makeshift studios, these 18 sides are the missing piece of the puzzle in absorbing Wolf's early pre-Chess period. It also helps that this just happens to be some of the nastiest sounding blues ever recorded. With no tracks being duplicated from the two Bear Family *Memphis Days* volumes, and sonics far surpassing all previous issues of this material (every last one of them horribly marred by an annoying 60 cycle hum), this is an essential part of any Wolf collection. Alternate take freaks will revel in the inclusion of two extra takes of "Riding in the Moonlight" from an earlier and different session than the issued version also included. While not *quite* as essential as his first two Chess albums (and if we were making a judgement call on just passionate perfomances alone, even *that* would be debatable), this is definitely the next stop along the way in absorbing the raw genius of Howlin' Wolf. — *Cub Koda*

Ain't Gonna Be Your Dog / 1994 / MCA/Chess ✦✦✦✦✦
This double-disc set features 42 rare and unissued performances, effectively cleaning out the Chess vaults of all but alternate takes of alternate takes. But these are no bottom-of-the-barrel scrapings here, quite the opposite. The first 14 tunes collect the remainder of his Memphis recordings for Sam Phillips while the rest does the bootleggers one better, compiling masters that were previously only available on bad-sounding '70s vinyl albums. There's another snippet from his 1968 interview along with four more acoustic numbers from that same session (done, it turns out, as a promotional piece of sorts to preview his "soon to be released psychedelic album," which Wolf always dismissed as "birds**t"), sadly the only time Chess ever tried to record him as a solo artist. A wonderful companion piece to any other Wolf collection you might own. —*Cub Koda*

★ **Howlin' Wolf/Moanin' in the Moonlight** / MCA/Chess ✦✦✦✦✦
Wolf's first and second Chess albums, released in 1959 and 1962 respectively, are essential listening of the highest order. Compiled—as were all early blues albums—from various single sessions (not necessarily a bad thing, either), blues fans will probably debate endlessly about which of these two albums is the perfect introduction to his music. But the MCA-Chess CD issue renders all arguments moot as both album appear on one disc, making this one of the true best buys around today. Wolf's debut opus—curiously tacked on here *after* his second album—features all of his early hits ("How Many More Years," "Moanin' at Midnight," "Smokestack Lightning," "Forty Four," "Evil," and "I Asked for Water [She Gave Me Gasoline]") and is a pretty potent collection in its own right. But it is the follow-up (always referred to as 'the rocking chair album' because of Don Bronstein's distinctive cover art) where the equally potent teaming of Willie Dixon and Wolf produced one Chicago Blues classic ("Spoonful," "The Red Rooster," "Back Door Man," and "Wang Dang Doodle") after another. It's also with this marvelous batch of sides that one can clearly hear lead guitarist Hubert Sumlin coming into his own as a blues picking legend. The number of blues acolytes, both Black and White, who wore the grooves down to mush learning the songs and guitar licks off these two albums would fill a book all by itself. If you have to narrow it down to just one Howlin' Wolf purchase for the collection, this would be the one to have and undoubtedly the place to start. This and *The Best of Muddy Waters* are the essential building blocks of any Chicago Blues collection. And seldom does the music come with this much personality and brute force. —*Cub Koda*

Live in Cambridge, 1966 / New Rose ✦
These are some absolutely horrible-sounding live recordings of a club date with Wolf and his band laying it down so tough and brutal that it almost negates this disc's woeful audio deficiencies. With Wolf, Hubert, and Eddie Shaw getting a high octane kick in

the pants from drummer Sam Lay, this thing rocks harder than most live blues albums have a right to. While it's a pity that it sounds so awful from a technical standpoint, it's even more amazing that it exists at all. Sumlin's playing on the slow blues "Tell Me What I've Done" is seven minutes of the wildest you'll ever hear out of him and the takes on "Dust My Broom" and "300 Pounds Of Joy" are no less explosive. For diehards, true believers and completists who have to have it all. —*Cub Koda*

Memphis Days: Definitive Edition, Vol. 2 / Bear Family ✦✦✦✦✦
The second volume in this series collects all the known Memphis recordings that were either issued or originally offered to Chess. As such, it stands as a marvelous collection of Wolf's early 78s for that label. But what truly puts it over is the added bonus of a newly discovered acetate featuring several unissued versions of "How Many More Years" and "Baby Ride With Me (Riding In The Moonlight)." Much of this volume is pulled from discs, but the overall sound is good and the performances make it yet another must-have. —*Cub Koda*

Joe Hughes

b. 1938, Houston, TX
Guitar, Vocals / Electric Texas Blues
Houston was homebase to a remarkable cadre of red-hot blues guitarists during the 1950s. Joe Hughes may not be known as widely as his peers Albert Collins and Johnny Copeland, but he's a solid journeyman with a growing discography.

Another of his Houston neighbors, Johnny "Guitar" Watson, lit a performing fire in a 14-year-old Hughes. Lone Star stalwarts T-Bone Walker and Gatemouth Brown also exerted their influence on Hughes' playing. His path crossed Copeland's circa 1953, when the two shared vocal and guitar duties in a combo called the Dukes of Rhythm. Hughes served as bandleader at a local blues joint known as Shady's Playhouse from 1958 through 1963, cutting a few scattered singles of his own in his spare time ("I Can't Go On This Way," "Ants in my Pants," "Shoe Shy"). In 1963, Hughes hit the road with the Upsetters, switching to the employ of Bobby "Blue" Bland in 1965 (he also recorded behind the singer for Duke) and Al "T.N.T." Braggs from 1967 to 1969.

A long dry spell followed, but Hughes finally came back to the spotlight with a fine set for Black Top in 1989, *If You Want to See the Blues* (by that time, he'd inserted a "Guitar" as his middle name, much like his old pal Watson). Hughes' latest set for Bullseye Blues, 1996's *Texas Guitar Slinger,* is a slashing blend of blues and soul with tightly arranged horns and more than enough axe to fulfill Hughes' adopted nickname. —*Bill Dahl*

Texas Guitar Master Craftsman / 1988 / Double Trouble ✦✦✦

● **If You Want to See These Blues** / 1989 / Black Top ✦✦✦✦✦
This contemporary of Albert Collins and Johnny Copeland only recently began accruing his own share of immortality—and it really started with this fine album, recorded in both New Orleans and Houston. Hughes' clean, crisp guitar work and hearty vocals may not be quite as distinctive as those of his Houston pals, but he's an authentic Texas blues guitarist all the way. —*Bill Dahl*

Texas Guitar Slinger / 1996 / Bullseye Blues ✦✦✦✦
The versatile Hughes at times slips a little soul influence into his Lone Star blues conception on this satisfying album. He stakes his undeniable claim as a "Texas Guitar Slinger" on one of the set's best songs, a gent who deserves enshrinement right alongside Johnny Copeland and Albert Collins. No argument there—he was there when they all got started. —*Bill Dahl*

Helen Humes

b. Jun. 23, 1913, Louisville, KY, **d.** Sep. 9, 1981, Santa Monica, CA
Vocals / Blues, Swing
Helen Humes was a versatile singer equally skilled on blues, swing standards, and ballads. Her cheerful style was always a joy to hear. As a child she played piano and organ in church and made her first recordings (ten blues in 1927) when she was only 13 and 14. In the 1930s she worked with Stuff Smith and Al Sears, recording with Harry James in 1937–38. In 1938 Humes joined Count Basie's Orchestra for three years. Since Jimmy Rushing specialized in blues, Helen Humes mostly got stuck singing pop ballads but she did a fine job. After freelancing in

New York (1941–43) and touring with Clarence Love (1943–44), Humes moved to Los Angeles. She began to record as a leader and had a hit in "Be-ba-ba-le-ba"; her 1950 original "Million Dollar Secret" is a classic. Humes sometimes performed with Jazz at the Philharmonic but was mostly a single in the 1950s. She recorded three superb albums for Contemporary during 1959–61 and had tours with Red Norvo. She moved to Australia in 1964, returning to the U.S. in 1967 to take care of her ailing mother. Humes was out of the music business for several years but made a full comeback in 1973 and stayed busy up until her death. Throughout her career Helen Humes recorded for such labels as Savoy, Aladdin, Mercury, Decca, Dootone, Contemporary, Classic Jazz, Black & Blue, Black Lion, Jazzology, Columbia, and Muse. —*Scott Yanow*

E-Baba-Le-Ba / Nov. 20, 1944–Nov. 20, 1950 / Savoy ◆◆◆◆
The rhythm and blues years, 1986 reissue of 1944 and 1950 sessions. Stomping, lusty cuts with Humes at her most down-and-dirty. Though she said she didn't sing blues, this is sure close to it. —*Ron Wynn*

Tain't Nobody's Biz-Ness If I Do / Jan. 5, 1959–Feb. 10, 1959 / Original Jazz Classics ◆◆◆◆◆
This Helen Humes date will lock in one's mind—because she was one of the immediately identifiable jazz stylists and because it was an excellent example, perhaps one of the best post-Count Basie days examples, of her work. Emotion, open, warm and swinging is what you've got here. —*Bob Rusch, Cadence*

★ **Songs I Like to Sing** / Sep. 6, 1960–Sep. 8, 1960 / Original Jazz Classics ◆◆◆◆◆
Nice, classy set from vocalist Helen Humes, who enjoyed success throughout her career singing everything from classic blues to jazz and gospel to rock. She sticks to jazz on this '60 date, doing both scat and sophisticated ballads. —*Ron Wynn*

Swingin' with Humes / Jul. 27, 1961–Jul. 29, 1961 / Original Jazz Classics ◆◆◆◆
A solid early '60s set by vocalist Helen Humes, doing a program of standards with a fine combo sparked by tenor saxophonist Teddy Edwards and trumpeter Joe Gordon. The four-member rhythm section includes pianist Wynton Kelly, guitarist Al Viola, bassist Leroy Vinnegar, and drummer Frank Butler. —*Ron Wynn*

Sneakin' Around / Mar. 16, 1974 / Classic Jazz ◆◆◆◆
Helen Humes did both bawdy, double-entendre-laden blues and R&B, and more sophisticated, jazz-tinged numbers during her career. This set, done with Gerald Badini, Gerry Wiggins, Major Holley, and Ed Thigpen, had a little of both, and was spiced up by Humes, singing with equal parts sass and grace. It was originally done for the Black and Blue label and was recently on CD. —*Ron Wynn*

On the Sunny Side of The Street / Jul. 2, 1974 / Black Lion ◆◆◆◆
Several major jazz personalities are heard on this Black Lion reissue CD, recorded live at the 1974 Montreux Jazz Festival. The fine singer Helen Humes sticks to standards and blues while accompanied by either Earl Hines or Jay McShann on piano, tenor saxophonist Buddy Tate, bassist Jimmy Woode, and drummer Ed Thigpen. Although Hines and McShann are not the ideal accompanists, Humes fares quite well, winning the audience over with her enthusiasm and sincerity. —*Scott Yanow*

Helen Humes: Talk of the Town / Feb. 18, 1975 / Columbia ◆◆◆◆
This Columbia session, done in 1975, came much closer to challenging Helen Humes, due largely to the sensitivity of producer John Hammond who truly understood Humes' musical element. Her "Talk Of The Town" was among the most memorable treatments of the tune since Coleman Hawkins' 1954 version for Vanguard. "Good For Nothing Joe" and "You've Changed" were nearly as impressive. Her renderings were straightfoward and totally unaffected, characteristics shared by the handful of great vocalists today. What gave them their unique mark, however, was the lilting innocence with which she graced even the most poignant lyric, lyrics that could sound self-pitying in lesser hands. —*John Mcdonough, Downbeat*

Helen Humes with Red Norvo and His Orchestra / Aug. 1975 / RCA ◆◆◆
This RCA LP, originally made in 1958, made re-available one of the finest vocal albums ever recorded, by Helen Humes or anyone else. Why was it so remarkable? First, the material was

superb, among the finest specimens of American popular music. And second, and most important, the arrangements by Shorty Rogers were among the most perfect matings of vocalist and orchestra ever devised. Norvo's sparkling vibes were the ideal compliment to Humes' lithe, light-timbred clarity. Rogers' reed voicings were cool, deft and softly reminiscent of The Four Brothers sound. Humes was also in particularly fine voice. In any case, this LP was the perfect Helen Humes session, the ideal marriage of performer, material, and the instrumental support. —*John Mcdonough, Downbeat*

Helen Humes and the Muse All Stars / Oct. 5, 1979+Oct. 8, 1978 / Muse ◆◆◆◆◆
Helen Humes' return to an active singing career was one of the happier events in jazz of the late '70s. Able to give great feeling and sensitivity to ballads but also a superb lowdown blues singer, Humes flourished musically during her last years. On this excellent release (the CD reissue adds two alternate takes to the original program), Humes matches wits with altoist/singer Eddie "Cleanhead" Vinson on "I'm Gonna Move to the Outskirts of Town" and is in top form throughout. Tenors Arnett Cobb and Buddy Tate (along with a fine rhythm section led by pianist Gerald Wiggins) don't hurt either. An enthusiastic "Loud Talking Woman" and "My Old Flame" are highpoints. —*Scott Yanow*

Helen / Jun. 17, 1980+Jun. 19, 1980 / Muse ◆◆◆◆◆
Helen Humes was one of the most appealing jazz singers of the late '30s, and of the late '70s. Her comeback in her last few years was a happy event and all of her recordings for Muse are recommended. This one finds her backed by a veteran sextet including tenorman Buddy Tate, trumpeter Joe Wilder, and pianist Norman Simmons. Her versions of "There'll Be Some Changes Made," "Easy Living" and "Draggin' My Heart Around" are particularly memorable. —*Scott Yanow*

Let the Good Times Roll / Aug. 1981 / Classic Jazz ◆◆◆◆
Triumphant, but sometimes ragged, mid-'70s performances featuring Humes doing new versions of prior hits she made during her stint with Count Basie and in the '40s and '50s. She's backed by a group that includes Arnett Cobb, Jay McShann, Gatemouth Brown, Milt Bruckner, and Major Holley, among others, but they don't always hit on all cylinders. This, originally cut for the Black and Blue label, has been reissued on CD. —*Ron Wynn*

Alberta Hunter

b. Apr. 1, 1895, Memphis, TN, d. Oct. 17, 1984, Roosevelt Island, NY
Vocals / Classic Female Blues
An early blues vocalist in the 1920s, a sophisticated supper club singer in the 1930s and a survivor in the '80s, Alberta Hunter had quite a career. Hunter actually debuted in clubs as a singer as early as 1912, starting out in Chicago. She made her first recording in 1921, wrote "Down Hearted Blues" (which became Bessie Smith's first hit) and used such sidemen on her recordings in the 1920s as Fletcher Henderson, Eubie Blake, Fats Waller, Louis Armstrong, and Sidney Bechet. She starred in *Showboat* with Paul Robeson at the London Palladium (1928–29), worked in Paris and recorded straight ballads with John Jackson's Orchestra. After returning to the U.S., Hunter worked for the USO during World War II and Korea, singing overseas. She retired in 1956 to become a nurse (she was 61 at the time) and continued in that field (other than a 1961 recording) until she was forced to retire in 1977 when it was believed she was 65; actually Hunter was 82! She then made a startling comeback in jazz, singing regularly at the Cookery in New York until she was 89, writing the music for the 1978 film *Remember My Name* and recording for Columbia. After the 1920s, Alberta Hunter recorded on an infrequent basis but her dates from 1935, 1939, 1940, and 1950 have been mostly reissued by Stash, her Bluesville album (1961) is out in the OJC series and her Columbia sets are still available. —*Scott Yanow*

Chicago: The Living Legends / 1961 / Riverside ◆◆◆
Chicago: The Living Legends captures a reunion between vocalist Alberta Hunter and pianist Lovie Austin in 1961. Although it doesn't have the immediate power of their original sessions, it's an enjoyable, low-key reunion with an engaging, relaxed vibe. —*Thom Owens*

Songs We Taught / Aug. 1961 / Original Blues Classics ◆◆◆
Songs We Taught is captures a trio of classic female blues

singers recording in 1964, which is rather late in their careers. Alberta Hunter is the standout, infusing "I Got a Mind to Ramble" with a simmering sensuality. This is smoky, late-night blues at its best. — *Thom Owens*

Alberta Hunter with Lovie Austin and Her Blues Se / Sep. 1962 / Riverside ◆◆◆◆◆

Amtrack Blues / 1988 / CBS ◆◆◆
Amtrack Blues is a good latter-day collection from Alberta Hunter, as she runs through a set of classics and newly written material—everything from "Sweet Georgia Brown" to the title track. It's not exceptional, but it is an entertaining slice of classic female blues singing. — *Thom Owens*

● **Young Alberta Hunter** / Vintage Jazz ◆◆◆◆◆
1921–1940. 23 classic tracks, both small and large backup bands (Fletcher Henderson). Good sound. — *Michael Erlewine*

Ivory Joe Hunter

b. Oct. 10, 1914, Kirbyville, TX, d. Nov. 8, 1974, Memphis, TN
Piano, Vocals / R&B
Bespectacled and velvet-smooth in the vocal department, pianist Ivory Joe Hunter appeared too much mild-mannered to be a rock & roller. But when the rebellious music first crashed the American consciousness in the mid-'50s, there was Ivory Joe, deftly delivering his blues ballad "Since I Met You Baby" right alongside the wildest pioneers of the era.

Hunter was already a grizzled R&B vet by that time who had first heard his voice on a 1933 Library of Congress cylinder recording made in Texas (where he grew up). An accomplished tunesmith, he played around the Gulf Coast region, hosting his own radio program for a time in Beaumont before migrating to California in 1942. It was a wise move; Hunter (whose real name was Ivory Joe, incidentally—perhaps his folks were psychic!) found plenty of work pounding out blues and ballads in wartime California. He started his own label, Ivory Records, to press up his "Blues at Sunrise" (with Johnny Moore's Three Blazers backing him), and it became a national hit when leased to Leon Rene's Exclusive imprint in 1945. Another Hunter enterprise, Pacific Records, hosted a major hit in 1948 when the pianist's "Pretty Mama Blues" topped the R&B charts for three weeks.

At whatever logo Hunter paused from the mid-'40s through the late '50s, his platters sold like hotcakes. For Cincinnati-based King in 1948–49, he hit with "Don't Fall in Love with Me," "What Did You Do to Me," "Waiting in Vain," and "Guess Who." At MGM, then new to the record biz, he cut his immortal "I Almost Lost My Mind" (another R&B chart-topper in 1950), "I Need You So" (later covered by Elvis), and "It's a Sin." Signing with Atlantic in 1954, he hit big with "Since I Met You Baby" in 1956 and the two-sided smash "Empty Arms"/"Love's A Hurting Game" in 1957.

Hunter's fondness for country music reared its head in 1958. Upon switching to Dot Records, he scored his last pop hit with a cover of Bill Anderson's "City Lights." Hunter's Dot encores went nowhere; neither did typically mellow outings for Vee-Jay, Smash, Capitol, and Veep. Epic went so far as to recruit a simmering Memphis band (including organist Isaac Hayes, trumpeter Gene "Bowlegs" Miller, and saxist Charles Chalmers) for an LP titled *The Return of Ivory Joe Hunter* that hoped to revitalize his career, but it wasn't meant to be. The album's cover photo—a closeup of Hunter's grinning face with a cigarette dangling from his lips—seems grimly ironic in the face of his death from lung cancer only a few years later. — *Bill Dahl*

The Return of Ivory Joe Hunter / Epic ◆◆◆
Commendable attempt to update Ivory Joe Hunter's sound for early-'70s consumption, with an all-star Memphis aggregation that included Isaac Hayes on organ, saxist Charlie Chalmers, and a sax section lifted from the Hi studios. The album worked reasonably well, producing updated remakes of Hunter's hits and tasty versions of Don Covay's "I'm Coming Down with the Blues" and Chuck Willis' "What Am I Living For." — *Bill Dahl*

Sixteen of his Greatest Hits / 1988 / King ◆◆◆
Other than ruining his 1949 smash "Guess Who" entirely with hideous stereo overdubs, King has done pretty well by the pianist on this collection of his post-war output for the Cincinnati firm. Hunter was primarily in a sentimental blues ballad bag back then, some of his hits displaying a tinge of country influence. Sound quality is okay if not superlative. — *Bill Dahl*

● **Since I Met You Baby: The Best of Ivory Joe Hunter** / 1994 / Razor & Tie ◆◆◆◆◆
Bespectacled pianist Ivory Joe Hunter's crooning blues balladry made him a hot commodity from the late '40s through the late '50s, but he could rock reasonably convincingly hard too. He does both on this wonderful survey of his 1949–1958 MGM and Atlantic sides—"I Need You So," "I Almost Lost My Mind," and the title item are sophisticated and mellow, while "Rockin' Chair Boogie," "Love Is a Hurting Game," and "Shooty Booty" find the pianist in decidedly unsentimental moods. — *Bill Dahl*

Jumping at the Dew Drop / Route 66 ◆◆◆
A European import slab of vinyl offering an overview of Hunter's 1947–1952 pre-Atlantic days. Emphasis on jump entries ("Are You Hep?," "She's a Killer," "We're Gonna Boogie," "Old Man's Boogie") is a welcome change-of-pace from Hunter's better-known propensity for velvety blues ballads. — *Bill Dahl*

Long John Hunter

b. LA
Guitar, Vocals / Texas Blues
For much too long, the legend of Long John Hunter has largely been a local one, limited to the bordertown region between El Paso, TX and Juarez, Mexico. That's where the guitarist reigned for 13 years (beginning in 1957) at Juarez's infamous Lobby Bar. Its riotous, often brawling clientele included locals, cowboys, soldiers from nearby Fort Bliss, frat boys, and every sort of troublemaking tourist in between. Hunter kept 'em all entertained with his outrageous showmanship and slashing guitar riffs.

The Louisiana native got a late start on his musical career. When he was 22 and toiling away in a Beaumont, TX box factory, he attended a B.B. King show and was instantly transfixed. The next day, he bought a guitar. A year later, he was starring at the same bar that B.B. had headlined.

Hunter's 1954 debut single for Don Robey's Houston-based Duke label, "She Used to Be My Woman"/"Crazy Baby," preceded his move to El Paso in 1957. Along the way, Phillip Walker and Lonnie Brooks both picked up on his licks. But Hunter's recording output was slim—a few hot but obscure singles waxed from 1961 to 1963 for the tiny Yucca logo out of Alamogordo, NM (standouts include "El Paso Rock," "Midnight Stroll," and "Border Town Blues"). Perhaps he was just too busy—he held court at the Lobby seven nights a week from sundown to sunup.

Fortunately, Hunter's reputation is finally outgrowing the Lone Star state. His 1992 set for the now-shuttered Spindletop imprint, *Ride With Me*, got the ball rolling. Now, his 1996 disc for Alligator, *Border Town Legend*, should expose this Texas blues great to a far wider (if not wilder) audience than ever before. — *Bill Dahl*

Texas Border Town Blues / 1988 / Double Trouble ◆◆◆

Ride With Me / 1992 / Spindletop ◆◆◆◆
After too many years of being a dusty, distant Texas blues rumor, Long John Hunter happily sprang to life with this 1993 comeback effort for short-lived Spindletop Records. While not as polished or as gloriously consistent as his recent Alligator disc, which should finally catapult him to national recognition, the album does an impressive job of showcasing Hunter's ringing, angular guitar work and twangy vocals. — *Bill Dahl*

★ **Border Town Legend** / Jan. 30, 1996 / Alligator ◆◆◆◆◆
For many years Long John Hunter played in clubs without much attention, but that time sweating it out in roadhouses has paid off. During that time, he developed a gutsy, forceful technique that was fully evident on his belated 1993 debut, *Ride With Me*. Although his second album, *Border Town Legend*, is a slicker, more accessible effort, Hunter hasn't lost any of his spicy, distinctive flavor. Working with a horn section, he still manages to make himself the most powerful element on the record—both his guitar playing and his heated vocals ensure that. Furthermore, Hunter's songwriting is growing stronger. Out of the nine songs he has written or co-written for the album, he has contributed some first-rate tunes that might not stretch beyond generic conventions, but still are mighty fine. — *Stephen Thomas Erlewine*

Mississippi John Hurt

b. Jul. 1, 1893, Teoc, MS, d. Nov. 2, 1966, Grenada, MS
Guitar, Harmonica, Vocals / Acoustic Blues
The history of Mississippi John Hurt reads like a real Cinderella

story. Born John Smith Hurt on July 3, 1893, in Teoc (Carroll Co.), MS, his family moved to Avalon, MS (where he grew up) when he was two years of age. One of ten children (who all played music of one sort or another), Hurt was the most into it and taught himself how to play. Years later, when his White landlord asked how he came up with his melodies, he replied, "Well sir, I just make it sound like I think it should."

Although he learned to read and write, he did not attend school past the fourth grade. As a young adult, he became a sharecropper or tenant farmer for many years, but finally gave that up and switched to day labor. For fun and extra cash, Hurt joined other local guitarists and fiddlers for church suppers and town dances in surrounding towns. Hurt soon became a popular favorite at these local functions.

In the late '20s, a well-known fiddler named Willie Narmour, with whom Hurt often played, was spotted by a talent scout for Okeh Phonograph, a division of Columbia Records. When asked about other talented local musicians, Narmour gave them the name of John Hurt and directions on how to find him. Okeh found and interviewed Hurt, had him play a few songs, and decided to record him, provided he was willing to travel to Memphis and New York.

Hurt recorded two songs in February of 1928 while in Memphis, "Frankie" and "Nobody's Dirty Business," and these were released by Okeh. That December, Hurt traveled to New York City to record five more sides. During that visit he met Lonnie Johnson, but made a point of declaring that he cribbed nothing from that great guitarist. Hurt's records did not sell in great numbers, perhaps in the hundreds. After his short musical excursion, John returned to Avalon and went back to sharecropping and playing music just about every Saturday night in the towns surrounding his home.

That could have been the end of Hurt's national career had two young blues musicians from Washington, D.C., Tom Hoskins and Mike Stewart, not come across the original Okeh recording of "Avalon Blues." This was in 1963. Intrigued by John's intricate finger-picking style, they came up with the idea of trying to locate some of the original artists, should they still be alive. They checked the Mississippi maps, but no town named Avalon could be found. However, after locating an 1878 atlas, sure enough, there was an Avalon marked on a rural road running between Greenwood and Grenada. On a hope and a whim, the two blues archivists headed south armed with a tape recorder. With the help of the old map, they found Avalon with its single gas station/store and inquired about John Hurt.

They were floored to see the attendant point down the road and say that Hurt's house was "About a mile down that road, third mail box up the hill. Can't miss it." Hurt, at 71 years of age, was waiting for them, alive and still able to sing and play about as well as he had before. They recorded John and returned to Washington with the precious taped results and the rediscovery of Mississippi John Hurt. He was a complete and instant success in the folk/blues scene.

From the Spring of 1963, when he was brought to Washington, D.C., to perform, until his death in 1966, Hurt played all over the Northeast at clubs and many folk festivals, including twice at the Newport Folk Festival. Much admired by his new-found audience, Hurt loved his late success and gave as much as he got. He was befriended by fellow performers like Doc Watson, Fred McDowell, and Elizabeth Cotten. In the end, he retired to a small home in Granada, MS, not far from his home town of Avalon. So much for a great story; the music is just as good.

Mississippi John Hurt is an exquisite country-blues singer/guitarist with a subtle voice and refined finger-picking guitar style. As mentioned, he recorded in the '20s and again in the '60s, and both periods are well worth hearing. Here is acoustic country-blues with real technical clarity that is also comforting and easy to listen to. There is a gospel flavor in Hurt's blues. Mississippi John Hurt projects a sense of dignity and kindness through all of his recordings. If you have trouble with the occasional heaviness of many blues players, you may find Hurt refreshing. — *Michael Erlewine*

Worried Blues / Apr. 1963 / Rounder ✦✦✦✦✦
This is some of the Vanguard material recorded in April of 1963, not long after Hurt's rediscovery. It contains ten tracks with "Worried Blues" and "Oh Mary Don't You Weep." —*Michael Erlewine*

Memorial Anthology / Dec. 1964 / Adelphi ✦✦✦✦✦
Mississippi John Hurt's mid-'60s performances were usually distinctive and sometimes staggering. His guitar work was crisp, attractive and frequently brilliant, although his vocals were the real hook. Hurt's narratives, storytelling ability, and general communicative powers were at their peak on this two-CD set, which has languished in a vault for nearly 30 years. Hurt covers such traditional numbers as "C.C. Rider" and "Staggerlee" with vigor, plays several originals, sometimes shifts to gospel, and does everything in an unassuming way that nevertheless grabs your attention. The set's treasure is a 31-minute interview with Pete Seeger in which Hurt lays bare his life, times, and personality, doing so in the same steady, casual, gripping fashion that underscored his singing and playing. —*Ron Wynn*

Avalon Blues / 1965 / Rounder ✦✦✦✦✦
Recorded in April of 1963, these are part of the legacy of Hurt after his rediscovery. Contains "Avalon Blues," "Candyman Blues"—11 cuts in all. Great. —*Michael Erlewine*

Mississippi John Hurt at Newport / 1965 / Vanguard ✦✦✦

Today / 1966 / Vanguard ✦✦✦✦
This is material recorded after his rediscovery in 1963. Includes classic Hurt tunes like "Candy Man" and "Coffee Blues." Wonderful listening. —*Michael Erlewine*

The Immortal / 1967 / Vanguard ✦✦✦✦✦
This is the best of Hurt's '60s "rediscovery-era" recordings. —*Mark A. Humphrey*

The Mississippi John Hurt / 1968 / Vanguard ✦✦✦
A great double-album collection of '60s Hurt. —*Michael Erlewine*

The Best of Mississippi John Hurt / 1968 / Vanguard ✦✦✦✦✦
Contrary to what its title would make one believe, this record is not a collection of previously available recordings by Mississippi John Hurt—rather, it is a complete concert from Oberlin College on April 15, 1965. Regardless, the title is justified, as the concert features Hurt in excellent form doing most of his best known classic songs from the 1920s as well as newer compositions. —*Bruce Eder*

Last Sessions / 1970 / Vanguard ✦✦✦✦✦
Recorded in New York during February and July of 1966, the 17 songs on this collection represent Mississippi John Hurt's final studio efforts. It is astonishing that this man, in the final months of his life, could do 17 songs that were the equal of anything he had done at his first sessions 45 years earlier, his playing (supported on some tracks with producer Patrick Sky on second guitar) as alluringly complex as ever and his voice still in top form. Hurt is brilliant throughout, his voice overpowering in its mixture of warmth, gentleness, and power, and in addition to the expected crop of standards and originals, he covers songs by Bukka White ("Poor Boy, Long Ways from Home") and Leadbelly ("Goodnight Irene")—all of it is worthwhile, with some tracks, such as "Let the Mermaids Flirt with Me" especially haunting. —*Bruce Eder*

★ **1928 Sessions** / 1988 / Yazoo ✦✦✦✦
The 13 original 1928 recordings of Hurt. Justifiably legendary, with gentle grace and power on these understated vocal and fingerpicking masterpieces. These are the ones to hear, although all Hurt is worth listening to. —*Michael Erlewine*

The Greatest Songsters: Complete Works (1927–1929) / 1990 / Document ✦✦✦✦
You can get a lot of arguments started about which Mississippi blues musician is the best, so let's just say that this is first-rate Mississippi John Hurt material and leave it at that. —*Ron Wynn*

J.B. Hutto (Joseph Benjamin Hutto)

b. Apr. 26, 1926, Blackville, SC, d. Jun. 12, 1983, Harvey, IL
Guitar, Vocals / Electric Chicago Blues
J.B. Hutto—along with Hound Dog Taylor—was one of the last great slide guitar disciples of Elmore James to make it into the modern age. Hutto's huge voice, largely incomprehensible diction and slash-and-burn playing was Chicago blues with a fierce, raw edge all its own. He entered the world of music back home in Augusta, GA, singing in the family-oriented group the Golden Crowns Gospel Singers. He came north to Chicago in the mid-'40s, teaching himself guitar and eventually landing his first paying job as a member of Johnny Ferguson and His Twisters. His

recording career started in 1954 with two sessions for the Chance label supported by his original combo the Hawks (featuring George Mayweather on harmonica, Porkchop Hines on washboard traps, and Joe Custom on rhythm guitar), resulting in six of the nine songs recorded being issued as singles to scant acclaim. After breaking up the original band, Hutto worked outside of music for a good decade, part of it spent sweeping out a funeral parlor! He resurfaced around 1964 with a stripped-down, two guitars-drums-no bass trio version of the Hawks, working regularly at Turner's Blue Lounge and recording blistering new sides for the first time in as many years. From there, he never looked back and once again became a full-time bluesman. For the next 12 years Hutto gigged and recorded with various groups of musicians—always billed as the Hawks—working with electric bass players for the first time and recording for small labels, both here and overseas. After fellow slide man Hound Dog Taylor's death in 1976, J.B. "inherited" his backup band, the Houserockers. Although never formally recorded in a studio, this short-lived collaboration of Hutto with guitarist Brewer Phillips and drummer Ted Harvey produced live shows that would musically careen in a single performance from smoldering-ly intense to utter chaos. Within a year, Hutto would be lured to Boston where he put together a mixed group of "New Hawks," recording and touring America and Europe right up until his death in the mid-'80s. Hutto was an incredibly dynamic live performer, dressed in hot pink suits with headgear ranging from a shriner's fez to high-plains-drifters' hats, snaking through the crowd and dancing on tabletops with his 50-foot guitar cord stretched to the max. And this good-time approach to the music held sway on his recordings as well, giving a loose, barroom feel to almost all of them, regardless of who was backing him. —*Cub Koda*

Masters of Modern Blues / 1966 / Testament ◆◆◆◆
1966 was a banner year for Hutto and his Hawks—in addition to laying down the lion's share of his killer Delmark album, the slide master also waxed a similarly incendiary set for Pete Welding's Testament logo. Vicious versions of "Pet Cream Man," "Lulubelle's Here," and "Bluebird" are but a few of its charms, with Big Walter Horton's unmistakable harp winding through the proceedings. —*Bill Dahl*

☆ **Chicago/The Blues/Today!, Vol. 1** / 1967 / Vanguard ◆◆◆◆◆
Hutto only has five tracks on this album, sharing it with great solo turns by Junior Wells and Otis Spann, but it's truly the place to start, because it doesn't get much better than this; "Too Much Alcohol," "Please Help," "Going Ahead," and "That's The Truth" are all classics and Hutto is in perfect form throughout with swinging support from the Turner's Blue Lounge version of The Hawks, bass-rhythm guitarist Herman Hassell and former Bo Diddley drummer Frank Kirkland. Sound is crystal clear. —*Cub Koda*

● **Hawk Squat!** / 1968 / Delmark ◆◆◆◆◆
The raw-as-an-open-wound Chicago slide guitarist outdid himself throughout an outrageously raucous album (most of it waxed in 1966) anchored by an impossible-to-ignore "Hip-Shakin'," the blar-ing title cut, and savage renditions of "20% Alcohol" and "Notoriety Woman." Sunnyland Slim augments Hutto's Hawks on organ, rather than his customary piano. —*Bill Dahl*

Slidewinder / 1973 / Delmark ◆◆◆
Disappointing Delmark encore from 1972 suffers from Bombay

Carter's frequently out-of-tune electric bass and a comparatively uninspired song selection. —*Bill Dahl*

Slideslinger / Apr. 1, 1982 / Evidence ◆◆◆
While he was not in top shape during the early '80s, J.B. Hutto could still bend strings, churn out whiplash chords, and offer exuberant shouts, which he did on this '82 set, reissued on a '92 CD with two bonus cuts. He did not always hit every note on the fretboard or maintain his vocal depth, but his spirit never flagged. Hutto's jagged lines, energized vocals, and inspiring presence made his originals standouts, while his covers of Little Walter Jacobs' "Tell Me Mama" and Elmore James' "Look At The Yonder Wall" resonated with the quality that only a genuine blues survivor could provide. The backing band of guitarist Steve Coveney, bassist Kenny Krumbholz, and drummer Leroy Pina gave Hutto good support, wisely yielding him the spotlight, where he belongs. —*Ron Wynn*

Slippin' & Slidin' / 1983 / Varrick ◆◆◆
Much smoother production by Scott Billington than was normal for Hutto's scathing output, but not alarmingly so. With pianist Ron Levy and the Roomful of Blues horn section augmenting Hutto's New Hawks, the slide guitarist did himself proud on covers of Fenton Robinson's "Somebody Loan Me a Dime" and Junior Parker's "Pretty Baby," alongside a passel of his own distinctive compositions. —*Bill Dahl*

And the Houserockers Live 1977 / 1991 / Wolf ◆◆◆
Culled from a couple of nights in a Boston jazz club and record-ed on a cassette deck with two microphones, this stunning document of Hutto with Hound Dog Taylor's band in support gives new meaning to the phrase raw 'n steamy. Although the trio is fleshed out at this point by the addition of a fairly obtrusive bass player (Mark Harris) and a guest piano man on a couple of tracks, the sheet metal tone of Phillips' and Hutto's twin Telecaster attack cuts through the murkiest of mixes and Ted Harvey swings mightily. —*Cub Koda*

Roy Hytower & Motif

Guitar / Modern Electric Blues
Well-regarded as a blues guitarist and soulful singer around Chicago, Roy Hytower has carved out an equally impressive niche as an actor in various Windy City musical productions. Among his starring roles: portraying Muddy Waters and Otis Redding.

After picking up some experience singing around Mobile, Hytower came to Chicago in 1962, replacing Mighty Joe Young as rhythm guitarist for Otis Rush. Often adopting a soul-slanted sound, Hytower cut 45s for Avin, Expo, Brainstorm, and Mercury's Blue Rock subsidiary (where he sang the fine "I'm In Your Corner" and "Undertaker" in 1969). Hytower's 1988 album *Root Doctor* (with his band, Motif) was issued on Diamond Gem Records. He still performs locally. —*Bill Dahl*

Root Doctor / Urgent! ◆◆◆
Hytower is a very competent blues guitarist, but you'll find too little proof of that on this synthesizer-heavy set, cut with his band, Motif. Earthier production values would have greatly ben-efitted the stop-time title cut, and blues content elsewhere is only intermittent and overly derivative. —*Bill Dahl*

J

Bullmoose Jackson (Benjamin Joseph Jackson)

b. Apr. 22, 1919, Cleveland, OH, **d.** Jul. 31, 1989, Cleveland, OH
Saxophone, Vocals / Electric Jump Blues

Allegedly, Benjamin Jackson resembled a bullmoose. At least, that's what a few wags in Lucky Millinder's band thought—and the colorful moniker stuck. Up until then, he was Benjamin Jackson, but it was as Bull Moose that he lit up the R&B charts repeatedly during the late '40s and early '50s. Jackson had a split musical personality—he sang "I Love You, Yes I Do" and "All My Love Belongs to You" like a pop crooner, then switched gears to belt out the double-entendre naughties "I Want a Bowlegged Woman" and "Big Ten Inch Woman" with total abandon. Record buyers loved both sides of the Moose.

Jackson was a childhood violinist prior to taking up the sax. He proved accomplished on the latter, blowing jazz in a variety of situations before latching on with Millinder's outfit in 1944 as both singer and saxist. His first 78 under his own name for Syd Nathan's fledgling Queen logo was "I Know Who Threw the Whiskey in the Well," an answer to a popular Millinder tune from the year before that became a smash in its own right. Jackson dubbed his combo the Buffalo Bearcats due to his frequent gigs at a Buffalo nitery.

Moose hit big for Nathan's King diskery in 1947 with "I Love You, Yes I Do"; in 1948 with "Sneaky Pete," "All My Love Belongs to You," "I Want a Bowlegged Woman," "I Can't Go On Without You," and two more; and in 1949 with "Little Girl, Don't Cry" and "Why Don't You Haul Off and Love Me" (the latter a cover of Wayne Raney's hillbilly hit, a popular cross-fertilizing practice at King). He also made an appearance in the 1948 film *Boarding House Blues* with Millinder's band.

Some of Jackson's hilariously risqué stuff—"Big Ten Inch Record" and the astonishingly raunchy "Nosey Joe" (penned by the young but obviously streetwise Jerry Leiber and Mike Stoller), both from 1952— were probably too suggestive to merit airplay, but they're stellar examples of jump blues at its craziest.

Jackson stayed at King into 1955. Six years later, he briefly reentered the charts by remaking "I Love You, Yes I Do" for 7 Arts, but it was an isolated occurrence (catering kept the bills paid during the lean years in Washington, D.C.). There was a belated outbreak of *Moosemania!* in 1985 when his LP of that name emerged in conjunction with a Pittsburgh band called the Flashcats, but Moose's heartwarming comeback was short—lung cancer felled him in 1989. *—Bill Dahl*

Big Fat Mamas Are Back in Style Again / 1980 / Route 66 ✦✦✦✦✦
A solid reissue of Jackson's best sides from 1945-1956. *—Cub Koda*

● **Badman Jackson That's Me** / 1991 / Charly ✦✦✦✦✦
The best representation of saxist Jackson's jump blues activities for King Records during the late '40s and early '50s. The Moose was a smooth ballad crooner, too, but you'll find none of his mellow stuff on this 22-tracker—just horn-leavened blasters, often with hilariously risque lyrics. "Big Ten Inch Record" (here in two takes), "I Want a Bowlegged Woman," the country-rooted "Why Don't You Haul Off and Love Me," and most of all the Leiber & Stoller-penned sleaze-o "Nosey Joe" are party records guaranteed to excite any gathering! *—Bill Dahl*

Final Recordings / 1992 / Bogus ✦✦
This attempt to recreate jump blues style succeeds intermittently. *—Bill Dahl*

George Jackson

b. MS
Songwriter / Soul Blues

This Mississippi songwriter has been one of the most consistent composers in both R&B and pop circles. He initially recorded for Pram in 1963 and later sang with The Ovations, writing "It's Wonderful To Be In Love," which reached #22 in 1965. He also recorded for Decca in 1968 as "Bart" Jackson. But it's his compositions that have earned Jackson fame; they include "Too Weak To Fight" for Clarence Carter, "A Man And A Half" for Wilson Pickett, "Down Home Blues" for Z.Z. Hill, "One Bad Apple" for The Osmond Brothers, and "Old Time Rock & Roll" for Bob Seger. He has been a staff writer for Malaco since the early '80s, and has provided songs to Hill, Bobby "Blue" Bland, Latimore, Denise LaSalle, and Johnnie Taylor, among others. *—Ron Wynn*

● **Sweet Down Home Delta Blues** / Amblin' ✦✦✦✦✦

Jim Jackson

b. 1890, Hernando, MS, **d.** 1937, Hernando, MS
Guitar / Acoustic Memphis Blues

Coming from the rich medicine-show tradition of the Memphis area, Jim Jackson veered toward a more pronounced blues feel than most of his songster and jug band contemporaries. Born in Hernando, MS in 1890, Jackson took an interest in music early on, learning the rudiments of guitar from his father. By the age of 15, he was already steadily employed in local medicine shows and by his 20s was working the country frolic and juke joint circuit, usually in the company of Gus Cannon and Robert Wilkins. After joining up with the Silas Green Minstrel Show, he settled in Memphis, working clubs with Furry Lewis, Cannon, and Will Shade. The entire decade known as the "roaring '20s" found him regularly working with his Memphis cronies, finally recording his best known tune, "Kansas City Blues" (one of the great classics of the idiom), and a batch of other classics by the end of the decade. He also appeared in one of the early talkies, *Hallelujah!*, in 1929. While Jackson's best work may seem a bit quaint by modern standards, he was a major influence on Chicago bluesman J.B. Lenoir and his "Kansas City Blues" was a regular fixture of Robert Nighthawk's set list.—*Cub Koda*

● **Kansas City Blues** / 1980 / Agram ✦✦✦✦
Sixteen tracks from Jackson's peak creative period. Includes many variations of the title track. *—Cub Koda*

Complete Recorded Works, Vols. 1-2 / Document ✦✦✦
Everything Jim Jackson recorded between 1927 and 1930 is collected on the two-volume *Complete Recorded Works* (both discs are available separately). Jackson wrote some fine songs and recorded some great performances, but his entire body of work is primarily of interest only to historians and country blues completists. In other words, fanatics will enjoy this set, even if they find some of the music a little tiresome, but listeners that just want a taste of Jackson should stick with single-disc collections. *—Thom Owens*

John Jackson (John H. Jackson)

b. Feb. 25, 1924, Woodville, VA
Banjo, Guitar, Vocals / Acoustic Country Blues

For much of his life, John Jackson played for country houseparties in Virginia, or around the house for his own amusement. Then in the '60s he encountered the folk revival, and since that time he has been the Washington, D.C. area's best-loved blues artist. Undoubtedly the finest traditional Piedmont guitarist active today, Jackson exemplifies the songster tradition at its best. His eclectic repertoire embraces the music of his guitar heroes Willie Walker (who once visited his father's house), Blind Boy Fuller, and—most notably—Blind Blake. Besides the blues, rags, and dance tunes associated with these masters, Jackson plays ballads, country songs, and what he terms "old folk songs," such as "The Midnight Special." His confident finger-picking, down-home Virginia accent, and contagious good humor mark his performances, live or on record, as something special. A world-class storyteller and party-thrower as well as a National Heritage Award-winning musician, Jackson has recorded a half-dozen albums and toured the world as often as he has wanted to. Today he often performs with his son James. —*Barry Lee Pearson*

Blues and Country Dance Tunes from Virginia / 1965 / Arhoolie ✦✦✦✦✦
John Jackson was an excellent country blues musician whose repertoire also included reels, mountain music, and folk tunes. This was an outstanding collection of vintage material done in what was about as contemporary a fashion as you could get in that genre in the mid-'60s. —*Ron Wynn*

● **Don't Let Your Deal Go Down** / 1970 / Arhoolie ✦✦✦✦✦
Fine compilation of Arhoolie sides. —*Bill Dahl*

Step It up & Go / 1979 / Rounder ✦✦✦✦
Virginia ragtime, blues, and hillbilly from this amiable singer/guitarist. —*Mark A. Humphrey*

Lil' Son Jackson

b. Aug. 17, 1916, Tyler, TX, d. Mar. 30, 1976, Dallas, TX
Guitar, Vocals / Acoustic Texas Blues
Lil' Son Jackson was a stylistic throwback from the moment he first turned up during the immediate postwar era. He was a Texas country bluesman of the highest order whose rustic approach appealed wholeheartedly to the early '50s blues marketplace.

Melvin Jackson's dad loved blues, while his mother played gospel guitar. Their son's initial experience came with a spiritual aggregation called the Blue Eagle Four. A mechanic by trade, he served in the Army during World War II before giving the idea of being a professional blues musician a shot.

In 1946, he shipped off a demo to Bill Quinn, who owned a Houston diskery called Gold Star Records. Quinn was suitably impressed, inking Jackson and enjoying a national R&B hit, "Freedom Train Blues," in 1948 for his modest investment. It would prove Jackson's only national hit, although his 1950-1954 output for Imperial Records must have sold consistently, judging from how many sides the L.A. firm issued by the Texas guitarist.

Jackson's best Imperial work was recorded solo. Later attempts to squeeze his style into a small band format (his idea, apparently) tended to emphasize his timing eccentricities. His "Rockin' and Rollin'," cut in December of 1950, became better-known through a raft of subsequent covers as "Rock Me Baby." He gave up the blues during the mid-'50s after an auto wreck, resuming work as a mechanic. Arhoolie Records boss Chris Strachwitz convinced Jackson to cut an album in 1960, but his comeback proved fleeting. —*Bill Dahl*

Papa Charlie Jackson (Charlie Carter)

b. 1885, New Orleans, LA, d. 1938, Chicago, IL
Banjo, Guitar, Ukulele, Vocals / Acoustic Country Blues
Papa Charlie Jackson was the first bluesman to record, beginning in 1924 with the Paramount label, playing a hybrid banjo-guitar (six strings tuned like a guitar but with a banjo body that gave it a lighter resonance) and ukelele. And apart from his records and their recording dates, little else is known for sure about this pioneering blues performer, other than his probable city of birth, New Orleans—even his death in Chicago during 1938 is more probable than established fact.

Jackson spent his teen years as a singer/performer in minstrel and medicine shows, picking up a repertory of bawdy but entertaining songs that would serve him well for decades. He is known to have busked around Chicago in the early '20s, playing for tips on Maxwell Street, as well as the city's West side clubs

beginning in 1924. In August of that year, Jackson made his first record, "Papa's Lawdy Lawdy Blues" and "Airy Man Blues," for a Paramount label. He followed this up a month later with "Salt Lake City Blues" and "Salty Dog Blues," which became one of his signature tunes—he later re-recorded this number as a member of Freddie Keppard's Jazz Cardinals, also for the Paramount label, a common practice in those days as the notion of contracts and exclusivity was almost unknown in blues recording. Jackson made his first duet records in 1925, "Mister Man, Parts 1 and 2," with singer Ida Cox, again for Paramount, and later cut duets with Ma Rainey and future Oscar-winning actress Hattie McDaniel.

He was already regarded as one of the Paramount label's more successful recording artists, and all but a handful of his recordings were done for Paramount over the next decade. Jackson had a wide diversity of material and voices in which he recorded—"Good Doing Papa Blues" and "Jungle Man Blues" presented Jackson as a ladies' man in playful settings, while "Ma and Pa Poorhouse Blues," cut in a duet with Ma Rainey, was a far more serious song, dealing with poverty and its attendant miseries. "Don't Break Down," by contrast, was a seductive love song with pop elements, while "Baby Please Loan Me Your Heart"—with its exquisite banjo strumming—is a sweetly romantic piece that could've come out of vaudeville. Whether he was strumming or finger-picking, his music was always of interest for its structure, content, and execution.

Jackson reached a musical peak of sorts in September of 1929 when he got to record with his longtime idol, Blind (Arthur) Blake, often known as the king of ragtime guitar during this period. "Papa Charlie and Blind Blake Talk About It" parts one and two are among the most unusual sides of the late '20s, containing elements of blues jam session, hokum recording, and ragtime, containing enough humor to make it the 1920s rival of tracks such as Bo Diddley's "Say Man" as well. More is the pity that better sources haven't survived for both sides, but what is here is beyond price—there may not be a dozen guitar records in any genre that are more important or more fascinating.

Jackson switched to guitar on some of his late '20s recordings, and occasionally played the ukelele as well, although he was back to using the five-string hybrid in 1934, when he cut his final sessions. For reasons that nobody has ever established, he parted company with Paramount after 1930, and never recorded for the label again, even though Paramount lasted another two years before going under amid the hardships of the Great Depression. His last sides for the label, "You Got That Wrong" and "Self Experience," were highly personal songs dealing with romance and an apparent brush with the law, after which he disappeared from recording for four years. Jackson continued performing, however, and he returned to the recording studio again in November of 1934 for sessions on the Okeh label, including three songs cut with his friend Big Bill Broonzy, which were never issued. Jackson was an important influence on Broonzy, who outlived his mentor by 20 years.

Papa Charlie Jackson remains a shadowy figure, considered a highly influential figure in the blues, though not quite a major blues figure, apart from the fact that he was the first male singer/guitarist who played the blues to get to record. His recordings are all eminently listenable, although most are not blues, but fall into such related areas as ragtime and hokum. At this writing, the only extant collections consist of three Austrian produced CDs. —*Bruce Eder*

● **Fat Mouth** / 1970 / Yazoo ✦✦✦✦✦
The best single-disc retrospective of this early country blues artist. —*Cub Koda*

Papa Charlie Jackson / 1972 / Biograph ✦✦✦✦✦
Jackson's mid-'20s material blended topical fare with hokum hilarity and blues laments, and Jackson's four- and six-string banjo accompaniment was among country blues' most striking. His guitar work wasn't bad either. —*Ron Wynn*

Complete Works, Vols. 1-3 / 1992 / Document ✦✦✦✦
Surprisingly good-sounding, with a few notable exceptions (especially "Papa Do Do Do Blues" and the two Blind Blake sides on volume three) that are almost inevitable. A complete output of Jackson's work, of which volume three, containing his duets with Blind Blake, is probably of greatest interest if a starting point is needed. —*Bruce Euer*

Colin James

b. 1964, Canada
Guitar, Vocals, Pennywhistle, Mandolin / Modern Blues
This Canadian guitarist, singer, and songwriter is Canada's answer to the U.S.'s Chris Duarte or Kenny Wayne Shepherd. Colin Munn grew up in Saskatchewan, listening to folk and blues. After learning the pennywhistle and mandolin, he quit school and worked with a succession of bands, among them, the Hoo Doo Men.

When he was 19 years old, he moved to Vancouver and joined the Night Shades. About two years later, performing under his changed name, Colin James, he was lucky enough to be noticed by the folks at Virgin Records, who signed him. James' 1988 self-titled debut was the fastest-selling album in Canadian history, and he followed that in 1990 with *Sudden Stop*, and *Colin James and the Little Big Band* in 1993. In 1995, James switched over to Warner Music Canada, and released *Bad Habits*. On *Bad Habits*, James is teamed with some good company: Bobby King and Terry Evans, Mavis Staples, guitarist Waddy Wachtel, Lenny Kravitz, and former Stevie Ray Vaughan and Double Trouble keyboardist Reese Wynans.

All of James' albums are well-recorded affairs. The only problem is, he doesn't tour the U.S. very much, and spends most of his time in Canada. In 1988, he toured with Steve Winwood, Little Feat and Keith Richards, but if he's ever going to become a truly international blues musician, he's going to have to start touring the U.S. a whole lot more. An accomplished guitarist, singer and songwriter who, as of this writing, hasn't yet turned 30, we'll be hearing more from James before the millennium is out. *—Richard Skelly*

● **Colin James** / 1988 / Virgin ♦♦♦♦♦
An impressive debut by the blues-drenched guitarist, it includes the wrenching gem, "Voodoo Thing." *—David Szatmary*

Sudden Stop / Oct. 1990 / Virgin ♦♦♦
A solid, stylistically varied followup by this Canadian guitarist. *—David Szatmary*

Bad Habits / 1996 / Elektra ♦♦♦
Canadian blues guitarist Colin James turns in a fine set of both original and cover material. Paring back the sound of his previous effort to the basic guitar, bass, and drums, James uses horns and keyboards to color and accentuate certain tracks rather than overwhelm. He works his blues magic on such covers as Robert Johnson's "Walkin' Blues" and Jerry Williams's "Standing On The Edge Of Love" while proving his own song writing capabilities on cuts like "Freedom" and "Better Days." A great return to form. *—James Chrispell*

Colin James & The Little Big Band / Virgin ♦♦♦♦
A tasty hybrid of rock & roll, jive, and blues, James' eponymous recording—a collection of standards from the late '40s-early '50s recorded live from the floor—takes a swingin' jump approach with horns and organ given equal billing to smooth, hollow-body guitar tones. Highlights: the finger-snapping, fedora-over-one-eye cool of "Evening" and a bopping, knockout version of "Train Kept A-Rollin." *—Roch Parisien*

Elmore James

b. Jan. 27, 1918, Richland, MS, **d.** May 24, 1963, Chicago, IL
Guitar, Vocals / Electric Chicago Blues
No two ways about it, the most influential slide guitarist of the postwar period was Elmore James, hands down. Although his early demise from heart failure kept him from enjoying the fruits of the '60s blues revival as his contemporaries Muddy Waters and Howlin' Wolf did, James left a wide influential trail behind him. And that influence continues to the present time— in approach, attitude, and tone—in just about every guitar player who puts a slide on his finger and wails the blues. As a guitarist, he wrote the book, his slide style influencing the likes of Hound Dog Taylor, Joe Carter, his cousin Homesick James, and J.B. Hutto, while his seldom-heard single-string work had an equally profound effect on B.B. King and Chuck Berry. His signature lick—an electric updating of Robert Johnson's "I Believe I'll Dust My Broom" and one that Elmore recorded in infinite variations from day one to his last session—is so much a part of the essential blues fabric of guitar licks that no one attempting to play slide guitar can do it without being compared to Elmore James. Others may have had more technique—Robert

Nighthawk and Earl Hooker immediately come to mind—but Elmore had the sound and all the feeling.

A radio repairman by trade, Elmore reworked his guitar amplifiers in his spare time, getting them to produce raw, distorted sounds that wouldn't resurface until the advent of heavy rock amplification in the late '60s. This amp on 11 approach was hot-wired to one of the strongest emotional approaches to the blues ever recorded. There is never a time when you're listening to one of his records that you feel—no matter how familiar the structure—that he's phoning it in just to grab a quick session check. Elmore James always gave it everything he had, everything he could emotionally invest in a number. This commitment of spirit is something that shows up time and again when listening to multiple takes from his session masters. The sheer repetitiveness of the recording process would dim almost anyone's creative fires, but Elmore always seemed to give it 100% every time the red light went on. Few blues singers had a voice that could compete with James'; it was loud, forceful, prone to "catch" or break up in the high registers, almost sounding on the verge of hysteria at certain moments. Evidently the times back in the mid-'30s when Elmore had first-hand absorption of Robert Johnson as a playing companion had deep influence on him, not only in his choice of material, but also in his presentation of it.

Backing the twin torrents of Elmore's guitar and voice was one of the greatest—and earliest—Chicago blues bands. Named after James' big hit, the Broomdusters featured Little Johnny Jones on piano, J.T. Brown on tenor sax, and Elmore's cousin Homesick James on rhythm guitar. This talented nucleus was often augmented by a second saxophone on occasion while the drumming stool changed frequently. But this was the band that could go toe to toe in a battle of the blues against the bands of Muddy Waters or Howlin' Wolf and always hold their own, if not walk with the show. Utilizing a stomping beat, Elmore's slashing guitar, Jones' two-fisted piano delivery, Homesick's rudimentary boogie bass rhythm, and Brown's braying nanny-goat sax leads, the Broomdusters were as loud and powerful and popular as any blues band the Windy City had to offer.

As urban as their sound was, it all had roots in Elmore's hometown of Canton, MS. He was born there on January 27, 1918, the illegitimate son of Leola Brooks and later given the surname of his stepfather, Joe Willie James. He adapted to music at an early age, learning to play bottleneck on a homemade instrument fashioned out of a broom handle and a lard can. By the age of 14, he was already a weekend musician, working the various country suppers and juke joints in the area under the names "Cleanhead" or Joe Willie James. Although he confined himself to a home-base area around Belzoni, he would join up and work with traveling players coming through like Robert Johnson, Howlin' Wolf, and Sonny Boy Williamson. By the late '30s he had formed his first band and was working the Southern state area with Sonny Boy until the second world war broke out, spending three years stationed with the Navy in Guam. When he was discharged, he picked off where he left off, moving for a while to Memphis, working in clubs with Eddie Taylor and his cousin Homesick James. Elmore was also one of the first "guest stars" on the popular *King Biscuit Time* radio show on KFFA in Helena, AR, also doing stints on the *Talaho Syrup* show on Yazoo City's WAZF and the *Hadacol* show on KWEM in West Memphis.

Nervous and unsure of his abilities as a recording artist, Elmore was surreptitiously recorded by Lillian McMurray of Trumpet Records at the tail end of a Sonny Boy session doing his now signature tune, "Dust My Broom." The legend has it that James didn't even stay around long enough to hear the playback, much less record a second side. Mrs. McMurray stuck a local singer (Bo Bo Thomas) on the flip side and the record became the surprise R&B hit of 1951, making the Top Ten and conversely making a recording star out of Elmore. With a few months left on his Trumpet contract, Elmore was recorded by the Bihari brothers for their Modern label subsidiaries, Flair and Meteor, but the results were left in the can until James' contract ran out. In the meantime, Elmore had moved to Chicago and cut a quick session for Chess, which resulted in one single being issued and just as quickly yanked off the market as the Biharis swooped in to protect their investment. This period of activity found Elmore assembling the nucleus of his great band the Broomdusters, and several fine recordings were issued over the next few years on a plethora of Bihari-owned labels, with several of them charting and most all of them becoming certified blues classics.

By this time James had established a beach-head in the clubs of Chicago as one of the most popular live acts and regularly broadcasting over WPOA under the aegis of disc-jockey Big Bill Hill. In 1957, with his contract with the Biharis at an end, he recorded several successful sides for Mel London's Chief label, all of them later being issued on the larger Vee-Jay label. His health—always in a fragile state due to a recurring heart condition—would send him back home to Jackson, MS, where he temporarily set aside his playing for work as a disc jockey or radio repair man. He came back to Chicago to record a session for Chess, then just as quickly broke contract to sign with Bobby Robinson's Fire label, producing the classic "The Sky Is Crying" and numerous others. Running afoul with the Chicago musician's union, he returned back to Mississippi, doing sessions in New York and New Orleans waiting for Big Bill Hill to sort things out. In August of 1963, Elmore returned to Chicago, ready to resume his on-again off-again playing career—his records were still being regularly issued and reissued on a variety of labels—when he suffered his final heart attack. His wake was attended by over 400 blues luminaries before his body was shipped back to Mississippi. He was elected to the Blues Foundation's Hall of Fame in 1980 and was later elected to the Rock & Roll Hall of Fame as a seminal influence. Elmore James may not have lived to reap the rewards of the blues revival, but his music and influence continues to resonate. —*Cub Koda*

Whose Muddy Shoes / 1969 / MCA/Chess ✦✦✦✦✦
Elmore had recorded a session for Chess in 1953 before settling down with the Bihari brothers and again in 1960, shortly before starting his final recordings for Bobby Robinson's Fire, Fury and Enjoy labels. This collects all of them on CD with the bonus addition of an alternate take of "The Sun Is Shining," which can be interpreted as a precursor to his later hit "The Sky Is Crying." The earlier sides from 1953 lack his inimitable slide, but the 1960 session produced classics like "Talk to Me Baby," "Madison Blues," and a powerful reading of T-Bone Walker's "Stormy Monday." These tracks of Elmore working with the Chess production team are delightfully fleshed out with a half dozen gems by the highly underrated John Brim, some of which include stellar harp work by Little Walter ("Rattlesnake," "Be Careful"—on which Walter stops playing in several spots to become an ad-lib backup vocalist— and "You Got Me") as well as the original version of "Ice Cream Man," better known to rock fans from Van Halen's cover version of it from their debut album. —*Cub Koda*

☆ **The Original Meteor & Flair Sides** / 1984 / Ace ✦✦✦✦✦
The best of James's early-'50s sides with stunning slide and driving band support. At the top of his form, this is a perfect introduction to his music. (Import) —*Cub Koda*

Rollin' & Tumblin': The Best of Elmore James / 1992 / Relic ✦✦✦✦✦
Although the Capricorn box set does a great job of rounding at least one take of everything James cut for Bobby Robinson's Fire and Enjoy labels, if you want (or need) to sweat it down to bare essentials, this is the one to grab out of the blues bin and take home. The remastering by Little Walter Devenne on this single disc is exemplary and for late period Elmore, this truly is the best of the best. —*Cub Koda*

☆ **King of the Slide Guitar** / 1992 / Warner Brothers ✦✦✦✦✦
Elmore's last great recordings occurred in the 1960s when he was signed by New York producer/label owner Bobby Robinson. Unlike many of his contemporaries, James seemingly got *better* as the years went by and while none of the sides feature a slide guitar anywhere near as nasty as his early Modern and Flair recordings, he's still obviously giving it all on each and every side. These recordings are the ones most commonly issued on James and have surfaced on so many different compilations—all with varying levels of sound quality—that it would be futile to list them all here. Fortunately, to make things easier we have this two-disc 50-song box set rounding up at least one extant take of everything Elmore recorded with Robinson at the helm. While some of the material are recuts of his best known tunes ("Dust My Broom" resurfaces here in two version from two different sessions and the version of "It Hurts Me Too" included here—it was originally cut for Chief in the late '50s—became a posthumous hit for him), the majority of it breaks new ground and stands as some of Elmore's most emotion-laden work. Nice

essays in the booklet make up for the disgusting art work that adorns the box. —*Cub Koda*

★ **The Sky Is Crying: The History of Elmore James** / 1993 / Rhino ✦✦✦✦✦
With the confusing plethora of Elmore James discs out on the market, this is truly the place to start, featuring the best of his work culled from several labels. Highlights include James' original recording of "Dust My Broom," "It Hurts Me Too," "T.V. Mama" (with Elmore backing Big Joe Turner), and the title track, one of the best slow blues ever created. Slide guitar doesn't get much better than this, making this particular compilation not only a perfect introduction to Elmore's music, but an essential piece for any blues collection. —*Cub Koda*

☆ **The Classic Recordings** / 1993 / Flair-Virgin ✦✦✦✦✦
After Elmore hit the national charts with his Trumpet recording of "Dust My Broom," he came to record for the Bihari brothers, first for their Meteor subsidiary, then later for their Flair and Modern labels. This multi-disc retrospective rounds up every existing master Elmore recorded for the Biharis, plus his backup work behind band members Johnny Jones and J.T. Brown. James' guitar tone is distorted and overamped to the extreme; *this* is the sound that changed the face of slide guitar forever, influencing everyone from Hound Dog Taylor to J.B. Hutto to George Thorogood and everybody in between. The intensity of James' vocals are nothing short of riveting and the material collected here (along with breakdowns, studio chat, etc.) is simply the best of Elmore's early-'50s sides and a box set well worth saving up for.—*Cub Koda*

Best Of Elmore James: Early Years / 1995 / Ace ✦✦✦
This breaks down Elmore's Modern recordings into a single disc retrospective and a damn fine one it is, too. This compiles the a and b sides of every single recorded for the Bihari brothers, with the original Trumpet recording of "Dust My Broom" standing in the place of "1839 Blues." If you really want to hear Elmore at his wildest and most unfettered and don't want to wade through a pile of alternate takes to get to it, we heartily suggest adding this one to the collection. Import. —*Cub Koda*

Dust My Broom: The Best of Elmore James, Vol. 2 / Relic ✦✦✦✦
A second Relic volume of classics from the Fire/Fury/Enjoy vaults that picks up where the company's first one left off. Even if you already own Capricorn's definitive two-disc collection of his Bobby Robinson-produced sides, you're missing one gem here: "Poor Little Angel Child," which features the robust vocal talent of harpist Sam Myers. Great sound quality throughout, with many stereo items. —*Bill Dahl*

Etta James (Jamesetta Hawkins)

b. Jan. 25, 1938, Los Angeles, CA
Vocals / Soul Blues
Few R&B singers have endured tragic travails on the monumental level that Etta James has and remain on earth to talk about it. The lady's no shrinking violet; her recent autobiography, *Rage to Survive*, describes her past (including numerous drug addictions) in sordid detail.

But her personal problems have seldom affected her singing. James has hung in there from the age of R&B and doo wop in the mid-'50s through soul's late-'60s heyday and right up to today (where her 1994 disc *Mystery Lady* paid loving jazz-based tribute to one of her idols, Billie Holiday). Etta James' voice has deepened over the years, coarsened more than a little, but still conveys remarkable passion and pain.

Jamesetta Hawkins was a child gospel prodigy, singing in her Los Angeles Baptist church choir (and over the radio) when she was only five years old under the tutelage of Professor James Earle Hines. She moved to San Francisco in 1950, soon teaming with two other girls to form a singing group. When she was 14, bandleader Johnny Otis gave the trio an audition. He particularly dug their answer song to Hank Ballard & the Midnighters' "Work with Me Annie."

Against her mother's wishes, the young singer embarked for L.A. to record "Roll with Me Henry" with the Otis band and vocalist Richard Berry in 1954 for Modern Records. Otis inverted her first name to devise her stage handle and dubbed her vocal group the Peaches (also Etta's nickname). "Roll with Me Henry," renamed "The Wallflower" when some radio programmers objected to the original title's connotations, topped the R&B charts in 1955.

The Peaches dropped from the tree shortly thereafter, but Etta James kept on singing for Modern throughout much of the decade (often under the supervision of saxist Maxwell Davis). "Good Rockin' Daddy" also did quite well for her later in 1955, but deserving follow-ups such as "W-O-M-A-N" and "Tough Lover" (the latter a torrid rocker cut in New Orleans with Lee Allen on sax) failed to catch on.

James landed at Chicago's Chess Records in 1960, signing with their Argo subsidiary. Immediately, her recording career kicked into high gear; not only did a pair of duets with her then-boyfriend (Moonglows lead singer Harvey Fuqua) chart, her own sides (beginning with the tortured ballad "All I Could Do Was Cry") chased each other up the R&B lists as well. Leonard Chess viewed James as a classy ballad singer with pop crossover potential, backing her with lush violin orchestrations for 1961's luscious "At Last" and "Trust in Me." But James' rougher side wasn't forsaken—the gospel-charged "Something's Got a Hold On Me" in 1962, a kinetic 1963 live LP (*Etta James Rocks the House*) cut at Nashville's New Era Club and a blues-soaked 1966 duet with childhood pal Sugar Pie De Santo, "In The Basement," ensured that.

Although Chess hosted its own killer house band, James traveled to Rick Hall's Fame studios in Muscle Shoals in 1967 and emerged with one of her all-time classics. "Tell Mama" was a searing slice of upbeat southern soul that contrasted markedly with another standout from the same sessions, the spine-chilling ballad "I'd Rather Go Blind." Despite the death of Leonard Chess, Etta James remained at the label into 1975, experimenting toward the end with a more rock-based approach.

There were some mighty lean years, both personally and professionally, for Miss Peaches. But she got back on track recording-wise in 1988 with a set for Island, *Seven Year Itch*, that reaffirmed her southern soul mastery. Her last few albums have been a varied lot—1990's *Sticking to My Guns* was contemporary in the extreme; 1992's Jerry Wexler-produced *The Right Time* for Elektra was slickly soulful, and her most recent outings have explored jazz directions.

In concert, Etta James is a sassy, no-holds-barred performer whose suggestive stage antics sometimes border on the obscene. She's paid her dues many times over as an R&B and soul pioneer; long may she continue to shock the uninitiated. —*Bill Dahl*

☆ **At Last** / 1961 / MCA/Chess ✦✦✦✦✦
Most of these are also on *Greatest Sides*. Those that are not are well worth hearing. —*George Bedard*

The Second Time Around / 1961 / MCA/Chess ✦✦✦✦
Etta James' second album isn't what you pull off the shelf when you want to hear her belt some soul. Like her debut, it found Chess presenting her as more or less a pop singer, using orchestration arranged and conducted by Riley Hampton, and mostly tackling popular standards of the '40s. If you're not a purist, this approach won't bother you in the least; James sings with gutso, proving that she could more than hold her own in this idiom as well. R&B isn't entirely neglected either, with the rousing "Seven Day Fool" (co-written by Berry Gordy, Jr.) a standout; "Don't Cry Baby" and "Fool That I Am" were R&B hits that made a mild impression on the pop charts as well. —*Richie Unterberger*

☆ **Rocks the House** / 1964 / MCA/Chess ✦✦✦✦✦
Simply one of the greatest live blues albums ever captured on tape. Cut in 1963 at the New Era Club in Nashville, the set finds Etta James in stellar shape as she forcefully delivers her own "Something's Got a Hold on Me" and "Seven Day Fool" interspersed with a diet of sizzling covers ("What'd I Say," "Sweet Little Angel," "Money," "Ooh Poo Pah Doo"). The CD incarnation adds three more great titles, including an impassioned reprise of her "All I Could Do Is Cry." Guitarist David T. Walker is outstanding whenever he solos. —*Bill Dahl*

Call My Name / 1967 / Cadet ✦✦✦✦
Still unavailable digitally, James' 1966 LP is dynamite Chicago soul, with the vaunted Chess house band in uplifting support. Among the many standouts are "I'm So Glad (I Found Love in You)," "It Must Be Your Love," and "Don't Pick Me for Your Fool." —*Bill Dahl*

Tell Mama / 1968 / MCA/Chess ✦✦✦✦✦
Leonard Chess dispatched Etta James to Muscle Shoals in 1967,

and the move paid off with one of her best and most soul-searing Cadet albums. Produced by Rick Hall, the resultant album boasted a relentlessly driving title cut, the moving soul ballad "I'd Rather Go Blind," sizzling covers of Otis Redding's "Security" and Jimmy Hughes' "Don't Lose Your Good Thing," and a pair of fine Don Covay copyrights. The skin-tight session aces at Fame Studios really did themselves proud behind Miss Peaches. —*Bill Dahl*

Losers Weepers / 1971 / Cadet ✦✦✦
Another vinyl-only LP from her Chess stint produced by Ralph Bass that traverses a wide range of material. Chess saxist Gene "Daddy G" Barge penned "I Think It's You," but his presence is matched by that of Duke Ellington ("I Got It Bad and That Ain't Good") and J. Fred Coots ("For All We Know") in the composers' credits. —*Bill Dahl*

Come a Little Closer / 1974 / MCA/Chess ✦✦
Bawdy, rocking R&B and soul from the great Etta James. This is one of several reissues and/or collections from her days on Chess, when she was arguably the most dynamic, energetic, and sassy female vocalist on the scene. The sound quality is good, and the selections featured outstanding. —*Ron Wynn*

R&B Dynamite / 1987 / Virgin ✦✦✦✦✦
The singer in her precocious formative years, headed by her 1955 R&B smash "Roll with Me Henry" (aka "The Wallflower"). James' followups included the driving "Good Rockin' Daddy," a bluesy "W-O-M-A-N," and the New Orleans raveup "Tough Lover," which found her backed by the gang at Cosimo's (notably saxman Lee Allen). Even though her tenure at Modern Records only produced a handful of hits, these 22 cuts are delightful artifacts of the belter's earliest days. —*Bill Dahl*

The Sweetest Peaches/Chess Years / 1988 / MCA/Chess ✦✦✦✦✦
A good 20-track survey of her Chess work on this double LP. All but two of the songs, however, are now available on the much more extensive CD *The Essential Etta James*, making this collection redundant. —*Richie Unterberger*

Stickin' to My Guns / Sep. 1990 / Island ✦✦
Contemporary-styled R&B effort that stays true to her roots. —*Bill Dahl*

The Right Time / 1992 / Elektra ✦✦
Many big names came together for the making of this album. Jerry Wexler produced it, sidemen include Steve Cropper and Lucky Peterson—but the final product is a disappointment. It's just too slickly rendered to come close to the knockout punch of her vintage Chess material. —*Bill Dahl*

How Strong Is a Woman: The Island Sessions / 1993 / 4th & Broadway ✦✦✦
How Strong Is a Woman collects the highlights from Etta James' late '80s and early '90s stint at Island Records. Although she didn't record any new classics while she was at the label, she demonstrated time and time again that she hadn't lost much of her vocal power and that she remained vital 40 years after she began recording. *How Strong Is a Woman* offers positive proof of that and is a good sampling of her work for Island. —*Thom Owens*

★ **The Essential Etta James** / Jun. 8, 1993 / MCA/Chess ✦✦✦✦✦
Forty-four tracks summarizing the long and brilliant Chess tenure of Miss Peaches, opening with her 1960 smash "All I Could Do Was Cry," encompassing her torchy, fully orchestrated ballads "At Last," "My Dearest Darling," and "Trust in Me," and continuing on through her 1961 gospel rocker "Something's Got a Hold On Me," the Chicago soul standouts "I Prefer You" and "842-3089," and her 1967 Muscle Shoals-cut smash "Tell Mama." A few of the '70s sides that conclude the two-disc set seem makeweight when compared to what preceded them, but most of the essentials are aboard. —*Bill Dahl*

Something's Got a Hold / 1994 / Charly ✦✦✦
It's not that the contents of this 20-song disc aren't terrific; until the last few songs, anyway, they are. After all, this is Etta James' Chess legacy we're talking about here. But compared to MCA's superior-sounding (and annotated) anthologies, this disc falls a bit flat. —*Bill Dahl*

Mystery Lady: Songs of Billie Holiday / Mar. 1, 1994 / Private Music ✦✦✦
The popular Etta James usually performs raunchy single-enten-

dre blues so this surprisingly subtle outing is a real change of pace. She sounds quite laid back on a set of ballads associated with Billie Holiday and utilizes a jazz rhythm section led by pianist Cedar Walton plus three horn players including the great Red Holloway on tenor and alto. James makes no attempts at exploring uptempo material or scatting, sticking to soulful interpretations of the classic ballads. Despite the lack of variety in tempos, the music is quite satisfying. —Scott Yanow

These Foolish Things / 1995 / MCA/Chess ✦✦✦✦
James has long been a masterful blues balladeer—a talent spotlighted throughout the course of this 14-song collection. Some tracks are cushioned by string-enriched arrangements, others—notably 1965's passionate "Only Time Will Tell"—are melodic Chicago soul. Four tracks are previously unreleased, including her reading of Billie Holiday's "Lover Man." —Bill Dahl

Skip James (Nehemiah Curtis James)

b. Jun. 9, 1902, Bentonia, MS, d. Oct. 3, 1969, Philadelphia, PA
Guitar, Vocals, Kazoo, Organ, Piano / Acoustic Mississippi Blues
Among the earliest and most influential Delta bluesmen to record, Skip James was the best-known proponent of the so-called Bentonia school of blues players, a genre strain invested with as much fanciful scholarly "research" as any. Coupling an oddball guitar tuning set against eerie, falsetto vocals, James' early recordings could make the hair stand up on the back of your neck. Even more surprising was when blues scholars rediscovered him in the '60s and found his singing and playing skills intact. Influencing everyone from a young Robert Johnson (Skip's "Devil Got My Woman" became the basis of Johnson's "Hellhound on My Trail") to Eric Clapton (who recorded James' "I'm So Glad" on the first Cream album), Skip James' music, while from a commonly shared regional tradition, remains infused with his own unique personal spirit. —Cub Koda

She Lyin' / 1964 / Genes ✦✦✦✦✦
By the time James had been rediscovered in the 1960s, he was still capable of playing entrancing, dynamic music, but was much less consistent and not as striking a vocalist. It was a testimony to his greatness that he still managed to make compelling records, and he was among the best storytellers and dramatic singers in the traditional realm. This mid-'60s CD features songs James recorded for the Adelphi label in 1964 that were never issued. It's hard to understand why this wasn't issued at the time it was recorded; it's just as solid as the albums James recorded for Columbia during the same period. —Ron Wynn

☆ **Skip James Today!** / 1965 / Vanguard ✦✦✦✦✦
As quiet as it was kept then, Skip James might have made the best music of anyone who resurfaced during the mid-'60s "rediscovery" era for Mississippi country blues types. Certainly, there weren't many albums made during that time as good as this one; wonderful vocals, superb guitar and a couple of tunes with tasty piano make this essential. —Ron Wynn

Devil Got My Woman / 1968 / Vanguard ✦✦✦
Fine blues-revival sides from a very influential artist. —Barry Lee Pearson

☆ **Complete 1931 Session** / 1986 / Yazoo ✦✦✦✦✦
A magnificent sampler of the '30s repertoire of a major Mississippi artist. Blues, ballads, and religious songs are included among the major songs from this idiosyncratic musical genius who has influenced current artists such as John Cephas. —Barry Lee Pearson

★ **Complete Early Recordings** / 1994 / Yazoo ✦✦✦✦✦
Complete Early Recordings collects 18 tracks Skip James recorded in the early '30s. The single-disc compilation features all of his classic songs in their original versions, including "I'm So Glad." It's a concise and thorough collection and it's essential to any blues library. —Thom Owens

Steve James

b. 1950, New York, NY
Vocals, Guitar / Modern Acoustic Blues
A native of New York City, James got into the blues via his father's guitar at age 13 and phonograph (thanks to his father's 78s by Leadbelly and Josh White). He was primarily self-taught, although he received tutelage from veterans such as Furry Lewis, Sam McGee and Lum Guffin, after moving to Tennessee in the early '70s. He also trained in luthiery at Gurian Guitars

(1970–71) and was a deejay at WEVL in Memphis. In 1977 he settled in San Antonio, where he played solo and sometimes with R&B sax legend Clifford Scott. After moving to Austin he signed with Antone's Records in 1991. In addition to his solo CDs, he has backed blues singers Gary Primich and Angela Strehli on record, as well as singer-songwriter James McMurtry and others. He is currently a contributing editor to *Acoustic Guitar* magazine. —Dan Forte

Two Track Mind / 1993 / Antone's ✦✦✦
A rarity in today's field of acoustic blues pickers; a guitarist with encyclopedic knowledge who never sounds academic. James embraces a wide scope of fingerpicking styles—Piedmont school ragtime, hokum ("Huggin' and Chalkin'"), country (Sam McGee is the source of two tunes here), and slide (his showstopping take on Sylvester Weaver's "Guitar Rag") with super technique, humor, and a relaxed ease that borders on cockiness. Only one original here, but that situation was to be rectified on Steve's follow-up. —Dan Forte

● **American Primitive** / 1994 / Antone's ✦✦✦✦✦
Utilizing a jug band of fellow Austinites Danny Barnes (tenor guitar and banjo), Mark Rubin (stand-up bass and Sousaphone—both of the Bad Livers), and harpist Gary Primich on some tracks, James sounds more mature here, evidenced by six originals (the John Hurt-esque "Talco Girl" is particularly nice) and one collaboration with bassist/songwriter Sarah Brown ("My Last Good Car") and effective rather than affected vocals. Stellar guitar throughout, with an added treat: James' blues mandolin on "Midnight Blues." —Dan Forte

Blind Lemon Jefferson

b. Jul. 11, 1897, Couchman, TX, d. Dec. 1929, Chicago, IL
Guitar, Vocals / Texas Acoustic Blues
One of the first blues-guitar stars, Blind Lemon Jefferson became the most famous bluesman of the Roaring Twenties. His 78s shattered racial barriers, becoming popular from coast to coast and influencing a generation of musicians. His best songs forged original, imagistic themes with inventive arrangements and brilliantly improvised solos. He was a serious showman, balancing a driving, unpredictable guitar style with a booming, two-octave voice. His guitar became a second voice that complemented rather than repeated his lyrics. He often halted rhythm at the end of vocal lines to launch into elaborate solo flourishes, and he could play in unusual meters with a great deal of drive and flash. A man well acquainted with booze, gambling, and heavy-hipped mamas, Blind Lemon lived the rough-and-tumble themes that dominate his songs. Portraits of Afro-American life during the early 1900s, his lyrics create a unique body of poetry—humorous and harrowing, jivey and risqué, a stunning view of society from the perspective of someone at the bottom. To this day, he ranks among the most gifted and individualistic artists in blues history. —Jas Obrecht

Blind Lemon Jefferson / Mar. 1961 / Milestone ✦✦✦✦✦
Solid collection (73 minutes' worth) of some of Lemon's best. "Jack O'Diamond Blues," "Match Box Blues," and "That Black Snake Moan" are all on board, and with the Sonic Solutions System employed on the audio restoration end, the result is about the best these surviving 60-year-old 78s have ever sounded. —Cub Koda

★ **King of the Country Blues** / 1985 / Yazoo ✦✦✦✦✦
King of the Country Blues compiles 28 of Blind Lemon Jefferson's finest songs, all presented in the original '20s versions. It is the finest introduction to the guitarist—as well as the most effective, concise retrospective—ever assembled. —Thom Owens

One Dime Blues / Aldabra ✦✦✦
One Dime Blues collects 16 tracks Blind Lemon Jefferson recorded for Paramount in the late '20s, including "Corinna Blues." While it isn't a definitive retrospective, the collection is a nice overview and offers a good sampling of Jefferson's sound. —Thom Owens

Complete Recorded Works, Vol. 1–4 / Document ✦✦✦
Over the course of four separate CDs, Document compiled everything Blind Lemon Jefferson recorded in the '20s. Although there is an immense amount of brilliant music here—he was one of the great bluesmen of the '20s, after all—the sequencing and presentation make the series useful only to completists and his-

torians. Other listeners will be better served by more concise collections. —*Thom Owens*

Big Jack Johnson

Guitar, Vocals / Modern Electric Blues
Contemporary Mississippi blues doesn't get any nastier than in Big Jack Johnson's capable hands. The ex-oil truck driver's axe cuts like a rusty machete, his rough-hewn vocals a siren call to Delta passion. But he's a surprisingly versatile songwriter; *Daddy, When Is Mama Comin' Home?*, his ambitious 1990 set for Earwig, found him tackling issues as varied as AIDS, wife abuse, and Chinese blues musicians in front of slick, horn-leavened arrangements!

Big Jack Johnson was a chip off the old block musically. His dad was a local musician playing both blues and country ditties at local functions; by the time he was 13 years old, Johnson was sitting in on guitar with his dad's band. At age 18, Johnson was following B.B. King's electrified lead. His big break came when he sat in with bluesmen Frank Frost and Sam Carr at the Savoy Theatre in Clarksdale. The symmetry between the trio was such that they were seldom apart for the next 15 years, recording for Phillips International and Jewel with Frost, the bandleader.

Chicago blues aficionado Michael Frank was so mesmerized by the trio's intensity when he heard them playing in 1975 at Johnson's Mississippi bar, the Black Fox, that Frank Frost eventually formed Earwig just to capture their steamy repertoire. That album, *Rockin' the Juke Joint Down*, came out in 1979 (as by the Jelly Roll Kings) and marked Johnson's first recordings as a singer.

Johnson's subsequent 1987 album for Earwig, *The Oil Man*, still ranks as his most intense and moving, sporting a hair-raising rendition of "Catfish Blues." The '90s have been good to Big Jack Johnson; in addition to *Daddy, When is Mama Comin' Home?* and an upcoming live album for Earwig, he appeared in the acclaimed film documentary *Deep Blues* and on its resulting soundtrack. —*Bill Dahl*

● **The Oil Man** / 1987 / Earwig ✦✦✦✦✦
With his barbed-wire guitar work and hearty vocal on a marathon rendition of "Catfish Blues," Johnson hauls the time-honored Delta tradition into contemporary blues. The entire album is an eminently solid, doggedly down-home affair, though nothing else quite measures up to the powerhouse attack of that one vicious workout. —*Bill Dahl*

Daddy, When Is Mama Comin' Home / 1991 / Earwig ✦✦✦
The precise opposite of the Mississippi guitarist's previous Earwig release. This one's slick, horn-leavened, and full of down-home ruminations on everything from AIDS and spousal abuse to Chinese blues musicians. Too weird for some purists, but definitely engaging in its singular approach. —*Bill Dahl*

Blind Willie Johnson

b. 1902, Temple, TX, **d.** 1947
Guitar, Vocals / Blues Gospel
A guitar-playing evangelist with a scary, emotion-charged voice, Blind Willie Johnson played the most exquisite slide ever heard. Void of frivolity or uncertainty, his 78s were clearly the work of a pained believer seeking streetcorner redemption with a guitar and a tin cup. He was gifted with an incomparable sense of timing and tone, using his pocket-knife slide to duplicate his vocal inflections or to produce an unforgettable phrase from a single strike of a string. With its wide, rough vibrato, his voice was as fierce as Charles Patton's or Son House's, but much easier to understand.

Little is known about his background, but thanks largely to the research of author Samuel Charters, who interviewed Johnson's widow and second wife Angeline Johnson and an old Texas preacher, Adam Booker, during the late '50s, some sketchy facts were unearthed. He was born around 1902 on the outskirts of Temple, TX. While still an infant, he and his father, George Johnson, moved to Marlin where the elder probably worked as a sharecropper. When Willie was about five, he told his father he wanted to become a preacher and made his first guitar out of a cigar box. Following the death of his mother, Johnson's father remarried. One day George Johnson caught her messing with another man and beat her up. She retaliated by throwing lye into the face of seven-year-old Willie to deliberately blind him. Later, when his father got a job in Hearne, a town about 35 miles

from Marlin, he would take young Johnson to town where he would sing religious songs and play his guitar every Saturday with a tin cup around his neck for tips.

As a young man, he lived in Marlin where he marrried Willie B. Harris in the mid-'20s and attended services at the Marlin Church of God in Christ on Commerce Street, where he often performed. Their marriage apparently dissolved in the early '30s. In 1927, Johnson became one of the first gospel guitarists on 78. Among his 30 recorded songs is the landmark instrumental "Dark Was the Night, Cold Was the Ground," described by Ry Cooder as "the most transcendent piece in all American music." Johnson spent most of his life singing for the Baptist Church or playing for tips on the streets of Beaumont, TX. He died of pneumonia in the late '40s after his wife made him sleep on wet bedding following a house fire. Decades later, his music echoed in the styles of Mississippi Fred McDowell and Mance Lipscomb. Still, he remains a slide guitarist without parallel, a player so perfect he's impossible to adequately imitate. —*Jas Obrecht & Sandra Brennan*

☆ **Praise God I'm Satisfied** / 1989 / Yazoo ✦✦✦✦✦
Pre-war gospel blues at its most harrowing and transcendental, this is unsurpassed slide guitar. —*Jas Obrecht*

Sweeter As the Years Go By / 1990 / Yazoo ✦✦✦✦✦
Blind Willie Johnson was perhaps the finest singing evangelist of all time. While the 16 tracks on this CD aren't as striking as those on the seminal *Praise God I'm Satisfied*, they're still invigorating and a vital part of his legacy. Johnson played acoustic rather than slide on several cuts, and didn't take flamboyant solos or add slashing counterpoint. But he demonstrated a skillful use of repetition and outstanding rhythmic and melodic skills. Johnson teamed with Willie B. Harris on several songs, and her rough, cutting voice proved an ideal match with his equally ragged sound. —*Ron Wynn*

★ **Complete Recordings of Blind Willie Johnson** / Apr. 27, 1993 / Columbia ✦✦✦✦✦
If you've never heard Blind Willie Johnson, you are in for one of the great, bone-chilling treats in music. Johnson played slide guitar, and sang in a rasping, false bass that could freeze the blood. But no bluesman was he; this was gospel music of the highest order, full of emotion and heartfelt commitment. Of all the guitar playing evangelists, Blind Willie Johnson may have been the very best. Though not related by bloodlines to Robert Johnson, comparisons in emotional commitment from both men cannot be helped. This two-CD anthology collects everything known to exist, and that's a lot of stark, harrowing emotional commitment no matter how you slice it. Not for the faint of heart, but hey, the good stuff never is. —*Cub Koda*

Buddy Johnson (Woodrow Wilson Johnson)

b. Jan. 10, 1915, Darlington, SC, **d.** Feb. 9, 1977, New York, NY
Piano / Jump Blues
With his sister Ella seductively serving for decades as his primary vocalist, pianist Buddy Johnson led a large jump blues band that enjoyed tremendous success during the 1940s and '50s. The suave bandleader spotlighted a series of talented singers, including balladeers Arthur Prysock, Nolan Lewis, and Floyd Ryland, but it was Ella's understated delivery (beautifully spotlighted on the sumptuous ballad "Since I Fell for You") and Buddy's crisply danceable "Walk-Em Rhythm" that made the aggregation so successful for so long.

Buddy began taking piano lessons at age four. Although he specialized professionally in tasty R&B, classical music remained one of his passions. In 1939, Buddy Johnson waxed his first 78 for Decca, "Stop Pretending (So Hep You See)." Shortly thereafter, Ella joined her older brother; her delicious vocal on "Please Mr. Johnson" translated into long-term employment.

Buddy had assembled a nine-piece orchestra by 1941 and visited the R&B charts often for Decca during wartime with "Let's Beat Out Some Love," "Baby Don't You Cry," the chart-topping "When My Man Comes Home," and "That's the Stuff You Gotta Watch." Ella cut her beloved rendering of "Since I Fell for You" in 1945, a year after Buddy waxed his jiving gem "Fine Brown Frame."

In addition to their frequent jaunts on the R&B hit parade, the Johnson organization barnstormed the country to sellout crowds throughout the '40s. Buddy moved over to Mercury Records in 1953 and scored more smashes with Ella's "Hittin' on Me" and

"I'm Just Your Fool," the latter a 1954 standout that was later purloined by Chicago harpist Little Walter.

Rock & roll eventually halted Buddy Johnson's momentum, but his band (tenor saxophonist Purvis Henson was a constant presence in the reed section) kept recording for Mercury through 1958, switched to Roulette the next year, and bowed out with a solitary session for Hy Weiss' Old Town label in 1964.

Singer Lenny Welch ensured the immortality of "Since I Fell for You" when his velvety rendition of the Johnson-penned ballad reached the uppermost reaches of the pop charts in 1963. It was a perfect match of song and singer; Welch's smooth, assured delivery would have fit in snugly with the Johnson band during its heyday a couple of decades earlier. —*Bill Dahl*

● **Go Ahead and Rock and Roll** / 1958 / Roulette ✦✦✦✦
Buddy Johnson was one of the top R&B bandleaders and composers in the '50s, as well as being an above-average vocalist. This was prototype '50s material, an era when swing-derived R&B was being mixed with country and gospel and rock was emerging from the stew. The songs are either raw, stirring uptempo tunes or steamy ballads, and they're done at a powerhouse pace. Johnson, like most great R&B acts, was a singles artist, but the songs featured here are good at worst and often magical despite clearly being from another era. —*Ron Wynn*

1953–1964 / Bear Family ✦✦✦✦✦
Four discs (104 tracks in all) that exhaustively document the Mercury, Roulette, and Old Town output of big-band veteran Buddy Johnson, whose eternally swinging outfit was seductively fronted by his sister Ella (along with several interchangeable male crooners). Buddy's band wasn't as big as it once was during his Mercury tenure (tenor saxman Purvis Henson was at the core of the blazing horn section), but the tightly arranged New York-style sizzle remained. —*Bill Dahl*

Jimmy Johnson

b. Nov. 25, 1928, Holly Springs, MS
Guitar, Harmonica, Keyboards, Vocals / Electric Chicago Blues
Chicago guitarist Jimmy Johnson didn't release his first full domestic album until he was 50 years old. He's determinedly made up for lost time ever since, establishing himself as one of the Windy City's premier blues artists with a twisting, unpredictable guitar style and a soaring, soul-dripping vocal delivery that stand out from the pack.

Born into a musical family (younger brother Syl Johnson's credentials as a soul star are all in order, while sibling Mack Thompson was Magic Sam's first call bassist), Jimmy Thompson moved to Chicago with his family in 1950. But his guitar playing remained a hobby for years—he toiled as a welder while Syl blazed a trail on the local blues circuit. Finally, in 1959, Jimmy Thompson started gigging with harpist Slim Willis around the West side. Somewhere down the line, he changed his surname to Johnson (thus keeping pace with Syl).

Since there was more cash to be realized playing R&B during the 1960s, Jimmy Johnson concentrated on that end of the stylistic spectrum for a while. He led polished house bands on the South and West sides behind Otis Clay, Denise LaSalle, and Garland Green, cutting an occasional instrumental 45 on the side. Johnson found his way back to the blues in 1974 as Jimmy Dawkins' rhythm guitarist. He toured Japan behind Otis Rush in 1975 (the journey that produced Rush's album *So Many Roads—Live in Concert*).

With the 1978 release of four stunning sides on Alligator's first batch of *Living Chicago Blues* anthologies and the issue of *Johnson's Whacks*, his first full domestic set on Delmark the next year, Jimmy Johnson's star began ascending rapidly. *North/South*, the guitarist's 1982 Delmark follow-up, and the 1985 release of *Barroom Preacher* by Alligator continued to propel Johnson into the first rank of Chicago bluesdom. Then tragedy struck: on December 2, 1988, Johnson was driving his band van when it swerved off the road in downstate Indiana, killing bassist Larry Exum and keyboardist St. James Bryant.

Understandably, Johnson, himself injured in the wreck, wasn't too interested in furthering his career for a time after the tragedy. But he's back in harness now, cutting a solid set for Verve in 1994, *I'm a Jockey*, that spotlights his blues-soul synthesis most effectively. —*Bill Dahl*

Johnson's Whacks / 1979 / Delmark ✦✦✦✦
Uncommon wit runs through the lyrics of this varied set, certainly one of the more intriguing Chicago blues albums of the late '70s. Johnson's high-pitched vocals are particularly soulful on the impassioned "I Need Some Easy Money" and "Ashes in My Ashtray," while "The Twelve Bar Blues" and "Poor Boy's Dream" are upbeat entries that don't sound as comfortable for the guitarist. Johnson gets away with a honky-tonk reprise of Ernest Tubb's country classic "Drivin' Nails in My Coffin," but his rehash of Dave Brubeck's "Take Five" should have stayed on the bandstand. —*Bill Dahl*

North/South / 1982 / Delmark ✦✦✦
Another lyrically challenging effort from Johnson (unfortunately not on CD yet), though some of the most daring musical aspects of his previous efforts have been smoothed off (for better or worse). Bassist Larry Exum was a bedrock of funky grooves for the guitarist's band. —*Bill Dahl*

● **Barroom Preacher** / 1983 / Alligator ✦✦✦✦✦
Unlike his Delmark sets, almost everything on this set (first issued in France on Black & Blue) is a cover (only the observant "Heap See" boasts original lyrics). Still, "Barroom Preacher" stands as the Chicago guitarist's most satisfying and consistent album, as he deals out gorgeous, shimmering versions of "Little by Little," "Cold, Cold Feeling," and "You Don't Know What Love Is" tailored to his soaring vocals and twisting guitar riffs (ominous minor keys often play a role in his rearrangements). —*Bill Dahl*

I'm a Jockey / 1995 / Verve ✦✦✦✦
It shouldn't have taken Johnson a full decade to find his way back into a studio, but such are the injustices of the record business. The wait was worth it, though—backed by his touring trio of the timeframe, Johnson mixes blues and soul, originals (a heartfelt "Black & White Wall" and the soaring ballad "My Ring") and covers (his takes on McKinley Mitchell's "End of a Rainbow" and Wilson Pickett's "Engine Number 9" hit home), in decidedly solid contemporary form. —*Bill Dahl*

Johnnie Johnson

b. Jul. 8, 1924, Fairmont, WV
Piano / R&B, Rock & Roll, Blues Piano
Legendary piano player Johnnie Johnson isn't exactly a household name, even among followers of blues music. That's because for 28 years, he worked as a sideman to one of rock & roll's most prominent performers, Chuck Berry. Berry joined Johnson's band, the Sir John Trio, on New Year's Eve, 1953, and after, Berry took over as the group's songwriter and frontman/guitar player. On the strength of a recommendation from Muddy Waters and an audition, Berry got a deal with Chess Records. Johnson's rhythmic piano playing was a key element in all of Berry's hit singles, a good number of which Johnson arranged. The pair's successful partnership lasted a lot longer than most rock & roll partnerships last these days.

Johnson began playing piano at age five, thanks to his mother, who provided the funds to purchase one and encouraged the young Johnson's interest. His parents had a good collection of 78-rpm records, including items by Bessie Smith and Ethel Waters. In his teens, he listened to the radio broadcasts of big bands, and taught himself based on what he heard from the likes of Art Tatum, Earl "Fatha" Hines, and Meade "Lux" Lewis. Johnson's goal in all of this listening and playing in his teenage years was to come up with his own distinctive style. His own somewhat ailing career got a shot in the arm with the Chuck Berry concert film, *Hail! Hail! Rock 'n' Roll*, and by his involvement in Keith Richards' solo release with Richards' band, the X-Pensive Winos.

In a 1995 interview, Johnson explains his abilities with piano as his mother did, a gift from God. "I can hear something and keep it in my mind until such point as I can get to a piano, and then I'll play it…that is a gift, the ability to do that."

Johnson's albums under his own name include *Blue Hand Johnny* for the St. Louis-based Pulsar label in 1987; *Johnnie B. Bad* in 1991 for the Elektra American Explorer label; *That'll Work* in 1993 for the same label; and most recently, *Johnnie Be Back* for the New Jersey-based MusicMasters label in 1995. All four are winners, and all are available on compact disc. —*Richard Skelly*

● **Blue Hand Johnnie** / 1988 / Evidence ✦✦✦✦
Johnnie Johnson's rolling, barrelling licks are as enticing as ever on this reissued Evidence CD of cuts from '90, but there are some other things that are not so grand. These include barely tolerable vocalists Barbara Carr and Stacy Johnson, whose enthusiasm is commendable, but whose vocals often get in the

way. Johnson's covers of Fats Washington's "O.J. Blues" and "Black Nights" are great, as are his versions of "Honky Tonk" and "See See Rider." But he falters on "Baby, What You Want Me To," in part because he does not convey either the original's loping stride or laconic quality, and also because it is not the kind of peppy arrangement and backbeat suited to his style. A decent effort that might have been a superior one with a couple of added touches. —*Ron Wynn*

Rockin' Eighty Eight / Apr. 1990 / Modern Blues ✦✦✦✦✦
Three underrated pianists, Clayton Love, Johnnie Johnson, and Jimmy Vaughn, typify the St. Louis Blues piano tradition on this solid sender. —*Bill Dahl*

Johnnie B. Bad / 1991 / Elektra/Nonesuch ✦✦✦✦
Keith Richards, Eric Clapton, and various NRBQ members guest on this pianist's inconsistent major-label debut. —*Bill Dahl*

Johnnie Be Back / Oct. 1995 / Music Masters ✦✦✦

L.V. Johnson

b. 1946
Vocals, Guitar / Modern Electric Blues
A mournful, often gripping singer and a good guitarist, Chicago performer L.V. Johnson actually did better as a writer than a lead artist. His songs "Are You Serious" and "True Love Is Hard To Find" were big hits for Tyrone Davis, while "Country Love" did moderately well for Bobby "Blue" Bland, and "Give Your Baby A Standing Ovation" was among The Dells' finest soul performances. Johnson played with Davis before going on his own in the '80s. The nephew of Elmore James, Johnson learned guitar from B.B. King. Besides working with Davis, Johnson was a staff guitarist at Stax, playing on sessions for The Barkays, Johnnie Taylor, and The Soul Children. He recorded for ICA, Phono, and Ichiban, although his sound and approach to soul were far too deep for the Urban marketplace. Johnson was also part-owner of a steakhouse and nightclub in Chicago. —*Ron Wynn*

● **Cold & Mean** / 1991 / Ichiban ✦✦✦✦
Although he enjoyed a sterling reputation around Chicago for his subtle, complex blues guitar style, the late L.V. Johnson seldom displayed his mastery of the genre on his albums for Ichiban. Instead, he trod an urban contemporary route that will hold little fascination for blues fans. —*Bill Dahl*

I Got the Touch / 1991 / Ichiban ✦✦✦

Unclassified / 1992 / Ichiban ✦✦✦

Lonnie Johnson (Alonzo Johnson)

b. Feb. 8, 1889, New Orleans, LA, d. Jun. 16, 1970, Toronto, Canada
Guitar, Vocals / Jazz Blues, Acoustic Blues
Blues guitar simply would not have developed in the manner that it did if not for the prolific brilliance of Lonnie Johnson. He was there to help define the instrument's future within the genre and the genre's future itself at the very beginning, his melodic conception so far advanced from most of his pre-war peers as to inhabit a plane all his own. For more than 40 years, Johnson played blues, jazz, and ballads his way; he was a true blues originator whose influence hung heavy on a host of subsequent blues immortals.

Johnson's extreme versatility doubtless stemmed in great part from growing up in the musically diverse Crescent City. Violin caught his ear initially, but he eventually made the guitar his passion, developing a style so fluid and inexorably melodic that instrumental backing seemed superfluous. He signed up with Okeh Records in 1925 and commenced to recording at an astonishing pace—between 1925 and 1932, he cut an estimated 130 waxings. The red-hot duets he recorded with White jazz guitarist Eddie Lang (masquerading as Blind Willie Dunn) in 1928–29 were utterly groundbreaking in their ceaseless invention. Johnson also recorded pioneering jazz efforts in 1927 with no less than Louis Armstrong's Hot Five and Duke Ellington's orchestra.

After enduring the Depression and moving to Chicago, Johnson came back to recording life with Bluebird for a five-year stint beginning in 1939. Under the ubiquitous Lester Melrose's supervision, Johnson picked up right where he left off, selling quite a few copies of "He's a Jelly Roll Baker" for old Nipper. Johnson went with Cincinnati-based King Records in 1947 and promptly enjoyed one of the biggest hits of his uncommonly

long career with the mellow ballad "Tomorrow Night," which topped the R&B charts for seven weeks in 1948. More hits followed posthaste: "Pleasing You (As Long As I Live)," "So Tired," and "Confused."

Time seemed to have passed Johnson by during the late '50s. He was toiling as a hotel janitor in Philadelphia when banjo player Elmer Snowden alerted Chris Albertson to his whereabouts. That rekindled a major comeback, Johnson cutting a series of albums for Prestige's Bluesville subsidary during the early '60s and venturing to Europe under the auspices of Horst Lippmann and Fritz Rau's American Folk Blues Festival banner in 1963. Finally, in 1969, Johnson was hit by a car in Toronto and died a year later from the effects of the accident.

Johnson's influence was massive, touching everyone from Robert Johnson, whose seminal approach bore strong resemblance to that of his older namesake, to Elvis Presley and Jerry Lee Lewis, who each paid heartfelt tribute with versions of "Tomorrow Night" while at Sun. —*Bill Dahl*

Losing Game / 1960 / Bluesville ✦✦✦✦
Johnson recorded prolifically for Prestige's Bluesville during his early-'60s comeback; this 1960 set is a typically gorgeous solo outing that ranges from torchy standards of the Tin Pan Alley species ("What a Difference a Day Makes," "Summertime") to bluesier pursuits of his own creation. —*Bill Dahl*

★ **Blues & Ballads** / Apr. 1960 / Bluesville ✦✦✦✦✦
Later Johnson, doing blues and ballads with jazz guitarist Elmer Snowden. Johnson's vocals are refined and sensitive. It is hard to hear him sing his own composition "I Found a Dream" and remain unmoved. Such a lovely album. —*Michael Erlewine*

Blues, Ballads & Jumpin' Jazz / Apr. 1960 / Bluesville ✦✦✦✦✦
This is an unusual CD. In 1960 guitarists Lonnie Johnson and Elmer Snowden (along with bassist Wendell Marshall) teamed up for *Blues and Ballads* which was primarily a showcase for Johnson's blues vocals. This previously unreleased set from the same session has six instrumentals and just four vocals with Snowden generally in the lead. The two guitarists are heard good-naturedly suggesting songs before launching into spontaneous improvisations and the results sound like an intimate concert. Highlights of this fun outing include "Lester Leaps In," "C-Jam Blues," and "Careless Love." —*Scott Yanow*

Idle Hours / Jul. 1961 / Bluesville ✦✦✦
Johnson and Victoria Spivey had known one another for decades (they duetted on the ribald "Toothache Blues" way back in 1928), so it's no surprise that their musical repartee on 1961's "Idle Hours" seems so natural and playful. Spivey guests on three tracks (including the title number) and plays piano on her one solo entry. Johnson does the majority of the disc without her, benefitting from pianistic accompaniment by Cliff Jackson. —*Bill Dahl*

The Complete Folkways Recordings / 1967 / Smithsonian/ Folkways ✦✦✦✦
An even two dozen solo performances from late in the legendary guitarist's amazing career (1967), but chock full of stellar moments all the same. Artists of Johnson's versatility were rare even then—he brings a multitude of shadings to "My Mother's Eyes," and "How Deep Is the Ocean," then delivers a saucy "Juice Headed Baby" with the same stunning complexity. —*Bill Dahl*

Sings 24 Twelve Bar Blues / 196 / King ✦
Avoid these edited versions of his King sides. —*Bill Dahl*

Tomorrow Night / 1976 / Gusto ✦✦✦✦✦
Here's a two-LP collection just begging for digital reissue. Its 22 sides from Johnson's King stay include the immortal blues ballad "Tomorrow Night," his definitive renditions of "Careless Love" and "Jelly Roll Baker," and the lightly jumping "Trouble Ain't Nothin' But the Blues"—none of which grace Charly's CD compilation by the late blues great. —*Bill Dahl*

Another Night to Cry / 1978 / Bluesville ✦✦✦
Lonnie Johnson, a talented vocalist and guitarist who chose to spend much of his life playing blues (although in the 1920s he recorded with some of the top jazz stars), had his fifth recording for Prestige/Bluesville (a solo set) reissued on this CD. "Blues After Hours" is an instrumental that shows off his jazz roots and many of the 11 songs (all of which are Johnson originals) have spots for his guitar. Since there are only around 34 minutes on this set (which could have been combined on one CD with the music from another LP) and none of the individual songs even

reach four minutes, this is not one of the more essential Lonnie Johnson releases but it does have its strong moments. —*Scott Yanow*

Mr. Johnson's Blues / 197 / Mamush ✦✦✦
Fourteen cuts from the late '20s to early '30s, with Eddie Lang, Victoria Spivey, Texas Alexander, Mooch Richardson, Katherine Baker, and Violet Green. Highlights include "Uncle Ned Don't Use Your Head" and "Winnie the Wailer." —*Barry Lee Pearson*

The Originator of Modern Guitar Blues / 1980 / Blues Boy ✦✦✦✦✦
Later Lonnie Johnson, demonstrating his proficiency on everything from pop to blues and R&B. It's excellently remastered, sequenced and presented, covering 1940s and '50s cuts. —*Ron Wynn*

★ **Steppin' on the Blues** / 1991 / Columbia/Legacy ✦✦✦✦✦
Groundbreaking guitar work of dazzling complexity that never fails to amaze—and this stuff was cut in the 1920s! Johnson's astonishingly fluid guitar work was massively influential (Robert Johnson, for one, was greatly swayed by his waxings), and his no-nonsense vocals (frequently laced with threats of violence—"Got the Blues for Murder Only" and "She's Making Whoopee in Hell Tonight" are prime examples on this 19-cut collection) are scarcely less impressive. Johnson's torrid guitar duets with jazzman Eddie Lang retain their sense of legend nearly seven decades after they were cut. —*Bill Dahl*

He's a Jelly Roll Baker / Sep. 1992 / Bluebird ✦✦✦✦✦
This 20-song collection covers 1930s and '40s material in which Johnson primarily performs blues tunes, doing salty, sassy, mournful and suggestive numbers in a distinctive, memorable fashion. His vocals on "Rambler's Blues," "In Love Again," the title cut and several others are framed by brilliant, creative playing and excellent support from such pianists as Blind John Davis, Lil Hardin Armstrong, and Joshua Altheimer. This is tight, intuitive music in which Johnson set the tone and dominated the songs. If you're unaware of Lonnie Johnson's brilliant blues material, here's an excellent introduction. —*Ron Wynn*

Stompin' At The Penny / 1995 / Columbia/Legacy ✦✦
Their archives filled to bursting with seminal pre-war sides by Lonnie Johnson, and what does Legacy hand us instead? This uniformly mediocre document of Johnson's dealings with a Canadian trad jazz band. Some of the disc doesn't even feature Johnson. One to avoid, unless you're into Dixieland. —*Bill Dahl*

Me & My Crazy Self / Charly ✦✦✦✦✦
With a firm emphasis on the less schmaltzy side of Johnson's 1947–1952 stint at Cincinnati's King Records, this 20-tracker finds the blues pioneer coming into the age of electric blues and R&B quite adroitly. His dignified vocal style similarly weathered the ensuing decades nicely—"You Can't Buy Love," "Friendless Blues," and the title track are bittersweet outings sporting multiple levels of subtlety. —*Bill Dahl*

Complete Recorded Works, Vols. 1–7 / Document ✦✦✦
A fantastic seven-CD collection of Johnson's earliest works. Includes "Bed of Sand," "Treat 'Em Right," "Woke Up with the Blues in My Fingers," "When a Man Is Treated like a Dog," "Have to Change Keys to Play These Blues," "Blues Is Only a Ghost," "Not the Chump I Used to Be," and the romantic "She's Making Whoopee in Hell Tonight." —*Cub Koda*

Complete Recorded Works, Vols. 1–3 / Document ✦✦✦
Three CDs from a full decade of Lonnie's best, featuring "Man Killing Broad," "I'm Nuts over You," and "Laplegged Drunk Again." —*Cub Koda*

Luther "Snake Boy" Johnson

b. Aug. 30, 1934, Davisboro, GA, d. Mar. 18, 1976, Boston, MA
Guitar / Chicago Blues
The confusing plethora of artists working under the name of Luther (nickname here) Johnson can leave even those with a decent knowledge of blues in a major state of confusion. But in this biographical entry, we concern ourselves with the life and times of Luther "Georgia Boy/Snake Boy" Johnson who, to make matters even *more* confusing, also worked and recorded under the names Little Luther and Luther King.

He was born in 1934 in Davisboro, GA, which explains at least one of his nicknames, but it turns out his real name wasn't even Luther, but Lucius. One of ten children working on a farm,

he started playing at the tender age of seven. He soon ran away from home and was placed in a reform school by 1947. A three year stint in the Army followed. Upon his discharge, he was picked as a member of the Milwaukee Supreme Angels gospel group, working the local church circuit. But the blues bug hit and he soon had his own little blues trio together, eventually settling in Chicago by the early '60s. He played for a while with Elmore James and was a regular fixture in the Muddy Waters band by the mid-'60s. He recorded as Little Luther for Chess in the mid-'60s ("The Twirl," available on the Ace anthology, *Houserockin' Blues*, listed in the compilation section) and by 1970 was relocated to Boston, MA, working as a solo artist. The next five years found him working steadily on the college and blues festival circuit before cancer overtook him on March 18, 1976, at a mere 41 years of age. —*Cub Koda*

Come on Home / 1969 / Douglas ✦✦✦

The Muddy Waters Blues Band / Dec. 1969 / Douglas ✦✦

Born in Georgia / 1972 / Black & Blue ✦✦✦

● **Lonesome in My Bedroom** / Dec. 18, 1975 / Evidence ✦✦✦✦✦
This was Johnson's final album before his death in 1976, and it was originally cut for Black and Blue (now reissued with three bonus tracks). While various tracks reflect the influence of Muddy Waters, Jimmy Reed, and John Lee Hooker, Johnson's own inimitable vocals, raspy lines and tart guitar eventually create his own aura. He is nicely backed by drummer Fred Below, bassist Dave Myers, guitar burner Lonnie Brooks, and the solid rhythm work of Hubert Sumlin. This was a fine session for a good, occasionally outstanding blues artist. —*Ron Wynn*

On the Road Again / 1976 / Black & Blue ✦✦✦
On the Road Again, an early-'70s outing, shows Johnson in fine form, assisted by a tough backing band. Cut in France. —*Bill Dahl*

Get Down to the Nitty Gritty / 1976 / New Rose ✦✦✦
Culled from a radio broadcast made for a Rochester, NY radio station in 1976, *Get Down to the Nitty Gritty* is a nifty set of hard-edged Chicago blues. Luther Johnson pays homage to his mentor and employer, Muddy Waters, throughout the album, playing classics like "Hoochie Coochie Man" and originals in the same vein. Although the sound quality of the recording is poor—there are dropouts and tape hiss all over the place—the performance is stellar. Johnson sings with passion and his guitar solos are blistering. *Get Down to the Nitty Gritty* is a rough gem that is worthwhile to any fan of Johnson or Muddy Waters. —*Thom Owens*

Luther "Guitar Junior" Johnson

b. Apr. 11, 1939, Itta Bena, MS
Guitar, Vocals / Modern Electric Blues
Of the three blues guitarists answering to the name of Luther Johnson, this West side-styled veteran is probably the best-known. Adding to the general confusion surrounding the triumvirate: like Luther "Georgia Boy" Johnson, "Guitar Junior" spent a lengthy stint in the top-seeded band of Muddy Waters (1972–1979).

Gospel and blues intersected in young Luther Johnson's life while he was still in Mississippi. But after he moved to Chicago in the mid-'50s, blues was his main passion, working with Ray Scott and Tall Milton Shelton before taking over the latter's combo in 1962. Magic Sam was a major stylistic inspiration to Johnson during the mid-'60s (Johnson spent a couple of years in Sam's band). The West side approach remains integral to Johnson's sound today, even though he moved to the Boston area during the early '80s.

Johnson's 1976 debut album, *Luther's Blues*, was cut during a European tour with Muddy Waters. By 1980, he was on his own, recording with the Nighthawks as well as four tracks on Alligator's second series of *Living Chicago Blues* anthologies. With his own band, the Magic Rockers, and the Roomful of Blues horn section, Johnson released *Doin' the Sugar Too* on Rooster Blues in 1984. Since 1990, Johnson has been signed to Ron Levy's Bullseye Blues logo; his three albums for the firm have been sizzling, soul-tinged blues (with a strong West Side flavor often slicing through). —*Bill Dahl*

Luther's Blues / Nov. 1, 1976 / Evidence ✦✦✦
The confidence that ex-Muddy Waters sideman Luther "Guitar Junior" Johnson exudes on his contemporary albums wasn't quite there in abundance yet when the French Black & Blue

imprint produced this album in 1976 with the rest of his Waters bandmates in tow. A few too many hoary covers ("Sweet Home Chicago," "Mother-In-Law Blues") also grate. But as his first solo album, it's an important chapter in his development. —*Bill Dahl*

Doin' the Sugar Too / 1984 / Rooster Blues ✦✦✦
A step in the right direction—much better production, savvier song selection, including a few snappy originals, and the five-piece Roomful of Blues horn section in staunch support. The guitarist's Magic Rockers include keyboardist Ron Levy, who would go on to produce Johnson's Bullsye Blues output. —*Bill Dahl*

I Want to Groove with You / 1990 / Bullseye Blues ✦✦✦✦✦
Now this is more like it. Johnson and his New England-based Magic Rockers sizzle the hide off the genre with tough West Side-styled grooves redolent of Johnson's Chicago upbringing but up-to-the-minute in their execution. With this set, Johnson fully came into his own as a recording artist. —*Bill Dahl*

It's Good to Me / 1992 / Bullseye Blues ✦✦✦✦
Another barn-burner mixing the guitarist's West-side roots with soul and blues shadings to present some of the fieriest contemporary blues on the market. Saxist Gordon Beadle and keyboardist Joe Krown distinguish themselves behind Johnson. —*Bill Dahl*

Country Sugar Papa / Mar. 30, 1994 / Bullseye Blues ✦✦✦✦
Johnson's third and final album for producer Ron Levy's Bullseye Blues diskery is every bit as spellbinding as the prior pair. Whether fronting his latest batch of Magic Rockers or going it alone, Johnson is totally convincing. —*Bill Dahl*

● **Slammin' on the West Side** / 1996 / Telarc ✦✦✦✦✦
Lousy title, great album. Johnson hasn't been based out of Chicago in years, but that sound remains at the heart of his approach—even when he's recording in Louisiana along a funky New Orleans rhythm section (bassist George Porter, Jr. and drummer Herman Ernest). Jump blues in the form of Buddy Johnson's "A Pretty Girl (A Cadillac and Some Money)," the Magic Sam tribute "Hard Times (Have Surely Come)," the solo acoustic "Get Up and Go," a soul-slanted "Every Woman Needs to Be Loved"—Johnson smokes 'em all. —*Bill Dahl*

Luther "Houserocker" Johnson

Guitar, Vocals / Modern Electric Blues
The latest Luther Johnson to add his name to the blues directory is an adept singer/guitarist who is a current favorite on the Atlanta blues scene. Proficient in various shadings of the electric blues idiom, Johnson has recently extended his repertoire from covers of blues standards to his own material, performed with the same '50s/'60s flavor.

Johnson taught himself how to play guitar when he was a teenager in Atlanta by listening to records. Soon, he began playing guitar in pickup bands, which gave him the opportunity to support such touring musicians as Johnny Winter. After several years playing in bar bands, Johnson formed his own group, the Houserockers.

The Houserockers played bars and clubs around Georgia for several years, eventually landing a record contract with Ichiban in 1989. That same year, Johnson released his debut album, *Takin' a Bite Outta the Blues.* Two years later, his second record, *Houserockin' Daddy,* appeared. Luther "Houserocker" Johnson continued to tour the US throughout the '90s. —*Jim O'Neal & Stephen Thomas Erlewine*

Takin' a Bite Outta the Blues / 1989 / Ichiban ✦✦✦
This tough, direct, small-group blues sounds hardened by years in bars, "giving people what they want." Included are covers of B.B. King, Jimmy Reed, Ray Charles, and Charles Brown. —*Niles J. Frantz*

● **Houserockin' Daddy** / 1991 / Ichiban ✦✦✦✦✦
Johnson is a traditional electric bluesman (now living and working in the Atlanta area) who was heavily influenced by Jimmy Reed. The album includes covers of Jimmy Reed, Lightnin' Slim, Howlin' Wolf, and Guitar Slim tunes. It's simple, driving, to the point, streamlined, no-frills blues. —*Niles J. Frantz*

Robert Johnson

b. May 8, 1911, Hazlehurst, MS, **d.** Aug. 16, 1938, Greenwood, MS
Guitar, Vocals / Acoustic Delta Blues
If the blues has a truly mythic figure, one whose story hangs

over the music the way a Charlie Parker does over jazz or a Hank Williams does over country, it's Robert Johnson, certainly the most celebrated figure in the history of the blues. Of course, his legend is immensely fortified by the fact that Johnson also left behind a small legacy of recordings that are considered the emotional apex of the music itself. These recordings have not only entered the realm of blues standards ("Love in Vain," "Crossroads," "Sweet Home Chicago," "Stop Breaking Down"), but have been adapted by rock & roll artists as diverse as the Rolling Stones, Steve Miller, Led Zeppelin, and Eric Clapton. While there are historical naysayers who would be more comfortable downplaying his skills and achievements (most of whom have never made a convincing case as where the source of his apocalyptic visions emanates from), Robert Johnson remains a potent force to be reckoned with. As a singer, a composer, and as a guitarist of considerable skills, he produced some of the genre's best music and the ultimate blues legend to deal with. Doomed, haunted, driven by demons, a tormented genius dead at an early age, all of these add up to making him a character of mythology who—if he hadn't actually existed—would have to be created by some biographer's overactive romantic imagination.

The legend of his life—which by now, even folks who don't know *anything* about the blues can cite to you chapter and verse—goes something like this: Robert Johnson was a young Black man living on a plantation in rural Mississippi. Branded with a burning desire to become great blues musician, he was instructed to take his guitar to a crossroad near Dockery's plantation at midnight. There he was met by a large Black man (the Devil) who took the guitar from Johnson, tuned it and handed it back to him. Within less than a year's time, in exchange for his everlasting soul, Robert Johnson became the king of the Delta blues singers, able to play, sing, and create the greatest blues anyone had ever heard.

As success came with live performances and phonograph recordings, Johnson remained tormented, constantly haunted by nightmares of hellhounds on his trail, his pain and mental anguish finding release only in the writing and performing of his music. Just as he was to be brought to Carnegie Hall to perform in John Hammond's first Spirituals to Swing concert, the news had come from Mississippi; Robert Johnson was dead, poisoned by a jealous husband while playing a jook joint. Those who were there swear he was last seen alive foaming at the mouth, crawling around on all fours, hissing and snapping at onlookers like a mad dog. His dying words (either spoken or written on a piece of scrap paper) were, "I pray that my redeemer will come and take me from my grave." He was buried in a pine box in an unmarked grave, his deal with the Devil at an end.

Of course, Johnson's influences in the real world were far more disparate than the legend suggests, no matter how many times it's been retold or embellished. As a teenage plantation worker, Johnson fooled with a harmonica a little bit, but seemingly had no major musical skills to speak of. Every attempt to sit in with local titans of the stature of Son House, Charlie Patton, Willie Brown and others brought howls of derision from the older bluesmen. Son House: "We'd all play for the Saturday night balls, and there'd be this little boy hanging around. That was Robert Johnson. He blew a harmonica then, and he was pretty good at that, but he wanted to play a guitar. He'd sit at our feet and play during the breaks and such another racket you'd never heard." He married young and left Robinsonville, wandering the Delta and using Hazlehurst as base, determined to become a full-time professional musician after his first wife died during childbirth. Johnson returned to Robinsonville a few years later and when he encountered House and Willie Brown at a juke joint in Banks, Mississippi, according to House, "When he finished all our mouths were standing open. I said, 'Well, ain't that fast! He's gone now!'" To a man, there was only one explanation as how Johnson had gotten *that* good *that* fast; he had sold his soul to the Devil.

But Johnson's skills were acquired in a far more conventional manner, born more of a concentrated Christian work ethic than a Faustian bargain with old Scratch. He idolized the Delta recording star Lonnie Johnson—sometimes introducing himself to newcomers as "Robert Lonnie, one of the Johnson brothers"—and the music of Scrapper Blackwell, Skip James, and Kokomo Arnold were all inspirational elements that he drew his unique style from. His slide style certainly came from hours of watching local stars like Charlie Patton and Son House, among others. Perhaps the biggest influence, however, came from an unrecorded bluesman named Ike Zinneman. We'll never really know what Zinneman's music sounded like (we do know from various reports that he liked to practice late at night in the local graveyard, sitting on tombstones while he strummed away) or how much of his personal muse he imparted to Johnson, if any. What *is* known is that after a year or so under Zinneman's tutelage, Johnson returned with an encyclopedic knowledge of his instrument, an ability to sing and play in a multiplicity of styles, and a very carefully worked out approach to song construction, keeping his original lyrics with him in a personal digest. As an itinerant musician, playing at country suppers as well as on the street, his audience demanded someone who could play and sing everything from blues pieces to the pop and hillbilly tunes of the day. Johnson's talents could cover all of that and more. His most enduring contribution, the boogie bass line played on the bottom strings of the guitar (adapted from piano players), has become part and parcel of the sound most people associate with down-home blues. It is a sound so very much of a part of the music's fabric that the listener cannot imagine the styles of Jimmy Reed, Elmore James, Eddie Taylor, Lightnin' Slim, Hound Dog Taylor or a hundred lesser lights existing without that essential component part. As his playing partner Johnny Shines put it, "Some of the things that Robert did with the guitar affected the way everybody played. He'd do rundowns and turnbacks. He'd do repeats. None of this was being done. In the early '30s, boogie on the guitar was rare, something to be heard. Because of Robert, people learned to complement theirselves, carrying their own bass as their own lead with this one instrument." While his music can certainly be put in context as part of a definable tradition, what he did with it and where he took it was another matter entirely.

Although Robert Johnson never recorded near as much as Lonnie Johnson, Charlie Patton, or Blind Lemon Jefferson, he certainly traveled more than all of them put together. After his first recordings came out and "Terraplane Blues" became his signature tune (a so-called "race" record selling over three or four thousand copies back in the early to mid-'30s was considered a hit), Johnson hit the road, playing anywhere and everywhere he could. Instilled with a seemingly unquenchable desire to experience new places and things, his wandering nature took him up and down the Delta and as far afield as St. Louis, Chicago, Detroit (where he performed over the radio on the *Elder Moten Hour*), and New York City, places Son House and Charlie Patton had only seen in the movies, if that. But the end came at a Saturday-night dance at a juke joint in Three Forks, Mississippi in August of 1938. Playing with Honeyboy Edwards and Sonny Boy Williamson (Rice Miller), Johnson was given a jug of moonshine whiskey laced with either poison or lye, presumably by the husband of a woman the singer had made advances toward. He continued playing into the night until he was too sick to continue, then brought back to a boarding house in Greenwood, some 15 miles away. He lay sick for several days, successfully sweating the poison out of his system, but caught pneumonia as a result and died on August 16th. The legend was just beginning.

In the early '60s, Columbia Records released *King of the Delta Blues Singers*, the first compilation of Johnson's music and one of the earliest collections of pure country blues. Rife with liner notes full of romantic speculation, little in the way of hard information and a painting standing for a picture, this for years was the world's sole introduction to the music and the legend, doing much to promote both. A second volume—collecting the other master takes and issuing a few of the alternates—was released in the '70s, giving fans a first-hand listen to music that had been only circulated through bootleg tapes and albums or cover versions by English rock stars. Finally in 1991—after years of litigation—a complete two-CD box set was released with every scrap of Johnson material known to exist plus the holy grail of the blues; the publishing of the only two known photographs of the man himself. Columbia's parent company, Sony, were hoping that sales would maybe hit 20,000. The box set went on to sell over a million units, the first blues recordings ever to do so.

In the intervening years since the release of the box set, Johnson's name and likeness has become a cottage growth merchandising industry. Posters, postcards, t-shirts, guitar picks, strings, straps and polishing cloths—all bearing either his likeness or signature (taken from his second marriage certificate)— have become available, making him the ultimate blues commodity with his image being reproduced for profit far more than any contemporary bluesman, dead or alive. Although the man himself (and his contemporaries) could never have imagined it in a million years, the music and the legend both live on. —*Cub Koda*

☆ **King of the Delta Blues Singers** / 1961 / Columbia ✦✦✦✦✦
Reading about the power inherent in Robert Johnson's music is one thing, but actually *experiencing* it is another matter entirely. Here's where you go to find it. The gold-disc edition of this album is certainly worth the extra money, as it was mastered off of newly discovered safety tapes of far superior quality to even that of the 1991 box set. If there is such a thing as a "greatest hits" package available on Johnson, this landmark album would come very close indeed. The majority of Johnson's best-known tunes are aboard; "Crossroads," "Terraplane Blues," "Me and the Devil Blues," "Come on in My Kitchen," and the apocalyptic visions contained in "Hellhound on My Trail" are the blues as its finest, the lyrics sheer poetry. If you are starting your blues collections, be sure to make this your first purchase. —*Cub Koda*

☆ **King of the Delta Blues Singers, Vol. 2** / 1970 / Columbia ✦✦✦✦✦
This second volume—although made somewhat superfluous by the arrival two decades later of the box set—contains the rest of the issued takes and some, but not all, of the alternate takes. The music is excellent, featuring the first album appearance of "Love in Vain." —*Cub Koda*

★ **The Complete Recordings** / 1990 / Columbia/Legacy ✦✦✦✦✦
A double-disc box set containing everything Robert Johnson ever recorded, *The Complete Recordings* is essential listening, but it is also slightly problematic. The problems aren't in the music itself, of course, which is stunning, and the fidelity of the recordings is the best it ever has been or ever will be. Instead, it's in the track sequencing. As the title implies, *The Complete Recordings* contains all of Johnson's recorded material, including a generous selection of alternate takes. All of the alternates are sequenced directly after the master, which can make listening to the album a little intimidating and tedious for novices. Certainly, the alternates can be programmed out with a CD player, but the set would have been more palatable if the alternate takes were presented on a separate disc. Nevertheless, this is a minor complaint—Robert Johnson's music retains its power no matter what context it is presented in. He, without question, deserves this kind of deluxe box-set treatment. —*Stephen Thomas Erlewine*

Tommy Johnson

b. 1896, Terry, MS, d. Nov. 1, 1956, Crystal Springs, MS
Guitar, Kazoo, Vocals / Acoustic Delta Blues
Next to Son House and Charlie Patton, no one was more important to the development of pre-Robert Johnson Delta blues than Tommy Johnson. Armed with a powerful voice that could go from a growl to an eerie falsetto range and a guitar style that had all of the early figures and licks of the Delta style clearly delineated, Johnson only recorded for two years—from 1928 to 1930—but left behind a body of work that's hard to ignore.

The legend of Tommy Johnson is even harder to ignore. The stories about his live performances—where he would play the guitar behind his neck in emulation of Charlie Patton's showboating while hollering the blues at full-throated level for hours without a break—are part of it. So is his uncontrolled womanizing and alcoholism, both of which constantly got him in trouble. Johnson's addiction to spirits was so pronounced that he was often seen drinking Sterno-denatured alcohol used for artificial heat—or shoe polish strained through bread for the kick each could offer when whiskey wasn't affordable or available in dry counties throughout the South. Then there's the crossroads story. Yes, years before the deal with the Devil at a deserted Delta crossroad was being used as an explanation of the otherworldly abilities of young Robert Johnson, the story was being told repeatedly about Tommy, often by the man himself to reinforce his abilities to doubting audiences.

Then there's the music. His "Cool Water Blues" got amped up in the '50s by one of his early admirers, Howlin' Wolf, and became "I Asked for Water (She Brought Me Gasoline)." Another signature piece, his "Maggie Campbell," came with a chord progression that was used for infinite variations by blues players dating all the way back to his contemporary Charlie Patton through Robert Nighthawk. Two of his best-known numbers have survived into modern times; "Big Road Blues" is probably best known to contemporary blues fans from adaptations by Floyd Jones and others, while his "Canned Heat Blues"—a bone-chilling account of his complete addiction to alcohol and his slavish attempts to score it by whatever means necessary—was the tune that gave a California blues-rock band their name. After awhile, all of the above starts adding up, no matter how you slice it. Tommy Johnson was one tough hombre, and a real piece of work.

He was born in 1896 in Hinds County, MS, on the George Miller plantation. Once the family moved to Crystal Springs in 1910, Tommy picked up the guitar, learning from his older brother, LeDell. By age 16, Johnson had run away from home to become a "professional" musician, largely supporting himself by playing on the street for tips. By the late teens-early '20s, Tommy was frequently playing in the company of rising local stars Charlie Patton, Dick Bankston, and Willie Brown. Their collective output planted seed, later becoming the first greening of the Mississippi Delta blues. Johnson spent most of the '20s drinking, womanizing, gambling, and playing in the company of Rubin Lacy, Charley McCoy, Son Spand, Walter Vincent, and Ishmon Bracey when the money got low and apparently, only when the mood struck him. By all acounts, Tommy felt no particular drive to relentlessly promote himself and—while he played music for pay till the very end of his life—he certainly wasn't as serious about his career as he was about his drinking. He cut his first records for the Victor (later RCA Victor, now BMG) label at sessions held in Memphis, TN, in 1928. Johnson's first releases hit the area hard, inspiring a raft of up-and-comers that reads like the proverbial who's who list; you could easily count Howlin' Wolf, Robert Nighthawk, Houston Stackhouse, Floyd Jones, Boogie Bill Webb, K.C. Douglas, Johnny "Geechie" Temple, and Otis Spann among his many disciples.

He cut one more stack of great records for the Paramount label in 1930, largely through the maneuvering of fellow drinking buddy Charlie Patton. Then the slow descent into alcoholism started taking its toll, the one too many nights of Sterno and shoe polish buzzes reducing his once prodigious talents to small, sporadic flickerings of former genius. He worked on a medicine show with Ishmon Bracey in the '30s, but mostly seemed to be a mainstay of the juke and small party dance circuit the rest of his days. He was playing just such a local house party in November of 1956 when he suffered a fatal heart attack and went out in probably the exact fashion he wanted to. Whether the story about the deal with the Devil at the crossroads was something he truly believed or just something Johnson said to drum up local interest in himself, it seems odd that you'll find him buried at the Warm Springs Methodist Church Cemetery in Crystal Springs. Maybe he mellowed out towards the end, maybe he found God. Some things about the blues you'll never know, no matter how many computers you hook up to it. —Cub Koda

★ **Complete Recorded Works** / Document ✦✦✦✦✦
The complete Victor and Paramount sides from 1928-1929 are sequenced in chronological order. —Jas Obrecht

Casey Jones

Drums / Electric Chicago Blues
Long recognized as one of the Chicago circuit's premier drummers, charismatic Casey Jones has moved out in front of his band over the last decade instead of hiding behind his kit. Casey discovered that beating his way through the world was fun while drilling with his high school marching band back in Greenville. He moved to Chicago in 1956. Before the end of the year, he was drumming professionally with an outfit called Otis Luke & the Rhythm Bombers (for a whopping five bucks a night). One auspicious 1959 night, Jones was forced to sing live for the first time when the pianist leading his band was tossed in jail. He found screaming like Little Richard was pretty enjoyable too.

Early '60s session work behind Earl Hooker, A.C. Reed, McKinley Mitchell, and Muddy Waters (1962's "You Need Love") kept Jones busy, as did playing on the South and West sides with the likes of Otis Rush and Freddy King. His profile rose markedly in 1978 when he slid into the drum chair with Albert Collins' hand-picked combo, the Icebreakers. His impeccable timekeep-

ing powered the band for six-and-a-half years, and he played on Collins' first six Alligator albums (notably *Ice Pickin'* and the '85 summit meeting *Showdown!* with Robert Cray and Johnny Copeland).

Casey Jones has been holding down Sunday nights at Chicago's popular Kingston Mines nightclub for nearly a decade—a period that's seen his own discography grow steadily. 1987's *Solid Blue* for Rooster Blues preceded the formation of his own label, Airwax Records (source of his last few CDs, including 1993's *The Crowd Pleaser* and *[I-94] On My Way to Chicago* in 1995). —Bill Dahl

Solid Blue / Jul. 1988 / Rooster Blues ✦✦✦✦
One of the Chicago drummer's best solo outings, still not yet available on CD. Eight originals, all of them well-done (especially the chunky "Mr. Blues" and a rocking "Hip Hip Hooray"). Jones' vocals are enthusiastic and his backing is expert—sidemen include harpist Billy Branch, guitarist Maurice Vaughn, and bassist Johnny B. Gayden (the latter Jones' former cohort in Albert Collins' band, the Icebreakers. —Bill Dahl

Crowd Pleaser / 1993 / Airwax ✦✦✦✦
A very enjoyable collection of new and recent (three songs, including "Tribute to the Boogie Men" and "Mr. Blues," stem from "Solid Blue") numbers on Jones' own Airwax logo. Of course, he handles his own timekeeping throughout. —Bill Dahl

● **(I-94) On My Way to Chicago** / 1995 / Airwax ✦✦✦✦✦
As good a place to begin your Casey Jones collection as any, since his vocals remain strong and his songwriting is as pleasing as ever. The title cut, "I Know I Got a Good Woman," and the sinuous "She Treats Me Right" all make highly favorable impressions. —Bill Dahl

Curtis Jones

b. Aug. 18, 1906, Naples, TX, **d.** Sep. 11, 1971, Munich, Germany
Piano, Vocals / Electric Chicago Blues, Piano Blues
The origins of the blues standard "Tin Pan Alley" can be traced directly back to pianist Curtis Jones, who also enjoyed considerable success in 1937 with his "Lonesome Bedroom Blues" for Vocalion (a song inspired by a breakup with his wife).

Jones started out on guitar but switched to the 88s after moving to Dallas. He arrived in Chicago in 1936 and recorded for Vocalion, Bluebird, and Okeh from 1937 to 1941. But the war ended his recording career until 1953, when powerful deejay Al Benson issued a one-off single by Jones, "Wrong Blues"/"Cool Playing Blues," on his Parrot label with L.C. McKinley on guitar. In 1960, Jones waxed his debut album, *Trouble Blues,* for Prestige's Bluesville subsidiary with a classy crew of New York session aces and Chicagoan Johnny "Big Moose" Walker on guitar. By then, his audience was shifting drastically, as he became a fixture on the Chicago folk circuit. His next LP, *Lonesome Bedroom Blues,* was a 1962 solo affair for Delmark offering definitive renditions of the title cut and "Tin Pan Alley." Jones left Chicago permanently in January of 1962, settling in Europe and extensively touring the continent until his 1971 death. —Bill Dahl

Lonesome Bedroom Blues / 1962 / Delmark ✦✦✦✦
Jones, solo and at the top of his powers on piano and vocally, on a set produced by Bob Koester. The pianist was an exceptional lyricist, evidenced by his classic "Tin Pan Alley" and several lesser-known numbers on this album (which awaits digital re-emergence). —Bill Dahl

● **Trouble Blues** / 1983 / Original Blues Classics ✦✦✦✦✦
The taciturn pianist in the company of a fine New York rhythm section and Johnny "Big Moose" Walker (but on guitar, not piano) made for a winning combination on this 1960 album. Jones delivers his downbeat "Suicide Blues," "Low Down Worried Blues," "Lonesome Bedroom Blues"... well, you get the picture. Jones wasn't exactly an upbeat kind of guy. The compilers did unearth a bonus for the CD version: Jones' treatment of "Pinetop Boogie." —Bill Dahl

1937-40 / Document ✦✦✦✦
A solid collection of Jones' earliest sides. —Cub Koda

Eddie "One String" Jones (Edward Hazelton)

Unitar / Acoustic Blues
In most blues reference books, the name Eddie Jones refers to the given handle of the New Orleans guitarist better known as

"Guitar Slim." But this time, we take pause to relate what little information exists on another Eddie Jones, this one a street musician situated in Los Angeles' Skid Row.

Eddie "One String" Jones was, by no stretch of the imagination, a professional musician. Nor, like his more famous namesake, was he even a guitar player. Had it not been for his chance discovery by folklorist and ethnic musicologist Frederick A. Usher in February of 1960, it's a pretty safe bet that no recorded document of him would probably exist.

Usher was in Los Angeles' Skid Row section on business with an associate when he was accosted by two panhandlers. One of those two men (Jones) was holding a rough cut 2'x4' plank, a homemade one-stringed instrument of the crudest construction. After a bit of cajoling from Usher, Jones reached into his pocket and fished out the other two working tools he used to make music with the board, a half pint whiskey bottle to slide with and a carefully whittled stick to bang the single string with in place of a guitar pick. The sound was raw, jangly, and chaotic, as far removed from normal slide or bottleneck techniques as Usher (or anyone else) had ever heard. This was evidently a direct tie to the African instrument known as the "diddleybow," but Jones' technique with the stick gave the music an otherworldly edge, multiple tones to be derived from a single note, and a total departure from what most folklorists had previously known about the instrument. Sensing that Jones was a modern-day link to an African art form long since dissipated, Usher was bowled over and ran back home as fast as he could to grab his portable tape recorder. After hooking up to a nearby store's electricity in a deserted back alley, Usher made the first recordings of Eddie "One String" Jones. But Jones' lifestyle as a homeless person made all attempts by Usher to mainstream him into folk music circles a virtual impossibility. "One String" was most secretive about his technique, the origin of the instrument, even his given name, which—it turns out—could have been Eddie Jones or Jessie Marshall. After scheduling two more informal recording sessions (one of which appears to be a no-show) and a chance to play for a group of Usher's friends in Hollywood, Jones slipped back into obscurity and has eluded all modern day blues detective work to even try and append his bio with a date of his death. If there's a romantic, mystery figure in blues history, Eddie "One String" Jones would certainly be at the top of the list. —*Cub Koda*

One String Blues / 1993 / Gazelle Documents ✦✦✦✦✦
Jones shares this 15-track compilation with harmonica street player Edward Hazelton, another one of Frederick Usher's elusive Skid Row discoveries, who contributes a half dozen sides featuring a stripped-down Sonny Terry style. The first nine tracks by Jones are primitive in the extreme, untouched by any commercial considerations whatsoever. His instrument—described on the front cover as "a home-made African derived Zither-Monochord"—delivers tones that border on somewhere between keening, rhythmic, and downright eerie. Even repeated listening to any of the early Delta blues slide greats will not prepare you for the sound on this recording, which is trebly, bordering on metallic. Blues as folklore, but a whole lot of fun to explore as well. —*Cub Koda*

Floyd Jones

b. Jul. 21, 1917, Marianna, AR, d. Dec. 19, 1989, Chicago, IL
Guitar, Vocals / Electric Chicago Blues
His sound characteristically dark and gloomy, guitarist Floyd Jones contributed a handful of genuine classics to the Chicago blues idiom during the late '40s and early '50s, notably the foreboding "Dark Road" and "Hard Times."

Born in Arkansas, Jones grew up in the blues-fertile Mississippi Delta (where he picked up the guitar in his teens). He came to Chicago in the mid-'40s, working for tips on Maxwell Street with his cousin Moody Jones and Baby Face Leroy Foster and playing local clubs on a regular basis. Floyd was right there when the postwar Chicago blues movement first took flight, recording with harpist Snooky Pryor for Marvel in 1947; pianist Sunnyland Slim for Tempo Tone the next year (where he cut "Hard Times"), JOB and Chess in 1952–53, and Vee-Jay in 1955 (where he weighed in with a typically downcast "Ain't Times Hard").

Jones remained active on the Chicago scene until shortly before his 1989 death, although electric bass had long since replaced the guitar as his main axe. He participated in Earwig Records' *Old Friends* sessions in 1979, sharing a studio with longtime cohorts Sunnyland Slim, Honeyboy Edwards, Big Walter Horton, and Kansas City Red. —*Bill Dahl*

● **Masters Of Modern Blues** / 1994 / Testament ✦✦✦✦✦
Eight priceless 1966 tracks by tragically underrecorded guitarist Floyd Jones are paired for this CD with eight more by sessionmate Eddie Taylor. Produced in both cases by Testament boss Pete Welding with Big Walter Horton on harp, pianist Otis Spann, and drummer Fred Below lending their collective hands, Jones recreates his dour, uncompromising "Dark Road," "Hard Times," and "Stockyard Blues" with an early-'50s sense of purpose. —*Bill Dahl*

"Little" Johnny Jones

b. Nov. 1, 1924, Jackson, MS, d. Nov. 19, 1964, Chicago, IL
Piano, Vocals / Chicago Blues, Piano Blues
In 40 short years on earth, Johnny Jones established himself as one of the greatest piano players ever to inhabit the Chicago blues scene. Best known for his rock-solid accompaniment to slide guitarist Elmore James both in the studio and as an onstage member of James' Broomdusters, "Little Johnny" also waxed a handful of terrific sides as a leader.

Jones arrived in Chicago from Mississippi in 1946 well-versed on the 88s. Influenced greatly by pianist Big Maceo Merriwether, Jones followed him into Tampa Red's band in 1947 after Maceo suffered a stroke. Johnny Jones' talents were soon in demand as a sideman—in addition to rolling the ivories behind Tampa Red for RCA Victor from 1949 to 1953, he backed Muddy Waters on his 1949 classic "Screamin' and Cryin'" and later appeared on sides by Howlin' Wolf.

But it's Elmore James that he'll forever be associated with; the indispensable pianist played on James' halcyon 1952-56 Chicago sessions for the Bihari brothers' Meteor, Flair, and Modern logos, as well as dates for Checker, Chief, and Fire. The Broomdusters (rounded out by saxist J.T. Brown and drummer Odie Payne, Jr.) held down a regular berth at the West Side blues club Sylvio's for five years.

When he got the chance to sit behind a microphone, Jones' insinuating vocal delivery was equally enthralling. Muddy Waters, Jimmy Rogers, and Leroy Foster backed Jones on his 1949 Aristocrat label classic "Big Town Playboy" (later revived by Eddie Taylor, another unsung Chicago hero), while Elmore James and saxist J.T. Brown were on hand for Jones' 1953 Flair coupling "I May Be Wrong"/ "Sweet Little Woman" (the latter a wonderfully risqué "dozens" number). The rocking "Hoy Hoy," his last commercial single, was done in 1953 for Atlantic and also featured James and his group in support. Jones continued to work in the clubs (with Wolf, Sonny Boy Williamson, Syl Johnson, Billy Boy Arnold, and Magic Sam, among others) prior to his 1964 death of lung cancer.

Ironically, Jones was reportedly the first cousin of another Chicago piano great, Otis Spann. —*Bill Dahl*

● **Johnny Jones With Billy Boy Arnold** / 1979 / Alligator ✦✦✦✦✦
Thank heaven Norman Dayron had the presence of mind to capture these sides by Chicago pianist Johnny Jones when he played at the Fickle Pickle in 1963—as little as remains on tape of his talents as a singer, we're eternally indebted to Dayron's actions. Jones' insinuating vocals and bedrock 88s are abetted by harpist Billy Boy Arnold on these performances, and that's it—he had no rhythm section to fall back on. —*Bill Dahl*

Paul "Wine" Jones

Blues, Modern Electric Blues
Another of the obscure Delta bluesmen brought to a wide audience via producer Robert Palmer's series of modern Delta blues for the Fat Possum label. Jones, from the small town of Belzoni, Mississippi, didn't make his debut until the age of 48, with 1995's *Mule*. He plays raw (by 1990s standards) electric jukejoint blues, with modern influences making themselves apparent in the occasional use of wah-wah guitar riffs. —*Richie Unterberger*

Mule / 1995 / Fat Possum ✦✦✦
Blues Jones' vocals and guitar pace a rough-and-ready quartet, which offers modern electric blues at its most spontaneous. The album was granted a very positive critical reception, but it must be noted that the songs themselves have an unfinished (as

opposed to merely unpolished) feel. That, combined with the similar-sounding material and arrangements, means that the album tends to drag after a while. —*Richie Unterberger*

Little Sonny Jones

b. New Orleans, LA, **d.** 1989, New Orleans, LA
Vocals / New Orleans Blues

When Black Top reissued Little Sonny Jones' 1975 album *New Orleans R&B Gems* recently, even some true blues fans probably shook their heads and wondered, "Who?" But rest assured: folks in the Crescent City recall Jones with great affection. He was born there and he died there, making some fine music in between.

Born Johnny Jones, the singer picked up his enduring nickname from his pal Fats Domino when they were both playing at the Hideaway Club in the ninth ward during the late '40s. Domino hit it big, but Jones' vinyl fortunes weren't as lucky: a 1953 single on Specialty ("Do You Really Love Me"/"Is Everything Allright") preceded a four-song session for Imperial the next year under Dave Bartholomew's direction (songs included "I Got Fooled" and "Winehead Baby"). All three 45s stiffed, but Fats kept him employed as a warmup act until 1961.

After seven years back home singing with the band of brothers David and Melvin Lastie, Jones retired until his 1975 album (first issued on Black Magic Records overseas). The set accurately recreated the Crescent City R&B sound of the '50s, thanks to Little Sonny Jones' rich singing and the efforts of veterans Dave "Fat Man" Williams on piano and vocals, saxists Clarence Ford and David Lastie, guitarist Justin Adams, bassist Frank Fields, and drummer Robert French.

Jones came out to play the annual Jazz & Heritage Festival until his 1989 death of heart failure. —*Bill Dahl*

● **New Orleans Rhythm & Blues** / 1995 / Black Magic ✦✦✦✦

Charley Jordan

b. 1890, Mabelvale, AR, **d.** Nov. 15, 1954, St. Louis, MO
Guitar, Vocals / Acoustic Blues

A fine St. Louis guitarist and vocalist, Charley Jordan teamed with many blues luminaries for some fine recordings in the '20s, '30s and '40s. After traveling throughout the Southeast as a hobo in the '30s, Jordan settled in St. Louis. He played with Memphis Minnie, Roosevelt Sykes, Casey Bill Weldon, Peetie Wheatstraw, and many others. Jordan overcame a permanent spine injury he suffered during a shooting incident in 1928. He recorded for Vocalion and Decca in the '30s, and also doubled as a talent scout for both labels. Jordan worked often with Big Joe Williams in the late '30s and the '40s. —*Ron Wynn*

● **Charley Jordan Vol. 1, 1930–31** / Document ✦✦✦✦✦
A fine St. Louis singer and guitarist, this was the first volume of songs Charley Jordan did in the early '30s. He could be very humorous or cuttingly poignant, and there are examples in both veins on this anthology. The sound quality ranges from good to awful. —*Ron Wynn*

Charley Jordan Vol. 2, 1931–34 / Document ✦✦✦
Charley Jordan Vol. 3, 1935–37 / Document ✦✦✦

Louis Jordan

b. Jul. 8, 1908, Brinkley, AR, **d.** Feb. 4, 1975, Los Angeles, CA
Saxophone, Vocals / Jump Blues

Effervescent saxophonist Louis Jordan was one of the chief architects and prime progenitors of the R&B idiom. His pioneering use of jumping shuffle rhythms in a small combo context was copied far and wide during the 1940s.

Jordan's sensational hit-laden run with Decca Records contained a raft of seminal performances, featuring inevitably infectious backing by his band, the Tympany Five, and Jordan's own searing alto sax and street corner jive-loaded sense of humor. Jordan was one of the first Black entertainers to sell appreciably in the pop sector; his Decca duet mates included Bing Crosby, Louis Armstrong, and Ella Fitzgerald.

The son of a musician, Jordan spent time as a youth with the Rabbit Foot Minstrels and majored in music later on at Arkansas Baptist College. After moving with his family to Philadelphia in 1932, Jordan hooked up with pianist Clarence Williams. He joined the orchestra of drummer Chick Webb in 1936 and remained there until 1938. Having polished up his singing abil-

ities with Webb's outfit, Jordan was ready to strike out on his own.

The saxist's first 78 for Decca in 1938, "Honey in the Bee Ball," billed his combo as the Elks Rendezvous Band (after the Harlem nightspot that he frequently played). From 1939 on, though, Jordan fronted the Tympany Five, a sturdy little aggregation often expanding over quintet status that featured some well-known musicians over the years: pianists Wild Bill Davis and Bill Doggett, guitarists Carl Hogan and Bill Jennings, bassist Dallas Bartley, and drummer Chris Columbus all passed through the ranks.

From 1942 to 1951, Jordan scored an astonishing 57 R&B chart hits (all on Decca), beginning with the humorous blues "I'm Gonna Leave You on the Outskirts of Town" and finishing with "Weak Minded Blues." In between, he drew up what amounted to an easily followed blueprint for the development of R&B (and for that matter, rock & roll—the accessibly swinging shuffles of Bill Haley & the Comets were directly descended from Jordan; Haley often pointing to his Decca labelmate as profoundly influencing his approach).

"G.I. Jive," "Caldonia," "Buzz Me," "Choo Choo Ch' Boogie," "Ain't That Just like a Woman," "Ain't Nobody Here but Us Chickens," "Boogie Woogie Blue Plate," "Beans and Cornbread," "Saturday Night Fish Fry," and "Blue Light Boogie"—every one of those classics topped the R&B lists, and there were plenty more that did precisely the same thing. Black audiences coast-to-coast were breathlessly jitterbugging to Jordan's jumping jive (and one suspects, more than a few Whites kicked up their heels to those same platters as well).

The saxist was particularly popular during World War II. He recorded prolifically for the Armed Forces Radio Service and the V-Disc program. Jordan's massive popularity also translated onto the silver screen—he filmed a series of wonderful short musicals during the late '40s that were decidedly short on plot but long on visual versions of his hits (*Caldonia, Reet Petite & Gone, Look Out Sister,* and *Beware,* along with countless soundies) that give us an enlightening peek at just what made him such a beloved entertainer. Jordan also cameoed in a big-budget Hollywood wartime musical, *Follow the Boys.*

A brief attempt at fronting a big band in 1951 proved an ill-fated venture, but it didn't dim his ebullience. In 1952, tongue firmly planted in cheek, he offered himself as a candidate for the highest office in the land on the amusing Decca outing "Jordan for President."

Even though his singles were still eminently solid, they weren't selling like they used to by 1954. So after an incredible run of more than a decade-and-a-half, Jordan moved over to the Mesner brothers' Los Angeles-based Aladdin logo at the start of the year. Alas, time had passed the great pioneer by—"Dad Gum Ya Hide Boy," "Messy Bessy," "If I Had Any Sense," and the rest of his Aladdin output sounds great in retrospect, but it wasn't what young R&B fans were searching for at the time. In 1955, he switched to RCA's short-lived "X" imprint, where he tried to remain up-to-date by issuing "Rock 'n' Roll Call."

A blistering Quincy Jones-arranged date for Mercury in 1956 deftly updated Jordan's classics for the rock & roll crowd, with hellfire renditions of "Let the Good Times Roll," "Salt Pork, West Virginia," and "Beware" benefiting from the blasting lead guitar of Mickey Baker and Sam "The Man" Taylor's muscular tenor sax. There was even time to indulge in a little torrid jazz at Mercury; "The JAMF," from a 1957 LP called *Man, We're Wailin',* was a sizzling indication of what a fine saxist Jordan was.

Ray Charles had long cited Jordan as a primary influence (he lovingly covered Jordan's "Don't Let the Sun Catch You Crying" and "Early in the Morning"), and paid him back by signing Jordan to the Genius' Tangerine label. Once again, the fickle public largely ignored his worthwhile 1962-64 offerings.

Lounge gigs still offered the saxman a steady income, though, and he adjusted his onstage playlist accordingly. A 1973 album for the French Black & Blue logo found Jordan covering Mac Davis' "I Believe in Music" (can't get much loungier than that!). A heart attack silenced this visionary in 1975, but not before he acted as the bridge between the big-band era and the rise of R&B.

His profile continues to rise posthumously, in large part due to the recent acclaimed Broadway musical *Five Guys Named Moe,* based on Jordan's bubbly, romping repertoire and charismatic persona. —*Bill Dahl*

☆ **Let the Good Times Roll: The Complete Decca Recordings 1938–54** / 1938–1954 / Bear Family ✦✦✦✦
The price of this multi-disc import boxed set is a hefty one, but it contains every track the pioneering saxman waxed for Decca—the multitude of hits that inexorably influenced the future of R&B and eventually rock & roll. Bear Family's attention to detail in its presentation is always immaculate, and sound quality follows suit. —*Bill Dahl*

★ **The Best of Louis Jordan** / Nov. 15, 1941–Jan. 1941 / MCA ✦✦✦✦✦
For the rest of us who can't quite finance the Bear Family extravaganza, here's the perfect introduction to the founding father of R&B. Twenty of his all-time classics, including the jumping "Choo Choo Ch'Boogie," "Let the Good Times Roll," "Caldonia," "Blue Light Boogie," and "Five Guys Named Moe," in their seminal Decca configurations. —*Bill Dahl*

Jazz Heritage: Greatest Hits, Vol. 2 (1941–1947) / Nov. 15, 1941–Apr. 23, 1947 / MCA ✦✦✦
Another package of Louis Jordan's R&B hits, this one covering the early and mid-'40s. Jordan was among the biggest stars in the nation during this period, and not only did he have smash songs for himself, others like Woody Herman, Ella Fitzgerald, and even Pearl Bailey and Moms Mabley covered his material. —*Ron Wynn*

Just Say Moe! Mo' Best of Louis / Jul. 21, 1942–1973 / Rhino ✦✦✦✦
A nice across-the-board compilation spanning his Decca, Aladdin, RCA, Mercury, and Tangerine label stints. The Decca standouts include "Don't Worry 'Bout That Mule" and the often-covered "Ain't That Just like a Woman," while his Mercury output includes "Big Bess" and "Cat Scratchin'." Could have done without the live "I Believe in Music" at the end, though—that isn't the way we want to remember this wonderful performer. —*Bill Dahl*

☆ **Five Guys Named Moe: Original Decca Recordings, Vol. 2** / Jul. 21, 1942–May 8, 1952 / Decca ✦✦✦✦
Another 18 of the saxist's Decca label classics (although "Five Guys Named Moe" turns up again, in deference to the hit Broadway production). "Is You Is or Is You Ain't (My Baby)," "Jack, You're Dead," "Texas and Pacific," "Boogie Woogie Blue Plate," and "G.I. Jive" are high on the list of gems this time, along with his persuasive 1952 campaign "Jordan for President." —*Bill Dahl*

● **1943–1945** / Nov. 22, 1943–Jul. 12, 1945 / Classics ✦✦✦✦
Although Louis Jordan's greatest hits are continually reissued, this Classics CD (the fourth in the series) gives listeners an opportunity to hear many of his lesser-known recordings, quite a few of which sound as if they could have been hits too. Jordan, a fine R&Bish altoist who was an underrated singer and a brilliant comedic talent who knew a good line when he heard one (there are many memorable ones throughout this program), is heard in peak form. The 23 performances are Decca sides (including five not originally released), some V-Discs and the privately recorded "Louis' Oldsmbile Song." Bing Crosby sings

duets with Jordan on "My Baby Said Yes" and "Your Socks Don't Match," there are two major hits ("G.I. Jive" and "Caldonia") and among the sidemen are the fine trumpeter Eddie Roane, the forgotten but talented pianist Tommy Thomas, trumpeter Idrees Sulieman (on the January 19, 1945 session) and (for the final two songs) pianist Wild Bill Davis. Other highlights include "You Can't Get That No More," "I Like 'Em Fat like That," "Deacon Jones" and "They Raided the House." Highly recommended. —*Scott Yanow*

Louis Jordan and His Tympany Five / 1944 / Circle ✦✦✦✦✦
Wondrous cuts that combined hip vocals, robust solos, and inventive lyrics into a sound that was later called R&B. These are also available in other collections on Charly and Jukebox Lil. —*Ron Wynn*

One Guy Named Louis / 1954 / Blue Note ✦✦✦
It is a strange fact that as rock & roll began to catch on, one of the artists who helped influence its birth was dropping rapidly in popularity. Singer/altoist Louis Jordan, who had had dozens of hits with his Tympani Five while on Decca, recorded 21 songs for Aladdin in 1954 (all of which are included on this CD) and none of them sold well. The strange part is that there is nothing wrong with the music. It compares quite well artistically with his earlier performances; it was just out of style. That fact should not trouble latter-day Jordan fans, for the formerly rare music on this set is witty, swinging and eternally hip. —*Scott Yanow*

Rock 'n Roll Call / 1955 / RCA ✦✦✦✦
Only a dozen numbers on this disc, but that's all the saxist made during his 1955–1956 pause at RCA's Vik and "X" subsidiaries. The saxist tried hard to keep up with the times, waxing a stomping title track written by Jack Hammer and Rudy Toombs and a Winfield Scott-penned "Slow, Smooth and Easy" and "Let's Do It Up Baby," but the teenagers just weren't buying. No reason we shouldn't! —*Bill Dahl*

Rock 'n' Roll / Oct. 22, 1956–Aug. 1957 / Verve ✦✦✦✦✦
Twenty-one-track French import that contains the best of Jordan's 1956–1957 stay at Mercury. Here are the rockin' remakes of his timeless hits, cut with a New York mob including Sam "The Man" Taylor on tenor sax and guitarist Mickey Baker, as well as fresh nuggets like "Big Bess," "Cat Scratchin'," and "Rock Doc." "The JAMF" is a scorching jazz showcase for Jordan's alto, and he does a nice easy-swinging job on "Got My Mojo Working." —*Bill Dahl*

I Believe in Music / Nov. 6, 1973 / Evidence ✦✦✦
Nice early '70s date with alto saxophonist and vocalist Louis Jordan doing more conventional blues and jazz material and very few comedy routines. As he became a celebrity, Jordan's instrumental prowess took a back seat to his quips and monologues. But this time, the music reigned. —*Ron Wynn*

Complete Recordings 1938–1941 / Affinity ✦✦✦✦
Just what it says—two discs' worth of Jordan's earliest Decca work, filled with jivey novelties and lusty sax work by the leader of the Tympany Five. Ends with a couple of his earliest hits, "Knock Me a Kiss" and "I'm Gonna Move to the Outskirts of Town." Forty-nine tracks in all. —*Bill Dahl*

K

Keb' Mo' (Kevin Moore)

b. , Los Angeles, CA
Guitar, Vocals / Modern Blues
Keb' Mo' draws heavily on the old-fashioned country blues style of Robert Johnson, but keeps his sound contemporary with touches of soul and folksy storytelling. He writes much of his own material and has applied his acoustic, electric, and slide guitar skills to jazz and rock-oriented bands in the past as well. Born Kevin Moore in Los Angeles to parents of Southern descent, he was exposed to gospel music at a young age. At 21, Moore joined an R&B band later hired for a tour by Papa John Creach and played on three of Creach's albums. Opening for jazz and rock artists such as the Mahavishnu Orchestra, Jefferson Starship, and Loggins & Messina helped broaden Moore's horizons and musical abilities. Moore cut an R&B-based solo album, *Rainmaker*, in 1980 for Casablanca, which promptly folded. In 1983, he joined Monk Higgins' band as a guitarist and met a number of blues musicians who collectively increased his understanding of the music. He subsequently joined a vocal group called the Rose Brothers and gigged around L.A. 1990 found Moore portraying a Delta bluesman in a local play called *Rabbit Foot* and he later played Robert Johnson in a docudrama called *Can't You Hear the Wind Howl?* He released his self-titled debut album as Keb' Mo' in 1994, featuring two Robert Johnson covers, eleven songs written or co-written by Moore, and his guitar and banjo work. Keb' Mo' performed a well-received set at the 1995 Newport Folk Festival. —*Steve Huey*

● **Keb' Mo'** / 1995 / OKeh/550/Epic ◆◆◆◆◆
Keb' Mo's self-titled debut is an edgy, ambitious collection of gritty country blues. Keb' Mo' pushes into new directions, trying to incorporate some of the sensibilites of the slacker revolution without losing touch of the tradition that makes the blues the breathing, vital art form it is. His attempts aren't always successful, but his gutsy guitar playing and impassioned vocals, as well as his surprisingly accomplished songwriting, make *Keb' Mo'* a debut to treasure. —*Thom Owens*

Tiny Kennedy

Vocals / Electric Jump Blues
Tiny Kennedy was anything but diminutive, either in stature or vocal range. "Big and fat" was how Trumpet Records boss Lillian McMurry vividly described him, and she should know: Trumpet recorded the shouter in 1951 and again in 1952.

The vocalist, born Jesse Kennedy, Jr., had recorded with the great Kansas City pianist Jay McShann for Capitol in 1949 prior to joining Tiny Bradshaw's jumping band as one of its featured front men. After a session with Elmore James in 1951 didn't result in anything releasable, McMurry sent Kennedy up to Sam Phillips' fledgling Memphis Recording Service in September of 1952. Musicians on the session, which produced the fine "Strange Kind of Feelin,'" "Early in the Mornin', Baby" (with overdubbed crowing by "Elmer, the Disc Jockey Rooster"), and "Blues Disease," included guitarist Calvin Newborn and saxist Richard Sanders. After a 1955 date for RCA's Groove subsidiary, Kennedy disappeared permanently from the R&B scene. —*Bill Dahl*

● **Strange Kind of Feeling** / Trumpet ◆◆◆◆◆
Three of the unsung heroes on Lillian McMurry's Trumpet label fill this anthology with their early-'50s work. Kennedy's sides were cut in Memphis under Sam Phillips' supervision in 1952.

"Strange Kind of Feelin'" and "Blues Disease" rate with the best things the rotund shouter waxed. —*Bill Dahl*

Willie Kent

b. Sep. 24, 1936, Mississippi
Bass, Vocals / Modern Electric Blues
Bassist Willie Kent and his band, the Gents, are among the last of a dying breed around Chicago: a combo that intuitively knows the meaning of ensemble playing, rather than functioning as a generic backdrop for endless guitar solos. The Mississippi-born Kent has been laying down bedrock bass lines for decades, and his uncommonly powerful vocals make him even more of a standout.

Kent hit Chicago during the '50s, weaned on Muddy Waters, John Lee Hooker, and Robert Nighthawk. He apprenticed long and hard on the West side, playing with the Hudson brothers, Ralph & the Red Tops, Eddie Taylor, Little Walter, Fenton Robinson, and plenty more before folks started taking notice of his bandleading skills. A 1987 heart bypass operation forced him to abandon his day job as a truck driver; from then on, music has been his full-time vocation. Two outstanding albums for Delmark, 1991's *Ain't It Nice* (with a guest vocal by frequent cohort Bonnie Lee) and 1994's *Too Hurt to Cry*, have solidified Kent's reputation. —*Bill Dahl*

● **Ain't It Nice** / 1991 / Delmark ◆◆◆◆◆
West-side bassist Kent and his Gents serve up Chicago blues the way it was meant to be played (but too often isn't nowadays): with tight ensemble passages that greatly enhance the power of Kent's gruff vocals. His first album for Delmark beautifully typifies his groove-heavy approach; whether digging into a slow grinding blues or an upbeat soul-inflected item, he and his comrades keep their business together. —*Bill Dahl*

● **Too Hurt To Cry** / 1994 / Delmark ◆◆◆
There's little newness anyone should expect to hear on a contemporary blues record. The only thing that makes them valuable is if the performer has their own notion of the blues and can state it in a distinctive manner. Willie Kent certainly can; his mournful, often powerful vocals are frequently memorable, even when he's mining the reliable formula of heartache and anguish. If his compositions aren't lyrically transcendent, Kent's rendering of the words elevates them. You never tire of hearing him sing, and he makes you feel and believe his messages, even as his backing band plugs in familiar progressions and lines behind him. Indeed, it's only when Kent covers someone else's music that things become less interesting. —*Ron Wynn*

Junior Kimbrough

b. Jul. 28, 1930, Hudsonville, MS
Guitar, Vocals / Modern Delta Blues
Cited as a prime early influence by rockabilly pioneer Charlie Feathers, Mississippi Delta bluesman Junior Kimbrough's modal, hypnotic blues vision remained a regional sensation for most of his career. He finally transcended the confines of his region in the early '90s, when he appeared in the 1991 movie *Deep Blues* and on its Anxious/Atlantic soundtrack, leading to his own debut for Fat Possum Records, *All Night Long.*

Junior Kimbrough was born and raised in Hudsonville, MS, where he learned how to play guitar by listening to records by Delta bluesmen. In 1968, he cut his first single, "Tramp," for the local Philwood label. For the next two decades, Kimbrough didn't have the opportunity to record frequently—he recorded a single, "Keep Your Hands Off Her," for High Water and his "All Night Long" was available on the various artists compilation, *National Downhome Festival, Vol. 2*, released on Southland Records.

During the '70s and '80s, Kimbrough played juke joints throughout Mississippi, which is where music journalist Robert Palmer discovered him in the late '80s. Palmer featured Kimbrough in his documentary film *Deep Blues.* The exposure in the movie led to a national record contract for Kimbrough—he signed with Fat Possum and released his first full-length album, *All Night Long,* in 1992. The record was critically-acclaimed by both blues and mainstream publications, as was *Deep Blues* and its accompanying soundtrack. All of the media attention led to performances outside of the Delta, including a few shows in England. After the flurry of activity in 1992, Junior Kimbrough returned to playing juke joints in the Delta, recording occasionally—he released his second album, *Sad Days, Lonely Nights,* in 1993. —*Bill Dahl & Stephen Thomas Erlewine*

● **All Night Long** / 1992 / Fat Possum ◆◆◆◆◆
Junior Kimbrough has been a regional sensation for years due to his Sunday afternoon juke-joint styled parties at his home in Holly Springs, Mississippi. It's the kind of honest, undiluted, country blues still heard in Deep South dirt-floor clubs but long since considered commercially dead. Kimbrough finally got a chance to cut a full album in 1992, following Robert Mugge's film *Deep Blues* and the similarly titled soundtrack release. The 10 cuts on *All Night Long* aren't uniformly great, but the really good ones like "Work Me Baby," "Stay All Night," and the title cut resonate with a gritty, searing intensity seldom captured on record. —*Ron Wynn*

Sad Days, Lonely Nights / 1993 / Fat Possum ◆◆

Albert King (Albert Nelson)

b. Apr. 25, 1923, Indianola, MS, **d.** Dec. 21, 1992
Guitar, Vocals / Modern Electric Blues
Albert King is truly a "King of the Blues," although he doesn't hold that title (B.B. does). Along with B.B. and Freddie King, Albert King is one of the major influences on blues and rock guitar players. Without him, modern guitar music would not sound as it does—his style has influenced both Black and White blues players from Otis Rush and Robert Cray to Eric Clapton and Stevie Ray Vaughan. It's important to note that while almost all modern blues guitarists seldom play for long without falling into a B.B. King guitar cliché, Albert King never does—he's had his own style and unique tone from the beginning.

Albert King plays guitar left handed, without re-stringing the guitar from the right-handed setup; this "upside-down" playing accounts for his difference in tone, since he pulls down on the same strings that most players push up on when bending the blues notes. King's massive tone and totally unique way of squeezing bends out of a guitar string has had a major impact. Many young White guitarists—especially rock & rollers—have been influenced by King's playing, and many players who emulate his style may never have heard of Albert King, let alone heard his music. His style is immediately distinguishable from all other blues guitarists, and he's one of the most important blues guitarists to ever pick up the electric guitar.

Born in Indianola, MS, but raised in Forrest City, AR, Albert King (b. Albert Nelson) taught himself how to play guitar when he was a child, building his own instrument out of a cigar box. At first, he played with gospel groups—most notably the Harmony Kings—but after hearing Blind Lemon Jefferson, Lonnie Johnson, and several other blues musicians, he solely played the blues. In 1950, he met MC Reeder, who owned the T-99 nightclub in Osceola, AR. King moved to Osceloa shortly afterward, joining the T-99's house band, the In The Groove Boys. The band played several local Arkansas gigs besides the T-99, including several shows for a local radio station.

After enjoying success in the Arkansas area, King moved to Gary, IN, in 1953, where he joined a band that also featured Jimmy Reed and John Brim. Both Reed and Brim were guitarists, which forced King to play drums in the group. At this time, he adopted the name Albert King, which he assumed after B.B. King's "Three O'Clock Blues" became a huge hit. Albert met Willie Dixon shortly after moving to Gary, and the bassist/songwriter helped the guitarist set up an audition at Parrot Records. King passed the audition and cut his first session late in 1953.

Five songs were recorded during the session and only one single, "Be On Your Merry Way" / "Bad Luck Blues," was released; the other tracks appeared on various compilations over the next four decades. Although it sold respectably, the single didn't gather enough attention to earn him another session with Parrot. In early 1954, King returned to Osceola and re-joined the In The Groove Boys; he stayed in Arkansas for the next two years.

In 1956, Albert moved to St. Louis, where he initially sat in with local bands. By the fall of 1956, King was headlining several clubs in the area. King continued to play the St. Louis circuit, honing his style. During these years, he began playing his signature Gibson Flying V, which he named Lucy. By 1958, Albert was quite popular in St. Louis, which led to a contract with the fledgling Bobbin Records in the summer of 1959. On his first Bobbin recordings, King recorded with a pianist and a small horn section, which made the music sound closer to jump blues than Delta or Chicago blues. Nevertheless, his guitar was taking a center stage and it was clear that he had developed a unique, forceful sound. King's records for Bobbin sold well in the St. Louis area, enough so that King Records leased the "Don't Throw Your Love on Me So Strong" single from the smaller label. When the single was released nationally late in 1961, it became a hit, reaching number 14 on the R&B charts. King Records continued to lease more material from Bobbin—including a full album, *The Big Blues,* which was released in 1963—but nothing else approached the initial success of "Don't Throw Your Love on Me So Strong." Bobbin also leased material to Chess, which appeared in the late '60s.

Albert King left Bobbin in late 1962 and recorded one session for King Records in the spring of 1963, which were much more pop-oriented than his previous work; the singles issued from the session failed to sell. Within a year, he cut four songs for the local St. Louis independent label Coun-Tree, which was run by a jazz singer named Leo Gooden. Though these singles didn't appear in many cities—St. Louis, Chicago, and Kansas City were the only three to register sales—they foreshadowed his coming work with Stax Records. Furthermore, they were very popular within St. Louis, so much so that Gooden resented King's success and pushed him off the label.

Following his stint at Coun-Tree, Albert King signed with Stax Records in 1966. Albert's records for Stax would bring him stardom, both within blues and rock circles. All of his '60s Stax sides were recorded with the label's house band, Booker T. & the MG's, which gave his blues a sleek, soulful sound. That soul underpinning gave King crossover appeal, as evidenced by his R&B chart hits—"Laundromat Blues" (1966) and "Cross Cut Saw" (1967) both went Top 40, while "Born Under a Bad Sign" (1967) charted in the Top 50. Furthermore, King's style was appropriated by several rock & roll players, most notably Jimi Hendrix and Eric Clapton, who copied Albert's "Personal Manager" guitar solo on the Cream song, "Strange Brew." Albert King's first album for Stax, 1967's *Born Under a Bad Sign,* was a collection of his singles for the label and became one of the most popular and influential blues albums of the late '60s. Beginning in 1968, Albert King was playing not only to blues audiences, but also to crowds of young rock & rollers. He frequently played at the Fillmore West in San Francisco and he even recorded an album, *Live Wire / Blues Power,* at the hall in the summer of 1968.

Early in 1969, King recorded *Years Gone By,* his first true studio album. Later that year, he recorded a tribute album to Elvis Presley (*King Does the King's Things*) and a jam session with Steve Cropper and Pops Staples (*Jammed Together*), in addition to performing a concert with the St. Louis Symphony Orchestra. For the next few years, Albert toured America and Europe, returning to the studio in 1971, to record the *Lovejoy* album. In 1972, he recorded *I'll Play the Blues for You,* which featured accompaniment from the Bar-Kays, the Memphis Horns, and the Movement. The album was rooted in the blues, but featured distinctively modern soul and funk overtones.

By the mid-'70s, Stax was suffering major financial problems, so King left the label for Utopia, a small subsidiary of RCA Records. Albert released two albums on Utopia, which featured some concessions to the constraints of commercial soul productions. Although he had a few hits at Utopia, his time there was essentially a transitional period, where he discovered that it was better to follow a straight blues direction and abandon contemporary soul crossovers. King's subtle shift in style was evident on his first albums for Tomato Records, the label he signed with in

1978. Albert stayed at Tomato for several years, switching to Fantasy in 1983, releasing two albums for the label.

In the mid-'80s, Albert King announced his retirement, but it was short-lived—Albert continued to regularly play concerts and festivals throughout America and Europe for the rest of the decade. King continued to perform until his sudden death in 1992, when he suffered a fatal heart attack on December 21. The loss to the blues was a major one—although many guitarists have tried, no one can replace King's distinctive, trailblazing style. Albert King is a tough act to follow. —*Daniel Erlewine & Stephen Thomas Erlewine*

★ **Born Under a Bad Sign** / 1967 / Stax ✦✦✦✦✦
One day this southpaw was playing little clubs in Osceola, AR, the next he was headlining rock ballrooms like the Fillmore. This is the album that changed everything—including seemingly 90% of the blues and rock guitarists on the landscape. Backed by Booker T. & the MG's and the Memphis Horns, Albert proved he was every bit as hip as they, not to mention flexible. In fact, as throughout his career, he used a relatively small vocabulary of licks, but gave them slightly different timing and English, depending on the groove and the surroundings. The result was a whole new language. This LP is one big classic from top to bottom. "Crosscut Saw," "Oh, Pretty Woman," "The Hunter," "As the Years Go Passing By," "Personal Manager," the title tune—every track is a must-have. —*Dan Forte*

Live Wire/Blues Power / 1968 / Stax ✦✦✦✦✦
Live Wire/Blues Power is one of Albert King's definitive albums. Recorded live at the Fillmore Auditorium in 1968, the guitarist is at the top of his form throughout the record—his solos are intense and piercing. The band is fine, but ultimately it's King's show—he makes Herbie Hancock's "Watermelon Man" dirty and funky and wrings out all the emotion from "Blues at Sunrise." —*Thom Owens*

Years Gone By / 1969 / Stax ✦✦✦✦✦
Years Gone By features typically inspired Stax work from The King of the Flying V. —*Bill Dahl*

Albert King: King of the Blues Guitar / 1969 / Atlantic ✦✦✦✦✦
No blues guitarist who emerged during the '60s wielded more influence. This incendiary collection contains his best '60s work-outs for Stax. —*Bill Dahl*

★ **King of the Blues Guitar** / 1969 / Atlantic ✦✦✦✦✦
Atlantic's original vinyl edition of this was comprised of Albert's Stax singles—a few from *Born Under a Bad Sign,* along with "Cold Feet," "I Love Lucy" (two of King's patented monologues), and the beautiful "You're Gonna Need Me." Great stuff. Even greater, though, is the CD reissue, which includes those singles (which didn't appear on any other LPs) and *all* of *Born Under a Bad Sign.* Need I say more? —*Dan Forte*

Blues for Elvis: Albert King Does the King's Things / 1970 / Stax ✦✦✦
A silly but surprisingly listenable Presley tribute. —*Bill Dahl*

The Lost Session / 1971 / Stax ✦✦
Lost Session is an interesting historical curiosity, but it is rather unsuccessful musically. John Mayall produced the record and he tried to move Albert King toward jazz. First of all, King's style isn't quite suited for jazz—he's too direct and forceful. Furthermore, the songs are simply skeletons—their only function is to let the band solo. And there are a couple of good solos, all of them from King. But ultimately, it's a forgettable exercise that should have been left in the vault. —*Thom Owens*

Lovejoy / 1971 / Stax ✦✦✦
Lovejoy is a rock-tinged departure from his usual Memphis sound. —*Bill Dahl*

I'll Play the Blues for You / 1972 / Stax ✦✦✦✦✦
A moody, R&B-influenced set with plenty of intensity. —*Bill Dahl*

I Wanna Get Funky / 1974 / Stax ✦✦✦
Another very solid, early-'70s outing. —*Bill Dahl*

Albert / 1976 / Tomato ✦✦
Albert is bit slick but reasonably satisfying. —*Bill Dahl*

Truckload of Lovin' / 1976 / Tomato ✦✦✦
The best of King's mid-'70s, slightly disco-fied period. —*Bill Dahl*

The Pinch / 1976 / Stax ✦✦✦
One of King's more soul-oriented efforts, from sessions recorded in 1973 and 1974. It's been retitled as *The Blues Don't Change* for its CD reissue. —*Richie Unterberger*

New Orleans Heat / 1978 / Rhino ✦✦
Allen Toussaint is one of the greatest R&B producers ever to grace New Orleans, but his touch as a blues producer is shaky at best. This attempt to update King's early classics is a snooze. —*Bill Dahl*

Chronicle (With Little Milton) / 1979 / Stax ✦✦✦
This compilation has a leftover feel; the liner notes provide no sources and dates, admitting only that these are "Stax recordings, some never before available on LP." If you're a big fan of one or both of the artists involved, though, it's not bad, with a quality that's generally consistent with their fully-baked Stax-era albums, though the King half of the program is somewhat superior to the Milton tracks. —*Richie Unterberger*

Albert King Live / 1979 / Tomato ✦✦✦
Albert King Live was in some ways the finest live blues album King ever made, although it wasn't as successful as the recordings he made at the Fillmore West. But it featured numerous spectacular solos, with King showing his complete guitar technique. Rhino's recent CD reissue unfortunately opted to trim the superb, lengthy cut, "Jam In A-Flat," which featured blistering solos by King, Rory Gallagher, and Louisiana Red. That dubious decision doesn't negate the CD's value, but certainly casts a pall over it, particularly since they retained Robert Palmer's exhaustive original notes and convey the impression that you're getting the total session intact. Still, King's versions of "Stormy Monday," "Kansas City," "Watermelon Man," and "I'll Play The Blues For You" are marvelous, as are "Matchbox Holds My Clothes," "As The Years Go Passing By," and "Don't Burn Down The Bridges." —*Ron Wynn*

Tomato Years / Rhino/Tomato ✦✦✦
Albert King enjoyed an erratic but memorable reign at Tomato in the 1970s. The label aimed to continue the success King had enjoyed at Stax mixing blues backing and vocals with pop/soul arrangements and lyrics. He recorded six LPs for Tomato; this anthology culls 14 cuts from his Tomato releases, among them the slashing numbers "Blues At Sunrise" and "I'm Gonna Call You Soon As The Sun Goes Down," which vividly illustrated King's guitar prowess. Others, like "Truckload Of Lovin'" and "We All Wanna Boogie," show how he skillfully crammed moments of inspiration into formulaic outings. —*Ron Wynn*

San Francisco '83 / 1983 / Fantasy ✦✦✦
Early-'80s studio LP, reissued in its entirety on CD under the title *Crosscut Saw: Albert King in San Francisco.* As that reissue adds two extra previously unreleased tracks, it's the recommended alternative to the original vinyl edition. —*Richie Unterberger*

In San Francisco: Crosscut Saw / Mar. 1983 / Stax ✦✦✦
A reissue of King's 1983 LP *San Francisco '83* (a studio album, not a live one), with the addition of two previously unreleased cuts. His first new release in five years, it wasn't one of King's better records. But it did represent a return to a basic five-piece sound, an improvement upon his over-produced outings of the late '70s. —*Richie Unterberger*

Blues at Sunrise: Live at Montreux / 1988 / Stax ✦✦✦
Recorded at Albert King's appearance at the 1973 Montreux Jazz Festival, *Blues at Sunrise: Live at Montreux* is a typically engaging live record from the guitarist. King is in good form and the set list is a little unpredictable, featuring standards like "Blues at Sunrise" and "I'll Play the Blues for You" as well as lesser-known items like "Little Brother (Make a Way)" and "Don't Burn Down the Bridge." —*Thom Owens*

Let's Have a Natural Ball / 1989 / Modern Blues ✦✦✦✦✦
Great compilation of King's Bobbin sides of the late '50s and early '60s. —*Bill Dahl*

Wednesday Night in San Francisco: Recorded Live at the Fillmore Auditorium / 1990 / Stax ✦✦✦
Wednesday Night was recorded in June of 1968—it's culled from the very same dates as *Live Wire/Blues Power.* It's slightly weaker than *Live Wire,* which isn't surprising since it consists of outtakes. Nevertheless, Albert King is in fine form throughout the record, throwing out stinging solos with passion. It's a necessary purchase for any King fan. —*Thom Owens*

Thursday Night in San Francisco: Recorded Live at the Fillmore Auditorium / 1990 / Stax ✦✦✦
Like *Wednesday Night, Thursday Night* consists of outtakes from

a 1968 Fillmore show that are just as scorching as the *Live Wire* album. —*Bill Dahl*

Door to Door / 1990 / MCA/Chess ✦✦✦
Half of *Door to Door* is devoted to early-'60s King, the other half to Otis Rush Chess efforts of the same era. —*Bill Dahl*

The Best of Albert King, Vol. 1 / 1991 / Stax ✦✦✦✦✦
"The best of Albert King"? More like the best material that he happened to record for Stax between 1968 and 1973. Even that's debatable, the 13 tracks including covers such as "Honky Tonk Woman," "Sky Is Crying," and "Hound Dog." It does present a reasonable cross-section of his soul-inflected work of the period, drawing from over a half-dozen LPs and a couple of singles, though you might be as well or better off with his more focused individual titles. And for the true "best of Albert King," Rhino's *Ultimate Collection* remains the hands-down winner. —*Richie Unterberger*

★ **Ultimate Collection** / 1993 / Rhino ✦✦✦✦✦
This two-disc set covers a few early songs, but concentrates on the inspired blend of soul, blues and rock that King made famous in the 1960s and '70s. Many songs, such as "Laundromat Blues," "Crosscut Saw," "I'll Play The Blues For You" and of course "Born Under A Bad Sign," featured simple riffs, catchy lyrics and solid grooves parlayed into memorable performances through King's confident vocals and soaring solos. To be sure, there were formulaic numbers, and after a time King's solos and note choices were as much show biz effect as they were exciting, but the anthology's live cuts show that King was always capable of surprise and invention on the bandstand. The later numbers aren't quite as powerful, but King's rendition of "Phone Booth" shows his successors and imitators what legitimate blues playing is all about. —*Ron Wynn*

Hard Bargain / Feb. 1996 / Stax ✦✦✦
A collection of B-sides, alternate takes, and previously unissued outtakes from King's Stax prime (1966–1972), some instrumental. It's not as good as King's best Stax material, but it's not far behind, often benefiting from house players like Booker T. & the MGs, Isaac Hayes, and the Bar-Kays. —*Richie Unterberger*

The Blues Don't Change / Stax ✦✦✦
Previously titled *The Pinch* when it was issued on LP in 1977, this material was actually recorded in 1973 and 1974. These are some of King's most soul-oriented sessions, with contributions from the Memphis Horns and a couple of the MG's. Blues-oriented fans may find this one of his lesser efforts, putting less emphasis on King's guitar work than usual, and more on the vocals and arrangements. This approach has its merits, though, as it's one of the more relaxed items in the King catalog, with none of the occasional excess that creeped into his blues guitar solos. —*Richie Unterberger*

B.B. King (Riley B. King)

b. Sep. 16, 1925, Itta Bena, MS
Guitar, Vocals / Modern Electric Blues
Universally hailed as the reigning king of the blues, the legendary B.B. King is without a doubt the single most important electric guitarist of the last half century. A contemporary blues guitar solo without at least a couple of recognizable King-inspired bent notes is all but unimaginable, and he remains a supremely confident singer capable of wringing every nuance from any lyric (and he's tried his hand at many an unlikely song—anybody recall his version of "Love Me Tender"?).

Yet B.B. King remains an intrinsically humble superstar, an utterly accessible icon who welcomes visitors into his dressing room with self-effacing graciousness. Between 1951 and 1985, King notched an amazing 74 entries on *Billboard*'s R&B charts, and he was one of the few full-fledged blues artists to score a major pop hit when his 1970 smash "The Thrill Is Gone" crossed over to mainstream success (engendering memorable appearances on *The Ed Sullivan Show* and *American Bandstand*!).

The seeds of King's enduring talent were sown deep in the blues-rich Mississippi Delta. That's where Riley B. King was sired—in Itta Bena, to be exact. By no means was his childhood easy. Young Riley was shuttled between his mother's home and his grandmother's residence. The youth put in long days working as a sharecropper and devoutly sang the Lord's praises at church before moving to Indianola—another town located in the very heart of the Delta—in 1943.

Country and gospel music left an indelible impression on King's musical mindset as he matured, along with the styles of blues greats T-Bone Walker and Lonnie Johnson and jazz geniuses Charlie Christian and Django Reinhardt. In 1946, B.B. King set off for Memphis to look up his cousin, rough-edged country blues guitarist Bukka White. For ten invaluable months, White taught his eager young relative the finer points of playing blues guitar. After returning briefly to Indianola and the sharecropper's eternal struggle with his wife Martha, King arrived in Memphis once again in late 1948. This time, he stuck around for a while.

King was soon broadcasting his music live via Memphis radio station WDIA, a frequency that had only recently switched to a pioneering all-Black format. Local club owners preferred that their attractions also held down radio gigs so they could plug their nightly appearances on the air. When WDIA deejay Maurice "Hot Rod" Hulbert exited his airshift, King took over his record-spinning duties. At first tagged "The Peptikon Boy" (an alcohol-loaded elixir that rivaled Hadacol) when WDIA put him on the air, King's on-air handle became the "Beale Street Blues Boy," later shortened to Blues Boy and then a far snappier B.B.

1949 was a four-star breakthrough year for King. He cut his first four tracks for Jim Bulleit's Bullet Records (including a number entitled "Miss Martha King" after his wife), then signed a contract with the Bihari brothers' Los Angeles-based RPM Records. King cut a plethora of sides in Memphis over the next couple of years for RPM, many of them produced by a relative newcomer named Sam Phillips (whose Sun Records was still a distant dream at that point in time). Phillips was independently producing sides for both the Biharis and Chess; his stable also included Howlin' Wolf, Rosco Gordon, and fellow WDIA personality Rufus Thomas.

The Biharis also recorded some of King's early output themselves, erecting portable recording equipment wherever they could locate a suitable facility. King's first national R&B chart-topper in 1951, "Three O'Clock Blues" (previously waxed by Lowell Fulson), was cut at a Memphis YMCA. King's Memphis running partners included vocalist Bobby Bland, drummer Earl Forest, and ballad-singing pianist Johnny Ace. When King hit the road to promote "Three O'Clock Blues," he handed the group, known as the Beale Streeters, over to Ace.

It was during this era that King first named his beloved guitar "Lucille." Seems that while he was playing a joint in a little Arkansas town called Twist, fisticuffs broke out between two jealous suitors over a lady. The brawlers knocked over a kerosene-filled garbage pail that was heating the place, setting the room ablaze. In the frantic scramble to escape the flames, King left his guitar inside. He foolishly ran back in to retrieve it, dodging the flames and almost losing his life. When the smoke had cleared, King learned that the lady who had inspired such violent passion was named Lucille. Plenty of Lucilles have passed through his hands since; Gibson has even marketed a B.B.-approved guitar model under the name.

The 1950s saw King establish himself as a perennially formidable hitmaking force in the R&B field. Recording mostly in L.A. (the WDIA airshift became impossible to maintain by 1953 due to King's endless touring) for RPM and its successor Kent, King scored 20 chart items during that musically tumultuous decade, including such memorable efforts as "You Know I Love You" (1952); "Woke Up This Morning" and "Please Love Me" (1953); "When My Heart Beats like a Hammer," "Whole Lotta' Love," and "You Upset Me Baby" (1954); "Every Day I Have the Blues" (another Fulson remake), the dreamy blues ballad "Sneakin' Around," and "Ten Long Years" (1955); "Bad Luck," "Sweet Little Angel," and a Platters-like "On My Word of Honor" (1956); and "Please Accept My Love" (first cut by Jimmy Wilson) in 1958. King's guitar attack grew more aggressive and pointed as the decade progressed, influencing a legion of up-and-coming axemen across the nation.

In 1960, King's impassioned two-sided revival of Joe Turner's "Sweet Sixteen" became another mammoth seller, and his "Got a Right to Love My Baby" and "Partin' Time" weren't far behind. But Kent couldn't hang onto a star like King forever (and he may have been tired of watching his new LPs consigned directly into the 99-cent bins on the Biharis' cheapo Crown logo). King moved over to ABC-Paramount Records in 1962, following the lead of Lloyd Price, Ray Charles, and before long, Fats Domino.

In November of 1964, the guitarist cut his seminal *Live at the Regal* album at the fabled Chicago theater and excitement virtually leaped out of the grooves. That same year, he enjoyed a minor hit with "How Blue Can You Get," one of his many signature tunes. 1966's "Don't Answer the Door" and "Paying the Cost to Be the Boss" two years later were Top Ten R&B entries, and the socially charged and funk-tinged "Why I Sing the Blues" just missed achieving the same status in 1969.

Across-the-board stardom finally arrived in 1969 for the deserving guitarist, when he crashed the mainstream consciousness in a big way with a stately, violin-drenched minor-key treatment of Roy Hawkins' "The Thrill Is Gone" that was quite a departure from the concise horn-powered backing King had customarily employed. At last, pop audiences were convinced that they should get to know King better–not only was the track a number three R&B smash, it vaulted to the upper reaches of the pop lists as well.

King was one of a precious few bluesmen to score hits consistently during the 1970s, and for good reason: he wasn't afraid to experiment with the idiom. In 1973, he ventured to Philadelphia to record a pair of huge sellers, "To Know You Is to Love You" and "I Like to Live the Love," with the same silky rhythm section that powered the hits of the Spinners and the O'Jays. In 1976, he teamed up with his old cohort Bland to wax some well-received duets. And in 1978, he joined forces with the jazzy Crusaders to make the gloriously funky "Never Make Your Move Too Soon" and an inspiring "When It All Comes Down." Occasionally, the daring deviations veered off-course–*Love Me Tender,* an album that attempted to harness the Nashville country sound, was an artistic disaster.

Although his concerts have long been as consistently satisfying as anyone now working in the field (and he remains a road warrior of remarkable resiliency who used to gig an average of 300 nights a year), King has tempered his studio activities. Still, his 1993 MCA disc *Blues Summit* was a return to form, as King duetted with his peers (John Lee Hooker, Etta James, Fulson, Koko Taylor) on a program of standards.

King's immediately recognizable guitar style, utilizing a trademark trill that approximates the bottleneck sound shown him by cousin Bukka White all those decades ago, has long set him apart from his contemporaries. Add his patented pleading vocal style and you have the most influential and innovative bluesman of the post-war period. There can be little doubt that B.B. King will reign as the genre's undisputed king (and goodwill ambassador) for as long as he lives. *–Bill Dahl*

My Kind of Blues / 1961 / Crown ✦✦✦
According to his biographer, Charles Sawyer, this is King's personal favorite among his recordings. Unlike most of his albums from this period (which are mostly collections of singles), this was recorded in one session and takes him out of his usual big-band setting, using only bass, drums, and piano for accompaniment. The result is a masterpiece: a sparse, uncluttered sound with nothing to mask King's beautiful guitar and voice. "You Done Lost Your Good Thing Now" (its unaccompanied guitar intro is a pure distillation of his style), "Mr. Pawn Broker," "Someday Baby" (R&B Top Ten, 1961), "Walkin' Dr. Bill," and a great version of "Drivin' Wheel" are highlights. (Out of print) — *George Bedard*

★ **King of the Blues** / Jul. 1961 / MCA ✦✦✦✦✦
No way can a mere four discs cover every facet of the blues king's amazing recording career, but MCA makes a valiant stab at it. The first two discs, as expected, are immaculate. Opening with his Bullet Records debut ("Miss Martha King"), the box continues with a handful of pivotal RPM/Kent masters before digging into his 1960s ABC-Paramount material ("I'm Gonna Sit in 'Til You Give In" and "My Baby's Comin' Home" are little-recalled gems). The hits—"The Thrill Is Gone," "Why I Sing the Blues," "To Know You Is to Love You"—are all here, and if much of the fourth disc is pretty disposable, it only mirrors King's own winding down in the studio. *–Bill Dahl*

★ **Live at the Regal** / 1965 / ABC/MCA ✦✦✦✦✦
This is one of the all-time classic live albums. Recorded in 1964, it captures King in his prime playing to a *very* enthusiastic Black audience. He stretches out on guitar in a way he doesn't on his studio recordings—his guitar sound (it's a joy to hear him switching around and playing with different settings and guitar tones) has a vibrancy and, sometimes, a wild edge that doesn't get captured in the studio. This is a must for B.B. King fans. *–George Bedard*

Lucille / 1968 / MCA ✦✦✦✦
A decent but short (nine songs) late '60s set, with somewhat sparser production than he'd employ with the beefier arrangements of the "Thrill Is Gone" era. Brass and stinging guitar plays a part on all of the songs, leading off with the eight-minute title track, a spoken narrative about his famous guitar. *–Richie Unterberger*

Live & Well / 1969 / MCA ✦✦✦
Although *Live & Well* wasn't a landmark album in the sense of *Live at the Regal*, it was a significant commercial breakthrough for King, as it was the first of his LPs to enter the Top 100. That may have been because recognition from rock stars such as Eric Clapton had finally boosted his exposure to the White pop audience, but it was a worthy recording on its own merits, divided evenly between live and studio material. King's always recorded well as a live act, and it's the concert tracks that shine brightest, although the studio ones (cut with assistance from studio musicians like Al Kooper and Hugh McCracken) aren't bad. *–Richie Unterberger*

Completely Well / 1969 / MCA ✦✦✦✦
Containing "The Thrill Is Gone," the violin-soaked minor-key blues that broke him permanently onto the pop circuit, this album is solid but hardly earthshattering, with a revival of Jay McShann's "Confessin' the Blues" and the heated "So Excited" to its credit. *–Bill Dahl*

Indianola Mississippi Seeds / 1970 / MCA ✦✦✦
B.B. King hasn't made many better pop-flavored albums than this. Besides making Leon Russell's "Hummingbird" sound like his own composition, King showed that you can put the blues into any situation and make it work. Carole King was one of several pop luminaries who did more than just hang on for the ride. *–Ron Wynn*

Live at Cook County Jail / 1971 / MCA ✦✦✦✦
Some veteran King aficionados have been known to tout this album as superior to the massively acclaimed *Live at the Regal*. Either way, it's a crisply paced concert recording for a very appreciative audience. *–Bill Dahl*

In London / 1971 / ABC ✦✦
The plodding rhythms laid down by a coterie of British rock stars for this set make one long for King's road-tested regular band. But it was the fashion in 1971 to dispatch American blues legends to London to record mediocre LPs with alleged rock royalty (the lineup here includes Ringo Starr, Peter Green, Alexis Korner, and Klaus Voormann). *–Bill Dahl*

Guess Who / 1972 / MCA ✦✦✦
When B.B. King is cajoled into covering the Lovin' Spoonful's "Summer in the City," you know material's in dangerously short supply. It's the lead number on this rather undistinguished album, cut with most of his road band of the time. One staple of his live show, the sentimental blues ballad "Guess Who," came from this set. *–Bill Dahl*

To Know You Is to Love You / 1973 / MCA ✦✦✦
The combination of King and the well-oiled Philly rhythm section that powered hits by the O'Jays, Spinners, and Stylistics proved a surprisingly adroit one. Two huge hits came from this album, the Stevie Wonder/Syreeta Wright-penned title track and "I Like to Live the Love," both of them intriguing updates of King's tried-and-true style. *–Bill Dahl*

Midnight Believer / 1978 / MCA ✦✦✦
Another collaboration that worked a lot better than one might have expected. King and the Crusaders blended in a marginally funky, contemporary style for the buoyant "Never Make Your Move Too Soon" and an uplifting "When It All Comes Down." *–Bill Dahl*

Live "Now Appearing" at Ole Miss / 1980 / MCA ✦✦
Surely the worst, most lethargic live album that King ever made. Rumor has long had it that after-the-fact enhancements were added to the live tapes to make them more palatable—if so, it didn't work! *–Bill Dahl*

Great Moments with B.B. King / 1981 / MCA ✦✦✦✦
Very solid 23-track package culled from some of King's best mid-to-late-'60s ABC-Paramount and BluesWay LPs. Some of the best cuts stem from a sizzling live album; "Gambler's Blues," "Waitin' on You," and a stunning "Night Life" find his reverb level rising to the boiling point. A brassy "That's Wrong Little Mama,"

"Dance with Me," and "Heartbreaker" connect like consecutive right hooks, and his rousing smash "Paying the Cost to Be the Boss" is also on board. —*Bill Dahl*

There Must Be a Better World Somewhere / 1981 / MCA ✦✦✦
One of King's more credible contemporary albums, with much of the material in a legitimately bluesy vein (no trace of any country crooning, thank goodness!). —*Bill Dahl*

Love Me Tender / 1982 / MCA ✦✦
B.B. King's extremely ill-advised foray into mushy Nashville cornpone. Hearing him croon the title track in front of an array of Music Row's most generic pickers is enough to drive one screaming into his or her record collection for a surefire antidote: some 1950s King on RPM! Ahh...—*Bill Dahl*

Do the Boogie! B.B. King's Early '50s Classics / 1988 / Flair ✦✦✦✦✦
20 killer tracks from B.B. King's 1950s heyday, including quite a few alternate takes and a few tough-to-locate items ("Bye Bye Baby," "Dark Is the Night," "Jump with You Baby"). Many of the titles are familiar ones—"Woke Up This Morning," "Every Day," "Please Love Me," "Whole Lotta Love"—but often as not, compiler Ray Topping unearthed contrasting versions from the same sessions that shed new, fascinating light on King's studio techniques. —*Bill Dahl*

The Best of B. B. King, Vol. 1 / 1991 / Flair ✦✦✦
A 20-track hits compilation that should have been a great deal better than it is. The disc embarrassingly uses an inferior remake of King's classic "Whole Lotta Love" instead of the original, while drums and electric bass have been clumsily overdubbed on the original takes of "You Upset Me Baby," "Every Day," and "Please Love Me," absolutely ruining them. What a shame, since two-thirds of the collection is just fine. —*Bill Dahl*

Spotlight on Lucille / 1991 / Flair ✦✦✦✦
From the contemporary-looking cover, this would appear to be recently recorded material. But wait—these are all 1950s/early-'60s instrumentals from the Modern/Kent vaults, spotlighting B.B. King's pristine lead guitar in an often jazzier mode than he usually adopted in the studio. His workout on Louis Jordan's "Just like a Woman" is a tour de force that's been reissued often, but much of the compilation is rare stuff that gives Lucille her full due. —*Bill Dahl*

The Fabulous B.B. King / 1991 / Flair ✦✦
The Best of B.B. King, Vol. 1, also on Flair, has 20 tracks from the same era covered by this collection, which only has 12. So you should really stick with the other Flair compilation, even if it's a bit more expensive. Which doesn't mean that this CD is bad; the 12 songs, all from the early and mid-'50s, include some of his most famous early classics, such as "Three O'Clock Blues," "Everyday I Have the Blues," and "Sweet Little Angel." —*Richie Unterberger*

Live at San Quentin / Jun. 1991 / MCA ✦✦

☆ **Singin' the Blues/The Blues** / 1992 / Flair ✦✦✦✦✦
Two great original Crown albums from the '50s appear on one import CD, including most of King's Top Ten R&B hits from the period: "3 O'Clock Blues," "Please Love Me," "You Upset Me Baby," "You Know I Love You," "Woke Up This Morning," and "Sweet Little Angel," plus one of his best, "Crying Won't Help You." This is the stuff that was so hugely influential to other blues guitarists and singers in its original recorded version. Here is lots of the real early, gritty stuff: "That Ain't the Way to Do It," "When My Heart Beats like a Hammer," "Don't You Want a Man like Me?" The guitar intro to "Early in the Morning" is one of the finest examples of King in a jazzy mode. Great guitar! —*George Bedard*

Heart & Soul / 1992 / Point Blank ✦✦✦
The Biharis harbored dreams of crossing the rich-voiced King over into the pop market during the '50s, trying him out on some of the dreariest ballads imaginable. Many of those limp outings turn up on this collection—hearing the king of the blues croon "On My Word of Honour" and "My Heart Belongs to You" like a refugee from the Platters ain't a good time by any means! Fortunately, not everything is so dire: "Story from My Heart and Soul," "Lonely and Blue," and the delicious "Sneakin' Around" sport a more edifying mix of blues and balladry. —*Bill Dahl*

Blues Summit / 1993 / MCA ✦✦✦
On this release, King comes close to equaling his past triumphs

on small independent labels in the '50s and '60s. He's ditched the psuedo-hip production fodder and cut a 12-song set matching him with blues peers. His duets with Buddy Guy, John Lee Hooker, and Albert Collins are especially worthy, while the songs with Koko Taylor, Ruth Brown, and Irma Thomas have some good-natured banter and exchanges, as well as tasty vocals. The master gives willing pupils Joe Louis Walker and Robert Cray valuable lessons on their collaborations. There's also a medley in which King invokes the spirit of his chitlin circuit days, taking the vocal spotlight while his Orchestra roars along underneath. —*Ron Wynn*

My Sweet Little Angel / Oct. 5, 1993 / Flair ✦✦✦✦
Another 21-track anthology chock full of alternate takes and previously unreleased masters from B.B. King's 1950s stint at RPM/Kent. A wild cross-section of material—signature items like "Sweet Little Angel" and "Please Accept My Love," an off-the-wall reading of Tony Bennett's "In the Middle of an Island," and best of all, a torrid jazzy instrumental called "String Bean" that finds King pulling some astounding guitar tricks out of a seemingly bottomless bag. —*Bill Dahl*

Lucille & Friends / 1995 / MCA ✦✦✦

Earl King

b. Feb. 7, 1934, New Orleans, LA
Guitar, Vocals / Electric New Orleans Blues
Unilaterally respected around his Crescent City homebase as both a performer and a songwriter, guitarist Earl King has been a prime New Orleans R&B force for more than four decades—and he shows no signs of slowing down.

Born Earl Johnson, the youngster considered the platters of Texas guitarists T-Bone Walker and Gatemouth Brown almost as fascinating as the live performances of local luminaries Smiley Lewis and Tuts Washington. King met his major influence and mentor, Guitar Slim, at the Club Tijuana, one of King's favorite haunts (along with the Dew Drop, of course), the two becoming fast friends. Still billed as Earl Johnson, the guitarist debuted on wax in 1953 on Savoy with "Have You Gone Crazy" (with pal Huey "Piano" Smith making the first of many memorable supporting appearances on his platters).

Johnson became Earl King upon signing with Specialty the next year (label head Art Rupe intended to name him King Earl, but the typesetter reversed the names). "A Mother's Love," Earl's first Specialty offering, was an especially accurate Guitar Slim homage produced by Johnny Vincent, who would soon launch his own label, Ace Records, with King one of his principal artists. King's first Ace single, the seminal two-chord south Louisiana blues "Those Lonely, Lonely Nights," proved a national R&B hit (despite a soundalike cover by Johnny "Guitar" Watson). Smith's rolling piano undoubtedly helped make the track a hit.

King remained with Ace through the rest of the decade, waxing an unbroken string of great New Orleans R&B sides with the unparalleled house band at Cosimo's studio. But he moved over to Imperial to work with producer Dave Bartholomew in 1960, cutting the classic "Come On" (also known as "Let The Good Times Roll") and 1961's humorous "Trick Bag" and managing a second chart item in 1962 with "Always a First Time." King wrote standout tunes for Fats Domino, Professor Longhair, and Lee Dorsey during the '60s.

Although a potential 1963 pact with Motown was scuttled at the last instant, King admirably rode out the rough spots during the late '60s and '70s. Since signing with Black Top, his performing career has been rejuvenated; 1990s *Sexual Telepathy* and *Hard River to Cross* three years later were both superlative albums. —*Bill Dahl*

New Orleans Rock 'n' Roll / 1977 / Sonet ✦✦

Earl King / 1981 / Vivid ✦✦✦

Street Parade / 1981 / Charly ✦✦✦
Funky 1972 tracks that should have fueled a comeback for the Crescent City mainstay but didn't (a lease deal with Atlantic fell through). Allen Toussaint was apparently in charge of the sessions, which produced updates of "Mama and Papa" and "A Mother's Love" as well as a bevy of fresh nuggets (notably the fanciful "Medieval Days," later revived by King on Black Top) and the two-part title item. —*Bill Dahl*

● **Trick Bag** / 1983 / EMI America ✦✦✦✦✦
Here's an extremely hard-to-find French LP that remains the only

place where King's wonderful early-'60s Imperial Records catalog was gathered in one place (a handful grace EMI's two-disc Dave Bartholomew set; he produced them). Earl changed his sound to fit the funkier Crescent City sound of the time on the two-part "Come On," the humorous "Trick Bag" and "Mama and Papa," and a passionate "You're More to Me than Gold." *—Bill Dahl*

Glazed / 1988 / Black Top ✦✦✦
The coupling of funky Crescent City guitarist Earl King with the East Coast-based Roomful of Blues wasn't exactly made in heaven (the band excels at jump blues; at second-line beats, they're fairly clueless), but it did mark the beginning of King's heartwarming comeback as a recording artist. King's songwriting skills were certainly in fine shape: "It All Went Down the Drain," "Iron Cupid," and "Love Rent" were typically well-observed originals. *—Bill Dahl*

Sexual Telepathy / 1990 / Black Top ✦✦✦✦✦
Reunited with a more sympathetic New Orleans rhythm section (bassist George Porter, Jr., and drummer Kenny Blevins) and a funkier horn section, King excelled handsomely on this uncommonly strong outing. As we've come to expect from him, he brought a sheaf of new originals to the sessions, from a saucy "Sexual Telepathy" to a heartwarming "Happy Little Nobody's Waggy Tail Dog." Remakes of his "Always a First Time" and "A Weary Silent Night" were welcome inclusions (especially since we can't easily lay our hands on the originals). *—Bill Dahl*

Hard River to Cross / 1993 / Black Top ✦✦✦✦✦
The quirky guitarist with the endlessly wavy hair made it two winners in a row with this one. Snooks Eaglin guests on guitar for three tracks (including the hilarious "Big Foot" and a joyous "No City like New Orleans") while Porter and drummer Herman Ernest III lay down scintillating grooves behind King's ringing axe and wise vocals. *—Bill Dahl*

● **Those Lonely, Lonely Nights** / 1993 / P-Vine ✦✦✦✦✦
Why must New Orleans guitarist Earl King's 1950s material be so difficult to locate on CD? This expensive Japanese import does the job handily, if you can find it—all eight of King's Guitar Slim-influenced Specialty sides (including "A Mother's Love" and its rocking flip, "I'm Your Best Bet Baby") and 17 of his terrific efforts for Ace, notably the hit title track, the equally moving "My Love Is Strong," and the jumping "Everybody's Carried Away," "Little Girl," and "I'll Take You Back Home." *—Bill Dahl*

Freddie King

b. Sep. 3, 1934, Gilmer, TX, **d.** Dec. 28, 1976, Dallas, TX
Guitar, Vocals / Modern Electric Blues
Guitarist Freddie King rode to fame in the early '60s with a spate of catchy instrumentals which became instant bandstand fodder for fellow bluesmen and White rock bands alike. Employing a more down-home (thumb and finger picks) approach to the B.B. King single-string style of playing, King enjoyed success on a variety of different record labels. Furthermore, he was one of the first bluesmen to employ a racially integrated group onstage behind him. Influenced by Eddie Taylor, Jimmy Rogers, and Robert Jr. Lockwood, King went on to influence the likes of Eric Clapton, Mick Taylor, Stevie Ray Vaughan, and Lonnie Mack, among many others.

Freddie King (who was originally billed as "Freddy" early in his career) was born and raised in Gilmer, TX, where he learned how to play guitar as a child; his mother and uncle taught him the instrument. Initially, King played rural acoustic blues, in the vein of Lightnin' Hopkins. By the time he was a teenager, he had grown to love the rough, electrified sounds of Chicago blues. In 1950, when he was 16 years old, his family moved to Chicago, where he began frequenting local blues clubs, listening to musicians like Muddy Waters, Jimmy Rogers, Robert Jr. Lockwood, Little Walter, and Eddie Taylor. Soon, the young guitarist formed his own band, the Every Hour Blues Boys, and was performing himself.

In the mid-'50s, King began playing on sessions for Parrott and Chess Records, as well as playing with Earlee Payton's Blues Cats and the Little Sonny Cooper Band. Freddie King didn't cut his own record until 1957, when he recorded "Country Boy" for the small independent label El-Bee. The single failed to gain much attention.

Three years later, King signed with Federal Records, a subsidiary of King Records, and recorded his first single for the label, "You've Got to Love Her with Feeling," in August of 1960. The single appeared the following month and became a minor hit, scraping the bottom of the pop charts in early 1961. "You've

Got to Love Her with Feeling" was followed by "Hide Away," the song that would become Freddie King's signature tune and most influential recording. "Hide Away" was adapted by King and Magic Sam from a Hound Dog Taylor instrumental and named after one of the most popular bars in Chicago. The single was released as the B-side of "I Love the Woman" (his singles featured a vocal A-side and an instrumental B-side) in the fall of 1961 and it became a major hit, reaching number five on the R&B charts and number 29 on the pop charts. Throughout the '60s, "Hide Away" was one of the necessary songs blues and rock & roll bar bands across America and England had to play during their gigs.

King's first album, *Freddy King Sings,* appeared in 1961 and it was followed later that year by *Let's Hide Away and Dance Away with Freddy King: Strictly Instrumental.* Throughout 1961, he turned out a series of instrumentals—including "San-Ho-Zay," "The Stumble," and "I'm Tore Down"—which became blues classics; everyone from Magic Sam and Stevie Ray Vaughan to Dave Edmunds and Peter Green covered King's material. "Lonesome Whistle Blues," "San-Ho-Zay," and "I'm Tore Down" all became Top Ten R&B hits that year.

Freddie King continued to record for King Records until 1968, with a second instrumental album (*Freddy King Gives You a Bonanza of Instrumentals*) appearing in 1965, although none of his singles became hits. Nevertheless, his influence was heard throughout blues and rock guitarists throughout the '60s—Eric Clapton made "Hide Away" his showcase number in 1965. King signed with Atlantic/Cotillion in late 1968, releasing two albums—*Freddie King Is a Blues Master* and *My Feeling for the Blues*—the following year; both collections were produced by King Curtis. After their release, King and Atlantic/Cotillion parted ways.

King landed a new record contract with Leon Russell's Shelter Records in the fall of 1970. King recorded three albums for Shelter in the early '70s, all of which sold well. In addition to respectable sales, his concerts were also quite popular with both blues and rock audiences. In 1974, he signed a contract with RSO Records—which was also Eric Clapton's record label—and he released *Burglar,* which was produced and recorded with Clapton. Following the release of *Burglar,* King toured America, Europe, and Australia. In 1975, he released his second RSO album, *Larger than Life.*

Throughout 1976, Freddie King toured America, even though his health was beginning to decline. On December 29, 1976, King died of heart failure. Although his passing was premature—he was only 42 years old—Freddie King's influence could still be heard in blues and rock guitarists 20 years after his death. *—Stephen Thomas Erlewine & Cub Koda*

Getting Ready / 1971 / Shelter ✦✦✦
The first of King's three albums for Leon Russell's Shelter label set the tone for his work for the company: competent electric blues with a prominent rock/soul influence. King sings and plays well, but neither the sidemen nor the material allowed him to scale significant heights. Part of the problem is that Freddie himself wrote none of the songs, which are divided between Chicago blues standards and material supplied by Leon Russell and Don Nix. The entire album is included on the compilation *King of the Blues. —Richie Unterberger*

Texas Cannonball / 1972 / Shelter ✦✦✦
Similar to his first Shelter outing (*Getting Ready*), but with more of a rock feel. That's due as much to the material as the production. Besides covering tunes by Jimmy Rogers, Howlin' Wolf, and Elmore James, King tackles compositions by Leon Russell and, more unexpectedly, Bill Withers, Isaac Hayes-David Porter, and John Fogerty (whose "Lodi" is reworked into "Lowdown in Lodi"). King's own pen remained virtually in retirement, as he wrote only one of the album's tracks. Reissued in its entirety on *King of the Blues. —Richie Unterberger*

Woman Across the River / 1973 / Shelter ✦✦✦
King's last Shelter album was his most elaborately produced, with occasional string arrangements and female backups vocals, although these didn't really detract from the net result. Boasting perhaps heavier rock elements than his other Shelter efforts, it was characteristically divided between blues standards (by the likes of Willie Dixon and Elmore James), Leon Russell tunes, and more R&B/soul-inclined material by the likes of Ray Charles and Percy Mayfield. It's been reissued, along with his other

Shelter albums, on the *King of the Blues* anthology. —*Richie Unterberger*

King of the Blues / 1995 / Shelter/EMI ✦✦✦
Double-CD compilation that includes all three of the albums King recorded for Leon Russell's Shelter label in the early 1970s, as well as some other cuts (half a dozen of which were previously unissued) recorded around the same period. King's vocal and guitar-playing skills remained intact when he joined Shelter, but these recordings aren't among his best. That's partially because he was playing with rock-oriented sidemen, and partially because the material–divided between covers of blues standards, contemporary rock and soul items, and songs written by Leon Russell–wasn't especially exciting or sympathetic. Most crucial was the near-total absence of material from the pen of King himself. Although this set isn't bad, when you want to turn to classic King, you'll go elsewhere, particularly to the sides he recorded for the King label in the '60s. —*Richie Unterberger*

Just Pickin' / 1986 / Modern Blues ✦✦✦✦✦
Both of Freddy's all-instrumental albums for the King label (*Let's Hide Away and Dance Away with Freddy King* and *Freddy King Gives You A Bonanza Of Instrumentals*) on one compact disc. "Hide Away", "The Stumble" and "San-Ho-Zay" are the numbers that made King's rep and influenced guitarists on both sides of the Atlantic. —*Cub Koda*

★ **Hide Away: The Best of Freddie King** / 1993 / Rhino ✦✦✦✦✦
Although not always placed in the upper echelon of blues performers alongside the other Kings (B.B. and Albert), Freddie King was a dynamo. He was both a powerhouse, imaginative guitarist and a glorious, soulful vocalist who could belt out come-ons, shout with gusto or wail in anguish. His instrumentals were also catchy, usually simply structured but vigorous and vividly articulated. This tremendous 20-cut sampler includes familiar hits like "Going Down" and the title cut, plus the shattering "Have You Ever Loved A Woman" and the poignant "Lonesome Whistle Blues." The tracks are exquisitely remastered and intelligently sequenced, and the notes are informative and thorough without being academic or fawning. —*Ron Wynn*

Live At The Electric Ballroom, 1974 / Feb. 1996 / Black Top ✦✦✦
An Atlanta concert that wasn't issued for two decades. Archival releases of this sort tend to be for collectors only, but this is a cut above the standard. The sound is very good, the band is pretty tight, and King solos with fire and sings with conviction, sticking mostly to covers of warhorses like "Dust My Broom," "Key to the Highway," and "Sweet Home Chicago." It's a better deal, in fact, than his studio albums for Shelter in the early '70s, boasting a far more suitable, no-frills small combo approach. As a neat bonus, it also contains two solo acoustic performances recorded at a Dallas radio station in the 1970s. —*Richie Unterberger*

Little Jimmy King (Manuel Gales)

b. Dec. 4, 1968
Guitar, Vocals / Modern Electric Blues
Memphis-based left-handed guitar player Little Jimmy King is certainly one of the most exciting of the new crop of blues players to emerge on the scene in the 1990s. King was born December 4, 1968, as Manuel Gales but renamed himself for his two favorite guitar heroes, Jimi Hendrix and Albert King. He got started as a rock & roller, but by the mid-'80s had switched to blues. By 1988, he had left the Memphis blues scene to go on the road with his hero as part of Albert King's band. The late Albert King called Little Jimmy his grandson, and the late Stevie Ray Vaughan also had high praise for the young guitarist. In a moment King will never forget, Vaughan reportedly told him: "Play on, brother, you've got it. Don't stop playing for nobody."

King's self-titled debut was released in 1991 on the Rounder Bullseye Blues label, and he followed it up in 1994 with *Something Inside of Me*, on which he's accompanied by former Double Trouble bassist Tommy Shannon and drummer Chris "Whipper" Layton. King can also be heard playing guitar on Ann Peebles' *Full Time Love* and Otis Clay's *I'll Treat You Right.*

Little Jimmy King's live shows, like his two highly praised recordings for Bullseye Blues, are full of fire and fury, passionate guitar playing within the context of his band, the Memphis Soul Survivors, great vocals and clever songs. When you realize

this guy still hasn't hit 30, you know why he's being called "the future of blues guitar." King is taking the idiom to a whole new generation of younger fans and he's also a key link in the music's required, ongoing evolution. —*Richard Skelly*

● **Little Jimmy King and the Memphis Soul Survivors** / 1991 / Bullseye Blues ✦✦✦✦✦
Hailing from the Jimi Hendrix and Stevie Ray Vaughan school of blues-rock, Little Jimmy King turns in a promising eponymous debut. Though he leans a little too heavily toward rock & roll for some tastes—at his rootsiest, he sounds like Albert King—there's no denying his skill. King runs through a number of rollicking uptempo tracks, shuffles, R&B grinders, smoldering slow blues and even funk in the form of a cover of Sly Stone's "Sex Machine." Though his songwriting isn't quite up to par, his conviction carries him through the weakest moments and he shows signs of developing into a more distinctive songwriter. On the whole, it's an exciting, promising debut. —*Thom Owens*

Something Inside of Me / Mar. 30, 1994 / Bullseye Blues ✦✦✦
Little Jimmy King's second Bullseye/Rounder session matches the slashing guitarist with the rhythm section that once backed Stevie Ray Vaughan. King soars on these 11 cuts; while he lacks Vaughan's speed and is more a straight blues technician, he plays with more imagination and drive than on his debut. He contributes six originals and does a competent job of reworking material by Elmore James, Albert King, and even Phil Collins. While there's nothing here startling or surprising, King effectively teams with Chris Layton and Tommy Shannon, and producer/organist Ron Levy crafts an entertaining program of contemporary blues-rock with vintage sensibilities and overtones. —*Ron Wynn*

Kinsey Report

Group / Modern Electric Blues
This family band consists of Donald Kinsey (b. May 12, 1953, Gary, IN), (vocal, guitar); Ralph "Woody" Kinsey, (drums); Kenneth Kinsey, (bass); Ronald Prince, (guitar). Solidly based in the blues as a result of lifelong training in The Big Daddy Kinsey household, The Kinsey scions are also versed in a broad range of music. The older brothers Donald and Ralph had an early blues-rock trio (White Lightnin') in the mid-'70s, long before they regrouped as The Kinsey Report in 1984 and began to launch new excursions into rock. Donald also recorded and toured with Albert King and with Bob Marley, and the influence of those giants (as well as that of Big Daddy Kinsey, naturally) show through in the music of The Kinsey Report. The band expertly covers all the bases from Chicago blues through reggae, rock, funk, and soul, and their recordings are also distinguished by the songwriting talents and self-contained production approach of The Kinseys. —*Jim O'Neal*

● **Edge of the City** / 1987 / Alligator ✦✦✦✦✦
An engaging, original blues-rock album comes from this family band. —*Niles J. Frantz*

Crossing Bridges / May 4, 1993 / Capitol ✦✦
Crossing Bridges is a disappointing set of rock meanderings. —*Bill Dahl*

Big Daddy Kinsey

b. Mar. 18, 1927, Pleasant Grove, MS
Guitar, Harmonica, Vocals / Modern Electric Blues, Chicago Blues
Long before Lester "Big Daddy" Kinsey and his clan hit the international blues circuit, he established himself as the modern-day blues patriarch of Gary, IN, and as the Steeltown's answer to Muddy Waters. A slide guitarist and harp blower with roots in both the Mississippi Delta and postwar Chicago styles, Kinsey worked with local bands only long enough for his sons to mature into top-flight musicians, and since 1984 (when Big Daddy recorded his debut album, *Bad Situation*) the family act has become one of the hottest attractions in contemporary blues. Big Daddy's material ranges from deep blues in the Muddy Waters vein to hard-rocking blues with touches of funk and even reggae, courtesy of sons Donald and Ralph (who venture even further afield in their own outings as The Kinsey Report). —*Jim O'Neal*

Bad Situation (with the Kinsey Report) / 1985 / Rooster Blues ✦✦✦
Crisp, funky, and modern, *Bad Situation* shows Big Daddy and the band in fine form. —*Bill Dahl*

Midnight Drive / 1989 / Alligator ✦✦✦
Big Daddy Kinsey attempts to expand the sonic palette of blues by adding elements of funk and hard rock. Although there are some interesting moments—primarily in the skillful solos—the music often falls flat and the songwriting isn't distinctive. Kinsey's attempts at diversity are admirable, but ultimately unsuccessful. —*Thom Owens*

● **Can't Let Go** / 1990 / Blind Pig ✦✦✦✦✦
Fine patriarchal blues from this little-known Chicago artist, backed by his sons (Kinsey Report). —*Cub Koda*

Powerhouse / 1991 / Point Blank ✦✦✦
This hard-rock album is spiced (lightly) with blues. —*Niles J. Frantz*

I Am the Blues / Jan. 1993 / Verve ✦✦
On this disappointingly pompous set, Kinsey seems to want to occupy Muddy Waters' shoes, even recruiting his old band here; it didn't work! —*Bill Dahl*

Can't Let Go / Blind Pig ✦✦✦✦✦
This decent encore LP has an emphasis on Kinsey's enduring delta roots. —*Bill Dahl*

Eddie Kirkland

b. Aug. 16, 1928, Jamaica
Guitar, Harmonica, Vocals / Modern Electric Blues
How many Jamaican-born bluesmen have recorded with John Lee Hooker and toured with Otis Redding? It's a safe bet there's only one: Eddie Kirkland, who's engaged in some astonishing onstage acrobatics over the decades (like standing on his head while playing guitar on TV's *Don Kirshner's Rock Concert*).

But you won't find any ersatz reggae grooves cluttering Kirkland's work. He was brought up around Dothan, AL, before heading north to Detroit in 1943. There he hooked up with Hooker five years later, recording with him for several firms as well as under his own name for RPM in 1952, King in 1953, and Fortune in 1959. Tru-Sound Records, a Prestige subsidiary, invited Kirkland to Englewood Cliffs, NJ, in 1961–62 to wax his first album, *It's the Blues Man!* The polished R&B band of saxist King Curtis crashed head on into Kirkland's intense vocals, raucous guitar and harmonica throughout the exciting set.

Exiting the Motor City for Macon, GA, in 1962, Kirkland signed on with Otis Redding as a sideman and show opener not long thereafter. Redding introduced Kirkland to Stax/Volt co-owner Jim Stewart, who flipped over Eddie's primal dance workout "The Hawg." It was issued on Volt in 1963, billed to Eddie Kirk. By the dawn of the 1970s, Kirkland was recording for Pete Lowry's Trix label. More recently, he's waxed three CDs for Deluge (his latest, an unpredictable *Where You Get Your Sugar?*, emerged in 1995). —*Bill Dahl*

● **It's the Blues Man!** / 1961 / Original Blues Classics ✦✦✦✦✦
Wildman guitarist/harpist Kirkland brought his notoriously rough-hewn attack to this vicious 1962 album for Tru-Sound, joined by a very accomplished combo led by saxman extraordinaire King Curtis and including guitarist Bill Doggett. As the crew honed in on common stylistic ground, the energy levels soared sky-high, Kirkland roaring "Man of Stone," "Train Done Gone," and "I Tried" with ferocious fervor. —*Bill Dahl*

The Devil & Other Blues Demons / Apr. 1975 / Trix ✦✦✦
Eddie Kirkland has long straddled the fence between bluesy soul and soulful blues. He was at a low point when he recorded for Trix in 1973, but this session recharged him musically, if not sales-wise. It is great to have it available again; whether Kirkland is doing silly numbers, offering taut blues licks or giving examples of his philosophy, he finds creative ways to utilize the standard 12-bar scheme. —*Ron Wynn*

Have Mercy / 1988 / Evidence ✦✦✦
Kirkland's roaring guitar and garbled, gospel-tinged vocals are pretty much submerged in the mix here, a hodge podge of standard blues readymades and hyperactive funk-blues workouts. —*Cub Koda*

● **Three Shades of the Blues** / 198 / Relic ✦✦✦✦✦
Kirkland's eight sides on this compilation are as hard-driving and intense as you could possibly ask for. It also includes four sides each from B.B. King disciple Mr. Bo and the Ohio Untouchables, with dazzling guitar work from Robert Ward on the latter. —*Cub Koda*

All Around The World / 1992 / Deluge ✦✦
All Around the World is a comparatively lackluster set. —*AMG*

Some Like It Raw / Sep. 1993 / Deluge ✦✦✦
Recorded live at a blues bar in Vancouver, British Columbia, this finds Kirkland in typical latter-day form, full of buzzy guitar, garbled vocals, and loads of intensity. Alternating between original material (most of it in a soul-funk vein) and blues classics (few of which bear much likeness to their original counterparts), Kirkland gets solid support from the young, white backing band here and the recording quality is quite good. —*Cub Koda*

Where You Get Your Sugar / Nov. 7, 1995 / Deluge ✦✦✦
Kirkland remains an amazingly raucous entertainer whose freeform sense of blues convention remains elusive to capture on records; perhaps he's best experienced live. This album's no exception—fiery at times, meandering and frustrating at others. To his credit, Kirkland's no moldy fig, mixing thoroughly contemporary rhythms and unusual chord changes into his rowdy musical stew. —*Bill Dahl*

Cub Koda

b. Oct. 1, 1948, Detroit, MI
Guitar, Vocals / Electric Chicago Blues
Best known as the leader of Brownsville Station and composer of their hit, "Smokin' in the Boys Room," Cub Koda has proven that his roots went far deeper, both before the band's formation, during its days in the sun, and long after its demise. His high school band, the Del-Tino's, was dipping into blues and rockabilly as far back as 1963—not only pre-Butterfield, but pre-Beatles. Similarly, he recorded legendary home tapes during his off hours from Brownsville, before the rockabilly revival had uttered its first hiccup, and later teamed with Hound Dog Taylor's former rhythm section, the HouseRockers to play the blues in the '80s. Along the way he cranked out a monthly column ("The Vinyl Junkie") and recorded a series of albums that kept roots music of all kinds alive without ever treating it like a museum piece.

Originally a drummer at age five, Cub switched over to guitar when he formed his first band, the Del-Tino's, a teenage garage combo equally influenced by rock & roll, blues, and rockabilly. The group cut their first single—Roy Orbison's "Go Go Go"—in the fall of 1963, and released two more 45s independently before they disbanded in 1966. By this time, Koda had become so immersed in the blues, that the last Del-Tino's single had the trio doing Muddy Waters' "I Got My Mojo Workin'" on one side and Robert Johnson's "Ramblin' on My Mind" on the other.

After a couple of bands in the late '60s that largely went unrecorded, Koda formed Brownsville Station in 1969. After playing local Midwest gigs and releasing a handful of singles, the band released their first album in 1970. But it wasn't until "Smokin' in the Boys Room" that Brownsville had a genuine hit. Released as a single in the Fall of 1973, "Smokin'" climbed all the way to number three, eventually selling 2 1/2 million copies.

But Cub began to back away from the group's loud, overdriven rock sound—at least in private. He purchased a multi-track tape recorder and started producing one-man-band tapes, where he overdubbed all the instruments and vocals. For the next several years, Cub made home recordings of rockabilly, blues, R&B, country, jazz, and early rock & roll—the exact opposite of Brownsville's heavy rock stance; the rockabilly tapes were eventually released as *That's What I Like About the South* in the early '80s, with other tracks showing up on compilations as late as 1993.

When Brownsville disbanded in 1979, Cub began writing a column—the "Vinyl Junkie"—for *Goldmine* magazine, now being published in *DISCoveries*. Through the column's success, Koda established himself as an expert record collector and critic—eventually, Cub would compile and write liner notes for a number of projects, including three volumes in Rhino's acclaimed *Blues Masters* series.

In 1980, Koda worked with Hound Dog Taylor's backing band, the Houserockers. Over the next 15 years, Koda, guitarist Brewer Phillips, and drummer Ted Harvey performed and recorded together, with their first album, *It's the Blues*, appearing in 1981 and their latest, *The Joint Was Rockin'* being released in 1996.

Throughout the '80s and '90s, Koda has continued to divide his time equally between touring, recording, and writing. 1993 saw the twin release of *Smokin' in the Boy's Room: The Best of Brownsville Station* on Rhino and *Welcome to My Job*, a retrospective of his non-Brownsville material on Blue Wave, followed a year later by *Abba Dabba Dabba—A Bonanza of Hits* on Schoolkids' Records. What's next—given Cub's eclectic tastes—is anyone's guess. *—Stephen Thomas Erlewine & Dan Forte*

It's the Blues / 1981 / Fan Club ♦♦♦
The addition of bass and special guests Left Hand Frank and Lefty Diz only distract from the chemistry beween Cub and the House Rockers (even more obvious on their belated live followup), but this is a strong session, with the ex-stadium boogie boy sounding totally at home with these blues veterans. His vocal duet with Brewer Phillips on J.B. Lenoir's "Talk to Your Daughter" is a joy, and thankfully not every note is perfectly in place—or in the case of Brewer's guitar, in tune. Added treats: Cub's big-toned harp on "Rockin' This Joint Tonight" and humorous dialog with Frank on "Dirty Duck Blues." *—Dan Forte*

● **Live at B.L.U.E.S. 1982** / 1991 / Wolf ♦♦♦♦♦
What's wrong with this picture? The sawed-off bespectacled singer/guitarist from Brownville Station fronting the late Hound Dog Taylor's ex-rhythm section, the House Rockers—blasphemy, you say? Get a life. Cub smokes like he's: 1) out to dispell any doubts about his legtimacy, and 2) having the time of his life. Opening with Howlin' Wolf's "Highway 49" (a rather tall order), the Cubmaster grabs the Chicago crowd by its collective neck and shakes it into submission. His guitar trade-offs with Brewer Phillips (no bass in this band) are a delight, and by "You Can't Sit Down" drummer Ted Harvey is blowing his police whistle—signalling that things be rockin'! Eddie Clearwater sits in on one tune, and Cub tips his hat to the guitarist with a stellar rendition of Eddie's "Hillbilly Blues." This is worthy of wider release, not to mention an encore. *—Dan Forte*

● **Welcome to My Job: the Cub Koda Collection 1963–93** / 1993 / Blue Wave ♦♦♦♦♦
Covering everything from his pre-Brownsville Station days to two brand-new songs, *Welcome to My Job* is the definitive collection of Cub Koda's versatile solo career. *—Stephen Thomas Erlewine*

● **The Joint Was Rockin'** / 1996 / Deluxe ♦♦♦♦♦
Recorded live in the Boston area in 1984 with the Houserockers and featuring a selection of blues classics like "The Sky Is Crying" and "Dust My Broom," as well as more obscure numbers like "Give Me Back My Wig," "Bad Boy," and Jimmy Roger's "That's All Right," *The Joint Was Rockin'* captures Cub Koda at his bluesiest. Koda simply burns on the slide guitar, turning out wild, frenetic licks and solos with flair. The Houserockers are equally exciting, creating a loose but in the pocket rhythm that exemplifies what greasy, gritty blues is all about (plus, Brewer Phillips turns in a terrific solo on "Whole Lotta Lovin'). *— Stephen Thomas Erlewine*

Koerner, Ray & Glover

Group / Acoustic Blues
In today's climate of a blues band seemingly on every corner with 'the next "Stevie Ray Vaughan" being touted every other minute, it's hard to imagine a time when being a White blues singer was considered kind of a novelty. But in those heady times of the early '60s and the folk and blues revival, that's *exactly* how it was. But into this milieu came three young men who knew it, understood it, and could play and sing it; their names were Koerner, Ray and Glover. They were folkies, to be sure, but the three of them did a lot—both together and separately—to bring the blues to a White audience and in many ways, set certain things in place that have become standards of the Caucasian presentation of the music over the years.

The three of them were college students attending the University of Minnesota, immediately drawn together by their common interests in the music and by the close-knit folk community that existed back then. As was their wont, they all decided to append their names with colorful nicknames; there was "Spider" John Koerner, the Jesse Fuller and Big Joe Williams of the group, Dave "Snaker" Ray, a 12-string playing Leadbelly aficionado, and Tony "Little Sun" Glover on harmonica, holding up the Sonny Terry end of things. This simple little act of reinven-

tion resonates up to the present day, with myriads of White practitioners throwing their mundane appellations out the window to recast themselves as something along the lines of Juke Joint Slim and the Boogie Blues Blasters.

They worked in various configurations within the trio unit, often doing solo turns and duets, but seldom all three of them together. Their breakthrough album, *Blues, Rags and Hollers*, released in 1963, sent out a clarion call that this music was just as accessible to White listeners—and especially players—as singing and strumming several choruses of "Aunt Rhody." While recording two excellent follow-ups for Elektra, both Koerner and Ray released equally fine solo albums. Tony Glover, for his part, put together one of the very first instructional books on how to play blues harmonica (*Blues Harp*) around this time, and its excellence and conciseness still make it the how-to book of choice for all aspiring harmonica players. Both Koerner and Ray still maintain an active performing schedule and every so often, the three of them get back together for a one-off concert. *—Cub Koda*

● **Lots More Blues Rags & Hollers** / 1964 / Elektra ♦♦♦♦♦
Return of Koerner, Ray & Glover / 1966 / Elektra ♦♦
Good Old Koerner, Ray & Glover / 1972 / Mill City ♦♦♦
Blues Rags and Hollers / 1995 / Audiophile ♦♦

Alexis Korner

b. Apr. 19, 1928, Paris, France, **d.** Jan. 1, 1984, London, England
Guitar, Vocals / British Blues
The cofounder of British blues (with Cyril Davies), guitarist Alexis Korner never achieved anything like the fame of the younger players who learned from him (among them Charlie Watts, who played in Blues Incorporated). Gifted though he was, Korner lacked the vocal skills or the commercial edge needed for mass success. After splitting up the last of his various incarnations of Blues Incorporated, he began popularizing the blues as the host of a children's TV show. He toured with The Rolling Stones in the mid-'70s, then formed his last (and best) band, Rocket 88, late in the decade, prior to his sudden death in the early '80s. *—Bruce Eder*

● **R&B from the Marquee** / 1962 / Ace Of Clubs ♦♦♦♦♦
Britain's first home-grown blues album to make the UK charts is a landmark with good playing, even if none of the flash associated with Korner alumni like The Rolling Stones or Yardbirds is present. (Import) *—Bruce Eder*

I Wonder Who / 1967 / BGO ♦♦
Recorded in a mere two sessions, this had the potential to be a decent, if hardly innovative, effort. At this point, Korner's group was in one its most stripped-down phases, featuring just Alexis on guitar, Danny Thompson on bass, and Terry Cox on drums. Very shortly after this disc, Thompson and Cox would form the rhythm section of Pentangle, so these cuts are somewhat akin to hearing the bare bones of Pentangle in a much more blues/jazz-based context. The musical backing is not the problem, nor is the material, divided between Korner originals and blues standards by the likes of Jimmy Smith, Percy Mayfield, Ma Rainey, and Jelly Roll Morton. The problem is that Korner elected to sing these himself in his gruff, scraggly croak. It's not like listening to Dylan or Buffy Sainte-Marie, who take some getting used to, but have considerable, idiosyncratic talent—Korner simply cannot, objectively speaking, sing. (His butchering of Herbie Hancock's "Watermelon Man" has to be heard to be believed.) And that makes this album downright difficult to bear, despite the fine, spare musical arrangements (the instrumental cover of Jimmy Smith's "Chicken Shack Back Home" is a major standout in this context). If Korner had the wisdom to employ even a minor-league British bluesman like, say, Duffy Power (who guested with him occasionally during this time) as his singer for these sessions, the results would have been immeasurably better. *— Richie Unterberger*

● **Bootleg Him!** / 1972 / Warner Brothers ♦♦♦♦♦
The best of all the Korner anthologies, boasting unreleased tapes and a lot of interesting one-off recordings from the various nooks and crannies of his career. *—Bruce Eder*

Rocket 88 / 1981 / Atlantic ♦♦♦♦♦
Arguably the best record ever for an offshoot of The Rolling Stones, with Korner on guitar, Ian Stewart on piano, Charlie

Watts on drums, and Jack Bruce on upright bass. This has tight, rippling, rollicking interpretations of blues and jazz standards and is a seminal part of any collection. —*Bruce Eder*

● **The Alexis Korner Collection** / 1988 / Castle ✦✦✦✦
A strong import anthology featuring Korner's various bands over the years. Probably the best extant collection. —*Bruce Eder*

The Smokin' Joe Kubek Band

Guitar, Vocals / Modern Electric Texas Blues
Another young Texas axeman from the old school, Smokin' Joe Kubek issued his band's debut disc in 1991 on Bullseye Blues, *Steppin' Out Texas Style*. Kubek was already playing his smokin' guitar on the Lone State chitlin circuit at age 14, supporting such musicians as Freddie King. Soon, he formed his own band and began playing a number of bars across Dallas. In the '80s, he met guitarist/vocalist B'nois King, a native of Monroe, LA, and the duo formed the first edition of the Smokin' Joe Kubek Band.

The Smokin' Joe Kubek Band began playing the rest of the southwest in the late '80s. In 1991, they signed to Bullseye Blues, releasing their debut *Steppin' Out Texas Style* the same year. Following its release, the band launched their first national tour. For the rest of the '90s, the Smokin' Joe Kubek Band toured the United States frequently. —*Bill Dahl & Stephen Thomas Erlewine*

● **Steppin' out Texas Style** / 1991 / Bullseye Blues ✦✦✦✦✦
Smokin' Joe Kubek's debut album is a delight. Kubek leads his band through a set of smoking hot Texas and Memphis blues, delivered with passion—they can play this music with precision, but they choose to be looser and more fun than most traditionalists. Kubek's a skillful guitarist and B'Nois King, his vocalist and rhythm guitarist, can play nearly as well and their duels are the high watermark of an already wonderful album. —*Thom Owens*

Chain Smokin' Texas Style / 1992 / Bullseye Blues ✦✦✦
Smokin' Joe Kubek is pure Texas blues—he's a forceful guitarist and his band rocks with a loose, greasy vibe. What makes the album so much fun is the combination of solid material and piledriving performances—it may follow a tradition, but it manages to be unpredictable. —*Thom Owens*

Texas Cadillac / 1993 / Bullseye Blues ✦✦✦✦✦
Smokin' Joe Kubek's third Rounder album juggles blues-rock originals with faithful, exuberant covers of Jimmy Reed, Willie Dixon, Muddy Waters, and Little Walter Jacobs, among others. Kubek is a good, sometimes captivating guitarist and entertaining singer, if not the greatest pure vocalist, and the band rips through the 11 cuts in a relaxed, yet passionate fashion. But it's hard for any longtime blues fan to get excited over hearing another version of "Little Red Rooster" or "Mean Old World"; it's impossible to reinvent Delta, urban, Texas or West Coast blues. The solution is probably to make the best music you can and hope you hook those willing to listen to contemporary blues rather than spurn it for the originals. —*Ron Wynn*

L

Sonny Landreth

b. Feb. 1, 1951, Canton, MS
Guitar, Vocals / Modern Electric Blues

Southwest Louisiana-based guitarist, songwriter and singer Sonny Landreth is a musician's musician. The blues slide guitar playing found on his two Zoo Entertainment releases, *Outward Bound* (1992) and *South of I-10* (1995), is distinctive and unlike anything else you've ever heard. His unorthodox guitar style comes from the manner in which he simultaneously plays slide and makes fingering movements on the fret board. Landreth, who has an easy going personality, can play it all, like any good recording-session musician. His distinctive guitar playing can be heard on recordings by John Hiatt, Leslie West, and Mountain, and other rock & rollers.

Landreth was born February 1, 1951, in Canton, MS, and his family lived in Jackson, MS, for a few years before settling in Lafayette, LA. Landreth, who still lives in southwest Louisiana, began playing guitar after a long tenure with the trumpet. His earliest inspiration came from Scotty Moore, the guitarist from Elvis Presley's band, but as time went on, he learned from the recordings of musicians and groups like Chet Atkins and the Ventures. As a teen, Landreth began playing out with his friends in their parents' houses.

"They would ping-pong us from one house to another, and though we were all awful at first, as time went on we got pretty good. It's an evolutionary process, just like songwriting is," Landreth explained in an interview on his 44th birthday in 1995. After his first professional gig with accordionist Clifton Chenier in the 1970s (where he was the only White guy in the Red Beans and Rice Revue for awhile), Landreth struck out on his own, but not before he recorded two albums for the Blues Unlimited label out of Crowley, LA, *Blues Attack* in 1981 and *Way Down in Louisiana* in 1985. If anyone is living proof of the need to press on in spite of obstacles, it is Landreth.

The second of those two albums got him noticed by some record executives in Nashville, which in turn led to his recording and touring work with John Hiatt. That led to still more work with John Mayall, who recorded Landreth's radio-ready "Congo Square." More recently, he's worked with New Orleans bandleader and pianist Allen Toussaint (who guests on several tracks on *South of I-10*, as does Dire Straits guitarist Mark Knopfler).

On both of Landreth's brilliant albums for Zoo, the lyrics draw the listener in to the sights, sounds, smells and heat of southwest Louisiana, and a strong sense of place is evident in many of Landreth's songs. Although his style is completely his own and his singing is more than adequate, Landreth admits that writers like William Faulkner have had a big influence on his lyric writing. The fact that it's taken so long for academics at American universities to recognize the great body of poetry that blues is concerns Landreth as well. Robert Johnson is Landreth's big hero when it comes to guitar playing. "When I finally discovered Robert Johnson, it all came together for me," Landreth said, noting that he also closely studied the recordings of Skip James, Mississippi John Hurt, and Charley Patton. *—Richard Skelly*

Outward Bound / 1992 / Zoo ♦♦

Sonny Landreth is the Louisiana-based slide-guitar master known for his work with John Hiatt and B.C.'s Sue Medley (both make back-up vocal appearances here). Like fellow ace Ry Cooder, Landreth's playing sizzles and slashes on his debut solo outing *Outward Bound* without idle wanking. There's lots of space where what isn't played is just as important as what is. "Back To Bayou Teche" echoes the performer's early days backing some of Louisiana's best known Cajun musicians; aboriginal rhythms grace "Sacred Ground;" commercial pop meets Southern boogie on "New Landlord;" Landreth borrows a lick or two from buddy Hiatt for "Common-Law Love." *—Roch Parisien*

Down In Louisiana / Mar. 23, 1993 / Epic ♦♦♦

This is the music from the Saturday-night dances in Louisiana. The hot and sweaty have a good time dancing, drinking, and looking at all the people. Do not look for the Royal Albert Hall production in this CD, as in his stunning *South of I-10*, with its myriad "guest artists." The feel for this music is shown by someone who grew up with it. Listen to the respect and feeling he gives to Clifton Chenier's "If I Ever Get Lucky." Try and keep your body and feet from bouncing to the beat of "Sugar Cane" or "Little Linda." Doesn't your eye just start to look around for a dance partner, even though you're in your living room? There is solid playing throughout even though the sound is at times a bit thin, and the big name "guest artists" are nowhere to be found on this CD. It is a solid effort that spans the musical boundaries of all of Louisiana. Cajun, zydeco, blues, and country are all blended together so they are no longer confining, but a homogenous mix. A solid effort. *—Bob Gottlieb*

● **South of I-10** / 1995 / Praxis/Zoo ♦♦♦♦♦

Screaming slide guitar plowing right into you and carrying you along on its feral journey into deeper recesses. This CD opens going for your guts and it never quits, though at times its touch is more caressing than careening, as in "Cajun Waltz." This CD got a lot of airplay yet never got tiring, the true test of good music. It stopped me in my tracks the first time I heard a cut come ripping out of speakers. I stopped at the first phone and called the station and demanded to know who it was. I remembered seeing him as a member of John Hiatt's band years ago and liking what I heard. A wide variety of slide guitar styles, backed by an extremely tight rhythm section and various other New Orleans musicians adds to the pleasure of the album. This music combines the best of zydeco, New Orleans R&B, Cajun, and rock & roll into one mood-elevating experience. Listen to "Mojo Boogie" next to "C'est Chaud," then go on to "Shootin' for the Moon," there is no letdown, but there is great variety. A must-buy. *—Bob Gottlieb*

Denise Lasalle

b. Jul. 16, 1939, MS
Vocals / Soul Blues

Unlike so many other blues vocalists who just re-interpret material given to them by songwriters, LaSalle is a seriously talented songwriter. Although her soul blues style has strong urban contemporary overtones at times, it's best to think of LaSalle as a modern-day Bessie Smith, because that's really what she is. She writes funny songs full of sassy attitude, and it's an attitude she carries with her on stage. Off stage, LaSalle accommodates all autograph seekers and gladly obliges journalists and radio disc jockeys.

The Jackson, TN-based LaSalle was raised in Belzoni, MS (also home to Joe Willie "PineTop" Perkins some years earlier), but she got started singing in local churches around Leflore County. She was born July 16, 1939 as Denise Craig. Growing up, she listened to the Grand Ole Opry radio broadcasts and then in Belzoni, lived across the street from a jukejoint. LaSalle's early influences, from the jukeboxes around Belzoni and over the radio, included Ruth Brown, Dinah Washington, and Laverne Baker. LaSalle moved north to Chicago when she was in her early 20s, and

157

would attend shows at the Regal Theatre, always returning home to write songs. She got to know blues musicians and began giving her songs to them, until one day a Chess Records executive stopped by at Mixer's Lounge, where LaSalle was working as a bar maid. He listened to one of her songs and took it down to Chess Records, and the company later signed her as a vocalist, but never recorded her. Two years later, LaSalle recorded and produced her own record with the help of Billy "The Kid" Anderson, the Chess executive who'd originally shown an interest in her. After the record made some waves on local radio, Chess stepped in and purchased the master and took it to Europe. Meanwhile, LaSalle continued writing songs and sitting in with blues musicians around the Chicago clubs.

LaSalle's first big hit came about in 1971 when her "Trapped by a Thing Called Love" broke on the radio in Chicago and then Detroit. That record was for the Westbound label, and then she signed with ABC Records in 1975, cutting three albums in three years, until the label was sold to MCA. After MCA dropped her because of the label's "difficulty in promoting Black acts" at that time, she continued performing as much as she could in Chicago and Memphis. In 1980, a Malaco executive called to ask her to write a song for Z.Z. Hill. She's been with Malaco ever since; "they pay their royalties on time" she said, and her Malaco sides are probably her most important recordings, other than the original of her early-'70s hit, "Trapped."

At Malaco, LaSalle hasn't slowed down a bit, and her specialty remains Southern soul-blues. Her records for the label include *Still Trapped*, *Lady in the Street*, *Right Place*, *Right Time*, *Love Talkin'*, *Hittin' Where It Hurts* and *Love Me Right*. —*Richard Skelly*

● **On the Loose** / 1973 / Westbound ✦✦✦✦✦
A prime example of her Memphis work, with Bowlegs Miller arrangements, this set features "Man Sized Job" and "Breaking up Somebody's Home." —*Bil Carpenter*

Hittin' Where It Hurts / 1986 / Malaco ✦✦✦
One of LaSalle's more recent Malaco outings, the company made a few tiny concessions in instrumentation and production in trying for the umpteenth time to break one of its acts beyond the South besides the late Z.Z. Hill. But LaSalle has been cutting downhome soul and country/blues material too many years to suddenly try to be uptown or city. She doesn't attempt that on this one either; her voice, manner, attitude, and style are defiantly Southern and soulful. —*Ron Wynn*

Lady in the Street / 1986 / Malaco ✦✦✦
The title track was among LaSalle's best Malaco tunes, a stomping, urgently sung, sassy bit that walked the line between confrontation, invitation, and remorse. The other tunes weren't quite as inspired, but were equally well performed. Few performers have ever staked out an area and remained loyal to it like LaSalle, who's been doing country/blues soul since the early '70s and seldom strayed from the path, despite numerous trends and changes on the black music scene. Some would call that suicidal; others would say it's commendable. —*Ron Wynn*

It's Lying Time Again / Malaco ✦✦
Denise LaSalle's Malaco albums have all been fine productions, usually featuring some sassy love songs, heartfelt bluesy ballads, and one or two numbers complete with spoken interludes in which the woman tells off the man. Unfortunately, none of them have matched her Westbound or ABC/MCA releases, mainly because soul no longer gets the same kind of widespread airplay outside the South. LaSalle has the kind of rough, tough yet vulnerable sound ideal for these songs, and her delivery has as much country and blues influence as soul and gospel. Her style and Malaco's productions may be dated, but they're the kind of vintage sound that anyone who grew up in the '50s and '60s will always revere. —*Ron Wynn*

Love Talkin' / Malaco ✦✦
As with all her Malaco albums, Denise LaSalle mixes things up nicely, going from hard-hitting, trash-talking tunes to heartfelt ballads, bluesy numbers, and country/soul wailers. She's had a string of regionally successful releases since joining Malaco in the '80s, but has never been able to break the embargo on Southern soul. She's been around too long to change at this point, and really shouldn't anyway. Her albums are reliable and enjoyable, even if they're a throwback. —*Ron Wynn*

Rain and Fire / Malaco ✦✦
Denise LaSalle has drawn some fire at times for her frank, no-

holds-barred dialogues and album cuts. She also has remained loyal to vintage soul and blues/country-tinged songs that will never get urban contemporary airplay and attention because they're thoroughly Southern in style, sound, and production values. Thus, each Malaco album is almost doomed from the beginning, other than as a regional proposition. That said, here's another one right in that same vein, and it's as fine as all the rest in what it does. —*Ron Wynn*

Right Place Right Time / Malaco ✦✦
The title cut came close to getting Denise LaSalle a little attention beyond the standard Southern boundaries. The rest of the album is her familiar litany of terse, crusty dialogues, country and blues-tinged wailers, and hard-hitting soul tunes. At times, LaSalle and others of her generation seem like illogical warriors, fighting to keep alive a sound that's long since faded as a viable commercial proposition. But as long as she keeps making records and putting her heart and soul into them, they deserve a listen by fans of the genre. —*Ron Wynn*

Sammy Lawhorn

b. Jul. 12, 1935, Little Rock, AR, **d.** Apr. 29, 1990, Chicago, IL
Guitar
Guitarist Sammy Lawhorn was born Samuel David Lawhorn. He was raised in the South by his grandparents after his mother and stepfather moved to Chicago. He first heard live guitar from blind guitar players on the street and soon was learning the instrument. Starting with a ukulele, graduating to an acoustic (Stella), and finally getting an electric (Supro), Lawhorn learned to play the guitar in about two years.

As a teenager he worked as a King Biscuit Boy for Sonny Boy Williamson II and learned slide guitar from Houston Stackhouse. After a stint in the service, Lawhorn returned to Arkansas and played and/or recorded with Willie C. Cobbs, the Five Royals, Eddie Boyd, and Roy Brown.

He moved to Chicago in the early '60s and became part of the house band at Theresa's, one of Chicago's main blues clubs. He worked on and off with Muddy Waters for about ten years and toured with that band. Lawhorn became best known as the resident guitarist at Theresa's club, where he played behind just about any great blues artist you could name. His influences were T-Bone Walker, Lightnin' Hopkins, Pee Wee Crayton, Lowell Fulson, and Muddy Waters. He was especially drawn to slide and Hawaiian-style guitar, and became well known for his use of the tremolo bar. He is considered one of finest examples of postwar style Chicago blues guitar. He can be heard on recordings of Muddy Waters, Big Mama Thornton, Otis Spann, Junior Wells, John Lee Hooker, Eddie Boyd and many others. Lawhorn died on April 29, 1990, in Chicago. —*Michael Erlewine*

Sam Lay

b. Mar. 20, 1935, Birmingham, AL
Drums, Vocals / *Chicago Blues*
Sam Lay began his career as a drummer in Cleveland in 1954, working with the Moon Dog Combo. In 1957 he joined the Original Thunderbirds and stayed with that group until 1959, when he left for Chicago to work with the legendary Little Walter. Lay began to work with Howlin' Wolf in 1960 and spent the next six years with that group. He and bassist Jerome Arnold were hired away from Wolf's band by Paul Butterfield in 1966 and became part of the Paul Butterfield Blues Band, recording that classic first album. Lay toured with Butterfield until he accidentally shot himself.

Sam Lay backed Bob Dylan at the historic 1965 Newport Folk Festival, when Dylan first introduced electric-rock to the folk crowd. He went on to record with Dylan on *Highway 61 Revisited*. He can be heard on more than 40 classic Chess blues recordings, and his famous double-shuffle is the envy of every would-be blues drummer. In 1969, Lay played drums for the Muddy Waters *Fathers and Sons* album, now a classic. He also was the original drummer for the James Cotton Blues Band.

Later in 1969, he also worked with the Siegel-Schwall Band. He went on to form the Sam Lay Blues Revival Band, which has involved many players over the years including Jimmy Rogers, George "Wild Child" Buttler, Eddie Taylor, and others.

Sam Lay was inducted into the Blues Hall of Fame in 1992 and received a nomination for a W.C. Handy award. He formed the Sam Lay Blues Band and has had recent recordings on

Appaloosa Records (*Shuffle Master, Sam Lay Live*) and on Alligator with the Siegel-Schwall Band, with whom he often plays. A 1996 release on Evidence is in the can. *—Michael Erlewine*

Sam Lay in Bluesland / 1968 / Blue Thumb ✦✦✦

● **Shuffle Master** / 1992 / Appaloosa ✦✦✦✦

Lazy Lester (Leslie Johnson)

b. Jun. 20, 1933, Torras, LA

Guitar, Harmonica, Percussion, Vocals, Washboard / Electric Louisiana Blues

His colorful sobriquet (supplied by prolific south Louisiana producer J.D. Miller) to the contrary, harpist Lazy Lester swears he never was all that lethargic. But he seldom was in much of a hurry either, although the relentless pace of his Excello Records swamp blues classics "I'm a Lover Not a Fighter" and "I Hear You Knockin'" might contradict that statement too.

While growing up outside of Baton Rouge, Leslie Johnson was influenced by Jimmy Reed and Little Walter. But his entree into playing professionally arrived quite by accident: while riding on a bus sometime in the mid-'50s, he met guitarist Lightnin' Slim, who was searching fruitlessly for an AWOL harpist. The two's styles meshed seamlessly, and Lester became Slim's harpist of choice.

In 1956, Lester stepped out front at Miller's Crowley, Louisiana studios for the first time. During an extended stint at Excello that stretched into 1965, he waxed such gems as "Sugar Coated Love," "If You Think I've Lost You," and "The Same Thing Could Happen to You." Lester proved invaluable as an imaginative sideman for Miller, utilizing everything from cardboard boxes and claves to whacking on newspapers in order to locate the correct percussive sound for the producer's output.

Lester gave up playing for almost two decades (and didn't particularly miss it, either), settling in Pontiac, MI, in 1975. But Fred Reif (Lester's manager, booking agent, and rubboard player) convinced the harpist that a return to action was in order, inaugurating a comeback that included a nice 1988 album for Alligator, *Harp & Soul*. His swamp blues sound remains as atmospheric (and dare we say it, energetic) as ever. *—Bill Dahl*

★ **True Blues** / Excello ✦✦✦✦✦

His original album collects the best of the early Excello sides. Includes "Sugar Coated Love," "I Hear You Knockin'," and "I'm a Lover, Not a Fighter." *—Cub Koda*

Harp & Soul / 1988 / Alligator ✦✦✦✦

After a lengthy hiatus from the music business, Lester was in the midst of his comeback when he waxed this album for Alligator. The overall sound is redolent of those Louisiana swamp blues classics, but with a cannily updated contemporary edge that works well. *—Bill Dahl*

Rides Again / 1988 / Sunjay ✦✦✦✦✦

His original rediscovery album pairs him with English blues musicians, with surprisingly great results. (Import) *—Cub Koda*

Lazy Lester / 1989 / Flyright ✦✦✦✦

Alternate takes and unissued titles from the cache of producer J.D. Miller, whose tiny Crowley, LA studio was the prime site for recording swamp blues during the '50s and '60s. A fine companion to AVI's essential Lester compilation. *—Bill Dahl*

★ **I Hear You Knockin'!!!** / 1995 / Excello/AVI ✦✦✦✦✦

Southern Louisiana swamp blues doesn't get more infectious or atmospheric than in the hands of Lazy Lester, whose late-'50s/early-'60s catalog for Excello Records (produced by the legendary J.D. Miller) is splendidly summarized with the 30 sides here. Lester's insistent harp and laconic vocals shine brightly on the rollicking "I'm a Lover, Not a Fighter," "Sugar Coated Love," "I Hear You Knockin'," and "If You Think I've Lost You," serving to help define the genre's timeless appeal. *—Bill Dahl*

Leadbelly (Huddie William Ledbetter)

b. Jan. 20, 1888, Mooringsport, LA, d. Dec. 6, 1949, New York, NY

Guitar, Piano, Accordion, Vocals / Acoustic Country Blues

Leadbelly was the first blues musician to achieve fame among White audiences. For this reason alone, and more for the sheer novelty of his career as an ex-convict-turned-singer than for any recognition of his abilities, he was the first bluesman to be treated as a major media figure in the mainstream press.

Leadbelly's life story could—and has—filled at least one book. Huddie Ledbetter was born on January 20, 1888, not far from

the Texas border. He remained in school until he was 12 or 13 and could read and write, and was a precocious child, serious and ambitious beyond his years.

Ledbetter's music making may have begun as early as age two or three, when he made his own primitive fife from twigs that he found. He was surrounded by a multitude of influences growing out of the post-slavery/post-Reconstruction era of the late 19th century, including blues, spirituals, and minstrel songs.

By the time he was 14, he was known for his ability with the guitar and his way with a song. He played before audiences on most Saturday nights, at parties and square dances in the area around Mooringsport, LA, but before he was far into his teens, he was attracted to the red-light district in Shreveport. Apart from the women, however, the district's main attraction to the teenager was its music.

He was married by the first decade of the 20th century, but the relationship and the marriage didn't last. The music, however, did, with an important new wrinkle—Ledbetter switched from the six-string to the 12-string guitar, a pivotal decision in the development of his own career.

He was already performing songs of his own and adapting others during the 1890s, and his abilities in this area grew with his experience. He first picked up a song known as "Irene" sometime in the first decade of the 20th century and "Goodnight, Irene," as it is better known, became one of Leadbelly's best-known songs.

Sometime around 1915 he made the acquaintance of Blind Lemon Jefferson, from whom he learned slide guitar. Despite some months of working together, Ledbetter was left behind by Jefferson, a result of his inability to stay clear of the law. Finally, in 1917, he was arrested for shooting a man and sentenced by the state of Texas to 30 years in prison.

On the Shaw State Prison Farm, Leadbelly's talents served him just as well as they had outside. His singing and guitar playing made him one of the more popular prisoners. He was ultimately released in 1925 after he played for the visiting Texas governor, Pat Neff, requesting a pardon. The pardon was signed by Neff on virtually his last day in office, and immortalized the man in the annals of the blues.

Leadbelly, as he was now known professionally, tried working regular jobs for the remainder of the 1920s, but was never able to stay far from the rambling life that had led him into trouble back in the previous decade. In 1930, he was arrested and convicted in Louisiana of assault with intent to commit murder, and sentenced to 30 years in the Louisiana State Penitentiary at Angola, a prison farm with a reputation as bad as, or worse, than the Texas prison from which he'd been released.

And it was there, in 1933, that he first met John Lomax, an ambitious researcher for the Library of Congress, who was traveling through the South with his son Alan, collecting blues and any other authentic American music that they could find. Leadbelly's reputation within the prison was well-known, and it was inevitable that he would meet the Lomaxes.

They found in Leadbelly a talent and a resource beyond anything they could have hoped for—the man was not only a gifted player who exuded a musical charisma that transcended the prison setting, but he was a veritable human jukebox, in the range of songs that he knew. Leadbelly dazzled the Lomaxes with his singing, playing, and songwriting, and Lomax recognized in his new discovery a talent that was very different from the makers of the commercial "race" records of the period. Leadbelly's style and repertory were unaffected by the currents running through commercial blues and country music, but a talent that was worth trying to develop commercially, into a valid and successful brand of Black American folk music.

Leadbelly was released in 1934 with help from John Lomax, and began an extended relationship with him and his son, serving as driver and valet while making recordings and preparing plans for concerts. It was Lomax's intention to make Leadbelly and—as his manager and "discoverer"—himself into stars.

On the positive side, this resulted in Lomax trying to get Leadbelly to record virtually every song he knew, an impossible task given the sheer range of music to which he'd been exposed since the 1890s, but one that resulted in dozens upon dozens of sides for the Library of Congress, cut on Lomax's relatively crude "portable" recording unit (which weighed about 300 pounds), and later many attempts at commercial recording as well.

On the negative side, however, it resulted in a terrible

exploitation of Leadbelly, who appeared in photos and on stage in striped prison uniforms, and whose violent past was emphasized along with his musical abilities. The result was a flurry of publicity that brought Leadbelly some exposure in the White community, but also made him give one the impression of a captured savage.

It would have been demeaning for any man, but was especially so for Leadbelly, and ultimately not terribly profitable for Lomax. The copyrights that he signed his name to as Leadbelly's songwriting "collaborator" ultimately proved to be worth a small fortune, but at the time, he quickly discovered that sensationalistic press didn't necessarily translate into large paying audiences. Moreover, Leadbelly quickly grew beyond Lomax's ability to control him, and later rebelled at their continued relationship. And Lomax found out as early as 1935, following Leadbelly's first commercial recording sessions for the American Record Company that Leadbelly's brand of blues was of virtually no interest to Black audiences, who had already moved to more modern sounds.

Ironically, the ARC sides contain some of Leadbelly's best music; brought into a real recording studio for the first time, he took to the new environment like a natural, his voice booming larger than life and his guitar captured more crisply than ever before.

Leadbelly moved to New York City, and subsequently split with Lomax, although they remained close. It was in New York that Leadbelly came to find some success, reaching a small, but dedicated, following of White listeners, mostly consisting of folk song enthusiasts and members of the city's uniquely Bohemian intelligentsia. Leadbelly did some sessions for Musicraft, and also for the Bluebird label, but his major activities during the early '40s were with Moe Asch, the founder of Folkways Records.

Leadbelly's music at any phase of his career was startling, but his sound also evolved, a process made all the more vivid by the many different versions of his songs that he recorded across his career. By the early '40s, he even began to develop a consciousness that prefigured the topical songwriters of the early '60s. This was all pretty strong stuff to do in the middle of World War II. And, yet, Leadbelly also did whole programs and concerts devoted to songs intended specifically to entertain children—he had a natural affinity for children and visa versa—and those recordings were among the most successful of the huge body of his work that Moe Asch recorded.

Leadbelly never gave up the hope that he might become a star in the music world, and recognized enough that was special in his life story that he even tried to interest Hollywood in signing him up. That didn't work, although a visit to California did result in a short-lived contract with Capitol Records in 1944, yielding a dozen sides.

Soon after this period, however, he began developing the health problems that would ultimately kill him. Leadbelly continued working into 1949, but it was too early for the folk revival boom that would have embraced him. He played his last concert at the University of Texas on June 15th of that year. The recording of that concert is very poignant—as he leaves the stage, he promises to come back, vowing—to get well now that he has a new doctor.

Instead, he was hospitalized a month later, and died in New York on December 6, 1949. Two years later, his one-time protégés the Weavers had a million-selling hit with their recording of "Goodnight Irene," starting the whole folk-song revival—and six years later, England's Lonnie Donegan had a hit with a version of "Rock Island Line," a song that Leadbelly adapted and brought to modern audiences.

Leadbelly's place in blues history is a peculiar one; unassailable as a source for much of the country-blues repertory as it has been passed down to us, and a major contributor to the folk music revival upon the 1950s, but virtually non-existent in terms of his effect upon the commercial blues market in his own lifetime or since. —*Bruce Eder*

Includes Legendary Performances Never Before Released / Mar. 21, 1952 / Columbia ✦✦✦✦✦
While one should always be suspicious about how "legendary" material can be that was originally withheld from circulation, there's little that Leadbelly did that isn't worth hearing. That holds true here. —*Ron Wynn*

☆ **Library of Congress Recordings [2 LPs]** / 1966 / Elektra ✦✦✦✦✦
These powerful performances date from 1939–43 when

Ledbetter had moved to New York City after his years in prison. He was a fluid performer and his command of his trademark 12-string guitar is evident. Recorded by John and Alan Lomax, these sessions include "BollWeevil," "The Titanic," "Tight like That," and "Henry Ford Blues." —*Richard Meyer*

Good Mornin' Blues (1936–1940) / 1969 / Biograph ✦✦✦✦✦
Wonderful mid-'30s and early-'40s material from Leadbelly, including some of his finest and most colorful blues tunes and good folk numbers as well. —*Ron Wynn*

Leadbelly Sings Folk Songs / 1990 / Smithsonian/Folkways ✦✦✦✦✦
Leadbelly was a consummate song stylist; not necessarily a blues artist, although he certainly could deliver the blues with earnestness and authority. His forte was taking all types of songs, whether they were simple, filled with chilling metaphors, funny stories, or tragic events, and making them unforgettable personal anthems. That's what he does on all 15 cuts on *Leadbelly Sings Folk Songs*, teaming with such fellow greats as Woody Guthrie, Cisco Houston, and Sonny Terry. Leadbelly made many great albums with Folkways; this was certainly among them. —*Ron Wynn*

Alabama Bound / 1990 / RCA ✦✦✦✦✦
Sixteen of the sides that Leadbelly cut for Victor's Bluebird label in the summer of 1940, many backed by the Golden Gate Singers. The mix of blues with a gospel chorus doesn't always work, although "Pick a Bale of Cotton," "Rock Island Line," and "Midnight Special" are appealing, and there are Leadbelly solo covers of "Roberta," "Easy Rider," "New York City," and so on. —*Bruce Eder*

☆ **Gwine Dig a Hole To Put the Devil In** / 1991 / Rounder ✦✦✦✦✦
An excellent sampling of material from Leadbelly's early Library of Congress sessions, including versions of some of the first songs he ever learned, "Green Corn" and "Po' Howard," his song to Governor Neff that helped secure his release from a Texas prison in 1925, his first recorded version of "If It Wasn't for Dickie" (later transformed into "Kisses Sweeter than Wine")—the master of which is, alas, somewhat damaged—and "C. C. Rider." —*Bruce Eder*

Let It Shine on Me / 1991 / Rounder ✦✦✦✦
The third volume of Leadbelly's incredible Library of Congress sessions includes several searing spiritual numbers, among them "Down In The Valley To Pray," "Must I Be Carried To The Sky," "Run Sinners," and "You Must Have That Religion, Halloo." The CD begins with an informative interview/performance segment that features Leadbelly answering questions about his life and stylistic influences, then demonstrating techniques and recounting the origins of particular songs. The disc also contains an interesting rendition of "When I Was A Cowboy" and the topical tunes "Mr. Hitler," "The Scottsboro Boys," and "The Roosevelt Song." Leadbelly's mournful, moving and authoritative vocals, plus his sometimes surging, sometimes reflective guitar playing, were never more moving or appealing than during the Library of Congress sessions. —*Ron Wynn*

☆ **Midnight Special** / 1991 / Rounder ✦✦✦✦
The earliest of Leadbelly's surviving Library of Congress recordings, from 1934, in surprisingly good sound. This is where it all started, and the power and sheer kinetic energy of these songs remains undiminished more than 60 years later. Includes "Irene," "Midnight Special," and "Matchbox Blues." —*Bruce Eder*

Leadbelly ("Irene Goodnight") / 1992 / Blues Encore ✦✦✦✦✦
The best anthology on Leadbelly to date—unfortunately, it's also a bootleg from Italy, where this material is considered fair game. Includes an excellent overview of Leadbelly's work from the 1930s to his final concert in 1949 ("Goodnight Irene"), with recordings from the Victor and ARC sessions as well. Excellent transfer, sketchy notes, decent sessionography. —*Bruce Eder*

Complete Studio Recordings, Vols. 4–5 / 1994 / Document ✦✦✦✦
These two European bootlegs cover a lot of material available elsewhere on legitimate American releases, but between them, they also contain the complete Leadbelly Capitol recording sessions of 1944, which have never surfaced on CD. The quality is superb, and the material is unique as the last commercial sides that Leadbelly ever cut. —*Bruce Eder*

Kisses Sweeter Than Wine / 1994 / Omega ✦✦✦✦✦
NOTE: This is actually a Weavers double CD, and if you buy it for the Leadbelly material, make sure that it has the third bonus disc with his stuff on it inside. A dozen songs cut by Leadbelly for Musicraft in 1947—not mentioned in any discography—and forgotten for the next 46 years, all found on tapes in the label owner's garage when he moved to Florida. The singing is good, the material is unique, and it includes his last recording of "If It Wasn't for Dickie," the Irish folk song that Leadbelly taught the Weavers that they turned into "Kisses Sweeter than Wine." —*Bruce Eder*

Nobody Knows the Trouble I've Seen, Vol. 5 / Mar. 30, 1994 / Rounder ✦✦✦✦✦
This is another excellent installment in Rounder's reissue of Leadbelly's Library of Congress recordings. —*AMG*

Pickup on This / Mar. 30, 1994 / Rounder ✦✦✦✦✦
Like the other volumes that came before it, *Pickup on This* is full of wonderful music and interviews from Leadbelly's Library of Congress recordings. —*AMG*

The Titanic, Vol. 4 / Mar. 30, 1994 / Rounder ✦✦✦✦
Later Leadbelly Library of Congress recordings, from 1939-43, including several children's songs and quasi-biographical and topical material, including "Mister Tom Hughes' Town." —*Bruce Eder*

Leadbelly's Last Sessions / 1995 / Smithsonian/Folkways ✦✦✦
Four CDs containing the best part of Leadbelly's only recordings on magnetic recording tape, which allowed him to stretch his songs to their usual length for the first time on record. The clarity of the recording, the presence of the between-song comments, and the selection of material makes this a seminal part of any serious collection. —*Bruce Eder*

Goodnight Irene / 1996 / Tradition ✦✦✦✦✦
The date of these recordings is unclear, and the sleeve is not of much help. The liner notes identify them as being taped in 1943 and 1944, while the back cover confidently refers to a 1939 date [though it seems much more likely that they were made in the 1940s]. At any rate, these are very good performances, with Leadbelly in fine voice. Most are performed solo on his 12-string guitar, although Sonny Terry and Josh White make cameos on one track each. "Goodnight Irene," "New Orleans" (essentially the same song as "House of the Rising Sun"), "John Hardy," and "When I Was a Cowboy" are all among the most famous tunes that he helped to popularize. But at a mere 28 minutes, this is pretty short on running time. —*Richie Unterberger*

Leadbelly In Concert / 1996 / Magnum ✦✦✦✦✦
Leadbelly's final concert from June 15, 1949, reissued on CD at last. The sound is very clean, the fidelity excellent, and the recording indispensible. —*Bruce Eder*

Where Did You Sleep Last Night / Feb. 20, 1996 / Smithsonian/Folkways ✦✦✦
The first of Folkways Records founder Moses Asch's original Leadbelly releases, from the best existing sources and remastered using the best mid-'90s technology, with some notable outtakes. The results are startlingly good, with an overall crisp sound, surprising delicacy in both the audio texture and Leadbelly's playing and singing, which is usually lost on the inferior reissues that have appeared on some of this work in the past. —*Bruce Eder*

★ **King of the 12-String Guitar** / Columbia/Legacy ✦✦✦✦✦
One of the greatest collections of Leadbelly's 1930's work, and his best commercial sides, done for ARC in 1935. It isn't quite complete, however, and one should also own the earlier Columbia Records CD, *Leadbelly*, as a companion. —*Bruce Eder*

Convict Blues / Aldabra ✦✦✦✦✦
Convict Blues collects a number of recordings he made for the American Record Corporation in 1935, which were, for the most part, never released. These 16 tracks are straight blues songs, delivered with passion. While it's not as essential as his Folkways or Library of Congress recordings, there's a wealth of terrific music here. —*Thom Owens*

Congress Blues / Aldabra ✦✦✦✦✦
Congress Blues collects a batch of folk songs that Leadbelly recorded in the early '40s. There is wonderful music here, to be sure, but it is available on better collections from Folkways and Rounder. —*Thom Owens*

Frankie Lee

b. Apr. 29, 1941, Mart, TX
Vocals / Soul Blues
Vocalist Frankie Lee has always been an engaging and energetic live performer, though his recorded output is still very small, given the number of years he's been around and how legendary his live shows have become. If Denise LaSalle is a modern day Bessie Smith, than Lee is a 1990s Otis Redding. One of Lee's live-show trademarks (like the late Albert Collins' guitar walks) is the point in the show in which he leaves his mic on stage and walks out into his audience, be it a festival of 10,000 people or a small club of 50. Lee's motto is, "whether it's one or 1,000, me and my band are gonna put on a show."

Lee was born April 29, 1941, in rural Mart, TX. His early influences included Sam Cooke, but before that, he sang in church groups. He recalled in several interviews that his grandmother made him sing, never realizing he'd end up singing blues, not gospel. He began recording in 1963 with Don Robey's Duke/Peacock label out of Houston. He recorded three singles that attracted regional attention: "Full Time Lover," "Taxi Blues," and "Hello, Mr. Blues." While he and Sonny Rhodes were living in Austin, Lee was heard by Ike Turner. That night, Turner invited him to join the Ike & Tina Turner road show. He was off with them the next day, gaining invaluable performing experience.

After returning from the road trips with their revue, Lee settled in Houston and had the chance to work with the people he admired, including Big Mama Thornton, Bobby "Blue" Bland, Clarence "Gatemouth" Brown, Ted Taylor, Junior Parker, O.V. Wright, James "Thunderbird" Davis, and Joe Hinton. Don Robey heard Lee in a Houston nightclub and offered him the chance to record. Later, Lee began working with guitarist Albert Collins, and the two became good friends, finally leaving Texas together in 1965 for California. Lee sang with Collins' band for the next six years. By 1971, Lee was in Los Angeles, working with his cousin Johnny "Guitar" Watson. (Watson passed away at age 61 on May 17, 1996.) He recorded for Elka Records, with Watson producing. In 1973, Lee moved north to the San Francisco Bay Area, and in the late '70s, he recruited a young guitarist, Robert Cray, to play in his back-up band. Finally Lee landed a contract with Hightone Records, a then developing label, and recorded his debut album, *The Ladies and the Babies* in 1984.

After successful performances with Sonny Rhodes at the Chicago Blues Festival, Lee moved to New Jersey in 1986, where he quickly established a following at clubs and festivals throughout the northeast. Lee was signed to record for the Flying Fish label in 1992, and *Sooner or Later*, with Doug Newby and the Virginia-based Bluzblasters, was the result. Lee's latest release, *Going Back Home*, is on the San Francisco-based Blind Pig label. The album was actually recorded back in the mid-'80s, but wasn't released until 1994.

Oddly enough, as of the mid-'90s, Lee's live clubs shows were as energetic as ever, and he's lost none of his enthusiasm for performing, despite the fact that he's now in his mid-50s. He's got a whole lot of talent and energy left, so there will be more recordings from this exciting vocalist and showman in the future. Records worth owning include *The Ladies and the Babies* and *Going Back Home*. Any of his singles for the Peacock or Elka labels, such as "Full Time Lover"/"Don't Make Me Cry," are collector's items, and should be snatched up without hesitation. —*Richard Skelly*

● **Ladies & the Babies** / Apr. 1986 / Hightone ✦✦✦✦✦
On these soul-styled contemporary blues, Lee's vocals exhibit a strong gospel influence. —*Bill Dahl*

Going Back Home / 1994 / Blind Pig ✦✦✦

Left Hand Frank (Frank Craig)

Guitar, Vocals / Modern Electric Chicago Blues
Southpaw guitarist Frank Craig (like many of his peers, he played an axe strung for a right-hander, strapping it on upside down) never really transcended his reputation as a trusty sideman instead of a leader—and that was just fine with him. But he stepped into the spotlight long enough to sing four fine tunes for Alligator's *Living Chicago Blues* anthologies in 1978.

Craig was already conversant with the guitar when he moved to Chicago at age 14. Too young to play inside the Club Zanzibar (where Muddy Waters, Little Walter, and Wolf held forth), Frank and his teenaged pals, guitarist Eddie King and bassist Willie Black, played outside the joint for tips instead. Legit gigs with harpist Willie Cobbs, guitarist James Scott, Jr., Jimmy Dawkins, Junior Wells, Good Rockin' Charles, Jimmy Rogers, and Hound Dog Taylor kept Frank increasingly active on the Chicago circuit from the mid-'50s to the late '70s. He moved to Los Angeles not too long after the Alligator session, eventually hanging up his guitar altogether due to health problems. —*Bill Dahl*

Live at the Knickerbocker Cafe / New Rose ✦✦✦

Legendary Blues Band

Group / Electric Chicago Blues

The Legendary Blues Band includes Calvin Jones (b. 1926, Greenwood, MS; bass, violin); Willie Smith (b. 1935, Helena, AR; drum); and various others on vocals, guitar, harmonica, piano. When the Muddy Waters band quit the master en masse in 1980, most of the sidemen stuck together and formed their own group. The Legendary Blues Band, as they were named, included Pinetop Perkins, Jerry Portnoy, Willie Smith, and Calvin Jones throughout its early years. Short-term member Louis Myers, another Muddy Waters alumnus, appeared as guitarist on the band's first album (Rounder, 1981). The band has since changed personnel with some regularity, and while its lineup has become progressively less "legendary" in name or historic associations, its music has remained solid and true to the mainstream Chicago style. In a later configuration, they even made the *Billboard* Black Music charts. Recent albums have featured guitarist Billy Flynn and harmonicist Madison Slim. The rhythm section of Jones and Smith has anchored the unit throughout the changes, never failing to deliver the Chicago blues with aplomb. —*Jim O'Neal*

Life of Ease / 1981 / Rounder ✦✦✦

● **Red Hot 'n Blue** / 1983 / Rounder ✦✦✦✦✦
Very solid vocals by Pinetop Perkins and Calvin Jones. Above-average LBB set. —*Bill Dahl*

Woke up with the Blues / 1989 / Ichiban ✦✦✦

Keepin' the Blues Alive / 1990 / Ichiban ✦✦✦✦✦
Only bassist Calvin Jones and drummer Willie Smith remain from Muddy Waters' old crew, but guitarist John Duich helps keep the traditional Chicago sound in place. —*Bill Dahl*

U B Da Judge / 1991 / Ichiban ✦✦
U B Da Judge is only an OK effort. —*Bill Dahl*

Money Talks / 1993 / Wild Dog ✦✦✦
All of a sudden, on their 1993's *Money Talks*, drummer Willie Smith has become a very credible singer. —*Bill Dahl*

Keri Leigh & the Blue Devils

Bass, Guitar, Harmonica, Drums / Modern Electric Blues

Vocalist, songwriter, record-producer, journalist, and author Keri Leigh is one of these multi-talented, accomplished individuals that the blues music world can't seem to get enough of. And the fact that she's barely 30 years old insures that she'll be around, pursuing her number one passion—singing the blues—for a long time.

Her latest album, *Arrival*, (1995), for the Jackson, MS-based Malaco Records label, isn't with her usual backing band, the Blue Devils, but it was recorded at Muscle Shoals Studios (which Malaco owns), and Leigh and her husband acted as co-producers of the record.

Leigh moved to Austin from her native Oklahoma with her guitarist/husband Mark Lyon, in 1990. Fortunately, they were welcomed for the most part with open arms by the Austin blues community, and certainly by Clifford Antone, owner of Antone's (blues nightclub), who booked them into his place every week for about a year. Within a year of so of her moving to Austin, she began work on her first book, *Stevie Ray: Soul to Soul*, (Taylor Books, Dallas), a passionate account of the ups and downs of the late guitarist's all-too-short life. Leigh first met Vaughan when she interviewed him in 1986, and after several interviews, they became friends. In May 1990, they began work on what was to be his autobiography, but in August of that year, Vaughan was killed in a helicopter accident in Wisconsin.

Leigh's recordings all have a Joplin-esque quality to them, and one way to describe her singing style is as a Janis Joplin for the 1990s; in fact, some critics have described her as the greatest voice to come out of Texas since Joplin.

Leigh has used her background as a radio and newspaper journalist to get publicity for the Blue Devils, and a glance at her overflowing press-clips folder shows what a hustler she is. But Leigh and her band work as hard as any of the other touring

blues musicians around the U.S., and they spend upwards of 150 nights a year on the road. Leigh's husband Lyon is one of the most naturally gifted slide guitarists you'll ever hear, and the ease with which he handles the instrument makes it look deceptively simple. In fact, good blues guitar is very difficult to play, but Lyon has all the moves down pat.

Leigh and her Blue Devils have two releases out on Amazing Records (a now-defunct label), *No Beginner* (1993) and *Blue Devil Blues*, their debut (1991), in addition to their latest Malaco album. *Arrival*, consisting of one-half originals and one-half cover tunes, is certainly the most accessible of her recordings. Leigh and her group have many more good years ahead of them; wherever they go, their affable ways earn them new friends and fans in the blues world. They also have a knack for making new blues converts out of rock & rollers. —*Richard Skelly*

Blue Devil Blues / 1991 / Amazing ✦✦✦
Keri Leigh's debut album isn't much more than standard Texas blues, but her passion for the music shines through every song, and that is what makes it a worthwhile listen. Leigh and guitarist Mark Lyon lead the band through eight covers and three fairly average originals, but they deliver the material with conviction, especially when they attack nuggets like Son House's "Preachin' Blues." Leigh's forceful, raspy voice sounds terrific and Lyon is a good guitarist, but the album is hampered by its predictability. —*Thom Owens*

● **No Beginner** / Jun. 8, 1993 / Amazing ✦✦✦✦
Keri Leigh's second album, *No Beginner*, is a more distinguished effort than her debut. Leigh and her guitarist/husband Lyon stake out a territory between Texas blues and blues-rock, much like their predecessors Stevie Ray Vaughan, Janis Joplin, and ZZ Top. Leigh's music doesn't have as many rock & roll overtones as her debut, but she and her band, the Blue Devils, play with a fiery rock energy and that energy comes across more clearly here than on their debut. —*Thom Owens*

J.B. Lenoir

b. May 5, 1929, Monticello, MS, d. Apr. 29, 1967, Urbana, IL
Guitar, Vocals / Electric Chicago Blues

Newcomers to his considerable legacy could be forgiven for questioning J.B. Lenoir's gender upon first hearing his rocking waxings. Lenoir's exceptionally high-pitched vocal range is a fooler, but it only adds to the singular appeal of his music. His politically charged "Eisenhower Blues" allegedly caused all sorts of nasty repercussions upon its 1954 emergence on Al Benson's Parrot logo (it was quickly pulled off the shelves and replaced with Lenoir's less controversially titled "Tax Paying Blues").

J.B. (that was his entire legal handle) fell under the spell of Blind Lemon Jefferson as a wee lad, thanks to his guitar-wielding dad. Lightnin' Hopkins and Arthur Crudup were also cited as early influences. Lenoir spent time in New Orleans before arriving in Chicago in the late '40s. Boogie grooves were integral to Lenoir's infectious routine from the get-go, although his first single for Chess in 1951, "Korea Blues," was another slice of topical commentary. From late 1951 to 1953, he waxed several dates for Joe Brown's JOB logo in the company of pianist Sunnyland Slim, drummer Alfred Wallace, and on the romping "The Mojo," saxist J.T. Brown.

Lenoir waxed his most enduring piece, the infectious (and often-covered) "Mama Talk to Your Daughter," in 1954 for Al Benson's Parrot label. Lenoir's 1954-55 Parrot output and 1955-58 Checker catalog contained a raft of terrific performances, including a humorously defiant "Don't Touch My Head" (detailing his brand-new process hairdo) and "Natural Man." Lenoir's sound was unique: saxes (usually Alex Atkins and Ernest Cotton) wailed in unison behind Lenoir's boogie-driven rhythm guitar as drummer Al Galvin pounded out a rudimentary backbeat everywhere but where it customarily lays. Somehow, it all fit together.

Scattered singles for Shad in 1958 and Vee-Jay two years later kept Lenoir's name in the public eye. His music was growing substantially by the time he hooked up with USA Records in 1963 (witness the 45's billing: J.B. Lenoir & his African Hunch Rhythm). Even more unusual were the two acoustic albums he cut for German blues promoter Horst Lippmann in 1965 and 1966. *Alabama Blues* and *Down in Mississippi* were done in Chicago under Willie Dixon's supervision, Lenoir now free to elaborate on whatever troubled his mind ("Alabama March," "Vietnam Blues," "Shot on James Meredith").

Little did Lenoir know his time was quickly running out. By the time of his 1967 death, the guitarist had moved to downstate Champaign—and that's where he died, probably as a delayed result of an auto accident he was involved in three weeks prior to his actual death. —*Bill Dahl*

Natural Man / 1968 / MCA/Chess ◆◆◆◆◆
This collection of J.B.'s mid-'50s tenure at the label—originally issued in the '70s—duplicates two songs from the Parrot collection (a label which Chess later acquired), but the rest of it is more than worth the effort to seek out. The rocking "Don't Touch My Head," the topical "Eisenhower Blues" and the sexually ambiguous, chaotic and cool title track are but a few of the magical highlights aboard. Either this or the Parrot sides will do in a pinch, but I can't imagine being without either one. —*Cub Koda*

★ **The Parrot Sessions, 1954–55: Vintage Chicago Blues** / 1989 / Relic ◆◆◆◆◆
Lenoir's sound really got locked in during this period, using twin saxes, himself on boogie rhythm guitar (with an occasional minimal solo), revolving piano and bass stools and Al Gavin-certainly the strangest of all Chicago drummers—constantly turning the beat around. This is J.B. at his creative and performing best, including his best known songs "Mama Talk To Your Daughter" (with the famous "one note for 12 bars" guitar solo), "Eisenhower Blues" and "Give Me One More Shot," where Gavin starts out the tune on the wrong beat, gets on the right beat by mistake, then 'corrects' himself! Lyrics as metaphorically powerful as any in the blues against grooves alternating between low-down slow ones and Lenoir's patented boogie. —*Cub Koda*

His J.O.B. Recordings 1951–54 / 1991 / Paula/Flyright ◆◆◆◆◆
These are Lenoir's earliest sides in a very stripped down setting compared to the Parrot and Chess sides. Over half of the 14 sides feature Lenoir on guitar with only Sunnyland Slim on piano and Alfred Wallace on drums in support, with J.T. Brown on tenor sax aboard for the next session. They all suffer from a curiously muffled sound, but early delights like "The Mojo (Boogie)" and "Let's Roll" make all audio points mute. This CD also includes seven tracks fronted by Sunnyland Slim recorded the same day with Lenoir in a supporting role. —*Cub Koda*

Vietnam Blues: The Complete L&R Recordings / 1995 / Evidence ◆◆◆◆◆
Recorded in September 1966, shortly before his death the following spring, this session was Lenoir's most effective fusion of acoustic blues, African percussion, and contemporary, topical songwriting."Round And Round," "Voodoo Music," and "Feelin' Good" bring the African influence to the fore, while J.B. addresses tough issues like Vietnam and discrimination more directly than any other bluesman of the time on cuts like "Down In Mississippi," "Shot On Meredith," and "Vietnam Blues." Supervised by Willie Dixon, this recording also featured top Chicago blues drummer Fred Below. —*Richie Unterberger*

Ron Levy's Wild Kingdom

b. May 29, 1951, Cambridge, MA
Piano, Organ / Modern Electric Blues
Ron Levy (b. Reuvin Zev ben Yehoshua Ha Levi) was born on May 29, 1951, in Cambridge, MA. Although Levy grew up playing clarinet, he switched to piano at age 13 after attending a Ray Charles concert. Then, influenced by Jimmy Smith, Booker T., and Billy Preston, he picked up on the Hammond organ. Within a few years he was working in the Boston area backing up blues acts. Albert King discovered and hired him in 1971 while still in high school. They worked together for 18 months. He then went on to B.B. King's band and worked with King for almost seven years. From 1976 until 1980, Levy worked with the Rhythm Rockers and it was here that he met guitarist Ronnie Earl. Levy joined the Roomful of Blues from 1983 to 1987. Levy's own band, Ron Levy's Wild Kingdom, has recorded a number of fine albums for Black Top, Rounder, and Bullseye. —*Michael Erlewine*

Ron Levy's Wild Kingdom / May 1987 / Black Top ◆◆◆
Ten tunes with an all-star cast including Ronnie Earl (guitar), Kim Wilson (harmonica), Greg Piccolo (sax), Wayne Bennett (guitar), and other excellent players. Plenty of fine guitar, keyboards, harmonica, and up-tempo blues music. —*Michael Erlewine*

Safari to New Orleans / 1988 / Black Top ◆◆◆
Ron Levy's piano playing shines throughout *Safari to New*

Orleans, but he fails to come up with enough strong songs to make the album memorable. —*Thom Owens*

★ **B-3 Blues & Grooves** / Apr. 1, 1993 / Bullseye Blues ◆◆◆◆
Ron Levy is one of the finest young masters of the Hammond B-3. Here are 11 soul-satisfying cuts that feature Levy's funky keyboard playing—many written by Levy himself. Those who look for B-3 jams in the soul-jazz vein that are as funky as can be will not be disappointed. This is a great CD to own. —*Michael Erlewine*

Paving the Way / Black Top ◆◆◆

Furry Lewis (Walter Lewis)

b. Mar. 6, 1893, Greenwood, MS, d. Sep. 14, 1981, Memphis, TN
Guitar, Harmonica, Vocals / Acoustic Memphis Blues
For 30 years, from 1930 until 1960, Furry Lewis was a forgotten man in Memphis to all but a handful of friends and neighbors for whom he played at parties and dances. But for 21 years after that, Furry Lewis was the living embodiment of Memphis blues, of whom Pete Welding once wrote, "his music, engagingly direct and sincere, typifies the best that the Memphis blues has to offer." And that from a city that also produced the likes of Frank Stokes, Howlin' Wolf, and Memphis Minnie.

Furry Lewis was the only blues singer of the 1920s to achieve major media attention in the 1960s and 1970s. One of the most recorded of Memphis-based guitarists of the late '20s, Lewis' subsequent fame 40 years later was based largely on the strength of those early sides. One of the very best blues storytellers, and an extremely nimble-fingered guitarist right into his seventies, he was equally adept at blues and ragtime, and made the most out of an understated, rather than an overtly flamboyant style.

Walter Lewis was born in Greenwood, MS, sometime between 1893 and 1900—the exact year is in dispute, as Lewis altered this more than once. The Lewis family moved to Memphis when he was seven years old, and Lewis made his home there for the remainder of his life. He got the name "Furry" while still a boy, bestowed on him by other children. He built his first guitar when he was still a child from scraps he found around the family's home, cigar boxes, beaverboard, nails, and wire from a screen door. Before long he was trying to really play, and coming up with instruments that could make musical sounds.

Lewis' only admitted mentor was a local guitarist whom he knew as "Blind Joe," who may have come from Arkansas, a denizen of Memphis' Brinkley Street, where the family resided. The already late-middle-aged Blind Joe was Lewis' source for the songs "Casey Jones" (or "Kassie Jones") and "John Henry," among other traditional numbers. The loss of a leg in a railroad accident in 1917 doesn't seem to have slowed his life or career down—in fact, it hastened his entry into professional music, because he assumed (luckily, wrongly as it turned out) that there was no gainful employment open to crippled, uneducated Blacks in Memphis. Lewis' real musical start took place on Beale Street in the late teens, where he began his career playing "East St. Louis Blues." He picked up bottleneck playing early on, and tried to learn the harmonica but never quite got the hang of it. Lewis started playing traveling medicine shows, and it was in this setting that he began showing off an uncommonly flashy visual style, including playing the guitar behind his head. He played for a time with the W.C. Handy Orchestra, and claimed that it was Handy himself that gave Lewis his first genuinely good guitar to play.

Lewis' recording career began in April 1927, with a trip to Chicago with fellow guitarist Landers (or Lannis) Walton to record for the Vocalion label, which resulted in five songs, also featuring mandolin player Charles Jackson (or Johnson) on three of the numbers. "Everybody's Blues," "Mr. Furry's Blues," "Sweet Papa Moan," "Jelly Roll," and "Rock Island Blues" proved that Lewis was a natural in the recording studio, playing to the microphone as easily as he did to audiences in person. Those first four songs were not, strictly speaking, representative of Lewis' usual sound, because they featured two backup musicians. In October of 1927 Lewis was back in Chicago to cut six more songs, this time with nothing but his voice and his own guitar—these included the bottleneck showcases "Fallin' Down Blues" and "Why Don't You Come Home?" and his cover of "Mean Old Bedbug Blues," a number first issued by Bessie Smith that same year.

Lewis seldom played with anyone else, partly because of his loose bar structures, which made it very difficult for anyone to follow him. The interplay of his voice and guitar, on record and in person, made him a very effective showman in both venues. Lewis' records, however, did not sell well, and he never developed more than a cult following in and around Memphis—he was never as popular locally as Memphis Minnie or Frank Stokes.

A few of his records, however, lingered in the memory far beyond their relatively modest sales. On August 28, 1928, at a session in Memphis for the Victor label, Lewis cut "Kassie Jones—Parts 1 and 2," arguably one of the great blues recordings of the 1920s. The song itself originated with a celebrated 1900 train wreck at Canton, MS, and had been a standard on the vaudeville boards since 1909. Lewis picked it up from Blind Joe sometime early in his life and had undoubtedly been playing it for many years before 1928. By that time, he had turned it into a guitar and vocal tour-de-force, a stripped-down epic that built in tension and excitement steadily for six minutes or more, and delighted the ear with all manner of word play as well. The producers obviously felt good enough about "Kassie Jones" (also known as "Casey Jones") that they agreed to make it a two-sided record to accommodate the dimensions of Lewis' treatment. More than 60 years later it still holds up, and is a necessary part of any blues collection, or any serious popular music collection, being one of the greatest records ever made by anybody.

Not far behind is Lewis' version of "John Henry," another song he picked up from Blind Joe. There are numerous versions of this song, about the legendary steel-driving man who sacrificed his life to prove that a man was better than a machine, including several by Leadbelly (who played accordion on his version), but Lewis' has a majesty, fury, and power that transcends all others, coupled with some dazzling string work.

Lewis gave up music as a profession during the mid-1930s, when the Depression reduced the market for country blues of his style. He never made a full living from his music—fortunately, he found work as a municipal laborer in Memphis during the 1920s, and continued in this capacity right into the 1960s. His brand of acoustic country blues was hopelessly out-of-style in Memphis during the postwar years, and Lewis didn't even try to revive his recording or professional performing career.

In the intervening years, he played for friends, relatives, and neighbors, living in obscurity and reasonably satisfied. At the end of the 1950s, however, folksong/blues scholar Sam Charters discovered Lewis and persuaded him to resume his music career. In the interim, all of the blues stars who'd made their careers in Memphis during the 1930s had passed on or retired, and Lewis was a living repository of styles and songs that, otherwise, were scarcely within living memory of most Americans.

Lewis returned to the studio under Charters' direction and cut two albums for the Prestige/Bluesville labels in 1961. These showed Lewis in excellent form, his voice as good as ever and his technique on the guitar still dazzling. Audiences—initially hardcore blues and folk enthusiasts, and later more casual listeners—were delighted, fascinated, charmed, and deeply moved by what they heard. Gradually, as the 1960s and the ensuing blues boom wore on, Lewis emerged as one of the favorite rediscovered stars of the 1930s, playing festivals, appearing on talk shows, and being interviewed. He proved to be a skilled public figure, regaling audiences with stories of his life that were both funny and poignantly revealing, claiming certain achievements (such as being the inventor of bottleneck guitar) in dubious manner, and delighting the public. After his retirement from working for the city of Memphis, he also taught in an antipoverty program in the city.

Furry Lewis became a blues celebrity during the 1970s, following a profile in *Playboy* magazine and appearances on *The Tonight Show*, and managed a few film and television appearances, including one as himself in the Burt Reynolds action/comedy *W.W. And the Dixie Dance Kings*. By this time, he had several new recordings to his credit, and if the material wasn't as vital as the sides he'd cut at the end of the twenties, it was still valid and exceptionally fine blues, and paid him some money for his efforts.

Lewis died in 1981 a beloved figure and a recognized giant in the world of blues. His music continues to sell well, and attract new listeners more than 15 years later. —*Bruce Eder*

Back on My Feet Again / 1961 / Bluesway ✦✦✦
An April 1961 session of traditional material such as "Shake 'Em

on Down," "John Henry," "Roberta," and "St. Louis Blues." The album has been combined with another 1961 LP, *Done Changed My Mind,* for the CD reissue compilation *Shake 'Em on Down.* —*Richie Unterberger*

Done Changed My Mind / 1962 / Bluesville ✦✦✦
A May 1961 session of traditional material along the lines of "Casey Jones" and "Frankie and Johnnie." It's been combined with a similar 1961 LP, *Back on My Feet Again,* onto one disc for the CD reissue compilation *Shake 'Em on Down.* —*Richie Unterberger*

☆ **Shake 'Em on Down** / 1972 / Fantasy ✦✦✦✦✦
A 20-song single CD reissue of Lewis' first modern commercial recordings, done for two Prestige/Bluesville albums (*Back On My Feet Again, Done Changed My Mind*) in April and May of 1961 at Sun Studios in Memphis. Lewis is in brilliant form throughout, his fingers nearly as fast and his voice as rich as they were 30-odd years earlier. His version of "John Henry" (not just Lewis' definitive version—*the* definitive version), one of the greatest vocal performances ever put on record and a guitar workout so dazzling that you'd swear there was more than one guy playing. What's more, with the extended running time available on tape (Lewis' sessions in the 1920s having been captured on 78 rpm discs with limited running times), he really stretched out here and obviously loves doing it. The slight reverb in the studio also gives Lewis a larger-than-life stature on this recording. —*Bruce Eder*

Fourth & Beale / 1975 / Lucky Seven ✦✦✦
Recorded in Memphis on March 5, 1969, with Lewis in bed—essentially an impromptu concert for the microphone and whoever happened to be there—these nine tracks show Lewis to fairly good advantage. They're more laidback than his work at the other end of the decade for Prestige/Bluesville, with Lewis playing more slowly and singing more roughly than those earlier sessions. His slide work is still stingingly effective, however, and his voice still highly expressive, and he knows how to put over a song even at this late date, playing his an almost hypnotic intensity—the songs include new renditions of "John Henry" and "Casey Jones," as well as "When the Saints Go Marching In" and W. C. Handy's "St. Louis Blues." —*Bruce Eder*

★ **In His Prime (1927–1928)** / 1988 / Yazoo ✦✦✦✦✦
The best overview of Lewis' classic late-'20s sides, containing 14 songs from the period (though not "John Henry"), all of which are crisply remastered, showing off both his superb guitar playing and his brilliantly expressive singing (the vocal performance on "Falling Down Blues" alone is worth the price of the disc) to excellent advantage. A seminal part of any blues collection, as well as any collection of Lewis' material. —*Bruce Eder*

☆ **Furry Lewis: Complete Works (1927–1929)** / 1990 / Document ✦✦✦✦✦
This Austrian import would be the finest single collection of Furry Lewis' work, covering his Vocalion and Victor sides, if it only included "Kassie Jones—Part 2," which it does not. But otherwise it is as comprehensive a collection as has been put together on Lewis' work. "John Henry" is included, as is the laidback "Mr. Furry's Blues," the latter featuring Charles Jackson (or Johnson) on mandolin. Some of the tracks have more noise than we might like, but overall this is as good as Lewis' work is represented. —*Bruce Eder*

Canned Heat Blues: Masters of Memphis Blues / 1992 / BMG ✦✦✦
This 21-song three-artist collection (with Tommy Johnson and Ishman Bracey) is a good introduction to Lewis' work (or that of the others) for those unwilling to spring for $15 for one of the Yazoo or Wolf releases. The mastering quality is generally excellent, and the eight Lewis songs on hand include both parts of "Kassie Jones," though not "John Henry." It's a beginning, and anyone who likes this sampling can go to the more serious collections. It's apparently out-of-print at this writing, but relatively easy to find. —*Bruce Eder*

Smiley Lewis (Overton Lemons)
b. Jul. 5, 1913, DeQuincey, LA, d. Oct. 7, 1966, New Orleans, LA
Guitar, Vocals / New Orleans R&B
Dave Bartholomew has often been quoted to the effect that Smiley Lewis was a "bad luck singer," because he never sold more than 100,000 copies of his Imperial singles. In retrospect,

Lewis was a lucky man in many respects—he enjoyed stellar support from New Orleans' ace sessioneers at Cosimo's, benefitted from top-flight material and production (by Bartholomew), and left behind a legacy of marvelous Crescent City R&B. We're lucky he was there, that's for sure.

Born with the unwieldy handle of Overton Lemons, Lewis hit the Big Easy in his mid-teens, armed with a big, booming voice and some guitar skills. He played clubs in the French Quarter, often with pianist Tuts Washington (and sometimes billed as "Smiling" Lewis). By 1947, his following was strong enough to merit a session for DeLuxe Records, which issued his debut 78, "Here Comes Smiley." Nothing happened with that platter, but when Lewis signed with Imperial in 1950 (debuting with "Tee-Nah-Nah"), things began to move.

As the New Orleans R&B sound developed rapidly during the early '50s, so did Lewis, as he rocked ever harder on "Lillie Mae," "Ain't Gonna Do It," and "Big Mamou." He scored his first national hit in 1952 with "The Bells Are Ringing," but enjoyed his biggest sales in 1955 with the exultant "I Hear You Knocking" (its immortal piano solo courtesy of Huey Smith). Here's where that alleged bad luck rears its head—pop chanteuse Gale Storm swiped his thunder for any pop crossover possibilities with her ludicrous whitewashed cover of the plaintive ballad.

But Storm wouldn't dare come near its roaring flip, the Joe Turnerish rocker "Bumpity Bump," or some of Smiley Lewis' other classic mid-'50s jumpers ("Down the Road," "Lost Weekend," "Real Gone Lover," "She's Got Me Hook, Line and Sinker," "Rootin' and Tootin'"). In front of the Crescent City's hottest players (saxists Lee Allen, Clarence Hall, and Herb Hardesty usually worked his dates), Lewis roared like a lion.

Strangely, Fats Domino fared better with some of Smiley Lewis' tunes than Lewis did ("Blue Monday" in particular). Similarly, Elvis Presley cleaned up the naughty "One Night" and hit big with it, but Lewis' original had already done well in 1956 (as had his melodic "Please Listen to Me"). His blistering "Shame, Shame, Shame" found its way onto the soundtrack of the steamy Hollywood potboiler Baby Doll in 1957 but failed to find entry to the R&B charts.

After a long and at least semi-profitable run at Imperial, Lewis moved over to Okeh in 1961 for one single, stopped at Dot in 1964 just long enough to make a solitary 45 (produced by Nashville deejay Bill "Hoss" Allen) and bowed out with an Allen Toussaint-produced remake of "The Bells Are Ringing" for Loma in 1965. By then, stomach cancer was eating the once-stout singer up. He died in the autumn of 1966, all but forgotten outside his New Orleans homebase.

The ensuing decades have rectified that miscarriage of justice, however Smiley Lewis' place as one of the greatest New Orleans R&B artists of the 1950s is certainly assured. —Bill Dahl

● **The Best of** / 1992 / Capitol ✦✦✦✦
Smiley Lewis made several fabulous singles, had a booming, terrific voice, and received the same great backing and support that defined the city's R&B sound. But Lewis' records seldom made it outside New Orleans, even though they were frequently brilliant. This great 24-track anthology contains the four that did make it to the charts, among them the signature song "I Hear You Knocking." It shows Lewis doing first-rate novelty tracks, ballads, weepers, uptempo wailers and blues, and making wonderful recordings. The set also includes a thorough discography and good notes and is superbly mastered. It's magnificent, exuberant R&B, and deserved a much better national fate than it enjoyed. —Ron Wynn

☆ **Shame Shame Shame** / 1993 / Bear Family ✦✦✦✦✦
Booming-voiced Smiley may have never enjoyed his share of breaks (as his producer Dave Bartholomew never tires of pointing out), but he sure left behind a legacy of blistering 1950s New Orleans R&B. This four-disc boxed set contains every track Lewis cut for Imperial, along with a handful of obscurities issued on Okeh, Dot, and Loma not long before his untimely demise. If EMI's single disc retrospective isn't enough for you, this exhaustively annotated, beautifully presented package is the ultimate source. —Bill Dahl

Jimmy Liggins

b. Oct. 14, 1922, Newby, OK, d. Jul. 18, 1983, Durham, NC
Guitar / Jump Blues
Another of the jump blues specialists whose romping output can

be pinpointed as a direct precursor of rock & roll, guitarist Jimmy Liggins was a far more aggressive bandleader than his older brother Joe, right down to the names of their respective combos (Joe led the polished Honeydrippers; Jimmy proudly fronted the Drops of Joy).

Inspired by the success of his brother (Jimmy toiled as Joe's chauffeur for a year), the ex-pugilist jumped into the recording field in 1947 on Art Rupe's Specialty logo. His "Tear Drop Blues" pierced the R&B Top Ten the next year, while "Careful Love" and "Don't Put Me Down" hit for him in 1949. But it's Liggins' rough-and-ready rockers—"Cadillac Boogie," "Saturday Night Boogie Woogie Man," and the loopy one-chord workout "Drunk" (his last smash in 1953)—that mark Liggins as one of rock's forefathers. His roaring sax section at Specialty was populated by first-rate reedmen such as Harold Land, Charlie "Little Jazz" Ferguson, and the omnipresent Maxwell Davis.

Liggins left Specialty in 1954, stopping off at Aladdin long enough to wax the classic-to-be "I Ain't Drunk" (much later covered by Albert Collins) before fading from the scene. —Bill Dahl

● **And His Drops of Joy** / 1989 / Specialty ✦✦✦✦✦
Guitarist Jimmy Liggins swung considerably harder than his brother Joe during his 1947-1953 Specialty stint, presaging rock's rise with his torrid jump blues "Cadillac Boogie," "Saturday Night Boogie Woogie Man," and the marvelously loopy "Drunk." Twenty-five of his best are right here. —Bill Dahl

Rough Weather Blues, Vol. 2 / 1992 / Specialty ✦✦✦✦✦
Twenty-five more Specialty cookers, including an undubbed version of "Drunk," plenty of horn-leavened jump blues outings, and several unissued artifacts (including a rare example of the Drops of Joy getting jazzy on "Now's the Time"). —Bill Dahl

Joe Liggins

b. 1915, Guthrie, OK, d. Aug. 1, 1987
Piano / Jump Blues
Pianist Joe Liggins and his band, the Honeydrippers, tore up the R&B charts during the late '40s and early '50s with their polished brand of polite R&B. Liggins scored massive hits with "The Honeydripper" in 1945 and "Pink Champagne" five years later, posting a great many more solid sellers in between.

Born in Oklahoma, Liggins moved to San Diego in 1932. He moved to Los Angeles in 1939 and played with various outfits, including Sammy Franklin's California Rhythm Rascals. When Franklin took an unwise pass on recording Liggins' infectious "The Honeydripper," the bespectacled pianist assembled his own band and waxed the tune for Leon Rene's Exclusive logo. The upshot: an R&B chart-topper. Nine more hits followed on Exclusive over the next three years, including the schmaltzy "Got a Right to Cry," the often-covered "Tanya" (Chicago guitarist Earl Hooker waxed a delicious version) and "Roll 'Em."

In 1950, Joe joined his brother Jimmy at Specialty Records. More hits immediately followed: "Rag Mop," the number one R&B smash "Pink Champagne," "Little Joe's Boogie," and "Frankie Lee." During this period, the Honeydrippers prominently featured saxists Willie Jackson and James Jackson, Jr. Liggins stuck around Specialty into 1954, later turning up with solitary singles on Mercury and Aladdin. But time had passed Liggins by, at least right then; later, his sophisticated approach came back into fashion, and he led a little big band until his death. —Bill Dahl

★ **And His Honeydrippers** / 1985 / Specialty ✦✦✦✦✦
Bouncy, danceable early-'50s jump blues by this pianist's brassy combo. The CD version has nine bonus cuts. —Bill Dahl

● **Joe Liggins & the Honeydrippers** / 1990 / Specialty ✦✦✦✦✦
Pianist Joe Liggins presented a fairly sophisticated brand of swinging jump blues to jitterbuggers during the early '50s, when his irresistible "Pink Champagne" scaled the R&B charts. Twenty-five of his very best 1950-1954 Specialty sides grace this collection, including a tasty remake of "The Honeydripper," "Rhythm in the Barnyard," and the syncopated "Going Back to New Orleans" (recently revived by Dr. John). —Bill Dahl

Dripper's Boogie, Vol. 2 / 1992 / Specialty ✦✦✦✦
An encore helping of 20 rarities by Joe Liggins from Specialty, dotted with unissued discoveries (including two versions of "Little Joe's Boogie" and "Hey, Betty Martin") from 1950-1954. —Bill Dahl

Papa George Lightfoot

b. Mar. 2, 1924, Natchez, MS, **d.** Nov. 28, 1971, Natchez, MS
Harmonica, Vocals / Electric Blues
Thanks to a handful of terrific 1950s sides, the name of Papa Lightfoot was spoken in hushed and reverent tones by 1960s blues aficionados. Then, producer Steve LaVere tracked down the elusive harp master in Natchez, cutting an album for Vault in 1969 that announced to the world that Lightfoot was still wailing like a wildman on the mouth organ. Alas, his comeback was short-lived; he died in 1971 of respiratory failure and cardiac arrest.

Sessions for Peacock in 1949 (unissued), Sultan in 1950, and Aladdin in 1952 preceded an amazing 1954 date for Imperial in New Orleans that produced Lightfoot's "Mean Old Train," "Wine Women Whiskey" (comprising his lone single for the firm) and an astonishing "When the Saints Go Marching In." Lightfoot's habit of singing through his harp microphone further coarsened his already rough-hewn vocals, while his harp playing was simply shot through with endless invention. Singles for Savoy in 1955 and Excello the next year (the latter billed him as "Ole Sonny Boy") closed out Lightfoot's '50s recording activities, setting the stage for his regrettably brief comeback in 1969. —*Bill Dahl*

Rural Blues, Vol. 2 / 1969 / Liberty ✦✦✦
● **Goin' Back To The Natchez Trace** / 1995 / Ace ✦✦✦✦✦
Until producer Steve LaVere rediscovered him in 1969, harp giant Papa Lightfoot was revered for a mere handful of '50s sides. This album for Vault served as his comeback announcement, a gloriously down-in-the-alley affair cut at then-fledgling Malaco studios in Jackson, MS. Six bonus tracks, including three minutes of spoken monologue, have been added to the import CD reissue, enhancing an already fine album. —*Bill Dahl*

Lightnin' Slim (Otis Hicks)

b. Mar. 13, 1913, St. Louis, MO, **d.** Jul. 24, 1974, Detroit, MI
Guitar, Vocals / Electric Louisiana Blues
The acknowledged kingpin of the Louisiana school of blues, Lightnin' Slim's style was built on his grainy but expressive vocals, and rudimentary guitar work, with usually nothing more than a harmonica and a drummer in support. It was down-home country blues edged two steps further into the mainstream; first by virtue of Lightnin's electric guitar, and secondly by the sound of the local Crowley musicians who backed him being bathed in simmering, pulsating tape echo. As the first great star of producer J.D. Miller's blues talent stable, the formula was a successful one, scoring him regional hits that were issued on the Nashville-based Excello label for over a decade, with one of them, "Rooster Blues," making the national R&B charts in 1959. Combining the country ambience of a Lightnin' Hopkins with the plodding insistency of a Muddy Waters, Slim's music remained uniquely his own, the perfect blues raconteur, even when reshaping other's material to his dark, somber style. He also possessed one of the truly great voices of the blues; unadorned and unaffected, making the world-weariness of a Sonny Boy Williamson sound like the second coming of Good Time Charlie by comparison. His exhortation to "blow your harmonica, son" has become one of the great, mournful catchphrases of the blues, and even on his most rockin' numbers, there's a sense that you are listening less to an uptempo offering than a slow blues just being played faster. Lightnin' always sounded like bad luck just moved into his home approximately an hour after his mother-in-law did.

He was born with the unglamorous handle of Otis Hicks in St. Louis, Missouri on March 15, 1913. After 13 years of living on a farm outside of the city, the Hicks family moved to Louisiana, first settling in St. Francisville. Young Otis took to the guitar early, first shown the rudiments by his father, then later by his older brother, Layfield. Given his recorded output, it's highly doubtful that either his father or brother knew how to play in any key other than E natural, as Lightnin' used the same patterns over and over on his recordings, only changing keys when he used a capo or had his guitar de-tuned a full step.

But the rudiments were all he needed, and by the late '30s/early '40s he was a mainstay of the local picnic/country supper circuit around St. Francisville. In 1946, he moved to Baton Rouge, playing on weekends in local ghetto bars, and started to make a name for himself on the local circuit, first working as a member of Big Poppa's band, then on his own.

The '50s dawned with harmonica player Schoolboy Cleve in tow, working club dates and broadcasting over the radio together. It was local disc jockey Ray "Diggy Do" Meaders who then persuaded Miller to record him. He recorded for 12 years as an Excello artist, starting out originally on Miller's Feature label. As the late '60s found Lightnin' Slim working and living in Detroit, a second career blossomed as European blues audiences brought him over to tour, and he also started working the American festival and hippie ballroom circuit with Slim Harpo as a double act. When Harpo died unexpectedly in 1970, Lightnin' went on alone, recording sporadically, while performing as part of the American Blues Legends tour until his death in 1974. Lazy, rolling and insistent, Lightnin' Slim is Louisiana blues at its finest. —*Cub Koda*

Bell Ringer / 1987 / Excello ✦✦✦✦✦
Superb early Slim Excello material. He never sang with more clarity or conviction, nor did his harmonica or guitar playing ever sound more electrifying than on these songs, many of which were more popular singles. Other than Rice Miller's (Sonny Boy Williamson II) definitive anthem, Slim's rendition of "Don't Start Me To Talking" was the finest. —*Ron Wynn*

★ **Rooster Blues** / 1987 / Excello ✦✦✦✦✦
Stark, sparse, swamp blues with the deepest tone in the South Louisiana genre's history. Lightnin' Slim was an Excello mainstay from the mid-'50s to the mid-'60s; 18 of his best J.D. Miller-produced sides reside here. The title track, "Hoo-Doo Blues," "GI Slim," "Tom Cat Blues," and the ribald "It's Mighty Crazy" rate with the guitarist's seminal efforts. —*Bill Dahl*

I'm Evil / 1995 / Excello/AVI ✦✦✦✦✦
A goldmine of 27 1950s/1960s obscurities from one of the lonesomest bayou blues greats ever. Filled with alternate takes and outright unissued efforts, *I'm Evil* reverberates with lowdown treatises that cut to the the heart and soul of the swamp. "Bad Luck," "Mean Ol' Lonesome Train," and "Rock Me Mama" are pure, unadulterated Louisiana blues of the highest order. —*Bill Dahl*

Lil' Ed & the Blues Imperials (Lil' Ed Williams)

Guitar, Vocals / Modern Electric Blues
Lil' Ed and the Blues Imperials are among the premiere party bands to have come out of Chicago during the '80s. Often compared to Elmore James and Hound Dog Taylor, firey, flamboyant slide guitarist Lil' Ed Williams and his group play dedicated, rough-edged and hard-rocking dance music and have established an international reputation. A native of Chicago, Williams was first inspired by renowned slide guitarist and Williams' uncle, J.B. Hutto, with whom he studied as a young teen. Hutto not only taught him slide, he also introduced Williams to bass and drums. William's half brother, James Young, was also a student of Hutto. Later he became the bassist for the Blues Imperials. The brother co-founded their group in the early '70s and went professional in 1975, playing at Big Duke's Blue Flame, on the West Side. The gig earned them a whopping six bucks, which the group members split evenly. In those early years, Williams worked days at a car wash while Young drove a school bus. Despite their humble start, Williams and the Blues Imperials kept performing at night and by the early '80s had developed a substantial regional following. Signing to Alligator in the mid-'80s, they released their debut album, *Roughhousin',* in 1986 and found themselves receiving national attention. They began playing urban clubs and festivals all over the country and eventually toured Canada, Europe, and Japan. They released their second album, *Chicken, Gravy & Biscuits,* in 1989 and the success continued as the Blues Imperials began appearing with such artists as Koko Taylor and Elvin Bishop during the Alligator Records 20th Anniversary Tour. They released their third album *What You See is What You Get* in 1992. If Ed, half brother Pookie Young, and the latest members of the revamped Blues Imperials never do much to modernize their blues or develop a new sound, that will be just fine with the band's growing legion of followers ("Ed Heads," no less), to whom the raucous, rocking slide guitar heritage of Hutto, Hound Dog Taylor, and Elmore James is blues nirvana. —*Jim O'Neal & Sandra Brennan*

Roughhousin' / 1986 / Alligator ✦✦✦
Wild & greasy blues at its best, a two-song session for an anthol-

ogy turned into an all-night, live-in-the-studio jam. Sounds like it was great fun. —*Niles J. Frantz*

● **Chicken Gravy & Biscuits** / 1989 / Alligator ✦✦✦✦✦
Wild, raw, rough-edged Chicago slide guitar blues, this is jumpin', partyin' music in the tradition of Hound Dog Taylor and J.B. Hutto (Lil' Ed's uncle). Recorded live in the studio with no overdubs, it includes nine original compositions plus covers of Hutto and Albert Collins tunes. —*Niles J. Frantz*

What You See is What You Get / 1992 / Alligator ✦✦✦
There's enough greasy slide guitar blues on *What You See Is What You Get* to satisfy fans of Lil' Ed Williams, but it doesn't rank as one of his best albums. Though there are a couple of ripping tracks—particularly the off-beat "Life Is like Gambling"—Williams sounds a little tired, and, ultimately, that flagging energy is what sinks the album. —*Thom Owens*

Charly Lincoln

b. Mar. 11, 1900, Lithonia, GA, **d.** Sep. 28, 1963, Cairo, GA
Guitar, Vocals / Country Blues
Aliases and pseudonyms aside, Charlie Hicks, aka Charley or Charlie Lincoln, was an above-average country blues vocalist. He teamed often with either his brother Robert Hicks (aka Barbecue Bob) or with Peg Leg Howell. His guitar voicings and style were influenced by Curley Weaver, but Hicks was a colorful singer and flashy player. Weaver's mother Savannah taught Lincoln the guitar as a teenager. Lincoln recorded with his brother for Columbia from 1927-1930; he continued playing with him into the '50s, though his performance and playing schedule was highly irregular. A murder conviction ended his career in 1955; he was in prison until his death in 1963. —*Ron Wynn*

Complete Recorded Works (1927–1930) / 1984 / Document ✦✦✦

Hip Linkchain (Willie Richard)

b. Nov. 10, 1936, Jackson, MS, **d.** 1989
Guitar, Vocals / Electric Chicago Blues
Cancer struck guitarist Hip Linkchain down before he could shed his status as a Chicago blues journeyman. With a fine album on the Dutch Black Magic logo, *Airbusters*, to his credit shortly before he died, Linkchain might have managed to move up a rung or two in the city's blues pecking order had he lived longer.
Born Willie Richard in Mississippi, his odd stage name stemmed from being dubbed "Hipstick" as a lad. (White residents of the area gave his seven-foot-tall dad the name Linkchain because he wore logging chains around his neck). Dad and older brother Jesse both played the blues, and Hip followed in their footsteps. He heard Elmore James, Little Milton, and Sonny Boy Williamson while living in the Delta before relocating to Chicago during the early '50s.
Linkchain made inroads on the competitive Chicago circuit during the '50s and '60s, playing with harpists Dusty Brown, Willie Foster, and Lester Davenport. His own band, the Chicago Twisters, was fronted by a very young Tyrone Davis in 1959. Linkchain cut a handful of very obscure 45s for the tiny Lola and Sanns logos prior to the emergence of his debut domestic album for Teardrop Records, *Change My Blues*, circa 1981. —*Bill Dahl*

Change My Blues / Jun. 1983 / Teardrop ✦✦
Anemic album by journeyman Chicago blues guitarist Linkchain that didn't come close to capturing his stinging sound. —*Bill Dahl*

● **Airbusters** / 1993 / Evidence ✦✦✦✦
Linkchain was a solid, no frills bluesman and this album (his last before his death in 1989) showcases him at his best. Loads of great original material, with the added bonus of top notch playing from Chicago's finest blues players. Standout tracks include "Blow Wind Blow," "I'll Overcome," and "Take Out Your False Teeth." —*Cub Koda*

Mance Lipscomb

b. Apr. 9, 1895, Navasota, TX, **d.** Jan. 30, 1976, Navasota, TX
Guitar, Violin, Vocals / Acoustic Country Blues, Acoustic Texas Blues
Like Leadbelly and Mississippi John Hurt, the designation as strictly a blues singer dwarfs the musical breadth of Mance Lipscomb. A sharecropper/tenant farmer all his life who didn't

record until 1960, "songster" fits what Lipscomb did best. A proud, yet unboastful man, Lipscomb would point out that he was an educated musician, his ability to play everything from classic blues, ballads, pop songs to spirituals in a multitude of styles and keys being his particular mark of originality. With a wide-ranging repertoire of over 90 songs, Lipscomb may have gotten a belated start in recording, but left a remarkable legacy (eight albums in fifteen years) to be enjoyed. —*Cub Koda*

★ **Texas Sharecropper & Songster** / 1960 / Arhoolie ✦✦✦✦✦
Included are '60s Texas blues, traditional songs, and jackknife slide by a country master. —*Jas Obrecht*

You Got to Reap What You Sow / 1964 / Arhoolie ✦✦✦✦✦
Mance Lipscomb was a great songster, someone who knew hundreds of songs and could deliver any and all of them in different but effective ways. He sang blues, spirituals, old folk numbers, and his own tunes. Lipscomb had few rivals when it came to telling stories, setting up situations, creating characters, and depicting incidents. This 24-song reissued disc from 1964 puts Lipscomb in a perfect context, ripping through various songs and talking about everything from drugs to domestic conflict and police worries to spiritual concerns. —*Ron Wynn*

Texas Songster, Vol. 4 / 1994 / Arhoolie ✦✦✦

Texas Songster, Vol. 6 / 1994 / Arhoolie ✦✦✦

Texas Songster, Vol. 5: Texas Blues / 1994 / Arhoolie ✦✦✦

Texas Songster, Vol. 2 (You Got to Reap What You Sow) / 1994 / Arhoolie ✦✦✦

Texas Songster, Vol. 3: Texas Songster in a Live Performance / 1994 / Arhoolie ✦✦✦

Little Buster and the Soul Brothers

b. Hertford, NC
Guitar, Vocals / Soul Blues
Anyone lucky enough to stumble across Little Buster's 1995 debut album for Bullseye Blues might well have been asking themselves, "Where's this guy been all this time?" The answer: for the last three decades or so, the blind guitarist has been serving up his soulful brand of blues around his adopted home of Long Island, NY, with his band, the Soul Brothers.
Edward "Little Buster" Forehand, born in Hertford, NC, left the North Carolina School for the Deaf and Blind when he was 16 years old, moving to New York and breaking into the local R&B scene almost immediately. Buster recorded sparingly during the '60s, waxing the Doc Pomus-penned "Young Boy Blues" for Jubilee in 1967. But the world-at-large remained ignorant of Buster's impressive command of the soul and blues lexicons until 1995, when *Right on Time!* blew onto the contemporary scene like an unexpected breath of fresh air. —*Bill Dahl*

● **Right on Time** / 1995 / Bullseye Blues ✦✦✦✦✦
This remarkable debut album by blind guitarist Little Buster and his combo came literally from out of nowhere (he's no stranger to the studio, though, with a handful of late-'60s 45s to his credit). Mixing blues and soul traditions with melismatic passion, Buster was responsible for one of 1995's best albums—debut or otherwise. —*Bill Dahl*

Little Charlie & the Nightcats

Group / Modern Electric Blues
Little Charlie and the Nightcats have been bringing West Coast club-goers to their feet with their eclectic blues-infused repertoire since the mid-'70s. Drawing from styles ranging from Chicago and jazzy West Coast blues to Texas Swing to rockabilly to surf music and R&B, the Nightcats sing mostly original songs and are noted for their wry, satirical lyrics. They also perform adaptations of obscure older tunes. Though they primarily perform in California and Oregon, the Nightcats frequently tour across the continent, and have even toured Europe. They feature a talented lineup that centers upon extraordinary harp player/songwriter/singer Rick Estrin and versatile guitarist Little Charlie Baty. Dobie Strange on drums and bass player Ronnie James Weber (who joined the Nightcats in the mid-'90s) round out the lineup. —*Sandra Brennan*

All the Way Crazy / 1987 / Alligator ✦✦✦
A very happening debut album; it's funny and danceable. —*Niles J. Frantz*

● **Disturbing the Peace** / 1988 / Alligator ✦✦✦✦✦
These are jumpin' blues with wild antics, a good sense of humor, tons of fun, often outrageous. Very, very good guitar comes from Charlie Baty and interesting harp from lead vocalist Rick Estrin. —*Niles J. Frantz*

The Big Break / 1989 / Alligator ✦✦✦
Here is another raucous, rollicking release. —*Niles J. Frantz*

Captured Live / 1991 / Alligator ✦✦✦
This enjoyable live set captures the group's manic energy. —*Niles J. Frantz*

Night Vision / 1993 / Alligator ✦✦✦
Unlike their previous efforts (where it sounded like the band pulled the van up to the studio, unloaded their gear, and played a set and split before someone hollered out for last call), this one sounds more like a real album. With Joe Louis Walker producing, the boys explore new twists on their wide-ranging bag of tricks. The band's humor is found in abundance on sleazy blues items like "I'll Never Do That No More" and the soul rocker opener "My Next Ex-Wife," while the boys truly get down to business on the rockabilly-tinged "Backfire" and the smokin' shuffle "Can't Keep It Up." Augmenting their basic lineup are guest appearances by Walker and a host of others in support, making this their most musical-sounding album yet. —*Cub Koda*

Straight Up! / 1995 / Alligator ✦✦
Straight Up! is a typically rollicking, humourous collection of updated Chicago blues from Little Charlie & the Nightcats. As with any of the of the band's albums, the quality of the material is slightly uneven, but the band's good-natured energy makes those shortcomings somewhat forgiveable, especially if you are already a fan. —*Stephen Thomas Erlewine*

Little Mike & the Tornadoes

Group / Modern Electric Blues
Harmonica player and keyboardist Mike Markowitz, born in Queens, NY, and raised in New York City's burgeoning 1980s blues club scene, has made his mark in the blues world through a lot of hard touring and a bit of good old fashioned New York salesmanship, or "chutzpah."

Born November 23, 1955, Markowitz cites his earliest influences as John Lee Hooker, Muddy Waters, and Little Walter Jacobs. In 1978, he formed his first blues band and began playing the blues bars around lower Manhattan, but his reputation began to grow when he began backing up legendary musicians like pianist Pinetop Perkins, Hubert Sumlin and Jimmy Rogers when they came to New York or New Jersey to perform. Markowitz's passion for blues, as a fan and as a performer, is legendary, and he carried it over into the producer's chair in 1988, when he recorded albums for Perkins and later for Sumlin.

In 1990, Little Mike and the Tornadoes got their own recording contract with Blind Pig, a San Francisco-based label, and his output has been quite prolific since then. The group's first album, *Heart Attack*, includes guest performances by Perkins, Paul Butterfield and Sumlin. Two years later, he recorded *Payday*, also for Blind Pig, before recording his debut for Flying Fish Records (a label that has since been acquired by Rounder Records), *Flynn's Place*.

Markowitz is an extremely hard-working, level-headed blues musician who will no doubt surface again and again on records, whether for Rounder or for some other label. All three of Markowitz's albums are available on compact disc, and worth seeking out. —*Richard Skelly*

● **Heart Attack** / 1990 / Blind Pig ✦✦✦✦✦
On this competent White-guy bar-band sort of blues, four cuts feature Paul Butterfield on harp (believed to be his last recordings). Other guests are Ronnie Earl, Pinetop Perkins, Big Daddy Kinsey, and Hubert Sumlin. —*Niles J. Frantz*

Payday / 1992 / Blind Pig ✦✦✦
Little Mike & the Tornadoes don't alter their musical approach on *Payday* at all, but they don't need to—they deliver driving Chicago blues with no frills and lots and lots of passion. The group doesn't just churn out the same old covers, either—they tear through a set of 12 originals that are written in the style of classic '50s and '60s blues. Occasionally their songwriting falters, but never their performances. Every song is delivered with con-

viction, and Little Mike positively wails on both the piano and harp. —*Thom Owens*

Flynn's Place / 1995 / Flying Fish ✦✦✦
Flynn's Place is another excellent collection of piledriving, good-time blues and boogie from Little Mike & the Tornadoes, featuring a fine selection of originals and smoking solos. —*Thom Owens*

Little Milton (Milton Campbell)

b. Sep. 7, 1934, Inverness, MS
Guitar, Vocals / Soul Blues
One of the great blues guitarists, singers, and composers of all time, Milton began his recording career in Memphis with Sun Records in 1953. Small-label singles followed for Meteor and Bobbin before he landed at Chess records in Chicago in 1961. He became one of the best-selling blues artists of the '60s, with many hit singles, including a #1 R&B hit "We're Gonna Make It" and items such as "Feel So Bad," "If Walls Could Talk," and "Baby I Love You." There may be soap-opera elements in much of Milton's work, but it is always done with flair and good humor. While the mold was pretty much established during his Checker period, it also worked with his later affiliations at Stax and Glades. His Malaco recordings (dating from 1984) bring the formula of strings, horns, and background vocals up to date, but the blues artistry of Milton still shines through. —*Bob Porter*

If Walls Could Talk / 1970 / MCA/Chess ✦✦✦✦✦
On *If Walls Could Talk* Little Milton continues to fuse blues with soul—if anything, the album leans toward soul more than blues. Supported by a band with a thick, wailing horn section, Little Milton sings and plays with power. Though there are a couple of wonderful solos, the focus of the record is on the songs, which all sound terrific, thanks to Milton's compassionate vocals. —*Thom Owens*

Grits Ain't Groceries / Jan. 1970 / Checker ✦✦✦
Grits Ain't Groceries is another set of soul and R&B songs from the blues guitarist Little Milton, highlighted by the scorching title track. —*Thom Owens*

Greatest Hits / 1972 / MCA/Chess ✦✦✦
Greatest Hits offers a good sampling of Little Milton's singles for Chess Records in the '60s, including the hits "We're Gonna Make It" and "If Walls Could Talk." It may be a little brief, but there are no bad songs on the record at all and it's an excellent introduction to the guitarist's talents. —*Thom Owens*

Waiting for Little Milton / 1973 / Stax ✦✦✦
Although Little Milton's Stax recordings aren't as blues-oriented as his classic Chess and Checker recordings, there are still plenty of things to recommend about them. Primarily, they're of interest because they focus on his soulful vocals and those vocals shine on *Waiting for Little Milton*. On the whole, the album is a little uneven—the songs aren't always first-rate and the production is a little too smooth—but the performances make it worthwhile for most dedicated fans. —*Thom Owens*

What It Is / 1973 / Stax ✦✦✦
What It Is captures Little Milton at the 1973 Montreux Blues and Jazz Festival, where the guitarist was in fine form. Throughout the concert, Milton sings and solos with flair, making it more than just another live album from the guitarist and turning it into something special. —*Thom Owens*

Blues 'n Soul / 1974 / Stax ✦✦✦
Blues 'n Soul is one of his best Stax sets. —*Bill Dahl*

Tin Pan Alley / 1975 / Stax ✦✦✦✦✦
Most of the guitarist's best soul/blues Stax sides of the 1970s with plenty of his crisp guitar. —*Bill Dahl*

☆ **Chess Blues Master Series** / 1976 / MCA/Chess ✦✦✦✦✦
Little Milton hit his creative and playing stride at Chess, at least in terms of blues. "Grits Ain't Groceries," "We're Gonna Make It" and many other gems were available on this LP anthology. It's no longer available except in used record stores, but is still worth pursuing. —*Ron Wynn*

Chronicle [with Albert King] / 1979 / Stax ✦✦✦
This compilation has a leftover feel; the liner notes provide no sources and dates, admitting only that these are "Stax recordings, some never before available on LP." If you're a big fan of one or both of the artists involved, though, it's not bad, with a quality that's generally consistent with their fully-baked Stax-era

albums. The Milton half of the program is somewhat inferior to the King tracks, the singer taking a misstep with his version of Charlie Rich's country smash "Behind Closed Doors." —*Richie Unterberger*

Raise a Little Sand / 1982 / Red Lightnin' ✦✦✦
Raise a Little Sand collects Little Milton's recordings for Sun and Bobbin Records, which rank as his rawest, most exciting work. Although the quality of this package isn't quite as good as it could have been—the sound and the presentation could have been more carefully considered—this is top-notch, essential music that should be heard in any form. —*Thom Owens*

The Blues Is Alright / Dec. 1982 / Evidence ✦✦
As the title suggests, *Blues Is Alright* leans toward the blues more than his late-'70s and early-'80s collections. However, the quality of Milton's performance isn't quite up to par, making the collection a bit of a disappointment. —*Thom Owens*

Age Ain't Nothin' But a Number / 1983 / Mobile Fidelity ✦✦✦
"Little Milton" Campbell made an excellent modern blues/soul album for MCA in the early '80s that languished due to inadequate promotional efforts. The failure of *Age Ain't Nothin' But A Number* convinced Campbell to move to Malaco. Mobile Fidelity's recent remastered CD reissue of this underrated session provides a perfect sonic framework for Milton's taut, tantalizing and nicely executed guitar, soulful, often biting vocals, and solid arrangements and songs. The title cut was a mild hit, one of the last times Milton reached the R&B charts, while other numbers such as "Why Are You So Hard To Please," "Don't Leave Me," and "Living On The Dark Side Of Love" were as expertly crafted as any of his best Chess dates. —*Ron Wynn*

Playing for Keeps / 1984 / Malaco ✦✦✦
Playing for Keeps is one of Little Milton's best latter-day albums, featuring a smooth, but not too slick production, impassioned vocals, and a generally strong set of songs, highlighted by "The Blues Is Alright." —*Thom Owens*

Greatest Sides / 1984 / MCA/Chess ✦✦✦✦✦
Greatest Sides contains a few of Little Milton's best cuts—including "We're Gonna Make It"—but the packaging isn't very good and the songs are presented haphazardly. There might be some good music on *Greatest Sides*, but there are far better compilations to purchase. —*Thom Owens*

Annie Mae's Cafe / 1987 / Malaco ✦✦✦
Annie Mae's Cafe is one of the strongest albums Little Milton recorded for Malaco. Milton's solos are crisp and stinging throughout the album and his vocals are impassioned. Because he's in top form, he can save the lesser material and that's what makes the album so consistent. —*Thom Owens*

★ **Sun Masters** / 1990 / Rounder ✦✦✦✦✦
While he was at Sun, Little Milton tried a variety of different sounds and styles—sounding like everybody from Elmore James and B.B. King to Fats Domino—which was all tied together by his raw, manic lead guitar. *The Sun Masters* collects many of Milton's absolute finest moments—he never again sounded quite as wild or reckless, either vocally or instrumentally, as he did here. —*Thom Owens*

Blues Is Alright / 1993 / Evidence ✦✦
Little Milton has not been playing much guitar in the '80s and '90s; his Malaco albums are mostly confessional and country soul numbers, geared to attract fans of romantic dialogues and misadventures. So this recently reissued Evidence CD of an '82 date originally done for Isabel is blessed relief for people who would like less yarn spinning and more string bending. They get plenty; Milton does not spare the flashy, jagged guitar lines. At the same time there was soul aplenty in his singing; it was assertive, raw and animated. By comparison, much of his recent output sounds dry and spent. —*Ron Wynn*

Greatest Hits / Sep. 5, 1995 / Malaco ✦✦✦
For fans of Little Milton's Chess, Checker, and Sun sides, his '80s records for Malaco aren't particularly attractive, since they are slicker and more polished. Nevertheless, he cut several first-rate songs for the label, songs that showcase his considerable guitar and vocal talents, and the majority of those songs are collected on *Greatest Hits*. It's a solid introduction to the latter part of Milton's career. —*Thom Owens*

We're Gonna Make It/Little Milton Sings Big Blues / MCA/Chess ✦✦✦✦✦
Two of Milton's classic mid-'60s Chess albums on one CD makes for a great value. —*Bill Dahl*

Little Sonny (Aaron Willis)

b. Oct. 6, 1932, Greensboro, AL
Harmonica, Vocals / Electric Blues
The Stax empire wasn't exactly renowned for its legion of blues harpists, but Little Sonny found the Memphis firm quite an agreeable home during the early '70s (he even appeared in the label's grandiose concert film, *Wattstax*, albeit very briefly).

Aaron Willis was a product of Detroit's blues scene. He moved to the Motor City in 1953 after growing up on his dad's farm in Alabama (his mom gave him his nickname). When Sonny wasn't working local haunts with John Lee Hooker, Eddie Burns, Eddie Kirkland, Baby Boy Warren, or Washboard Willie (who gave him his first paying gig), he was snapping photos of the patrons for half a buck a snap.

Sonny Boy Williamson rambled through town in 1955 and gave Willis some valuable pointers. In 1958, Sonny made his blues recording debut, cutting for both Duke ("I Gotta Find My Baby") and local entrepreneur Joe Von Battle, who leased Sonny's "Love Shock" to Nashville's Excello imprint.

The harpist acquired a two-track tape machine and took matters into his own hands during the early '60s, helming his tiny Speedway label. He leased "The Creeper" and "Latin Soul" to Detroit's Revilot Records (his labelmates included Darrell Banks and George Clinton's Parliaments) in 1966. That set the stage for his joining Stax's Enterprise label in 1970; his first album was the largely instrumental *New King of the Blues Harmonica*—a rather brash boast for a relative unknown!

Two more Enterprise sets that more effectively featured Sonny's vocal talents soon followed: *Black & Blue* and 1973's *Hard Goin' Up*, the latter distinguished by the Bettye Crutcher-penned "It's Hard Goin' Up (But Twice as Hard Coming Down)" and a variety of other soul-inflected tracks.

Not much was heard of the harpist in recent years until the British Sequel imprint released *Sonny Side Up* in 1995. His backing crew included keyboardist Rudy Robinson and guitarist Aaron Willis, Jr., both of whom graced *Hard Goin' Up* more than two decades before. —*Bill Dahl*

● **New Orleans R&B Gems** / 1995 / Black Top ✦✦✦✦
Little known outside his Crescent City homebase, singer Little Sonny Jones' pipes deserved wider acclaim. Thanks to the efforts of Black Top, who recently reissued this collection on CD, maybe he'll finally receive a little posthumously. Though cut in 1975, the set sounds as though it was done a couple of decades earlier. Pianist Dave "Fat Man" Williams (who handles a few vocals as well), saxists Clarence Ford and David Lastie, and guitarist Justin Adams were all vets of that bygone era, and their love for the genre shines through every infectious track. —*Bill Dahl*

Ann Arbor Blues & Jazz Festival, Vol. 2: Blues With a Feeling / 1995 / Schoolkids ✦✦✦
One of a series of compilations from John Sinclair's stash of tapes from the Ann Arbor fests, this 1972 performance caught Sonny at his funk-tinged finest. He pleased the youthful throng with a few of his own numbers—"The Creeper Returns," "They Want Money"—and harp standards first done by Little Walter and Jimmy Reed. —*Bill Dahl*

Sonny Side Up / Glynn ✦✦✦
It's unequivocally nice to have Little Sonny back in harness after a long recording hiatus, but the harpist's comeback offering suffers from backing that feels too mechanical to really do his supple harp justice. A little more earthiness would have suited the project much better. —*Bill Dahl*

● **New King of Blues Harmonica/Hard Goin' Up** / Ace ✦✦✦✦✦
A import coupling of the harpist's first and third LPs for Stax's Enterprise subsidiary and the best spot to inaugurate a Little Sonny CD collection. 1970's *New King* is mostly instrumental and places Sonny in a funky, contemporary setting; 1973's *Hard Goin' Up* was his best album for the firm, benefitting from excellent material spotlighting his vocal talents in a soul-slanted format. Stax offers *New King* by itself as a domestic CD. —*Bill Dahl*

Little Walter (Marion Walter Jacobs)

b. May 1, 1930, Marksville, LA, **d.** Feb. 15, 1968, Chicago, IL
Harmonica, Guitar, Vocals / Electric Chicago Blues
Who's the king of all postwar blues harpists, Chicago division or otherwise? Why, the virtuosic Little Walter, without a solitary

doubt. The fiery harmonica wizard took the humble mouth organ in dazzling amplified directions that were unimaginable prior to his ascendancy. His daring instrumental innovations were so fresh, startling, and ahead of their time that they sometimes sported a jazz sensibility, soaring and swooping in front of snarling guitars and swinging rhythms perfectly suited to Walter's pioneering flights of fancy.

Marion Walter Jacobs was by most accounts an unruly but vastly talented youth who abandoned his rural Louisiana home for the bright lights of New Orleans at age 12. Walter gradually journeyed north from there, pausing in Helena (where he hung out with the wizened Sonny Boy Williamson), Memphis, and St. Louis before arriving in Chicago in 1946.

The thriving Maxwell Street strip offered a spot for the still-teenaged phenom to hawk his wares. He fell in with local royalty—Tampa Red and Big Bill Broonzy and debuted on wax that same year for the tiny Ora-Nelle logo ("I Just Keep Loving Her") in the company of Jimmy Rogers and guitarist Othum Brown. Walter joined forces with Muddy Waters in 1948; the resulting stylistic tremors of that coupling are still being felt today. Along with Rogers and Baby Face Leroy Foster, this super-confident young group became informally known as the Headhunters. They would saunter into South side clubs, mount the stage, and proceed to calmly "cut the heads" of whomever was booked there that evening.

By 1950, Walter was firmly entrenched as Waters' studio harpist at Chess as well (long after Walter had split the Muddy Waters band, Leonard Chess insisted on his participation in waxings—why split up an unbeatable combination?). That's how Walter came to record his breakthrough 1952 R&B chart-topper "Juke"—the romping instrumental was laid down at the tail end of a Waters session. Suddenly Walter was a star on his own, combining his stunning talents with those of the Aces (guitarists Louis and David Myers and drummer Fred Below) and advancing the conception of blues harmonica another few light years with every session he made for Checker Records.

From 1952 to 1958, Walter notched 14 Top Ten R&B hits, including "Sad Hours," "Mean Old World," "Tell Me Mama," "Off the Wall," "Blues with a Feeling," "You're So Fine," a threatening "You Better Watch Yourself," the mournful "Last Night," and a rocking "My Babe" that was Willie Dixon's secularized treatment of the traditional gospel lament "This Train." Throughout his Checker tenure, Walter alternated spine-chilling instrumentals with gritty vocals (he's always been underrated in that department; he wasn't Muddy Waters or the Wolf, but who was?).

Walter utilized the chromatic harp in ways never before envisioned (check out his 1956 free-form instrumental "Teenage Beat," with Robert Jr. Lockwood and Luther Tucker manning the guitars, for proof positive). 1959's determined "Everything's Gonna Be Alright" was Walter's last trip to the hit lists; Chicago blues had faded to a commercial non-entity by then unless your name was Jimmy Reed.

Tragically, the '60s saw the harp genius slide steadily into an alcohol-hastened state of unreliability, his once-handsome face becoming a roadmap of scars. In 1964, he toured Great Britain with the Rolling Stones, who clearly had their priorities in order, but his once-prodigious skills were faltering badly. That sad fact was never more obvious than on 1967's disastrous summit meeting of Waters, Bo Diddley, and Walter for Chess as the Super Blues Band; there was nothing super whatsoever about Walter's lame remakes of "My Babe" and "You Don't Love Me."

Walter's eternally vicious temper led to his violent undoing in 1968. He was involved in a street fight (apparently on the losing end, judging from the outcome) and died from the incident's after-effects at age 37. His influence remains inescapable to this day—it's unlikely that a blues harpist exists on the face of this earth who doesn't worship Little Walter. —*Bill Dahl*

★ **Best** / 1958 / MCA/Chess ✦✦✦✦✦
If there's a blues harmonica player alive today who *doesn't* have a copy of this landmark album in their collection, they're either lying or had their copy of it stolen by another harmonica player. This 12-song collection is the one that every harmonica player across the board cut their teeth on. All the hits are here; "My Babe," "Blues with a Feeling," "You Better Watch Yourself," "Off the Wall," "Mean Old World" and the instrumental that catapulted him from the sideman chair in Muddy Waters' band to the top of the R&B charts in 1952, "Juke." Walter's influence to this very

day is so pervasive over the landscape of the instrument that this collection of singles is truly: 1) one of the all-time greatest blues harmonica albums, 2) one of the all-time greatest Chicago blues albums, and 3) one of the first ten albums you should purchase if you're you're building your blues collection from the ground up. —*Cub Koda*

Hate to See You Go / 1969 / MCA/Chess ✦✦✦✦
Another solid collection of tracks recorded between 1952 and 1960 that originally appeared in 1969 as part of the short-lived Chess Vintage Blues Masters series. Three of the tracks overlap with the budget compilation *The Best of Little Walter, Volume 2,* but the other 12 are just too good to pass by because of a minor programming gaffe. Standout cuts abound just about anywhere the laser beam falls, but the set closer, the minor-key masterpiece "Blue and Lonesome," just may be the most emotionally terrifying masterpiece of Walter's illustrious career. —*Cub Koda*

Boss Blues Harmonica / 1980 / MCA/Chess ✦✦✦
For quite a while this double LP (also available for a while, with identical contents, as part of the Chess *Blues Masters* series) was the best Little Walter compilation, but now virtually all of the cuts are available on CD. As for the music, it's very fine, the 24 selections including much of his most famous and best material. —*Richie Unterberger*

The Blues World of Little Walter / 1988 / Delmark ✦✦✦
If you really want to hear what Little Walter sounded like in his pre-amplified days and early stages of development with the Muddy Waters band, this is the one to get. The title is a bit of a misnomer as Walter is featured more as a sideman to Baby Face Leroy, Muddy Waters, and others on early Parkway, Regal and Savoy sides, but it's clear that Walter at this stage of the game should have been paying royalties to both Sonny Boys and Walter Horton in particular. One of the high points features explosive slide work from Waters on a pre-Chess version of "Rollin' & Tumblin'," as crude as a version as you'll ever hear and certainly not to be missed. Although many of these sides have appeared on other compilations (usually taped up off of old scratchy 78s), this one features superior sound taken from the original lacquer masters. —*Cub Koda*

☆ **The Best of Little Walter, Vol. 2** / 1989 / MCA/Chess ✦✦✦✦✦
This ten-song budget compilation continues the overview of Walter's enormous output for the Chess label. For rock fans, the most familiar track on here is the original version of "Boom Boom (Out Go the Lights)." But there's more where that came from, including the smoking uptempo "It Ain't Right," the blistering instrumental "Boogie," and the soulful strut of "I Don't Play." Another bonus is the inclusion of an early Muddy Waters instrumental featuring Walter on acoustic harp, "Evans' Shuffle." A great, cost-effective way to add some more Walter to the collection. —*Cub Koda*

☆ **The Chess Years 1952–1963** / 1992 / Charly ✦✦✦✦✦
Damn near everything (*Blues with a Feeling* popped any semblance of absolute completion) that the Chicago harp genius ever waxed for Chess (95 sides in all), spread over four generously programmed discs. Particularly revealing are the lengthy snippets of studio chatter on the final rarities disc—Sonny Boy had nothing on Walter when it came to verbally sparring in the studio with Leonard Chess! —*Bill Dahl*

★ **The Essential** / Jun. 8, 1993 / MCA/Chess ✦✦✦✦✦
In many ways, this supplants the original single disc, *Best of Little Walter,* and appends it with 35 more classics of Chicago blues harp genius, although one track from the original 12-song lineup is (perhaps purposely) left off. If you want to start your Walter collection with a nice generous helping of his best, this one runs the entire gamut of his solo career, from the classic 1952 instrumental "Juke" up to the Willie Dixon-penned "Dead Presidents." 46 tracks, one dynamite booklet, nice remastering, a great value for the cash outlay involved and best of all, an album title that truly delivers the goods. —*Cub Koda*

Blues With a Feeling / Oct. 24, 1995 / MCA/Chess ✦✦✦✦
Blues with a Feeling is a two-CD, 40-track compilation which makes the perfect audio bookend to *The Essential Little Walter* (or the single disc *The Best of Little Walter* for those on a budget) by systematically combing the Chess vaults and rounding up the best stuff. No bottom-of-the-barrel scrapings here; this comp effectively renders all '70s Euro vinyl bootlegs null and void, both from a sound and selection standpoint. While not as

exhaustive as the European nine-CD retrospective (in and out of print as of this writing), there are *still* things on this compilation that are left off the box set on Charly. The rarities (including the low down "Tonight with a Fool," possibly the rarest Walter Checker single of all and one whose title never shows up in the lyrics) are all noteworthy by their inclusion. But the alternate takes are the real motherlode here; every one has got some kind of major screwup to 'em while showing Walter's penchant for putting a new spin on a tune every time the engineer hit the record button. Like Charles Brown's "Drifting Blues," where he decides to start up his solo by playing the bump and grind part from "Night Train," leaving the entire band in the dust trying to figure out what changes to play once Walter changes his mind or "Blues with a Feeling," where halfway thru his solo the cord on Walter's harp mike unexplainably shorts out, just crackling away like a bowl of Rice Krispies. Or "You're Sweet," where he mangles the first line of the vocal ("you sweet, as any apple on a fruit") thus immediately relegating it to the unissued file, regardless of how great the solo in the middle is. By far the most interesting instrumental here is the previously unissued "That's It" (formerly only a discographical sighting) where Walter honks mind-altering stuff that I've never heard him do anywhere else on record. The alternate of "My Babe" doesn't sound *anything* like the hit version, making it another minor revelation, while the storming uptempo reading of "Going Down Slow"—with the track fueled by a particularly nasty riff courtesy of Robert Jr. Lockwood, whose acerbic comments punctuate the liner notes throughout—is a prime candidate for the repeat button mode on the CD player, featuring the groove from Hell that refuses to abate. Bottom line is, this is one very cool release that even I've-heard-it-all-before hardliners are gonna want to add to the collection. Little Walter was a blues genius and once you've absorbed the influential hits, here's exactly where you go next to get the rest of the story. —*Cub Koda*

Bluesmasters / Tomato ✦✦
These live performances have been circulating around bootleg channels under a plethora of titles on vinyl and cassette for over a decade and a half. The Otis Rush cuts fare okay, although the sound quality is pretty awful and will generally make any decent stereo playback system sound like there's a pile of blankets draped over the speakers. The Walter cuts are another matter entirely. On one of its earlier vinyl bootleg incarnations, these tracks were purported to be recorded live at Pepper's Lounge in Chicago sometime in the late '60s. If they were, it must have been amateur night. The backing band heard here behind Walter are a bunch of rhythmically challenged ham-fisted hacks who sound like every blues lover's worst nightmare; buzzing obtrusive bass lines, clumsy, lumbering drums that sound like the guy's building a house and a lead guitar that sounds like he's plugged into a 100-watt kazoo. As for Walter himself, he's in the absolute worst recorded form ever documented. His harp playing is raggedy and short-winded (to be fair, by this time he *was* trying to blow with one collapsed lung) and he forgets lyrics left and right, letting out frustrated yelps as he keeps losing his place mid-song, breaking time constantly. —*Cub Koda*

Blue Midnight / Le Roi du Blues ✦✦✦✦
It's hard to determine the worth of Le Roi du Blues' Little Walter rarity compilations these days. Not only has much of the material been reissued on CD; it's sometimes hard to determine what's been reissued elsewhere and what hasn't, given the minimal differences between some of these alternate takes. It's reasonably certain that *Blue Midnight*, the third and final volume of the series, had the rarest material of the lot, and the most songs that remained unused on Chess' CD compilations. The material is good, but not as impressive as the previous two Le Roi du Blues volumes (*Blue and Lonesome* and *Southern Feeling*), drawing more from his '60s recordings than the other installments. —*Richie Unterberger*

Blue and Lonesome / Le Roi du Blues ✦✦✦✦
Although its legality was dubious, the three-volume Le Roi du Blues series of rare Little Walter recordings was a model example of rare material being made available to collectors who could simply not locate it otherwise. The first of these, *Blue and Lonesome* is much less desirable than it was pre-1990, though, because most of the songs are now available on domestic Chess CDs. The music is certainly excellent, only slightly less impressive than his greatest hits compilation, collecting some rare sin-

gles and unissued takes that had been confined to the vaults for decades. —*Richie Unterberger*

Southern Feeling / Le Roi du Blues ✦✦✦✦✦
Virtually all of this came out on *The Essential Little Walter* and *Blues with a Feeling*, making it unnecessary to hunt this down, despite the high quality of its contents. Diehard collectors, though, might want to do so because of the presence of two very rare tracks by the Coronets, an obscure doo wop group whose 1954 single included harmonica work by Walter. —*Richie Unterberger*

Little Willie Littlefield

b. Sep. 16, 1931, Houston, TX
Piano, Vocals / Electric Jump Blues
Before he was 21 years old, Texas-born pianist Little Willie Littlefield had etched an all-time classic into the blues lexicon. Only trouble was, his original 1952 waxing of "Kansas City" (here titled "K.C. Loving") didn't sell sufficiently to show up on the charts (thus leaving the door open for Wilbert Harrison to invade the airwaves with the ubiquitous Jerry Leiber/Mike Stoller composition seven years later).

Influenced by Albert Ammons, Charles Brown, and Amos Milburn, Little Willie was already a veteran of the R&B recording wars by the time he waxed "K.C. Loving," having made his debut 78 in 1948 for Houston-based Eddie's Records while still in his teens. After a few sides for Eddie's and Freedom, he moved over to the Bihari brothers' Los Angeles-headquartered Modern logo in 1949. There he immediately hit paydirt with two major R&B hits, "It's Midnight" and "Farewell" (he added another chart entry, "I've Been Lost," in 1951).

Littlefield proved a sensation upon moving to L.A. during his Modern tenure, playing at area clubs and touring with a band that included saxist Maxwell Davis. At Littlefield's first L.A. session for King's Federal subsidiary in 1952, he cut "K.C. Loving" (with Davis on sax), but neither it nor several fine Federal follow-ups returned the boogie piano specialist to the charts.

Other than a few 1957–58 singles for Oakland's Rhythm logo, little was heard from Little Willie Littlefield until the late '70s, when he began to mount a comeback at various festivals and on the European circuit. While overseas, he met a Dutch woman, married her, and settled in the Netherlands, where he remains active musically. —*Bill Dahl*

● **It's Midnight** / 1979 / Route 66 ✦✦✦✦
Nice compilation of Littlefield's best sides, 1949–57. (Import) —*Cub Koda*

Johnny Littlejohn (John Funchess)

b. Apr. 16, 1931, Lake, MS, **d.** Feb. 1, 1994, Chicago IL
Guitar, Vocals / Electric Chicago Blues
Johnny Littlejohn's stunning mastery of the slide guitar somehow never launched him into the major leagues of bluesdom. Only on a handful of occasions was the Chicago veteran's vicious bottleneck attack captured effectively on wax, but anyone who experienced one of his late-night sessions as a special musical guest on the Windy City circuit will never forget the crashing passion in his delivery.

Delta-bred John Funchess first heard the blues just before he reached his teens at a fish fry where a friend of his father's named Henry Martin was playing guitar. He left home in 1946, pausing in Jackson, MS, Arkansas, and Rochester, NY, before winding up in Gary, IN. In 1951, he began inching his way into the Gary blues scene, his Elmore James-influenced slide style making him a favorite around Chicago's south suburbs in addition to steel mill-fired Gary.

Littlejohn waited an unconscionably long time to wax his debut singles for Margaret (his trademark treatment of Brook Benton's "Kiddio"), T-D-S, and Weis in 1968. But before the year was out, Littlejohn had also cut his debut album, *Chicago Blues Stars*, for Chris Strachwitz's Arhoolie logo. It was a magnificent debut, the guitarist blasting out a savage Chicago/Delta hybrid rooted in the early '50s rather than its actual timeframe.

Unfortunately, a four-song 1969 Chess date remained in the can. After that, another long dry spell preceded Littlejohn's 1985 album *So-Called Friends* for Rooster Blues, an ambitious but not altogether convincing collaboration between the guitarist and a humongous horn section that sometimes grew to eight pieces.

The guitarist had been in poor health for some time prior to his 1994 passing. —*Bill Dahl*

So-Called Friends / 1985 / Rooster Blues ✦✦✦
Surrounding Littlejohn with a huge horn section probably wasn't the greatest idea in retrospect; the booming brass detracts at times from his pungent slide work, rather than enhancing it. But hearty renditions of his signature "Chips Flying Everywhere," a sturdy "She's Too Much," and several songs written by bassist Aron Burton recommend the vinyl-only LP nonetheless. —*Bill Dahl*

● **Chicago Blues Stars** / 1991 / Arhoolie ✦✦✦✦✦
Slide guitar master Littlejohn was already overdue for the full-length album treatment when he waxed this stellar set for Arhoolie in 1969 (enhanced by three bonus cuts on the CD version). A sizzling Chicago combo provides sterling backing as Littlejohn sears the strings on "Dream," "Shake Your Moneymaker," and a rough-edged adaptation of Brook Benton's "Kiddeo," his powerhouse vocals consistently stunning. —*Bill Dahl*

Robert Jr. Lockwood

b. Mar. 27, 1915, Marvell, AR
Guitar, Harmonica, Vocals / Chicago Blues, Electric Delta Blues, Acoustic Delta Blues
Robert Jr. Lockwood learned his blues first-hand from an unimpeachable source: the immortal Robert Johnson. Lockwood can still conjure up the bone-chilling Johnson sound whenever he so desires, but he's never been one to linger in the past for long—which accounts for the jazzy swing he often brings to the licks he plays on his 12-string electric guitar.

Now past the age of 80, Lockwood is one of the last living links to the glorious Johnson legacy. When Lockwood's mother became romantically involved with the charismatic rambler in Helena, AR, the quiet teenager suddenly gained a role model and a close friend—so close that Lockwood considered himself Johnson's stepson. Robert Jr. learned how to play guitar very quickly with Johnson's expert help, assimilating Johnson's technique inside and out.

Following Johnson's tragic murder in 1938, Lockwood embarked on his own intriguing musical journey. He was among the first bluesmen to score an electric guitar in 1938 and eventually made his way to Chicago, where he cut four seminal tracks for Bluebird. Jazz elements steadily crept into Lockwood's dazzling fretwork, although his role as Sonny Boy Williamson's musical partner on the fabled KFFA *King Biscuit Time* radio broadcasts during the early '40s out of Helena, AR, probably didn't emphasize that side of his dexterity all that much.

Settling in Chicago in 1950, Lockwood swiftly gained a reputation as a versatile in-demand studio sideman, recording behind harp genius Little Walter, piano masters Sunnyland Slim and Eddie Boyd, and plenty more. Solo recording opportunities were scarce, though Lockwood did cut fine singles for Mercury in 1951 ("I'm Gonna Dig Myself a Hole") and JOB in 1955 ("Sweet Woman from Maine"/"Aw Aw Baby").

Lockwood's best modern work as a leader was done for Pete Lowry's Trix label, including some startling workouts on the 12-string axe that he daringly added to his arsenal in 1965. He later joined forces with fellow Johnson disciple Johnny Shines for two eclectic early-'80s Rounder albums. Intent on satisfying his own instincts first and foremost, the sometimes taciturn Lockwood is a priceless connection between past and present. —*Bill Dahl*

Steady Rollin' Man / 1967 / Delmark ✦✦✦
Sophisticated, mellow set cut in 1970 that occasionally gets a little too laidback. Lockwood's complex lead guitar work and aged-in-the-wool vocals are a delight, but guitarist Louis Myers asserts himself as soloist more than he should have in such a situation, making one yearn for more Robert Jr. riffs. —*Bill Dahl*

Contrasts / 1974 / Trix ✦✦✦✦✦
Robert Jr. Lockwood has never been a conventional musician or blues artist. This was one of a pair of spectacular albums done for Trix in the 1970s. Johnson's version of "Driving Wheel" maintains the spirit of Roosevelt Sykes' familiar rendition, but has his own compelling twists. Otherwise, the session featured Lockwood songs, and he demonstrated the probing, animated qualities that made him a legend and a survivor. —*Ron Wynn*

Does 12 / 1977 / Trix ✦✦✦✦✦
Robert Jr. Lockwood made two excellent albums for the Trix label that didn't get the publicity or distribution they merited, which quickly disappeared. Muse has recently begun reissuing Trix material, but thus far hasn't gotten to this Lockwood date or its companion. Grab it if you can. —*Ron Wynn*

Hangin' On / 1979 / Rounder ✦✦✦
Two of the principal keepers of the Robert Johnson flame joined forces for a Rounder LP that's stunning in its non-conformity to what purists might like to hear from the two veterans. Jazz and swing influences invest much of the LP, the pair sharing vocal and guitar duties. —*Bill Dahl*

Mr. Blues Is Back to Stay (with Johnny Shines) / 1980 / Rounder ✦✦✦
Another pairing of the venerable Delta blues vets, and it's even less traditional than their previous outing. Utilizing a jazz-steeped two-piece sax section, Lockwood swings with impugnity. Shines had recently suffered a serious stroke that left him unable to play guitar, so his contributions are limited to vocals only. —*Bill Dahl*

● **Plays Robert and Robert** / Nov. 28, 1982 / Black & Blue ✦✦✦✦✦
Lockwood in a beautifully recorded solo context (cut in France in 1982 for Black & Blue), doing what he does best—his own songs and those of his legendary mentor, Robert Johnson. Purists may quiver at Lockwood's use of the 12-string guitar as his primary axe, but he long ago made the instrument his own blues tool of choice, and he handles its nuances expertly. —*Bill Dahl*

Robert Lockwood / 1991 / Paula ✦✦✦✦✦
All 20 of these tracks were recorded for JOB in the early '50s, but only half feature Lockwood; the others are Johnny Shines solo sides. The title is a bit misleading; the Lockwood tracks, recorded in 1951 and 1955, mix genuine Lockwood solo performances with sides on which he supported Sunnyland Slim and Alfred Wallace. It's decent sparse, early Chicago blues, though not as good as the preceding Shines tracks on the disc. —*Richie Unterberger*

Cripple Clarence Lofton (Albert Clemens)

b. Mar. 28, 1887, Kingsport, TN, d. Jan. 9, 1957, Chicago, IL
Piano, Vocals / Piano Blues
Cripple Clarence Lofton is one of those colorful names that adorned many an album collection of early boogie-woogie piano 78s in the early days of the '60s folk-blues revival. An early practitioner of the form, along with his fellow contemporaries Cow Cow Davenport, Meade Lux Lewis, Pine Top Smith, and Jimmy Yancey, Lofton was one of the originators who spread the word in Chicago in the early '20s.

The physically challenged nicknamed he used—seen by modern audiences as a tad exploitative, to say the least—was a bit of a ringer. Although he suffered a birth defect in his leg that made him walk with a pronounced limp, it certainly didn't stop him from becoming an excellent tap dancer, his original ticket into show business. He quickly developed a stage act that consisted of pounding out the boogie-woogie on the piano while standing up, dancing, whistling, and vocalizing while—as one old bluesman put it—"carrying on a lotta racket." Lofton's technique—or lack of it—stemmed more from a tent show background and those listening to his earliest and most energetic recordings will quickly attest that hitting every note or making every chord change precisely were not exactly high priorities with him. But this wild, high energy act got the young showman noticed quickly, and by the early '30s, he was so much a fixture of Chicago night life firmament that he had his own Windy City nightclub, the oddly named Big Apple. Lofton remained on the scene, cutting sides for the Gennett, Vocalion, Solo Art, Riverside, Session, and Pax labels into the '40s. When the boogie-woogie craze cooled off and eventually died down in the late '40s, Lofton went into early retirement, staying around Chicago until his death in 1957 from a blood clot in the brain. —*Cub Koda*

Honky-Tonk and Boogie-Woogie Piano / 1954 / Riverside ✦✦✦

Cripple Clarence Lofton / Jul. 14, 1954 / Riverside ✦✦✦

Cripple Lofton & Walter Davis / Yazoo ✦✦✦✦✦
Marvelous blues piano and singing from Cripple Clarence Lofton, and nearly as fine an effort from Walter Davis. —*Ron Wynn*

● **Cripple Clarence Lofton, Vol. 1** / RST ✦✦✦✦✦
Some of Lofton's best, with the selections "Strut That Thing,"
"Monkey Man Blues," and "Pitchin' Boogie" being particular
standouts. (Import) —*Cub Koda*

Complete Works, Vol. 1 (1935–1939) / Document ✦✦✦✦

Complete Works, Vol. 2 (1939–1943) / Document ✦✦✦

Lonesome Sundown

b. Dec. 12, 1928, Donaldsville, LA
Guitar, Vocals / Electric Louisiana Blues
Unlike many of his swamp blues brethren, the evocatively mon-
ickered Lonesome Sundown (the name was an inspired gift from
producer J.D. Miller) wasn't a Jimmy Reed disciple. Sundown's
somber brand of blues was more in keeping with the gruff
sound of Muddy Waters. The guitarist was one of the most powerful members of Miller's south Louisiana stable, responsible for
several seminal swamp standards on Excello Records.

The former Cornelius Green first seriously placed his hands
on a guitar in 1950, Waters and Hooker providing early inspiration. Zydeco pioneer Clifton Chenier hired the guitarist as one of
his two axemen (Phillip Walker being the other) in 1955. A demo
tape was enough proof for Miller—he began producing him in
1956, leasing the freshly renamed Sundown's "Leave My Money
Alone" to Excello.

There were plenty more where that one came from. Over the
next eight years, Sundown's lowdown Excello output included "My
Home Is a Prison," "I'm a Mojo Man," "I Stood By," "I'm a Samplin'
Man," and a host of memorable swamp classics preceded his 1965
retirement from the blues business to devote his life to the church.
It was 1977 before Sundown could be coaxed back into a studio
to cut a blues LP; *Been Gone Too Long*, co-produced by Bruce
Bromberg and Dennis Walker for the Joliet imprint, was an excellent comeback entry but did disappointing sales (even after being
reissued on Alligator). Scattered live performances were about all
that was heard of the swamp blues master after that. —*Bill Dahl*

Been Gone Too Long / 1977 / Hightone ✦✦✦
The Louisiana blues vet's 1977 comeback album was a well-done
affair, capturing some of the flavor of his '50s material (but with
a modern edge). Producers Bruce Bromberg and Dennis Walker
(who doubled on bass) recruited guitarist Phillip Walker, a long
time Sundown cohort, to handle some of the fret load, and the
predominantly original songlist was worthy of Sundown's lowdown sound. —*Bill Dahl*

Lonesome Sundown / 1990 / Flyright ✦✦✦✦
Twenty-one sides for producer J.D. Miller's Crowley, LA vaults,
dominated by alternate takes of the guitarist's best-known sides
and some otherwise unreleased numbers. Backing musicians
include keyboardist Katie Webster, harpist Lazy Lester, and
drummer Warren Storm. Tough stuff! —*Bill Dahl*

● **I'm A Mojo Man: The Best Of The Excello Singles** / 1995 /
AVI-Excello ✦✦✦✦✦
One of the swamp blues stalwarts in south Louisiana, producer
J.D. Miller's stable receives the deluxe treatment with a 24-song
anthology spanning his 1956–1964 Excello tenure. Sundown's
sparse, nasty sound was influenced by Muddy Waters as much
as the prevailing bayou beat, giving an extra discernible tang to
his "Leave My Money Alone," "My Home Is My Prison," and the
title cut. —*Bill Dahl*

Big Joe Louis & His Blues Kings

Group / British Blues
Playing and writing electric blues in the mold of the classic '50s
Chess Records prototype, Big Joe Louis and his crew suffer the
same mixed blessing common to many White (and some British)
blues bands. Their command of their instruments and genuine
love of the music is offset by mediocre if energetic vocals (from
guitarist/singer Louis) and a revivalist mindset that recreates
with precision, but lacks original vision. They get credit for writing most of the material on their 1996 CD, *Big Sixteen*, and exe-
cuting it with assured competence, though they fall into the huge
category of bands that could produce a high old time seen live,
but aren't anything special on disc. —*Richie Unterberger*

● **Big Sixteen** / 1996 / Ace ✦✦✦
Fair modern White blues, distinguished from the bar-band norm
by arrangements which consciously echo vintage Chess Records,
down to the standup bass and Little George Sueref's able

approximations of Little Walter's harmonica style. —*Richie
Unterberger*

Joe Hill Louis (Lester Hill)

b. Sep. 23, 1921, Raines, TN, d. Aug. 5, 1957, Memphis, TN
Guitar, Harmonica, Drums, Vocals / Electric Memphis Blues
Joe Hill Louis created quite a racket as a popular one-man blues
band around Memphis during the 1950s. If not for his tragic premature demise, his name would surely be more widely revered.

Lester (or Leslie) Hill ran away from home at age 14, living
instead with a well-heeled Memphis family. A fight with another youth that was won by young Hill earned him the "Joe Louis"
appellation. Harp came first for the multi-instrumentalist; by the
late '40s, his one-man musical attack was a popular attraction in
Handy Park and on WDIA, the groundbreaking Memphis radio
station where he hosted a 15-minute program billed as *The
Pepticon Boy.*

Also known as the Be-Bop Boy, Louis made his recording
debut in 1949 for Columbia, but the remainder of his output was
issued on R&B indies large and small, including Phillips (Sam
Phillips' first extremely short-lived logo), Modern, Sun, Checker,
Meteor, Big Town (where he cut the blistering "Hydramatic
Woman," a tune he'd cut previously for Sun in 1953 with Walter
Horton on harp, but Phillips never released it), and House of
Sound. Louis was only 35 when he died of tetanus, contracted
when a deep gash on his thumb became infected. —*Bill Dahl*

● **The Be-Bop Boy with Walter Horton and Mose Vinson** / Bear
Family ✦✦✦✦✦
Raw, chaotic, one-man band blues of the highest order. Highlights
include the original version of "Tiger Man," and Louis' scorching
lead guitar work on "She Treats Me Mean and Evil." Compiling virtually all the recordings he made for Sam Phillips in Memphis in
the early '50s, this CD also features astonishing harmonica work
from Big Walter Horton on several tracks. (Import) —*Cub Koda*

Louisiana Red

b. Mar. 23, 1936, Vicksburg, MS
*Guitar, Vocals, Harmonica / Modern Electric Blues, Modern
Acoustic Blues*
Louisiana Red (born Iverson Minter) is a flamboyant guitarist,
harmonica player and vocalist. He lost his parents early in life
through multiple tragedies; his mother died of pneumonia a
week after his birth, and his father was lynched by the Klu Klux
Klan when he was five. Red began recording for Chess in 1949,
then joined the Army. After his discharge, he played with John
Lee Hooker in Detroit for almost two years in the late '50s. Since
then he's maintained a busy recording and performing schedule,
having done sessions for Chess, Checker, Atlas, Glover, Roulette,
L&R and Tomato among others. —*Ron Wynn*

● **Lowdown Back Porch Blues** / 1963 / Collectables ✦✦✦✦✦
Still his best album, these early-'60s sides provided an attractive
showcase for the guitarist's eclectic talent. —*Bill Dahl*

Midnight Rambler / 1982 / Tomato ✦✦✦
At times harrowing, this is one of Red's more intense efforts. —
Bill Dahl

The Best Of Louisiana Red / 1995 / Evidence ✦✦✦✦✦

Billy Love

b. MS
Piano, Vocals / Electric Memphis Blues
There is not a whole lot of tangible information to convey about
pianist Billy "Red" Love, who signed to record for fledgling producer Sam Phillips in 1951. Phillips passed off an early Love performance, "Juiced," to Chess as the latest effort by Jackie
Brenston (then red-hot as a result of "Rocket 88").

Love's own debut record, "Drop Top," came out on Chess and
reportedly did fairly well regionally, but after a 1952 Chess
encore, "My Teddy Bear Baby," Chess dropped him. He stuck
around Sun through 1954, working sessions behind Rufus
Thomas and Willie Nix and recording a wealth of unissued sides
of his own.

Love left plenty of jumping blues behind in the Sun vaults—
enough to fill half an LP on Charly that he shared with Little
Junior Parker. Love's rocking "Gee I Wish," one of those long-
delayed masters, has been revived by guitarist Duke Robillard.
Love left Memphis in 1955 for parts unknown. —*Bill Dahl*

Clayton Love

b. Nov. 15, 1927, Mattson, MS
Piano, Vocals / Electric Blues
Pianist Clayton Love was a prominent member of Ike Turner's Kings of Rhythm during the mid-'50s, making some of his finest platters with the legendary band. But Love made his first vinyl appearance on Lillian McMurry's Jackson, MS-based Trumpet Records in 1951 with his own jump band, the Shufflers.

The combo was a fixture around Vicksburg, where Love was attending Alcorn A&M as a pre-med student. Love's cousin, Natchez bandleader Earl Reed, had recorded for Trumpet and recommended his young relative to McMurry. Love's 1951 debut, "Susie"/ "Shufflin' with Love," exhibited infectious enthusiasm if not a great deal of polish. From there, Love moved over to Aladdin in 1952 (with saxist Raymond Hill's band backing him), Modern (with Turner on guitar) and Groove in 1954, and in 1957, Love fronted and played the 88s with Turner and the Kings of Rhythm on their Federal platters "Do You Mean It," "She Made My Blood Run Cold," and "The Big Question."

Turner had nothing to do with Love's pair of 1958 singles for St. Louis-based Bobbin Records; bassist Roosevelt Marks led the backing band for the clever coupling "Limited Love"/ "Unlimited Love." Long settled in the Gateway City, Love made an album for Modern Blues Recordings in 1991 with fellow ivories aces Johnnie Johnson and Jimmy Vaughn, *Rockin' Eighty-Eights.* —*Bill Dahl*

Willie Love

b. Nov. 4, 1906, Duncan, MS, d. Aug. 19, 1953, Jackson, MS
Piano, Vocals / Acoustic Delta Blues, Electric Delta Piano Blues
Harpist Rice Miller, known to his legion of fans across the Delta as Sonny Boy Williamson, first encountered pianist Willie Love in Greenville, MS, in 1942. The talented pair played regularly on Nelson Street, the main drag of the Black section of Greenville, musically intertwining with remarkable empathy. And it was Williamson who brought Love into the fold at Trumpet Records (the label responsible for Love's entire recorded legacy as a leader).

Love was deeply influenced by Leroy Carr and equally conversant on boogies and down-in-the-alley blues. He played piano on several of Sonny Boy Williamson's Trumpet sessions, but Love didn't utilize his pal on any of his own 1951-1953 dates for the Jackson, MS, firm. Love's debut, "Take It Easy, Baby," was a rollicking boogie outing, and he followed it up with the equally sturdy "Everybody's Fishing," "Vanity Dresser Boogie," and "Nelson Street Blues." Love's last session in April of 1953 found him backed by a White bassist and drummer—certainly a rarity for the era. Four months later, Love, who had long suffered from alcoholism, was dead. —*Bill Dahl*

● **Clownin' With the World** / 1993 / Alligator ♦♦♦♦♦
Instead of assembling a single disc highlighting this Delta piano great, Alligator has spread pianist Willie Love's Trumpet catalog over three marvelous anthologies drawn from the early-'50s archives of Lillian McMurry's Trumpet Records. After eight terrific sides by Sonny Boy, Love pounds out "Take It Easy, Baby," "Little Car Blues," "Feed My Body to the Fishes," and five more, conjuring up a steamy Delta juke joint ambience. —*Bill Dahl*

Delta Blues: 1951 / 1993 / Alligator ♦♦♦
Six more classic 1951 performances by Love from Trumpet's vaults, including the romping "Everybody's Fishing," "My Own Boogie," and "Vanity Dresser Boogie." The pianist shares this disc with country bluesmen Luther Huff and the omnipresent Big Joe Williams; both turned in some inspired work for Lillian McMurry's logo. —*Bill Dahl*

● **Trumpet Masters, Vol. 1: Lonesome World Blues** / Collectables ♦♦♦♦♦
Willie Love played exciting, if sometimes unorganized piano and sang in an equally unpredictable and galvanizing fashion. This is how Mississippi juke joints sounded during the early '50s (they're not that different now). —*Ron Wynn*

Shout Brother Shout / Oldie Blues ♦♦♦♦
A more varied mix of musical styles than on the first two anthologies (everything from Wally Mercer's rocking R&B to Beverly White's schmaltzy lounge sounds). Love leads three more solid sides from 1953: the title item, "Way Back," and "Willie Mae." —*Bill Dahl*

M

Willie Mabon

b. Oct. 24, 1925, Hollywood, TN, **d.** Apr. 19, 1985, Paris, France
Piano, Vocals / Piano Blues
The sly, insinuating vocals and chunky piano style of Willie
Mabon won the heart of many an R&B fan during the early
'50s. His salty Chess waxings "I Don't Know," "I'm Mad," and
"Poison Ivy" established the pianist as a genuine Chicago blues
force, but he faded as an R&B hitmaker at the dawn of rock &
roll.

Mabon was already well-grounded in blues tradition from his
Memphis upbringing when he hit Chicago in 1942. Schooled in
jazz as well as blues, Mabon found the latter his ticket to stardom. His first sides were a 1949 78 for Apollo as Big Willie and
some 1950 outings for Aristocrat and Chess with guitarist Earl
Dranes as the Blues Rockers.

But Mabon's asking price for a night's work rose dramatically
when his 1952 debut release on powerful Windy City deejay Al
Benson's Parrot logo, "I Don't Know," topped the R&B charts for
eight weeks after being sold to Chess. From then on, Mabon was
a Chess artist, returning to the top R&B slot the next year with
the ominous "I'm Mad" and cracking the Top Ten anew with the
Mel London-penned "Poison Ivy" in 1954. Throughout his Chess
tenure, piano and sax were consistently to the fore rather than
guitar and harp, emphasizing Mabon's cool R&B approach.
Mabon's original version of Willie Dixon's hoodoo-driven "The
Seventh Son" bombed in 1955, as did the remainder of his fine
Chess catalog.

Mabon never regained his momentum after leaving Chess. He
stopped at Federal in 1957, Mad in 1960, Formal in 1962 (where
he stirred up some local sales with his leering "Got to Have
Some"), and USA in 1963-64. Mabon sat out much of the late
'60s but came back strong after moving to Paris in 1972, recording and touring Europe prolifically until his death. —*Bill Dahl*

Chicago 63 / 1974 / America ♦♦♦♦♦
Stylish piano and vocals ranging from clever to cranky to
anguished. Willie Mabon is seldom powerful, but can convey
more shadings and nuances than many blues vocalists or singers
in several other genres as well. —*Ron Wynn*

The Seventh Son [LP] / 1981 / Crown Prince ♦♦♦♦♦
18 sensational Chess sides from 1952-1956 collected on import
vinyl, quite a few of which unfortunately don't appear on the
Charly CD: "Wow I Feel So Good," "Would You Baby," "Say Man"
(not the Bo Diddley routine), "Cruisin'," and "Late Again," for
starters. —*Bill Dahl*

Original USA Recordings / 1981 / Flyright ♦♦♦
More Mabon sides, these from 1963-64 and the USA label, that
haven't made it to the digital domain yet (at least domestically).
The USA stuff wasn't as consistent as his early Chess work, but
there are some nice moments—the salacious "Just Got Some," a
chunky "I'm the Fixer" and Willie's mouth organ workout
"Harmonica Special." —*Bill Dahl*

● **Seventh Son** / 1993 / Charly ♦♦♦♦♦
Since MCA hasn't gotten around to this insinuating character's
splendid Chess catalog as yet, we'll have to opt for a 16-song
import that encompasses his three major hits "I Don't Know,"
"I'm Mad" (here in alternate take form, for whatever reason), and
the Mel London-penned "Poison Ivy." Mabon's urban R&B
approach was something of a departure for the Delta-rooted
blues prevalent at Chess at the time, but his laconic vocals on

"The Seventh Son," "Knock on Wood," and "Got to Have It" made
him a star (albeit briefly). —*Bill Dahl*

Chicago Blues Session! / 1995 / Evidence ♦♦♦

Lonnie Mack

b. Jul. 18, 1941, Harrison, IN
Guitar, Vocals / Modern Electric Blues
When Lonnie Mack sings the blues, country strains are sure to
infiltrate. Conversely, if he digs into a humping rockabilly groove,
strong signs of deep-down blues influence are bound to invade.
Par for the course for any musician who cites both Bobby Bland
and George Jones as pervasive influences.

Fact is, Lonnie Mack's lightning-fast, vibrato-enriched, whammy bar-hammered guitar style has influenced many a picker
too—including Stevie Ray Vaughan, who idolized Mack's early
singles for Fraternity and later co-produced and played on Mack's
1985 comeback LP for Alligator, *Strike like Lightning.*

Growing up in rural Indiana not far from Cincinnati, Lonnie
McIntosh was exposed to a heady combination of R&B and hillbilly. In 1958, he bought the seventh Gibson Flying V guitar ever
manufactured and played the roadhouse circuit around Indiana,
Ohio, and Kentucky. Mack has steadfastly cited another local legend, guitarist Robert Ward, as the man whose watery-sounding
Magnatone amplifier inspired his own use of the same brand.

Session work ensued during the early '60s behind Hank
Ballard, Freddy King, and James Brown for Cincy's principal
label, Syd Nathan's King Records. At the tail end of a 1963 date
for another local diskery, Fraternity Records, Mack stepped out
front to cut a searing instrumental treatment of Chuck Berry's
"Memphis." Fraternity put the number out, and it leaped all the
way up to the Top Five on *Billboard*'s pop charts!

Its hit follow-up, the frantic "Wham!," was even more amazing
from a guitaristic perspective with Mack's lickety-split whammy-
bar-fired playing driven like a locomotive by a hard-charging
horn section. Mack's vocal skills were equally potent; R&B stations began to play his soul ballad "Where There's a Will" until
they discovered Mack was Caucasian, then dropped it like a hot
potato (its flip, a sizzling vocal remake of Jimmy Reed's "Baby,
What's Wrong," was a minor pop hit in late 1963).

Mack waxed a load of killer material for Fraternity during the
mid-'60s, much of it not seeing the light of day until later on. A deal
with Elektra Records inspired by a 1968 *Rolling Stone* article pro-
filing Mack should have led to major stardom, but his three Elektra
albums were less consistent than the Fraternity material. (Elektra
also reissued his only Fraternity LP, the seminal *The Wham of That
Memphis Man.*) Mack cameoed on the Doors' *Morrison Hotel*
album, contributing a guitar solo to "Roadhouse Blues," and
worked for a while as a member of Elektra's A&R team.

Disgusted with the record business, Lonnie Mack retreated to
Indiana for a while, eventually signing with Capitol and waxing
a couple of obscure country-based LPs. Finally, at Vaughan's
behest, Mack abandoned his Indiana comfort zone for hipper
Austin, TX, and began to reassert himself nationally. Vaughan
masterminded the stunning *Strike like Lightning* in 1985; later
that year, Mack co-starred with Alligator labelmates Albert
Collins and Roy Buchanan at Carnegie Hall (a concert marketed
on home video as *Further on Down the Road*).

Mack's Alligator encore, *Second Sight*, was a disappointment
for those who idolized Mack's playing—it was more of a
singer/songwriter project. He temporarily left Alligator in 1988

for major-label prestige at Epic, but *Roadhouses and Dancehalls* was too diverse to easily classify and died a quick death. Mack's most recent album from 1990, *Live! Attack of the Killer V,* was captured on tape at a suburban Chicago venue called FitzGerald's and once again showed why Lonnie Mack is venerated by anyone who's even ventured into savage guitar playing. *—Bill Dahl*

★ **The Wham of That Memphis Man** / 1964 / Alligator ✦✦✦✦✦
This is a vinyl reissue of Lonnie's first album for the Fraternity in 1964, the one thousands of guitarists cut their teeth on. Muddy Waters once sang, "the blues had a baby and they named the baby rock & roll." This is the album that proves it. Instrumental versions of R&B hits ("Memphis," "Susie Q," "The Bounce") rebound against heartfelt soul numbers ("Farther Down The Road," "Why?") right next to dazzling fretboard blues romps both slow and fast ("Wham!," "Down And Out"). Lonnie sings his rear end off, the band–with saxes and Hammond organ and pumping soul bass–is right in there and Mack's vibrato drenched guitar stings, wounds, and amazes. It remains his defining moment. *—Cub Koda*

Glad I'm in the Band / 1969 / Elektra ✦✦✦
With the exception of his comeback album for Alligator, *Strike like Lightning,* nothing Mack has done since leaving Fraternity Records has come close to the wham-fisted brilliance of those seminal sides. This LP isn't bad at all, though–besides passable remakes of "Memphis" and "Why," Mack attacks Frankie Ford's "Roberta," Ted Taylor's "Stay Away from My Baby," and Little Willie John's "Let Them Talk" with a slightly rockier edge than his previous stuff. R&B vet Maxwell Davis did the horn charts. *—Bill Dahl*

Whatever's Right / 1969 / Elektra ✦✦✦
With a passel of familiar faces in the cast (ex-James Brown bassist Tim Drummond, pianist Dumpy Rice, harpist Rusty York), the reclusive Mack rocks up some memorable dusties his way–the Falcons' "I Found a Love," Bobby Bland's "Share Your Love with Me," Little Walter's "My Babe," and Jimmy Reed's chestnut "Baby What You Want Me to Do," along with his own "Gotta Be an Answer." *—Bill Dahl*

Lonnie Mack with Pismo / 1977 / Capitol ✦✦
Country-rock (mostly) from the versatile and unpredictable master picker. Pismo's members included bassist Tim Drummond and keyboardist Stan Szelest (frequent Mack cohorts), while Troy Seals, Graham Nash, and David Lindley contributed to the product as well. The unabashed rockers "Lucy" and "Rock and Roll like We Used To" have some life in them, but some of this stuff is dreary. *—Bill Dahl*

Strike Like Lightning / 1985 / Alligator ✦✦✦
Co-produced by Stevie Ray Vaughn, this was Lonnie's ticket back to the show after a few years on the sidelines. To say it was an inspired date would be putting it mildly. With his batteries recharged, Mack was in peak form, playing and singing better than ever. A major highlight is an inspired duet between Stevie and Lonnie on "Wham (Double Whammy)," going toe to toe for several exciting choruses. *—Cub Koda*

Second Sight / 1987 / Alligator ✦✦✦
After the sizzle of *Strike like Lightning,* this mellow set was a major disappointment. Yes, Mack is an exceptional vocalist, but the pop crossover ambience exploited here came at the expense of his unequalled guitar work–not a fair trade at all. *—Bill Dahl*

Attack of the Killer V: Live / 1990 / Alligator ✦✦✦
Cut in front of an appreciative throng at FitzGerald's in suburban Chicago, Mack cuts loose the way he so often does in concert, sticking almost exclusively to his Alligator-era tunes ("Satisfy Suzie," "Cincinnati Jail," the tortured soul ballad "Stop") and never looking too far backwards. *—Bill Dahl*

Lonnie on the Move / Ace ✦✦✦✦✦
Criminally, Mack's seminal LP *The Wham of That Memphis Man* remains unavailable on CD. But that doesn't mean Mack's Fraternity work is totally unrepresented in the digital racks. These 19 Flying V-soaked sides pack the same punch and hail from the same mid-'60s timeframe. He unleashes his vibrato-drenched axe on the torrid "Soul Express," "Lonnie on the Move," "Florence of Arabia," and an astonishing instrumental version of "Stand by Me" that'll send aspiring guitarists' jaws crashing to the floor. For a change of pace, "Men at Play" mines a jazzy walking groove to equally satisfying ends. *—Bill Dahl*

Road Houses & Dance Halls / Epic ✦✦
The folks at Columbia had no idea how to market Mack, so this

fairly undistinguished album died a quick and practically unnoticed death. *—Bill Dahl*

Magic Sam (Samuel Maghett)

b. Feb. 14, 1937, Grenada, MS, **d.** Dec. 1, 1969, Chicago, IL
Guitar, Vocals / Electric Chicago Blues
No blues guitarist better represented the adventurous modern sound of Chicago's West side than Sam Maghett. He died tragically young (at age 32 of a heart attack), right when he was on the brink of climbing the ladder to legitimate stardom–but Magic Sam left behind a thick legacy of bone-cutting blues that remains eminently influential around his old stomping grounds to this day.

Mississippi Delta-born Sam Maghett (one of his childhood pals was towering guitarist Morris Holt, who received his Magic Slim handle from Sam). In 1950, Sam arrived in Chicago, picking up a few blues guitar pointers from his new neighbor, Syl Johnson (whose brother Mack Thompson served as Sam's loyal bassist for much of his professional career). Harpist Shakey Jake Harris, sometimes referred to as the guitarist's uncle, encouraged Sam's blues progress and gigged with him later on, when both were West side institutions.

Sam's tremolo-rich staccato finger-picking was an entirely fresh phenomenon when he premiered it on Eli Toscano's Cobra label in 1957. Prior to his Cobra date, the guitarist had been gigging as Good Rocking Sam, but Toscano wanted to change his nickname to something old-timey like Sad Sam or Singing Sam. No dice, said the newly christened Magic Sam (apparently Mack Thompson's brainstorm).

His Cobra debut single, "All Your Love," was an immediate local sensation; its unusual structure would be recycled time and again by Sam throughout his tragically truncated career. Sam's Cobra encores "Everything Gonna Be Alright" and "Easy Baby" borrowed much the same melody but were no less powerful; the emerging West side sound was now officially committed to vinyl. Not everything Sam cut utilized the tune; "21 Days in Jail" was a pseudo-rockabilly smoker with hellacious lead guitar from Sam and thundering slap bass from the ubiquitous Willie Dixon. Sam also backed Shakey Jake Harris on his lone 45 for Cobra's Artistic subsidiary, "Call Me If You Need Me."

After Cobra folded, Sam didn't follow labelmates Otis Rush and Magic Slim over to Chess. Instead, after enduring an unpleasant Army experience that apparently landed him in jail for desertion, Sam opted to go with Mel London's Chief logo in 1960. His raw-boned West side adaptation of Fats Domino's mournful "Every Night About This Time" was the unalloyed highlight of his stay at Chief; some other Chief offerings were less compelling.

Gigs on the West side remained plentiful for the charismatic guitarist, but recording opportunities proved sparse until 1966, when Sam made a 45 for Crash Records. "Out of Bad Luck" brought back that trademark melody again, but it remained as shattering as ever. Another notable 1966 side, the plaintive "That's Why I'm Crying," wound up on Delmark's *Sweet Home Chicago* anthology, along with Sam's stunning clippity-clop boogie instrumental "Riding High" (aided by the muscular tenor sax of Eddie Shaw).

Delmark Records was the conduit for Magic Sam's two seminal albums, 1967's *West Side Soul* and the following year's *Black Magic.* Both LPs showcased the entire breadth of Sam's West side attack: the first ranged from the soul-laced "That's All I Need" and a searing "I Feel So Good" to the blistering instrumental "Lookin' Good" and definitive remakes of "Mama Talk to Your Daughter" and "Sweet Home Chicago," while *Black Magic* benefitted from Shaw's jabbing, raspy sax as Sam blasted through the funky "You Belong to Me," an impassioned "What Have I Done Wrong," and a personalized treatment of Freddy King's "San-Ho-Zay."

Sam's reputation was growing exponentially. He wowed an overflow throng at the 1969 Ann Arbor Blues Festival, and Stax was reportedly primed to sign him when his Delmark commitment was over. However, heart problems were taking their toll on Sam's health. On the first morning of December of 1969, he complained of heartburn, collapsed, and died.

Even now, more than a quarter century after his passing, Magic Sam remains the king of West side blues. That's unlikely to change as long as the sub-genre is alive and kicking. *—Bill Dahl*

Magic Touch / 1966 / Black Top ✦✦✦✦
Another rare glimpse at Magic Sam hard at work, this time at another fabled West side haunt, Sylvio's, in 1966. No saxes this time, but uncle Shakey Jake was around for a few guest shots,

while bassist Mac Thompson and drummer Odie Payne provide supple backing as Sam launches into another terrific set of numbers that for the most part he never recorded in the studio—songs by Freddy King, Albert Collins, James Robins, Junior Parker, and Jimmy McCracklin that brilliantly suited his soaring pipes and singular guitar style. —*Bill Dahl*

★ **West Side Soul** / 1968 / Delmark ✦✦✦✦✦
One of the truly essential Chicago blues albums of the 1960s. There's not a weak piece of filler on it—Sam exudes West side sizzle as he busts loose on "I Don't Want No Woman," "I Need You So Bad," definitive covers of "Sweet Home Chicago" and "Mama Talk to Your Daughter," the clippity-clop finger-twisting instrumental "Lookin' Good," and a soul-slanted "That's All I Need." —*Bill Dahl*

Black Magic / 1969 / Delmark ✦✦✦✦✦
With the key addition of raspy saxist Eddie Shaw to urge him on, Sam's Delmark encore was another instant classic, containing his R&B-slanted "You Belong to Me" and "What Have I Done Wrong," the bandstand favorites "Just a Little Bit" and "Same Old Blues," and a personalized treatment of Freddy King's "San-Ho-Zay." The album also proved his swan song; he was dead a year later. —*Bill Dahl*

Late Great Magic Sam / 1984 / Evidence ✦✦✦
The ten 1963-1964 sides that make up the majority of this set have sort of fallen through the historical cracks over the years. They didn't deserve such shoddy treatment—Sam didn't record "Back Door Friend" or "Hi-Heel Sneakers" anywhere else, and he's in top shape throughout. Two live tracks at the set's close from 1969 don't add much to the overall package. —*Bill Dahl*

Magic Sam Legacy / 1989 / Delmark ✦✦✦✦
Alternate takes and unissued surprises from the *West Side Soul* and *Black Magic* sessions, along with a couple of welcome 1966 sides ("I Feel So Good" and "Lookin' Good") that didn't see the light of day when they were recorded. Sam's versions of Jimmy Rogers' "Walkin' by Myself" and "That Ain't It" are important additions to his immortal legacy. —*Bill Dahl*

Live at Ann Arbor & in Chicago / 1990 / Delmark ✦✦✦✦
For the first half of this frequently amazing disc, Magic Sam plays for his West side homefolks at the Alex Club. The time is 1963-64, he's backed by saxists A.C. Reed and Eddie Shaw and his longtime bassist, Mac Thompson, and he's blasting the hits of the day with a joyous abandon. A little over six years later, Sam wowed the Ann Arbor Blues Festival with a sensational trio set just as inordinately powerful in its own way. Sound quality is rough on both artifacts, but no matter. —*Bill Dahl*

★ **1957-1966** / 1991 / Paula ✦✦✦✦✦
Never mind Otis Rush and Buddy Guy—this is the bedrock document of Chicago's West side blues guitar movement. Ten seminal numbers that constitute Sam's complete Cobra stash (notably "All Your Love," "Easy Baby," and the rockabilly-tinged "21 Days in Jail"), another pair by his harp-blowing uncle Shakey Jake, five numbers from 1960 that first appeared on Mel London's Chief logo (a tortured cover of Fats Domino's "Every Night About This Time" is the killer), and a couple of solid 1966 outings that reinforce Sam's standing as the king of the West side prior to his untimely demise. —*Bill Dahl*

Give Me Time / 1991 / Delmark ✦✦✦
We now adjourn to Sam's West side living room, where he's holding court in 1968 with only a few friends and family members on hand. Some of the tunes are familiar—"That's All I Need," "You Belong to Me"—but there are other originals only available here, and the super-intimate atmosphere brings out the intimate side of the late guitarist. —*Bill Dahl*

Otis Rush & Magic Sam / 1991 / Paula ✦✦✦✦✦
A pair of blues giants, each given ample room. While you can find better Rush and Sam, that's no slam on what's here. What you're getting are excellent songs that didn't make it onto the first reissue of Magic Sam/Shakey Jake material, plus powerhouse Rush that didn't make *Groaning The Blues*. In other words, this isn't exactly fodder. —*Ron Wynn*

Magic Slim (Morris Holt)

b. Aug. 7, 1937, Grenada, MS
Guitar, Vocals / Modern Electric Blues
Magic Slim & the Teardrops proudly uphold the tradition of what a Chicago blues band should sound like. Their emphasis

on ensemble playing and a humongous repertoire that allegedly ranges upwards of a few hundred songs give the towering guitarist's live performances an endearing off-the-cuff quality—you never know what obscurity he'll pull out of his oversized hat next.

Born Morris Holt, the Mississippi native was forced to give up playing the piano when he lost his little finger in a cotton gin mishap. Boyhood pal Magic Sam bestowed his magical monicker on the budding guitarist (times change; Slim's no longer slim). Holt first came to Chicago in 1955, but found that breaking into the competitive local blues circuit was a tough proposition. Although he managed to secure a steady gig for a while with Robert Perkins' band (Mr. Pitiful & the Teardrops), Slim wasn't good enough to progress into the upper ranks of Chicago bluesdom.

So he retreated to Mississippi for a spell to hone his chops. When he returned to Chicago in 1965 (with brothers Nick and Lee Baby as his new rhythm section), Slim's detractors were quickly forced to change their tune. Utilizing the Teardrops name and holding onto his Magic Slim handle, the big man cut a couple of 45s for Ja-Wes and established himself as a formidable force on the South side—his guitar work dripped vibrato-enriched nastiness, and his roaring vocals were as gruff and uncompromising as anyone's on the scene.

All of a sudden, the recording floodgates opened up for the Teardrops in 1979 when they cut four tunes for Alligator's *Living Chicago Blues* anthology series. Since then, a series of nails-tough albums for Rooster Blues, Alligator, Blind Pig, and a slew for the Austrian Wolf logo have fattened Slim's discography considerably. The Teardrops recently weathered a potentially devastating change when longtime second guitarist John Primer cut his own major-label debut for Code Blue, but with Slim and bass-wielding brother Nick Holt still on board, it's doubtful the quartet's overall sound will change dramatically in Primer's likely absence. —*Bill Dahl*

Highway Is My Home / Nov. 19, 1978 / Evidence ✦✦✦
Magic Slim's style is a full-speed-ahead, hard-edged, ragged one, with a deep, sometimes sloppy vocal approach and an equally cutting guitar approach. It is not pretty, flashy, pop-oriented, or even particularly appealing, but it is genuine. The stripped-down Slim sound was mostly on target throughout the 10 tracks (one bonus cut) on this late '70s date originally recorded for Black and Blue. This Evidence CD features Slim being assertive, as close to romantic as he can get, and otherwise powering straight ahead. Only on Elmore James' "The Sky Is Crying" does he sound overwhelmed, more by the song's litany (Albert King's equally transcendent version also looms in the background). Otherwise, blues for the non-crossover set. —*Ron Wynn*

Live at the Zoo Bar / 1980 / Candy Apple ✦✦
The towering guitarist and his Teardrops were only hinting at their future greatness when they cut this live set at the Zoo Bar in Nebraska. —*Bill Dahl*

Raw Magic / 1982 / Alligator ✦✦✦
A more consistent studio collection that first came out over in France and translated well to domestic consumption. Only seven titles, including Slim's lusty "Mama Talk to Your Daughter," a crowd-pleasing "Mustang Sally," and three tunes of the quartet's own making (which is rather rare with this cover-heavy combo). —*Bill Dahl*

● **Grand Slam** / 1982 / Rooster Blues ✦✦✦✦✦
Still absent from the CD shelves, this raw-boned LP captures Slim's unpretentious houserocking sound about as well as any studio set possibly could. Among its highlights: the hard shuffling "Early Every Morning," a surreal "Scuffling," and Slim's tribute to his late pal Magic Sam, "She Belongs to Me." —*Bill Dahl*

Live at B.L.U.E.S. / 1987 / B.L.U.E.S. R&B ✦✦✦✦
Captured at Chicago's intimate B.L.U.E.S. nightclub, this is surely one of the best live sets the quartet ever committed to tape. The vinyl time constraints limited the program to eight songs, but apart from a marathon "Mother Fuyer," they're not his usual standards—Chuck Willis' grinding "Keep a Drivin'," a resigned "Poor Man But a Good Man," and Slim's own "Help Yourself." —*Bill Dahl*

Gravel Road / 1990 / Blind Pig ✦✦✦
Another solid Slim set with an additional emphasis on the con-

siderable contributions of second guitarist John Primer, who handles vocals on three cuts (including covers of Otis Redding's "Hard to Handle" and Eugene Church's "Pretty Girls Everywhere"). This was a particularly potent edition of Teardrops, pounding through Slim's own title cut and "Please Don't Waste My Time" and Albert King's shuffling "Cold Women with Warm Hearts" with barroom bravado. —*Bill Dahl*

Taj Mahal (Henry Saint Clair Fredericks)
b. May 17, 1942, New York, NY
Banjo, Bass, Guitar, Piano, Vocals / Modern Acoustic Blues
Since the mid-'60s, Taj Mahal has played a vital role in the preservation of traditional blues and African-American roots music. He is a singer, songwriter, composer, and a noted musicologist who through intensive research creates authentic, rootsy compositions that, while remaining true to tradition, are still relevant to modern audiences and always bear his own unique stamp. Though he frequently ventures into different genres, Mahal's heart and soul belongs to the old-time country blues.

Born Henry Saint Clair Fredericks in New York City (but raised in Springfield, MA) to a gospel-singing South Carolinian schoolteacher and a piano-playing West Indian jazz arranger, his passion for the blues began while he was attending the University of Massachusetts in the early '60s. Though there was a folk music revival going on, many Black performers were more interested with exploring new musical venues and attempted to get away from the old ways, but for Fredericks (who claims the name Taj Mahal was inspired by a dream) the blues were anything but old hat. He fell in love with the music of such performers as T-Bone Walker. In that music he saw an important African musical tradition that represented every aspect of life. By keeping the music alive, he would be preserving the African heritage he cherished. In addition to his regular studies, Mahal began to delve into blues history. This led him to explore other forms of Black folk as well including West African music, Caribbean, and zydeco in addition to R&B, rock, and jazz. He already knew how to play the bass, but soon also learned to play the instruments used by old-time musicians including piano, acoustic guitar, banjo, mandolin, dulcimer, harmonica, and assorted flutes. Armed with new knowledge, he began playing the Boston folk circuit.

Following graduation with a BA in Agriculture in 1964, Mahal went to Los Angeles and teamed up with guitarist Ry Cooder to form the Rising Sons. The band broke up just before they were to record. Mahal made his own recording debut for Columbia in 1968 with a self-titled album. He recorded several more albums for the label through the early '70s and at the same time established himself as a popular, charismatic, yet laidback performer, known for his adventurousness, gentle wit, and intelligence. As the years have passed, Mahal has become known as a musical chameleon changing and mixing up genres to suit his current interests. He has even recorded children's albums that are anything but childish in their content. Many albums, such as *Like Never Before* (1991) contain an eclectic assortment of styles covering both old songs and his new compositions.

In addition to performing and album work, Mahal has also composed movie soundtracks *(Sounder and Sounder II)*, television scores for such shows as *The Man Who Broke a Thousand Chains*, and *Brer Rabbit.* In 1991 he composed authentic music for the Broadway production of *Mule Bone*, a Langston Hughes, Zora Neale Hurston play that had been lost since the mid-'30s. As the '90s progress, Mahal continues to contribute and add to his over 35-album discography. —*Sandra Brennan*

Taj Mahal / 1968 / Columbia ◆◆◆◆
His self-titled debut, with Ry Cooder and Jesse Ed Davis, is first and foremost. —*Mark A. Humphrey*

Natch'l Blues / 1968 / Columbia ◆◆◆◆◆
For some reason, Taj Mahal gets the back-of-the-hand treatment from a lot of blues purists. Sure, his records can get very self-indulgent, but when he turns to blues, you can hear a lot worse than Mahal. This was among his best LPs, with both strong originals and good remakes. —*Ron Wynn*

Giant Step/De Old Folks at Home / 1969 / Columbia ◆◆◆
This two-record set features one album of Delta blues that was recorded with a full electric band and one album of solo acoustic blues. The electric record is the better collection, but only by a small margin—the acoustic record suffers from poor production

that prevents a listener from completely connecting with Taj Mahal's blues. Nevertheless, there are terrific moments on both records and, on the whole, it is one of his finest albums. —*Thom Owens*

The Real Thing / 1971 / Columbia ◆◆
The Real Thing is double-live album featuring a new batch of songs as well as some old favorites augmented by, oddly enough, a four-piece tuba section. The change in arrangements may be a point of curiosity, but in the end, the album is bogged down by directionless jamming. —*AMG*

Happy Just to Be Like I Am / 1971 / Mobile Fidelity ◆◆◆◆
With *Happy Just to Be Like I Am*, Taj Mahal offers another (possibly his most effective) course in roots music, this time dabbling in Caribbean rhythms in addition to his more-or-less standard take on acoustic country blues. While his good intentions and craftsmanlike execution can't be denied, one hopes the listener will eventually decide to seek out the inspirations for these recordings. —*AMG*

Recycling the Blues & Other Related Stuff / 1972 / Mobile Fidelity ◆◆◆
The title certainly sums up the album quite well—that's exactly what Taj Mahal has been doing for several years by this point. The first side features laidback in-the-studio work with some nice gospel-inflected back-up from the Pointer Sisters. The second (and preferable) side offers a good look at Mahal's stage show. —*AMG*

Sounder / 1973 / Columbia ◆◆
On his first film score, *Sounder,* Taj Mahal mixes a handful of originals with fragmented sound effects and incidental passages. Certainly not an easy listen, this is one of his more indulgent studies. —*AMG*

Ooh So Good 'n' Blues / 1973 / Columbia ◆◆◆
Ooh So Good 'n' Blues takes a more straight-ahead approach that, with the exception of the jazzy misstep titled "Teacup's Jazzy Blues Tune," keeps the experimentation down to a minimum. As a result, this is one of his most consistently enjoyable and even albums. —*AMG*

Mo' Roots / Apr. 1974 / Columbia ◆◆◆
Mo' Roots finds Mahal stepping away from the blues, choosing instead to focus on reggae. While he can often be faulted for his all-too-academic approach, with *Mo' Roots* he turns in an album that truly expresses his appreciation and connection with the music. —*AMG*

Music Keeps Me Together / 1975 / Columbia ◆◆

Satisfied 'n Tickled Too / 1976 / Columbia ◆◆

● **Anthology, Vol. 1** / 1976 / Columbia ◆◆◆◆◆
Taj Mahal's often-indulgent experimentations have flawed most of his albums to different degrees; *The Taj Mahal Anthology, Vol. 1* rights these self-inflicted wrongs by compiling a coherent look at his early career (1966–1971). Though this collection is currently out-of-print, it provides the best introduction to his easygoing take on the blues. —*AMG*

Music Fuh Ya / 1977 / Warner Brothers ◆◆◆

Brothers / 1977 / Warner Brothers ◆◆

Evolution / 1977 / Warner Brothers ◆◆

● **The Best of Taj Mahal, Vol. 1** / 1981 / Columbia ◆◆◆◆◆
Best of Taj Mahal provides a concise career overview with a broader scope than *Anthology, Vol. 1.* —*AMG*

Taj / 1987 / Gramavision ◆◆◆

Live & Direct / 1987 / Laserlight ◆◆

Shake Sugaree / Sep. 1988 / Music For Little People ◆◆◆
Shake Sugaree is a wonderful children's album. Taj Mahal leads kids through a musical journey, taking them through the Caribbean, Africa, and the Deep South, telling stories and singing songs all the while. Some of the tracks feature a choir composed of his own children, and every song and story is not only entertaining, but educational as well. Simply a delightful record. —*Thom Owens*

Peace Is The World Smiling / 1989 / ◆◆◆
A sweet, good-natured project by Taj Mahal, Pete Seeger, Holly Near, Sweet Honey in the Rock, and many others that is directed toward world peace. Some of the tracks are bland, but it is hard to criticize the musician's intentions. Besides, there a handful of very nice songs on the album. —*Thom Owens*

Brer Rabbit And The Wonderful Tar Baby / 1990 / Windham Hill ++

Don't Call Us / 1991 / Atlantic ++

Like Never Before / Oct. 1991 / Private Music +++
After a string of children's albums and other side projects, Taj Mahal returns to his roots with *Like Never Before*—an eclectic assortment of styles featuring traditional covers and a new batch of originals. —*AMG*

Mule Bone / Nov. 1, 1991 / Gramavision +++
Taj Mahal won a Grammy nomination with this music from the Broadway production of the Hurston/Hughes play. —*Mark A. Humphrey*

Taj's Blues / Jun. 16, 1992 / Columbia/Legacy ++++
Taj's Blues is an entertainingly diverse record, featuring a variety of blues and roots-music styles, all fused together into a distinctive sound of its own. Half of the album is played on acoustic, the other with an electric band (which includes guitarists Ry Cooder and Jesse Davis on a handful of tracks), which gives a pretty good impression of the range of Mahal's talents. It's a good collection, featuring many of his best performances for Columbia, including "Statesboro Blues" and "Leaving Trunk," as well as the unreleased "East Bay Woman." —*Thom Owens*

Dancing the Blues / 1993 / Private Music +++
Taj Mahal has always been a more inclusive, eclectic musician than even some admirers understand; his work was never simply or totally blues, even though that strain was at the center and seldom far from anything he performed. That's the case with this collection, a 12-song set that includes splendid covers of Muddy Waters and Howlin' Wolf tunes, but also equally respectful, striking renditions of soul standards such as "Mockingbird," with special guest Etta James, and "That's How Strong My Love Is." There are also strong Mahal originals like "Blues Ain't Nothin'" and "Strut," with Mahal singing and playing in his wry, delicate, yet forceful way. —*Ron Wynn*

World Music / Jun. 1, 1993 / Columbia +++

Phantom Blues / Feb. 27, 1996 / Private Music ++
An eclectic bluesman would seem to be a contradiction in terms, but Taj Mahal, who has moved through the worlds of folk, rock, and pop to reach his present categorization, fits the description, and here he takes several pop and R&B oldies that came from blues roots—"Ooh Poo Pah Doo," "Lonely Avenue," "What Am I Living For?," "Let the Four Winds Blow"—and returns them to those roots. He also calls in such guest stars as Eric Clapton and Bonnie Raitt, who have more than a nodding acquaintance with the blues, to assist him. The result is progressive blues hybrid that treats the music not as a source, but as a destination. — *William Ruhlmann*

Shake It to the One . . . / Music For Little People +++
This is the only blues hero doing real children's music. Parents will like this music almost as much as their children. For ages three to eight. —*Bob Hinkle*

Harvey Mandel

b. 1945
Guitar / Modern Electric Blues
In the mold of Jeff Beck, Carlos Santana, and Mike Bloomfield, Mandel is an extremely creative rock guitarist with heavy blues and jazz influences. Like those guitarists, his vocal abilities are basically nonexistent, though Mandel, unlike some similar musicians, has always known this, and concentrated on recordings that are entirely instrumental, or feature other singers. A minor figure most known for auditioning unsuccessfully for the Rolling Stones, he recorded some intriguing (though erratic) work on his own that anticipated some of the better elements of jazz-rock fusion, showcasing his concise chops, his command of a multitude of tone pedal controls, and an eclecticism that found him working with string orchestras and country steel guitar wizards.

Mandel got his first toehold in the fertile Chicago White blues-rock scene of the mid-'60s (which cultivated talents like Paul Butterfield, Mike Bloomfield, and Steve Miller), and made his first recordings as the lead guitarist for harmonica virtuoso Charlie Musselwhite. Enticed to go solo by Blue Cheer producer Abe Kesh, Harvey cut a couple of nearly wholly instrumental albums for Phillips in the late '60s that were underground FM radio favorites, establishing him as one of the most versatile

young American guitar lions. He gained his most recognition, though, not as a solo artist, but as a lead guitarist for Canned Heat in 1969 and 1970, replacing Henry Vestine and appearing with the band at Woodstock. Shortly afterwards, he signed up for a stint in John Mayall's band, just after the British bluesman had relocated to California.

Mandel unwisely decided to use a vocalist for his third and least successful Philips album. After his term with Mayall (on *USA Union* and *Back to the Roots*) had run its course, he resumed his solo career, and also formed Pure Food & Drug Act with violinist Don "Sugarcane" Harris (from the '50s R&B duo Don & Dewey), which made several albums. In the mid-'70s, when the Rolling Stones were looking for a replacement for Mick Taylor, Mandel auditioned for a spot in the group; although he lost to Ron Wood, his guitar does appear on two cuts on the Stones' 1976 album, *Black & Blue*. Recording intermittently since then as a solo artist and a sessionman, his influence on the contemporary scene is felt via the two-handed fretboard tapping technique that he introduced on his 1973 album *Shangrenede*, later employed by Eddie Van Halen, Stanley Jordan, and Steve Vai. —*Richie Unterberger*

Cristo Redentor / 1968 / EG +++
Mandel's debut remains his best early work, introducing an accomplished blues-rock guitarist capable of producing smooth, fluid lines and a variety of tasteful distortion and buzzing via an assortment of tone pedals and customized amplifiers. He augmented his flash with an adventurous appetite for orchestrated, quasi-classical strings (especially in the eerie symphonic title cut), jazz-blues-rock fusion in the mold of The Electric Flag (as on "Before Six"), and even a bit of country in the presence of top steel guitarist Pete Drake. Available in its entirety on the reissue compilation *The Mercury Years*. —*Richie Unterberger*

Righteous / 1969 / Philips ++++
Not as consistent as his debut, due to the presence of a few pedestrian blues-rock numbers. The better tracks, though, show Mandel continuing to expand his horizons with imagination, particularly on the cuts with string and horn arrangements by noted jazz arranger Shorty Rogers. Harvey's workout on Nat Adderley's "Jazz Samba" is probably his best solo performance, and an obvious touchstone for the Latin-rock hybrid of Carlos Santana (whose own debut came out the same year); on the other side of the coin, "Boo-Bee-Doo" is one of his sharpest and snazziest straight blues-rockers. Available in its entirety on the reissue compilation *The Mercury Years*. —*Richie Unterberger*

Games Guitars Play / 1970 / Philips +++
Feeling that he needed a singer to compete commercially, Mandel decided to abandon his instrumental format, taking on multi-instrumentalist Russell Dashiel as his lead vocalist for a good share of the tracks. Alas, Dashiel was a mediocre singer who typified some of the lesser White blues-rock stylings of the period, and the material (with a higher percentage of blues and soul covers) was not up to the level of Mandel's first two efforts, although Harvey's playing remained accomplished and imaginative (as is evident on the original instrumental "Ridin' High," and the cover of Horace Silver's "Senor Blues"). Available in its entirety on the reissue compilation *The Mercury Years*. —*Richie Unterberger*

● **Baby Batter** / 1971 / Janus +++++
Fiery, jazz-influenced, blues-based rock by a former Canned Heat guitarist. —*David Szatmary*

Get Off in Chicago / 1972 / Ovation ++

The Snake / 1972 / Janus +++
Mandel shares more similarities with Jeff Beck than he's probably willing to admit. Both are stunning virtuoso guitarists who can't write consistently first-rate material or sing. Mandel's fifth album, like Beck's best '70s efforts, adds bluesy, jazzy shadings to a rock base. But *The Snake* is more firmly entrenched in blues-rock than, say, *Blow by Blow*. Harvey's playing (occasionally augmented by violinist Don "Sugarcane" Harris) is always impressive, but the compositions (all but one instrumental) aren't gripping, and, like much of the genre, meander too much. It's not as good as Mandel's late-'60s recordings for Philips, but it's still one of the better early rock-based fusion recordings. — *Richie Unterberger*

● **Mercury Years** / Oct. 24, 1995 / Mercury ✦✦✦✦✦
Double-CD reissue repackages the entire contents of his first three LPs (1968's *Cristo Redentor*, 1969's *Righteous*, 1970's *Games Guitars Play*) in their original track sequence, with extensive, informative liner notes. It could be that a more selective, single-disc distillation of the best Mercury material that weeded out the more generic blues-rock tunes would have been more effective. Still, it's a good retrospective of the early work of a somewhat overlooked '60s guitar hero, who helped lay the groundwork for the better elements of fusion and Latin-rock cross-fertilization. —*Richie Unterberger*

Martin, Bogan, & Armstrong

Group / Acoustic Blues
Only violinist, storyteller, and philosopher Howard Armstrong remains to tell of the exploits of this remarkable African-American string band. Virginia-born guitar and mandolin blues artist Carl Martin died in 1979, and guitarist Ted Bogan passed away a few years ago. But in their prime, Martin, Bogan, and Armstrong enjoyed multiple incarnations, first (in the '30s) as The Four Keys, The Tennessee Chocolate Drops, and the Wandering Troubadours. They played individually and collectively throughout the mid-South on radio, with medicine shows, and at country jukes before making it to Chicago in the late '30s and '40s, where they made records but mostly supported themselves by what Armstrong calls "pulling doors." This meant going into different cafes and taverns and playing for tips if they weren't thrown out. Playing various ethnic neighborhoods, the group took advantage of Armstrong's gift with languages and learned to sing in a variety of tongues. Best described as an acoustic string band (violin, guitar, mandolin, bass), the group played blues, jazz, pop, country, and various non-English favorites. As skilled musicians eager to earn tips by playing whatever their audiences wanted, they built a necessarily large repertoire.

After years of separation the group reunited as Martin, Bogan, & Armstrong in the early 70s and enjoyed substantial blues revival acclaim. After Carl Martin died, Bogan and Armstrong continued. When I worked with them in 1986, Bogan and Armstrong were still the greatest living exponents of the African-American string-band style, equally at home playing blues, swing, jazz, ragtime, or older Black string-band material. Armstrong, who speaks seven languages and is a painter and a sculptor, was a National Heritage Award winner in 1990. What made their music so wonderful, besides its energy and flawless presentation and their personable good humor, was their ability to remind us that good music transcends classifications and a skilled artist can draw from many streams. —*Barry Lee Pearson*

● **Martin, Bogan, & Armstrong** / Flying Fish ✦✦✦✦✦
A fine Black string band. —*Barry Lee Pearson*

That Old Gang of Mine / Flying Fish ✦✦✦
A mixed repertoire for all ethnic audiences. —*Barry Lee Pearson*

Barnyard Dance / Rounder ✦✦✦

Sara Martin

b. May 18, 1884, Louisville, KY, d. May 24, 1955, Louisville, KY
Vocals / Classic Female Blues
Known in her heyday as "the blues sensation of the West," the big-voiced Sara Martin was one of the best of the classic female blues singers of the '20s.

Martin began her career as a vaudeviller performer, switching to blues singing in the early '20s. In 1922, she began recording for Okeh Records, cutting a number of bawdy blues like "Mean Tight Mama." She continued recording until 1928. During this time, Martin became a popular performer on the southern Theater Owners' Booking Association circuits, eventually playing theaters and clubs on the east coast as well.

In the early '30s, Sara Martin retired from blues singing and settled in her hometown of Louisville, Kentucky. While she was in Louisville, she ran a nursing home and occasionally sang gospel in church. Sara Martin died after suffering a stroke in 1955. —*Cub Koda & Stephen Thomas Erlewine*

1922–1928 / Best of Blues ✦✦✦✦✦
All of Martin's best, featuring fine support from Fats Waller and Clarence Williams. —*Cub Koda*

John Mayall

b. Nov. 29, 1933, Manchester, England
Guitar, Harmonica, Keyboards, Vocals, Harmonium, Harpsichord, Organ, Piano, Tambourine, Ukulele / British Blues
The elder statesman of British blues, it is Mayall's lot to be more renowned as a bandleader and mentor than a performer in his own right. Throughout the '60s, his band, The Bluesbreakers, acted as a finishing school for the leading British blues-rock musicians of the era. Guitarists Eric Clapton, Peter Green, and Mick Taylor joined his band in a remarkable succession in the mid-'60s, honing their chops with Mayall before going on to join Cream, Fleetwood Mac, and the Rolling Stones, respectively. John McVie and Mick Fleetwood, Jack Bruce, Aynsley Dunbar, Dick Heckstall-Smith, Andy Fraser (of Free), John Almond, and Jon Mark also played and recorded with Mayall for varying lengths of times in the '60s.

Mayall's personnel have tended to overshadow his own considerable abilities. Only an adequate singer, the multi-instrumentalist was adept at bringing out the best in his younger charges (Mayall himself was in his thirties by the time The Bluesbreakers began to make a name for themselves). Doing his best to provide a context in which they could play Chicago-style electric blues, Mayall was never complacent, writing most of his own material (which ranged from good to humdrum), revamping his lineup with unnerving regularity, and constantly experimenting within his basic blues format. Some of these experiments (with jazz-rock and an album on which he played all the instruments except drums) were forgettable; others, like his foray into acoustic music in the late '60s, were quite successful. Mayall's output has caught some flak from critics for paling next to the real African-American deal, but much of his vintage work—if weeded out selectively—is quite strong, especially his legendary 1966 LP with Eric Clapton, which launched Clapton into stardom and kick-started the blues boom into full gear in England. Mayall had relocated to the United States by the beginning of the 1970s, and although he's released many albums since and remained a prodigiously busy and reasonably popular live act, little of his post-1970 output is worthy of discussion. —*Richie Unterberger*

John Mayall Plays John Mayall / Mar. 26, 1965 / Decca ✦✦✦
Recorded live at the British club Klooks Kleek in late 1964 before Clapton joined (Roger Dean plays lead guitar), this is a fine set of early British R&B with a more pronounced rock feel (akin to the Rolling Stones) than Mayall's other '60s work. Mayall wrote all but one of the songs on this overlooked but driving, highly enjoyable LP that is recommended to connisseurs of early British blues-rock. —*Richie Unterberger*

★ **Bluesbreakers with Eric Clapton** / Jul. 1966 / Deram ✦✦✦✦✦
One of the seminal blues albums of the '60s with The Bluesbreakers, capturing Clapton on a series of blues standards, after the pop leanings of The Yardbirds and before the heavy indulgence of Cream. —*William Ruhlmann*

Raw Blues / Jan. 1967 / Deram ✦✦
This is not, strictly speaking, a John Mayall album, but rather a various artists album containing among its 14 selections six recorded by Mayall, plus four tracks by Otis Spann, two by Champion Jack Dupree, and two by Curtis Jones. The three expatriate Americans had been recorded in sessions with British backup musicians, including Eric Clapton and Mayall himself. The Mayall tracks include two solo performances, one credited to the duo of Mayall and "Steve Anglo" (Steve Winwood), two pairing Mayall and Clapton, and one with Peter Green. Most of the playing is low-key blues, and Mayall holds his own with the homegrown competition. —*William Ruhlmann*

A Hard Road / Feb. 17, 1967 / Deram ✦✦✦
Eric Clapton is usually thought of as Mayall's most important right-hand man, but the case could also be made for his successor, Peter Green. The future Fleetwood Mac founder leaves a strong stamp on his only album with The Bluesbreakers, singing a few tracks and writing a couple, including the devastating instrumental "Supernatural." Green's use of thick sustain on this track clearly pointed the way to his use of this feature on Fleetwood Mac's hits "Albatross" and "Black Magic Woman," as well as providing a blueprint for Carlos Santana's style. Mayall acquaints himself fairly well on this mostly original set (with

occasional guest horns), though some of the material is fairly mundane. Highlights include the uncharacteristically rambunctious "Leaping Christine" and the cover of Freddie King's "Someday After a While (You'll Be Sorry)." *—Richie Unterberger*

Crusade / Sep. 1, 1967 / London ✦✦✦✦✦
The personnel changes in John Mayall's Bluesbreakers continued on his fourth album, and although Mayall had vowed not to, he had added two permanent horn players. Perhaps because he was putting out his second album within a year, Mayall wasn't able to fill up the record with his own compositions and turned to blues standards, which certainly didn't hurt the record overall. Mayall's heroes included Buddy Guy, Otis Rush, Freddie King, and Sonny Boy Williamson, and he did them proud. The album became his third straight U.K. Top Ten and, following The Bluesbreakers' first U.S. tour in the summer of 1967, his first charting album in America. *—William Ruhlmann*

The Blues Alone / Nov. 1967 / Deram ✦✦✦
The Blues Alone was the first Mayall "solo" album (without The Bluesbreakers). Mayall played and overdubbed all instruments except drums, which were handled by Bluesbreaker Keef Hartley. It also tried to serve notice that, despite his band being a spawning ground for several British stars by now, the real star of the group was its leader. But it didn't quite prove that, since Mayall, while certainly competent on harmonica, keyboards, and guitars, doesn't display the flair of an Eric Clapton or Peter Green, and the overdubbing, as is so often the case, robs the recording of any real sense of interplay. *—William Ruhlmann*

Blues from Laurel Canyon / 1968 / Deram ✦✦✦
This release has a couple of nice passages, but the album suffers from poor songwriting and indulgent solos, both from Mayall and his newly acquired L.A. sidemen. *—Thom Owens*

Bare Wires / Jun. 21, 1968 / Deram ✦✦✦
Bare Wires was the first Bluesbreakers album of new studio material since *A Hard Road*, released 16 months before. In that time, the band had turned over entirely, expanding to become a septet. Mayall's musical conception had also expanded—the album began with a 23-minute "Bare Wires Suite," which included more jazz influences than usual and featured introspective lyrics. In retrospect, all of this is a bit indulgent, but at the time it helped Mayall out of what had come to seem a blues straitjacket (although he would eventually return to a strict blues approach). It isn't surprising that he dropped the "Bluesbreakers" name after this release. (The album was Mayall's most successful ever in the U.K., hitting number 3.) *—William Ruhlmann*

The Turning Point / 1969 / Deram ✦✦✦✦✦
Recorded just after Mick Taylor departed for the Stones, Mayall eliminated drums entirely on this live recording. With mostly acoustic guitars and John Almond on flutes and sax, Mayall and his band, as his typically overblown liner notes state, "explore seldom-used areas within the framework of low-volume music." But it does work. The all-original material is flowing and melodic, with long jazzy grooves that don't lose sight of their bluesy underpinnings. Lyrically, Mayall stretches out a bit into social comment on "The Laws Must Change" on this fine, meditative mood album. *—Richie Unterberger*

Looking Back / Aug. 1969 / Deram ✦✦✦
Reasonably interesting collection of non-LP singles from 1964 to 1968, featuring almost all of the notable musicians that passed through The Bluesbreakers throughout the decade. "Sitting In The Rain" (with Peter Green) showcases fine fingerpicking, the haunting "Jenny" is one of Mayall's best originals, and "Stormy Monday" is one of the few cuts from the 1966 lineup that briefly featured both Eric Clapton and Jack Bruce. The rest is largely passably pleasant and doesn't rank among Mayall's finest work. *—Richie Unterberger*

Empty Rooms / 1970 / Polydor ✦✦✦
This was John Mayall's studio-recorded followup to the live *The Turning Point*, featuring the same drumless quartet of himself, guitarist Jon Mark, reed player Johnny Almond, and bassist Steve Thompson. Mayall was at a commercial and critical peak with this folk-jazz approach; the album's lead-off track, "Don't Waste My Time," had become his sole singles chart entry prior to the LP's release, and although his former label, London, confused matters by releasing the two-year-old *Diary of a Band, Vol. 1* in the U.S. just before this new album appeared in early 1970, the new crop of fans he'd found with *The Turning Point* stuck

with him on this gentle, reflective release. *Empty Rooms* hit number 33 in the U.S.; in the U.K. it got to number nine. *—William Ruhlmann*

USA Union / Jul. 1970 / Polydor ✦✦
John Mayall's *Turning Point* band—Jon Mark, Johnny Almond, and Steve Thompson—broke up in June 1970 after a European tour. Mayall then assembled his first all-American band and recorded this album in July. It had more drive than the previous outfit, and Mayall turned to environmentalism on the leadoff track, "Nature's Disappearing." But much of his low-volume, reflective approach remained on an album that was still more of a jazz-pop outing than the blues sessions of his early career. *USA Union* had the highest U.S. chart peak of his career, hitting number 22. But in the U.K., where its title confirmed Mayall's U.S. leanings, the album showed a big dropoff from his usual sales. *—William Ruhlmann*

Back to the Roots / 1971 / Polydor ✦✦✦
For this double LP, recorded in November, 1970, John Mayall gathered together prominent musicians who had played in his bands during the past several years, including Sugarcane Harris, Eric Clapton, Johnny Almond, Harvey Mandel, Keef Hartley, and Mick Taylor. Mayall's compositions aren't all that impressive, but the sidemen frequently shine, especially Clapton. *Back To The Roots* hit number 52 in the U.S. and number 31 in the U.K., where it was Mayall's final album to reach the charts. It was reissued in altered form under the title *Archives to Eighties* in 1988. (See separate entry.) *—William Ruhlmann*

Thru the Years / 1971 / Deram ✦✦✦✦✦
A grab-bag of rare tracks from the '60s, some of which stand among Mayall's finest. His debut 1964 single "Crawling up a Hill" is one of his best originals; this comp also includes a couple of 1964–65 flipsides that were never otherwise issued in the U.S. The eight songs featuring Peter Green include some topnotch material that outpaces much of the only album recorded by the Green lineup (*A Hard Road*), particularly the Green originals "Missing You" and "Out of Reach," a great B-side with devastating, icy guitar lines, and downbeat lyrics that ranks as one of the great lost blues-rock cuts of the '60s. The set is filled out with a few songs from the Mick Taylor era, the highlight being the vicious instrumental "Knockers Step Forward." Look for the CD reissue and not the early-'70s double U.S. album of the same name, which includes a lot of superfluous material and omits the three 1964–65 songs from British 45s. *—Richie Unterberger*

Memories / Dec. 1971 / Polydor ✦✦✦
Having gone *Back To The Roots*, John Mayall returned to his forward-looking musical explorations with 1971's *Memories*, the true followup to *USA Union*, on which he retained bassist Larry Taylor, replaced Harvey Mandel with guitarist Jerry McGee of The Ventures, and dropped Sugarcane Harris, for an unusually small trio session. Actually, he was still looking back on a set of autobiographical lyrics about growing up, starting with the title track, and including "Grandad," and "Back From Korea." (Forced to compete with the simultaneous release of the London Records compilation *Thru The Years*, *Memories* managed to reach only number 179 in the U.S. charts.) *—William Ruhlmann*

Ten Years Are Gone / 1973 / Polydor ✦✦✦
Mayall returned to the studio in 1973 for this double album. The ten years Mayall had in mind, of course, were the previous ten, which had seen him start as a local musician in Manchester, England, and emerge a decade, almost two dozen albums, and nearly as many lineups later with an evolved jazz-blues style and an international following. The album allows the ensemble considerable room to solo on Mayall's typically simple, blues-based song structures, and the approach is perhaps excessively casual. The second LP is a live date recorded at the Academy of Music in New York, and here things stretch out even more: "Harmonica Free Form" clocks in at 12 minutes and "Dark of the Night" runs 17:41. *—William Ruhlmann*

Latest Edition / 1974 / Polydor ✦✦✦
The title makes a virtue of necessity, as John Mayall introduces another all-new lineup (actually, bassist Larry Taylor is returning from an older edition). Two guitarists, Hightide Harris and Randy Resnick, lead the band in more of an uptempo R&B style than has been used in much of Mayall's music during the past several years, starting with the timely "Gasoline Blues" (1974 was the year of the gas lines, remember?) and going on to

"Troubled Times" (which advises impeaching President Nixon). Still, this was a lackluster set, which is only appropriate since it was Mayall's swan song with Polydor, and the album became his first to miss the charts in the U.S. since 1967. —*William Ruhlmann*

Primal Solos / 1977 / Deram ♦♦
Fuzzy live tapes from 1966 and 1968 of dubious quality, in both sonics and performance. Side one has Clapton on lead and Bruce on bass on familiar Chicago blues standards by the likes of John Lee Hooker, Willie Dixon, and Sonny Boy Williamson. Side two is from a couple of 1968 gigs with Mick Taylor, with three lengthy tracks that have little to recommend them. For fanatics only. —*Richie Unterberger*

Last of the British Blues / 1978 / One Way ♦♦♦
This was the last of the six albums John Mayall originally made for Blue Thumb/ABC Records between 1975 and 1978, about which he has said, "ABC released six of my albums as a tax write-off. A week after they were released you couldn't find them in any store." It's a live album on which Mayall fronts a quartet consisting of guitarist James Quill Smith (who sings lead on several songs), bassist Steve Thompson, and drummer Soko Richardson. The approach is rock-oriented, and the set list includes such Bluesbreakers favorites as Mose Allison's "Parchman Farm" and Freddie King's "Hideaway" (taken at a frantic tempo), along with the usual complement of generic Mayall originals, among them, a remake of "The Bear" from *Blues From Laurel Canyon.* —*William Ruhlmann*

Behind the Iron Curtain / 1985 / GNP ♦♦
On his first new album in four years (and first new U.S. release in seven years), John Mayall reclaims the "Bluesbreakers" name for the first time in 18 years to highlight a quintet featuring two lead guitarists, Coco Montoya and Walter Trout, along with a rhythm section of Bobby Haynes (bass) and Joe Yuele (drums). The album was recorded in concert in Hungary in June, 1985, and takes a fairly bluesy approach with lots of space for the guitarists to shine, a format similar to that of The Bluesbreakers lineups of 1965–1968. Sound quality is only fair, and this is not an inspired performance, but Mayall has latched onto a cohesive unit here, and the results are encouraging for the future. —*William Ruhlmann*

The Collection / 1986 / Castle ♦♦♦♦
This two-LP set is a compilation of John Mayall's Decca recordings, 1964–1968. It's a good, 22-track selection starting with songs from The Bluesbreakers album that featured Eric Clapton and pulling selections from other notable albums and from Mayall singles. This was a prolific period for the bandleader, and he is well-served by a coherent best-of that highlights his own compositions and some significant covers. —*William Ruhlmann*

Some of My Best Friends are Blues / 1986 / Decal/Charly ♦♦♦
The title is a giveaway that this compilation of John Mayall's Decca recordings of 1966–1967 is devoted to cover versions of blues standards rather than his own compositions. A thematically consistent set, it gathers together tracks from singles and EPs as well as relying heavily on Mayall's *Crusade* album, which was intended to showcase the blues masters. Four of the 11 tracks come from that album, and they include songs like "Oh, Pretty Woman" and "I Can't Quit You Baby." The guitar playing is by Peter Green, who provides some biting blues runs. —*William Ruhlmann*

Chicago Line / Aug. 1988 / Island ♦♦
John Mayall's first new studio album to be released in the U.S. in more than a decade shows that his current crop of Bluesbreakers—Coco Montoya, Walter Trout, Bobby Haynes, and Joe Yuele—who have been together longer than any previous outfit, play like a seasoned blues band, sparking each other (especially guitarists Montoya and Trout), and never falling into complacency. Mayall presides over the music without dominating it, which makes The Bluesbreakers more of a group than they've been since the '60s. —*William Ruhlmann*

Crocodile Walk / 1990 / Lost Rose ♦♦
Pretty fair, if hardly revelatory, compilation of 1965–67 BBC sessions with Mayall's best lineups, variously featuring Roger Dean, Eric Clapton, and Peter Green on guitar. A few of the songs ("Cheating Woman," "Nowhere To Run," "Bye Bye Bird") were never recorded officially by Mayall during this period. Clapton actually doesn't shine particularly brightly on the few tracks that feature his playing, but the fidelity is good and the material pretty strong. The three closing tracks, recorded live with Mick Taylor in 1968, are a waste: lousy sound, tedious jamming. —*Richie Unterberger*

A Sense of Place / Mar. 1990 / Island ♦♦♦
A Sense Of Place represents Mayall's full-fledged return to major-label record-making, with all the good and bad things that implies, from a high-profile producer, R.S. Field, to the introduction of such cover material as Wilbert Harrison's "Let's Work Together" and J.J. Cale's "Sensitive Kind." Field uses a spare production style, light on atmosphere and heavy on unusual percussion. This makes for an identifiable sound, to be sure, but you can't help thinking that it isn't what The Bluesbreakers sound like on a good night in a small club. The result, as intended, was Mayall's first chart appearance in 15 years, but as a commercial comeback, the record ultimately failed. —*William Ruhlmann*

● **London Blues (1964–1969)** / 1992 / PolyGram ♦♦♦♦♦
Featuring forty tracks over two discs, *London Blues* is an excellent collection of most of the best moments from Mayall and the Bluesbreakers' early recordings, a time when Eric Clapton, Peter Green, and Mick Taylor all passed through the band. —*Stephen Thomas Erlewine*

Room to Move (1969–1974) / 1992 / Polydor ♦♦♦♦♦
The majority of Mayall and The Bluesbreakers' best material from the early '70s is collected on this 29-track, double-disc set. Although Clapton appears on a couple of songs, the playing on *Room to Move* isn't as universally breathtaking as it is on *London Blues*, but the collection is thoroughly listenable, and it does feature many fine musicians. —*Stephen Thomas Erlewine*

Wake Up Call / 1993 / Jive/Novus ♦♦♦
Fuelled by Coco Montoya's searing but economical string-slashing, drummer Joe Yuele, and bassist Rick Cortes, John Mayall has managed to keep a stable core of Bluesbreakers together in recent years. Mayall rarely does the same album twice, and *Wake Up Call* finds him returning to a basic, physical sound after 1990's more progressive/highly produced *A Sense Of Place*. The harp whiz has rarely flirted with the pop charts over the decades, a track record that will likely handicap the title track—a potential hit featuring guest vocalist Mavis Staples and some take-charge riffing from former mate Mick Taylor. For pure guitar joy though, Montoya turns the trick all on his own with barnburners "Loaded Dice" and "Nature's Disappearing". —*Roch Parisien*

Percy Mayfield

b. Aug. 12, 1920, Minden, LA, d. Aug. 11, 1984, Los Angeles, CA
Piano, Vocals / West Coast Blues
A masterful songwriter whose touching blues ballad "Please Send Me Someone to Love," a multi-layered universal lament, was a number one R&B hit in 1950, Percy Mayfield had the world by the tail until a horrific 1952 auto wreck left him facially disfigured. That didn't stop the poet laureate of the blues from writing in prolific fashion, though. As Ray Charles' favorite scribe during the '60s, he handed the Genius such gems as "Hit the Road, Jack" and "At the Club."

Like so many of his postwar L.A. contemporaries, Mayfield got his musical start in Texas but moved to the coast during the war. Surmising that Jimmy Witherspoon might like to perform a tune he'd penned called "Two Years of Torture," Mayfield targeted Supreme Records as a possible buyer for his song. But the bosses at Supreme liked his own gentle reading so much that they insisted he wax it himself in 1947 with an all-star band that included saxist Maxwell Davis, guitarist Chuck Norris, and pianist Willard McDaniel.

Art Rupe's Specialty logo signed Mayfield in 1950 and scored a solid string of R&B smashes over the next couple of years. "Please Send Me Someone to Love" and its equally potent flip "Strange Things Happening" were followed in the charts by "Lost Love," "What a Fool I Was," "Prayin' for Your Return," "Cry Baby," and "Big Question," cementing Mayfield's reputation as a blues balladeer of the highest order. Davis handled sax duties on most of Mayfield's Specialty sides as well. Mayfield's lyrics were usually as insightfully downbeat as his tempos; he was a true master at expressing his innermost feelings, laced with vulnerability and pathos (his "Life Is Suicide" and "The River's Invitation" are two prime examples).

Even though his touring was drastically curtailed after the accident, Mayfield hung in there as a Specialty artist through 1954, switching to Chess in 1955–56 and Imperial in 1959.

Charles proved thankful enough for Mayfield's songwriting genius to sign him to his Tangerine logo in 1962; over the next five years, the singer waxed a series of inexorably classy outings, many with Brother Ray's band (notably "My Jug and I" in 1964 and "Give Me Time to Explain" the next year).

It's a rare veteran blues artist indeed who hasn't taken a whack at one or more Mayfield copyrights. Mayfield himself persisted into the '70s, scoring minor chart items for RCA and Atlantic while performing on a limited basis until his 1984 death. —Bill Dahl

My Jug and I / 1962 / Tangerine ✦✦✦✦✦
Mayfield's gentle vocal delivery and the big, brassy sound of Ray Charles' orchestra were a match made in heaven. Mayfield brought some first-class material to this party (which begs for CD reissue): "My Jug and I," "Stranger in My Own Home Town" (later covered by Elvis Presley), the untypically jumping "Give Me Time to Explain," and a handful of Specialty remakes. —Bill Dahl

Bought Blues / 1969 / Tangerine ✦✦✦✦
Another elegant, beautifully arranged collection fraught with brilliant, sometimes heartbreaking material: "Ha Ha in the Daytime," "We Both Must Cry," "My Bottle Is My Companion." —Bill Dahl

★ **Poet of the Blues** / 1990 / Specialty ✦✦✦✦✦
The insightful songwriting skills of this West Coaster were matched by his wry, plaintive vocal delivery (Mayfield was usually his own best interpreter). The 25 sides here date from his hit-laden 1950–1954 stay at Art Rupe's Specialty logo and include his univesal lament "Please Send Me Someone to Love," the resolutely downbeat "Strange Things Happening" and "Lost Love," and an ironic "The River's Invitation." Saxman Maxwell Davis led the horn-powered combos providing sympathetic support behind Mayfield. —Bill Dahl

Memory Pain / Specialty ✦✦✦✦✦
Twenty-five more nuggets from the voluminous Specialty vaults, including alternate takes of some of his biggest smashes, a plethora of unissued stuff, both sides of his 1957 single for the firm that showed him coping subtly with the rocking changes sweeping the R&B world, and ending with a 1960 demo of his classic "Hit the Road, Jack." —Bill Dahl

For Collectors Only / Specialty ✦✦✦
As the title suggests, this gives a deeper look at Mayfield's early career. Alternate takes and unissued material are included. —Hank Davis

Jerry McCain

b. Jun. 18, 1930, Gadsden, AL
Guitar, Harmonica, Vocals, Drums, Trumpet, Jew's Harp / Modern Electric Blues

Not only is Alabama-born Jerry McCain a terrific amplified harpist, he's also one of the funniest songwriters working the genre. Has been for more than four decades, as anyone who's dug his out-of-control 1950s Excello rockers "My Next Door Neighbor" and "Trying to Please" will gladly testify.

Little Walter was McCain's main man on harp, an instrument McCain began playing at age five. Walter passed through Gadsden one fateful night in 1953 with his Aces, offering encouragement and a chance to jam at a local nightpot. That same year, "Boogie" McCain made his vinyl debut for Lillian McMurry's Trumpet label in Jackson, MS, with "East of the Sun"/"Wine-O-Wine." His brother Walter played drums on the sides. McCain's 1954 Trumpet encore, "Stay Out of Automobiles"/"Love to Make Up," was solid Southern blues but barely hinted at the galvanic energy of his subsequent output.

Jerry McCain signed with Ernie Young's Nashville-based Excello logo in 1955, cutting "That's What They Want" with his usual sidekick, Christopher Collins, on guitar. "Run, Uncle John! Run," "Trying to Please," the torrid "My Next Door Neighbor" (a prior homemade demo version of the track that surfaced much later was even crazier)," and "The Jig's Up" ranked with McCain's best 1955–57 Excello efforts.

The harpist is probably best-known for his two-sided 1960 gem for Rex Records, "She's Tough"/"Steady." The Fabulous Thunderbirds later appropriated the insinuating mid-tempo A-side, while McCain's harp chops were strikingly showcased on

the flip. McCain waxed three 45s for Okeh in Nashville in 1962, utilizing Music Row mainstays Floyd Cramer, Grady Martin, and Boots Randolph as his backup for "Red Top" and "Jet Stream." A series of 1965–68 sides for Stan Lewis' Shreveport-based Jewel Records included a tailor-made tribute to the company, "728 Texas (Where the Action Is)" (Jewel's address).

After too many years spent in relative obscurity, McCain rejuvenated his fortunes in 1989 by signing with Ichiban Records and waxing a series of outings that displayed both his irreverent wit and a social conscience rare on the contemporary circuit. —Bill Dahl

Blues 'n' Stuff / 1967 / Ichiban ✦✦✦
There's nothing aboard this okay outing that would suggest how amazing McCain's early work for Trumpet, Excello, and Rex was. —Bill Dahl

Strange Kind of Feelin' / 1990 / Acoustic Archives ✦✦✦
These are McCain's earliest sides, cut in 1953 and 1954 for Lillian McMurray's Trumpet label in Jackson, Mississippi. Both sides of his two Trumpet 78s plus the addition of three previously unissued tracks make up his total output for the label, so the collection is filled out with five tracks by Tiny Kennedy, plus two by pianist Clayton Love. Although longtime axeman Christopher Collins is well to the fore on these tracks, McCain's harp is somewhat underrecorded, giving a lopsided effect to the music. But minor gems like "Stay Out Of Automobiles," "Fall Guy," "Middle Of The Night," and "Crazy 'Bout That Mess" are all sign pointers to the Excello material and make this a collection well worth seeking out. —Cub Koda

Struttin' My Stuff / 1992 / Ichiban ✦✦✦
Alabaman Jerry McCain is a veteran of the blues and in fact recorded for the Trumpet label in Jackson, MS, at the same time as Elmore James and Sonny Boy Williamson. As one would expect, his harp work is both traditional and solid. Although original, his instrumental style bears resemblance to the work of past masters—The Sonny Boys and The Walters—while his original lyrics reflect modern life. This is a fine set of funky, urban blues—a standout from the Ichiban catalogue. —Larry Hoffman

Love Desperado / 1992 / Ichiban ✦✦✦
The Alabama harpist's contemporary releases for Ichiban are certainly competent, but that insane energy level that marked his Excello output of the '50s is ancient history—and so too, for the most part, is the gleeful irreverence that made his early sides such a delight. —Bill Dahl

I've Got the Blues All over Me / 1993 / Wild Dog ✦✦✦

That's What They Want: The Best Of Jerry McCain / 1995 / AVI-Excello ✦✦✦✦
McCain has always marched to the beat of a different drummer and the proof of it is right here, 23 recordings that define the place where the blues and rock & roll meet at the end of a dark alley. The first 12 tracks are McCain's complete singles output for Excello Records, the sides upon which most of his reputation rests. From the cold hearted bravado of the the title track to the rocking insanity of "Trying To Please," this music is as special as it comes. The following 11 tracks come from homemade demo tapes circa.1955 that were cut in Jerry's living room with a single mike, one track home tape recorder. Featuring grinding, massively distorted guitars, crashing drums and lyrical texts concerning themselves with going crazy to rock & roll, rock & roll as salvation ("Rock & Roll Ball," "Geronimo's Rock"), or going crazy from outside worldly pressures ("Bell In My Heart," "My Next Door Neighbors"), these masterpieces answer the musical question: what would a rock & roll album by Little Walter have sounded like? —AMG

Cash McCall (Morris Dollison, Jr.)

b. Jan. 28, 1941, New Madrid, MO
Guitar, Vocals / Modern Electric Blues

Guitarist Cash McCall has segued from gospel to soul to blues over a distinguished career spanning more than three decades. Born Morris Dollison, Jr., he found that the best way to exit his rural existence was to enlist in the Army. After completing his hitch, he relocated in Chicago (where his family lived for a time when he was a child). Gospel was Dollison's initial passion—he sang with the Gospel Songbirds (he also played guitar with the group, recording with them for Excello in 1964 with fellow future R&B hitmaker Otis Clay singing lead) and the Pilgrim Jubilee Singers.

He waxed his first secular single, the two-part workout "Earth Worm," for One-derful Records' M-Pac! subsidiary in 1963 as Maurice Dollison. In 1966, he made a demo of a soul number called "When You Wake Up" that he had penned with producer Monk Higgins. He was doubtless shocked to learn of its subsequent release on the Thomas label, billed to one Cash McCall! The tune proved a national R&B hit, sending the newly christened McCall on the road with Dick Clark's Caravan of Stars (others on the bill: Lou Christie and Mitch Ryder).

Similarly tasty R&B follow-ups for Thomas and Checker failed to hit the same commercial heights. McCall was a valuable session guitarist and composer at Chess, learning the business end of his trade from Chess in-house legend Willie Dixon. McCall's blues leanings grew more prominent during the next decade. He cut an LP for Paula in 1973 called *Omega Man* before relocating to L.A. in 1976, his ties to Dixon growing ever stronger. McCall co-produced Dixon's Grammy-winning *Hidden Charms* in 1988 and worked as a sideman with Dixon's band, the All-Stars. McCall currently tours as a solo blues artist. *—Bill Dahl*

No More Doggin' / 1983 / Evidence ◆◆◆
While he rightfully earned his share of renown on the Chicago soul scene of the 1960s as a writer/producer/singer/sideman, guitarist McCall has re-invented himself as a bluesman in recent years. This 1983 outing blends both genres on a predominantly original set (the lone cover is an update of Rosco Gordon's "No More Doggin'"). *—Bill Dahl*

● **Cash Up Front** / 1987 / Stony Plain ◆◆◆◆◆
An excellent, varied blues and R&B album, it has ten original compositions. Top-notch session musicians give this the sheen of studio perfection rather than bar-band rawness. Yet McCall can still get down in the alley, as he does on the cheatin' story "Girlfriend, Women, and Wife." *—Niles J. Frantz*

Tommy McClennan

b. Apr. 8, 1908, Yazoo City, MS, **d.** Chicago, IL
Guitar, Vocals / Acoustic Delta Blues
A gravel-throated back-country blues growler from the Mississippi Delta, McClennan was part of the last wave of downhome blues guitarists to record for the major labels in Chicago. His rawboned 1939–1942 Bluebird recordings were no-frills excursions into the blues bottoms. He left a powerful legacy that included "Bottle It Up and Go," "Cross Cut Saw Blues," "Deep Blue Sea Blues" (aka "Catfish Blues"), and others whose lasting power has been evidenced through the repertoires and re-recordings of other artists. Admirers of McClennan's blues would do well to check out the 1941–1942 Bluebird sessions of Robert Petway, a McClennan associate who performed in a similar, but somewhat more lyrical vein. McClennan never recorded again and reportedly died destitute in Chicago; blues researchers have yet to even trace the date or circumstances of his death. *—Jim O'Neal*

★ **Travelin' Highway Man** / 1990 / Travelin' Man ◆◆◆◆◆
Paint-peelin' Delta blues, 1939-1942. *—Jas Obrecht*

Tommy McClennan (1939–1942) / Travelin' Man ◆◆◆◆◆

Tommy McClennan, Cotton Patch Blues, 1939–1942 / Travelin' Man ◆◆◆

Delta Blues in Chicago, Mississippi Country Blues, V. 2 / Document ◆◆◆

Delbert McClinton

b. Nov. 4, 1940
Harmonica, Vocals / Modern Electric Blues
A Texas music institution, McClinton honed his musical chops to razor sharpness as a teenage harmonica man learning firsthand from blues legends traveling through the area. His harp work on Bruce Channel's hit, "Hey Baby," got him on the big time circuit, making it over to tour England and eventually giving harmonica lessons to a young John Lennon. Much behind-the-scenes work throughout the '60s ensued with McClinton fronting the Rondells, who hit the Hot 100 with "If You Really Want Me To, I'll Go." He hit the charts again in the '70s with Glen Clark as Delbert & Glen. Around this period, McClinton's songs started getting covered by country acts, Waylon Jennings and Emmylou Harris both having hits with his material. The Blues Brothers

used his "B-Movie Box Car Blues" on their first album and their hit movie. He has released idiosyncratic solo efforts up to the present time and guested on albums with everyone from Roy Buchanan to Bonnie Raitt. A Texas music treasure, we've not heard the last of Delbert McClinton. *—Cub Koda*

Second Wind / 1978 / Mercury ◆◆◆
McClinton lays on the grease with two great originals, "B Movie" and "Maybe Someday Baby" (featuring a wailing support vocal by Clydie King). Also included is a decent collection of covers ("Spoonful" and "Big River"). *—Rick Clark*

● **The Best of Delbert McClinton** / 1989 / Curb ◆◆◆◆◆
This adequate overview contains mostly familiar material but lacks the cohesiveness of his best early albums. *—Rick Clark*

Honky Tonkin' [Alligator] / 1989 / Alligator ◆◆◆

Live from Austin / 1989 / Alligator ◆◆◆
This rock-solid, gritty roadhouse R&B is performed with a no nonsense spirit. *—Rick Clark*

Never Been Rocked Enough / 1992 / Curb ◆◆◆
One of those influential "musician's musician" types, vocalist/harpplayer Delbert McClinton was able to call on the likes of Bonnie Raitt, Tom Petty, and Melissa Etheridge for support on *Never Been Rocked Enough.* The results cover the whole checkerboard while remaining vintage McClinton: his harp wails on "Everytime I Roll the Dice;" "Can I Change My Mind" flirts with Motown soul; "Blues As Blues Can Get" defines the confessional blues ballad; "I Used To Worry" and the title track chug into Band/Little Feat territory. The disc also includes the performer's Grammy winning duet with Bonnie Raitt, "Good Man, Good Woman." *—Roch Parisien*

Jimmy McCracklin

b. Aug. 13, 1921, St. Louis, MO
Piano, Vocals / Electric West Coast Blues
More than a half-century from when he started out in the blues business, Jimmy McCracklin is still touring, recording, and acting like a much younger man. In fact, he vehemently disputes his commonly accepted birthdate—but since he began recording back in 1945, it seems reasonable.

McCracklin grew up in Missouri, his main influence on piano being Walter Davis (little Jimmy's dad introduced him to the veteran pianist). McCracklin was also a promising pugilist, but the blues eventually emerged victorious. After a stint in the Navy during World War II, he bid St. Louis adieu and moved to the West Coast, making his recorded debut for the Globe logo with "Miss Mattie Left Me" in 1945. On that platter, J.D. Nicholson played piano; most of McCracklin's output found him handling his own 88s.

McCracklin recorded for a daunting array of tiny labels in Los Angeles and Oakland prior to touching down with Modern in 1949-50, Swing Time the next year, and Peacock in 1952-54. Early in his recording career, McCracklin had Robert Kelton on guitar, but by 1951, Lafayette "Thing" Thomas was installed as the searing guitarist with McCracklin's Blues Blasters and remained invaluable to the pianist into the early '60s.

By 1954, the pianist was back with the Bihari brothers' Modern logo and really coming into his own with a sax-driven sound. "Couldn't Be a Dream" was hilariously surreal, McCracklin detailing his night out with a woman sent straight from hell, while a 1955 session found him doubling credibly on harp.

A series of sessions for Bay Area producer Bob Geddins' Irma label in 1956 (many of which later turned up on Imperial) preceded McCracklin's long-awaited first major hit. Seldom had he written a simpler song than "The Walk," a rudimentary dance number with a good groove that Checker Records put on the market in 1958. It went Top Ten on both the R&B and pop charts, and McCracklin was suddenly rubbing elbows with Dick Clark on network TV.

The nomadic pianist left Chess after a few more 45s, pausing at Mercury (where he cut a torrid "Georgia Slop" in 1959, later revived by Big Al Downing) before returning to the hit parade with the tough R&B workout "Just Got to Know" in 1961 for Art-Tone Records. A similar follow-up, "Shame, Shame, Shame," also did well for him the next year. Those sides eventually resurfaced on Imperial, where he hit twice in 1965 with "Every Night, Every Day" (later covered by Magic Sam) and the uncompromising "Think" and with "My Answer" in 1966.

McCracklin's songwriting skills shouldn't be overlooked as an integral factor in his enduring success. He penned the funky "Tramp" for guitarist Lowell Fulson and watched his old pal take it to the rarified end of the R&B lists in 1967, only to be eclipsed by a sassy duet cover by Stax stalwarts Otis Redding and Carla Thomas a few months later. Ever the survivor, McCracklin made a string of LPs for Imperial, even covering "These Boots Are Made for Walkin'" in 1966, and segued into the soul era totally painlessly.

Two recent discs for Bullseye Blues prove that McCracklin still packs a knockout punch from behind his piano—no matter what his birth certificate says. —*Bill Dahl*

Twist With / 1961 / Crown ✦✦✦✦
Undoubtedly it was a mite difficult to twist to jump blues records from the mid-'50s, but this budget LP at least gave McCracklin's Modern catalog renewed life in the Crown catalog. Some of his best 1950s rockers: the hilarious "Couldn't Be a Dream," "You Don't Seem to Understand," "Reelin' and Rockin'," "I'm Gonna Tell Your Mother." Overdue for CD reissue. —*Bill Dahl*

I Just Gotta Know / 1961 / Imperial ✦✦✦✦✦
It's always a "Shame, Shame, Shame" (to quote one of this LP's best numbers) when a 35-year-old slab of vinyl must be cited as what may be an artist's finest collection—but since no one has yet touched McCracklin's massive '60s Imperial catalog for CD reissue, here you go! Contains his definitive soul-tinged ballad "Just Got to Know," the Amos Milburn-derived jump blues "Club Savoy," and several more late-'50s rockers that Imperial acquired from various small concerns after he began to hit with regularity. —*Bill Dahl*

Jimmy McCracklin Sings / 1961 / MCA/Chess ✦✦✦✦✦
Great late-'50s rocking R&B. —*Bill Dahl*

Everynight Everyday / 1965 / Imperial ✦✦✦✦
Another vintage LP by the ex-boxer that's well worth the search. Along with the hit title track, there's a remake of "The Walk," his sturdy "Looking for a Woman," and an energetic "Let's Do It All." —*Bill Dahl*

Think / 1965 / Imperial ✦✦✦✦
There's a ton of great McCracklin material patiently awaiting reissue—this LP boasts the infectious title item, a sinuous "Steppin' Up in Class," and a driving "My Best Friend," for starters. —*Bill Dahl*

● **My Answer** / 1966 / Imperial ✦✦✦✦✦
Conveniently enough, Imperial slapped together what amounts to a greatest-hits set here, and it serves as the best available introduction to the pianist's '60s catalog. Contains "Just Got to Know," "Every Night, Every Day," "Think," "Steppin' Up in Class," and the title item—every one of them occupying an intriguing island midway between blues and soul. —*Bill Dahl*

High on the Blues / 1971 / Stax ✦✦✦
Given that this was co-produced by Al Jackson (of Booker T. & the MGs) and Willie Mitchell (of Hi Records), and adds embellishment by the Memphis Horns, it's unsurprising that this is very much a soul-blues record. It's a workmanlike effort with an early-'70s Stax period feel, including remakes of two of his past R&B singles, "Think" and "Just Got to Know." The CD reissue adds a couple of previously unreleased bonus tracks. —*Richie Unterberger*

My Story / 1991 / Bullseye Blues ✦✦✦✦✦

Jimmy McCracklin: The Mercury Recordings / 1992 / Bear Family ✦✦✦✦
McCracklin's liaison with Mercury was relatively brief, from late 1958 to the fall of 1960, and Bear Family has only managed to locate 13 songs for this CD. But it's a rewarding chapter in the pianist's endlessly nomadic recording career, featuring his original dance tunes "Georgia Slop" and "Let's Do It (The Chicken Scratch)," a New Orleans-cut cover of Johnny Cash's "Folsom Prison Blues," and some smoothly arranged (by Clyde Otis, Brook Benton's collaborator) pop/R&B outings that suggest Mercury had big plans for McCracklin that never quite panned out. —*Bill Dahl*

Taste Of The Blues / 1994 / Bullseye Blues ✦✦✦
Now these are the sort of cameos that make a contemporary blues disc work! Lowell Fulson, Larry Davis, Smokey Wilson, Barbara Lynn, and Johnny Otis all guested on McCracklin's most recent album for Bullseye Blues, making it clear that the pianist

is no museum piece with their swinging grooves and sharp solos. —*Bill Dahl*

Roots of Rhythm & Blues / Roots ✦✦✦✦
The country of origin of this disc remains murky, but its 18 McCracklin tracks, from his 1957-58 layover at Chess (there was a belated 1962 date as well), are in dire need of domestic reissue—so until that happens, this one (shared with Paul Gayten) will just have to do. McCracklin's smash dance tune "The Walk" is here, along with the amusing playlet "He Knows the Rules" (immaculate axe by Lafayette Thomas), a jumping "Everybody Rock," and another workout that didn't fare as well, "The Wobble." —*Bill Dahl*

Blast 'Em Dead! / Ace ✦✦✦✦
McCracklin's vast catalog is perhaps more fully appreciated overseas than in his home. British Ace assembled 18 of the piano-pounder's Duke waxings for this searing LP, which features frequent interjections from guitarist Lafayette Thomas. Jumping stuff! —*Bill Dahl*

Larry McCray

b. Apr. 5, 1960, Magnolia, AR
Guitar, Vocals / Modern Electric Blues
If contemporary blues has a longterm future as we boldly venture into the 21st century, it's very likely that guitarist Larry McCray will play a recurring role in its ongoing development. His first two albums, *Ambition* and *Delta Hurricane*, signal both a strong commitment to the tradition and the vision to usher the genre in exciting new directions.

McCray's first influence on guitar was none other than his sister, Clara, who toured regionally around Arkansas with her own combo, the Rockets. Clara never got to record her Freddy King-styled blues for posterity—but her little brother has at least partially made up for that omission. Larry followed Clara up to Saginaw, MI, in 1972. She turned him on to the joys of the three Kings (B.B., Freddy, and Albert), Albert Collins, and Magic Sam, and Larry added superheated rock licks (à la Jimi Hendrix and the Allman Brothers) to his arsenal as he began playing the local circuit with his brothers Carl on bass and Steve on drums.

Working on General Motors' assembly line occupied a great deal of Larry McCray's time after he finished high school. But he eventually found enough free hours to put together *Ambition*, his 1991 debut album for Pointblank, in a Detroit friend's basement studio. The stunning set was a convincing hybrid of blues, rock, and soul, McCray combining the interrelated idioms in sizzling fashion. Suddenly, the stocky young guitarist was touring with label-mate Albert Collins. His 1993 Pointblank encore, *Delta Hurricane*, was a slicker affair produced by veteran British blues maven Mike Vernon that McCray much prefers to his homemade debut. —*Bill Dahl*

● **Ambition** / 1990 / Charisma ✦✦✦✦✦
Burly Larry McCray crashed the consciousness of the blues world with his stunning debut album, comprised of equal parts blues, soul, and rock. Guitar fanatics will no doubt wax rhapsodic about McCray's blazing pyrotechnics on "Nobody Never Hurt Nobody with the Blues," but it's the mellower R&B material buried toward the end of the CD—"Secret Lover," "Me and My Baby"—that best displays the warmth of the young bluesman's voice. Tab him for 21st-century blues stardom! —*Bill Dahl*

Delta Hurricane / 1993 / Point Blank ✦✦✦
Blues guitarist and vocalist Larry McCray's second Pointblank CD gets off to a dreary start with the title track, a tune with neither interesting lyrics nor a good arrangement. But after that flop fades, the remaining ten cuts are almost as powerful as the material on his critically acclaimed debut. McCray has the kind of tough, down-in-the-dirt voice you can neither fake nor acquire. His guitar work is equally authentic; there aren't any flashy phrases or flamboyant riffs, just pile-driving lines, barreling statements and energetic support for his vocals. There aren't many better contemporary blues albums being made by major labels; McCray is the real deal. —*Ron Wynn*

Mississippi Fred McDowell

b. Jan. 12, 1904, Rossville, TN, d. Jul. 3, 1972, Memphis, TN
Guitar, Vocals / Acoustic Delta Blues
When Mississippi Fred McDowell proclaimed on one of his last albums, "I do not play no rock & roll," it was less a boast by an

aging musician swept aside by the big beat than a mere statement of fact. As a stylist and purveyor of the original Delta blues, he was superb; equal parts Charlie Patton and Son House coming to the fore through his roughed-up vocals and slashing bottleneck style of guitar playing. McDowell *knew* he was the real deal and while others were diluting and updating their sound to keep pace with the changing times and audiences, Mississippi Fred stood out from the rest of the pack simply by not changing his style one iota. Though he scorned the amplified rock sound with a passion matched by few country bluesmen, he certainly had no qualms about passing any of his musical secrets along to his young White acolytes, prompting several of them—including a young Bonnie Raitt—to develop slide guitar techniques of their own. Although generally lumped in with other blues "rediscoveries" from the '60s, the most amazing thing about him was that this rich repository of Delta blues had never recorded in the '20s or early '30s, didn't get "discovered" until 1959, and didn't become a full-time professional musician until the mid-'60s.

McDowell was playing the guitar by the age of 14 with a slide hollowed out of a steer bone. His parents died when Fred was a youngster, and the wandering life of a traveling musician soon took hold. The 1920s saw him playing for tips on the street around Memphis, TN, and the hoboing life eventually setting him down in Como, MS, where he lived the rest of his life. There McDowell split his time between farming and keeping up with his music by playing weekends for various fish fries, picnics, and house parties in the immediate area. This pattern stayed largely unchanged for the next 30 years until he was discovered in 1959 by folklorist Alan Lomax. Lomax was the first to record this semi-professional bluesman, the results of which were released as part of a American folk music series on the Atlantic label. McDowell, for his part, was happy to have some sounds on record, but continued with his farming and playing for tips outside of Stuckey's candy store in Como for spare change. It wasn't until Chris Strachwitz—folk blues enthusiast and owner of the fledgling Arhoolie label—came searching for McDowell to record him that the bluesman's fortunes began to change dramatically.

Two albums, *Fred McDowell, Volume 1 and Volume 2,* were released on Arhoolie in the mid-'60s, and the shock waves were felt throughout the folk-blues community. Here was a bluesman with a repertoire of uncommon depth, putting it over with great emotional force and to top it all off, who had seemingly slipped through the cracks of late-'20s/early-'30s field recordings. No scratchy, highly prized 78s on Paramount or Vocalion to use as a yardstick to measure his current worth, no romantic stories about him disappearing into the Delta for decades at a time to become a professional gambler or a preacher. No, Mississippi Fred McDowell had been in his adopted home state, farming and playing all along, and the world coming to his doorstep seemed to ruffle him no more than the little boy down the street delivering the local newspaper.

The success of the Arhoolie recordings suddenly found McDowell very much in demand on the folk and festival circuit, where his quiet, good-natured performances left many a fan utterly spellbound. Working everything from the Newport Folk Festival to coffeehouse dates to becoming a member of the American Folk Blues Festival in Europe, McDowell suddenly had more listings in his resume in a couple of years than he had in the previous three decades combined. He was also well documented on film, with appearances in *The Blues Maker* (1968), his own documentary *Fred McDowell* (1969), and *Roots of American Music: Country and Urban Music* (1970) being among them. By the end of the decade, he was signed to do a one-off album for Capitol Records (the aforementioned *I Do Not Play No Rock 'n' Roll*) and his tunes were being mainstreamed into the blues-rock firmament by artists like Bonnie Raitt (who recorded several of his tunes, including notable versions of "Write Me a Few Lines" and "Kokomo") and the Rolling Stones, who included a very authentic version of his classic "You Got to Move" on their *Sticky Fingers* album. Unfortunately, this career largess didn't last much longer, as McDowell was diagnosed with cancer while performing dates into 1971. His playing days suddenly behind him, he lingered for a few months into July of 1972, finally succumbing to the disease at age 68. And right to the end, the man remained true to his word; he *didn't* play any rock & roll, just the straight, natural blues. *—Cub Koda*

★ **Mississippi Delta Blues** / Aug. 1964 / Arhoolie ✦✦✦✦✦
With 19 great tracks (1964–1965) of bottleneck slide guitar, the release also features excellent liner notes. *—Jas Obrecht*

My Home Is in the Delta / Sep. 1964 / Testament ✦✦✦✦✦
Mississippi Fred McDowell's home may have been in the Delta, but his music belonged to the world. This is heartfelt, raw, glorious country blues, delivered without an ounce of pretension or nostalgia. *—Ron Wynn*

Mississippi Blues / Dec. 1965 / Black Lion ✦✦✦
"Mississippi" Fred McDowell played simple, haunting blues with vivid, demonstrative passion and power. He wasn't a great guitarist, but his voicings and backings were always memorable, while his singing never lacked intensity or conviction or failed to hold interest. This 1965 set contains mostly McDowell compositions, with the exception of the set's final number, a nearly seven-minute exposition of Big Bill Broonzy's "Louise" Assisted at times by his wife Annie, Fred McDowell makes every song entertaining, whether they're humorous, poignant, reflective, or bemused. *—Ron Wynn*

Mississippi Delta Blues 2 / 1966 / Arhoolie ✦✦✦✦✦

Long Way from Home / 1966 / Original Blues Classics ✦✦✦
Good no-frills set of acoustic solo blues on bottleneck guitar. The accent is on traditional material, including "Milk Cow Blues," "John Henry," "Big Fat Mama," and the title track. *—Richie Unterberger*

● **Amazing Grace** / 1966 / Testament ✦✦✦✦✦
The connection between rural blues and spiritual music is sometimes overlooked. This 1966 recording, featuring McDowell, his guitar, and the Hunter's Chapel Singers of Como, MS (including his wife Annie Mae), is one of the best illustrations of how closely the styles can be linked. McDowell and company perform what the record subtitle calls "Mississippi Delta spirituals" on this stark and moving set, which includes a version of one of his signature tunes, "You Got to Move." The CD reissue adds three previously unreleased tracks. *—Richie Unterberger*

Fred McDowell / 1966 / Flyright ✦✦✦
This is another well-rounded collection. *—Jas Obrecht*

I Do Not Play No Rock 'n' Roll / 1969 / Capitol ✦✦✦✦✦
Blues purists were disappointed to hear McDowell pick up an electric guitar for the first time on this LP, as well as work with a young White rhythm section. To the rest of us, this session sounds pretty good. Fred's vocals, guitar playing, and integrity coming through just as strongly as it had on his acoustic work. The title track, and the rap that opens it up, is a mini-classic in its own right—if McDowell does not play no rock'n'roll, as he claims, he certainly keeps a beat pretty well. The album, as well as a second one cut at the same sessions (released on the Just Sunshine label) and some previously unreleased tracks, was released as an expanded double CD by Capitol in 1995. *—Richie Unterberger*

Mississippi Fred McDowell and Johnny Woods / 1977 / Rounder ✦✦✦
A nice, laidback set from guitar legend McDowell and his old harmonica sidekick, Johnny Woods. *—Barry Lee Pearson*

I Do Not Play No Rock 'n' Roll: Complete Sessions / Oct. 24, 1995 / Capitol ✦✦✦✦✦
A reissue of his popular 1969 electric album, expanded into a double CD with the addition of other material recorded at the same sessions (most of which was issued on an LP on the Just Sunshine label). It makes more sense to pick this up rather than the original vinyl album, as it rounds up all the material recorded at the *I Do Not Play No Rock 'n' Roll* sessions in November, 1969, and adds lengthy liner notes. *—Richie Unterberger*

Brownie McGhee (Walter McGhee)

b. Nov. 30, 1915, Knoxville, TN, **d.** Feb. 23, 1996, Oakland, CA
Guitar, Piano, Kazoo, Vocals / Acoustic Country Blues, Piedmont Blues
Brownie McGhee's death represents an enormous and irreplaceable loss to the blues field. Although he had been semi-retired and suffering from stomach cancer, the guitarist was still the leading Piedmont-style bluesman on the planet, venerated worldwide for his prolific activities both on his own and with his longtime partner, the blind harpist Sonny Terry.
Together, McGhee and Terry worked for decades in an

acoustic folk-blues bag, singing ancient ditties like "John Henry" and "Pick a Bale of Cotton" for appreciative audiences world-wide. But McGhee was capable of a great deal more. Throughout the immediate postwar era, he cut electric blues and R&B on the New York scene, even enjoying a huge R&B hit in 1948 with "My Fault" for Savoy (Hal "Cornbread" Singer handled tenor sax duties on the 78).

Walter Brown McGhee grew up in Kingsport, TN. He contracted polio at the age of four, which left him with a serious limp and plenty of time away from school to practice the guitar chords that he'd learned from his father, Duff McGhee. Brownie's younger brother, Granville McGhee, was also a talented guitarist who later hit big with the romping "Drinkin' Wine Spo-Dee-O-Dee"; he earned his nickname, "Stick," by pushing his crippled sibling around in a small cart propelled by a stick.

A 1937 operation sponsored by the March of Dimes restored most of McGhee's mobility. Off he went as soon as he recovered, traveling and playing throughout the Southeast. His jaunts brought him into contact with washboard player George "Oh Red" (or "Bull City Red") Washington in 1940, who in turn introduced McGhee to talent scout J. B. Long. Long got him a recording contract with Okeh/Columbia in 1940; his debut session in Chicago produced a dozen tracks over two days.

Long's principal blues artist, Blind Boy Fuller, died in 1941, precipitating Okeh to issue some of McGhee's early efforts under the sobriquet of Blind Boy Fuller No. 2. McGhee cut a moving tribute song, "Death of Blind Boy Fuller," shortly after the passing. McGhee's third marathon session for Okeh in 1941 paired him for the first time on shellac with whooping harpist Terry for "Workingman's Blues."

The pair resettled in New York in 1942. They quickly got connected with the city's burgeoning folk music circuit, working with Woody Guthrie, Pete Seeger, and Leadbelly. After the end of World War II, McGhee began to record most prolifically, with and without Terry, for a myriad of R&B labels: Savoy (where he cut "Robbie Doby Boogie" in 1948 and "New Baseball Boogie" the next year), Alert, London, Derby, Sittin' in With and its Jax subsidiary in 1952, Jackson, Bobby Robinson's Red Robin logo (1953), Dot, and Harlem, before crossing over to the folk audience during the late '50s with Terry at his side. One of McGhee's last dates for Savoy in 1958 produced the remarkably contemporary "Living with the Blues," with Roy Gaines and Carl Lynch blasting away on lead guitars and a sound light years removed from the staid folk world.

McGhee and Terry were among the first blues artists to tour Europe during the 1950s, and they often ventured overseas after that. Their plethora of late-'50s/early-'60s albums for Folkways, Choice, World Pacific, Bluesville, and Fantasy presented the duo in acoustic folk trappings only, their Piedmont-style musical interplay a constant (if gradually more predictable) delight.

McGhee didn't limit his talents to concert settings. He appeared on Broadway for three years in a production of playwright Tennessee Williams' *Cat on a Hot Tin Roof* in 1955 and later put in a stint in the Langston Hughes play *Simply Heaven*. Films (*Angel Heart, Buck and the Preacher*) and an episode of the TV sitcom *Family Ties* also benefited from his dignified presence.

The wheels finally came off the partnership of McGhee and Terry during the mid-'70s. Toward the end, they preferred not to share a stage with one another (Terry would play with another guitarist, then McGhee would do a solo), let alone communicate. One of McGhee's final concert appearances came at the 1995 Chicago Blues Festival; his voice was a tad less robust than usual, but no less moving, and his rich, full-bodied acoustic guitar work cut through the cool evening air with alacrity. His like won't pass this way again. —*Bill Dahl*

Brownie McGhee & Sonny Terry Sing / 1958 / Smithsonian/Folkways ✦✦✦✦
One of the duo's best acoustic folk-blues collaborations, originally issued in 1958. They convincingly run through a very enjoyable series of collaborations marked by affectionate interplay, with drummer Gene Moore adding rhythmic power. —*Bill Dahl*

Back Country Blues / Nov. 1958 / Savoy ✦✦✦✦✦
Brownie McGhee's solo material had a certain charm and compelling quality missing from his collaborations with Terry. For whatever reason, he tended to try more things alone and vary

his approach, sound, and delivery. This is first-rate country and topical material, delivered without the forced humor that eventually made his dates with Terry more camp than substance. —*Ron Wynn*

At the 2nd Fret / Mar. 1963 / Bluesville ✦✦✦✦✦
Brownie McGhee and Sonny Terry were the ultimate blues duo; McGhee's stylized singing and light, flickering guitar was wonderfully contrasted by Terry's sweeping, whirling harmonica solos and intense, country-tinged singing. They were in great form during the ten tunes featured on this live date, recently reissued on CD. Sometimes, as on "Custard Pie" or "Barking Bull Dog," they're funny; at other times, they were prophetic, chilling, or moving. This is Piedmont blues at its best, and this disc's tremendous remastering provides a strong sonic framework. —*Ron Wynn*

Hometown Blues / 1990 / Mainstream ✦✦✦✦
Plenty of delightful interplay between McGhee and Terry recommends these 18 1948–1951 sides for producer Bobby Shad for his Sittin' in With label, but they predate the duo's later folk period by a longshot. Back then, they were still aiming their output solely at the R&B crowd—meaning "Man Ain't Nothin' But a Fool," "Bad Blood," "The Woman Is Killing Me," and "Dissatisfied Woman" are straight-ahead, uncompromising New York-style blues. —*Bill Dahl*

● **Folkways Years, 1945–1959** / 1991 / Smithsonian/Folkways ✦✦✦✦✦
Brownie McGhee was among the last generation of blues musicians with deep country and traditional ties who maintained some level of popularity into the '50s. The onslaught of electrified urban blues would change the music's direction and result in many Delta and country artists losing stature among the genre's core constituency. But McGhee managed to continue working, both with longtime musical companion Sonny Terry and as a solo act. The 17 cuts presented on this reissued CD were taken from six McGhee albums and include ballads, folk tunes, originals, and comedic numbers depicting the versatility and idiomatic range that was commonplace in McGhee's music. —*Ron Wynn*

Brownie McGhee & Sonny Terry (at the 2nd Fret) / 1993 / Prestige ✦✦✦✦✦
Prototype Piedmont-style blues from that genre's finest guitar/harmonica duo. They were so tight and interconnected that it's no wonder they got so vicious when things soured. There's plenty of familiar material, but they were in a groove at this point and sounded fantastic. —*Ron Wynn*

★ **Complete Brownie McGhee** / 1994 / Columbia/Legacy ✦✦✦✦
Well, complete as far as his pre-war country blues waxings for Okeh sans Sonny Terry (except for one or two where the whooping harpist provided accompaniment). McGhee was working firmly in the Piedmont tradition by 1940, when he signed with Okeh and began cutting the 47 enlightening sides here, which represent some of the purest country blues he ever committed to posterity. —*Bill Dahl*

Stick McGhee

b. Mar. 23, 1917, Kingsport, TN, d. Aug. 15, 1961, New York, NY
Guitar, Vocals / Electric Blues
He may have not been as prolific or celebrated as his brother Brownie, but guitarist Stick McGhee cut some great boozy blues and R&B from 1947 to 1960—including the immortal "Drinkin' Wine Spo-Dee-O-Dee" (a tune that Jerry Lee Lewis, for one, picked up on early in life and has revived often since).

Young Granville McGhee earned his nickname by pushing his polio-stricken older brother Brownie through the streets of Kingsport, TN, on a cart that he propelled with a stick. McGhee was inspired to pen "Drinkin' Wine" while in Army bootcamp during World War II; it was apparently a ribald military chant that the McGhees cleaned up for public consumption later on. Stick McGhee's first recorded version of the tune for J. Mayo Williams' Harlem logo made little impression in 1947, but a rollicking 1949 remake for Atlantic (as Stick McGhee & his Buddies) proved a massive R&B hit (brother Brownie chiming in on guitar and harmony vocal). The tune has attracted countless covers over the years—everyone from Jerry Lee Lewis and Johnny Burnette to Wynonie Harris and Larry Dale has taken a sip from this particular wine flask.

After one more smash for Atlantic, 1951's "Tennessee Waltz Blues," McGhee moved along to Essex, King (where he waxed some more great booze numbers from 1953 to 1955–"Whiskey Women and Loaded Dice," "Head Happy with Wine," "Jungle Juice," "Six to Eight," "Double Crossin' Liquor"), Savoy, and Herald, where he made his last 45 in 1960 before lung cancer cut him down the following year. —*Bill Dahl*

Highway of Blues / 1959 / Deluxe ♦♦
Contains sone of his fine '50s jump blues tracks for King. —*Bill Dahl*

● **Stick McGhee & his Spo-Dee-O-Dee Buddies** / Ace ♦♦♦♦♦
The British Ace label—long a prime source for quality compilations—has done Brownie's little brother proud, collecting his dozen 1953-1955 jump blues sides for the King logo, many of them detailing the effects of booze. Also aboard are four country blues styled numbers by Ralph Willis, and four more by the pseudonymous Big Tom Collins (two of them feature Brownie McGhee's vocals, the other pair Champion Jack Dupree). —*Bill Dahl*

Big Jay McNeely

b. Apr. 29, 1927, Watts, CA
Saxophone / West Coast Blues
His mighty tenor sax squawking and bleating with wild-eyed abandon, Big Jay McNeely blew up a torrid R&B tornado from every conceivable position—on his knees, on his back, and being wheeled down the street on an auto mechanic's "creeper" like a modern-day pied piper. As one of the titans who made tenor sax the solo instrument of choice during rock's primordial era, Big Jay McNeely could peel the paper right off the walls with his sheets of squealing, honking horn riffs.

Cecil McNeely and his older brother Bob (who blew baritone sax lines with Jay in unison precision on some of Jay's hottest instrumentals) grew up in Los Angeles, where jazz reigned on Watts' bustling nightlife strip. Inspired by Illinois Jacquet and tutored by Jack McVea, McNeely struck up a friendship with Johnny Otis, co-owner of the popular Barrelhouse nitery. Ralph Bass, a friend of Otis, produced McNeely's debut date for Savoy Records in 1948 (Savoy boss Herman Lubinsky tagged the saxist Big Jay, in his eyes a more commercial name than Cecil). McNeely's raucous one-note honking on "The Deacon's Hop" gave him and Savoy an R&B chart-topper in 1949, and his follow-up, "Wild Wig," also hit big for the young saxist with the acrobatic stage presence.

From Savoy, McNeely moved to Exclusive in 1949, Imperial in 1950-51, King's Federal subsidiary in 1952-54 (where he cut some of his wildest waxings, including the mind-boggling "3-D"), and Vee-Jay in 1955. McNeely's live shows were the stuff that legends are made of—he electrified a sweaty throng of thousands packing L.A.'s Wrigley Field in 1949 by blowing his sax up through the stands and then from home plate to first base on his back! A fluorescently painted sax that glowed in the dark was another of his showstopping gambits.

In 1958, McNeely cut his last hit in a considerably less frantic mode with singer Little Sonny Warner. The bluesy "There Is Something on Your Mind" was committed to tape in Seattle but came out on deejay Hunter Hancock's Swingin' imprint the next year. McNeely's original was a huge smash, but it was eclipsed the following year by New Orleans singer Bobby Marchan's dramatic R&B chart-topping version for Fire. Since then, it's been covered countless times, including a fine rendition by Conway Twitty!

Honking saxists had fallen from favor by the dawn of the '60s, so McNeely eventually became a mailman and joined Jehovah's Witnesses (no, that's not the name of a combo). Happily, his horn came back out of the closet during the early '80s. Today, McNeely records for his own little label and tours the country and overseas regularly. This deacon's still hopping! —*Bill Dahl*

Big Jay in 3-D / Aug. 26, 1952–Apr. 8, 1954 / Federal ♦♦♦♦
Honking R&B tenor-sax giant McNeely blows his brains out on these early-'50s stompers for King. Truly astonishing is the torrid "3-D," where Big Jay and his baritone sax-blowing brother Bob play some incredibly complex riffs over one of the fastest tempos imaginable. —*Bill Dahl*

The Deacon Rides Again / 1957 / Marconi ♦♦♦
Hot tenor licks, sweltering vocals from Jesse Belvin, and bluesy inflections courtesy of Mercy Dee. —*Ron Wynn*

From Harlem to Camden / Aug. 1983–Sep. 1983 / Ace ♦♦♦
An album of lusty, robust honking sax on standard R&B arrangements. —*Ron Wynn*

Meets the Penguins / Oct. 1983 / Ace ♦♦♦
This reissue of raucous, upbeat R&B cuts also includes the doo-wop harmony ensemble the Penguins. —*Ron Wynn*

● **Nervous** / 1995 / Saxophile ♦♦♦♦♦
A thorough 19-track examination of McNeely's early heyday, incorporating a live 1951 reprise of his signature "Deacon's Hop," the King label classics "3-D," "Nervous Man Nervous," and "Texas Turkey," a handful of live 1957 efforts that include the crazed "Insect Ball," and McNeely's original hit version of the incendiary blues ballad "There Is Something on Your Mind" (with Little Sonny Warner handling the Ray Charles-influenced lead vocal). —*Bill Dahl*

Swingin' / Collectables ♦♦♦♦
Gymnastic sax maniac's output for L.A. deejay Hunter Hancock's Swingin' logo during the late '50s and early '60s. Naturally, his smash "There Is Something on Your Mind" is front and center, alongside the oddly titled "Back...Shack...Track," "Psycho Serenade," and "Blue Couch Boogie." Little Sonny Warner is the vocalist on some sides. —*Bill Dahl*

Live at Birdland: 1957 / Collectables ♦♦♦♦
An amazing artifact from 1957, when live recordings like this one didn't happen very often. A Seattle engineer with a spanking-new stereo tape recorder captured the contents of this disc while McNeely and his swinging combo were working out at a Seattle nightspot called the Birdland. He gets plenty of room to peel the paper from the gin joint's walls as he wails on "Flying Home," "How High the Moon," and "Let It Roll." —*Bill Dahl*

Blind Willie McTell (William Samuel McTell)

b. May 5, 1901, Thomson, GA, **d.** Aug. 19, 1959, Milledgeville, GA
Guitar, Harmonica, Accordion, Vocals / Acoustic Country Blues
Willie Samuel McTell was one of the blues' greatest guitarists, and also one of the finest singers ever to work in blues. A major figure with a local following in Atlanta from the 1920s onward, he recorded dozens of sides throughout the 1930s under a multitude of names—all the better to juggle "exclusive" relationships with many different record labels at once—including Blind Willie, Blind Sammie, Hot Shot Willie, and Georgia Bill, as a back-up musician to Ruth Mary Willis, and even in utter anonymity as the partner in "Curley Weaver and partner." And those may not have been all of his pseudonyms—we don't even know what he chose to call himself, although "Blind Willie" was his preferred choice among friends. Much of what we do know about him was learned only years after his death, from family members and acquaintances.

His family name was, so far as we know, McTier or McTear, and the origins of the "McTell" name are unclear. What is clear is that he was born into a family filled with musicians—his mother and his father both played guitar, as did one of his uncles, and he was also related to Georgia Tom Dorsey (a close associate of Tampa Red, who later achieved his widest recognition, after abandoning the blues in favor of gospel music, as the Reverend Thomas Dorsey, whose protégés included Aretha Franklin), Buddy Moss, Barbecue Bob, and Bob's brother Charlie Lincoln.

He was born in Thomson, GA, near Augusta, and raised near Statesboro. Willie was probably born blind, although early in his life he could perceive light in one eye. His blindness never became a major impediment, however, and it was said that his sense of hearing and touch were extraordinary. He could make his way around Atlanta, up and down the East coast, and even through New York City with astonishing ease and certainty. His first instruments were the harmonica and the accordion, but as soon as he was big enough he took up the guitar and showed immediate aptitude on the new instrument. He played a standard six-string acoustic until the mid-'20s, and never entirely abandoned the instrument, but from the beginning of his recording career, he used a 12-string acoustic in the studio almost exclusively.

Willie's technique on the 12-string instrument was unique. Unlike virtually every other bluesman who used one, he relied not on its resonances as a rhythm instrument but, instead, displayed a nimble, elegant slide and finger-picking style that made it sound like more than one guitar at any given moment. He studied at a number of schools for the blind, in Georgia, New

York, and Michigan, during the early '20s, and probably picked up some formal musical knowledge. He worked medicine shows, carnivals, and other outdoor venues, and was a popular attraction, owing to his sheer dexterity and a nasal singing voice that could sound either pleasant or mournful, and incorporated some of the characteristics normally associated with White hillbilly singers. In that regard, Willie can be said, to some degree, to have been the distant popular antecedent to Chuck Berry, whose earliest records were thought by many listeners to be the work of a White country artist.

Willie's recording career began in late 1927 with two sessions for Victor records, eight sides including "Statesboro Blues," arguably his early masterpiece, which became an internationally known rock standard in the hands of the Allman Brothers Band at the end of the 1960s. McTell's earliest sides were superb examples of storytelling in music, coupled with dazzling guitar work. All of McTell's music showed extraordinary power, some of it delightfully raucous ragtime, other examples evoking darker, lonelier sides of the blues, all of it displaying astonishingly rich guitar work.

He worked under a variety of names, and with a multitude of partners, including his one-time wife Ruthy Kate Williams (who recorded with him under the name Ruby Glaze), and also Buddy Moss and Curley Weaver, two guitarists whose abilities were the equal of his own, although so far as is known, he never worked with Moss or Weaver as part of one of their various pseudonymous groups, such as the Georgia Browns or the Georgia Cotton Pickers. McTell cut some of his best songs more than once in his career—"Talkin' to Myself" and "Broke Down Engine Blues" turn up in different parts of his discography and different decades. Like many bluesmen, he recorded under different names simultaneously, and was even signed to Columbia and Okeh Records, two companies that merged at the end of the 1930s, at the same time under two names.

His recording career never gave Willie quite as much success as he had hoped, partly due to the fact that some of his best work appeared during the depths of the Depression, a period when sales of many fine records were limited by peoples' lack of disposable income, although until close to the end of his career he never entirely gave up trying. He was uniquely popular in Atlanta, where he continued to live and work throughout most of his career, and, in fact, was the only blues guitarist of any note from the city to remain active in the city until well after World War II—Barbecue Bob died at the beginning of the 1930s, Charlie Lincoln went to prison, and most of the other major names left for points north (especially Chicago) or left music altogether.

Willie was well-known enough that Library of Congress archivist John Lomax felt compelled to record him in 1940, although during the war, like many other acoustic country bluesmen, his recording career came to a halt. Luckily for Willie and generations of listeners after him, however, there was a brief revival of interest in acoustic country blues after World War II that brought him back into the studio. Amazingly enough, the newly founded Atlantic Records—which was more noted for its recordings of jazz and R&B—took an interest in Willie and cut 15 songs with him in Atlanta during 1949. The one single released from these sessions, however, didn't sell, and most of those recordings remained unheard for more than 20 years after they were made. A year later, however, he was back in the studio, this time with his longtime partner Curley Weaver (who may have been playing on some of the Atlantic sides with Willie), cutting songs for the Regal label. None of these records sold especially well, however, and while Willie kept playing to anyone who would listen, the bitter realities of life had finally overtaken him, and he began drinking on a more regular basis. He was rediscovered in 1956, just in time to get one more historic session down on tape. He left music soon after, to become a pastor of a local church, and he died of a brain hemorrhage in 1959, his passing so unnoticed at the time that certain reissues in the 1970s referred to Willie as still being alive in the 1960s.

Blind Willie McTell was one of the giants of the blues, as a guitarist and as a singer and recording artist. Hardly any of his work passed down to us on record is less than first rate, and this makes most any collection of his music (only the postwar Atlantic, Regal, and Prestige releases can be considered as proper "albums"—virtually everything else was cut four songs, or two singles, at a time) worthwhile. A studious and highly skilled musician whose skills transcended the blues, he was equally adept at ragtime, spirituals, story-songs, hillbilly numbers, and popular tunes (he was doing brilliant covers of 1920s pop tunes in the late '40s), excelling in all of these genres. He could read and write music in braille, which gave him an edge on many of his sighted contemporaries, and was also a brilliant improvisor on the guitar, as is evident from his records. Willie always gave an excellent account of himself, even in his final years of performing and recording (and, in particular, any rock listeners looking into Willie's work based on the Allman Brothers' version of "Statesboro Blues" will find someone here to be in awe of, even more so than Duane, God bless him). —Bruce Eder

☆ **Atlanta Twelve String** / 1949 / Atlantic ♦♦♦♦♦
In 1949, a brief flurry of interest in old-time country blues resulted in this 15-song session by McTell for the newly formed Atlantic Records during 1949. Only two songs, "Kill It Kid" and "Broke Down Engine Blues," were ever issued on a failed single, and the session was forgotten until almost 20 years later. McTell is mostly solo here, vividly captured on acoustic 12-string (his sometime partner Curley Weaver may have been present on some tracks), and in excellent form. The playing and the repertory are representative of McTell as he was at this point in his career, a blues veteran rolling through his paces without skipping a beat and quietly electrifying the listener. Songs include "Dying Crapshooter's Blues," "The Razor Ball," and "Ain't I Grand to Live a Christian." —Bruce Eder

☆ **Pig 'n Whistle Red** / 1950 / Biograph ♦♦♦♦♦
This collection of 20 songs, cut by McTell with Curley Weaver on second guitar and sharing the vocals, was left out of many McTell biographical accounts until it resurfaced in 1993. Cut for Regal Records in 1950, it's a remarkable document, capturing McTell and Weaver in vivid modern sound, and includes remakes of McTell's 1933 "Talkin' to You Mama" and "Good Little Thing" as well as more recent material that the two had been doing, and even outtakes, showing very different interpretations of the 1920's pop standard "Pal of Mine" and the gospel number "Sending Up My Timber." The sheer diversity of material makes this an indispensable (as well as a delightful) recording, and except for some minor fate damage on "A to Z Blues" and one other cut, there are few technical flaws here. The playing is so sharp and crisp, and the vocals so delicate in their textures, that this has to be considered essential to any serious blues collection. McTell and Weaver were a legendary duo in Atlanta from before World War II, and it is nothing less than a gift to have them still together and in excellent form on this postwar recording. —Bruce Eder

Last Session / 1956 / Bluesville ♦♦♦♦♦
This recording has a less-than-stellar reputation, principally because it was done so late in McTell's career, and it is true that he lacks some of the edge, especially in his singing, that he showed on his other postwar recordings. On the other hand, his 12-string playing is about as nimble as ever and a real treat. McTell cut these sides for record store owner Ed Rhodes, who had begun taping local bluesmen at his shop in Atlanta in the hope of releasing some of it—McTell took to the idea of recording only slowly, then turned up one night and played for the microphone and anyone who happened to be listening, finishing a pint of bourbon in the process—the result was a pricelessly intimate document, some of the words slurred here and there, but brilliantly expressive and stunningly played. No apologies are needed for "The Dyin' Crapshooter's Blues," "Don't Forget It," or "Salty Dog," however. McTell lived a few more years but never recorded again, which is a pity, because based on this tape he still had a lot to show people. Rhodes never did anything with the tapes, and might've junked them if he hadn't remembered how important the McTell material was—they turned out to be the only tapes he saved, out of all he'd recorded. —Bruce Eder

Legendary Library of Congress Session / Jun. 1967 / Elektra ♦♦♦

Complete Library of Congress Recordings (1940) / 1969 / Document ♦♦♦♦♦
Included are songs and autobiographical monologues. —Jas Obrecht

Blind Willie McTell / 1989 / Yazoo ♦♦♦
This is one of the few Yazoo records that cannot be recommended as a potential first choice, because it was done relatively early. The sound is okay, but the song selection—all made up

of pre-World War II material, as usual for Yazoo—is rather paltry compared with McTell collections that have come out since. It's not a bad choice, just not as good as some others, and it does include a decent, if limited, cross-section of early material, including "Statesboro Blues." —*Bruce Eder*

☆ **Complete Recorded Works, Vol. 1 (1927–1931)** / 1990 / Document ✦✦✦✦
Of all the compilations of McTell's early work, this is probably the most rewarding, because it includes both his Victor songs (including "Statesboro Blues") and his Columbia sides (which have been issued separately by Columbia-Legacy), and RCA-BMG seems to be in no hurry to put any of the Victor material out as a comprehensive collection. The songs all have some noise—there are no "masters" to speak of on acoustic blues of this vintage—but none of it is overly obtrusive, and the orderly chronology is very illuminating. Subsequent volumes from Document are also worthwhile, but Sony-Legacy does have superior workmanship in dealing with much of the same material. —*Bruce Eder*

Complete Recorded Works, Vol. 2 (1931–1933) / 1990 / Document ✦✦✦✦
Complete Recorded Works, Vol. 3 (1933–1935) / 1990 / Document ✦✦✦✦
Complete Recorded Works (1949–1950) / 1990 / Document ✦✦✦

★ **The Early Years 1927–1933** / 1990 / Yazoo ✦✦✦✦
A good sampler, it emphasizes 12-string guitar. —*Jas Obrecht*

☆ **The Complete Blind Willie McTell** / 1994 / Columbia ✦✦✦✦
All of the recordings Blind Willie McTell made for Columbia, Okeh, and Vocalion between 1929 and 1933 are collected on this essential two-disc set. —*Stephen Thomas Erlewine*

Definitive / 1994 / Columbia Legacy ✦✦✦✦
This double-CD set is a little misleading. It is definitive, but only in terms of McTell's Columbia and Okeh sides—you won't find "Statesboro Blues" or his other earliest sides here, because they were done for Victor. But the material that is here is all worthwhile, and this is the best single source for McTell's work for those labels (done under a variety of names) from the mid-'30s, very nicely remastered and thoroughly annotated, although producer Lawrence Cohn concedes that even Sony-Legacy was unable to locate sources on a handful of songs that McTell is known to have recorded. —*Bruce Eder*

The Complete Victor Recordings, 1927–1932 / Oct. 1995 / Victor ✦✦✦
Doing That Atlanta (1927–1935) / Yazoo ✦✦✦
Blind Willie McTell 1927–1949 / Wolf ✦✦✦
This is a first-rate collection of sides the guitarist recorded in the early '30s. These songs are impassioned and positively haunting, ranking among the best music he ever made. —*Thom Owens*

Mellow Fellows

Group / Modern Electric Chicago Blues
Now known as The Chicago Rhythm And Blues Kings, The Mellow Fellows held their personnel together after the 1990 death of singer Larry "Big Twist" Nolan. Saxist Terry Ogolini and guitarist Pete Special, co-founders of the group, recruited Twist's pal Martin Allbritton to front the band, and they cut the buoyant *Street Party* for Alligator in 1990 with part-time member Gene "Daddy G" Barge helping out on sax and vocals. When Special split, the band switched to its current regal billing. —*Bill Dahl*

Street Party / 1990 / Alligator ✦✦✦✦
Martin Allbritton, a melismatic and undeniably more powerful vocalist than the finesse-oriented Twist, proves an eminently worthy successor to the beloved big man on this highly enjoyable effort. Barge also pitches in with a few lead vocals as the group attacks a handful of joyous originals ("We'll Be Friends," "Street Party," "Broad Daylight") and storming R&B classics by Sam & Dave and Harold Burrage. —*Bill Dahl*

Memphis Jug Band

Group / Acoustic Memphis Blues
One of the definitive jug bands of the '20s and early '30s, this seminal group was comprised of Will Shade, Will Weldon, Hattie Hart, Charlie Polk, Walter Horton, and others, in various configurations.

Guitarist/harpist Will Shade formed the Memphis Jug Band in the Beale Street section of Memphis in the mid-'20s. A few years after their formation, Shade signed a contract with Victor Records in 1927. Over the next seven years, Shade and the Memphis Jug Band recorded nearly 60 songs for the record label. During this time, a number of musicians passed through the group, including Big Walter Horton, Furry Lewis, and Casey Bill Weldon. Throughout all of the various lineup incarnations, Shade provided direction for the group. The Memphis Jug Band played a free-wheeling mixture of blues, ragtime, vaudeville, folk, and jazz, which was all delivered with good-time humor. That loose spirit kept the group and its records popular throughout the early '30s.

Although the group's popularity dipped sharply in the mid-'30s, Will Shade continued to lead the group in various incarnations until his death in 1966. —*Cub Koda & Stephen Thomas Erlewine*

Complete Recorded Works (1932–1934) / 1990 / Document ✦✦✦
American Skiffle Bands / Jul. 16, 1990 / Smithsonian/Folkways ✦✦✦
Complete Recorded Works, Vols. 1–3 / Document ✦✦✦✦
A definitive three-CD set with all the issued material from this groundbreaking jug band. Includes "Cocaine Habit Blues," "Cave Man Blues," the original "He's in the Jailhouse Now," and the always wonderful "I Whipped My Woman with a Single Tree." —*Cub Koda*

★ **Memphis Jug Band** / Yazoo ✦✦✦✦
This definitive 28-song collection by the city's finest jug band spans their output from 1927 to 1934. —*John Floyd*
Associates and Alternate Takes (1927–30) / Wolf ✦✦✦✦

Memphis Minnie (Lizzie Douglas)

b. Jun. 3, 1897, Algiers, LA, d. Aug. 6, 1973, Memphis, TN
Banjo, Guitar, Vocals / Acoustic Memphis Blues
Tracking down the ultimate woman blues guitar hero is problematic because woman blues singers seldom recorded as guitar players and woman guitar players (such as Rosetta Tharpe and Sister O.M. Terrell) were seldom recorded playing blues. Excluding contemporary artists, the most notable exception to this pattern was Memphis Minnie. The most popular and prolific blueswoman outside the vaudeville tradition, she earned the respect of critics, the support of record-buying fans, and the unqualified praise of the blues artists she worked with throughout her long career. Despite her Southern roots and popularity, she was as much a Chicago blues artist as anyone in her day. Big Bill Broonzy recalls her beating both him and Tampa Red in a guitar contest and claims she was the best woman guitarist he had ever heard. Tough enough to endure in a hard business, she earned the respect of her peers with her solid musicianship and recorded good blues over four decades for Columbia, Vocalion, Bluebird, Okeh, Regal, Checker, and JOB. She also proved to have as good taste in musical husbands as music and sustained working marriages with guitarists Casey Bill Weldon, Joe McCoy, and Ernest Lawlers. Their guitar duets span the spectrum of African-American folk and popular music, including spirituals, comic dialogs, and old-time dance pieces, but Memphis Minnie's best work consisted of deep blues like "Moaning the Blues." More than a good woman blues guitarist and singer, Memphis Minnie holds her own against the best blues artists of her time, and her work has special resonance for today's aspiring guitarists. —*Barry Lee Pearson*

★ **Hoodoo Lady (1933–1937)** / 1933–1937 / Columbia ✦✦✦✦
Great early stuff. —*Mark A. Humphrey*

Blues Classics by Memphis Minnie / Oct. 1965 / Blues Classics ✦✦✦✦
Shaking, volcanic material from the great Memphis Minnie. There weren't many stylists, male or female, who could match Lizzie Douglas when it came to conveying a lyric. She was in peak form on every selection here. —*Ron Wynn*

I Ain't No Bad Gal / 1988 / Portrait ✦✦✦
Minnie was the toughest guitar-picking femme of bluesdom, with plugged-in 1941 performances that included "Me and My Chauffeur Blues." —*Mark A. Humphrey*

Complete Recorded Works, Vol. 1 (1935–1941) / 1991 / Document ✦✦✦✦
A five-volume CD set of Memphis Minnie's entire output from

1935–1941. Highlights include "Me and My Chauffeur Blues," "Good Biscuits," "You Can't Rule Me," "If You See My Rooster," and "Selling My Porkchops." An essential collection by the greatest female blues guitarist ever. —*Cub Koda*

Complete Recorded Works, Vol. 2 (1935–1941) / 1991 / Document ✦✦✦

Complete Recorded Works, Vol. 3 (1935–1941) / 1991 / Document ✦✦✦

Complete Recorded Works, Vol. 4 (1935–1941) / 1991 / Document ✦✦✦

Complete Recorded Works, Vol. 5 (1935–1941) / 1991 / Document ✦✦✦✦

☆ **And Kansas Joe: 1929–1934** / 1991 / Document ✦✦✦✦✦
Minnie's earliest recordings with first husband Kansas Joe McCoy. Includes "I Want That," "Bumble Bee," "Squat It," "I Don't Want That Junk Outta You," and the original version of "When the Levee Breaks," later covered by (and re-credited to) Led Zeppelin. —*Cub Koda*

Travelling Blues / Aldabra ✦✦✦✦✦
Travelling Blues collects a number of sessions recorded with Kansas Joe McCoy, Memphis Minnie's second husband. Make no mistake about it—with her impassioned vocals, Memphis Minnie controls these recordings. This album sounds fine and contains a wealth of terrific music. —*Thom Owens*

1934–1942 / Biograph ✦✦✦✦✦
You can't go wrong with Memphis Minnie at almost any point in her estimable career. During the 1930s and early '40s, she made the adjustment to changing styles, but in the early '30s she *made* the style. The sound quality is pretty good throughout the set, although it's better on the later tunes. —*Ron Wynn*

With Kansas Joe / Blues Classics ✦✦✦✦✦
When she was married to Kansas Joe McCoy, Memphis Minnie was making wailing blues, memorable laments, and brilliant double-entendre tunes. He supplied her with excellent accompaniment and nice complementary vocals. These are simply marvelous songs. —*Ron Wynn*

Memphis Slim (Peter Chatman)

b. Sep. 3, 1915, Memphis, TN, **d.** Feb. 24, 1988, Paris, France
Piano, Vocals / Urban Blues
An amazingly prolific artist who brought a brisk air of urban sophistication to his frequently stunning presentation, Memphis Slim assuredly ranks with the greatest blues pianists of all time. He was smart enough to take Big Bill Broonzy's early advice about developing a style to call his own to heart, instead of imitating that of his idol, Roosevelt Sykes. Soon enough, other 88s pounders were copying Slim rather than the other way around—his thundering ivories attack set him apart from most of his contemporaries, while his deeply burnished voice possessed a commanding authority.

As befits his stage name, John Chatman was born and raised in Memphis—a great place to commit to a career as a bluesman. Sometime in the late '30s, he resettled in Chicago and began recording as a leader in 1939 for Okeh, then switched over to Bluebird the next year. Around the same time, Slim joined forces with Broonzy, then the dominant force on the local blues scene. After serving as Broonzy's invaluable accompanist for a few years, Slim emerged as his own man in 1944.

After the close of World War II, Slim joined Hy-Tone Records, cutting eight tracks that were later picked up by King. Lee Egalnick's Miracle label reeled in the pianist in 1947; backed by his jumping band, the House Rockers (its members usually included saxists Alex Atkins and Ernest Cotton), Slim recorded his classic "Lend Me Your Love" and "Rockin' the House." The next year brought the landmark "Nobody Loves Me" (better known via subsequent covers by Lowell Fulson, Joe Williams, and B.B. King as "Everyday I Have the Blues") and the heartbroken "Messin' Around (With the Blues)."

The pianist kept on label-hopping, moving from Miracle to Peacock to Premium (where he waxed the first version of his uncommonly wise down-tempo blues "Mother Earth") to Chess to Mercury before staying put at Chicago's United Records from 1952 to 1954. This was a particularly fertile period for the pianist; he recruited his first permanent guitarist, the estimable Matt Murphy, who added some serious fretfire to "The Come Back," "Sassy Mae," and "Memphis Slim U.S.A."

Before the decade was through, the pianist landed at Vee-Jay Records, where he cut definitive versions of his best-known songs with Murphy and a stellar combo in gorgeously sympathetic support (Murphy was nothing short of spectacular throughout).

Slim exhibited his perpetually independent mindset by leaving the country for good in 1962. A tour of Europe in partnership with bassist Willie Dixon a couple of years earlier had so intrigued the pianist that he permanently moved to Paris, where recording and touring possibilities seemed limitless and the veteran pianist was treated with the respect too often denied African-American blues stars at home back then. He remained there until his 1988 death, enjoying his stature as expatriate blues royalty. —*Bill Dahl*

At The Gate of Horn / 1959 / Vee-Jay ✦✦✦✦✦
Only this disc's short length (34 minutes) qualifies as something worthy of complaint; otherwise this is seminal blues piano, performed by a great player and singer, Memphis Slim. This 1959 session had everything: super piano solos, a strong lineup of horn players, clever, well-written and sung lyrics, and a seamless pace that kept things moving briskly from beginning to end. Other than Slim, instrumental honors go to guitarist Matt Murphy, a marvelous accompanist who was able to blend sophistication, technique, and earthiness into one dynamic package. Even at its bargain-basement length, *At The Gate of Horn* belongs in any blues fan's library. —*Ron Wynn*

Blue This Evening / Jul. 1960 / Black Lion ✦✦✦
Another artifact from the same historic tour of England. These 19 numbers, many of them the storied standards that long comprised Slim's repertoire, feature backing by guitarist Alexis Korner and drummer Stan Greig (who may be involved in the other CD from the same British tour). The same criticism applies: they weren't Murphy and Stepney, and the difference grates. —*Bill Dahl*

Memphis Slim / 1961 / MCA/Chess ✦✦✦✦
A straight CD reissue of a vintage Chess LP, its contents dating back to the early '50s and most tracks originally issued on the Premium logo. Includes an early and very nice reading of "Mother Earth;" also sharp as a tack is "Rockin' the Pad." In an unusual move, Slim is joined by a smooth vocal group, the Vagabonds, for "Really Got the Blues." —*Bill Dahl*

Memphis Slim: U.S.A. / 1962 / Candid ✦✦✦✦✦
By 1954, when these 12 tracks were laid down for Chicago's United Records, amazing young guitarist Matt Murphy had joined Slim's House Rockers, taking the band in fascinating modern directions on the title cut, "Sassy Mae," and the astonishing jazz-based instrumental "Backbone Boogie." Now, if Delmark would only reissue this terrific album on CD! —*Bill Dahl*

All Kinds Of Blues / 1963 / Bluesville ✦✦✦
A good-natured 1961 solo piano session, with Slim's mastery of boogie-woogie styles to the fore on both instrumentals and tunes punctuated by folky monologues. The material's mostly traditional in origin, though Slim wrote the lyrics for the most memorable performance, "Mother Earth." —*Richie Unterberger*

Steady Rollin' Blues / 1964 / Bluesville ✦✦✦
Like Slim's other Bluesville work, this is a characteristic and very consistent effort, though not what you would single out as the cream of his recorded work. He varies the program between originals and covers of standards like "Mean Mistreatin' Mama," "Rock Me Baby," and "Goin' Down Slow," providing a touch of unpredictability by switching from the piano to the organ on a few tracks. —*Richie Unterberger*

The Real Folk Blues / 1966 / MCA/Chess ✦✦✦✦
Lots of duplication with the other Chess reissue CD here, so take your pick. Or pick 'em both up—you can't go wrong with either one of these early-'50s collections. —*Bill Dahl*

Mother Earth / 1969 / Buddah ✦✦✦
Excellent singing and rousing, sparkling barrelhouse, boogie-woogie, and straight blues piano playing from a certified legend. Memphis Slim wasn't shy about making records, and they were seldom not worth hearing. This one didn't break the string of quality efforts. —*Ron Wynn*

Messin' Around with the Blues / 1970 / King ✦✦✦✦
He wasn't messing around with either his singing or playing

here. Memphis Slim made dozens of albums; most were good, some were very good, and a handful were great. This was among the handful. —*Ron Wynn*

★ **Rockin' the Blues** / 1981 / Charly ✦✦✦✦✦
The most complete gathering of Slim's 1958-1959 Vee-Jay output available on disc (16 songs to the even dozen on the *Gate of Horn* domestic disc) and the best-sounding too. This is the crowning achievement in Memphis Slim's massive legacy—he delivers his classics one right after another, backed by his unparalleled combo that was anchored by Matt "Guitar" Murphy's startlingly fresh solos. Along with the standbys—"Messin' Around," "Mother Earth," "Wish Me Well"—there's the catchy instrumental "Steppin' Out," later covered by Eric Clapton; the romping "What's the Matter," and a blistering "Rockin' the House" where the band nearly sails right out of the studio! —*Bill Dahl*

Memphis Heat / 1981 / IMS ✦✦
The combination of Memphis Slim and Canned Heat didn't generate much in the way of sparks when they were brought together for this set in 1974. And a five-strong edition of the Memphis Horns, brought in at some point to add a little punch to the proceedings, actually seem to get in the way. Safe to skip this one, with so much prime Slim available on CD. —*Bill Dahl*

I Just Keep on Singing the Blues / 1981 / Muse ✦✦✦
He kept singing and playing the blues with gusto and distinction his entire career. This came a bit later in The Memphis Slim legacy, when he was more of an established artist than a maverick performer, but it's still almost as essential as his landmark recordings from the 1950s. —*Ron Wynn*

1960 London Sessions / 1993 / Sequel ✦✦✦
The pianist was quite an attraction when he first ventured overseas, and he received plenty of offers to record while he was there. The uncredited combo on these 15 rare tracks is too timid to give Slim what he needed out of a band, but his irrepressible power saves the show. —*Bill Dahl*

Lonesome / 1994 / Drive Archive ✦✦✦✦
Sound quality isn't exactly superb here on this 1961 album, first out on Strand, but the contents are. Another House Rockers album featuring Murphy, saxists John Calvin and Johnny Board, bassist Sam Chatman, and drummer Billie Stepney flying high on "Let the Good Times Roll Creole" (likely the only time Slim and Bill Haley battled it out for bragging rights on a tune), the crackling title track, and a very oddly titled "What Is the Mare-Rack." Slim wouldn't make any more albums with this band (after all, they didn't relocate to Paris with him), making it all the more precious. —*Bill Dahl*

Live at the Hot Club / 1994 / Milan ✦✦
Recorded live in 1980 in Paris, this is not the Memphis Slim that you want for your collection, unless you're the type that has to have everything in a discography just because it's there. Slim is actually in decent enough form. The problems are that his only accompanist is a clunky drummer, and that the fidelity is fairly funky (although not truly grating). And with so many other Memphis Slim recordings available, this ranks pretty far down the list. —*Richie Unterberger*

Together Again One More Time/Still Not Ready For.. / Antone's ✦✦✦
A modern-day reunion of the revered pianist and his favorite guitarist at Austin, TX-based Antone's nightclub, preserved for posterity. They sound mighty happy to see one another. —*Bill Dahl*

Life Is Like That / Charly ✦✦✦✦✦
Some of Slim's earliest post-war sides for Miracle and King (1946-1949), and some of his best. He'd already assembled his little combo with saxists Alex Atkins and Ernest Cotton by that time (interchangeable bassists included Willie Dixon and Big Crawford; no drums necessary), and the classics were flowing: "Lend Me Your Love," "Nobody Loves Me" (adapted by Lowell Fulson as "Every Day I Have the Blues"), and the luxurious "Messin' Around with the Blues." —*Bill Dahl*

Memphis Willie B. (Willie Borum)

b. Nov. 4, 1911, Shelby County, TN
Vocals, Guitar, Harmonica / Acoustic Memphis Blues
Willie Borum, better known under his recording sobriquet of Memphis Willie B., was a mainstay of the Memphis blues and jug band circuit. Adept at both harmonica and guitar, Borum could add pep to any combination he worked in, as well as leaving a striking impression as a solo artist.

He was born in 1911 in Shelby County, TN. He took to the guitar early in his childhood, taught principally by his father and Memphis medicine show star Jim Jackson. By his late teens, he was working with Jack Kelly's Jug Busters, and working for tips on the street, with the occasional house party and country supper rounding out his meager paycheck. This didn't last long, as Borum joined up with the Memphis Jug Band, one of two professional outfits in existence at that time. The group frequently worked what later became W.C. Handy Park in Memphis, their touring stretching all the way down to New Orleans during the Mardi Gras. Sometime in the '30s he learned to play harmonica, being taught by no less a master than Noah Lewis, the best harp blower in Memphis and mainstay of Gus Cannon's Jug Stompers. As his style began to move further away from a strict jug band approach, Willie B. began working on and off with various traveling Delta bluesmen, performing at various functions with Rice Miller, Willie Brown, Garfield Akers, and Robert Johnson. He finally got to make some records in New York under his own name in 1934 for Vocalion, but quickly moved back into playing juke joints and gambling houses with Son Joe, Joe Hill Louis, and Will Shade until around 1943, when he became a member of the U.S. Army.

It was a much different world he returned to and after a brief fling at trying to pick up where he left off, Borum soon cashed in his chips and started looking for a day job. That would have been the end of the story, except in 1961—with the folk and blues revival in full hootenanny steam—Borum was tracked down and recorded an absolutely marvelous session at the Sun studios for Prestige's Bluesville label. It turned into a little bit of a career upswing for the next few years; Willie B. started working the festival and coffeehouse circuit with old Memphis buddies Gus Cannon and Furry Lewis. But then just as quickly, he dropped out of the music scene and eventually out of sight altogether. The reports of his death in the early '70s still remain unconfirmed as of press time. —*Cub Koda*

Introducing Memphis Willie B. / 1961 / Bluesville ✦✦

● **Bluesville Years, Vol. 3** / Prestige ✦✦✦✦
"Beale Street Get-Down" is the folksiest of the bunch, most of it recorded at the Sun studios in Memphis with country blues guitarists Furry Lewis and Memphis Willie B. (Borum) and pianist Memphis Slim all contributing to the fray. —*Cub Koda*

Big Maceo Merriweather (Major Merriweather)

b. Mar. 31, 1905, Atlanta, GA, d. Feb. 26, 1953, Chicago, IL
Piano, Vocals / Chicago Blues, Piano Blues
The thundering 88s of Big Maceo Merriweather helped pave the way for the great Chicago blues pianists of the 1950s—men like Johnny Jones, Otis Spann, and Henry Gray. Unfortunately, Merriweather wouldn't be around to enjoy their innovations—he died a few years after suffering a debilitating stroke in 1946.

Major Merriweather was already a seasoned pianist when he arrived in Detroit in 1924. After working around the Motor City scene, he ventured to Chicago in 1941 to make his recording debut for producer Lester Melrose and RCA Victor's Bluebird subsidiary. His first day in the studio produced 14 tracks—six of his own and eight more as accompanist to renowned Chicago guitarist Tampa Red. One of his initial efforts, "Worried Life Blues," has passed into blues standard status (Chuck Berry was hip to it, covering it for Chess).

Merriweather remained Tampa Red's favorite pianistic accompanist after that, gigging extensively with him and Big Bill Broonzy on Chicago's South side. The pianist cut a series of terrific sessions as a leader for Bluebird in 1941-42 and 1945 (the latter including his tour de force, "Chicago Breakdown") before the stroke paralyzed his right side. He tried to overcome it, cutting for Victor in 1947 with Eddie Boyd assuming piano duties and again for Specialty in 1949 with Johnny Jones, this time at the stool. His health fading steadily after that, Merriweather died in 1953. —*Bill Dahl*

☆ **Chicago Breakdown** / Oct. 1975 / Bluebird ✦✦✦✦✦
Worth searching out for the seven extra songs, including "It's All Up to You," "Why Should I Hang Around," "Come on Home," and "It's All Over Now." Mike Rowe's fascinating liner notes are uti-

lized for both packages, so there's no clear-cut advantage in that department. —*Bill Dahl*

Volume One / 1976 / RCA ✦✦✦✦✦
Chicago Blues is synonymous with Muddy Waters to most, but the 1930s saw the growth of a superb style based on piano and acoustic guitar. Leroy Carr and Scrapper Blackwell were two of the giants. Big Maceo Merriweather and Tampa Red matched them in a slightly more robust style with greater country links. These are some of the blues' greatest moments. —*John Storm Roberts, Original Music*

The Best of Big Maceo / 1992 / Arhoolie ✦✦✦✦✦
Thundering Chicago boogie and blues piano, this is essential. —*Bill Dahl*

★ **King of Chicago Blues Piano, Vols. 1 & 2** / Arhoolie ✦✦✦✦✦
A slightly truncated CD version of the RCA two-record set that first anthologized the thundering 1940s RCA Bluebird sides of pianist Big Maceo (25 cuts on the CD, 32 on the vinyl). The CD opens with Maceo's immortal blues "Worried Life Blues," closes with his instrumental tour de force "Chicago Breakdown," and boasts a great deal of blues piano magic in between. —*Bill Dahl*

Amos Milburn

b. Apr. 1, 1927, Houston, TX, **d.** Jan. 3, 1980, Houston, TX
Piano, Vocals / Electric Jump Blues
Boogie piano master Amos Milburn was born in Houston, and he died there a short 52 years later. In between, he pounded out some of the most hellacious boogies of the postwar era, usually recording in Los Angeles for Aladdin Records and specializing in good-natured upbeat romps about booze and its effects (both positive and negative) that proved massive hits during the immediate pre-rock era.

The self-taught 88s ace made a name for himself as the "He-Man Martha Raye" around Houston before joining the Navy and seeing overseas battle action in World War II. When he came out of the service, Milburn played in various Lone Star niteries before meeting the woman whose efforts would catapult him to stardom.

Persistent manager Lola Anne Cullum reportedly barged into Aladdin boss Eddie Mesner's hospital room, toting a portable disc machine with Milburn's demo all cued up. The gambit worked—Amos Milburn signed with Aladdin in 1946. His first date included a thundering "Down the Road Apiece" that presaged the imminent rise of rock & roll. But Milburn was capable of subtler charms too, crooning mellow blues ballads in a Charles Brown-influenced style (the two would later become close friends, playing together frequently).

The first of Milburn's 19 Top Ten R&B smashes came in 1948 with his party classic "Chicken Shack Boogie," which paced the charts and anointed his band with a worthy name (the Aladdin Chickenshackers, natch). A velvet-smooth "Bewildered" displayed the cool after-hours side of Milburn's persona as it streaked up the charts later that year, but it was rollicking horn-driven material such as "Roomin' House Boogie" and "Sax Shack Boogie" that Milburn was renowned for. Milburn's rumbling 88s influenced a variety of famous artists, notably Fats Domino.

With the ascent of "Bad, Bad Whiskey" to the peak of the charts in 1950, Milburn embarked on a string of similarly boozy smashes: "Thinking and Drinking," "Let Me Go Home Whiskey," "One Scotch, One Bourbon, One Beer" (an inebriating round John Lee Hooker apparently enjoyed), and "Good Good Whiskey" (his last hit in 1954). Alcoholism later brought the pianist down hard, giving these numbers a grimly ironic twist in retrospect. Milburn's national profile rated a series of appearances on the Willie Bryant-hosted mid-'50s TV program *Showtime at the Apollo* (where he gave out with a blistering "Down the Road Apiece").

Aladdin stuck with Milburn long after the hits ceased, dispatching him to New Orleans in 1956 to record with the vaunted studio crew at Cosimo's. There he recut "Chicken Shack Boogie" in a manner so torrid that it's impossible to believe it didn't hit (tenor saxist Lee Allen and drummer Charles "Hungry" Williams blast with atomic power as Milburn happily grunts along with his pounding boogie piano solo). In 1957, he left Aladdin for good.

Amos contributed a fine offering to the R&B Yuletide canon in 1960 with his swinging "Christmas (Comes but Once a Year)" for King. Berry Gordy gave Milburn a comeback forum in 1962,

issuing an album on Motown predominated by remakes of his old hits that doesn't deserve its extreme rarity today (even Little Stevie Wonder pitched in on harp for the sessions).

Nothing could jump-start the pianist's fading career by then, though. His health deteriorated, a string of strokes limited his mobility, and his left leg was eventually amputated. Not too long after, one of the greatest pioneers in the history of R&B was dead. —*Bill Dahl*

☆ **The Complete Aladdin Recordings of Amos Milburn** / 1994 / Mosaic ✦✦✦✦✦
Seven discs tracing the entire 1946-1957 Aladdin Records legacy of jump blues pioneer Amos Milburn, whose rippling boogie-based piano talent and predilection for songs about booze made him a postwar R&B superstar. 145 tracks in all (including plenty of unissued goodies) tab this as the ultimate collection for Milburn fans. He boogied like a champ at his first L.A. date for Aladdin with a thundering "Down Road Apiece" and rocked equally hard a decade later down in New Orleans when he was recutting "Chicken Shack Boogie" with the crew at Cosimo's. Mosaic does their usual elegant presentational job on this R&B legend, not skimping on a thing. Fabulous boxed set. —*Bill Dahl*

★ **Down the Road Apiece: The Best of Amos Milburn** / Jan. 11, 1994 / EMI America ✦✦✦✦✦
Pianist Amos Milburn mixed boogie-woogie with vocal energy and intensity to forge a style that was among early R&B's most exciting and appealing. Milburn's 1940s and '50s singles were sometimes fiery and sometimes silly, ranging from drinking songs and celebratory uptempo numbers to stomping instrumentals and an occasional blues or love tune. This excellent 26-track anthology contains such classic Milburn anthems as "ChickenS hack Boogie," "One Scotch, One Bourbon, One Beer," "Let's Have A Party," and "Bad, Bad Whiskey," as well as lesser-known but just as spirited romps. The mastering bolsters the sound, but doesn't deaden it, while Joseph Laredo's liner notes clearly and completely outline Milburn's musical and cultural/historical significance. —*Ron Wynn*

Blues, Barrelhouse & Boogie Woogie: The Best of Amos Milburn, 1946–1955 / 1996 / Capitol ✦✦✦✦✦
Here's a very reasonable compromise between the pricey Mosaic box and EMI's incomplete single-disc treatment of Milburn's Aladdin legacy: a three-disc, 66-song package that's heavy on boogies and blues and slightly deficient in the ballad department (to that end, his smash "Bewildered" was left off). Everything that is aboard is top-drawer, though—the booze odes, many a party rocker, and a plethora of the double-entendre blues that Milburn reveled in during his early years. The absent 1956 remake of "Chicken Shack Boogie" is a humongous omission, though. —*Bill Dahl*

The Motown Sessions, 1962–1964 / Feb. 1996 / Motown ✦✦✦✦✦
Signed to Motown years after his peak as an R&B star, Milburn's association with the label turned out to be something of a non-event, producing only an obscure album and flop single. A commercial non-event, that is; Milburn's skills were still intact, resulting in some fine if somewhat uncharacteristic performances. This compilation reissues that album (*Return of the Blues Boss*) and adds seven unreleased tracks. Milburn may still have been singing blues/R&B, but he was with Motown, which meant that a fair amount of soul-pop flavor inevitably seeped through. You can hear it in the occasional female backup vocals, swinging brass arrangements, and even a brief harmonica solo by Stevie Wonder on "Chicken Shack Boogie"; the arrangement on "I'll Make It Up to You Somehow" wouldn't have been out of place on an early Mary Wells single. The results are pleasantly surprising, updating Milburn's sound (which would have been quite anachronistic in the early 1960s) into the early soul era. The material is pretty strong, including both bluesy ballads and more uptempo numbers that don't totally smother his boogie-woogie roots. —*Richie Unterberger*

Lizzie Miles (Elizabeth Mary [Née Landreaux] Pajaud)

b. Mar. 31, 1895, New Orleans, LA., **d.** Mar. 17, 1963, New Orleans, LA.
Vocals / Classic Female Blues
Lizzie Miles was a fine classic blues singer from the 1920s who survived to have a full comeback in the 1950s. She started out singing in New Orleans during 1909-11 with such musicians as King Oliver, Kid Ory, and Bunk Johnson. Miles spent several years touring the South in minstrel shows and playing in the-

aters. She was in Chicago during 1918–20 and then moved to New York in 1921, making her recording debut the following year. Her recordings from the 1922–30 period mostly used lesser-known players, but Louis Metcalf and King Oliver were on two songs apiece and she recorded a pair of duets with Jelly Roll Morton in 1929. Miles sang with A.J. Piron and Sam Wooding, toured Europe during 1924–25 and was active in New York during 1926–31. Illness knocked her out of action for a period but by 1935 she was performing with Paul Barbarin. She sang with Fats Waller in 1938, and recorded a session in 1939. Lizzie Miles spent 1943–49 outside of music but in 1950 began a comeback and she often performed with Bob Scobey or George Lewis during her final decade. —*Scott Yanow*

● **Queen Mother of the Rue Royale** / 1955 / Cook ✦✦✦✦✦
An unjustly forgotten name in classic blues annals. Lizzie Miles was a great entertainer and versatile song stylist who could handle everything from vaudeville to classic blues to traditional New Orleans jazz. She had passed her prime by these recordings, but was still able to retain her grit and intensity while relying on experience rather than power. —*Ron Wynn*

Roy Milton
b. Jul. 31, 1907, Wynnewood, OK, **d.** Sep. 18, 1983, Los Angeles, CA
Drums, Vocals / Electric Jump Blues
As in-the-pocket drummer of his own jump blues combo, the Solid Senders, Roy Milton was in a perfect position to drive his outfit just as hard or soft as he desired. With his stellar sense of swing, Milton did just that; his steady backbeat on his 1946 single for Art Rupe's fledgling Juke Box imprint, "R.M. Blues," helped steer it to the uppermost reaches of the R&B charts (his assured vocal didn't hurt either).

Milton spent his early years on an Indian reservation in Oklahoma (his maternal grandmother was a Native American) before moving to Tulsa. He sang with Ernie Fields' territory band during the late '20s and began doubling on drums when the band's regular trapsman got arrested one fateful evening. In the mood to leave Fields in 1933, Milton wandered west to Los Angeles and formed the Solid Senders. 1945 was a big year for him—along with signing with Juke Box (soon to be renamed Specialty), the band filmed three soundies with singer June Richmond.

"R.M. Blues" was such a huge seller that it established Specialty as a viable concern for the long haul. Rupe knew a good thing when he saw it, recording Milton early and often through 1953. He was rewarded with 19 Top Ten R&B hits by the Solid Senders, including "Milton's Boogie," "True Blues," "Hop, Skip and Jump," "Information Blues," "Oh Babe" (a torrid cover of Louis Prima's jivey jump), and "Best Wishes." Milton's resident boogie piano specialist, Camille Howard, also sang on several Milton platters, including the 1947 hit "Thrill Me," concurrently building a solo career on Specialty.

After amassing a voluminous catalog as one of Specialty's early bedrocks, Milton moved on to Dootone, King (there he cut the delectable instrumental "Succotash"), and Warwick (where he eked out a minor R&B hit in 1961, "Red Light") with notably less commercial success. Sadly, even though he helped pioneer the postwar R&B medium, rock & roll had rendered Roy Milton an anachronism.

The drummer remained active nonetheless, thrilling the throng at the 1970 Monterey Jazz Festival as part of Johnny Otis' all-star troupe. It's a safe bet he was swinging until the very end. —*Bill Dahl*

★ **Roy Milton & His Solid Senders** / 1990 / Specialty ✦✦✦✦✦
Certainly this is the place to go for Milton's most popular and influential material—a whopping 18 of the 25 cuts made the R&B Top Ten in the late '40s and early '50s. These include such classics as "R.M. Blues," "The Hucklebuck," and "Hop, Skip & Jump" (given a great rockabilly treatment in the 1950s by the Collins Kids). All of the tracks are prime jump blues, Milton occasionally slowing down the boogies into ballads; one number ("Thrill Me") features fellow jump blues star Camille Howard on vocals. —*Richie Unterberger*

Groovy Blues, Vol. 2 / 1992 / Specialty ✦✦✦✦✦
The rarities and unissued material begin to pop up on *Vol. 2*, making it even more of a feast for collectors. Milton's Solid Senders, featuring pianist/singer Camille Howard, guitarist

Johnny Rogers, and a crew of roaring saxmen, were one of the tightest and most respected on the Coast. —*Bill Dahl*

Blowin' with Roy / 1994 / Specialty ✦✦✦✦✦
The third and presumably final entry in Specialty's exhaustive Milton reissue series is by no means a makeweight affair. Even when the Solid Senders tackled Tin Pan Alley fare like "Along the Navajo Trail," "Coquette," and "When I Grow Too Old to Dream," they swung 'em. More late-'40s/early-'50s rarities and unissued items galore. —*Bill Dahl*

Mississippi Sheiks
Group / Acoustic Country Blues
One of the classic string bands of the late '20s and early '30s, this group featured the talents of Walter Vinson, Bo Carter, and Lonnie Chatmon in various configurations.

Based in Jackson, MS, the group took their name from the Rudolph Valentino movie *The Sheik*. Several years after they began performing, the group recorded their first session in 1930. Over the next five years, they cut nearly 70 songs, which ranged from old-timey string songs to racy blues. During this time, the core of the group consisted of fiddler Lonnie Chatmon and guitarist Walter Vinson, with guitarists Bo Carter and Sam Chatmon joining the group frequently; both Carter and Sam also had successful solo careers, which occasionally prevented them from performing with the group.

The Mississippi Sheiks retained their popularity until the end of the '30s, when they slowly faded from view. —*Cub Koda & Stephen Thomas Erlewine*

☆ **Mississippi Sheiks, Vols. 1–4** / Document ✦✦✦✦✦
There's absolutely no way you can go wrong with this superlative four-CD import set of this seminal blues band. Covers everything they ever recorded from 1930 to 1936. —*Cub Koda*

★ **Stop and Listen** / Yazoo ✦✦✦✦✦
Stop and Listen collects 20 tracks the Mississippi Sheiks recorded in the early '30s, gathering together most of their best-known material (including "Sitting on Top of the World"), plus the previously unreleased "Livin' in a Strain." These records are of significant historical importance and this is the definitive compilation of this groundbreaking—and popular—string band. —*Thom Owens*

Mr. B. (Mark Lincoln Braun)
Piano / Piano Blues
Mark Lincoln Braun (aka Mr. B) plays boogie-woogie piano the traditional way, with blues and jazz elements. The Detroit-based artist has released six albums since 1984: *B's Bounce, Detroit Special* (1985), *Shining the Pearls* (1986), *Partners in Time* (1988), *My Sunday Best* (1991), and *Blue Ivory* (1991), a compilation with Roosevelt Sykes, Henry Gray, and Boogie-Woogie Red. —*John Bush*

Shining the Pearls / May 1987 / Blind Pig ✦✦✦
Mr. B's *Shining the Pearls* has some fine moments, especially when the pianist sticks to the blues. However, the album suffers from somewhat meandering arrangements and the lack of a rhythm section to keep the whole thing in focus. —*Thom Owens*

My Sunday Best / 1991 / Schoolkids ✦✦✦
Mr. B. (Mark Braun) is an exciting boogie-woogie pianist inspired by Little Brother Montgomery, Boogie Woogie Red, and Sunnyland Slim who also sounds a bit like Ray Bryant in spots. His 1991 live recording (taken from several performances) puts the emphasis on the blues either at romping tempos or as slow drags. Roy Brooks plays drums on half of the dozen numbers (including a spot on musical saw during "Blues for a Carpenter"), Mr. B. sings effectively on Blind John Davis' "When I Lost My Baby" and "Roll 'Em Pete," and there is enough variety during this spirited set to hold one's interest throughout. The last selection is a bit odd, for when Mark Hynes suddenly starts playing tenor, the performance quickly fades out! But other than that minor (and unexplained) fault, this is a fine set recommended to fans of blues piano. —*Scott Yanow*

Hallelujah Train / Sep. 3, 1994+Jan. 7, 1995 / Schoolkids ✦✦✦✦✦
Mr. B. (Mark Braun) is a talented boogie-woogie pianist who, on this CD, teams up successfully with bassist Paul Keller's Bird of Paradise orchestra, a seven-year-old big band from Michigan. The arrangements smoothly integrate Mr. B. into the orchestra and these enthusiastic live performances are often quite memorable. Although largely a "no-name" big band, the many soloists are consistently talented (with the standouts being Mark Hynes

on tenor, altoist Scott Peterson, and trumpeter Paul Finkbeiner) and the pianist is in consistently inspired form. Highlights include "Hallelujah Train," "Brauny," tributes to Little Brother Montgomery, Horace Silver, and Eddie Palmieri, an exciting rendition of "Down the Road Apiece," "Air Mail Special," and a lengthy "B's Boogie Woogie." Highly recommended. —Scott Yanow

● **Partners in Time** / Blind Pig ◆◆◆◆◆

McKinley Mitchell

b. Dec. 25, 1934, Jackson, MS, **d.** Jan. 18, 1986
Vocals / Soul Blues
Blessed with an extraordinary set of soaring pipes, McKinley Mitchell waxed a series of superb Chicago soul platters during the 1960s, later veering stylistically closer to contemporary blues in his last years of performing.

At age 16, Mitchell was already fronting a gospel group, the Hearts of Harmony, in Jackson. After spending time singing spirituals in Springfield, MS, and Philadelphia, Mitchell hit Chicago in 1958 and went secular. A rocking debut for the tiny Boxer label the next year preceded his signing with George Leaner's fledgling One-derful logo in 1961.

His first single for the firm, the gorgeous soul ballad "The Town I Live In," proved a national R&B hit and launched the imprint in high style. Mitchell's One-derful follow-ups, including the imaginative "A Bit of Soul," failed to equal the heights of his first single; neither did 45s for Chess (produced by Willie Dixon) and a variety of Dixon-owned labels.

Finally, in 1977, Mitchell returned to the R&B charts with "The End of the Rainbow," another beautiful R&B ballad, for Malaco's Chimneyville subsidiary. An eponymous LP for the label the next year stunningly showcased Mitchell's still-potent voice on a program that combined blues and soul material. A 1984 LP for Retta's, *I Won't Be Back for More*, was among the singer's last releases (by then, he was livingback in Jackson). —Bill Dahl

● **Complete Malaco Collection** / Waldoxy ◆◆◆◆◆
The former Chicago soul singer found new life and a second chance at the brass ring at Malaco during the late '70s. The gent with the soaring pipes wrote the touching ballad "The End of the Rainbow" himself; seldom have singer and song matched any closer. —Bill Dahl

Featuring 12 Great Songs / P-Vine ◆◆◆◆
Until someone sorts out precisely who owns the masters originally on Chicago's One-derful label, we'll have to make do (if we can find it, of course) with this Japanese vinyl collection of Mitchell's early-'60s R&B gems. Includes his haunting first hit, "The Town I Live In," and a clever "A Bit of Soul." —Bill Dahl

Prince Phillip Mitchell

b. 1945
Vocals, Guitar, Piano / Soul Blues
A veteran composer, vocalist, guitarist, and pianist, Prince Phillip Mitchell's roots are in vintage R&B, although he's better known for soul tunes. Mitchell sang with both The Premiers and The Checkmates in the late '50s and early '60s. He was also a dancer with The Bean Brothers in Los Angeles. Mitchell had hits recorded by Mel & Tim, Millie Jackson, Norman Connors, Joe Simon, and Candi Staton, but hasn't had as much luck on his own as a vocalist. His only moderate hit was "One On One" for Atlantic in 1978, and it only cracked the R&B Top 40. Mitchell has also recorded for Event and Ichiban. —Ron Wynn

Loner / Ichiban ◆◆
Vocalist/composer Prince Phillip Mitchell sings a mix of bluesy soul and soulful blues on this early '90s date for Ichiban, the Atlanta-based Southern soul and blues label. Mitchell, always a fine, exuberant, earthy vocalist, sounded strong and convincing, but this album did little beyond the South, as has been the case with the bulk of Ichiban material. Fans who preferred the rough songs Mitchell cut in the '60s and early '70s before joining Norman Connors will enjoy hearing him back in that style. —Ron Wynn

● **Top of the Line** / Atlantic ◆◆◆◆◆

Little Brother Montgomery (Eurreal Montgomery)

b. Apr. 18, 1906, Kentwood, LA, **d.** Sep. 6, 1985, Champaign, IL
Piano, Vocals / Piano Blues
A notable influence on the likes of Sunnyland Slim and Otis

Spann, pianist "Little Brother" Montgomery's lengthy career spanned both the earliest years of blues history and the electrified Chicago scene of the 1950s.

By age 11, Montgomery had given up on attending school to instead play in Louisiana juke joints. He came to Chicago as early as 1926 and made his first 78s in 1930 for Paramount (the booty that day in Grafton, WI, included two of Montgomery's enduring signature items, "Vicksburg Blues" and "No Special Rider"). Bluebird recorded Montgomery more prolifically in 1935–36 in New Orleans.

In 1942, Little Brother Montgomery settled down to a life of steady club gigs in Chicago, his repertoire alternating between blues and traditional jazz (he played Carnegie Hall with Kid Ory's Dixieland band in 1949). Otis Rush benefited from his sensitive accompaniment on several of his 1957–58 Cobra dates, while Buddy Guy recruited him for similar duties when he nailed Montgomery's "First Time I Met the Blues" in a supercharged revival for Chess in 1960. That same year, Montgomery cut a fine album for Bluesville with guitarist Lafayette "Thing" Thomas that remains one of his most satisfying sets.

With his second wife, Janet Floberg, Montgomery formed his own little record company, FM, in 1969. The first 45 on the logo, fittingly enough, was a reprise of "Vicksburg Blues," with a vocal by Chicago chanteuse Jeanne Carroll (her daughter Karen is following in her footsteps around the Windy City). —Bill Dahl

● **Tasty Blues** / 1960 / Original Blues Classics ◆◆◆◆
Unfortunately not available on CD, here's a very attractive example of a pianist with roots dug deep in pre-war tradition updating his style just enough to sound contemporary for 1960. With a little help from bassist Julian Euell and Lafayette Thomas (better known as Jimmy McCracklin's guitarist), Montgomery swoops through his seminal "Vicksburg Blues" and "No Special Rider" with enthusiasm and élan. —Bill Dahl

● **Chicago: The Living Legends (South Side Blues)** / 1962 / Original Blues Classics ◆◆◆◆
This album features '60s recordings by this venerable blues pianist. —Mark A. Humphrey

Goodbye Mister Blues / 1973–1976 / Delmark ◆◆◆
While Eurreal "Little Brother" Montgomery was among blues' greatest barrelhouse and boogie pianists, he was also well versed in traditional jazz. This disc's 13 cuts feature him working with the State Street Swingers, an early jazz unit, doing faithful recreations of such chestnuts as "South Rampart St. Parade," "Riverside Blues," and "Panama Rag." Montgomery's vocals are stately, yet exuberant, while his piano solos were loose and firmly in the spirit, showing the link between early jazz and blues. While the emphasis is more on interaction and ensemble playing than individual voices, players expertly maximized their solo time. This is a fine example of a vintage style. —Ron Wynn

At Home / 1990 / Earwig ◆◆◆
Very informally recorded for the most part in the latter days of the fabulous pianist's career, these tapes provide a glimpse at what Montgomery played to please himself (and wife Jan, of course). —Bill Dahl

Complete Recorded Works (1930–1936) / 1991 / Document ◆◆◆◆◆

John Mooney

b. , Rochester, NY
Guitar, Vocals / Modern Acoustic Blues
John Mooney is an slide guitarist, working primarily in a traditionalist Delta acoustic style. Originally hailing from Rochester, NY, Mooney learned his craft first-hand from country blues legend Son House. Later in his career, he moved to New Orleans, switched to electric guitar and began enlivening his music with Second Line rhythms indigenous to the area.

Born in New Jersey but raised in Rochester, NY, John Mooney began playing guitar following a meeting with Son House, who also lived in Rochester. Mooney learned the basics of blues guitar from House and he returned the favor by supporting the guitarist during the mid-'70s. In 1976, Mooney relocated to New Orleans and within a year of his arrival, he landed a contract with Blind Pig in 1977. He released his debut album, *Comin' Your Way*.

After performing straight acoustic Delta blues for several years, Mooney changed his musical direction in 1983, when he formed Bluesiana, a more eclectic—and electric—outfit. During the '80s, he toured and recorded with Bluesiana, opening for the likes of Albert King, Bonnie Raitt, and Clarence "Gatemouth" Brown. After a few years of touring, Mooney was able to sign another record contract, releasing *Telephone King* on the Powerhouse label. Throughout the late '80s and early '90s, Mooney toured consistently and released albums on a variety of different record labels. —*Cub Koda & Stephen Thomas Erlewine*

Comin' Your Way / 1979 / Blind Pig ✦✦✦
This album features acoustic guitar and arresting vocals on high-energy blues. —*AMG*

Late Last Night / 1980 / Bullseye Blues ✦✦
A mixture of solo (acoustic) and band (electric) tracks, this album is fun, but not too heavy or self important —*Niles J. Frantz*

● **Telephone King** / 1991 / Blind Pig ✦✦✦✦✦
Contemporary blues musicians tend to sound more reverential than stirring, but not John Mooney. He's not doing tributes, he's having a party, and that's the spirit that makes this session both intriguing and enjoyable. —*Ron Wynn*

Testimony / Domino ✦✦✦✦✦
Testimony captures the driving intensity of John Mooney's live shows. Recorded with a stellar supporting band—featuring drummer Johnny Vidcovich and the Meters' bassist George Porter, Jr.—*Testimony* featuring seven covers (including cuts by Robert Johnson and Son House) and seven originals, which are easily among the best that Mooney has ever written. But the key to the record is the sound—not only is Mooney's guitar playing hot and greasy, but there's a tense fury to his vocals that brings the whole thing to a boil. *Testimony* is a gripping listen and one of the best albums Mooney ever recorded. —*Thom Owens*

Alex Moore

b. Nov. 22, 1899, Dallas, TX, **d.** Jan. 20, 1989, Dallas, TX
Piano, Vocals / Piano Blues
One of the last of the old-time Texas barrelhouse pianists, Alex Moore was an institution in Dallas, his lifelong home. A colorful entertainer with a poetic gift for rambling improvisations, Moore had one of the longest recording careers in blues history (his first sides for Columbia were made in 1929; his final session was in 1988). Yet it was hardly one of the most prolific, as there were usually lengthy gaps between sessions. The spontaneous, auto-biographical nature of his latter-day recordings imbue his albums with a special charm.

Moore began performing in the early '20s, playing clubs and parties around his hometown of Dallas; he usually performed under the name Whistlin' Alex. In 1929, he recorded his first sessions, which were for Columbia Records. The sides didn't gain much attention and Moore didn't record again until 1937, when he made a few records for Decca. Between his first and second sessions, he continued to play clubs in Dallas. The time span between his second session in 1937 and his third was even longer than the time between his first and second—Moore didn't record again until 1951, when RPM/Kent had him cut several songs. Throughout the '40s and '50s, Moore performed in clubs throughout Dallas, occasionally venturing to other parts of Texas.

Alex Moore's national break coincided with the blues revival of the early '60s. Arhoolie Records signed the pianist in 1960 and those records helped make him a national name. For the rest of the '60s, he played clubs and festivals in America, as well as a handful of festival dates in Europe.

Although he didn't make many records in the '70s and '80s, Moore continued to perform until his death in 1989. The year before his death, he recorded a final session for Rounder Records, which was released as the *Wiggle Tail* album. —*Jim O'Neal & Stephen Thomas Erlewine*

● **Wiggle Tail** / 1988 / Rounder ✦✦✦✦✦
These are late recordings by this venerable Texas blues pianist. —*Mark A. Humphrey*

From North Dallas to the East Side / 1994 / Arhoolie ✦✦✦

Gary Moore

b. , Belfast, Ireland
Guitar / Blues-Rock
Belfast native Gary Moore first achieved renown as the lead guitarist of hard rockers Thin Lizzy. Moore's first band, Skid Row,

featured bassist Brendan Shields, drummer Noel Bridgeman, and singer Phil Lynott, who left to form Thin Lizzy while Moore remained to pursue a record deal with the help of Fleetwood Mac guitarist Peter Green. Skid Row recorded three albums before Moore left for a solo career, releasing his first album, *Grinding Stone*, in 1973. Lynott then invited Moore to join Thin Lizzy as a replacement for guitarist Eric Bell; Moore stayed for a short time before leaving to pursue session work, which he has continued off and on throughout his career. Moore joined the fusion outfit Colosseum II in 1975 and stayed there as a full-time member, appearing on their 1979 album *Black Rose*. In the middle of a 1979 American tour, Moore left Thin Lizzy again to form the unsuccessful G-Force; his single "Parisienne Walkways," from the solo LP *Back on the Streets*, became a U.K. hit that May.

Moore recorded a series of moderately successful albums during the 1980s and had popular U.K. numbers "Empty Rooms" in 1985 and a collaboration with Lynott, "Out in the Fields." 1989's *After the War* showed the influence of Celtic music, but Moore's breakthrough came with the following year's *Still Got the Blues*. Toning down the hard rock feel of many of his previous recordings, Moore mixed traditional blues standards with a sprinkling of originals and delivered a superb performance vocally and instrumentally, and the album became a critical and commercial success. Moore followed his surprise success with *After Hours*, which featured guest spots from B.B. King and Albert Collins and solidified Moore's reputation as a blues-rocker of note. Moore recorded a side project called BBM in 1994 with former Cream rhythm section Jack Bruce and Ginger Baker, and in 1995, he released a tribute album to his idol, Peter Green, composed entirely of Green originals played on a guitar Green had given him years ago. —*Steve Huey*

Back on the Streets / 1979 / Grand Slamm ✦✦

Corridors of Power / 1982 / Mirage ✦✦✦

After the War / 1989 / Virgin ✦✦✦

● **Still Got the Blues** / 1990 / Charisma ✦✦✦✦✦
Relieved from the pressures of having to record a hit single, he cuts loose on some blues standards as well as some newer material. Moore plays better than ever, spitting out an endless stream of fiery licks that are both technically impressive and soulful. It's no wonder *Still Got the Blues* was his biggest hit. —*David Jehnzen*

After Hours / 1992 / Charisma ✦✦✦✦✦
Not wanting to leave a good thing behind, Moore reprises *Still Got the Blues* on its follow-up, *After Hours*. While his playing is just as impressive, the album feels a little calculated. Nevertheless, Moore's gutsy, impassioned playing makes the similarity easy to ignore. —*David Jehnzen*

The Early Years / Jan. 1992 / WTG ✦✦

Blues For Greeny / 1995 / Virgin ✦✦✦
Gary Moore's tribute to Fleetwood Mac guitarist Peter Green, *Blues for Greeny,* is more of a showcase for Moore's skills than Green's songwriting. After all, Green was more famous for his technique than his writing. Consequently, Moore uses Green's songs as a starting point, taking them into new territory with his own style. And Moore positively burns throughout *Blues for Greeny,* tearing off licks with ferocious intensity. If anything, the album proves that Moore is at his best when interpreting other people's material—it easily ranks as one of his finest albums. —*Stephen Thomas Erlewine*

● **Ballads & Blues 1982–1994** / Mar. 21, 1995 / Charisma ✦✦✦

Johnny B. Moore

b. Jan. 24, 1950, Clarksdale, MS
Guitar, Vocals / Electric Chicago Blues
Very few young Chicago bluesmen bring the depth and knowledge of tradition to the table that Johnny B. Moore does. His sound is a slightly contemporized version of what's been going down on the West Side for decades, emblazoned with Moore's sparkling rhythmic lead guitar lines and growling vocals.

Moore first met the legendary Jimmy Reed in Clarksdale, when he was only eight years old. By the time he was 13 or so, Moore was sharing a bandstand or two with Reed up in Chicago. Letha Jones, widow of piano great Johnny Jones, took an interest in Moore's musical development, spinning stacks of blues wax for the budding guitarist.

Moore joined Koko Taylor's Blues Machine in 1975, touring and recording with the Chicago blues queen (on her 1978 LP for Alligator, *The Earthshaker*). He went out on his own around the turn of the '80s, waxing a fine 1987 album for B.L.U.E.S. R&B, *Hard Times*, that impressively spotlighted his versatility.

After some rough spots, Moore is now more visible than ever on the Chicago circuit, with two new albums (one for Austrian Wolf, the other, *Live at Blue Chicago*, for Delmark). In addition to playing as a leader, Moore is likely to turn up on local stages as a sideman behind everyone from Mary Lane and Karen Carroll to rock-solid bassist Willie Kent. If Johnny B. Moore isn't a star in the making, there's no justice in the blues world. —*Bill Dahl*

● **Johnny B. Moore** / Feb. 6, 1996 / Delmark ◆◆◆◆

Matt Murphy

b. Dec. 29, 1927, Sunflower, MS
Guitar, Vocals / Electric Chicago Blues
Probably best-known for playing behind the Blues Brothers (and appearing prominently in their 1980 hit movie), Matt "Guitar" Murphy deserves enshrinement in the blues guitar hall of fame anyway. His jazz-tinged, stunningly advanced riffing behind Memphis Slim elevated the towering pianist's 1950s output for United and Vee-Jay Records to new heights.

Guitar playing ran in the Murphy household (which moved from Mississippi to Memphis when Matt was a toddler). Matt and his brother Floyd both made a name for themselves on the early-'50s Memphis scene (that's Floyd on Little Junior Parker & the Blue Flames' 1953 Sun waxings of "Feelin' Good" and "Mystery Train"). Matt played with Howlin' Wolf as early as 1948 (harpist Little Junior Parker was also in the band at the time). Murphy added hot licks to early sides by Parker and Bobby Bland for Modern before latching on with Memphis Slim's House Rockers in 1952. Normally, the veteran pianist eschewed guitarists altogether, but Murphy's talent was so prodigious that he made an exception.

Murphy's consistently exciting guitar work graced Slim's United waxings from 1952-54 and his 1958-59 platters for Vee-Jay. Another solid Memphis Slim LP for Strand in 1961 and dates with Chuck Berry, Otis Rush, Sonny Boy Williamson, Etta James, and the Vibrations at Chess preceded Murphy's memorable appearance on the 1963 American Folk Blues Festival tour of Europe (along with Slim, Sonny Boy Williamson, Muddy Waters, Lonnie Johnson, Big Joe Williams, Victoria Spivey, and Willie Dixon). On that pioneering tour (promoted by Lippmann and Rau), Murphy commanded the spotlight with a thrilling "Matt's Guitar Boogie" that showcased his ultra-clean rapid-fire picking.

Harpist James Cotton was the sweaty beneficiary of Murphy's prowess during much of the 1970s. Murphy's crisp picking matched Cotton's high-energy blowing on the harpist's 1974 Buddah album *100% Cotton* (the guitarist penned a non-stop "Boogie Thing" for the set). From there, it was on to aiding and abetting John Belushi and Dan Aykroyd's antic mugging, both on stage and in *The Blues Brothers* flick (where he played Aretha Franklin's guitarist hubby, convinced to come out of retirement by the boys in black).

Murphy has toured as a bandleader in recent years, and recorded an album of his own in 1990, *Way Down South*, for Antone's (with brother Floyd on rhythm guitar). His repertoire encompasses blues, funk, jazz, R&B, and even a few of those Blues Brothers chestnuts (he usually carries someone in the entourage to sing 'em Belushi-style). Murphy's latest disc, *The Blues Don't Bother Me!*, recently emerged on Roesch Records. —*Bill Dahl*

● **Way Down South** / 1990 / Antone's ◆◆◆◆◆
The dazzling guitarist has recorded very sparingly as a leader over the course of his long career, preferring the relative anonymity of sideman duties behind Memphis Slim, James Cotton, and the Blues Brothers. But he acquits himself most competently here, mixing blues, funk, R&B, and a little jazz into his sparkling fretwork. His brother Floyd Murphy, a Memphis blues guitar legend himself, is on hand for a family reunion. —*Bill Dahl*

Charlie Musselwhite

b. Jan. 31, 1944, Kosciusko, MS
Guitar, Harmonica, Vocals / Electric Chicago Blues
Harmonica wizard Norton Buffalo can recollect a leaner time

when his record collection had been whittled down to only the bare essentials: *The Paul Butterfield Blues Band* and *Stand Back! Here Comes Charley Musselwhite's South Side Band*. Butterfield and Musselwhite will probably be forever linked as the two most interesting, arguably most important, products of the "White blues movement" of the mid-to-late '60s—not only because they were near the forefront chronologically, but because they stand out as being especially faithful to the style. Each certainly earned the respect of his legendary mentors. The late Big Joe Williams said, "Charlie Musselwhite is one of the greatest living harp players of country blues. He is right up there with Sonny Boy Williams [I], and he's been my harp player ever since Sonny Boy got killed."

It's interesting that Big Joe specifies "country" blues, because, even though he made his mark leading electric bands in Chicago and San Francisco, Musselwhite began playing blues with people he'd read about in Sam Charters' *Country Blues*—Memphis greats like Furry Lewis, Will Shade, and Gus Cannon. It was these rural roots that set him apart from Butterfield, and decades later Charlie began incorporating his first instrument, guitar.

Born in Kosciusko, MS, in 1944, Charlie's family moved north to Memphis, where he went to high school. Musselwhite migrated north in search of the near mythical $3.00-an-hour job (the same lure that set innumerable Blacks on the same route), and became a familiar face at blues haunts like Pepper's, Turner's, and Theresa's, sitting in with and sometimes playing alongside harmonica lords such as Little Walter, Shakey Horton, Good Rockin' Charles, Carey Bell, Big John Wrencher, and even Sonny Boy Williamson. Before recording his first album, Musselwhite appeared on LPs by Tracy Nelson and John Hammond and dueted (as "Memphis Charlie") with Shakey Horton on Vanguard's *Chicago/The Blues/Today* series.

When his aforementioned debut LP became a standard on San Francisco's underground radio, Musselwhite played the Fillmore Auditorium and never returned to the Windy City. Leading bands that featured greats like guitarists Harvey Mandel, Freddie Roulette, Luther Tucker, Louis Myers, Robben Ford, Fenton Robinson, and Junior Watson, Charlie played steadily around Bay Area bars and mounted somewhat low-profile national tours. It wasn't until the late '80s, when he conquered a career-long drinking problem, that Musselwhite began touring worldwide to rave notices. Today he is busier than ever. —*Dan Forte*

★ **Stand Back Here Comes Charlie Musselwhite's Southside Band** / 1967 / Vanguard ◆◆◆◆
Here was a harpist every bit as authentic, as emotional, in some ways as adventuresome, as Paul Butterfield. Similarly leading a Chicago band with a veteran Black rhythm section (Fred Below on drums, Bob Anderson on bass) and rock-influenced soloists (keyboardist Barry Goldberg, guitarist Harvey Mandel), Musselwhite played with a depth that belied his age—only 22 when this was cut! His gruff vocals were considerably more affected than they would become later (clearer, more relaxed), but his renditions of "Help Me," "Early in the Morning," and his own "Strange Land" stand the test of time. He let his harmonica speak even more authoritatively on instrumentals like "39th and Indiana" (essentially "It Hurts Me Too" sans lyrics) and "Cha Cha the Blues," and his version of jazz arranger Duke Pearson's gospel-tinged "Cristo Redentor" has become his signature song—associated with Musselwhite probably more so than with trumpeter Donald Byrd, who originally recorded the song for Blue Note. Goldberg is in fine form (particularly on organ), but Mandel's snakey, stuttering style really stands out—notably on "Help Me," his quirky original "4 P.M.," and "Chicken Shack," where he truly makes you think your record is skipping. —*Dan Forte*

Louisiana Fog / 1968 / Cherry Red ◆◆◆
The first disappointment in the Musselwhite catalog, this hodgepodge of material and sidemen still has some standouts, especially Little Richard's R&B ballad "Directly from My Heart"—which features the Ford brothers and Tim Kaihatsu and Clay Cotton (back in the lineup from the *Stone Blues* days). "Big Legged Woman" and "Takin' Care of Business" are respectable, but overall the album ranges from uneven to subpar. —*Dan Forte*

★ **Tennessee Woman** / 1969 / Vanguard ◆◆◆◆◆
The addition of jazz pianist Skip Rose gave a new dimension to

the ensemble sound, and provided a perfect foil to Charlie's own soloing—especially on the re-take of "Cristo Redentor," extended to 11 minutes, shifting to double-time in spots. Rose's instrumental, "A Nice Day for Something," is a welcome change of pace, and Musselwhite's "Blue Feeling Today" compares favorably to fine covers of Little Walter and Fenton Robinson tunes. —*Dan Forte*

Memphis Charlie / 1969 / Arhoolie ✦✦✦✦
The 14 performances on *Memphis Charlie* include some loose live sides and even a taste of slide guitar from Musselwhite. They're the work of a more mature artist than the brash kid on *Stand Back.* —*AMG*

Takin' My Time / 1974 / Arhoolie ✦✦✦✦✦
Another highly talented and original ensemble—Rose still on piano, with the Ford brothers (Pat and Robben) on drums and guitar, respectively. Again, Rose contributes an original departure, the solo piano ballad "Two Little Girls"—and, as usual, it is to Charlie's credit that he welcomed such far-from-blues mood swings. Otherwise, the band's (especially Robben's) jazzier leanings were checked at the studio door, and Robben's guitar is mixed too low throughout. At this stage, Charlie was changing personnel too quickly to give any unit a second chance in the studio, which would have been especially interesting with this outfit. —*Dan Forte*

Goin' Back Down South / 1975 / Arhoolie ✦✦✦
Combining two leftovers from *Takin' My Time* with a much later session featuring Chicago pianist Lafayette Leake didn't do much for this LP's continuity, but it was nice to see the tracks see the light of day (especially Robben Ford's jazz instrumental "Blue Stu," a rare recorded example of him on alto sax). Musselwhite and Leake together proves a natural, especially on "On the Spot Boogie," with Musselwhite quoting Charlie Parker's "Now's the Time." Musselwhite's guitar playing makes its first appearance on vinyl here: the primitive country blues of "Taylor, Arkansas" and a nod to Earl Hooker's slide playing, "Blue Steel." —*Dan Forte*

Leave the Blues to Us / 1975 / Capitol ✦✦
Musselwhite's major-label debut was unfortunately a lackluster runthrough. This isn't a bad album; it's just that there's nothing very special about it. His working band centered around Kaihatsu and Sevareid (again, from *Stone Blues*), with the addition of saxophonist Ray Arvizu, a honking tenor as opposed to Robben Ford's jazzy alto. Cameos by Barry Goldberg and Mike Bloomfield only add to an inexplicably cacophonous mix; Goldberg's organ on "Keys to the Highway" is especially obnoxious. Charlie's singing and harp playing are good, but this sounds surprisingly low-budget compared to his previous independent releases. —*Dan Forte*

Times Gettin' Tougher Than Tough / 1978 / Crystal Clear ✦✦✦
Cutting an audiophile session direct-to-disc (meaning that each entire side of the LP is recorded live in the studio, with the band literally pausing between tunes, then forging ahead), someone came up with the bright idea of teaming Charlie with a band that he (mostly) had never played with, including a three-piece horn section. Under normal circumstances (retakes, overdubs, mixing—Charlie's vocals should be louder) this could have been a killer; as it is, it's yet another interesting side of this complex bluesman. Horns and piano (Skip Rose returns) give "Help Me" a whole new wrinkle, and Mose Allison's "Nightclub" is channeled through "Got My Mojo Working." Interesting, yes; definitive, no. —*Dan Forte*

Harmonica According to Charlie / 1979 / Kicking Mule ✦✦✦
Ostensibly an instructional blues harp album (with an exhaustive accompanying book penned by Charlie), this is emotional and listenable rather than academic. Charlie covers a wide range of blues styles (and harp positions), and ventures to the outer fringes of the genre for the instrumentals "Hard Times" (from Ray Charles' sax man David "Fathead" Newman) and his Latin original "Azul Para Amparo" (backed only by guitarist Sam Mitchell). The English studio band is sympathetic, especially pianist Bob Hall. —*Dan Forte*

Dynatones Live—Featuring Charlie Musselwhite / 1982 / War Bride ✦✦
After several years without a new record, this confusing item appeared—in hindsight, looking like a scam to launch Charlie's backup band into a career of its own. Musselwhite gets second billing, even though he sings five of the seven vocal tunes—the lone instrumental being a so-so version of his by-now signature piece "Cristo Redentor"—and the crowd that came to this live gig no doubt didn't see "Dynatones" on the marquee. Confusing. But around this time that had become the norm in Charlie's recording career. —*Dan Forte*

Memphis Tennessee / 1984 / Mobile Fidelity ✦✦✦✦✦
Though steel guitarist Freddie Roulette was pictured on *Tennessee Woman,* he did not play on the album; luckily he is given ample space here, and the combination of his eerie vocal-like sound, Jack Myers' solid but adventurous bass playing, and Skip Rose's jazz piano voicings made this edition of the Musselwhite band one of the most original blues outfits ever. Charlie is in fine form as well, on a rock-solid cover of Muddy's "Trouble No More," a lyrical reading of "Willow Weep for Me," and his harp tour de force "Arkansas Boogie." —*Dan Forte*

Tell Me Where Have All the Good Times Gone / 1984 / Blue Rock-It ✦✦✦✦
Drummer/label head Pat Ford reunited with Charlie and brought along brother Robben on guitar, producing this return to form. Charlie is up to the task in all departments—singing, playing (great tone), and especially songwriting (the title tune and "Seemed Like the Whole World Was Crying," inspired by Muddy Waters' death)—but it had been a while since Robben had played lowdown blues (touring with Joni Mitchell, putting in countless hours in L.A. studios). Pianist Clay Cotten is in fine form, and it may have been wiser to give the guitar chair to Tim Kaihatsu, who by this time had seniority (in terms of hours on the bandstand with Musselwhite) over any of Charlie's alumni. The to-be-expected-by-now deviations this time out: Don and Dewey's "Stretchin' Out," an impressive chromatic harp rendering of "Exodus," and Charlie's solo guitar outing, "Baby-O." Easily Charlie's best-engineered album (nice job, Greg Goodwin). —*Dan Forte*

Mellow-Dee / 1986 / Crosscut ✦✦
By this time Charlie was confident enough to include four acoustic guitar vehicles—one ("Baby Please Don't Go") with overdubbed harp, one ("I'll Get a Break") from his old pal Will Shade of the Memphis Jug Band. The ensemble numbers feature a German backup band with expatriate Jim Kahr on guitar. A more expansive workout (than the Chicago BlueStars' version) on "Coming Home Baby" is nice, and "Cristo Redentor" (Charlie's fourth recording of the song, this time subtitled "Slight Return") gets a beautiful piano-harp duet treatment. Unfortunately, the proceedings are sabotaged by completely inappropriate engineering—mechanical-sounding drums, tons of reverb, way too much high-end. Ouch! —*Dan Forte*

Ace of Harps / 1990 / Alligator ✦✦✦
"This is the best band I've ever had," Musselwhite proclaims on the back of this LP; longtime fans would find that debatable. Rather than schooled on the Chess sounds that provided Charlie with his foundation, these guys play a Malako strain of blues, and Tommy Hill is simply one of the busiest (read: obnoxious) drummers anywhere. A "Boogie Chillen" takeoff ("River Hip Mama") is surprisingly *not* just same-old, same-old, but for the most part the funkified blues contrasts sharply with the album's two most poignant numbers, the jazz standard "Yesterdays" (with Charlie on chromatic, borrowing from trumpeter Clifford Brown's "strings" album) and "My Road Lies in Darkness"—just Charlie and his acoustic guitar. —*Dan Forte*

Signature / Oct. 1991 / Alligator ✦✦✦
Signature is a typically engaging release from Charlie Musselwhite. The harpist runs through a set of modern blues, complete with jazz and funk overtones—indeed, there are two straight jazz instrumentals, "Catwalk" and "What's New?," which showcase his astonishing technique. Not only is Musselwhite in fine form, his band is tight, soulful, and sympathetic, making *Signature* a worthwhile listen for most blues fans. —*Thom Owens*

In My Time / 1993 / Alligator ✦✦✦✦✦
Charlie Musselwhite takes four different approaches on this Alligator release. On two tracks, he turns to guitar, proving a competent instrumentalist and convincing singer in a vintage Delta style. He also does two gospel numbers backed by the legendary Blind Boys of Alabama, which are heartfelt, but not exactly triumphs. Musselwhite reveals his jazz influence on three

tracks, making them entertaining harmonica workouts. But for blues fans, Musselwhite's biting licks and spiraling riffs are best featured on such numbers as "If I Should Have Bad Luck" and "Leaving Blues." Despite the diverse strains, Musselwhite retains credibility throughout while displaying the wide range of sources from which he's forged his distinctive style. —*Ron Wynn*

Cambridge Blues / Big Beat ✦✦✦
Yet another intriguing setting: Musselwhite in an essentially acoustic trio format, backed by pianist Bob Hall and acoustic guitarist Dave Peabody, both from England, live at that country's Cambridge Folk Festival. The crowd's thunderous response says it all—a rare and satisfying night by three great blues players, each skilled in the art of supportive interplay. —*Dan Forte*

Blues Never Die / Vanguard ✦✦✦✦
This may be an overview of Musselwhite's career (from the late '60s to the present—with some previously unreleased tracks, including the title cut), but it is not the best introduction to the artist. For that, his Vanguard '60s output is still recommended, along with the 1984 session on Blue Rock'it and Alligator's *In My Time.* —*Dan Forte*

Louis Myers

b. Sep. 18, 1929, Byhalia, MS, **d.** Sep. 5, 1994, Chicago, IL
Guitar, Harmonica, Vocals / Electric Chicago Blues
Though he was certainly capable of brilliantly fronting a band, remarkably versatile guitarist/harpist Louis Myers will forever be recognized first and foremost as a top-drawer sideman and founding member of the Aces—the band that backed harmonica wizard Little Walter on his immortal early Checker waxings.

Along with his older brother David—another charter member of the Aces—Louis left Mississippi for Chicago with his family in 1941. Fate saw the family move next door to blues great Lonnie Johnson, whose complex riffs caught young Louis' ear. Another Myers brother, harp-blowing Bob, hooked Louis up with guitarist Othum Brown for house party gigs. Myers also played with guitarist Arthur "Big Boy" Spires before teaming with his brother David on guitar and young harpist Junior Wells to form the first incarnation of the Aces (who were initially known as the Three Deuces). In 1950, drummer Fred Below came on board.

In effect, the Aces and Muddy Waters traded harpists in 1952, Wells leaving to play with Waters while Little Walter, just breaking nationally with his classic "Juke," moved into the front man role with the Aces. Myers and the Aces backed Walter on his seminal "Mean Old World," "Sad Hours," "Off the Wall," and "Tell Me Mama" and at New York's famous Apollo Theater before Louis left in 1954 (he and the Aces moonlighted on Wells' indispensable 1953-54 output for States).

Plenty of sideman work awaited Myers—he played with Otis Rush, Earl Hooker, and many more. But his own recording career was practically non-existent; after a solitary 1956 single for Abco, "Just Whaling"/"Bluesy," that found Myers blowing harp in Walter-like style, it wasn't until 1968 that two Myers tracks turned up on Delmark.

The Aces reformed during the 1970s and visited Europe often as a trusty rhythm section for touring acts. Myers cut a fine set for Advent in 1978, *I'm a Southern Man,* that showed just how effective he could be as a leader (in front of an L.A. band, no less). Myers was hampered by the effects of a stroke while recording his last album for Earwig, 1991's *Tell My Story Movin'.* He courageously completed the disc but was limited to playing

harp only. His health soon took a turn for the worse, ending his distinguished musical career. —*Bill Dahl*

● **I'm a Southern Man** / 1978 / Advent ✦✦✦✦✦
Despite his vaunted reputation as a versatile standout on the Windy City circuit, Louis Myers seldom recorded as a leader. This is the best set he did as a front man; cut in 1978, it was ironically recorded in Hollywood. Fellow ex-Little Walter sideman Freddy Robinson shared guitar duties with Myers (who also played harp) on a well-produced set strong on tradition but with one eye cocked toward contemporary developments (witness Myers' stylish diatribe on "Women's Lib"). —*Bill Dahl*

Tell My Story Movin' / 1992 / Earwig ✦✦✦
Since a serious stroke had largely robbed Myers of his revered ability to play guitar, this effort really isn't indicative of his vast talent. But you've got to give him points for courage—Myers summoned up the strength to play harp and sing on what would be his final release. A nice Chicago combo that included guitarists Steve Freund and John Primer undoubtedly put Myers' mind at ease. —*Bill Dahl*

Sam Myers (Sammy Myers)

b. Mar. 19, 1936, Laurel, MS
Harmonica, Drums, Vocals / Electric Harmonica Blues
Sam Myers got a second chance at the brass ring, and he's happily made the most of it. As frontman for Anson Funderburgh & the Rockets, the legally blind Myers' booming voice and succinct harp work have enjoyed a higher profile recently.

Although he was born and mostly raised in Mississippi, Myers got into the habit of coming up to visit Chicago as early as 1949 (where he learned from hearing Little Walter and James Cotton). Myers joined a band, King Mose & the Royal Rockers, after settling in Jackson, MS, in 1956. Myers' 1957 debut 45 for Johnny Vincent's Ace logo, "Sleeping in the Ground"/"My Love Is Here to Stay," featured backing by the Royal Rockers.

Myers played both drums and harp behind slide guitar great Elmore James at a 1961 session for Bobby Robinson's Fire label in New Orleans. Myers cut a standout single of his own for Robinson's other logo, Fury Records, the year before that coupled his appealing remake of Jimmy Reed's "You Don't Have to Go" with "Sad, Sad Lonesome Day."

Myers made some albums with a loosely-knit group called the Mississippi Delta Blues Band for TJ during the early '80s before teaming up with young Texas guitar slinger Funderburgh, whose insistence on swinging grooves presents the perfect backdrop for Myers. Their first collaboration for New Orleans-based Black Top Records, 1985's *My Love is Here to Stay,* was followed by several more albums—*Sins, Rack 'Em Up, Tell Me What I Want to Hear,* 1995's *Live at the Grand Emporium*—each one confirming that this is one of the most enduring blues partnerships of the 1990s. —*Bill Dahl*

● **My Love Is Here to Stay** / 1986 / Black Top ✦✦✦✦✦
Young Texas guitarist Anson Funderburgh and veteran harpist Sam Myers got along so well during the making of this fine set that they got their act together and took it on the road. Happily, it remains there, with Myers deftly fronting Funderburgh's Rockets. Myers' booming voice and rocking harp and Funderburgh's crisp, tradition-laden lead guitar mesh beautifully here—the disc features brash remakes of Myers' past triumphs "My Love Is Here to Stay" and "Poor Little Angel Child" and a host of fresh titles. —*Bill Dahl*

N

Mark Naftalin

b. 1944, Minneapolis, MN

Piano, Organ, Guitar, Accordion, Vibes

Blues musician, composer and producer Mark Naftalin played keyboards with the original Paul Butterfield Blues Band from 1965 to 1968. Since then he has recorded with top blues players like John Lee Hooker, Otis Rush, Percy Mayfield, James Cotton, Michael Bloomfield, Lowell Fulson, Big Joe Turner, and dozens of others—a sideman on over 100 albums.

Naftalin is sought after for his elegant, understated keyboard accompaniment and tasty solos. Although first known as an organist, he has also recorded on piano, guitar, accordion, vibes, and various electric keyboards. In his solo concerts he plays mostly acoustic piano.

Born in Minneapolis, MN, in 1944, Naftalin moved to Chicago in 1961 and enrolled at the University of Chicago, where he jammed along on piano at many of the campus "twist parties," the rage at the time. It was at these parties that Naftalin had his first opportunity to play with harmonica player Paul Butterfield and guitarist Elvin Bishop, the nucleus of what was to become the Paul Butterfield Blues Band.

In 1964, Naftalin moved to New York City, where he spent a year at the Mannes College of Music, and it was there that he sat in with the Butterfield band during a recording session warmup song, playing the Hammond organ (for the first time!). Michael Bloomfield had recently joined the band. The group liked the organ sound (and his playing) and Naftalin went on to record eight of the 11 songs on the first Butterfield album that very day. Butterfield asked Naftalin to join the group during that first session.

In the late '60s, after the first four Butterfield albums, Naftalin went out on his own, settling in the San Francisco Bay area. There he put together the Mark Naftalin Rhythm & Blues Revue and has been active in blues and rock recording sessions, solo gigs and revue shows, and as a producer of concerts, festivals and radio shows. He also played with Michael Bloomfield as a duo and in a band (most often called Mike Bloomfield & Friends) from the late '60s through the mid-'70s, and hosted *Mark Naftalin's Blue Monday Party,* a weekly blues show (1979-1983) that featured over 60 blues artists and groups and was the scene of 86 live radio broadcasts and three TV specials.

More recently, Naftalin has produced the Marin County Blues Festival (1981 to the present) and has been the associate producer of the Monterey Jazz Festival's Blues Afternoon (1982-1991). His weekly radio show, *Mark Naftalin's Blues Power Hour* has been on the air almost continuously since 1979 on San Francisco's KALW-FM.

Currently, Naftalin heads up the Blue Monday Foundation and produces recordings for his label, Winner Records, whose most recent releases are the Paul Butterfield Blues Band's *Strawberry Jam*—live nightclub recordings of the Butterfield band in their heyday—and the classic *Percy Mayfield Live.* He performs, both solo and ensemble, in the Bay Area and elsewhere, often with slide guitar virtuoso Ron Thompson, a long-time associate.

Upcoming for Mark Naftalin as we go to press is the Winner album *East-West Live,* which documents the Butterfield band performing that historic composition in three venues. (See: The Paul Butterfield Blues Band) *—Michael Erlewine*

Steve Nardella

Guitar, Harmonica, Vocals / Modern Blues

Nardella is a strong, American roots-music performer, equally adept at rockabilly and low-down blues. His first known recording behind Detroit bluesman Bobo Jenkins on "Shake 'Em on Down" also featured the debut work of Austin, TX, mainstay Sarah Brown and Fran Christina of the Fabulous Thunderbirds. He formed local Boogie Brothers band with Brown, Christina, and John Nicholas (Asleep at the Wheel, Guitar Johnny & the Guitar Rockers), backing every blues legend who came into their native Ann Arbor, appearing on Atlantic's 1972 Ann Arbor Blues & Jazz Festival behind Johnny Shines, and doing their own solo turn. After the nucleus of band moved to Boston with Nicholas, Nardella formed the Silvertones with local guitar hot-shot George Bedard, recording one fine album for the Blind Pig label. He has continued on his own since then, expanding his musical genres beyond just straight blues forms and turning out some interesting music along the way. *—Cub Koda*

It's All Rock & Roll / 1979 / Blind Pig ♦♦♦

Extraordinary rock, R&B, and rockabilly influences all come out of Nardella's love for blues. As well as possessing a strong voice, Nardella is also an electrifying guitarist in the Chuck Berry mold. Nardella's a rare bird, with more talent than he can harvest. *—Michael G. Nastos*

● **Daddy Rollin' Stone** / 1993 / Schoolkids ♦♦♦♦♦

Hard rocking music from a mix of rock, rockabilly, and R&B on Silvertones member Nardella's solo outing. *—AMG*

Kenny Neal

b. Oct. 14, 1957, Los Angeles, CA

Bass, Guitar, Harmonica, Piano, Vocals / Modern Electric Blues

The future of Baton Rouge swamp blues lies squarely in multi-instrumentalist Kenny Neal's capable hands. Along with a few others (Larry Garner, for one), the second-generation southern Louisiana bluesman is entirely cognizant of the region's venerable blues tradition and imaginative enough to steer it in fresh directions—as his five albums for Alligator confirm.

Neal was exposed to the swamp blues sound from day one. His dad, harpist Raful Neal, was a Baton Rouge blues mainstay whose pals included Buddy Guy and Slim Harpo (the latter handed three-year-old Kenny an old harp one day as a toy, and that was it). At age 13, Neal was playing in his father's band, and he picked up a bass at 17 for Buddy Guy.

The guitarist recruited some of his talented siblings to form the Neal Brothers Blues Band in Toronto (brother Noel later played bass behind James Cotton; five other Neal brothers also play in various bands) before returning stateside. In 1987, Kenny Neal cut his debut LP for Florida producer Bob Greenlee—a stunningly updated swamp feast initially marketed on King Snake Records as *Bio on the Bayou.* Alligator picked it up the following year, retitled it *Big News from Baton Rouge!!,* and young Neal was on his way.

Neal's sizzling guitar work, sturdy harp, and gravelly, aged-beyond-his-years vocals have served him well ever since. An acclaimed 1991 stint on Broadway in a production of *Mule Bone* found him performing acoustic versions of Langston Hughes' poetry set to music by Taj Mahal. His last Alligator set, 1994's *Hoodoo Moon,* rates as one of his most satisfying outings to date. *—Bill Dahl*

Big News from Baton Rouge!! / 1987 / Alligator ✦✦✦✦
The debut release for the second-generation bayou blues gui-
tarist/harpist, whose gruff-before-their-time vocals retain their
swamp sensibility while assuming a bright contemporary feel
that tabs him as a leading contender for future blues stardom. –
Bill Dahl

Bio on the Bayou / Jul. 1988 / King Snake ✦✦✦

Devil Child / 1988 / Alligator ✦✦✦✦
Backed by a punchy horn section and sizzling rhythms, Neal did-
n't suffer from any sophomore jinx. Between Neal, his bass-play-
ing co-producer Bob Greenlee, and drummer Jim Payne, there's
some very crafty songwriting going on here–"Any Fool Will Do,"
"Bad Check," and "Can't Have Your Cake (And Eat It Too)" are
among the standouts. –*Bill Dahl*

Walking on Fire / 1991 / Alligator ✦✦✦✦
Another in the remarkably consistent Alligator catalog of Kenny
Neal that strikingly captures his contemporary Baton Rouge blues
sound. He gets a little hot help from the Horny Horns–alto saxist
Maceo Parker and trombonist Fred Wesley–who once filled a similar role behind the Godfather of Soul himself, James Brown. Two
songs find Neal going the unplugged route, just as he had performed them in the Broadway musical *Mule Bone*. –*Bill Dahl*

● **Bayou Blood** / 1992 / Alligator ✦✦✦✦✦
You really can't go wrong with any of the guitarist's fine
Alligator albums, but this one sparkles as brightly as any, with
memorable outings like "Right Train, Wrong Track," "That Knife
Don't Cut No More," and the steamy title track. Neal's albums
are invariably dominated by well-chosen originals–no small
feat these days. –*Bill Dahl*

Hoodoo Moon / 1994 / Alligator ✦✦✦✦
Neal is one of the most impressive young blues artists on the
scene today–a fact borne out by the contents of this collection.
Ably backed by a band that includes his brother Noel on bass
and keyboardist Lucky Peterson, Neal indulges in a couple of
covers this time, but the majority of the disc is original and
incendiary. –*Bill Dahl*

Raful Neal

b. Jun. 6, 1936, Baton Rouge, LA
Harmonica, Vocals / Modern Electric Blues
When he wasn't busy siring progeny (the Neal household produced ten kids, most of them seemingly now playing the blues),
Raful Neal was staking his claim as one of the top harpists on
the Baton Rouge blues front. Unfortunately, until recently, his
discography didn't reflect that status–but albums for Alligator
and Ichiban have righted that injustice.
    Neal took up the harp at age 14, tutored by a local player
named Ike Brown and influenced by Chicago mainstay Little
Walter. Neal's first band, the Clouds, also included guitarist
Buddy Guy. The harpist debuted on vinyl in 1958 with a 45 for
Don Robey's Houston-headquartered Peacock Records. But
"Sunny Side of Love," fine though it was, didn't lead to an encore
for Peacock or anywhere else until much later, when Neal turned
up with 45s on Whit, La Louisiane, and Fantastic.
    Neal's debut album, the aptly titled *Louisiana Legend*, first
emerged on Bob Greenlee's King Snake Records and was picked
up by Alligator in 1990. *I Been Mistreated*, Neal's equally
swampy follow-up, was released on Ichiban the following year;
sons Noel (on bass) and Raful Jr. (on guitar) pitched in to help
their old man out. –*Bill Dahl*

● **Louisiana Legend** / 1990 / Alligator ✦✦✦✦✦
Kenny Neal's dad Raful is a longtime Baton Rouge swamp blues
stalwart whose own discography is way sparser than it should
be. This album, first out on Bob Greenlee's King Snake logo, is
an atmospheric indication of what the elder Neal can do with a
harmonica, mixing covers ("Steal Away," "Honest I Do," "No
Cuttin' Loose") with spicy originals. –*Bill Dahl*

I Been Mistreated / 1991 / Ichiban ✦✦✦✦
Neal wrote the majority of the sides on this satisfying disc him-
self. His supple band includes two sons, Raful, Jr. on guitar and
Noel on bass, and Lucky Peterson on keys. –*Bill Dahl*

Jimmy Nelson

b. Apr. 17, 1928, Philadelphia, PA
Vocals / Texas Blues
Heavy-voiced Jimmy Nelson was very briefly a star in 1951,

when his downbeat "T-99 Blues" topped the R&B charts for
Modern Records' RPM subsidiary. Strangely, he was unable to
ever return to hitdom, despite some very worthy follow-ups.
    Though he was based out of Houston, Nelson did most of his
early recording in California. After debuting on wax in 1948
with a single for Olliet, he cut his only smash, the aforementioned "T-99 Blues," at the Clef Club in Richmond, TX, in 1951,
with backup from pianist Peter Rabbit's trio. (The exultant slow
blues was covered by bandleader Tiny Bradshaw for King.)
    From then on, Nelson did his studio work for RPM in L.A.
with a cadre of the city's top session men: saxist Maxwell Davis,
pianist Willard McDaniel, guitarist Chuck Norris, bassists Red
Callender and Ted Brinson, and drummer Lee Young. For
unknown reasons, the ominous "Meet Me with Your Black Dress
On," "Second Hand Fool," "Sweetest Little Girl," and the rest
failed to repeat for the singer.
    Nelson made a single for Chess in Houston in 1955 (the typi-
cally laidback "Free and Easy Mind"), ventured next to Ray
Dobard's Bay Area-based Music City diskery in 1957 to wax "The
Wheel," and tried his luck with a variety of tiny Texas labels during the mid-'60s with no further success. At last report, Nelson
was still active vocally. –*Bill Dahl*

● **Jimmy Mr T99 Nelson** / 1981 / Ace ✦✦✦✦✦
No CD exists containing Texas shouter Nelson's early-'50s output
for Modern, but Ace did assemble a nice vinyl collection of his
best material that'll have to suffice (if you can find it) until they
get around to issuing it digitally. –*Bill Dahl*

Watch That Action! / Ace ✦✦✦✦✦

Tracy Nelson

b. Dec. 27, 1947, CA
Vocals / Modern Blues
A very versatile and talented vocalist, Tracy Nelson is better
known for her role as lead singer of Mother Earth. The Nashville
sextet had three albums in a country-rock vein on the charts in
the late '60s and early '70s. But Nelson is just as capable in soul,
R&B, and blues, though she hasn't released many records in that
style. Her albums for Flying Fish were more indicative of her
eclecticism, but her R&B and blues roots are really evident on
her 1993 release, *In the Here And Now*, and 1995's *I Feel So
Good*–both on Rounder Records.
    Born in California but raised in Madison, WI, Nelson began
playing music when she was a student at the University of
Wisconsin. Nelson began singing folk and blues at coffeehouses
and R&B and rock & roll at parties with a covers band called the
Fabulous Imitators. In 1964, she recorded an album for Prestige,
Deep Are the Roots, which was produced by Sam Charters.
    Two years after recording *Deep Are the Roots*, Nelson headed
out to the West Coast, spending some time in Los Angeles before
settling in San Francisco. After arriving in San Francisco, she
formed Mother Earth in 1968. The band stayed together for five
years, recording several albums for Mercury Records, among a
handful of other labels. Nelson left the band in the mid-'70s,
embarking on a solo career that saw her release albums for a
variety of labels, including Columbia, Atlantic, and Flying Fish.
    Tracy Nelson continued to record and perform into the '90s. In
1993, she released *In the Here and Now*, her first album for
Rounder Records and, not coincidentally, her first straight blues
record since she began recording in the '60s. –*Ron Wynn &
Stephen Thomas Erlewine*

Homemade Songs / 1978 / Flying Fish ✦✦✦
This album features gospel-tinged blues from this big-voiced,
intense singer. –*AMG*

Come See About Me / 1980 / Flying Fish ✦✦
This second album features R&B music. –*AMG*

● **In the Here & Now** / Jun. 1, 1993 / Rounder ✦✦✦✦✦
Tracy Nelson's lack of commercial success has always been baffling, even though her voice and style are too eclectic to be
pigeonholed into any trend. This Rounder release features her in
a suitable forum–singing blues and R&B with strength, depth,
and passion. Nelson doesn't just cover such songs as Elmore
James' "It Hurts Me Too" or Willie Dixon's "Whatever I Am (You
Made Me)"; she probes, tears, stretches, and extends them, making the lyrics and sentiments her own through intense, animated singing and phrasing. The final number, a first-rate cover of
Percy Mayfield's "Please Send Me Someone To Love," matches

her with the great Irma Thomas, another blues and R&B survivor. It's a fitting conclusion to an album that comes quite close to displaying Tracy Nelson's complete skills and persona. —*Ron Wynn*

I Feel So Good / 1995 / Rounder ♦♦♦

Robert Nighthawk (Robert McCollum)

b. Nov. 30, 1909, Helena, AR, **d.** Nov. 5, 1967, Helena, AR
Guitar, Harmonica, Vocals / Electric Chicago Blues, Acoustic Chicago Blues

A true master of the slide guitar, Robert Nighthawk was a major influence on Muddy Waters, Elmore James, and Earl Hooker but never managed to parlay his bottleneck elegance into record sales. Nevertheless, Nighthawk made some sensational records for Aristocrat/Chess and United during the late '40s and early '50s.

Born Robert McCullum, he picked up some of his early guitar technique from his cousin, Houston Stackhouse. The pair made money playing for parties and dances in Mississippi before Nighthawk left for St. Louis after a mid-'30s shooting incident. He changed his name to Robert McCoy at this time. The guitarist began recording in 1937 for Bluebird in the company of Big Joe Williams and Sonny Boy Williamson, billed as Robert Lee McCoy or Rambling Bob. He switched over to Decca in 1940.

After playing for a time in Chicago, the guitarist began broadcasting over KFFA in Helena, performing under the evocative sobriquet of Robert Nighthawk (after the title of his popular number "Prowling Nighthawk"). Stackhouse, Ike Turner, Earl Hooker, and Pinetop Perkins all passed through Nighthawk's band at one point or another.

Muddy Waters helped Nighthawk gain a toehold at Aristocrat in 1948. He spent a couple of commercially uneventful years recording for the Chess brothers, laying down the brilliant "Black Angel Blues," "Jackson Town Gal," and "Return Mail Blues" in front of a series of fine pianists: Sunnyland Slim, Ernest Lane, and Pinetop Perkins.

When nothing much happened for him at Chess, Nighthawk defected to United in 1951. There he waxed a storming "Kansas City Blues" and "Take It Easy Baby" and the luxurious "Crying Won't Help You," his immaculate slide work riding over the boogie piano of Bob Call or Roosevelt Sykes and a solid rhythm section. United shuttled Nighthawk over to its States subsidiary for his other session there, which produced the remarkably supple "Maggie Campbell" and a lowdown "The Moon Is Rising." After that, Nighthawk indulged his penchant for rambling, not returning to the studio until 1964. That year, he made up for lost time, recording for Pete Welding's Testament label as well as Chess.

He was also captured in action on Maxwell Street in 1964 by Norman Dayron for eventual issue on Rounder. Nighthawk also made a memorable appearance in filmmaker Mike Shea's documentary *And This Is Free*, playing "Goin' Down to Eli's" for his faithful followers on Maxwell Street. His health fading, Nighthawk returned to Helena to live out his last few years. —*Bill Dahl*

Bricks in My Pillow / 1977 / Pearl Flapper ♦♦♦
A very nice compilation of at least one extant take of Nighthawk's complete output for the Chicago based United label, recorded in 1951 and 1952. Similar in feel to the Chess sides with the addition of Jump Jackson's rock-sock drumming, these 12 sides find Nighthawk exploring familiar turf on the slow ones ("Crying Won't Help You" and "The Moon Is Rising" are two of his best) while kicking up his heels on the fast boogies like Jim Jackson's "(Gonna Move To) Kansas City" and "Take It Easy Baby." Of particular interest is the adaption of an old Delta solo piece "Maggie Campbell," here treated to a full band rhumba beat arrangement that actually works. —*Cub Koda*

Complete Recorded Works (1937–1940) / 1985 / Wolf ♦♦♦♦
For a glimpse into Nighthawk's earliest sides for the Victor label, this is the place to go. The sound–all of it taken off old 78s with little regard for modern noise reduction–is less than stellar, but the performances are nothing but. This includes the tune that gave his permanent non de plume, "Prowling Night Hawk." —*Cub Koda*

★ **Live on Maxwell Street** / 1988 / Rounder ♦♦♦♦♦
Recorded by Norman Dayron live on the street (one can actually hear cars driving by) in 1964 with just Robert Whitehead on drums and John Lee Granderson on rhythm guitar in support, Nighthawk's slide playing (and single-string soloing, for that matter) are nothing short of elegant and explosive. Highlights

include "The Maxwell Street Medley" which combines his two big hits "Anna Lee" and "Sweet Black Angel," a mind-altering 12-bar solo on "The Time Have Come" which proves that Nighthawk's lead playing was just as well developed as his slide work and a couple of wild instrumentals with Carey Bell sitting in on harmonica. Nighthawk sounds cool as a cucumber, presiding over everything with an almost genial charm while laying the toughest sounds imaginable. One of the top three greatest live blues albums of all time. —*Cub Koda*

The Nighthawks

Group / Modern Blues

A hard-driving DC-based bar band with strong Chicago blues roots. Formed in 1972 by harpist and vocalist Mark Wenner and guitarist Jimmy Thackery, the band earned a reputation as a solid outfit through more than a decade of touring and recording projects with John Hammond and former members of Muddy Waters' band. Thackery left in 1986, but Wenner regrouped around longtime members Jan Zukowski on bass and Pete Ragusa on drums. *Trouble*, their recent release on Powerhouse, is a blend of blues, R&B, and rock influences, with a typically energetic sound born in thousands of one-night stands across the country. —*Bill Dahl*

● **Open All Nite** / 1976 / Mobile Fidelity ♦♦♦♦♦
This longtime Washington D.C. blues-rock aggregation made one of its more complete and satisfying albums with this date. Everything, from the vocals to the good mix of bar-band arrangements and explosive solos, clicked. —*Ron Wynn*

Jacks & Kings / 1977 / Genes ♦♦♦♦♦
Classic material and stirring playing. A must-find. —*Michael G. Nastos*

Side Pocket Shot / 1977 / Adelphi ♦♦♦
A studio album with the Rhythm King's Horns. Another solid album. —*Michael G. Nastos*

10 Years Live / 1982 / Varrick ♦♦♦
A highly recommended two-fer that celebrates their decade together. —*Michael G. Nastos*

Rock This House / Big Mo ♦♦♦
Typical roadhouse rocking blues. —*Bill Dahl*

Ollie Nightingale

b. Batesville, TN
Vocals / Soul Blues

Call him a blues singer if you prefer, but Ollie Nightingale will likely always be recalled most readily for the emotionally charged Memphis soul he cut from 1968 to 1970 as front man for Ollie & the Nightingales.

Like most great soul singers, Ollie Hoskins came straight out of church musically. He was the lead singer of the Dixie Nightingales, a Memphis spiritual group, by 1958, when they made their vinyl debut on tiny Pepper Records. Influenced by gospel greats Kylo Turner and Ira Tucker, Hoskins hung in with the group as they moved to Nashboro in 1962 before signing with Stax's short-lived Chalice gospel logo.

Stax exec Al Bell convinced the group to go pop in 1968, though that sanctified spirit rings through melismatically on their R&B hits "I Got a Sure Thing," "You're Leaving Me," and "I've Got a Feeling." Hoskins went solo at the turn of the decade, billing himself as Ollie Nightingale and scoring a couple of R&B chart items ("It's a Sad Thing" and "May the Best Man Win") in 1971–72. The Nightingales soldiered on, recruiting singer Tommy Tate to replace him in the studio.

Nightingale remains a popular blues and soul singer around Memphis. He recently did a performing cameo in *The Firm*, a movie thriller starring Tom Cruise. —*Bill Dahl*

● **I'll Drink Your Bathwater, Baby** / 1995 / Ecko ♦♦♦♦

Hammie Nixon (Hammie Nickerson)

b. Jan. 22, 1908, Brownsville, TN, **d.** Aug. 17, 1984, Jackson, TN
Harmonica, Guitar

Harmonica player Hammie Nixon was born on January 22, 1908, in Brownsville, TN. An orphan at a young age, he was raised by foster parents. He began his career as a professional harmonica player in the 1920s, but also played the kazoo, guitar, and jug. He performed with Sleepy John Estes for more than 50 years, first recording with Estes in 1929 for the Victor label.

He also recorded with Little Buddy Doyle, Lee Green, Charlie Pickett, and Son Bonds.

Nixon helped to pioneer the use of the harmonica as an accompaniment instrument with a band in the 1920s. Before that time, it had been mostly a solo instrument. He played with many jug bands. After Estes died, Nixon played with the Beale Street Jug Band (also called the Memphis Beale Street Jug Band) from 1979 onward. Hammie Nixon died August 17, 1984. — *Michael Erlewine*

Darrell Nulisch & Texas Heat

Vocals, Harmonica / Electric Blues
Vocalist/harpist Darrell Nulisch debuted his own band, Texas

Heat, in 1991 with their Black Top release *Business As Usual.* The big-voiced Dallas native surfaced in 1981 as lead singer with Anson Funderburgh and the Rockets, staying with the band long enough to cut a pair of Black Top albums. He moved on to front Ronnie Earl and the Broadcasters, where he cut three more sets for the firm before going solo. Nulisch also contributed guest vocals to Hubert Sumlin's Black Top output. —*Bill Dahl*

Business As Usual / 1991 / Black Top ✦✦✦
Darrell Nulisch burns throughout *Business as Usual,* but his band fails to give him the needed rhythmic support that would have made this album great. As it is, it's merely a good set of contemporary blues, made worthwhile by Nulisch's dynamic harp. — *Thom Owens*

O

St. Louis Jimmy Oden (James Burke Oden)

b. Jun. 26, 1903, Nashville, TN, **d.** Dec. 30, 1977, Chicago, IL
Piano, Vocals / Piano Blues
Few blues songs have stood the test of time as enduringly as "Goin' Down Slow." Its composer, St. Louis Jimmy Oden, endured rather impressively himself—he recorded during the early '30s and was still at it more than three decades later.

If not for a fortuitous move to St. Louis circa 1917, James Oden might have been known as Nashville Jimmy. He fell in with pianist Roosevelt Sykes on the 1920s Gateway City blues circuit (the two remained frequent musical partners through the ensuing decades). Oden enjoyed a fairly prolific recording career during the 1930s and '40s, appearing on Champion, Bluebird (where he hit with "Goin' Down Slow" in 1941), Columbia, Bullet in 1947, Miracle, Aristocrat (there he cut "Florida Hurricane" in 1948 accompanied by pianist Sunnyland Slim and a young guitarist named Muddy Waters), Mercury, Savoy, and Apollo.

Scattered singles for Duke (with Sykes on piano) and Parrot (a 1955 remake of "Goin' Down Slow") set the stage for Oden's 1960 album debut for Prestige's Bluesville subsidiary (naturally, it included yet another reprise of "Goin' Down Slow"). Oden was backed by guitarist Jimmie Lee Robinson and a swinging New York rhythm section. As much a composer as a performer, Oden wrote "Soon Forgotten" and "Take the Bitter with the Sweet" for Muddy Waters. —*Bill Dahl*

● **1932–1948** / Story Of Blues ✦✦✦✦✦
A solid sixteen-track import collection of Oden's earliest and best sides. —*Cub Koda*

Andrew Odom

b. Dec. 15, 1936, Denham Springs, LA, **d.** Dec. 23, 1991, Chicago IL
Vocals / Modern Electric Chicago Blues
Capable of serving up spot-on imitations of both Bobby "Blue" Bland and B.B. King, Andrew Odom was also a man of many interrelated nicknames: Big Voice, B.B., Little B.B., B.B. Junior. Perhaps his chameleonic talents held him back; Odom was a journeyman Chicago singer who recorded relatively sparingly.

Like the majority of his peers, Odom started out singing spirituals but fell in with Albert King and Johnny O'Neal on the St. Louis blues scene of the mid-'50s and began plying his trade there. He made an unobtrusive recording debut in 1961, singing "East St. Louis" with the band of one Little Aaron for the obscure Marlo imprint. He arrived in Chicago around 1960, hooking up with Earl Hooker as the slide guitar wizard's vocalist. A single for Nation Records in 1967 (as Andre Odom) preceded his debut album for ABC-BluesWay (cut in 1969, it remained in the can for quite a while before the label finally issued it).

A guest spot on Jimmy Dawkins' encore Delmark LP, *All for Business,* was a highlight of the '70s for the singer. He cut his own album for the French Isabel label in 1982 in the company of Magic Slim & the Teardrops (reissued by Evidence in 1993), but it was a 1992 set for Flying Fish, *Goin' to California* (co-produced by guitarist Steve Freund), that probably captured his considerable vocal charms the best.

Odom was a popular attraction on the Windy City circuit right up until the fateful night when he suffered a heart attack while driving from Buddy Guy's Legends to another local blues mecca, the Checkerboard Lounge. He's been missed ever since. —*Bill Dahl*

Farther on the Road / 1969 / Bluesway ✦✦
Disappointing debut album by the Chicago singer with the mellifluous pipes. Even with Earl Hooker on lead guitar, the spark just wan't there. —*Bill Dahl*

● **Going to California** / 1991 / Flying Fish ✦✦✦✦✦
Not long before he died, Odom made the album of his life with a combo called the Gold Tops, who provided precisely the right backing to properly spotlight his booming voice. A few overdone standards—"Rock Me Baby," "Woke Up This Morning," "Next Time You See Me"—intrude a bit, but Odom's own "Bad Feelin'," "Why Did You Leave Me," and "Come to Me" make impassioned amends. Steve Freund, best-known for his long stint with Sunnyland Slim, contributes stellar lead guitar. —*Bill Dahl*

Omar & the Howlers

Group / Modern Texas Blues
European blues fans adore Austin, TX-based guitarist, singer and songwriter Omar Kent Dykes. That's because he fits the stereotypical image many of them have of the American musician: he's tall, wears cowboy boots, and has a deep voice with a Southern accent. However, Dykes does not carry a gun, and though he looks rough and tough, he's actually an incredibly peaceful and intelligent musician, and a veteran at working a crowd in a blues club or a festival. While Dykes still has a sizeable American audience, owing to his albums for Columbia Records, he still spends a good portion of his touring year at festivals and clubs around Europe.

Among White blues musicians, Dykes is truly one of a kind, a fact that Columbia Records recognized in the 1980s, when he recorded for them. These days, Dykes and his band, the Howlers, record for the Austin, TX-based Watermelon Records label. Since being dropped by Columbia Records after the company was bought by Sony, Dykes' independent-label output since 1990 has been nothing short of extraordinary. His albums since 1990 include *Monkey Land* (1990, Antone's); *Live at Paradiso, Blues Bag,* and *Courts of Lulu,* (all for Rounder); as well as *Muddy Springs Road* (1995), and *World Wide Open* (1996). Dykes' 1987 debut for Columbia, *Hard Times in the Land of Plenty,* sold upwards of 500,000 copies, excellent numbers for a blues album.

Omar Kent Dykes was born in 1950, in McComb, MS, the same town from which Bo Diddley hails. He first set foot into neighborhood juke joints at age 12, he recalled. After he'd been playing guitar for awhile, he went back into the juke joint. After graduating from high school, Dykes lived in Hattiesburg and Jackson, MS, for a few years before relocating to Austin in 1976. He'd heard the blues scene in Texas was heating up. At that time, Stevie Ray Vaughan was still playing with Paul Ray and the Cobras.

"I know Stevie Ray had a big impact on me, 'cause he was such a great guy. But I think everybody in the blues scene around here influenced everyone else," he said in a 1994 interview. "The blues scene is tight and loose at the same time, everybody is rooting for everybody else, because it helps everybody else out when one artist is on the radio," he added.

To hear how Dykes has developed as a songwriter in the 1990s, check out *Muddy Springs Road* or *World Wide Open,* his two recent releases for Watermelon Records. To hear the finesse, fury and excitement of one of his live shows, pick up *Live at Paradiso* (Rounder) recorded at the club by the same name in Amsterdam. —*Richard Skelly*

Big Leg Beat / 1980 / Amazing ✦✦✦
Omar & the Howler's debut *Big Leg Beat* is an impressive piece
of work. "Omar" Kent "Dykes" was an imposing, forceful vocalist
from the start and the Howlers are a tough, exciting band, slamming through gritty Chicago blues with passion. Although they
made better albums later in their career, *Big Leg Beat* remains
an invigorating listen. —*Thom Owens*

● **I Told You So** / 1984 / Austin ✦✦✦✦✦
This is one of the finest records Omar & the Howlers ever
released, filled with roaring, impassioned performances and a
sharp set of material. —*Thom Owens*

Hard Times in the Land of Plenty / 1987 / Columbia ✦✦✦✦✦
For their major-label debut, Omar & the Howlers were trimmed
down to a trio, but that didn't decrease their power. If anything,
the group sounds leaner and meaner. *Hard Times in the Land of
Plenty* is one of their finest releases for this reason—it's a rough
and tumble collection that is driven as much by fine original
songwriting as it is by the band's edgy sound. —*Thom Owens*

Live at Paradiso / Sep. 1991 / Bullseye Blues ✦✦
For a band that usually sounds alive and vibrant on record, *Live
at Paradiso* is a disappointingly sedate live album from Omar &
the Howlers. Although there are a couple of fine moments scattered throughout the album, there's not enough to make the
album a captivating listen. —*Thom Owens*

Courts of Lulu / 1992 / Bullseye Blues ✦✦✦
Omar & the Howlers' misadventures at the majors began when
they trimmed the blues and padded the rock. Since returning to
Rounder/Bullseye, they have smartly managed to keep the balance, and that's the case on their latest. The 13 tracks alternate
between boogie shuffles, swaggering wailers, and heartache tes-
timonies, with Omar's flailing guitar and spiraling harmonica
nicely backed by his trio and such assistants as organist Reese
Wynans, vocalist Kris McKay, and saxophonist John Mills. Plenty
of blues and more than enough rock fervor. —*Ron Wynn*

World Wide Open / 1996 / Watermelon ✦✦✦
Supported by a new batch of Howlers, Omar Dykes doesn't show
any signs of wear and tear on *World Wide Open*. The band continues to turn out a gut-busting mixture of blues and dirty rock
& roll, occasionally sounding like Howlin' Wolf, other times like
the Stones or Creedence Clearwater Revival. As always, the quality of songs is slightly inconsistent but the band never sounds
tired—they perform with as much energy, if not more, than they
ever have. —*Thom Owens*

Monkey Land / Antone's ✦✦✦
A solid effort, it benefits from its excellent label. —*David
Szulmary*

Johnny Otis (John Veliotes)

b. Dec. 28, 1921, Vallejo, CA
Piano, Drums, Vocals, Vibes / West Coast Blues
Johnny Otis has modeled an amazing number of contrasting
musical hats over a career spanning more than half a century.
Bandleader, record producer, talent scout, label owner, nightclub
impresario, disc jockey, TV variety show host, author, R&B pioneer, rock & roll star—Otis has answered to all those descriptions and quite a few more. Not bad for a Greek-American who
loved jazz and R&B so fervently that he adopted the African-
American culture as his own.
California-born John Veliotes changed his name to the black-
er-sounding Otis when he was in his teens. Drums were his first
passion—he spent time behind the traps with the Oakland-based
orchestra of Count Otis Matthews and kept time for various
Midwestern swing outfits before settling in Los Angeles during
the mid-'40s and joining Harlan Leonard's Rockets, then resident
at the Club Alabam.
It wasn't long before the Alabam's owner entreated Otis to
assemble his own orchestra for house-band duties. The group's
1945 debut sides for Excelsior were solidly in the big-band jazz
vein and included an arrangement of the moody "Harlem
Nocturne" that sold well. Shouter Jimmy Rushing fronted the
band for two tracks at the same date. Otis' rep as a drummer was
growing; he backed both Wynonie Harris and Charles Brown
(with Johnny Moore's Three Blazers) that same year.
The Otis outfit continued to record for Excelsior through 1947
(one date featured Big Jay McNeely on sax), but his influence on
L.A.'s R&B scene soared exponentially when he and partner

Bardu Ali opened the Barrelhouse Club in Watts. R&B replaced
jazz in Otis' heart; he pared the big band down and discovered
young talent such as the Robins, vocalists Mel Walker and Little
Esther Phillips, and guitarist Pete Lewis that would serve him
well in years to come.
Otis signed with Newark, NJ-based Savoy Records in 1949,
and the R&B hits came in droves: "Double Crossing Blues,"
"Mistrustin' Blues," and "Cupid's Boogie" all hit number one that
year (in all, Otis scored ten Top Ten smashes that year alone!);
"Gee Baby," "Mambo Boogie," and "All Nite Long" lit the lamp
in 1951, and "Sunset to Dawn" capped his amazing run in 1952
(vocals were shared by Esther, Walker, and other members of the
group). By then, Otis had branched out to play vibes on many
waxings.
In late 1951, Otis moved to Mercury, but apart from a Walker-
led version of Floyd Dixon's "Call Operator 210," nothing found
pronounced success with the public. A 1953–55 contract with
Don Robey's Peacock logo produced some nice jump blues sides
but no hits (though the Otis orchestra backed one of his many
discoveries, Big Mama Thornton, on her chart-topping "Hound
Dog," as well as a young Little Richard while at Peacock). Otis
was a masterful talent scout; among his platinum-edged discoveries were Jackie Wilson, Little Willie John, Hank Ballard,
and Etta James (he produced her debut smash "Roll with Me
Henry").
In 1955, Otis took studio matters into his own hands, starting
up his own label, Dig Records, to showcase his own work as well
as his latest discoveries (including Arthur Lee Maye & the
Crowns, Tony Allen, and Mel Williams). Rock & roll was at its
zenith in 1957, when the multi-instrumentalist signed on with
Capitol Records; billed as the Johnny Otis Show, he set the R&B
and pop charts ablaze in 1958 with his shave-and-a-haircut beat,
"Willie and the Hand Jive," taking the vocal himself (other
singers then with the Otis Show included Mel Williams and the
gargantuan Marie Adams & the Three Tons of Joy). During the
late '50s, Otis hosted his own variety program on L.A. television,
starring his entire troupe (and on one episode, Lionel Hampton),
and did a guest shot in a 1958 movie, *Juke Box Rhythm*.
After cutting some great rock & roll for Capitol from 1957 to
1959 with only one hit to show for it, Otis dropped anchor at
King Records in 1961-62 (in addition to his own output, Otis'
band also backed Johnny "Guitar" Watson on several sides).
Later in the decade, Otis recorded some ribald material for Kent
and watched as his young son Shuggie built an enviable reputation as a blues guitarist while recording for Columbia. Father
and son cut an album together for Alligator in 1982, accurately
entitled *The New Johnny Otis Show*.
In recent years, the multi-talented Otis added operating a
California health-food emporium to his endless list of wide-ranging accomplishments. If blues boasts a renaissance man
amongst its ranks, Johnny Otis surely fills that bill. —*Bill Dahl*

The Johnny Otis Show / 1958 / Savoy ✦✦✦✦✦
Some of the R&B bandleader's earliest and best work (1945-51)
for Savoy. The cast includes singers Little Esther and Mel Walker,
The Robins, and guitarist Pete Lewis. —*Bill Dahl*

Live at Monterey / 1971 / Epic ✦✦✦✦✦
An R&B oldies show with a difference, the artists represented
the cream of the crop of jump blues, and in 1970, they were still
in fine form. The disc stars Otis, Esther Phillips, Eddie Vinson,
Joe Turner, Ivory Joe Hunter, Roy Milton, Roy Brown, Pee Wee
Crayton, and Johnny's guitar-wielding son, Shuggie. —*Bill Dahl*

The Capitol Years / 1988 / Capitol ✦✦✦✦✦
Unfortunately now out-of-print, this set anthologizes Otis' late-
'50s rise to rock & roll fame, thanks to his shave-and-a-haircut
special "Willie and the Hand Jive." Like every other style of R&B
Otis drifted into, he excelled at it—"Castin' My Spell," "Crazy
Country Hop," "Willie Did the Cha Cha," and "Three Girls
Named Molly" are catchy rockers. Otis had a terrific band—guitarist Jimmy Nolen (later James Brown's main axeman), pianist
Ernie Freeman, drummer Earl Palmer, and a tight horn section
(along with singers Marie Adams and Mel Williams) gave him
all the help he could possibly need. —*Bill Dahl*

Be Bop Baby Blues / 1989 / Night Train ✦✦✦
A bit skimpy at 14 songs, this disc casts Otis mostly in a bandleader role on late-'40s sides culled from the Excelsior, Supreme,
and Swing Time labels. Vocalists fronting the Otis outfit include
the extremely obscure Joe Swift, Earl Jackson, Clifford "Fat Man"

Blivens, and Johnny Crawford. Swinging, horn-leavened jump blues all the way. —*Bill Dahl*

★ **The Original Johnny Otis Show** / 1994 / Savoy Jazz ✦✦✦✦✦
Twenty-seven of the Otis aggregation's best early sides for Savoy and Excelsior, including a slew of the group's early-'50s Little Esther and/or Mel Walker-fronted R&B smashes ("Mistrustin' Blues," "Cry Baby," "Sunset to Dawn"). Jimmy Rushing and the Robins also share vocal duties, as does Otis himself on a jumping "All Nite Long." This is one time when the bonus cuts are on the vinyl version—it contained 32 cuts appearing on a *Completer Disc* that Savoy Jazz reissued at the same time as this CD. The original artwork and liner notes have been reduced so much for the CD that they're unreadable (Pete Welding's essay deserves more respect). *Bill Dahl*

Too Late to Holler / 1995 / Night Train ✦✦✦✦
A more generous selection of late-'40s Swing Time and Excelsior sides, again featuring Swift (who dominates the compilation), Jackson, and Blivens in front of the powerful Otis orchestra. Very little duplication exists between the two discs. —*Bill Dahl*

Let's Live It Up / Charly ✦✦✦
Otis stopped off at King Records for a while during the early '60s, making clever 45s that no one paid much attention to. Twenty-two of them are here, including five by the late Johnny "Guitar" Watson (whose "In the Evenin'" is chillingly direct). It's a mixed bag—vocal group stuff, twist workouts, and the inevitable sequel "Hand Jive One More Time" (alas, nobody did). —*Bill Dahl*

Creepin' with the Cats: The Legendary Dig Masters / Ace ✦✦✦
Twenty-two tracks, almost half previously unreleased, from circa 1956–57 that Otis recorded for his own short-lived Dig label. Not as vivacious as the sides he recorded for Capitol in the late '50s, this is spirited but generic jump blues/R&B, divided evenly between vocals and instrumentals. Occasional cuts like the silly novelty instrumental "Ali Baba's Boogie" stand out from the pack. The one commanding greatest interest is "Hey! Hey! Hey!," which served as the model for Little Richard's version, which in turned was covered by the Beatles in the mid-'60s (as "Kansas City"). —*Richie Unterberger*

Jack Owens

b. Bentonia, MS
Guitar, Vocals / Acoustic Country Blues, Acoustic Mississippi Blues

Like Skip James, Owens hails from Bentonia, MS. Owens is much less famous than James, but he's often compared to Skip due to his high, rich vocals and intricate guitar styles, which finds him using several tunings and occasional minor keys. His material, it must be noted, is not nearly as strong or tightly constructed as James', although it draws from some of the same sources. Noted folklorist and blues scholar David Evans made several recordings with Owens in the late '60s and early '70s. —*Richie Unterberger*

It Must Have Been the Devil / 1971 / Testament ✦✦✦
Although this album is credited to Owens and Bud Spires, it's really Owens' show; Spires adds some harmonica accompaniment to Jack's playing and singing. Although David Evans (who produced these recordings) intimates that Owens is better than Skip James in his liner notes, it's really not that hard to figure out why James is better known; James' songs are simply better written, more gripping, and more memorable, and Owens tends to ramble pleasantly. If you're looking for the Bentonia sound, though, this is certainly a down-home, well-recorded representation, and has an advantage over those vintage James (or any vintage blues) sides in that the fidelity is much, much clearer. Recorded in 1970, the 1995 CD reissue adds five previously unreleased tracks. —*Richie Unterberger*

P

Hot Lips Page (Oran Thaddeus Page)

b. Jan. 27, 1908, Dallas, TX, **d.** Nov. 5, 1954, New York, NY
Trumpet, Vocals / Blues, Dixieland, Swing

One of the great swing trumpeters in addition to being a talented blues vocalist, Hot Lips Page's premature passing left a large hole in the jazz world; virtually all musicians (no matter their style) loved him. Page gained early experience in the 1920s performing in Texas, playing in Ma Rainey's backup band. He was with Walter Page's Blue Devils during 1928–31 and then joined Bennie Moten's band in Kansas City in time to take part in a brilliant 1932 recording session. Page freelanced in Kansas City and in 1936 was one of the stars in Count Basie's orchestra but, shortly before Basie was discovered, Joe Glaser signed Hot Lips as a solo artist. Although Page's big band did all right in the late '30s (recording for Victor), if he had come east with Basie he would have become much more famous. Page was one of the top sidemen with Artie Shaw's Orchestra during 1941–42 and then mainly freelanced throughout the remainder of his career, recording with many all-star groups and being a welcome fixture at jam sessions. —*Scott Yanow*

★ **The Chronological Hot Lips Page (1938–1940)** / Mar. 10, 1938–Dec. 3, 1940 / Classics ◆◆◆◆◆

After Hours in Harlem / 1941 / Onyx ◆◆◆◆

Dr. Jazz Series, Vol. 6 / Dec. 21, 1951–Mar. 7, 1952 / Storyville ◆◆◆◆◆

There are not that many recordings from the later part of Page's career, which makes this CD (comprised of radio broadcasts) of great interest. Page is heard on a variety of Dixieland and swing standards with quite an assortment of all-stars including cornetist Wild Bill Davison; trombonists Lou McGarity and Sandy Williams; clarinetists Pee Wee Russell, Bob Wilber, Eddie Barefield, Cecil Scott, and Peanuts Hucko; pianists Red Richards, Dick Cary, Joe Sullivan, and Charlie Queener; and drummer George Wettling (who was actually the leader of these groups). Page is in exuberant form, whether singing tunes such as "When My Sugar Walks Down the Street" and a riotous "St. Louis Blues" or leading the ensembles. This is one of his best recordings currently available and is often quite exciting. —*Scott Yanow*

Bobby Parker

b. Aug. 31, 1937, Lafayette, Louisiana
Guitar, Vocals / Modern Blues

Guitarist, singer, and songwriter Bobby Parker is one of the most exciting performers in modern blues, and it's quite apparent he'll inherit the top blues spots left open by the unfortunate, early passings of people like Albert King, Johnny "Guitar" Watson, and others. That's because Parker can do it all: he writes brilliant songs, he sings well, and he backs it all up with powerful, stinging guitar. But things weren't always so good for Parker, and much of his newfound success is the result of years of hard work and struggling around the bars in Washington, D.C. and Virginia.

Parker has two brilliant albums out on the Black Top label out of New Orleans (distributed by Rounder), *Shine Me Up* (1995) and *Bent Out of Shape* (1993).

He was born August 31, 1937, in Lafayette, LA, but raised in Southern California after his family moved to Los Angeles when he was six. Going to school in Hollywood, the young Parker decided he wanted to be in show business. At the Million Dollar Theatre, he saw big stage shows by Count Basie, Duke Ellington,

Billy Eckstine, and Lionel Hampton. Although he had an early interest in jazz, the blues bit him when artists like T-Bone Walker, Lowell Fulson, Johnny "Guitar" Watson, and Pee Wee Crayton came to town.

He began playing in the late '50s as a guitarist with Otis Williams and the Charms after winning a talent contest sponsored by West Coast blues and R&B legend Johnny Otis. Later, he backed Bo Diddley, which included an appearance on *The Ed Sullivan Show* before joining the touring big band of Paul "Hucklebuck" Williams. He settled in Washington, D.C. in the 1960s, dropping out of Williams' band and making a go of it on his own.

He is perhaps best-known for his 1961 song, "Watch Your Step," a single for the V-Tone label that became a hit on British and U.S. R&B charts. Parker's song was later covered by several British blues groups, most prominent among them the Spencer Davis Group. And though Parker may not yet be a name as familiar to blues fans as, say, Eric Clapton or B.B. King, he's been cited as a major musical influence by Davis, John Mayall, Robin Trower, Clapton, Jimmy Page, drummer Mick Fleetwood, John Lennon, and, most importantly, Carlos Santana. Parker's style has been described by his protege Bobby Radcliff as Guitar Slim meets James Brown, and that's not that far off the mark. In the summer of 1994, Santana was so happy about Parker's comeback on the Black Top/Rounder label that he took him on the road for some arena shows on the East and West coasts.

"Carlos likes to tell people that he saw me playing in Mexico City when he was a kid, and that inspired him to pick up the guitar," Parker explained in a recent interview. Santana pays homage to Parker on his *Havana Moon* album, on which he covers "Watch Your Step." Dr. Feelgood also covered the tune in the 1970s.

For the rest of the 1990s, Parker is destined to be one of the major players on the blues circuit, provided his stellar output and rigorous touring schedules continue. Unlike so many other blues musicians, Parker's live shows are almost entirely his own songs. He does very few covers.

"Unless the music of the day has some kind of substance to it, the blues always comes back," Parker says, adding, "I think Stevie Ray Vaughan had a lot to do with bringing the blues to White audiences, and Z.Z. Hill helped bring the Black audience back to the blues." —*Richard Skelly*

● **Bent Out of Shape** / 1993 / Black Top ◆◆◆◆◆
The best blues album of 1993 featured soulful vocals, stunning guitar, and crisp, polished backing. —*Bill Dahl*

Shine Me Up / 1995 / Black Top ◆◆◆◆◆
Guitarist Bobby Parker continued his '90s comeback with *Shine Me Up*, an album filled with fiery leads and gritty, soulful R&B-based material. —*Thom Owens*

Junior Parker (Herman Parker)

b. May 27, 1932, Clarksdale, MS, **d.** Nov. 18, 1971, Chicago, IL
Harmonica, Vocals / Electric Memphis Blues, Soul Blues

His velvet-smooth vocal delivery to the contrary, Junior Parker was a product of the fertile postwar Memphis blues circuit whose wonderfully understated harp style was personally mentored by none other than regional icon Sonny Boy Williamson.

Herman Parker, Jr. only traveled in the best blues circles from the outset. He learned his initial licks from Williamson and gigged with the mighty Howlin' Wolf while still in his teens. Like so many young blues artists, Little Junior (as he was known then) got his first recording opportunity from talent scout Ike Turner, who brought him to Modern Records for his debut session as a leader in 1952. It produced the lone single "You're My Angel," with Turner pounding the 88s and Matt Murphy deftly handling guitar duties.

Parker and his band, the Blue Flames (including Floyd Murphy, Matt's brother, on guitar), landed at Sun Records in 1953 and promptly scored a hit with their rollicking "Feelin' Good" (something of a Memphis response to John Lee Hooker's primitive boogies). Later that year, Little Junior cut a fiery "Love My Baby" and a laidback "Mystery Train" for Sun, thus contributing a pair of future rockabilly standards to the Sun publishing coffers (Hayden Thompson revived the former, Elvis Presley the latter).

Before 1953 was through, the polished Junior Parker had moved on to Don Robey's Duke imprint in Houston. It took a while for the harpist to regain his hitmaking momentum, but he scored big in 1957 with the smooth "Next Time You See Me," an accessible enough number to even garner some pop spins.

Criss-crossing the country as headliner with the Blues Consolidated package (his support act was labelmate Bobby Bland), Parker developed a breathtaking brass-powered sound (usually the work of trumpeter/Duke-house-bandleader Joe Scott) that pushed his honeyed vocals and intermittent harp solos with exceptional power. Parker's updated remake of Roosevelt Sykes' "Driving Wheel" was a huge R&B hit in 1961, as was the surging "In the Dark" (the R&B dance workout "Annie Get Your Yo-Yo" followed suit the next year).

Parker was exceptionally versatile—whether delivering "Mother-In-Law Blues" and "Sweet Home Chicago" in faithful downhome fashion, courting the teenage market with "Barefoot Rock," or tastefully howling Harold Burrage's "Crying for My Baby" (another hit for him in 1965) in front of a punchy horn section, Parker was the consummate modern blues artist, with one foot planted in Southern blues and the other in uptown R&B.

Once Parker split from Robey's employ in 1966, though, his hitmaking fortunes declined. His 1966-68 output for Mercury and its Blue Rock subsidiary deserved a better reception than it got, but toward the end, he was covering the Beatles ("Taxman" and "Lady Madonna") for Capitol. A brain tumor tragically silenced Junior Parker's magic-carpet voice in late 1971 before he reached his 40th birthday. —*Bill Dahl*

Driving Wheel / 1962 / Duke ✦✦✦✦
Junior's emerging from his fin-tailed Cadillac on the front of this vintage LP, which contains all kinds of gems not on MCA's CD. For example: an irresistibly upbeat "How Long Can This Go On," the richly arranged blues ballads "I Need Love So Bad" and "Someone Somewhere," Junior's dance hit "Annie Get Your Yo Yo" (all done with Duke's brassy house band), and the New Orleans-cut "The Tables Have Turned" and "Foxy Devil." —*Bill Dahl*

Baby Please / 1967 / Mercury ✦✦✦
Parker traveled back to his old Memphis stomping grounds to cut this quality set for Mercury under Bobby Robinson's supervision with a coterie of the city's hotter young R&B-oriented studio hands: guitarists Reggie Young and Tommy Cogbill, organist Bobby Emmons, and Willie Mitchell's horn section. "Just like a Fish," "Cracked Up over You," and "Sometimes I Wonder" are among its smooth highlights. —*Bill Dahl*

Honey-Drippin' Blues / 1969 / Blue Rock ✦✦✦✦
Junior Parker a Chicago soul singer? Yeah, on at least four cuts of this fine LP for Mercury's Blue Rock R&B subsidiary. "I'm So Satisfied" (penned by Cash McCall), "Ain't Gon' Be No Cutting Aloose" (later covered by James Cotton for Alligator), "You Can't Keep a Good Woman Down," and "Easy Lovin'" stem from a soulful 1969 date in the Windy City. Also aboard: considerably bluesier remakes of Lowell Fulson's "Reconsider Baby" and Percy Mayfield's "What a Fool I Was." —*Bill Dahl*

Sometime Tomorrow / 1973 / Bluesway ✦✦✦
Cobbled together from mostly unissued performances out of the Duke vaults, we have here a nice Parker LP anthology emphasizing his early-to-mid-'60s soul-inflected sound. He whoops it up like Little Richard on the torrid "If You Can't Take It (You Sure Can't Make It)" (sensible, since Richard wrote it), and gives a warm reading to "Today I Sing the Blues" (generally associated

with female singers, primarily Helen Humes amd Aretha Franklin). —*Bill Dahl*

The ABC Collection / 1976 / ABC ✦✦✦✦
Housed in something that looks vaguely like a square gray envelope that's guaranteed to wear out if you're not careful, this album is still one of the only places to locate many of Parker's best 1958-1966 Duke sides (unless you've got the 45s salted away somewhere). "Man or Mouse," "Dangerous Woman," the two-part "These Kind of Blues," and "I'll Forget About You" are prime vehicles for Parker's uncommonly smooth vocals and occasional harp blasts. —*Bill Dahl*

Mystery Train / 1990 / Rounder ✦✦✦✦✦
This excellent little compilation features at least one extant take of everything Junior and his original band, the Blue Flames, recorded at Sun Records between 1952 to 1954. His debut single for the label and his first hit, the classic "Feelin' Good," is aboard as well as the equally fine (but originally unissued) "Feelin' Bad." His leanings toward smoother Roy Brown stylings are evident with tracks like "Fussing and Fighting Blues" and "Sitting and Thinking," but the follow-up to his first Sun single, the original version of "Mystery Train" and two takes of the flip side, "Love My Baby," are the must-hears on this collection. Fleshing out Parker's meager output for Sun are essential early tracks from James Cotton. Cotton doesn't blow harp on any of these, but the sax-dominated "My Baby," and especially "Cotton Crop Blues" and "Hold Me in Your Arms" with Pat Hare on super-distorted blistering guitar are Memphis-'50s blues at its apex. Hare himself also rounds out the compilation with two tracks, the prophetic "I'm Gonna Murder My Baby" (Hare did exactly that and spent the rest of his life behind bars as a result) and the previously unissued "Bonus Pay." Don't let the short running time of this CD stop you from picking this one up; the music is beyond excellent. —*Cub Koda*

★**Junior's Blues/the Duke Recordings, Vol. 1** / 1992 / MCA ✦✦✦✦✦
After the non-success of "Mystery Train" on the R&B charts, Parker jumped contract and signed with Don Robey's Houston-based Duke Records. With his smooth vocal approach, Parker clearly envisioned himself as the next Roy or Charles Brown. But from the evidence of these early sides, it's clear that Robey wanted to piggyback off the success of the Sun sound. Tracks like "I Wanna Ramble" were virtual carbon copies of the "Feelin' Good" riff and Parker's recasting of old favorites like Robert Johnson's "Sweet Home Chicago," Roosevelt Sykes' "Driving Wheel," "Yonder's Wall" and "Mother-In-Law Blues," were all clearly in the down-home vein that Parker felt was too "old timey" for an up-to-date musician/vocalist of his caliber. His first big hit for the label, the horn-driven "Next Time You See Me" is here with others in the same vein, but this otherwise excellent collection is curiously missing "Pretty Baby," Parker's version of Howlin' Wolf's "Riding in the Moonlight," certainly one of his best. —*Cub Koda*

Charley Patton

b. 1887, Edwards, MS, d. Apr. 28, 1934, Indianola, MS
Guitar, Vocals / Acoustic Delta Blues
If the Delta country blues has a convenient source point, it would probably be Charley Patton, its first great star. His hoarse, impassioned singing style, fluid guitar playing and unrelenting beat made him the original king of the Delta blues. Much more than your average itinerant musician, Patton was an acknowledged celebrity and a seminal influence on musicians throughout the Delta. Rather than bumming his way from town to town, Patton would be called up to play at plantation dances, juke joints and the like. He'd pack them in like sardines everywhere he went, and the emotional sway he held over his audiences caused him to be tossed off of more than one plantation by the ownership, simply because workers would leave crops unattended to listen to him play any time he picked up a guitar. He epitomized the image of a '20s "sport" blues singer; rakish, raffish, easy to provoke, capable of downing massive quantities of food and liquor, a woman on each arm, and a flashy, expensive-looking guitar fitted with a strap and kept in a traveling case by his side, only to be opened up when there was money or good times involved. His records—especially his first and biggest hit, "Pony Blues"—could be heard on phonographs throughout the South. Although he was certainly not the first Delta bluesman to

record, he quickly became one of the genre's most popular. By late-'20s Mississippi plantation standards, Charley Patton was a star, a genuine celebrity.

Although Patton was roughly five foot, five inches tall and only weighed a spartan 135 pounds, his gravelly, high-energy singing style (even on ballads and gospel tunes it sounded this way) made him sound like a man twice his weight and half again his size. Sleepy John Estes claimed he was the loudest blues singer he ever heard and it was rumored that his voice was loud enough to carry outdoors at a dance up to 500 yards away without amplification. His vaudeville-style vocal asides—which on record give the effect of two people talking to each other—along with the sound of his whiskey- and cigarette-scarred voice would become major elements of the vocal style of one of his students, a young Howlin' Wolf. His guitar playing was no less impressive, fueled with a propulsive beat and a keen rhythmic sense that would later plant seeds in the boogie style of John Lee Hooker. Patton is generally regarded as one of the original architects of putting blues into a strong, syncopated rhythm, and the strident tone he achieves on record was achieved by tuning his guitar a step to a step and a half above standard pitch instead of using a capo. His compositional skills on the instrument are illustrated by his penchant for finding and utilizing several different themes as background accompaniment in a single song. His slide work—either played in his lap like a Hawaiian guitar and fretted with a pocket knife or in the more conventional manner with a brass pipe for a bottleneck—was no less inspiring, finishing vocal phrases for him and influencing contemporaries like Son House and up and coming youngsters like Robert Johnson. He also popped his bass strings (a technique he developed some 40 years before funk bass players started doing the same thing), beat his guitar like a drum, and stomped his feet to reinforce certain beats or to create counter rhythms, all of which can be heard on various recordings. Rhythm and excitement were the bywords of his style.

The second, and equally important, part of Patton's legacy handed down to succeeding blues generations was his propensity for entertaining. One of the reasons for Charlie Patton's enormous popularity in the South stems from him being a consummate barrelhouse entertainer. Most of the now-common guitar gymnastics modern audiences have come to associate with the likes of a Jimi Hendrix, in fact, originated with Patton. His ability to "entertain the peoples" and rock the house with a hell-raising ferociousness left an indelible impression on audiences and fellow bluesmen alike. His music embraced everything from blues, ballads, and ragtime to gospel. And so keen were Patton's abilities in setting mood and ambience, that he could bring a barrelhouse frolic to a complete stop by launching into an impromptu performance of nothing but religious-themed selections and still manage to hold his audience spellbound. Because he possessed the heart of a bluesman with the mindset of a vaudeville performer, hearing Patton for the first time can be a bit overwhelming; it's a lot to take in as the music and performances careen from emotionally intense to buffoonishly comic, sometimes within a single selection. It is all strongly rooted in '20s Black dance music and even on the religious tunes in his repertoire, Patton fuels it all with a strong rhythmic pulse.

He first recorded in 1929 for the Paramount label and within a year's time, he was not only the largest-selling blues artist but—in a whirlwind of recording activity—also the most prolific. Patton was also responsible for hooking up fellow players Willie Brown and Son House with their first chances to record. It is probably best to issue a blanket audio disclaimer of some kind when listening to Patton's total recorded legacy, some 60-odd tracks total, his final session done only a couple of months before his death in 1934. We will never know what Patton's Paramount masters really sounded like. When the company went out of business, the metal masters were sold off as scrap, some of it used to line chicken coops! All that's left are the original 78s—rumored to have been made out of inferior pressing material commonly used to make bowling balls—and all of them are scratched and heavily played, making all attempts at sound retrieval by current noise-reduction processing a tall order indeed. That said, it is still music well worth seeking out and not just for its place in history. Patton's music gives us the first flowering of the Delta blues form, before it became homogenized with turnarounds and 12-bar restrictions, and few humans went at it so aggressively. —*Cub Koda*

★ **Founder of the Delta Blues** / 1969 / Yazoo ◆◆◆◆◆
A cornerstone of any blues collection, this is where you start. As compilations go, this originally started life as a double record set featuring all of Patton's best known titles and sound wise was miles above all previous versions. Its compact disc incarnation here trims the tune list to 24 tracks, but all the seminal tracks are here: "Pony Blues," "High Water Everywhere," "Screamin' And Hollerin' The Blues," "A Spoonful Blues," "Shake It And Break It," and the wistful "Poor Me," recorded at his final session in 1934, a scant two months before he died. —*Cub Koda*

☆ **King of the Delta Blues** / 1991 / Yazoo ◆◆◆◆◆
This excellent companion volume to the above pulls together 23 more Patton tracks (including some alternate takes that were for years thought to be lost) to give a much more complete look at this amazing artist. It's interesting here to compare the tracks from his final session to his halcyon output from 1929. Highlights include "Mean Black Cat Blues," Patton's adaptation of "Sitting On Top of the World" ("Some Summer Day"), and both parts of "Prayer of Death," originally issued under the non de plume of "Elder J.J. Hadley." The sound on this collection is vastly superior from a noise reduction standpoint to its companion volume. —*Cub Koda*

Complete Recorded Works, Vols. 1–3 / Document ◆◆◆
This is a 61-track, three-CD set that encompasses a complete chronological run of Patton's recorded output. All of his solo sides are here, as well as his duets with Bertha Lee and Henry Sims and his backup work behind both of them. All previous incarnations of this material don't sound near as good as they do on these three volumes, all of them given the full deluxe Cedarization noise reduction treatment from the Document folks. This is as nice as this stuff's probably ever gonna sound, thus justifying the usual hefty import price. —*Cub Koda*

Odie Payne

b. Aug. 27, 1926, Chicago, IL, **d.** Mar. 1, 1989, Chicago, IL
Drummer
Fascinated by music as a child, Odie Payne listened to everything he could get his hands on—classical, pop, musicals, and big band. Even as a teen he would sneak into clubs to watch and listen to what the drummers were doing. He studied music through high school and was drafted into the Army when his schoolwork fell off. After release from the military, Payne studied drums and graduated with high honors from the Roy C. Knapp School of Percussion. While playing with pianist Johnny Jones in 1949, Payne met Tampa Red and soon joined Red's band. They played and recorded together for several years. Payne states that he apprenticed himself to Red.

In 1952 Payne and pianist Johnny Jones became part of Elmore James' dance band, the Broomdusters. Payne stayed with the band for three years, but recorded with James until 1959—recording some 31 singles. He became a highly sought after studio musician and, in the later 1950s, played on many essential recordings for the Cobra label, for artists like Otis Rush, Magic Sam, and Buddy Guy. Odie Payne developed the famous double-shuffle, later used by Fred Below and Sam Lay to great effect. Payne recorded for Chess, including a number of classic Chuck Berry tunes like "Nadine" and "No Particular Place to Go." He recorded with most of the great Chicago blues artists: Otis Rush, Sonny Boy Williamson II, Muddy Waters, Jimmy Rogers, Eddie Taylor, Magic Sam, Yank Rachell, Sleepy John Estes, Little Brother Montgomery, Memphis Minnie, and many others.

Much watched and admired by other Chicago drummers, Payne was perhaps most famous for his trademark use of the cowbell, lightning-fast bass drum pedal, and extended cymbal and drum rolls. Odie Payne died March 1, 1989, in Chicago. Loved and respected by those who knew him, Payne served as a role model for many working musicians. —*Michael Erlewine*

Peg Leg Sam

b. Dec. 18, 1911, Jonesville, SC, **d.** Nov. 27, 1977, Jonesville, SC
Harmonica, Vocals / Acoustic Country Blues
Peg Leg Sam was a performer to be treasured, a member of what may have been the last authentic traveling medicine show, a harmonica virtuoso, and an extraordinary entertainer. Born Arthur Jackson, he acquired his nickname after a hoboing accident in 1930. His medicine show career began in 1938, and his repertoire—finally recorded only in the early '70s—reflected the

rustic nature of the traveling show. "Peg" delivered comedy routines, bawdy toasts, and monologues; performed tricks with his harps (often playing two at once); and served up some juicy Piedmont blues (sometimes with a guitar accompanist, but most often by himself). Peg Leg Sam gave his last medicine-show performance in 1972 in North Carolina and was still in fine fettle when he started making the rounds of folk and blues festivals in his last years. —*Jim O'Neal*

Joshua / Sep. 1990 / Tomato ✦✦✦✦✦
These are rootsy '70s performances by this Southeastern country-blues harmonica player and singer. —*Mark A. Humphrey*

Peg Leg Sam / Tomato ✦✦✦✦
Recorded shortly before his death, this album features Peg Leg Sam with Louisiana Red performing a set of old-timey, traditional blues—the kind of that was frequently heard at travelling medicine shows. Although it was recorded late in his career, the album captures the essence of Peg Leg Sam. —*Thom Owens*

Pinetop Perkins

b. Jul. 13, 1913, Belzoni, MS
Guitar, Piano, Vocals / Piano Blues
He admittedly wasn't the originator of the seminal piano piece "Pinetop's Boogie Woogie," but it's a safe bet that more people associate it nowadays with Pinetop Perkins than with the man who devised it in the first place, Clarence "Pinetop" Smith.

Although it seems as though he's been around Chicago forever, the Mississippi native actually got a relatively late start on his path to Windy City immortality. It was only when Muddy Waters took him on to replace Otis Spann in 1969 that Perkins' rolling mastery of the ivories began to assume outsized proportions.

Perkins began his blues existence primarily as a guitarist, but a mid-'40s encounter with an outraged chorus girl toting a knife at a Helena, AR, nightspot left him with severed tendons in his left arm. That dashed his guitar aspirations, but Joe Willie Perkins came back strong from the injury, concentrating solely on piano from that point on.

Perkins traveled to Helena with Robert Nighthawk in 1943, playing with the elegant slide guitarist on Nighthawk's KFFA radio program. Perkins soon switched over to rival Sonny Boy Williamson's beloved *King Biscuit Time* radio show in Helena, where he remained for an extended period. Perkins accompanied Nighthawk on a 1950 session for the Chess brothers that produced "Jackson Town Gal," but Chicago couldn't hold him at the time.

Nighthawk disciple Earl Hooker recruited Perkins during the early '50s. They hit the road, pausing at Sam Phillips' studios in Memphis long enough for Perkins to wax his first version of "Pinetop's Boogie Woogie" in 1953. He settled in downstate Illinois for a spell, then relocated to Chicago. Music gradually was relegated to the back burner until Hooker coaxed him into working on an LP for Arhoolie in 1968. When Spann split from Muddy Waters, the stage was set for Pinetop Perkins' reemergence.

After more than a decade with the Man, Perkins and his bandmates left en masse to form the Legendary Blues Band. Their early Rounder albums (*Life of Ease, Red Hot 'n' Blue*) prominently spotlighted Perkins' rippling 88s and rich vocals. He had previously waxed an album for the French Black & Blue logo in 1976 and four fine cuts for Alligator's *Living Chicago Blues* anthologies in 1978. Finally, in 1988, he cut his first domestic album for Blind Pig, *After Hours*.

Ever since then, Pinetop Perkins has made up for precious lost time in the studio. Discs for Antone's, Omega (*Portrait of a Delta Bluesman*, a solo outing that includes fascinating interview segments), Deluge, Earwig, and several other firms ensure that his boogie legacy won't be forgotten in the decades to come. —*Bill Dahl*

Boogie Woogie King / Nov. 1, 1976 / Evidence ✦✦✦
Although he did not have an album issued under his name as a leader until 1988, pianist Pine Top Perkins actually should have had one released in 1976, when he cut the eight tracks on this recently reissued Evidence CD for the Black & Blue label. They did not appear until 1992, which is a shame. Perkins' trademark boogie-woogie riffs, rumbling rhythms, left-hand lines, and spinning phrases were in fine form. His accompaniment and supporting phrases behind guitarist/vocalist Luther Johnson Jr. are equally tasty and inviting. Johnson, as erratic a performer as any in contemporary blues, came ready to play and sing on this date.

His vocals had plenty of grit, conviction, and energy, while his playing had no excesses and was delivered with zip and flair. —*Ron Wynn*

● **After Hours** / 1986 / Blind Pig ✦✦✦✦✦
Easy-grooving blues and boogie is backed by the competent New York City-based blues band Little Mike and the Tornadoes. Though Perkins followed Otis Spann as the piano player in the Muddy Waters band, these are the first domestically available recordings under his own name. —*Niles J. Frantz*

Pinetop's Boogie Woogie / 1992 / Antone's ✦✦✦✦
The maze of new and recent discs by this veteran Chicago piano man can be daunting, but rest assured that this is one of his best to date. Many of the songs are Perkins standbys—"Kidney Stew," "Caldonia," and of course, "Pinetop's Boogie Woogie"—but the backing here is stellar (sidemen include harpists James Cotton and Kim Wilson, guitarists Matt Murphy, Jimmy Rogers, Hubert Sumlin, and Duke Robillard), and several driving rhythm sections—that the project rises above most of Perkins' output. —*Bill Dahl*

On Top / Jan. 1992 / Deluge ✦✦✦
Solid entry in Perkins' ever-growing discography of contemporary CDs. —*Bill Dahl*

Portrait of a Delta Bluesman / 1993 / Vanguard ✦✦✦✦✦
Considerably more ambitious than just another Perkins set, this solo disc intersperses key songs from his storied history with interview segments that reveal much about the man himself, from his Delta beginnings to when he replaced Otis Spann in Muddy Waters' vaunted band. —*Bill Dahl*

Live Top / 1995 / Deluge ✦✦✦
A very competent combo offers incendiary support behind the veteran Chicago pianist throughout the album, recorded live before an appreciative gathering. —*Bill Dahl*

With the Blue Ice Band / 1995 / Earwig ✦✦
The pianist is as charming and effervescent as ever on this live/studio outing—but he's often undermined by the presence of mediocre harpist Chicago Beau and an Icelandic band that doesn't know the meaning of the words subtlety or taste. Rock-drenched guitar solos fly with abandon, destroying any semblance of Chicago-style ambience. —*Bill Dahl*

Bill Perry

b. Chester, NY
guitar, vocals / Modern Blues
Although guitarist, songwriter, and singer Bill Perry may seem like a newcomer to the blues scene to some, he's actually put in a long apprenticeship with folk-rock singer Richie Havens. Perry was Havens' main guitarist for shows he performed with a band through the 1980s.

Signed in 1995 to an unprecedented five-album deal with the Pointblank/Virgin label, Perry's future looks bright because he's a sharp songwriter, an adequate singer, and a fiery guitar player. Perry's style could best be characterized as hard-driving blues for the 1990s. Perry's song, "Fade to Blue," is covered by Havens on his recent album, *Cuts to the Chase.*

Perry was born in the upstate town of Chester, NY, and grew up in a music-filled household. His grandmother played organ in the church, but a young Perry was attracted to his father's Jimmy Smith albums, which featured guitarist Kenny Burrell. Perry began playing guitar at age six and played in his first talent show at 13. By high school, he led bands as vocalist and lead guitarist before graduation. After graduating, he lived in California and Colorado, all the while honing his distinctive guitar playing. He moved back to upstate New York and accompanied Havens on most of his shows with a band through the 1980s. Perry toured with the Band's Garth Hudson and Levon Helm at the same time he was working with Havens, and all that traveling spurred him on to form his own band, which he did in the early '90s.

Look for more brilliant albums and a whole lot of live shows from this guitarist for the rest of the 1990s. He loves playing live, and he knows how to pace his sets to get maximum audience response. —*Richard Skelly*

James Peterson

b. Nov. 4, 1937, Russell County, AL
Guitar, Vocals / Modern Electric Blues
Florida-based guitarist, singer and songwriter, James Peterson

plays a gritty style of southern-fried blues that is at times reminiscent of Howlin' Wolf and other times more along the lines of Freddie King. He formed his first band while he was living in Buffalo, NY, and running Governor's Inn, House of Blues in the 1960s. He and his band would back up the traveling musicians who came through, including blues legends like Muddy Waters, Howlin' Wolf, Big Joe Turner, Freddie King, Lowell Fulson, and Koko Taylor.

Peterson was born November 4, 1937 in Russel County, AL. Peterson was strongly influenced by gospel music in the rural area he grew up in, and he began singing in church as a child. Thanks to his father's juke joint, he was exposed to blues at an early age, and later followed in his footsteps in upstate New York. After leaving home at age 14, he headed to Gary, IN, where he sang with his friend John Scott. While still a teen, he began playing guitar, entirely self-taught. Peterson cites musicians like Muddy Waters, Howlin' Wolf (Chester Burnett), Jimmy Reed, and B.B. King as his early role models. After moving to Buffalo, NY, in 1955, he continued playing with various area blues bands, and ten years later, he opened his own blues club.

In 1970, Peterson recorded his first album, *The Father, Son, and the Blues* on the Perception/Today label. While he ran his blues club at night, he supplemented his income by running a used-car lot during the day. Peterson's debut album was produced and co-written with Willie Dixon, and it featured a then-five-year-old Lucky Peterson on keyboards. Peterson followed it up with *Tryin' to Keep the Blues Alive* a few years later. Peterson's other albums include *Rough and Ready* and *Too Many Knots* for the Kingsnake and Ichiban labels in 1990 and 1991, respectively.

The album that's put Peterson back on the road as a national touring act is his 1995 release, *Don't Let the Devil Ride* for the Jackson, MS-based Malaco Records. A master showman who has learned from the best and knows how to work an audience, he's also a crafty songwriter endowed with a deep, gospel-drenched singing style. Fans can expect more great albums from Peterson throughout the 1990s. —*Richard Skelly*

Rough and Ready / 1977 / Kingsnake ✦✦✦✦✦
A pleasant album of original compositions by this Alabama-born bluesman, it features James' son Lucky Peterson (Alligator recording artist) on guitar and keyboards. —*Niles J. Frantz*

Too Many Knots / Ichiban ✦✦✦

Lucky Peterson

b. Dec. 13, 1964, Buffalo, NY
Organ, Bass, Guitar, Piano, Drums, Vocals / Modern Electric Blues
Child-prodigy status is sometimes difficult to overcome upon reaching maturity. Not so for Lucky Peterson—he's far bigger (in more ways than one) on the contemporary blues circuit than he was at the precocious age of six, when he scored a national R&B hit with the Willie Dixon-produced "1-2-3-4."

Little Lucky Peterson was lucky to be born into a musical family. His dad, James Peterson, owned the Governor's Inn, a popular Buffalo, NY, blues nightclub that booked the biggies: Jimmy Reed, Muddy Waters, and Bill Doggett. The latter's mighty Hammond B-3 organ fascinated the four-and-a-half-year-old lad, and soon Peterson was on his way under Dixon's tutelage. "1-2-3-4" got Peterson on *The Tonight Show* and *The Ed Sullivan Show*, but he didn't rest on his laurels—he was doubling on guitar at age eight, and at 17, he signed on as Little Milton's keyboardist for three years.

A three-year stint with Bobby Bland preceded Peterson's solo career launch, which took off when he struck up a musical relationship with Florida-based producer Bob Greenlee. Two Greenlee-produced albums for Alligator, 1989's *Lucky Strikes!* and the following year's *Triple Play*, remain his finest recorded offerings. Extensive session work behind everyone from Etta James and Kenny Neal to Otis Rush also commenced during this period.

In 1993, Peterson's first Verve label album, *I'm Ready*, found him boldly mixing contemporary rock and soul into his simmering blues stew. Two more high-energy Verve sets have followed, making it clear that Peterson's luck remains high (as does his father's, who's fashioned his own career as a bluesman in recent years with albums for Ichiban and Waldoxy). —*Bill Dahl*

● **Ridin'** / Mar. 1984 / Evidence ✦✦✦✦✦
As a child prodigy, keyboardist and organist Lucky Peterson's exploits were legendary. The stories grew even more widespread as he became a teen and stints with Little Milton and Bobby "Blue" Bland only added to his fame. But Peterson's records have not always justified or reaffirmed his reputation. That is not the case with the cuts on this 1984 set, recently reissued by Evidence. The spiraling solos, excellent bridges, turnbacks, pedal maneuvers, and soulful accompaniment are executed with a relaxed edge and confident precision. If you have wondered whether Lucky Peterson deserves the hype and major label bonanza, these songs are the real deal. —*Ron Wynn*

Lucky Strikes / 1989 / Alligator ✦✦✦✦
Peterson's real coming-out party as a mature blues triple threat: his guitar and keyboard skills are prodigious (though he's no longer a child prodigy), and his vocals on "Pounding of My Heart," "Can't Get No Loving on the Telephone," and "Heart Attack" (all written by producer/bassist Bob Greenlee) served notice that more than luck was involved in Peterson's adult rise to fame. —*Bill Dahl*

● **Triple Play** / 1990 / Alligator ✦✦✦✦✦
Even more impressive than his previous Alligator set, thanks to top-flight material like "Don't Cloud Up on Me," "Let the Chips Fall Where They May," and "Locked Out of Love," the fine house band at Greenlee's King Snake studios, and Peterson's own rapidly developing attack on two instruments. —*Bill Dahl*

I'm Ready / Aug. 1992 / Verve ✦✦✦
Lucky Peterson is a smooth operator, cool and always in control with a guitar tone reminiscent of the more restrained sides of Roy Buchanan or Carlos Santana. He's capable of lashing out, though, as the livewire showstopper "Don't Cloud Up On Me" ably proves. But this versatile musician is most distinctive with his Hammond organ and Wurlitzer electric piano sound, instruments that he's been playing professionally since the age of five. Check out the heady swirl of instrumental workout "Junk Yard" on this front, although comparisons to Billy Preston will be inevitable. —*Roch Parisien*

Beyond Cool / 1994 / Verve ✦✦
Once Peterson arrived at Verve, his taste in material seemed to sail right out the window. This disc is confusingly unfocused (rock influences are as prominent as blues) and a far cry indeed from his fine Alligator sets of a precious few years before. —*Bill Dahl*

Brewer Phillips

b. Coila, MS
Guitar, Vocals / Chicago Blues
Brewer Phillips is one of the more unique sidemen in Chicago blues history. His guitar playing combines the rhythmic sense of an Eddie Taylor (an early childhood friend and fishing buddy) with the stinging lead work of a Pat Hare. Born on a plantation in Coila, MS, he came under the early tutelage of Memphis Minnie and grew up with the legends of the blues all around him, seeing many of them perform first-hand. After leaving Mississippi, he moved to Memphis, becoming a professional musician and making his first recordings as a member of Bill Harvey's band, with a session behind pianist Roosevelt Sykes that has yet to surface. Best known for his work as a member of the Houserockers (see Hound Dog Taylor entry), his backup work behind Taylor—a trio with no bass player—finds him alternating between the icepick-in-your-ear sheet-metal lead tones produced from his battered Telecaster to comping bass lines while simultaneously combining chords, all of it executed with a thumbpick and bare fingers. It's a sound totally rooted in the juke joint sounds of Phillips' Mississippi upbringing and there's simply no equal to it in the blues today. Since Taylor's death in 1976, he has recorded on his own and worked sporadically with J.B. Hutto, Lil Ed, Cub Koda, and others while remaining a largely shadowy figure in Chicago blues circles. —*AMG*

Good Houserockin' / 1995 / Wolf ✦✦✦✦✦
This combines various late-'70s and early-'80s recordings into one package. The first 11 tracks are from Phillips's 1982 solo album for the label, *Ingleside Blues*. The next six tracks were recorded live in 1977 in Vienna and Boston, featuring Brewer fronting J.B. Hutto and the Houserockers. The last two sides are unissued leftovers from the 1980 Cub Koda and the

Houserockers' *It's the Blues!* album. Phillips' longtime playing partner, drummer Ted Harvey, is present on all 19 tracks and shares billing with him on this disc. Some of the recording quality (especially on the live Hutto tracks) is unbelievably crude and harsh sounding, making the overall sound of this disc very spotty and uneven. This album is probably the most complete—though not necessarily the best—collection of Phillips's solo work. *—AMG*

Gene Phillips
....
b. Jul. 25, 1915
Guitar, Vocals / West Coast Blues
A West Coast session stalwart who appeared on a myriad of jump blues waxings during the late '40s and early '50s, guitarist Gene Phillips faded from view even before the dawn of rock & roll. Any serious collector of the Bihari brothers' budget-priced Crown albums (you know, the ones with those ubiquitous cheesy cover illustrations by artist "Fazzio") should be intimately familiar with Phillips' LP—it's one of the best Crown acquisitions you can possibly make (especially since there's no CD equivalent yet).

The T-Bone Walker-influenced Phillips recorded extensively for the Biharis' Modern Imprint from 1947 through 1950. His often-ribald jump blues gems for the firm included "Big Legs," "Fatso," "Rock Bottom," "Hey Now," and a version of Big Bill Broonzy's witty standard "Just a Dream." Phillips' bandmates were among the royalty of the L.A. scene: trumpeter Jake Porter; saxists Marshall Royal, Maxwell Davis, and Jack McVea; and pianist Lloyd Glenn were frequently on hand. Phillips returned the favor in Porter's case, singing and playing on the trumpeter's 1947 dates for Imperial.

After a 78 of his own for Imperial in 1951 ("She's Fit 'n Fat 'n Fine"), Phillips bowed out of the recording wars as a leader with a solitary 1954 effort for Combo, "Fish Man," backed by McVea's band. *—Bill Dahl*

I Like 'Em Fat / Ace ✦✦✦✦
● **Gene Phillips** / Ace ✦✦✦✦✦
No CD presence for late-'40s/early-'50s Los Angeles guitar stalwart Phillips yet, but Ace was kind enough to assemble a nice cross-section of his jumping R&B sides a while back. *—Bill Dahl*

Piano Red (William Lee Perryman)
....
b. Oct. 19, 1911, Hampton, GA, **d.** Jul. 25, 1985, Decatur, GA
Piano, Vocals / Piano Blues
Willie Perryman went by two nicknames during his lengthy career, both of them thoroughly apt. He was known as Piano Red because of his albino skin pigmentation for most of his performing life. But they called him Doctor Feelgood during the '60s, and that's precisely what his raucous, barrelhouse-styled vocals and piano were guaranteed to do: cure anyone's ills and make them feel good.

Like his older brother, Rufus Perryman, who performed and recorded as Speckled Red, Willie Perryman showed an aptitude for the 88s early in life. At age 12, he was banging on the ivories, influenced by Fats Waller, but largely his own man. He rambled some with blues greats Barbecue Bob, Curley Weaver, and Blind Willie McTell during the 1930s (and recorded with the latter in 1936), but mostly worked as a solo artist.

In 1950, Red's big break arrived when he signed with RCA Victor. His debut Victor offering, the typically rowdy "Rockin' with Red," was a huge R&B hit, peaking at number five on *Billboard's* charts. It's surfaced under a variety of guises since: Little Richard revived it as "She Knows How to Rock" in 1957 for Specialty, Jerry Lee Lewis aced it for Sun (unissued at the time), and pint-sized hillbilly dynamo Little Jimmy Dickens beat 'em both to the punch for Columbia.

"Red's Boogie," another pounding rocker from the pianist's first RCA date, also proved a huge smash, as did the rag-tinged "The Wrong Yo-Yo" (later covered masterfully by Carl Perkins at Sun), "Just Right Bounce," and "Laying the Boogie" in 1951. Red became an Atlanta mainstay in the clubs and over the radio, recording prolifically for RCA through 1958 both there and in New York. There weren't any more hits, but that didn't stop the firm from producing a live LP by the pianist in 1956 at Atlanta's Magnolia Ballroom that throbbed with molten energy. Chet Atkins produced Red's final RCA date in Nashville in 1958, using Red's touring band for backup.

A 1959 single for Checker called "Get Up Mare" and eight tracks for the tiny Jax label preceded the rise of Red's new guise, Dr. Feelgood & the Interns, who debuted on Columbia's Okeh subsidiary in 1961 with a self-named rocker, "Doctor Feel-Good," that propelled the aging piano pounder into the pop charts for the first time. Its flipside, "Mister Moonlight" (penned and ostensibly sung by bandmember Roy Lee Johnson), found its way into the repertoire of the Beatles. A subsequent remake of "Right String but the Wrong Yo-Yo" also hit for the good doctor in 1962. The Doc remained with Okeh through 1966, recording with veteran Nashville saxist Boots Randolph in his band on five occasions.

Red remained ensconced at Muhlenbrink's Saloon in Atlanta from 1969 through 1979, sandwiching in extensive European tours along the way. He was diagnosed with cancer in 1984 and died the following year. *—Bill Dahl*

Piano Red in Concert / 1956 / Groove ✦✦✦
On this pioneering live set cut at Atlanta's Magnoia Ballroom, the sound is suprisingly clean and Red rocks the house! *—Bill Dahl*

Jump Man, Jump / 1956 / Groove ✦✦✦✦✦
Raucous barrelhouse blues and boogies with a hot R&B combo on these swinging sides. *—Bill Dahl*

Atlanta Bounce / 1992 / Arhoolie ✦✦✦
Two distinct timeframes are represented on this slightly schizophrenic disc. Much of it is comprised of latter-day barrelhouse and blues waxed by Arhoolie, but there's also a thrilling handful of raucous live items from a 1956 concert at Atlanta's Magnolia Ballroom that capture the albino 88s ace at his most enthralling. *—Bill Dahl*

● **The Doctor's In!** / 1993 / Bear Family ✦✦✦✦✦
As usual, Bear Family does Piano Red up right: four discs packed to the brim with everything you'd ever want or need—the entirety of his 1950-1958 stint at RCA and Groove (including his smashes "Rockin' with Red" and "Right String But the Wrong Yo Yo"); subsequent dates for Checker (six of eight tracks from this 1958 date were previously unreleased), Jax, and Okeh, where he was musically reborn as Dr. Feelgood & the Interns in 1961 and rocked unrepentantly on his signature "Doctor Feel-Good," "What's Up Doc," and "Bald-Headed Lena." A non-stop good time—no easy task over four jam-packed discs! *—Bill Dahl*

● **Wildfire** / Matchbox ✦✦✦✦✦
A dozen tracks of Red at his poundin' best. (Import) *—Cub Koda*

Rod Piazza
....
Harmonica, Vocals / Modern Electric Blues
A California-based blues bandleader, harmonica player, and singer, Rod Piazza's stratospheric harmonica wailings owe a heavy debt to both Little Walter and George "Harmonica" Smith.

Piazza began his professional career as a member of the Dirty Blues Band in the mid-'60s. The Dirty Blues Band recorded two albums for ABC/Bluesway—an eponymous debut in 1967 and 1968's *Stone Dirty*. Rod left the band after the release of *Stone Dirty*, choosing to hit the road with his idol, George "Harmonica" Smith instead. Over the next decade and a half, Piazza and Smith performed together frequently under the name Bacon Fat; they also recorded the occasional album. In 1969, Bacon Fat released their debut album on Blue Horizon.

While he was performing with Smith, Piazza released his own solo albums, the first of which—*Rod Piazza Blues Man*—appeared on LMI in 1973. The second, *Chicago Flying Saucer Band*, was released in 1979 on Gangster Records.

As Smith's health began to decline in the early '80s, Piazza assembled the Mighty Flyers—which featured his wife Honey Alexander on keyboards—which began playing clubs in 1980. Between 1981 and 1985, the Mighty Flyers released three albums—*Radioactive Material* (1981), *File Under Rock* (1984), and *From the Start to the Finish* (1985). During the early '80s, Piazza became a session musician, working with artists as diverse as Pee Wee Crayton and Michelle Shocked. In the mid-'80s, he began a full-fledged solo career, releasing *Harp Burn* on Murray Brothers in 1986 and *So Glad to Have the Blues* in 1988.

Piazza and the Mighty Flyers signed a contract with Black Top Records in 1991; the label later re-released the group's albums on CD. Throughout the '90s, Piazza continued to record and perform with the Mighty Flyers, releasing the occasional solo album. *—Cub Koda & Stephen Thomas Erlewine*

Harpburn / 1986 / Black Top ✦✦✦
So Glad to Have the Blues / 1988 / Murray Bros ✦✦✦
Blues in the Dark / 1991 / Black Top ✦✦✦✦✦
A contemporary band, led by harmonica player/vocalist Piazza, has nice piano from Honey Alexander. —*Niles J. Frantz*
Alphabet Blues / 1992 / Black Top ✦✦✦✦✦
Another fine effort from Rod Piazza and the Mighty Flyers, *Alphabet Blues* alternates between first-rate slow blues and cooking uptempo boogies and shuffles, both of which showcase their versatile, many-sided talents. There are a few weak songs, but the album on the whole is quite entertaining. —*Thom Owens*
● **The Essential Collection** / 1992 / Hightone ✦✦✦✦✦
Compilation of fairly recent sides by the powerhouse West Coast harpist; like most of his work, it smokes! —*Bill Dahl*
Live at B.B. King's Blues Club / 1994 / Big Mo ✦✦✦

Greg Piccolo

b. May 10, 1951, Westerly, RI
Sax (Tenor), Vocals / Modern Electric Jump Blues
Former Roomful of Blues vocalist and sax man Greg Piccolo was born May 10, 1951, in Westerly, RI. At the age of 13 he was playing sax with a six-piece rock band, the Rejects. Two years later he joined Duke Robillard as a vocalist for the Variations, a British Invasion cover band. Piccolo rejoined Robillard in 1970 to create that first Roomful of Blues, inspired by the R&B band, the Buddy Johnson Orchestra. The group was further modified in 1971 and Piccolo began playing sax. The band worked throughout the Northeast, gradually building up a national following. Robillard left the group in 1979 and was replaced by blues guitarist Ronnie Earl. By this time, Piccolo was the de facto leader. *Dressed Up to Get Messed Up* features a number of his compositions. The group stayed together until the early '90s when Piccolo went out on his own.
Piccolo has released two solo albums in the acid-jazz vein, *Heavy Juice* on Black Top Records (1990) and *Acid Blue* (1995) on Fantasy. He lives in Rhode Island and records for Fantasy. (See: Roomful of Blues) —*Michael Erlewine*
● **Heavy Juice** / May 9, 1990–May 13, 1990 / Black Top ✦✦✦✦✦
These stomping tenor sax instrumentals come from the jazz and R&B repertoire of the '40s and '50s. Many Roomful of Blues alumni, such as Duke Robillard (guitar) and Al Copley (piano), contribute. It doesn't rock any harder than this. —*Bob Porter*
Acid Blue / Nov. 1995 / Fantasy ✦✦✦✦

Dan Pickett

b. Alabama
Guitar, Vocals / Acoustic Country Blues
Reissuers have unearthed little information about Dan Pickett: he may have come from Alabama, he played a nice slide guitar in a Southeastern blues style, and he did one recording session for the Philadelphia-based Gotham label in 1949. That session produced five singles, all of which have now been compiled along with four previously unreleased sides on a reissue album that purports to contain Pickett's entire recorded output—unless, of course, as some reviewers have speculated, Dan Pickett also happens to be Charlie Pickett, the Tennessee guitarist who recorded for Decca in 1937. As Tony Russell observed in *Juke Blues*, both Picketts recorded blues about lemon-squeezing, and Dan uses the name Charlie twice in the lyrics to "Decoration Day." 'Tis from such mystery and speculation that the minds of blues collectors dissolve. —*Jim O'Neal*
1949 Country Blues / 1990 / Collectables ✦✦✦✦✦
A CD reissue of beautiful, ragtime-esque acoustic blues, it is generally very lighthearted. —*Niles J. Frantz*
Dan Pickett & Tarheel Slim—1949 / Flyright ✦✦✦✦

Cousin Joe Pleasant

b. Dec. 20, 1907, Wallace, LA, d. Oct. 2, 1989, New Orleans, LA
Vocals, Guitar / New Orleans R&B, Blues
Few blues legends have the presence of mind to write autobiographies. Fortunately, Pleasant Joseph did, spinning fascinating tales of a career in his 1987 tome *Cousin Joe: Blues from New Orleans* that spanned more than half a century.
Growing up in New Orleans, Pleasant began singing in church before crossing over to the blues. Guitar and ukulele were his

first axes. He eventually prioritized the piano instead, playing Crescent City clubs and riverboats. He moved to New York in 1942, gaining entry into the city's thriving jazz scene, where he played with Dizzy Gillespie, Sidney Bechet, Charlie Parker, Billie Holiday, and a host of other luminaries.
He recorded for King, Gotham, Philo (in 1945), Savoy, and Decca along the way, doing well on the latter logo with "Box Car Shorty and Peter Blue" in 1947. After returning to New Orleans in 1948, he recorded for DeLuxe and cut a two-part "ABCs" for Imperial in 1954 as Smilin' Joe under Dave Bartholomew's supervision. But by then, his recording career had faded.
The pianist was booked on a 1964 *Blues and Gospel Train* tour of England, sharing stages with Muddy Waters, Otis Spann, Brownie McGhee and Sonny Terry, and Sister Rosetta Tharpe, and appearing on BBC-TV with the all-star troupe. He cut a 1971 album for the French Black & Blue label, *Bad Luck Blues*, that paired him with guitarists Gatemouth Brown and Jimmy Dawkins and a Chicago rhythm section—hardly the ideal situation, but still a reasonably effective showcase for the ebullient entertainer (it was reissued in 1994 by Evidence). —*Bill Dahl*
● **Bad Luck Blues** / Nov. 1971 / Evidence ✦✦✦✦✦
The New Orleans pianist ventured overseas in 1971 and waxed this CD along the way with a mighty unlikely band: guitarists Gatemouth Brown and Jimmy Dawkins and a Chicago rhythm section (bassist Mac Thompson and drummer Ted Harvey). A lesser musician might have wilted with players so unfamiliar with his basic approach, but Pleasant's bubbly ebullience and the strength of his "Box Car Shorty," "Life Is a One Way Ticket," and "Railroad Porter Blues" saved the day. —*Bill Dahl*
● **Bluesman from New Orleans** / 1974 / Big Bear ✦✦✦✦✦
Gospel Wailing / 1982 / Big Bear ✦✦✦
Relaxin' in New Orleans / Great Southern ✦✦✦
Cousin Joe From New Orleans in His Prime / Oldie Blues ✦✦✦

Jerry Portnoy

Harmonica, Vocals / Modern Electric Harmonica Blues
Another ex-Muddy Waters employee, Jerry Portnoy's biting, flailing harmonica style rivals any within contemporary blues circles for fluency or emotional range. His vocals are effective enough, especially when punctuated by his harp accompaniment and solos.
Portnoy began his professional musical career as part of Muddy Waters' backing band in the early '70s. Jerry replaced Mojo Buford in 1974 and he stayed with the band for six years. During his tenure with Waters, he appeared on the albums *I'm Ready*, *Muddy "Mississippi" Waters Live*, and *King Bee*. In 1980, Portnoy, bassist Calvin Jones, pianist Pinetop Perkins, and drummer Willie Smith all left Muddy to form the Legendary Blues Band.
Throughout the early '80s, Portnoy stayed with the Legendary Blues Band, recording the albums *Life of Ease* and *Red Hot & Blue*. In 1986, he left the band and he briefly retired. By the end of 1987, he had returned to the scene, founding the Broadcasters with Ronnie Earl. Two years later, he and Earl had a falling out, causing Jerry to leave the group. Portnoy formed his own band, the Streamliners in 1989. Two years later, the band released their debut, *Poison Kisses*, on Modern Blues Recordings. Between 1991 and 1993, Portnoy was part of Eric Clapton's All-Star Blues Band. After leaving Clapton's band in 1993, he played a number of concerts, releasing his second album, *Home Run Hitter*, in 1995. —*Ron Wynn & Stephen Thomas Erlewine*
● **Poison Kisses** / 1991 / Modern Blues ✦✦✦✦✦
Jerry Portnoy's debut album, *Poison Kisses*, is a fine set of rollicking Chicago blues. Portnoy is at his best when he is blowing away on the harp, and there's no exception to the rule here—the whole album can fall apart when he's simply singing, but when he's playing the harp, the music catches fire. Worthwhile for harmonica fans. —*Thom Owens*
Home Run Hitter / 1995 / Indigo ✦✦✦

Powder Blues Band

Group / Modern Blues
Guitarist Tom Lavin, bassist Jack Lavin, and a keyboard player formed Powder Blues Band in 1978, later adding trumpeter Mark Hasselbach, drummer Duris Maxwell, and saxophonists Wayne Kozak, Gordie Bertram, and David Woodward. The group signed with Capitol, which released *Uncut* and *Powder Blues* in 1980. Other albums include *Thirsty Ears* (1981), *Party Line*

(1982), *Red Hot/True Blue* (1983), *First Decade-Greatest Hits* (1990), and *Let's Get Loose* (1993). —*John Bush*

Uncut / 1980 / RCA ◆◆◆

Thirsty Ears / 1981 / ◆◆◆

Powder Blues / 1983 / Liberty ◆◆◆◆◆

Red Hot/True Blue / Sep. 1986 / Flying Fish ◆◆◆

Duffy Power

His best recordings, as noteworthy for the players on the album as himself. Laid down sometime in the mid-'60s, Power (who sings and plays occasional guitar and harp) is backed by a rotating ensemble including, at various points, John McLaughlin and Jack Bruce (before they gained fame), as well as future Pentangle members Danny Thompson and Terry Cox. Neither as rock-oriented as The Stones nor as strictly revivalist as Alexis Korner (with whom Power played for a time), this is one of the best British blues recordings, cutting straight down the middle between gutbucket blues and soulful R&B. Divided equally between Power originals and R&B blues covers, the material and performances are spare, powerful, and as consistent as any '60s British blues album. Unfortunately, these sessions were unissued for several years, surfacing briefly under the title *Innovations* in 1970 on the British Transatlantic label. This reissue on another tiny British label is equally obscure, but should not be missed by fans of '60s British R&B. —*Richie Unterberger*

● **Little Boy Blue** / 1992 / Edsel ◆◆◆◆
His best recordings, as noteworthy for the players on the album as Power himself. Laid down sometime in the mid-'60s, Power (who sings and plays occasional guitar and harp) is backed by a rotating ensemble including, at various points, John McLaughlin and Jack Bruce (before they gained fame), as well as future Pentangle members Danny Thompson and Terry Cox. Neither as rock-oriented as The Stones nor as strictly revivalist as Alexis Korner (with whom Power played for a time), this is one of the best British blues recordings, cutting straight down the middle between gutbucket blues and soulful R&B. Divided equally between Power originals and R&B blues covers, the material and performances are spare, powerful, and as consistent as any '60s British blues album. Unfortunately, these sessions were unissued for several years, surfacing briefly under the title *Innovations* in 1970 on the British Transatlantic label. This reissue on another tiny British label is equally obscure, but should not be missed by fans of '60s British R&B. —*Richie Unterberger*

Elvis Presley (Elvis Aron Presley)

b. Jan. 8, 1935, Tupelo, MS, d. Aug. 16, 1977, Memphis, TN
Vocals, Guitar / Rock & Roll

Elvis Presley listed in a book on the blues? Why not, he's listed and/or mentioned in any development of the music that mentions White people playing it and doing it with enough success that the world just happened to take notice. His is the one story in this book that doesn't really need to be embellished or listed in even the most cursory detail; there are tons of books, movies for television, videotapes, and magazines devoted to exploring that subject in beyond-finite detail. He has become an American icon, having been transformed from a White hillbilly musician who sang the blues to a cultural concept, from a human being to a wine decanter. If you don't know who Elvis was, we can only assume that your spaceship landed from Mars just a few hours ago. His emotional link to the blues and its basis to the development of his style, therefore, will be supported by two salient quotes that nicely and emphatically validate his presence between these covers. One comes from ace writer (and Elvis biographer) Peter Guralnick's liner notes to an all-blues Elvis compilation, *Reconsider Baby*: "I remember the first time I met the great bluesman, Howlin' Wolf, in 1966. He started talking about White blues singers, a new concept at the time. He liked Paul Butterfield, he said, also 'that other boy—what's his name? Somewhere out in California, that 'Hound Dog' number.' He was talking about Elvis Presley. But surely Elvis couldn't be considered strictly a blues singer, somebody pointed out. Maybe not, conceded Wolf in that great hoarse growl of his, but 'he started from the blues. If he stopped, he stopped. It's nothing to laugh at. He made his pull from the blues.'"

The second quote comes from the man himself in June of 1956, one of the few interviews where he ever discussed his musical roots, seemingly amazed by all the fuss his version was causing at the time: "The colored folks been singing it and playing it just like I'm doin' it now, man, for more years than I know. They played it like that in their shanties and their juke joints, and nobody paid it no mind 'til I goosed it up. I got it from them. Down in Tupelo, Mississippi, I used to hear old Arthur Crudup bang his box the way I do now, and I said if I ever got to the place where I could feel all old Arthur felt, I'd be a music man like nobody ever saw." Needless to say that at a very real level, he connected big time and that the world saw and heard his message. On the strength of the two above quotes, the defense rests. The rest is not only history, but the history of rock 'n' roll as well. —*Cub Koda*

☆ **Reconsider Baby** / 1985 / RCA ◆◆◆◆◆
A 12-song, budget-priced compilation of Elvis' most notable blues sides for the label. A good place to start digging Elvis' commitment to the music—always returning to it right up through the '70s like an old friend, whenever he needed a quick fix of the real thing—as he takes on everything from R&B slices like Tommy Tucker's "High Heel Sneakers" to Percy Mayfield's "Stranger in My Own Home Town." Major highlights on this collection are Elvis playing acoustic rhythm guitar and driving the band through a take of the Lowell Fulson title track, blistering versions of two Arthur Crudup songs, an unreleased Sun recording of Lonnie Johnson's "Tomorrow Night," and the R-rated take of Smiley Lewis' "One Night (of Sin)." —*Cub Koda*

★ **The Sun Sessions CD** / 1987 / RCA ◆◆◆◆◆
This is it, your perfect starting point to understanding how Elvis—as Howlin' Wolf so aptly put it—"made his pull from the blues." All the source points are there for the hearing; Arthur Crudup's "That's All Right (Mama)," Roy Brown's "Good Rockin' Tonight," Kokomo Arnold's "Milkcow Blues Boogie," Arthur Gunter's "Baby, Let's Play House," and Junior Parker's "Mystery Train." Modern day listeners coming to these recordings for the first time will want to reclassify this music into a million subgenres, with all the hyphens firmly in place. But what we ultimately have here is a young Elvis Presley, mixing elements of blues, gospel and hillbilly music together and getting ready to unleash its end result—rock 'n' roll—on an unsuspecting world. —*Cub Koda*

☆ **The King of Rock 'n' Roll: Complete 50's Masters** / 1992 / RCA ◆◆◆◆◆
A casual Elvis fan wanting to assemble a decent overview of The King's '50s sides could probably sweat it down to the *Sun Sessions* CD and Volume 1 of the *Top Ten Hits* compilation. But for those of you who take your '50s Presley seriously, *The King of Rock 'n' Roll: The Complete 50's Masters* is absolutely essential. For the hardcore Elvis fan, the booklet and CD graphics for this five-disc set provide incentive enough to justify its purchase. The liner notes by Presley expert Peter Guralnick are passionate, contagious in their enthusiasm, and filled with a real sense of history, time, and place. The treasure-trove of unpublished photos, session information, and Elvis memorabilia accompanying the booklet text is no less inspiring. But it's the music (140 tracks in all) that's the real meat and potatoes of this set. Every studio track cut during the '50s—the seminal Sun sides, the early RCA hits, movie soundtracks, alternates, live performances, rarities (including both sides of the long-lost acetate he cut for his mother back in 1953)—it's all here in one gorgeous package. Soundwise, this box makes any of the previous issues of this material pale by comparison, the proper (non-reverbed) inclusion of the Sun masters being a particular treat. This is no mere rehash of what's been around a dozen times before—there's a lot of thought and care behind this package, and no serious fan of American rock 'n' roll should consider a collection complete without it. —*Cub Koda*

Elvis Presley '56 / Mar. 5, 1996 / RCA ◆◆◆◆◆
Sure the music on here's great. How could it not be? It has 22 of his hottest tracks from his first year at RCA, including not only the hits "Heartbreak Hotel," "Hound Dog," "Don't Be Cruel," and "Too Much," but such noted early rockers as "My Baby Left Me," "Blue Suede Shoes," "Money Honey," and "So Glad You're Mine." From a collector's viewpoint, though, you have to wonder whether it was really necessary. The only previously unreleased item is a sparser earlier take of "Heartbreak Hotel." Everything else has been widely available (even on CD) for years, and it's a good bet that many of the Elvis fans who buy this already have

virtually all of the contents on the *King of Rock 'n' Roll* box set. —*Richie Unterberger*

Jimmy Preston

Saxophone / Electric Jump Blues
Alto sax blower Jimmy Preston is another one of the legion of postwar R&B figures that can accurately be cited as a genuine forefather of rock 'n' roll. His chief claim to fame: the blistering 1949 smash "Rock the Joint," which inspired a groundbreaking cover by Bill Haley & the Comets in 1952.

"Rock the Joint" wasn't Preston's first trip to the R&B Top Ten. Earlier in 1949, he'd hit with "Hucklebuck Daddy." Both were cut for Ivin Ballen's Philadelphia-based Gotham logo. The scorching sax breaks on "Rock the Joint" weren't Preston's doing, but tenor saxist Danny Turner's. Preston cut rather prolifically for Gotham through much of 1950 (including a session with jazzman Benny Golson on tenor sax) before switching to Derby Records and scoring his last hit, "Oh Babe" (with a vocal by Burnetta Evans). The 1950 date for the New York label was apparently his last. —*Bill Dahl*

Jimmy Preston / Collectables ◆◆◆◆
Jump blues pioneer Preston, a solid alto saxist, with some of his 1949-1950 outings for Philadelphia's Gotham imprint. The titles tell it all: "Swingin' in the Groove," "Hang Out Tonight," "Estellina Bim Bam." —*Bill Dahl*

● **Rock the Joint, Vol. 2** / Collectables ◆◆◆◆◆
Saxman Preston waxed one of the first legitimately traceable rock 'n' roll singles with his scorching jumper "Rock the Joint" for Philadelphia-based Gotham Records in 1949. It's here, along with his inexorably swinging "Hucklebuck Daddy," "Messin' with Preston," and "They Call Me the Champ." —*Bill Dahl*

Lloyd Price

b. Mar. 9, 1933, Kenner, LA, d. 1988
Vocals / New Orleans R&B
Not entirely content with being a 1950s R&B star on the strength of his immortal New Orleans classic "Lawdy Miss Clawdy," singer Lloyd Price yearned for massive pop acceptance. He found it, too, with a storming rock 'n' roll reading of the ancient blues "Stagger Lee" and the unabashedly pop-slanted "Personality" and "I'm Gonna Get Married" (the latter pair sounding far removed indeed from his Crescent City beginnings).

Growing up in Kenner, a suburb of New Orleans, Price was exposed to seminal sides by Louis Jordan, the Liggins brothers, Roy Milton, and Amos Milburn through the jukebox in his mother's little fish fry joint. Lloyd and his younger brother Leo (who later co-wrote Little Richard's "Send Me Some Lovin'") put together a band for local consumption while in their teens. Bandleader Dave Bartholomew was impressed enough to invite Specialty Records boss Art Rupe to see the young singer (this was apparently when Bartholomew was momentarily at odds with his longtime employers at rival Imperial).

At his very first Specialty date in 1952, Price sang his classic eight-bar blues "Lawdy Miss Clawdy" (its rolling piano intro courtesy of a moonlighting Fats Domino). It topped the R&B charts for an extended period, making Lloyd Price a legitimate star before he was old enough to vote. Four more Specialty smashes followed: "Oooh, Oooh, Oooh," "Restless Heart," "Tell Me Pretty Baby," "Ain't It a Shame"—before Price was drafted into the Army and deposited most unhappily in Korea.

When he finally managed to break free of the military, Lloyd Price formed his own label, KRC Records, with partners Harold Logan and Bill Boskent and got back down to business. "Just Because," a plaintive ballad Price first cut for KRC, held enough promise to merit national release on ABC-Paramount in 1957 (his ex-valet, Larry Williams, covered it on Price's former label, Specialty).

"Stagger Lee," Price's adaptation of the old Crescent City lament "Stack-A-Lee," topped both the R&B and pop lists in 1958. By now, his sound was taking on more of a cosmopolitan bent, with massive horn sections and prominent pop background singers. Dick Clark insisted on toning down the violence inherent to the song's storyline for the squeaky-clean *American Bandstand* audience, accounting for the two different versions of the song you're likely to encounter on various reissues.

After Lloyd Price hit with another solid rocker, "Where Were You (On Our Wedding Day)?," in 1959, the heavy brass-and-choir sound became his trademark at ABC-Paramount. "Personality," "I'm Gonna Get Married," and "Come Into My Heart" all shot up the pop and R&B lists in 1959, and "Lady Luck" and "Question" followed suit in 1960.

Always a canny businessman, Price left ABC-Paramount in 1962 to form another firm of his own with Logan. Double L Records debuted Wilson Pickett as a solo artist and broke Price's Vegas lounge-like reading of "Misty" in 1963. Later, he ran yet another diskery, Turntable Records (its 45s bore his photo, whether on his own sizable 1969 hit "Bad Conditions" or when the single was by Howard Tate!), and operated a glitzy New York nightspot by the same name.

But the music business turned sour for Price when his partner, Logan, was murdered in 1969. He got as far away from it all as he possibly could, moving to Africa and investing in nonmusical pursuits. Perfect example: He linked up with electric-haired Don King to promote Muhammad Ali bouts in Zaire (against George Foreman) and Manila (against Joe Frazier). He indulged in a few select oldies gigs (including an appearance on NBC-TV's *Midnight Special*), but overall, little was seen of Lloyd Price during the 1970s.

Returning to America in the early '80s, he largely resisted performing until a 1993 European tour with Jerry Lee Lewis, Little Richard, and Gary U.S. Bonds convinced him there was still a market for his bouncy, upbeat oldies. Price's profile has been on the upswing ever since—he recently guested on a PBS-TV special with Huey Lewis & the News, and regularly turns up to headline the Jazz & Heritage Festival in his old hometown. —*Bill Dahl*

Mr. Personality / 1959 / ABC/Paramount ◆◆◆
Recorded in absolutely breathtaking stereo that greatly enhances the brass-heavy arrangements, this LP is worth grabbing any time you run across it. Sure, Lloyd Price sounds offkey on the Tin Pan Alley chestnuts "I Only Have Eyes for You" and "Time After Time," but a forceful "I Want You to Know," the torchy "Dinner for One," and a rocking "Is It Really Love?" make up for the intrusions. —*Bill Dahl*

Mr. Personality Sings the Blues / 1960 / ABC/Paramount ◆◆◆◆
Blues was no big stretch for the vocalist—his Crescent City output was solidly rooted in the idiom. On this LP, he does a fine job on Eddie Vinson's "Kidney Stew," Paul Perryman's "Just to Hold My Hand," and his own blasting "I've Got the Blues and the Blues Got Me." —*Bill Dahl*

Sings the Million Sellers / 1961 / ABC/Paramount ◆◆◆
Lloyd Price sang the hits of the immediate timeframe on this long out-of-print album, doing particular justice to "Ain't That Just like a Woman" (then a minor seller for Fats Domino), the Miracles' "Shop Around," the Midnighters' "The Hoochie Coochie Coo," and the Drifters' "I Count the Tears." Uptown soul arrangements by future Motown staffer Gil Askey give Price full-bodied support. —*Bill Dahl*

Greatest Hits / 1990 / Curb ◆◆◆
Inadequately shallow peek at the New Orleans singer's biggest hits, largely the pop ones—"Personality," "Stagger Lee." Doesn't even make a tiny dent in Lloyd Price's vast catalog. —*Bill Dahl*

★ **Lawdy!** / 1991 / Specialty ◆◆◆◆◆
Twenty-five stellar 1952-1956 examples of why Lloyd Price ranks with the greatest R&B performers ever to emerge from the Crescent City. Beginning with his debut smash "Lawdy Miss Clawdy," Price wails the rocking "Mailman Blues," "Where You At?," "Rock 'n' Roll Dance," and "Baby Please Come Home" in front of fat sax cushions, rolling pianos, and steamy rhythm sections. —*Bill Dahl*

Heavy Dreams, Vol. 2 / 1993 / Specialty ◆◆◆◆
No discernible artistic dropoff on Specialty's encore Price retrospective, distinguished by his classics "Oooh-Oooh-Oooh," "Tell Me Pretty Baby," "Ain't It a Shame?" (not Fats Domino's hit), "Country Boy Rock," and "Why" (he later recut the latter for ABC-Paramount). —*Bill Dahl*

● **Greatest Hits** / 1994 / MCA ◆◆◆◆◆
Price wasn't content with R&B fame; he yearned for pop acceptance, too. He got plenty at ABC-Paramount from 1957 to 1960 (the timeframe this 18-song retro addresses). Creating a brassy, accessible sound, Price hit huge with his rock 'n' roll rendition of "Stagger Lee" (here in two versions—original and *American*

Bandstand-sanitized) and went all the way pop with the undeniably catchy "Personality." Innovative arrangements and Price's earnest vocals greatly distinguish "Have You Ever Had the Blues?," "Lady Luck," "Three Little Pigs," and "Where Were You (On Our Wedding Day)," and there's a previously unissued "That's Love" to further up the ante. —*Bill Dahl*

● **Lloyd Price Sings His Big Ten** / Feb. 8, 1994 / Capitol/Curb ✦✦✦✦✦

Like all standard Curb anthologies, this is too skimpy, numbering ten tracks. It does, however, include all of Price's major hits— "Stagger Lee," "Personality," "I'm Gonna Get Married," "Where Were You (On Our Wedding Day)", and "Lady Luck." And in its favor, it also includes the most famous of his pre-ABC hits, "Lawdy Miss Clawdy." —*Richie Unterberger*

Sammy Price

b. Oct. 6, 1908, Honey Grove, TX, **d.** Apr. 14, 1992, New York, NY
Piano / Piano Blues
Sammy Price had a long and productive career as a flexible blues and boogie-woogie-based pianist. He studied piano in Dallas and was a singer and dancer with Alphonso Trent's band during 1927–30. In 1929 he recorded one solitary side under the title of "Sammy Price and his Four Quarters." After a few years in Kansas City he spent time in Chicago and Detroit. In 1938 Price became the house pianist for Decca in New York and appeared on many blues sides with such singers as Trixie Smith and Sister Rosetta Tharpe. He led his own band on records in the early '40s, which included (on one memorable session) Lester Young. Price worked steadily on 52nd Street, in 1948 played at the Nice Festival with Mezz Mezzrow, spent time back in Texas, and then a decade with Red Allen; he was also heard on many rock 'n' roll-type sessions in the 1950s. In later years he recorded with Doc Cheatham. Sammy Price was active until near his death, 63 years after his recording debut. —*Scott Yanow*

● **Sam Price 1929–1941** / Sep. 29, 1929–Dec. 10, 1941 / Classics ✦✦✦✦✦

Rib Joint/Roots of Rock & Roll / Oct. 17, 1956–Mar. 24, 1959 / Savoy ✦✦✦✦✦
Here's a two-LP set that truly deserves immediate CD reissue. Price led a mighty New York R&B combo through three Savoy Records sessions in 1956–57 that elicited some sizzling instrumentals: "Rib Joint" (here in two takes), "Back Room Rock," "Juke Joint," "Chicken Out," "Ain't No Strain" (sidemen included guitarist Mickey Baker and saxman King Curtis). A slightly more restrained 1959 date sans sax that comprises the second LP is no less joyful. —*Bill Dahl*

Blues and Boogies / Nov. 14, 1969 / Black & Blue ✦✦✦✦✦
Price is heard here on solo piano and vocal, playing eight Price originals and "See See Rider." It is good to hear him alone on this rare solo album, recorded in France. —*Michael G. Nastos*

King of the Boogie Woogie / 1995 / Storyville ✦✦✦

● **And the Blues Singers** / Wolf ✦✦✦✦✦
When the Austrian Wolf logo decided to pay tribute to pianist Sammy Price's prolific legacy as both leader and sideman, they really did it up right. Ninety-four sides on four discs dating from 1929 to 1950 spotlight Price's rippling ivories behind a plethora of vocalists—Peetie Wheatstraw, Harmon Ray, Bea Booze, Johnnie Temple, Monette Moore, Scat Man Bailey, and a great many more—as well as some very tasty instrumentals of his own. —*Bill Dahl*

John Primer

b. Mar. 3, 1945, Camden, MS
Guitar, Vocals / Modern Electric Chicago Blues
By any yardstick, Chicago guitarist John Primer has paid his dues. Prior to making what he's hoping will be his breakthrough for Mike Vernon's Atlantic-distributed Code Blue label, *The Real Deal*, Primer spent 13 years as the ever-reliable rhythm guitarist with Magic Slim & the Teardrops. Before that, he filled the same role behind Chicago immortals Muddy Waters and Willie Dixon.
All that grounding has paid off handsomely for Primer. His sound is rooted in the classic Windy City blues sound of decades past: rough-edged and uncompromising and satisfying in the extreme. He's one of the last real traditionalists in town.
By the time he came to Chicago in 1963, Primer was thor-

oughly familiar with the lowdown sounds of Waters, Wolf, Jimmy Reed, B.B. and Albert King, and Elmore James. He fronted a West Side outfit for a while called the Maintainers, dishing out a mix of soul and blues, before joining the house band at the South side blues mecca Theresa's Lounge for what ended up a nine-year run. Elegant guitarist Sammy Lawhorn proved quite influential on Primer's maturing guitar approach during this period.
Always on the lookout for aspiring talent, Willie Dixon spirited him away for a 1979 gig in Mexico City. After a year or so as one of Dixon's All-Stars, Primer was recruited to join the last Muddy Waters band, playing with the Chicago blues king until his 1983 death. Right after that, Primer joined forces with Magic Slim; their styles interlocked so seamlessly that their partnership seemed like an eternal bond.
But Primer deserved his own share of the spotlight. In 1992, Michael Frank's Chicago-based Earwig logo issued Primer's debut domestic disc, *Stuff You Got to Watch*. It was a glorious return to the classic '50s Chicago sound, powered by Primer's uncommonly concise guitar work and gruff, no-nonsense vocals. With the 1996 emergence of *The Real Deal*—produced by Vernon and featuring all-star backing by harpist Billy Branch, pianist David Maxwell, and bassist Johnny B. Gayden, Primer's star appears ready to ascend at last. —*Bill Dahl*

Poor Man Blues: Chicago Blues Session, Vol. 6 / 1991 / Wolf ✦✦✦✦✦

Stuff You Got to Watch / 1993 / Earwig ✦✦✦✦
Chicago guitarist Primer's domestic debut album was doubtless an eye-opener for anyone not familiar with his searing slide work and sturdy vocal abilities. Apart from a very ill-advised cover of Glen Campbell's "Rhinestone Cowboy" (yuck!), the album resonates with mean, lowdown guitar work and fine ensemble backing. —*Bill Dahl*

● **The Real Deal** / 1995 / Code Blue ✦✦✦✦✦
Thought they didn't make traditional Chicago blues albums worthy of the name anymore? Guess again: Primer's major-label bow is an entirely satisfying affair produced by Mike Vernon that's long on intensity and devoid of pretention. Lots of originals; a handful of well-chosen covers, and a vicious band (pianist David Maxwell and harpist Billy Branch solo stunningly) help make the set go, while Primer grabs hold of the opportunity with a vise-like grip and makes believe it's the 1950s all over again. —*Bill Dahl*

Gary Primich

b. Apr. 20, 1958, Chicago, IL
Harmonica, Vocals / Modern Electric Harmonica Blues
Don't let his intelligence, charm and self-effacing manner fool you: Gary Primich is one bad-ass harmonica player. And he's more than competent guitar player, too.
Primich was born April 20, 1958 in Chicago and raised in nearby Gary, IN. He learned harmonica from the masters at the Maxwell Street Market in nearby Chicago as a teen. By the early '80s, however, Primich became dissatisfied with the blues scene in Chicago, and in 1984, shortly after he earned his degree in radio and television from Indiana University, he moved to Austin, TX.
After landing a job at the University of Texas doing electrical work, he began to work as a sideman at Austin area clubs. In 1987, he ran into former Frank Zappa/Mothers of Invention drummer Jimmy Carl Black, who had also relocated to Austin, and the two formed a band, the Mannish Boys. Their debut album on the now-defunct Amazing Records label was called *A L'il Dab'll Do Ya*. Though Black left the band, Primich led the Mannish Boys through another album for Amazing, *Satellite Rock*. Both albums attracted sufficient attention to Primich that he was able to record under his own name for the Amazing label, and in 1991 he cut his self-titled debut for the label. He followed it up with *My Pleasure* in 1992. After Amazing Records folded, he was picked up by the Chicago-based Flying Fish label. Primich recorded two equally brilliant albums for Fish, and they include *Travelin' Mood* (1994) and *Mr. Freeze* (1995).
On his last two albums for Flying Fish (a label that has since been acquired by Rounder Records), Primich's talents as a songwriter really start to come through, and as of this writing, he was without a label, but still nurturing his fan base through almost constant touring. —*Richard Skelly*

Company Man / 1996 / Black Top ✦✦✦

Mr. Freeze / 1995 / Flyng Fish ✦✦✦

Gary Primich / 1991 / Amazing ✦✦✦
Gary Primich's eponymous album is an uneven collection, hampered by a handful of rote, by-the-book tracks but its best moments are vibrant, eclectic and quite exciting. Unfortunately, the album gets off to a weak start, running through a bunch of uptempo blues-rockers. After those are through, Primich begins to open up his sound, diving deep into New Orleans R&B, as well as some jump blues and Latin-tinged rhythms. It's on these numbers that Primich reveals his talents as a vocalist and harpist, not on the conventional numbers. — *Thom Owens*

● **My Pleasure** / 1992 / Amazing ✦✦✦✦✦
My Pleasure is pretty much straight-up Chicago blues, delivered with authority by Gary Primich. Fellow harpist James Harman produced the record, and he tames Primich's more adventurous qualities. However, he does bring out the grease and grit of Primich's straightforward blues that was lacking on the previous record, which makes this a very enjoyable, if predictable, album. — *Thom Owens*

Travelin' Mood / 1994 / Flying Fish ✦✦

Hot Harp Blues / Amazing ✦✦✦✦✦

Professor Longhair (Henry Roeland Byrd)

b. Dec. 19, 1918, Bogalusa, LA, d. Jan. 30, 1980, New Orleans, LA
Piano, Vocals / New Orleans R&B
Justly worshipped a decade-and-a-half after his death as a founding father of New Orleans R&B, Roy "Professor Longhair" Byrd was nevertheless so down-and-out at one point in his long career that he was reduced to sweeping the floors in a record shop that once could have moved his platters by the boxful.

That Fess made such a marvelous comeback testifies to the resiliency of this late legend, whose Latin-tinged rhumba-rocking piano style and croaking, yodeling vocals were as singular and spicy as the second-line beats that power his hometown's musical heartbeat. Byrd brought an irresistible Caribbean feel to his playing, full of rolling flourishes that every Crescent City ivories man had to learn inside out (Fats Domino, Huey Smith, and Allen Toussaint all paid homage early and often).

Roy Byrd grew up on the streets of the Big Easy, tap dancing for tips on Bourbon Street with his running partners. Local 88s aces Sullivan Rock, Kid Stormy Weather, and Tuts Washington all left their marks on the youngster, but Byrd brought his own conception to the stool. A natural-born card shark and gambler, Longhair began to take his playing seriously in 1948, earning a gig at the Caldonia Club. Owner Mike Tessitore bestowed Byrd with his nickname (due to Byrd's shaggy coiffure).

Longhair debuted on wax in 1949, laying down four tracks (including the first version of his signature "Mardi Gras in New Orleans," complete with whistled intro) for the Dallas-based Star Talent label. His band was called the Shuffling Hungarians, for reasons lost to time! Union problems forced those sides off the market, but Longhair's next date for Mercury the same year was strictly on the up-and-up. It produced his first and only national R&B hit in 1950, the hilarious "Bald Head" (credited to Roy Byrd & his Blues Jumpers).

The pianist made great records for Atlantic in 1949, Federal in 1951, Wasco in 1952, and Atlantic again in 1953 (producing the immortal "Tipitina," a romping "In the Night," and the lyrically impenetrable boogie "Ball the Wall"). After recuperating from a minor stroke, Longhair came back on Lee Rupe's Ebb logo in 1957 with a storming "No Buts—No Maybes." He revived his "Go to the Mardi Gras" for Joe Ruffino's Ron imprint in 1959; this is the version that surfaces every year at Mardi Gras in New Orleans.

Other than the ambitiously arranged "Big Chief" in 1964 for Watch Records, the '60s held little charm for Longhair. He hit the skids, abandoning his piano playing until a booking at the fledgling 1971 Jazz & Heritage Festival put him on the comeback trail. He made a slew of albums in the last decade of his life, topped off by a terrific set for Alligator, *Crawfish Fiesta*.

Longhair triumphantly appeared on the PBS-TV concert series *Soundstage* (with Dr. John, Earl King, and the Meters), co-starred in the documentary *Piano Players Rarely Ever Play Together* (which became a memorial tribute when Longhair died in the middle of its filming; funeral footage was included), and saw a group of his admirers buy a local watering hole in 1977 and rechristen it Tipitina's after his famous song. He played there regularly when he wasn't on the road; it remains a thriving operation.

Longhair went to bed on January 30, 1980, and never woke up. A heart attack in the night stilled one of New Orleans' seminal R&B stars, but his music is played in his hometown so often and so reverently, you'd swear he was still around. — *Bill Dahl*

Rock 'n Roll Gumbo / 1977 / Dancing Cat ✦✦✦✦
It features great renditions of New Orleans standards such as "Junco Partner" and "Rockin' Pneumonia" with an all-star band that features Clarence "Gatemouth" Brown on guitar and violin. — *Bruce Boyd Raeburn*

Crawfish Fiesta / 1980 / Alligator ✦✦✦✦✦
Probably the best of all the many albums Longhair waxed during his comeback. A tremendously tight combo featuring three horns and Dr. John on guitar delightfully back the Professor every step of the way as he recasts Solomon Burke's "Cry to Me" and Fats Domino's "Whole Lotta Loving" in his own indelible image and roars, yodels, and whistles out wonderful remakes of his own oldies "Big Chief" and "Bald Head." — *Bill Dahl*

Mardi Gras in New Orleans / 1981 / Nighthawk ✦✦✦✦✦
Plenty of rarities are featured on this valuable cross-section of the Professor's early releases. Both sides of the pianist's first two 78s for Star Talent Records are aboard, as well as sides he cut for Mercury, Federal ("Curly Haired Baby," "Gone So Long"), Wasco ("East St. Louis Baby"), Atlantic, and Ebb. — *Bill Dahl*

House Party / 1987 / Rounder ✦✦✦
A classic pairing, Professor Longhair meets New Orleans guitar-legend Snooks Eaglin and drummer "Zig" Modeliste of The Meters. — *Bruce Boyd Raeburn*

New Orleans Piano / 1989 / Atlantic ✦✦✦✦✦
All 16 of the Atlantic sides from 1949 and 1953 (including a handful of alternate takes) on one glorious disc. Longhair's work for the label was notoriously marvelous—this version of "Mardi Gras in New Orleans" reeks of revelry in the streets of the French Quarter; "She Walks Right In" and "Walk Your Blues Away" ride a bedrock boogie, and "In the Night" bounces atop a parade-beat shuffle groove and hard-charging saxes. — *Bill Dahl*

Mardi Gras in Baton Rouge / 1991 / Rhino ✦✦✦✦
Some of the earliest sides from Longhair's rediscovery period (1971–72), featuring a lot of tunes inexorably associated with him through previous versions and a few ("Jambalaya," "Sick and Tired") that weren't. An added bonus is the magical presence of guitarist Snooks Eaglin, whose approach is every bit as singular as the Professor's was. — *Bill Dahl*

★ **Fess: Professor Longhair Anthology** / 1993 / Rhino ✦✦✦✦✦
The rhumba-rocking rhythms of Roy "Professor Longhair" Byrd live on throughout Rhino's 40-track retrospective of the New Orleans icon's amazing legacy. Most of the seminal stuff arrives early on: "Bald Head," the rollicking ode Byrd cut for Mercury in 1950, is followed by a raft of classics from his 1949 and 1953 Atlantic dates ("Tipitina," "Ball the Wall," "Who's Been Fooling You"), the storming 1957 "No Buts—No Maybes" and "Baby Let Me Hold Your Hand" for Ebb, and his beloved "Go to the Mardi Gras" as waxed for Ron in 1959. The second disc is a hodge-podge of material from his 1970s comeback, all of it wonderful in its own way but not as essential as the early work. — *Bill Dahl*

Houseparty New Orleans Style / 1994 / Rounder ✦✦✦✦✦
Boiling blues and trademark Afro-Latin and boogie-woogie riffs were the menu when Professor Longhair brought his Crescent City music show to Baton Rouge and Memphis in 1971 and 1972, respectively. The 15 numbers on this set matched the great pianist with an esteemed array of musicians that included outstanding guitarist Snooks Eaglin on both sessions, and fine rhythm sections as well. Eaglin's flashy, inventive solos were excellent contrasts to Longhair's rippling keyboard flurries and distinctive mix of yodels, yells, cries, and shouts. — *Ron Wynn*

Professor's Blues Revue/Karen Carroll

Group / Modern Electric Blues
"Professor" Eddie Lusk worked frequently as a session keyboardist during the 1970s and '80s on the Chicago blues scene. His own revue showcased several singers over the years, notably

Gloria Hardiman (featured on their "Meet Me With Your Black Drawers On" on Alligator's 1987 anthology, *The New Bluebloods*) and Karen Carroll, principal singer on the band's 1992 Delmark album, *Professor Strut*. Tragically, Lusk took his own life by plunging into the Chicago River. —*Bill Dahl*

Professor Strut / 1989 / Delmark ✦✦✦
Eddie Lusk's only solo album is a blues revue, as he leads a variety of singers through several classic blues songs from all of the music's subgenres. The concept is good one, but the performance is decidedly uneven—several of the singers are mediocre and the fidelity on the release is poor. For those who want to sit through the rough spots, they'll find a handful of good solos, but not much more. —*Thom Owens*

Snooky Pryor (James Edward Pryor)

b. Sep. 15, 1921, Lambert, MS
Harmonica, Drums, Vocals / Electric Chicago Blues
Only in the last few years has Snooky Pryor finally begun to receive full credit for the mammoth role he played in shaping the amplified Chicago blues harp sound during the postwar era. He's long claimed he was the first harpist to run his sound through a public-address system around the Windy City—and since nobody's around to refute the claim at this point, we'll have to accept it! He's still quite active musically, having cut two potent discs for Austin, TX-based Antone's Records in recent years.

James Edward Pryor was playing harmonica at the age of eight in Mississippi. The two Sonny Boys were influential to Pryor's emerging style, as he played around the Delta. He hit Chicago for the first time in 1940, later serving in the Army at nearby Fort Sheridan. Playing his harp through powerful Army PA systems gave Pryor the idea to acquire his own portable rig once he left the service. Armed with a primitive amp, he dazzled the folks on Maxwell Street in late 1945 with his massively amplified harp.

Pryor made some groundbreaking 78s during the immediate postwar Chicago blues era. Teaming with guitarist Moody Jones, he waxed "Telephone Blues" and "Boogie" for Planet Records in 1948, encoring the next year with "Boogy Fool"/"Raisin' Sand" for JOB with Jones on bass and guitarist Baby Face Leroy Foster in support. Pryor made more more classic sides for JOB (1952–53), Parrot (1953), and Vee-Jay ("Someone to Love Me"/"Judgment Day") in 1956, but commercial success never materialized. He wound down his blues-playing in the early '60s, finally chucking it all and moving to downstate Ullin, IL, in 1967.

For a long while, Pryor's whereabouts were unknown. But the 1987 Blind Pig album, *Snooky,* produced by guitarist Steve Freund, announced to the world that the veteran harpist was alive and well, his chops still honed. A pair of solid discs for

Antone's, *Too Cool to Move* and *In This Mess Up to My Chest,* followed. Pryor stays just as busy as he cares to nowadays, still ensconced in Ullin (where life is good and the fishing is easy). —*Bill Dahl*

★ **Snooky Pryor** / 1969 / Paula/Flyright ✦✦✦✦✦
If anyone doubts the longevity and journeyman greatness of Snooky Pryor, this collection of sides should do much to quiet them. Starting with the 1947 Floyd Jones (the classic "Stockyard Blues") and Johnny Young sessions for Old Swingmaster with Snooky in support and running right from the early '50s into the early '60s sides for the JOB label with "Boogie Twist" (his Vee-Jay and Parrot sides are not here), this is ground floor Chicago blues one step removed from Maxwell Street. Lots of unissued sides—all of them great—plus the inclusion of the instrumental "Boogie," which became the blueprint for Little Walter's hit "Juke." Pryor's finest moments on wax. —*Cub Koda*

Do It If You Want / 1973 / Bluesway ✦✦

Homesick James & Snooky Pryor / 1974 / Caroline ✦✦✦

Snooky / 1987 / Blind Pig ✦✦✦✦
An outstanding comeback effort by Chicago harp pioneer Snooky Pryor, whose timeless sound meshed well with a Windy City trio led by producer/guitarist Steve Freund for this set. Mostly Pryor's own stuff—"Why You Want to Do Me Like That," "That's the Way To Do It," "Cheatin' and Lyin'"—with his fat-toned harp weathering the decades quite nicely. —*Bill Dahl*

Too Cool to Move / 1992 / Antone's ✦✦✦✦
Another excellent recent set from the veteran harpist, cut in Austin with a mixture of Texans and Chicagoans in support: pianist Pinetop Perkins, guitarists Duke Robillard and Luther Tucker, and drummer Willie "Big Eyes" Smith. Pryor's made quite a substantial addition to his long-dormant discography in the last few years. —*Bill Dahl*

In This Mess Up To My Chest / 1994 / Antone's ✦✦✦✦
Pryor reaffirms his mastery of postwar blues harp over the course of this sturdy set, again done with the help of some fine Texas and Chicago players. Pryor's downhome vocals shine on the distinctive "Bury You in a Paper Sack" and "Stick Way Out Behind." —*Bill Dahl*

Hand Me Down Blues / Relic ✦✦✦✦✦
A nice 16-track compilation of rare blues material from the Parrot label, this features both sides of Snooky's lone single for the label, "Crosstown Blues" and "I Want You For Myself." Also features obscure and unissued tracks by Little Willie Foster ("Four Day Jump"), Dusty Brown ("Yes She's Gone"), John Brim ("Gary Stomp"), Sunnyland Slim ("Devil Is a Busy Man"), early Albert King ("Little Boy Blue") and the title track), plus Henry Gray with four previously unissued sides, all of them sloppy and great. —*Cub Koda*

R

Yank Rachell

b. Mar. 16, 1910, Brownsville, TN
Guitar, Harmonica, Mandolin, Vocals / Acoustic Country Blues
Best known for his down-home mandolin playing, guitarist, vocalist, and songwriter Yank Rachell played a central role in several of the most exciting chapters in blues history. Born in either Mississippi or Tennessee, he took up mandolin as a youngster and was soon making the rounds with the Brownsville, TN, blues crowd: John Estes, John Lee "Sonny Boy" Williamson, Jab Jones, and Homesick James Williamson. During the '30s he was part of the vibrant St. Louis blues community, working with Henry Townsend and Big Joe Williams before moving on to Chicago. For the past 30 years he has resided in Indianapolis, presiding over still another blues community, which once included Shirley Griffith, J. T. Adams, and guitarist Pete Franklin. When I met Rachell in the early '70s, he had put an electric band together with his son-in-law and some local R&B players. Although much of his recording career with Victor, ARC, Bluebird, and Delmark was spent accompanying others, he composed and sang powerful songs such as "Lake Michigan Blues" and "Gravel Road Woman." When he visited my classroom in 1976, he told the students he coauthored the classic "Schoolgirl" with his onetime partner Sonny Boy Williamson. Explaining his music, he said: "I learned the hard way, out in the country all by myself—so far back in the woods my breath smelled like cord wood." Throughout his lengthy career, his music changed little, holding a country dance flavor. At the same time, he demonstrated a remarkable ability to play with other musicians—the mark of a seasoned string-band veteran. For 60 years Rachell worked in various ensemble formats, but his heart remained with his string-band roots. *—Barry Lee Pearson*

Blues Mandolin Man / 1902 / Blind Pig ✦✦✦
This contains fine material by one of the few great mandolin bluesmen. *—Barry Lee Pearson*

Mandolin Blues / 1986 / Delmark ✦✦✦

● **Chicago Style** / 1987 / Delmark ✦✦✦✦✦
While Yank Rachell was past his prime when he began recording for Delmark in the 1960s, he was still an effective, often exciting vocalist and mandolin player. He seldom sounded more striking and enjoyable than on the nine cuts that comprised *Chicago Style*, recently reissued on CD. Rachell sang with a spirited mix of irony, anguish, dismay and bemusement on such numbers as "Depression Blues," "Diving Duck," and "Going To St. Louis." *—Ron Wynn*

Complete Recorded Works..., **Vol. 2: 1938–1941** / Wolf ✦✦✦✦✦

James "Yank" Rachell, Vol. 1 (1934–38) / Wolf ✦✦✦

Bobby Radcliff

b. Sep. 22, 1951, Bethesda, MD
Guitar, Vocals / R&B, Modern Electric Blues
Although Bobby Radcliff has spent the last 25 years honing his craft in bars around his native Washington, D.C., and in New York City and Chicago, the 45-year old guitarist, singer, and songwriter is just now coming into his prime.
Born September 22, 1951, Radcliff grew up in Bethesda, MD and had easy access to Washington, D.C., blues clubs, where he learned from people like Bobby Parker. Before graduating from high school, he'd already made several trips to Chicago to meet his idol, Magic Sam Maghett, owing to a small but growing blues club scene in Washington. Radcliff began playing when he was 12, and he started taking classical guitar lessons. After his guitar teacher showed him some blues, he began buying every blues guitar album he could get his hands on.
In 1977, Radcliff moved to New York City and worked in a bookstore by day until 1987, when he realized he was making enough money playing in clubs to give up his day job. Since he hooked up his recording deal with Black Top Records, Radcliff has toured the U.S., Canada, and Europe more than a dozen times, and his fiery guitar playing is always a festival crowd-pleaser.
Parker has three excellent albums out on the Black Top label that showcase his songwriting, guitar playing and soulful singing. They include his debut, *Dresses Too Short* (1989), *Universal Blues* (1991), and *There's a Cold Grave in Your Way* (1994). Collectors will seek out his 1985 vinyl release, *Early in the Morning*, on the A-Okay label. *—Richard Skelly*

● **Dresses Too Short** / Oct. 1989 / Black Top ✦✦✦✦
Bobby Radcliff turns in a tight, tough update of Magic Sam-style Chicago blues with *Dresses Too Short*. The songs are either too familiar or a weak approximation of the genre, but the playing throughout is terrific—his guitar playing is alternately subtle and ferocious. Best of all is the handful of tracks cut with Ronnie Earl & the Broadcasters who spur Radcliff on to his best performances. *—Thom Owens*

Universal Blues / 1991 / Black Top ✦✦✦
Universal Blues is another successful reworking of Chicago blues from Bobby Radcliff. It's less flashy than the previous *Dresses Too Short*, but that's a plus—without all the pyrotechnics, Radcliff's guitar actually sounds more powerful and versatile, which makes the album quite entertaining. *—Thom Owens*

There's A Cold Grave / 1994 / Black Top ✦✦✦✦✦

Ma Rainey (Gertrude Rainey)

b. Apr. 26, 1886, Columbus, GA, **d.** Dec. 22, 1939, Columbus, GA
Vocals / Classic Female Blues
Ma Rainey wasn't the first blues singer to make records, but by all rights she probably should have been. In an era when women were the marquee names in blues, Ma Rainey was once the most celebrated of all—the "Mother of the Blues" had been singing the music for more than 20 years before she made her recording debut (Paramount, 1923). With the advent of blues records, she became even more influential, immortalizing such songs as "See See Rider," "Bo-Weavil Blues," and "Ma Rainey's Black Bottom." Like the other classic blues divas, she had a repertoire of pop and minstrel songs as well as blues, but she maintained a heavier, tougher vocal delivery than the cabaret blues singers who followed. Ma Rainey's records featured her with jug bands, guitar duos, and bluesmen such as Tampa Red and Blind Blake, in addition to the more customary horns-and-piano jazz-band accompaniment (occasionally including such luminaries as Louis Armstrong, Kid Ory, and Fletcher Henderson).
Born and raised in Columbus, Georgia, Ma Rainey (b. Gertrude Pridgett) began singing professionally when she was a teenager, performing with a number of minstrel and medicine shows. In 1904, she married William "Pa" Rainey and changed her name to "Ma" Rainey. The couple performed as "Rainey and

Rainey, Assassinators of the Blues" and toured throughout the south, performing with several minstrel shows, circuses, and tent shows. According to legend, she gave a young Bessie Smith vocal lessons during this time. By the early '20s, Ma Rainey had become a featured performer on the Theater Owners' Booking Association circuit.

In 1923, Ma Rainey signed a contract with Paramount Records. Although her recording career lasted only a mere six years—her final sessions were in 1928—she recorded over 100 songs and many of them, including "C.C. Rider" and "Bo Weavil Blues," became genuine blues classics. During these sessions, she was supported by some of the most talented blues and jazz musicians of her era, including Louis Armstrong, fletcher Henderson, Coleman Hawkins, Buster Bailey, and Lovie Austin.

Rainey's recordings and performances were extremely popular among Black audiences, particularly in the south. After reaching the height of her popularity in the late '20s, Rainey's career faded away in the early '30s as female blues singing became less popular with the blues audience. She retired from performing in 1933, settling down in her hometown of Columbus. In 1939, Ma Rainey died of a heart attack. She left behind an immense recorded legacy, which continued to move and influence successive generations of blues, country, and rock 'n' roll musicians. In 1983, Rainey was inducted into the Blues Foundation's Hall of Fame; seven years later, she was inducted into the Rock & Roll Hall of Fame. —*Jim O'Neal & Stephen Thomas Erlewine*

★ **Ma Rainey** / Jun. 1975 / Milestone ◆◆◆◆◆
The archetypical "classic" blues femme belter on 1924-1928 recordings, with Fletcher Henderson on piano and Coleman Hawkins bass sax on two tracks. —*Mark A. Humphrey*

Bonnie Raitt

b. Nov. 8, 1949, Cleveland, OH
Guitar, Vocals / Modern Acoustic Blues, Modern Electric Blues
While some blues critics like to act as if *all* White practitioners of the music—especially those who achieve any kind of mainstream success—are little more than modern-day carpetbaggers, few artists on the charts today have earned or come by their success more honestly or in a more hard-won manner than Ms. Bonnie Raitt. Purists and naysayers will quickly point out that she's never made an album of just straight blues, but if it took Eric Clapton 30 plus years to get around to doing one, it's almost a certainty that the prolific redhead won't make blues lovers wait *quite* that long. As a vocalist, she's never been any less than soulful and as a guitarist—especially on slide, her specialty—she reduces the old macho saw of "she plays pretty for a girl" into the same antiquated thought processes as expecting all women to look and act like June Cleaver.

Born in 1949 into a show business family (her Dad is bigvoiced Broadway star John Raitt) Bonnie started guitar early on, but really got the blues bug when she attended college in Cambridge, MA in the '60s. Learning the ropes first-hand from blues legends Son House, Mississippi Fred McDowell (her twin inspirations on slide), and classic blues woman vocalist Sippie Wallace, she started doing the local coffeehouse circuit (usually opening for John Hammond, Jr.), catching the eye of Dick Waterman, who managed all three artists and was soon managing her as well. She soon was appearing with all three performers, appearing on every folk and blues festival in existence, establishing herself as the little hippie girl who was undoubtedly the real deal. A recording contract with Warner Brothers soon followed and her eponymously titled debut opus featured the talents of Chicago blues legends Junior Wells and A.C. Reed. But with eclectic tastes in abundance, Raitt was soon flexing her interpretive muscles on future outings, showing her love for the work of great modern songwriters of all genres. Dividing her time equally with more pop-oriented albums while playing smaller venues as a solo act, the years of trying to party hearty with the older bluesmen finally caught up with her and the mid-'80s found her overweight with an alcohol and drug problem to boot. To make matters even worse, Warner Brothers—her label of 15 years—unceremoniously dumped her. But her turnaround—both personally and professionally—couldn't have been more dramatic if she had hired a Hollywood scriptwriter to orchestrate it. With her booze and drug problems clearly behind her, she suddenly became the comeback kid with the 1989 Grammy-winning success of the aptly titled *Nick of Time*. She

continued the run for the gold (or in this case, platinum) with the follow-ups *Luck of the Draw* and *Longing in Their Hearts*. But rather than kick back and hobnob with industry swells, her excellent contributions to John Lee Hooker's 1990 album *The Healer* and her tireless efforts on behalf of the Rhythm & Blues Foundation clearly illustrated that she hadn't left her blues roots in the trunk of the limo. No matter what eclectic path she follows from here on out, Bonnie Raitt remains one hell of a blues lady. —*Cub Koda*

Bonnie Raitt / 1971 / Warner Brothers ◆◆◆
By the time Raitt recorded this impressive self-titled debut, she had developed quite a set of blues chops playing with artists like Mississippi Fred McDowell, Howlin' Wolf, and other blues greats. In fact, she enlisted Chicago-bluesmen Junior Wells and A.C. Reed to aid in the proceedings, which are relaxed and earthy. —*Rick Clark*

● **Give It Up** / Sep. 1972 / Warner Brothers ◆◆◆◆◆
Raitt's sophomore release is a classic. Of all the albums from her days with Warner, this is the one that put together her folky singer/songwriter sensitivities with her love for country blues. *Give It Up*, which took 13 years to go gold, showcased an intelligent song selection, with tracks by Jackson Browne ("Under the Falling Sky"), Eric Kaz ("Love Has No Pride"), and Joel Zoss ("Been Too Long at the Fair"). Her self-penned "Love Me like a Man" highlighted her impressive guitar technique. —*Rick Clark*

Moses Rascoe

b. 1917, Windsor, NC
Guitar, Vocals / Modern Acoustic Blues
Moses Rascoe got his first guitar in North Carolina at the age of 13 and turned professional in Pennsylvania some 50-odd years later. In between, he traveled the roads as a day laborer and truck driver, playing guitar only for "a dollar or a drink," as he told Jack Roberts in *Living Blues*. But he'd picked up plenty of songs over the years, from old Brownie McGhee Piedmont blues to Jimmy Reed's '50s jukebox hits, and when he retired from trucking at the age of 65, he gave his music a shot. The local folk-music community took notice, as did blues and folk festivals from Chicago to Europe. Rascoe recorded his first album live at Godfrey Daniels, a Pennyslvania coffeehouse, in 1987. —*Jim O'Neal*

Blues / 1987 / Flying Fish ◆◆◆◆◆
A former truck driver turned touring bluesman, Rascoe primarily covers other people's tunes and classic blues themes. There is much Jimmy Reed and "traditional" material. —*Niles J. Frantz*

Sugar Ray & the Bluetones

Harmonica, Vocals / Modern Electric Blues
East Coast based blues band fronted by singer/harmonica man Ray Norcia and featuring guitar work over the years by Ronnie Earl (Roomful of Blues, Ronnie Earl & the Broadcasters) and Kid Bangham (The Fabulous Thunderbirds). —*AMG*

● **Knockout** / 1989 / Varrick ◆◆◆◆◆
A surprisingly tasteful and solidly swinging album, Sugar Ray is a powerhouse vocalist and a more-than-respectable harp player. There are some good songs, too, especially the slow blues "I'm Tortured." —*Niles J. Frantz*

Don't Stand in My Way / 1990 / Bullseye Blues ◆◆◆
There's more swagger and less swing; it's still quite good. —*Niles J. Frantz*

A.C. Reed (Aaron Cortler)

b. May 9, 1926, Wardell, MO
Saxophone, Vocals / Electric Chicago Blues
To hear tenor saxist A.C. Reed bemoan his fate onstage, one might glean the impression that he truly detests his job. But it's a tongue-in-cheek complaint—Reed's raspy, gutbucket blowing and laidback vocals belie any sense of boredom.

Sax-blowing blues bandleaders are scarce as hen's teeth in Chicago; other than Eddie Shaw, Reed's about all there is. Born in Missouri, young Aaron Corthen (whether he's related to blues legend Jimmy Reed remains hazy, but his laconic vocal drawl certainly mirrors his namesake) grew up in downstate Illinois. A big-band fan, he loved the sound of Paul Bascomb's horn on an obscure Erskine Hawkins 78 he heard tracking on a tavern jukebox so much that he was inspired to pick up a sax himself.

Arriving in Chicago during the war years, he picked up steady gigs with Earl Hooker and Willie Mabon before the '40s were over. In 1956, he joined forces with ex-Ike Turner cohort Dennis "Long Man" Binder, gigging across the Southwest for an extended period. Reed became a valuable session player for producer Mel London's Age and Chief labels during the early '60s; in addition to playing on sides by Lillian Offitt, Ricky Allen, and Hooker, he cut a locally popular 1961 single of his own for Age, "This Little Voice."

More gems for Age—"Come on Home," "Mean Cop," "I Stay Mad"—followed. He cut 45s for USA in 1963 ("I'd Rather Fight than Switch"), Cool ("My Baby Is Fine," a tune he's recut countless times since) and Nike ("Talkin' 'Bout My Friends") in 1966, and "Things I Want You to Do" in 1969 for T.D.S.

Reed joined Buddy Guy's band in 1967, visiting Africa with the mercurial guitarist in 1969 and, after harpist Junior Wells teamed with Guy, touring as opening act for the Rolling Stones in 1970. He left the employ of Guy and Wells for good in 1977, only to hook up with Alligator acts Son Seals and then the Master of the Telecaster, Albert Collins. Reed appeared on Collins' first five icy Alligator LPs, including the seminal *Ice Pickin'*.

During his tenure with Collins, Reed's solo career began to reignite, with four cuts on the second batch of Alligator's *Living Chicago Blues* anthologies in 1980 and two subsequent LPs of his own, 1982's *Take These Blues and Shove 'Em!* (on Ice Cube Records, a logo co-owned by Reed and drummer Casey Jones) and *I'm in the Wrong Business!* five years later for Alligator (with cameos by Bonnie Raitt and Stevie Ray Vaughan). Reed remains an active force on the Chicago circuit with his band, the Spark Plugs (get it? AC sparkplugs? Sure you do!). —*Bill Dahl*

Take These Blues and Shove 'Em / 1982 / Rooster Blues ✦✦✦
The first of the saxist's humorous diatribes detailing his tongue-in-cheek hatred of his life's calling. His argument doesn't hold water, though, since the LP is so refreshingly funky ("I Am Fed Up with This Music" remains a bandstand staple for him) and enjoyable. Drummer Casey Jones, Reed's longtime bandmate behind Albert Collins, co-produced with the sardonic horn man. —*Bill Dahl*

● **I'm in the Wrong Business** / 1987 / Alligator ✦✦✦✦✦
Solid, soulful blues, often with humorous, self-deprecating lyrics, come from the well-respected vocalist, tenor player, composer, and veteran of the bands of Albert Collins, Buddy Guy, Magic Sam, and Son Seals. Reed has been called "the definitive Chicago blues sax player." This album features Reed's band, with guests Bonnie Raitt and Stevie Ray Vaughan. —*Niles J. Frantz*

Dalton Reed

b. 1952, Lafayette, LA, **d.** Sep. 24, 1994
Vocals / Modern Louisiana Blues
Dalton Reed attempted to keep the sweet sound of deep soul alive in the '90s. The Lafayette, LA, singer comes from a gospel background—a prerequisite for success in the genre—and cut his first single for his own little label in 1986.

When he was a child, Dalton Reed sang gospel in church and played trumpet in his high school marching band. Reed fell in love with R&B and soul as a teenager, prompting him to join a few local bands. Soon, he formed his own group, Dalton Reed and the Musical Journey Band. In a short while, the band was playing bars and clubs throughout Louisiana, Alabama, and Texas.

Reed founded his own record label, Sweet Daddy Records, in 1986, releasing his debut single, "Givin' on in to Love," that same year. Within a few years after the formation of Sweet Daddy, Dalton and his brother Johnny Reed formed another independent lable, Reed Brothers Records.

In 1990, Bullseye Blues signed Dalton Reed and the label released his debut album, *Louisiana Soul Man*, the following year. Three years later, his second album, *Willing & Able*, appeared. When he wasn't recording, Reed toured, playing concerts throughout America. —*Bill Dahl*

Louisiana Soul Man / Dec. 1991 / Bullseye Blues ✦✦✦
Dalton Reed's *Louisiana Soul Man* establishes the singer as an heir to the deep Southern soul of such artists as Otis Redding, Arthur Conley, and Percy Sledge. Despite the title, there's no hint of cajun music or zydeco on the record—it's pure testifying from start to finish. The new material is usually quite good, and it should be with songwriters like Doc Pomus, Dr. John, Dan Penn, and Delbert McClinton involved. *Louisiana Soul Man* is for anyone who believed that pure Southern soul died with Otis Redding. —*Thom Owens*

● **Willing & Able** / Mar. 30, 1994 / Bullseye Blues ✦✦✦✦
Dalton Reed is a classic gospel-based soul vocalist. There's nothing sophisticated in his approach, staid in his delivery, or polite and detached in his sound. He explodes, attacks, and rips through the 10 tracks on his second Bullseye blues LP, his voice full of animation and expressiveness. These songs are done in the vivid, overwrought manner considered too intense by the urban contemporary tastemakers; you won't hear trendy backgrounds or drum machines on these numbers. This is unapologetic soul from a vocalist who will never appeal to the crossover audience, but is making some of the better R&B in today's market. —*Ron Wynn*

Jimmy Reed (Mathis James Reed)

b. Sep. 6, 1925, Dunleith, MS, **d.** Aug. 29, 1976, Oakland, CA
Guitar, Harmonica, Vocals / Electric Chicago Blues
There's simply no sound in the blues as easily digestible, accessible, instantly recognizable, and as easy to play and sing as the music of Jimmy Reed. His best-known songs—"Baby, What You Want Me to Do," "Bright Lights, Big City," "Honest I Do," "You Don't Have to Go," "Going to New York," "Ain't That Lovin' You Baby," and "Big Boss Man"—have become such an integral part of the standard blues repertoire, it's almost as if they have existed forever. Because his style was simple and easily imitated, his songs were accessible to just about everyone from high school garage bands having a go at it to Elvis Presley, Charlie Rich, Lou Rawls, Hank Williams, Jr., and the Rolling Stones, making him—in the long run—perhaps the most influential bluesman of all. His bottom-string boogie rhythm guitar patterns (all furnished by boyhood friend and longtime musical partner Eddie Taylor), simple two-string turnarounds, countryish harmonica solos (all played in a neck rack attachment hung around his neck), and mush-mouthed vocals were probably the first exposure most White folks had to the blues. And his music—lazy, loping, and insistent and constantly built and reconstructed single after single on the same sturdy frame—was a formula that proved to be enormously successful and influential, both with middle-aged Blacks and young White audiences for a good dozen years. Jimmy Reed records hit the R&B charts with amazing frequency and crossed over onto the pop charts on many occasions, a rare feat for an unreconstructed bluesman. This is all the more amazing simply because Reed's music was nothing special on the surface; he possessed absolutely no technical expertise on either of his chosen instruments and his vocals certainly lacked the fierce declamatory intensity of a Howlin' Wolf or a Muddy Waters. But it was *exactly* that lack of in-your-face musical confrontation that made Jimmy Reed a welcome addition to everybody's record collection back in the '50s and '60s. And for those aspiring musicians who wanted to give the blues a try, either vocally or instrumentally, perhaps Billy Vera said it best in his liner notes to a Reed greatest hits anthology: "Yes, anybody with a range of more than six notes could sing Jimmy's tunes and play them the first day Mom and Dad brought home that first guitar from Sears & Roebuck. I guess Jimmy could be termed the '50s punk bluesman."

Reed was born on September 6, 1925, on a plantation in or around the small burg of Dunleith, MS. He stayed around the area until he was 15, learning the basic rudiments of harmonica and guitar from his buddy Eddie Taylor, who was then making a name for himself as a semi-pro musician, working country suppers and juke joints. Reed moved to Chicago in 1943, but was quickly drafted into the Navy, where he served for two years. After a quick trip back to Mississippi and marriage to his beloved wife Mary (known to blues fans as "Mama Reed"), he relocated to Gary, IN, and found work at an Armour Foods meat packing plant while simultaneously breaking into the burgeoning blues scene around Gary and neighboring Chicago. The early '50s found him working as a sideman with John Brim's Gary Kings (that's Reed blowing harp on Brim's classic "Tough Times" and its instrumental flipside, "Gary Stomp") and playing on the street for tips with Willie Joe Duncan, a shadowy figure who played an amplified, homemade one-string instrument called a Unitar. After failing an audition with Chess Records (his later chart success would be a constant thorn in the side of the firm), Brim's drummer at the time—improbably enough, future blues guitar legend Albert King—brought him over to the newly formed Vee-Jay Records where his first recordings were made. It was during this time that he was reunited and started playing again with Eddie Taylor, a musical partnership that would last off and on until Reed's death. Success was slow in coming, but when his third single, "You Don't Have to Go" backed with "Boogie in the Dark," made the number five slot on *Billboard's* R&B charts, the hits pretty much kept on coming for the next decade.

But if selling more records than Muddy Waters, Howlin' Wolf, Elmore James, or Little Walter brought the rewards of fame to his doorstep, no one was more ill-equipped to handle it than Jimmy Reed. With signing his name for fans being the total sum of his literacy, combined with a back-breaking road schedule once he became a name attraction, and his self-description as a "liquor glutter," Reed started to fall apart like a cheap suit almost immediately. His devious schemes to tend to his alcoholism—and the just plain aberrant behavior that came as a result of it—quickly made him the laughing stock of his show business contemporaries. Those who shared the bill with him in top-of-the-line R&B venues like the Apollo Theater—where the story of him urinating on a star performer's dress in the wings has been repeated verbatim by more than one oldtimer—still shake their heads and wonder how Jimmy could actually stand up straight and perform, much less hold the audience in the palm of his hand. Other stories of Jimmy being "arrested" and thrown into a Chicago drunk tank the night before a recording session also reverberate throughout the blues community to this day. Little wonder then that when he was stricken with epilepsy in 1957, it went undiagnosed for an extended period of time, simply because he had experienced so many attacks of delirium tremens. Eddie Taylor would relate how he sat directly in front of Reed in the studio, instructing him while the tune was being recorded, exactly when to start to start singing, when to blow his harp, and when to do the turnarounds on his guitar. He also appears, by all accounts, to have been unable to remember the lyrics to new songs—even ones he had composed himself—and Mama Reed would sit on a piano bench and whisper them into his ear, literally one line at a time. Blues fans who doubt this can clearly hear the proof on several of Jimmy's biggest hits, most notably "Big Boss Man" and "Bright Lights, Big City," where she steps into the fore and starts singing along with him in order to keep him on the beat.

But seemingly none of this mattered. While revisionist blues historians like to make a big deal about either the lack of variety of his work or how later recordings turned him into a mere parody of himself, the public just couldn't get enough of it. Jimmy Reed placed 11 songs on the *Billboard* Hot 100 pop charts and a total of 14 on the R&B charts, a figure that even a much more sophisticated artist like B.B. King couldn't top. To paraphrase the old saying, nobody liked Jimmy Reed but the people.

Reed's slow descent into the ravages of alcoholism and epilepsy roughly paralleled the decline of Vee-Jay Records, which went out of business at approximately the same time that his final 45 was released, "Don't Think I'm Through." His manager, Al Smith, quickly arranged a contract with the newly formed ABC-Bluesway label and a handful of albums were released into the '70s, all of them lacking the old charm, sounding as if they were cut on a musical assembly line. Jimmy did one last album, a horrible attempt to update his sound with funk beats and wah-wah pedals, before becoming a virtual recluse in his final years. He finally received proper medical attention for his epilepsy and quit drinking, but it was too late and he died trying to make a comeback on the blues festival circuit on August 29, 1976.

All of this is sad beyond belief, simply because there's so much joy in Jimmy Reed's music. And it's that joy that becomes evident every time you give one of his classic sides a spin. Although his bare-bones style influenced everyone from British Invasion combos to the entire school of Louisiana swamp blues artists (Slim Harpo and Jimmy Anderson in particular), the simple indisputable fact remains that—like so many of the other originators in the genre—there was only one Jimmy Reed. —*Cub Koda*

Best of Jimmy Reed / 1961 / Vee-Jay ♦♦♦♦♦
Another tough-to-beat old album full of Reed's finest and most influential work. —*Bill Dahl*

★ **Live at Carnegie Hall/Best of Jimmy Reed** / 1961 / Mobile Fidelity ♦♦♦♦♦
Not a live album at all, this is actually two LPs of Reed's finest studio efforts for Vee-Jay. —*Bill Dahl*

Jimmy Reed / 1965 / Paula/Flyright ♦♦♦
With so much attention paid to Jimmy's seminal Vee-Jay sides,

it's hard to realize that he had a recording career that extended past the label's demise in the mid-'60s. But with manager Al Smith producing, Reed turned out a bushelbascket of albums for the ABC-Bluesway and Exodus labels, the best of which are collected here. These 21 tracks recorded between 1966 and 1971 vary quite a bit from the original vinyl issues, which were edited and sometimes retitled for release. Not Reed at his best, but for a complete picture of the man and his music, you'll definitely want to add this one to the pile. —*Cub Koda*

Ride 'Em on Down / 1989 / Charly ♦♦♦♦♦
Reed shares this compilation with Eddie Taylor (with Reed in support on four tracks) and features a dozen tracks from Reed's early days. Good sound throughout (this has the most listenable disc transfer of Reed's first single "High & Lonesome") and the perfect companion piece to the above. —*Cub Koda*

Classic Recordings / 1995 / Tomato ♦♦♦♦♦
This three-CD, 55-song box is the most comprehensive domestic retrospective of Reed's career (a six-CD box is available on import). The material is fine and consistent, but this isn't the best deal for either the average fan or the completist. Reed is one of the most homogenous blues greats, and unless your interest is deep, three CDs at once will become monotonous; you're better off with one of the several fine single-disc compilations available. Also, this has no information whatsoever on release dates or sessions, and inexplicably omits one of his two Top 40 hits, "Honest I Do" (covered by The Rolling Stones on their first album). —*Richie Unterberger*

★ **Speak The Lyrics To Me, Mama Reed** / Vee-Jay ♦♦♦♦♦
Although many *Best Of Jimmy Reed* compilations exist on the market (most with variable sound quality and maddening duplication), this 25-tracker is currently the one to beat. Including all the influential hits and a few of the best rare ones ("You Upset My Mind" and the single version of "Little Rain," different than the take on his debut album), this features impeccable sound (except on the disc transfer of Reed's first single, "High & Lonesome") and is the perfect place to start. —*Cub Koda*

Lula Reed

Vocals / Electric R&B
A longtime cohort of pianist/producer Sonny Thompson, singer Lula Reed recorded steadily for Cincinnati-based King Records during the mid-'50s after debuting on wax in 1951 to sing Thompson's original version of the moving ballad "I'll Drown in My Own Tears" (a 1956 smash for Ray Charles as "Drown in My Own Tears").

After serving as Thompson's vocalist at first, the attractive chanteuse was sufficiently established by 1952 to rate her own King releases. She was versatile, singing urban blues most of the time but switching to gospel for a 1954 session. Reed's strident 1954 waxing "Rock Love" was later revived by labelmate Little Willie John. She briefly moved to the Chess subsidiary Argo in 1958–59 but returned to the fold in 1961 (as always, under Thompson's direction) on King's Federal imprint. While at Federal, she waxed a series of sassy duets with guitarist Freddy King in March of 1962. Another move—to Ray Charles' Tangerine logo in 1962–63—soon followed. After that, her whereabouts are unknown. —*Bill Dahl*

● **Blue and Moody** / 1959 / King ♦♦♦♦♦
The longtime protégé of King Records house pianist/arranger/producer Sonny Thompson possessed a sultry style well-suited to blues ballads in the urban vein and lighthearted upbeat fare—both of which reside on this reissue of her vintage King album. —*Bill Dahl*

Sonny Rhodes

b. Nov. 3, 1940, Smithville, TX
Bass, Guitar, Guitar (Steel), Vocals / Modern Electric Blues
Blues guitarist, singer, and songwriter Sonny Rhodes is such a talented songwriter, so full of musical ideas, that he's destined to inherit the seats left open by the untimely passing of blues greats like Albert King and Albert Collins.

Rhodes was the sixth and last child of Le Roy and Julia Smith, who were sharecroppers. Rhodes began playing seriously when he was 12, although he got his first guitar when he was eight as a Christmas present. He began performing around Smithville and nearby Austin in the late '50s, while still in his teens. He listened to a lot of T-Bone Walker when he was young, and it shows in his playing today. Other guitarists he credits as being influences include Pee Wee Crayton and B.B. King. Rhodes' first band, Clarence Smith and the Daylighters, played the Austin area blues clubs, until Rhodes decided to join the Navy after graduating from high school.

In the Navy, he moved west to California, where he worked for awhile as a radio man and closed-circuit Navy ship disc-jockey, telling off-color jokes in between the country and blues records he would spin for the entertainment of the sailors.

Rhodes recorded a single for Domino Records in Austin, "I'll Never Let You Go When Something Is Wrong," in 1958, and also learned to play bass. He played bass behind Freddie King and his friend Albert Collins. After his stint in the Navy, Rhodes returned to California while in his mid-20s, and lived in Fresno for a few years before hooking up a deal with Galaxy Records in Oakland. In 1966, he recorded a single, "I Don't Love You No More" backed with "All Night Long I Play the Blues." He recorded another single for Galaxy in 1967 and then in 1978, out of total frustration with the San Francisco Bay Area record companies, he recorded "Cigarette Blues" backed with "Bloodstone Beat" on his own label. Rhodes toured Europe in 1976, and that opened a whole new European market to him, and he was recorded by several European labels, but without much success. His European recordings include *I Don't Want My Blues Colored Bright* and a live album, *In Europe*. In desperation again, Rhodes went into the studio to record an album in 1985, *Just Blues*, on his own Rhodesway label.

Fortunately, things have been on track for Rhodes since the late '80s, when he began recording first for the Ichiban label and later for King Snake. His albums for Ichiban include *Disciple of the Blues* (1991) and *Living Too Close to the Edge* (1992).

More recently, Rhodes has gotten better distribution of his albums with the Sanford, Florida-based King Snake label. Aside from his self-produced 1985 release *Just Blues* (now available on compact disc through Evidence Music), his best albums include the ones he's recorded for King Snake, because these are the records that have gotten Rhodes and his various back-up bands out on the road together throughout the U.S., Canada and Europe. They include *The Blues Is My Best Friend* and his 1995 release, *Out of Control*. On these albums we hear Rhodes, the fully developed songwriter, and not surprisingly, both releases drew high marks from blues critics. —*Richard Skelly*

Disciple of the Blues / 1991 / Ichiban ✦✦✦✦✦
This beturbaned bluesman plays lap steel guitar. This is a good one, but he's got an even better one in him. —*Niles J. Frantz*

● **Livin' Too Close to the Edge** / 1992 / Ichiban ✦✦✦✦✦
This is an exciting, blistering set of contemporary blues, drivin by Sonny Rhodes' innovative lap steel playing. —*Thom Owens*

The Blues Is My Best Friend / 1994 / King Snake ✦✦✦

In Europe / Appaloosa ✦✦✦

Just Blues / Evidence ✦✦✦

Tommy Ridgley

b. Oct. 30, 1925, New Orleans, LA
Piano, Vocals / Electric New Orleans Blues
Tommy Ridgley was on the Crescent City R&B scene when it first caught fire, and he remains a proud part of that same scene today. That's a lot of years behind a microphone, but Ridgley doesn't sound the slightest bit tired; his 1995 Black Top album *Since the Blues Began* rates with his liveliest outings to date.

Ridgley cut his debut sides back in 1949 for Imperial under Dave Bartholomew's direction. His "Shrewsbury Blues" and "Boogie Woogie Mama" failed to break outside of his hometown, though. Sessions for Decca in 1950 and Imperial in 1952 (where he waxed the wild "Looped") preceded four 1953–55 sessions for Atlantic that included a blistering instrumental, "Jam Up," that sported no actual Ridgley involvement but sold relatively well under his name (incomparable tenor saxist Lee Allen was prominent).

New York's Herald Records was Ridgley's home during the late '50s. The consistently solid singer waxed "When I Meet My Girl" for the firm in 1957, encoring with a catchy "Baby Do-Liddle." From there, it was on to his hometown-based Ric logo, where he laid down the stunning stroll-tempoed "Let's Try and

Talk It Over" and a bluesy "Should I Ever Love Again" in 1960. He recorded intermittently after leaving Ric in 1963, waxing a soulful "I'm Not the Same Person" in 1969 for Ronn.

Ridgley always remained a hometown favorite even when recording opportunities proved scarce. Happily, *Since the Blues Began* ranked with 1995's best albums, Ridgley sounding entirely contemporary but retaining his defining Crescent City R&B edge. —*Bill Dahl*

● **The New Orleans King of the Stroll** / 1988 / Rounder ✦✦✦✦✦
Tommy Ridgley was a solid R&B vocalist who was quite successful with novelty tunes and silly songs, but was also a good romantic balladeer. This 15-track collection mostly covers Ridgley material from 1960 to 1964 for the Ric label, and ranges from laments like "Please Hurry Home" and "I Love You Yes I Do" to such comic material and dance-based numbers as "Double-Eyed Whammy" and "The Girl From Kooka Monga." Ridgley wasn't as booming or dynamic as some other Crescent City vocalists, but made several nice period pieces and soul tunes, several of which are included on this set. —*Ron Wynn*

She Turns Me on / 1992 / Modern Blues ✦✦✦
Competent contemporary effort that proved Ridgley's voice was still in excellent shape, albeit a less-engaging outing overall than his subsequent Black Top release. —*Bill Dahl*

Since The Blues Began / 1995 / Black Top ✦✦✦✦
The veteran New Orleans singer remains a contemporary force to be reckoned with. Guitarist Snooks Eaglin, bassist George Porter, Jr., and saxist Kaz Kazanoff help Ridgley out on what's easily his finest contemporary release. There are a handful of remakes of his earlier triumphs, but for the most part, he is commendably living in the present, incorporating funk-tinged rhythms into his delectable musical gumbo. —*Bill Dahl*

The Herald Recordings / Collectables ✦✦✦✦
There are some very nice late-'50s New Orleans R&B recommending this 17-track collection, along with a few superfluous instrumental backing tracks that could have safely been jettisoned altogether. Ridgley's stint at Herald included the sizzling "When I Meet My Girl," "Baby Do Little," and several more impressive rocking efforts, backed by the esteemed crew at Cosimo's Crescent City studio—saxist Lee Allen, etc. —*Bill Dahl*

Paul Rishell

Guitar, Vocals / Modern Acoustic-Electric Blues
Boston-area blues guitarist and singer Paul Rishell specializes in the country blues, but in recent years, he's been proving his mettle on occasional gigs with an electric band as well. Rishell has been riding the wave of renewed interest in acoustic music in general, and he's taken his style of acoustic country blues to festivals and clubs around the U.S., often accompanied by his harmonica-playing partner, Little Annie Raines.

Before he ever entered the recording studio, Rishell spent many years studying his craft, and he's shared stages with good people: Son House, Johnny Shines, Howlin' Wolf, Sonny Terry and Brownie McGhee, Buddy Guy and Junior Wells, John Lee Hooker and Bonnie Raitt.

Rishell has two albums out on the Tone-Cool label, *Blues on Holiday* (1990) and *Swear to Tell the Truth* (1993). Both are distributed by Rounder Records, are readily available, and are excellent albums. —*Richard Skelly*

Swear to Tell the Truth / 1993 / Tone-Cool ✦✦✦
The tendency to be snide and cynical whenever encountering contemporary versions of vintage country blues is great, mainly because there is no way anyone singing Skip James or Son House tunes in the 1990s could possibly best the originals. Paul Rishell's versions of their songs are neither faceless covers nor spectacular reworkings; they are merely Rishell's earnest attempt to communicate the music he loves. Sometimes it works and other times it doesn't, but it is never pretentious or solemn. The better tracks are the jumping version of Earl Hooker's "Do You Swear To Tell The Truth," with guitar by Ronnie Earl, and Rishell's own "I'm Gonna Jump and Shout." This is not Hall of Fame stuff, but it also should not be curtly dismissed or unfairly ridiculed. —*Ron Wynn*

Blues on a Holiday / Tone-Cool ✦✦✦✦✦
Blues on a Holiday is divided between full-band numbers and songs guitarist Paul Rishell performed on a solo guitar. Both sides are exciting, offering invigorating updates of Delta and Chicago blues. Although the solo numbers—which were all per-

formed on a National Steel—are raw and exciting, the songs recorded with a full band give a good idea of the depths of Rishell's talent. It is on these songs that he really tears loose, demonstrating what a versatile guitarist he is. —*Thom Owens*

Duke Robillard

Guitar, Vocals / Modern Blues

Duke Robillard is one of the founding members of Roomful of Blues, as well as one of the guitarists that replaced Jimmie Vaughan in the Fabulous Thunderbirds in 1990. Between that time, Robillard pursued a solo career that found him exploring more musically adventurous territory than either Roomful of Blues or the T-Birds. On his solo recordings, the guitarist dips into blues, rockabilly, jazz, and rock 'n' roll, creating a unique fusion of American roots musics.

In 1967, Duke Robillard formed Roomful of Blues in Westerly, Rhode Island. For the next decade, he led the band through numerous lineup changes before he decided that he had grown tired of the group. Robillard left the band in 1979, initially signing on as rockabilly singer Robert Gordon's lead guitarist. After his stint with Gordon, Robillard joined the Legendary Blues Band.

In 1981, the guitarist formed a new group, the Duke Robillard Band, which soon evolved into Duke Robillard & the Pleasure Kings. After a few years of touring, the group landed a contract with Rounder Records, releasing their eponymous debut album in 1984. For the rest of the decade, Robillard and the Pleasure Kings toured America and released a series of albums on Rounder Records. Occasionally, the guitarist would release a jazz-oriented solo album.

In 1990, Robillard joined the Fabulous Thunderbirds. Even though he had become a member of the Austin group, the guitarist continued to record and tour as a solo artist, signing with the major label Point Blank/Virgin in 1994. —*Stephen Thomas Erlewine*

Duke Robillard & the Pleasure Kings / 1984 / Rounder ✦✦✦✦✦

Featuring fine T-Bone Walker-influenced guitar and vocals from the leader, these trio recordings mostly contain original compositions. This is good for what it is, but it seems to lack the punch that larger instrumentation might provide. —*Bob Porter*

Too Hot to Handle / 1985 / Rounder ✦✦✦

Rockin' Blues / 1988 / Rounder ✦✦✦

Robillard, both a good blues guitarist and knowledgeable swing player, displays his rocking side on this '88 date. There are flashier solos, more uptempo cuts, and an aggressive, frenetic quality that's missing on Robillard's jazz-oriented releases. —*Ron Wynn*

You Got Me / 1988 / Rounder ✦✦✦

Duke Robillard's sessions have alternated between jazzy, sophisticated, low-key ventures and bluesy, more energetic, rousing dates. This was on the robust side, matching Robillard's guitar and good-natured, celebratory vocals with the talents of a great guest corps that included Dr. John and Ron Levy on keyboards, guitarist Jimmie Vaughan, bassist Thomas Enright and drummer Tommy DeQuattro (The Pleasure Kings). These weren't always musical triumphs, but even the songs that didn't quite work were entertaining, while the more inspirational offerings like "You're the One I Adore" and "Don't Treat Me Like That" nicely balance tremendous instrumental support with energetic vocal performances. —*Ron Wynn*

Swing / Oct. 1988 / Rounder ✦✦✦

While he makes his fame and fortune cutting blues-rock, guitarist Duke Robillard periodically issues albums of stylish, restrained, subtly swinging jazzy material. This date included guest appearances from swing-influenced contemporary instrumentalists, such as tenor saxophonist Scott Hamilton and guitarist Chris Flory, who teams with Robillard on "Glide On" for some excellent twin guitar fireworks. Otherwise, it's Jim Kelly who matches licks with Robillard on "Jim Jam" and "What's Your Story, Morning Glory." It's relaxed, elegant music, with just enough grit to keep things interesting. —*Ron Wynn*

Turn It Around / 1990 / Rounder ✦✦✦

Guitarist Duke Robillard emphasized the rocking blues and barrelhouse side of his musical personality on this '91 session that highlighted what was then his band. Vocalist Susan Forrest pro-

vided a lusty, sensual quality while bassist Scott Appelrough and drummer Doug Hinman laid down sparse rhythmic backgrounds. Robillard provided the lead guitar presence and energy, adding more flashy chords, riffs, licks, and driving solos than on his more restrained jazz-based material. It was an effective session, though Forrest's vocals weren't always as hard-hitting as the material demanded. But Robillard and his mates provided instrumental cover when Forrest didn't quite hit the mark, and were even more on target when she did. —*Ron Wynn*

● **After Hours Swing Session** / May 1990 / Rounder ✦✦✦✦✦

While guitarist Duke Robillard has won widespread popularity for his facility with rocking blues and barrelhouse numbers, he also loves understated, quietly swinging jazz fare. He got a chance to demonstrate his proficiency in this style on this intimate combo session. The eight songs featured on the CD include brisk workouts, as well as light-hearted numbers that showcase Robillard's decent, if not great, voice, along with his fluid, tasty fills and crisp, clean acoustic and electric guitar solos. Here's another side of Duke Robillard, one that deserves equal billing with the flashy, burning one. —*Ron Wynn*

Minor Swing / 1992 / North Star ✦✦✦

Temptation / 1994 / Capitol ✦✦✦✦✦

Duke's Blues / Jan. 23, 1996 / Point Blank ✦✦✦

With *Duke's Blues*, guitarist Duke Robillard pays tribute to his blues idols, such as Albert Collins, T-Bone Walker, Guitar Slim, and Lowell Fulson. As expected, it's an affectionate and professional tribute. Robillard works with an augmented blues combo, featuring a second guitarist, piano, and a small horn section. The band runs through the material precisely and efficiently. Although there's plenty of fine musicianship throughout *Duke's Blues*, it's the record to admire, not love—it's expertly executed, but it never catches fire. —*Thom Owens*

Fenton Robinson

b. Sep. 23, 1935, Minter City, MS

Guitar, Vocals / Modern Electric Blues

His Japanese fans reverently dubbed Fenton Robinson "the mellow blues genius" because of his ultra-smooth vocals and jazz-inflected guitar work. But beneath the obvious subtlety resides a spark of constant regeneration—Robinson tirelessly strives to invent something fresh and vital whenever he's near a bandstand.

The soft-spoken Mississippi native got his career going in Memphis, where he'd moved at age 16. First, Rosco Gordon used him on a 1956 session for Duke that produced "Keep on Doggin'" The next year, Fenton made his own debut as a leader for the Bihari brothers' Meteor label with his first reading of "Tennessee Woman." His band, the Dukes, included mentor Charles McGowan on guitar; T-Bone Walker and B.B. King were Robinson's idols.

In 1957, Fenton teamed up with bassist Larry Davis at the Flamingo Club in Little Rock. Bobby Bland caught the pair there and recommended them to his boss, Duke Records prexy Don Robey. Both men made waxings for Duke in 1958, Robinson playing on Davis' classic "Texas Flood" and making his own statement with "Mississippi Steamboat." Robinson cut the original version of the often-covered Peppermint Harris-penned slow blues "As the Years Go Passing By" for Duke in 1959 with New Orleans prodigy James Booker on piano. The same date also produced a terrific "Tennessee Woman" and a marvelous blues ballad, "You've Got to Pass This Way Again."

Fenton moved to Chicago in 1962, playing South side clubs with Junior Wells, Sonny Boy Williamson, and Otis Rush and laying down the swinging "Say You're Leavin'" for USA in 1966. But it was his stunning slow blues "Somebody Loan Me a Dime," cut in 1967 for Palos, that insured his blues immortality. Boz Scaggs liked it so much that he covered it for his 1969 debut LP. Unfortunately, he initially also claimed he wrote the tune; much litigation followed.

John Richbourg's Sound Stage 7/Seventy 7 labels, it's safe to say, didn't really have a clue as to what Fenton Robinson's music was all about. The guitarist's 1970 Nashville waxings for the firm were mostly horrific—Robinson wasn't even invited to play his own guitar on the majority of the horribly unsubtle rock-slanted sides. His musical mindset was growing steadily jazzier by then, not rockier.

Robinson fared a great deal better at his next substantial stop: Chicago's Alligator Records. His 1974 album *Somebody Loan Me a Dime* remains the absolute benchmark of his career, spotlighting his rich, satisfying vocals and free-spirited, understated guitar work in front of a rock-solid horn-driven band. By comparison, 1977's *I Hear Some Blues Downstairs* was a trifle disappointing despite its playful title track and a driving T-Bone tribute, "Tell Me What's the Reason."

Alligator issued *Nightflight*, another challenging set, in 1984, then backed off the guitarist. His most recent disc, 1989's *Special Road*, first came out on the Dutch Black Magic logo and was reissued by Evidence Music not long ago. Robinson now resides in downstate Illinois, visiting his old stomping grounds only sporadically. —*Bill Dahl*

★ **Somebody Loan Me a Dime** / 1974 / Alligator ♦♦♦♦♦
One of the most subtly satisfying electric blues albums of the 1970s. Robinson never did quite fit the "Genuine Houserocking Music" image of Alligator Records—his deep, rich baritone sounds more like a magic carpet than a piece of barbed wire, and he speaks in jazz-inflected tongues, full of complex surprises. The title track hits with amazing power, as do the chugging "The Getaway," a hard-swinging "You Say You're Leaving," and the minor-key "You Don't Know What Love Is." In every case, Robinson had recorded them before, but thanks to Bruce Iglauer's superb production, a terrific band, and Robinson's musicianship, these versions reign supreme. —*Bill Dahl*

I Hear Some Blues Downstairs / 1977 / Alligator ♦♦♦
A disappointment in its inconsistency following such a mammoth triumph as his previous set, yet not without its mellow delights. The title track is atypically playful; Robinson's revisiting of the mournful "As the Years Go Passing By" is a moving journey, and his T-Bone Walker tribute "Tell Me What's the Reason" swings deftly. On the other hand, a superfluous remake of Rosco Gordon's "Just a Little Bit" goes nowhere, and nobody really needed another "Killing Floor." —*Bill Dahl*

Blues in Progress / 1984 / Black Magic ♦♦♦
Smooth and jazzy. —*Bill Dahl*

Nightflight / 1984 / Alligator ♦♦♦
For the most part, another easy-going trip to the mellower side of contemporary blues, Robinson's jazzy tone and buttery vocals applied to a couple of his '50s-era numbers ("Crazy Crazy Lovin'" and "Schoolboy") along with some intriguing new items and Lowell Fulson's mournful "Sinner's Prayer." Tasty backing helps too. —*Bill Dahl*

Special Road / Apr. 1989 / Evidence ♦♦♦
Fenton Robinson is among the second-line blues musicians who have come close but never made it over the hump. He has certainly got the guitar goods, and his vocals are often memorable and anguished. The 13 songs he did on this 1989 date were mostly good but not as intense as he has delivered on other occasions. Neither is the instrumental work on this Evidence CD; his solos are firmly articulated, often elaborately constructed and paced, but they lack impact. Too many times Robinson falls just short of turning in a triumphant or exciting number, either through a less-than-emphatic vocal or a mundane solo. This is not necessarily a bad session, just a disappointing one. —*Ron Wynn*

Mellow Fellow / Charly ♦♦
Clearly, the folks at Sound Stage 7 Records had no idea what Fenton Robinson was all about during his 1970-1971 stay there. They even took the guitar out of his hands altogether at one dreadful session reproduced on this 19-track retrospective in its entirety, entrusting the lead work instead to some pitiful rock players better left anonymous. The last few sides are much better—"Little Turch" actually sounds like Robinson, his elegant guitar work back up front where it belongs. —*Bill Dahl*

Freddy Robinson

b. Feb. 24, 1939
Guitar / Modern Blues
Blues fans know him as one of harp genius Little Walter's studio accompanists during the latter portion of his tenure at Chess. Jazz aficionados are aware of him for the albums he did for World Pacific. Freddy Robinson has been one versatile guitarist across the decades.

Robinson played both bass and guitar behind Walter at Chess circa 1959-60. His own recording career commenced in 1962 with a jazz-laced instrumental pairing, "The Buzzard"/"The Hawk," for King's short-lived Queen subsidiary. He gave singing

a try in 1966, cutting "Go-Go Girl" for Checker (with Barbara Acklin and Mamie Galore helping out as background vocalists). By 1968, he was recording with pianist Monk Higgins and the Blossoms (Darlene Love's vocal group) in Los Angeles for Cobblestone.

Blues fans may find the material Robinson cut for a Stax LP in 1972 noteworthy; "At the Drive-In" and "Bluesology" are in-the-alley blues efforts that hark back to the guitarist's early days in Chicago. Robinson later recorded for Al Bell's ICA logo. —*Bill Dahl*

The Coming Atlantis / Apr. 1970 / World Pacific ♦♦♦

At the Drive In / 1972 / Enterprise ♦♦♦
It's rather hard to get a handle on this phase of Robinson's career—there are some reasonably lowdown blues with the guitarist speaking the lyrics as much as singing them here, but he was mainly a jazz musician by then. —*Bill Dahl*

Off the Cuff / Mar. 1974 / Enterprise ♦♦

Ikey Robinson

b. Jul. 28, 1904, Dublin, VA, **d.** Oct. 25, 1990, Chicago, IL
Banjo, Guitar, Vocals / Blues, Classic Jazz
Ikey Robinson was an excellent banjoist and singer who was versatile enough to record both jazz and blues from the late '20s into the late '30s. Unfortunately, he spent long periods off records after the swing era, leading to him being less known than he should be. After working locally, Robinson moved to Chicago in 1926, playing and recording with Jelly Roll Morton, Clarence Williams and (most importantly) Jabbo Smith during 1928–29. He led his own recording sessions in 1929, 1931, 1933, and 1935 (all have been reissued on a CD from the Austrian label RST). Robinson played with Wilbur Sweatman, Noble Sissle, Carroll Dickerson, and Erskine Tate in the 1930s, recorded with Clarence Williams and led small groups from the 1940s on. In the early '60s he was with Franz Jackson, and in the 1970s (when he was rediscovered) he had an opportunity to tour Europe and be reunited with Jabbo Smith. —*Scott Yanow*

● **"Banjo" Ikey Robinson** / Jan. 4, 1929–May 19, 1937 / RST ♦♦♦♦♦
It would not be an understatement to call this CD definitive of Ikey Robinson's work since it includes every selection (except for two songs that have Half Pint Jaxon vocals) ever led by the banjoist/vocalist. The diversity is impressive, for Robinson is heard (on "Got Butter on It" and "Ready Hokum") with a hot group featuring cornetist Jabbo Smith, singing the blues, performing with The Hokum Trio And The Pods of Pepper (both good-time bands), backing singer Charlie Slocum and heading his own Windy City Five (a fine swing group) in 1935; he even plays clarinet on one song. This consistently enjoyable Austrian import is well worth searching for. —*Scott Yanow*

Jimmy Lee Robinson

b. Apr. 30, 1931, Chicago, IL
Guitar / Chicago Blues
Unlike many of his Chicago blues contemporaries, Jimmie Lee Robinson wasn't a Mississippi Delta emigre. The guitarist was born and raised right in the Windy City—not far from Maxwell Street, the fabled open-air market on the near-West side where the blues veritably teemed during the 1940s and '50s.

Robinson learned his lessons well. He formed a partnership with guitarist Freddy King in 1952 for four years (they met outside the local welfare office), later doing sideman work with Elmore James and Little Walter and cutting sessions on guitar and bass behind Little Walter, Eddie Taylor, Shakey Jake, and St. Louis Jimmy Oden. Robinson cut three singles for the tiny Bandera label circa 1959-60; the haunting "All My Life" packed enough power to be heard over in England, where John Mayall faithfully covered it. Another Bandera standout, "Lonely Traveller," was revived as the title track for Robinson's 1994 Delmark comeback album.

Europe enjoyed a glimpse of Robinson when he hit the continent as part of Horst Lippmann and Fritz Rau's 1965 American Folk Blues Festival alongside John Lee Hooker, Buddy Guy, and Big Mama Thornton. After that, his mother died, and times grew tough. Robinson worked as a cabbie and security guard for the Board of Education for a quarter century or so until the members of the Ice Cream Men—a young local band with an overriding passion for 1950s blues—convinced Robinson that he was much too young to be retired. They've been proven right ever since. —*Bill Dahl*

Lonely Traveller / 1994 / Delmark ♦♦♦♦♦
Jimmie Lee Robinson doesn't do everything in the standard 12-bar blues form; sometimes he half-sings, half-talks through songs, or varies the tempo, breaks up the rhythms, and paces the performances in an unusual manner. His solos also aren't the usual piercing or flashy phrases and riffs, but sometimes more decorative or sparse underneath the words. His diverse style and unpredictable vocal manner make this one of the more striking modern blues outings in quite some time, despite the fact that he's neither a great vocalist nor a spectacular instrumentalist. But he's written much of the material, and those songs that he covers, such as Lightnin' Hopkins' "Can't Be Successful" or Big Bill Broonzy's "Key to the Highway," are certainly not reflective of their original creators. —*Ron Wynn*

Tad Robinson

Vocals / Soul Blues
Tad Robinson would have fit in snugly with the blue-eyed soul singers of the 1960s. His vocals virtually reeking of soul, he's capable of delving into a straightahead Little Walter shuffle or delivering a vintage O.V. Wright R&B ballad. Add his songwriting skills and exceptional harp technique and you have quite the total package.

Robinson grew up in New York City on a nutritious diet of Stax, Motown, and Top 40, digging everyone from Otis Redding and Arthur Alexander to Eric Burdon and Joe Cocker. He matriculated at Indiana University's school of music in 1980, fronting a solid little combo on the side called the Hesitation Blues Band that made it up to Chicago now and then (where he soon relocated).

Long respected locally, his reputation outside the city limits soared when he took over as vocalist with Dave Specter & the Bluebirds. Their 1994 Delmark disc, *Blueplicity*, was an inspiring marriage of Robinson's soaring vocals and Specter's tasty, jazz-laced guitar and featured the striking Robinson-penned originals "What's Your Angle," "Dose of Reality," and "On the Outside Looking In."

Delmark granted Tad Robinson his own album later that year. *Ode to Infinity* escorted him even further into soul territory (guests on the set included Mighty Flyers guitarist Alex Schultz, the mystical Robert Ward, and Specter). Now living once more in Indiana, Robinson still makes it into Chicago on a regular basis (but never frequently enough for his followers). —*Bill Dahl*

● **One to Infinity** / 1994 / Delmark ♦♦♦♦♦
Harpist Robinson displays his multi-faceted talents, exploring a multitude of shades of blues and soul. The backing on each song neatly fits the piece—guitarist Robert Ward briefly turns up as a sideman as Robinson proves he's one of the top young vocalists on the contemporary circuit. —*Bill Dahl*

Rogers & Buffalo

Guitar, Harmonica / Acoustic Blues
Slide guitarist/producer Roy Rogers and harmonica maestro Norton Buffalo teamed up for a one-off side project with surprisingly down-home results. —*Cub Koda*

● **R & B** / 1991 / Blind Pig ♦♦♦♦♦
R&B is straight out of the Sonny Terry and Brownie McGee book—a set of stripped-down acoustic blues. Roy Rogers and Norton Buffalo both play with surprising grit and unsurprising affection, making it a very pleasurable tribute. —*Thom Owens*

Travellin' Tracks / 1992 / Blind Pig ♦♦♦

Jimmy Rogers (James A. Lane)

b. Jun. 3, 1924, Ruleville, MS
Guitar, Harmonica, Piano, Vocals / Electric Chicago Blues
Guitarist Jimmy Rogers is the last living connection to the groundbreaking first Chicago band of Muddy Waters (informally dubbed the Headhunters for their penchant of dropping by other musicians' gigs and "cutting their heads" with a superior onstage performance). Instead of basking in worldwide veneration, he's merely a well-respected Chicago elder boasting a seminal 1950s Chess Records catalog, both behind Waters and on his own.

Born James A. Lane (Rogers was his stepdad's surname), the guitarist grew up all over: Mississippi, Atlanta, West Memphis, Memphis, and St. Louis. Rogers started out on harp as a teenager. Big Bill Broonzy, Joe Willie Wilkins, and Robert Jr. Lockwood all influenced Rogers, the latter two when he passed through Helena. Rogers settled in Chicago during the early '40s and began playing professionally around 1946, gigging with Sonny Boy Williamson, Sunnyland Slim, and Broonzy.

Rogers was playing harp with guitarist Blue Smitty when Muddy Waters joined them. When Smitty split, Little Walter was welcomed into the configuration, Rogers switched over to second guitar, and the entire postwar Chicago blues genre felt the stylistic earthquake that followed. Rogers made his recorded debut as a leader in 1947 for the tiny Ora-Nelle logo, then saw his efforts for Regal and Apollo lay unissued.

Those labels' monumental errors in judgment were the gain of Leonard Chess, who recognized the comparatively smooth-voiced Rogers' potential as a blues star in his own right. (He first played with Muddy Waters on an Aristocrat 78 in 1949 and remained his indispensable rhythm guitarist on wax into 1955.) With Walter and bassist Big Crawford laying down support, Rogers' debut Chess single in 1950, "That's All Right," has earned standard status after countless covers, but his version still reigns supreme.

Rogers' artistic quality was remarkably high while at Chess. "The World Is in a Tangle," "Money, Marbles, and Chalk," "Back Door Friend," "Left Me with a Broken Heart," "Act like You Love Me," and the 1954 rockers "Sloppy Drunk" and "Chicago Bound" are essential early-'50s Chicago blues.

In 1955, Rogers left Muddy Waters to venture out as a band-leader, cutting another gem, "You're the One," for Chess. He made his only appearance on *Billboard*'s R&B charts in early 1957 with the driving "Walking by Myself," which boasted a stunning harp solo from Big Walter Horton (a last-second stand-in for no-show Good Rockin' Charles). The tune itself was an adaptation of a T-Bone Walker tune, "Why Not," that Rogers had played rhythm guitar on when Walker cut it for Atlantic.

By 1957, blues was losing favor at Chess, the label reaping the rewards of rock via Chuck Berry and Bo Diddley. Rogers' platters slowed to a trickle, though his 1959 Chess farewell, "Rock This House," ranked with his most exciting outings (Reggie Boyd's light-fingered guitar wasn't the least of its charms).

Rogers virtually retired from music for a time during the 1960s, operating a West side clothing shop that burned down in the aftermath of Dr. Martin Luther King's assassination. He returned to the studio in 1972 for Leon Russell's Shelter logo, cutting his first LP, *Gold-Tailed Bird* (with help from the Aces and Freddie King). There have been a few more fine albums since then, notably *Ludella*, a 1990 set for Antone's—but Rogers hasn't fattened his discography nearly as much as some of his contemporaries have. Jimmy's son, Jimmy D. Lane, plays rhythm guitar in his dad's band and fronts a combo of his own on the side. —*Bill Dahl*

Gold Tailed Bird / 1971 / Shelter ♦♦♦
Rogers' attempt to break through to a new, younger audience was less exciting than his Chess years but plausible nonetheless. —*Bill Dahl*

Sloppy Drunk / Dec. 8, 1973–Dec. 15, 1973 / Black & Blue ♦♦♦
Blues legend Jimmy Rogers had not worked steadily prior to cutting these early '70s tracks since 1960. His return on this session's 16 tracks, originally recorded for Black & Blue and now reissued on CD by Evidence, was not a heralded one because there was not much mainstream attention paid to blues at the time. But Rogers' voice was in above-average shape; his sound, range, and tone were anguished and expressed with vigor and clarity. While Willie Mabon's tinkling piano chords and figures moved in and out of loping arrangements, Rogers played easy, penetrating fills, never trying for spectacular effects but nicely punctuating his leads. —*Ron Wynn*

★ **Chicago Bound** / 1976 / MCA/Chess ♦♦♦♦♦
The logical place to inaugurate any Rogers collection is this perennially acclaimed 14-song retrospective of the guitarist's 1950s Chess years. Most of the big ones are here for your perusal: "That's All Right," "Sloppy Drunk," "You're the One," "Walking by Myself," and the thundering title track. Peerless band support from the likes of Muddy Waters, Little Walter, Otis

Spann, and Walter Horton. This is a cornerstone of Chicago blues history. —*Bill Dahl*

Living The Blues / 1976 / Vogue ✦✦

Live / 1982 / JSP ✦✦

Feelin Good / 1985 / Murray Bros ✦✦✦

☆ **That's All Right** / 1989 / Charly ✦✦✦✦✦
Quite a few important items from Rogers' classic Chess catalog that aren't on *Chicago Bound* turn up on this 24-track British import (along with the prerequisite hits,), notably a torrid "Rock This House" (Reggie Boyd's mercurial guitar solos are stunning), the downcast "The World's in a Tangle," a rhumba-beat "My Baby Don't Love Me No More" with a tremendous Walter Horton harp solo, and the bizarre "My Last Meal." —*Bill Dahl*

Ludella / 1990 / Antone's ✦✦✦✦
One of the most enriching contemporary items in Rogers' growing album catalog. Combining studio tracks with live performances, the set trods heavily on the past with loving renditions of "Rock This House," "Ludella," "Sloppy Drunk," and "Chicago Bound." Kim Wilson proves a worthy harp disciple of Little Walter, while bassist Bob Stroger and drummer Ted Harvey lay down supple grooves behind the blues great. —*Bill Dahl*

Chicago's Jimmy Rogers Sings the Blues / 1990 / DCC ✦✦✦

With Ronnie Earl and the Broadcasters / 1993 / ✦✦✦
Despite Earl's love and mastery of the '50s Chicago sound and Rogers' still-sharp talents, there's something about this live set that never really takes flight. Maybe it was just a matter of the two factions not being totally familiar with one another, but something's missing in the sparks department. —*Bill Dahl*

Blue Bird / 1994 / Analogue ✦✦

Chicago Blues Masters, Vol. 2 / 1995 / Capitol ✦✦✦✦
Rogers reemerged after a long layoff with a 1972 album for Leon Russell's Shelter label called *Gold Tailed Bird*. It wasn't the equivalent of his immortal Chess stuff, but the Shelter sides, here in their entirety, are pretty decent themselves (and no wonder, with the Aces, Freddy King, and reliable Chicago pianist Bob Riedy all involved). A few extra numbers not on the original Shelter LP make this 18-song set even more solid. —*Bill Dahl*

Complete Shelter Recordings / Oct. 24, 1995 / Capitol ✦✦✦✦✦

Roy Rogers

Guitar, Vocals / Modern Acoustic Blues
A northern California-based blues guitarist, Roy Rogers works firmly out of a Delta blues acoustic style and is particularly good with a slide. A member of John Lee Hooker's '80s Coast to Coast band, Rogers produced and played on Hooker's Grammy-winning album, *The Healer* and its follow-up, *Mr. Lucky*.
During the early '70s, Rogers played with a variety of Bay Area bar bands. In 1976, he and harpist David Burgin recorded *A Foot in the Door*, which was released on Waterhouse Records. For the next few years, he played in various bands before he formed his own, the Delta Rhythm Kings, in 1980. Two years later, John Lee Hooker asked Rogers to join his Coast to Coast band and the guitarist accepted.
Rogers stayed with Hooker for four years, leaving in 1986. That same year, he released his debut album, *Chops Not Chaps*, on Blind Pig Records. The record was successful with blues audiences and was nominated for a W.C. Handy Award. In 1987, he released his second solo album, *Slidewinder*, which was followed two years later by *Blues on the Range*. In 1990, Rogers produced John Lee Hooker's Grammy-winning comeback album, *The Healer*. The following year, he produced Hooker's *Mr. Lucky*, which also won a Grammy.
In 1991, Roy Rogers recorded a duet album, *R&B*, with harmonica player Norton Buffalo. The following year, the duo released another record, *Travellin' Tracks*. Rogers continued to pursue a solo career, performing concerts across America and occasionally recording an album. —*Stephen Thomas Erlewine*

Chops Not Chaps / Sep. 1986 / Blind Pig ✦✦✦
Roy Rogers' debut album *Chops Not Chaps* is a fine blues-rock album, driven by his dynamite slide guitar. The album alternates between covers of blues classics and originals that are effective, but not particularly remarkable. Nevertheless, the quality of Rogers' performance makes this an impressive and memorable debut. —*Thom Owens*

● **Slidewinder** / 1988 / Blind Pig ✦✦✦✦✦
One of Roy Rogers' best albums, this is a collection of smoking hot contemporary blues, ranging from jacked-up rocking boogie numbers and dirty Chicago blues to stripped-down acoustic numbers. It all works equally well, especially the two stellar duets with pianist Allen Toussaint. —*Thom Owens*

Blues on the Range / 1989 / Blind Pig ✦✦✦
Blues on the Range is a nice, but not particularly noteworthy, set of traditional blues. What makes the album worth a listen is Rogers' facility as a slide player—he can make his guitar sing. However, the quality of the songs and performances are slightly uneven, making it only of interest to diehard fans. —*Thom Owens*

R&B / 1991 / Blind Pig ✦✦

The Rolling Stones

Group / British Blues, Rock & Roll
The Rolling Stones are the definitive rock 'n' roll band and, by now, the longest-lived rock 'n' roll band to remain consistently popular throughout their (30-year) career. The group came together in London, where singer Mick Jagger (b. Jul 26, 1943) and guitarist Keith Richards (b. Dec 18, 1943), who had been grade school classmates, joined with guitarist Brian Jones (b. Feb 28, 1942–d.Jul 3, 1969) and a rhythm section then consisting of pianist Ian Stewart, bassist Dick Taylor, and drummer Mick Avory (later of The Kinks) at a debut show at the Marquee on July 12, 1962. Taylor was replaced soon after by Bill Wyman (b. Oct 24, 1936), and Avory eventually by jazz drummer Charlie Watts (b. Jun 2, 1941).
The Rolling Stones played an eight-month residency at the Crawdaddy Club in 1963, during which they signed a management contract with Andrew "Loog" Oldham (who demoted Ian Stewart to road manager) and a recording contract with Decca. The group was devoted to playing Chicago blues and its offshoots, notably the rock 'n' roll of Chuck Berry, and its early records were either covers of such music or extremely derivative originals. The Stones' first single, for example, was a cover of Berry's "Come On." It was followed by "I Wanna Be Your Man," a song written for The Stones by John Lennon and Paul McCartney.
The Stones' first really successful single, however, was a version of Buddy Holly's "Not Fade Away," which reached number 3 in England and became their first American chart entry. Their next five U.K. singles all hit number 1, and by 1965 they had established themselves as second only to the Beatles as the most popular British rock group, a position they held until the Beatles broke up.
The important factor setting the Stones apart from their lesser competition was that they successfully moved from being a blues-rock cover band to being a band that performed primarily original pop/rock material with a blues base. Jagger and Richards turned into a songwriting team as early as 1964, and by 1965 such Stones hits as "The Last Time" and "(I Can't Get No) Satisfaction" were scoring on both sides of the Atlantic.
The Stones toured extensively in the mid-'60s, with their success partially attributable to frontman Mick Jagger, who became the most prominent lead singer in rock. They followed many of the trends of the '60s as the decade wore on, and their involvement with drugs curtailed their ability to play in the U.S. after 1966. By that time, like the Beatles and others, their musical horizons had expanded to include a variety of eclectic styles. Unlike the Beatles, however, the Stones were never really comfortable with psychedelia, and after their 1967 *Sgt. Pepper* knock-off, *Their Satanic Majesties Request*, they returned to a more basic hard rock style on the single "Jumpin' Jack Flash" and the album *Beggars Banquet*.
In 1969, The Stones re-emerged as a concert attraction after firing Brian Jones (who died shortly after) and hiring guitarist Mick Taylor (b. Jan 17, 1948), who in turn was replaced by Ron Wood (b. Jun 1, 1947) in 1976. They released the single "Honky Tonk Women" and the album *Let it Bleed*, and embarked on an American concert tour that culminated in the disastrous Altamont Festival. Despite that debacle, after the Beatles' split the following year, the Stones were undisputed in their claim to being "the greatest rock 'n' roll band in the world."
In the '70s, the Stones toured every three years and released a series of million-selling, chart-topping albums, despite guitarist

Keith Richards' descent into heroin addiction. The drug problem came to a head when Richards was arrested in Toronto in 1977. He subsequently cleaned up, however, and took a more active role in The Stones' creative efforts, resulting in improved albums in the late '70s and early '80s.

The band played a world tour in 1981–1982 and continued actively into the mid-'80s, but when Jagger made a solo album in 1985 and then refused to tour behind the Stones' 1986 *Dirty Work* album, their long career together seemed to be over. Richards reluctantly began work on a solo album and publicly voiced his anger. Jagger released a second solo album in 1987 and toured Japan in 1988, but by the time of the release of Richards' solo album, *Talk Is Cheap*, the Stones were in discussions about a reunion. A new album, *Steel Wheels*, was recorded and released in 1989, accompanied by another world tour lasting into 1990.

Bill Wyman left the group for good after the *Steel Wheels* tour. For a couple of years, The Stones had no bassist; they signed a multi-million dollar deal with Virgin Records in 1992 as a four-piece. After all four members released solo records in 1992 and 1993, the band began auditioning bassists during rehearsals for their new album. Released in the summer of 1994, *Voodoo Lounge* was recorded with former Miles Davis and Sting bassist Darryl Jones; after the album's release, he was named as Wyman's permanent replacement. — *William Ruhlmann*

Rolling Stones [British import] / Apr. 16, 1964 / London ✦✦✦✦✦
The imported edition of the group's first album is superior in sound to the American version, with some curious differences in the songs as well ("Tell Me" runs longer). — *Bruce Eder*

The Rolling Stones (England's Newest Hitmakers) / May 30, 1964 / ABKCO ✦✦✦✦
The group's debut album, a bit bluesier and more acoustically textured than the sound they later became famous for, with the influence of Slim Harpo and Muddy Waters getting equal time with Chuck Berry and Bo Diddley. "Carol," "King Bee," and "Route 66" are just a few of the indispensable highlights. — *Bruce Eder*

☆ **12 X 5** / Oct. 17, 1964 / ABKCO ✦✦✦✦✦
A much more rock-oriented album than their debut, *12 X 5* is the album that solidified the group's Chuck Berry and Bo Diddley-based sound, and on which guitarists Keith Richards and Brian Jones first flexed their muscles. — *Bruce Eder*

The Rolling Stones Now! / Apr. 1965 / ABKCO ✦✦✦✦✦
The group's second album is a louder blues record, moving toward rock, with Mick Jagger beginning to stretch out as a vocalist and the band hardening its sound. "Everybody Needs Somebody to Love" and "Mona" are among the best parts of a near-perfect record. — *Bruce Eder*

Out of Our Heads / Aug. 1965 / ABKCO ✦✦✦✦
The first of the American patchwork albums, assembled from sessions on two continents and some London concerts, and it all works. "Satisfaction" was the hit, but "I'm Alright" was a concert favorite for years. — *Bruce Eder*

December's Children / Dec. 1965 / ABKCO ✦✦✦✦✦
A much more artful release, compiled from various singles and album sessions. The blues material is subservient to rock numbers like "Get off of My Cloud" and elegant R&B such as "You Better Move On." — *Bruce Eder*

Big Hits High Tide and Green Grass / Mar. 1966 / ABKCO ✦✦✦✦✦
Big Hits—Vol. 1 (High Tide & Green Grass) is a concise collection of the group's early hits, without any surprises. — *Bruce Eder*

☆ **Aftermath** / Jun. 1966 / ABKCO ✦✦✦✦✦
The group's most accomplished studio record of the '60s, and the first to feature all Jagger-Richards originals. The sound also expands here to embrace the mild psychedelic/Eastern sound of "Paint It Black," and the barrier-bursting 10-minute-plus "Goin' Home," highlighted by Brian's workout on blues harp. — *Bruce Eder*

● **Hot Rocks 1964–1971** / Jan. 1972 / ABKCO ✦✦✦✦✦
This import double-disc anthology contains their biggest hits on London, as well as many of their most popular album tracks. A stereo version of "Satisfaction" is the highlight, and worth the price, even though the U.S. mono version is also pretty cool. — *Bruce Eder*

● **More Hot Rocks (Big Hits and Fazed Cookies)** / Nov. 1972 / ABKCO ✦✦✦✦✦
Highlighted by a unique stereo edition of "It's All Over Now." Often thought of as secondary, this anthology is really a lot more interesting than *Hot Rocks*. — *Bruce Eder*

☆ **Singles Collection: the London Years** / 1989 / ABKCO ✦✦✦✦✦
The best individual collection of their classic hits ever assembled, for sound and content. — *Bruce Eder*

Bright Lights, Big City / Bootleg ✦✦✦✦✦
As you'd expect, there are a ton of Rolling Stones bootlegs, but there isn't a great deal of essential material from the '60s to be found on them. The exceptions are these outtakes from 1963 and 1964, which have popped up under quite a few guises, but most frequently under the *Bright Lights, Big City* title. The five early-1963 demos were cut shortly before they signed with Decca, and capture the band at their bluesiest and blackest; when Brian Jones was being frozen out of The Stones in the late '60s, it's said that he would play these for listeners as examples of the purity of the group's original vision. With clear fidelity, the standards of these performances are well up to official release; "Baby What's Wrong," "Road Runner," and "I Want to Be Loved" are downright electrifying. The four 1964 cuts were recorded at Chess Studios, and again (with the possible exception of the jam "Stewed And Keefed") are well up to release quality, with fine, spare readings of "Hi-Heel Sneakers," Howlin' Wolf's "Down in the Bottom," and Big Bill Broonzy's "Tell Me Baby." Essential for serious fans. — *Richie Unterberger*

BBC Sessions / Bootleg ✦✦✦
The Rolling Stones' BBC sessions haven't been accorded the same deluxe bootleg treatment as those of the Beatles, for two big reasons: they didn't record nearly as much for the Beeb as The Fab Four, and (unlike The Beatles) didn't record many tracks that they didn't release on record. Good fidelity tapes exist of a few dozen of their mid-'60s BBC airshots, and fans will find them worth picking up. Heavy on R&B covers (the Stones, like the Beatles, didn't record for the BBC after 1965), the tracks, as is par for the course on radio sessions, don't better or usually even equal the studio renditions, but have an interesting rougher live feel. They did manage to let rip on a half-dozen or so unreleased covers, and these items are naturally the most interesting, especially their takes on "Memphis, Tennessee" and their incendiary "Roll Over Beethoven," which is perhaps even better than the well-known Beatle version. — *Richie Unterberger*

Roomful of Blues

Group / Modern Jump Blues
This nine piece blues/jump band from Providence, Rhode Island, formed in 1967, has recorded and toured tirelessly for over two decades, while eschewing the standard Chicago blues band/Muddy Waters approach for a horn-dominated style that owes more to jazz leanings and late-'40s blues masters like Wynonie Harris, Roy Brown, and Big Joe Turner. More than capable of backing artists like Turner, Eddie "Cleanhead" Vinson (both of whom had Roomful back them for complete albums) as well as delivering the goods on their own, major players who have come through the ranks over the years have included guitarists Duke Robillard and Ronnie Earl, bassist Preston Hubbard, and drummer Fran Christina (Fabulous Thunderbirds). — *AMG*

Roomful of Blues / 1979 / Island ✦✦✦

● **Let Have a Party** / Nov. 1979 / Antilles ✦✦✦✦✦
Decent to good R&B-influenced jump and party blues. This group has always been great live; their albums have always been mixed affairs, and this is no different. — *Ron Wynn*

Hot Little Mama / 1981 / Varrick ✦✦✦

Live at Lupo's Heartbreak Hotel / Nov. 1987 / Varrick ✦✦✦
Live at Lupo's Heartbreak Hotel is a fine, but unremarkable, set Roomful of Blues recorded in the late '80s. The source material—Fats Domino, Howlin' Wolf, etc.—is fine and there are good solos scattered throughout the album, but the entire record never quite catches fire. — *Thom Owens*

Dance All Night / May 28, 1994 / Bullseye Blues ✦✦✦✦
This incarnation of Roomful of Blues includes vocalist and harmonica player Sugar Ray Norcia taking the singing spotlight, Matt McCabe now their pianist, and Chris Vachon principal guitarist. This CD blends blues and R&B classics with a couple of

originals; highlights include a fine reading of Smiley Lewis' "Lillie Mae," a remake of "Hey Now" originally done by Ray Charles, and Norcia's fiery vocal and torrid harmonica solo on Little Walter Jacobs' "Up The Line." This is faithful to the classic tradition, but contains enough contemporary qualities to have a fresh and inviting sound. —*Ron Wynn*

Turn It On, Turn It Up / Oct. 3, 1995 / Bullseye Blues ✦✦✦
Roomful of Blues' *Turn It On, Turn It Up* is a typically infectious set of bar-room burners from the popular blues-rockers. Not all of the songs are particularly memorable, but they play with a joyous energy that makes the shortcomings easy to accept. — *Sara Sytsma*

Dressed Up to Get Messed Up / Varrick ✦✦

First Album / Varrick ✦✦✦

Otis Rush

b. Apr. 29, 1934, Philadelphia, MS
Guitar, Vocals / Electric Chicago Blues
Breaking into the R&B Top Ten his very first time out in 1956 with the startlingly intense slow blues "I Can't Quit You Baby," southpaw guitarist Otis Rush subsequently established himself as one of the premier bluesmen on the Chicago circuit. He remains so today.

Rush is often credited with being one of the architects of the West side guitar style, along with Magic Sam and Buddy Guy. It's a nebulous honor, since Otis Rush played clubs on Chicago's South side just as frequently during the sound's late-'50s incubation period. Nevertheless, his esteemed status as a prime Chicago innovator is eternally assured by the ringing, vibrato-enhanced guitar work that remains his stock-in-trade and a tortured, super-intense vocal delivery that can force the hairs on the back of your neck upwards in silent salute.

If talent alone were the formula for widespread success, Rush would be Chicago's leading blues artist. But fate, luck, and the guitarist's own idiosyncrasies have conspired to hold him back on several occasions when opportunity was virtually begging to be accepted.

Rush came to Chicago in 1948, met Muddy Waters, and knew instantly what he wanted to do with the rest of his life. The omnipresent Willie Dixon caught Rush's act and signed him to Eli Toscano's Cobra Records in 1956. The frighteningly intense "I Can't Quit You Baby" was the maiden effort for both artist and label, streaking to number six on *Billboard*'s R&B chart.

His 1956-58 Cobra legacy is a magnificent one, distinguished by the Dixon-produced minor-key masterpieces "Double Trouble" and "My Love Will Never Die," the nails-tough "Three Times a Fool," and "Keep on Loving Me Baby," and the rhumba-rocking classic "All Your Love (I Miss Loving)." Rush apparently dashed off the latter tune in the car en route to Cobra's West Roosevelt Road studios, where he cut it with the nucleus of Ike Turner's combo.

After Cobra closed up shop, Rush's recording fortunes mostly floundered. He followed Dixon over to Chess in 1960, cutting another classic (the stunning "So Many Roads, So Many Trains") before moving on to Duke (one single, 1962's "Homework"), Vanguard, and Cotillion (there he cut the underrated Mike Bloomfield-Nick Gravenites-produced 1969 album *Mourning in the Morning*, with yeoman help from the house rhythm section in Muscle Shoals).

Typical of Rush's horrendous luck was the unnerving saga of his *Right Place, Wrong Time* album. Laid down in 1971 for Capitol Records, the giant label inexplicably took a pass on the project despite its obvious excellence. It took another five years for the set to emerge on the tiny Bullfrog label, blunting Rush's momentum once again (the album is now available on HighTone).

An uneven but worthwhile 1975 set for Delmark, *Cold Day in Hell,* and a host of solid live albums that mostly sound very similar kept Rush's gilt-edged name in the marketplace to some extent during the 1970s and '80s, a troubling period for the legendary southpaw.

In 1986, he walked out on an expensive session for Rooster Blues (Louis Myers, Lucky Peterson, and Casey Jones were among the assembled sidemen), complaining that his amplifier didn't sound right and thereby scuttling the entire project. Alligator picked up the rights to an album he had done overseas for Sonet originally called *Troubles, Troubles.* It turned out to be

a prophetic title: much to Rush's chagrin, the firm overdubbed keyboardist Lucky Peterson and chopped out some masterful guitar work when the set as *Lost in the Blues* in 1991.

Finally, in 1994, the career of this Chicago blues legend began traveling in the right direction. *Ain't Enough Comin' In,* his first studio album in 16 years, was released on Mercury and ended up topping many blues critics' year-end lists. Produced spotlessly by John Porter with a skin-tight band, Rush roared a set of nothing but covers—but did them all his way, his blistering guitar consistently to the fore.

Once again, a series of personal problems threatened to end Rush's long-overdue return to national prominence before it got off the ground. But he's been in top-notch form lately, fronting a tight band that's entirely sympathetic to the guitarist's sizzling approach. Rush recently signed with the House of Blues' fledgling record label, instantly granting that company a large dose of credibility and setting himself up for another large-scale career push when the album is completed.

It still may not be too late for Otis Rush to assume his rightful throne as Chicago's blues king. —*Bill Dahl*

Mourning in the Morning / Aug. 1969 / Atlantic ✦✦✦
Panned by many a critic upon its 1969 release, Otis Rush's trip to Muscle Shoals sounds pretty fine now (with the obvious exceptions of "My Old Lady" and "Me," which no amount of time will ever save). The house band (including Duane Allman and drummer Roger Hawkins) picks up on Rush's harrowing vibe and runs with it on the stunning "Gambler's Blues," a chomping "Feel So Bad," and a shimmering instrumental treatment of Aretha Franklin's "Baby I Love You." —*Bill Dahl*

Door to Door (With Albert King) / Jun. 1970 / MCA/Chess ✦✦✦✦✦
Although Albert King is pictured on the front cover and has the lion's share of tracks on this excellent compilation, six of the 14 tracks come from Rush's shortlived tenure with the label and are some of his very best. Chronologically, these are his next recordings after the Cobra sides and they carry a lot of the emotional wallop of those tracks, albeit with much of it recorded in early stereo. Oddly enough, some of the material ("All Your Love," "I'm Satisfied [Keep On Loving Me Baby]") were remakes—albeit great ones—of tunes that Cobra had already released as singles! But Rush's performance of "So Many Roads" (featuring one of the greatest slow blues guitar solos of all time) should not be missed at any cost. —*Cub Koda*

Screamin' & Cryin' / Nov. 26, 1974 / Evidence ✦✦✦
Otis Rush's crunching guitar and vocals were never more emphatic than during the '70s when it seemed that he would actually find the pop attention and mass stardom that he deserved. These mid-'70s tracks were originally cut for the Black & Blue label, with Rush playing grinding, relentless riffs and creating waves of sonic brilliance through creatively repeated motifs, jagged notes, and sustained lines and licks, while hollering, screaming, moaning, and wailing. Jimmy Dawkins, an outstanding lead artist in his own right, has also long been one of Chicago's great rhythm artists and shows it by adding plenty of tinkling, crackling figures and lines in the backgrounds. While not as consistently riveting as his live Evidence date, this one is also a valuable Rush document. —*Ron Wynn*

Cold Day in Hell / 1976 / Delmark ✦✦✦
Inconsistent but sometimes riveting 1975 studio set that hits some high highs (a crunchy "Cut You a Loose," the lickety-split jazzy instrumental "Motoring Along") right alongside some incredibly indulgent moments. But that's Otis—the transcendent instants are worth the hassle. —*Bill Dahl*

Right Place, Wrong Time / Feb. 1976 / Hightone ✦✦✦✦✦
Among the undisputed high points in Rush's checkered career is this 1971 studio set, originally done for Capitol (who astonishingly took a pass on the finished product). Rush has seldom sounded more convincing vocally than on the downtrodden title track, and his surging reading of Ike Turner's "I'm Tore Up" rates with his best up-tempo vehicles. —*Bill Dahl*

Lost in the Blues / Oct. 1977 / Alligator ✦✦✦
The powers-that-be at Alligator were subjected to a fair amount of criticism for taking a 1977 album of standards that Rush had cut in Sweden and overdubbing Lucky Peterson's keyboards to make the thing sound fuller and more contemporary. History,

after all, should not be messed with. But it's still a reasonably successful enterprise; Rush imparting his own intense twist to "I Miss You So," "You Don't Have to Go," and "Little Red Rooster." —*Bill Dahl*

Live in Europe / Oct. 1977 / Evidence ✦✦✦✦
Recorded in France in 1987, this 10-song set finds Otis backed by strong trio support throughout in a delightfully engaged performance. Though several live albums exist, seldom has his declamatory vocals and stinging left-handed upside down guitar style been so well documented. Rush puts forth solo after solo, each with its own unique set of twists and turns, making this a veritable textbook of what he does best. Inspired listening and highly recommended. —*Cub Koda*

Tops / 1985 / Blind Pig ✦✦✦
There are simply too many live albums by Rush on the market to keep track of anymore. This was one of the earlier entries, cut in 1985 with a West Coast combo following Rush pretty well. Since the same basic set list turns up on most every one of these things, there's not really a whole lot of difference between any of 'em (but go with Delmark's *So Many Roads* first). —*Bill Dahl*

★ **Cobra Recordings, 1956–1958** / 1989 / Paula/Flyright ✦✦✦✦✦
Otis Rush's debut recordings for the Cobra label are defining moments of Chicago blues. Seldom had a young Windy City artist recorded with this much harrowing emotion in both his singing and playing, simultaneously connecting with the best that Delta blues had to offer while plunging headlong into the electric future. These are the songs that continue to be the building blocks of his legend; "All Your Love," "Double Trouble," "I Can't Quit You, Baby," "Groaning The Blues," "It Takes Time," and "Checking On My Baby" are all singular masterpieces. This single-disc collection features all sixteen Cobra sides issued as singles plus the bonus of four alternate takes, all presented here with the best sound to date. These are milestone recordings in the history of the blues and an essential part of anyone's collection. —*Cub Koda*

Ain't Enough Comin' In / 1994 / This Way Up ✦✦✦✦✦
With sympathetic production from John Porter, a great lineup of players who follow him every bluesy turn of the way, and a dozen well-chosen pieces of material, Rush wipes the uninspired album slate clean with this one. Everything that makes Otis a unique master of his form is here to savor, from his passionate vocals to the shimmering finger vibrato he applies to the liquid tones of his Fender Stratocaster. While Rush has tackled some of this material on other outings, never has it been served up so passionately as it is here. Even the re-cut of his famous Duke 45 "Homework" burns with a new intensity that makes you believe that this is one opportunity that Rush–at least this time–refused to let go by the boards. —*Cub Koda*

So Many Roads: Live / Aug. 1, 1995 / Delmark ✦✦✦✦
There's a pile of Otis Rush live albums in the bins now, but this was the one that made everybody sit up and take notice and it's still his best. Recorded live outdoors in a Tokyo park in the Summer of 1975 with thousands of fans hanging on every note and word, Otis digs deep and delivers some of the most inspired singing and playing he's ever committed to magnetic tape. All the performances are of a nice, comfortable length with none of the interminable soloing that mars other Rush live sets. This is the one to have. —*Cub Koda*

Jimmy Rushing

b. Aug. 26, 1903, Oklahoma City, OK, **d.** Jun. 8, 1972, New York
Vocals / Blues, Swing
A huge, striking artist, Jimmy Rushing defined and transcended jazz-based blues shouting. His voice was dominating and intricately linked to the beat. He could maintain his intonation regardless of volume, and could sing sensitively one moment, then bellow and yell in almost frightening fashion the next, making both styles sound convincing. Rushing's parents were musicians, and he studied music theory in high school. He attended Wilberforce University, but dropped out. He moved to the West Coast, and did odd jobs while sometimes singing at house parties. Composer and pianist Jelly Roll Morton was among the people he met while making these appearances. Rushing joined Walter Page's Blue Devils in the late '20s. He left them to work in his father's cafe in Oklahoma City, but returned to Page's group in 1928. He made his first records with them in 1929. Rushing toured with Bennie Moten from 1929–1935, recording with Moten in 1931, then joined Count Basie in 1936. Basie has credited Rushing with helping hold things together when times got tough. At an early 1936 session with John Hammond producing, things came together. This marked Lester Young's debut with the band. The songs "Boogie-Woogie" (better known as "I May Be Wrong") and "Evenin'" were instant classics. Rushing's booming voice and the Basie orchestra proved a perfect fit until 1950; they recorded for Columbia and RCA, cutting everything from steamy blues to joyous stomps and novelty tunes like "Did You See Jackie Robinson Hit That Ball." When Basie disbanded the orchestra in 1950, Rushing briefly tried retirement. He ended it a short time later, forming his own band. He'd made some solo recordings in 1945, and continued in the mid-'50s and early '60s, this time for Vanguard. Rushing recreated Basie classics, worked with some of his sidemen and even accompanied himself on piano. He cut other sessions with Buck Clayton, Dave Brubeck, and Earl Hines and frequently had reunions with Basie and/or his sidemen. Rushing appeared in both film shorts and features, among them "Take Me Back, Baby," "Air Mail Special," "Choo Choo Swing," and "Funzapoppin'" between 1941 and 1943. He participated in the historic 1957 television show "The Sound of Jazz," and was featured on the sixth episode of a 13-part series "The Subject Is Jazz" in 1958. He was also in the 1973 film "Monterey Jazz," which profiled the '70 festival. Rushing also had a singing and acting role in the '69 film "The Learning Tree." He died three years later. —*Ron Wynn and Bob Porter*

★ **The Essential Jimmy Rushing** / Dec. 1, 1954–Mar. 5, 1957 / Vanguard ✦✦✦✦✦
Fine anthology collecting material done by the great blues shouter for Vanguard during the mid-'50s. Songs included a remake of "Going to Chicago," plus other combo dates, and he was backed by such Basie comrades as Jo Jones and Buddy Tate. This has been reissued on CD. —*Ron Wynn*

Dave Brubeck and Jimmy Rushing / Jan. 29, 1960–Aug. 4, 1960 / Columbia ✦✦✦✦✦
Pairing of divergent styles proves effective. —*Ron Wynn*

Gee, Baby, Ain't I Good to You / Oct. 30, 1967 / Master Jazz ✦✦
This is a decent session that, considering the lineup, does not live up to its potential. At what was essentially a jazz party held in a recording studio, the musicians (trumpeter Buck Clayton, trombonist Dickie Wells, tenor saxophonist Julian Dash, pianist Sir Charles Thompson, bassist Gene Ramey, and drummer Jo Jones) are all veterans of the famous series of Buck Clayton jam sessions held in the 1950s and, along with singer Jimmy Rushing, the majority are alumni of the Count Basie Orchestra. The problem is that their renditions of the blues and swing standards are often quite loose, and there is a generous amount of missteps and, although Clayton is heroic under the circumstances (this was one of his final recordings before ill health caused his retirement), most of the musicians would have benefited from running through the songs an additional time. It's recommended only to completists. —*Scott Yanow*

The You and Me That Used to Be / 1971 / RCA/Bluebird ✦✦✦✦
Late-period Jimmy Rushing vehicle in which he was weighted down by lavish production and a slick setting and also wasn't near his peak. Still, there are times when the powerful Rushing sound and dramatic style do come forth. —*Ron Wynn*

Everyday I Have the Blues / Bluesway ✦✦✦✦✦
A CD reissue of the great blues shouter Jimmy Rushing singing recreated versions of his classics with the Basie band. This originally came out in the mid-'50s, when Rushing had left Basie and was heading his own band. While these versions aren't the definitive ones, they're far from bad. —*Ron Wynn*

S

Saffire

Group / Modern Acoustic Blues
The ladies from Saffire at one point in the early '90s just considered themselves blues historians, but since their performing career has gotten launched on the festival circuit, they've become much more than that. All three have developed into talented songwriters. Since blues fans are always looking for fresh themes or new twists on old themes, this trio is a sought-after club and festival act. The core members of this Virginia-based group include pianist Ann Rabson (b. April 12, 1945) and Gaye Adegbalola (b. March 21, 1944), and while the trio was accompanied for a while by bassist Earlene Lewis, she has since left the group. Lewis was replaced by mandolinist Andra Faye McIntosh, also from the Washington, D.C./Virginia area. Rabson worked as a computer programmer and Adegbalola was an award-winning teacher before they gave up their day jobs to play blues full-time for a living.

Saffire has no shortage of fresh ideas. The group has recorded five albums for the Chicago-based Alligator Records label since 1990, and their two more recent albums *Cleaning House* (1996) and *Old, New Borrowed and Blue* (1994) showcase the trio's songwriting skills, although there are also a few covers, reinterpreted in their own distinctive way. These acoustic musicians inject a sense of humor into their songs and take it with them on stage. The group's other albums for Alligator include their 1990 debut, *Saffire: The Uppity Blues Women* (1990), *Hot Flash* (1991), and *Broadcasting* (1992). Their prolific output as songwriters is matched only by their desire to tour, and they perform everywhere and anywhere, having already made several U.S., Canadian, and European tours.

The group's fundamental appeal is their original songs and their ability to dig up and reinterpret old blues gems from the 1920s and '30s. They specialize in songs made by the sassy original blues divas including Bessie Smith, Ma Rainey, Memphis Minnie, and Ida Cox. *—Richard Skelly*

The Uppity Blues Women / 1990 / Alligator ✦✦✦
Saffire's debut album, takes the best moments from their independently released tape and adds a number of songs that weren't on the cassette. The result is a stronger, funnier and heartfelt record. It doesn't hurt that Alligator gives the group a clean production, where their voices simply leap out from the speakers. The result is an album that provides a boisterous and thought-provoking listen. *—Thom Owens*

● **Hot Flash** / 1991 / Alligator ✦✦✦✦✦
In many ways, *Hot Flash* is the definitive Saffire album. Racy and sassy—and to some tastes cutesy—the album is a fun, free-thinking update of classic female blues, performed with gusto and verve. The instrumentation is sparse—a piano, guitar, bass, harmonica, and kazoo provide the foundation of the music—but the focus of these songs is solely on the vocals, which are vigorous and humorous. If you share Saffire's sense of humor, it's a rollicking good time. *—Thom Owens*

Broadcasting / 1992 / Alligator ✦✦
Between *Hot Flash* and *Broadcasting,* Saffire lost a bassist, but added a mandolin, fiddler, an organist, and an electric guitarist, which gives *Broadcasting* a fuller, richer sound. Fortunately, that hasn't distracted attention from the bawdy, sassy vocals of Ann Rabson and Gaye Adegbalola, who still exhibit a raw, natural charisma. And the material—which ranges from fresh interpretations of warhorses from Louis Jordan and Hank Williams to

clever originals—is all first-rate, helping make the album one of the group's best efforts. *—Thom Owens*

Old, New, Borrowed, & Blue / 1994 / Alligator ✦✦
This album finds Saffire's sound bordering on the formulaic—songs like "Bitch with a Bad Attitude" and "There's Lighting in These Thunder Thighs" are simply too cutesy and too predictable—but there is still plenty for their fans to treasure on the record. *—Thom Owens*

The Middle Aged Blues / Saffire ✦✦✦
As Saffire's debut tape, the vocal trio has already developed a distinctive style. Although some listeners might find their material a bit too jokey, it's clear that the group is having fun with their material. They have respect for blues traditions, particularly classic female blues, but they don't merely regurgitate the same songs in the same fashion—Saffire makes them loose and fun, like you were eavesdropping on a party. *Middle Aged Blues* isn't as fully formed as their later albums for Alligator, but it still has plenty of good times. *—Thom Owens*

Curtis Salgado & the Stilettos

Harmonica, Vocals / Modern Electric Blues
Reportedly a primary inspiration for John Belushi's "Joliet Jake" character in *The Blues Brothers*, Salgado was a prominent early member of Robert Cray's band during their formative years around Eugene, OR. Salgado has also worked with Roomful of Blues. He currently fronts his own group, The Stilettos. *—Bill Dahl*

Curtis Salgado & the Stilettos / 1991 / JRS ✦✦✦✦✦
The blues, spiked with '60s soul, delivered by West Coast singer Curtis Salgado. *—David Szatmary*

Satan & Adam

Group / Modern Acoustic Blues
The blues duo of guitarist, singer, and songwriter Sterling Magee and harmonica player Adam Gussow have paid their dues. They began their career on the street, on the corner of Seventh Avenue and 125th Street, to be exact. Within a matter of weeks, they were drawing crowds to their corner, people pausing on their way home from work to stop and listen. For five years, nearly every afternoon that weather permitted, the pair would meet on the corner and Magee would set up his simple stool, drum kit, guitar and amplifier. Using a combination of foot stomps, tambourines, hi-hat cymbals, and his guitar, Magee gives the duo a full sound.

Magee and Gussow specialize in funky, gritty, electric urban blues, and there are few groups or artists anywhere who sound anything remotely like them. Gussow's exquisite harmonica solos complement the driving, open-toned guitar playing of Magee, who prefers to be called Mr. Satan, and who frequently refers to Gussow in live performances as Mr. Gussow.

The pair have such a unique sound, it seems they're destined for a major label, given their knowledge and experience with blues. Magee, born May 20, 1936 in Mississippi and raised in Florida, began his career playing piano in churches in both states. Since the early '80s, he's played on Harlem streets, but in the 1960s he was a key session guitarist, playing on recordings by James Brown, King Curtis, George Benson, and others. Adam Gussow, born April 3, 1958 and raised in Rockland County, NY, was a Princeton-educated harmonica player who had a little uptown apartment, and in passing Magee one day on the street in 1985, he asked if he could sit in on harmonica. That was the start of a musical and social relationship between the two that continues to this day.

The pair have recorded several critically acclaimed albums for the now-defunct Flying Fish label, and they include *Harlem Blues* (1991) and *Mother Mojo* (1993). Satan and Adam also performed in U2's *Rattle and Hum* movie. On their *Mother Mojo*, the group reinterprets and funkifies well-known songs like Herbie Hancock's "Watermelon Man" and Joe Turner's "Crawdad Hole." Their most recent recording *Living on the River* (1996) is on the New York state-based Rave On Records label.

Satan and Adam have redefined and shaped the sound of modern blues so much that "I Want You" from their *Harlem Blues* debut was included on a Rhino Records release, *Modern Blues of the 1990s*. Look for more great albums from this duo for years to come. —*Richard Skelly*

● **Harlem Blues** / 1991 / Flying Fish ✦✦✦✦✦
Harlem Blues sounds exactly like how Satan & Adam would sound playing on a street corner—it's raw and tough, with a surprisingly adventurous streak. Satan and Adam stick to a basic acoustic blues duo, but their rhythms and techniques occasionally stray into funkier, jazzier territory. And that sense of careening unpredictability is what makes *Harlem Blues* so entertaining—they might be playing blues in a traditional style, but the end result is anything but traditional. —*Thom Owens*

Mother Mojo / Jan. 1993 / Flying Fish ✦✦✦
Mother Mojo was an excellent follow-up to Satan & Adam's first-rate debut, *Harlem Blues*. The duo hasn't abandoned their minimalist guitar and harp blues, but there is a loose energy that keeps the music fresh and consistently engaging. —*Thom Owens*

Buddy Scott

b. 1935, Jackson, MS, **d.** Feb. 5, 1994, Chicago, IL
Guitar, Vocals / Electric Chicago Blues
Chicago guitarist Kenneth "Buddy" Scott hailed from an extended musical brood, to put it mildly. His brothers, singer Howard and guitarist Walter, are mainstays on the local scene; his son, guitarist Thomas "Hollywood" Scott, leads Tyrone Davis' Platinum Band, and even his grandmother Ida knew her way around a guitar—she played on the South side with the likes of Little Walter and Sonny Boy Williamson back in the 1950s.

Buddy Scott left Mississippi for Chicago at age seven. Both his mom and local legend Reggie Boyd tutored him as a guitarist. Like several of his brothers, Buddy was a member of a local doo wop vocal group, the Masqueraders, during the early '60s and recorded a few singles with his siblings as the Scott Brothers later in the decade. He was best known as leader of Scotty & the Rib Tips, who were staples of the South and West side blues circuit; they were featured on Alligator's second batch of *Living Chicago Blues* anthologies in 1980.

By the time Scott caught his big major-label break with Verve in 1993 with his debut domestic album, *Bad Avenue*, it was too late for him to capitalize on his belated good fortune. The stomach cancer that had been gaining on him did him in shortly after its release. —*Bill Dahl*

● **Bad Avenue** / Oct. 19, 1993 / Verve ✦✦✦✦✦
Not the perfect vehicle for the late Chicago blues guitarist—it's a tad too slick, and some of the song choices fall into the realm of overworked cliche—but Scott's major-label debut album was a credible swan song, his enthusiastic vocals and clean guitar work ringing through well. —*Bill Dahl*

Son Seals (Frank Seals)

b. Aug. 13, 1942, Osceola, AR
Guitar, Drums, Vocals / Electric Chicago Blues
It all started with a phone call from Wesley Race, who was at the Flamingo Club on Chicago's South side, to Alligator Records owner Bruce Iglauer. Race was raving about a new find, a young guitarist named Son Seals. He held the phone in the direction of the bandstand, so Iglauer could get an on-site report. It didn't take long for Iglauer to scramble into action. Alligator issued Seals' 1973 eponymous debut album, which was followed by six more.

Son Seals, born Frank Seals, was born into the blues. His dad operated a juke joint called the Dipsy Doodle Club in Osceola, AR, where Sonny Boy Williamson, Robert Nighthawk, and Albert King cavorted up front while little Frank listened intently in back. Drums were the youth's first instrument; he played them behind

Nighthawk at age 13. But by the time he was 18, Son Seals turned his talents to guitar, fronting his own band in Little Rock.

While visiting his sister in Chicago, he hooked up with Earl Hooker's Roadmasters in 1963 for a few months, and there was a 1966 stint with Albert King that sent him behind the drumkit once more. But with the death of his father in 1971, Seals returned to Chicago, this time for good. When Alligator signed him up, his days fronting a band at the Flamingo Club and the Expressway Lounge were numbered.

Seals' jagged, uncompromising guitar riffs and gruff vocals were showcased very effectively on his 1973 debut set, which contained "Your Love Is Like a Cancer" and a raging instrumental called "Hot Sauce." *Midnight Son*, his 1976 encore, was by comparison a much slicker affair, with tight horns, funkier grooves, and a set list that included "Telephone Angel" and "On My Knees." Seals cut a live LP in 1978 at Wise Fools Pub; another studio concoction, *Chicago Fire*, in 1980; and a solid set in 1984, *Bad Axe*, before having a disagreement with Iglauer that was patched up in 1991 with the release of his sixth Alligator set, *Living in the Danger Zone*. *Nothing but the Truth* followed in 1994, sporting some of the worst cover art in CD history, but a stinging lineup of songs inside. Another live recording was planned for June of 1996 at Buddy Guy's Legends.

Seals prefers to remain close to his Chicago home these days, holding his touring itinerary to an absolute minimum. That means that virtually every weekend he can be found somewhere on the North side blues circuit, dishing up his raw-edged brand of bad blues axe to local followers. —*Bill Dahl*

The Son Seals Blues Band / 1973 / Alligator ✦✦✦✦
The Chicago mainstay's debut album was a rough, gruff, no-nonsense affair typified by the decidedly unsentimental track "Your Love Is Like a Cancer." Seals wasn't all that far removed from his southern roots at this point, and his slashing guitar work sports a strikingly raw feel on his originals "Look Now, Baby," "Cotton Picking Blues," and "Hot Sauce" (the latter a blistering instrumental that sounds a bit like the theme from *Batman* played sideways). —*Bill Dahl*

● **Midnight Son** / Jun. 1977 / Alligator ✦✦✦✦✦
A much more polished set than its predecessor, *Midnight Son* is a particularly effective effort with several numbers that remain in Seals' onstage repertoire to this day—"Telephone Angel," "On My Knees," the jumping "Four Full Seasons of Love." The addition of a brisk horn section enhanced his staccato guitar attack and uncompromising vocals, rendering this his best set to date. —*Bill Dahl*

Live & Burning / 1978 / Alligator ✦✦✦✦
Lives up to its billing. Seals' smoking set, caught live at Chicago's long-gone (and definitely lamented) Wise Fools Pub, finds him attacking a sharp cross-section of material—Detroit Junior's deliberate "Call My Job," Elmore James' "I Can't Hold Out," his own "Help Me, Somebody"—with an outstanding band in tow—saxist A.C. Reed, guitarist Lacy Gibson, pianist Alberto Gianquinto, bassist Snapper Mitchum, and drummer Tony Gooden. —*Bill Dahl*

Chicago Fire / 1980 / Alligator ✦✦✦
Son Seals in an experimental mood, utilizing chord progressions that occasionally don't quite fit together seamlessly (but give him an A for trying to expand the idiom's boundaries). Less innovative but perhaps more accessible are his smoking covers of Albert King's "Nobody Wants a Loser" and Junior Parker's "Goodbye Little Girl." —*Bill Dahl*

Bad Axe / 1984 / Alligator ✦✦✦✦
One of Son Seals' finest collections, studded with vicious performances ranging from covers of Eddie Vinson's "Person to Person" and Little Sonny's "Going Home (Where Women Got Meat on Their Bones)" to his own "Can't Stand to See Her Cry" and swaggering "Cold Blood." Top-drawer Windy City studio musicians lay down skin-tight grooves throughout. —*Bill Dahl*

Living in the Danger Zone / 1991 / Alligator ✦✦✦
The guitarist keeps his string of consecutive fine releases alive with a studio-cut disc that sizzles with bandstand-level velocity (until its last cut, anyway). "Frigidaire Woman," "Woman in Black," and "Bad Axe" rate with the highlights; the self-pitying ballad closer "My Life" is the worst thing Seals has ever put on tape for Alligator. —*Bill Dahl*

Nothing But the Truth / 1994 / Alligator ✦✦✦✦
The grotesque cover illustration is an abomination, but the con-

tents are right in the growling grizzly bear style that we've come to expect. Only four Seals-penned originals, but the R&B-laced "Life Is Hard" and "I'm Gonna Take It All Back" are quality efforts. So is his heartfelt tribute to Hound Dog Taylor, "Sadie." —*Bill Dahl*

Eddie Shaw

b. Mar. 20, 1937, Stringtown, MS
Saxophone / Electric Chicago Blues
When it comes to blues, Chicago's strictly a guitar and harmonica town. Saxophonists who make a living leading a blues band in the Windy City are scarce as hen's teeth. But Eddie Shaw has done precisely that ever since his longtime boss, Howlin' Wolf, died in 1976.

The powerfully constructed tenor saxist has rubbed elbows with an amazing array of luminaries over his 40-plus years in the business. By the time he was age 14, Shaw was jamming with Ike Turner's combo around Greenville, MS. At a gig in Itta Bena where Shaw sat in, Muddy Waters extended the young saxman an invitation he couldn't refuse: a steady job with Waters' unparalleled band in Chicago. After a few years, Shaw switched his onstage allegiance to Waters' chief rival, the ferocious Howlin' Wolf, staying with him until the very end and eventually graduating to a featured role as Wolf's bandleader.

Eddie Shaw also shared a West side bandstand or two along the way with Freddy King, Otis Rush, and Magic Sam. The saxist did a 1966 session with Sam that produced his first single, the down-in-the-alley instrumental "Blues for the West Side" (available on Delmark's *Sweet Home Chicago* anthology). Shaw also blew his heart out on Sam's 1968 Delmark encore LP, *Black Magic.*

Shaw's own recording career finally took off during the late '70s, with a standout appearance on Alligator's *Living Chicago Blues* anthologies in 1978, his own LPs for Simmons and Rooster Blues, and fine recent discs for Rooster Blues (*In the Land of the Crossroads*) and Austrian Wolf (*Home Alone*). Eddie Shaw, who once operated the hallowed 1815 Club on West Roosevelt Road (one of Wolf's favorite haunts), has sired a couple of high-profile sons: diminutive Eddie Jr., known as Vaan, plays lead guitar with Eddie's Wolf Gang and has cut a pair of his own albums for Wolf, while husky Stan Shaw is a prolific character actor in Hollywood. —*Bill Dahl*

Movin' and Groovin' Man / May 14, 1982 / Evidence ✦✦✦
Tenor saxophonist Eddie Shaw is a rarity in blues circles—a first-class instrumentalist who is not a guitarist or pianist. Shaw is a soulful, exuberant player whose lusty licks make a solid counterpoint to his rough-hewn vocals and narratives. While Shaw carries the majority of the load on this 10-cut date from 1982 previously recorded for Isabel (reissued on CD by Evidence), it is guitarist Melvin Taylor who is the revelation as second soloist. Between his work with Lucky Peterson, his own CD, and his brisk, sizzling solos and accompaniment here, Taylor merits high praise as a workmanlike, flexible contributor. The others, with the exception of the great Eddie "Cleanhead" Vinson, are heavy pros capably handling limited support duties. —*Ron Wynn*

King of the Road / Sep. 1986 / Rooster Blues ✦✦✦✦
A revealing compilation of the ballsy Chicago saxist's earlier work (1966–1984) that certainly deserves to be on CD but isn't yet. "Blues for the West Side" and "Lookin' Good," both with Magic Sam on guitar, are highlights of Shaw's entire career, while his vocal talents are well-served on "It's All Right," an amusing "I Don't Trust Nobody," and his touching tribute "Blues Men of Yesterday." —*Bill Dahl*

● **In the Land of the Crossroads** / 1992 / Rooster Blues ✦✦✦✦✦
The best contemporary Shaw offering, cut in his old Mississippi stomping grounds with his trusty combo, the Wolf Gang. Lots of lyrically unusual originals—"Dunkin' Donut Woman," "Wine Head Hole," and "She Didn't Tell Me Everything," for starters— and Shaw's usual diamond-hard horn lines and commanding vocals make this a standout selection. —*Bill Dahl*

Trail Of Tears / 1994 / Wolf ✦✦✦✦✦
Home Alone / 1995 / Wolf ✦✦✦✦
Although it's pressed on an Austrian logo, Eddie Shaw's rollicking recent disc was waxed in his Chicago hometown with the Wolf Gang (son Vaan on guitar, longtime bassist Shorty Gilbert, and drummer Tim Taylor) summoning up solid support. Once

again, Shaw tackles some interesting subjects—he fantasizes about "Blues in Paris," decried being "Home Alone," and searches out an endorsement deal with "Motel Six" via his sprightly musical tribute to the budget chain. —*Bill Dahl*

The Blues Is Nothing But Good News! / Wolf ✦✦✦

Robert Shaw

b. Aug. 9, 1908, Stafford, TX, d. May 18, 1985, Austin, TX
Piano, Vocals / Texas Blues
He didn't record much at all—a marvelous 1963 album for Almanac, reissued on Chris Strachwitz's Arhoolie label, remains his principal recorded legacy—but barrelhouse pianist Robert Shaw helped greatly to establish a distinctive regional style of pounding the 88s around Houston, Fort Worth, and Galveston during the 1920s and '30s.

Those decades represented Shaw's playing heyday, when he forged a stunning barrelhouse style of his own in the bars, dance halls, and whorehouses along the route of the Santa Fe railroad. Shaw got around—in 1933, he had a radio program in Oklahoma City. But by the mid-'30s, Shaw relegated his playing to the back burner to open a grocery store. Mack McCormick coaxed him back into action in 1963 and the results as collected on Arhoolie were magnificent; "The Cows" was a piece of incredible complexity that would wilt anything less than a legitimate ivories master. Shaw continued to perform stateside and in Europe intermittently during the 1970s, turning up unexpectedly in California in 1981 to help Strachwitz celebrate Arhoolie's 20th anniversary. —*Bill Dahl*

● **The Ma Grinder** / 1963 / Arhoolie ✦✦✦✦✦
Stunning solo Texas blues and barrelhouse piano by the late pianist. The most amazing material, produced by Mack McCormick in Austin, dates from 1963—the rhythmically and technically complex "The Cows" is a tour de force, and "The Ma Grinder" and "The Clinton" aren't far behind. Later numbers from 1973 and 1977 prove that Shaw's skills didn't degenerate with time. —*Bill Dahl*

Texas Barrelhouse Piano / Dec. 1980 / Arhoolie ✦✦✦✦

Kenny Wayne Shepherd

b. Jun. 12, 1977, Shreveport, LA
Guitar, Vocals / Modern Electric Blues
Kenny Wayne Shepherd and his group have exploded on the scene in the mid-'90s and garnered huge amounts of radio airplay on commercial radio, which historically has not been a solid home for blues and blues-rock music, with the exception of Stevie Ray Vaughan in the mid-'80s.

Shepherd began playing at age 7, figuring out Muddy Waters licks from his father's record collection (he has never taken a formal lesson). At age 13, he was invited onstage by New Orleans bluesman Brian Lee and held his own for several hours; thus proving himself, he decided on music as a career. He formed his own band, which featured lead vocalist Corey Sterling, gaining early exposure through club dates and, later, radio conventions. Shepherd's father/manager used his own contacts and pizazz in the record business to help land his son a major label record deal with Irving Azoff's Giant Records. *Ledbetter Heights,* his first album, was released two years later in 1995. *Ledbetter Heights* was an immediate hit, selling over 500,000 by early 1996. Most blues records never achieve that level of commercial success, much less ones released by artists that are still in their teens.

Although Shepherd—who has been influenced by (and has played with) guitarists Stevie Ray Vaughan, Albert King, Slash, Robert Cray, and Duane Allman—is definitely a performer who thrives in front of an audience, *Ledbetter Heights* is impressive for its range of styles: acoustic blues, rockin' blues, Texas blues, and Louisiana blues. The only style that he doesn't tackle is Chicago blues, owing to Shepherd's home base smack dab in the middle of the Texas triangle. —*Steve Huey & Richard Skelly*

Ledbetter Heights / Oct. 1995 / Giant ✦✦✦✦✦
You would never guess from Kenny Wayne Shepherd's fiery playing that the guitarist is still only in his teens. On his debut, *Ledbetter Heights,* Shepherd burns through a set of rather generic blues-rock ravers that are made special by his exceptional technique. It may still be a while before he says something original, but he plays with style, energy, and dedication, which is more than enough for a debut album. —*Thom Owens*

Johnny Shines (John Ned Shines)

b. Apr. 26, 1915, Frayser, TN, **d.** Apr. 20, 1992, Chicago, IL
Guitar, Vocals / Electric Delta Blues, Acoustic Delta Blues
There was much more to Johnny Shines than his inexorable link to the legacy of the immortal Robert Johnson. Yes, Johnson was a very important influence on Shines, but only one of several. Moreover, Shines was never content to live in the past; his contemporary recordings ran the gamut from acoustic blues in the best Johnson tradition to up-to-the-minute contemporary stylings.

Before Shines fell in with Johnson in 1935, he listened to Blind Lemon Jefferson, Lonnie Johnson, and Charlie Patton. Shines had first picked up a guitar in 1932; a year or two later he was playing professionally. After meeting in Helena, AR, Johnson and Shines rambled and played together through Tennessee, Missouri, and Arkansas until 1937.

Shines moved to Chicago in 1941 and established himself on the South side club scene. He made his debut recordings in 1946 under the aegis of producer Lester Melrose, but Columbia sat on the four tracks at the time. Chess issued his 1950 coupling "Joliet Blues"/"So Glad I Found You" (with accompaniment from harpist Little Walter and guitarist Jimmy Rogers) under the unfortunate billing of Shoe Shine Johnny.

The guitarist's finest '50s recordings were done for JOB in 1952–53. His keening slide work and booming vocals were brilliantly spotlighted on "Ramblin'," "Cool Driver," "Evening Sun," and "Brutal Hearted Woman" (the latter pair featuring Big Walter Horton's equally inspired harmonica). Unfortunately, none of them made Shines any money, and he blew off the music business during the late '50s for the stability of construction work.

Shines made a triumphant return during the mid-'60s, recording for Vanguard and Testament, and again in 1968 for Blue Horizon. The hiatus hadn't dulled Shines' attack any; if anything, he'd become more musically imaginative than ever. It was an admirable trait that continued throughout the rest of his career—sets for Advent (in 1970) and (paired with fellow Robert Johnson disciple Robert Jr. Lockwood) two albums for Rounder during the early '80s showed him moving freely between various blues styles that swung and occasionally bordered on soul.

A 1980 stroke greatly limited his guitar playing, but his voice never failed to rattle the floorboards wherever he roamed until the end of his life in 1992. —*Bill Dahl*

Back to the Country / 1960 / Blind Pig ♦♦♦

Master of the Modern Blues, Vol. 1 / 1966 / Testament ♦♦♦♦♦

Last Night Dream / 1968 / Warner Brothers ♦♦♦♦♦
It's no wonder that this album, cut in 1968 with British blues maven Mike Vernon at the helm, works so well. When you team a rejuvenated Shines with his longtime compadres Horton, Spann, bassist Willie Dixon, and drummer Clifton James, a little blues history was bound to be made. —*Bill Dahl*

Johnny Shines with Big Walter Horton / Nov. 1969 / Testament ♦♦♦♦♦
Outstanding late-'60s Shines material matching him with a sterling lineup. Big Walter Horton is awesome on harmonica, a young Luther Allison doesn't dissipate his brilliance on haphazard soul and funk, and pianist Otis Spann and drummer Fred Below are super on their cuts. The date combines 1966 and 1969 sessions; there's another LP with a full collection culled from 1966. —*Ron Wynn*

Johnny Shines [Advent] / 1974 / Advent ♦♦♦
Johnny Shines made this good, if not great, LP for Advent during a period when he was ignored despite still being in solid form. There are strong vocals, fine arrangements, and guitar support, but the production and the songs are too inconsistent to label this a significant session. —*Ron Wynn*

Johnny Shines [Hightone] / 1976 / Hightone ♦♦♦

Hey Ba-Ba-Re-Bop / 1978 / Rounder ♦♦♦♦♦
Delta blues vocalist, guitarist, and composer Johnny Shines hadn't yet encountered the physical difficulties that made his final years so troubling when he recorded the 13 selections on this CD. He could still sing and moan with intensity and passion, hold a crowd hypnotized with his remembrances and asides, and play with a mix of fury and charm. While the menu includes oft-performed chestnuts "Sweet Home Chicago," "Terraplane Blues"

and "Milk Cow Blues," there wasn't anything staid or predictable about the way Shines ripped through the lyrics and presented the music. If you missed it the first time around, grab this one immediately. —*Ron Wynn*

★ **Johnny Shines & Robert Lockwood** / 1979 / Paula/Flyright ♦♦♦♦♦
Shines has half of this 20-track disc, the remainder being devoted to sides from the same era featuring Robert Lockwood. Recorded in 1952 and 1953 for the JOB label, this is Shines at his most primal, working with a drumless trio; Big Walter Horton plays harmonica on the 1953 sides. These tracks decidedly outshine the Lockwood efforts (also recorded for JOB in the early '50s), some of which only feature Robert as a sideman. —*Richie Unterberger*

Traditional Delta Blues / 1991 / Biograph ♦♦♦♦♦
Robert Johnson's pal pays homage on acoustic recordings from 1972–1974. —*Jas Obrecht*

Mr. Cover Shaker / 1992 / Biograph ♦♦♦

Masters Of Modern Blues / 1994 / Testament ♦♦♦♦♦
After stepping away from the music business altogether for a while, Shines came back strong during the mid-'60s, recording far more prolifically than his first time around. This 1966 date is one of his best, spotlighting his booming pipes and sturdy guitar in front of an all-star Chicago crew: Walter Horton on harp, pianist Otis Spann, and drummer Fred Below. —*Bill Dahl*

Standing at the Crossroads / Testament ♦♦♦

J.D. Short

b. Dec. 26, 1902, Port Gibson, MS, **d.** Oct. 21, 1962, St. Louis, MO
Harmonica / Acoustic Blues
Gifted with a striking and almost immediately identifiable vocal style characterized by an amazing vibrato, J.D. Short was also a very versatile musician. He played piano, saxophone, guitar, harmonica, clarinet and drums. Growing up in the Mississippi Delta, Short learned guitar and piano. He was a frequent performer at house parties before he moved to St. Louis in the '20s. Short played with the Neckbones, Henry Spaulding, Honeyboy Edwards, Douglas Williams, and Big Joe Williams from the '30s until the early '60s. He recorded for Vocalion, Delmark, Folkways, and Sonet. Short was in the 1963 documentary "The Blues," but died before it was released. —*Ron Wynn*

Stavin' Chain Blues / Jul. 1965 / Delmark ♦♦♦♦♦
He could sing, wail, holler, or moan traditional Delta blues with a lot of names that were much bigger. J.D. Short didn't make a lot of records, but the few he cut during the 1930s should be heard over and over to truly appreciate their quality. —*Ron Wynn*

Siegel-Schwall Band

Group / Modern Electric Blues, Electric Chicago Blues
Paul Butterfield and Elvin Bishop were not the only White dudes that formed a blues band in Chicago in the early '60s. Corky Siegel and Jim Schwall formed the Siegel-Schwall Band in the mid-'60s in Chicago and worked as a duo playing blues clubs like Pepper's Lounge, where they were the house band. All of the great blues players would sit in—all the time. Corky Siegel played harp and electric Wurlitzer piano, with an abbreviated drum set stashed under the piano; Jim Schwall played guitar and mandolin. Both sang.

Corky Siegel was born in Chicago on October 24, 1943; Jim Schwall was born on November 11, 1942, also in Chicago. Corky Siegel met Jim Schwall in 1964, when they were both music students at Roosevelt University—Schwall studying guitar, Siegel studying classical saxophone and playing in the University Jazz Big Band. Corky Siegel first became interested in the blues that same year. Schwall's background ran more to country and bluegrass. The Siegel-Schwall Band approach to music (and blues) was lighter than groups like Butterfield or Musselwhite, representing more of a fusion of blues and more country-oriented material. They seldom played at high volume, stressed group cooperation, and shared the solo spotlight.

When the Butterfield band left their in gig at Big John's on Chicago's North Side, it was the Siegel-Schwall Band that took their place. Signed by Vanguard scout Sam Charters in 1965, they released their first album in 1966, the first of five they would do with that label. Bass player Jack Dawson, formerly of the Prime Movers Blues Band, joined the band in 1967.

In 1969 the band toured, playing the Fillmore West, blues/folk festivals, and many club dates—one of several White blues bands that introduced the blues genre to millions of Americans during that era. They were, however, the first blues band to record with a full orchestra, performing *Three Pieces for Blues Band and Symphony Orchestra* in 1971 with the San Francisco Orchestra. Later that year, the band signed with RCA (Wooden Nickel) and produced five albums in the next four years. The band broke up in 1974.

In 1987, the band reformed and produced a live album on Alligator, *The Siegel-Schwall Reunion Concert.* Jim Schwall is a university professor of music in Kalamazoo, MI. Corky Siegel has been involved in many projects over the years that fuse classical music with blues, including his current group *Chamber Blues*—a string quartet, with a percussionist (tabla), and Siegel on piano and harmonica. And on rare occasions, the old band still gets together and performs. —*Michael Erlewine*

Siegel-Schwall Band / 1966 / Vanguard ✦✦✦
Their debut album is played a little too timidly to stand up to repeated listenings in today's noisy world, but their takes on Jimmy Reed's "Going to New York" and others are fascinating nonetheless. A different way of approaching any color blues, period. —*Cub Koda*

Say Siegel Schwall / 1967 / Vanguard ✦✦✦✦
For all parties concerned, this was the group's breakthrough album. Corky Siegel's emotional harp work and foxy, sly (almost cutesy) vocals, coupled with a hot rhythm section and Jim Schwall's cardboard-sounding acoustic with a pickup guitar work made this the one that connected big with White audiences. Some of it rocks, some of it boogies, some of it's downright creepy and eerie. Worth seeking out. —*Cub Koda*

Shake / 1968 / Vanguard ✦✦✦
Shake! was probably the group's second best album and certainly the one that came the closest to representing their live act. The major highlight is their take on Howlin' Wolf's "Shake for Me." Lots of fun and fireworks on this one, the sound of a band at the top of their game. —*Cub Koda*

Three Pieces for Blues & Orchestra / 1974 / Polydor ✦✦
This is not an album—or a piece of music—to be neutral about. Collaborations between the high brow and the low down have always been dicey (anyone ever heard Albert King playing with a symphony orchestra?), but this one will definitely leave you on one side of the debate or the other; either you'll hail it as the blues brought "uptown" or as an experiment gone terrible awry. —*Cub Koda*

The Best of Siegel-Schwall / Dec. 1974 / Vanguard ✦✦✦✦
Vinyl best-of compilation that hits a few (but not all) of the high notes of their tenure with Vanguard Records. —*Cub Koda*

Reunion Concert / 1988 / Alligator ✦✦
The coziness the band always had on their good nights seems totally lost on this live radio broadcast. Proof positive that you can't go home again. File under "guess you had to be there." —*Cub Koda*

● **Where We Walked (1966–1970)** / 1991 / Vanguard ✦✦✦✦
A very nice, fairly thorough, compilation that supersedes the old vinyl collection on several levels; nice mastering, better notes, and nicer selection. For a basic introduction to their sound, this one's hard to beat. —*Cub Koda*

Frankie Lee Sims

b. Apr. 30, 1917, New Orleans, LA, **d.** May 10, 1970, Dallas, TX
Guitar, Vocals / Electric Texas Blues
A traditionalist who was a staunch member of the Texas country blues movement of the late '40s and early '50s (along with the likes of his cousin Lightnin' Hopkins, Lil' Son Jackson, and Smokey Hogg), guitarist Frankie Lee Sims developed a twangy, ringing electric guitar style that was irresistible on fast numbers and stung hard on the downbeat stuff.

Sims picked up a guitar when he was 12 years old. By then, he had left his native New Orleans for Marshall, TX. After World War II ended, he played local dances and clubs around Dallas and crossed paths with T-Bone Walker. Sims cut his first 78s for Herb Rippa's Blue Bonnet Records in 1948 in Dallas, but didn't

taste anything resembling regional success until 1953, when his bouncy "Lucy Mae Blues" did well down south.

The guitarist recorded fairly prolifically for Los Angeles-based Specialty into 1954, then switched to Johnny Vincent's Ace label (and its Vin subsidiary) in 1957 to cut the mighty rockers "Walking with Frankie" and "She Likes to Boogie Real Low," both of which pounded harder than a ballpeen hammer.

Sims claimed to play guitar on King Curtis' 1962 instrumental hit "Soul Twist" for Bobby Robinson's Enjoy label, but that seems unlikely. It is assumed that he recorded for Robinson in late 1960 (the battered contents of three long-lost acetates emerged in 1985 on the British Krazy Kat label).

Sims mostly missed out on the folk-blues revival of the early '60s that his cousin Lightnin' Hopkins cashed in on handily. When he died at age 53 in Dallas of pneumonia, Sims was reportedly in trouble with the law due to a shooting incident and had been gripped by drinking problems. —*Bill Dahl*

Lucy Mae Blues / 1970 / Specialty ✦✦✦✦✦
This collection of Sims' Specialty sides, primarily in a drums and electric guitar format, is pretty hard to beat. It combines all of the original singles, the extra tracks from his lone album plus unissued material and, until further alternate takes come to light, the best overview of his tenure with the label. Some tracks are augmented with harmonica and/or string bass, but it's Frankie Lee's guitar and sly vocals that drive things along. Until his early Bluebonnet and later Ace material is cobbled together to complete the picture, this compilation is all you'll need. —*Cub Koda*

Hal "Cornbread" Singer

b. Oct. 8, 1919, Tulsa, OK
Saxophone / Jazz Blues
Equally at home blowing scorching R&B or tasty jazz, Hal "Cornbread" Singer has played and recorded both over a career spanning more than half a century. Singer picked up his early experience as a hornman with various Southwestern territory bands, including the outfits of Ernie Fields, Lloyd Hunter, and Nat Towles. He made it to Kansas City in 1939, working with pianist Jay McShann (whose sax section also included Charlie Parker) before venturing to New York in 1941 and playing with Hot Lips Page, Earl Bostic, Don Byas, and Roy Eldridge (with whom he first recorded in 1944). After the close of the war, Singer signed on with Lucky Millinder's orchestra.

Singer had just fulfilled his life's ambition—a chair in Duke Ellington's prestigious reed section—in 1948 when a honking R&B instrumental called "Cornbread" that he'd recently waxed for Savoy as a leader began to take off. That presented a wrenching dilemma for the young saxist, but in the end, his decision to go out on his own paid off—"Cornbread" paced the R&B charts for four weeks and gave him his enduring nickname. Another of his Savoy instrumentals, "Beef Stew," also cracked the R&B lists.

Singer recorded rocking R&B workouts for Savoy 1956 (the cuisine motif resulting in helpings of "Neck Bones," "Rice and Red Beans," and "Hot Bread"), working with sidemen including pianists Wynton Kelly and George Rhodes, guitarist Mickey Baker, bassist Walter Page, and drummer Panama Francis. One of his last dates for the firm produced the torrid "Rock 'n Roll," which may have featured Singer as singer as well as saxist!

By the late '50s, Singer had abandoned rock 'n' roll for a life as a jazz saxist. He recorded for Prestige in a more restrained manner in 1959 and stayed in that general groove. Singer relocated to Paris in 1965, winning over European audiences with his hearty blowing and engaging in quite a bit of session work with visiting blues and jazz luminaries. The old R&B fire flared up temporarily in 1990, when he cut *Royal Blue* for Black Top with boogie piano specialist Al Copley. —*Bill Dahl*

● **Rent Party** / Jun. 1948–May 3, 1956 / Savoy ✦✦✦✦✦
This is an essential LP (now out of print, as are all U.S. Savoys) of Hal Singer's honkin', screamin' tenor sax instrumentals. Singer was in Ellington's reed section when his 1948 "Cornbread" hit big, and he left the band to pursue the beat-heavy music that would soon be driving teens crazy. Several of these cuts are in the hand-clappin', toe-tappin' vein, while others are more thoughtful jazz and blues numbers. Sax-heavies Buddy Lucas and Sam "The Man" Taylor join in, as does Mickey Baker. It's all vintage stuff (1948–1956). —*Roots & Rhythm Newsletter*

● **Blue Stompin'** / Feb. 20, 1959 / Prestige ✦✦✦✦✦
This is a fun set of heated swing with early R&B overtones. The title cut is a real romp with tenor saxophonist Hal Singer and trumpeter Charlie Shavers not only constructing exciting solos but riffing behind each other. With the exception of the standard "With a Song in My Heart," Singer and Shavers wrote the remainder of the repertoire and, with the assistance of a particularly strong rhythm section (pianist Ray Bryant, bassist Wendell Marshall, and drummer Osie Johnson), there are many fine moments on this easily enjoyable set. Recommended. —*Scott Yanow*

Royal Blue / Black Top ✦✦✦
There's no way that this collaboration between the veteran saxist and boogie piano specialist Al Copley could equal the searing power of Singer's late-'40s/early-'50s sides for Savoy; a few too many years had passed for Singer to play in the same searing fashion. But his jazzy riffs and Copley's keyboard antics are enjoyable enough in their own right. —*Bill Dahl*

TV Slim

b. Feb. 10, 1916, Houston, TX, **d.** Oct. 21, 1969, Klingman, AZ
Guitar, Vocals / Electric Blues
Oscar "TV Slim" Wills' hilarious tale of a sad sack named "Flat Foot Sam" briefly made him a bankable name in 1957. Sam's ongoing saga lasted longer than Slim's minute or two in the spotlight, but that didn't stop him from recording throughout the 1960s.
Influenced by DeFord Bailey and both Sonny Boy Williamsons on harp and Guitar Slim on axe while living in Houston, Wills sold one of his early compositions, "Dolly Bee," to Don Robey for Junior Parker's use on Duke Records before getting the itch to record himself. To that end, he set up Speed Records, his own label and source for the great majority of his output over the next dozen years.
The first version of "Flat Foot Sam" came out on a tiny Shreveport logo, Cliff Records, in 1957. Local record man Stan Lewis, later the owner of Jewel/Paula Records, reportedly bestowed the colorful nickname of "TV Slim" on Wills; he was a skinny television repairman, so the handle fit perfectly.
"Flat Foot Sam" generated sufficient regional sales to merit reissue on Checker, but its ragged edges must have rankled someone at the Chicago label enough to convince Slim to recut it in much tighter form in New Orleans with the vaunted studio band at Cosimo's. This time, Robert "Barefootin'" Parker blew a strong sax solo, Chess A&R man Paul Gayten handled piano duties, and Charles "Hungry" Williams laid down a brisk secondline beat. It became Slim's biggest seller when unleashed on another Chess subsidiary, Argo Records.
Slim cut a torrent of 45s for Speed, Checker, Pzazz, USA, Timbre, Excell, and Ideel after that, chronicling the further adventures of his prime mealticket with "Flatfoot Sam Made a Bet," "Flat Foot Sam Met Jim Dandy," and "Flat Foot Sam #2." Albert Collins later covered Slim's Speed waxing of the surreal "Don't Reach Cross My Plate." Wills died in a car wreck outside Klingman, AZ, in 1969 en route home to Los Angeles after playing a date in Chicago. —*Bill Dahl*

Drink Small

b. 1933, Bishopville, SC
Guitar, Vocals / Acoustic Blues
The breadth of Drink Small's repertoire is fascinating in itself, but what's even more impressive is his depth as a performer in any of his chosen genres. His records may suddenly shift from a solo acoustic blues-guitar track to a smooth soul ballad with horns to who-knows-what, yet Small never seems to be caught out of place. He can be gruff and rough, clean and modern, or light and bouncy, altering his voice and guitar to suit the mood. Rated one of America's top gospel guitarists before he turned to blues in the late '50s, the South Carolina "Blues Doctor" for years had only one 45 on the market (Sharp, 1959). His discography has recently begun to grow considerably, finally revealing the extent of his songwriting and performing talents. —*Jim O'Neal*

I Know My Blues Are Different / 1976 / Southland ✦✦
● **The Blues Doctor** / 1990 / Ichiban ✦✦✦✦✦
Drink's own special blend of Delta, Chicago, and Carolina blues,

it includes some band stuff, some solo stuff. Particularly wonderful is Drink's rich, gospel-influenced bass voice. A truly unique artist sharing his unique point of view, Drink includes a couple of saucy items ("Tittie Man" and "Baby, Leave Your Panties Home") along with covers of "Little Red Rooster" and "Stormy Monday Blues." —*Niles J. Frantz*

Round Two / 1991 / Ichiban ✦✦✦
With more good stuff, it's much like the first. Highlights: the cautionary "D.U.I." and the funky "Don't Let Nobody Else." —*Niles J. Frantz*

Bessie Smith

b. Apr. 15, 1894, Chattanooga, TN, **d.** Sep. 26, 1937, Clarksdale, MS
Vocals / Classic Female Blues
The first major blues and jazz singer on record and one of the most powerful of all time, Bessie Smith rightly earned the title of "The Empress of the Blues." Even on her first records in 1923, her passionate voice overcame the primitive recording quality of the day and still communicates easily to today's listeners (which is not true of any other singer from that early period). At a time when the blues were in and most vocalists (particularly vaudevillians) were being dubbed "blues singers," Bessie Smith simply had no competition.
Back in 1912, Bessie Smith sang in the same show as Ma Rainey, who took her under her wing and coached her. Although Rainey would achieve a measure of fame throughout her career, she was soon surpassed by her protégé. In 1920 Bessie had her own show in Atlantic City and in 1923 she moved to New York. She was soon signed by Columbia and her first recording (Alberta Hunter's "Downhearted Blues") made her famous. Bessie worked and recorded steadily throughout the decade, using many top musicians as sidemen on sessions including Louis Armstrong, Joe Smith (her favorite cornetist), James P. Johnson, and Charlie Green. Her summer tent show, Harlem Frolics, was a big success during 1925–27 and Mississippi Days in 1928 kept the momentum going.
However by 1929 the blues were out of fashion and Bessie Smith's career was declining despite being at the peak of her powers (and still only 35). She appeared in *St. Louis Blues* that year (a low-budget movie short that contains the only footage of her) but her hit recording of "Nobody Knows You When You're Down and Out" predicted her leaner Depression years. Although she was dropped by Columbia in 1931 and made her final recordings on a four-song session in 1933, Bessie Smith kept on working. She played the Apollo in 1935 and substituted for Billie Holiday in the show *Stars over Broadway*. The chances are very good that she would have made a comeback, starting with a Carnegie Hall appearance at John Hammond's upcoming "From Spirituals to Swing" concert, but she was killed in a car crash in Missouri. Columbia has reissued all of her recordings, first in five two-LP sets and more recently on five two-CD boxes that also contain her five alternate takes, the soundtrack of *St. Louis Blues* and an interview with her niece Ruby Smith. "The Empress of the Blues," based on her recordings, will never have to abdicate her throne! —*Scott Yanow*

● **The Complete Recordings, Vol. 1** / Feb. 16, 1923–Apr. 8, 1924 / Columbia/Legacy ✦✦✦✦✦
In the 1970s Bessie Smith's recordings were reissued on five double LPs. Her CD reissue series also has five volumes (the first four are double-CD sets) with the main difference being that the final volume includes all of her rare alternate takes (which were bypassed on LP). The first set (which, as with all of the CD volumes, is housed in an oversize box that includes an informative booklet) contains her first 38 recordings. During this early era, Bessie Smith had no competitors on record and she was one of the few vocalists who could overcome the primitive recording techniques; her power really comes through. Her very first recording (Alberta Hunter's "Down Hearted Blues") was a big hit and is one of the highlights of this set along with "'Tain't Nobody's Bizness If I Do" (two decades before Billie Holiday), "Jail-House Blues" and "Ticket Agent, Ease Your Window Down." Smith's accompaniment is nothing special (usually just a pianist and maybe a weak horn or two) but she dominates the music anyway, even on two vocal duets with her rival Clara Smith. All of these volumes reward close listenings and are full of timeless recordings. —*Scott Yanow*

★ **The Complete Recordings, Vol. 2 (1924–1925)** / Apr. 8, 1924–Nov. 18, 1925 / Columbia/Legacy ◆◆◆◆◆
Bessie Smith, even on the evidence of her earliest recordings, well deserved the title "Empress of the Blues." In the 1920s there was no one in her league for emotional intensity, honest blues feeling, and power. The second of five volumes finds her accompaniment improving rapidly with such sympathetic sidemen as trombonist Charlie Green, cornetist Joe Smith, and clarinetist Buster Bailey often helping her out. However they are overshadowed by Louis Armstrong whose two sessions with Smith (nine songs in all) fall into the time period of this second set; particularly classic are their versions of "St. Louis Blues," "Careless Love Blues," and "I Ain't Goin' to Play Second Fiddle." Other gems on this essential set include "Cake Walkin' Babies from Home," "The Yellow Dog Blues," and "At the Christmas Ball." — *Scott Yanow*

The Complete Recordings, Vol. 3 / Nov. 20, 1925–Feb. 16, 1928 / Columbia/Legacy ◆◆◆◆◆
On the third of five volumes that reissue all of her recordings, the great Bessie Smith is greatly assisted on some of the 39 selections by a few of her favorite sidemen: cornetist Joe Smith, trombonist Charlie Green, and clarinetist Buster Bailey. But the most important of her occasional musicians is pianist James P. Johnson, who makes his first appearance in 1927 and can be heard on four duets with Bessie including the monumental "Back Water Blues." Other highlights of this highly recommended set (all five volumes are essential) include "After You've Gone," "Muddy Water," "There'll Be a Hot Time in the Old Town Tonight," "Trombone Cholly," "Send Me to the 'Lectric Chair" and "Mean Old Bedbug Blues." The power and intensity of Bessie Smith's recordings should be considered required listening; even 70 years later they still communicate. — *Scott Yanow*

The Complete Recordings, Vol. 4 / Feb. 21, 1928–Jun. 11, 1931 / Columbia/Legacy ◆◆◆◆◆
The fourth of five volumes that reissue all of Bessie Smith's recordings traces her career from a period when her popularity was at its height down to just six songs away from the halt of her recording career. But although her commercial fortunes might have slipped, Bessie Smith never declined and these later recordings are consistently powerful. The two-part "Empty Bed Blues" and "Nobody Knows You When You're Down and Out" (hers is the original version) are true classics and none of the other 40 songs (including the double-entendre "Kitchen Man") are throwaways. With strong accompaniment during some performances by trombonist Charlie Green, guitarist Eddie Lang, Clarence Williams' band, and on ten songs (eight of which are duets) the masterful pianist James P. Johnson, this volume (as with the others) is quite essential. — *Scott Yanow*

Complete Recordings, Vol. 5: The Final Chapter / May 6, 1925–Nov. 24, 1933 / Sony Legacy ◆◆◆◆◆
Bessie Smith cut 160 sides for the Columbia and Okeh labels between 1923 and 1933, and the four previous two-CD/cassette boxed sets of her complete recordings released in the 1990s covered 154 of them; which introduces the question, what can a fifth two-CD/cassette boxed set contain in addition to the remaining six cuts? First, there are five previously unreleased alternate takes; second, there is the 15-minute low-fi soundtrack to the two-reel short *St. Louis Blues*, which constitutes the only film of Smith; and third, taking up all of the second CD/cassette, there are 72 minutes of interview tapes of Ruby Smith, Bessie Smith's niece, who traveled as part of her show. The box contains a "Parental Advisory—Explicit Lyrics" warning because of the nature of Ruby Smith's reminiscences. You won't learn much about Bessie Smith's music from her niece's remarks, but you will learn a lot about her sexual preferences. — *William Ruhlmann*

The Bessie Smith Collection [Deja Vu] / 1985 / Deja Vu ◆◆
Bessie Smith Collection contains some good music, but it's a haphazardly compiled budget-priced collection—stick with Columbia's sets for a more complete picture. — *Thom Owens*

★ **The Bessie Smith Collection [Columbia Jazz Masterpieces]** / Dec. 1989 / Columbia ◆◆◆◆◆
While there's no denying the importance and quality of Columbia/Legacy's *Complete Recordings* series, nine discs may seem a bit intimidating to the newcomer. *Collection*, a mid-priced, 16-track collection which spans most of Smith's career,

ultimately does a better service to the casual listener with a limited budget. This is probably the best introduction—undoubtedly many will seek out the more comprehensive packages afterwards. — *Chris Woodstra*

Byther Smith

b. Apr. 17, 1933, Monticello, MS
Bass, Guitar, Vocals / Modern Electric Blues, Chicago Blues
Strictly judging from the lyrical sentiment of his recordings to this point, it might be wise not to make Chicago guitarist Byther Smith angry. Smitty's uncompromising songs are filled with threats of violence and ominous menace (the way blues used to be before the age of political correctness), sometimes to the point where his words don't even rhyme. They don't have to, either—you're transfixed by the sheer intensity of his music.

Smitty came to Chicago during the mid-'50s after spending time toiling on an Arizona cattle ranch. He picked up guitar tips from J.B. Lenoir (his first cousin), Robert Jr. Lockwood, and Hubert Sumlin, then began playing in the clubs during the early '60s. Theresa's Lounge was his main haunt for five years as he backed Junior Wells; he also played with the likes of Big Mama Thornton, George "Harmonica" Smith, and Otis Rush.

A couple of acclaimed singles for C.J. (the two-part "Give Me My White Robe") and BeBe ("Money Tree"/"So Unhappy") spread his name among aficionados, as did a 1983 album for Grits, *Tell Me How You Like It*. But it's only been during the last few years that the rest of the country has begun to appreciate Smitty, thanks to a pair of extremely solid albums on Bullseye Blues: 1991's *Housefire* (first out on Grits back in 1985) and *I'm a Mad Man* two years later. With a new set on Delmark and a stepped-up touring itinerary on the horizon, Smitty's just hitting his stride. — *Bill Dahl*

Tell Me How You Like It / Oct. 1985 / Grits ◆◆◆◆◆
Fine guitar from this longtime Chicago bluesman, including four originals. — *Barry Lee Pearson*

Addressing the Nation with the Blues / 1989 / JSP ◆◆◆
Smith was so far outside the domestic blues loop that this Chicago-cut set only found release on a British logo, JSP. It was our loss—Smith is typically brusque and ominous, threatening to "Play the Blues on the Moon" and "Addressing the Nation with the Blues" as only he can. Nothing derivative about his lyrical muse—he's intense to the point of allowing his words not to rhyme to make his points, while his lead guitar work is inevitably to the point. — *Bill Dahl*

Housefire / 1991 / Bullseye Blues ◆◆◆◆
An unheralded gem that fell through the cracks during its initial issue in 1985 and definitely deserved its higher Bullseye Blues profile six years later. Except for a stinging cover of Detroit Junior's "Money Tree" that leads off, Smitty wrote the entire disc, and it's typically singular stuff: a paranoid "The Man Wants Me Dead," a promise to "Live On and Sing the Blues," all solidly backed by a sympathetic combo. — *Bill Dahl*

● **I'm a Mad Man** / 1993 / Bullseye Blues ◆◆◆◆◆
Smitty is not mellowing with age. This set finds him physically threatening some poor slob in "Get Outta My Way" and generally living up to the boast of the title track. As his profile finally rises, Smith is receiving a little high-profile assistance—Ron Levy produced the set and handles keyboards, while the Memphis Horns add their punchy interjections wherever appropriate. — *Bill Dahl*

Blues Knights (with Larry Davis) / 1994 / Evidence ◆◆◆
Davis and Smith both acquit themselves well and are backed by the same band. — *Bill Dahl*

Funny Papa Smith (John T. Smith)

b. 1890, TX
Guitar, Vocals / Acoustic Texas Blues
J.T. "Funny Papa" Smith acquired the name Howling Wolf from the title of his first record in 1930. Any influence on the more famous Chester "Howlin' Wolf" Burnett from Mississippi was probably in name only, but Smith was an influential musician within the Texas blues idiom. In fact, the liner notes of his Yazoo reissue album refer to his recordings as "practically definitive of what is known as Texas blues-playing." The notes also tout Smith's originality as a composer and his skill as an instrumentalist, "despite the fact that his guitar was chronically out of

tune." Little biographical information has been published on Smith; blues guitarist Tom Shaw remembered him as the overseer of an Oklahoma plantation who was sent to prison for murder. He made his last recordings in 1935, presumably after his release. According to *Blues Who's Who*, Smith toured with Texas Alexander in 1939; "whereabouts unknown thereafter." —*Jim O'Neal*

● **The Howling Wolf (1930–1931)** / 1971 / Yazoo ✦✦✦✦✦
This is fine guitar-based Texas country blues by an artist completely unlike the later Howlin' Wolf. —*Mark A. Humphrey*

True Texas Blues / 1995 / Collectables ✦✦✦

George Harmonica Smith

b. Apr. 22, 1924, Helena, AR, d. Oct. 2, 1983, Los Angeles, CA
Harmonica, Vocals / Electric Harmonica Blues
George Smith was born on April 22, 1924 in Helena, AR, but was raised in Cairo, IL. At age four, Smith was already taking harp lessons from his mother, a guitar player and a somewhat stern taskmaster—it was a case of get-it-right-or-else. In his early teens, he started hoboing around towns in the South and later joined Early Woods, a country band with Early Woods on fiddle and Curtis Gould on spoons. He also worked with a gospel group in Mississippi called the Jackson Jubilee Singers.

Smith moved to Rock Island, IL, in 1941 and played with a group that included Francis Clay on drums. There is evidence that he was one of the first to amplify his harp. While working at the Dixie Theater, he took an old 16mm cinema projector, extracted the amplifier/speaker, and began using this on the streets.

His influences include Larry Adler, and later Little Walter. Smith would sometimes bill himself as Little Walter Jr. or Big Walter. He played in a number of bands, including one with a young guitarist named Otis Rush, and later went on the road with the Muddy Waters Band, replacing Henry Strong.

In 1954, he was offered a permanent job at the Orchid Room in Kansas City where, early in 1955, Joe Bihari of Modern Records (on a scouting trip), heard Smith, and signed him to Modern. These recording sessions were released under the name Little George Smith, and included "Telephone Blues" and "Blues in the Dark." The records were a success.

Smith traveled with Little Willie John and Champion Jack Dupree on one of the Universal Attractions tours. While on the tour, he recorded with Champion Jack Dupree in November of 1955 in Cincinnati, producing "Sharp Harp" and "Overhead Blues." The tour ended in Los Angeles and Smith settled down, spending the rest of his life in that city.

In the late '50s he recorded for J&M, Lapel, Melker, and Caddy under the names Harmonica King or Little Walter Junior. He also worked with Big Mama Thornton on many shows.

In 1960, Smith met producer Nat McCoy who owned Soloplay and Carolyn labels, with whom he recorded ten singles under the name of George Allen. In 1966, while Muddy Waters was on West Coast, he asked Smith to join him and they worked together for a while, recording for Spivey Records.

Smith's first album on World Pacific, *A Tribute to Little Walter*, was released in 1968. In 1969, Bob Thiele produced an excellent solo album of Smith on Bluesway, and later made use of Smith as a sideman for his Blues Times label, covering sets with T-Bone Walker, and Harmonica Slim. Smith met Rod Piazza, a young White harp player, and they formed the Southside Blues Band, later known as Bacon Fat.

In 1969, Smith signed with U.K. producer Mike Vernon and did the *No Time for Jive* album. Smith was less active in the 1970s appearing with Eddie Taylor and Big Mama Thornton. Around 1977, Smith became friends with William Clarke and they began working together. Their working relationship and friendship continued until Smith died on October 1, 1983.

William Clarke, Smith's protégé, writes, "He had a technique on the chromatic harp where he would play two notes at once, but one octave apart. He would get an organ-type sound by doing this. George really knew how to make his notes count by not playing too much and taking his time by letting the music unfold easily. He could also swing like crazy and was a first-class entertainer. I have heard from a friend that they had seen George Smith in the 1950s playing a club in Chicago, tap dancing around everybody's drinks on top of the bar while playing his harp. "

"I have been with him in church and seen him play amplified harmonica by himself. This was very soulful. I have never heard George play a song the same way twice. He was very creative and played directly from his heart. He admired all great musicians but had his own sound and style. He was a true original. Mr. Smith would always give 100% on stage whether or not there were 1 or 1,000 people listening. This was his performing style, always.

"George Smith greatly admired harmonica player Larry Adler, and although Adler used the octave technique on the harp also, George really was the one that developed this to its full potential. Before Mr. Smith, nobody in blues had used this octave technique.

"An extremely kind and gentle man, George always went all out to help other harmonica players. Everybody liked George Smith. He played a huge role in advancing blues harmonica and should never be forgotten. You can hear the influence of George Smith in most everyone playing blues harmonica today, whether directly or indirectly. He also was a great blues singer. He had a huge baritone voice that conveyed great emotion and soulfulness."

Recommended Smith recordings include *Blowin' the Blues* (1960) on Pea Vine, *Tribute to Little Walter* (1968) on Liberty, *No Time for Jive* (1970) on Blue Horizon, *Of the Blues* (1973) reissued on Crosscut Records, and *Little George Smith* (1991) on Ace Records. —*Michael Erlewine*

● **Tribute to Little Walter** / 1968 / World Pacific ✦✦✦✦✦
The L.A. harp ace pays tribute to one of his peers and influences with a well-conceived set of Little Walter covers. —*Bill Dahl*

No Time to Jive / 1970 / Blue Horizon ✦✦✦
Laidback L.A. session from 1969 produced by Mike Vernon for his Blue Horizon label that's dominated by a mellow feel. There are a few upbeat items—"Before You Do Your Thing (You'd Better Think)" and "Soul Feet"—but mostly George sits back and blows with a relaxed ease. His sidemen include guitarists Pee Wee Crayton and Marshall Hooks, pianist J.D. Nicholson, and drummer Richard Innes. —*Bill Dahl*

Arkansas Trap / 1971 / Deram ✦✦

George Smith of the Blues / 1973 / Bluesway ✦✦✦

Oopin' Doopin' Doopin' / Ace ✦✦✦

Mamie Smith

b. May 26, 1883, Cincinnati, OH, d. Aug. 16, 1946, New York, NY
Piano, Vocals / Classic Female Blues
A pillar in the classic female blues tradition, Mamie Smith is generally recognized as the first to record in the genre. Her version of "Crazy Blues" on Okeh Records was the first major hit of the blues, which led other record labels to record the previously neglected blues musicians. In the process, "Crazy Blues" and its success created the first market for blues records.

Biographical information about Mamie Smith is incomplete, but it is confirmed that she danced for Tutt-Whitney's Smart Set Company when she was a teenager. Before 1920, she moved from her birthplace of Cincinnati, OH, and began singing in Harlem nightclubs. Smith cut her first records in 1920, after songwriter Perry Bradford—who wrote nearly all of the songs Mamie sang—persuaded Okeh Records that there was a Black audience that would buy recordings by Black musicians. Initially, Smith cut "That Thing Called Love" and "You Can't Keep a Good Man Down." The singles sold well and Okeh had her cut another session in August, during which she recorded "Crazy Blues." Within its first month of release, "Crazy Blues" sold 75,000 copies and within a year, it sold nearly a million copies.

For the next three years, Mamie Smith recorded a number of songs for Okeh, which all featured instrumental support by the Jazz Hounds. Soon after her 1920 recordings, Smith's music recalled vaudeville more than blues. Following her final 1923 session for Okeh, Smith stopped performing regularly and slowly faded away from the blues scene. She died October 30, 1946, in New York, NY. —*Cub Koda & Stephen Thomas Erlewine*

★ **In Chronological Order, Vol. 1** / Document ✦✦✦✦✦
This first volume of a five-volume import set of her complete recordings features her earliest and best sides, including the classic "Crazy Blues." —*Cub Koda*

Chris Smither

b. New Orleans
Guitar, Vocals / Modern Acoustic Blues, Blues Rock
Like John Hammond and a handful of other musicians whose careers began in the 1960s blues revival, guitarist, singer, and songwriter Chris Smither can take pride in the fact that he's been there since the beginning. Except for a few years when he was away from performing in the 1970s, Smither has been a mainstay of the festival, coffeehouse, and club circuits around the U.S., Canada and Europe since his performing career began in earnest in the coffee houses in Boston in the spring of 1966.

Smither is best known for his great songs, items like "Love You like a Man" and "I Feel the Same," both of which have been recorded by guitarist Bonnie Raitt. Raitt and Smither got started at about the same time in the coffeehouse scene around Boston, though Smither was born and raised in New Orleans, the son of university professors.

Smither's earliest awareness of blues and folk music came from his parents' record collection. In a 1992 interview, he recalled that it included albums by Josh White, Susan Reed and Burl Ives. After a short stint taking piano lessons, Smither switched to ukulele after discovering his mother's old instrument in a closet. The young Smither was passionately attached to the ukulele, and now, years later, it helps to explain the emotion and expertise behind his unique finger-picking guitar style. Smither discovered blues music when he was 17 and heard a Lightnin' Hopkins album, *Blues in the Bottle.* The album was a major revelation to him and he subsequently spent weeks trying to figure out the intricate guitar parts he'd heard on that record. Smither moved to Boston after realizing he was a big fish in a small pond in the New Orleans folk/coffeehouse circuit of the mid-'60s. Also, acoustic blues pioneer Ric Von Schmidt had recommended Smither check out the Boston folk/blues scene.

Smither recorded his first couple of albums for the Poppy label in 1970 and 1971, *I'm a Stranger Too* and *Don't It Drag On.* In 1972, Smither recorded a third album, *Honeysuckle Dog,* for United Artists, that was never released. On the sessions for that album, he was joined in the studio by his old friends Bonnie Raitt and Mac Rebennack, a.k.a. Dr. John. After a long bout with alcohol, Smither launched his recording career again in the late '80s, although he was performing through the whole time he wasn't sober.

His return to a proper recording career, due to a deal with Flying Fish Records, didn't happen until 1991, when the label released *Another Way to Find You,* a folk blues album. Smither did record for Adelphi label in 1984, *It Ain't Easy,* which has since been re-released on compact disc. Since then, he's more than proved his mettle as an enormously gifted songwriter, releasing albums of mostly his own compositions for the Flying Fish and Hightone labels. Smither's other albums include *Happier Blue* (1993, Flying Fish) and *Up on the Lowdown* (1995, HighTone Records).

Any of Smither's Flying Fish releases or his HighTone release are worthy of careful examination by guitarists and students of all schools of blues music. Smither is still to some extent an unheralded master of modern acoustic blues. Fortunately, his festival bookings through the 1990s have elevated his profile to a higher level than he's ever enjoyed previously. *—Richard Skelly*

Don't It Drag on / 1972 / Poppy ✦✦

It Ain't Easy / 1983 / Adelphi ✦✦

Another Way to Find You / 1991 / Flying Fish ✦✦✦✦✦
Recorded live in the studio in Boston in 1989 with an audience of friends and guests, Smither is a very talented folk/blues singer/songwriter and a very good guitarist. He has an attractive low-key, introspective way about the blues. *—Niles J. Frantz*

● **Happier Blue** / 1993 / Flying Fish ✦✦✦✦✦
All the elements of Chris Smither's distinctive style are here: passionate vocals, his cool songs, and some covers. *—Richard Meyer*

Smoky Babe

b. 1927, Itta Bena, MS, d. 1975
Guitar, Vocals / Acoustic Louisiana Blues
Robert Brown, a.k.a. Smoky Babe, is a shadowy figure from the early days of the '60s folk-blues revival. The scant details of his life read like a prototypical country bluesman's bio; born in Itta

Bena, MS, in 1927, raised on a plantation, had a hard life of sharecropping, picked up the guitar along the way, spent several years hoboing throughout the South, moved to the big city and found life no better there. He apparently only worked sporadically as a semi-pro musician in New Orleans in the '50s returning to his adopted home base of Scotlandville to work as a garage mechanic at the time of his discovery. His brief recording career was limited to a pair of album-length releases recorded as "in the field" location sessions in 1960 and 1961 for the Folk Lyric and Bluesville labels. His few recordings display a strong rhythmic sense in his guitar playing with a strong thumping bass line with the occasional fore into slide guitar. His vocals were nothing less than rich, strong, and authoritative. After a few years of playing at picnics and local parties for friends around Baton Rouge in the early '60s, he seemingly disappeared, never to be seen or heard from again. His death in 1975 remains unconfirmed at the time of this writing. *—Cub Koda*

● **Louisiana Country Blues** / Arhoolie ✦✦✦✦
A reissue (on compact disc) of a reissue (on Arhoolie) of an album originally released on the Folk Lyric label, this combines two albums of Louisiana country blues material on one CD. Smoky Babe may have been a semi-pro musician, but the feel of the 12 sides suggests that he was full command of his powers when folklorist Dr. Harry Oster hit the "record" button. Combined with another album's worth of material from the equally obscure Herman E. Johnson (who performs four tracks on electric guitar in a most chaotic manner), this is back porch country blues of the highest order. Just because neither is a "famous name," don't let that keep you checking this superlative release out. *—Cub Koda*

Little Smokey Smothers

b. Jan. 2, 1939, Tchula, MS
Guitar, Vocals / Electric Chicago Blues
Not to be confused with his late older brother Big Smokey, Albert "Little Smokey" Smothers began to transcend his journeyman status in 1993 with a superlative Dick Shurman-produced album for the Dutch Black Magic label, *Bossman: The Chicago Blues of Little Smokey Smothers.* The set happily reunited him with his ex-guitar pupil Elvin Bishop and his cousin, singer Lee Shot Williams.

Little Smokey rolled into Chicago during the mid-'50s, landing gigs with guitarist Arthur "Big Boy" Spires and pianist Lazy Bill Lucas and playing with Howlin' Wolf on the 1959 Chess session that produced "I've Been Abused" and "Mr. Airplane Man." Smothers fell in with young White harpist Paul Butterfield when the latter was just starting out in the early '60s and is still fondly recalled as a major influence by his buddy Bishop, who would go on to make history as Butterfield's slashing axeman after Smothers left the harpist's employ.

There was a time during the '70s when Little Smokey pretty much gave up music, but he slid back into playing gradually during the next decade with the Legendary Blues Band. Heart problems temporarily shelved Smothers for a spell not too long ago, but he's back in action now. *—Bill Dahl*

● **Bossman—Chicago Blues of 1993** / 1993 / Black Magic ✦✦✦✦✦
Sizzling and long-overdue debut album by the veteran Chicago bluesman, whose approach is considerably more contemporary than that of his late older brother. Producer Dick Shurman recruited vocalist Lee Shot Williams (Smokey's cousin) and Elvin Bishop (who Smokey tutored during the early '60s) for this project, a fine showcase for Smothers' hearty vocals and expressive guitar. *—Bill Dahl*

Otis Smokey Smothers

b. Mar. 21, 1929, Lexington, MS, d. Jul. 23, 1993, Chicago, IL
Guitars, Vocals / Electric Chicago Blues
The Chicago blues scene boasted its own pair of Smothers Brothers, but there was nothing particularly amusing about their tough brand of blues music. The older of the two by a decade, Otis "Big Smokey" Smothers was first to arrive in the Windy City from Mississippi in the mid-'40s. Howlin' Wolf liked the way he played enough to invite him into the Chess studios as his rhythm guitarist on several 1956-57 sessions (songs included "Who's Been Talking," "Tell Me," "Going Back Home," and "I Asked for Water").

Federal Records found Smothers' simple shuffle sound immensely appealing in 1960, recording 12 tracks by the good-natured bluesman with labelmate Freddy King handling lead guitar duties (King, Federal's parent logo, even issued a Smothers LP that's worth a pretty penny today). A four-song 1962 session that included "Way Up in the Mountains of Kentucky" and an updated version of the Hank Ballard & the Midnighters classic "Work With Me Annie" ("Twist With Me Annie") completed his Federal tenure.

Apart from a 1968 single for Gamma ("I Got My Eyes on You"), Smothers didn't make it back onto wax until 1986, when Red Beans Records, a small Chicago outfit run by pianist Erwin Helfer and guitarist Pete Crawford, brought him back to the record racks with an LP called *Got My Eyes on You* that showed his style hadn't changed a whit with the decades. Smokey Smothers was a beloved Chicago traditionalist until the very end. *—Bill Dahl*

● **Sings the Backporch Blues** / 1961 / King ♦♦♦♦♦
Lowdown Chicago blues album that's exceedingly rare on vinyl but well worth the search. Smothers was a master of the slow-grinding shuffle, and some tracks sport the presence of Freddy King on lead guitar. *—Bill Dahl*

Drivin' Blues / King ♦♦♦♦♦
Uncompromising Chicago blues. *—Bill Dahl*

Got My Eyes on You / May 1987 / Red Beans ♦♦♦
The guitarist's only other album was a decent representation of his gutbucket sound, backing him with a crew of sympathetic young traditionalists that didn't update his basic shuffles a bit. *—Bill Dahl*

Otis Spann

b. Mar. 21, 1930, Jackson, MS, **d.** Apr. 24, 1970, Chicago, IL
Piano, Vocals / Electric Chicago Blues
An integral member of the nonpareil Muddy Waters band of the 1950s and 1960s, pianist Otis Spann took his sweet time in launching a full-fledged solo career. But his own discography is a satisfying one nonetheless, offering ample proof as to why so many aficionados considered him then and now as Chicago's leading postwar blues pianist.

Spann played on most of Waters' classic Chess waxings between 1953 and 1969, his rippling 88s providing the drive on Waters' seminal 1960 live version of "Got My Mojo Working" (cut at the prestigious Newport Jazz Festival, where Spann dazzled the assembled throng with some sensational storming boogies).

The Mississippi native began playing piano by age eight, influenced by local ivories stalwart Friday Ford. At 14, he was playing in bands around Jackson, finding more inspiration in the 78s of Big Maceo, who took the young pianist under his wing once Spann migrated to Chicago in 1946 or 1947.

Spann gigged on his own and with guitarist Morris Pejoe before hooking up with Waters in 1952. His first Chess date behind the Chicago icon the next year produced "Blow Wind Blow." Subsequent Waters classics sporting Spann's ivories include "Hoochie Coochie Man," "I'm Ready," and "Just Make Love to Me."

Strangely, Chess failed to recognize Spann's vocal abilities. His own Chess output was limited to a 1954 single, "It Must Have Been the Devil," that featured B.B. King on guitar, and sessions in 1956 and 1963 that remained in the can for decades. So Spann looked elsewhere, waxing a stunning album for Candid with guitarist Robert Jr. Lockwood in 1960, a largely solo outing for Storyville in 1963 that was cut in Copenhagen, a set for British Decca the following year that found him in the company of Waters and Eric Clapton, and a 1964 LP for Prestige where Spann shared vocal duties with bandmate James Cotton. Testament and Vanguard both recorded Spann as a leader in 1965.

The Blues Is Where It's At, Spann's enduring 1966 album for ABC-Bluesway, sounded like a live recording but was actually a studio date enlivened by a gaggle of enthusiastic onlookers that applauded every song (Waters, guitarist Sammy Lawhorn, and George "Harmonica" Smith were among the support crew on the date). A Bluesway encore, *The Bottom of the Blues* followed in 1967 and featured Otis' wife, Lucille Spann, helping out on vocals.

Spann's last few years with Muddy Waters were memorable

for their collaboration on the Chess set *Fathers and Sons*, but the pianist was clearly ready to launch a solo career, recording a set for Blue Horizon with British blues-rockers Fleetwood Mac that produced Spann's laidback "Hungry Country Girl." He finally turned the piano chair in the Waters band over to Pinetop Perkins in 1969, but fate didn't grant Spann long to achieve solo stardom. He was stricken with cancer and died in April of 1970. *—Bill Dahl*

Otis Spann Is the Blues / Aug. 1960 / Candid ♦♦♦♦♦
He may not have been *the* blues, but he was sure close to being *the blues pianist*. Spann provided wonderful, imaginative, tasty piano solos and better-than-average vocals, and was arguably the best player whose style was more restrained than animated. Not that he couldn't rock the house, but Spann's forte was making you think as well as making you dance. *—Ron Wynn*

● **Complete Candid Recordings—Otis Spann/Lightnin' Hopkins Sessions** / Aug. 23, 1960 / Mosaic ♦♦♦♦♦
With Robert Lockwood, Jr. Two classic Spann albums: *Otis Spann Is the Blues* and *Walkin' the Blues*. Early, potent Spann with flawless liner notes and a complete discography. Also included are the Candid sessions of Lightnin' Hopkins. *—Michael Erlewine*

The Blues Never Die / Oct. 1969 / Original Blues Classics ♦♦♦♦♦

Blues of Otis Spann . . . Plus / 1993 / See For Miles ♦♦♦
A Mike Vernon-produced British album from 1964 that was one of Spann's first full-length dates as a leader. Nice band, too: Muddy Waters on guitar, bassist Ransom Knowling, and drummer Willie "Big Eyes" Smith, along with a young Eric Clapton playing on a couple of cuts. Spann plays a harpsichord on a few items; needless to say, they aren't the album's shining moments! *—Bill Dahl*

Otis Spann's Chicago Blues / 1994 / Testament ♦♦
Recorded in 1965 and 1966, these 15 tracks are divided between solo piano performances and pieces with a full band, with support from guitarist Johnny Young and members of the Muddy Waters Band. The variation in approach means that this isn't the most consistent Spann album. The material and performances don't rank among his best either, although they're reasonably solid. Included are some of the rare tracks on which Spann played organ rather than piano. *—Richie Unterberger*

Down To Earth / 1995 / MCA ♦♦♦♦♦
Both of the great Chicago pianist's albums for ABC-Bluesway, characterized with rippling piano and ruminative vocals. Backed in style by his mates in the Muddy Waters band (including the man himself), Spann responds to a studio full of people on "Popcorn Man," "Steel Mill Blues," and "Nobody Knows Chicago like I Do." Spann's 1967 encore LP united him in the studio with wife Lucille for several vocals. *—Bill Dahl*

Speckled Red (Rufus Perryman)

b. Oct. 23, 1892, Monroe, LA, **d.** Jan. 2, 1973, St. Louis, MO
Piano, Organ / Piano Blues
Pianist Speckled Red was born in Monroe, LA, but he made his reputation as part of the St. Louis and Memphis blues scenes of the '20s and '30s. Red was equally proficient in early jazz and boogie woogie—his style is similar to Roosevelt Sykes and Little Brother Montgomery.

Speckled Red was raised in Hampton, GA, where he learned how to play his church's organ. In his early teens, his family—including his brother Willie Perryman, who is better-known as Piano Red—moved to Atlanta, GA. Throughout his childhood and adolescence he played piano and organ and by the time he was a teenager, he was playing house parties and juke joints. Red moved to Detroit in the mid-'20s and while he was there, he played various night clubs and parties. After a few years in Detroit, he moved back south to Memphis. In 1929, he cut his first recording sessions. One song from these sessions, "The Dirty Dozens," was released on Brunswick and became a hit in late '29. He recorded a sequel, "The Dirty Dozens, No. 2," the following year, but it failed to become a hit.

After Red's second set of sessions failed to sell, the pianist spent the next few years without a contract—he simply played local Memphis clubs. In 1938, he cut a few sides for Bluebird, but they were largely ignored.

In the early '40s, Speckled Red moved to St. Louis, where he played local clubs and bars for the next decade and a half. In 1954, he was rediscovered by a number of blues afficionados and record label owners. By 1956, he had recorded several songs for the Tone record label and began a tour of America and Europe. In 1960, he made some recordings for Folkways. By this time, Red's increasing age was causing him to cut back the number of concerts he gave. For the rest of the '60s, he only performed occasionally. Speckled Red died in 1973. —*Stephen Thomas Erlewine & Michael G. Nastos*

Dirty Dozens / Delmark ✦✦✦✦✦
If you have trouble keeping track of the "Reds," Rufus G. Perryman was "Speckled Red," while William Lee Perryman was either "Piano Red" or "Doctor Feelgood." In addition, Speckled Red's style contained more rag and folk elements than Piano Red's, as this set reveals. But both Reds talked a lot trash, and Speckled Red had a lighter barrelhouse approach than his younger brother. —*Ron Wynn*

Dave Specter w/ Bill Smith

b. May 21, 1963, Chicago IL
Guitar, Vocals / Modern Electric Blues
In a relatively short time, Chicago guitarist Dave Specter has found his way onto the blues equivalent of the fast track. Just over a decade ago, the towering guitarist with the carefully coiffed hair first made his presence felt as a good-natured bouncer at B.L.U.E.S., a Windy City blues mecca. Now, he's got four acclaimed albums in the Delmark catalog, every one a satisfying, challenging mix of blues (Specter lists influences including T-Bone Walker, Pee Wee Crayton, Magic Sam, and Otis Rush) and jazz (Kenny Burrell's another of his main men).

The native of Chicago's Northwest side didn't even grab a guitar until he was 18 years old, inspired by his harp-blowing older brother Howard. In 1985, he hired on at B.L.U.E.S., making valuable contacts on the job that led to sideman gigs with Johnny Littlejohn, Son Seals, and the Legendary Blues Band before he assembled his own outfit, the Bluebirds, in 1989.

Since Specter doesn't sing, he recruited deep-voiced crooner Barkin' Bill Smith as his first vocalist. The two shared the spotlight on Specter's alluring 1991 Delmark debut, *Bluebird Blues*. After Smith departed, Specter latched on to another West side veteran, Jesse Fortune, backing the singer on his 1993 Delmark set *Fortune Tellin' Man*. Dazzling harpist Tad Robinson took over front-man duties for the Bluebirds' 1994 disc *Blueplicity* and *Live in Europe* the next year. Currently, California harpman Lynwood Slim is the band's resident singer.

Jazz is growing increasingly prominent in Specter's evolving guitar attack. He imported legendary organist Brother Jack McDuff to provide a Hammond B-3 cushion for his latest Delmark project. Squeezing frequent European tours in between a myriad of local gigs, Specter wears his love for swinging blues tradition on his sleeve—and it fits him well. —*Bill Dahl*

Bluebird Blues with Ronnie Earl / 1991 / Delmark ✦✦✦✦
There wasn't any musical generation gap between young Chicago guitarist Specter and his much older front man Barkin' Bill Smith. Specter's love for the electrified 1950s styles of Magic Sam, T-Bone Walker, and B.B. King blended well with Smith's deep, almost crooning baritone pipes on what was the debut album for both men. Lots of breezy swing informs the retro-styled set. —*Bill Dahl*

● **Blueplicity** / 1993 / Delmark ✦✦✦✦✦
Sometimes conviction, charm, and humor can be as important as performing proficiency. While there's little in the playing or singing of guitarist Dave Specter or vocalist/harmonica player Tad Robinson that you haven't heard before, they so obviously enjoy what they're doing and communicate it so well that you eventually overlook their familiar material and become engrossed in their performances. This disc has a gritty, rough-edged sound often missing from modern blues dates. The menu ranges from jazzy tunes to lowdown wailers, soul-tinged pieces, and uptempo instrumentals. —*Ron Wynn*

Live in Europe / 1995 / Delmark ✦✦✦✦
Specter, Tad Robinson, and his swinging Bluebirds ventured over to Germany on tour in 1994, cutting this fine set over two memorable evenings. Robinson, now on his own, was an exceptional match for Specter's concise, crisp guitar style; equally conversant in blues and soul, Robinson is also an exceptional songwriter

who penned three of the disc's highlights ("On the Outside Looking In," "Sweet Serenity," "Dose of Reality"). More straight blues than on *Blueplicity:* "Little by Little," "Bad Boy," "Kidney Stew," Little Walter's "It's Too Late Brother." —*Bill Dahl*

Victoria Spivey (Victoria Regina Spivey)

b. Oct. 15, 1906, Houston, TX, **d.** Oct. 3, 1976, New York, NY
Vocals / Classic Female Blues
Although primarily a blues singer, Victoria Spivey often crossed over into jazz during her lengthy career. She learned piano early on and was singing professionally when she was 12. She worked locally (most notably with Blind Lemon Jefferson) and then in 1926 had a major hit with her first recording, "Black Snake Blues." A major attraction for the remainder of the decade, Spivey was one of the stars in the all-black MGM musical *Hallelujah* in 1929. She recorded in the late '20s (among her sidemen were Louis Armstrong and Red Allen) and in the mid-'30s, worked in vaudeville and toured with the *Hellzapoppin'* show in the late '40s although by then her years of fame had passed. However in the 1960s she started her Spivey label, recorded for several companies (including with Lonnie Johnson), and remained a constant force in the blues scene until her death in 1976. —*Scott Yanow*

And Her Blues, Vol. 2 / Jun. 10, 1961–Jun. 4, 1972 / Spivey ✦✦✦
Victoria Spivey, a classic blues singer of the 1920s, started her own label Spivey in 1961 and kept it going for 15 years. This LP, released posthumously, has three solo performances from 1961 (on which the singer plays either piano or ukulele), a trio rendition of "The Rising Sun" from 1962 with clarinetist Eddie Barefield, four numbers from 1972 in small combos and a loose three-song live performance from 1963 with a guitarist and a kazoo player. Although not essential, the music on this set is enjoyable and should be of interest to jazz historians. —*Scott Yanow*

● **1926–1931** / Document ✦✦✦✦✦
Spivey is in marvelous form throughout. This album features the classics "Steady Grind," "Black Snake Blues," and "Blood Thirsty Blues." —*Cub Koda*

Frank Stokes

b. Jan. 1, 1888, Whitehaven, TN, **d.** Sep. 12, 1955, Memphis, TN
Guitar, Vocals / Acoustic Memphis Blues
Frank Stokes and partner Dan Sain recorded as The Beale Street Shieks, a Memphis answer to the musical Chatmon family string band, The Mississippi Shieks. According to local tradition, Stokes was already playing the streets of Memphis by the turn of the century, about the same time the blues began to flourish. As a street artist, he needed a broad repertoire of songs and patter palatable to Blacks and Whites. A medicine show and houseparty favorite, Stokes was remembered as a consummate entertainer who drew on songs from the 19th and 20th centuries with equal facility. Solo or with Sain and, sometimes, fiddler Will Batts, Stokes recorded 38 sides for Paramount and Victor. These treasures include blues as well as older pieces: "Chicken You Can't Roost Too High for Me," "Mr. Crump Don't Like It," an outstanding version of "You Shall" (commonly known as "You Shall Be Free"), and "Hey Mourner," a traditional comic anticlerical piece. Stokes possessed a remarkable declamatory voice and was an adroit guitarist. His duets with Sain merit special attention because of their subtle interplay and propulsive rhythm. —*Barry Lee Pearson*

★ **The Victor Recordings** / Document ✦✦✦✦✦
Declamatory deep blues, Memphis style, it was recorded in 1928–1929. —*Jas Obrecht*

The Beale Street Sheiks / 1990 / Document ✦✦✦
This contains his Paramount 1927–1929 sides with Dan Sain. —*Jas Obrecht*

The Memphis Blues / Yazoo ✦✦✦✦✦
No one in the Memphis minstrel/traveling show or early blues tradition had a more distinguished career than Frank Stokes. This is marvelous, inspiring guitar, done in such a spry and captivating manner that you forget Stokes got his start working alongside a blackface comedian in the early '20s, or that much of this material by even 1950s standards was borderline offensive at best. —*Ron Wynn*

Angela Strehli

b. Nov. 22, 1945, Lubbock, TX
Vocals / Modern Electric Blues

Don't let her lack of albums fool you: vocalist Angela Strehli is an immensely gifted singer and songwriter, a Texas blues historian, impressario and fan. Born November 22, 1945 in Lubbock, TX, Strehli comes out of the same school of hippie folksingers that gave rise to some of Americana music's most gifted writers, people like Jimmie Dale Gilmore and her brother Al Strehli.

Raised in Lubbock and inspired by the mix of blues, country and rock 'n' roll she heard on West Texas early-'60s radio, she learned harmonica and played bass before becoming a full-time vocalist. Despite the fact that her recordings are scant, Strehli spends a good portion of each year performing live shows in Europe and around the U.S. and Canada.

You can hear Strehli, who's now based in San Francisco, in all her glory on *Soul Shake* (1989, Antone's Records), *Dreams Come True*, with Lou Ann Barton and Marcia Ball (Antone's, 1990), and *Blonde and Blue* (1994, Rounder Records). Of these, *Blonde and Blue* seems to best showcase her talents as a vocalist and writer of quality songs. Strehli, an avid student of the blues, and a sharp blues historian who helped build the Austin blues scene with club-owner Clifford Antone and musicians like Kim Wilson and the Vaughan brothers, knows enough about the state of the art to know there's an awful lot of albums out there. As a result, she takes her time writing and weeding out less than top-notch songs and records albums of lasting significance.

"My thinking has always been that volume is not so great, what's more important is the quality of the material," she explained in a 1995 interview in Austin. —*Richard Skelly*

● **Soul Shake** / Nov. 1987 / Antone's ✦✦✦✦✦
Soul Shake is an excellent album that effectively captures Angela Strehli's gritting, hard-edged roadhouse blues. Not only is her singing gutsy and powerful, the band is tough and the songs are first-rate, making *Soul Shake* a welcome reminder of the power of straight-ahead Texas blues-rock. —*Thom Owens*

Blonde and Blue / 1993 / Rounder ✦✦✦✦✦
The danger for modern blues performers is turning into a parody of what you're allegedly celebrating or honoring. Vocalist Angela Strehli avoids that trap by simply being herself; her honesty and individuality makes her cover of Major Lance's "Um, Um, Um, Um, Um" a legitimate treatment. Strehli's tough-talking personna was tailor-made for such songs as "Two Bit Texas Town" and "Go On," while she managed to register pain without pathos on "Can't Stop These Teardrops" and "I'm Just Your Fool." Only on Elmore James "The Sun Is Shining" did she falter, more because Albert King has established a credible alternate vision of that number. But she makes up for that with the remarkable closing tune "Going To That City." While she doesn't eclipse Sister O.M. Terrell's transcendent original, she comes as close as anyone possibly could to providing a treatment that's just as valid. —*Ron Wynn*

Hubert Sumlin

b. Nov. 16, 1931, Greenwood, MS
Guitar, Vocals / Electric Chicago Blues

Quiet and extremely unassuming off the bandstand, Hubert Sumlin played a style of guitar incendiary enough to stand tall beside the immortal Howlin' Wolf. The Wolf was Sumlin's imposing mentor for more than two decades, and it proved a mutually beneficial relationship; Sumlin's twisting, darting, unpredictable lead guitar constantly energized the Wolf's 1960s Chess sides, even when the songs themselves (check out "Do the Do" or "Mama's Baby" for conclusive proof) were less than stellar.

Sumlin started out twanging the proverbial broom wire nailed to the wall before he got his mitts on a real guitar. He grew up near West Memphis, AR, briefly hooking up with another young lion with a rosy future, harpist James Cotton, before receiving a summons from the mighty Wolf to join him in Chicago in 1954.

Sumlin learned his craft nightly on the bandstand behind Wolf, his confidence growing as he graduated from rhythm guitar duties to lead. By the dawn of the '60s, Sumlin's slashing axe was a prominent component on the great majority of Wolf's waxings, including "Wang Dang Doodle," "Shake for Me," "Hidden Charms" (boasting perhaps Sumlin's greatest recorded solo), "Three Hundred Pounds of Joy," and "Killing Floor."

Although they had a somewhat tempestuous relationship, Sumlin remained loyal to Wolf until the big man's 1976 death.

But there were a handful of solo sessions for Sumlin before that, beginning with a most unusual 1964 date in East Berlin that was produced by Horst Lippmann during a European tour under the auspices of the American Folk Blues Festival (the behind-the-Iron Curtain session also featured pianist Sunnyland Slim and bassist Willie Dixon).

Only in the last few years has Sumlin allowed his vocal talents to shine. He's recorded solo sets for Black Top and Blind Pig that show him to be an understated but effective singer—and his guitar continues to communicate most forcefully. —*Bill Dahl*

My Guitar & Me / Dec. 1975 / Evidence ✦✦
Sumlin's exceptionally low-key vocals and unexceptional backing by two-thirds of the Aces, pianist Willie Mabon, and rhythm guitarist Lonnie Brooks render this 1975 session pretty disposable overall. Sumlin cops plenty of solo space, but there's too little of the unpredictable fire that greatly distinguished his work with Howlin' Wolf. —*Bill Dahl*

Groove / 1976 / Black & Blue ✦✦✦

Blues Party / 1987 / Black Top ✦✦✦
Sumlin still wasn't totally prepared for solo stardom by the time of this disc, relying on the hearty contributions of guitarist Ronnie Earl and soul-searing singer Mighty Sam McClain to get over. —*Bill Dahl*

Blues Anytime! / 1994 / Evidence ✦✦✦✦
A remarkable 1964 session, produced by Horst Lippmann behind the Iron Curtain in East Germany, that found Sumlin trying for the first time on record to sing. He played both electric and acoustic axe on the historic date, sharing the singing with more experienced hands Willie Dixon and Sunnyland Slim (Clifton James is on drums). All three Chicago legends acquit themselves well. —*Bill Dahl*

Healing Feeling / Black Top ✦✦✦
An improvement over his previous Black Top disc, especially on Sumlin's two vocal showcases, "Come Back Little Girl" and "Honey Dumplins." James "Thunderbird" Davis is also on board in a guest role, though he has to share his mic time with the considerably less remarkable Darrell Nulisch, who dominates the vocals. —*Bill Dahl*

● **Heart & Soul** / Blind Pig ✦✦✦✦✦
The veteran guitarist sounds more confident and expressive vocally here than on any other of his contemporary recordings. Backing by harpist James Cotton, along with Little Mike & the Tornadoes, is nicely understated, affording Sumlin just enough drive without drowning out his easygoing vocals (no small feat). —*Bill Dahl*

Sunnyland Slim (Albert Luandrew)

b. Sep. 5, 1907, Vance, MS, **d.** Mar. 17, 1995, Chicago, IL
Piano, Vocals / Piano Blues

Exhibiting longevity commensurate with his powerful, imposing physical build, Sunnyland Slim's status as a beloved Chicago piano patriarch endured long after most of his peers had perished. For more than 50 years, the towering Sunnyland had rumbled the ivories around the Windy City, playing with virtually every local luminary imaginable and backing the great majority in the studio at one time or another.

He was born Albert Luandrew in Mississippi and received his early training on a pump organ. After entertaining at juke joints and movie houses in the Delta, Luandrew made Memphis his home base during the late '20s, playing along Beale Street and hanging out with the likes of Little Brother Montgomery and Ma Rainey.

He adopted his colorful stage name from the title of one of his best-known songs, the mournful "Sunnyland Train." The downbeat piece immortalized the speed and deadly power of a St. Louis-to-Memphis locomotive that mowed down numerous people unfortunate enough to cross its tracks at the wrong instant.

Slim moved to Chicago in 1939 and set up shop as an in-demand piano man, playing for a spell with John Lee "Sonny Boy" Williamson before waxing eight sides for RCA Victor in 1947 under the somewhat misleading handle of "Doctor Clayton's Buddy." If it hadn't been for the helpful Sunnyland, Muddy Waters may not have found his way onto Chess; it was at the pianist's 1947 session for Aristocrat that the Chess brothers made Waters' acquaintance.

Aristocrat (which issued his harrowing "Johnson Machine

Gun") was but one of a myriad of labels that Sunnyland recorded for between 1948 and 1956: Hytone, Opera, Chance, Tempo-
Tone, Mercury, Apollo, JOB, Regal, Vee-Jay (unissued), Blue Lake,
Club 51, and Cobra all cut dates on Slim, whose vocals thun-
dered with the same resonant authority as his 88s. In addition,
his distinctive playing enlivened hundreds of sessions by other
artists during the same timeframe.

In 1960, Sunnyland Slim traveled to Englewood Cliffs, NJ, to
cut his debut LP for Prestige's Bluesville subsidiary with King
Curtis supplying diamond-hard tenor sax breaks on many cuts.
The album, *Slim's Shout*, ranks as one of his finest, with defini-
tive renditions of the pianist's "The Devil Is a Busy Man," "Shake
It," "Brown Skin Woman," and "It's You Baby."

Like a deep-rooted tree, Sunnyland Slim persevered despite
the passing decades. For a time, he helmed his own label,
Airway Records. As late as 1985, he made a fine set for the Red
Beans logo, *Chicago Jump,* backed by the same crack combo that
shared the stage with him every Sunday evening at a popular
North side club called B.L.U.E.S. for some 12 years.

There were times when the pianist fell seriously ill, but he
always defied the odds and returned to action, warbling his
trademark Woody Woodpecker chortle and kicking off one more
exultant slow blues as he had done for the previous half century. Finally, after a calamitous fall on the ice coming home from
a gig led to numerous complications, Sunnyland Slim finally
died of kidney failure in 1995. He's sorely missed. —*Bill Dahl*

House Rent Party / 1949 / Delmark ✦✦✦✦✦
From deep in the vaults of Apollo Records comes this sensational collection of 1949 artifacts by the veteran pianist, along
with sides by singer St. Louis Jimmy, young pianist Willie
Mabon, and two unissued sides by guitarist Jimmy Rogers
(including a pre-Chess rendition of his seminal "That's All
Right"). Slim's mighty roar shines on "Brown Skin Woman," "I'm
Just a Lonesome Man," and "Bad Times (Cost of Living)," all
from the emerging heyday of the genre. —*Bill Dahl*

● **Slim's Shout** / 1969 / Prestige ✦✦✦✦✦
You wouldn't think that transporting one of Chicago's reigning
piano patriarchs to Englewood Cliffs, NJ, would produce such a
fine album, but this 1960 set cooks from beginning to end. His
swinging New York rhythm section has no trouble following
Slim's bedrock piano, and the estimable King Curtis peels off
diamond-hard tenor sax solos in the great Texas tradition that
also mesh seamlessly. Slim runs through his standards—"The
Devil Is a Busy Man," "Shake It," "It's You Baby"—in gorgeous
stereo, and two unissued bonus cuts (including another of his
best-known tunes, "Everytime I Get to Drinking") make the CD
reissue even more appealing. —*Bill Dahl*

Chicago Jump / Apr. 1986 / Evidence ✦✦✦✦
The last of Slim's great band-backed albums, cut with yeoman
help from his longtime combo (guitarist Steve Freund and drummer Robert Covington share the vocals) at the heart of the matter are Slim's rolling 88s and still-commanding vocals, invested
with experience beyond all comprehension. —*Bill Dahl*

Be Careful How You Vote / 1989 / Earwig ✦✦✦
Latter-day work originally issued on the pianist's own poorly-dis-
tributed Airway logo and given a decent rebirth by Earwig.
Slim's timely advice on voting rates a listen, as does the remainder of the set. —*Bill Dahl*

Sunnyland Train / 1995 / Evidence ✦✦✦
There are definite signs of Slim's increasing frailty on this solo
outing from the 1980s, but the majestic power of his aging
frame comes through frequently nevertheless. —*Bill Dahl*

Live at the D.C. Blues Society / Mapleshade ✦✦✦
Sunnyland Slim's brand of weary blues, punctuated by rolling
piano accents and boogie riffs, predates the rise and fall of
Delta blues and the emergence of its urban successor. Slim
toured the South in the '20s, '30s, and early '40s, then left for
Chicago and has been there ever since. This blend of Delta and
urban sensibilities has been infused in his songs since he began
recording and permeates the 14 selections on the 1987 CD *Live
at the D.C. Blues Society.* Although long since past his vocal
peak, Slim still spins a nifty yarn and mournful lament. —*Ron
Wynn*

Live in Europe / Airway ✦✦✦
A labor of love project by Slim's longtime saxman Sam
Burckhardt, who assembled this collection of informally taped

performances from the pianist's Germany stopover on April 23,
1975. Burckhardt wasn't playing his horn that day; instead, he
laid down a simple backbeat on drums and let Sunnyland do the
rest. Sturdy versions of many of the pianist's signature numbers
grace the disc. —*Bill Dahl*

Sunnyland Slim / Flyright ✦✦✦✦✦
This vinyl compendium of the pianist's work as leader and sideman for the JOB label from 1951 to 1955 contains some of his
hardiest sides. His vocal roar on the jumping "When I Was
Young" and a lowdown "Worried About My Baby" and "Down
Home Child" is exemplary, while the swinging instrumental
"Bassology" verges on a Count Basie motif. Slim's 88s anchor
sides by J.B. Lenoir, Johnny Shines, and drummer Alfred Wallace
to complete the LP. —*Bill Dahl*

Roosevelt Sykes

b. Jan. 31, 1906, Elmar, AR, **d.** Jul. 17, 1983, New Orleans, LA
Piano, Vocals / Piano Blues
Next time someone voices the goofball opinion that blues is simply too depressing to embrace, sit 'em down and expose 'em to
a heady dose of Roosevelt Sykes. If he doesn't change their
minds, nothing will.

There was absolutely nothing downbeat about this roly-poly,
effervescent pianist (nicknamed "Honeydripper" for his youthful
prowess around the girls), whose lengthy career spanned the
pre-war and postwar eras with no interruption whatsoever.
Sykes' romping boogies and hilariously risqué lyrics (his double-
entendre gems included "Dirty Mother for You," "Ice Cream
Freezer," and "Peeping Tom") characterize his monumental contributions to the blues idiom—he was a pioneering piano-
pounder responsible for the seminal pieces "44 Blues," "Driving
Wheel," and "Night Time Is the Right Time."

Sykes began playing while growing up in Helena. At age 15,
he hit the road, developing his rowdy barrelhouse style around
the blues-fertile St. Louis area. Sykes began recording in 1929
for Okeh and was signed to four different labels the next year
under four different names (he was variously billed as Dobby
Bragg, Willie Kelly, and Easy Papa Johnson)! Sykes joined Decca
Records in 1935, where his popularity blossomed.

After relocating to Chicago, Sykes inked a pact with Bluebird
in 1943 and recorded prolifically for the RCA subsidiary with his
combo, the Honeydrippers, scoring a pair of R&B hits in 1945
(covers of Cecil Gant's "I Wonder" and Joe Liggins' "The
Honeydripper"). The following year, he scored one more national chart item for the parent Victor logo, the lowdown blues
"Sunny Road." He also often toured and recorded with singer St.
Louis Jimmy Oden, the originator of the classic "Going Down
Slow."

In 1951, Sykes joined Chicago's United Records, cutting more
fine sides over the next couple of years. A pair of Dave
Bartholomew-produced 1955 dates for Imperial in New Orleans
included a rollicking version of "Sweet Home Chicago" that presaged all the covers that would surface later on. A slew of
albums for Bluesville, Folkways, Crown, and Delmark kept
Sykes on the shelves during the 1960s (a time when European
tours began to take up quite a bit of the pianist's itinerary). He
settled in New Orleans during the late '60s, where he remained
a local treasure until his death.

Precious few pianists could boast the thundering boogie
prowess of Roosevelt Sykes—and even fewer could chase away
the blues with his blues as the rotund cigar-chomping 88s ace
did. —*Bill Dahl*

The Return of Roosevelt Sykes / 1960 / Bluesville ✦✦✦✦
Sykes' lyrical images are as vivid and amusing as ever on this
1960 set, with titles like "Set the Meat Outdoors" and
"Hangover" among its standouts. Other than drummer Jump
Jackson, the quartet behind the pianist is pretty obscure, but they
rock his boogies with a vengeance. Contains a nice remake of his
classic "Drivin' Wheel." —*Bill Dahl*

The Honeydripper / 1961 / Prestige ✦✦✦✦✦
Roosevelt Sykes expertly fit his classic downhome piano riffs
and style into a fabric that also contained elements of soul, funk
and R&B. The nine-cut date, recently reissued by Original Blues
Classics, included such laments as "I Hate To Be Alone," "Lonely
Day," and "She Ain't For Nobody," as well as the poignant "Yes
Lawd" and less weighty "Satellite Baby" and "Jailbait." Besides
Sykes' alternately bemused, ironic and inviting vocals, there's

superb tenor sax support from King Curtis, Robert Banks' tasty organ and steady, nimble bass and drum assistance by Leonard Gaskins and drummer Belton Evans. —*Ron Wynn*

Roosevelt Sykes Sings the Blues / 1962 / Crown ✦✦✦
Long out-of-print LP on the cheaply pressed Crown logo that nevertheless impressively captured Sykes' rough-and-tumble boogie and blues prowess in a band setting. —*Bill Dahl*

Roosevelt Sykes in Europe / 1969 / Delmark ✦✦✦
This 1966 solo set was recently reissued on CD as *Gold Mine*. —*Bill Dahl*

The Country Blues Piano (1929–1932) / 1972 / Yazoo ✦✦✦✦✦
Featured is this Arkansas-born pianist/songster in some of his best early outings. —*Mark A. Humphrey*

Raining in My Heart / 1987 / Delmark ✦✦✦✦
Amazingly, this fine collection of Sykes' early-'50s sides for Chicago's United Records still awaits its reincarnation. That's a shame, since it contains some of the pianist's finest work with his jumping combo, the Honeydrippers (with unusual augmentation from violinist Remo Biondi on one 1952 date). "Toy Piano Blues" finds Sykes switching over to celeste, but "Too Hot to Handle," "Walking the Boogie," and "Fine and Brown" are in the customary Sykes mode. —*Bill Dahl*

Gold Mine: Live in Europe / 1991 / Delmark ✦✦✦
Solid 1966 solo set, cut during one of the effervescent piano pounder's frequent overseas jaunt and originally issued on Delmark as *In Europe*. A winning combination of material ancient even back then ("44 Blues," the jaunty boogie "Boot That Thing") and fresh numbers. —*Bill Dahl*

Blues by Roosevelt "The Honey-Dripper" Sykes / 1995 / Smithsonian/Folkaways ✦✦✦✦
Other than a cameo piano appearance by his producer (and peer) Memphis Slim on the appropriately titled "Memphis Slim Rock," this is a stellar solo outing by the prolific pianist from 1961. He belts out a booming "Sweet Old Chicago," takes a trip to Chicago's South side on "47th Street Jive," and indulges in a little ribald imagery for "The Sweet Root Man." —*Bill Dahl*

Complete Recorded Works, Vol. 1-7 / Document ✦✦✦
All of Roosevelt Sykes' recordings between 1929 and 1942 are collected on this seven-volume series; it is essential for hardcore fans of blues piano. —*AMG*

● **Boogie Honky Tonk** / Oldie Blues ✦✦✦✦✦
Vinyl compilation of the pianist's 1944–1947 output for RCA with his jumping little combo, the Honeydrippers, all of it cut in Chicago. Backed by a myriad of swinging Windy City sidemen (saxists Leon Washington, J.T. Brown, and Bill Casimir; bassist Ransom Knowling, drummers Jump Jackson and Judge Riley), Sykes rips through "Peeping Tom," the wonderfully titled "Flames of Jive," and his often-covered "Sunny Road" with ebullient charm. —*Bill Dahl*

T

Tampa Red (Hudson Whittaker)

b. Jan. 8, 1904, Smithville, GA, d. Mar. 19, 1981, Chicago, IL
Guitar, Piano, Kazoo, Vocals / Electric Chicago Blues, Acoustic Chicago Blues
Out of the dozens of fine slide guitarists who recorded blues, only a handful—Elmore James, Muddy Waters, and Robert Johnson, for example—left a clear imprint on tradition by creating a recognizable and widely imitated instrumental style. Tampa Red was another influential musical model. During his heyday in the '20s and '30s, he was billed as "The Guitar Wizard," and his stunning slide work on steel National or electric guitar shows why he earned the title. His 30-year recording career produced hundreds of sides: hokum, pop, and jive, but mostly blues (including classic compositions "Anna Lou Blues," "Black Angel Blues," "Crying Won't Help You," "It Hurts Me Too," and "Love Her with a Feeling"). Early in Red's career, he teamed up with pianist, songwriter, and latter-day gospel composer Georgia Tom Dorsey, collaborating on double entendre classics like "Tight Like That."

Listeners who only know Tampa Red's hokum material are missing the deeper side of one of the mainstays of Chicago blues. His peers included Big Bill Broonzy, with whom he shared a special friendship. Members of Lester Melrose's musical mafia and drinking buddies, they once managed to sleep through both games of a Chicago White Sox doubleheader. Eventually alcohol caught up with Red, and he blamed his latter-day health problems on an inability to refuse a drink.

During Red's prime, his musical venues ran the gamut of blues institutions: down-home jukes, the streets, the vaudeville theater circuit, and the Chicago club scene. Due to his polish and theater experience, he is often described as a city musician or urban artist in contrast to many of his more limited musical contemporaries. Furthermore, his house served as the blues community's rehearsal hall and an informal booking agency. According to the testimony of Broonzy and Big Joe Williams, Red cared for other musicians by offering them a meal and a place to stay and generally easing their transition from country to city life.

Today's listener will enjoy Tampa Red's expressive vocals and perhaps be taken aback by his kazoo solos. His songwriting has stood the test of time, and any serious slide guitar student had better be familiar with Red's guitar wizardry. —*Barry Lee Pearson*

★ **Bottleneck Guitar (1928–1937)** / 1974 / Yazoo ♦♦♦♦♦
Prime cuts from one of the greatest guitarists ever to strap on a slide. —*Cub Koda*

Guitar Wizard (1935–1953) / 1975 / Blues Classics ♦♦♦♦♦
Thirty-two of Red's premier tracks from his RCA Bluebird days dating from 1934–1953 (talk about longevity!) on two slabs of vinyl (with exhaustive liner notes by Jim O'Neal). Red's rousing kazoo blasts power many of these essential sides, which feature legends like pianists Black Bob, Blind John Davis, and Johnny Jones in support roles. Red's last few Victor sides were right in the stylistic heart of the later Chicago sound; the remarkable Latin-tinged "Rambler's Blues" boasts a spine-tingling amplified harp solo from Big Walter Horton. —*Bill Dahl*

☆ **Tampa Red: Guitar Wizard** / Oct. 1975 / RCA ♦♦♦♦♦
A 32-song collection of great slide guitar from 1934–1953, featuring sidemen Carl Martin, Black Bob, Blind John Davis, Johnnie Jones, and Walter Horton. Produced by Frank Driggs, this captures the full range of blues, hokum, and pop from a most popular and influential blues player. —*Barry Lee Pearson*

It's Tight Like That / 1976 / Blues Document ♦♦♦♦♦
Superb slide and suggestive hokum from 1928–1942. —*Jas Obrecht*

Bawdy Blues / 1977 / Bluesville ♦♦♦
Latter-day Tampa, from the late '50s to early '60s, with Memphis Slim and Lonnie Johnson. —*Jas Obrecht*

Tampa Red / 1982 / Bluesville ♦♦

Don't Tampa with the Blues / 1982 / Bluesville ♦♦♦
The kazoo-toting bluesman wasn't as powerful a presence when he came back in 1960 to record this set in a solo setting as he was in his Bluebird heyday, but it's hard to resist these agreeable versions of "Let Me Play with Your Poodle," "Love Her with a Feeling," and "It's Tight like That" nonetheless. —*Bill Dahl*

Complete Recorded Works, Vol. 1–5 / 1991 / Document ♦♦♦
Tampa Red's complete recordings from 1928 to 1934 are collected on this five-disc series. —*AMG*

The Guitar Wizard [CD] / 1994 / Columbia/Legacy ♦♦♦♦
Some of the earliest work (1928–1934) by the slide guitar great, ranging from the irresistible hokum he served up with piano-playing partner "Georgia Tom" Dorsey ("Dead Cats on the Line," "No Matter How She Done It") to the gorgeous "Black Angel Blues" (eventually known as "Sweet Little Angel") and the solo guitar masterpieces "Things 'Bout Comin' My Way" and "Denver Blues." —*Bill Dahl*

★ **It Hurts Me Too: The Essential Recordings** / 1995 / Indigo ♦♦♦♦♦
A magnificent primer on the catalog of this prolific guitar/kazoo ace that spans 1928–1942. Opening with his immortal hokum duet with "Georgia Tom" Dorsey, the bawdy "It's Tight Like That," the disc makes clear just how seminal Red's Chicago-cut output was—here are the original versions of "It Hurts Me Too," "Love with a Feeling," "Don't You Lie to Me," and the double-entendre hoots "She Wants to Sell My Monkey" and "Let Me Play with Your Poodle." —*Bill Dahl*

The Complete Bluebird Recordings, Vol. 1 1934–1936 / Oct. 1995 / Columbia/Legacy ♦♦♦♦♦

Tampa Red (1928–1942) / Story Of Blues ♦♦♦♦♦
Tampa Red sang and played the guitar and kazoo with a joy and flair that made almost every tune he did instantly unforgettable. His early work has been reissued and repackaged so often that it's easy to get caught in the mire. These are marvelous cuts, matching him with various accompanists, including Georgia Tom (later Dr. Thomas A. Dorsey), and offering the best in double-entendre, rags, topical, and novelty material. —*Ron Wynn*

Tarheel Slim (Alden Bunn)

b. Sep. 24, 1924, Wilson, NC, d. Aug. 21, 1977
Guitar, Vocals / Electric Blues
Talk about a versatile musician: Alden Bunn recorded in virtually every postwar musical genre imaginable. Lowdown blues, gospel, vocal group R&B, poppish duets, even rockabilly weren't outside the sphere of his musicianship.

Spirituals were Bunn's first love. While still in North Carolina during the early '40s, the guitarist worked with the Gospel Four and then the Selah Jubilee Singers, who recorded for Continental and Decca. Bunn and Thurman Ruth broke away in 1949 to form their own group, the Jubilators. During a single day in New York in 1950, they recorded for four labels under four different names!

One of those labels was Apollo, who convinced them to go secular. That's basically how the Larks, one of the seminal early R&B vocal groups whose mellifluous early-'50s Apollo platters rank with the era's best, came to be. Bunn sang lead on a few of their bluesier items ("Eyesight to the Blind," for one), as well as doing two sessions of his own for the firm in 1952 under the name of Allen Bunn. As Alden Bunn, he encored on Bobby Robinson's Red Robin logo the next year.

Bunn also sang with another R&B vocal group, the Wheels. And with his future wife, Anna Sanford, Bunn recorded as the Lovers; "Darling It's Wonderful," their 1957 duet for Aladdin's Lamp subsidiary, was a substantial pop seller. (Ray Ellis did the arranging.)

Tarheel Slim made his official entrance in 1958 with his wife, now dubbed Little Ann, in a duet format for Robinson's Fire imprint ("It's Too Late," "Much Too Late"). Then old Tarheel came out of the gate like his pants were on fire with a pair of rockabilly raveups of his own, "Wildcat Tamer" and "No. 9 Train," with Jimmy Spruill on blazing lead guitar.

After a few years off the scene, Tarheel Slim made a bit of a comeback during the early '70s, with an album for Pete Lowry's Trix label that harked back to Bunn's Carolina blues heritage. It would prove his last. —Bill Dahl

Number 9 Train / 1980 / Charly ✦✦✦

● **Red Robin & Fire Years** / Collectables ✦✦✦✦✦
Slim was quite an eclectic soul during his 1950s tenure with Bobby Robinson's Red Robin and Fire imprints (as this set conclusively shows). New York blues, pop/R&B duets with Little Ann, even blistering rockabilly-tinged outings ("Number 9 Train," and "Wildcat Tamer") were all well within the versatile guitarist's stylistic scope. —Bill Dahl

Baby Tate (Charles Henry Tate)

b. Jan. 28, 1916, Elberton, GA, **d.** Aug. 17, 1972, Columbia, SC
Guitar, Vocals / Piedmont Acoustic Blues
In the course of his nearly 50-year career, guitarist Baby Tate recorded only a handful of sessions. The bulk of his life was spent as a sideman, playing with musicians like Blind Boy Fuller, Pink Anderson, and Peg Leg Sam.

Born Charles Henry Tate, he was raised in Greenville, SC. When he was 14 years old, Tate taught himself how to play guitar. Shortly afterward, he began playing with Blind Boy Fuller, who taught Tate the fundamentals of blues guitar. When he was in his late teens, Baby began playing with Joe Walker and Roosevelt Brooks; the trio played clubs throughout the Greenville area.

In 1932, Tate stopped working with Walker and Brooks, hooking up with Carolina Blackbirds. The duo played a number of shows for the radio station WFBC. For most of the '30s, Baby played music as a hobby, performing at local parties, celebrations, and medicine shows.

Tate served in the U.S. Army in the late '30s and early '40s. While he was stationed in Europe, he played local taverns and dances. In 1942, he returned to Greenville, SC, where he earned a living doing odd jobs around the town. Tate picked up music again in 1946, setting out on the local blues club circuit. In 1950, he cut several sessions for the Atlanta-based Kapp label.

In the early '50s, Baby moved to Spartanburg, SC, where he performed both as a solo act and as a duo with Pink Anderson. Tate and Anderson performed as duo into the '70s.

In 1962, Tate recorded his first album, *See What You Done*. The following year, he was featured in the documentary film, *The Blues*. For the rest of the decade, Baby Tate played various gigs, concerts, and festivals across America. With the assistance of harmonica player Peg Leg Sam, Baby Tate recorded another set of sessions in 1972. Later that year, Tate suffered a fatal heart attack. He died on August 17, 1972. —Stephen Thomas Erlewine

See What You Done Done / 1994 / Prestige ✦✦✦

Eddie Taylor

b. Jan. 29, 1923, Benoit, MS, **d.** Dec. 25, 1985, Chicago, IL
Guitar, Vocals / Electric Chicago Blues
When you're talking about the patented Jimmy Reed laconic shuffle sound, you're talking about Eddie Taylor just as much as Reed himself. Taylor was the glue that kept Reed's lowdown grooves from falling into serious disrepair. His rock-steady rhythm guitar powered the great majority of Reed's Vee-Jay sides

during the 1950s and early '60s, and he even found time to wax a few classic sides of his own for Vee-Jay during the mid-'50s.

Eddie Taylor was as versatile a blues guitarist as anyone could ever hope to encounter. His style was deeply rooted in Delta tradition, but he could snap off a modern funk-tinged groove just as convincingly as a straight shuffle. Taylor saw Delta immortals Robert Johnson and Charlie Patton as a lad, taking up the guitar himself in 1936 and teaching the basics of the instrument to his childhood pal Reed. After a stop in Memphis, he hit Chicago in 1949, falling in with harpist Snooky Pryor, guitarist Floyd Jones, and—you guessed it—his old homey Reed.

From Jimmy Reed's second Vee-Jay date in 1953 on, Eddie Taylor was right there to help Reed through the rough spots. Taylor's own Vee-Jay debut came in 1955 with the immortal "Bad Boy" (Reed returning the favor on harp). Taylor's second Vee-Jay single coupled two more classics, "Ride 'Em on Down" and "Big Town Playboy," and his last two platters for the firm, "You'll Always Have a Home" and "I'm Gonna Love You," were similarly inspired. But Taylor's records didn't sell in the quantities that Reed's did, so he was largely relegated to the role of sideman (he recorded behind John Lee Hooker, John Brim, Elmore James, Snooky Pryor, and many more during the '50s) until his 1972 set for Advent, *I Feel So Bad*, made it abundantly clear that this quiet, unassuming guitarist didn't have to play second fiddle to anyone. When he died in 1985, he left a void on the Chicago circuit that remains apparent even now. They just don't make 'em like Eddie Taylor anymore. —Bill Dahl

I Feel So Bad / 1972 / Hightone ✦✦✦✦
One of the Chicago guitarist's most satisfying contemporary albums, this 1972 set (first issued on Advent) was cut not in the Windy City, but in L.A. in 1972 with a combo featuring Phillip Walker on second guitar and George Smith on harp. Taylor was no strict traditionalist; he was as conversant with funk-tinged modern rhythms as with Delta-based styles—and he exhibits both sides of his musical personality on this one. —Bill Dahl

Still Not Ready for Eddie / Jul. 1988 / Antone's ✦✦✦
Shows signs of the brilliance that we've long come to expect from the uncommonly versatile Taylor, but clearly not the equal of some of the other Taylor sets on the market. —Bill Dahl

★ **Bad Boy** / 1993 / Charly ✦✦✦✦✦
The Delta-rooted mid-'50s Vee-Jay label classics by perennially underrated Chicago guitarist Eddie Taylor, who stepped out of Jimmy Reed's shadow long enough to leave behind "Bad Boy," "Big Town Playboy," "Ride 'Em on Down," the bouncy "I'm Gonna Love You," and several more brilliant sides. Fifteen songs in all, including five from 1964 that are scarcely less impressive than his previous stuff. —Bill Dahl

My Heart is Bleeding / 1994 / Evidence ✦✦✦
Credible set from 1980 mostly cut in Chicago but first out on the German L+R logo. Taylor's in typically solid form, and his tough backing includes the marvelous Sunnyland Slim on piano and harpist Carey Bell. Taylor pays homage to his pal Jimmy Reed with a loping "Going to Virginia" and Muddy Waters on "Blow Wind Blow," but "Soul Brother" rides a chunky R&B groove that's a long way from Reed's rudimentary rhythms. The last five sides stem from a 1980 European tour (with Hubert Sumlin and Bell handling some of the vocals) and don't add much to the package. —Bill Dahl

Long Way From Home [Live] / Nov. 1995 / Blind Pig ✦✦✦
Okay effort from the venerable Chicago guitarist's later days that's not as essential as Taylor's prior recording activities. —Bill Dahl

★ **Ride 'Em on Down** / Charly ✦✦✦✦✦
An absolutely essential 24-track collection which alternates 12 of Eddie's classic Vee-Jay sides (including "Bad Boy," "Big Town Playboy," "Find My Baby," "Looking For Trouble," and the title track) with a dozen more early Jimmy Reed sides with Taylor in support. As a collection of Taylor's best solo sides, it's as complete as any on the market. As a sample of Taylor's impeccable backup work behind Reed, it stands as a very nice collection of rarities that shows off both artists to good advantage, although it contains no hits. As a document of early '50s Chicago blues, it's a major brick in the wall. As seamless blues groove listening, consider it a must have. —Cub Koda

Hound Dog Taylor (Theodore Roosevelt Taylor)

b. Apr. 12, 1915, Natchez, MS, **d.** Dec. 17, 1975, Chicago, IL
Guitar, Vocals / Electric Chicago Blues
Alligator Records, Chicago's leading contemporary blues label, might never have been launched at all if not for the crashing, slashing slide guitar antics of Hound Dog Taylor. Bruce Iglauer, then an employee of Delmark Records, couldn't convince his boss, Bob Koester, of Taylor's potential, so Iglauer took matters into his own hands. In 1971, Alligator was born for the express purpose of releasing Hound Dog's debut album. We all know what transpired after that.

Named after President Theodore Roosevelt, Mississippi native Taylor took up the guitar when he was 20 years old. He made a few appearances on Sonny Boy Williamson's fabled KFFA *King Biscuit Time* radio broadcasts out of Helena, AR, before coming to Chicago in 1942. It was another 15 years before Taylor made blues his full-time vocation, though. Taylor was a favorite on the South and West sides during the late '50s and early '60s. It's generally accepted that Freddy King copped a good portion of his classic "Hide Away" from an instrumental he heard Taylor cranking out on the bandstand.

Taylor's pre-Alligator credits were light—only a 1960 single for Cadillac baby's Bea & Baby imprint ("Baby Is Coming Home"/"Take Five"), a 1962 45 for Carl Jones' Firma Records ("Christine"/"Alley Music"), and a 1967 effort for Checker ("Watch Out"/"Down Home") predated his output for Iglauer.

Taylor's relentlessly raucous band, the HouseRockers, consisted of only two men, though their combined racket sounded like quite a few more. Second guitarist Brewer Phillips, who often supplied buzzing pseudo-bass lines on his guitar, had developed such an empathy with Taylor that their guitars intertwined with ESP-like force, while drummer Ted Harvey kept everything moving along at a brisk pace.

Their eponymous 1971 debut LP contained the typically rowdy "Give Me Back My Wig," while Taylor's first Alligator encore in 1973, *Natural Boogie*, boasted the hypnotic "Sadie" and a stomping "Roll Your Moneymaker." *Beware of the Dog*, a live set, vividly captured the good-time vibe that the perpetually beaming guitarist emanated, but Taylor didn't live to see its release—he died of cancer shortly before it hit the shelves.

Hound Dog Taylor was the obvious inspiration for Alligator's "Genuine Houserocking Music" motto, a credo Iglauer's firm still tries to live up to today. He wasn't the most accomplished of slide guitarists, but Hound Dog Taylor could definitely rock any house he played at. —*Bill Dahl*

★ **Hound Dog Taylor & the Houserockers** / 1971 / Alligator ◆◆◆◆◆
The first album and the perfect place to start. Wild, raucous, crazy music straight out of the South Side clubs. The incessant drive of Hound Dog's playing is best heard on "Give Me Back My Wig," "55th Street Boogie," and "Taylor's Rock," while the sound of Brewer Phillips' Telecaster on "Phillips' Theme" gives new meaning to the phrase "sheet metal tone." One of the greatest slide guitar albums of all time. —*Cub Koda*

Natural Boogie / 1973 / Alligator ◆◆◆◆◆
Hound Dog's second album was every bit as wild as the first, bringing with it a fatter sound and a wider range of emotions and music. A recut here of Hound Dog's first single, "Take Five," totally burns the original while the smoldering intensity of "See Me In The Evening" and "Sadie" take this album to places the first one never reached. —*Cub Koda*

Beware of the Dog / 1975 / Alligator ◆◆◆◆◆
This was Hound Dog's posthumous live album containing performances that are even steamier than the first two studio albums, if such a notion is possible. For lowdown slow blues, it's hard to beat the heartfelt closer "Freddie's Blues" and for surreal moments on wax, it's equally hard to beat the funkhouse turned looney bin dementia of "Let's Get Funky" or the hopped up hillbilly fever rendition of "Comin' Around The Mountain." —*Cub Koda*

Genuine Houserocking Music / 1982 / Alligator ◆◆◆
With Alligator label prexy Bruce Iglauer recording some 20 or 30 tracks over two nights everytime the band went into the studio, there were bound to be some really great tracks lurking in the vaults and these are them. Noteworthy for the great performance of Robert Johnson's "Crossroads" (previously only available as a Japanese 45) but also for the "rock 'n' roll" inclusion of "What'd I Say" and Brewer Phillips' take on "Kansas City." No bottom of the barrel scrapings here. —*Cub Koda*

Live at Joe's Place / 1992 / New Rose ◆◆◆◆◆
A 1972 live recording in Boston. They're drunk, they're out of tune, but the crowd goes nuts and the overall vibe cancels out any musical inconsistencies. Doesn't really add anything to the Alligator legacy, as it's extremely loose and chaotic, but it's great fun anyway. —*Cub Koda*

Have Some Fun / 1992 / Wolf ◆◆◆
More 1972 live recordings from Joe's Place. Different song selection, somewhat better fidelity. Confusingly for people who'll want to order this as an import, it's issued under the name "The Houserockers" with only Hound Dog's photo on the front! —*Cub Koda*

Freddie's Blues / 1993 / Wolf ◆◆◆
This is the third volume of live recordings from Joe's Place in Cambridge, Massachusetts in 1972. Six of the 11 tunes here are instrumentals (four of them featuring the lead guitar of Brewer Phillips), and while Taylor and the Houserockers are generally in rare form here, some chaotic moments ("Let's Get Funky") do abound, but that's half the fun and charm of it all. —*Cub Koda*

Koko Taylor

b. Sep. 28, 1935, Memphis, TN
Vocals / Electric Chicago Blues
She's the undisputed queen of Chicago blues, and has been for decades. And truthfully, no one has even mounted a serious challenge to Koko Taylor's magnificent reign in recent memory.

Born and raised on a Memphis farm, young Cora Walton was urged to sing gospel by her folks but found the blues she heard on B.B. King's local radio show too powerful to resist. Big Mama Thornton and Bessie Smith were influential to her developing singing style, but so were Muddy Waters and Howlin' Wolf.

Along with her future husband, Robert "Pops" Taylor, she moved to the Windy City at age 18 and found work cleaning houses in the suburbs. Meanwhile, she and Pops made the South side scene, checking out her idols in person. Naturally, Taylor grabbed any chance to sit in that came her way.

In 1962, Willie Dixon caught Taylor's act and took over as her mentor. He produced her 1963 debut 45 for USA, "Honky Tonky," then got her signed to Chess. There she enjoyed one of the last legitimate Chicago blues hits with her rousing rendition of the Dixon-penned party classic "Wang Dang Doodle." It went all the way to number four on *Billboard's* R&B charts in 1966. Dixon's role as writer/producer was a prominent one on Taylor's eponymous Chess debut LP, but none of her encores enjoyed the same success level as "Wang Dang Doodle" (still her enduring signature song).

After a dry spell, Taylor joined Bruce Iglauer's Alligator Records in 1975 (she was the fledgling firm's first female artist). Her Grammy-nominated Alligator album debut, *I Got What It Takes*, catapulted Koko Taylor back into the blues limelight, and six more sets for the label have kept her there. She's got a skintight band called the Blues Machine, a closet full of Handy Awards, a 1984 Grammy, and made a memorable singing cameo in David Lynch's bizarre film, *Wild at Heart*.

Koko Taylor's raspy growl is a beloved Chicago fixture, just like deep-dish pizza and Michael Jordan. A recent attempt to market a nightclub under her name didn't pan out for long, but that setback was momentary; the queen's reign continues. —*Bill Dahl*

Koko Taylor / 1968 / MCA/Chess ◆◆◆◆◆
Straight digital reissue of Taylor's debut Chess album from 1969. Produced by Willie Dixon (who can intermittently be heard as a duet partner), the set is one of the strongest representations of the belter's Chess days available, with her immortal smash "Wang Dang Doodle," the chunky "Twenty-Nine Ways," "I'm a Little Mixed Up," and "Don't Mess with the Messer." Top-flight session musicians on Taylor's 1965-1969 output included guitarists Buddy Guy, Matt Murphy, and Johnny Shines and saxman Gene "Daddy G" Barge. —*Bill Dahl*

Basic Soul / 1972 / MCA/Chess ◆◆◆

Koko Taylor / 1972 / MCA/Chess ◆◆◆◆◆
A funky blues set. —*Bil Carpenter*

South Side Lady / Dec. 1, 1973 / Evidence ✦✦✦
Cut during the period when she was between Chess and Alligator, this 15-song selection, cut in a French studio and live in the Netherlands in 1973, is a potent set that finds her ably backed by the Aces, guitarist Jimmy Rogers, and pianist Willie Mabon. Lots of familiar titles—a live "Wang Dang Doodle," studio remakes of "I'm a Little Mixed Up" and "Twenty-Nine Ways"—and a few numbers that aren't usually associated with Chicago's undisputed blues queen. —*Bill Dahl*

Southside Baby / 1975 / Black & Blue ✦✦✦
Taylor's first Alligator album is as tough and uncompromising as any she's done for the the firm. —*Bill Dahl*

I Got What It Takes / 1975 / Alligator ✦✦✦✦✦
The queen's first album for Alligator, and still one of her very best to date. A tasty combo sparked by guitarists Mighty Joe Young and Sammy Lawhorn and saxist Abb Locke provide sharp support as the clear-voiced Taylor belts Bobby Saxton's "Trying to Make a Living," Magic Sam's "That's Why I'm Crying," her own "Honkey Tonkey" and "Voodoo Woman," and Ruth Brown's swinging "Mama, He Treats Your Daughter Mean." —*Bill Dahl*

Queen of the Blues / 1975 / Alligator ✦✦✦✦
Co-producer Bruce Iglauer anticipated a future trend by making this a set filled with cameos, but the presence of Lonnie Brooks, James Cotton, Albert Collins, and Son Seals is entirely warranted and the contributions of each work quite well in the context of the whole. Taylor's gritty "I Cried like a Baby" and a snazzy remake of Ann Peebles' "Come to Mama" are among the many highlights. —*Bill Dahl*

★ **What It Takes: The Chess Years** / 1977 / MCA/Chess ✦✦✦✦✦
With 18 tracks spanning 1964-1971, this compilation receives the nod over the shorter *Koko Taylor* (eight cuts double off anyway). Opening with her nails-tough "I Got What It Takes," the disc boasts "Wang Dang Doodle," several sides never before on album, and the strange previously unissued "Blue Prelude." Four 1971 tracks from Taylor's tough-to-find second Chess album, *Basic Soul*, are also aboard (including "Bills, Bills, and More Bills" and her queenly version of "Let Me Love You Baby"). Producer Willie Dixon's guiding hand is apparent everywhere. —*Bill Dahl*

The Earthshaker / 1978 / Alligator ✦✦✦✦✦
Koko Taylor's Alligator encore harbored a number of tunes that still pepper her set list to this day—the grinding "I'm a Woman" and the party-down specials "Let the Good Times Roll" and "Hey Bartender." Her uncompromising slow blues "Please Don't Dog Me" and a sassy remake of Irma Thomas' "You Can Have My Husband" also stand out, as does the fine backing by guitarists Sammy Lawhorn and Johnny B. Moore, pianist Pinetop Perkins, and saxman Abb Locke. —*Bill Dahl*

From the Heart of a Woman / Jan. 1981 / Alligator ✦✦✦
Another very credible outing, though Taylor's not quite convincing on the jazzily swinging "Sure Had a Wonderful Time Last Night." Far more suited to her raspy growl are her own "It Took a Long Time," a funky "Something Strange Is Going On," and Etta James' moving soul ballad "I'd Rather Go Blind" (beautifully complemented by Criss Johnson's liquidic guitar). —*Bill Dahl*

An Audience Wit / 1987 / Alligator ✦✦✦
Growling and slightly lacking in dynamics. —*Bill Dahl*

Live from Chicago / 1987 / Alligator ✦✦✦
Unfortunately, Koko Taylor's only domestic live album to date was cut with one of the lesser incarnations of her band, the Blues Machine, whose work could have displayed considerably more subtlety and swing than it does. Still, the set offers a vivid portrait of Chicago's blues queen in action, with faithful recitals of "Wang Dang Doodle," "I'm a Woman," and "Let the Good Times Roll." —*Bill Dahl*

Jump for Joy / 1990 / Alligator ✦✦✦
A slightly slicker Koko Taylor than we've generally been accustomed to, with nice horn arrangements by Gene Barge that frame the blues queen's growl effectively. A Taylor duet with Lonnie Brooks would normally be something to savor, but they're saddled here with an extremely corny "It's a Dirty Job" that's beneath both their statures. Taylor wrote four of that disc's best numbers herself, including "Can't Let Go" and the title cut. —*Bill Dahl*

Force of Nature / 1993 / Alligator ✦✦✦✦
A solid contemporary blues album that ranges from Taylor's

own "Spellbound" and "Put the Pot On," a rendition of Toussaint McCall's tender soul lament "Nothing Takes the Place of You," and a saucy revival of the old Ike & Tina Turner R&B gem "If I Can't Be First." Gene Barge once again penned the horn charts, Carey Bell contributes his usual harp mastery to Taylor's remake of Little Milton's "Mother Nature," and only Buddy Guy's over-the-top guitar histrionics on "Born Under a Bad Sign" grate. Long may the queen reign! —*Bill Dahl*

Little Johnny Taylor (Johnny Lamar Taylor)

b. Feb. 11, 1943, Memphis, TN
Vocals / Soul Blues
Some folks still get them mixed up, so let's get it straight from the outset. Little Johnny Taylor is best-known for his scorching slow blues smashes "Part Time Love" (for Bay Area-based Galaxy Records in 1963) and 1971's "Everybody Knows About My Good Thing" for Ronn Records in Shreveport, LA. He's definitely not the suave Sam Cooke protégé that blitzed the charts with "Who's Making Love" for Stax in 1968; that's Johnnie Taylor, who added to the confusion by covering "Part Time Love" for Stax.

Another similarity between the two Taylors is that both hailed from strong gospel backgrounds. Little Johnny came to Los Angeles in 1950 and did a stint with the Mighty Clouds of Joy before going secular. Influenced by Little Willie John, he debuted as an R&B artist with a pair of 45s for Hunter Hancock's Swingin' logo, but his career didn't soar until he inked a pact with Fantasy's Galaxy subsidiary in 1963 (where he benefited from crisp production by Cliff Goldsmith and Ray Shanklin's arrangements).

The gliding mid-tempo blues "You'll Need Another Favor," firmly in a Bobby Bland mode, was Taylor's first chart item. He followed it up with the tortured R&B chart-topper "Part Time Love," which found him testifying in gospel-fired style over Arthur Wright's biting guitar and a grinding, horn-leavened downbeat groove. The singer also did fairly well with "Since I Found a New Love" in 1964 and "Zig Zag Lightning" in 1966.

Taylor's tenure at Stan Lewis' Ronn imprint elicited the slow blues smash "Everybody Knows About My Good Thing" in 1971, and a similar witty hit follow-up, "Open House at My House," the next year (both were covered later by Z.Z. Hill for Malaco). While at Ronn, Little Johnny cut some duets with yet another Taylor, this one named Ted (no, they weren't related either). He hasn't recorded much of late, but Little Johnny Taylor remains an active performer. —*Bill Dahl*

● **Greatest Hits** / Fantasy ✦✦✦✦✦
The gospel-tinged and decidedly soul-inflected 1963-1968 blues sides of Little Johnny Taylor on Galaxy Records benefited from marvelous horn-powered arrangements by Ray Shanklin that brilliantly pushed Taylor's melismatic vocals. Naturally, the impassioned "Part Time Love" is included, along with the Bobby Bland-tinged mid-tempo groover "You'll Need Another Favor," a delicious "Since I Found a New Love," and the blistering "You Win, I Lose." Seventeen tracks in all, many of them bolstered by Arthur Wright's stinging guitar. —*Bill Dahl*

Everybody Knows About My Good Thing / 1970 / Ronn ✦✦✦✦
A great simmering soul-blues album crying out for digital reincarnation. Two R&B hits—"It's My Fault Darling" and the ironic two-part title cut, later revived by Z.Z. Hill—share microgroove space with eight more solid efforts, supervised by Miles Grayson (who co-wrote a good deal of the album). —*Bill Dahl*

Super Taylors / 1974 / Ronn ✦✦✦
Now here's a relic from Taylor's prolific early '70s Ronn tenure, with Ted Taylor, that is available on CD. Although they weren't related (except by label), Little Johnny and Ted shared this album like long-lost brothers. Four duets find the two complementing one another most soulfully; otherwise, the album is comprised of solo sides by both (including Little Johnny's "Everybody Knows About My Good Thing"). —*Bill Dahl*

I Shoulda Been a Preacher / 1981 / Red Lightnin' ✦✦✦✦✦
Only his pastor knows that for sure, but this is one wailing collection. It contains the hottest gospel-tinged singles Taylor cut for Galaxy, and anyone turned off by the tepid material coming out for Ichiban should consult these before hopping off the bandwagon. —*Ron Wynn*

Stuck in the Mud / 1988 / Ichiban ✦✦✦
Ugly Man / 1989 / Ichiban ✦✦✦
Frankly, Taylor's voice isn't what it used to be, but this contemporary effort isn't without its merits. —*Bill Dahl*

Melvin Taylor

Guitar
Taylor grew up hearing the songs of Muddy Waters and other bluesmen being played around the house. When he grew older, but was still too young to go to the clubs, he would hang around outside local blues bars, just listening and learning. As a teen, he joined the Transitors, an R&B-oriented teen quartet managed by the man who was to become his father-in-law. This band ended in the early '80s.

He was then invited by blues piano great Pinetop Perkins to join the Legendary Blues Band, which had been Muddy Waters' backup band. He was flattered, said yes, and they toured the West Coast and then Europe. His guitar playing so impressed European audiences that Taylor has been invited back, year after year. He grew to love the European audiences and recorded two albums for the French label Isabel, *Blues on the Run* and *Plays the Blues for You*. These are now available on Evidence. He has also backed Lucky Peterson and Eddie Shaw in the recording studio.

When he wasn't in Europe, he played in the many remaining Chicago blues clubs (backing a variety of acts) and finally settled in Rosa's Lounge in Chicago as his main venue. In recent years he has been influenced by jazz guitarists Kenny Burrell, Wes Montgomery, and George Benson and has integrated some of that great tradition into his playing. A fusion of blues and jazz guitar styles with some rock (Jimi Hendricks) thrown in, Taylor plays some funky direct blues with a lot of the wah-wah pedal and effects thrown in. —*Michael Erlewine*

• **Blues on the Run** / Apr. 1982 / Evidence ✦✦✦✦✦
Blues on the Run is Taylor's best disc to date. —*Bill Dahl*

Plays the Blues for You / Mar. 21, 1984 / Isabel ✦✦✦✦
Guitarist Melvin Taylor's fluid, smartly constructed solos and understated yet winning vocals are surprises on this 1984 nine-track set recorded for Isabel and recently reissued by Evidence on CD. Taylor is not a fancy or arresting singer but succeeds through his simple, effective delivery of lyrics, slight inflections, and vocal nuances. His guitar work is impressive, with skittering riffs, shifting runs, and dashing solos. Organist/pianist Lucky Peterson is an excellent second soloist, adding cute background phrases at times, then stepping forward and challenging or buttressing Taylor's playing with his own dazzling lines. —*Ron Wynn*

Johnnie "Geechie" Temple

b. Oct. 18, 1906, Canton, MS, d. Nov. 22, 1968, Jackson, MS
Guitar, Vocals / Delta Blues
Johnnie Temple is one of the great unsung heroes of the blues. A contemporary of Skip James, Son House, and other Delta legends, Temple was one of the very first to develop the now-standard bottom-string boogie bass figure, generally credited to Robert Johnson.

Born and raised in Mississippi, Temple learned to play guitar and mandolin as a child. By the time he was a teenager, he was playing house parties and various other local events. Temple moved to Chicago in the early '30s, where he quickly became part of the town's blues scene. Often, he performed with Charlie and Joe McCoy. In 1935, Temple began recording, releasing "Louise Louise Blues" the following year on Decca Records.

Although he never achieved stardom, Temple's records—which were released on a variety of record labels—sold consistently throughout the late '30s and '40s. In the '50s, his recording career stopped, but he continued to perform, frequently with Big Walter Horton and Billy Boy Arnold. Once electrified post-war blues overtook acoustic blues in the mid-'50s, Temple left Chicago and moved to Mississippi. After he returned to his homestate, he played clubs and juke joints around the Jackson area for a few years before he disappeared from the scene. Johnny Temple died in 1968. —*Cub Koda & Stephen Thomas Erlewine*

1935–39 / Document ✦✦✦✦✦
A solid collection of Temple's earliest sides, including the killer "Lead Pencil Blues." —*Cub Koda*

Sonny Terry & Brownie McGhee

b. Oct. 24, 1911, Greensboro, GA, d. Mar. 11, 1986, Mineola, NY
Harmonica, Vocals / Acoustic Country Blues
The joyous whoop that Sonny Terry naturally emitted between raucous harp blasts was as distinctive a signature sound as can possibly be imagined. Only a handful of blues harmonicists wielded as much of a lasting influence on the genre as did the sightless Terry (Buster Brown, for one, copied the whoop and all), who recorded some fine urban blues as a bandleader in addition to serving as guitarist Brownie McGhee's longtime duet partner.

Saunders Terrell's father was a folk-styled harmonica player who performed locally at dances, but blues wasn't part of his repertoire (he blew reels and jigs). Terry wasn't born blind—he lost sight in one eye when he was five, the other at age 18. That left him with extremely limited options for making any sort of feasible living, so he took to the streets armed with his trusty harmonicas. Terry soon joined forces with Piedmont pioneer Blind Boy Fuller, first recording with the guitarist in 1937 for Vocalion.

Terry's unique talents were given an extremely classy airing in 1938 when he was invited to perform at New York's Carnegie Hall at the fabled From Spirituals to Swing concert. He recorded for the Library of Congress that same year and cut his first commercial sides in 1940. Terry had met McGhee in 1939, and upon the death of Fuller, they joined forces, playing together on a 1941 McGhee date for Okeh and settling in New York as a duo in 1942. There they broke into the folk scene, working alongside Leadbelly, Josh White, and Woody Guthrie.

While Brownie McGhee was incredibly prolific in the studio during the mid-'40s, Terry was somewhat less so as a leader (perhaps most of his time was occupied by his prominent role in *Finian's Rainbow* on Broadway for approximately two years beginning in 1946). There were sides for Asch and Savoy in 1944 before three fine sessions for Capitol in 1947 (the first two featuring Stick McGhee rather than Brownie on guitar) and another in 1950.

Terry made some nice sides in an R&B mode for Jax, Jackson, Red Robin, RCA Victor, Groove, Harlem, Old Town, and Ember during the '50s, usually with Brownie close by on guitar. But it was the folk boom of the late '50s and early '60s that made Brownie and Sonny household names (at least among folk aficionados). They toured long and hard as a duo, cutting a horde of endearing acoustic duet LPs along the way, before scuttling their decades-long partnership amidst a fair amount of reported acrimony during the mid-'70s. —*Bill Dahl*

★ **The Folkways Years, 1944–1963** / Smithsonian/Folkaways ✦✦✦✦✦
While he's best known as guitarist Brownie McGhee's longtime partner, harmonica ace, and vocalist Sonny Terry made many excellent recordings as a solo act, and also recorded with Blind Boy Fuller and others. The 17 songs on this anthology include Terry playing with McGhee's brother Sticks, Pete Seeger, and others, as well as several featuring Terry's biting harmonica and wry leads relating stories of failure, triumph, and resiliency, backed by McGhee's flickering but always audible guitar. The title is a bit misleading, since the earliest date for any session is 1946 (one number), and most are done between 1955 and 1959. —*Ron Wynn*

Sonny's Story / 1960 / Original Blues Classics ✦✦✦

Sonny & Brownie at Sugar Hill / Dec. 1961 / Original Blues Classics ✦✦✦

Whoopin' / 1984 / Alligator ✦✦✦✦✦
The textbook charge usually levelled against Alligator sessions are that they're sanitized. You couldn't lodge that one against this set with a straight face; if anything, somebody turned Sonny Terry loose. It didn't hurt that Johnny Winter was around on guitar and piano, playing gritty blues with a passion. It didn't help that Terry didn't put any amplified muscle behind his harmonica, however. Otherwise, this is a strong session. —*Ron Wynn*

Sonny Terry / 1987 / Collectables ✦✦✦✦✦
Harmonica player and vocalist Sonny Terry cut some stunning material for Gotham in the early '50s. Some of it was issued, and much of it wasn't. This is a healthy chunk of things that were and weren't released, with good remastering embellishing Terry's cutting vocals and splintering harmonica. —*Ron Wynn*

Blowin' the Fuses: Golden Classics / 1989 / Collectables ✦✦✦
California Blues / 1990 / Fantasy ✦✦✦
Po' Boys / 1994 / Drive Archive ✦✦✦
McGhee and Terry in their folkie mode again, most of the ten selections stemming from a 1960 LP for Vee-Jay. One of their anthems, "Walk On," receives a spirited reading, as do "Down by the Riverside" and "Trouble in Mind." —*Bill Dahl*

Sonny Terry / 1995 / Capitol ✦✦✦✦
Some of the whooping harmonicist's finest stuff as a bandleader, dating from his 1947–1950 Capitol Records tenure. Brownie McGhee handles the guitar on two sessions, his brother Stick on the other two, but Terry is front and center on all. Contains all 16 numbers Terry did for the major label, notably "Whoopin' the Blues," "Custard Pie Blues," and "Beer Garden Blues." —*Bill Dahl*

Whoopin' The Blues: The Capitol Recordings, 1947–1950 / Oct. 1995 / Capitol ✦✦

Henry Thomas

b. 1874, Big Sandy, TX?
Pan Quill Pipes, Vocals / Acoustic Country Blues
Texas songster Henry Thomas remains a relative stranger who made some great recordings, then returned to obscurity. Evidence suggests he was an itinerant street musician, a musical hobo who rode the rails across Texas and possibly to the World Fairs in St. Louis and Chicago just before and after the turn of the century. Most agree he was the oldest African-American folk artist to produce a significant body of recordings. His projected 1874 birthdate would predate Charley Patton by a good 17 years. Like Patton and a handful of other musicians generally termed songsters (including John Hurt, Jim Jackson, Mance Lipscomb, Furry Lewis, and Leadbelly), Thomas' repertoire bridged the 19th and 20th centuries, providing a compelling glimpse into a wide range of African-American musical genres. The 23 songs he cut for Vocalion between 1927 and 1929 include a spiritual, ballads, reels, dance songs, and eight selections titled blues. Obviously dance music, his songs were geared to older dance styles shared by Black and White audiences.

Thomas' sound, like his repertoire, is unique. He capoed his guitar high up the neck and strummed it in the manner of a banjo, favoring dance rhythm over complex fingerwork. On many of his pieces, he simultaneously played the quills or panpipes, a common but seldom-recorded African-American folk instrument indigenous to Mississippi, Louisiana, and Texas. Combining the quills, a limited-range melody instrument, with his banjo-like strummed guitar produced one of the most memorable sounds in American folk music. For example, his lead-in on "Bull Doze Blues" still worked as a hook when recycled 40 years later by blues/rockers Canned Heat in their version of "Going Up the Country." "Ragtime Texas," as Thomas was known, provides a welcome inroad to 19th-century dance music, but his music is neither obscure nor merely educational: it has a timeless quality, and while it may be an acquired taste, once you catch on to it, you're hooked. —*Barry Lee Pearson*

★ **Texas Worried Blues** / Yazoo ✦✦✦✦
Songster Thomas plays a cross-section of blues and pre-blues with a unique guitar-and-panpipes instrumentation. Although it may sound archaic to the beginner, given time it will get your toes tapping and quickly become a favorite. —*Barry Lee Pearson*

James "Son" Thomas

b. Oct. 14, 1926, Eden, MS
Guitar, Vocals / Delta Blues
One of the last great traditional Delta blues musicians, James "Son" Thomas style conveyed the power, earnesty and integrity of masterful country artists like Arthur "Big Boy" Crudup. Thomas grew up on a farm in Mississippi and played in juke joints and barrelhouses before he began recording in the late '60s. He appeared in the films *Delta Blues Singer: James "Sonny Ford" Thomas* in 1970 and *Give My Poor Heart Ease: Mississippi Delta Bluesmen* in 1975, plus the short *Mississippi Delta Blues* in 1974. Thomas also made festival appearances in the '70s and '80s. He recorded for Transatlantic, Matchbox, Southern Folklore, and regional labels in the '60s, '70s, and '80s. —*Ron Wynn*

● **Son Thomas: Son Down on the Delta** / 1981 / Flying High ✦✦✦✦✦

Ramblin' Thomas

Guitar, Vocals / Texas Blues
A fine Texas blues guitarist who was also an effective singer, Ramblin' Thomas made some tremendous recordings for Paramount and Victor in the '20s and '30s. He was a brilliant slide technician though he didn't use it all that often, and his singing was riveting and distinctive. —*Ron Wynn*

Ramblin' Mind Blues / Biograph ✦✦✦✦✦
His name probably came more from his life than his playing style, but Ramblin' Thomas also roamed within his songs. Still, there are plenty of fine vocals and old-time guitar work on this session. —*Ron Wynn*

● **1928–1932** / Document ✦✦✦✦✦
Solid but thematically unvarying country blues from a fine practitioner. Ramblin' Thomas told great stories and backed himself just as nicely. —*Ron Wynn*

Rockin' Tabby Thomas

b. Baton Rouge, LA
Vocals, Piano, Guitar / Electric Louisiana Blues
A solid Louisiana vocalist who plays both guitar and piano, Rockin' Tabby Thomas has been cutting stirring recordings since the mid-'50s. He's teamed often with harmonica players Whispering Smith and Lazy Lester, and has done several sessions for Maison De Soul and various labels owned by Jay Miller.

Thomas began his musical career in San Francisco, where he was stationed while he was in the Army. After he completed his time in the service, Thompson stayed in San Francisco, playing shows and talent contests. He happened to win a talent contest, which led to a record contract with Hollywood Records. Hollywood issued "Midnight Is Calling," which gained no attention, and the label dropped Thomas.

After the failure of "Midnight Is Calling," Tabby Thomas returned to Baton Rouge. He began playing local clubs with his supporting band the Mellow, Mellow Men. In 1953, the group recorded two songs—"Thinking Blues" and "Church Members Ball"—for the Delta label. After those songs didn't gain much attention, Thomas went through a number of record labels—including Feature, Rocko, and Zynn—before having a hit on Excello Records in 1962 with "Voodoo Party."

Thomas wasn't able to record a hit followup to "Voodoo Party" and by the end of the '60s, he retired from performing music. His retirement was short-lived—in 1970, he founded his own record label, Blue Beat. In addition to releasing Thomas' own recordings, Blue Beat spotlighted emerging Baton Rouge talent. Within a few years, the label was very successful and Thomas began his own blues club, Tabby's Blues Box and Heritage Hall. By the mid-'80s, the club was the most popular blues joint in Baton Rouge.

Although he had become a successful businessman in the late '70s, Thomas continued to perform and record. All of his efforts—from his recordings and concerts, to his label and nightclub—made Tabby Thomas the leading figure of Baton Rouge's blues scene for nearly three decades. Thomas was still active in the '90s, although he wasn't performing as frequently as he had in the past. —*Ron Wynn & Stephen Thomas Erlewine*

● **King of Swamp Blues** / Maison de Soul ✦✦✦✦✦
Good, hard-rocking Louisiana blues with just a tinge of swamp from "Rockin'" Tabby Thomas. What he lacks in vocal range, he compensates for with exuberance. The backing band is no all-star unit, but they provide some solid grooves behind Thomas' surging leads. —*Ron Wynn*

Rockin' with the Blues / Maison de Soul ✦✦✦

Ron Thompson

b. Oakland, CA
Guitar, Vocals / Modern Electric Blues, Boogie-Woogie
After honing his chops behind Little Joe Blue and John Lee Hooker, guitarist Ron Thompson went solo in 1980, forming his own blues/roots-rock trio, The Resisters. *Just Like a Devil*, a 1990 release on pianist Mark Naftalin's Winner label, was culled from Thompson's appearances on Naftalin's "Blue Monday Party" radio program.

Born and raised in Oakland, CA, Thompson began playing guitar when he was 11, picking up slide guitar shortly afterward. When he was in his late teens, he was playing slide guitar with Little Joe Blue. For about five years, he worked in local Bay Area clubs, both as a solo artist and a supporting musician. In 1975, John Lee Hooker asked Thompson to join his backing band and the guitarist accepted. For the next three years, he played with Hooker, developing a national reputation.

Thompson left Hooker in 1978. Two years later, he formed his own band, the Resistors, and landed a contract with Takoma Records. Thompson's debut album, *Treat Her Like Gold,* appeared in 1983. Although he launched a solo career, Thompson continued to play with a number of other musicians, including Lowell Fulson, Etta James, and Big Mama Thornton. In 1987, his second album, *Resister Twister,* was released; it was followed shortly afterward by *Just Like A Devil.* Thompson continued to perform throughout the late '80s and '90s, although he didn't record quite as frequently. *—Bill Dahl & Stephen Thomas Erlewine*

● **Resister Twister** / 1987 / Blind Pig ✦✦✦✦✦
Rockin' blues from a former John Lee Hooker sideman. *—Robert Gordon*

Just Like a Devil / 1987 / Winner ✦✦✦

Treat Her Like Gold/No Bad Days / Takoma ✦✦✦

Big Mama Thornton (Willie Mae Thornton)

b. Dec. 11, 1926, Montgomery, AL, d. Jul. 25, 1984, Los Angeles, CA
Harmonica, Drums, Vocals / Electric West Coast Blues
Willie Mae "Big Mama" Thornton only notched one national hit in her lifetime, but it was a true monster. "Hound Dog" held down the top slot on *Billboard*'s R&B charts for seven long weeks in 1953. Alas, Elvis Presley's rocking 1956 cover was even bigger, effectively obscuring Thornton's chief claim to immortality.

That's a damned shame, because Thornton's menacing growl was indeed something special. The hefty belter first opened her pipes in church but soon embraced the blues. She toured with Sammy Green's Hot Harlem Revue during the 1940s. Thornton was ensconced on the Houston circuit when Peacock Records boss Don Robey signed her in 1951. She debuted on Peacock with "Partnership Blues" that year, backed by trumpeter Joe Scott's band.

But it was her third Peacock date with Johnny Otis' band that proved the winner. With Pete Lewis laying down some truly nasty guitar behind her, Big Mama shouted "Hound Dog," a tune whose authorship remains a bone of contention to this day (both Otis and the team of Jerry Leiber and Mike Stoller claim responsibility) and soon hit the road a star.

But it was an isolated incident. Though Thornton cut some fine Peacock follow-ups—"I Smell a Rat," "Stop Hoppin' on Me," "The Fish," "Just like a Dog"—through 1957, she never again reached the hit parade. Even Elvis was apparently unaware of her; he was handed "Hound Dog" by Freddie Bell, a Vegas lounge rocker. Early-'60s 45s for Irma, Bay-Tone, Kent, and Sotoplay did little to revive her sagging fortunes, but a series of dates for Arhoolie that included her first vinyl rendition of "Ball and Chain" in 1968 and two albums for Mercury in 1969-70 put her back in circulation (Janis Joplin's overwrought but well-intentioned cover of "Ball and Chain" didn't hurt either). Along with her imposing vocals, Thornton began to emphasize her harmonica skills during the 1960s.

Thornton was a tough cookie. She dressed like a man and took no guff from anyone. During the last years of her life the pounds fell off her once-ample frame and she became downright scrawny. Medical personnel found her lifeless body in an L.A. rooming house in 1984. *—Bill Dahl*

Ball 'N Chain / 1968 / Arhoolie ✦✦✦

They Call Me Big Mama / 1991 / MCA ✦✦✦✦✦

● **Hound Dog: The Peacock Recordings** / 1992 / MCA ✦✦✦✦✦
Let's face it, Big Mama Thornton will always be chiefly recalled for her growling 1952 reading of the classic "Hound Dog." But the other 17 sides on this collection of her 1952-1957 output for Don Robey's Peacock Records aren't exactly makeweight. Thornton's mighty roar was backed by the jumping combos of Johnny Otis and saxist Bill Harvey, producing additional gems in

"My Man Called Me," "They Call Me Big Mama," "The Fish," and a duet with the ill-fated Johnny Ace, "Yes Baby." *—Bill Dahl*

George Thorogood & the Destroyers
Guitar, Vocals / Modern Blues Rock
A blues-rock guitarist who draws his inspiration from Elmore James, Hound Dog Taylor, and Chuck Berry, George Thorogood was never earned much respect from blues purists, but he became a popular favorite in the early '80s through repeated exposure on FM radio and the arena rock circuit. Thorogood's music was always loud, simple, and direct—his riffs and licks were taken straight out of '50s Chicago blues and rock 'n' roll—but his formulaic approach helped him gain a rather large audience in the '80s, when his albums regularly went gold. Although his audience shrunk in the '90s, he never changed his musical attack and continued to tour the club circuit rather successfully.

Originally, Thorogood intended to become a professional baseball player, and he even reached the minor leagues, but decided to become a musician in 1970 after seeing John Paul Hammond in concert. Three years later, he assembled the Destroyers in his home state of Delaware; in addition to Thorogood, the band featured bassist Michael Lenn, second guitarist Ron Smith, and drummer Jeff Simon. Shortly after the group was formed, he moved them to Boston, where they became regulars on the blues club circuit, frequently supporting acts as they came to town. In 1974, they cut a batch of demos which were later released in 1979 as the *Better than the Rest* album. Within a year of recording the demos, Thorogood and the Destroyers were discovered in the Cambridge, MA club Joe's Place by John Forward, who helped them secure a contract with Rounder Records. Before they made their first album, Lenn was replaced by Billy Blough.

Thorogood and the Destroyers' eponymous debut was finally released in early 1977. The group's second album, *Move It on Over,* was released in 1978. The title track, a cover of Hank Williams' classic, was pulled as a single and it received heavy FM airplay, helping the album enter the American Top 40 and go gold. Its success led to MCA's release of *Better than the Rest,* which the band disdained. In 1980, Ron Smith left the band and the group added a saxophonist, Hank Carter and released their third album, *More George Thorogood and the Destroyers.* The following year, they opened for the Rolling Stones on several stadium dates.

Following the release of *More George Thorogood,* the guitarist signed with EMI Records, releasing his major-label debut *Bad to the Bone* in 1982. The title track of the album became his first major crossover hit, thanks to MTV's saturation airplay of the song's video; one of Thorogood's idols, Bo Diddley, appeared in the video. The album went gold and spent nearly a full year on the charts. Thorogood's next three albums after *Bad to the Bone—Maverick* (1985), *Live* (1986), *Born to Be Bad* (1988)—all went gold. Between *Bad to the Bone* and Thorogood's next album, 1985's *Maverick,* the Destroyers added a second guitarist, Steve Chrismar. In 1985, the Destroyers supported Albert Collins at Live Aid.

By the beginning of the '90s, Thorogood's audience began to decrease. None of the albums he released—1991's *Boogie People,* 1992's hits compilation *The Baddest of George Thorogood and the Destroyers,* 1993's *Haircut—*went gold, even though *Haircut*'s title track was a number-two album rock hit. Despite his declining record sales, Thorogood continued to tour blues and rock clubs and he usually drew large crowds. *—Stephen Thomas Erlewine*

George Thorogood & the Destroyers / 1978 / Rounder ✦✦✦✦✦
Contains Thorogood's crowd-pleasing rendition of John Lee Hooker's "One Bourbon, One Scotch, One Beer." Its basic approach—heavy on Thorogood's bluesy guitar playing—serves as the prototype for every Destroyers record that followed. *—William Ruhlmann*

Move It on Over / Jan. 1979 / Rounder ✦✦✦
In 1978, George Thorogood was just beginning to make some noise on the blues-rock circuit. This was his second album, and what's now almost a cliche then sounded fresh and vital. Thorogood's energy, rousing vocals, and driving guitar playing came roaring through on inspired covers of Elmore James' "The Sky Is Crying," Bo Diddley's "Who Do You Love," and Chuck Berry's "It Wasn't Me." He even did a credible Piedmont blues on

Brownie McGhee's "So Much Trouble." While Thorogood went on to make more commercially succesful albums, the spirit and innocence in his early releases has seldom been duplicated. This Rounder CD reissue returns him to a simpler, and in some ways superior, period. —*Ron Wynn*

More George Thorogood and the Destroyers / 1980 / Rounder ◆◆

George Thorogood was honing his focus and getting the Destroyers concept down pat on this 1980 album. He hadn't yet become so established and comfortable that his rocking blues licks and vocals were more show business than intensity and energy. Thorogood's playing and singing on such tracks as "House of Blue Lights," "Night Time," and "I'm Wanted" were earnest enough to make the treatments convincing, and retain interest. While this wasn't quite as memorable as his earlier dates, George Thorogood still had the hunger that fueled his breakout sessions. —*Ron Wynn*

Bad to the Bone / 1982 / EMI America ◆◆◆◆

Though songs such as "Back to Wentzville" are credited to G. Thorogood, he'd be the first to admit that they are proudly derivative of Chuck Berry and his other mentors. The title track, another Thorogood copyright, has become ubiquitous in *Terminator 2* and the *Problem Child* movies and elsewhere, but it's still terrific. —*William Ruhlmann*

● **The Baddest of George Thorogood and the Destroyers** / 1992 / EMI America ◆◆◆◆

Aptly-titled, this album offers a dozen tracks that cleanse the church of rock 'n' roll of all but its most basic elements: guitar, bass, drums, and a pile of Chuck Berry, Bo Diddley, and Rolling Stones licks. Delaware's George Thorogood has never quite captured his wildman live presence in the studio, but having all his best material gathered on one disc—including "Bad to the Bone," "Move It on Over," and "One Bourbon, One Scotch, One Beer"—makes for a great party. Steve Morse's liner notes are brief but, like the songs, get right to the point…cut to the bone, you might say. —*Roch Parisien*

Haircut / 1993 / EMI America ◆◆

You wouldn't expect any changes from George Thorogood, whose pile-driving rocking-blues and boogie have maintained their appeal despite the emergence of numerous similar-sounding ensembles. Thorogood's rough-hewn singing and always tantalizing playing are on target through the usual mix of originals and covers (this time including Bo Diddley and Willie Dixon). Besides the bonus of major label engineering and production, Thorogood's work has never lost its edge because he avoids becoming indulgent or a parody, and continues to sound genuinely interested in and a fan of the tunes he's doing. —*Ron Wynn*

Henry Townsend (Too Tight Henry)

b. Oct. 27, 1909, Shelby, MS
Guitar, Piano, Vocals / Acoustic Country Blues, Piano Blues
Influenced by Roosevelt Sykes and Lonnie Johnson, Henry Townsend was a commanding musician, adept on both piano and guitar. During the '20s and '30s, Townsend was one of the musicians that helped make St. Louis one of the blues centers of America.

Townsend arrived in St. Louis when he was around ten years old, just before the '20s began. By the end of the '20s, he had landed a record contract with Columbia, cutting several sides of open-tuning slide guitar for the label. Two years later, he made some similar recordings for Paramount. During this time, Townsend began playing the piano, learning the instrument by playing along with Roosevelt Sykes records. Within a few years, he was able to perform concerts with pianists like Walter Davis and Henry Brown.

During the '30s, Townsend was a popular session musician, performing with many of the era's most popular artists. By the late '30s, he had cut several tracks for Bluebird. Those were among the last recordings he ever made as a leader. During the '40s and '50s, Townsend continued to perform and record as a session musician, but he never made any solo records.

In 1960, he led a few sessions, but they didn't receive much attention. Toward the end of the '60s, Townsend became a staple on the blues and folk festivals in America, which led to a comeback. He cut a number of albums for Adelphi and played shows throughout America. By the end of the '70s, he had switched from Adelphi to Nighthawk Records.

Townsend had become an elder statesmen of St. Louis blues by the early '80s, recording albums for Wolf and Swingmaster and playing a handful of shows every year. *That's The Way I Do It,* a documentary about Townsend, appeared on public television in 1984. During the late '80s, Townsend was nearly retired, but he continued to play the occasional concert. —*Cub Koda & Stephen Thomas Erlewine*

Mule / 1980 / Nighthawk ◆◆◆◆

Venerable St. Louis guitarist and pianist Henry Townsend mostly stuck to the keyboard on this outstanding session. It was forceful, wonderfully sung and alternately moving, impressive and inspiring. —*Ron Wynn*

● **Henry Townsend & Henry Spaulding** / 1986 / Wolf ◆◆◆◆

Topflight country-blues from Townsend, with the bonus of two cuts from the seldom-heard Henry Spaulding. —*Cub Koda*

Bessie Tucker

Vocals / Classic Female Blues
Though gifted with a huge voice which she used extremely effectively, Bessie Tucker's not among the most well-known "classic" blues singers. But she was certainly one of the hottest and bawdiest vocalists who worked during that era, recording in the late '20s in Memphis with pianist K.D. Johnson. Her sessions were eventually reissued by Magpie. —*Ron Wynn*

★ **Complete Works (1928–1929)** / 1991 / Document ◆◆◆◆

Luther Tucker

b. Jan. 20, 1936, Memphis, TN, d. Jun. 18, 1993, Greenbrae, CA
Guitar / Chicago Blues
Guitarist Luther Tucker was born on January 20, 1936, in Memphis, TN, but relocated to Chicago's South side when Tucker was around seven years of age. His father, a carpenter, built Tucker his first guitar and his mother, who played boogie-woogie piano, introduced him to Big Bill Broonzy around that time. He went on to study guitar with Robert Jr. Lockwood, for whom he had the greatest admiration and respect. Tucker worked with Little Walter Jacobs for seven years and played on many of Walter's classic sides. He also recorded with Otis Rush, Robben Ford, Sonny Boy Williamson II, Jimmy Rogers, Snooky Prior, Muddy Waters, John Lee Hooker, Elvin Bishop, and James Cotton.

In the mid-'60s, Tucker was featured in the James Cotton Blues Band and traveled with that band extensively. He relocated to Marin County, CA, in 1973 and formed the Luther Tucker Band. He played in clubs in the San Francisco Bay Area until his death on June 18, 1993, in Greenbrae, CA. Luther Tucker, who was soft-spoken and even shy, was one of a handful of backup artists (the Four Aces/Jukes were others) who helped to create and shape the small combo sound of Chicago blues. Unfortunately, they seldom get much credit. Yet, as the history of Chicago blues gets written, there will be more and more time to discover the wonderful understated rhythmic guitar mastery of Luther Tucker. —*Michael Erlewine*

Sad Hours / Antone's ◆◆◆◆

Sadly, this disc was issued posthumously. —*Bill Dahl*

Tommy Tucker (Robert Higginbotham)

b. Mar. 5, 1933, Springfield, OH, d. Jan. 17, 1982, Newark, NJ
Piano, Vocals / Electric R&B
When Tommy Tucker ordered his lady to "put on her high-heel sneakers" in 1964, the whole world was listening, judging from the myriad of covers and sequels that followed in its wake.

Robert Higginbotham (Tucker's legal handle) grew up in Springfield, getting his little fingers accustomed to the ivories by age seven. Tucker joined saxist Bobby Wood's band in the late '40s as its piano player. When vocal groups became the rage, the band switched gears and became the Cavaliers, a doo wop outfit that remained intact into the late '50s. Tucker put together his own combo after that to play bars in Dayton, his personnel including guitarist Weldon Young and bassist Brenda Jones.

The trio eventually relocated to Newark, NJ, setting Tucker up for his debut solo session in 1961 for Atco. "Rock and Roll Machine" was issued as by Tee Tucker and already exhibited the gritty, Ray Charles-inflected vocal delivery that Tucker later used to great advantage. His traveling companions did pretty well for themselves, too: renamed Dean & Jean, they hit big in 1963–64 with the lighthearted duets "Tra La La La Suzy" and "Hey Jean, Hey Dean" for Rust Records.

Tommy Tucker fortuitously hooked up with Atlantic Records co-founder Herb Abramson, who was working as an independent R&B producer during the early '60s. Among their early collaborations was the lowdown Jimmy Reed-style shuffle "Hi-Heel Sneakers" (Dean Young was the nasty lead guitarist). Abramson leased it to Checker Records and watched it sail to the upper reaches of the pop charts in early 1964. A terrific Checker LP and a trip to Great Britain were among the immediate upshot for the organist.

R&B star Don Covay co-wrote Tucker's follow-up, "Long Tall Shorty," an amusing tune in a similar groove. It barely scraped the lower end of the charts, and Tucker never scored another hit. That didn't stop Abramson from trying, though—he produced Tucker singing a soulful "That's Life" in 1966 for his own Festival label, while "Alimony," another standout Checker 45, certainly deserved a better reception than it got in 1965.

Although the majority of his waxings were under Abramson's supervision, Tucker did travel to Chicago in 1966 to record with producer Willie Dixon in an effort to jump-start his fading career. "I'm Shorty" had Dixon contributing harmony vocals and Big Walter Horton on harp, but it didn't do the trick.

Abramson admirably stuck by his protégé, recording him for at least another decade, but most of the mixed results just gathered dust in his vaults. Tucker was still musically active when he died, a relatively young man, in 1982. —Bill Dahl

● **Hi Heel Sneakers** / 1964 / Checker ✦✦✦✦✦
Until some enterprising CD reissue label assembles a decent Tucker package, this ancient slab of vinyl will remain a prime collector's item. A dozen of his best blues and soul outings for producer Herb Abramson, including the two hits, the grinding soul rockers "Just for a Day," "I Don't Want 'Cha," and "I Warned You About Him" (oodles of Ray Charles influence on all of 'em), and an absolutely stunning "Come Rain or Come Shine." —Bill Dahl

Mother Tucker / 1974 / Red Lightnin' ✦✦✦
Leftovers from deep in the Abramson archives. A precious few tracks—"Lean Greens," "Drunk"—possess the same gritty charm that invested Tucker's greatest hit, "Hi-Heel Sneakers" (here in longer, unedited form with Tucker's faltering organ solo intact). Most of the 16-song LP is comprised of demo tapes and other flotsam that doesn't present the keyboardist in the best light. —Bill Dahl

Big Joe Turner

b. May 18, 1911, Kansas City, MO, d. Nov. 24, 1985, Inglewood, CA
Vocals / Jump Blues, Jazz
The premier blues shouter of the postwar era, Big Joe Turner's roar could rattle the very foundation of any gin joint he sang in—and that's without a microphone. Turner was a resilient figure in the history of blues; he effortlessly spanned boogie-woogie, jump blues, even the first wave of rock 'n' roll, enjoying great success in each genre.

Turner, whose powerful physique certainly matched his vocal might, was a product of the swinging, wide-open Kansas City scene. Even in his teens, the big-boned Turner looked mature enough to gain entry to various K.C. niteries. He ended up simultaneously tending bar and singing the blues before hooking up with boogie piano master Pete Johnson during the early '30s. Theirs was a partnership that would endure for 13 years.

The pair initially traveled to New York at John Hammond's behest in 1936. On December 23, 1938, they appeared on the fabled Spirituals to Swing concert at Carnegie Hall on a bill with Big Bill Broonzy, Sonny Terry, the Golden Gate Quartet, and Count Basie. Big Joe and Johnson performed "Low Down Dog" and "It's All Right, Baby" on the historic show, kicking off a boogie-woogie craze that landed them a long-running slot at the Cafe Society (along with piano giants Meade Lux Lewis and Albert Ammons).

As 1938 came to a close, Turner and Johnson waxed the thundering "Roll 'Em Pete" for Vocalion. It was a thrilling up-tempo number anchored by Johnson's crashing 88s, and Turner would re-record it many times over the decades. Turner and Johnson

waxed their seminal blues "Cherry Red" the next year for Vocalion with trumpeter Hot Lips Page and a full combo in support. In 1940, the massive shouter moved over to Decca and cut "Piney Brown Blues" with Johnson rippling the ivories. But not all of Turner's Decca sides teamed him with Johnson; Willie "The Lion" Smith accompanied him on the mournful "Careless Love," while Freddie Slack's Trio provided backing for "Rocks in My Bed" in 1941.

Turner ventured out to the West Coast during the war years, building quite a following while ensconced on the L.A. circuit. In 1945, he signed on with National Records and cut some fine small combo platters under Herb Abramson's supervision. Turner remained with National through 1947, belting an exuberant "My Gal's a Jockey" that became his first national R&B smash. Contracts didn't stop him from waxing an incredibly risqué two-part "Around the Clock" for the aptly named Stag imprint (as Big Vernon) in 1947. There were also solid sessions for Aladdin that year that included a wild vocal duel with one of Turner's principal rivals, Wynonie Harris, on the ribald two-part "Battle of the Blues."

Few West Coast indie labels of the late '40s didn't boast at least one or two Turner titles in their catalogs. The shouter bounced from RPM to Down Beat/Swing Time to MGM (all those dates were anchored by Johnson's piano) to Texas-based Freedom (which moved some of their masters to Specialty) to Imperial in 1950 (his New Orleans backing crew there included a young Fats Domino on piano). But apart from the 1950 Freedom 78, "Still in the Dark," none of Big Joe's records were selling particularly well. When Atlantic Records bosses Abramson and Ahmet Ertegun fortuitously dropped by the Apollo Theater to check out Count Basie's band one day, they discovered that Turner had temporarily replaced Jimmy Rushing as the Basie band's front man, and he was having a tough go of it. Atlantic picked up his spirits by picking up his recording contract, and Big Joe Turner's heyday was about to commence.

At Turner's first Atlantic date in April of 1951, he imparted a gorgeously world-weary reading to the moving blues ballad "Chains of Love" (co-penned by Ertegun and pianist Harry Van Walls) that restored him to the uppermost reaches of the R&B charts. From there, the hits came in droves: "Chill Is On," "Sweet Sixteen" (yeah, the same downbeat blues B.B. King's usually associated with; Turner did it first), and "Don't You Cry" were all done in New York, and all hit big.

Big Joe Turner had no problem adapting his prodigious pipes to whatever regional setting he was in. In 1953, he cut his first R&B chart-topper, the storming rocker "Honey Hush" (later covered by Johnny Burnette and Jerry Lee Lewis), in New Orleans, with trombonist Pluma Davis and tenor saxman Lee Allen in rip-roaring support. Before the year was through, he stopped off in Chicago to record with slide guitarist Elmore James' considerably rougher-edged combo and hit again with the salacious "T.V. Mama."

Prolific Atlantic house writer Jesse Stone was the source of Turner's biggest smash of all, "Shake, Rattle and Roll," which proved his second chart-topper in 1954. With the Atlantic braintrust reportedly chiming in on the chorus behind Turner's rumbling lead, the song sported enough pop possibilities to merit a considerably cleaned-up cover by Bill Haley & the Comets (and a subsequent version by Elvis Presley that came a lot closer to the original leering intent).

Suddenly, at the age of 43, Big Joe Turner was a rock star. His jumping follow-ups—"Well All Right," "Flip Flop and Fly," "Hide and Seek," "Morning, Noon, and Night," "The Chicken and the Hawk"—all mined the same goodtime groove as "Shake, Rattle, and Roll," with crisp backing from New York's top session aces and typically superb production by Ertegun and Jerry Wexler.

Turner turned up on a couple episodes of the groundbreaking TV program *Showtime at the Apollo* during the mid-'50s, commanding center stage with a joyous rendition of "Shake, Rattle and Roll" in front of saxman Paul "Hucklebuck" Williams' band. Nor was the silver screen immune to his considerable charms: Turner mimed a couple of numbers in the 1957 film *Shake Rattle & Rock* (Fats Domino and Mike "Mannix" Connors also starred in the flick).

Updating the pre-war number "Corrine, Corrina" was an inspired notion that provided Turner with another massive seller in 1956. But after the two-sided hit "Rock a While"/"Lipstick Powder and Paint" later that year, his Atlantic output swiftly faded from commercial acceptance. Atlantic's recording strategy wisely involved recording Turner in a jazzier setting for the adult-oriented album market; to that end, a Kansas City-styled set (with his former partner Johnson at the piano stool) was laid down in 1956 and remains a linchpin of his legacy.

Turner stayed on at Atlantic into 1959, but nobody bought his violin-enriched remake of "Chains of Love" (on the other hand, a revival of "Honey Hush" with King Curtis blowing a scorching sax break from the same session was a gem in its own right). The '60s didn't produce too much of lasting substance for the shouter—he actually cut an album with longtime admirer Haley and his latest batch of Comets in Mexico City in 1966!

But by the tail end of the decade, Big Joe Turner's essential contributions to blues history were beginning to receive proper recognition; he cut LPs for BluesWay and Blues Time. During the '70s and '80s, Turner recorded prolifically for Norman Granz's jazz-oriented Pablo label. These were super-relaxed impromptu sessions that often paired the allegedly illiterate shouter with various jazz luminaries in what amounted to loose-ly-run jam sessions. Turner contentedly roared the familiar lyrics of one or another of his hits, then sat back while somebody took a lengthy solo. Other notable album projects included a 1983 collaboration with Roomful of Blues, *Blues Train*, for Muse. Although health problems and the size of his humongous frame forced him to sit down during his latter-day performances, Turner continued to tour until shortly before his death in 1985. They called him the Boss of the Blues, and the appellation was truly a fitting one: when Big Joe Turner shouted a lyric, you were definitely at his beck and call. —*Bill Dahl*

★ **Big, Bad & Blue: The Big Joe Turner Anthology** / Dec. 30, 1938–Jan. 26, 1983 / Rhino ✦✦✦✦
Rhino has done a stellar job of cross-licensing to present an exhaustive three-disc, 62-track compilation that traces the booming jump blues belter's recording career from its Kansas City-bred beginnings with pianist Pete Johnson in 1938 through the postwar years with the National, Aladdin, Down Beat, and Freedom labels and on into his R&B heyday on Atlantic from 1951 to 1959. Of course, all the great prototypical rockers are aboard—"Honey Hush," "Shake, Rattle, and Roll," "Flip Flop and Fly," "Corrina, Corrina"—and the set closes with three far more recent entries that are the weakest tracks on the entire anthology. The sheer power of Big Joe's pipes was overwhelming, his combos cooked mercilessly, and this set is one to get. —*Bill Dahl*

☆ **Complete 1940–1944** / Nov. 11, 1940–Nov. 13, 1944 / Official ✦✦✦✦✦
Big Joe Turner's 25 Decca recordings are all included on this excellent set. The music is consistently exciting and finds the blues singer in prime form. His accompaniment is quite varied and always colorful with such pianists as Art Tatum, Pete Johnson, Willie "the Lion" Smith (a perfect match), Sam Price and the surprisingly effective Freddie Slack all getting their spots. Turner had a remarkably long and commercially successful career considering that he never changed his basic approach; he just never went out of style. —*Scott Yanow*

Every Day in the Week / Sep. 8, 1941–Apr. 13, 1967 / Decca ✦✦✦
Most of the material on this grab bag dates from early- and mid-'40s sessions for Decca. Rather muted and jazzy in feel, they're made more interesting or tedious, depending on your perspective, by the inclusion of many alternate takes (some previously unissued). As these are grouped together one after another, it can make tough listening for the general fan, although Turner completists will appreciate the attention to detail. Rounding out the collection are four 1963–64 tracks, which awkwardly update Turner's R&B with modern soul and pop touches, and a track from a 1967 Bluesway LP. —*Richie Unterberger*

Tell Me Pretty Baby / Nov. 1947–1949 / Arhoolie ✦✦✦✦
Lusty, romping jump blues and boogies from 1947–1949 that teams Big Joe Turner with his longtime piano partner Pete Johnson and a coterie of solid L.A. sessioneers. The two dozen entries include party rockers like "Wine-O-Baby Boogie," "Christmas Date Boogie," "I Don't Dig It," and an incredibly raunchy two-part "Around the Clock Blues" (where Turner spends his time in a by-the-hour sexual tryst). —*Bill Dahl*

Jumpin' the Blues / 1948 / Arhoolie ✦✦✦✦✦
Superb collection of Turner tracks cut with Pete Johnson in jump

blues, jive, boogie, and Kansas City swing style. Turner is at his shouting, hollering best, while Johnson pounds out the boogie woogie riffs and licks with a vengeance. —*Ron Wynn*

★ **Greatest Hits** / Apr. 19, 1951–Jan. 22, 1958 / Atlantic ✦✦✦✦✦
The best single-disc collection available of Turner's seminal 1950s Atlantic sides (21 sides in all). Most of the essential stuff is here—the world-weary blues ballads "Chains of Love" and "Sweet Sixteen," the rockers "Shake, Rattle and Roll," "Flip Flop and Fly," and "Boogie Woogie Country Girl," and a lusty "Well All Right" that rates with Turner's best jump blues outings ever. —*Bill Dahl*

Texas Style / Apr. 26, 1971 / Evidence ✦✦✦
Big Joe Turner was well beyond his prime when he recorded these eight tracks for the Black and Blue label in 1971, but even at less than peak strength he could still shout, roar, and wail the blues with resonance and presence. This Evidence CD reissue features him backed by a small combo with the great "Papa" Jo Jones striding on drums, Milt Buckner adding rollicking piano licks, and bassist Slam Stewart keeping things steadily moving. Turner's treatment of "TV Mama" was not as majestic as the original with Elmore James; nor were "Cherry Red" or "Rock Me Baby" definitive versions. But they were nonetheless emphatic, rugged, and rocking, with Turner's projection, delivery, and tone alternately defiant, menacing (in a showman-like way), and suggestive. —*Ron Wynn*

Nobody in Mind / 1975 / Original Jazz Classics ✦✦✦✦✦
Blues singer Big Joe Turner is in good form on this late-period session. In addition to his usual rhythm section (featuring guitarist Pee Wee Crayton), Turner is joined by two notable soloists: trumpeter Roy Eldridge (whose determination makes up for his occasional misses) and vibraphonist Milt Jackson. Other than "Red Sails in the Sunset" (which is largely turned into a blues), the music is fairly typical for Turner but the spirit and sincerity of the singer and his sidemen make this CD reissue worth picking up. —*Scott Yanow*

Things That I Used to Do / Feb. 8, 1977 / Original Jazz Classics ✦✦✦✦✦
This is one of Big Joe Turner's best albums of his last period. Turner is in fine form and joined by some superb blues and jazz musicians. Altoist Eddie "Cleanhead" Vinson (pity that he didn't have a vocal duet with Turner) and trumpeter Blue Mitchell get some solo space as does the veteran R&B tenor Wild Bill Moore, pianist Lloyd Glenn and guitarist Gary Bell. Mitchell can be heard on many of the tunes setting hot ensemble riffs. There are some loose spots but the spirit is definitely there and Turner's voice can be heard still in its prime on such tunes as "Jelly Jelly Blues," "Shake It and Break It," and "St. Louis Blues." Fun music. —*Scott Yanow*

Patcha, Patcha All Night Long / Apr. 11, 1985 / Original Jazz Classics ✦✦✦
This CD reissue, which is subtitled "Joe Turner Meets Jimmy Witherspoon," does not quite deliver on its promise. Turner (who would pass away within a year) and Witherspoon only actually meet up on the first two numbers and, other than some interplay on "Patcha, Patcha," the matchup generates few sparks. However the individual features (two songs apiece) are excellent, particularly Witherspoon's "You Got Me Runnin'" and Turner's "The Chicken and the Hawk." In addition there are many fine solos from altoist Red Holloway, Lee Allen on tenor, and guitarist Gary Bell. This is a worthwhile and obviously historic set, recommended as much to blues as jazz collectors. —*Scott Yanow*

Rhythm & Blues Years / 1986 / Atlantic ✦✦✦✦✦
This album picks up the rest of the 1950s Atlantic Records motherlode. The Chicago-cut double-entendre gem "TV Mama" (with Elmore James on guitar), the lighthearted rockers "Rock a While," "Morning Noon & Night," and "Lipstick, Powder, & Paint," and a rip-snorting remake of Turner's classic "Roll 'Em Pete," here titled "(We're Gonna) Jump for Joy," that in its own way rivals the original (King Curtis' blistering sax solo doesn't hurt), are among the many highlights on the 28-song collection. —*Bill Dahl*

I've Been to Kansas City, Vol. 1 / 1990 / Decca/MCA ✦✦✦✦
Sixteen of Big Joe's earliest sides (1940–1941) for Decca, many but not all with the immortal pianist Pete Johnson rolling the ivories behind the Kansas City shouter (other sidemen include pianists Art Tatum, Sammy Price, and Willie "The Lion" Smith,

guitarist Oscar Moore, and trumpet ace Hot Lips Page). Big Joe sounds young and virile on "Piney Brown Blues," "Wee Baby Blues," and "Nobody in Mind," and there's an early reading of "Corrine, Corrina" that's considerably different from his subsequent rock 'n' roll hit version. —*Bill Dahl*

Have No Fear, Big Joe Turner is Here / 1994 / Savoy Jazz ✦✦✦✦
Producer Herb Abramson's first encounters with Big Joe Turner weren't at Atlantic, but for the National logo, where Turner paused from 1945 to 1947 and cut the 26 swinging numbers on this collection. For once, the CD format limits the amount of selections rather than enlarging it; the original two-LP version of this package boasted a few more cuts. Pete Johnson returns to run the 88s on the first seven numbers (including a two-part cover of Saunders King's "S.K. Blues"), and familiar names like saxman Wild Bill Moore and drummer Red Saunders also turn up. "Sally Zu-Zazz," "I Got Love for Sale," and "My Gal's a Jockey" capture the peerless shouter at his ribald best. —*Bill Dahl*

Jumpin' with Joe: the Complete Aladdin & Imperial Recordings / Jan. 11, 1994 / EMI America ✦✦✦✦✦
Big Joe Turner's remarkable recordings for Atlantic and Decca have been frequently reissued and evaluated. But his singles for other labels haven't gotten similar treatment, which makes this 18-cut single-disc anthology of Aladdin and Imperial material so welcome. These were recorded in the late '40s and early '50s and were closer to the Kansas City swing Turner had done earlier in his career; there was more emphasis on lyric interpretation, swing, and timing than sheer volume and volcanic, non-stop hollering. Although these songs aren't remembered as fondly as the landmark Atlantic numbers, they're just as important a part of Turner's legacy. —*Ron Wynn*

Jazz Heritage: Early Big Joe (1940–1944) / MCA ✦✦✦✦✦
Vital early '40s Joe Turner when he was ripping and shouting the blues, doing Kansas City Swing numbers and working with long-time friend and musical companion Pete Johnson. These are tracks cut for Decca, among them a pre-hit version of "Corrina, Corrina" and the tremendous composition "Wee Baby Blues." —*Ron Wynn*

Ike Turner

b. Nov. 5, 1931
Guitar, Piano, Vocals / Soul Blues, R&B
It is arguably true that Ike Turner would have never amounted to more than a footnote of rock history if he hadn't joined forces

with Tina Turner in 1960. But as a solo artist, he's an important footnote. In 1951, he made a lasting contribution to the music by playing piano on Jackie Brenston's "Rocket 88," which is often cited as one of the very first rock 'n' roll records. That session was one of the first blues/R&B/rock 'n' roll dates produced in Sun Studios in Memphis; Turner learned guitar shortly afterwards, and backed up other R&B artists at Sun in the early '50s. Throughout the decade, the guitarist and piano player was a prolific session player, contributing to records by blues legends Elmore James, Howlin' Wolf, and Otis Rush.

Ike also backed a host of obscure R&B artists in his early years, occasionally issuing discs under his name. Not much of a singer, both his own records and the ones he contributed to and/or produced often showcased his stinging, bluesy licks, and the best of his solo outings tended to be his instrumentals. He continued to put out the occasional solo session and work with other artists after he hooked up with Tina, sometimes under the name Ike Turner's Kings of Rhythm. His career has lurched along in obscurity since he broke up with Tina in the mid-'70s, though he remains active. —*Richie Unterberger*

● **I Like Ike! The Best of Ike Turner** / 1994 / Rhino ✦✦✦✦✦
18 songs spotlighting Turner's work as a bandleader, guitarist, and solo artist from 1951 to 1972, concentrating heavily on his work in the 1950s and early '60s. Leading off with Jackie Brenston's classic "Rocket 88," it includes rare singles featuring Turner by Dennis Binder, the Sly Fox, Willie King, and others, along with rare Turner solo recordings, some under the pseudonym Icky Renrut, and a 1958 45 with Tina, then known as Annie Mae Bullock, on backing vocals. These singers are usually journeymen, frankly, and the material is rather standard-issue R&B; better are the instrumentals, which give Ike a chance to really strut his distinctive tone. —*Richie Unterberger*

Rhythm Rockin' Blues / Nov. 1995 / Ace ✦✦✦

1958–1959 / Paula ✦✦✦✦✦
Ever the hustler, Ike Turner found himself picking up some extra money on a road trip through Chicago recording for Cobra Records both as a bandleader and sideman. After contributing the sparkle to several Otis Rush classics (an alternate of one of them, "Keep On Loving Me Baby," is found here) and some early Buddy Guy sides, Turner also recorded a handful of sides, scant few of them seeing release until now. This CD collects them all up, including surviving alternate versions and is a delightful fly-on-the-wall invite to a 1950s Chicago blues session. —*Cub Koda*

255

V

Vaughan Brothers

Group / Modern Electric Blues

Brothers Jimmie and Stevie Ray Vaughan got together for what would tragically be their first and last studio collaboration in the spring of 1990. That August, just before the release of the album, Stevie was killed in a helicopter crash. The public heard "Tick Tock" for the first time at Stevie's funeral in Dallas. *—Dan Forte*

Family Style / Jan. 1990 / Epic ✦✦✦

With slick production from Nile Rodgers and employing neither guitarist's band (Double Trouble nor the Fabulous Thunderbirds), this is bluesy, but far from purist. Jimmie makes his vocal debut on "White Boots" and "Good Texan," and the brothers blur the lines between their expected guitar styles—Stevie sometimes going for a less sustainy twang, Jimmie moving into Albert King territory. When standard blues is the order of the day (the slow instrumental "Brothers"), the key word is "standard"—bordering on run-of-the-mill. Instrumentals "D/FW" and "Hillbillies from Outer Space" fare better—offering ZZ Top crunch and Santo & Johnny steel, respectively. *—Dan Forte*

Jimmie Vaughan

b. Mar. 20, 1951, Dallas, TX

Guitar, Vocals / Modern Electric Blues

As a founding member of the Fabulous Thunderbirds, Jimmie Vaughan was one of the leading Austin, TX, guitarists of the late '70s and '80s, responsible for opening the national market up for gritty roadhouse blues and R&B. Influenced by guitarists like Freddie King, B.B. King, and Albert King, Vaughan developed a tough, lean sound that became one of the most recognizable sounds of '70s and '80s blues and blues-rock. For most of his career, Vaughan co-led the Fabulous Thunderbirds with vocalist Kim Wilson. It wasn't until 1994 that he launched a full-fledged solo career.

Born and raised in Dallas, TX, Jimmie Vaughan began playing guitar as a child. Initially, Vaughan was influenced by both blues and rock 'n' roll. While he was in his teens, he played in a number of garage rock bands, none of which attained any success. At the age of 19, he left Dallas and moved to Austin. For his first few years in Austin, Vaughan played in a variety of blues bar bands. In 1972, he formed his own group, the Storm, which supported many touring blues musicians.

In 1974, Vaughan met a vocalist and harmonica player named Kim Wilson. Within a year, the pair had formed the Fabulous Thunderbirds along with bassist Keith Furguson and drummer Mike Buck. For four years, the T-Birds played local Texas clubs, gaining a strong fan base. By the end of the decade, the group had signed a major label contract with Chrysalis Records and seemed bound for national stardom. However, none of their albums became hits and they were dropped by Chrysalis at the end of 1982.

At the same time the T-Birds were left without a recording contract, Jimmie's younger brother, Stevie Ray Vaughan, came storming upon the national scene with his debut album, *Texas Flood.* For the next few years, Stevie Ray dominated not only the Texan blues scene, but the entire American scene, while Jimmie and the Thunderbirds were struggling to survive. The T-Birds finally received a new major label contract in 1986 with Epic/Associated and their first album for the label, *Tuff Enuff,* was a surprise hit, selling over a million copies and spawning a Top Ten hit title track.

The Fabulous Thunderbirds spent the rest of the '80s trying to replicate the success of *Tuff Enuff,* often pursuing slicker, more commercially-oriented directions. By 1989, Jimmie Vaughan was frustrated by the group's musical direction and left the band. Before launching a solo career, he recorded a duet album with his brother, Stevie Ray, *Family Style.* Following the completion of the record, Stevie Ray Vaughan died in a tragic helicopter crash in August of 1990. *Family Style* appeared just a few months later, in the fall of 1990.

After Stevie Ray's death, Jimmie took a couple of years off, in order to grieve and recoup. After a couple of years, he began playing the occasional concert. In 1994, he returned with his first solo album, *Strange Pleasures,* which received good reviews and sold respectably. Vaughan supported *Strange Pleasures* with a national tour. *—Stephen Thomas Erlewine*

● **Strange Pleasure** / 1994 / Epic ✦✦✦✦

Vaughan's solid solo debut is loaded with good-time Austin roadhouse blues-influenced rock. Guest artists include Lou Ann Barton, Dr. John and Nile Rodgers. Lovers of a good earthy groove and fine economical guitar work should pick up on this. *—Rick Clark*

Stevie Ray Vaughan

b. Oct. 3, 1954, Dallas, TX, **d.** Aug. 27, 1990, East Troy, WI

Guitar / Modern Electric Blues

With his astonishingly accomplished guitar style, Stevie Ray Vaughan ignited the blues revival of the '80s. Vaughan drew equally from bluesmen like Albert King, Otis Rush, and Muddy Waters, and rock 'n' roll players like Jimi Hendrix and Lonnie Mack, as well as the stray jazz guitarist like Kenny Burrell, developing a uniquely eclectic and fiery style that sounded like no other guitarist, regardless of genre. Vaughan bridged the gap between blues and rock like no other artist had since the late '60s. For the next seven years, Stevie Ray was the leading light in American blues, consistently selling out concerts while his albums regularly went gold. His tragic death in 1990 only emphasized his influence in blues and American rock 'n' roll and how much he changed the country's musical landscape.

Born and raised in the Oak Cliff section of Dallas, Stevie Ray Vaughan began playing guitar as a child, influenced by older brother Jimmie. Stevie Ray learned how to play by listening to Jimmie and stacks of blues and rock 'n' roll records, ranging from Otis Rush to Lonnie Mack. When he was in junior high school, he began playing in a number of garage bands, which occasionally landed gigs in local nightclubs. By the time he was 17, he had dropped out of high school to concentrate on playing music. Vaughan's first real band was the Cobras, who played clubs and bars in Austin during the mid-'70s. Following that group's demise, he formed Triple Threat in 1975, which was designed to cover only blues and R&B songs. Triple Threat also featured bassist Jackie Newhouse, drummer Chris Layton, and vocalist Lou Ann Barton. After a few years of playing Texas bars, clubs, and roadhouses, Barton left the band in 1978. The group decided to continue performing under the name Double Trouble, which was inspired by the Otis Rush song of the same name; Stevie Ray became the band's lead singer.

For the next few years, Stevie Ray Vaughan and Double Trouble played the Austin area, becoming one of the most popular bands in Texas. In 1982, the group finally began gathering some national recognition. First, Mick Jagger invited the band to play a private party for the Rolling Stones after witnessing a videotape of Vaughan in action. More importantly, Vaughan and Double Trouble played the Montreux Festival that year, and their performance caught the attention of David Bowie and Jackson Browne. After Double Trouble's performance, Bowie asked Vaughan to play on his forthcoming album, while Browne offered Double Trouble free recording time at his Los Angeles studio, Downtown; both offers were accepted. Stevie Ray laid down the lead guitar tracks for what became Bowie's *Let's Dance* album in late 1982. Shortly afterward, John Hammond, Sr. landed Vaughan and Double Trouble a record contract with Epic and the band recorded their debut album in less than a week at Downtown.

Vaughan's debut album, *Texas Flood*, was released in the summer of 1983, a few months after Bowie's *Let's Dance* appeared. On its own, *Let's Dance* earned Vaughan quite a bit of attention, but *Texas Flood* was a blockbuster blues success, receiving positive reviews in both blues and rock publications, reaching number 38 on the charts, and crossing over to album rock radio stations; the album was nominated for two Grammy awards, Best Traditional Blues Recording and Best Rock Instrumental Performance ("Rude Mood"), the following year. Bowie offered Vaughan the lead guitarist role for his 1983 stadium tour, but Stevie Ray turned him down, preferring to play with Double Trouble.

Stevie Ray and Double Trouble set off on a successful tour and quickly recorded their second album, *Couldn't Stand the Weather*, which was released in May of 1984. The album was more successful than its predecessor, reaching number 31 on the charts; by the end of 1985, the album went gold. In 1985, Vaughan won his first Grammy for his version of "Texas Flood" on the anthology *Blues Explosion*. Double Trouble added keyboardist Reese Wynans in 1985, before they recorded their third album, *Soul To Soul*. The record was released in August, 1985 and was also quite successful, reaching number 34 on the charts. Around the same time as *Soul to Soul*'s release, Vaughan began guesting on a number of records by other artists, as well as producing albums, most notably *Strike Like Lightning* by Lonnie Mack.

Although his professional career was soaring, Vaughan was sinking deep into alcoholism and drug addiction, culminating with his onstage collapse in London in 1986. Despite the collapse, Stevie Ray continued to push himself, releasing the double live album *Live Alive* in October of 1986 and launching an extensive American tour in early 1987. Following the tour, Vaughan checked into a rehabilitation clinic in 1987 along with bassist Tommy Shannon. The guitarist's time in rehab was kept fairly quiet and for the next year, Stevie Ray and Double Trouble were fairly inactive.

Vaughan performed a number of concerts in 1988, including a headlining gig at the New Orleans Jazz & Heritage Festival. During this time, he was writing and recording material for his fourth studio album. The resulting record, *In Step*, was released in June and became his most successful album, spawning the number one album rock hit "Crossfire," peaking at number 33 on the charts, earning a Grammy for Best Contemporary Blues Recording, and going gold just over six months after its release. In the fall of 1989, Vaughan and Double Trouble embarked on a co-headlining American tour with Jeff Beck.

In the spring of 1990, Stevie Ray recorded an album with his brother Jimmie, which was scheduled for release in the fall of the year. After appearing at the 1990 New Orleans Jazz Festival in May, Vaughan and Double Trouble launched a co-headlining tour with Joe Cocker that lasted two months. After it was completed, Double Trouble set out on their own headlining tour. On August 26, 1990, their East Troy, WI, gig concluded with an encore jam featuring guitarists Eric Clapton, Buddy Guy, Jimmie Vaughan, and Robert Cray. After the concert, Stevie Ray Vaughan boarded a helicopter bound for Chicago. Minutes after its 12:30 AM takeoff, the helicopter crashed, killing Vaughan and the other four passengers. Vaughan was only 35 years old.

Family Style, Stevie Ray's duet album with Jimmie Vaughan, appeared in October and entered the charts at number seven; it would later win two Grammy awards, Best Rock Instrumental ("D/FW") and Best Contemporary Blues Recording. *Family Style* began a series of posthumous releases that were as popular as the albums Stevie Ray released during his lifetime. *The Sky is Crying*, a collection of studio outtakes compiled by Jimmie

Vaughan, was released in October of 1991; it entered the charts at number ten and went platinum three months after its release. *In the Beginning*, a recording of a Double Trouble concert in 1980, was released in the fall of 1992 and the compilation *Greatest Hits* was released in 1995. *— Stephen Thomas Erlewine*

Texas Flood / May 1983 / Epic ✦✦✦
A late-arriving star, Vaughan did not make his first album until the age of 28. By that time he had become a seasoned player, so this doesn't really sound like a debut album; rather, it sounds like a blues guitar master at the top of his form. Highlights include "Pride & Joy," "Love Struck Baby," "Lenny," and the hard blues title cut. *— William Ruhlmann*

Couldn't Stand the Weather / May 1984 / Epic ✦✦✦✦✦
Vaughan does not ease up on this second set, even taking on Jimi Hendrix in a rendition of "Voodoo Chile (Slight Return)," and handling it beautifully. *— William Ruhlmann*

Soul to Soul / Aug. 1985 / Epic ✦✦✦✦
Soul to Soul shows that Vaughan is a great guitarist, but everybody already knew that. What makes this album different from his two previous efforts is the inspired backing of Double Trouble—who finally sound like they aren't intimidated by their leader—and Vaughan's considerably more soulful and assertive vocals. *— Stephen Thomas Erlewine*

Live Alive / Oct. 1986 / Epic ✦✦✦
Live Alive not only covers many of Vaughan's most popular album tracks, but it also showcases a version of Stevie Wonder's "Superstition." Other standout tracks include "Look at Little Sister," "Willie the Wimp," and "Cold Shot." *— Rick Clark*

In Step / Jun. 1989 / Epic ✦✦✦✦✦
Vaughan sounds just as fierce sober as he did before, and he is beginning to bloom as a songwriter, a fact most notable on the driving "The House Is Rockin'" and the confessional "Wall of Denial." *— William Ruhlmann*

The Sky Is Crying / 1991 / Epic ✦✦✦✦✦
The posthumously released *The Sky Is Crying*, assembled out of tracks recorded between 1984 and 1989, is a lovingly assembled tribute to Vaughan's brilliance as a guitarist. Arguably this is Vaughan's finest album. The first-rate playing is unforced and natural in execution. On the songs, from his impeccable version of Hendrix's "Little Wing" to the hard blues shuffle of "Empty Arms," Vaughan's execution is unforced and his phrasing is relaxed. The release contains great liner notes and track information. Fans of hard blues-rock should check this one out. *— Rick Clark*

In the Beginning / Oct. 6, 1992 / Epic ✦✦
Although this is a very rough early concert from 1980, this album captures an energetic Stevie Ray Vaughan still developing his signature style, which makes it essential for fans. *— Stephen Thomas Erlewine*

★ **Greatest Hits** / Nov. 21, 1995 / Epic ✦✦✦✦
Stevie Ray Vaughan was a great guitarist, but he had trouble making consistent albums. *Greatest Hits* rectifies that problem by collecting all of his best-known tracks, from "Pride and Joy" to "Crossfire." Not only is it a terrific introduction, it's his most consistent album, demonstrating exactly why he was one of the most important guitarists of the '80s. *— Stephen Thomas Erlewine*

Maurice John Vaughn

b. Nov. 6, 1952, Chicago, IL
Guitar, Saxophone, Vocals / Modern Electric Blues
Maurice John Vaughn's 1984 debut set, *Generic Blues Album*, came packaged in a plain white jacket, its title unceremoniously stamped on its front like a package of no-brand rice on a grocer's shelf. It looked like the cleverest of publicity ploys, but in reality, it was a simple economic necessity—Vaughn's own Reecy label was operating on a shoestring.

Vaughn is no longer a blues unknown. With a challenging 1993 album on Alligator (*In the Shadow of the City*) melding blues, soul, funk, and other contemporary influences, he's grown into one of Chicago's most interesting and versatile younger blues artists. Fluent on both guitar and sax, Vaughn played both in sideman roles prior to stepping out on his own.

Sax came first. Vaughn grew up on Chicago's South side, blowing his horn with various R&B groups and recording with the Chosen Few for Chi-Sound Records in 1976. When sax gigs grew scarce, Vaughn began to emphasize his guitar skills. Blues guitarist Phil Guy recruited him and his band for a 1979 Canadian tour, and the genre appealed to him. Vaughn later held down sideman spots with Luther Allison, Son Seals, Valerie Wellington, and A.C. Reed.

Alligator Records retained the no-frills packaging when it reissued *Generic Blues Album* after Vaughn sang "Nothing Left to Believe In" on the label's 1987 anthology *The New Bluebloods. In the Shadow of the City* came in 1993. And despite the cover art on his first LP, there's nothing generic at all about Maurice Vaughn's brand of soulful blues. —*Bill Dahl*

● **Generic Blues Album** / Apr. 1986 / Alligator ✦✦✦✦✦
Anything but generic, this is actually powerful, contemporary, funky Chicago blues. With excellent musicianship, Vaughn performs interesting songs focusing on the trials of modern urban life and work. Vaughn, a top session player, sings and plays guitar and sax. —*Niles J. Frantz*

In the Shadow of the City / 1993 / Alligator ✦✦✦✦
The Chicago guitarist/saxist spreads his stylistic wings considerably further than he did on his debut, embracing funk more fully than his first time around but offering enough tasty contemporary blues to keep everyone happy. The prolific triple threat (he's also an engaging singer) wrote all but three tracks himself (one of the covers is the shuffling "Small Town Baby"; its composer, veteran pianist Jimmy Walker, plays on the cut). —*Bill Dahl*

Eddie "Cleanhead" Vinson

b. Dec. 18, 1917, Houston, TX, **d.** Jul. 2, 1988, Los Angeles, CA
Saxophone, Vocals / R&B, Blues, Electric Jump Blues, Bop, Jazz, Early R&B
An advanced stylist on alto saxophone who vacillated throughout his career between jump blues and jazz, bald-pated Eddie "Cleanhead" Vinson (he lost his hair early on after a botched bout with a lye-based hair-straightener) also possessed a playfully distinctive vocal delivery that stood him in good stead with blues fans.

Vinson first picked up a horn while attending high school in Houston. During the late '30s, he was a member of an incredible horn section in Milton Larkin's orchestra, sitting next to Arnett Cobb and Illinois Jacquet. After exiting Larkin's employ in 1941, Vinson picked up a few vocal tricks while on tour with bluesman Big Bill Broonzy. Vinson joined the Cootie Williams Orchestra from 1942 to 1945. His vocals on trumpeter Williams' renditions of "Cherry Red" and "Somebody's Got to Go" were in large part responsible for their wartime hit status.

Vinson struck out on his own in 1945, forming his own large band, signing with Mercury, and enjoying a double-sided smash in 1947 with his romping R&B chart-topper "Old Maid Boogie" and the song that would prove his signature number, "Kidney Stew Blues" (both songs featured Vinson's instantly identifiable vocals). A 1949–52 stint at King Records produced only one hit, the amusing sequel "Somebody Done Stole My Cherry Red," along with the classic blues "Person to Person" (later revived by another King artist, Little Willie John).

Vinson's jazz leanings were probably heightened during 1952–53, when his band included a young John Coltrane. Somewhere along about here, Vinson wrote two Miles Davis classics, "Tune Up" and "Four." Vinson steadfastly kept one foot in the blues camp and the other in jazz, waxing jumping R&B for Mercury (in 1954) and Bethlehem (1957), jazz for Riverside in 1961 (with Cannonball Adderley), and blues for Blues Time and ABC-BluesWay. A 1969 set for Black & Blue, cut in France with pianist Jay McShann and tenor saxophonist Hal Singer, beautifully recounted Vinson's blues shouting heyday (it's available on Delmark as *Kidney Stew is Fine*). A much later set for Muse teamed him with the sympathetic little big band approach of Rhode Island-based Roomful of Blues. Vinson toured the States and Europe frequently prior to his 1988 death of a heart attack. —*Bill Dahl*

Back in Town / Sep. 1957 / Bethlehem ✦✦✦
Although he had achieved a certain amount of popularity in the late '40s with his blues vocals and boppish alto, Eddie "Cleanhead" Vinson's Bethlehem album was one of only two recordings he made as a leader between 1956–66. With arrangements by Ernie Wilkins, Manny Albam, and Harry Tubbs, and his sidemen including several members (past and present) of the

Count Basie Orchestra, the blues-oriented music (which gives Vinson a chance to sing such material as "It Ain't Necessarily So," "Is You Is or Is You Ain't My Baby" and "Caledonia") is quite enjoyable and really rocks; pity that this record did not catch on. —*Scott Yanow*

Kidney Stew Is Fine / Mar. 28, 1969 / Delmark ✦✦✦
Although its programming has been juggled a bit and the CD has been given liner notes, this Delmark release is a straight reissue of the original LP. Clocking in at around 38 minutes, the relatively brief set is the only recording that exists of Vinson, pianist Jay McShann and guitarist T-Bone Walker playing together; the sextet is rounded out by the fine tenor Hal Singer, bassist Jackie Sampson, and drummer Paul Gunther. Vinson, whether singing "Please Send Me Somebody to Love," "Just a Dream," and "Juke Head Baby," or taking boppish alto solos, is the main star throughout this album (originally on Black & Blue), a date that helped launch Vinson's commercial comeback. —*Scott Yanow*

You Can't Make Love Alone / Jun. 18, 1971 / Mega ✦✦✦
Eddie "Cleanhead" Vinson was in inspired form at the 1971 Montreux Jazz Festival. He stole the show when he sat in with Oliver Nelson's big band during their "Swiss Suite" and played a brilliant blues alto solo. The same day he recorded this Mega album but, due to its extreme brevity (under 24 minutes), perhaps this label should have changed its name to "Mini." Despite the low quantity, the quality of his performance (on which Vinson is joined by the guitars of Larry Coryell and Cornell Dupree, pianist Neal Creque, bassist Chuck Rainey, and drummer Pretty Purdie) makes this album still worth acquiring, although preferably at a budget price. Vinson takes "Straight No Chaser" as an instrumental and does a fine job of singing "Cleanhead Blues," "You Can't Make Love Alone," "I Had a Dream," and "Person to Person." —*Scott Yanow*

● **Cherry Red Blues** / 1976 / King/Gusto ✦✦✦✦
Somehow, amidst all the CD reissues from the King Records vaults unleashed by Charly, Ace, Rhino, and King's current ownership, this versatile alto saxist has fallen through the cracks. Thus, this two-LP collection, boasting all but a handful of his jumping 1949–1952 outings for King, remains your best introduction to the Cleanheaded one's R&B output (along with the 1945–1947 sides he waxed for Mercury, which grace the seven-disc anthology *Blues, Boogie, & Bop: The 1940s Mercury Sessions*). —*Bill Dahl*

The Clean Machine / Feb. 22, 1978 / Muse ✦✦✦
What makes this album different from many of Eddie "Cleanhead" Vinson's is that four of the seven selections are taken as instrumentals. Vinson's alto playing has long been underrated due to his popularity as a blues singer, so this release gives one the opportunity to hear his bop-influenced solos at greater length. With the assistance of a strong rhythm section led by pianist Lloyd Glenn and some contributions from trumpeter Jerry Rusch and Rashid Ali on tenor, Vinson is in excellent form throughout this enjoyable set. —*Scott Yanow*

Hold It Right There! / Aug. 25, 1978–Aug. 26, 1978 / Muse ✦✦✦✦✦
After years of neglect, Eddie "Cleanhead" Vinson was finally receiving long overdue recognition at the time of this live session—one of six albums recorded during a week at Sandy's Jazz Revival. Two of these albums featured tenors Arnett Cobb and Buddy Tate in lead roles. While Vinson has fine blues vocals on "Cherry Red" and "Hold It," it is his boppish alto solos on "Cherokee," "Now's the Time," and "Take the 'A' Train" (the latter also having spots for Cobb and Tate) that make this set recommended to blues and bop fans alike. —*Scott Yanow*

Live at Sandy's / Aug. 25, 1978–Aug. 26, 1978 / Muse ✦✦✦✦
Muse recorded six albums during one week at Sandy's Jazz Revival, a club in Beverly, MA; two of them (this one and *Hold It Right There*) feature the blues vocals and alto solos of Eddie "Cleanhead" Vinson. Some of the songs also have the tenors of Arnett Cobb and Buddy Tate in a supporting role, but this album is largely Vinson's show. Backed by a superb rhythm section (pianist Ray Bryant, bassist George Duvivier, and drummer Alan Dawson), Vinson takes four fine vocals and plays many swinging alto solos including one on "Tune Up," a song he wrote that has been mistakenly credited to Miles Davis for decades. —*Scott Yanow*

● **I Want a Little Girl** / Feb. 10, 1981 / Pablo ✦✦✦✦✦

Eddie "Cleanhead" Vinson, 64 at the time of this Pablo recording, is in superior form on the blues-oriented material. With Art Hillery (on piano and organ) and guitarist Cal Green leading the rhythm section, and trumpeter Martin Banks and the tenor of Rashid Ali offering contrasting solo voices, this is a particularly strong release. It is true that Vinson had sung such songs as "I Want a Little Girl," "Somebody's Got to Go," and "Stormy Monday" a countless number of times previously but he still infuses these versions with enthusiasm and spirit, making this set a good example of Cleanhead's talents in his later years. — *Scott Yanow*

★ **And Roomful of Blues** / Jan. 27, 1982 / Muse ✦✦✦✦✦

If there were justice in the world, Eddie "Cleanhead" Vinson would have been able to tour with this type of group throughout much of his career. Roomful of Blues, a popular five-horn nonet, has rarely sounded more exciting than on this musical meeting with the legendary singer/altoist. Vinson himself is exuberant on some of the selections, particularly "House of Joy," one of five instrumentals among the eight selections. Whether one calls it blues, bebop, or early rhythm & blues, this accessible music is very enjoyable and deserves to be more widely heard. Among the supporting players, tenorman Greg Piccolo, trumpeter Bob Enos, and guitarist Ronnie Earl (in one of his earliest recordings) win honors. — *Scott Yanow*

Mose Vinson

b. Aug. 7, 1917, Mississippi Delta
Piano, Vocals / Piano Blues

A Memphis piano institution for more than half a century, Mose Vinson recorded a handful of unreleased sides for Sun in 1953 (recently liberated by Bear Family) and did scattered session work for Sam Phillips as well. He remains an active performer.

Vinson began playing piano as a child in the Mississippi Delta, initially playing in his local church. By his teens, he had begun playing jazz and blues. In 1932, he moved to Memphis, TN, where he played local juke joints and parties throughout the '30s and '40s. In the early '50s, Sam Phillips had Vinson accompany a number of Sun Records blues artists, most notably James Cotton in 1954. During that time, Phillips also had Vinson cut some tracks, but they remained unreleased until the '80s.

For the next three decades, Vinson continued to perform at local Memphis clubs. However, he didn't play as frequently as he did in the previous two decades. In the early '80s, the Center for Southern Folklore hired Vinson to perform at special cultural festivals, as well as local schools. For the next two decades, he played concerts, educational, and cultural festivals associated with the Center for Southern Folklore. — *Bill Dahl & Stephen Thomas Erlewine*

● **Memphis Piano Blues Today** / 1990 / Wolf ✦✦✦✦✦

Walter Vinson

b. Feb. 2, 1901, Bolton, MS, **d.** Apr. 22, 1975, Chicago, IL
Guitar, Violin, Vocals / Memphis Blues

A outstanding guitarist and violinist, Walter Jacobs Vinson played with many blues immortals from the '20s to the '70s. He began playing music as a child, and worked at parties and picnics as a teen in Mississippi. Vinson worked with Rubin Lacy, Charlie McCoy, and Son Spand during the '20s, and teamed with Lonnie Chatmon in 1928. He recorded with Chatmon's Mississippi Hot Footers, the Carter Brothers, and Bo Chatmon and the Mississippi Sheiks in the late '20s and early '30s. Vinson made recordings as a leader for Okeh, Paramount, Bluebird, Riverside, and Rounder, while also doing sessions with Tommy Griffin and Harry Chatmon. He made many club appearances in the early '40s, but then took a lengthy absence from music until 1960. Vinson made festival and club appearances in the '60s and '70s. — *Ron Wynn*

● **Complete Recorded Works in Chronological Order** / Document ✦✦✦✦

W

Joe Louis Walker

b. Dec. 25, 1949, San Francisco, CA
Guitar, Vocals / Modern Electric Blues
Without a doubt one of the most exciting and innovative artists gracing contemporary blues, guitarist Joe Louis Walker has glowed like a shining blue beacon over the last decade. His 1986 debut album for HighTone, *Cold Is the Night*, announced his arrival in stunning fashion; his subsequent output on HighTone and Verve has only served to further establish Walker as one of the leading younger bluesmen on the scene.

Walker traveled a circuitous route to get to where he is today. At age 14, he took up the guitar, playing blues (with an occasional foray into psychedelic rock) on the mushrooming San Francisco circuit. For a while, Walker roomed with Mike Bloomfield, who introduced him to Jimi Hendrix and the Grateful Dead and taught him some very useful licks. Walker even made a brief pilgrimage to Chicago to check out the blues scene there.

But by 1975, Walker was burned out on blues and turned to God, singing for the next decade with a gospel group, the Spiritual Corinthians. When the Corinthians played the 1985 New Orleans Jazz & Heritage Festival, Walker was inspired to embrace his blues roots again. He assembled a band, the Boss Talkers, and wrote some stunning originals that ended up on *Cold Is the Night* (co-produced by Bruce Bromberg and Dennis Walker).

More acclaimed albums for HighTone—1988's *The Gift, Blue Soul* the next year, and two riveting sets cut live at Slim's in 1990—preceded a switch to the major Verve imprint and three more discs that were considerably more polished than their grittier HighTone counterparts.

Joe Louis Walker is quite the total package, as tremendously assured on a down-in-the-alley acoustic solo outing as he is performing a thoroughly modern R&B-laced number with his latest crew of Boss Talkers. Expect more great things from him in years to come. *—Bill Dahl*

Cold Is the Night / 1986 / HighTone ✦✦✦✦
The Bay Area blues guitarist's debut album sounds underproduced compared to what would soon follow—and that's no knock. Walker's gritty, expressive vocals and ringing, concise guitar work shine through loud and clear in front of his band, the Boss Talkers. Walker and his producers Dennis Walker and Bruce Bromberg wrote virtually the entire set, including the slashing "Cold Is the Night," "Don't Play Games," and "One Woman." *—Bill Dahl*

● **The Gift** / 1988 / HighTone ✦✦✦✦✦
Although it didn't enjoy the major label hype that his current output does, Walker's HighTone encore just may be his finest album of all, filled with soulful vocal performances, bone-cutting guitar work, and tight backing from the Boss Talkers and the Memphis Horns. Honestly, you can't go wrong with any of Walker's remarkably consistent HighTone discs—but give this one the slightest of edges over the rest. *—Bill Dahl*

Blue Soul / 1989 / HighTone ✦✦✦✦✦
Another winner sporting memorable songs ("T.L.C.," "Personal Baby," "City of Angels," "Prove Your Love"), sinuous grooves, and a whole lot of vicious guitar from one of the hottest relatively young bluesmen on the circuit. He goes it alone on the finale, "I'll Get to Heaven on My Own," sounding as conversant with the country blues tradition as he does with the contemporary stuff. *—Bill Dahl*

Live at Slim's / May 1991 / HighTone ✦✦✦✦✦
Joe Louis Walker has always been a more probing and exciting blues musician than Robert Cray, although I wouldn't pick him in a singing contest. This live set features Walker at his hottest, and it clicks despite some occasional engineering difficulties. *—Ron Wynn*

Live at Slim's, Vol. 1 / 1991 / HighTone ✦✦✦✦
Walker was hot enough over the course of a two-day stand at Slim's in San Francisco to warrant the issue of two full albums from the dates. The first is a sizzling combination of past triumphs, new items, and covers of Clifton Chenier's "Hot Tamale Baby," Junior Wells' "Little By Little" (with Huey Lewis, no less, on harp), and a saucy duet with Angela Strehli on the old Fontella Bass/Bobby McClure rocker "Don't Mess Up a Good Thing." *—Bill Dahl*

Live at Slim's, Vol. 2 / Nov. 1992 / HighTone ✦✦✦✦
More from that searing Slim's engagement, including Joe Louis ripping through Ray Charles' "Don't You Know," Little Milton's "Love at First Sight," and Rosco Gordon's overworked "Just a Little Bit," along with his own gems. Huey Lewis turns up again as the harpist on Walker's version of Haskell Sadler's "747." *—Bill Dahl*

Blues Survivor / Oct. 19, 1993 / Verve ✦✦✦
By no means a bad album, Walker's major-label debut just wasn't quite as terrific as what directly preceded it. The studio atmosphere seems a bit slicker than before, and the songs are in several cases considerably longer than they need to be (generally in the five-to-seven-minute range). A reworking of Howlin' Wolf's "Shake for Me" is the only familiar entry. *—Bill Dahl*

JLW / 1994 / PolyGram ✦✦✦
Another overly polished effort that nevertheless packs a punch on many selections. Walker's songwriting is considerably less prominent, with only three self-penned tunes on the disc this time. Otis Blackwell's pulsating "On That Power Line" and the Don Gardner & Dee Dee Ford dusty "I Need Your Lovin'" receive spirited revivals, and there's an acoustic duet with James Cotton, "Going to Canada." *—Bill Dahl*

Blues of the Month Club / Sep. 12, 1995 / Verve ✦✦✦
Walker's latest is, alas, also his weakest to date—strange, since he shares production credit this time with the legendary Steve Cropper. Once again, some songs drag on far after their logical conclusions; also, Walker doesn't quite possess the pipes to effectively belt the old Jackie Brenston rouser "You've Got to Lose." The title track, with Cropper co-featured on guitar, is a clever piece of material, but overall, the slick production values strip some of the grit from Walker's incendiary attack. *—Bill Dahl*

Phillip Walker

b. Feb. 11, 1937, Welsh, LA
Guitar, Vocals / Modern Electric Blues
Despite recording somewhat sparingly since debuting as a leader in 1959 on Elko Records with the storming rocker "Hello My Darling," Louisiana-born guitarist Phillip Walker enjoys a sterling reputation as a contemporary blues guitarist with a distinctive sound honed along the Gulf Coast during the 1950s.

A teenaged Walker picked up his early licks around Port Arthur, TX, from the likes of Gatemouth Brown, Long John

Hunter, Lightnin' Hopkins, and Lonnie "Guitar Junior" Brooks. Zydeco king Clifton Chenier hired Walker in 1953 as his guitarist, a post he held for three-and-a-half years.

In 1959, Walker moved to Los Angeles, waxing "Hello My Darling" for producer J.R. Fulbright (a song he's revived several times since, most effectively for the short-lived Playboy logo). Scattered 45s emerged during the '60s, but it wasn't until he joined forces with young producer Bruce Bromberg in 1969 that Walker began to get a studio foothold. Their impressive work together resulted in a 1973 album for Playboy, *Bottom of the Top*, that remains Walker's finest to date.

Walker cut a fine follow-up set for Bromberg's Joliet label, *Someday You'll Have These Blues*, that showcased his tough Texas guitar style (it was later reissued by Alligator). Sets for Rounder and HighTone were high points of the 1980s for the guitarist. His 1995 set for Black Top, *Working Girl Blues*, shows that Walker remains at peak operating power, combining attractively contrasting tracks waxed in New Orleans and Los Angeles. *—Bill Dahl*

Blues / 1973 / HighTone ✦✦✦
Contains a rich, reassuring reading of "Don't Be Afraid of the Dark," a tune generally associated with HighTone stablemate Robert Cray (Walker's version was reportedly waxed the day before Cray's), with the Memphis Horns adding extra punch. *— Bill Dahl*

Someday You'll Have These Blues / 1977 / HighTone ✦✦✦
Recorded in 1975-76 and initially out on the short-lived Joliet logo (later Alligator picked it up; it's now out on HighTone), this collection wasn't quite the masterpiece that its predecessor was ("Breakin' Up Somebody's Home" and "Part Time Love" were hardly inspired cover choices), the set does have its moments—the uncompromising title track and "Beaumont Blues," to cite a couple. *—Bill Dahl*

From L.A. to L.A. / 1982 / Rounder ✦✦✦
Walker's tunes from 1969, 1970, and 1976 sessions, were produced by Bruce Bromberg and recorded with Lonesome Sundown. They're very nice. *—Niles J. Frantz*

Tough As I Want to Be / 1984 / Rounder ✦✦✦✦
Hotter and fiercer than other recordings, these originals and covers come from Lowell Fulson and Jimmy McCracklin. *—Niles J. Frantz*

● **Bottom of the Top** / 1990 / HighTone ✦✦✦✦✦
There weren't many blues albums issued during the early '70s that hit harder than this one. First out on the short-lived Playboy logo, the set firmly established Walker as a blistering axeman sporting enduring Gulf Coast roots despite his adopted L.A. homebase. Of all the times he's cut the rocking "Hello My Darling," this is indeed the hottest, while his funky, horn-driven revival of Lester Williams' "I Can't Lose (With the Stuff I Lose)" and his own R&B-drenched "It's All in Your Mind" are irresistible. After-hours renditions of Sam Cooke's "Laughing & Clowning" and Long John Hunter's "Crazy Girl" are striking vehicles for Walker's twisting, turning guitar riffs and impassioned vocal delivery. *—Bill Dahl*

Working Girl Blues / 1995 / Black Top ✦✦✦✦
Walker remains in fine form on this recent set, a mix of remakes of past triumphs ("Hello, My Darling," "Hey, Hey Baby's Gone") and fresh explorations. Two distinct bands were utilized—a New Orleans crew populated by bassist George Porter, Jr., and his funky cohorts, and an L.A. posse with more of a straight-up swinging feel. *—Bill Dahl*

Big Blues from Texas / JSP ✦✦✦
Nice comeback set after a lengthy absence from the recording scene that was cut in London under the direction of guitarist Otis Grand (who shares axe duties throughout). Why this Louisiana-born guitarist hasn't been recorded more heavily is a mystery; he seldom fails to connect, and this import is no exception to the rule. *—Bill Dahl*

T-Bone Walker (Aaron Thibeaux Walker)

b. May 28, 1910, Linden, TX, d. Mar. 16, 1975, Los Angeles, CA
Guitar, Vocals / Electric Texas Blues
Modern electric blues guitar can be traced directly back to this Texas-born pioneer, who began amplifying his sumptuous lead lines for public consumption circa 1940 and thus initiated a revolution so total that its tremors are still being felt today.

Few major postwar blues guitarists come to mind that don't owe T-Bone Walker an unpayable debt of gratitude. B.B. King has long cited him as a primary influence, marveling at Walker's penchant for holding the body of his guitar outward while he played it. Gatemouth Brown, Pee Wee Crayton, Goree Carter, Pete Mayes, and a wealth of other prominent Texas-bred axemen came stylistically right out of Walker during the late '40s and early '50s. Walker's nephew, guitarist R.S. Rankin, went so far as to bill himself as T-Bone Walker, Jr. for a 1962 single on Dot, "Midnight Bells Are Ringing" (with his uncle's complete blessing, of course; the two had worked up a father-and-son-type act long before that).

Aaron Thibeault Walker was a product of the primordial Dallas blues scene. His stepfather, Marco Washington, stroked the bass fiddle with the Dallas String Band, and T-Bone followed his stepdad's example by learning the rudiments of every stringed instrument he could lay his talented hands on. One notable visitor to the band's jam sessions was the legendary Blind Lemon Jefferson. During the early '20s, Walker led the sightless guitarist from bar to bar as the older man played for tips.

In 1929, Walker made his recording debut with a single 78 for Columbia, "Wichita Falls Blues"/"Trinity River Blues," billed as Oak Cliff T-Bone. Pianist Douglas Fernell was his musical partner for the disc. Walker was exposed to some pretty outstanding guitar talent during his formative years; besides Jefferson, Charlie Christian—who would totally transform the role of the guitar in jazz with his electrified riffs much as Walker would with blues—was one of his playing partners circa 1933.

T-Bone Walker split the Southwest for Los Angeles during the mid-'30s, earning his keep with saxist Big Jim Wynn's band with his feet rather than his hands as a dancer. Popular bandleader Les Hite hired Walker as his vocalist in 1939. Walker sang "T-Bone Blues" with the Hite aggregation for Varsity Records in 1940, but didn't play guitar on the outing. It was about then, though, that his fascination with electrifying his axe bore fruit; he played L.A. clubs with his daring new toy after assembling his own combo, engaging in acrobatic stage moves—splits, playing behind his back—to further enliven his show.

Capitol Records was a fledgling Hollywood concern in 1942, when Walker signed on and cut "Mean Old World" and "I Got a Break Baby" with boogie master Freddie Slack hammering the 88s. This was the first sign of the T-Bone Walker that blues guitar aficionados know and love, his fluid, elegant riffs and mellow, burnished vocals setting a standard that all future blues guitarists would measure themselves by.

Chicago's Rhumboogie Club served as Walker's home away from home during a good portion of the war years. He even cut a few sides for the joint's house label in 1945 under the direction of pianist Marl Young. But after a solitary session that same year for Old Swingmaster that soon made its way onto another newly established logo, Mercury, Walker signed with L.A.-based Black & White Records in 1946 and proceeded to amass a stunning legacy.

The immortal "Call It Stormy Monday (But Tuesday Is Just as Bad)" was the product of a 1947 Black & White date with Teddy Buckner on trumpet and invaluable pianist Lloyd Glenn in the backing quintet. Many of Walker's best sides were smoky after-hours blues, though an occasional up-tempo entry—"T-Bone Jumps Again," a storming instrumental from the same date, for example—illustrated his nimble dexterity at faster speeds.

Walker recorded prolifically for Black & White until the close of 1947, waxing classics like the often-covered "T-Bone Shuffle" and "West Side Baby," though many of the sides came out on Capitol after the demise of Black & White. In 1950, Walker turned up on Imperial. His first date for the L.A. indie elicited the after-hours gem "Glamour Girl" and perhaps the penultimate jumping instrumental in his repertoire, "Strollin' with Bones" (Snake Sims' drum kit cracks like a whip behind Walker's impeccable licks).

Walker's 1950-54 Imperial stint was studded with more classics: "The Hustle Is On," "Cold Cold Feeling," "Blue Mood," "Vida Lee" (named for his wife), "Party Girl," and, from a 1952 New Orleans jaunt, "Railroad Station Blues," which was produced by Dave Bartholomew. Atlantic was T-Bone Walker's next stop in 1955; his first date for them was an unlikely but successful collaboration with a crew of Chicago mainstays (harpist Junior Wells, guitarist Jimmy Rogers, and bassist Ransom Knowling among them). Rogers found the experience especially useful; he later adapted Walker's "Why Not" as his own Chess hit "Walking by Myself."

With a slightly more sympathetic L.A. band in staunch support, Walker cut two follow-up sessions for Atlantic in 1956–57. The latter date produced some amazing instrumentals ("Two Bones and a Pick," "Blues Rock," "Shufflin' the Blues") that saw him duelling it out with his nephew and jazzman Barney Kessel (Walker emerged victorious in every case).

Unfortunately, the remainder of Walker's discography isn't of the same sterling quality for the most part. As it had with so many of his peers from the postwar R&B era, rock's rise had made Walker's classy style an anachronism (at least during much of the 1960s). He journeyed overseas on the first American Folk Blues Festival in 1962, starring on the Lippmann & Rau-promoted bill across Europe with Memphis Slim, Willie Dixon, and a host of other American luminaries. A 1964 45 for Modern and an obscure LP on Brunswick preceded a pair of BluesWay albums in 1967–68 that restored this seminal pioneer to American record shelves.

European tours often beckoned. A 1968 visit to Paris resulted in one of his best latter-day albums, *I Want a Little Girl*, for Black & Blue (and later issued stateside on Delmark). With expatriate tenor saxophonist Hal "Cornbread" Singer and Chicago drummer S.P. Leary picking up Walker's jazz-tinged style brilliantly, the guitarist glided through a stellar set list.

Good Feelin',' a 1970 release on Polydor, won a Grammy for the guitarist, though it doesn't rank with his best efforts. A five-song appearance on a 1973 set for Reprise, *Very Rare*, was also a disappointment. Persistent stomach woes and a 1974 stroke slowed Walker's career to a crawl, and he died in 1975.

No written accolades can fully convey the monumental importance of what T-Bone Walker gave to the blues. He was the idiom's first true lead guitarist, and undeniably one of its very best. —*Bill Dahl*

☆ **T Bone Blues** / 1959 / Atlantic ✦✦✦✦✦
Walker's finest mid-period album. Classics abound any place you look, and T-Bone's guitar work is nothing short of extraordinary. —*Cub Koda*

Sings the Blues / 1959 / Imperial ✦✦✦✦✦
These early-'50s Imperial sides find the Texas guitar pioneer in top form. —*Bill Dahl*

Singing the Blues / 1960 / Imperial ✦✦✦✦✦
More early-'50s gems. —*Bill Dahl*

I Get So Weary / 1961 / Imperial ✦✦✦✦✦
Still another LP of Walker's elegant guitar and smooth vocals. —*Bill Dahl*

I Want a Little Girl / 1967 / Delmark ✦✦✦✦✦
This pioneering artist had more influence in the shaping of modern blues guitar styles than anyone on the planet. His was a cross-genre genius that skirted the boundaries of blues, R&B, jump, jazz, and pop. He appears on nearly 50 labels in a studio career that spanned over 30 years, and very little of this output falters even slightly. This tasty set made originally for the Black and Blue label in 1968 features him with a like-minded unit of tenor sax, piano, bass, and drums that provides a solid and excellent groove throughout. Musically, this is truly the genius at home, calling the shots. —*Larry Hoffman*

Dirty Mistreater / 1973 / Bluesway ✦✦✦
A reissue of a 1973 Bluesway album, it shows T-Bone near the end. —*Hank Davis*

T-Bone Walker / 1974 / Blue Note ✦✦✦
A scholarly 17-track compilation, it has great photos and notes, and features selections from 1929 to 1953. For the serious collector. —*Hank Davis*

Classics of Modern Blues / Aug. 1975 / Blue Note ✦✦✦✦✦
This two-LP set contains most of Walker's seminal sides for Imperial (cut in 1952–53). —*Bill Dahl*

Original 1945–50 Performances / 1976 / EMI ✦✦✦✦✦
A deep look into T-Bone's roots, it features 12 classic performances, including the original "Stormy Monday Blues." —*Hank Davis*

Jumps Again / 1981 / Charly ✦✦✦✦✦
1942–47 sides, early and terrific. —*Bill Dahl*

Natural Blues / 1983 / Charly ✦✦✦✦✦
More '40s Walker classics. —*Bill Dahl*

Inventor of the Electric Guitar Blues / 1983 / Blues Boy ✦✦✦✦✦
Some formative and masterful recordings by Aaron T-Bone Walker, among the greatest pure vocalists in modern blues history. The find is a side with Walker playing 1929 country blues and sounding just as comfortable and exciting as he does on the 16 other 1940s and '50s numbers. —*Ron Wynn*

☆ **The Complete Recordings of T-Bone Walker 1940–1954** / Oct. 1990 / Mosaic ✦✦✦✦✦
A 1940–1954 six-CD boxed set—an education in the lineage of urban blues. It appears that T-Bone Walker had a greater influence on urban blues players than any other single talent. His guitar, vocals, song selection, and sheer style live on today in nearly every blues performer. He is the master. —*Michael Erlewine*

● **The Complete Imperial Recordings** / 1991 / EMI America ✦✦✦✦✦
Another essential T-Bone Walker stake, this time a two-disc dish with 52 sensational tracks from his stint at Lew Chudd's Imperial Records. Whether waxing with his own jump blues unit in L.A. or Dave Bartholomew's hard-drivers in New Orleans, Walker always stayed true to his vision, and the proof was in the grooves: "Glamour Girl," "The Hustle Is On," "Tell Me What's the Reason," "High Society," "Cold, Cold Feeling," and the immaculate jumping instrumental "Strollin' with Bones" all date from this historic period of Walker's legacy. —*Bill Dahl*

★ **Complete Capitol/Black & White Recordings** / 1995 / Capitol ✦✦✦✦✦
Three-CD, 75-track box of T-Bone Walker's recordings for the Capitol and Black & White labels in the 1940s. From a historical perspective, this is perhaps the most important phase of Walker's evolution. It was here where he perfected his electric guitar style, becoming an important influence on everyone from B.B. King down. It was also here where he acted as one of the key players in small combo West Coast bands' transition from jazz to a more jump blues/R&B-oriented sound (though most of these sides retain a pretty strong jazz flavor). These sessions, which include the original version of his most famous tune ("Call It Stormy Monday"), have previously been chopped up into small morsels for reissue, or incorporated into the mammoth limited-edition Mosaic box set; this isolates them more conveniently. At the same time, it may be too extensive for some listeners, especially with the abundance of alternate takes (which are placed right after the official versions). Excellent liner notes, although the discographical information is surprisingly inconsistent. —*Richie Unterberger*

● **T-Bones Blues** / Atlantic ✦✦✦✦✦
The last truly indispensable disc of the great guitar hero's career, and perhaps the most innately satisfying of all—these mid-'50s recordings boast magnificent presence, with Walker's axe so crisp and clear it seems as though he's sitting right next to you as he delivers a luxurious remake of "Call It Stormy Monday." Atlantic took some chances with Bone, dispatching him to Chicago for a 1955 date with Junior Wells and Jimmy Rogers that produced "Why Not" and "Papa Ain't Salty." Even better were the 1956–57 L.A. dates that produced the scalding instrumentals "Two Bones and a Pick" (the latter finding Walker duelling it out with nephew R.S. Rankin and jazzman Barney Kessel). —*Bill Dahl*

Sippie Wallace (Beulah Wallace)

b. Nov. 1, 1898, Houston, TX, **d.** Nov. 1, 1986, Detroit, MI
Vocals / Classic Female Blues
A classic female blues singer from the '20s, Wallace kept performing and recording until her death. She was a major influence on a young Bonnie Raitt, who recorded several of Wallace's songs and performed live with her.

The daughter of a Baptist deacon, Sippie Wallace (b. Beulah Thomas) was born and raised in Houston. As a child, she sang and played piano in church. Before she was in her teens, she began performing with her pianist brother Hersal Thomas. By the time she was in her mid-teens, she had left Houston to pursue a musical career, singing in a number of tent shows and earning a dedicated fan base. In 1915, she moved to New Orleans with her pianist brother Hersal Thomas. Two years later, she married Matt Wallace.

In 1923, Sippie, Hersal, and their older brother George moved to Chicago, where Sippie became part of the city's jazz scene. By the end of the year, she had earned a contract with Okeh Records. Her first two songs for the label, "Shorty George" and "Up the Country Blues," were hits and Sippie soon became a star. Throughout the '20s, she produced a series of singles that were nearly all hits. Wallace's Okeh recordings featured a number of celebrated jazz musicians, including Louis Armstrong, Eddie Heywood, King Oliver, and Clarence Williams; both Hersal and George Thomas performed on Sippie's records as well, in addition to supporting her at concerts. Between 1923 and 1927, she recorded over 40 songs for the Okeh. Many of the songs were Wallace originals or co-written by Sippie and her brothers.

In 1926, Hersal Thomas died of food poisoning, but Sippie Wallace continued to perform and record. Within a few years, however, she stopped performing regularly. After her contract with Okeh was finished in the late '20s, she moved to Detroit in 1929. In the early '30s, Wallace stopped recording, only performing the occasional gig. In 1936, both George Thomas and her husband Matt died. Following their deaths, Sippie joined the Leland Baptist Church in Detroit, where she was an organist and vocalist; she stayed with the church for the next 40 years.

Between 1936 and 1966, Sippie Wallace was inactive on the blues scene—she only performed a handful of concerts and cut a few records. In 1966, she was lured out of retirement by her friend Victoria Spivey, who convinced Sippie to join the thriving blues and folk festival circuit. Wallace not only joined the circuit, she began recording again. Her first new album was a collection of duets with Spivey, appropriately titled *Sippie Wallace and Victoria Spivey*, which was recorded in 1966; the album wasn't released until 1970. Also in 1966, Wallace recorded *Sippie Wallace Sings the Blues* for Storyville, which featured support from musicians like Little Brother Montgomery and Roosevelt Sykes. The album was quite popular, as were Sippie's festival performances.

In 1970, Sippie Wallace suffered a stroke, but she was able to continue recording and performing, although not as frequently as she had before. In 1982, Bonnie Raitt—who had claimed Sippie as a major influence—helped Wallace land a contract with Atlantic Records. Raitt produced the resulting album, *Sippie*, which was released in 1983. *Sippie* won the WC Handy Award for best blues album of the year and was nominated for a Grammy. The album turned out to be Sippie Wallace's last recording—she died in 1986, when she was 88 years old. — *Stephen Thomas Erlewine & Cub Koda*

Women Be Wise / 1992 / Alligator ✦✦✦
Recorded on Halloween night, 1966, in Copenhagen, Denmark, this one of the few great "blues rediscovery" albums that comes by its reputation honestly. With Roosevelt Sykes and Little Brother Montgomery sharing the piano stool, Sippie clearly shows that the intervening years had, indeed, been kind to her, belting out one great tune after another. Listing highlights is superfluous, simply because every track's a gem. The no-frills production is warm and cozy enough to make you feel like you're hearing the world's greatest one-woman concert right in your living room. And you're glad you bought a ticket. — *Cub Koda*

Sippie Wallace Sings the Blues / Storyville ✦✦✦
● **1923–1929** / Document ✦✦✦✦✦
Sippie's earliest and best sides, including "I'm a Mighty Tight Woman." (Import) — *Cub Koda*

Mercy Dee Walton

b. Aug. 3, 1915, Waco, TX, d. Dec. 2, 1962, Stockton, CA
Piano, Vocals / Piano Blues
Mose Allison certainly recognized the uncommon brilliance of pianist Mercy Dee Walton. The young jazz-based Allison faithfully covered Walton's downtrodden "One Room Country Shack" in 1957, four years after Walton had waxed the original for Los Angeles-based Specialty Records (his original was a huge R&B smash).

Walton was a Texas émigré, like so many other postwar California R&B pioneers, who had played piano around Waco from the age of 13 before hitting the coast in 1938. Once there, the pianist gigged up and down the length of the Golden State before debuting on record in 1949 with "Lonesome Cabin Blues" for the tiny Spire logo, which became a national R&B hit. Those sides were cut in Fresno, but Los Angeles hosted some of the

pianist's best sessions for Imperial in 1950 and Specialty in 1952-53.

Walton, who usually recorded under the handle of Mercy Dee, was a talented songsmith whose compositions ran the gamut from lowdown blues to jumping R&B items. A half dozen tracks for the Bihari brothers' Flair imprint in 1955 included "Come Back Maybellene," a rocking sequel to Chuck Berry's then-current hit.

After a lengthy layoff, Walton returned to the studio in a big way in 1961, recording prolifically for Chris Strachwitz's Arhoolie label with his northern California compatriots: K.C. Douglas on guitar, harpist Sidney Maiden, and drummer Otis Cherry (some of this material ended up on Prestige's Bluesville subsidiary). It's very fortunate that Strachwitz took an interest in documenting Walton's versatility, for in December of 1962, the pianist died. — *Bill Dahl*

One Room Country Shack / 1952–1953 / Specialty ✦✦✦
Unlike many other blues performers who migrated to California, Mercy Dee Walton didn't change or rework his style to fit the new environment. Rather than becoming a more sophisticated singer or a more jazz-oriented instrumentalist, Walton kept making the same countrified, intimate, simple songs, replete with down-home imagery and sung in a weary, cautionary tone, backed by sparse piano accompaniment. The material on *One Room Country Shack*, a 24-song collection of Walton originals, could have been cut in Texas or Mississippi for that matter. It includes a remake of his landmark 1949 number "Lonesome Cabin Blues" and the marvelous title cut, which was later covered by Mose Allison. — *Ron Wynn*

Troublesome Mind / 1961 / Arhoolie ✦✦✦✦
Fine 16-song selection from the California-based pianist's 1961 sessions for Chris Strachwitz's Arhoolie logo. A trio of sympathetic cohorts (harpist Sidney Maiden, guitarist K.C. Douglas, and drummer Otis Cherry) give the music a rough-edged barroom feel as Dee pounds out "After the Fight," "Call the Asylum," and a nice remake of his dour "One Room Country Shack." — *Bill Dahl*

Mercy Dee Walton & His Piano / 1961 / Arhoolie ✦✦✦
● **Mercy Dee** / Aug. 1962 / Original Blues Classics ✦✦✦✦✦
Whether you know him as Mercy Dee Walton, Mercy Dee or just plain Mercy, there was no doubt that he could write some incredible songs and spin some wonderful yarns. The playing wasn't bad either, and these early-'60s recordings are among his finest. — *Ron Wynn*

Robert Ward

b. Oct. 15, 1938, Georgia
Guitar, Vocals / Soul, R&B, Soul Blues
Comeback tales don't come any more heartwarming (or unlikely) than Robert Ward's. Totally off the scene and thought by many aficionados to be dead, Ward's chance encounter with guitar-shop owner Dave Hussong in Dayton, OH, set off a rapid chain of events that culminated in Ward's 1990 debut album for Black Top, *Fear No Evil*, and a second chance at the brass ring.

Ward's first taste of stardom came as leader of the Ohio Untouchables (who later mutated into the Ohio Players long after Ward's departure) during the early '60s. Born into impoverished circumstances in rural Georgia, Ward picked up his first guitar at age ten. Singles by Sister Rosetta Tharpe, B.B. King, and Muddy Waters left their mark on the youth. After a stint in the Army, Ward came home in 1959 and joined his first band, the Brassettes (who also included Roy Lee Johnson, soon to join Piano Red's band and croon "Mister Moonlight").

Tired of seeing little monetary reward for opening for the likes of James Brown and Piano Red with the Brassettes, Ward moved to Dayton, OH, in 1960. Inspired by hard-bitten FBI man Eliott Ness on TV's *The Untouchables*, Ward recruited bassist Levoy Fredrick and drummer Cornelius Johnson to form the first edition of the Ohio Untouchables. Ward's trademark vibrato-soaked guitar sound was the direct result of acquiring a Magnatone amplifier at a Dayton music store. Lonnie Mack was so entranced by the watery sound of Ward's amp that he bought a Magnatone as well; both still utilize the same trademark sound to this day.

Detroit producer Robert West signed the Untouchables to his LuPine logo in 1962. Ward's quirky touch was beautifully exhibited on the hard-bitten "I'm Tired," a chilling doo wop-tinged

"Forgive Me Darling," and the exotic "Your Love Is Amazing" for LuPine. In addition, the Untouchables backed Wilson Pickett and the Falcons on their gospel-charged 1962 smash "I Found a Love."

Ward and his band also briefly recorded for Detroit's Thelma Records, waxing the driving blues "Your Love Is Real" and a soul-sending "I'm Gonna Cry a River." Ward left the Untouchables in 1965 (to be replaced by Leroy "Sugarfoot" Bonner), stopping at Don Davis' Groove City label long enough to cut a super Detroit soul pairing, "Fear No Evil" (the original version) and "My Love Is Strictly Reserved for You," circa 1966–67.

During the early '70s, Ward worked as a session guitarist at Motown, playing behind the Temptations and the Undisputed Truth (he was an old pal of Joe Harris, lead singer of the latter group). But when his wife died in 1977, Ward hit the skids. He moved back to Georgia, and served a year in jail at one point (ironically, one of his prison mates was singer Major Lance, whose career was at similarly low ebb).

In 1990, that auspicious encounter with Hussong started the ball rolling for Ward's return to action. Black Top boss Hammond Scott signed the guitarist and produced the amazing *Fear No Evil* and a credible 1993 follow-up, *Rhythm of the People*. The label recently issued a third set, *Black Bottom*, that once again captured Ward's curiously mystical appeal. Today, Ward lives in tiny Dry Branch, GA, with his second wife Roberta, who contributed background vocals to his encore album. —*Bill Dahl*

★ **Fear No Evil** / 1991 / Black Top ◆◆◆◆◆
One of the most amazing comeback stories of the modern blues era was ignited by this astonishing album. Robert Ward hadn't recorded as a leader in close to a quarter century, but his melismatic, almost mystical vocal quality and quirky, vibrato-enriched guitar sound utterly vital and electrifying as he revives some of his own obscure oldies ("Your Love Is Amazing," "Forgive Me Darling," "Strictly Reserved for You") and debuts a few new compositions for good measure. One of the classic blues/soul albums of the '90s. —*Bill Dahl*

Rhythm of the People / 1993 / Black Top ◆◆◆
Disappointing sequel to Ward's magnificent first Black Top disc—his vocals don't sound nearly as hearty this time around, and a some of the songs just aren't up to par ("All Proud Races" is downright stupid). There's a taste of gospel in "What a Friend We Have in Jesus," Ward's own take on "I Found a Love," and a steamy remake of James Brown's "And I Do Just What I Want." —*Bill Dahl*

Hot Stuff / 1995 / Relic ◆◆◆◆◆
These are the first magnificent 1960s waxings of guitarist Robert Ward & the Ohio Untouchables for the tiny LuPine, Thelma, and Groove City logos; full of fiery soul, watery, vibrato-enhanced axe, and sinuous rhythms. Ward's piercing vocals on "I'm Tired," "Your Love Is Amazing," and "Fear No Evil" are mesmerizing. Also aboard are four classic cuts by the Wilson Pickett-led Falcons from 1962 with the Untouchables in support (the gospel-soaked "I Found a Love" was a legit smash, while Ward sears the strings on their "Let's Kiss and Make Up"). —*Bill Dahl*

Black Bottom / Oct. 17, 1995 / Black Top ◆◆◆◆
Now this is more like it. Ward is back in top form for his third Black Top outing, with better songs (most of them originals), skin-tight support from the Black Top house band, and plenty of that singularly gurgly guitar that inspired Lonnie Mack to follow Ward's lead and buy a Magnatone amp when he was starting out. —*Bill Dahl*

Baby Boy Warren

b. Aug. 13, 1919, Lake Providence, LA, **d.** Jul. 1, 1977, Detroit, MI
Guitar, Vocals / Electric Blues
The denizens of Detroit's postwar blues scene never really received their due (except for John Lee Hooker, of course). Robert "Baby Boy" Warren compiled a sterling discography from 1949 to 1954 for a variety of Motor City firms without ever managing to transcend his local status along Hastings Street.

After honing his blues guitar approach in Memphis (where he was raised), Warren came to Detroit in 1942 to work for General Motors and gig on the side. The fruits of his first recording session in 1949 with pianist Charley Mills supporting him came out on several different logos: Prize, Staff, Gotham, even King's Federal subsidiary. A second date in 1950 that found him backed by pianist Boogie Woogie Red was split between Staff and

Sampson; Swing Time snagged "I Got Lucky"/"Let's Renew Our Love" and pressed it for West Coast consumption.

One of his most memorable sessions took place in 1954, when wizened harpist Sonny Boy Williamson came to Detroit and backed Warren on "Sanafee" and "Chuc-A-Luck," which found their way to Nashville's Excello label. Joe Von Battle's JVB imprint unleashed Warren's "Hello Stranger" and "Baby Boy Blues" from the same date. That same year, a single for powerful Chicago deejay Al Benson's Blue Lake Records coupled "Mattie Mae" and "Santa Fe."

The 1970s brought Baby Boy Warren a taste of European touring, though nothing substantial, before he passed away in 1977. —*Bill Dahl*

● **Baby Boy Warren** / BBW ◆◆◆◆◆
This may be a bootleg vinyl album (issued at various times with different covers ranging from a mocked-up newspaper headline to a grotesque, sloppy cartoon impressionistic rendering of the bluesman) taped off of old scratchy 78s, but it's the only place you're going to hear the recorded output of this marvelous Detroit bluesman. Recording for JVB, Excello, Drummond, Staff, and Gotham, Warren's sense of song structure owes a strong debt to Robert Johnson and his lyrics are full of wry humor and mordant wit. As the leader of the first great band to emerge from the Detroit blues scene, the lineup of players on these sides include Boogie Woogie Red on piano, Calvin Frazier (another running buddy of Robert Johnson) on lead guitar, the self describable Washboard Willie, and, on four tracks, Sonny Boy Williamson, moonlighting away from the King Biscuit Boys. Highlights include "Not Welcome Anymore," "Baby Boy Blues," the stomping instrumental "Chuck-a-Luck," "Mattie Mae," "Hello Stranger" (a different version of "Mattie Mae" from a later session), and a driving take on Robert Johnson's "Stop Breaking Down." Next to the early work of John Lee Hooker and a stray anthology, this is Detroit blues at its finest. —*Cub Koda*

Washboard Sam (Robert Brown)

b. Jul. 15, 1910, Walnut Ridge, AR, **d.** Nov. 13, 1966, Chicago, IL
Vocals, Washboard / Acoustic Chicago Blues
A popular hokum blues artist, Washboard Sam recorded hundreds of records in the late '30s and '40s, usually with singer/guitarist Big Bill Broonzy. Of all the washboard players of the era, Sam was the most popular, due not only to his to his washboard talent, but his skills as a songwriter, as well as his strong voice. As an accompanist, Washboard Sam played with Broonzy, and with bluesmen like Bukka White, Memphis Slim, Willie Lacey, and Jazz Gillum.

Washboard Sam (b. Robert Brown) is the illegitimate son of Frank Broonzy, who also fathered Big Bill Broonzy. Sam was raised in Arkansas, working on a farm. He moved to Memphis in the early '20s to play the blues. While in Memphis, he met Sleepy John Estes and Hammie Nixon and the trio played street corners, collecting tips from passer-bys. In 1932, Washboard Sam moved to Chicago. Initially he played for tips, but soon he began performing regularly with Big Bill Broonzy. Within a few years, Sam was supporting Broonzy on the guitarist's Bluebird recordings. Soon, he was supporting a number of different musicians on their recording sessions, including pianist Memphis Slim, bassist Ransom Knowlin, and a handful of saxophone players, who all recorded for Bluebird

In 1935, Washboard Sam began recording for both Bluebird and Vocalion Records, often supported by Big Bill Broonzy. Throughout the rest of the '30s and the '40s, Sam was one of the most popular Chicago bluesmen, selling numerous records and playing to packed audiences. After World War II, his audience began to shrink, largely because he had difficulty adapting to the new electric blues. In 1953, Washboard Sam recorded a session for Chess Records and then retired. In the early '60s, Williie Dixon and Memphis Slim tried to persuade Sam to return to the stage to capitalize on the blues revival. Initially, he relented, but in 1963, he began performing concerts in clubs and coffeehouses in Chicago; he even played a handful of dates in Europe in early 1964.

Washboard Sam made his final recordings for the small Chicago-based label Spivey in 1964. The following year, his health quickly declined and he stopped recording and playing shows. In November of 1966, he died of heart disease. —*Stephen Thomas Erlewine & Cub Koda*

Feeling Lowdown / 1971 / RCA Victor ✦✦✦✦✦
Washboard Sam (1935–1947) / Jan. 1991 / Story Of Blues ✦✦✦
Forget the washboard, which was almost more a prop than an instrument. Robert Brown was a captivating vocalist and an expert at working off his sidemen, and he coaxed creditable riffs out of that washboard, even if they all sounded the same. This is peak material, done when he was in excellent voice and hadn't yet gotten stagnant in his material or approach. —*Ron Wynn*

● **Blues Classics by Washboard Sam 1935–1941** / Blues Classics ✦✦✦✦✦
This still ranks as the best collection of Washboard Sam's finest, or at least popularly known pieces. —*Ron Wynn*

Washboard Sam, Vol. 1 / Document ✦✦✦✦✦
Eighteen sides from the classic Bluebird period, with solid support from Big Bill Broonzy, Black Bob, and Blind John Davis. Includes "Who Pumped the Wind in My Doughnut" and "He's a Creepin' Man." —*Cub Koda*

Dinah Washington (Ruth Lee Jones)

b. Aug. 29, 1924, Tuscaloosa, AL, **d.** Dec. 14, 1963, Detroit, MI
Vocals / Blues, Standards
One of the most versatile and gifted vocalists in American popular music history, Dinah Washington made extraordinary recordings in jazz, blues, R&B, and light pop contexts, and could have done the same in gospel had she chosen to record in that mode. But the former Ruth Jones didn't believe in mixing the secular and spiritual, and once she'd entered the non-religious music world professionally, refused to include gospel in her repertoire. Washington's penetrating, high-pitched voice, incredible sense of drama and timing, crystal clear enunciation, and equal facility with sad, bawdy, celebratory or rousing material enabled her to sing any and everything with distinction. Washington played piano and directed her church choir growing up in Chicago. For a while she split her time between clubs and singing and playing piano in Salle Martin's gospel choir as Ruth Jones. There's some dispute about the origin of her name. Some sources say the manager of the Garrick Stage Bar gave her the name Dinah Washington; other say it was Hampton who selected it. It is undisputed Hampton heard and was impressed by Washington, who'd been discovered by manager Joe Glaser. She worked in Hampton's band from 1943 to 1946. Some of her biggest R&B hits were written by Leonard Feather, the distinguished critic who was a successful composer in the '40s. Washington dominated the R&B charts in the late '40s and '50s, but also did straight jazz sessions for EmArcy and Mercury, with horn accompanists including Clifford Brown, Clark Terry, and Maynard Ferguson, and pianists Wynton Kelly, a young Joe Zawinul, and Andrew Hill. She wanted to record what she liked, irregardless of whether it was considered suitable, and in today's market would be a crossover superstar.

"What A Difference A Day Makes." From that point forward nearly all of her recordings were slow ballads with accompaniment from faceless orchestras that would not have been out of place on a country record! Although she did have a few more hits (including some duets with Brook Benton), Washington's post-1958 output has not dated well at all, unlike the music from her first 15 years of recordings. However she was only 39 and still in peak musical form when she died from an accidental overdose of diet pills and alcohol in 1963. Dinah Washington remains the biggest influence on most black female singers (particularly in R&B and soul) who have come to prominence since the mid-1950s. Virtually all of her recordings are currently in print on CDs including a massive reissue series of her Mercury and EmArcy sessions. —*Ron Wynn and Dan Morgenstern*

Slick Chick: R&B Years / Dec. 29, 1943–Nov. 17, 1954 / Emarcy ✦✦✦✦✦
This double LP has the cream of Dinah Washington's early recordings. She recorded extensively for Mercury and EmArcy and all of the performances are available on multi-disc sets but, for those listeners who want just a sampling of Dinah Washington at her best, this two-fer is the one to get. All 16 of her R&B hits from 1949–54 are here plus her very first recording session (which is highlighted by the original version of "Evil Gal Blues") and seven other selections. Whether backed by the Gerald Wilson Orchestra, Tab Smith, Cootie Williams, an all-star unit headed by drummer Jimmy Cobb, or studio orchestras, she is in superb form. —*Scott Yanow*

Wise Woman Blues / 1943–Aug. 26, 1963 / Rosetta ✦✦✦✦
This Rosetta LP draws its material from three sources. Eight of the 15 recordings are from Dinah Washington's Apollo sessions of December 1945 (all of which are included on Delmark's CD). Six songs are taken from live performances with Lionel Hampton's orchestra and "Do Nothing Till You Hear from Me" is a real rarity with Washington backed by Duke Ellington's Orchestra in 1963. The extensive liner notes (which have ten pictures of the singer from various stages of her career) are a major plus. —*Scott Yanow*

Mellow Mama / Dec. 10, 1945–Dec. 13, 1945 / Delmark ✦✦✦✦✦
Dinah Washington's first solo recordings (with the exception of a session supervised by Lionel Hampton in 1943) are included on this Delmark repackaging of her Apollo sides. Recorded in Los Angeles during a three-day period, the 12 selections feature the singer with a swinging jazz combo that has tenor saxophonist Lucky Thompson, trumpeter Karl George, vibraphonist Milt Jackson, and bassist Charles Mingus among its eight members. The 21-year-old Washington was already quite distinctive at this early stage and easily handles the blues and jive material with color and humor. Recommended despite the brevity (34 minutes) of the CD. —*Scott Yanow*

☆ **The Complete Dinah Washington on Mercury, Vol. 1 (1946–1949)** / Jan. 14, 1946–Sep. 27, 1949 / Mercury ✦✦✦✦
All of Dinah Washington's studio recordings from 1946–61 have been reissued in definitive fashion by Polygram on seven three CD sets. *Volume 1* finds the youthful singer (who was 21 on the earliest sessions) evolving from a little-known but already talented singer to a best-selling R&B artist. Ranging from jazz and spirited blues to middle-of-the-road ballads, this set (as with the others in the *Complete* series) includes both gems and duds but fortunately the great majority fall into the former category. The backup groups include orchestras led by Gerald Wilson, Tab Smith, Cootie Williams, Chubby Jackson, and Teddy Stewart and there are a dozen strong numbers with just a rhythm section. The first five volumes in this series are highly recommended. — *Scott Yanow*

☆ **The Complete Dinah Washington on Mercury, Vol. 2 (1950–1952)** / Feb. 7, 1950–May 6, 1952 / Mercury ✦✦✦✦
Dinah Washington was a best-selling artist on the R&B charts during this period but she was also a very versatile singer who could easily handle swinging jazz, schmaltzy ballads, blues and novelties with equal skill. The second of these seven three-CD sets in Mercury's *Complete* program mostly finds Washington being accompanied by studio orchestras although The Ravens join her on two numbers and drummer Jimmy Cobb heads a couple of jazz groups (including one with both Ben Webster and Wardell Gray on tenors). Not every selection is a classic but the quality level is quite high and the packaging is impeccable. Recommended. —*Scott Yanow*

☆ **Complete Dinah Washington on Mercury, Vol. 3 (1952–1954)** / 1952–Aug. 14, 1954 / Mercury ✦✦✦✦
Of the seven three-CD sets in Mercury's *Complete* series of Dinah Washington recordings, this is the most jazz-oriented one. The versatile singer participates in a very memorable jam session with an all-star group (featuring Clifford Brown, Maynard Ferguson, and Clark Terry on trumpets), meets up with Terry and tenor saxophonist Eddie Lockjaw Davis on another spontaneous date (highlighted by uptempo bops on "Bye Bye Blues" and "Blue Skies"), and has several classic collaborations with the warm Lester Youngish tenor of Paul Quinichette. There are a few commercial sides with studio orchestras that are included (since they took place during the same period) but those are in the great minority on this essential volume. —*Scott Yanow*

☆ **Complete Dinah Washington on Mercury, Vol. 4 (1954–1956)** / Nov. 2, 1954–Apr. 25, 1956 / Mercury ✦✦✦✦✦
The fourth of seven three-CD sets in Mercury's *Complete* series alternates between strong swinging jazz with the likes of trumpeter Clark Terry, tenor saxophonist Paul Quinichette, pianist Wynton Kelly and altoist Cannonball Adderley, and middle-of-the-road pop performances with studio orchestras. The third volume is the strongest in this series but the first five sets all contain more than enough jazz to justify their purchase. *Vol. 4* really attests to Dinah Washington's versatility. —*Scott Yanow*

☆ **Complete Dinah Washington on Mercury, Vol. 5 (1956–1958)** / Jun. 25, 1956–Jul. 6, 1958 / Mercury ✦✦✦✦✦
Mercury has given the great singer Dinah Washington the com-

plete treatment with seven three-CD sets that contain all of her recordings during the 1946–61 period, practically her entire career. *Vol. 5* is the final volume to be highly recommended, since it has her final jazz recordings. On many of these performances she is backed by orchestras led by Quincy Jones, Ernie Wilkins (including a tribute to Fats Waller), or Eddie Chamblee in arrangements that often leave room for short statements from some of the sidemen; one of the albums with Chamblee has a full set of songs associated with Bessie Smith. *Vol. 5* (which contains only a few commercial sides) concludes with her strong performance at the 1958 Newport Jazz Festival. —*Scott Yanow*

The Bessie Smith Songbook / Dec. 30, 1957–Jan. 20, 1958 / Emarcy ✦✦✦
It was only natural that the "Queen of the Blues" should record songs associated with the "Empress of the Blues." The performances by the septet/octet do not sound like the 1920s and the purposely ricky-tick drumming is insulting, but Dinah Washington sounds quite at home in this music. "Trombone Butter" (featuring trombonist Quentin Jackson in Charlie Green's role), "You've Been a Good Ole Wagon," "After You've Gone" and "Back Water Blues" are highpoints as she overcomes the cornball arrangements. —*Scott Yanow*

What a Diff'rence a Day Makes! / Feb. 19, 1959–Aug. 1959 / Mercury ✦✦✦✦
Dinah Washington's career reached a turning point with this album. A very talented singer who could interpret jazz, blues, pop, novelties and religious songs with equal skill, Washington had an unexpected pop hit with her straightforward version of "What a Diff'rence a Day Makes." From then on she would only record with commercial studio orchestras and stick to middle-of-the-road pop music. This 1959 set is not as bad as what would follow, with such songs as "I Remember You," "I Thought About You," "Manhattan," and "A Sunday Kind of Love" all receiving tasteful melodic treatment (although no chances are taken) by Washington and an orchestra conducted and arranged by Belford Hendricks. —*Scott Yanow*

Complete Dinah Washington on Mercury, Vol. 6 (1958–1960) / Feb. 19, 1959–Nov. 12, 1960 / Mercury ✦✦
Up until 1959, Dinah Washington was able to excel in every musical setting that she found herself. A strong jazz/blues vocalist who had many R&B hits, Washington always sounded confident and soulful even when backed by insipid studio orchestras. However, after her Feb. 19, 1959 recording of "What a Diff'rence a Day Makes" became a major hit and she gained fame, Dinah Washington stuck to safely commercial pop music. Even when she was singing superior songs during the 1959–63 period, Washington was always backed by large orchestras outfitted with extremely commercial charts better suited to country pop stars. The sixth in Mercury's series of three-CD sets starts with the Feb. 19 session and covers 21 months in Dinah Washington's career. Most of the 73 performances are difficult to sit through. —*Scott Yanow*

Unforgettable / Aug. 1959–Jan. 15, 1961 / Mercury ✦✦
After her hit of "What a Diff'rence a Day Makes" in 1959, Dinah Washington largely discarded her blues and jazz roots (at least on recordings) and played the role of a pop star. This CD (which has the original LP program of 12 songs joined by six others) finds Washington singing brief (mostly under three-minute) versions of standards in hopes of gaining another hit. The backing is strictly commercial and, although some may enjoy "This Bitter Earth," "The Song Is Ended," and "A Bad Case of the Blues," the music is consistently predictable and disappointingly forgettable. —*Scott Yanow*

Complete Dinah Washington on Mercury, Vol. 7 (1961) / 1961 / Mercury ✦✦
The seventh and final volume in Mercury's *Complete* series of Dinah Washington's recordings has impeccable packaging and largely inferior music, at least from the jazz standpoint. After recording a surprising hit version of "What a Diff'rence a Day Makes" in 1959, the singer stuck exclusively to middle-of-the-road pop music with large string orchestras on her recordings. This three-CD set (which contains Washington's final 67 recordings for Mercury plus a recently discovered alternate take from 1947) is often difficult to sit through for it totally lacks surprises, suspense or spontaneity. For completists only, but get the first five volumes. —*Scott Yanow*

In Love / May 1962–Aug. 1962 / Roulette ✦✦
Dinah Washington's final four years of recordings (1959–63) were purely commercial. Even her mannerisms and phrasing leaned closer to middle-of-the-road pop than to her roots in jazz and blues. For this so-so Roulette CD, Washington interprets standards and current pop tunes in very predictable fashion. Everything has the impression of being planned in advance and the accompanying orchestra (arranged by Don Costa) is quite anonymous. Pass on this and get Dinah Washington's earlier jazz sides instead. —*Scott Yanow*

Dinah '63 / 1963 / Roulette ✦✦
It is fairly easy to evaluate Dinah Washington's recordings. Before 1959 virtually everything she recorded (even when in a commercial setting) is worth acquiring but the opposite is true of the records from her final period (1959–63). As a pop artist, Washington was better than many but only a shadow of what she had been. Her preplanned emotions and exaggerated mannerisms on her Roulette recordings (of which *Dinah '63* was one of her last) get tiring very fast. —*Scott Yanow*

Tuts Washington (Isidore Washington)
b. 1907, **d.** 1984, New Orleans, LA
Piano / Boogie-Woogie
Isidore "Tuts" Washington (also widely known as "Papa Yellow") was 76 years old at the time of the release of his first solo recording. He began playing piano at age ten and worked with a number of famed New Orleans bandsmen—Kid Rena, Papa Celestin, Kid Punch Miller—over the course of his long career. In the late '30s he made trips to California and in 1950 joined the Tab Smith Orchestra in St. Louis for a time. During the better part of the '40s, he worked in a trio backing up blues singer Smiley Lewis, which took him to various locations from Oklahoma to Florida. In 1958 he was with the Clyde Kerr Orchestra in New Orleans, and a decade later made several excursions up the Mississippi River on the Delta Queen. From 1968 to 1973 Tuts held forth at the Court of Two Sisters Restaurant in the French Quarter, then moving on to the piano bar at the Pontchartrain Hotel in the early '80s. He died while performing on stage at the 1984 New Orleans World's Fair.

Tuts Washington identified Joseph Louis "Red" Cayou, an itinerant New Orleans pianist, as a prime influence on his early playing. He developed his repertoire by following the brass bands on the streets of New Orleans, memorizing the tunes and working out his own versions at home. He was self-taught at first but eventually took lessons at age 18; apparently his "professor" felt that Tuts was already too advanced to benefit from basic instruction, and at that point he turned to "Red" Caillou, whose hands he described as "like lightning." Washington specialized in instrumental pieces, but he also maintained a number of bawdy blues songs which he delivered with an impish relish. As the recognized "dean" of New Orleans piano players by the mid-century, he is credited frequently as a major influence on Fats Domino, Professor Longhair, James Booker, Dr. John, and Allen Toussaint. —*Bruce Boyd Raeburn*

● **New Orleans Piano Professor** / Apr. 1984 / Rounder ✦✦✦✦✦
Venerable New Orleans pianist Tuts Washington didn't get many chances to record during his lifetime. This 1983 session, now available on CD, was his most extensive project, with 23 songs covering everything from spirituals to traditional jazz numbers, pop pieces, novelty tunes, blues and country. Washington played them all in a seamless manner, displaying the mix of boogie-woogie and barrelhouse riffs, R&B, blues, and gospel elements, Afro-Latin and Caribbean rhythmic accents, and jazz phrasing and licks mastered through many decades of playing in bars and clubs. This was his chance in the spotlight, and Washington didn't waste it. —*Ron Wynn*

Walter "Wolfman" Washington
b. New Orleans, LA
Guitar, Vocals / Soul, R&B, Soul Blues
Walter Washington became a local legend in the Black clubs of New Orleans in the '70s and '80s and worked his way up to national status with a series of well-received albums and appearances. His recording affiliations have likewise moved from local to national independent to major label. An innovative guitarist and fine singer who has also done some excellent work with vocalist Johnny Adams, Washington does not perform in the

classic New Orleans R&B mold but incorporates soul, funk, jazz, and blues with fluency and power.

Washington was born and raised in New Orleans, where he performed in his mother's church choir as a child. As he grew older, he fell in love with blues and R&B and he learned how to play guitar. His first big break came in the form of a supporting role for vocalist Johnny Adams, working with the singer in the late '50s. In the early '60s, Washington became a member of Lee Dorsey's touring band; after that engagement was through, he worked with Irma Thomas.

In the mid-'60s, Washington formed his own band, the All Fools Band, and began headlining at local New Orleans clubs. By the early '70s, his popularity had grown enough to earn him a slot on a European package tour of New Orleans R&B acts. In the late '70s, he toured Europe on his own with his new band, the Roadmasters.

Washington began his recording career relatively late, cutting his first album in 1981. The record, *Rainin' In My Heart*, appeared on a small independent lable called Hep Me; it was later re-released on Maison de Soul. Four years after his debut, Washington landed a contract with Rounder Records, releasing *Wolf Tracks* in 1986. The guitarist recorded two more albums for Rounder—*Out of the Dark* (1988) and *Wolf at the Door*—before moving to the major-label Point Blank/Charisma in 1991. Throughout the '90s, Washington continued to perform regularly, particularly in New Orleans clubs, and he recorded occasionally. —*Jim O'Neal & Stephen Thomas Erlewine*

Wolf Tracks / 1986 / Rounder ✦✦✦
Guitarist/vocalist Walter "Wolfman" Washington didn't get his shot on a national label until his 1986 debut for Rounder. While the album wasn't flawless, he possessed a strong, often compelling voice and was a skilled guitarist who could play effectively in a blues, R&B or jazz mode. Washington turned in a competent cover of the Tyrone Davis hit "Can I Change My Mind," spun a good yarn on "You Got Me Worried," and sounded weary, forlorn and anguished on various cuts. Although his songs weren't exactly lyrical triumphs, they were earnestly performed, and Washington displayed more than enough talent to justify subsequent followups. —*Ron Wynn*

Out of the Dark / 1988 / Rounder ✦✦✦✦
Walter "Wolfman" Washington's second Rounder session mixed Crescent City R&B and jazz licks with contemporary and vintage songs and production. Washington's cover of "Ain't That Loving You," while not quite as dramatic as Bobby "Blue" Bland's, was still outstanding; he was appropriately ironic and bemused on "You Can Stay But The Noise Must Go" and vividly soulful on "Save Your Love For Me" and "Steal Away." Only on "Feel So Bad," a questionable song at best, did he sound strained and unfocused. Washington's guitar playing was sharp, creative and tasty without being self-indulgent. It wasn't the kind of glossy, trendy work that garners the pop spotlight, but Washington showed progress and fine skills. —*Ron Wynn*

● **Wolf at the Door** / 1991 / Rounder ✦✦✦✦✦
This release was arguably Washington's finest; it contained riveting, steamy ballads and fiery uptempo originals written by Washington, and featured his most mature, convincing leads. He did credible covers of "Is It Something You've Got (I Had It All The Time)" and the Doc Pomus/Dr. John number "Hello Stranger," but it was on his own numbers that Washington demonstrated a much improved, more dynamic approach. His band was tasty, tight, and funky, especially saxophonist Tom Fitzpatrick. —*Ron Wynn*

Sada / 1991 / Point Blank ✦✦✦
Walter Washington's *Sada* is a blues album only in the loosest sense of the term—Washington draws from Southern soul and funk as much as Chicago blues. Even so, he and his band are accomplished professionals, capable of negotiating every twist and turn in the music. The uptempo numbers are fun, but the best parts about the record are the ballads—Washington is a smooth, seductive singer and he makes all of his slow ones sound heartfelt and genuine. —*Thom Owens*

Ethel Waters

b. Oct. 31, 1896, Chester, PA, d. Sep. 1, 1977, Chatsworth, CA
Vocals / Blues, Swing, Classic Jazz
Ethel Waters had a long and varied career and was one of the first true jazz singers to record. Defying racism with her talent and bravery, Waters became a stage and movie star in the 1930s and '40s without leaving the U.S. She grew up near Philadelphia

and, unlike many of her contemporaries, developed a clear and easily understandable diction. Originally classified as a blues singer (and she could sing the blues almost on the level of a Bessie Smith), Waters' jazz-oriented recordings of 1921-28 swung before that term was even coined. A star early on at theatres and nightclubs, Waters introduced such songs as "Dinah," "Am I Blue" (in a 1929 movie) and "Stormy Weather." She made a smooth transition from jazz singer of the 1920s to a pop music star of the '30s and she was a strong influence on many vocalists including Mildred Bailey, Lee Wiley and Connee Boswell. Waters spent the latter half of the 1930s touring with a group headed by her husband-trumpeter Eddie Mallory and appeared on Broadway (*Mamba's Daughter* in 1939) and in the 1943 film *Cabin in the Sky;* in the latter she introduced "Taking a Chance on Love," "Good for Nothing Joe," and the title cut. In later years Waters was seen in nonmusical dramatic roles and after 1960 she mostly performed performances to religious work for the evangelist Billy Graham. The European Classics label has reissued all of Ethel Waters' prime recordings and they still sound fresh and lively today. —*Scott Yanow*

Ethel Waters 1921-1923 / Mar. 21, 1921-Mar. 1923 / Classics ✦✦✦✦
Ethel Waters was one of the few singers from the early '20s whose early recordings are still quite listenable. This CD from the Classics label has her first 22 sides (many previously rare, including five interesting instrumentals by Waters' band) and, although not on the same level as her performances from a few years later, the music is quite good for the time period. The sidemen are mostly obscure but include pianist Fletcher Henderson and cornetists Gus Aiken and Joe Smith with the highlights being "The New York Glide," "Down Home Blues," "There'll Be Some Changes Made," and "Midnight Blues." —*Scott Yanow*

1923-1925 / Mar. 1923-Jul. 28, 1925 / Classics ✦✦✦✦
The European Classics label's Ethel Waters program completely wipes out all of the other Waters reissues–it reissues all of her recordings from her prime years in chronological order. Since the singer was very consistent, there are very few duds and many gems in these sets. This particular CD traces Ethel Waters during a two year period. Both the recording quality and her accompaniment greatly improve during this time; cornetist Joe Smith is a standout and pianist Fats Waller is present on "Pleasure Mad" and "Back-Bitin' Mamma." Highlights includes "You Can't Do What My Last Man Did," "Sweet Georgia Brown," "Go Back Where You Stayed Last Night," and "Sympathetic Dan." —*Scott Yanow*

Ethel Waters' Greatest Years / Apr. 29, 1925-Mar. 30, 1934 / Columbia ✦✦✦✦✦
When this two-LP set was originally released, it was the definitive Ethel Waters reissue although now it has been succeeded by Classics' more complete CD program. However this two-fer is still the best single package ever released of the singer. The first album (covering 1925-28) focuses on her jazz years and has particularly strong contributions from cornetist Joe Smith and pianist James P. Johnson among others; "Sweet Georgia Brown," "Go Back Where You Stayed Last Night," "You Can't Do What My Last Man Did," "Sweet Man," "I've Found a New Baby," "Sugar," "Guess Who's in Town," and "My Handy Man" all qualify as classics. The second album mostly dates from 1929-34 and finds Waters joined by studio orchestras on most tracks. The emphasis is on ballads and sweet melodies but Waters still excels, particularly on "Waiting at the End of the Road," "Porgy," and "A Hundred Years from Today." This set is highly recommended to listeners who do not have the Classics CDs. —*Scott Yanow*

★ **1925-1926** / Aug. 25, 1925-Jul. 29, 1926 / Classics ✦✦✦✦
This CD in the Classics *Complete* Ethel Waters series contains plenty of gems including "You Can't Do What My Last Man Did," the original version of "Dinah," "Shake That Thing," "I've Found a New Baby" (which has some memorable cornet playing from Joe Smith), "Sugar," and "Heebies Jeebies." On "Maybe Not at All" Ethel Waters does eerie imitations of both Bessie Smith and Clara Smith. She had few competitors as a jazz singer during this era and the mostly intimate recordings (12 of the 23 tracks find her backed by just a pianist) feature Waters at her best. —*Scott Yanow*

Ethel Waters on Stage/Screen (1925-1940) / Oct. 20, 1925-Nov. 7, 1940 / Columbia ✦✦✦
The Columbia LP features Ethel Waters performing 16 songs

that debuted in shows or movies. With the exception of "Dinah" (this 1925 version is the original one) and "I'm Coming Virginia," all of the music dates from the 1929-40 era when Waters was better known as a musical comedy star than as a jazz singer. However, although the backing is generally a bit commercial, her performances of such numbers as "You're Lucky to Me," "Stormy Weather," "Taking a Chance on Love," and "Cabin in the Sky" are consistently memorable and definitive. —*Scott Yanow*

☆ **1926–1929** / Sep. 14, 1926–May 14, 1929 / Classics ♦♦♦♦♦
Few female jazz singers were on Ethel Waters' level during this period, just Bessie Smith and Annette Hanshaw and all three were quite different from each other. Waters has rarely sounded better than on the four numbers in which she is backed rather forcefully by pianist James P. Johnson (particularly "Guess Who's in Town" and "Do What You Did Last Night") but she is also in fine form on the other small-group sides. "I'm Coming Virginia," "Home," "Take Your Black Bottom Outside," "Someday Sweetheart," and "Am I Blue" (which she introduced) are among the many gems on this highly recommended entry in Classics' complete series. —*Scott Yanow*

1929–1931 / Jun. 6, 1929–Jun. 16, 1931 / Classics ♦♦♦♦♦
During the period covered in this CD from Classics' *Complete Ethel Waters* series, the singer was quickly developing into a top musical comedy and Broadway star. Although her backup was not as jazz-oriented as previously (despite the presence of such players as clarinetist Benny Goodman, trombonist Tommy Dorsey, Jimmy Dorsey on clarinet and alto, and trumpeter Manny Klein), Waters' renditions of many of these future standards are definitive, particularly "True Blue Lou," "Waiting at the End of the Road," "Porgy," "You're Lucky to Me," and "When Your Lover Has Gone." Superior jazz-oriented singing from one of the very best. —*Scott Yanow*

1931–1934 / Aug. 10, 1931–Sep. 5, 1934 / Classics ♦♦♦♦♦
Ethel Waters was one of the very few Black performers who was able to keep working in music during the early years of the Depression; in fact her fame grew during the period covered by this excellent CD from Classics' *Complete* series. Among her back-up musicians on these consistently excellent sides are violinist Joe Venuti, the Dorsey Brothers, trumpeter Bunny Berigan, trombonist Jack Teagarden, clarinetist Benny Goodman, members of the Chick Webb big band, and the entire Duke Ellington orchestra (the latter on "I Can't Give You Anything but Love" and "Porgy"). Highpoints include the Ellington tracks, "St. Louis Blues" (with The Cecil Mack Choir), the original version of "Stormy Weather," "A Hundred Years from Today," and a remake of "Dinah." Highly recommended as are all of the Ethel Waters Classics discs. —*Scott Yanow*

Foremothers, Vol. 6 / Nov. 9, 1938–Aug. 15, 1939 / Rosetta ♦♦♦♦
This very attractive Rosetta LP (which has definitive liner notes and numerous pictures) includes all of singer Ethel Waters' 16 Bluebird recordings of 1938-39. She is accompanied by two different bands led by her husband (trumpeter Eddie Mallory) with Benny Carter on alto and clarinet and trombonist Tyree Glenn (doubling on vibes) among the sidemen. Waters was not a major part of the swing era but her own career (on stage and in films) was booming around this period. Her voice is heard in its prime on a variety of period pieces which are highlighted by "Old Man Harlem," "Georgia on My Mind," "Jeepers Creepers," and "They Say." —*Scott Yanow*

Muddy Waters (McKinley Morganfield)

b. Apr. 4, 1915, Rolling Fork, MS, **d.** Apr. 30, 1983, Westmont, IL
Guitar, Vocals / Electric Chicago Blues
A postwar Chicago blues scene without the magnificent contributions of Muddy Waters is absolutely unimaginable. From the late '40s on, he eloquently defined the city's aggressive, swaggering, Delta-rooted sound with his declamatory vocals and piercing slide guitar attack. When he passed away in 1983, the Windy City would never quite recover.

Like many of his contemporaries on the Chicago circuit, Waters was a product of the fertile Mississippi Delta. Born McKinley Morganfield in Rolling Fork, he grew up in nearby Clarksdale on Stovall's Plantation. His idol was the powerful Son House, a Delta patriarch whose flailing slide work and intimidating intensity Waters would emulate in his own fashion.

Musicologist Alan Lomax traveled through Stovall's in August of 1941 under the auspices of the Library of Congress, in search of new talent for purposes of field recording. With the discovery of Morganfield, Lomax must have immediately known he'd stumbled across someone very special.

Setting up his portable recording rig in the Delta bluesman's house, Lomax captured for Library of Congress posterity Waters' mesmerizing rendition of "I Be's Troubled," which became his first big seller when he recut it a few years later for the Chess brothers' Aristocrat logo as "I Can't Be Satisfied." Lomax returned the next summer to record his bottleneck-wielding find more extensively, also cutting sides by the Son Simms Four (a string band that Waters belonged to).

Waters was renowned for his blues-playing prowess across the Delta, but that was about it until 1943, when he left for the bright lights of Chicago. A tiff with "the bossman" apparently also had a little something to do with his relocation plans. By the mid-'40s, Waters' slide skills were becoming a recognized entity on Chicago's South side, where he shared a stage or two with pianists Sunnyland Slim and Eddie Boyd and guitarist Blue Smitty. Producer Lester Melrose, who still had the local recording scene pretty much sewn up in 1946, accompanied Waters into the studio to wax a date for Columbia, but the urban nature of the sides didn't electrify anyone at the label's hierarchy and remained unissued for decades.

Sunnyland Slim played a large role in launching the career of Muddy Waters. The pianist invited him to provide accompaniment for his 1947 Aristocrat session that would produce "Johnson Machine Gun." One obstacle remained beforehand: Waters had a day gig delivering venetian blinds. But he wasn't about to let such a golden opportunity slip through his talented fingers. He informed his boss that a fictitious cousin had been murdered in an alley, so he needed a little time off to take care of business.

When Sunnyland was finished that auspicious day, Waters sang a pair of numbers, "Little Anna Mae" and "Gypsy Woman," that would become his own Aristocrat debut 78. They were rawer than the Columbia stuff, but not as inexorably down-home as "I Can't Be Satisfied" and its flip, "I Feel like Going Home" (the latter was his first national R&B hit in 1948). With Big Crawford slapping the bass behind Waters' gruff growl and slashing slide, "I Can't Be Satisfied" was such a local sensation that even Muddy Waters himself had a hard time buying a copy down on Maxwell Street.

He assembled a band that was so tight and vicious on stage that they were informally known as the Headhunters; they'd come into a bar where a band was playing, ask to sit in, and then "cut the heads" of their competitors with their superior musicianship. Little Walter, of course, would single-handedly revolutionize the role of the harmonica within the Chicago blues hierarchy; Jimmy Rogers was an utterly dependable second guitarist; and Baby Face Leroy Foster could play both drums and guitar. On top of their instrumental skills, all four men could sing powerfully.

1951 found Waters climbing the R&B charts no less than four times, beginning with "Louisiana Blues," and continuing through "Long Distance Call," "Honey Bee," and "Still a Fool." Although it didn't chart, his 1950 classic "Rollin' Stone" provided a certain young British combo with a rather enduring name. Leonard Chess himself provided the incredibly unsubtle bass-drum bombs on Waters' 1952 smash "She Moves Me."

"Mad Love," his only chart bow in 1953, is noteworthy as the first hit to feature the rolling piano of Otis Spann, who would anchor the Waters aggregation for the next 16 years. By this time, Foster was long gone from the band, but Rogers remained, and Chess insisted that Walter—by then a popular act in his own right—make nearly every Waters session into 1958 (why break up a winning combination?). There was one downside to having such a peerless band; as the ensemble work got tighter and more urbanized, Waters' trademark slide guitar was largely absent on many of his Chess waxings.

Willie Dixon was playing an increasingly important role in Muddy Waters' success. In addition to slapping his upright bass on Waters' platters, the burly Dixon was writing one future bedrock standard after another for him: "I'm Your Hoochie Coochie Man," "Just Make Love to Me," and "I'm Ready"; seminal performances all, and each blasted to the uppermost reaches of the R&B lists in 1954.

When labelmate Bo Diddley borrowed Waters' swaggering beat for his strutting "I'm a Man" in 1955, Muddy turned around and did him tit for tat by reworking the tune ever so slightly as

"Mannish Boy" and enjoying his own hit. "Sugar Sweet," a piledriving rocker with Spann's 88s anchoring the proceedings, also did well that year. 1956 brought three more R&B smashes: "Trouble No More," "Forty Days & Forty Nights," and "Don't Go No Farther."

But rock 'n' roll was quickly blunting the momentum of veteran blues aces like Waters; Chess was growing more attuned to the modern sounds of Chuck Berry, Bo Diddley, the Moonglows, and the Flamingos. Ironically, it was Muddy Waters that had sent Berry to Chess in the first place.

After that, there was only one more chart item, 1958's typically uncompromising (and metaphorically loaded) "Close to You." But Waters' Chess output was still of uniformly stellar quality, boasting gems like "Walking Thru the Park" (as close as he was likely to come to mining a rock 'n' roll groove) and "She's Nineteen Years Old," among the first sides to feature James Cotton's harp instead of Walter's, in 1958. That was also the year that Muddy Waters and Spann made their first sojourn to England, where his electrified guitar horrified sedate Britishers accustomed to the folksy homilies of Big Bill Broonzy. Perhaps chagrined by the response, Waters paid tribute to Broonzy with a solid LP of his material in 1959.

Cotton was apparently the bandmember that first turned Muddy on to "Got My Mojo Working," originally cut by Ann Cole in New York. Waters' 1956 cover was pleasing enough but went nowhere on the charts. But when the band launched into a supercharged version of the same tune at the 1960 Newport Jazz Festival, Cotton and Spann put an entirely new groove to it, making it an instant classic (fortuitously, Chess was on hand to capture the festivities on tape).

As the 1960s dawned, Muddy Waters' Chess sides were sounding a trifle tired. Oh, the novelty thumper "Tiger in Your Tank" packed a reasonably high-octane wallop, but his adaptation of Junior Wells' "Messin' with the Kid" (as "Messin' with the Man") and a less-than-timely "Muddy Waters Twist" were a long way removed indeed from the mesmerizing Delta sizzle that Waters had purveyed a decade earlier.

Overdubbing his vocal over an instrumental track by guitarist Earl Hooker, Waters laid down an uncompromising "You Shook Me" in 1962 that was a step in the right direction. Drummer Casey Jones supplied some intriguing percussive effects on another 1962 workout, "You Need Love," which Led Zeppelin liked so much that they purloined it as their own creation later on.

In the wake of the folk blues boom, Waters reverted to an acoustic format for a fine 1963 LP, *Folk Singer*, that found him receiving superb backing from guitarist Buddy Guy, Dixon on bass, and drummer Clifton James. In October, he ventured overseas again as part of the Lippmann & Rau-promoted American Folk Blues Festival, sharing the bill with Sonny Boy Williamson, Memphis Slim, Big Joe Williams, and Lonnie Johnson.

The personnel of the Waters band was much more fluid during the 1960s, but he always whipped them into first-rate shape. Guitarists Pee Wee Madison, Luther "Snake Boy" Johnson, and Sammy Lawhorn; harpists Mojo Buford and George Smith; bassists Jimmy Lee Morris and Calvin "Fuzz" Jones; and drummers Francis Clay and Willie "Big Eyes" Smith (along with Spann, of course) all passed through the ranks.

In 1964, Waters cut a two-sided gem for Chess, "The Same Thing"/"You Can't Lose What You Never Had," that boasted a distinct 1950s feel in its sparse, reflexive approach. Most of his subsequent Chess catalog, though, is fairly forgettable. Worst of all were two horrific attempts to make him a psychedelic icon. 1968's *Electric Mud* forced Waters to ape his pupils via an unintentionally hilarious cover of the Stones' "Let's Spend the Night Together" (session guitarist Phil Upchurch still cringes at the mere mention of this album). *After the Rain* was no improvement the following year.

Partially salvaging this barren period in his discography was the *Fathers and Sons* project, also done in 1969 for Chess, which paired Muddy Waters and Spann with local youngbloods Paul Butterfield and Mike Bloomfield in a multi-generational celebration of legitimate Chicago blues.

After a period of steady touring worldwide but little standout recording activity, Waters' studio fortunes were resuscitated by another of his legion of disciples, guitarist Johnny Winter. Signed to Blue Sky, a Columbia subsidiary, Waters found himself during the making of the first LP, *Hard Again*—backed by pianist

Pinetop Perkins, drummer Willie Smith, and guitarist Bob Margolin from his touring band, Cotton on harp, and Winter's slam-bang guitar, Waters roared like a lion who had just awoken from a long nap.

Three subsequent Blue Sky albums continued the heartwarming back-to-the basics campaign. In 1980, his entire combo split to form the Legendary Blues Band; needless to note, he didn't have much trouble assembling another one (new members included pianist Lovie Lee, guitarist John Primer, and harpist Mojo Buford).

By the time of his death in 1983, Muddy Waters' exalted place in the history of blues (and 20th-century popular music, for that matter) was eternally assured. The Chicago blues genre that he turned upside down during the years following World War II would never recover—and that's a debt we'll never be able to repay. —*Bill Dahl*

☆ **Muddy Waters at Newport** / 1960 / MCA/Chess ✦✦✦✦
For many back in the early '60s, this was their first exposure to live recorded blues and it's still pretty damn impressive some 30-plus years down the line. Muddy, with a band featuring Otis Spann, James Cotton and guitarist Pat Hare, lays it down tough and cool with a set that literally had 'em dancing in the aisles by the set-closer, a ripping version of "Got My Mojo Working," reprised again in a shorter encore version. Kicking off with a version of "I've Got My Brand on You" that positively burns the relatively tame, in comparison, studio take, Waters heads full bore through impressive versions of "Hoochie Coochie Man," Big Bill Broonzy's "Feel So Good," and "Tiger in Your Tank." A great breakthrough moment in blues history, preserved for posterity. —*Cub Koda*

Muddy Waters Sings Big Bill Broonzy / 1964 / MCA/Chess ✦✦✦✦
Waters' tribute album to the man who gave him his start on the Chicago circuit, this stuff doesn't sound much like Broonzy so much as a virtual recasting of his songs into Muddy's electric Chicago style. Evidently the first time Waters and his band were recorded in stereo, the highlights include high voltage takes on "When I Get to Drinkin'" and "The Mopper's Blues," with some really great harp from James Cotton as an added bonus. —*Cub Koda*

The Real Folk Blues / 1965 / MCA/Chess ✦✦✦✦✦
Once Chess discovered a White folk-blues audience ripe and ready to hear the real thing, they released a series of albums under the *Real Folk Blues* banner. This is one of the best entries in the series, a mixed bag of early Chess sides from 1949–1954, some of it hearkening back to Muddy's first recordings for Aristocrat with only Big Crawford on string in support with some wonderful full band sides rounding out the package to give everyone the big picture. A couple of highlights to pay special attention to are the cha cha/shuffle strut of the band charging through "Walkin' Through the Park" and the "I'm a Man"-derived nastiness of "Mannish Boy." —*Cub Koda*

Blues from Big Bill's Copacabana / 1967 / MCA/Chess ✦✦✦✦
Originally released as *Folk Festival of the Blues* on Chess' Argo subsidiary, the reissue gets the title right the second time around, a live document of a steamy night in a Chicago blues club. Chicago blues disc jockey Big Bill Hill intros the band and the assembled stars (one of whom, Little Walter, is nowhere to be found on this disc), then Buddy Guy's band rips into "Wee Wee Baby," sung in three-part harmony by Buddy, Muddy Waters, and Willie Dixon. Some of the tracks here are ringers; Sonny Boy Williamson's "Bring It On Home" and a stray Buddy Guy track are actually studio takes with fake applause dubbed on. But the two from Howlin' Wolf and everything here from Muddy are real as it gets; funky, out of tune in spots, with the crowd literally sweating all over the tape. Muddy's versions (with Otis Spann sitting in with the band) of "Clouds In My Heart" and "She's 19 Years Old" are nothing short of brilliant and the only thing better than this aural document would be to have actually been there right down front. Simply raw and amazing. —*Cub Koda*

More Real Folk Blues / 1967 / MCA/Chess ✦✦✦✦✦
The companion volume to the first Waters entry in the series is even more down home than the first. Featuring another brace of early Chess sides from 1948–1952, this release features some essential tracks not found on *The Chess Box*. With the blud-

geoning stomp of "She's Alright" featuring Elgin Evans' kickass drumming and the moody introspection of "My Life Is Ruined" to be counted among the numerous highlights, this is a fine budget package that Muddy (and lovers of early Chicago blues) fans certainly shouldn't overlook. —*Cub Koda*

Super Super Blues Band / 1968 / MCA/Chess ✦✦
Featuring Bo Diddley stubbing his toe on a wah-wah pedal, Wolf and Muddy clearly ill at ease trying to sing songs they don't know, and a super annoying female chorus giving out banshee shrieks approximately every 45 seconds, this is one very chaotic, untogether super session to try and wade through. —*Cub Koda*

Super Blues / Nov. 1968 / MCA/Chess ✦✦
This is the first of two super session albums that Chess produced in the late '60s. Time has been a bit kinder to this one, featuring Muddy, Bo Diddley and Little Walter, than the one cut a year later with Howlin' Wolf standing in for Walter. It's loose and extremely sloppy, the time gets pushed around here and there and Little Walter's obviously in bad shape, his voice rusted to a croak and trying to blow with a collapsed lung. But there are moments where Bo's heavily tremoloed guitar sounds just fine, the band kicks it in a few spots and Muddy seems to be genuinely enjoying himself. Granted, these moments are few and way too far between, but at least nobody's playing a wah-wah pedal on here. —*Cub Koda*

They Call Me Muddy Waters / 1970 / MCA/Chess ✦✦✦
Upon its original 1970 release, this was a Grammy winner for Best Ethnic/Traditional Recording. A quarter of a century later, it seems like an interesting, but diffuse, collection of Muddy Waters tracks, running chronologically from 1951 up to 1967. Excepting the title track and a couple others, there's nothing really indispensable here. A good one to add to the collection after you've picked up on a half dozen others. —*Cub Koda*

The London Muddy Waters Sessions / 1971 / MCA/Chess ✦✦
If you like hearing '70s British rock stars attempting to jam with one of the originators of the form, then you'll probably like the results from this tepid 1971 session. Only the late Irish guitarist Rory Gallagher seems to be interacting with the old master here (and guitarist Sammy Lawhorn) while Stevie Winwood, Georgie Fame and Mitch Mitchell seem to be totally lost. —*Cub Koda*

Live at Mister Kelly's / Jun. 1971 / MCA/Chess ✦✦✦
Pretty decent live set, taped at a legendary and now-defunct Chicago nightspot not exactly known for presenting blues. Muddy Waters had one of his finer bands for the 1971 sessions—harpists James Cotton and Paul Oscher, guitarists Pee Wee Madison and Sammy Lawhorn, bassist Calvin Jones, and drummer Willie Smith push the Chi-town blues king as he tries his hand at "Boom Boom," "You Don't Have to Go," and "Nine Below Zero" (along with a few of his own classics). —*Bill Dahl*

Muddy & the Wolf / 1974 / MCA/Chess ✦✦✦
The title is a bit of a ringer, since this isn't a collaborative effort in any way, shape or form. This contains a half dozen live Waters tracks with Mike Bloomfield, Paul Butterfield, and Otis Spann culled from the *Father & Sons* sessions and also features tracks by Howlin' Wolf from his London sessions with Eric Clapton and Ringo Starr. File under 'just ok.' —*Cub Koda*

Hard Again / May 1977 / Blue Sky ✦✦✦
By the mid-'70s Muddy Waters was all but forgotten as a viable recording entity. But one person who hadn't forgotten—and was willing to put his rock stardom on the line for it—was Johnny Winter. He assembled a crack backing unit with himself, Pinetop Perkins, and James Cotton blowing their brains out and fueled the fire even further with top-notch material like "The Blues Had a Baby and They Named It Rock 'n' Roll." The end result was the finest latter-day album of Muddy's long career and the only one that can sit comfortably on the shelf next to his Chess classics. —*Cub Koda*

I'm Ready / Jun. 1978 / Blue Sky ✦✦✦
Another fine latter-day effort. —*Bill Dahl*

Muddy "Mississippi" Waters: Live / 1979 / Blue Sky ✦✦✦✦
Featuring fierce, declamatory vocals and an otherworldly slide, this documents a bluesman at the height of his powers. —*Jas Obrecht*

King Bee / 1981 / Blue Sky ✦✦✦
Waters' 1981 swan song was recorded with Johnny Winter. —*Jas Obrecht*

Rare & Unissued / 1984 / MCA/Chess ✦✦✦✦
Compiler Dick Shurman rummaged around in the voluminous Chess vaults long enough to emerge with this sterling 14-song collection of unissued and rare sides, most of them dating from Waters' 1947-1954 heyday. "Little Anna Mae," "Feel like Going Home," and "You're Gonna Miss Me" spotlight his stark Delta roots; "Stuff You Gotta Watch," "Smokestack Lightnin'," and "Born Lover" boast fuller Waters bands of immense power and drive. —*Bill Dahl*

Fathers and Sons / 1987 / Vogue ✦✦✦
This is a 1969 "super session" that actually works, teaming up Muddy with Paul Butterfield, Michael Bloomfield, Duck Dunn, Otis Spann, and Buddy Miles and Sam Lay sharing the drum stool. Originally issued as a double album, one disc featured studio remakes while the other disc featured the whole gang live in concert in front of a super-enthusiastic audience. No new material to speak of, but some really great performances and the "youngsters" give the old man the backing he deserves. —*Cub Koda*

★ **The Best of Muddy Waters** / 1987 / MCA/Chess ✦✦✦✦
If you're building your Muddy Waters collection from the ground up, you can do no better than this compact disc reissue of his first album featuring 12 tightly compacted gems of seminal Chicago blues. This release features the original versions of "I'm Your Hoochie-Coochie Man," "Long Distance Call," "I'm Ready," "Honey Bee," "I Just Wanna Make Love to You," "Still a Fool," and a song called "Rollin' Stone," which provided the name inspiration for a hippie rock magazine and a group of British musicians. 30-plus years after its original release, it still stands as the perfect introduction to his music and one of the top five greatest Chicago blues albums of all time. —*Cub Koda*

Trouble No More/Singles (1955–1959) / 1989 / MCA/Chess ✦✦✦✦
This is an excellent compilation of some of Muddy Waters' lesser-anthologized singles, all of them dating from the late '50s. Some of these were surprisingly hard to acquire in any form until this appeared; the original version of "Got My Mojo Working," for instance, as well as some of his higher-profile tracks, like "Rock Me," "Trouble No More," "Close to You," and "Don't Go No Further." All of these tracks appear on the *Chess Box*, so if you have that one, you don't need this one. But if you don't, you do. —*Richie Unterberger & Cub Koda*

★ **The Chess Box** / Mar. 1990 / MCA/Chess ✦✦✦✦
Multi-disc box sets are a nettlesome proposition for the casual blues fan and even some hardliners. Most folks just don't have the time or the attention span to stay with one artist over the course of three to four hours of material and because the very best sides are usually spread out over the various discs, just popping one in might not give you the artistic quick fix you're seeking. But if you've decided that Muddy's your main man and you want to build a Chicago blues collection that's comprehensive and expansive, this three-disc box just might be your first stop. While there's a European box that's far more exhaustive (and expensive, sporting both dodgy sound quality and dubious legality), this one is far easier to digest. If you want to go for the big one, this is it. —*Cub Koda*

Can't Get No Grindin' / 1991 / MCA/Chess ✦✦✦
One of Waters' last salvos for Chess, first issued in 1973. The title track boasts a nice easy swing reminiscent of past glories, and the lowdown "Garbage Man" has taken on a life of its own through subsequent covers. But some of the other tunes are fairly makeweight. —*Bill Dahl*

The Complete Muddy Waters 1947–1967 / 1992 / Charly ✦✦✦✦
No, this mammoth nine-disc compilation—205 tracks in all—isn't actually complete, since alternate takes have since turned up on a couple of items. Further, the sound quality is decidedly spotty, and Charly's legal right to put Chess material on the market at all has long been in question. But this is the only place CD enthusiasts are currently going to find more than a few indispensable 1950s sides that MCA hasn't gotten around to releasing quite yet. And the final disc holds some enlightening alternate takes (including a whopping eight runthroughs of "Woman Wanted" and nine versions of "Read Way Back") that may never see domestic light of day. For aficionados only, make no mistake! —*Bill Dahl*

Blues Sky / Jun. 16, 1992 / Columbia/Legacy ✦✦✦✦
This is a nice collection pairing down the best of the material
Waters recorded for the Blue Sky label between 1976 to 1980. With
Johnny Winter in the producer's chair, the backings are sympathet-
ic, and the songs are great (some of them remakes of earlier Chess
material). These are the tracks that garnered three consecutive
Grammy Awards (for Best Ethnic or Traditional Recording) for
Waters. And that can't be all bad. Not the place to start by any
means, but definitely worth a listen or two.—*Cub Koda*

Live In 1958 / 1993 / MW ✦✦✦
In the fall of 1958, Muddy Waters came to England to perform for
the first time. With his regular pianist Otis Spann along for the ride
and backed by the jazzy, horn-dominated Chris Barber band,
Muddy's declamatory vocals and electric slide guitar (set at Chicago
blues tavern levels) proved to be too much reality for purist British
audiences to handle. He immediately toned down his approach to
appease the straight-laced Brits, and what survives here is the complete concert from the following night at the Manchester Free Trade
Hall, dubbed from the only existing acetate. (Import)— Cub Koda

☆ **The Complete Plantation Recordings** / Jun. 8, 1993 / MCA
✦✦✦✦✦
At long last, Muddy's historic 1941–1942 Library of Congress
field recordings are all collected in one place, with the best fidelity that's been heard thus far. Waters performs solo pieces (you
can hear his slide rattling against the fretboard in spots) and
band pieces with the Son Sims Four, "Rosalie" being a virtual
blueprint for his later Chicago style. Of particular note are the
inclusion of several interview segments with Muddy from that
embryonic period and a photo of Muddy playing on the porch of
his cabin, dressed up and looking sharper than any Mississippi
sharecropper on Stovall's plantation you could possibly imagine.
This much more than just an important historical document; this
is some really fine music imbued with a sense of place, time and
loads of ambience. Beyond essential. —*Cub Koda*

One More Mile / 1994 / MCA/Chess ✦✦✦✦✦
A double CD of 41 tracks, none of which are found on the box
set. With only three exceptions, none of them have ever been
available on an American album before, and quite a few were
never previously released anywhere. During most of his stay at
Chess, Muddy's output was remarkably prolific and consistent. If
you are interested enough in him to own more than one of his
albums, you'll like what you hear on this collection, which
matches or nearly matches the standards of his best work. Lots
of rarities spanning the late '40s to the early '70s, with some special points of interest: the original 1955 version of "I Want To Be
Loved," covered by The Rolling Stones on the B-side of their very
first single, finally makes its first appearance on an American LP,
and the final 11 songs are from a previously unreleased 1972
Swiss radio broadcast, showcasing Muddy in a drummerless trio.
—*Richie Unterberger*

Johnny "Guitar" Watson

b. Feb. 3, 1935, Houston, TX, d. May 17, 1996, Japan
Guitar, Vocals / Soul, R&B
"Reinvention" could just as easily have been Johnny "Guitar"
Watson's middle name. The multi-talented performer parlayed
his stunning guitar skills into a vaunted reputation as one of the
hottest blues axemen on the West Coast during the 1950s. But
that admirable trait wasn't paying the bills as the 1970s rolled in.
So he totally changed his image to that of a pimp-styled
funkster, enjoying more popularity than ever before for his
down-and-dirty R&B smashes "A Real Mother for Ya" and
"Superman Lover."
Watson's roots were in the fertile blues scene of Houston. As
a teen, he played with fellow Texas future greats Albert Collins
and Johnny Copeland. But he left Houston for Los Angeles when
he was only 15 years old. Back then, Watson's main instrument
was piano; that's what he played with Chuck Higgins' band
when the saxist cut "Motorhead Baby" for Combo in 1952
(Watson also handled vocal duties).
He was listed as Young John Watson when he signed with
Federal in 1953. His first sides for the King subsidiary found him
still tinkling the ivories, but by 1954, when he dreamed up the
absolutely astonishing instrumental "Space Guitar," the youth
(he was two days short of his 17th birthday) had switched over
to guitar. "Space Guitar" ranks with the greatest achievements of
its era—Watson's blistering rapid-fire attack, done without the

aid of a pick, presages futuristic effects that rock guitarists still
hadn't mastered another 15 years down the line.
Watson moved over to the Bihari brothers' RPM label in 1955
and waxed some of the toughest upbeat blues of their timeframe
(usually under saxist Maxwell Davis' supervision). "Hot Little
Mama," "Too Tired," and "Oh Baby" scorched the strings with
their blazing attack; "Someone Cares for Me" was a churchy Ray
Charles-styled slow-dragger, and "Three Hours Past Midnight"
cut bone-deep with its outrageous guitar work and laidback
vocal (Watson's cool phrasing as a singer was scarcely less distinctive than his playing). He scored his first hit in 1955 for RPM
with a note-perfect cover of New Orleanian Earl King's two-chord
swamp ballad "Those Lonely Lonely Nights."
Though he cut a demo version of the tune while at RPM,
Watson's first released version of "Gangster of Love" emerged in
1957 on Keen. Singles for Class ("One Kiss"), Goth, Arvee (the
rocking introduction "Johnny Guitar"), and Escort preceded a
hookup with Johnny Otis at King during the early '60s. He recut
"Gangster" for King, reaching a few more listeners this time, and
dented the R&B charts again in 1962 with his impassioned, violin-enriched blues ballad "Cuttin' In."
Never content to remain in one stylistic bag for long, Watson
landed at Chess just long enough to cut a jazz album in 1964
that placed him back behind the 88s. Along with longtime pal
Larry Williams, Watson rocked England in 1965 (their dynamic
repartee was captured for posterity by British Decca). Their partnership lasted stateside through several singles and an LP for
Okeh; among their achievements as a duo was the first vocal hit
on "Mercy, Mercy, Mercy" in 1967 (predating the Buckinghams
by a few months).
Little had been heard of this musical chameleon before he
returned decked out in funk threads during the mid-'70s. He hit
with "I Don't Want to Be a Lone Ranger" for Fantasy before
putting together an incredible run at DJM Records paced by "A
Real Mother for Ya" in 1977 and an updated "Gangster of Love"
the next year.
After a typically clever "Strike on Computers" nicked the R&B
lists in 1984, Watson again seemed to fall off the planet. But
counting this remarkable performer out was always a mistake.
Bow Wow, his 1994 album for Al Bell's Bellmark logo, returned
him to prominence and earned a Grammy nomination for best
contemporary blues album, even though its contents were pure
old school funk. Sadly, in the midst of a truly heartwarming
comeback campaign, Watson passed away while touring Japan
in 1996. —*Bill Dahl*

★ **Gangster of Love** / Charly ✦✦✦✦✦
Here's the innovative guitar wizard when he was young and
wearing his Texas blues roots prominently on his sleeve. Watson
spent two stints at King/Federal, both of them sampled here: his
1953–54 output includes the incomparable "Space Guitar," a sizzling "Half Pint of Whiskey," and a woozy "Gettin' Drunk." The
1961–63 King stuff is headed by the definitive version of
"Gangster of Love," the searing soul-tinged "Cuttin' In," and a
chunky "Broke and Lonely." —*Bill Dahl*

Johnny Guitar Watson / 1963 / King ✦✦✦✦✦
Fine collection of the guitarist's innovative 1950s and '60s stuff.
—*Bill Dahl*

I Cried for You / 1963 / Cadet ✦✦
Watson was highly versatile on this jazz piano set, but *I Cried for
You* is no big thrill. —*Bill Dahl*

Blues Soul / 1965 / MCA/Chess ✦✦✦
This 1964 album, later reissued under the title of *I Cried for You*,
displays an entirely different facet of the multitalented R&B
star's musical personality. Here he's an accomplished jazz pianist
in a trio setting, giving old standards like "Witchcraft" and
"Misty" his own vocal twist. Lowell Fulson's "Reconsider Baby"
is the only blues number on the LP. —*Bill Dahl*

Gangster Is Back / 1975 / Red Lightnin' ✦✦✦
Digital reissue of an old Red Lightnin' bootleg covering Watson's
1950s output that was revered back in the pre-CD era but
sounds very rough now. One thing in its favor: the disc sports
Watson's otherwise digitally unavailable 1957 version of
"Gangster of Love" for Keen. —*Bill Dahl*

Ain't That a Bitch / 1976 / Collectables ✦✦✦✦
The first of Watson's monstrously popular funk-based albums for
DJM, and in all likelihood, the best of the lot. The title cut of the

1976 album is a sardonic gem, Watson's sinuous guitar licks a far cry from his brash '50s sound. The intimate "I Want to Ta-Ta You Baby," "Superman Lover," and "I Need It" also rate with Watson's most alluring old school R&B output. —*Bill Dahl*

Funk Beyond the Call of Duty / Feb. 1977 / Collectables ✦✦✦
Less consistent than its immediate predecessors but still a reasonably good funky time, as Johnny Guitar once again displays his streetwise humor on "It's About the Dollar Bill" and "Barn Door" on the 1977 set. —*Bill Dahl*

Love Jones / 1980 / Collectables ✦✦
Watson's once-innovative funk formula was showing major signs of wear and tear by the time this 1980 album hit the charts. Weird and spacy in spots, and seldom interesting. —*Bill Dahl*

I Heard That / 1985 / Charly ✦✦✦✦✦
King-Federal sides from the 1950s and '60s includes the amazing "Space Guitar." —*Bill Dahl*

Three Hours Past Midnight / 1991 / Flair ✦✦✦✦
Watson's mid-'50s catalog for the Bihari brothers' Flair logo is unassailable with searing rockers like "Oh Baby," "Hot Little Mama," and "Ruben" and the blistering slow blues title cut. Unfortunately, this 16-song collection utilizes inferior alternate takes on several of the most important titles. On the positive side, it contains both sides of his rare 1959 single for Class, "One Kiss"/"The Bear." —*Bill Dahl*

● **Gonna Hit That Highway: The Complete RPM Recordings** / 1992 / P-Vine ✦✦✦✦✦
No omissions with this two-disc Japanese set—not only are the official versions of all of Watson's vicious RPM sides here, so are a plethora of alternate takes and extreme rarities (including a demo version of "Gangster of Love" as "Love Bandit"). Could be tough to locate, but for anyone seriously into this brilliant guitarist's early blues output, absolutely essential! —*Bill Dahl*

Listen/I Don't Want To Be Alone, Stranger / 1992 / Ace ✦✦✦✦
Watson's first two funk-slanted albums, combined conveniently on one disc. *Listen* dates from 1973, *I Don't Want to Be Alone* from two years later, and both are very together funk outings with a heady dose of modern blues at their core. —*Bill Dahl*

Real Mother / 1994 / Collectables ✦✦✦
Obviously, the storming funk workout that gives this 1977 gold album its title is the album's principal draw (it's been covered countless times, but never duplicated). As was his wont by this time, the multitalented Watson plays everything except drums and horns. —*Bill Dahl*

Giant / 1994 / Collectables ✦✦✦
Disco rhythms rear their repetitive head on much of this 1978 set, making it a whole lot less likable than Watson's earlier DJM albums. But his updated "Gangster of Love" packs a killer groove and sports some nice, very concise blues guitar work by the man. —*Bill Dahl*

Junior Watson (Michael Watson)

Guitar, Vocals / West Coast Blues
Despite playing the role of sideman, often in fine bands that left much to be desired in the visibility department, Mike "Junior" Watson was, and is, one of the most influential blues guitarists of his generation. In fact, following Robben Ford's defection into fusion, Watson was rivaled only by Hollywood Fats as king of the hill in California and only by Jimmie Vaughan anywhere else. While he and Vaughan have radically different approaches, Watson's arch-top-cheapo-through-reverb-tank sound has much in common with Hollywood Fats', as does his ability to nail seemingly every traditional electric blues style. But whereas Fats was a master of mimicry, Watson has a spontaneous, original bent laced with his oddball sense of humor. After starting out with harpist Gary Smith in Northern California in the early '70s, he teamed with Rod Piazza's Mightly Flyers (née Flying Saucer Band) for 11 years, where he was instrumental in injecting the Chicago-styled blues band (and countless others in its wake) with ample doses of swing, culling licks from guitarists Bill Jennings, Tiny Grimes, and Billy Butler. Along the way he gigged with Charlie Musselwhite, Jimmy Rogers, Luther Tucker, and others, eventually joining the '80s edition of Canned Heat, with whom he continues to tour. —*Dan Forte*

● **Long Overdue** / Jan. 24, 1994 / Black Top ✦✦✦✦✦
Giving jump blues and early R&B a kick in its baggy pants,

Watson's aptly-titled solo debut revealed what only guitarists (the more conscientious of them) had known for more than a decade: Here is a 6-stringer of rare talent, with the unique ability to play authentically and spontaneously—all-too-often contradictory paths in the late '70s blues revival. The best and most fitting compliment one could give a Watson solo is that it makes you laugh; this is blues of the rent party variety and Watson never lapses into the maudlin. Along with singers Brenda Burns and Lynwood Slim (on harp as well), Watson favors us with half a dozen surprisingly confident vocals. In fact, the only criticism is that his voice is sometimes too low in the mix. —*Dan Forte*

Noble Watts

b. Feb. 17, 1926, DeLand, FL
Saxophone / Electric Blues
The 1950s R&B scene was rife with fire-breathing tenor sax honkers. Noble "Thin Man" Watts was one of the most incendiary. Watts enrolled at Florida A&M University in 1942 (his mates in the school marching band included future jazz luminaries Nat and Cannonball Adderly). The Griffin Brothers, one of Dot Records' top R&B acts (obviously, this was before the days when Randy Wood's label provided safe haven for the hopelessly pale likes of Pat Boone and Gale Storm) hired young Noble Watts after he got out of college. Watts joined baritone saxist Paul "Hucklebuck" Williams in 1952, recording with him for Jax and taking sax solos behind Dinah Washington, Amos Milburn, and Ruth Brown on the groundbreaking mid-'50s TV program *Showtime at the Apollo* (Williams led the house band for the Willie Bryant-hosted extravaganza). Later, there was a stint with Lionel Hampton.

Watts' own discography commenced in 1954 with a tasty coupling for DeLuxe ("Mashing Potatoes"/"Pig Ears and Rice"). A 1956 single for Vee-Jay with Williams' band ("South Shore Drive") came just prior to Watts' salad days on the New York-based Baton label. With his band, the Rhythm Sparks, in support, Watts wailed "Easy Going," "Blast Off," "Shakin'," "Flap Jack," and quite a few more searing instrumentals for Baton from 1957 to 1959, the biggest of all being "Hard Times (The Slop)," which propelled the saxist onto the pop charts in December of 1957. Guitar twanger Duane Eddy must have dug what he heard—he covered the grinding shuffle for Jamie a few years later. That wasn't Noble Watts' only connection to rock 'n' roll—he played behind Jerry Lee Lewis, Buddy Holly, Chuck Berry, the Everly Brothers, and many more on various late-'50s package tours.

Boxer Sugar Ray Robinson managed Watts during the late '50s and early '60s, recruiting the saxist to lead the house band at the pugilist's Harlem lounge. Things got thin for the Thin Man during the '60s (45s for Sir, Cub, Enjoy, Peanut, Jell, Clamike, and Brunswick came and went without much notice) and '70s, but he mounted a comeback bid in 1987 with a fresh album, *Return of the Thin Man*, for Bob Greenlee's King Snake logo (later picked up by Alligator). *King of the Boogie Sax* followed in 1993 for Ichiban's Wild Dog imprint. Watts continues to work as a session saxist for Greenlee when he's not pursuing his own interests. —*Bill Dahl*

● **Return of the Thin Man** / 1987 / Alligator ✦✦✦✦
Much more jazz-oriented than his savage R&B honking instrumentals for Baton Records during the late '50s. —*Bill Dahl*

Noble & Nat / 1990 / Kingsnake ✦✦✦✦✦

King of The Boogie Sax / 1993 / Wild Dog ✦✦✦
A less inspired follow-up to Watts' previous outings for King Snake. —*Bill Dahl*

Carl Weathersby

b. 1955, Meadville, MS
Guitar
Since 1982, guitarist Carl Weathersby has been a prominent part of harpist Billy Branch's uncommonly hard-hitting Chicago combo, Sons of Blues. Folks have been wondering for much of that time why Weathersby hasn't stepped out on his own, since his stinging guitar work and rich vocals are far more satisfying than much of what passes for contemporary blues. Finally he has, with a 1996 debut album, *Don't Lay Your Blues on Me*, for Evidence Music.

Weathersby grew up in tiny Meadville, MS. Though his family moved to East Chicago, IN, when Weathersby was eight, he summered in Mississippi. He boasts some interesting bloodlines—he was related to Leonard "Baby Doo" Caston, Willie Dixon's longtime pianist, and his cousins include Leonard Caston, Jr. (an ex-member of the Radiants) and soul singer G.C.

Cameron. Influenced and encouraged by Albert King (a pal of his dad's), Weatherby got his chops together in East Chicago. King eventually hired him as rhythm guitarist for road stints in 1979, 1980, and 1982.

Weathersby's East Chicago residency kept him totally in the dark about the blazing blues scene just over the border in Chicago. Finally, he went to check out the SOBs one fateful night, sat in, and was hired on the spot. He's played with the combo ever since, but don't be surprised if he's out on his own before too long—he's too solid not to. —*Bill Dahl*

Curley Weaver

b. Mar. 26, 1906, Newton County, GA, **d.** Sep. 20, 1962, Covington, GA

Guitar, Vocals / Acoustic Country Blues

Curley Weaver, who was known for much of his life as "the Georgia Guitar Wizard," is only just beginning to be appreciated as one of the best players ever to pick up a six-string instrument. Although he recorded a fair number of sides on his own during the 1920s and 1930s, Weaver was most commonly heard in performances and recordings in association with his better-known colleagues Blind Willie McTell (with whom he worked from the 1930s until the early 1950s), Barbecue Bob, and Buddy Moss.

Weaver was born in Newton County, GA, in Covington, and was raised on a cotton farm. His mother, Savanah Shepard, encouraged him to sing from a very early age and also taught him to play the guitar, beginning when he was ten years old. Savanah Shepard was a renowned guitarist in her own right around Newton County, and also taught guitar legends Robert "Barbecue Bob" Hicks and his brother, Charlie Lincoln, to play the instrument when they were children. Her musical interests lay in gospel—she played accompaniment to the singers at Sunday church services—but, as in the case of Hicks and Lincoln, her son gravitated in the opposite direction, toward the blues.

Curley Weaver learned to play slide guitar from two legendary (and, alas, never-recorded) local bluesmen, Nehemiah Smith and Blind Buddy Keith. He showed extraordinary aptitude and, at age 19, teamed up with harmonica player Eddie Mapp, and moved to Atlanta. There he hooked up with Barbecue Bob and Charlie Lincoln, who quickly showed their younger friend the ins-and-outs of life, busking on Decatur Street, the heart of Atlanta's Black entertainment district, with its bars, restaurants, clubs, and theaters.

The association between the three guitarists was to prove providential. Barbecue Bob emerged as a local star first and, as a consequence, was also the first to go into the recording studio for the Columbia Records label in 1927—his first releases sold well, and he, in turn, arranged for his brother and Curley Weaver to make their debuts in the studio the following year. Weaver paid his first visit to the recording studio in Atlanta on October 26, 1928, laying down two tracks, "Sweet Petunia" and "No No Blues." The former was a cheerfully lazy, romantic blues, boasting a strained but honestly mournful vocal and very clean, tasteful guitar that sounded effectively like a second voice under the ends of each line, while the latter showcased Weaver's already formidable slide playing in a faster, ragtime-style number.

Weaver's debut led to more recording work, both as a solo act and in the company of Eddie Mapp, as well as Barbecue Bob. It was also through the recording studio, appearing as the Georgia Cotton Pickers in association with Barbecue Bob, that Weaver first made the acquaintance of Buddy Moss, a 16-year-old harmonica player who learned guitar from Weaver and Bob and later emerged as a major star on the instrument himself. The two were to work together throughout the decade.

Although many of Weaver's recording sessions in the 1930s were in New York, he kept his home base in Atlanta for his entire life, and it was while playing at clubs, parties, dances, picnics, and even on streetcorners in the early part of the decade that he struck up the most important professional relationship of his life, with Blind Willie McTell. A renowned 12-string guitarist, McTell had begun his recording career in 1927, and was a local legend around Atlanta. The two played and recorded together for 20 years or more, and comprised one of the most important and celebrated East Coast blues teams in history.

Weaver's most renowned recordings were done in association either with McTell or Moss, the latter under the guise of the Georgia Browns, during the mid-'30s. His playing was nothing less than dazzling—these men complemented each other perfectly in any setting they chose, from authentic blues to ragtime

and popular music adaptations. Weaver could make an acoustic guitar practically sing, and not just when playing slide, and his recordings showcased this ability brilliantly.

It wasn't possible for Weaver to sustain his brilliance, though not for lack of his ability or trying. The mid-'30s were a trying time for most blues players. The boom years of the late '20s and very early '30s had seen lots of opportunities to perform and record. The sales of records in those days had been booming in some instances—some estimates have records by artists such as Blind Lemon Jefferson selling in the hundreds of thousands of units (precise figures were almost never kept, especially given that there were no royalties based on sales such as we know today). The Great Depression destroyed much of the marketplace that had led to these successes, and sales by the mid-'30s had, for most bluesmen—especially acoustic country players—dried up considerably from their former levels, and most labels also cut back on the chances they were offering to record.

For Weaver, the decade was an even more bitter period. Barbecue Bob had died of pneumonia at the beginning of the 1930s. Eddie Mapp was killed, and Buddy Moss ended up in prison at age 21 on a five-year stretch that halted his career, essentially permanently. Weaver continued playing with McTell across the South, at clubs, restaurants, on street corners, and in outdoor markets, but the onset of the Second World War saw even a lot of this activity dry up. He continued to play around Atlanta, and in 1950 cut an album's worth of material with McTell for the Regal label. He continued playing whenever he could, and was reunited with Buddy Moss in a trio that performed in northern Georgia but, alas, never recorded.

Weaver's performing career was brought to a halt only by the failure of his eyesight. He passed away three years later, in 1962, remembered around Atlanta and by serious blues enthusiasts elsewhere, but largely unheralded during the blues revival that he'd just missed being a part of.

Curley Weaver was, by virtue of his virtuosity and the associations that he kept throughout his life and career, a guitarist's guitarist, a virtuoso among a small coterie of Atlanta-based guitar wizards. He never had the renown of Blind Willie McTell, but he was Willie's equal and match in just about every conceivable respect as a player and singer, his six-string being perfectly mated to Willie's 12-string. When he was playing or recording with McTell, Buddy Moss, or Barbecue Bob, the results were the blues equivalent of what rock people later would've called a "super-session" except that, as a listen to the surviving records reveals, the results were more natural and overpowering—these guys genuinely liked each other, and loved playing together, and it shows beyond the virtuosity of the music, in the warmth and elegance of the playing and the sound.

Note: In addition to the recordings credited to Curley Weaver, his work can also be heard on Blind Willie McTell's *Pig 'n Whistle Blues*. —*Bruce Eder*

☆ **Georgia Guitar Wizard (1928–1935)** / 1987 / Story Of Blues ✦✦✦✦

These are 16 of the greatest blues sides ever to come out of Atlanta, and a match for the best work of Blind Willie McTell, Barbecue Bob, and Buddy Moss (whose harmonica playing on the Georgia Browns' "Decatur Street 81" reveals him to be an equally formidable talent on that instrument), who are all over these sides as well. The sound is a little rough at times and there are some major gaps between 1929 and 1933—including his renowned "Guitar Rag"—but none of the flaws do violence to the music, and all that is here is worth the price of admission. One important bonus—the presence of "Oh Lawdy Mama," the song that later, in Willie Dixon's hands, evolved into the blues standard "Down in the Bottom" (an unreleased version was cut by the Rolling Stones, in what might be their best early blues side); it was also cut by Buddy Moss a year earlier as a solo number. —*Bruce Eder*

☆ **Complete Studio Recordings** / 1990 / Document ✦✦✦✦✦
Weaver's complete recordings, taking into account all of the sessions for Moss, McTell, et al. where he played guitar, would comprise a lot more than the 19 tracks here, but that's no reason not to spring for this slightly more expensive collection, which doesn't entirely overlap with the Story of Blues disc. —*Bruce Eder*

Sylvester Weaver

Guitar, Vocals / Acoustic Country Blues
The pioneering guitarist from the early days of the blues, Weaver

created the enduring classic "Guitar Rag," later popularized as "Steel Guitar Rag." He was adept at everything from ragtime to slide guitar stylings, all performed with great technical skill and a marvelous sense of time. —*Cub Koda*

● **Smoketown Strut** / Agram ✦✦✦✦
Weaver's earliest and best sides, including "Guitar Rag." The sound is horrible in spots, but every note of the music is great. —*Cub Koda*

"Boogie" Bill Webb

b. 1926, Jackson, MS, **d.** Aug. 23, 1990, New Orleans, LA
Guitar, Vocals / Electric Country Blues
Although he lived in New Orleans most of his life, and none other than Fats Domino brought him to Imperial Records for his recording debut in 1953, Boogie Bill Webb was never much a part of the New Orleans R&B scene. Webb's music grew out of the Jackson area country-blues tradition of Tommy Johnson and others, and he retained a down-home, idiosyncratic approach to a wide range of material from C&W to R&B and traditional jazz. Beginning in 1966, Webb recorded occasionally for folklorists and field researchers, finally recording his first full album in 1989 with funding from the Louisiana Endowment for the Humanities. Album producer Ben Sandmel, who also played drums with Webb for five years, described Boogie Bill's approach as "quirky, often anarchic," but it is appealing in its very unpredictability, humor, and warmth. —*Jim O'Neal*

● **Drinkin' & Stinkin'** / 1989 / Flying Fish ✦✦✦✦
Houseparty, juke-joint blues. —*Niles J. Frantz*

Katie Webster

b. Jan. 9, 1939, Houston, TX,
Organ, Piano, Vocals, Harmonica / Electric New Orleans Blues
A piano-pounding institution on the southern Louisiana swamp blues scene during the late '50s and early '60s, Katie Webster later grabbed a long-deserved share of national recognition with three recent Alligator albums.

Kathryn Thorne had to deal with deeply religious parents that did everything in their power to stop their daughter from playing R&B. But the rocking sounds of Fats Domino and Little Richard were simply too persuasive. Local guitarist Ashton Savoy took her under his wing, sharing her 1958 debut 45 for the Kry logo ("Baby Baby").

Webster rapidly became an invaluable studio sessioneer for Louisiana producers J.D. Miller in Crowley and Eddie Shuler in Lake Charles. She played on sides by Guitar Junior (Lonnie Brooks), Clarence Garlow, Jimmy Wilson, Lazy Lester, and Phil Phillips (her gently rolling 88s powered his hit "Sea of Love").

The young pianist also waxed some terrific sides of her own for Miller from 1959 to 1961 for his Rocko, Action, and Spot labels (where she introduced a dance called "The Katie Lee"). Webster led her own band, the Uptighters, at the same time she was spending her days in the studio. In 1964, she guested with Otis Redding's band at the Bamboo Club in Lake Charles and so impressed the charismatic Redding that he absconded with her. For the next three years, Webster served as his opening act!

The 1970s were pretty much a lost decade for Katie Webster as she took care of her ailing parents in Oakland, CA. But in 1982 a European tour beckoned, and she journeyed overseas for the first of many such jaunts. The Alligator connection commenced in 1988 with some high-profile help: Bonnie Raitt, Robert Cray, and Kim Wilson all made guest appearances on *The Swamp Boogie Queen*. The lovably extroverted boogie pianist encored with *Two-Fisted Mama!* and *No Foolin'* before suffering a 1993 stroke. —*Bill Dahl*

I Know That's Right (CD) / 1987 / Arhoolie ✦✦✦
I Know That's Right is an okay step in the venerable boogie pianist's comeback bid, but the mediocre band backing she receives on most cuts doesn't add much to the swampy brew. —*Bill Dahl*

Swamp Boogie Queen / 1988 / Alligator ✦✦✦✦
Lovable Katie Webster had some high-profile help for this impressive comeback album—Bonnie Raitt shares the vocal on "Somebody's on Your Case" and plays guitar on "On the Run"; Kim Wilson duets with Webster for a cover of Johnnie Taylor's "Who's Making Love" (a track that Robert Cray contributes crisp guitar to). Throughout, Webster's vocals are throatier than they

used to be (she soulfully covers one-time mentor Otis Redding's "Fa-Fa-Fa-Fa-Fa [Sad Song]" and "Try a Little Tenderness"), while her driving left hand still lays down some powerhouse boogie rhythms. —*Bill Dahl*

Two-Fisted Mama! / 1990 / Alligator ✦✦✦✦
Another impressive showcase for Katie Webster's rollicking 88s and earthy vocals. Other than the Memphis Horns, no special guests this time—just Webster and her tight trio (anchored by guitarist Vasti Jackson). —*Bill Dahl*

● **Katie Webster** / 1991 / Paula ✦✦✦✦✦
Webster is at her full bayou-bred boogie-blues best here, when she was the queen of south Louisiana's swamp sessioneers. Webster's own late-'50s/early-'60s output for producer J.D. Miller was no less captivating; her self-named dance number "The Katie Lee" and "Mama Don't Allow" which uproots the Gary U.S. Bonds party vibe to New Orleans are two of the best items on the 20-track disc. There's also her blues-drenched "No Bread, No Meat" and a nice version of "Sea of Love" (Webster added the gently rolling piano to Phil Phillips' original hit). —*Bill Dahl*

No Foolin'! / 1991 / Alligator ✦✦✦
Webster's last Alligator disc before a serious stroke sidelined her. Vasti Jackson again handles the guitar solos behind her, while fellow Gulf Coast émigré Lonnie Brooks teams with the pianist for a duet on Earl King's seminal two-chord blues ballad "Those Lonely, Lonely Nights." A four-piece Chicago horn section is populated by saxists Gene "Daddy G" Barge and Hank Ford. —*Bill Dahl*

Casey Bill Weldon

b. Jul. 10, 1909, Pine Bluff, AR
Guitar, Vocals / Acoustic Blues, Acoustic Country Blues, Prewar Country Blues
Among the premier "Hawaiian" guitarists, Will "Casey Bill" Weldon's voicings, fluidity and tunings were creative and imaginative, as were his arrangements. He was married to Memphis Minnie in the '20s, and they made some superb recordings together in the late '20s. Weldon played in medicine shows before beginning his recording career in 1927 for Victor. There were later dates for Champion, Vocalion, and Bluebird. Weldon recorded and played with The Memphis Jug Band, Charlie Burse and the Picaninny Jug Band, and the Brown Bombers of Swing. He moved to the West Coast in the '40s and purportedly recorded for several soundtracks. Weldon moved to Detroit and left the music world in the '60s. —*Ron Wynn*

Bottleneck Guitar Trendsetters of the 1930's / Yazoo ✦✦✦✦
Outstanding bottleneck guitar and above-average singing from Casey Bill Weldon, one of the least publicized but tremendous prewar stylists. —*Ron Wynn*

Valerie Wellington

b. Nov. 14, 1959, Chicago, IL, **d.** Jan. 3, 1991
Vocals / Modern Electric Blues
Valerie Wellington took the Chicago blues scene by surprise in 1982, perhaps not forgoing her classical training as an opera singer as much as using it to enhance her work in the blues. As a blueswoman she fit right in, not only becoming a regular in the blues clubs but also compiling an impressive theatrical resume for her portrayals of Ma Rainey and Bessie Smith—women who, like opera singers, learned to project their voices without microphones. The influence of Koko Taylor has also been evident in Wellington's blues approach, which combines classic vaudeville-era blues with hard-driving Chicago sounds. Her power-packed voice has been heard on only a few record releases but has been featured frequently in TV and radio commercials. —*Jim O'Neal*

● **Million Dollar $ecret** / Oct. 1984 / Flying Fish ✦✦✦✦✦
Wellington is a powerful yet subtle vocalist, backed by some of the best Chicago blues players, including Sunnyland Slim, Billy Branch, Casey Jones, and Magic Slim & the Teardrops. The CD reissue contains two bonus tracks. —*Niles J. Frantz*

Junior Wells (Amos Blackmore)

b. Dec. 9, 1934, Memphis, TN
Harmonica, Vocals / Electric Chicago Blues
He's one bad dude, strutting across the stage like a harp-toting gangster, mesmerizing the crowd with his tough-guy antics and

rib-sticking Chicago blues attack. And amazingly, Junior Wells has been at precisely this sort of thing since the dawn of the 1950s.

Born in Memphis, Wells learned his earliest harp licks from another future legend, Little Junior Parker, before he came to Chicago at age 12. In 1950, the teenager passed an impromptu audition for guitarists Louis and David Myers at a house party on the South side, and the Deuces were born. When drummer Fred Below came aboard, they changed their name to the Aces.

Little Walter left Muddy Waters in 1952 (in the wake of his hit instrumental, "Juke"), and Wells jumped ship to take his place with Waters. That didn't stop the Aces (who joined forces with Little Walter) from backing Wells on his initial sessions for States Records, though—his debut date produced some seminal Chicago blues efforts, including his first reading of "Hoodoo Man," a rollicking "Cut That Out," and the blazing instrumentals "Eagle Rock" and "Junior's Wail."

More fireworks ensued the next year when he encored for States with a mournful "So All Alone" and the jumping "Lawdy! Lawdy!" (Muddy Waters moonlighted on guitar for the session). Already Wells was exhibiting his tempestuous side—he was allegedly AWOL from the Army at the time.

In 1957, Wells hooked up with producer Mel London, who owned the Chief and Profile logos. The association resulted in many of Wells' most enduring sides, including "I Could Cry" and the rock 'n' rolling "Lovey Dovey Lovely One" in 1957; the grinding national R&B hit "Little by Little" (with Willie Dixon providing vocal harmony) in 1959, and the R&B-laced classic "Messin' with the Kid" in 1960 (sporting Earl Hooker's immaculate guitar work). Wells' harp was de-emphasized during this period on record in favor of his animated vocals.

With Bob Koester producing, the harpist cut an all-time classic LP for Delmark in 1965. *Hoodoo Man Blues* vividly captured the feel of a typical Wells set at Theresa's Lounge, even though it was cut in a studio. With Buddy Guy (initially billed as "Friendly Chap" due to his contract with Chess) providing concise lead guitar, Wells laid down definitive versions of "Snatch It Back and Hold It," "You Don't Love Me," and "Chitlin' Con Carne."

The harpist made his second appearance on the national R&B lists in 1968 with a funky James Brown-tinged piece, "You're Tuff Enough," for Mercury's feisty Blue Rock logo. Wells had been working in this bag for some time, alarming the purists but delighting R&B fans; his brass-powered 1966 single for Bright Star, "Up in Heah," had previously made a lot of local noise.

After a fine mid-'70s set for Delmark (*On Tap*), little was heard from Wells on vinyl for an extended spell, though he continued to enjoy massive appeal at home (Theresa's was his principal haunt for many a moon) and abroad (whether on his own or in partnership with Guy; they opened for the Rolling Stones on one memorable tour and cut an inconsistent but interesting album for Atco in the early '70s).

A pair of recent sets for Telarc have been major disappointments; Wells just doesn't seem to be into recording anymore. Live, though, he still cuts the same swaggering figure as ever, commanding the attention of everyone in the room with one menacing yelp or a punctuating blast from his amplified harmonica. He's still bad—and that's mighty good! —*Bill Dahl*

★ **Hoodoo Man Blues** / 1965 / Delmark ✦✦✦✦✦
One of the truly classic blues albums of the 1960s, and one of the first to fully document the smoky ambience of a night at a West side nightspot in the superior acoustics of a recording studio. Wells just set up with his usual cohorts—guitarist Buddy Guy (billed as "Friendly Chap" on first vinyl pressings), bassist Jack Myers, and drummer Billy Warren—and proceeded to blow up a storm, bringing an immediacy to "Snatch It Back and Hold It," "You Don't Love Me," "Chitlin Con Carne," and the rest that is absolutely mesmerizing. —*Bill Dahl*

It's My Life, Baby / 1966 / Vanguard ✦✦✦
Partly live from Pepper's Lounge in Chicago, with Buddy Guy and Freddy Below. Junior's first Vanguard album. —*Barry Lee Pearson*

On Tap / 1966 / Delmark ✦✦✦
Underrated collection boasting a contemporary, funky edge driven by guitarists Phil Guy and Sammy Lawhorn, keyboardist Big Moose Walker, and saxman A.C. Reed. Especially potent is

the crackling "The Train I Ride," a kissin' cousin to Little Junior Parker's "Mystery Train." —*Bill Dahl*

You're Tuff Enough / 1968 / Blue Rock ✦✦✦✦
Another period of the veteran Chicago harp man's career that awaits CD documentation—and one of the most exciting. Wells' late-'60s output for Bright Star and Mercury's Blue Rock subsidiary frequently found him mining funky James Brown grooves (with a bluesy base, of course) to great effect—"Up in Heah" and his national smash "You're Tuff Enough" are marvelous examples of his refusal to bend to purists' wishes (though there's a glorious version of Bobby Bland's blues-soaked "You're the One" that benefits handily from Sammy Lawhorn's delicate guitar work). —*Bill Dahl*

Comin' at You / 1968 / Vanguard ✦✦✦
Another eminently solid outing by the legendary harpist that captures his trademark barroom bravado in a studio setting. The band is quite tight—Buddy Guy and Lefty Dizz are the guitarists, Douglas Fagan plays sax, and Clark Terry, believe it or not, occupies a third of the trumpet section—and the set list is dominated by oldies from both Sonny Boys, Willie Dixon, and John D. Loudermilk (Junior invests his "Tobacco Road" with a lights-out toughness that the Nashville Teens could never even imagine). —*Bill Dahl*

South Side Jam / 1969 / Delmark ✦✦✦
You can't go wrong with any Wells mid-'60s release. This had hard-driving, powerful uptempo tunes and equally impressive slow wailers. Wells was joined by the likes of Buddy Guy and Fred Below, among others, and there were absolutely no stylistic excesses or LP padding. —*Ron Wynn*

Live at the Golden Bear / Dec. 1969 / Blue Rock ✦✦✦
The swaggering harpman took his act on the road to Huntington Beach, CA to do this live set with his touring quartet of the moment. Virtually nothing but blues and soul standards that show his wide stylistic range—alongside tunes by Muddy Waters, both Sonny Boys, and the Wolf resides an impassioned reading of James Brown's "Please, Please, Please." —*Bill Dahl*

In My Younger Days / 1971 / Red Lightnin' ✦✦
Good collection of 16 early sides from 1953-62. The earliest tracks are straight blues, and Wells at his most conventional. Starting with the late-'50s performances, he began to broaden his influences into his trademark blend of blues, R&B, rock, and even some Latin music. Earl Hooker lends his guitar to the early-'60s tracks, which are highlighted by the original version of his signature tune, "Messin' with the Kid." —*Richie Unterberger*

Play the Blues / 1972 / Atlantic ✦✦✦
Buddy Guy and Junior Wells seldom made more effective records than this celebrated album (reissued on CD in 1992). There were none of the erratic vocals, questionable song selection, or rambling solos that sometimes plagued their live shows. Wells was sizzling and aggressive as lead vocalist, Guy's solos were controlled and disciplined, yet strikingly effective in uptempo and ballad situations, while saxophonist A.C. Reed provided soulful and shattering fills and solos behind the vocalists and during the interludes. They were helped by assorted rock luminaries from Eric Clapton, J. Geils, and Magic Dick to Dr. John. This deserves a place among the other tremendous items in the Rhino/Atlantic R&B Masters series. —*Ron Wynn*

Blues Hit Big Town / 1977 / Delmark ✦✦✦✦✦
Why isn't this seminal collection of the harpist's earliest 1953-1954 sides for States Records available on CD? Its Chicago blues treasures include Wells' first waxing of "Hoodoo Man," a jumping "Cut That Out" and "Tomorrow Night," and slashing showcases for the young bluesman's amplified harp: "Eagle Rock," "Junior's Wail." Junior's sidemen are the absolute cream of the crop—Muddy Waters, the Aces, Elmore James, pianists Otis Spann and Johnny Jones—making these 12 sides all the more indispensable. —*Bill Dahl*

Pleading the Blues / Oct. 31, 1979 / Isabel ✦✦✦
Recorded on Halloween night in 1979, this pairs up Wells and Guy in a fashion that hasn't been heard since Hoodoo Man Blues, their first, and best collaboration. Solid backing by the Philip Guy band (Buddy's brother) makes this album a rare treat. —*Cub Koda*

Drinkin' TNT 'n' Smokin' Dynamite / Jun. 1982 / Blind Pig ✦✦✦
Live at Montreux, featuring Junior and Buddy. —*Bill Dahl*

Harp Attack! / 1990 / Alligator ✦✦✦✦
Along with his Windy City peers James Cotton, Carey Bell, and
Billy Branch, Wells trades harp solos and vocals on this raucous
meeting of the minds. Junior's front and center on a fine rendition of Sonny Boy II's "Keep Your Hands Out of My Pockets" and
the tailor-made "Somebody Changed the Lock" and "Broke and
Hungry," obviously relishing the camaraderie between himself
and his fellow harmonica giants. —*Bill Dahl*

● **1957–1966** / 1991 / Paula ✦✦✦✦✦
The indispensable sides for Mel London's Profile, Chief, and Age
labels (and a few for USA Records that directly followed). Backed
by a modern-sounding crew that included immaculate guitarist
Earl Hooker, saxist A.C. Reed, and keyboardist Johnny "Big
Moose" Walker. Wells enjoyed a considerable R&B hit with the
grinding "Little by Little," glides atop a rocking rhythm groove
on the original "Messin' with the Kid," rocks "Lovey Dovey
Lovely One" and the hokey-but-fun "I Need Me a Car," and blows
some husky amplified harmonica on "Cha Cha Cha in Blue" and
"Calling All Blues." —*Bill Dahl*

Alone & Acoustic / 1991 / Alligator ✦✦✦

Undisputed Godfather of the Blues / Dec. 1992 / Gbw ✦✦✦
About half is a decent Junior Wells album. The other half's mired
in hopelessly overdone standards that we've heard a few too
many times before—but every once in a while, he exhibits signs
of the old fire. —*Bill Dahl*

Better Off with the Blues / Jun. 1993 / Telarc ✦✦
Remarkably mundane effort that leaves one with the impression
that Wells didn't care a whole lot about making this disc. Even
the presence of Buddy Guy, Lucky Peterson, and bassist Johnny
B. Gayden can't save the overly slick set, where Wells waxes one
more "Messin' with the Kid," a dire reading of the country/soul
standby "Today I Started Loving You Again," and a way-too-long
title track. —*Bill Dahl*

Everybody's Gettin' Some / Telarc ✦✦
Makes his prior Telarc offering look like a masterpiece by com-
parison. A passel of superfluous guest stars—Bonnie Raitt, Carlos
Santana, Sonny Landreth—unite to produce the most worthless
Wells album ever down in Louisiana rather than in Wells'
Chicago stomping grounds. Why he wanted to remake songs
from the songbooks of War and Bill Withers is a mystery better
left for future generations to ponder. —*Bill Dahl*

The Devil's Son-In-Law (Peetie Wheatstraw)

b. Dec. 21, 1902, Ripley, TN, **d.** Dec. 21, 1941, East St. Louis,
IL
Piano, Vocals / Piano Blues
A very popular bluesman in the '30s and early '40s, pianist
Peetie Wheatstraw's signature vocal phrase, "Oh well well," was
adapted by several bluesmen, Muddy Waters among them.
Born William Bunch, Peetie Wheatstraw arrived in East St.
Louis around 1929, when he was about 27 years old; not much
is known his life before that date, although it is speculated that
he was raised in Cotton Plant, AR. When he arrived in East St.
Louis, the pianist adopted the Peetie Wheatstraw name, which
derives from an old folk story.
Inspired by the success of the guitar/piano duets of Scrapper
Blackwell and Leroy Carr, Wheatstraw set out to find a guitarist
to collaborate with. He wound up playing with a number of different musicians—including Kokomo Arnold, Charlie McCoy,
Bumble Bee Slim, Casey Bill, Weldonand, and Charley Jordan—
but his primary collaborator was Lonnie Johnson. Wheatstraw
recorded with all of these guitarists, releasing records on Decca,
Vocalion, and Bluebird throughout the '30s. His records were
quite popular, largely due to his unique, laidback singing and his
provocative lyrics.
At the height of his popularity in 1941, Peetie Wheatstraw was
killed when his car was hit by an oncoming train at a railroad
crossing. After his death, his distinctive vocal phrasing lived on
in the music of everyone from Big Bill Broonzy and Champion
Jack Dupree to Muddy Waters and Johnny Shines. —*Cub Koda
& Stephen Thomas Erlewine*

● **The Devil's Son-in-Law** / Blues Document ✦✦✦✦✦
A 20-track import compilation of Wheatstraw's best. Includes "I
Want Some Seafood" and "Fairasee Woman." —*Cub Koda*

Whispering Smith

b. Jan. 25, 1932, Brookhaven, MS, **d.** Apr. 28, 1984, Baton Rouge,
LA
Harmonica, Vocals / Electric Louisiana Blues
Harpist Whispering Smith made it in on the tail end of the
swamp blues movement that swept the Baton Rouge region,
working with Lightnin' Slim and Silas Hogan before making his
own fine singles for Crowley, LA, producer J.D. Miller.
Alternating down-in-the-bayou entries such as "Mean Woman
Blues" (not the Elvis Presley/Roy Orbison rocker), "I Tried So
Hard," and "Don't Leave Me Baby" with the storming instru-
mentals "Live Jive" (also featuring the fleet guitar of Ulysses
Williams) and "Hound Dog Twist," Smith was an excellent performer who arrived in Crowley just a trifle late, after the heyday
of the swamp blues sound.
Excello decided to give swamp music another try in 1970
without Miller's expert supervision, inviting Smith back to cut an
LP in Baton Rouge that just didn't live up to his former glory. —
Bill Dahl

Over Easy / 1991 / P-Vine ✦✦✦✦

Artie White

b. Apr. 16, 1937, Vicksburg, MS
Vocals / Soul, R&B, Soul Blues
Very few Chicago blues artists were able to pierce the R&B
charts during the 1970s, when interest in the genre was at rock-
bottom. But smooth-voiced Artie "Blues Boy" White managed
the rare feat with his 1977 single for Altee, "Leanin' Tree."
Gospel was White's initial musical pursuit. He sang with a
spiritual aggregation, the Harps of David, at the age of 11 prior
to coming to Chicago in 1956. More church singing was in
store for White with the Full Gospel Wonders. The singer
claims that he was lured into singing the devil's music by a
well-heeled gent who drove up to an unsuspecting White in a
flashy Cadillac and promised him $10,000 to record some
blues songs!
White's '70s singles for PM and Gamma stiffed, but with the
advent of "Leanin' Tree," White was able to command a nice asking price on the Chicago circuit (and still does). For a while,
White tried his hand at running a blues club, Bootsy's Lounge.
But performing and recording won out; White waxed a terrific
debut LP in 1985 for Shreveport-based Ronn Records called
Blues Boy.
White signed with Ichiban in 1987 and waxed six fine sets in
the soul-blues vein (enough to merit a *Best Of* CD in 1991,
which made seven), utilizing Chicago songwriter Bob Jones (the
composer of "Leanin' Tree") and labelmate Travis Haddix as
chief sources of material. On 1989's *Thangs Got to Change,*
White enjoyed the presence of Little Milton Campbell, one of his
prime influences, on lead guitar. —*Bill Dahl*

Blues Boy / 1985 / Ronn ✦✦✦✦
Blues Boy's first album, dating back to the mid-'80s, also ranks
as one of his most soulfully satisfying, thanks to the contempo-
rary grooves of a Chicago outfit called Amuzement Park and
White's smoky, Little Milton-influenced vocal delivery. He deliv-
ers a fine remake of his own modern blues "Leaning Tree" and
Little Beaver's "Jimmie" and adapts Aretha Franklin's "Chain of
Fools" to his own rich vocal range. —*Bill Dahl*

Nothing Takes the Place of You / 1987 / Ichiban ✦✦✦
Artie White's Ichiban debut is typically confident and soulful.
Along with standards by Toussaint McCall and Willie Nelson,
White does a solid job on a sheaf of original material and Z.Z.
Hill's anguished "I Need Someone." —*Bill Dahl*

Where It's at / 1989 / Ichiban ✦✦✦
Sam Cooke, Clarence Carter, and Al Green receive the cover
treatment this time, but White and his usual cohorts (writers Bob
Jones and Travis Haddix, in addition to the singer himself)
penned the majority of the fine blues-soul set. A fine band helps,
too: guitarists Criss Johnson and Pete Allen and a six-piece horn
section led by Willie Henderson frame White's husky vocals
beautifully. —*Bill Dahl*

Thangs Got to Change / 1989 / Ichiban ✦✦✦
Little Milton Campbell—one of Artie White's principal influences
and advisors—wrote a good portion of this typically solid soul-
blues collection, and White covers numbers by Lowell Fulson,
Brook Benton, and B.B. King for flavor. —*Bill Dahl*

Tired of Sneaking Around / 1990 / Ichiban ✦✦✦✦✦
White is a B.B. King-sounding singer, with an original overall sound, who makes great records with big-band feel. There are lots of horns and stuff. —*Niles J. Frantz*

Dark End of the Street / 1991 / Ichiban ✦✦✦✦
Whether it's blues, soul, or something between the two, White does a fine job throughout this disc. Travis Haddix, once White's Ichiban labelmate, contributes three nice tunes, Bob Jones a couple more, and White dips into past triumphs by B.B. King, Ike Turner, James Carr, and Little Milton for the rest. —*Bill Dahl*

Hit & Run / 1992 / Ichiban ✦✦✦✦
Without a great deal of fanfare, Artie White released a steady stream of quality contemporary releases on Ichiban, each straddling the sometimes imperceptible fence between blues and deep soul. This one's no exception—backed by a Chicago combo called Masheen Co., White delivers originals penned by Travis Haddix, Bob Jones (the title cut), and himself in assured, smooth style. —*Bill Dahl*

● **The Best of Artie White** / Ichiban ✦✦✦✦✦
A well-selected 12-song overview of White's prolific tenure at Ichiban. His delivery, pitched somewhere between blues and soul, is equally effective on the contemporary blues-based items "Hattie Mae" and "Jodie" and the soul-slanted "Dark End of the Street" (though he can't give James Carr a run for his money in the intensity department) and Toussaint McCall's tender "Nothing Takes the Place of You." —*Bill Dahl*

Bukka White (Booker T. Washington White)
b. Nov. 12, 1906, Houston, TX, d. Feb. 26, 1977, Memphis, TN
Guitar, Harmonica, Piano, Vocals / Acoustic Delta Blues
Achieving a distinctive musical voice is a highly prized blues value, yet few artists develop an easily recognizable vocal and instrumental style that is uniquely theirs. Bukka White was one of those remarkable artists with an overall approach and composition style that were unusual, yet he was a popular house party musician and a successful recording artist. Although he had a second career during the blues revival and remained a powerful performer, his best work was on his 1937 and 1940 Vocalion sides, reissued by Columbia. They feature down-home country-blues at its best, personal, moving, and instrumentally compelling. White's percussive approach to his open G-tuned steel National can be imitated but not duplicated. Like other Delta artists, White's sound was melodically simple but rhythmically complex. Sporting an attack vaguely reminiscent of Big Joe Williams, White worked his guitar like a drum, adding rhythmic nuances with his chording hand on the guitar neck. On his '40s session, he added further percussive rhythm. Many of White's pieces employ spoken or chanted passages, especially his train songs, which combined talking blues and train effects. His compositions generally either fall outside mainstream blues or bridge sacred and secular traditions, as in his classic "Fixing to Die." Moody and introspective, his songs let you into his life, detailing his experiences as a prisoner at Mississippi's notorious Parchman Farm or as a hobo riding the rails. His dance songs, such as "Bukka's Jitterbug Swing," aptly demonstrate his skills as a houseparty performer and bear out his reputation as a breakdown artist, which means people danced so hard to his beat that they literally broke the floors down at the jukes and plantation balls over which he reigned. —*Barry Lee Pearson*

☆ **Parchman Farm** / 1970 / Columbia ✦✦✦✦✦
Brilliant country blues from Bukka White, whose churning, rousing vocal approach was complemented by a crackling guitar style. —*Ron Wynn*

☆ **The Complete Sessions 1930–1940** / 1976 / Travelin' Man ✦✦✦✦✦
Delta blues as propulsive as a runaway freight train. It's not for the weakhearted. —*Jas Obrecht*

Three Shades of Blues / 1989 / Biograph ✦✦✦
Three Shades of Blues comprises a selection of tracks cut by Bukka White, Skip James, and Blind Willie McTell, all recorded during different eras. James' tracks were made in 1964, the first he cut since 1931. James fares the worst—he sounds unsure of himself and several of the songs are painful to listen to. The five White tracks were recorded in 1974, after he was released from prison; while his voice does sound worn, they're fascinating historical items. McTell's recordings are taken from the last com-

merical sessions he made in 1949, and they're more than historical curiosities—he sounds as haunted and powerful as he ever has. —*Thom Owens*

Shake 'Em on Down / 1993 / ROIR ✦✦✦✦✦
This fine collection supplants *Parchman Farm* as the definitive set spotlighting Bukka White's Vocalion country blues recordings. —*Ron Wynn*

★ **The Complete Bukka White** / 1994 / Columbia ✦✦✦✦✦
All of Bukka White's landmark recordings for Vocalion and Okeh Records are collected on this brilliant single disc. —*AMG*

Aberdeen Mississippi Blues / Travelin' Man ✦✦✦
This album collects some of the sessions he cut in 1937 for Vocalion. Although the music is superb, it is available in better collections. —*Thom Owens*

Josh White
b. Feb. 11, 1908, Greenville, MS, d. Sep. 5, 1969
Guitar, Vocals / Folk Blues
Most blues enthusiasts think of Josh White as a folk revival artist. It's true that the second half of his music career found him based in New York playing to the coffeehouse and cabaret set and hanging out with Burl Ives, Woody Guthrie, and fellow transplanted folk revival artists Sonny Terry and Brownie McGhee. When I saw him in Chicago in the 1960s his shirt was unbuttoned to his waist a la Harry Belafonte and his repertoire consisted of folk revival standards such as "Scarlet Ribbons." He was a show business personality—renowned for his sexual magnetism and his dramatic vocal presentations. What many people don't know is that Josh White was a major figure in the Piedmont blues tradition. The first part of his career saw him as apprentice and lead boy to some of the greatest blues and religious artists ever, including Willie Walker, Blind Blake, Blind Joe Taggert (with whom he recorded), and allegedly even Blind Lemon Jefferson. On his own, he recorded both blues and religious songs, including a classic version of "Blood Red River." A fine guitar technician with an appealing voice, he became progressively more sophisticated in his presentation. Like many other Carolinians and Virginians who moved north to urban areas, he took up city ways, remaining a fine musician if no longer a down-home artist. Like several other canny blues players, he used his roots music to broaden and enhance his life experience, and his talent was such that he could choose the musical idiom that was most lucrative at the time. —*Barry Lee Pearson*

Jazz, Ballads & Blues / 1986 / Rykodisc ✦✦✦
Josh White, Jr., son of the distinguished folksinger, displays an eclectic nature and stylistic adaptability on this 1986 set. The 10 selections range from folk tunes like "Frankie and Johnny" to pre-rock standards like "You'd Be So Nice To Come Home To" and "House of the Rising Sun," written by White's father, who also supplied the original arrangements. White doesn't have his father's sheer power or personality, but sings and plays in a resolute, affable manner. He's well supported by violinist Robin Batteau and bassist Jerry Burnham, and the trio does a nice job of showing the links between the three forms covered in the session's title. —*Ron Wynn*

● **Blues Singer 1932–1936** / 1996 / Columbia/Legacy ✦✦✦✦✦
The suave and debonair blues sex symbol in his earliest and purest period, when the Piedmont influence was at its peak in his playing. This is strong stuff, eons away from the collegiate crowd-pleasing folkie stuff he engaged in during the '60s: "Milk Cow Blues," "Lazy Black Snake Blues," and "Silicosis Is Killin' Me" are acoustic solo blues of a consistently high quality, and there are a few religious tunes thrown in to spotlight the other side of White's early recording activities. —*Bill Dahl*

★ **The Legendary Josh White** / MCA ✦✦✦✦✦
This is a two-record set that has a good sampling of White's major songs. —*Michael Erlewine*

Lavelle White
b. Texas
Vocals / Chicago Blues
Texas-based vocalist and songwriter "Miss" Lavelle White has a significant discography of singles, most dating back to the 1950s and '60s, but she only recently released her first full length album, *Miss Lavelle*, on the Austin, Texas-based Antone's label.

To say the album has been a long time coming would be the understatement of the year, for White's talents as a songwriter and singer were well-known in 1950s Houston, where she recorded several singles for the Duke/Peacock labels. In the late '50s, her labelmates included Bobby "Blue" Bland, B.B. King, and Junior Parker. *Miss Lavelle* was White's first recording of any kind, in fact, in 30 years. The fact that it's a gorgeous album helped White play some large blues festivals in the last couple of years across the U.S., Canada and Europe, but for a number of years when she had no record deal, White continued to enterain club crowds with her singing in Chicago, Texas, Louisiana, and Florida.

White's first big break as a vocalist came about with something she wrote for herself, "If I Could Be with You," and a procession of other singles followed for the Duke/Peacock label, including "Just Look at You Fool," "Stop These Teardrops," and "The Tide of Love." Unlike many other blues singers, White didn't get started recording until she was 25, thanks to fellow Houstonian Johnny "Clyde" Copeland, who brought White to Duke/Peacock owner Don Robey's attention.

White, now in her fifties, began writing poems and songs when she was 12, she said in a 1994 interview.

"Hardships in life made me start to write," she explained, "and the first record I cut was with a gospel group, 'Precious Lord, Lead Me On.'" When she was 16, White moved to Houston and fell into the city's burgeoning blues club scene with Clarence Hollimon, who now records with his wife Carol Fran for the Rounder label.

Today, more than 30 years after she got her humble start in the blues clubs in Houston, White sings as well as she ever did, and though she's had time off from the road over the years, she's never stopped singing or writing songs. All of this is apparent with one listen to *Miss Lavelle*. The dignified manner in which White conducts herself on stage, dressed in flashy outfits and walking about confidently, is something that was instilled in her from an early age. This stage presence that is apparent when Miss Lavelle White performs is something the younger generation of blues players (and many rock 'n' rollers) seem to lack. — *Richard Skelly*

Johnny Wicks

b. Louisville, KY
Group / Jump Blues
An unbelievably obscure outfit from Louisville, KY, who cut one session for Chicago's United Records in 1952, Johnny Wicks' Swinging Ozarks were partially rescued from historical oblivion by Delmark boss Bob Koester, who bucked the commercial odds by issuing an LP of their United material. Wicks played bass; Preacher Stephens blew tuba and sang. — *Bill Dahl*

● **Swingin' Ozarks** / Delmark ◆◆◆◆
This early-'50s R&B/jazz with a singing tuba player is hopelessly obscure, but intriguing. — *Bill Dahl*

Robert Wilkins (Rev. Robert Timothy Wilkins)

b. Jan. 16, 1896, Hernando, MS, **d.** May 26, 1987, Memphis, TN
Guitar, Vocals / Acoustic Country Blues, Acoustic Memphis Blues
A superior guitarist, Robert Wilkins projected a relaxed ease on his exquisite country-blues 78s. He was working as a Pullman porter in Memphis when he was hired by Victor to record in 1928. He was soon back in the studio for Brunswick and Vocalion. The 1929 "That's No Way to Get Along," the most famous of his pre-war 78s, was covered by the Rolling Stones as "Prodigal Son."

Wilkins' great Mississippi vibrato was similar to that of Frank Stokes and Joe Callicott, and his records show considerable finesse with rag and blues guitar. Ungoverned by standard 12-bar conventions, Wilkins created his own structures and was especially strong in open *E*, as heard in "That's No Way to Get Along" and the spooky one-chord "Rollin' Stone." He crafted lyrics into coherent narratives, carefully avoiding any hint of the risqué. He showed up at the Chicago World's Fair but did most of his playing in Memphis and Hernando. Unnerving violence at a houseparty prompted him to quit the blues in 1936 and find Jesus. In 1964 a rediscovered Rev. Robert Wilkins, spiritual singer and minister of the Church of God in Christ, hit the folk circuit and made some deeply moving records. He refused to

play blues but did recycle some old riffs. Near the end of his life, Rev. Wilkins was seen working as a root doctor on a Memphis side street. He lived to be 91. — *Jas Obrecht*

Memphis Blues 1928–1935 / 1901 / Document ◆◆◆
Wilkins' complete works also include sides by Tom Dickinson and Allen Shaw. — *Jas Obrecht*

Remember Me / 1971 / Genes ◆◆◆
Although he left the world of blues for gospel, Rev. Robert Wilkins never abandoned his guitar or toned down his brillant instrumental tendencies; he simply took his rampaging playing style and used it in the service of the Lord. While he wasn't in peak form for this newly discovered and released 1971 concert, he was far from second-rate. He performed 13 cuts and sang with passion, power, and conviction. Robert Palmer's liner notes outline Wilkins' contributions and style. — *Ron Wynn*

● **The Original Rolling Stone** / 1980 / Yazoo ◆◆◆◆◆
These 14 pre-war tracks include adequate liner notes. — *Jas Obrecht*

Big Joe Williams

b. Oct. 16, 1903, Crawford, MS, **d.** Dec. 17, 1982, Macon, MS
Guitar, Vocals / Electric Delta Blues, Acoustic Delta Blues
Big Joe Williams may have been the most cantankerous human being who ever walked the earth with guitar in hand. At the same time, he was an incredible blues musician: a gifted songwriter, a powerhouse vocalist, and an exceptional idiosyncratic guitarist. Despite his deserved reputation as a fighter (documented in Michael Bloomfield's bizarre booklet *Me and Big Joe*), artists who knew him well treated him as a respected elder statesman. Even so, they may not have chosen to play with him, because, as with other older Delta artists, if you played with him you played by his rules.

As protégé David "Honeyboy" Edwards described him, Williams in his early Delta days was a walking musician who played work camps, jukes, store porches, streets, and alleys from New Orleans to Chicago. He recorded through five decades for Vocalion, Okeh, Paramount, Bluebird, Prestige, Delmark, and many others. As a youngster, I met him in Delmark owner Bob Koester's store, the Jazz Record Mart. At the time, Big Joe was living there when not on his constant travels. According to Charlie Musselwhite, he and Big Joe kicked off the blues revival in Chicago in the '60s.

When I saw him playing at Mike Bloomfield's "blues night" at the Fickle Pickle, Williams was playing an electric nine-string guitar through a small ramshackle amp with a pie plate nailed to it and a beer can dangling against that. When he played, everything rattled but Big Joe himself. The total effect of this incredible apparatus produced the most buzzing, sizzling, African-sounding music I have ever heard.

Anyone who wants to learn Delta blues must one day come to grips with the idea that the guitar is a drum as well as a melody-producing instrument. A continuous, African-derived musical tradition emphasizing percussive techniques on stringed instruments from the banjo to the guitar can be heard in the music of Delta stalwarts Charley Patton, Fred McDowell, and Bukka White. Each employed decidedly percussive techniques, beating on his box, knocking on the neck, snapping the strings, or adding buzzing or sizzling effects to augment the instrument's percussive potential. However, Big Joe Williams, more than any other major recording artist, embodied the concept of guitar-as-drum, bashing out an incredible series of riffs on his *G*-tuned nine-string for over 60 years. — *Barry Lee Pearson*

Piney Woods Blues / 1958 / Delmark ◆◆◆
Fine Delmark cuts from the late-50s rediscovery phase of Big Joe's career. — *Barry Lee Pearson*

Nine String Guitar Blues / 1961 / Delmark ◆◆◆◆◆
The title says it all—Big Joe Williams plays a custom-made nine-string guitar, which sounds like no other instrument in existence. That alone would give his stripped-down acoustic Delta blues a new spin, but he brings so much grit and passion to his performances, they would have sounded fresh and vital anyway. — *Thom Owens*

Blues on Highway 49 / 1961 / Delmark ◆◆◆
One of Big Joe Williams' better releases, *Blues on Highway 49* is a tense, gritty set of roadhouse blues. Williams' stinging playing and singing brings out the best in such songs as "Tijuana Blues"

and "45 Blues"—he shows exactly how Delta blues could be updated. —*Thom Owens*

Walking Blues / Oct. 1961 / Fantasy ✦✦✦
Blues for 9 Strings / Mar. 1963 / Bluesville ✦✦✦
Back to the Country / 1964 / Testament ✦✦✦✦✦
Fellow Mississippians Jimmy Brown on fiddle and Willie Lee Harris on harmonica augment Big Joe's down-home Delta blues from the blues revival of the '70s. —*Barry Lee Pearson*

● **Early Recordings 1935–41** / 1965 / Mamlish ✦✦✦✦✦
This blues legend and guitar wizard's best initial Bluebird recordings, including the best versions of "49 Highway" and "Baby Please Don't Go" from 1935. —*Barry Lee Pearson*

Classic Delta Blues / 1966 / Milestone ✦✦✦
Big Joe Williams cut these twelve tracks in 1964. For these recordings, he played a standard six-string guitars instead of hauling out his custom nine-string and the effects are pleasant, but not revelatory. —*Thom Owens*

Stavin' Chain Blues / 1966 / Delmark ✦✦✦✦✦
A CD reissue of 1958 recordings, it includes four previously unreleased tracks. This is raw but beautiful country blues, featuring the otherworldly sound of Big Joe's nine-string guitar. —*Niles J. Frantz*

● **Shake Your Boogie** / 1990 / Arhoolie ✦✦✦✦✦
Arhoolie reissued two of Big Joe Williams' seminal rediscovery albums on one disc in 1990. The first, 1960's *Tough Times*, ranks among his best; the second, 1969's *Thinking of What They Did*, isn't as strong, but the two albums provide an excellent introduction to this Delta bluesman. —*Stephen Thomas Erlewine*

Delta Blues: 1951 / 1991 / Trumpet ✦✦✦✦✦
Although the early '50s were not a great time for Delta blues musicians, there remained some proficient players performing in this vein throughout the South. The three presented on this collection of classic Trumpet recordings include Big Joe Williams, known for his nine-string guitar and robust singing, Luther Huff, a good, if derivative vocalist/guitarist, and the spry pianist and vocalist Willie Love, an exuberant performer whose Three Aces band at various times contained Elmore James and Little Milton. This anthology includes 18 selections that show the link between older, traditional blues and the urban, electric sounds that emerged as the idiom's dominant form later in the decade. —*Ron Wynn*

Complete Works, Vol. 1 (1935–1941) / 1991 / Document ✦✦✦
Complete Works, Vol. 2 (1945–1949) / 1991 / Document ✦✦✦

Jody Williams

b. Feb. 3, 1935, Mobile, AL
Guitar, Vocals / Electric Chicago Blues
Retired from the Chicago blues business for decades, Jody Williams' stinging lead guitar work is still stirringly felt every time someone punches up Billy Boy Arnold's "I Was Fooled," Bo Diddley's "Who Do You Love," Otis Spann's "Five Spot," or Williams' eerie minor-key instrumental masterpiece, "Lucky Lou."

Born in Alabama, Joseph Leon Williams moved to Chicago at age six. He grew up alongside Bo Diddley, the two trading licks as kids and playing for real by 1951. By the mid-'50s, Williams was ensconced as a Chicago session guitarist of high stature, but he began to grow disenchanted when the signature lick he created for newcomer Billy Stewart's Argo waxing of "Billy's Blues" was appropriated by Mickey Baker for the Mickey & Sylvia smash "Love Is Strange." Baker apparently caught Williams playing the riff in Washington, D.C., at the Howard Theatre. When the legal smoke had cleared, Bo Diddley's wife owned the writing credit for "Love Is Strange" and Jody Williams had zipola for monetary compensation.

Williams made his recording debut (singing as well as playing) as a leader for powerhouse deejay Al Benson's Blue Lake imprint in 1955: "Looking for My Baby" was credited to Little Papa Joe. That alias pattern held in 1957, when Argo unleashed "Lucky Lou" and its sumptuous slow blues vocal flip "You May" as by Little Joe Lee (quite a band here—saxists Harold Ashby and Red Holloway, keyboardist Lafayette Leake, and bassist Willie Dixon). In 1960, Herald Records labeled him Sugar Boy Williams on "Little Girl." 1960s outings for Nike, Jive, Smash, and Yulando round out Williams' slim discography.

At last report, Jody Williams was working as a computer maintenance technician and burglar alarm installer, his salad days as one of Chicago's hottest young guitar slingers in the regrettably distant past. —*Bill Dahl*

● **Leading Brand [6 Track]** / 1977 / Red Lightnin' ✦✦✦✦✦
A bootleg LP, very welcome nevertheless in its day, spotlighting two of Chicago's most advanced blues pickers of the '50s and early '60s. Earl Hooker's brilliant stuff for producer Mel London dominates, but the last six sides showcase Jody Williams' taut, ringing guitar lines (especially on 1957's West Side-styled minor-key "Lucky Lou") and smooth vocals on "You May," and "Looking for My Baby." —*Bill Dahl*

Joe Williams (Joseph Goreed)

b. Dec. 12, 1918, Cordele, GA
Vocals / Blues, Swing, Standards
Joe Williams was possibly the last great big band singer, following in the tradition of Jimmy Rushing but carving out his own unique identity. Equally skilled on blues (including double entendre ad-libs), ballads, and standards, Williams has always been a charming and consistently swinging performer. In the late '30s he performed regularly with Jimmie Noone. Williams gigged with Coleman Hawkins and Lionel Hampton in the early '40s and toured with Andy Kirk during 1946–47. After stints with Red Saunders and Hot Lips Page and recordings with King Kolax (including a 1951 version of "Every Day I Have the Blues"), Williams joined Count Basie's Orchestra in 1954. During the next seven years he and Basie had a mutually satisfying relationship, both making each other more famous! His version of "Every Day" with Count became his theme song while many other pieces (such as "Goin' to Chicago" and "Smack Dab in the Middle") became permanent parts of Williams' repertoire. After leaving Basie in 1961, the singer worked with the Harry Edison quintet for a couple of years and has freelanced as a leader ever since, having occasional reunions with the Basie band. His collaborations with Cannonball Adderley and George Shearing were successful as was an album with the Thad Jones-Mel Lewis Orchestra. Joe Williams has remained one of the most popular and talented singers in jazz. —*Scott Yanow*

Everyday I Have the Blues / 1951–Sep. 28, 1953 / Savoy ✦✦✦✦
From the Roulette catalog, this superior Joe Williams/Count Basie collaboration finds the singer concentrating on the blues with consistently excellent results. In addition to a remake of the title cut, Williams is heard at his best on the classic "Going to Chicago" and such numbers as "Just a Dream," "Cherry Red," and "Good Mornin' Blues." This LP is well worth searching for. —*Scott Yanow*

★ **Count Basie Swings / Joe Williams Sings** / Jul. 17, 1955–Jul. 26, 1955 / Verve ✦✦✦✦✦
This is the definitive Joe Williams record, cut shortly after joining Count Basie's orchestra. Included are his classic versions of "Every Day I Have the Blues," "The Comeback," "Alright, Okay, You Win," "In the Evening," and "Teach Me Tonight." Williams' popularity was a major asset to Basie and getting to sing with that swinging big band on a nightly basis certainly did not harm the singer. This gem belongs in everyone's jazz collection. —*Scott Yanow*

A Swingin' Night at Birdland / Jun. 1962 / Roulette ✦✦✦✦
In 1961, after six years as one of the main attractions of Count Basie's orchestra, Williams (with Basie's blessing) went out on his own. One of his first sessions was this live recording cut at Birdland with a strong quintet that featured trumpeter Harry "Sweets" Edison and Jimmy Forrest on tenor. Williams mostly sings standards and ballads but also tosses in a few of his popular blues (including "Well Alright, OK, You Win" and "Goin' to Chicago") during a well-rounded and thoroughly enjoyable set. —*Scott Yanow*

Me and the Blues / Jan. 2, 1963–Dec. 5, 1963 / RCA ✦✦✦✦✦
This CD is a straight reissue of the original LP and features singer Joe Williams backed by a studio orchestra headed and arranged by Jimmy Jones. Williams mostly sticks to blues-oriented material but there is a surprising amount of mood variation on the dozen selections along with short solos by trumpeters Thad Jones and Clark Terry, altoist Phil Woods and Seldon Powell on tenor; Ben Webster has a guest spot on "Rocks in My Bed." Williams, heard at the peak of his powers, is at his best on

"Me and the Blues," "Rocks in My Bed," "Work Song," and "Kansas City." —*Scott Yanow*

● **The Overwhelmin'** / Feb. 6, 1963–Jun. 18, 1965 / Bluebird ✦✦✦✦✦

A CD sampler taken from five former LPs, this fine CD features Joe Williams doing three songs from Duke Ellington's play *Jump for Joy*, five numbers at the 1963 Newport Jazz Festival (during which he is joined by trumpeters Clark Terry and Howard McGhee and tenor greats Coleman Hawkins, Zoot Sims, and Ben Webster), four blues backed by an all-star jazz group and five ballads in front of an orchestra. Although it would be preferable to have each of the five original albums intact, this superb collection features Joe Williams on a wide variety of material, and he is heard close to his peak throughout. —*Scott Yanow*

☆ **And the Thad Jones/Mel Lewis Orchestra** / Sep. 1966 / Blue Note ✦✦✦✦✦

This CD reissues one of Joe Williams' finest recordings. Accompanied by the Thad Jones/Mel Lewis Orchestra, the singer is heard at the peak of his powers. The big band primarily functions as an ensemble (Snooky Young gets off some good blasts on "Nobody Knows the Way I Feel This Morning") but the inventive Thad Jones arrangements insure that his illustrious sidemen have plenty to play. Many of the selections (half of which have been in the singer's repertoire ever since) are given definitive treatment on this set (particularly a humorous "Evil Man Blues," "Gee Baby Ain't I Good to You?" and "Smack Dab in the Middle") and Williams scats at his best on "It Don't Mean a Thing." Get this one. —*Scott Yanow*

Joe Williams Live / Aug. 7, 1973 / Fantasy ✦✦✦✦

Williams meets the Cannonball Adderley Septet on this rather interesting session. The expanded rhythm section (which includes keyboardist George Duke and both acoustic bassist Walter Booker and the electric bass of Carol Kaye) gives funky accompaniment to Williams while altoist Cannonball and cornetist Nat have some solo space. Actualy the singer easily steals the show on a rather searing version of "Goin' to Chicago Blues," his own "Who She Do" and a few unusual songs, including Duke Ellington's "Heritage." —*Scott Yanow*

Prez Conference / 1979 / GNP ✦✦✦✦✦

Dave Pell's Prez Conference was to Lester Young what Supersax is to Charlie Parker. Pell's short-lived group featured harmonized Lester Young solos recreated by three tenors and a baritone; their matchup with singer Joe Williams is quite enjoyable. Since Young was in Count Basie's orchestra when Jimmy Rushing was the vocalist, Joe Williams has a rare opportunity to give his own interpretation to Rushing and Billie Holiday classics like "I May Be Wrong," "You Can Depend on Me," "If Dreams Come True," and "Easy Living." A delightful and swinging date. —*Scott Yanow*

Nothin' But the Blues / Nov. 16, 1983–Nov. 17, 1983 / Delos ✦✦✦✦

Sticking to blues, Joe Williams is in prime form on this special session. His backup crew includes such all-stars as tenor saxophonist Red Holloway, organist Brother Jack McDuff and (on alto and one lone vocal) the great Eddie "Cleanhead" Vinson. The many blues standards are familiar but these versions are lively and fresh. —*Scott Yanow*

I Just Wanna Sing / Jun. 29, 1985–Jun. 30, 1985 / Delos ✦✦✦✦

For this session, Joe Williams is backed by such master jazzmen as trumpeter Thad Jones, the contrasting tenors of Eddie "Lockjaw" Davis and Benny Golson and guitarist John Collins. The material varies from the dated humor of "It's Not Easy Being White" to classic versions of "Until I Met You" and "I Got It Bad." Joe Williams is in prime form and this is one of his better sessions from his later years. —*Scott Yanow*

Ballad and Blues Master / May 7, 1987–May 8, 1987 / Verve ✦✦✦✦

Taken from the same sessions that had previously resulted in *Every Night*, the identical adjectives apply. Joe Williams was in superior form for this live date, putting a lot of feeling into such songs as "You Can Depend on Me," "When Sunny Gets Blue" and "Dinner for One Please, James." A closing blues medley is particularly enjoyable and the backup by a quartet that includes pianist Morman Simmons and guitarist Henry Johnson is tasteful and swinging. —*Scott Yanow*

Every Night: Live at Vine St. / May 7, 1987–May 8, 1987 / Verve ✦✦✦✦✦

The focus is entirely on Joe Williams (who is backed by a standard four-piece rhythm section) during this live session from Vine Street. Then 69, Williams had not lost a thing and his voice has rarely sounded stronger. This version of "Every Day I Have the Blues" is transformed into Miles Davis' "All Blues," Williams revives Eubie Blake's "A Dollar for a Dime" and sounds wonderful on such songs as "Too Marvelous for Words," "I Want a Little Girl," and "Roll 'Em Pete." This is the best of Joe Williams' records from the '80s. —*Scott Yanow*

In Good Company / Jan. 19, 1989–Jan. 21, 1989 / Verve ✦✦✦✦

A bit of a grab-bag, this CD finds Joe Williams joined by Supersax on two numbers, doing a pair of vocal duets with Marlena Shaw ("Is You Is or Is You Ain't My Baby" is excellent), teaming up with vocalist/pianist Shirley Horn for two ballads and being joined by the Norman Simmons Quartet for the remainder. Sticking mostly to standards, Joe Williams shows that at 70 he still had the magic. —*Scott Yanow*

Live at Orchestra . . . / Nov. 20, 1992 / Telarc ✦✦✦✦

Joe Williams is so closely associated with the Count Basie Orchestra that it is difficult to believe that this Telarc CD was his first recording with jazz's great institution in over 30 years. Williams (in generally fine form despite an occasionally raspy voice) performs a well-rounded set of blues, ballads and standards with the Frank Foster-led Basie orchestra, combining some of his older hits with a few newer songs such as Grady Tate's "A Little at a Time" and "My Baby Upsets Me." Foster's sidemen are mostly heard in an ensemble role with all of the instrumental solos being rather brief; there is little interaction with the vocalist. That fault aside, this is one of Joe Williams' better recordings of the past decade. —*Scott Yanow*

Juanita Williams

Vocals / Modern Blues

Although Juanita Williams may seem like a new face on the blues scene, one listen to her brilliant debut album on the Big Mo label, *Introducing Juanita Williams*, and you realize this woman is a pro. In fact, she's spent the last 20 years as lead vocalist for the Airmen of Note, a prestigious Air Force Big Band originally founded by Glenn Miller.

The comparisons to Aretha Franklin are inevitable, and her debut features a wide-ranging sample of modern and classic blues tunes, everything from Ike and Tina Turner's "Crazy About You Baby" to Freddie King's "That Will Never Do" and Bobby Bland's "Two Steps from the Blues."

Williams began singing in the church, but her secular influences eventually stole her heart, and they included singers like Etta James and Aretha Franklin, yet Williams' voice, passion and energy are completely unique. Anybody who has doubts about the future of women blues vocalists should pick up Williams' impressive debut. —*Richard Skelly*

● **Introducing Juanita Williams** / 1994 / Big Mo ✦✦✦✦

Lee "Shot" Williams

b. May 21, 1938, Lexington, MS
Vocals / Soul Blues

A journeyman southern soul-blues singer, Williams has made about 20 singles since the early '60s, as well as three albums (two of those appearing in the 1990s). Through the years he's toured with the likes of Earl Hooker and Bobby Bland, the latter of whom (along with B.B. King) is one of the gospel-influenced singer's most visible points of reference. On his latest effort, *Cold Shot* (recorded in Chicago in 1994), he's backed by guitarist Little Smokey Smothers, an occasional associate since the 1950s. —*Richie Unterberger*

Cold Shot / 1994 / Black Magic ✦✦✦

Competent modern soul-blues with a friendly, non-threatening tone, augmented by a three-man brass section, the Chicago Playboy Horns. —*Richie Unterberger*

Robert Pete Williams

b. Mar. 14, 1914, Zachary, LA, d. Dec. 31, 1980, Rosedale, LA
Guitar, Vocals / Acoustic Louisiana Blues

Discovered in the Louisiana State Penitentiary, Robert Pete Williams became one of the great blues discoveries during the folk boom of the early '60s. His disregard for conventional patterns, tunings, and structures kept him from a wider audience, but his music remains one of the great, intense treats of the blues.

Williams was born in Zachary, LA, the son of sharecropping parents. While he was a child, he worked the fields with his family; he never attended school. Williams didn't begin playing blues until his late teens, when he made himself a guitar out of a cigar box. Playing his homemade guitar, Williams began performing at local parties, dances, and fish fries at night while he worked during the day. Even though he was constantly working, he never made quite enough money to support his family, which caused considerable tension between him and his wife—according to legend, she burned his guitar one night in a fit of anger.

Despite all of the domestic tension, Williams continued to play throughout the Baton Rouge area, performing at dances and juke joints. In 1956, he shot and killed a man in a local club. Williams claimed the act was in self-defense, but he was convicted of murder and sentenced to life in prison. He was sent to Angola prison, where he served for two years before being discovered by ethnomusicologists Dr. Harry Oster and Richard Allen. The pair recorded Williams performing several of his own songs, which were all about life in prison. Impressed with the guitarist's talents, Oster and Allen pleaded for a pardon for Williams. The pardon was granted in 1959, after he had served a total of three and a half years. For the first five years after he left prison, Williams could only perform in Lousiana, but his recordings—which appeared on Folk-Lyric, Arhoolie, and Prestige, among other labels—were popular and he received positive word-of-mouth reviews.

In 1964, Williams played his first concert outside of Louisiana—it was a set at the legendary Newport Folk Festival. Williams' performance was enthusiastically received and he began touring the Untied States, often playing shows with Mississippi Fred McDowell. For the remainder of the '60s and most of the '70s, Robert Pete Williams constantly played concerts and festivals across America, as well a handful of dates in Europe. Along the way, he recorded for a handful of small independent labels, including Fontana and Storyville. Williams slowed down his work schedule in the late '70s, largely due to his old age and declining health. The guitarist died on December 31, 1980, at the age of 66. —*Cub Koda & Stephen Thomas Erlewine*

★ **Angola Prisoner's Blues** / Mar. 1961 / Arhoolie ✦✦✦✦✦
Not enough great things to say about this one, one of the finest field recordings ever done anywhere. If Robert Pete's "Prisoner's Talking Blues" doesn't move you, check your heart into your refrigerator's freezer section. —*Cub Koda*

Free Again / Nov. 1961 / Original Blues Classics ✦✦✦✦✦

Rural Blues (With Snooks Eaglin) / Storyville ✦✦✦✦✦
Not only does Snooks Eaglin prove a fine partner for Robert Pete Williams, but his vocals and playing have seldom been more disciplined and exciting. —*Ron Wynn*

Those Prison Blues / 1981 / Arhoolie ✦✦✦✦✦

Robert Pete Williams, Vol. 1 / 1994 / Arhoolie ✦✦✦
Robert Pete Williams' music had the striking lyricism and highly individualized sound of the great Delta blues masters, but it was made well after the heyday of that style. Williams improvised considerably in his performances, using blues' language but varying his approach. These songs were mostly recorded at the Angola State Penitentiary. While Williams sings mournful, anguished blues with spectacular impact, he also can turn around and do more joyous fare effectively. His vigorous accompaniment, especially on six-string guitar, is just as creative and stunning as his vocals. This 15-cut disc, which has five bonus cuts, is most welcome. —*Ron Wynn*

Robert Pete Williams, Vol. 2 / 1994 / Arhoolie ✦✦✦
This second volume of newly released (on CD) Robert Pete Williams material was mostly recorded in Louisiana in 1959, shortly after Williams was paroled from Angola by Governor Earl Long. The cuts recorded during this time reflect both his appreciation for being out of jail and his understanding that he was still not completely free. The searing "All Night Long," "I Got The Blues So Bad" and "This Train Is Heaven Bound" are punctuated by equally gripping guitar accompaniment on either 6- or 12-string. There's also material recorded later in his career in

Berkeley. The three cuts from 1970 show Williams in a more reflective mode, though no less powerful. These are two of nine previously unissued cuts comprising the majority of the disc. —*Ron Wynn*

When a Man Takes the Blues / 1994 / Arhoolie ✦✦✦✦✦
Important collection of Williams' best early work. —*Bill Dahl*

I'm as Blue as a Man Can be / 1994 / Arhoolie ✦✦✦✦✦
More classic early sides. —*Bill Dahl*

Homesick James Williamson

b. Apr. 3, 1910, Somerville, TN
Guitar, Vocals / Electric Chicago Blues
His correct age may remain in doubt (he's claimed he was born as early as 1905), but the slashing slide guitar skills of Homesick James Williamson have never been in question. Many of his most satisfying recordings have placed him in a solo setting, where his timing eccentricities don't disrupt the proceedings (though he's made some fine band-backed waxings as well).

Williamson was playing guitar at age ten and soon ran away from his Tennessee home to play at fish fries and dances. His travels took the guitarist through Mississippi and North Carolina during the 1920s, where he crossed paths with Yank Rachell, Sleepy John Estes, Blind Boy Fuller, and Big Joe Williams.

Settling in Chicago during the 1930s, Williamson played local clubs and recorded for RCA Victor in 1937. The miles and gigs had added up before Williamson made some of his finest sides in 1952-53 for Art Sheridan's Chance Records (including the classic "Homesick" that gave him his enduring stage name).

James also worked extensively as a sideman, backing harp great Sonny Boy Williamson in 1945 at a Chicago gin joint called the Purple Cat, and during the 1950s with his cousin, slide master Elmore James (to whom Homesick is stylistically indebted). He also recorded with James during the 1950s. Homesick's own output included crashing 45s for Colt and USA in 1962, a fine 1964 album for Prestige, and four tracks on a Vanguard anthology in 1965.

Williamson has never stopped recording and touring; he's done recent albums for Appaloosa and Earwig. No matter what his current chronological age, there's nothing over-the-hill about the blues of Homesick James Williamson. —*Bill Dahl*

● **Blues on the South Side** / 1965 / Prestige ✦✦✦✦✦
Probably the best album the slide guitarist ever laid down (originally for Prestige in 1964). His stylistic similarities to his cousin, the great Elmore James, are obvious, but Homesick deviates repeatedly from the form. Tough as nails with a bottleneck, he goes for the jugular on "Goin' Down Swingin'," "Johnny Mae," and "Gotta Move," supported by pianist Lafayette Leake, guitarist Eddie Taylor, and drummer Clifton James. —*Bill Dahl*

Goin Back In The Times / 1994 / Earwig ✦✦✦
A credible, reflective return to the slide guitar veteran's country blues days. —*Bill Dahl*

Sonny Boy Williamson [II] (Aleck Ford "Rice" Miller)

b. Dec. 5, 1899, Glendora, MS, **d.** May 25, 1965, Helena, AR
Harmonica, Vocals / Electric Delta Blues, Electric Chicago Blues
Sonny Boy Williamson was, in many ways, the ultimate blues legend. By the time of his death in 1965, he had been around long enough to have played with Robert Johnson at the start of his career and Eric Clapton, Jimmy Page, and Robbie Robertson at the end of it. In between, he drank a lot of whiskey, hoboed around the country, had a successful radio show for 15 years, toured Europe to great acclaim, and simply wrote, played and sang some of the greatest blues ever etched into black phonograph records. His delivery was sly, evil, and world-weary, while his harp playing was full of short, rhythmic bursts one minute and powerful, impassioned blowing the next. His songs were chock-full of mordant wit, with largely autobiographical lyrics that hold up to the scrutiny of the printed page. Though he took his namesake from another well-known harmonica player, no one really sounded like him. A moody, bitter, and suspicious man, no one wove such a confusing web of misinformation as Sonny Boy Williamson II. Even his birth date (either 1897 or 1909) and real name (Aleck or Alex or Willie "Rice"—which may or may not be a nickname—Miller or Ford) cannot be verified with absolute certainty. Of his childhood days in Mississippi, absolutely nothing is known. What *is* known is that by the mid-

'30s, he was traveling the Delta working under the alias of Little Boy Blue. With blues legends like Robert Johnson, Robert Nighthawk, Robert Jr. Lockwood, and Elmore James as interchangeable playing partners, he worked the juke joints, fish fries, country suppers, and ballgames of the era. By the early '40s, he was the star of KFFA's *King Biscuit Time,* the first live blues radio show to hit the American airwaves. As one of the major ruses to occur in blues history, his sponsor—the Interstate Grocery Company—felt they could push more sacks of their King Biscuit Flour with Miller posing as Chicago harmonica star John Lee "Sonny Boy" Williamson. In today's everybody-knows-everything video age, it's hard to think that such an idea would work, much less prosper. After all, the real Sonny Boy was a national recording star, and Miller's vocal and harmonica style was in no way derivative of him. But Williamson had no desire to tour in the South, so prosper it did, and when John Lee was murdered in Chicago, Miller became—in his own words—"the original Sonny Boy." Among his fellow musicians, he was usually still referred to as Rice Miller, but to the rest of the world he did, indeed, become *the* Sonny Boy Williamson.

The show was an immediate hit, prompting IGC to introduce Sonny Boy Corn Meal, complete with a likeness of Williamson on the front of the package. With all this local success, however, Sonny Boy was not particularly anxious to record. Though he often claimed in his twilight years that he had recorded in the '30s, no evidence of that appears to have existed. Lillian McMurray, the owner of Trumpet Records in Jackson, MS, had literally tracked him down to a boarding house in nearby Belzoni and enticed him to record for her. The music Sonny Boy made for her between 1951 to 1954 show him in peak form, his vocal, instrumental, and songwriting skills honed to perfection. Williamson struck paydirt on his first Trumpet release, "Eyesight to the Blind," and though the later production on his Chess records would make the Trumpet sides seem woefully underrecorded by comparison, they nonetheless stand today as classic performances, capturing juke-joint music in one of its finest hours.

Another major contribution to the history of the blues occurred when Sonny Boy brought *King Biscuit Time* guest star Elmore James into the studio for a session. With Williamson blowing harp, a drummer keeping time, and the tape machine running surreptitiously, Elmore recorded the first version of what would become his signature tune, Robert Johnson's "Dust My Broom." By this time Sonny Boy had divorced his first wife (who also happened to be Howlin' Wolf's sister) and married Mattie Gordon. This would prove to be the longest and most enduring relationship of his life outside of music, with Mattie putting up with the man's rambling ways, and living a life of general rootlessness in the bargain. On two different occasions Sonny Boy moved to Detroit, taking up residence in the Baby Boy Warren band for brief periods, and contributed earth-shattering solos on Warren sides for Blue Lake and Excello in 1954.

By early 1955, after leasing a single to Johnny Vincent's Ace label, McMurray had sold Williamson's contract to Buster Williams in Memphis, who in turn sold it to Leonard Chess in Chicago. All the pieces were finally tumbling into place, and Sonny Boy finally had a reason to take up permanent residence north of the Mason-Dixon line; he now was officially a Chess recording artist. His first session for Chess took place on August 12, 1955, and the single pulled from it, "Don't Start Me to Talkin'," started doing brisk business on the R&B charts. By his second session for the label, he was reunited with longtime musical partner Robert Jr. Lockwood. Lockwood—who had been one of the original King Biscuit Boys—had become *de facto* house guitarist for Chess, as well as moonlighting for other Chicago labels. With Lockwood's combination of Robert Johnson rhythms and jazz chord embellishments, Williamson's harp and parched vocals sounded fresher than ever and Lockwood's contributions to the success of Sonny Boy's Chess recordings cannot be overestimated.

For a national recording artist, Williamson had a remarkable penchant for pulling a disappearing act for months at a time. Sometimes, when Chicago bookings got too lean, he would head back to Arkansas, fronting the *King Biscuit* radio show for brief periods. But in 1963 he was headed to Europe for the first time, as part of the American Folk Blues Festival. The folk music boom was in full swing and Europeans were bringing over blues artists, both in and past their prime, to face wildly appreciative

White audiences for the first time. Sonny Boy unleashed his bag of tricks and stole the show every night. He loved Europe and stayed behind in Britain when the tour headed home. He started working the teenage beat club circuit, touring and recording with the Yardbirds and Eric Burdon's band, whom he always referred to as 'de Mammimals.' On the folk blues tours, Sonny Boy would be very dignified and laidback. But in the beat club setting, with young, White bands playing on eleven behind him, he'd pull out every juke-joint trick he used with the King Biscuit Entertainers and drive the kids nuts. "Help Me" became a surprise hit in Britain and across Europe. Now in his mid-60s (or possibly older), Williamson was truly appreciative of all the attention, and contemplated moving to Europe permanently. But after getting a harlequin, two-tone, city gentleman's suit (complete with bowler hat, rolled umbrella and attaché case full of harmonicas) made up for himself, he headed back to the States—and the Chess studios—for some final sessions. When he returned to England in 1964, it was as a conquering hero. One of his final recordings, with Jimmy Page on guitar, was entitled "I'm Trying to Make London My Home."

In 1965, he headed home, back to Mississippi one last time, and took over the *King Biscuit* show again. Still wearing his custom-made suit, he regaled the locals with stories of his travels across Europe. Some were impressed, others who had known him for years felt he could have just as well substituted the name "Mars" for Europe in explaining his exploits, so used were they to Sonny Boy's tall tales. But after hoboing his way around the United States for thirty-odd years, and playing to appreciative audiences throughout Europe, Sonny Boy had a perfectly good reason for returning to the Delta; he had come home to die. He would enlist the help of old friends like Houston Stackhouse and Peck Curtis to take him around to all the back-road spots he had seen as a boy, sometimes paying his respects to old friends, other days just whiling away an afternoon on the banks of a river fishing.

When Ronnie Hawkins' ex-bandmates, the Hawks, were playing in the area, they made a special point of seeking out Sonny Boy and spent an entire evening backing him up in a juke joint. All through the night, Williamson kept spitting into a coffee can beside him. When Robbie Robertson got up to leave the bandstand during a break, he noticed the can was filled with blood. On May 25, 1965, Curtis and Stackhouse were waiting at the KFFA studios for Sonny Boy to do the daily *King Biscuit* broadcast. When Williamson didn't show, Curtis left the station and headed to the rooming house where Sonny Boy was staying, only to find him lying in bed, dead of an apparent heart attack. He was buried in the Whitfield Cemetery in Tutwiler, MS, and his funeral was well-attended. As Houston Stackhouse said, "He was well thought of through that country." He was elected to the Blues Foundation Hall of Fame in 1980. *—Cub Koda*

Down & Out Blues / 1959 / MCA/Chess ✦✦✦✦✦
Retaining photographer Don Bronstein's cover shot of a disheveled bum lying on the sidewalk (some former Chess artist, perhaps?) Sonny Boy Williamson's original 1959 album made it to digital reissue but has now been supplanted by MCA's exhaustive *The Essential Sonny Boy Williamson.* Still, for a budget price, there's a dozen unforgettable tracks: "Don't Start Me to Talkin'," his Checker debut; "All My Love in Vain," "Wake Up Baby," "99," "Cross My Heart," "Let Me Explain," and "The Key (To Your Door)." *—Bill Dahl*

The Real Folk Blues / 1965 / MCA/Chess ✦✦✦✦✦
With the exception of "Dissatisfied," cut in 1957, everything on this dozen-track comp dates from 1960-63 and holds "One Way Out," "Checkin' Up on My Baby," "Trust My Baby," and the catchy, country-tinged "Peach Tree," which drives along with a pronounced bounce. *—Bill Dahl*

More Real Folk Blues / Sep. 1967 / MCA/Chess ✦✦✦✦✦
More good early-'60s Chess recordings from Sonny Boy Williamson. "Help Me," "Bye Bye Bird," and "Nine Below Zero" have been covered by numerous blues and rock acts. Most of the songs, however, show up on the *Essential* best-of collection. *— Richie Unterberger*

One Way Out / 1968 / MCA/Chess ✦✦✦✦
Sly son-of-a-gun that he was, old Sonny Boy Williamson found a way to weld the twist to the blues with his rousing 1961 title track, with guitarists Robert Jr. Lockwood and Luther Tucker positively blazing in supple support. Fourteen more gems make

this one a must: 1955's "Good Evening Everybody," "Work with Me," and "You Killing Me," all with Muddy Waters and Jimmy Rogers in support; the sturdy "Keep It to Yourself" from the next year, and a forceful "This Is My Apartment." —*Bill Dahl*

Bummer Road / 1969 / MCA/Chess ✦✦✦✦
Yes, this is the album where Williamson and Leonard Chess get down to some serious cussing during their hilariously heated exchange while recording "Little Village." But there are plenty more reasons to pick up this CD than that one: his lascivious Yuletide ditty "Santa Claus;" the stirring "Unseen Eye" and "Keep Your Hand Out of My Pocket," the leering "She Got Next to Me." Everything here was done between 1957 and 1960—prime years for the wily harpist at Chess. —*Bill Dahl*

★ **King Biscuit Time** / 1989 / Arhoolie ✦✦✦✦
Sonny Boy's early Trumpet sides, 1951. The original "Eyesight To The Blind", "Nine Below Zero," and "Mighty Long Time" are Sonny Boy at his very best. Added bonuses include Williamson backing Elmore James on his original recording of "Dust My Broom" and a live KFFA broadcast from 1965. —*Cub Koda*

Clownin' with the World / 1989 / Trumpet ✦✦✦✦
This batch of mostly unreleased Trumpet blues cuts from the early '50s offers some sizzling, if sometimes uneven, material by Sonny Boy Williamson II (Rice Miller) and Willie Love. Each gets eight numbers, with Williamson's being recorded both in Houston and Jackson, Mississippi, while Love did all of his in Jackson. Williamson's ripping, searing harmonica and craggy vocals were then becoming popular, while Love's equally decisive singing and wild, carefree tunes were also attracting big audiences. This is undiluted, frequently chaotic, and always enjoyable music. —*Ron Wynn*

The Chess Years / 1991 / Charly ✦✦✦✦
This import multi-disc boxed set of Williamson's Chess sides (1955-1964) is a definitive overview. —*Cub Koda*

Keep It to Ourselves / 1992 / Alligator ✦✦✦
An intimate 1963 collection of Sonny Boy Williamson in solo and duet (with guitarist Matt Murphy) formats; on three tracks, pianist Memphis Slim hops aboard. This delightful addendum to Williamson's electric output of the same era was cut in Denmark and first issued on Storyville. —*Bill Dahl*

★ **The Essential Sonny Boy Williamson** / Jun. 8, 1993 / MCA/Chess ✦✦✦✦
Two-disc compilation offering 45 of the wizened harmonica genius' best efforts for the Chess brothers, this is the best domestic Williamson package you'll find. Not everything you might want, but pretty close to it: "Don't Start Me to Talkin'," "Let Me Explain," "The Key (To Your Door)" (an alternate take), "Bring It on Home," "Help Me," "One Way Out," "Your Funeral and My Trial," and plenty more. With Robert Jr. Lockwood and Luther Tucker peeling off sizzling guitar riffs behind him, Williamson always had a trick or two up his sleeve until the end. —*Bill Dahl*

Goin' in Your Direction / 1994 / Trumpet ✦✦✦✦
Alligator continues its Trumpet reissue series with an excellent 15-cut anthology covering early Rice Miller (Sonny Boy Williamson II) material, some of it also including guitarist Arthur "Big Boy" Crudup and guitarist Bobo "Slim" Thomas. Miller was honing the uncanny technique that made him a harmonica legend, playing long overtones, spitting lines, droning, and angular phrases that are now part of blues lore. His voice was gaining strength and stature, and he repeatedly demonstrated the kind of vocal character and instrumental acumen later immortalized on his Chess sessions. Alligator has found a genuine treasure chest with this series. —*Ron Wynn*

In Europe with Clapton, Dixon and Spann / 1995 / Evidence ✦✦✦
More highlights from Sonny Boy Williamson's overseas travels, in a wide variety of settings—during the 1963 and 1964 American Folk Blues Festivals with old friends like Willie Dixon, Sunnyland Slim, Hubert Sumlin and Matt Murphy behind him, and for nine tracks, with the Yardbirds in support. The latter combination works pretty well—Clapton and company offer reverent, laidback rhythms that seldom intrude and often mesh nicely. —*Bill Dahl*

Trumpet Masters, Vol. 5: From the Bottom / Collectables ✦✦✦✦✦
As you would expect, Sonny Boy Williamson II's Trumpet sides

were rough, raspy and combative, punctuated by biting harmonica and accented by his piercing vocals. This CD cleans up the sound a bit, but not enough to rob it of its energy or grit. —*Ron Wynn*

Sonny Boy Williamson [I] (John Lee Williamson)

b. Mar. 30, 1914, Jackson, TN, **d.** Jun. 1, 1948, Chicago, IL
Harmonica, Vocals / Chicago Blues, Acoustic Chicago Blues
Easily the most important harmonica player of the pre-war era, John Lee Williamson almost single-handedly made the humble mouth organ a worthy lead instrument for blues bands—leading the way for the amazing innovations of Little Walter and a platoon of others to follow. If not for his tragic murder in 1948 while on his way home from a Chicago gin mill, Williamson would doubtless have been right there alongside them, exploring new and exciting directions.

Williamson made the most of his limited time on the planet. Already a harp virtuoso in his teens, the first Sonny Boy (Rice Miller would adopt the same monicker down in the Delta) learned from Hammie Nixon and Noah Lewis and rambled with Sleepy John Estes and Yank Rachell before settling in Chicago in 1934.

Williamson's extreme versatility and consistent ingenuity won him a Bluebird recording contract in 1937. Under the direction of the ubiquitous Lester Melrose, Sonny Boy Williamson recorded prolifically for Victor both as a leader and behind others in the vast Melrose stable (including Robert Lee McCoy and Big Joe Williams, who in turn played on some of Williamson's sides).

Williamson commenced his sensational recording career with a resounding bang. His first vocal offering on Bluebird was the seminal "Good Morning School Girl," covered countless times across the decades. That same auspicious date also produced "Sugar Mama Blues" and "Blue Bird Blues," both of them every bit as classic in their own right.

The next year brought more gems, including "Decoration Blues" and "Whiskey Headed Woman Blues." The output of 1939 included "T.B. Blues" and "Tell Me Baby," while Williamson cut "My Little Machine" and "Jivin' the Blues" in 1940. Jimmy Rogers apparently took note of Williamson's "Sloppy Drunk Blues," cut with pianist Blind John Davis and bassist Ransom Knowling in 1941; Rogers adapted the tune in storming fashion for Chess in 1954. 1941's motherlode also included "Ground Hog Blues" and "My Black Name," while the popular "Stop Breaking Down" (1945) found the harpist backed by guitarist Tampa Red and pianist Big Maceo.

Sonny Boy cut more than 120 sides in all for RCA from 1937 to 1947, many of them turning up in the postwar repertoires of various Chicago blues giants. His call-and-response style of alternating vocal passages with pungent harmonica blasts was a development of mammoth proportions that would be adopted across-the-board by virtually every blues harpist to follow in his wake.

But Sonny Boy Williamson wouldn't live to reap any appreciable rewards from his inventions. He died at the age of 34, while at the zenith of his popularity (his romping "Shake That Boogie" was a national R&B hit in 1947 on Victor), from a violent bludgeoning about the head that occurred during a strong-arm robbery on the South side. "Better Cut That Out," another storming rocker later appropriated by Junior Wells, became a posthumous hit for Williamson in late 1948. It was the very last song he had committed to posterity. Wells was only one young harpist to display his enduring allegiance; a teenaged Billy Boy Arnold had recently summoned up the nerve to knock on his idol's door to ask for lessons. The accommodating Sonny Boy Williamson was only too happy to oblige, a kindness Arnold has never forgotten (nor does he fail to pay tribute to his eternal main man every chance he gets). Such is the lasting legacy of the blues' first great harmonicist. —*Bill Dahl*

Throw a Boogie Woogie (With Big Joe Williams) / Apr. 1990 / RCA ✦✦✦✦
Eight indispensable Bluebird sides dating from 1937-38—right at the very beginning of his reign as king of blues harpists—that display precisely why Williamson was such a revered innovator (and continues to be even now). Highlights include his classic "Good Morning School Girl" and "Sugar Mama Blues." He shares the disc with itinerant rambler Big Joe Williams, whose eight 1937-41 selections include six featuring Sonny Boy playing harp behind the nine-string guitarist. —*Bill Dahl*

★ **Sugar Mama** / 1995 / Indigo ✦✦✦✦✦
A well-researched 24-track compendium of the first Sonny Boy
Williamson's massively influential Bluebird catalog that spans
1937–1942. Besides being such an innovator on the mouth
organ, Williamson's songs themselves have stood the test of time
strikingly—"Good Morning School Girl," "Blue Bird Blues,"
"Decoration Blues," "Sloppy Drunk Blues," and many more on
the collection are recognized classics. —*Bill Dahl*

Complete Recorded Works, Vols. 1–5 / Document ✦✦✦✦✦
His complete works 1937–1947 in chronological order. Sonny
Boy was a major influence (both harmonica and vocals) on
many of the younger Chicago bluesmen, in particular Junior
Wells. —*Michael Erlewine*

Sonny Boy Williamson, Vol. 1; 1937–39 / Qualiton ✦✦✦✦✦
This artist was perhaps the most significant pioneer of the city-
styled, horn-oriented blues harp—a style brought to perfection
by Little Walter. Williamson adapted the country-styled, chordal-
rhythmic technique that he learned from Noah Lewis and
Hammie Nixon to suit the demands of the evolving urban blues
styles. These 24 tracks include Sonny Boy's first six records cut
in 1937 and sport an imposing list of sidemen: Robert
Nighthawk, Big Joe Williams, Henry Townsend, Walter Davis,
Yank Rachel, Big Bill Broonzy, and Speckled Red. This is a definitive collection. —*Larry Hoffman*

Chick Willis

b. Sep. 29, 1934, Atlanta, GA
Vocals, Guitar / R&B, Modern Electric Blues
Cousin to the late blues ballad singer Chuck Willis, Robert
"Chick" Willis is primarily beloved for his ribald, dozens-based
rocker "Stoop Down Baby." The guitarist cut his original version
in 1972 for tiny La Val Records of Kalamazoo, MI, selling a ton
of 45s for the jukebox market only (the tune's lyrics were way
too raunchy for airplay).
  The Atlanta-born Willis left the military in 1954, hiring on as
valet and chauffeur to cousin Chuck, then riding high with his
many R&B hits for Okeh Records. At that point, Chick's primary
role on the show was as a singer (he made his own vinyl debut
in 1956 with a single, "You're Mine," for Lee Rupe's Ebb Records
after winning a talent contest at Atlanta's Magnolia Ballroom),
but he picked up the guitar while on the road with his cousin
(Chick cites Guitar Slim as his main man in that department).
  When Chuck died of stomach problems in 1958, Willis soldiered on, pausing in Chicago to work as a sideman with slide
guitar great Elmore James. A few obscure 45s ("Twistin' in the
Hospital Ward," cut for Alto in 1962, sounds promising) preceded the advent of "Stoop Down Baby," which Willis has freshened
up for countless sequels ever since (he developed the song by
teasing passerby with his ribald rhymes while working in a car-
nival variety show).
  Risqué material has remained a staple of Willis' output in
recent years. He cut several albums for Ichiban, notably 1988's
Now!, *Footprints in My Bed* in 1990, and *Back to the Blues* in
1991. —*Bill Dahl*

● **Stoop Down Baby . . . Let Your Daddy See** / 1972 / Collectables
✦✦✦✦✦
Here's the signifyin' original "Stoop Down Baby" in its long,
unexpurgated version as issued on the tiny La Val label in 1972.
"Mother Fuyer" travels the same salacious route, but Chick Willis
has a serious side too—a pair of Guitar Slim covers spotlight
Willis' stinging guitar and sturdy singing. —*Bill Dahl*

Back to the Blues / 1991 / Ichiban ✦✦✦
Willis takes things a little more seriously than usual, concentrating largely on covers of material by Percy Mayfield, Howlin'
Wolf, Clarence Carter, and Guitar Slim. His own contributions
include "I Ain't Jivin' Baby" and "Bow-Legged Woman" (he
couldn't resist the raunchy stuff entirely!). —*Bill Dahl*

Footprints in My Bed / Ichiban ✦✦✦✦
One of the few real blues LPs to post a warning about explicit
lyrics, though it seems pretty tame in these rap-hardened times.
Nevertheless, "Jack You Up," "Nuts for Sale," and "Big Red
Caboose" are firmly in the best risque Willis tradition—and very
well produced and played to boot. —*Bill Dahl*

Now / Ichiban ✦✦
Willis updates his biggest seller with a "Stoop Down '88," and
there's a leering "I Want to Play with Your Poodle" and "I Want

a Big Fat Woman" for those who like their blues blue. —*Bill
Dahl*

Chuck Willis

b. Jan. 31, 1928, Atlanta, GA, **d.** Apr. 10, 1958, Atlanta, GA
Vocals / R&B
There were two distinct sides to Chuck Willis. In addition to
being a convincing blues shouter, the Atlanta-born Willis har-
bored a vulnerable blues balladeer side. In addition, he was a
masterful songwriter who penned some of the most distinctive
R&B numbers of the 1950s. We can't grant him principal credit
for his 1957 smash adaptation of "C.C. Rider," an irresistible
update of a classic folk-blues, but Willis did write such gems as
"I Feel So Bad" (later covered by Elvis Presley, Little Milton, and
Otis Rush), the anguished ballads "Don't Deceive Me (Please
Don't Go)" and "It's Too Late" (the latter attracting covers by
Buddy Holly, Charlie Rich, and Otis Redding) and his swan song,
"Hang Up My Rock and Roll Shoes."
  Harold Willis (he adopted Chuck as a stage handle) received
his early training singing at YMCA-sponsored "Teenage
Canteens" in Atlanta and fronting the combos of local band-
leaders Roy Mays and Red McAllister. Powerful deejay Zenas
"Daddy" Sears took an interest in the young vocalist's career,
hooking him up with Columbia Records in 1951. After a solitary
single for the major firm, Willis was shuttled over to its recently
reactivated Okeh R&B subsidiary.
  In 1952, he crashed the national R&B lists for Okeh with a
typically plaintive ballad, "My Story," swiftly encoring on the hit
parade with a gentle cover of Fats Domino's "Goin' to the River"
and his own "Don't Deceive Me" the next year and "You're Still
My Baby" and the surging Latin-beat "I Feel So Bad" in 1954.
Willis also penned a heart-tugging chart-topper for Ruth Brown
that year, "Oh What a Dream."
  Willis moved over to Atlantic Records in 1956 and immediately enjoyed another round of hits with "It's Too Late" and
"Juanita." Atlantic strove mightily to cross Willis over into pop
territory, inserting an exotic steel guitar at one session and
chirpy choirs on several more. The strategy eventually worked
when his 1957 revival of the ancient "C.C. Rider" proved the perfect number to do the "Stroll" to; *American Bandstand* gave the
track a big push, and Willis had his first R&B number one hit as
well as a huge pop seller (Gene "Daddy G" Barge's magnificent
sax solo likely aided its ascent).
  Barge returned for Willis' similar follow-up, "Betty and
Dupree," which also did well for him. But the turban-wearing
crooner's time was growing short—he had long suffered from
ulcers prior to his 1958 death from peritonitis. Much has been
made of the ironic title of his last hit, the touching "What Am I
Living For," but it was no more a clue to his impending demise
than its flip, the joyous "Hang Up My Rock and Roll Shoes." Both
tracks became massive hits upon the singer's death, and his
posthumous roll continued with "My Life" and a powerful "Keep
A-Driving" later that year.
  Willis' cousin, Robert "Chick" Willis, who began his career as
a backup singer for Chuck, remains active nationally. —*Bill Dahl*

My Story / 1980 / Columbia ✦✦✦✦
Not as exhaustive as Legacy's subsequent look at Willis' early-to-
mid-'50s hitmaking stint at Okeh, but this 14-tracker still gets
the job done with the smooth ballads "Going to the River,"
"Don't Deceive Me," and "My Story" and Willis' surging, Latin-
tempoed original "I Feel So Bad." —*Bill Dahl*

Let's Jump Tonight! The Best of Chuck Willis 1951–56 / 1994
/ Epic/Legacy ✦✦✦✦✦
Before his brief turn as a rock 'n' roll star with Atlantic, Willis
cut a lot of material for Okeh in much more of an R&B/jump
blues vein. This 26-cut collection includes all of his early and
mid-'50s R&B hits—"My Story," "Goin' To The River," "Don't
Deceive Me," "You're Still My Baby," and his most famous number from this period, "I Feel So Bad" (revived by Elvis Presley,
among others). The influence of Joe Turner, Charles Brown, early
Lloyd Price, and similar performers is strongly felt; Willis could
shout competently, but was much better on the emotional R&B
ballads. Not as strong or distinctive as his Atlantic material, this
includes several cuts that were previously unreleased or previously unavailable in the U.S. —*Richie Unterberger*

★ **Stroll On: The Chuck Willis Collection** / ✦✦✦✦✦
All 25 of the versatile Atlanta-bred singer's Atlantic Records

sides, presented beautifully (every R&B reissue on CD should be packaged so well, with plenty of brilliant stereo). Willis really hit his stride at Atlantic, doing the Stroll with his easy-going "C.C. Rider" and "Betty and Dupree" (both boasting darting sax breaks from Gene Barge), baring his tender soul on a devotional "What Am I Living For," and taking R&B into fresh directions with a jumping "Kansas City Woman," the relentless "Keep A-Drivin," and a buoyant "Hang Up My Rock and Roll Shoes." —*Bill Dahl*

Little Sonny Willis

b. Oct. 6, 1932, Greensboro, AL
Harmonica, Guitar / Electric Harmonica Blues
Detroit's blues circuit spawned harpist Little Sonny, whose real name was Aaron Willis. He cut scattered singles for Duke and Excello ("Love Shock") in 1958 and Revilot in '66 before coming into his own with three albums for Stax's Enterprise logo during the early '70s. —*Bill Dahl*

● **New King of Blues Harmonica** / 1970 / Stax ✦✦✦✦✦
This is harmonica-driven, small-band electric blues. —*Niles J. Frantz*

Hard Goin' Up / Mar. 1974 / Enterprise ✦✦✦
This soul-inflected blues makes for his best LP. —*Bill Dahl*

Black & Blue / 198 / Stax ✦✦✦✦
Sonny's second Enterprise LP was an impressive affair showcasing both his sinuous harp and rich vocals. Includes the Al Bell-produced "Where Women Got Meat on Their Bones" (later covered by Son Seals) and a fine rendition of "Wade in the Water." —*Bill Dahl*

Hop Wilson (Harding Wilson)

b. Apr. 27, 1927, Grapeland, TX, d. Aug. 27, 1975, Houston, TX
Table Steel Guitar, Vocals / Electric Texas Blues
Slide guitar blues with an Elmore James flavor played on an eight-string table (non-pedal) steel guitar was the trademarked sound of Houston blues legend Hop Wilson. Strictly a local phenomenon, Wilson recorded fitfully and hated touring. Though he also played fine down-home blues on conventional electric guitar and was a powerful singer as well, it is Wilson's unique slide stylings that remain a signature influence on Johnny Winter and Jimmie Vaughan, to name a few.

Wilson learned how to play guitar and harmonica as a child. By the time he was 18, he received his first steel guitar and began playing it at local Houston juke joints and clubs. His musical career was interrupted when he served in World War II. After his discharge from the Army, he decided to pursue a serious career as a blues musician, performing with Ivory Semien's group in the late '50s. Wilson and Semien recorded a number of sides for Goldband Records in 1957.

Hop Wilson didn't lead his own sessions until 1960, when he signed with the Ivory record label. Wilson only recorded for the label for two years—his final sessions were in 1961. After 1961, Wilson concentrated on playing local Houston clubs and bars. He continued to perform in Houston until his death in 1975. —*Cub Koda & Stephen Thomas Erlewine*

● **Steel Guitar Flash!** / 1988 / Ace ✦✦✦✦✦
Although the majority of the recordings collected here already show up on Bullseye Blues' 1991 reissue, *Houston Ghetto Blues*, this is the one to get. The main reason for this is the inclusion of all the known extant tracks cut in the '50s for the Lake Charles, LA Goldband label, where Hop's versions of "Chicken Stuff" and "Rockin' in the Coconut Top" became tri-state biggies, giving him his 15 seconds of fame and influencing the likes of a young Johnny Winter and other young Texan slideslingers in the process. With his drummer/sometimes-vocalist King Ivory Lee Semien banging the daylights out of a set that sounds like Salvation Army rejects (check out the floor-tom intro on the Goldband version of "Rockin' in the Coconut Top" and you'll see what I mean), a string bass played by the ubiquitous "Ice Water" Jones and a crackling, wires sticking out of it steel guitar going to places Elmore James could only think of after watching a bad sci-fi movie, Hop Wilson's dour singing delivery combined with his wild-ass playing becomes a whole genre of blues in and of itself and one well worth investigating. With a full generous 29 tracks aboard (including Hop and the boys backing up Fenton Robinson and Larry Davis on newly discovered cuts) covering all the Goldband, Trey and Ivory takes known to exist, this is now

the definitive Hop Wilson collection and reason enough to start haunting the blues import bins to track it down. Programming tip; for full frontal assault, program up tracks 13 and 25-29 first and prepare yourself for something real special. There was only one Hop Wilson and here's where you check in to get his message. —*Cub Koda*

Houston Ghetto Blues / Nov. 1993 / Bullseye Blues ✦✦✦✦
This collects 18 early-'60s sides for the Houston-based Ivory label, owned by fellow bandmate, drummer King Ivory Lee Semien. Not really the place to start, as the Goldband sides are vastly superior. —*Cub Koda*

Kim Wilson

b. Jan. 6, 1951, Detroit, MI
Harmonica, Vocals / Electric Texas Blues
Harmonica player, songwriter, and singer Kim Wilson is as much a student and historian of classic blues as he is one of the U.S.'s top harmonica players. Simply put, Wilson has taste; when he enters the recording studio, he has a clear vision of what he wants his next record to sound like. Aside from all this, he's also an extremely hard worker and a major road hog, spending upwards of 200 nights a year on the road, playing festivals and clubs throughout the U.S., Canada and Europe with his own Kim Wilson band and leading the Fabulous Thunderbirds.

Although he's long been known as the charismatic frontman for the Fabulous Thunderbirds, Wilson's solo albums—which feature bands of his own choosing for different tracks—is where the genius in his work shows through most clearly. Born January 6, 1951 in Detroit, Wilson grew up in California. His parents were singers who sang popular standards on the radio, and while Wilson took trombone and guitar lessons, he didn't discover blues until he was a senior in high school. Wilson's father later worked for General Motors and raised his family in Goleta, CA, he recalled in a 1994 interview in his adopted hometown of Austin.

"We weren't rich, but we were alright," he recalled. Wilson dropped out of college and began playing blues full time in 1970. Wilson had a rented room and lived the hippie existence, getting his harmonica chops together by playing with traveling blues musicians like Eddie Taylor. Even though Wilson had only switched to harmonica in his senior year in high school, his progress on the instrument was rapid and every bit as all-consuming as his blues record-buying habit. Charlie Musselwhite, John Lee Hooker, and Sonny Rhodes were among the other Bay Area musicians Wilson befriended and worked with in clubs. But Wilson didn't meet his biggest mentor until after he moved to Austin in the mid-'70s.

"Muddy Waters was my biggest mentor. He really made my reputation for me, and that was a fantastic time of my life, being associated with that man," he recalled of his early days with the Fabulous Thunderbirds in Austin. There, at Antone's blues nightclub, Wilson and his Thunderbirds would back up whoever came into town, and it didn't take long for the band to realize they had Waters' blessing.

As a songwriter, Wilson takes his cue from long-forgotten names like Tampa Red, Roosevelt Sykes, and Lonnie Johnson. His 1993 solo album, *Tigerman*, for the Austin-based Antone's label, features just three of his own tunes. Being the student of the blues that he is, Wilson was understandably hesitant to record too many of his own tunes when he'd already had a vision in his head of how he was going to rework classics like Joe Hill Louis' "Tiger Man," the album's title track. He followed up his debut with the equally brilliant *That's Life* (1994), also for Antone's, and again this recording contains just three self-penned songs.

Both of Wilson's solo albums are solid productions, highly recommended for harmonica students and fans of classic Texas blues and rhythm & blues. Meanwhile, in recent years, Wilson's career has taken a boost with a major-label deal with Private Music/BMG for the Fabulous Thunderbirds and with his frequent concert appearances with Bonnie Raitt. —*Richard Skelly*

Tigerman / 1993 / Antone's ✦✦
Tigerman, the first solo effort from the Fabulous Thunderbirds' frontman, Kim Wilson, is an uneven album, hampered by the uncertainness of Wilson and his band. They run through a standard set of blues-rock, plus Texas- and Chicago-style shuffles and boogies, but they never really let loose. Consequently, there are

pleasant, enjoyable spots on the album, but never anything truly memorable. — *Thom Owens*

● **That's Life** / 1994 / Antone's ✦✦✦✦
On *That's Life*, Kim Wilson's second solo album, the vocalist/harpist hits on the right formula of Texas roadhouse blues and gritty blues-rock, turning out a uniformly satisfying album. Some of the original songs are a little weak, but the performances are convincing and enjoyable, even if they don't offer a new spin on Texas blues-rock. — *Thom Owens*

Smokey Wilson

b. Glen Allen, MS
Guitar, Vocals / Electric West Coast Blues
When Los Angeles-based guitarist Smokey Wilson really got serious about setting a full-fledged career as a bluesman in motion, it didn't take him long to astound the aficionados with an incendiary 1993 set for Bullseye Blues, *Smoke n' Fire*, that conjured up echoes of the Mississippi Delta of his youth.

Robert Lee Wilson lived and played the blues with Roosevelt "Booba" Barnes, Big Jack Johnson, Frank Frost, and other Mississippi stalwarts before relocating to L.A. in 1970 when he was 35 years old. But instead of grabbing for the gold as a touring entity, he opened the Pioneer Club in Watts, leading the house band and nobly booking the very best in blues talent (all-star attractions at the fabled joint included Joe Turner, Percy Mayfield, Pee Wee Crayton, Albert Collins, and plenty more).

Wilson recorded sparingly at first, his LPs for Big Town not doing the man justice. A 1983 set for Murray Brothers (recently reissued on Blind Pig) with harpist Rod Piazza and Hollywood Fats on rhythm guitar may have been the turning point; clearly, he was gearing up to leave his Mississippi mark on Southern California blues.

Smoke n' Fire and its 1995 encore, *The Real Deal* (a title now used for three contemporary blues albums in a year's time: John Primer and Buddy Guy have also claimed it), nominate Smokey Wilson as one of the hottest late-bloomers in the blues business. — *Bill Dahl*

● **Smoke 'n Fire** / 1993 / Bullseye Blues ✦✦✦✦✦
Transplanted Mississippian Smokey Wilson has made plenty of records, but usually for poorly distributed regional labels. So although he is far from a newcomer, he might as well be a fledgling rookie to the average listener. The songs, aside from the lyrically commendable but awkward *Don't Burn Down L.A.*, are primarily his own urgent expositions on love, life's unfairness, and pain. His playing blends slamming fills, chunky riffs, and sonic barrages mixed with expert uses of distortion, bent notes, and flashy chords. This is the kind of no-nonsense set that has earned Rounder/Bullseye its exemplary reputation. — *Ron Wynn*

The Real Deal / 1995 / Bullseye Blues ✦✦✦✦
More steady-burning blues sparked by Wilson's unyielding guitar work and mean vocals. One difference—he goes the unplugged route on solo versions of Muddy Waters' "Feel Like Going Home" and his own "Son of A...Blues Player." Elsewhere, it's electric juke-joint nirvana, Wilson cutting close to the bone on "Rat Takin' Your Cheese," "I Wanna Do It to You Baby," and "House in Hollywood." — *Bill Dahl*

88th Street Blues / Nov. 1995 / Blind Pig ✦✦✦
The barbed-wire vocals and slashing guitar of Mississippi-bred Smokey Wilson blend well with harpist Rod Piazza and company on this 1983 set first out on Murray Bros. Records. Not quite as stunning as his more recent work for Bullseye Blues, but definitely has some incendiary moments. — *Bill Dahl*

Johnny Winter

b. Feb. 23, 1944, Leland, MS
Guitar, Vocals / Blues Rock
Blues guitarist Winter became a major star in the late '60s and early '70s. Since that time, he's confirmed his reputation in the blues by working with Muddy Waters and continuing to play in the style, despite musical fashion. Winter formed his first band at 14 with his brother Edgar in Beaumont, TX, and spent his youth recording studios cutting regional singles and in bars playing the blues. His discovery on a national level came via an article in *Rolling Stone* in 1968, which led to a management contract with New York club owner Steve Paul and a record deal with Columbia. His debut album (there are numerous albums of

juvenilia), *Johnny Winter*, reached the charts in 1969. Starting out with a trio, Winter later formed a band with former members of The McCoys, including second guitarist Rick Derringer. It was called Johnny Winter And. He achieved a sales peak in 1971 with the gold-selling *Live/Johnny Winter and.* He returned in 1973 with *Still Alive and Well*, his highest-charting album. His albums became more overtly blues-oriented in the late '70s and he also produced several albums for Muddy Waters. In the '80s he switched to the blues label Alligator for three albums, and has since recorded for the labels MCA and Virgin. — *William Ruhlmann*

Johnny Winter / 1969 / Columbia ✦✦✦✦✦
Winter's stunning debut features his fiery blues playing in both electric and acoustic settings, with backup that includes Willie Dixon. — *William Ruhlmann*

Captured Live! / 1976 / Blue Sky ✦✦✦

Nothin' but the Blues / 1977 / Blue Sky ✦✦✦✦
After a long period making rock records, Winter fronts the Muddy Waters band (with Waters singing) on this Chicago blues workout. He sounds happier than ever before. — *William Ruhlmann*

Guitar Slinger / 1984 / Alligator ✦✦✦✦
The first of three blues albums recorded after a four-year studio hiatus finds Winter as fleet-fingered as before and sounding more vocally involved than in some of the later Columbia material. — *William Ruhlmann*

Serious Business / 1985 / Alligator ✦✦

Third Degree / 1986 / Alligator ✦✦✦

Birds Can't Row Boats / 1988 / Relix ✦✦✦✦✦
Aside from "Ice Cube" (a 1959 instrumental), these tracks date from 1965–68. Many are previously unissued or only available on rare 45s. Those accustomed to his more famous recordings are in for a jolt, as this shows Johnny in several unexpected settings: grinding Texas psych-punk, the British Invasion-cum-folk-rock garage single "Gone for Bad," blue-eyed R&B/soul, and Everly Brothers cover, a *Highway 61*-era Dylan imitation, and even a shit-kickin' C&W tune. There are also some straight, predominantly acoustic blues numbers. — *Richie Unterberger*

Let Me In / 1991 / Point Blank ✦✦✦✦✦
Let Me In is a star-studded all-blues set from Johnny Winter, featuring cameos from Dr. John, Albert Collins, and several others. Though the set focuses on blues material, Winters can never leave his rock roots behind—the sheer volume and pile-driving energy of his performances ensures that. For most of the record, his enthusiasm is contagious, but there are a couple of bland, generic exercises that fail to work up a head of steam. But there is a lovely acoustic number called "Blue Mood," which shows Winter trying to stretch a bit by playing jazzy licks. It's a refreshing change of pace. — *Thom Owens*

Scorchin' Blues / Jun. 16, 1992 / Epic ✦✦
Scorchin' Blues marries tracks from Johnny Winter's early Columbia albums—including the classic National steel-driven "Dallas" from his 1969 debut—with material from his return-to-roots Blue Sky-period in the late '70s. The aggressive playing and raunchy vocals will appeal to both blues and rock fans, and Ben Sandmel crams an authoritative biography into seven pages, complete with interesting Winter quotes. The one downside: a miserly ten tracks spread over only 45 minutes of playing time. — *Roch Parisien*

Blues to The Bone / Aug. 29, 1995 / Relix ✦✦

Jimmy Witherspoon (James Witherspoon)

b. Aug. 8, 1923, Gurdon, AK
Vocals / Jazz Blues
Vocalist Jimmy Witherspoon has seen more than his fair share of record company ups and downs throughout his 40-odd-year career. But even without a record deal, he's managed to continue to tour throughout the U.S. and Europe for a number of years.

He was forced to slow down a little bit in the early '80s owing to a bout with throat cancer that was cured, but it left him with a slightly raspier voice. In 1995, however, Witherspoon was back on top, with a live album *Live at the Mint*, out on the On the Spot subsidiary of Private Music/BMG. On the album, he's accompanied by Los Angeles-area guitarist Robben Ford and his band.

Witherspoon got his start, like so many others from the South, singing in the church. He began singing at age six and by the time he was in his teens, he had moved to Los Angeles. After a tour in the merchant marines, during which he sat in with Teddy Weatherford's big band, he returned to California in 1944. He was hired as a replacement for Walter Brown in Jay McShann's big band in the mid-'40s, and one of a few blues vocalists enjoying success at that time was Witherson's prime influence, Big Joe Turner. The young Witherspoon modeled himself after Turner, but later in his career, he began recording soul jazz and blues-heavy jazz.

His first big recording break came about with his version of "Ain't Nobody's Business" that he cut in 1949 for the Supreme label. The song rose to number one on the rhythm & blues charts, and remained there for 34 weeks, longer than any earlier blues or R&B record. Later in 1949, he recorded LeRoy Carr's "In the Evenin'," and that rose to number five. As rock 'n' roll became the dominant music of the day in the 1950s, Witherspoon moved in a jazzier direction, and by 1959, his performance at the Monterey Jazz Festival helped to put him back in the spotlight. Until well into the 1970s, Witherspoon recorded and performed with musicians like Earl Hines, Roy Eldridge, Coleman Hawkins and Ben Webster. In 1971, "Spoon," as he was affectionately called by a host of British blues musicians, recorded *Guilty* with Eric Burdon, and toured with the former Animals vocalist. Spoon's 1975 release for Capitol Records, *Love Is a Five Letter Word*, sold extremely well for a blues album, and after recovering from throat cancer with radiation treatments in the early '80s, he recorded an album in 1986 with Dr. John and songwriter Jerome Felder, a.k.a. Doc Pomus. He joined guitarist Ford in the early '90s for a live album, *Live at the Norodden Blues Festival* and cut a 1992 album, *The Blues, The Whole Blues and Nothin' But the Blues* for Indigo Records, a new label formed by longtime British blues producer/impresario Mike Vernon.

For newcomers to Spoon and his artistry, his *Live at the Mint* album is a good reflection of his present state; the album contains live versions of his most definitive pieces and serves as a good introduction to the singer, despite the raspiness of his voice. *Live at the Mint* includes live, spontaneous takes of tunes he popularized, all of which have become signature songs for him, items like "Goin' Down Slow," "Stormy Monday," "Money Is Getting Cheaper," "Big Boss Man," and of course, "Ain't Nobody's Business." Another good introduction to Witherspoon for younger blues fans is *Blowin' in from Kansas City* (1993, Capitol), an album that pairs Spoon with Jay McShann, Tiny Webb, Ben Webster, Chuck Norris and others.

Witherspoon still lives in Los Angeles, and continues to tour internationally. —*Richard Skelly*

Jimmy Witherspoon & Jay McShann / 1947–1949 / DA ✦✦✦✦✦
Vintage blues shouting, jump blues, and boogie piano performed by two giants at their performance peaks. Vocalist Jimmy Witherspoon hollered, roared, and strutted with authority, while pianist Jay McShann not only headed a superb combo and backed Weatherford stylishly, but when given the spotlight, supplied connecting riffs, offered emphatic solos, and helped keep things roaring. There are 24 numbers on this 1992 CD reissue, and they illustrate the potency and appeal of Weatherford and McShann, while also revealing the links between swing, blues, and early R&B. —*Ron Wynn*

Goin' to Kansas City Blues / 1958 / RCA ✦✦✦✦✦
A reunion of sorts with McShann, with whom Witherspoon had sung for four years in the late '40s. A relaxed, swinging set that bisects jazz and blues, it holds no great surprises, but 'Spoon fans will find this an enjoyable and accomplished record. About half of the material is penned by McShann or Witherspoon, including a remake of "Confessin' the Blues," and "Blue Monday Blues," Jimmy's adaptation of "Kansas City Blues." —*Richie Unterberger*

The 'Spoon Concerts / 1959 / Fantasy ✦✦✦✦✦

Roots / 1962 / Reprise ✦✦✦ ✦
Roots is a nice duet session between vocalist Jimmy Witherspoon and saxophonist Ben Webster. The mood is laid back and relaxed—it's perfect music for late-night listening. Webster provides full-bodied, rounded licks, while Witherspoon's vocals are subtly textured and rich. It's a small gem of a record. —*Thom Owens*

Baby Baby Baby / 1963 / Original Blues Classics ✦✦✦
Veteran singer Jimmy Witherspoon is in good voice on this CD reissue, performing a dozen two- to four-minute songs that include such blues standards as Duke Ellington's "Rocks in My Bed," "Bad Bad Whiskey," "One Scotch, One Bourbon, One Beer," and "It's a Lonesome Old World." He is joined by a quintet featuring altoist Leo Wright and guitarist Kenny Burrell on the first eight numbers and a background septet (with trumpeter Bobby Bryant and Arthur Wright on harmonica) for the remainder of the set. The music is enjoyable if not classic and should please Witherspoon's many fans. —*Scott Yanow*

Blues Around the Clock / Nov. 5, 1963 / Original Blues Classics ✦✦✦
Veteran singer Jimmy Witherspoon (who bridges the gap between jazz and blues) mostly sticks to the latter on this spirited set. His backup group (organist Paul Griffin, guitarist Lord Westbrook, bassist Leonard Gaskin, and drummer Herbie Lovelle) is fine in support, but the spotlight is almost entirely on Witherspoon throughout these ten concise performances, only one of which exceeds four minutes. Highlights include "No Rollin' Blues," "S.K. Blues," and "Around the Clock." Witherspoon is in fine voice and, even if nothing all that memorable occurs, the music is enjoyable. —*Scott Yanow*

Some of My Best Friends Are the Blues / 1964 / Prestige ✦✦✦
Jimmy Witherspoon is accompanied by a large orchestra arranged by Benny Golson for a set emphasizing slow tempos (even on "And the Angels Sing" and "Who's Sorry Now"), ballads and blues. Nothing all that memorable occurs, but the singer is in strong voice and his fans will want to pick up this interesting CD reissue. —*Scott Yanow*

Evenin' Blues / 1964 / Original Blues Classics ✦✦✦✦✦
A good relaxed (but not laidback) session, and one of his bluesier ones, with organ, Clifford Scott (who played on Bill Doggett's "Honky Tonk") on sax, and T-Bone Walker on guitar. Nothing too adventurous about the song selection, including well-traveled items like "Good Rockin' Tonight" and "Kansas City," but Witherspoon sings them with ingratiating soul, reaching his peaks on his cover of "Don't Let Go" (perhaps better than the hit version by Roy Hamilton) and the late-night ambience of the title track. The CD reissue adds previously unissued alternate takes of four of the songs. —*Richie Unterberger*

● **Hey Mr. Landlord** / 1965 / Route 66 ✦✦✦✦✦
This is a thorough import survey of Witherspoon's earlier (1945–56) blues shoutin' days. *Hank Davis*

Ain't Nobodys Business / 1967 / Polydor ✦✦✦✦✦
It is unfortunate that the recording dates and personnel are not given on this budget CD for the performances (although not always all that well-recorded) are excellent. Singer Jimmy Witherspoon is heard near the beginning of his career. Five songs (the third through the seventh) are taken from a Pasadena concert that took place May 9, 1949. Backed by pianist Gene Gilbeaux's quartet (with Donald Hill featured on alto), Witherspoon is in happy form entertaining the enthusiastic crowd; on "New Orleans Woman" a few unidentified horns honk away to the audience's enjoyment. Of the other five songs, two are from 1950 ("I Done Found Out" and "Fickle Woman") and have Witherspoon backed by a nonet including pianist Jay McShann and tenor saxophonist Maxwell Davis, "Good Jumpin'" is with the Buddy Floyd sextet in 1948 and two others are not listed in discographies. But details aside, the music (which straddles the boundary between blues, early R&B and jazz) is easy to enjoy. —*Scott Yanow*

The Spoon Concerts / 1972 / Fantasy ✦✦✦✦✦
A classic Monterey Jazz Festival date, it featured Ben Webster, Roy Eldridge, and Coleman Hawkins. —*Hank Davis*

Spoonful / 1975 / Blue Note ✦✦
Spoonful finds Jimmy Witherspoon stretching out a bit, exploring soul and funk rhythms rather heavily. In fact, many fans of his jazz and blues recordings will find that this concentrates too much on the rhythm, to the detriment of the songs and performances. Consequently, *Spoonful* doesn't rank as much more than an interesting experiment. —*Thom Owens*

Live / 1979 / MCA ✦✦✦
Jimmy Witherspoon sticks exclusively to the blues during this Los Angeles club date from 1976. Guitarist Robben Ford's fiery Chicago blues playing is consistently exciting and imaginative,

often stealing the show from 'Spoon. This CD can easily be enjoyed by fans of both blues and swinging jazz. —*Scott Yanow*

Mean Old Frisco / Prestige ♦♦♦
These small combo sides swing solidly. —*Bill Dahl*

Spoon's Life / Oct. 1980 / Evidence ♦♦♦
Pair the K.C. shouter with a Chicago band and the results from this 1980 set aren't half bad. —*Bill Dahl*

Rockin' L.A. / 1988 / Fantasy ♦♦♦
Rockin' L.A. is an enjoyable latter-day record from Jimmy Witherspoon that finds the singer still in solid form, even if the power of his voice has somewhat declined over the years. —*Thom Owens*

Spoon So Easy: the Chess Years / 1990 / MCA/Chess ♦♦♦♦
This is an excellent retrospective of Jimmy Witherspoon's stint at Chess Records. During this time, he was moving closer to jump blues and R&B than jazz, but his music wasn't suffering at all—he sounds vigorous throughout these sessions. It's a brief sampler—there are only 12 songs on the disc—but it collects the cream of a somewhat checkered era for Witherspoon. —*Thom Owens*

Call Me Baby / 1991 / Night Train ♦♦♦♦♦
Call Me Baby captures Jimmy Witherspoon at an early stage of his career, when he was singing with bands led by Buddy Tate and Jay McShann. —*Thom Owens*

★ **Blowin' in from Kansas City** / 1993 / Capitol ♦♦♦♦♦
These 20 tunes pair the great Mr. Witherspoon with the finest jazz, jump, and blues talent around. Jay McShann, Maxwell Davis, Tiny Webb, and Chuck Norris are only a few of the first-rate session-men and arrangers who grace the tracks of this essential CD. A special mention must be made of tenor sax legend Ben Webster, whose solo on "I'm Going Around in Circles" is simply magnificent. This is quintessential Kansas City blues. Of all the shouters, Witherspoon is perhaps the greatest singer. —*Larry Hoffman*

Jays Blues / Charly ♦♦♦♦♦
Jays Blues is a fine collection of early-'50s jump blues sides that Jimmy Weatherspoon cut for Federal Records. This 23-track collection offers a good retrospective of one of Weatherspoon's most neglected—and admittedly, uneven—periods. —*Thom Owens*

Mitch Woods & His Rocket 88's

b. 1951, Brooklyn, NY
Piano, Vocals / Blues, Electric Jump Blues, Boogie-Woogie
Dubbing his swinging approach "rock-a-boogie," pianist Mitch Woods and his Rocket 88s have revived the jump-blues approach of the '40s and '50s on three Blind Pig albums.

Originally from Brooklyn, NY, Mitch Woods moved to San Francisco in 1970. While he was growing up in Brooklyn, he studied both jazz and classical music, but when he relocated to the Bay Area, he primarily played jump blues and R&B. San Franciscan guitarist HiTide Harris introduced Woods to the joyous jive of Louis Jordan, and the pianist's musical tastes were transformed. Between 1970 and 1980, Woods performed as a solo artist, gigging at a number of local clubs. In 1980, he formed the Rocket 88s—which featured Harris on guitar—and four years later, the band released their debut album, *Steady Date*, on Blind Pig. The album led to concerts at national blues clubs and festivals, as well as several European dates in 1987.

In 1988, Woods and the Rocket 88s released their second album, *Mr. Boogie's Back In Town*, and embarked on another round of shows in America, Canada, and Europe. Three years later, their third album, *Solid Gold Cadillac*, appeared. Woods and the Rocket 88s continued to tour and perform in the '90s, releasing their fourth album, *Shakin' the Shack*, in 1993. —*Bill Dahl & Stephen Thomas Erlewine*

Steady Date With / Apr. 1986 / Blind Pig ♦♦

Mr. Boogie's Back in Town / 1988 / Blind Pig ♦♦♦
Jump-blues and boogie with a rockabilly edge. —*Niles J. Frantz*

● **Solid Gold Cadillac** / 1991 / Blind Pig ♦♦♦♦♦
With West Coast jump blues and boogie-woogie piano. This is tasty, if not particularly original. Charlie Musselwhite guests on harp. —*Niles J. Frantz*

Shakin' the Shack / 1993 / Blind Pig ♦♦
Woods—a boogie-woogie pianist of first order—is rooted in good-timey rock, with interesting tangents into the Louisiana bayou

("Zydeco Boogie") and New Orleans Mardi Gras ("Hattie Queen"). "Boogie" is the operative word here, with the lead track, "Honkin', Shoutin', Pumpin', Poundin'," accurately setting the tone. —*Roch Parisien*

Big John Wrencher

b. Feb. 12, 1923, Sunflower County, MS, **d.** Jul. 15, 1977, Clarksdale, MS
Harmonica, Vocals / Electric Chicago Blues
The Maxwell Street open air market was a seven-to-ten-block area in Chicago that, from the 1920s to the middle '60s played host to various blues musicians—both professional and amateur—who performed right on the street for tips from passerbys. Most of them who started their careers there (like Little Walter, Earl Hooker, Hound Dog Taylor and others) moved up to the more comfortable confines of club work. But one who stayed and became a most recognizable fixture of the area was a marvelous harmonica player and singer named One-Arm or Big John Wrencher.

Wrencher was born in Sunflower County, MS, in 1923 on a plantation. His youthful interest in music—particularly the harmonica—kept him on the move as a traveling musician, playing throughout Tennessee and neighboring Arkansas from the late '40s to the early '50s. In 1958, Big John lost his left arm in a car crash in Memphis. By the early '60s, he had moved North to Chicago and quickly became a regular fixture on Maxwell Street, always working on Sundays from 10:00 a.m. to nearly 3:00 in the afternnon virtually non-stop, as Sundays were the big payday for most busking musicians working the area.

Although cupping both harmonica and bulky microphone in one hand (which he also sang through), Wrencher's physical challenge seemingly did little to alter the hugeness of his sound or the slurring attack he brought to the instrument. Usually backed by nothing more than an electric guitar and a drummer, Big John's sound and style was country juke joint blues brought to the city and amplified to the maximum. A flamboyant showman, he'd put on quite a show for the people on the street, moving and dancing constantly while the cigar box was passed around for tips. By all accounts, no one was ever disappointed by the show or the music.

But despite his enormous playing and performing talents, the discography on Wrencher, unfortunately, remains woefully thin. He appears to have played on a session with Detroit bluesman Baby Boy Warren in the '50s, but this tape appears to be lost to the ravages of time. His first official recordings surfaced on a pair of Testament albums in the '60s, featuring Big John in a sideman role behind slide legend Robert Nighthawk. His only full album of material surfaced in the early '70s on the Barrelhouse label. Producer George Paulus also used him as a backing musician behind slide guitarist but these sides laid unissued until recently, showing up piecemeal on various compilations.

After years of vacillating between his regular Maxwell Street gig and a few appearances on European blues festivals, Wrencher decided to go back to Mississippi to visit family and old friends in July of 1977. While swapping stories of his travels with some buddies at bluesman Wade Walton's barber shop in Clarksdale, he suddenly dropped dead from a heart attack at the age of 54. As a heartfelt (and somewhat surreal) memorial to his old pal, Big John's final bottle of whiskey is permanently ensconced on a shelf at Walton's barbershop.—*Cub Koda*

● **Maxwell Street Alley Blues** / Blue Sting ♦♦♦♦♦
While most blues albums bear romantic-sounding titles like the one used here, this is the real deal. Wrencher's one-armed amplified harp playing is perfectly supported by the lone guitar of Little Buddy Scott and the bar-bones basic drumming of Playboy Vinson. Listing titles is superfluous, since the feel and the ambience is the important thing. But blues albums seldom capture that elusive quality the way it is here, and that's the secret of its charm. Superlative in every regard, this is a great album by a very under-recorded artist. —*Cub Koda*

Billy Wright

b. May 21, 1932, Atlanta, GA, **d.** Oct. 27, 1991, Atlanta, GA
Vocals / R&B
A prime influence on Little Richard during his formative years, "Prince of the Blues" Billy Wright's hearty shouting delivery was an Atlanta staple during the postwar years.

Wright was a regular at Atlanta's 81 Theatre as a youth, soaking up the vaudevillians before graduating to singing and dancing status there himself. Saxist Paul "Hucklebuck" Williams caught Wright's act when they shared a bill with Charles Brown and Wynonie Harris at Atlanta's Auditorium, recommending the teenaged singer to Savoy Records boss Herman Lubinsky.

Wright's 1949 Savoy debut, "Blues For My Baby," shot up to number three on *Billboard*'s R&B charts, and its flip, "You Satisfy," did almost as well. Two more of Wright's Savoy 78s, "Stacked Deck" and "Hey Little Girl," were also Top Ten R&B entries in 1951. The flamboyant Wright set his pal Little Richard up with powerful WGST deejay Zenas Sears, who scored the newcomer his first contract with RCA in 1951. It's no knock on Richard to note that his early sides sound very much like Billy Wright.

Wright recorded steadily for Savoy through 1954, the great majority of his sessions held in his hometown with hot local players (saxist Fred Jackson and guitarist Wesley Jackson were often recruited). After he left Savoy, Wright's recording fortunes plummeted—a 1955 date for Don Robey's Peacock diskery in Houston and sessions for Fire (unissued) and Carrollton in 1959

ended his discography. Wright later emceed shows in Atlanta, remaining active until a stroke in the mid-'70s slowed him down. *—Bill Dahl*

Stacked Deck / 1980 / Route 66 ◆◆◆◆
The title track was a major R&B hit for Wright in 1951, and there are 13 more gems by the animated blues shouter on this import piece of vinyl. Everything's from the Savoy vaults except for an ultra-rare Wright cover of Billy Ward & the Dominoes' "Do Something for Me" that was cut live at Atlanta's Harlem Theatre in 1952. *—Bill Dahl*

Goin' Down Slow (Blues, Soul & Early R 'n' R, Vol. 1) / 1984 / Savoy ◆◆◆◆
Crying and pleading the blues, Wright's early-'50s Savoy output was very influential. *—Bill Dahl*

● **Billy Wright** / 1994 / Savoy Jazz ◆◆◆◆◆
15 of the Atlanta jump blues shouter's very best outings for Savoy, spanning 1949–1954. Wright's pleading style, a large influence indeed on a developing Little Richard, is irresistibly spotlighted on "After Awhile," "I Remember," and the romping "Billy's Boogie Blues." *—Bill Dahl*

Y

Jimmy Yancey

b. 1894, Chicago, IL, **d.** Sep. 17, 1951, Chicago, IL
Piano / Blues, Boogie-Woogie
One of the pioneers of boogie-woogie piano, Jimmy Yancey was generally more subtle than the more famous Albert Ammons, Pete Johnson and Meade Lux Lewis, falling as much into the blues genre as in jazz. Yancey, who could romp as well as anyone, made many of his most memorable recordings at slower tempos. No matter what key he played in, Yancey ended every song in E flat, leading to some hilarious conclusions to some recordings. He worked in vaudeville as a singer and tap dancer starting at age six and in 1915 settled in Chicago as a pianist. But Yancey spent his last 26 years (from 1925 on) earning his living as a groundskeeper at Comiskey Park for the Chicago White Sox. He played part-time in local clubs and began recording in 1939, on a few occasions backing his wife, singer Mama Yancey. Jimmy Yancey never achieved the fame of his contemporaries but he remained a major influence on all practioners in the genre. — *Scott Yanow*

In the Beginning / May 4, 1939 / Solo Art ✦✦✦✦✦
In the Beginning collects the first recordings Jimmy Yancey ever recorded. While the sound is a little rough, these are exciting performances, especially if you are overly familiar with his widely circulated, popular RCA recordings. Not all of the performances are as accomplished as his later work, but there's no denying the historical value of this collection—it's necessary listening for completists. — *Thom Owens*

★ **Vol. 1 (1939–1940)** / May 4, 1939+Sep. 6, 1940 / Document ✦✦✦✦✦
Yancey's earliest and best sides for the Solo Art label. Beautiful and sensitive performances. — *Cub Koda*

● **Complete Recorded Works, Vol. 2 (1939–1950)** / Feb. 23, 1940–Dec. 1943 / Document ✦✦✦✦
On the second of three CDs that trace virtually his entire recording career, pianist Jimmy Yancey is showcased on a variety of solo tracks. Two number from February 1940 are highlighted by the classic "Bear Trap Blues." There are a couple of numbers made for the tiny Art Center Jazz Gems label, a four-song (plus two alternate takes) definitive set cut for Bluebird (which includes "Death Letter Blues" and "Yancey's Bugle Call") and nine songs (five previously unissued) from 1943; on one version of "How Long Blues," Mama Yancey sings while Jimmy switches to the spooky sounding harmonium. This set also has Jimmy Yancey's only four recorded vocals, which are quite effective even though his voice is limited. All three volumes in this series are highly recommended for the subtle pianist, who made expert use of space and ended every tune in E flat. — *Scott Yanow*

The Yancey-Lofton Sessions, Vol. 1 / Dec. 1943 / Storyville ✦✦✦✦

The Yancey-Lofton Sessions, Vol. 2 / Dec. 1943 / Storyville ✦✦✦✦✦

Vol. 2 (1939-1950) / Dec. 1943+Dec. 23, 1950 / Document ✦✦✦✦✦

Vol. 3 (1943-1950) / Dec. 1943–Dec. 23, 1950 / Document ✦✦✦✦✦
The third of three CDs tracing the recording career of the unique boogie-woogie pianist Jimmy Yancey, whose subtlety could often result in some dramatic music, completes his December 1943

session and also has his December 23, 1950 solo set; his final recordings from July 1951 are available on an Atlantic release. The 1943 titles, three of which were previously unreleased, include two with Mama Yancey vocals (on one Jimmy switches to harmonium) and is highlighted by "White Sox Stomp," "Yancey Special" and two versions of "Pallet on the Floor." After the six fine titles from 1950, this CD finishes off with the only four numbers that Jimmy's older brother, the more ragtime-oriented Alonzo Yancey, ever recorded. Although his style was different, on "Ecstatic Rag" Alonzo does sound a bit like Jimmy. All three of these Document CDs, plus the Atlantic set, are highly recommended and preferable to the piecemeal domestic Bluebird reissues. — *Scott Yanow*

★ **Chicago Piano, Vol. 1** / Jul. 18, 1951 / Atlantic ✦✦✦✦✦
Jimmy Yancey was one of the pioneer boogie-woogie pianists but, unlike many of the other pacesetters, he had a gentle and thoughtful style that also crossed over into the blues. This Atlantic CD, a straight reissue of the 1972 LP, contains Yancey's final recordings, cut just eight weeks before his death from diabetes. The pianist is in fine form on these introspective and often emotional performances which, with the exception of Meade Lux Lewis' "Yancey Special" and the traditional "Make Me a Pallet on the Floor," are comprised entirely of Yancey's originals. His wife Mama Yancey takes five memorable vocals on this memorable set of classic blues. — *Scott Yanow*

The Yardbirds

Group / British Blues
Formed in 1963, The Yardbirds are one of the most influential groups in the history of rock 'n' roll. (The term "Yardbird" came from the designation given to hobos in a Jack Kerouac novel.) During the course of their career, The Yardbirds featured three of rock's greatest guitarists: Eric Clapton, Jeff Beck, and Jimmy Page. During their early period with Clapton, they pursued a highly charged style of electric blues, highlighted best on *Five Live Yardbirds*. Clapton split when he sensed the band was getting too pop with the release of their first single, "For Your Love."

Jeff Beck brought on phase two of the band's development with a highly experimental style that pioneered the application of feedback, fuzz, and unusual melodic scales. It was here that The Yardbirds achieved their creative peak, with songs like "I'm a Man," "Heart Full of Soul," "Evil Hearted You," "Lost Woman," and the masterly "Shapes of Things."

Around the time Beck began unraveling at the seams, Jimmy Page came on board. For a very brief time, The Yardbirds had a dream twin-lead guitar lineup, best chronicled on the hits "Happenings Ten Years Time Ago" and "Stroll On," from the movie *Blow Up*.

After Beck left, Page hung on for a little over a year, recording the rather lightweight album *Little Games*. Shortly afterwards, the band fell apart, when Page formed Led Zeppelin. Lead singer Keith Relf helped form the art-rock group Renaissance and bassist Paul Samwell-Smith went on to a successful production career for artists like Cat Stevens and Carly Simon. Even though The Yardbirds weren't among the most commercially successful bands of the '60s British Invasion, their profound impact on rock laid the groundwork for hard blues-based rock and heavy metal.

Of particular note to those seeking out the best-sounding Yardbirds discs: none of their CD reissues uses the original first-generation masters. EMI England has them but won't license them out, due to an unpaid studio bill dating back from the mid-'60s. On the other hand, the Edsel import of *Roger the Engineer* sounds impeccable. The reason: the band owns the original masters. —*Rick Clark*

Five Live Yardbirds / Dec. 1964 / Rhino ♦♦♦♦♦
Recorded live at London's Marquee Club, *Five Live Yardbirds* is the best document of Eric Clapton's work with the band. Tracks like "Too Much Monkey Business," "Got Love If You Want It," and "Smokestack Lightning" were good representations of The Yardbirds' "rave-ups," which were open-ended improvisations that helped lay the groundwork for groups like Cream and the Jimi Hendrix Experience. —*Rick Clark*

Roger the Engineer / 1966 / Edsel ♦♦♦♦
Roger the Engineer is a classic Yardbirds studio album, thanks to tracks like "Lost Woman," "Over Under Sideways Down," "What Do You Want?," "Psycho Daisies," and "Ever Since the World Began." Not available in the States, this British import (on Edsel) is the best-sounding Yardbirds CD by a long shot and a must-own for fans of this band. —*Rick Clark*

With Sonny Boy Williamson / 1966 / Mercury ♦♦
★ **Greatest Hits, Vol. 1: 1964–1966** / 1986 / Rhino ♦♦♦♦♦
Sonically, these tracks fail to match the brilliance and warmth of the original vinyl pressings, but *Greatest Hits* has more punch. "For Your Love" is an exception, with the record version sounding extremely compressed. Of the various Yardbird collections that exist, this is still the most intelligently chosen, even though it lacks key tracks from *Roger the Engineer*. —*Rick Clark*

On Air / 1991 / Band Of Joy ♦♦♦
Like most of the major British Invasion bands, The Yardbirds recorded many sessions for the BBC during their heyday. *On Air* contains 27 of these, recorded between 1965 and 1968; 21 of them feature Jeff Beck, the rest Jimmy Page (Eric Clapton is not featured on any). The BBC sessions offered listeners the opportunity to hear groups in a relatively live setting with relatively good sound quality, and that's basically what you get here. Most of their major hits—"For Your Love," "Heart Full of Soul," "Shapes of Things," "Over Under Sideways Down," "Still I'm Sad"—are included. By and large, these versions don't differ enormously from the studio cuts, with slightly different arrangements and guitar solos. One could argue, of course, that with a band so responsible for pushing rock guitar to the stratosphere, different guitar solos are a tasty discovery. And they are interesting, but they don't outdo the stellar studio renditions. Of most interest, if not highest quality, are a few covers never waxed by the group on their official releases: "Dust My Blues," "The Sun Is Shining," Garnett Mimms' "My Baby," and Dylan's "Most Likely You'll Go Your Way." On cuts like "I'm Not Talking" and "Too Much Monkey Business," Beck's pyrotechnics are truly breathtaking. But generally this release is more for Yardbirds fans than novices. —*Richie Unterberger*

Vol. 1: Smokestack Lightning / 1991 / Sony ♦♦♦♦
This double-disc set focuses on tracks from *For Your Love* and *Having a Rave-Up with the Yardbirds*. Included are live tracks recorded at the Crawdaddy Club while touring with Sonny Boy Williamson. Most of these tracks on *Smokestack Lightning* (as well as *Blues, Backtracks*) were mastered off of safety tapes, as opposed to the original masters, since EMI England has possession of them. Considering that EMI won't release the masters to anyone, this is a respectable sound—though not as good as the first vinyl pressings. —*Rick Clark*

Vol. 2: Blues, Backtrack's and Shapes of Things / 1991 / Sony ♦♦♦♦♦
Another double-disc set, this covers some later hits (including the classic future-rock of "Shapes of Things"), *Roger the Engineer* outtakes, and various other oddities. The sound on some of the outtakes is pretty respectable, considering some of them were taken from the original acetates. —*Rick Clark*

The Yardbirds Little Games Sessions & More / 1992 / EMI America ♦♦♦
This digitally remastered 39-track, double-disc set covers Jimmy Page's tenure with The Yardbirds. This period didn't contain the band's best work, mainly because Mickie Most's poppish production reined in the band's experimental strengths. Nevertheless, tracks like "Little Games," "Puzzles," "Smile on Me," "Drinking Muddy Water," and a wonderful acoustic version of Jimmy Page's "White Summer" make this a good overview of

The Yardbirds' final stretch as a band. This set includes extensive liner notes and discography—a real treat for fans. —*Rick Clark*

Johnny Young (John O. Young)
b. Jan. 1, 1918, Mississippi, d. Apr. 18, 1974, Chicago, IL
Guitar, Mandolin, Vocals / Electric Chicago Blues, Acoustic Chicago Blues
Although the mandolin is not an instrument commonly associated with Chicago blues, it has been used by Chicago-based string bands or on Chicago-made recordings by artists such as Carl Martin, Charles and Joe McCoy, and Yank Rachell. However, the only artist to use it successfully in the later electric blues format was Mississippi-born bluesman Johnny Young. An important figure in blues history, Young loved the rough-and-tumble string-band tradition of the Delta, a style that readily coexisted with blues.

Young's initial 1947 Chicago classic, "Money Taking Women," exhibits the same exuberant down-home sound, fusing blues with the older country breakdown traditions. The string-band ensemble sound suited street performance as well, whether in Memphis or in Chicago's open-air Maxwell Street Market, where Young and his cronies were brought in off the streets to record. Over the years, Young's mandolin activity declined as Chicago's African-American blues audience demanded a more modern and urban sound. Since Young was also a skilled guitarist and a fine vocalist, he easily weathered the transition.

During the late '60s, an emerging White blues-revival audience proved eager for Young's mandolin styling. Unlike Yank Rachell, whose mandolin playing retained an older string-band feel, Young's style was firmly grounded in a more contemporary postwar blues idiom, and he interacted well with other electric blues artists. Through his life, he had worked with the major figures of blues history, including Sonny Boy Williamson, Muddy Waters, Walter Horton, and Otis Spann. He was, he insisted, born to be a musician. When I interviewed him shortly before he died, he told me how he had struggled all his life trying to make it in the music business. An emotional man, he hoped he would live long enough to make enough money to buy a house. He never made it. —*Barry Lee Pearson*

Chicago Blues Band / 1966 / Arhoolie ♦♦♦♦♦
James Cotton nearly blew the roof off on harmonica, and Otis Spann added some wonderful rumbling piano. Johnny Young's spirited guitar, vocals and occasional mandolin provided the final elements for a superb mid '60s date. —*Ron Wynn*

Chicago/ the Blues/ Today!, Vol. 3 / 1967 / Vanguard ♦♦♦♦♦
● **Chicago Blues** / 1968 / Arhoolie ♦♦♦♦♦
This is an excellent '60s recording by the down-home urban singer, guitarist, and mandolinist, accompanied by Otis Spann on piano and James Cotton and Big Walter Horton on harmonicas. —*Mark A. Humphrey*

I Can't Keep My Foot from Jumping / 1973 / Bluesway ♦♦
Johnny Young and His Friends / 1994 / Testament ♦♦♦
Recorded in informal settings between 1962 and 1966, this presents Young with various configurations, with major Chicago blues talents like Otis Spann, Robert Nighthawk, Little Walter, and Walter Horton lending a hand at different points (Young also plays solo on a couple of numbers). Only three cuts feature drums, so this is usually at the midpoint between Delta blues and the electric Chicago sound; Young usually plays guitar, but also brings out his mandolin for a couple of songs. Warm performances, though not especially noteworthy. The CD reissue adds four previously unreleased bonus cuts. —*Richie Unterberger*

Mighty Joe Young
b. Sep. 23, 1927, Shreveport, LA
Guitar, Vocals / Electric Chicago Blues
Although physical problems have curtailed his guitar playing in recent years, there was a time during the late '70s and early '80s when Mighty Joe Young was one of the leading blues guitarists on Chicago's budding North side blues circuit.

The Louisiana native got his start not in the Windy City, but in Milwaukee, where he was raised. He earned a reputation as a reliable guitarist on Chicago's West side with Joe Little & his Heart Breakers during the mid-'50s, later changing his onstage allegiance to harpist Billy Boy Arnold. Young recorded with

Arnold for Prestige and Testament during the '60s and backed Jimmy Rogers for Chess in 1958.

After abortive attempts to inaugurate a solo career with Jiffy Records in 1955 and Chicago's Atomic-H label three years later, Young hit his stride in 1961 with the sizzling "Why Baby"/"Empty Arms" for Bobby Robinson's Fire label. Young gigged as Otis Rush's rhythm guitarist from 1960 to 1963 and cut a series of excellent Chicago blues 45s for a variety of firms: "I Want a Love," "Voo Doo Dust," and "Something's Wrong" for Webcor during the mid-'60s; "Something's Wrong" for Webcor in 1966; "Sweet Kisses" and "Henpecked" on Celtex; and "Hard Times (Follow Me)" for USA (all 1967); and "Guitar Star" for Jacklyn in 1969. Young even guested on Bill "Hoss" Allen's groundbreaking 1966 syndicated R&B TV program *The Beat* in Dallas. Late-'60s session work included dates with Tyrone Davis and Jimmy Dawkins.

Delmark issued Young's solo album debut, *Blues with a Touch of Soul,* in 1970, but a pair of mid-'70s LPs for Ovation (1974's *Chicken Heads* and an eponymous set in 1976) showcased the guitarist's blues-soul synthesis far more effectively. Young's main local haunt during the '70s and early '80s was Wise Fools Pub, where he packed 'em in nightly (with Freddy King's brother, Benny Turner, on bass). — *Bill Dahl*

Blues with a Touch of Soul / Delmark ♦♦

Soporific album debut for the Chicago guitarist—only seven songs, many of them way too long (10:40 of "Somebody Loan Me a Dime" being the worst offender), that sport little of the excitement of Young's '60s 45s for a variety of local firms. Young doesn't sound like he was prepared for the opportunity, and the stiff two-piece horn section doesn't help either. — *Bill Dahl*

Chicken Heads / 1974 / Ovation ♦♦♦♦

One of Mighty Joe Young's best efforts (and one that's not out on CD), an up-to-the-minute effort that combines soul and blues most effectively. Predominantly original material that suits his booming vocals and stinging guitar well. Nice band, too: bassist Louis Satterfield, drummer Ira Gates, and keyboardist Floyd Morris were all veterans of the '60s soul session scene. — *Bill Dahl*

● Mighty Joe Young / 1976 / Ovation ♦♦♦♦♦

Another out-of-print collection that's the crown jewel in Young's album discography. Many of Young's finest originals—"Need a Friend," "Takes Money," "Take My Advice (She Likes the Blues and Barbecue)"—reside in their most memorable recorded forms on this worthwhile LP. — *Bill Dahl*

Bluesy Josephine / Nov. 28, 1976 / Evidence ♦♦♦

Not exactly the most incendiary outing that Chicago guitarist Mighty Joe Young has ever cut. This 1976 album was cut in France for Black & Blue with a handful of Chicago stalwarts, but the excitement that Young routinely summoned up back home is in short supply as he walks through "Sweet Home Chicago" and "Five Long Years." Young's own "Takes Money" and "Need a Friend" are a definite improvement on those shopworn standards, but with only seven lengthy selections ("Teasing the Blues" runs 10:27), there isn't a lot to choose from. — *Bill Dahl*

Live at the Wise Fools / 1990 / Quicksilver ♦♦

For much of the 1970s and '80s, guitarist Mighty Joe Young "owned" Chicago's cozy Wise Fools Pub—at least musically speaking. He was the club's top draw, but this live disc, caught at the late and still-lamented Wise Fools, finds him sticking to the tiredest of warhorses. "Stormy Monday," "Turning Point," "That's All Right," and "I Can't Quit You Baby" may have wowed the homefolks, but they don't hold up all that well when transferred to the digital format. Young's quartet features Freddie King's brother, Benny Turner, on bass, and Lafayette Leake on piano. — *Bill Dahl*

Z

ZZ Top

Group / Blues Rock
This sturdy American blues-rock trio from Texas consists of Billy Gibbons (guitar), Dusty Hill (bass), and Frank Beard (drums). They were formed in 1970 in and around Houston from rival bands the Moving Sidewalks (Gibbons) and the American Blues (Hill and Beard). Their first two albums reflected the strong blues roots and Texas humor of the band. Their third album (*Tres Hombres*) gained them national attention with hit "La Grange," a signature riff tune to this day, based on John Lee Hooker's "Boogie Chillen." Their success continued unabated throughout the '70s, culminating with the year-and-a-half-long Worldwide Texas Tour.

Exhausted from the overwhelming work load, they took a three-year break, then switched labels and returned to form with *Deguello* and *El Loco*, both harbingers of what was to come. By their next album, *Eliminator*, and its worldwide smash follow-up, *Afterburner*, they had successfully harnessed the potential of synthesizers to their patented grungy blues-groove, giving their material a more contemporary edge while retaining their patented Texas style. Now sporting long beards, golf hats, and boiler suits, they met the emerging video age head-on, reducing their "message" to simple iconography. Becoming even more popular in the long run, they moved with the times while simultaneously bucking every trend that crossed their path. As genuine roots musicians, they have few peers; Gibbons is one of America's finest blues guitarists working in the arena rock idiom—both influenced by the originators of the form and British blues-rock guitarists like Peter Green—while Hill and Beard provide the ultimate rhythm section support. The only rock 'n' roll group that's out there with its original members still aboard after 20-plus years, ZZ Top's music is always instantly recognizable, eminently powerful, profoundly soulful, and 100% American in derivation. They have continued to support the blues through various means, perhaps the most visible when they were given a piece of wood from Muddy Waters' shack in Clarksdale, MS. The group members had it made into a guitar, dubbed the "Muddywood," then sent it out on tour to raise money for the Delta Blues Museum. ZZ Top's support and link to the blues remains as rock solid as the music they play. —*Cub Koda*

ZZ Top's First Album / 1970 / Warner Brothers ✦✦✦
This Texas trio's debut was a gritty exercise in bare-boned blues boogie. Tracks like "Brown Sugar," "Neighbor Neighbor," and "Shakin' Your Tree" helped establish them as a regionally successful act in the South. —*Rick Clark*

Rio Grande Mud / 1972 / Warner Brothers ✦✦✦
Rio Grande Mud possessed a beefier sound than its predecessor. The "Brown Sugar"-style "Francene" became their first hit at number 69. Other highlights included "Chevrolet" and "Just Got Paid." —*Rick Clark*

Tres Hombres / 1973 / Warner Brothers ✦✦✦✦✦
Constant touring and favorable radio exposure made *Tres Hombres* ZZ's first hit album, thanks in no small part to "La Grange" (number 41), an ode to a whorehouse. By this album, Billy Gibbons had practically perfected his distinctively dirty electric-guitar sound. His riffs and chordal voicings were also more memorable. Highlights included "Beer Drinkers & Hell Raisers," "Precious & Grace," "Waitin' for the Bus," and "Jesus Just Left Chicago." —*Rick Clark*

Fandango / 1975 / Warner Brothers ✦✦✦
Fandango is a half-studio/half-live effort. The concert side is a fairly straight-ahead, no-nonsense affair, which includes a version of "Jailhouse Rock." The studio side featured their first Top 40 hit, "Tush" (number 20). The hyper-boogie of "Heard It on the X" was another popular track off of this release. —*Rick Clark*

Takin' Texas to the People / 1976 / London ✦✦

Tejas / 1976 / Warner Brothers ✦✦

★ **The Best of ZZ Top** / 1977 / Warner Brothers ✦✦✦✦✦
The sound may be a little muddy, but this anthology is still the best representation of ZZ's early work. It contains classic rude, riff-heavy blues rockers like "Just Got Paid," "Jesus Just Left Chicago," "Heard It on the X," "Tush," and "La Grange." —*Rick Clark*

Deguello / 1979 / Warner Brothers ✦✦✦✦✦
Deguello was ZZ's best album from their pre-robotic blues-rock period—the last reminder of what a tough ensemble this trio could be. It was the first time they infused their lunkhead approach to fast cars, kinky girls, and partying with some bizarre humor. Their version of Sam & Dave's "I Thank You" (number 34) became their first Top 40 hit in five years. Other highlights included the oddball "Manic Mechanic," a rip-roaring version of Elmore James' "Dust My Broom," the funky boogie of "Cheap Sunglasses," and "Fool for Your Stockings," a down-and-dirty fetish blues. —*Rick Clark*

Six Pack / 1987 / Warner Brothers ✦✦
The idea of compiling albums one through five, plus their seventh effort, onto a three-disc set seemed like a good one. After all, there's a load of great playing on these discs. Unfortunately, the first five albums were hastily remixed from the original multitracks. The sound might have more definition and punch, but the effort to update the drum sounds with triggered samples, re-amped guitars, and cold digital reverbs gave some of the music a stiff, clinical quality. Why a band that touts the power of an organic genre like the blues would so insensitively plunder the recordings they made when they really were a real live band, makes one wonder if the sequencers had finally gone to their brains. That ZZ's management and Warner allowed such a half-baked job on the market seems to support that assertion. —*Rick Clark*

Greatest Hits / 1992 / Warner Brothers ✦✦✦
An 18-song compilation, it features the greatest hits of ZZ Top's MTV era, including "Gimme All Your Lovin'," "Sharp Dressed Man," "Tush," "Pearl Necklace," "Cheap Sunglasses," "Sleeping Bag," "Rough Boy," and a remixed version of "Legs." It's a good, fun collection that should have been better sequenced and, unfortunately, omits a few good songs. —*AMG*

One Foot In The Blues / 1994 / Warner Brothers ✦✦
Before they sweated their image down to beards, babes and hot rods, ZZ Top were a down 'n' dirty blues-rock trio with a bonafide hot guitar player in Billy Gibbons. On this 14-track offering Warners goes back through the back ZZ catalog and cobbles together an interesting collection of the Texas trio's bluesier sides that originally appeared on their earliest albums. Highlights include "Brown Sugar," "A Fool for Your Stockings," "My Head's in Mississippi," "Apologies to Pearly," and Gibbons' storming stringwork on "Bar-B-Q." —*Cub Koda*

VARIOUS ARTISTS

All Night Long They Play the Blues / 1992 / Specialty ✦✦✦✦✦
This excellent soul-blues '60s anthology comes from the Galaxy label vaults. —*Bill Dahl*

Alley Special / 1990 / Collectables ✦✦✦✦✦
These are blues of various styles and consistently high quality, released on the Gotham and 20th Century labels, with three previously unreleased cuts. Raw, early electric blues from the late '40s and early '50s. Includes Muddy Waters' first commercial recording. —*Niles J. Frantz*

The Alligator Records Christmas Collection / 1992 / Alligator ✦✦✦
To really get that Christmas party smoking, throw *The Alligator Records Christmas Collection* on the disc player and another log on the fire. The legendary blues label dishes up the goods and turns up the heat with a set of mostly original compositions. Koko Taylor peels wallpaper with "Merry, Merry Christmas," William Clarke's wailing harp drives "Please Let Me Be Your Santa Claus," Charles Brown sets the tone with "Boogie Woogie Santa Claus," and Lonnie Brooks serves the seasonal gumbo with "Christmas On The Bayou." For an updated traditional, just try sitting still for Katie Webster's "Deck The Halls with Boogie Woogie." —*Roch Parisien*

Alligator 20th Anniversary / 1991 / Alligator ✦✦✦
This is the way contemporary blues is meant to be played: loud, live, and electric. Alligator Records celebrates its 20th anniversary with a tour featuring several of the roots label's flagship artists, and this two-disc snapshot of the event makes for a solid primer. Highlight is "Two-Headed Man," where Brooks serves up the steak with lots of sonic sizzle. As for Koko Taylor and her Blues Machine Band—suffice to say that your stereo speakers will get a good workout from her deep, gravel-laden vocals. She delivers possibly the definitive version of Willie Dixon's "Wang Dang Doodle." The set closes with the entire cast jamming on "Sweet Home Chicago," each principal taking a well-deserved turn in the solo spotlight. —*Roch Parisien*

Alligator Records—25th Anniversary Collection / Mar. 1996 / Alligator ✦✦✦✦✦
It's hard to believe that Alligator Records has been around for 25 years, but indeed it's true. Yet, it's a bit hard to remember a time in the blues biz when Alligator wasn't on the scene. It's also pretty amazing to realize the state of the indie blues label way back then and how much label prexy Bruce Iglauer has changed the whole ballgame in the intervening years. And they couldn't have pulled it off if the music wasn't great to begin with. Here's where you go to get a real nice sampling of it. This is a specially priced two CDs for the price of one photocube set, loaded with great stuff from Charlie Musselwhite, Koko Taylor, Lonnie Brooks, Johnny Winter, Billy Boy Arnold, Lonnie Mack, and a host of others who've trotted their wares on the label over the years. Besides giving the novice a great introduction to the label (as the music runs from traditional to modern), the big bonus here is a treasure trove of previously unissued tracks from Roy Buchanan (a chaotic version of Link Wray's "Jack the Ripper"), Floyd Dixon (a recut of his Blues Brothers-approved hit "Hey Bartender"), Albert Collins and Johnny Copeland in a marvelous outtake from the *Showdown!* album ("Something to Remember You By") and the band that started it all, Hound Dog Taylor & the HouseRockers, with a crazed version of Elmore James's "Look on

Yonder's Wall," as sloppy as it is cool. While some naysayers in the blues community tend to diss Alligator for being too slick, this double set shows that Iglauer and company have done more than any other in promoting and fostering the music while simultaneously moving it away from the mummified scholarly leanings of other labels. Very good stuff and at these prices, a bargain and then some. —*Cub Koda*

The Alligator Records 20th Anniversary Tour / 1993 / Alligator ✦✦✦
Recorded live on Alligator Records' 20th Anniversary Tour, this double disc set is a showcase for the label's artists. Featuring an array of their most popular acts—Koko Taylor, Lonnie Brooks, Lil' Ed and the Blues Imperials, and Elvin Bishop—the record doesn't deliver any surprises, yet these performances are frequently more exciting than the studio versions. —*Stephen Thomas Erlewine*

Alternate Blues / Mar. 10, 1980 / Original Jazz Classics ✦✦✦
This CD is a straight reissue of a Pablo LP. Norman Granz teamed the very distinctive trumpeters Dizzy Gillespie, Freddie Hubbard, and Clark Terry with pianist Oscar Peterson, guitarist Joe Pass, bassist Ray Brown, and drummer Bobby Durham for a "Trumpet Summit." This particular release features (with one exception) unissued material from the session. There are four versions of a slow blues (only the fourth was released before), all of which have very different solos from the three trumpeters. In addition they interact on "Wrap Your Troubles in Dreams" and share the spotlight on a three-song ballad medley; Hubbard's "Here's That Rainy Day" is hard to beat. This release is not quite essential, but fans of the trumpeters will want to pick it up. —*Scott Yanow*

Angels in Houston / Rounder ✦✦✦✦✦
Great Duke recordings from the late '50s and '60s of Bobby Bland, James Davis, Larry Davis, and Fenton Robinson. Includes Bland's classic "Yield Not to Temptation." —*Barry Lee Pearson*

Ann Arbor Blues & Jazz Festival, Vol. 3: "Grind It!" Roosevelt Sykes and Victoria Spivey / Schoolkids ✦✦✦
Like the previous two installments in Schoolkids Records' Ann Arbor Blues & Jazz Festival series, the sound on Vol. 3 is pretty poor. There are plenty of poor fades and mixes, not to mention dropouts. When you're dealing with historical recordings such as this, you can handle poor fidelity if you're getting good music, which is the case here. Both Roosevelt Sykes and Victoria Spivey are captured at the top of the form, playing with vigor and style, even though they were nearing the end of their careers. And that's what makes this music special–these are among the last recordings Sykes or Spivey made, and they prove that the musicians remained vital until the very end. That revelation alone makes the poor sound quality tolerable. —*Thom Owens*

Ann Arbor Blues & Jazz Festival, Vol. 4: "Well All Right!" King Biscuit Boys/Big Walter Horton / Schoolkids ✦✦✦
The entries in this series have been a dodgy affair thus far; some volumes hit the bullseye, while others distinctly fall into that "guess you had to be there" category. All of the performances are worth documenting. Some of them suffer from obtrusive, too-loud funk bands cluttering up everything, and Schoolkids is still having problems with assigning proper song titles and credits, which is something you would expect out of a negligent foreign label like Wolf. And yes, these should all come with historical importance/audio disclaimers; even if these are

multi-track mobile unit masters, there's still that fluctuating in-and-out mix that comes from the old late '60s/early '70s mentality of taking a hit off a joint while simultaneously pushing a fader on a recording console and going, "I wonder what this one does?" Now don't get me wrong, I'm no audio snob, but a little forewarning on the tray card or at least in the notes might not be a bad idea. Okay, that's the bad part, now on to the good stuff.

If low-down gut-bucket juke joint blues floats your boat, then the nine selections (two of them, "Me and the Devil Blues" and "Down So Long" both only accessible on this disc as track three, even though they're not a medley) by the King Biscuit Boys is just the thing you've been waiting to hear. The King Biscuit Boys were a group of gentlemen who all worked the famous radio show back in the '50s. At this stage of the game they were fronted by Houston Stackhouse and Joe Willie Wilkins on guitars and Sonny Blake on harmonica with jake-legged "what are we doing here" support (?) from the truly clueless Melvin Lee on bass and Homer Jackson on drums. But Joe Willie, Stack, and Sonny are just too real, too down home to be worried about anything except flat laying it out, so if they aren't paying any attention, then why should we? There are goof-ups galore, like the bass player taking a chorus-and-a-half to figure the song isn't in the key he thinks it's in ("Me and the Devil"), the whole band trying to figure what key Joe Willie's in on "It's Too Bad;" yeah, if it's perfection you're after, you came to the wrong address, but the stuff is just so potent and utterly charming, it sets all malfunctions squarely in the "take the hairy with the smooth" file. You want to hear some blues, check this out. Scary.

The Walter Horton set brings back a flood of positive memories for this writer; Hey, I was there, I saw this set as it went down and it was a killer. Volume and fader fluctuations aside, Horton was having the time of his life and the backing band of Johnny Nicholas on guitar, Fran Christina on drums, and Sarah Brown on bass from Nicholas' band, the Boogie Brothers, were following Big Walter's every crazy musical move without ever letting go of the groove, no small feat, believe me. If you're even a little bit of a blues harp aficionado, put this one in your CD player and prepare to be astounded. Big Walter Horton on an inspired night with a good backup unit and a fresh harp was a musical force to be reckoned with. This is a nice place to start checking out what all the fuss is all about. The man could blow, oh Lord, how the man could blow. —*Cub Koda*

Antone's—Bringing You the Best in Blues / 1989 / Antone's ✦✦✦✦✦
A sampler of artists on this Austin, TX label, it includes a variety of Texas blues and R&B, originally released 1987-1990. Featured are Otis Rush, Angela Strehli, Doug Sahm, Matt "Guitar" Murphy, and several others. —*Niles J. Frantz*

Antone's 10th Anniversary Anthology, Vol. 1 / 1986 / Antone's ✦✦✦✦
Chicago blues living legends were recorded live at a popular Austin, TX club in July 1985. Included are Buddy Guy, Jimmy Rogers, Eddie Taylor, James Cotton, Snooky Pryor, Otis Rush, Albert Collins, and more. The CD has three bonus cuts. Good sound and very good performances. —*Niles J. Frantz*

Antone's 10th Anniversary Anthology, Vol. 2 / 1991 / Antone's ✦✦✦✦
This very consistent live package was cut at the Austin club. It includes incendiary tracks by Buddy Guy and Matt "Guitar" Murphy. —*Bill Dahl*

The Atlantic Blues Box / 1986 / Atlantic ✦✦✦✦
The Atlantic Blues Box includes four discs, with each focusing on a different style—vocalists, Chicago, guitar, and piano (each available separately as well). If you've got the money, this is a worthwhile addition to any blues collection. —*Bill Dahl*

Atlantic Blues: Chicago / 1986 / Atlantic ✦✦✦
Disappointing, but Johnnie Jones, Freddy King, and Otis Rush are solid. —*Bill Dahl*

Atlantic Blues: Guitar / 1986 / Atlantic ✦✦✦
This interesting anthology has a few valuable obscurities. —*Bill Dahl*

Atlantic Blues: Piano / 1986 / Atlantic ✦✦✦
This fine anthology features the ivories greats from Atlantic's vaults. —*Bill Dahl*

Atlantic Blues: Vocalists / 1986 / Atlantic ✦✦✦✦✦
Varied and very worthwhile. —*Bill Dahl*

Back Against the Wall: The Texas Country . . . / Collectables ✦✦
Very uneven; a few vintage gems alternate with truly mediocre contemporary sides. —*Bill Dahl*

Bad, Bad Whiskey (The Galaxy Masters) / 1994 / Specialty ✦✦✦✦✦
A subsidiary of Fantasy, the Galaxy label recorded a diverse assortment of soul and R&B in the 1960s and early '70s. This is a 26-track compilation of highlights from the company's output, covering 1962 to 1972. Landing the occasional minor R&B chart hit, Galaxy couldn't be said to have an especially distinctive label sound, though their efforts were on the whole bluesier than much soul of the era. But this is still a decent grab bag of odds and ends from soul's vintage period, with obscure sides by well-known performers like Betty Everett, Little Johnny Taylor, Lenny Williams, Charles Brown, Johnny "Guitar" Watson, Merl Saunders, and a host of unknowns. Especially good are the three sides by Rodger Collins, whose 1966 single "She's Looking Good" (which leads off the CD) was one of the better regional soul hits of the '60s, and was covered by Wilson Pickett a couple of years later. —*Richie Unterberger*

The Beauty of the Blues / 1991 / Columbia/Legacy ✦✦✦✦✦
This is a beautiful 18-track collection from a sampling of Columbia/Legacy's *Roots 'N' Blues* series. The recordings, from 1929-1947, include a wide variety of traditional blues and blues-related styles. Excellent sound, with music from Robert Johnson, Big Bill Broonzy, and others. —*Niles J. Frantz*

Best of Chess Blues / MCA ✦✦✦✦
This continuing series, six volumes to date, documents rare and obscure '50s tracks by Chess blues stalwarts, including Howlin' Wolf, Little Walter, Sonny Boy Williamson, and many more. —*Hank Davis*

The Best of Chicago Blues / 1973 / Vanguard ✦✦✦✦✦
These mostly '60s recordings of tough Chicago blues were produced by Samuel Charters and feature James Cotton, Junior Wells, Otis Spann, Buddy Guy, J.B. Hutto, Homesick James, Big Walter Horton, and Johnny Young. They're very successful snapshots of what was happening in the Chicago blues bars at that time. —*Niles J. Frantz*

The Best of Duke-Peacock Blues / 1992 / MCA ✦✦✦✦
Interesting collection of sides from this seminal Texas label. Highlights include tracks by Bobby Bland ("Stormy Monday," "Turn On Your Lovelight"), Otis Rush ("Homework"), Junior Parker ("Driving Wheel"), and Larry Davis' original version of "Texas Flood," made popular to a new audience by Stevie Ray Vaughan. —*Cub Koda*

Best of The Blues / 1993 / K-Tel ✦✦✦
Budget 10-track compilation of classic tracks from the genre's biggest stars. Hardcore fans will already have these, but this makes a perfect primer for those beginning to investigate the roots of rock. —*Cub Koda*

Big Road Blues: The Real Thing from Mississippi . . . / 1992 / Collectables ✦✦✦
Another uneven Collectables collection, it has some rough but atmospheric (and totally obscure) early-'50s material mixed with later efforts by Houston Stackhouse. —*Bill Dahl*

Black Top Blues Cocktail Party / 1991 / Black Top ✦✦✦
This features non-album tracks from the label's roster. —*Robert Gordon*

Black Top Blues-A-Rama: A Budget Sampler / 1990 / Black Top ✦✦✦✦
This 21-track sampler of Black Top Records music is a very good example of contemporary blues, with a focus on Texas and Louisiana. —*Niles J. Frantz*

Black Top Blues-A-Rama, Vol. 1 / Black Top ✦✦✦
1988 live sides by Anson Funderburgh, Sam Myers, organist Ron Levy, and sax wailer Grady Gaines. Typically hot and sweaty. —*Bill Dahl*

Black Top Blues-A-Rama, Vol. 2 / 1988 / Black Top ✦✦✦
Three R&B vets (Nappy Brown, Earl King, James Davis) and relative newcomer Ronnie Earl live in '88. —*Bill Dahl*

Black Top Blues-A-Rama, Vol. 3 / Black Top ✦✦✦
One of the weaker entries in the series; James Davis is top notch, Ron Levy and Bobby Radcliff somewhat less so. —*Bill Dahl*

Black Top Blues-A-Rama, Vol. 4: Down & Dirty / 1990 / Black Top ◆◆◆
All Houston saxman Grady Gaines and his Texas Upsetters. Cut live in '89 at Tipitina's. —*Bill Dahl*

Black Top Blues-A-Rama, Vol. 5 / Black Top ◆◆◆

Black Top Blues-A-Rama, Vol. 6: Live at Tipitina's / 1992 / Black Top ◆◆◆
Very strong lineup; stunning Snooks Eaglin sides, four wild efforts by guitarist Hubert Sumlin and reliably rocking Anson Funderburgh and Sam Myers. —*Bill Dahl*

Black Top Blues-A-Rama, Vol. 7: Live at Tipitina's / Black Top ◆◆◆
Robert Ward makes his live recording debut on this simmering '92 *Blues a Rama* set. Also aboard are bluesy zydeco export Lynn August and three numbers by Carol Fran and Clarence Holliman. —*Bill Dahl*

Blind Pig Sampler / 1990 / Blind Pig ◆◆◆◆
This is a representative collection of the prolific label's bluesy catalog. —*Bill Dahl*

Blow It Til You Like It / Charly ◆◆◆◆◆
More blues and R&B harmonica is included on this generous 24-track import sampler. —*Hank Davis*

☆ **Blue Flames: Sun Blues Collection** / 1990 / Rhino ◆◆◆◆◆
A skimpy (18 songs) but tremendous set of Sam Phillips's gut-bucket blues recordings, all are of early-'50s vintage and exquisitely remastered. Most of the big names are here. —*John Floyd*

Blue Ladies / Mar. 7, 1921–Oct. 28, 1925 / Memphis Archives ◆◆◆◆
This collector's CD has 18 selections from early classic blues singers. In addition to Bessie Smith, Mamie Smith, Clara Smith, Ida Cox, Trixie Smith, Ma Rainey, and Ethel Waters, a variety of lesser-known vocalists are represented: Edith Wilson, Clementine Smith, Sara Martin, Maggie Jones, Margaret Johnson, Rosa Henderson, Lucille Hegamin, Dora Carr, Mary Stafford, Viola McCoy, and Ethel Ridley. The majority of the selections were formerly rare (including Mary Stafford's "I'm Gonna Jazz My Way Straight Through Paradise") and the sidemen include Johnny Dunn, Coleman Hawkins, Charlie Green, Louis Metcalf, Tommy Ladnier, Cow Cow Davenport, Joe Smith, and even Louis Armstrong, making this a CD worth picking up by 1920s collectors. —*Scott Yanow*

1923–1933 / Jan. 31, 1923–Jul. 7, 1933 / Onyx Classix ◆◆◆
This CD from the Robert Parker series (in which the renowned engineer "enhances" early recordings by adding a slight echo and the feel of stereo) contains 16 performances that cover a wide range of styles. Most of the music is from the jazz side of the blues world and rarities are programmed next to more familiar selections. Despite the hodgepodge nature of the program, this one is worth picking up. Such singers as Ida Cox, Ma Rainey, Bessie Smith, Mamie Smith, Victoria Spivey, Ethel Waters, and even Jimmy Rodgers (along with nine others) are heard on one song apiece and most collectors will be missing at least a few of these recordings. —*Scott Yanow*

The Blues, Vol. 4 / Chess ◆◆◆◆
More classic Chess blues. —*Bill Dahl*

The Blues, Vol. 5 / Chess ◆◆◆◆
Classic Chess hits and a few obscurities (Jimmy Nelson, Percy Mayfield). —*Bill Dahl*

Blues As Big As Texas, Vol. 1 / 1991 / Collectables ◆◆◆◆◆
Previously unreleased Texas blues were digitally remastered from the original tapes. Various artists recorded between 1958 and 1971 in Houston (one cut in Beaumont, TX) include Johnny Copeland, Gatemouth Brown, Percy Mayfield, and more. It's a good and varied set. —*Niles J. Frantz*

Blues at the Newport Folk Festival / 1959 / Vanguard ◆◆◆
Blues at Newport—Newport Folk Festival 1959–64 offers fine performances by John Hurt, Skip James, Rev. Gary Davis, Robert Wilkins, and others. —*Mark A. Humphrey*

The Blues Came Down from Memphis / Charly ◆◆◆◆◆
Nice overview of Sun Records' early '50s blues recordings on a single-disc CD, primarily sticking to an issued singles format. Perfect place to start. —*Cub Koda*

Blues Deluxe / 1989 / Alligator ◆◆◆◆
A 1989 reissue, this budget CD (only 39 minutes long) was

recorded live at the 1980 Chicagofest. Included are Muddy Waters, Koko Taylor, Willie Dixon, and three others. —*Niles J. Frantz*

Blues Dimension / 1969 / Decca ◆◆◆◆
This is a very good collection of in-concert recordings from Stevie Ray Vaughan, Sugar Blue, and more. —*Niles J. Frantz*

Blues from "Big Bill's Copacabana" Live / Chess ◆◆◆◆◆
Classic 1963 Chicago blues. —*Bill Dahl*

Blues from the Montreux Jazz Fest. / 1991 / Malaco ◆◆◆◆
Recorded at the Montreux Jazz Festival in Switzerland, during the Malaco Records European Tour in 1989, it features Bobby Bland, Denise LaSalle, Johnnie Taylor, and Mosley & Johnson. Anything LaSalle does lately is worth listening to, and it's nice to have a snapshot of her in-concert style. —*Niles J. Frantz*

Blues Hangover / 1995 / AVI/Excello ◆◆◆◆
This two-disc, 43-track collection collects a treasure trove of rare and unissued performances from the vaults of Excello Records. All but one of the 17 tracks collected on the first disc were produced by Jay Miller in his Crowley, Louisiana studio, home of Excello's unmistakable "swamp blues" sound. The first 10 tracks are by Jimmy Anderson, who impersonates the vocal and harmonica style of Jimmy Reed so pervasively, it's downright eerie. Three tracks from Whispering Smith, a stray Lightnin' Slim cut, and both sides of the mysterious Blue Charlie single are aboard, as well as rare singles from the equally mysterious Ole Sonny Boy, Little Al (Gunter) and Little Sonny. But the true find here is the first-time release of 15 tracks from a 1966 audition tape by one Early Drane. For all intents and purposes, this appears to be the same "Earl Draines" that recorded for the label as part of The Blues Rockers ("Calling All Cows") in the mid '50s. But these remarkable tapes are the man alone in his living room, singing and playing a quirky collection of original material, blues, and gospel covers that career from brilliant to downright loony. Add to this lineup four tracks by Detroit bluesman Baby Boy Warren (featuring Sonny Boy Williamson on harmonica) and two early '60s stereo swingers by the little-known James Stewart and you've got an Excello rarities package that's pretty hard to beat. —*AMG*

Blues Harmonica Spotlight / Black Top ◆◆◆◆
Blues Harmonica Spotlight focuses on the New Orleans label's generous array of blues-harp talent. —*Bill Dahl*

Blues in D Natural / 1979 / Red Lightnin' ◆◆◆
Bootleg-quality sound, but no quarrel with selections by Earl Hooker, Robert Nighthawk, Frankie Lee Sims, and Sly Williams. —*Bill Dahl*

Blues in the Mississippi Night / Jul. 13, 1991 / Rykodisc ◆◆◆◆◆
This pioneering, documentary-style recording was produced by Alan Lomax and was unissued for decades after its 1946 recording, due to its frank discussion of racism by Big Bill Broonzy, Sonny Boy Williamson, and Memphis Slim. —*Bill Dahl*

Blues in the Night / May 26, 1992 / Laserlight ◆◆◆
More of a live jazz set than blues, with organists Jimmy McGriff and Groove Holmes. Only harpist Jr. Parker really qualifies as straight blues. —*Bill Dahl*

Blues Is Killin' Me / 1991 / Paula/Flyright ◆◆◆◆◆
20-track, rock-solid collection of classic blues sides from Chicago's JOB label, primarily focusing on both sides of original issue 78s by Floyd Jones, Memphis Minnie, Baby Face Leroy, and Little Hudson's Red Devil Trio with a few unissued surprises rounding out the already excellent package. —*Cub Koda*

Blues Is Killing Me / Feb. 1978 / Juke Joint ◆◆◆
Solid LP of '50s Chicago blues from job masters. —*Bill Dahl*

☆ **Blues Masters, Vol. 1: Urban Blues** / 1992 / Rhino ◆◆◆◆◆
While more horn-driven and less guitar-reliant than other forms of blues, the urban style nonetheless provides its own spectacular highlights, some of the best of which are right here. The first volume in this 15-volume series features classic performances by Eddie "Cleanhead" Vinson, Dinah Washington, T-Bone Walker, Charles Brown, Joe Turner, and Jimmy Witherspoon. Where the blues meets the jazz and heads uptown for a party. —*Cub Koda*

☆ **Blues Masters, Vol. 2: Post-War Chicago Blues** / 1992 / Rhino ◆◆◆◆◆
Excellent 18-track compendium of all the major movers and shakers who helped shape the Chicago blues scene in the '50s.

Everyone is well represented here, and major stars like Muddy Waters and Howlin' Wolf stand next to behind-the-scenes geniuses like Earl Hooker and Jody Williams for an interesting, and accurate, blend. —*Cub Koda*

☆ **Blues Masters, Vol. 3: Texas Blues** / 1992 / Rhino ♦♦♦♦♦
The best that the Lone Star state has had to offer over a 60-year period is right here, from Blind Lemon Jefferson's "Match Box Blues" (1927) to Stevie Ray Vaughan's live version of "Flood Down In Texas (Texas Flood)" from 1986. This compilation also features great sides by The Fabulous Thunderbirds, Lightnin' Hopkins, T-Bone Walker, and Albert Collins. As a introduction to the Texas blues style, this is a pretty darn good one. —*Cub Koda*

★ **Blues Masters, Vol. 4: Harmonica Classics** / 1992 / Rhino ♦♦♦♦♦
If massive amplified harp tone is what you're looking for, then step up to the volume control and crank it for Jerry McCain's instrumental "Steady." This excellent collection also includes seminal tracks from Little Walter, Big Walter Horton, Paul Butterfield, Jimmy Reed, Lazy Lester, Slim Harpo, Junior Wells, and Charlie Musselwhite. —*AMG*

☆ **Blues Masters, Vol. 5: Jump Blues Classics** / 1992 / Rhino ♦♦♦♦♦
Jump blues, of course, was crucial to the birth of R&B and rock & roll. More important, the infectious swing, grit, and humor were great in themselves. *Jump Blues Classics* collects 18 tracks from the golden days of the genre in the late '40s and 1950s. Most of the pioneers of the style are here—Joe Turner, Wynonie Harris, Roy Brown, Ruth Brown, Roy Milton, Big Jay McNeely, and others, even Louis Prima. The collection includes several cuts that were revived to become rock & roll classics, including "The Train Kept A-Rollin" (Tiny Bradshaw), "Shake, Rattle, And Roll" (Joe Turner), "Good Rockin' Tonight" (Wynonie Harris), "Hound Dog" (Big Mama Thornton), and the little-known original, pre-Muddy Waters version of "Got My Mojo Working" (Ann Cole). This is, of course, just the surface of a genre that was hugely successful in its time, producing hundreds of memorable recordings. This well-annotated anthology is a good starting point and a good representative sampling for those who only want the cream of the crop in their collection. —*Richie Unterberger*

Blues Masters, Vol. 10: Blues Roots / 1993 / Rhino ♦♦♦
Expertly compiled, annotated, and in most cases recorded by pioneering blues researcher Samuel Charters, this volume explores all areas of the blues' origins. Featuring devastating recordings of prison work hands, native African music, and Texas prison songs, this is as hardcore a collection as you're likely to find, yet still very accessible to the average fan. —*Cub Koda*

★ **Blues Masters, Vol. 6: Blues Originals** / 1993 / Rhino ♦♦♦♦♦
It's unfortunate, but it's true: the original versions of many blues classics aren't nearly as well known as their hit covers by (usually White) rock groups. That's not to say that some of these covers aren't great as well, but it's both educational and enjoyable to hear them from the source's mouth. *Blues Originals* contains 18 original versions of classics that went on to reach a wide audience via covers by the Stones, Yardbirds, Elvis, Led Zeppelin, the Doors, and others. The Chess stable of Howlin' Wolf, Muddy Waters, Bo Diddley, Little Walter, and Sonny Boy Williamson is represented here, of course, along with standards by Elmore James, Otis Rush, Robert Johnson, Slim Harpo, and Jimmy Reed. Mixed in with great and fairly available performances like Bo Diddley's "I'm A Man" and Howlin' Wolf's "Back Door Man" are some quite obscure and collectable delights. Arthur Crudup's original version of "That's All Right," covered by Elvis Presley for his first single, has been surprisingly hard to find over the years; ditto for Muddy Waters' "You Need Love," which formed the blueprint for Led Zeppelin's "Whole Lotta Love." Even most Yardbirds fanatics are unaware that the prototype for "Lost Woman" was taken from (and retitled from) an obscure Snooky Pryor single, "Someone To Love Me." And even many Chicago blues fanatics will be surprised to find the original version of "Got My Mojo Working," which was not recorded by Muddy Waters, but little-known jump blues singer Ann Cole. A fine collection, mixing together famous standards and obscure gems with thorough liner notes. —*Richie Unterberger*

Blues Masters, Vol. 7: Blues Revival / 1993 / Rhino ♦♦♦♦♦
It's hard to believe from the vantage point of a period when

blues songs are used for network television commercials, but it wasn't so long ago that the blues was, though hardly in danger of extinction, certainly limited to a pretty specialized audience. The blues revival of the early '60s brought the music back into the spotlight through its prominence at major folk festivals and college concerts, the rediscovery of lost legends like Skip James and Mississippi John Hurt, and the efforts of several musicians and record labels to popularize the work of the form's originators. *Blues Revival* covers a lot of these bases. This 17-track collection includes some of the biggest hit blues singles of the '60s (by Jimmy Reed, John Lee Hooker, Slim Harpo, and B.B. King), '60s recordings by acoustic Delta blues giants like Mississippi Fred McDowell and Son House, hot electric Chicago blues by Junior Wells and Muddy Waters, and White, rock-oriented revivalists like Paul Butterfield, John Mayall, and Canned Heat. Seasoned collectors won't find anything too obscure here, but it's a handy primer to some of the best blues recorded during an era in which the idiom reestablished itself as a vital and living form. —*Richie Unterberger*

Blues Masters, Vol. 8: Mississippi Delta Blues / 1993 / Rhino ♦♦♦
The title for this volume is a bit of a misnomer. While there is easily half a compilation's worth of authentic acoustic material here (including classics by Tommy Johnson, Charlie Patton, Willie Brown, and Robert Johnson), the inclusion of tracks by B.B. and Albert King and recorded-in-Chicago sides by Howlin' Wolf, Elmore James, and Robert Nighthawk do much to blur the distinctiveness of this package. —*Cub Koda*

Blues Masters, Vol. 9: Postmodern Blues / 1993 / Rhino ♦♦♦♦♦
A wonderful compendium of artists and styles illustrating the coming of blues into the mainstream. This volume features representative tracks by B.B. King, Albert Collins, Albert King, George Thorogood, Stevie Ray Vaughan, Johnny Winter, and the Fabulous Thunderbirds. The modern sound at its best, and most diverse. —*Cub Koda*

☆ **Blues Masters, Vol. 11: Classic Blues Women** / 1993 / Rhino ♦♦♦♦♦
Although it is now a male-dominated field, the earliest to record and have success in the blues field were women. This volume not only collects many of the great recordings by these women (Mamie, Trixie and Bessie Smith, Billie Holiday, Sippie Wallace, Ma Rainey), but also holds the distinction in the series of being one of the few that offers multiple selections by some of these artists. Highly recommended. —*Cub Koda*

☆ **Blues Masters, Vol. 12: Memphis Blues** / 1993 / Rhino ♦♦♦♦♦
Running the blues history of America's craziest city from early offerings by Cannon's Jug Stompers and the Memphis Jug Band to early Sun recordings from the '50s by Junior Parker, Rufus Thomas and Joe Hill Louis, this is undoubtedly one of the best-compiled volumes in the series. —*Cub Koda*

Blues Masters, Vol. 13: New York City Blues / 1993 / Rhino ♦♦♦♦♦
While other volumes in the series showcase the down-home aspects of the music, this one highlights the big band sound. Great sides by Lionel Hampton ("Hamp's Boogie Woogie"), Duke Ellington, Buddy Johnson, Count Basie, Sam "The Man" Taylor ("Oo-Wee"), and Lucky Millinder showcase a side to the music that is seldom heard. —*Cub Koda*

★ **Blues Masters, Vol. 14: More Jump Blues** / 1993 / Rhino ♦♦♦♦♦
Just as essential as the previous Rhino jump blues collection (volume five of the *Blues Masters* series), this has classics by Floyd Dixon ("Hey Bartender"), Joe Liggins ("Pink Champagne"), Joe Turner, Wynonie Harris, Ruth Brown, Big Maybelle, and Louis Jordan. It also takes some chances by presenting cuts by performers not strictly identified with the style, like Louis Prima, Bobby Charles (the original version of Bill Haley's "See You Later Alligator"), Little Richard, and Faye Adams, whose rousing "I'll Be True" is a touchstone of early R&B. —*Richie Unterberger*

☆ **Blues Masters, Vol. 15: Slide Guitar Classics** / 1993 / Rhino ♦♦♦♦♦
The final volume in the series (at least for now) features seminal and classic tracks from Elmore James ("Dust My Broom"), Muddy Waters ("Honey Bee") and Hound Dog Taylor to modern-day disciples like Johnny Winter and Ry Cooder. Blind Willie

Johnson's "Dark Was The Night, Cold Was The Ground" is worth the price of admission alone. —*Cub Koda*

☆ **Blues Masters, Vol. 1–15** / Rhino ✦✦✦✦✦
Spanning 15 volumes while covering pretty much the entire history of the genre, the Rhino *Blues Masters* series is the one blues collection that both neophytes and long-time fans can heartily embrace. Subtitled "the essential blues collection," it is all of that and more. With each volume devoted to the diverse styles the music entails, the series boasts both thoughtful selection and excellent sound and annotation, utilizing some of the best authorities on the subject. While the compilation form has existed as long as the microgroove long playing record, this is the first time that a comprehensive series has been launched, licensing from a myriad of other labels. While other record companies tend to keep the best material for their own anthologies, Rhino went all out in this endeavor and many of the important tracks in this series are seeing their first issuance in the compilation format (Robert Johnson, for example), while others are being reissued for the first time since the advent of the 78-RPM phonograph record. All in all, a series that will stand for decades to come as an essential building block for anyone's blues collection. —*Cub Koda*

Blues Piano Orgy / 1972 / Delmark ✦✦✦✦✦
A sensational keyboard anthology with great cuts by Speckled Red, Roosevelt Sykes, and Little Brother Montgomery. —*Ron Wynn*

Bluesiana Hot Sauce / 1993 / Shanachie ✦✦✦
Joe Ferry brought Art Blakey, David Newman, and Dr. John together for the concept album *Bluesiana Triangle* in 1989. This latest project, conceived as a tribute to the prior Bluesiana records, again links jazz, R&B, and rock players doing both pop and improvisational material, with the funds again going to the homeless. The assembled cast included trombonist Ray Anderson, harmonica ace Toots Thielemans at his bluesiest on "Brickyard Blues," and soulful tenor from Mike Brecker. Living Colour drummer Will Calhoun was once more funky and in the groove, contributing a solid vocal on "Ruby's Flowers," his own composition. This group does an admirable job of saluting the original cast while also making its own effective statement. —*Ron Wynn*

The Bluesville Years, Vol. 1: Big Blues Honks and Wails / 1995 / Prestige ✦✦✦✦✦
For almost a decade, Bluesville operated as a subsidiary label to the indie jazz pioneer Prestige Records. With a chaotic catalog, they issued everything from barrelhouse piano players working with hipster jazz combos to semi-pro street singers to tons of Lightnin' Hopkins albums. What we have here are the beginnings of the modern blues album as we know it. The Bluesville label captured that awkward moment in time where the blues first lost its commercial restraints and started making music of a different power, and a nice cross-section of it is here on all four of these volumes. There's a decidedly acoustic air to everything here, even the wilder Chicago sides. If you've been brought up on a steady blues album diet of electric guitars and heavy drumming, some of this will sound almost quaint by comparison, but it's well worth a listen. The first entry in the series, *Big Blues, Honks and Wails* features tracks by piano giants Sunnyland Slim and Roosevelt Sykes and uptown blues belters Mildred Anderson, Jimmy Witherspoon and Al Smith paired with small, jazz-oriented combos with sax legends King Curtis, Eddie "Lockjaw" Davis and Clifford Scott honkin' away. —*Cub Koda*

The Bluesville Years, Vol. 2: Feelin' Down on the South Side / 1995 / Prestige ✦✦✦✦✦
Feelin' Down on the South Side culls the best of the albums that were cut in Chicago with top flight selections by Billy Boy Arnold, Homesick James, Otis Spann, and James Cotton. Cotton's "One More Mile To Go," with its voodoo backup chorus from the Muddy Waters band, is downright bone chilling and eerie. —*Cub Koda*

The Bluesville Years, Vol. 3: Beale Street Get-Down / 1995 / Prestige ✦✦✦✦✦
Beale Street Get-Down is the folksiest of the bunch, most of it recorded at the Sun studios in Memphis with country blues guitarists Furry Lewis and Memphis Willie B. (Borum) and pianist Memphis Slim all contributing to the fray. —*Cub Koda*

The Bluesville Years, Vol. 4: In the Key of Blues / 1995 / Prestige ✦✦✦✦✦
The final volume, *In the Key of Blues,* features an all piano fest with boogies and blues from Mercy Dee Walton, Little Brother Montgomery, Curtis Jones, and still more from Sykes and Memphis Slim. —*Cub Koda*

Boogie Blues: Women Sing & Play / Mar. 1930–Oct. 31, 1961 / Rosetta ✦✦✦
All 16 performances on this LP are boogie-blues and put the spotlight on female singers and/or pianists. There is a wide variety of material ranging from a Lil Armstrong piano solo from the soundtrack of the TV show *Chicago & And That Jazz* in 1961 to Memphis Minnie, Ella Fitzgerald ("Cow Cow Boogie"), and Dorothy Donegan in 1942. Other performers include Georgia White, Helen Humes, Lucille Bogan, Hazel Scott, Merline Johnson, Sweet Georgia Brown, Gladys Bentley, Christine Chatman, Hadda Brooks, Myrtle Jenkins, Sister Rosetta Tharpe, and Mary Lou Williams. As usual with Rosetta's albums, this obvious labor of love has informative liner notes, colorful pictures and many rare recordings that have not yet been reissued on CD. —*Scott Yanow*

Boogie Woogie Blues / Sep. 1922–Apr. 1927 / Biograph ✦✦✦
Biograph has come out with many releases of piano rolls through the years. This CD has some by Cow Cow Davenport, James P. Johnson, Clarence Williams, Jimmy Blythe, Hersal Thomas, Lemuel Fowler, and two totally forgotten names: Everett Robbins and Clarence Johnson. As is usual with piano rolls, the rhythms are inflexible and the touch a bit unnatural, so it may take listeners a while to get used to these performances. The emphasis is more on blues than on boogie-woogie, but in general the music is fine for this idiom, although not as lively as real piano solos. —*Scott Yanow*

Bullseye Blues Christmas / Nov. 1995 / Bullseye Blues ✦✦✦
A slightly low-key, funky brand of blues is served up on *Bullseye Blues Christmas,* combining new and previously released flavorful seasonings from the likes of Champion Jack Dupree, Luther Guitar Junior Johnson, and the Persuasions. —*Roch Parisien*

Canadian Blues Masters / K-Tel ✦✦✦
"20 Explosive Heavy Power Dynamic Hits!" Anyone alive from the late '60s to mid '70s will recall those omnipresent K-Tel Records compilations, heavy on hyperbole, cramming 20 radio-ready pop tunes that ranged in quality from the wretched to the exquisite onto one disc. Well, K-Tel is still around, somehow latching onto the idea of compiling a Canadian blues sampler. Many of the obvious veterans are represented by recent material, including Downchild Blues Band, The Powder Blues, Dutch Mason, and King Biscuit Boy. As one might expect from a Canuck blues compilation, K-Tel shamelessly plunders the Stony Plain vaults, with no fewer than six tracks originating from the Edmonton-based label. —*Roch Parisien*

☆ **Chess Blues** / 1992 / MCA ✦✦✦✦✦
Superlative four-CD box set, featuring important tracks by all the main stars of the label (Muddy Waters, Howlin' Wolf, Little Walter, Sonny Boy Williamson), as well as much previously unreleased material. A well-done retrospective of Chicago blues in its heyday, as recorded by America's greatest blues label, Chess. —*Cub Koda*

☆ **Chicago: The Blues Today!, Vol. 1** / Oct. 1966 / Vanguard ✦✦✦✦✦
Junior Wells, J.B. Hutto, and Otis Spann are all superlative on this groundbreaking 1966 anthology. —*Bill Dahl*

☆ **Chicago: the Blues Today!, Vol. 2** / 1966 / Vanguard ✦✦✦✦✦
This series (three volumes) is one of the enduring gems from producer Sam Charters' tenure with Vanguard Records in the '60s. James Cotton's vocals and harp playing are both in top form on his five tracks; among them Ike Turner's "Rocket 88" and a make-over of Charles Brown's "Black Night." Slide guitarist Homesick James and his Dusters are fierce in Elmore's "Dust My Broom" and "Set a Date," and Otis Rush is simply magnificent on his five tracks, which include "It's a Mean Old World" and "I Can't Quit You, Baby." This disc is certain to climb to the Top Ten of any blues fan's collection. —*Larry Hoffman*

☆ **Chicago: The Blues Today!, Vol. 3** / 1966 / Vanguard ✦✦✦✦✦
This is one of the all-time great blues series ever recorded. Aside from the classic Chess albums (Muddy Waters, Little Walter, Howlin' Wolf, etc.), there is no better introduction to Chicago-

style blues than this three-volume set. Each one is incredible. This third album contains the Johnny Shines Blues Band, Johnny Young's South Side Blues Band, and Big Walter Horton's Blues Harp Band with Memphis Charlie Musselwhite. Here are the original Chicago artists who have grown up and played together for most of their lives, so the musical time is spacious—wide open. This is South side Chicago blues with a trace of country at its best. Big Walter Horton plays some of the best harmonica of his career on this album. Listening to Horton on backup and solo harp is an education. This album is definitive. —*Michael Erlewine*

Chicago Ain't Nothin' But a Blues Band / 1972 / Delmark ✦✦✦✦✦
Solid collection of sides from Chicago's Atomic H label with JoJo Williams, J.T. Brown, and Eddie Clearwater's earliest recordings being among the highlights. —*AMG*

☆ **Chicago Blues: Early 50s** / Blues Classics ✦✦✦✦✦
At the time of its release, it was an important examination of pioneering post-war Chicago blues. Now, the LP's worth has been superseded by better-sounding CD reissues. —*Bill Dahl*

Chicago Blues Anthology / 1984 / Chess ✦✦✦✦✦
A wonderful 24-cut set of raw, early Chicago blues from the Chess label. Delta blues influences are evident in the work of Johnny Shines, Robert Nighthawk, and Floyd Jones. A more modern, urban style is shown by Buddy Guy and Otis Rush on this worthwhile collection. —*Niles J. Frantz*

Chicago Blues Harmonicas / 1990 / Paula/Flyright ✦✦✦✦✦
The four remaining JOB sides by Pryor ("Boogy Fool," "Raisin' Sand," "Cryin' Shame" and "Eighty Nine Ten") are to be found here on this compilation, with Snooky also found in support on two tracks from a 1949 Baby Face Leroy session. With the other 13 tracks including John Lee Henley's "Rhythm Rockin' Boogie," Walter Horton's "Have A Good Time," and rare but notable sides by Sonny Boy Williamson, Little Willie Foster and Louis Myers and the Aces, this is a harmonica rarities package that's pretty tough to beat. —*Cub Koda*

Chicago Boogie: 1947 / 1983 / St. George ✦✦✦✦
All the earliest Maxwell Street acetate recordings from the short-lived Ora Nelle label, featuring the earliest sides of Little Walter, Jimmy Rogers, Johnny Young, and Othum Brown. Delta bluesman Johnny Temple's "Olds 98 Blues", done Robert Johnson-style with an electric guitar, is a particular standout. —*Cub Koda*

Chicago Boss Guitars / 1991 / Paula ✦✦✦
Otis Rush shares this compilation with Buddy Guy's early Artistic sides and five alternate takes from Magic Sam. The nine Cobra alternates by Rush are raw and even awkward in spots when compared to the issued versions, but chock full of emotional intensity. If you're a Cobra Records alternate take freak, here's the motherlode. —*Cub Koda*

Chicago South Side, Vol. 2: 1927–29 / Jul. 20, 1927–Jul. 27, 1931 / Historical ✦✦✦✦✦
This consistently enjoyable LP has a variety of performances recorded in Chicago during 1927-31. The songs in this collection are not reissued as complete sessions but what is here is often quite memorable: three numbers from Jimmy Noone; two apiece by Tiny Parham, the Dixie Rhythm Kings, the Chicago Footwarmers, the State Street Ramblers, and Jimmy Blythe's Washboard Wizards; and one song from Willie Hightower. With the sidemen including pianists Earl Hines and Jimmy Blythe, cornetists Punch Miller and Natty Dominique and the great clarinetist Johnny Dodds, the music is often quite special and always spirited. —*Scott Yanow*

Chicago South Side, 1927–31 / May 1926–Mar. 1932 / Historical ✦✦✦✦✦
Although the music on this sampler does not contain complete sessions, this LP is well worth searching for. The performances are quite spirited, featuring music from J.C. Cobb's Grains of Corn, Roy Palmer's Alabama Rascals, Jimmy Wade's Dixielanders, Jimmy Bertrand's Washboard Wizards, Harry Dial's Blusicians, and Jimmie Noone. Among the star soloists are cornetist Punch Miller, Junie Cobb on reeds, clarinetist Darnell Howard and Johnny Dodds, the great trombonist Roy Palmer, Louis Armstrong (on two of the Bertrand performances), and pianists Jimmy Blythe and Earl Hines. These performances are consistently joyful and essential to 1920s collectors in one form or another. —*Scott Yanow*

Clownin' with the World / 1989 / Acoustic Archives ✦✦✦✦✦
A wonderful CD from the vaults of Trumpet Records. Features unissued Sonny Boy Williamson sides and great tracks by his piano playin' buddy, Willie Love. —*AMG*

The Cobra Records Story / Apr. 26, 1993 / Warner Brothers ✦✦✦✦✦
A fine two-disc retrospective of the Chicago Blue label, it includes all of its 39 singles by such seminal figures as Magic Sam, Otis Rush, Buddy Guy, Ike Turner, Sunnyland Slim, and Walter Horton. —*AMG*

The Copulatin' Blues Compact Disc / Apr. 29, 1929–Feb. 5, 1940 / Stash ✦✦✦
The Stash label began in 1976 with a dozen or so LPs that featured subject matter from the 1930s that was considered risque for the period. In the case of this album, the 16 selections all have to do with sex; several cuts were previously unreleased and few had very wide circulation. Such top jazz and blues artists as Sidney Bechet, Lil Johnson, Bessie Smith ("Do Your Duty" and "I Need a Little Sugar in My Bowl"), The Harlem Hamfats, Merline Johnson, Tampa Red, Grant & Wilson, Jelly Roll Morton ("Winin' Boy"), and Lucille Bogan (an absolutely filthy "Shave 'Em Dry") are heard from. Some of this music has been reissued by Stash through its subsidiary Jass on CD but not in the same format. —*Scott Yanow*

The Copulatin' Blues, Vol. 2 / Jan. 26, 1929–1955 / Stash ✦✦✦
This collection contains a truthful warning and description: "A Party Record for Adults—Screen Before Airplay." It is doubtful if more than a couple of these 15 selections could be played on the radio, even now. Mostly dating from the 1930s, the risque performances include several (including a very profane "parody" by The Clovers in the 1950s) that were previously unissued. Best is "The Duck's Yas Yas" by Eddie Johnson and his Crackerjacks, "It Feels So Good" by The Hokum Boys, and the classic "Pussy" by Harry Roy's Bat Club Boys. —*Scott Yanow*

☆ **Country Blues Bottleneck Guitar Classics** / 1972 / Yazoo ✦✦✦✦✦
The first and possibly best anthology of pre-war bottleneck guitar (1926-1937), this includes the singing slides of Robert Johnson, Bukka White, Memphis Minnie, and—although scarcely country blues—a stunning "St. Louis Blues" by Jim and Bob, The Genial Hawaiians! —*Mark A. Humphrey*

Dapper Cats, Groovy Tunes & Hot Guitars / 1992 / Ace ✦✦✦
Sizzling blues and R&B from the mid-'50s vaults for Johnny Otis's Dig Records. —*Bill Dahl*

Dark Muddy Bottom Blues / 197 / Specialty ✦✦✦✦
Most of the 12 tracks on this 1972 blues compilation were previously unissued. Artists include John Lee Hooker, Lightnin' Hopkins, Mercy Dee, Big Joe Williams, and others. —*AMG*

Dealing with the Devil: Immediate Blues Story, Vol. 2 / 1980 / CBS ✦✦✦
Early British blues, featuring Eric Clapton, Jeff Beck, Jon Lord, Ron Wood, and other not-yet superstars in some rough, raw performances. —*Bruce Eder*

Deep Blue: 25 Years of Blues on Rounder Records / Sep. 12, 1995 / Rounder ✦✦✦
Over the course of two CDs, *Deep Blue: 25 Years of Blues on Rounder Records* rounds up the highlights of Rounder's blues catalog, including tracks from Professor Longhair, Clarence "Gatemouth" Brown, Lowell Fulson, Robert Nighthawk, Champion Jack Dupree, Luther "Guitar Junior" Johnson, Ronnie Earl, and Smokin' Joe Kubek, among many others. It's a fairly consistent collection, giving a good representation of the record label's catalog. —*Stephen Thomas Erlewine*

Deep in the Soul of Texas / 1991 / Collectables ✦✦✦✦
Texas soul from the '60s and '70s includes some previously unissued material. —*Niles J. Frantz*

Deep in the Soul of Texas, Vol. 2 / Collectables ✦✦✦✦
More one-star obscurities. —*Bill Dahl*

Delmark Records 40th Anniversary Blues / 1993 / Delmark ✦✦✦
Delmark's jazz anthology deserves praise despite the fundamental problems inherent within the sampler concept; the same holds true for its blues collection. This is a good 19-cut retrospective item containing exceptional cuts by Robert Jr. Lockwood, Otis Rush, J.B. Hutto, Roosevelt Sykes, and Magic

Sam; plus nice ones from Jimmy Johnson, Arthur Crudup, Yank Rachell, and Big Joe Williams. But no Eddie "Cleanhead" Vinson? —*Ron Wynn*

Delta Blues: 1951 / 1990 / Acoustic Archives ✦✦✦✦✦
Great compilation from Jackson, Mississippi's Trumpet Records. Features early '50s sides by Big Joe Williams, wonderful acoustic duets by the Huff Brothers, and the last recordings of original King Biscuit Boy Willie Love. A wonderful document. —*AMG*

Detroit Blues: Early 1950s / Blues Classics ✦✦✦✦✦
Tough, raw-edged and primitive urban blues from the Motor City. —*Bill Dahl*

Dig These Blues: The Legendary Dig Masters / Ace ✦✦✦✦✦
Johnny Otis produced these hot R&B sides for his Dig label during the mid-'50s. —*Bill Dahl*

Don't Leave Me Here / Yazoo ✦✦✦✦✦
Don't Leave Me Here—Blues of Texas, Arkansas & Louisiana is a 14-track country-blues collection of recordings from 1927-1932. This contains a variety of traditional acoustic blues styles from the Gulf Coast area. Highlights include King Solomon Hill and Little Hat Jones. —*Niles J. Frantz*

Drop Down Mama / 1970 / Chess ✦✦✦✦✦
Nighthawk's early sides for Chess back when they were still called Aristocrat. Includes the original "Sweet Black Angel," which later became a hit for B.B. King as "Sweet Little Angel" and "Anna Lee," two of his very best. Even with minimal band support on these sides, Nighthawk's voice and slide guitar resonate like an orchestra. This wonderful compilation also features seminal tracks by Johnny Shines ("So Glad I Found You"), Floyd Jones ("Dark Road"), Big Boy Spires ("One Of These Days"), and Honeyboy Edwards doing the title track with a full band. Truly a compilation that should be residing in everyone's collection. —*Cub Koda*

Drove from Home Blues / Flyright ✦✦✦✦✦
This is an interesting collection of tunes recorded by artists who are virtually unknown. The music is excellent, finding its niche in the stylish, pre-rockabilly/R&B world—a reflection of the work being done in the late '40s and early '50s by artists such as Arthur Crudup, Lightnin' Hopkins, Tommy McClennan, and Blind Boy Fuller. The music of Wright Holmes, for example, is cast in a Lightnin' Hopkins' mold, but his imaginative guitar style is very wild and unconventional. In addition, harpist Sonny Boy Johnson emerges from the John Lee "Sonny Boy" Williamson school. Also present is Muddy Waters' very first commercial recording. —*Larry Hoffman*

☆ **The Earliest Negro Vocal Quartets (1894–1928)** / Document ✦✦✦✦✦
A strong collection of mostly religious sides by some pioneering a cappella groups, beginning with an 1894 cylinder by The Standard Quartet. —*Kip Lornell*

East Coast Blues: 1926–1935 / Yazoo ✦✦✦✦✦
A fine assortment from Carl Martin, Willie Walker, William Moore, Blind Blake, Bayless Rose, and other East Coast guitarists. There are several very traditional blues like "Black Dog Blues" and "Crow Jane," plus lots of good ragtime guitar. For serious guitar players and Piedmont blues fans. —*Barry Lee Pearson*

Essential Blues / 1995 / House of Blues ✦✦✦✦
Essential Blues is an attempt to trace the evolution of the music from the Mississippi Delta to Chicago and other modern, urban cities. It does a fairly good job of providing a brief history, but the main strength of the collection simply comes from the music. Featuring cuts from Lightnin' Hopkins, Howlin' Wolf, B.B. King, Slim Harpo, Junior Parker, Elmore James, Albert Collins, and many, many others, it's a quick and effective way to sample a variety of different blues styles. For neophytes, *Essential Blues* does offer a splendid introduction to the genre. —*Stephen Thomas Erlewine*

Evidence Blues Sampler / Evidence ✦✦✦
Evidence's blues reissue campaign has been exhaustive and diverse in its artistic and stylistic range, something that is reflected in this 15-cut sampler culled from various sessions. There is vintage material from John Lee Hooker, J.B. Hutto, and the tandem of Junior Wells and Buddy Guy, plus classic R&B by Louis Jordan and Big Joe Turner and contemporary blues by Magic Slim, Lonnie Brooks, and Luther Johnson Jr. You can also hear

Otis Rush and Luther Allison at their best or Pinetop Perkins offering prototypical boogie-woogie and rumbling piano licks. —*Ron Wynn*

Excello Harmonica Blues Variety / 1994 / AVI/Excello ✦✦✦✦
This is a 39-track, double-CD package collecting various stray cuts in the Excello vaults by artists who didn't leave enough tracks behind to justify having compilations under their own names. The highlights include nine tracks by Jimmy Reed soundalike Jimmy Anderson, Lightnin' Slim sideman Lazy Lester, and 10 tracks by Jerry McCain And His Upstarts. Add to this stray singles by Baby Boy Warren (with Sonny Boy Williamson), Little Sonny, Whispering Smith, and the obscure Ole Sonny Boy and you have a package that fills up the holes in your Excello collection quite nicely. Over half of the tracks are dubbed from disc, but the music's fine just the same. —*Cub Koda*

The Fifties Juke Joint Blues / Capitol ✦✦✦✦
This is a valuable look at some of the toughest Delta and West Coast blues sides issued by Modern Records in the 1950s. —*Bill Dahl*

Frank Stokes' Dream: The Memphis Blues / Yazoo ✦✦✦✦✦
Early Memphis gems; pre-war acoustic. —*Bill Dahl*

Genuine Houserockin' Music, Vol. 1 / 1986 / Alligator ✦✦✦✦✦
These virtually interchangeable samplers of good-time, high-energy, modern R&B were produced by Chicago's Alligator label. Lonnie Brooks, Lonnie Mack, Koko Taylor, Fenton Robinson, Albert Collins, and others are included. Slick and well-produced. —*Hank Davis*

Genuine Houserockin' Music, Vol. 2 / 1987 / Alligator ✦✦✦✦

Genuine Houserockin' Music, Vol. 3 / 1988 / Alligator ✦✦✦

Genuine Houserockin' Music, Vol. 4 / Alligator ✦✦✦

Gonna Head for Home / Flyright ✦✦✦✦✦
Nice compendium of rare and unissued Excello sides by lesser-known names (Boogie Jake, Mr. Calhoun, Silas Hogan, and Jimmy Anderson) who recorded for the label. Excellent Louisiana swamp blues, crude and low down. —*AMG*

Good Time Blues: Harmonicas, Kazoos, Washboards / 1991 / Columbia/Legacy ✦✦✦✦✦
This small-group acoustic blues, dance, and washboard band music was recorded between 1930 and 1941. *Good Time Blues—Harmonicas, Kazoos, Washboards* is happy, generally uptempo party music and lots of fun. —*Niles J. Frantz*

Got Harp If You Want It / Blue Rock-It ✦✦✦
A decent overview of postwar blues harmonica, but hardly comprehensive. —*Ron Wynn*

Got My Mojo Working / 1991 / Flyright ✦✦✦✦✦
Collection of blues sides recorded for New York's Baton label in the mid-to-late '50s, featuring Chris Kenner's first recording and Ann Cole's original, pre-Muddy Waters version performance of the title track. —*Cub Koda*

Great Blues Guitarists: String Dazzlers / Aug. 1991 / Columbia/Legacy ✦✦✦
A high-quality survey of some of the finest blues guitar players, these were recorded from 1924-1940. It includes, among others, Tampa Red, Blind Willie Johnson, and Big Bill Broonzy. Highlights include three instrumental duets featuring Lonnie Johnson and Eddie Lang. They take your breath away. —*Niles J. Frantz*

☆ **The Great Bluesmen at Newport** / 1976 / Vanguard ✦✦✦✦✦
These performances come from 1959-1965 by rediscovery legends Son House, Mississippi John Hurt, Skip James, Sleepy John Estes, and other compelling singers and guitarists such as Robert Pete Williams, John Lee Hooker, and Mississippi Fred McDowell. —*Mark A. Humphrey*

● **The Greatest in Country Blues (1929–1956), Vol. 1** / Story Of Blues ✦✦✦✦✦
Story of the Blues has provided one of the best introductions to acoustic country blues with its three-volume *Greatest in Country Blues* series. While it collects most of the major figures as well as the obscure and their finest performances, there are a certain number of odd omissions, such as Reverend Gary Davis and Robert Nighthawk, that prevent it from being the definitive country blues set. Nevertheless, each of the three volumes is an invaluable reference as well as an interesting listen for both the specialist and the novice. —*Chris Woodstra*

● **The Greatest in Country Blues (1927–1936), Vol. 2** / Story Of Blues ✦✦✦✦✦

● **The Greatest in Country Blues (1929–1956), Vol. 3** / Story Of Blues ✦✦✦✦✦

Anyone interested in a survey of early blues will be thrilled with having any of these three historical volumes, suited to both novice and connoisseur alike. Each provides a dazzling, panoramic survey of artists both famous and obscure and covers every region known to have nurtured the music. *Volume 2* features Skip James's "Devil Got My Woman," Robert Johnson's "Preachin' Blues," and Kokomo Arnold's "Paddlin' Madeline Blues." From Texas Alexander there is a version of "Levee Camp Moan Blues," which is made timeless by the incomparable guitar of Lonnie Johnson. Great instrumentals like Palmer McAbee's "Railroad Piece" and The Dallas String Band's "Dallas Rag" add spice, and there are also first-rate entries by more obscure giants like King Solomon Hill, George "Bullet" Williams, "Hi" Henry Brown, and Blind Joe Taggart. —*Larry Hoffman*

Grinder Man Blues: Masters of Blues Piano / 1990 / RCA ✦✦✦✦✦

Six tracks each come from Little Brother Montgomery (1935–1936), Memphis Slim (1940–1941), and Big Maceo Merriweather (1941–1945). With piano blues and boogie-woogie, it's wonderful listening from beginning to end. —*Niles J. Frantz*

Guitar Player Presents Electric Blues, Vol. 1 / 1992 / Rhino ✦✦✦✦

Excellent 18-track CD compilation featuring definitive sides by Muddy Waters, Otis Rush, Hound Dog Taylor, Albert King, Eddie Taylor, and many more. —*Cub Koda*

Guitar Player Presents Electric Blues, Vol. 2 / 1992 / Rhino ✦✦✦✦

Companion volume to the above with excellent selections from B.B. King, Albert Collins, Eric Clapton, Michael Bloomfield, Magic Sam, Buddy Guy and a dozen others. —*Cub Koda*

Guitar Wizards: 1926–1935 / Yazoo ✦✦✦✦✦

This is an excellent collection of great pre-war blues guitarists. —*Mark A. Humphrey*

Gulf Coast Blues, Vol. 1 / 1990 / Black Top ✦✦✦✦

Contemporary Texas and Louisiana blues come from four artists deserving wider attention. Carol Fran, Joe "Guitar" Hughes, and Grady Gaines each contribute two cuts, with four from Teddy Reynolds. Fran and Reynolds are the highlights, and each deserve their own full releases. —*Niles J. Frantz*

Hand Me Down Blues Chicago Style / 1990 / Relic ✦✦✦✦✦

One of the finest 1950s Chicago Blues compilations in existence, taken from the vaults of Parrot-Blue Lake Records. Unissued sides and rare singles create an incredible ambience here. Essential listening. —*Cub Koda*

Harlem Rock 'n Blues, Vol. 3 / Collectables ✦✦✦

This continues the theme. Material that either influenced or reflected evolutionary trends in blues and R&B. —*Ron Wynn*

Harmonica Blues / 1991 / Yazoo ✦✦✦✦✦

This is a fine collection of pre-war harp performances. —*Mark A. Humphrey*

Harmonica Blues Kings / 1986 / Delmark ✦✦✦✦✦

Featuring a side each of Big Walter Horton and Alfred "Blues King" Harris in primarily supporting roles behind various vocalists from the vaults of United/States Records, 1954. Raw, lively harmonica and another missing piece of the early Chicago blues puzzle. —*AMG*

Harp Attack! / 1991 / Alligator ✦✦✦✦✦

This 11-track CD spotlights four Chicago harmonica players—Carey Bell, Billy Branch, James Cotton, and Junior Wells—in new recordings. All have played with Muddy Waters or Willie Dixon's Chicago Blues All-Stars (or both). This is solid electric-band-style Chicago blues. —*Niles J. Frantz*

Harps, Jugs, Washboards & Kazoos / Jun. 1926–Oct. 10, 1940 / RST ✦✦✦✦

Included on this fun CD from the Austrian RST label are all of the recordings done by the Five Harmaniacs (which date from 1926–27), the Salty Dog Four (from 1930–31 and also known as the Red Devils), the Scorpion Washboard Band (1933) and Rhythm Willie and his Gang (1940). While Rhythm Willie's group is an acoustic blues quartet led by a harmonica player,

Scorpion has a kazoo and washboard (along with more conventional instruments), the Salty Dog Four uses kazoo, violin, and sometimes mandolin, and the Harmaniacs have harmonica, kazoo and washboard. The goodtime music overall falls between jazz and blues and is difficult to resist, particularly tunes such as "Sadie Green, The Vamp of New Orleans," "Coney Island Washboard," "What Did Romie-O Juliet (When He Climbed Her Balcony)," and "Bedroom Stomp!" —*Scott Yanow*

House Rockin' Blues / 1995 / Ace ✦✦✦✦

Compilations of vintage Chess material seem to be plentiful these days, but this excellent collection of strictly uptempo material should not be passed by at any cost. With a healthy 27 tracks aboard, the highlights are numerous with the label's stars and second-stringers like Howlin' Wolf, J.B. Lenoir, John Brim, Billy Boy Arnold, Bo Diddley, Willie Mabon, Elmore James, and Otis Rush all present and accounted for. But rather than opt for the same tracks that have been around the block time and again, true obscurities like the anonymous Little Luther's "The Twirl," G.L. Crockett's "Look Out Mabel," the previously unissued Robert Nighthawk with Buddy Guy shuffle, "Someday," "Tired of Crying over You" by Morris Pejoe, and "He Knows the Rules" by Jimmy McCracklin pepper the mix to keep the collectors happy as well. If the boogie side of the Chess cannonade is your particular cup of coffee, this collection is the one you'll keep going back to time and again. Great! —*Cub Koda*

How Blue Can You Get?: Great Blues Vocals in the Jazz Tradition / Jun. 29, 1938–Nov. 20, 1963 / Bluebird ✦✦✦

Most of the 19 vocals on this interesting but not essential sampler feature jazz singers performing blues including Louis Armstrong, Jack Teagarden, Mildred Bailey, Wingy Mamnone, Fats Waller, Billy Eckstine, Jimmy Rushing, Joe Williams, Helen Humes, and Hot Lips Page. There are a couple of ringers tossed in, particularly Leadbelly doing his classic version of "Good Morning Blues" and Little Richard starting his recording career with a Leonard Feather blues. The music mostly falls into the swing tradition; only two selections are more recent than 1951. —*Scott Yanow*

If It Ain't a Hit . . . / Zu-Zazz ✦✦✦✦✦

X-rated blues is the theme here with selections ranging from totally raunchy to mildly titillating with great listening and a full dollop of humor throughout. Features under-the-counter performances by Jackie Wilson, LaVern Baker, Chick Willis, the Clovers, and The Fred Wolff Combo. Blues with a nudge and a wink to it. —*Cub Koda*

The Immediate Blues, Vol. 1: Stroll On / 1991 / Sony ✦✦✦

The Yardbirds, Eric Clapton, and a brace of early British bluesmen playing on what were intended as demos. Not profound, but entertaining. —*Bruce Eder*

Independent Women's Blues, Vol. 1: Mean Mothers / Rosetta ✦✦✦✦

Independent Women's Blues is an excellent, four-disc series of early blues and jazz recordings by women—all come highly recommended for not only the abundance of rarities but also for the quality of the music. *Vol. 1,* subtitled *Mean Mothers,* includes selections from Billie Holiday, Ida Cox, and Bessie Brown. —*Chris Woodstra*

Independent Women's Blues 2: Big Mamas / Apr. 1925–1953 / Rosetta ✦✦✦

Despite the title of this LP, many of the 16 blues and jazz singers heard here were not necessarily "big" physically but women in control of their situations, at least on these records. There is one song apiece from Ethel Waters, Edith Johnson, Viola McCoy, Hattie McDaniel (the same person as the actress), Issie Ringgold, Gussie Williams, Clara Smith, Ida Cox, Julia Lee, Susie Edwards, Martha Copeland, Ora Alexander, Rosa Henderson, Bea Foote, Billie Holiday, and Ella Johnson, and the majority are still quite rare. All of the Rosetta releases are worth searching for and this attractive album is no exception. —*Scott Yanow*

Independent Women's Blues 3: Super Sisters / Apr. 9, 1927–May 3, 1955 / Rosetta ✦✦✦

The third of four LPs issued by Rosetta in its *Independent Women's Blues* series has 16 blues and jazz recordings, one apiece from Ida Cox, Bertha Idaho, Helen Humes (in 1927), Sara Martin, Mildred Bailey, Sweet Peas Spivey, Lil Johnson, Trixie Smith, Susie Edwards, Lucille Bogan, Cleo Gibson, Martha Copeland, Edith Johnson, Albennie Jones, Lizzie Miles, and Ella

Fitzgerald. Many of these valuable performances are still quite rare and have not yet been reissued on CD. —*Scott Yanow*

Independent Women's Blues 4: Sweet Petunias / Jun. 20, 1929–Jun. 5, 1956 / Rosetta ✦✦✦
There is a wide variety of vocals on this Rosetta LP which, with one exception (O'Neil Spencer's "Sweet Patootie" with Sidney Bechet), features female singers. Such fine vocalists as June Richmond, Annisteen Allen, Mary Dixon, Etta Jones ("The Richest Guy In The Graveyard"), Monette Moore, Mae West, Stella Johnson, Ella Johnson, Bea Foote, Chippie Hill, Victoria Spivey, the Bandanna Girls, Betty Hall Jones, Helen Humes, and Big Mama Thornton perform one song apiece. Most of the recordings are rare and this appealing set, *Vol. 4* of Rosetta's *Independent Women's Blues* series, is easily recommended. — *Scott Yanow*

Jackson Blues: 1928–1938 / Yazoo ✦✦✦✦✦
Featured are Tommy Johnson and the school of Delta blues he inspired in Jackson, MS. —*Mark A. Humphrey*

Jewel/Paula Records Box / 1993 / Capricorn ✦✦✦
Jewel and Paula were started by Stan Lewis, a record store owner and mail-order operator specializing in the kind of vital R&B, blues, soul, and gospel tunes that many people enjoyed, but were highly undervalued by most major record labels. Lewis moved into the record business during the mid-'60s, signing raw artists who made music light-years away from slick pop fare. This two-disc anthology features prime Jewel and Paula acts from the 1960s, '70s and '80s. The first disc includes urgent soul tunes from Toussaint McCall and Ted Taylor, Delta blues from Frank Foster, classic shouting R&B from Joe Turner, the smoother R&B sound of Charles Brown, Lightnin' Hopkins, John Lee Hooker, and others. The second disc is just as distinguished, featuring Little Johnny Taylor, Fontella Bass, Ike and Tina Turner, Buster Benton and Ted Taylor, then-budding stars Bobby Rush and Artie "Blues Boy" White, plus other regional attractions. —*Ron Wynn*

Jump 'n Shout! (New Orleans Blues) / Pearl Flapper ✦✦✦
Solid New Orleans anthology. —*Bill Dahl*

Keys to the Crescent City / 1991 / Rounder ✦✦✦
The revelation on this CD anthology spotlighting three New Orleans greats and one West Coast blues legend (Charles Brown) was the late Willie Tee. Tee, who died in 1993, was known for his soulful vocals and skillful writing, but was undervalued as a pianist. He demonstrated with his voicings and solos on "Can It Be Done" and "In The Beginning" that he also merited attention as a keyboard stylist. Charles Brown turned in his customary polished, first-rate vocal and instrumental job on his three tunes, while Eddie Bo's singing exceeded his piano playing and Art Neville demonstrated again why he should do more recording outside the arenas of the Neville Brothers and the Meters. —*Ron Wynn*

Legends of Guitar: Electric Blues, Vol. 1 / Rhino ✦✦✦✦✦
This very consistent post-war blues-guitar collection includes Muddy Waters, T-Bone Walker, B.B. King, Guitar Slim, Earl Hooker, and Otis Rush contributing their vintage classics. —*Bill Dahl*

Legends of Guitar: Electric Blues, Vol. 2 / 1991 / Rhino ✦✦✦
Slightly less consistent than its predecessor, it's still loaded with gems—18 tracks including Clarence Gatemouth Brown, Albert Collins, Lowell Fulson, Magic Sam, etc. —*Bill Dahl*

Legends of the Blues, Vol. 2 / Columbia ✦✦✦✦✦
Volume 2 is just as diverse and entertaining as *Volume 1,* though the artists included are, in general, somewhat less well known. This collection (featuring recordings from 1929 to 1941, presented in chronological order) includes piano blues from Roosevelt Sykes, Charlie Spand, and Champion Jack Dupree; guitar greats Tampa Red, Buddy Boss, and Casey Bill Weldon; and "classic" blues from Lil' Johnson, Victoria Spivey, and Bessie Jackson. Also here is one of T-Bone Walker's first-ever recordings (as "Oak Cliff T-Bone" from 1929) as well as 13 sides previously unissued by Columbia or are alternate takes of issued recordings. —*Niles J. Frantz*

Living Chicago Blues, Vol. 1 / 1978 / Alligator ✦✦✦✦✦
Arguably the best entry in this pioneering anthology series, this features excellent sides by guitarist Jimmy Johnson and saxophonist Eddie Shaw. —*Bill Dahl*

Living Chicago Blues, Vol. 2 / 1978 / Alligator ✦✦✦
This set is almost as incendiary as Vol. 1, thanks to four sides each from Magic Slim, Lonnie Brooks, and Pinetop Perkins. —*Bill Dahl*

Living Chicago Blues, Vol. 3 / 1980 / Alligator ✦✦✦
Laconic saxman A. C. Reed and crisp guitarist Lacy Gibson are standouts. —*Bill Dahl*

Living Chicago Blues, Vol. 4 / 1980 / Alligator ✦✦✦
Not quite as strong, although witty pianist Detroit Jr and guitarist Andrew Brown contribute strong tracks. —*Bill Dahl*

Living Chicago Blues, Vol. 5 / Alligator ✦✦✦✦✦

Living Chicago Blues, Vol. 6 / Alligator ✦✦✦

Lonesome Road Blues: 15 Years in the Mississippi Delta, 1926–1941 / Yazoo ✦✦✦✦✦
Tommy Johnson's influence is again here on *Lonesome Road Blues: 15 Years in the Mississippi Delta,* which includes other fine pre-war Delta blues. —*Mark A. Humphrey*

Long Man Blues / Pearl Flapper ✦✦✦✦✦
Chicago blues obscurities from the '50s United/States vaults, including highlights Dennis Binder, Harold Burrage, Arbee Stidham, Jack Cooley, and Cliff Butler. —*Bill Dahl*

Louisiana Blues / 1970 / Arhoolie ✦✦✦✦✦
This is distinctive swamp blues by Henry Gray, Silas Hogan, Whispering Smith, and Guitar Kelley. —*Hank Davis*

Louisiana Scrapbook / 1987 / Rykodisc ✦✦✦
Contemporary Louisiana sounds were presented on this 18-track compilation, culled from various albums. While veteran stylists like Irma Thomas, Tuts Washington, and Johnny Adams were included, the disc contained cuts by other acts not so readily identified with the state (Marcia Ball) and sorely neglected artists (Phillip Walker, James Booker, Lonesome Sundown), as well as then-emerging stars (The Dirty Dozen Brass Band, Beausoleil), and both zydeco (Buckwheat Zydeco) and Cajun performers (D.L. Menard, Jo-El Sonnier). —*Ron Wynn*

Low Blows / Rooster Blues ✦✦✦✦✦
Low Blows—Anthology of Chicago Blues is a scatter-gun compilation of great early-'70s recordings by Chicago's better-known (Walter Horton, Carey Bell) and lesser-known (Big John Wrencher, Good Rockin' Charles Edwards) harmonica men. A missing chapter in blues history. —*Cub Koda*

☆ **Mama Let Me Lay It On You (1926–1936)** / Yazoo ✦✦✦✦✦
A fine collection of East Coast blues, including vintage Josh White, Pink Anderson, and guitarists Blind Blake and Willie Walker. —*Barry Lee Pearson*

Masters of Modern Blues / Testament ✦✦✦✦✦
This compilation of sides culled from three different sessions featuring Robert Nighthawk, Johnny Young, and Houston Stackhouse mark the first official recordings of Big John Wrencher. Although he's relegated to a sideman role here behind Nighthawk and Young, he appears on nine of the 18 tracks on this excellent collection. While the addition of a drummer would have placed the Nighthawk-Young-Wrencher trio in a less deliberate folk-blues setting, the music (which also includes Nighthawk's last session from 1967, playing bass behind Delta blues legend Houston Stackhouse with King Biscuit Boy drummer Peck Curtis) is just about as superb as one can expect from mid-'60s collector-oriented recordings and helps to flesh out Wrencher's meager discography. —*Cub Koda*

☆ **Masters of the Delta Blues: The Friends of Charlie Patton** / 1991 / Yazoo ✦✦✦✦✦
This CD perfectly anthologizes some of the best and rarest tracks by early Delta blues legends like Son House, Tommy Johnson and Bukka White. Rough sounds in spots, but indispensable nonetheless. —*Cub Koda*

Mean Mothers, Vol. 1 / May 17, 1926–Aug. 17, 1949 / Rosetta ✦✦✦
The Rosetta label specializes in prebop recordings from jazz women. This LP, Rosetta's initial release, features 16 different singers interpreting lyrics that in one way or another claim their independence from unreliable men: Martha Copeland, Bessie Brown, Maggie Jones ("You Ain't Gonna Feed in My Pasture Now"), Susie Edwards, Bernice Edwards, Gladys Bentley, Mary Dixon, Bertha Idaho, Rosa Henderson, Harlem Hannah, Lil Armstrong, Blue Lou Barker ("I Don't Dig You Jack"), Rosetta

Howard, Ida Cox, Lil Green (the original version of "Why Don't You Do Right"), and Billie Holiday ("Baby Get Lost"). The album is a good introduction to the classic blues singers of the 1920s and '30s. —*Scott Yanow*

☆ **Mean Old World: The Blues from 1940 to1994** / 1996 / Smithsonian Institution Press ✦✦✦✦✦
This four-disc set is just what you might expect from Smithsonian—comprehensive and well conceived. It contains representative major blues figures for each time period for the years 1940 through 1994—everyone from Ma Rainey to Taj Mahal. For most periods, the selection is excellent. The only downside to this approach is that for time periods with great blues activity, some major artists have been dropped from the collection, while for other time periods with low blues activity, minor artists are included. This approach results in biographies and selections for artists like Earl Hooker, Big Walter Horton, and J.B. Hutto missing from the collection. Aside from the above complaint, this is the best collection for its size (four discs) that has been produced to date. The artists selected and the selections for each of the artists are in most cases excellent—the best of the best, so to speak. This is a veritable tour of the best in recorded blues. The 90-page liner notes by Larry Hoffman contain copious notes on the various selections, including artist biographies (and photos), comments on the takes, etc.—perhaps the most thorough liner notes of its kind. The introductory essay focuses more on race relations than on the blues music. —*Michael Erlewine*

☆ **Memphis Masters: Early American Blues Classics** / 1994 / Yazoo ✦✦✦✦✦
A companion to Yazoo's excellent *Mississippi Masters* collection, this time focusing on Memphis artists recorded between 1927 to 1934. The tracks collected here offer up a musical ambience that accurately depicts time and place with classic selections from acknowledged area kingpins Frank Stokes, Furry Lewis, Gus Cannon's Jug Stompers, Memphis Minnie, Joe McCoy, and Jack Kelly. Like its companion volume, this 20 track compilation is mastered direct from extremely rare old 78s–in some cases, the only copies known to exist–and the sound varies wildly from track to track. But the music is so great and of such major historical significance, the 78 surface noise that remains only seems to add to the charm and romance of it all. *Cub Koda*

Mississippi Blues [Takoma] / 1969 / Takoma ✦✦✦
The best of White's "rediscovery phase" recordings. —*Barry Lee Pearson*

Mississippi Blues (1927–1941) / Yazoo ✦✦✦✦✦
This is another well-programmed anthology. —*Mark A. Humphrey*

Mississippi Burnin' Blues, Vol. 2 / 1995 / ✦✦
A collection of urban Delta blues from artists like Eddie Raspberry and Melvin "Smokehouse" Moore, *Mississippi Burnin' Blues, Vol. 2* is a fitfully entertaining disc, but it doesn't provide any true highlights. —*Stephen Thomas Erlewine*

Mississippi Delta Blues in the 1960s, Vol. 2 / 1994 / Arhoolie ✦✦✦
The second of a two-disc Arhoolie collection featuring late-'60s Delta blues again mixes tracks from familiar names and under-recorded performers. There are 11 cuts from Joe Callicot, among them the superb "Traveling Mama Blues" and "Fare Thee Well Blues," both of which Callicot originally performed in 1930, when he was at his vocal and playing peak. R.L. Burnside is revered inside the Mississippi Delta, but has a very low profile beyond it. He's featured on nine late-'60s tunes, four previously unissued. Burnside's ragged guitar riffs and dynamic voice rip through a variety of material from the novelty cut "Skinny Woman" to the double-entendre "See My Jumper Hangin' Out on the Line" and masterful "Walking Blues." Houston Stackhouse concludes the session with four interesting tunes, three previously unissued on Arhoolie. —*Ron Wynn*

Mississippi Delta Blues Jam in Memphis, Vol. 1 / 1993 / Arhoolie ✦✦✦
Field recording from 1967-68 is best known for Robert Nighthawk. —*Bill Dahl*

Mississippi Delta Blues Jam In Memphis, Vol. 2 / 1993 / Arhoolie ✦✦✦
The more satisfying of the pair, cut in 1967-68. Some of R.L. Burnside's best solo work, impressive country blues by Joe

Callicott (along with sides of his 1930 78) and four items by guitarist Houston Stackhouse and his combo. —*Bill Dahl*

Mississippi Delta Blues, Vol. 1: Blow My Blues Away / 1994 / Arhoolie ✦✦✦✦
George Mitchell recorded several vibrant, distinctive Delta blues performances here. The artists he chronicled ranged from such legendary greats as Robert Nighthawk, Johnny Woods and Fred McDowell to obscure but exciting performers such as Napoleon Strickland, Peck Curtis and Do-Boy Diamond. Their songs were quite simple; many were reworked tunes they had heard and/or played all their lives. They performed with no fanfare, sophisticated support to cover flaws, or pretension. The songs were about heartbreak, anguish, disappointment and indignation, and sometimes about getting drunk, sexual potency, or whatever else came to mind. There are 12 unreleased cuts among these 23 numbers, and the mastering and notes provide an added bonus to this nice set. —*Ron Wynn*

☆ **Mississippi Girls** / Sep. 1991 / Story Of Blues ✦✦✦✦✦
This is an important collection, because it helps fill the gap in the recorded history of blueswomen who played and sang outside of the well-known sphere of the "classic singers" such as Ma Rainey and Bessie Smith. The highlights here are the two recordings of Mattie Delaney, a wonderful singer/guitarist about whom almost nothing is known. Fine also are the more rough-hewn offerings of Rosie Mae Moore, who is accompanied by talented veterans Charlie McCoy and Ishmon Bracey. Although the Geechie Wiley/Elvie Thomas duets are marred by a scratchy background, they also are well worth hearing. —*Larry Hoffman*

Mister Charlie's Blues: 1926–1938 / Yazoo ✦✦✦✦✦
A fascinating exploration of blues-drenched, pre-war hillbilly recordings includes the great fingerpicked guitar of Sam McGee. —*Mark A. Humphrey*

Modern Blues Legends / Jan. 16, 1996 / ORC ✦✦✦
Modern Blues Legends is a solid collection of some of the most popular blues-rock artists of the late '80s and '90s. Featuring favorites like Johnny Winter, Robben Ford, Buddy Guy, Danny Gatton, and the Fabulous Thunderbirds, the album might lean too heavily on rock influences—Big Head Todd & the Monsters and Paul Rodgers contribute tracks, after all—but the music is fine and the disc does give a good feeling of the era. —*Stephen Thomas Erlewine*

Modern Chicago Blues / Testament ✦✦✦✦
Big John Wrencher never recorded much and so *any* documentation on this elusive artist is most welcome. On this compilation, he only appears on two tracks; the first, "Blues Before Sunrise," is a leftover from the October 1964 trio session with Robert Nighthawk and Johnny Young. The other, "I'm Going to Detroit," is another trio effort, but this time featuring Young on mandolin and John Lee Granderson on guitar, and sounds like it could have been taken from a late-'40s Maxwell Street recording session. Comparing this track to Wrencher's solo album shows that the intervening time had done much to coarsen up his approach, especially in the vocal department. Nice photo on the inside of the booklet of Big John playing on the street with Johnny Young, too. —*Cub Koda*

☆ **Mojo Working: The Best Of Ace Blues** / 1995 / Ace ✦✦✦✦✦
This 20-track collection puts together essential cuts by some of the biggest names in the genre. Elmore James, John Lee Hooker, Smokey Hogg, B.B. King, Slim Harpo, Albert King, Lowell Fulson, Lonesome Sundown, Howlin' Wolf, Johnny "Guitar" Watson, Arthur Gunter, Lazy Lester, Pee Wee Crayton, Ike Turner, and Lazy Lester are all represented by at least one track apiece and, in most cases, some of their representative work. A pretty great primer that not only serves as something of a greatest hits package for the novice, but just plain great listening for the hardliners as well. —*Cub Koda*

New Bluebloods / 1987 / Alligator ✦✦✦✦✦
An attempt to document "the next generation of Chicago blues," this is generally a very exciting and successful collection, including the Kinsey Report, Lil' Ed and the Blues Imperials, Valerie Wellington, and several more. —*Niles J. Frantz*

New Orleans Blues: Troubles Troubles / Rounder ✦✦✦✦✦
This is a sampler of late-'50s and early-'60s Ric and Ron label music by Edgar Blanchard, Mercy Baby, and Eddie Lang. —*Hank Davis*

New Orleans Jazz & Heritage Festival: 1976 / 1976 / Rhino ✦✦✦
This features Hopkins live on three tracks, playing a Stratocaster, raw and distorted, dragging a rhythm section by the scruff of the neck. Worth it for these three tracks alone. —*Cub Koda*

News & Blues: Telling It Like It Is / Feb. 1991 / Columbia ✦✦✦✦✦
Like any form of popular music, the blues has reflected the social conditions of the times, sometimes quite explicitly. *News & the Blues* offers 20 songs from the Columbia vaults from between 1927 and 1947. The Depression is reflected often, as expected, but there are also songs about natural disasters, public figures like Joe Louis, World War II, and even the atomic bomb. Memphis Minnie and Bill Gaither even take the step of recording specific tributes to other blues singers (Ma Rainey and Leroy Carr respectively). Many of the performers are well-known—Bessie Smith, Mississippi John Hurt, Big Bill Broonzy, Charlie Patton, Memphis Minnie, Bukka White—and several others are unknown to any but blues scholars (Jack Kelly, Homer Harris, Alfred Fields). Like several of Columbia's anthologies that are loosely grouped under a theme, you don't necessarily have to have a keen interest in the album concept to appreciate the music, which is an above-average gathering of early blues tracks of various styles. —*Richie Unterberger*

Oakland Blues / Arhoolie ✦✦✦✦✦
Fine album spotlighting Bay Area standouts Jerry Wilson, Jimmy McCracklin, and K.C. Douglas in a 1950 performance. —*Bill Dahl*

Old Town Blues, Vol. 1: Downtown Sides / 1993 / Ace ✦✦✦
Twenty-two blues tracks recorded in the 1950s for New York's Old Town label, most of which were unissued at the time. The core of this anthology is the 11 songs by Sonny Terry & Brownie McGhee, who do electrified city blues with an audible influence from Chicago performers like Bo Diddley and Jimmy Reed. It's not the style they're most renowned for, perhaps, but the results are pretty good. The rest of the CD is a hodgepodge of miscellany, including decent raw electric blues from James Wayne, fairly anonymous sides by Little Willie and Bob Gaddy, and a couple of rare Willie Dixon items from an unissued acetate of demos. —*Richie Unterberger*

Old Town Blues Vol. 2: The Uptown Sides / 1994 / Ace ✦✦
A grab-bag of blues sides with a strong R&B influence, recorded for New York's Old Town label between the mid-'50s and mid-'60s. This is aimed squarely at the blues collector/completist. There's nothing especially inept about these sides, but nothing especially captivating either. Nor is there a strong stylistic or instrumental thread connecting the tracks. It's period stuff, by obscure artists like Hal Paige, Ursula Reed, Lester Young (not the jazz great), Larry Dale, and Sam Baker. Wild Bill Moore and Buddy & Ella Johnson, represented by some of their least-known work, are the most recognizable of the bunch. —*Richie Unterberger*

Orig. American Folk Blues Festival / 1962 / PolyGram ✦✦✦✦✦
Recorded live in a studio in Hamburg, Germany, in October 1962. Includes artists involved with that year's American Folk Blues Festival tour, with generally relaxed and reflective performances. The artists include T-Bone Walker, Sonny Terry, and John Lee Hooker. —*Cub Koda*

Original Blues Classics / Original Blues Classics ✦✦✦✦
This 15-track compilation serves as a fine sampler of the OBC label. Included are "Trouble in Mind" (King Curtis), "I've Got Mine" (Pink Anderson), "The Dyin' Crapshooter's Blues" (Blind Willie McTell), and "Say No to the Devil" (Rev. Gary Davis). —*Roundup Newsletter*

Out of the Blue / 1985 / Rykodisc ✦✦✦✦✦
A 17-cut sampler of some of Rounder's blues and blues-related releases of the period, it features "straight" blues from J.B. Hutto, Phillip Walker, and Johnny Copeland; blues-rock from the Nighthawks and George Thorogood; soulful blues from Johnny Adams and Ted Hawkins; plus cuts from Buckwheat Zydeco, piano great James Booker, John Hammond, Solomon Burke, and several more. The Adams, Walker, and Copeland cuts are particularly nice, as is one entry from Marcia Ball and the Legendary Blues Band. —*Niles J. Frantz*

Planet Blues: the World of Blues-Rock / 1993 / Rhythm Safari ✦✦✦
There are so many blues anthologies and samplers currently

available that most, if not all, of the music contained here can be found elsewhere. The disc succeeds in its objective—to show the links between urban blues and modern rock. Indeed, songs like Eric Clapton's "Tribute To Elmore" or Canned Heat's "Dimple" are literally electric blues done by rockers. Likewise, the Bo Diddley, Howlin' Wolf, and Muddy Waters numbers were blueprints fully studied and absorbed by the entire first wave of British invaders. These are fun tracks and worth having, whether you get them here or somewhere else. —*Ron Wynn*

☆ **Play My Juke Box: East Coast Blues (1943–1954)** / Flyright ✦✦✦✦✦
Bruce Bastin's English Flyright label—only one of the magnificent tributaries of his Interstate Music Company—has consistently demonstrated a union of fine scholarship and great music. This collection of mostly little-known East Coast blues artists is no exception. There are seven tracks of singer/guitarists, four harp/guitar duets, four piano/guitar pairings, two guitar duos, and one arresting cut featuring three harps plus vocal. Artists such as Skoodle-Dum-Doo & Sheffield, Boy Green, Robert Lee Westmoreland, Marilyn Scott, and Sonny Jones serve up a startling reminder of all the amazing talent that has gone unrecognized over the years. —*Larry Hoffman*

Pot, Spoon, Pipe And Jug / May 19, 1924–Dec. 1975 / Stash ✦✦✦
The Stash label made its original reputation by releasing around a dozen LPs filled with mostly little-known vintage recordings of jazz and blues artists discussing (often in veiled ways) drugs and sex. This album sticks to the former and is (with two exceptions) from the 1927–41 period. Highlights include a test-pressing version of Cab Calloway's classic "Kickin' the Gong Around," Cab's famous "Reefer Man," Stuff Smith's humorous "You'se a Viper," Lil Green's "Knockin' Myself Out," and Blue Lu Barker's "Don't You Make Me High." —*Scott Yanow*

Prime Chops: Blind Pig Sampler / 1990 / Blind Pig ✦✦✦✦
A 14-track sampler, it has a variety of contemporary blues sounds. —*Niles J. Frantz*

Prime Chops: Blind Pig Sampler, Vol. 2 / 1993 / Blind Pig ✦✦✦✦
Plenty of choice blues, roots rock, gospel, and zydeco. You can sample 19 tracks from the Blind Pig catalogue at a budget price here, including Jimmy Thackery and The Drivers, Joanna Connor, Roy Rogers, Little Mike And The Tornadoes, and more. —*Roch Parisien*

Rare Chicago Blues / May 1, 1993 / Bullseye Blues ✦✦✦✦
Recorded between 1962 and 1968 by Norman Dayron, *Rare Chicago Blues* is an enthralling collection of rare blues from artists like Otis Spann, Little Brother Montgomery, Big Joe Williams, and Robert Pete Williams, as well as several others. Captured live in clubs and on the street, these tracks give a good taste of what real, gritty urban blues sounded like in the '60s and is worthwhile for true blues aficionados. —*Stephen Thomas Erlewine*

Raunchy Business: Hot Nuts & Lollypops / Aug. 1991 / Columbia ✦✦✦✦✦
This is a sampler of risque blues. —*Mark A. Humphrey*

RCA Victor Blues & Rhythm Revue / Dec. 1987 / RCA ✦✦✦✦✦
A great 25-cut cross-section of Nipper's R&B activities 1940–59, the set includes everyone from Count Basie to Little Richard to The Dew Droppers to The Isley Brothers. —*Bill Dahl*

The Real Blues Brothers / 1987 / DCC ✦✦✦✦
This is a nice Vee-Jay collection with representative cuts from Pee Wee Crayton, John Lee Hooker, Jimmy Reed, Lightnin' Hopkins, Billy Boy Arnold, Memphis Slim, and a stray track from Brownie McGhee and Sonny Terry. The big ticket for collectors on this one, however, is the inexplicable bonus of a previously unissued Eddie Taylor number, "Leave This Neighborhood," reason enough for hardcore fans to want to add this one to the collection. —*Cub Koda*

Reefer Madness / Feb. 8, 1924–1944 / Stash ✦✦✦
By the time Stash came out with this LP, its 20th release, one would think that the label had run out of vintage drug and sex songs to reissue. However the quality of these performances is still pretty high and, although some of the musicians were quite obscure, there are also selections from Cow Cow Davenport, Buck Washington, Louis Armstrong (1928's "Muggles"), Mills

Blue Rhythm Band, Mezz Mezzrow, Fats Waller, and Django Reinhardt. This collection is not essential but remains quite fun. —*Scott Yanow*

Reefer Songs: Original Jazz & Blues Vocals / Jun. 17, 1932–Nov. 2, 1945 / Stash ✦✦✦✦✦
This LP was the very first release by the Stash label and, as with its first dozen or so collections, it features vintage material that deals with illicit subject matter. Many of the best marijuana and drug-based recordings are on this set, including Stuff Smith's "Here Comes the Man with the Jive" (which features some hot Jonah Jones trumpet), Trixie Smith's "Jack I'm Mellow," Barney Bigard's "Sweet Marijuana Brown" (which has Art Tatum on piano), Andy Kirk's "All the Jive Is Gone," and Harry "The Hipster" Gibson's classic "Who Put the Benzedrine in Mrs. Murphy's Ovaltine?" Other performers include Cab Calloway, Benny Goodman, Buster Bailey, Sidney Bechet, the Harlem Hamfats, Chick Webb, and Clarence Williams. Some of this material has since been reissued on CD but the original set is still the best. —*Scott Yanow*

☆ **Riot in Blues** / Mobile Fidelity ✦✦✦✦✦
Excellent Lightnin' Hopkins, Sonny Terry, Brownie McGhee, James Wayne, and early Ray Charles scat singing. Partially field-recorded by Bob Shad in the early '50s. The best cuts include "Wayne's Junco Partner" and "Hopkins' Buck Dance Boogie." —*Barry Lee Pearson*

Risky Blues (R&B) / 1971 / King ✦✦✦✦✦
Old King LP boasting ribald early-'50s jump blues by Wynonie Harris, Bull Moose Jackson, etc. —*Bill Dahl*

Rockin' the Blues / ✦✦✦
Terrific 1955 all-R&B lineup includes performances by the Harptones, Linda Hopkins, the Hurricanes, Pearl Woods, Connie Carroll, and the Wanderers in this brisk black & white feature, which clocks in at just over an hour. Lame comedy bits are provided by the ubiquitous F. E. Miller and Mantan Moreland, stars of countless Black films during the '40s. —*Bill Dahl*

Roots 'n Blues/the Retrospective 1925–1950 / Jun. 30, 1992 / Columbia/Legacy ✦✦✦✦✦
Roots 'n Blues: the Retrospective presents five hours of music over four discs, covering the traditional recordings made by Columbia Records and its associated labels from 1925 to 1950. As an all-inclusive survey of American roots music, this set is an invaluable library piece and a good reference, but where this collection really stands out is in its presentation. The collection does a better service than the more academic studies by including a variety of styles—including early string band recordings, spirituals, jugbands, blues, cajun and country music, mixing the better-known artists with the more obscure— and in the end, the diversity makes for good listening as well as a good learning experience. —*Chris Woodstra*

Roots of Rhythm & Blues: A Tribute to the Robert Johnson Era / Sep. 1, 1992 / Columbia/Legacy ✦✦✦✦✦
This live program featured some of the late legend's old partners—Honeyboy Edwards, Johnny Shines, Robert Jr. Lockwood—and some of his contemporary successors, such as Lionel Pitchford, and Cephas and Wiggins paying heartfelt tribute. —*Bill Dahl*

☆ **Roots of Robert Johnson** / 1990 / Yazoo ✦✦✦✦✦
Robert Johnson's small body of recordings have become almost larger than life. Many novice listeners probably think the Delta blues began and ended with him. This 14-song collection traces the origins of Johnson's music, uncovering the roots of his tormented, anguished lyrics, and the origins of his wildly influential guitar style. Some of the finest songs by luminaries like Skip James, Charlie Patton, Son House, Kokomo Arnold, and Lonnie Johnson are included. It's not only of use for Johnson archivists but for anyone interested in the greatest pre-war Delta blues. —*Bruce Boyd Raeburn*

Roots of the Blues / 1977 / New World ✦✦✦
This fine concept recording by Alan Lomax compares an American and a Senegalese (Africa) holler. It also includes elements of work songs, Black string bands, church music, and other styles that fed into the blues before moving on to early blues styles themselves. The rarity of most of the cuts would make this a gem, even without Lomax's analysis. —*David L. Mayers*

St. Louis Blues (1929–1935) / Yazoo ✦✦✦
More fine pre-war blues. —*Mark A. Humphrey*

Screaming Saxophones: Have a Ball / Swingtime ✦✦✦
Most of the tenor saxophonists do not actually scream on this LP but there are plenty of honks, squeals, and roars during a variety of early R&Bish performances. Such colorful players as Joe Houston, Charlie Singleton, Joe Thomas (one of his songs is called "Tearing Hair"), Morris Lane, Paul Bascomb, Bumps Myers, and baritonist Leo Parker are heard at their most exuberant. Accessible and frequently exciting music. —*Scott Yanow*

The Shouters / Savoy ✦✦✦
1940s and 1950s jump blues from Gatemouth Moore, H-Bomb Ferguson, Eddie Mack, and Nappy Brown, whose scorching rockers are among the highlights of this two-LP set. —*Bill Dahl*

Shoutin' Swingin' & Makin' Love / MCA ✦✦✦✦✦
Included are Jimmy Witherspoon, Al Hibbler, and other urbane blues-jazz belters in full cry on Chess. —*Mark A. Humphrey*

Shouting the Blues / 1992 / Specialty ✦✦✦✦✦
Jump blues feast; Joe Turner, etc... —*Bill Dahl*

Sissy Man Blues: Str't & Gay Blues / Vintage Jazz ✦✦✦
Twenty-five straight and gay blues from 1924–1941 are featured, by various artists. —*Jas Obrecht*

☆ **The Slide Guitar: Bottles, Knives, & Steel** / Feb. 1991 / Columbia/Legacy ✦✦✦✦✦
A super collection of slide guitar pieces in such styles as blues, hokum, gospel, and dance songs from Blind Willie Johnson, Tampa Red, Bukka White, and other bottleneck masters. The Leadbelly cut, "Packing Trunk Blues," shows off his masterful slide style. For every blues guitarist. —*Barry Lee Pearson*

Bottles, Knives & Steel, Vol. 2 / Columbia/Legacy ✦✦✦✦✦
This is another excellent volume of various styles of blues slide guitar from Columbia's *Roots & Blues* series. —*AMG*

Slidin' ... Some Slide / 1948–1993 / Rounder ✦✦✦
Rounder's recent anthology of vintage and modern slide guitar playing is neither a disposable batch of recent hits nor merely a showcase for guitar freaks; it is a wonderful collection documenting the way bottleneck and slide styles have evolved. The sampler contains classics from Muddy Waters, Elmore James, Earl Hooker, J.B. Hutto, Hop Wilson, and Hound Dog Taylor that are either transcendent or delightful. They have also chosen songs from contemporary acts that demonstrate real craft and appreciation for the style; George Thorogood's nearly eight-minute workout on "Delaware Slide" and Sonny Landreth's "Zydeco Shuffle" are grinding, stunning treatments. This is one sampler with real musical and historical value. —*Ron Wynn*

Smackin' That Wax: the Kangaroo Records Story... / Collectables ✦✦✦✦
Obscure but solid '50s and '60s Texas blues and R&B, it includes a very early Albert Collins single. —*Bill Dahl*

Sorry But...: Women's RR Blues / Dec. 4, 1923–Feb. 9, 1942 / Rosetta ✦✦✦
Subtitled "Women's Railroad Blues," this LP consists of 15 songs that feature female vocalists singing about trains. Often the subject matter has to do with boyfriends who were able to escape the South while the females were stuck home. Although there is a certain amount of repetition, there are many rarities on this album with generally fine performances from Trixie Smith, Clara Smith, Bessie Smith, Ada Brown, Sippie Wallace, Martha Copeland, Bessie Jackson, Lucille Bogan, Blue Lou Barker, Sister Rosetta Tharpe, and Nora Lee King. An interesting set with colorful liner notes. —*Scott Yanow*

The Soul of R & B Revue: Live at the Lonestar Roadhouse / Dec. 1992 / Shanachie ✦✦✦
OK recreation of '60s soul sound. —*Bill Dahl*

The Soul of Texas Blues Women / 1991 / Collectables ✦✦✦
This very interesting, although uneven collection includes female blues and soul vocalists recorded between 1961 and 1970. —*Niles J. Frantz*

The Sound of the Delta / Jun. 1966 / Testament ✦✦✦✦
Blues scholar Pete Welding assembled these 19 recordings—most solo, all acoustic, most prominently featuring guitar and vocal—between 1963 and 1965, just as the blues revival was gathering steam. This isn't the best Delta blues compilation, as an introduction or a general sampler. If you can't get enough of

the stuff, though, it certainly stands up well. Big Joe Williams and Fred McDowell are the only well-known performers, but the others—obscure names like Arthur Weston and the delightfully raw-voiced Ruby McCoy—are generally in the same league. It's well recorded, and contains a reasonable variety of styles. The CD reissue adds bonus tracks by Williams and Avery Brady that were not included on the original version. —*Richie Unterberger*

Southern Blues / Savoy ✦✦✦✦✦
A wide-ranging 1950s blues/R&B two-LP set, including Billy Wright, John Lee Hooker, Huey Smith, Earl King. —*Bill Dahl*

Southern Rhythm & Rock / Rhino ✦✦✦
Southern Rhythm & Rock (The Best of Excello Records—Vol. 2) is the second volume of the Excello Records collection, with its companion *Sound of the Swamp*. This volume rounds up some wild and woolly R&B obscurities. —*John Floyd*

1929–1937 / 1989 / Story Of Blues ✦✦✦✦✦
St. Louis's red-light district became a magnet for many of the greatest blues pianists and singers of the era. This 19-track CD features many of the best of them. Well-known and accomplished ticklers such as Roosevelt Sykes, Henry Brown, Aaron "Pinetop" Sparks, and the High Sheriff himself, Peetie Wheatstraw, play host to singers such as Mary Johnson, Elizabeth Johnson, Dorothy Trowbridge, and Alice Moore—who, despite their relative obscurity, are quite talented and turn in more than a few minor classics. Spicing the instrumental mix are trombonist Ike Rodgers and guitarist Lonnie Johnson. Despite the poor sound quality of the first four tracks, this music is well chosen and highly recommended. —*Larry Hoffman*

Stars of British Blues, Vol. 1 / 1992 / K-Tel ✦✦✦
Back before Clapton was declared to be God and Rod to be the Bod and Jimmy Page was still a session player, each was making a name for himself in the fledgling British blues movement. This disc looks at some of the lesser-known projects by these and other players. Clapton is represented by "I'm Your Witchdoctor" (from his Bluesbreaker days), "Draggin' My Tail" (a duet with Jimmy Page), and a solo track, "A Tribute to Elmore (James)". The disc also includes cuts by Jeff Beck, Rod Stewart, and the Savoy Brown Blues Band. This album really deserves liner notes, but... —*Jim Worbois*

Stars of British Blues, Vol. 2 / 1993 / K-Tel ✦✦✦
More fun from the British blues movement of the early '60s. In addition to more from Clapton, Beck and Page, this disc includes tracks by future Rolling Stones sideman Nicky Hopkins and the influential Cyril Davies. Again, this disc would have benefitted from liner notes but that doesn't detract from the music. —*Jim Worbois*

The Stax Blues Brothers / 1970 / Stax ✦✦✦✦✦
A decent collection of Stax blues artists of the '70s, it includes Albert King, Johnnie Taylor, and others. —*Dan Heilman*

Stax Blues Mast / Stax ✦✦✦
A decent overview of Stax blues artists; inferior to individual records by Albert King and Little Milton. —*Ron Wynn*

Stompin' / ✦✦✦✦✦
So far there are nine volumes of *Stompin'* which are all collections of very raw blues records from the '40s–'60s with artists such as Screamin' Joe Neal, Smokey Smothers, Nat The Cool Cat. These are on LP and great records, don't pass them up if you can find 'em. (Import from England) *Stompin' Records: Vol. 1–9*—released over the last five years or so. —*Richard Meyer*

Stone Rock Blues / 1994 / MCA/Chess ✦✦✦✦
"The original recordings of songs covered by the Rolling Stones" is understandably heavy on the blues, R&B, and early rock & roll chestnuts they gleaned from Chess Records. Chuck Berry and Muddy Waters are, unsurprisingly, the most heavily represented artists here; seven Chuck tunes, five by Muddy (one of which, "Rollin' Stone," wasn't actually recorded by the Stones, but is included because it inspired their name). This 18-song collection is filled out by a couple of Bo Diddley tracks, Howlin' Wolf's "Little Red Rooster," and three songs outside of Chess' Black music axis: Dale Hawkins' rockabilly classic "Suzie Q," Buddy Holly's "Not Fade Away" (which of course relied heavily on the Bo Diddley beat), and Arthur Alexander's early soul ballad "You Better Move On." What this collection doesn't have are the early soul classics by Otis Redding, Sam Cooke, Wilson Pickett, Marvin Gaye, and more obscure singers like Barbara Lynn and Gene

Allison that formed another vital component of their early cover material. It's missing a few stray tracks by Slim Harpo, Rufus Thomas, Hank Snow, Larry Williams, and others that were covered by the Stones on their early albums. And it doesn't have Berry's "Let It Rock," which was available (albeit briefly) on a British maxi-single in the early '70s. But Chuck, Muddy, and Bo were their greatest influences, when you get down to it, and this is a handy basic primer of the blueprints for The Stones' early repertoire, with decent liner notes. —*Richie Unterberger*

☆ **The Story of the Blues** / Columbia ✦✦✦✦✦
An excellent blues sampler, it ranges from pre-war to the '60s, offering a broader palette of "shades of blue" than most. —*Mark A. Humphrey*

Straight and Gay / Dec. 10, 1924–Jun. 30, 1941 / Stash ✦✦✦
The Stash label had, by the release of this LP in 1979, almost totally exhausted its collection of vintage recordings dealing with the subject matters of drug and sex. However with titles such as "Anybody Here Want to Try My Cabbage" (featuring singer Maggie Jones accompanied by Louis Armstrong), "Take Your Hand Off It," "Sissy Man," and "Two Old Maids in a Folding Bed," there were obviously still a few fiery titles left to be reissued. Highlights include Sippie Wallace's famous "I'm a Mighty Tight Woman" and Victoria Spivey's initial recording "Black Snake Blues"; the other important performers are Lonnie Johnson, Lil Johnson, Washboard Sam, Mae Glover, Blanche Calloway, the Hokum Boys, Papa Charlie Jackson, Josh White, Ma Rainey (with Doc Cheatham on soprano in 1926), Monette Moore, Blind Willie McTell, and Lucille Bogan. —*Scott Yanow*

Streetwalking Blues / Dec. 9, 1924–1956 / Stash ✦✦✦
One of many Stash LPs that reissued vintage recordings dealing with sexual topics, this album has performances by many fine blues and jazz singers including Memphis Minnie, Maggie Jones ("Good Time Flat Blues" with Louis Armstrong), Virginia Liston, Lil Johnson, Sam Theard, Billie Pierce (from 1956), Clarence Williams, Lonnie Johnson (1941's "Crowin' Rooster Blues"), Georgia White, Ma Rainey, Clara Smith, Irene Scruggs, Bertha "Chippie" Hill, and Lucille Bogan. With titles such as "I've Got What It Takes," "I'm in the Racket," "Kitchen Mechanic Blues," and "Shave 'Em Dry," one gets the idea what this album is about pretty quickly. Most of these formerly rare performances (some of which have been reissued by Stash on their Jass subsidiary) are quite enjoyable. —*Scott Yanow*

Sun Records: The Blues Years / Charly ✦✦✦✦✦
Gigantic nine-record box with a 44-page booklet, this comes the closest to documenting the wide breadth of blues recordings done by Sam Phillips at the Sun studios in Memphis during the early '50s. A landmark achievement. —*Cub Koda*

Sun Records Harmonica Classics / 1990 / Rounder ✦✦✦✦✦
Brilliant compilation of blues sides cut at the Sun studios in the early '50s, featuring indispensable tracks by Walter Horton ("Easy" being one of the greatest harmonica instrumentals of all time), Joe Hill Louis and Doctor Ross. —*Cub Koda*

Superblues: All-Time Classic Blues Hits, Vol. 1 / 1990 / Stax ✦✦✦✦✦
The three-volume *Superblues* series may not have enough rare/unusual items for the collector, or enough of a solid connecting thread for the more general listener. For those who just want a varied assortment of top-notch blues hits (mostly from the '50s and '60s) in their collection, though, they're good deals. They cover a pretty wide territory of both top blues stars and lesser-known singers, and draw more from urban R&B- and jump blues-influenced cuts than most similar compilations. They also have generous playing times, and offer enough liner notes to provide a context for non-experts. Vol. 1 has classics by B.B. King, Ike & Tina Turner, Jimmy Reed, Koko Taylor, Bobby "Blue" Bland, Albert King, Little Milton, Howlin' Wolf, and others. —Richie Unterberger

Superblues: All-Time Classic Blues Hits, Vol. 2 / 1991 / Stax ✦✦✦✦✦
More soul and R&B influences are heard on this volume than the first, though it's not a detriment. The 18 tracks include prize items by Guitar Slim, Lloyd Price, Lowell Fulson, Elmore James, and Sonny Boy Williamson, with some bluesy Southern soul by O.V. Wright and Johnnie Taylor. Also has some little-anthologized gems, most notably Gene Allison's "You Can Make It If You Try" (covered by the Rolling Stones on their first album) and

Jimmy Hughes's magnificent bluesy soul ballad, "Steal Away." —
Richie Unterberger

Superblues: All-Time Classic Blues Hits, Vol. 3 / 1995 / Stax
✦✦✦✦✦
Another solid outing in the *Superblues* series. The 19 cuts
include classics by Little Walter, Elmore James, Jimmy Reed, and
Billy Boy Arnold ("I Wish You Would"); vintage jump blues by
Jimmy Liggins, Joe Liggins, and Camille Howard; and soul blues
by Little Johnny Taylor and Little Milton. This has a significantly higher percentage of obscure names than the previous two
volumes, with worthy items (some of which were one-shot R&B
hits) by Mercy Dee Walton, Larry Dale, Eddie Taylor, Larry
Birdsong, Larry Davis, Ted Taylor, Frankie Lee Sims, and others.
— *Richie Unterberger*

Sweet Home Chicago / Nov. 1988 / Delmark ✦✦✦✦✦
Solid '60s sides by Magic Sam, Eddie Shaw, Luther Allison, Louis
Myers. — *Bill Dahl*

Talkin' Trash / 1990 / Greasy ✦✦✦
A very obscure R&B compilation with great irreverent jump and
jivey blues from 1954-1963. The title cut is worth the price, but
check out "Your Wire's Been Tapped" and "Roll Dem Bones." —
Richard Meyer

A Taste of the Blues, Vol. 1 / 1993 / Vee-Jay ✦✦✦✦✦
At 25 tracks, 69 minutes of running time, and musician-histori-
an Billy Vera doing the compilation, there's little to quibble
about here, as all the selections are first-rate. Kicking off with the
one-two punch of Jimmy Reed's "Boogie in the Dark" and Eddie
Taylor's "Bad Boy," other highlights include J.B. Lenoir's thinly
veiled rewrite of Ray Charles' classic ("Do What I Say") and the
hopelessly obscure Morris Pejoe's "Hurt My Feelings," while Billy
(The Kid) Emerson's "Every Woman I Know (Is Crazy About an
Automobile)" just may be one of the finest car songs of all time.
Add to the mix Snooky Pryor's "Judgement Day," a pair of
Elmore James classics (the original versions of "It Hurts Me Too"
and "The 12 Year Old Boy"), Billy Boy Arnold's "Rockinitis," John
Lee Hooker's live at Newport performance of "Tupelo," and Pee
Wee Crayton's scorching guitar solo on "The Telephone Is
Ringing," and you have a compilation that's mighty hard to beat.
Sound quality on all this is first-rate, thanks to the digital remas-
tering work of Bob Fisher. — *Cub Koda*

A Taste of the Blues, Vol. 2 / Oct. 1993 / Vee-Jay ✦✦✦✦
A 26-track comp of more obscure and rare Vee-Jay sides, this
time featuring a previously unissued Snooky Pryor track, "You
Tried To Ruin Me." Also includes tracks from Elmore James,
Eddie Taylor, and Pee Wee Crayton, plus the added bonus of the
first time CD issue of Jimmy Reed's "I'm Gonna Ruin You." — *Cub
Koda*

Texas Blues / 1992 / Arhoolie ✦✦✦✦✦
This excellent collection features eight little-known blues artists
who recorded for Bill Quinn's Gold Star label in Houston. There
are 27 tracks in all—split unequally between acoustic
guitar/vocal (16) and piano/vocal (11). Lil' Son Jackson is perhaps the best known, and his ten tracks are all good, rocking
acoustic blues. There are also tunes by L.C. Williams, a polished
and imaginative guitarist, and one magnificent track by the
obscure Buddy Chiles. — *Larry Hoffman*

Texas Country Blues 1948-1951 / 1994 / Flyright ✦✦✦✦✦
Another entry in Flyright's ongoing quest to present the rare and
the wonderful, this collects some impossibly hard-to-find Texas
78s originally released on short-lived, dime-store labels like
Talent, Freedom, Nucraft, ARC, Bluebonnet, and the colorfully
named Oklahoma Tornado! Honeyboy Edwards and Frankie Lee
Sims are the only "big names" aboard, but the remainder of the
tracks featuring Rattlesnake Cooper, James Tisdom, Andrew
Thomas, Willie Lane, Monister Parker, Leroy "Country" Johnson
and others clearly illustrate how big the looming presence (both
commercially and artistically) of Lightnin' Hopkins already was
at this early stage of the game. — *Cub Koda*

Texas Guitar Greats / 1991 / Collectables ✦✦✦
Texas blues, boogie, and blues-rock recorded from 1962-1988,
this release includes several previously unreleased cuts, with
Johnny Winter, Freddie King, Gatemouth Brown, and Johnny
Copeland, among others. — *Niles J. Frantz*

☆ **Texas Piano Blues 1929-48** / Story Of Blues ✦✦✦✦✦
This is a good collection of piano-accompanied vocals sporting

bluesmen who worked the lumber camps and oil fields of rural
Texas, as well as the red-light districts of cities like Galveston
and Houston. Big Boy Knox shows a strong city influence in his
decorative right-hand work, as does Robert Cooper, whose playing points to the influence of Fats Waller. Joe Pullem is on board
with his hit, "Black Gal," which is perhaps overstated by three
takes and a variation. The vocals are good, however, and the
piano playing is uniformly excellent. Stylistically, this music falls
somewhere between ragtime, blues, and vaudeville. — *Larry
Hoffman*

Texas Sax Greats / Collectables ✦✦✦✦✦
Slightly inconsistent but rewarding R&B sax compilation; Big
Sambo, Link Davis, and Henry Hayes provide best moments. —
Bill Dahl

Them Dirty Blues / Jass ✦✦✦
The thin line between provocative and obscene, suggestive and
disgusting, gets examined and stretched throughout the 50
tracks presented on the 1989 two-disc set *Them Dirty Blues*.
Many of these songs could be deemed sexist using a '90s mea-
suring stick; on the other hand, many are also quite funny, language notwithstanding. They are reflective of a time when audiences were willing to accept songs with either overt carnal
themes or with an implicit, yet rather pronounced sexuality. —
Ron Wynn

Tomato Delta Blues Package / 1994 / Tomato/Rhino ✦✦
While there's no denying the greatness of the performers spotlighted on this 16-track anthology, Tomato/Rhino played a bit
loose with its definition of "Delta blues." Leadbelly, for example,
was more of a classic folk singer with blues ties, while Sonny
Terry and Brownie McGhee were Piedmont blues performers,
and the songs by Howlin' (not Howling) Wolf and the Little
Walter/Otis Rush duo aren't Delta blues either. Licensing problems probably reared their heads here; witness the absence of
Charlie Patton, Robert Johnson, Son House, Tommy Johnson, or
Sonny Boy Williamson (John Lee). There's still some good material, notably Arthur "Big Boy" Crudup, Mississippi Fred
McDowell, Johnny Shines, Mississippi John Hurt, and decent
(though hardly sensational) Lightnin' Hopkins and John Lee
Hooker. — *Ron Wynn*

Tuesday's Just As Bad / K-Tel ✦✦✦
Companion volume to K-Tel's *Best of the Blues*, this one fea-
tures 10 more indispensable cuts from Muddy Waters, Howlin'
Wolf, Elmore James, B.B. King, and others. Great listening even
if you already have the songs on other compilations. — *Cub
Koda*

Voice of the Blues . . . / Dec. 1976 / Yazoo ✦✦✦✦
Voice of the Blues—Bottleneck Guitar Masterpieces contains an
eclectic hodgepodge of pre-war slide-guitar styles, encompassing
everything from blues and Hawaiian to ragtime and country. —
John Floyd

Wake Up Dead Man: Black Convict Worksongs from Texas /
Rounder ✦✦✦✦✦
African-American worksongs were more than a functional tool
or a root of the blues. They were a monument to the
indomitability of the human spirit, and African survival into the
20th century. They're long gone now, but not forgotten by any-
body who's heard these superb examples from the 1960s, or
Alan Lomax's earlier recordings from Parchman Farm in
Mississippi. Fine notes are included, too. — *John Storm Roberts,
Original Music*

We Love You Bobby: A Tribute To Bobby Bland / 1992 /
Collectables ✦✦✦
There's not much Bland influence on many of them, but these
mostly '60s Texas R&B sides are soulful nonetheless. — *Bill Dahl*

Weed: A Rare Batch / Oct. 1928-Nov. 1947 / Stash ✦✦✦
As is usual with most of Stash's earliest releases, much of the
music on this LP refers in one way or another to drugs in its
lyrics but these jazz and blues performances from the swing era
are most notable for the fine playing by a wide variety of artists.
There is one selection apiece from Chick Webb (Ella Fitzgerald
singing "When I Get Low I Get High"), Tampa Red, Oscar's
Chicago Swingers, Carl Martin, the Harlem Hamfats, Julia Lee,
Sammy Price, Cootie Williams (a hot version of "Ol' Man River"),
Adrian Rollini, Lorraine Walton, Yack Taylor ("Knockin' Myself
Out"), Blue Steele, and Lucille Bogan ("Pot Hound Blues"). Many
of these selections have yet to be reissued on CD. — *Scott Yanow*

☆ **White Country Blues, 1926–1938...** / Apr. 27, 1993 / Columbia/Legacy ✦✦✦✦✦
Country artists sing pre-war blues-influenced songs. —*Bill Dahl*

Wizards from the Southside / Chess ✦✦✦✦✦
This is a great sampler of the finest in classic Chicago blues—perfect for those listeners who are looking for a taste of the best of the genre. Included are "Evil" by Howlin' Wolf (two wolf-tracks in all); "Rollin' and Tumblin'" by Muddy Waters (five); "Walkin' the Boogie" by John Lee Hooker (one); "Bring It on Home" by Sonny Boy Williamson (one); "I'm a Man" by Bo Diddley (two); and "Mellow Down Easy" by Little Walter (two). All of these fabulous sides were cut between 1950-61—the Golden Era of South side Chicago blues. —*Larry Hoffman*

Wrapped in My Baby / 1989 / Pearl Flapper ✦✦✦✦✦
Basement rehearsal recordings from the early '50s for the United/States labels, featuring Morris Pejoe's raw 'n rockin' "Let's Get High" from a full unissued session, plus four amazing sides from Arthur "Big Boy" Spires. Another missing chapter of Chicago Blues history brought to light, simply incredible. —*Cub Koda*

GROOVE AND BLUES IN JAZZ

By Michael Erlewine

Music is food for the soul. It is one of the best medicines that I know of and the better the music, the better I feel. Hearing the good stuff makes all the difference. And that is what this book is all about–how to locate the best blues music. Blues is so radical–such a root music–that it fuses with and gives rise to other music genres with ease. Jazz critics point out that the roots of jazz can be found in the blues. This article is about where in jazz blues lovers can hear and feel those roots–the blues in jazz.

A little background on where I am coming from: I have been a blues and jazz lover for over 37 years. In the late '50s and very early '60s there was a strong jazz scene in Ann Arbor, MI, where I grew up. This was before liquor by the glass became legal in 1963, after which a lot of the jazz scene moved into the clubs. Most any night of the week, but in particular on weekends, there was live jazz played in houses and apartments. Teenagers like myself were tolerated and we hung out. Players like Bob James, Ron Brooks, Bob Pozar, and Bob Detwiler were playing straight-up bop and exploring some cool jazz. The music and the parties often went on all night. On occasion, I heard Cannonball Adderley play in one of the many Detroit clubs like the Minor Key. Jazz records were big, too. I can remember staying up all night listening to John Coltrane's *My Favorite Things* album over and over when it first came out. This was about 1960.

I fell in with the folk scene in the early '60s and managed to hitchhike all over the country several times. A fantastic guitarist by the name of Perry Lederman, a young singer/songwriter by the name of Bob Dylan, and I hitched together for a stretch. Later I helped to put on the first Bob Dylan concert in Ann Arbor. During that time, I hung out with the New Lost City Ramblers, Ramblin' Jack Elliot, the Country Gentlemen, Joan Baez, and some other great folk artists that you may never have heard of.

It was in those years that I got introduced to blues and gospel music. The Swan Silvertones, an a cappella gospel group of infinite beauty, had an enormous effect on me in 1964 when I first heard their records. I had also been listening to classical music for a number of years, but had no real guidance. I spent all of 1964 listening to and learning in depth about classical music from a real expert. Then in 1965 I helped to form a band called the Prime Movers. Although we never recorded, we were no slouch. Iggy Pop was our drummer, avant-garde composer "Blue" Gene Tyranny our keyboardist, music columnist Dan Erlewine played lead guitar, Jack Dawson (later in the Siegel-Schwall Blues Band) was on bass, and I sang and played amplified harmonica.

Sometime in 1965 we heard the Paul Butterfield Blues Band live. That changed my life. We got to know those guys and they introduced us to all of the blues we had not yet found out for ourselves. We became, in an instant, the Prime Movers Blues Band. That was a time.

The net effect of all of this was that, during the 1960s, I listened to blues records day and night trying to learn to play the licks. And I just loved the music. In the mid-'60s, thanks to Bob Koester of Delmark Records, I heard players like Little Walter, Magic Sam, Junior Wells, and many others live in the Chicago clubs. Later, working with various blues and jazz festivals, I had the good fortune to interview (audio and video) just about any blues player you could name that was around back then, and most of them still were.

This article is about blues in jazz, and I am getting to that. My main love is the blues and it took me some time to get much into jazz. In the beginning about the only way I could hear jazz was through a blues filter, so any jazz I got into had to have those blues elements. Now that I know my way around the jazz catalog, I know that it contains some real treasures for blues lovers. But don't expect the standard 12-bar blues progression. Blue notes are found in jazz, but seldom in the form we are used to in blues recordings. It is the blues as a feeling, the soulful experience of the blues and gospel elements that can be found in jazz. So, I am writing this for blues lovers who may want to explore jazz through the same blues doorway I went through.

The jazz I love is the blues in jazz, whether that means bluesy jazz, funky jazz, original funk, or soul jazz–terms which I will explain in due course. I tend not to like (very much) jazz that does not have some kind of blues or modal element in it. Swing and bop, to the degree that they lack the roots sound of blues and gospel, fail to hold my attention. I like my jazz with blues, please.

Something I realized some time ago is that jazz (and most kinds of music) are either energizing or calming in their overall effect. If you are the kind of person who needs something to get you moving (to energize you), then you will be attracted to music that is agitating and energizing, like marches, Dixieland, bop, free jazz, and other forms of progressive jazz. It appeals to those who need that cup of coffee in life–get a move on! It stirs you up.

However, if you are a person (like me) who tends to be very active and sometimes even hyper, then you need music to relax and calm you, like blues, original funk, soul jazz–groove music. It helps to get you in a soothing groove that dissipates energy–relief! Regardless of the fact that as a person we may (in general) be drawn to music that either stimulates or calms us, at times all of us may need some pick-me-up music and at other times some slow-me-down stuff.

You will find that the above (admittedly simplistic) concept works very well. Blues and the blues that is in jazz (for the most part) has to do with the release and expression of feelings. The effect is calming to the system. It is "get down" and relaxin' music. Here is a brief tour of the bluesy stuff in jazz.

An Abbreviated History of Blues in Jazz

This is an abbreviated history because I want to just skip over the standard playing-the-blues-progression in jazz stuff. There is not much of it anyway. If you like blues, you already know that by now. For now, we will also pass on all of the old-time blues found in traditional jazz–the early New Orleans jazz. There is plenty of great old blues and blues-like music to hear there, and you will want to hear it someday. But it is just too much like the blues that you already know. The same goes for what few blues tunes came out of the swing and big-band era. You don't need a guide to check swing blues tunes out because there are not that many of them. When you can find them, they are pretty much straight-ahead blues songs or tunes played with a big band. Further, the arranged feeling of the big band is not up to the impromptu kind of blues feeling you may be used to, so let's pass on that too.

When I speak of blues in jazz, I mean some get-down funky blues sounds in jazz that you have not heard before, so let's just get to that. If this history stuff bores you, skip over it and just read the recommended albums list. Start finding and listening to some of the picks. As mentioned, we will pass over the earlier forms of jazz including the New Orleans varieties, Dixieland, and swing. However, since a lot of the bluesier jazz that may interest you grew out of bop (bebop), you will need to know what bop is and how that musical style came to be. We will start there.

Bop (bebop)–Bop distinguished itself from the popular big-band swing music out of which it emerged by the fact that it is most often played in small groups. You can hear each of the players as separate sounds. And while swing can have a groove that soothes you, bop is wake-me-up music. Its faster tempos, more elaborate melodies, and complex harmonies do not tend to establish a groove. It is more frenetic, even frantic, than swing. In other words, this is not relaxin' music. Bop has an attitude.

Unlike the large swing bands where there were a few featured soloists, most members of the small combo could and did solo–democratic. In addition to an increase in improvisation and solo virtuosity, there was little dependence on arrangements. And fast tempos too. Bop is more energetic (read agitating) than swing, with the rhythm section keeping the time on the ride cymbal. Bop tunes can be very fast, often with elaborate harmonies and complex chord changes that take an expert player to negotiate. In fact, fluency in bop became the benchmark of the young jazz musician. Bop is sophisticated music that can be, for many, somewhat of an acquired taste. In this respect it resembles classical music. Here are some bop artists and sample albums of them at their best:

Bop originators:

Charlie Parker (just about any album; the box sets are the best)
Dizzy Gillespie, *Dizziest*/Bluebird
Thelonious Monk, *Thelonious with John Coltrane*/OJC
Bud Powell, *Genius of Powell Vol. 1*/Polygram
Dexter Gordon, *Our Man in Paris*/Blue Note
Miles Davis, *First Miles*/Savoy
Fats Navarro, *The Fabulous Fats Navarro, Vol 1–2*/Blue Note

Sonny Stitt, *Constellation*/Muse
J.J. Johnson, *The Eminent Jay Jay Johnson Vol. 1*/Blue Note
Max Roach, *Freedom Now Suite*/Columbia
Lucky Thompson, *Lucky Strikes!*/Prestige
Tad Dameron, *Mating Call*/Prestige

1950s Bop Players:

Sonny Rollins, *Newk's Time*/Blue Note
Jackie McLean, *Let Freedom Ring*/Blue Note
Oscar Peterson, *The Trio*/Pablo
Clifford Brown, *Brownie*/Emarcy
Phil Woods, *Pairing Off*/Prestige
Kenny Dorham, *Una Mas*/Blue Note
Barry Harris, *Live in Tokyo*/Xanadu
Tommy Flanagan, *Thelonica*/Enja

1970-1980s Bop Revival:

Richie Cole, *New York Afternoon-Alto Madness*/Muse
Chris Hollyday, *Ho, Brother*/Jazzbeat

Blues in Bop:

Thelonious Monk, *The Thelonious Monk Trio*/Prestige
Miles Davis & Milt Jackson, *Bag's Groove*/Prestige
Miles Davis, *Walkin'*/Prestige
Horace Silver, *Senor Blues*/Blue Note

Hard Bop–Hard bop was a reaction to the somewhat brittle and intellectual nature of straight bop. Hard bop distinguished itself from bop by its simple melodies, slower tempos, and avoidance of the (by then) cliched bop chord changes. The constant uptempo frenetic quality of bop pieces is absent. Tunes are often in the minor mode, much slower paced, and often moody–more feeling and thoughtful. Hard bop reaches into the blues and gospel tradition for substance to slow the up-tempo bop music down, stretch the time out, and imbue the music with more feeling. It was as if jazz had once again found its roots and been nourished. The public thought so too, because it was more approachable than bop. Hard bop is one big step toward establishing a groove, but it lacks what has come to be known as a groove, as in "groove" music. Blues lovers will appreciate the more bluesy nature of hard bop, but probably still yearn for more blues yet.

Hard Bop Pioneers:

Horace Silver, *Pieces of Silver*/Blue Note
Art Blakey and the Jazz Messengers, *Moanin'*/Blue Note
Cannonball Adderley Quintet, *Quintet at the Lighthouse*/Landmark
Nat Adderley, *Work Song*/Riverside
Art Farmer, *Meet the Jazztet*/Chess
Crusaders, *Freedom Sounds*/Atlantic
Lou Donaldson, *Blues Walk*/Blue Note
Kenny Dorham, *Trumpet Toccata*/Blue Note
Donald Byrd, *House of Byrd*/Prestige

Coltrane-Influenced Hard Bop:

Wayne Shorter, *Native Dancer*/Columbia
Freddie Hubbard, *Hub-Tones*/Blue Note
McCoy Tyner, *Sahara*/Milestone
Herbie Hancock, *Maiden Voyage*/Blue Note
Joe Henderson, *Page One*/Blue Note
Weather Report (Joe Zawinul), *Mysterious Traveler*/Columbia

Mainstream Hard Bop:

Sonny Rollins, *Saxophone Colossus and More*/OJC
John Coltrane, *Blue Trane*/Blue Note
Wynton Kelly, *Kelly Blue*/Riverside
Clifford Jordan, *Glass Bead Game*/Strata-East
Booker Ervin, *The Book Cooks*/Affinity
George Coleman, *Amsterdam After Dark*/Timeless
Charlie Rouse, *Two Is One*/Strata-East
Harold Land, *The Fox*/Contemporary
Blue Mitchell, *The Thing to Do*/Blue Note
Kenny Dorham, *Afro-Cuban*/Blue Note
Oliver Nelson, *Soul Battle*/Prestige
Hank Mobley, *Soul Station*/Blue Note
Wes Montgomery, *Incredible Jazz Guitar of Wes Montgomery*/Riverside

Funky Jazz–Some hard-bop players, like pianist Horace Silver, began to include even more feeling in their playing by adding blues riffs and various elements from gospel music to their playing. Silver, considered by many to be the father of funk, describes funk: "Funky means earthy, blues-based. It may not be blues itself, but it has that down-home feel to it. Playing funky has nothing to do with style; it's an approach to playing ... 'Soul' is the same basically, but there's an added dimension of feeling and spirit to soul–an in-depth-ness. A soulful player might be funky or he might not be."

The hard bop jazz that they were playing became, in Silver's hands, still more earthy, bluesy or, as it was called, "funky". This was jazz, but with a funky flavor. It is quite easy to distinguish this funky jazz from the all-out jazz funk described below. I really like funky jazz because it sometimes has a groove, but I love jazz funk better because in that music there is a total groove.

Horace Silver, *Song for My Father*/Blue Note
Cannonball Adderley, *Somethin' Else*/Blue Note
Nat Adderley, *Work Song*/Riverside
Bobby Timmons, *Moanin'*/Milestone

The Blues Groove—Groove Music

The whole thing about groove music is that everything exists to establish and maintain the groove. Solos, egos, instruments–what have you–only exist to lay down the groove and to get in it. There is a steady constant beat that can become drone-like or trance-like. You get in a groove and you stay in the groove and that feels good. There are no absolute rules about what makes groove music. Anything can happen as long as the effect is to put you in and keep you in the groove. It often has a Hammond organ in the sound, but not always. It can have any number of instruments doing all kinds of solos and whatnot as long as these things don't break the groove. Everything exists to create and maintain the groove. Blues lovers tend to like groove music because the blues is nothing but a groove.

Groove music can be uptempo or slow, bright or dark, but the net effect of getting in a groove is always to satisfy and relax. There is always a constant rhythm section driving the groove, invariably danceable. Grooves have a funky, earthy flavor and blues and gospel elements are essential. All grooves are bluesy, by definition. It can be as funky and nasty as you want to be, but groove is not stir-it-up music. It is always cool-you-down music. If it is not relaxing, then it is not groove. Which is not to say that groove is not energetic or fast paced. It may sound wild, but the final effect is a groove. Although I hesitate to characterize it

this way, groove music is almost a little trance-like. The result of the funkiest, baddest piece of groove music is a bit of clear sailing–relaxation. Get in the groove! That's the place to BE.

Original Funk/Soul Jazz–The transformation of bop did not always stop with hard bop or even funkified jazz. Some players dove rather than dipped into the roots music and an even more bluesy music was born that came to be called funk or soul jazz. For the first time, we are talking real groove music.

Funkified jazz, also called soul jazz, jazz funk, original funk, or just plain funk, is a form of jazz that originated in the mid-'50s–a type of hard bop. It is often played by small groups–trios led by a tenor or alto sax, pianist, guitar and the Hammond organ. Funk music is very physical, usually "down and dirty."

Funk or soul jazz emerged as a reaction to the bop/cool jazz (cool, intellectualized) prevalent at the time. Funky music is everything that bop/cool jazz is not. It is hot, sweaty and never strays far from its blues roots. The term "soul" is a link to gospel roots; "funk" links to blues roots. This fusion of jazz with blues and gospel elements became known as "soul jazz" during the 1950s, partly through the promotion of the Cannonball Adderley Quintet as a "soul-jazz" group.

Fast-paced funk pieces have a bright melodic phrasing set against a hard, percussive dance rhythm. Funk ballads are never more than a few steps from the blues. Above all, this is dynamic relaxin' music that is easy to listen to–the groove. Those of you who like blues and R&B (and gospel), but find some jazz just a touch remote, may well like original funk. There is no better music to kick back to than this.

Jazz funk is sometimes called "original funk" to distinguish it from the contemporary funk sound of the James Brown/George Clinton variety. Along with blues and gospel, original funk or soul jazz had some R&B (soul music) elements thrown into the mix and the resulting fusion was even more to the public's taste. Soul jazz has remained one of the most popular and successful forms of jazz to this very day. Bop is stir-it-up music while funk or soul jazz (no matter how uptempo or percussive) is at heart calm-you-down or groove music. Here are some classic funk albums:

Eddie Lockjaw Davis, *Cookbook, Vol. 1–3*/OJC
Gene Ammons, *Gene Ammons Story: Organ Combos*/Prestige
Arnett Cobb, *Smooth Sailing*/OJC
Red Holloway, *Cookin' Together*/OJC
Willis Jackson, *Bar Wars*/Muse
Ike Quebec, *Blue and Sentimental*/Blue Note
Bobby Timmons, *Soul Man*/Prestige
Johnny Hammond Smith, *Breakout*/Kudu
Harold Vick, *Steppin' Out*/Blue Note
Harold Mabern, *Rakin' & Scrapin'*/Prestige
Stanley Turrentine, *Comin' Your Way*/Blue Note
Houston Person, *Soul Dance*/Prestige
Grover Washington, *Mister Magic*/Motown
Harold Mabern, *Rakin' and Scrapin'*/OJC
Cornell Dupree, *Coast to Coast*/Antilles
Les McCann, *Swiss Movement*/Atlantic (soul jazz)

Organ Combos–At the heart of original funk and soul jazz sits the Hammond organ, 400 pounds of musical joy. This unwieldy piece of equipment can do it all–work by itself, as a duo, trio, quartet, or with a full band. It is a full band. More important is the fact that the Hammond organ sound pretty much defines real funk. There is something about the percussive sound and the adjustable attack/decay effects that, coupled with the famed (rotating horns) Leslie speakers, epitomizes that music called funk.

Whatever the reason, you will find a Hammond organ at the center (or as backup) of the majority of soul jazz recordings, not to mention contemporary funk and R&B recordings. Jimmy Smith is the man who tamed the great beast and turned the Hammond from a roller-rink calliope into a serious jazz instrument. The story is that Smith locked himself in a warehouse with a Hammond for almost a year and came out playing that sound we all love.

And Smith is just the tip of the iceberg. There are many fine Hammond players that are every bit as great in their own way, names like Richard Groove Holmes, Jimmy McGriff, Shirley Scott, Charles Earland, John Patton, Larry Young, and others. Put a Hammond organ and some drums together with a tenor sax or guitar and you have all you need for some real funky music. This is groove music par excellence.

Jimmy Smith, *Back at the Chicken Shack*/Blue Note
Jimmy McGriff, *At the Apollo*/Collectables
Jack McDuff, *Live!*/Prestige
Richard Groove Holmes, *After Hours*/Pacific Jazz
Don Patterson, *Genius of the B-3*/Music
John Patton, *Let em' Roll*/Blue Note
Shirley Scott, *Blue Flames*/OJC
Charles Earland, *Black Talk*/Prestige
Charles Kynard, *Reelin' with the Feeling*/Prestige
Larry Young, *The Complete Blue Note Larry Young*/Mosaic
Joey DeFrancisco, *All of Me*/Columbia

The Commercialization of Soul Jazz

–Soul jazz sometimes gets a not-so-great rap. Anything so potent and popular lends itself to misuse and a great many so-called soul jazz albums were recorded that had no "soul"–bad commercial funk. On the theory that you never know what is enough until you have more than enough, artists sought to increase their popularity by making their music more and more commercial until, in the end, they lost touch with the roots of the music–the soul.

To make matters worse, the advent of bop and the various forms of progressive jazz that grew out of bop, gave birth to a somewhat elitist, conservative, and overly intellectualized attitude–the jazz purist. This purist looks down on jazz that partakes too much of its blues and gospel roots, and any R&B influences are really frowned upon. These mainstream jazz purists used the overt commercialism aspect of soul jazz as grounds to dismiss the entire music offhand. Funk and soul jazz was somehow (in their opinion) not as worthy of respect as the bop or progressive jazz they admired. The fact that soul jazz is the most successful and popular form of jazz was cited as further proof of its commonness. This elitist attitude is now on the decline and soul jazz is beginning to take its place in the history of jazz as a legitimate form. Soul jazz reissues are a hot item. It is a fact that most great jazz performers also have a funky or soul side and albums to prove it. Often very little is written about the soul jazz side of these artists.

Well, there you have a quick tour of the funkier side of jazz–groove music. It is important to point out that soul jazz, although always popular with the people, has received short shrift from the jazz elite. The attitude is that groove music is something, like the blues, which should be kept in the closet. That time has passed.

Groove Masters

We are coming out of a time when jazz has been measured by how outstanding the soloist is–how high can they fly? Critics only seem to know how to rate what stands out. This won't work for groove music. In groove, the idea is to lay down a groove, get in it, and deepen it. Groove masters always take us deeper into the groove. These artists are our windows into the groove, and their hearts become the highway over which the groove can run. They reinvest. And we ride the groove.

This is why jazz critics have either passed (never got it) over groove masters like Grant Green and Stanley Turrentine or heard something without knowing what to make of what they heard (and felt). If music is not viewed as such an intellectual thing (something to see) but rather more of a feeling kind of thing, then groove masters can be appreciated. You may not see the groove masters, but you sure can feel them. In groove, the solo (and all else) only exists if it adds to the groove. Witness Grant Green's incredible single-note repetitions. Who would ever think to do that? You wouldn't dare think of that. It is done by pure feeling. It feels good and you keep doing it. Nothing to think about.

Stanley Turrentine has been laying down grooves for many a year for all to hear. I am surprised at how many books don't even mention him. Grant Green has received even shorter shrift. There have been a few voices crying in the wilderness of soul jazz criticism. Producer Bob Porter of Atlantic Records and Bob Rusch of *Cadence* magazine have always known and told us about the groove. Recording engineer Rudy Van Gelder is another pre-eminent groove expert. More than half of all great soul jazz sessions were recorded by Van Gelder. The next time you hear some real groove music, particularly if there is a Hammond organ on it, just check the album for this engineer's name.

Grant Green: THE Groove Master–All that I can say about Grant Green is that he is *the*-groove master. Numero uno. He is so deep in the groove that most people have no idea what's up with him. Players like Stanley Turrentine, Jimmy Smith, Kenny Burrell, and many other really great soul jazz artists are also groove masters. But the main man is Grant Green. He is so far in the groove that it will take decades for us to bring him out in full. He is just starting to be discovered.

To get your attention and make clear that I am saying something here, consider the singing voice of Bob Dylan. A lot of people say the guy can't sing. But it's not that simple. He is singing. The problem is that he is singing so far in the future that we can't yet hear the music. Other artists can sing his tunes and we can hear that all right. Given enough time, enough years, that gravel-like voice will sound as sweet to our ears as any velvet-toned singer. Dylan's voice is all about microtones and inflection. For now that voice is hidden from our ears in time so tight that there is no room (no time) yet to hear it. Some folks can hear it now. I, for one, can hear the music in his voice. I know many of you can too. Someday everyone will be able to hear it, because the mind will unfold itself until even Dylan's voice is exposed for just what it is–a pure music. But by then our idea of music will also have changed. Rap is changing it even now.

Billie Holiday is another voice that is filled with microtones that emerge through time like an ever-blooming flower. You (or I) can't hear the end or root of her singing, not yet anyway. As we try to listen to Holiday (as we try to grasp that voice), we are knocked out by the deep information there. We try to absorb it, and before we can get a handle on her voice (if we dare listen!) she entrances us in a delightful dream-like groove and we are lost to criticism. Instead we groove on and reflect about this other dream that we have called life. All great musicians do this to us.

Grant Green's playing at its best is like this too. It is so recursive that instead of taking the obvious outs we are used to hearing, Green instead chooses to reinvest–to go in farther and deepen the groove. He opens up a groove and then opens up a groove and then opens a groove, and so on. He never stops. He opens a groove and then works to widen that groove until we can see into the music, see through the music into ourselves. He puts everything back into the groove that he might otherwise get out of it. He knows that the groove is the thing and that time will see him out and his music will live long. That is what grooves are about and why Grant Green is *the* groove master.

Blues in Jazz and R&B

There are forms of blues in jazz other than the groove music presented above. Here are a few notes on some of the major styles:

Blues Shouters and Singers–There are blues singers who tend toward jazz, and almost all jazz singers sing some blues. This is not the place to point these out since they are more-or-less straight-ahead blues singers when they sing blues. The one exception, of course, is Billie Holiday. Holiday is probably the most seminal singer ever recorded. But is her music the blues? Everything she sings is way beyond blues and blues is supposed to be the root music. Holiday is the equivalent of Delta blues singer Robert Johnson in that she is seminal–pure source. Period.

If you have not listened to Billie Holiday and gotten into her music to the point of real distraction (being moved!), then you have missed one of the premiere music experiences of a lifetime. Enough said.

Bluesy Jazz–There is also a style of blues-laden jazz that is not so much funky as downright bluesy. Kenny Burrell is perhaps the chief exponent of this style of jazz. Bluesy jazz has a slow or mid-tempo and is easy to listen to–relaxing. It makes great background or dinner music and yet is integral and stands on its own merits as a music. A lot of artists play bluesy jazz; some play it often. Much bluesy jazz can establish a groove.

Kenny Burrell, *Midnight Blue*/Blue Note
The Three Sounds (Gene Harris), *Introducing the Three Sounds*/Blue Note
Ron Carter, *Jazz: My Romance*/Blue Note
Grant Green, *Born to be Blue*/Blue Note
Ray Bryant, *All Blues*/Pablo
Red Garland, *Soul Junction*/Prestige
Wynton Kelly, *Kelly Blue*/Riverside

Blues/Funk Sax: Honkers, Screamers & Bar Walkers– Although the emergence of blues sax can be traced all the way back to the great Ben Webster, the honkin', screaming tenor sax of the bar-walking variety originated with Illinois Jacquet and was carried to its logical conclusion with the R&B sax of King Curtis. The term "bar walkin'" came from the habit of emotionally driven sax players walking on the top of a bar among the customers playing at a frenzied pitch–often in contests with another sax player walking from the other end of the bar. This honkin' blues-drenched sax style was as much performance bravado as sheer music. As Cannonball Adderley said about the funky big-toned sax, "It's the moan inside the tone." Since many of

the main players in this style hailed from the Southwest, players in this style are often referred to as "Texas tenors." Some of the main artists in this style include Al Sears, Big Jay McNeely, Willis Jackson, Sil Austin, Lee Allen, Rusty Bryant, Hal Singer, and Sam "The Man" Taylor. Most of these players came out of the large swing bands and either formed their own groups or found work in various R&B settings. This raunchy honkin' music scratches that blues itch and satisfies. This is often groove material.

Since many of these sax players can (and often had to) play it all–blues, R&B, honkin' sax, soul jazz, straight jazz, etc.–they are listed here together. I have made some notes to guide you as to their main directions. If you can find the three-CD collection called *Giants of the Blues and Funk Tenor Sax* (Prestige 3PCD-2302-2), you will get a superb 23-cut collection with many extended solos and liner notes by Bob Porter. Worth ordering or searching for.

Sax: Blues, R&B, Funk: Honkers and Bar Walkers

Lee Allen (R&B) *Walkin' with Mr. Lee*/Collectables
Gene Ammons (R&B, bop, soul jazz) *Boss Tenors– Straight Ahead from Chicago 1961*/Verve
Sil Austin (blues) *Slow Rock Rock*/Wing
Earl Bostic (R&B) *Best of Earl Bostic*/Deluxe
Rusty Bryant (R&B, soul jazz) *Rusty Bryant Returns*/ OJC
Arnett Cobb (blues, soul jazz) *Smooth Sailing*/OJC
King Curtis (R&B, soul jazz) *Soul Meeting*/Prestige
Hank Crawford (soul jazz) *Soul Survivors*/Milestone
Eddie Lockjaw Davis (blues, soul jazz) *Cookbook, Vol. 1–3*/OJC
Jimmy Forrest (blues, bop, soul jazz) *Out of the Forest*/ Prestige
Frank Foster (blues) *Soul Outing*/Prestige
Johnny Griffin (bop, hard bop, blues) *Big Soul Band*/ OJC
Eddie Harris (soul jazz) *Best of*/Atlantic
Coleman Hawkins (blues, hard bop)
Red Holloway (soul jazz) *Cookin' Together*/Prestige
Joe Houston (R&B Honker, blues)
Willis Jackson (R&B, funk) *Bar Wars*/Muse
Illinois Jacquet (Honker, blues, R&B) *Blues: That's Me!*/OJC
Big Jay McNeely (R&B, Honker, blues)
Wild Bill Moore (blues) (Look for him as a sideman)
Oliver Nelson (blues, out) *Soul Battle*/OJC
David Fathead Newman (R&B, soul jazz) *Lonely Avenue*/Atlantic
Harold Ousley (blues, soul jazz) *Sweet Double Hipness*/Muse
Houston Person (soul jazz) *Goodness*/OJC
Ike Quebec (blues, soul jazz) *Blue and Sentimental*/ Blue Note
Al Sears (blues) *The Swingville All-Stars*/Swingville
Hal Singer (blues) *Blue Stompin'*/Prestige
Sonny Stitt (bop, soul jazz) *Soul Summit*/Prestige
Buddy Tate (blues) *Tate's Date*/Swingville
Sam "The Man" Taylor (blues, R&B)
Eddie Cleanhead Vinson (blues) *Kidney Stew*/Black & Blue
Ernie Watts (blues, bop, soul jazz) *Ernie Watts Quartet*/JVC

Blues in Free Jazz–Blues in free jazz are present; the notes are there. The problem is that the constant beat is missing and thus the groove never gets laid down. More important, most free jazz is stir-it-up music rather than cool out. While this is great music, it is not groove music. Here are some outstanding examples of some blues in free jazz.

Archie Shepp, *Attica Blues*/Impulse
Oliver Nelson, *Screamin' the Blues*/New Jazz
Charles Mingus, *Charles Mingus Presents Charles Mingus*/Candid
John Coltrane, *Love Supreme*/Impulse
Sun Ra, *The Heliocentric Worlds of Sun Ra*/ESP
Ornette Coleman, *Tomorrow is the Question*/Contemporary

Blues in Jazz Rock & Fusion–The same is true for most jazz rock as for free jazz. The notes occur but the energy is more agitating than not and the groove is seldom established.

Crusaders, *Crusaders 1*/Blue Thumb
David Sanborn, *Backstreet*/Warner Brothers
Mahavishnu Orchestra, *The Inner Mounting Flame*/Columbia
Miles Davis, *Star People*/Columbia

I hope that some of what I have written here will help blues lovers push off from the island of blues out into the sea of jazz. You can always head back to the solid ground of blues if you can't get into the jazz. Blues and jazz are not mutually exclusive. Blues in jazz has been a thrilling ride (groove) for me and I have found a whole new music that satisfies much like the blues satisfy. I listen to groove music all the time. If you find some great groove styles that I have not mentioned here, drop me a line. I want to hear them.

Thanks.

Michael Erlewine
c/o All-Music Guide
315 Marion Avenue
Big Rapids, MI 49307
Phone: (616) 796-3437
e-mail: Michael@TheNewAge.com

THE GROOVE GUIDE
TO BLUES IN JAZZ

Here is something that I wished I had when I first started to get into groove and blues jazz–a quick guide to the best recordings. It can save you both time and money. These are some of the main jazz (and R&B) artists with a strong blues content. You will want to hear them out. In each case I have tried to point out key albums that are worth a listen from a blues or groove perspective. The albums are rated and reviewed (where possible) to give you insight into why these might or might not interest you. A short biography is also included and sometimes additional notes on how to approach the artist from a blues perspective. We would need a whole book to do this right, and the *All Music Guide to Jazz* (2nd edition) is available when you are. I am sorry to say that many of the albums listed below are not available on CD. Some probably never will be. Although I love CDs, I have had to get back into vinyl to hear a lot of this music. Many of you will also–back to the old record bins. It's worth it if the music is there. And it is. I hope you enjoy this short guide to groove music. —*Michael Erlewine*

Cannonball Adderley (Julian Edwin Adderley)

b. Sep. 15, 1928, Tampa, Florida, **d.** Aug. 8, 1975, Gary, IN
Sax (Alto) / Soul Jazz, Hard Bop
One of the great alto saxophonists, Cannonball Adderley had an exuberant and happy sound (as opposed to many of the more serious stylists of his generation) that communicated immediately to listeners. His intelligent presentation of his music (often explaining what he and his musicians were going to play) helped make him one of the most popular of all jazzmen.

Adderley already had an established career as a high-school band director in Florida when, during a 1955 visit to New York, he was persuaded to sit in with Oscar Pettiford's group at the Cafe Bohemia. His playing created such a sensation that he was signed to Savoy and persuaded to play jazz full-time in New York. With his younger brother, cornetist Nat, Cannonball formed a quintet that struggled until its breakup in 1957. Adderley then joined Miles Davis, forming part of his super sextet with John Coltrane and participating on such classic recordings as *Milestones* and *Kind of Blue*. Adderley's second attempt to form a quintet with his brother was more successful for in 1959 with pianist Bobby Timmons he had a hit recording of "This Here." From then on, Cannonball was able to work steadily with his band.

During its Riverside years (1959-63), the Adderley Quintet primarily played soulful renditions of hard bop and Cannonball really excelled in the straight-ahead settings. During 1962-63 Yusef Lateef made the group a sextet and pianist Joe Zawinul was an important new member. The collapse of Riverside resulted in Adderley signing with Capitol and his recordings became gradually more commercial. Charles Lloyd was in Lateef's place for a year (with less success) and then with his departure the group went back to being a quintet. Zawinul's 1966 composition "Mercy, Mercy, Mercy" was a huge hit for the group, Adderley started doubling on soprano and the Quintet's later recordings emphasized long melody statements, funky rhythms and electronics. However during his last year, Cannonball Adderley was revisiting the past a bit and on *Phenix* he recorded new versions of many of his earlier numbers. But before he could evolve his

music any further, Cannonball Adderley died suddenly from a stroke. –*Scott Yanow*
Groove: Cannonball is one of the pioneers of soul jazz, in the sense of jazz played with a funky soul flavor, so don't look for your standard organ-combo groove music. It was the Cannonball Adderley Quintet that was first refered to by critics as a "soul jazz" group. Cannonball jazz is sunny, not dark. It is bright and clear. The album *Somethin' Else* is a good place to start. –*Michael Erlewine*

★ **Somethin' Else** / Mar. 9, 1958 / Blue Note ✦✦✦✦✦
Shortly after Adderley broke up his original quintet and joined Miles Davis' sextet, he recorded this LP with Davis in the rare role of a sideman. Actually Davis dominates several of the selections (including "Autumn Leaves," "Love for Sale," and "One for Daddy-o") but both hornmen (backed by pianist Hank Jones, bassist Sam Jones and drummer Art Blakey) sound quite inspired by each other's presence. –*Scott Yanow*

☆ **Things Are Getting Better** / 1958 / Riverside ✦✦✦✦✦
First pairing of Milt Jackson with Cannonball for an all-star blowin' session. This one works. With Wynton Kelly (p), Milt Jackson (vib), Percy Heath (b), and Art Blakey (d). Recorded while Adderley was a sideman with the classic Miles Davis Sextet. –*Michael Erlewine*

● **Cannonball and Coltrane** / Feb. 3, 1959 / EmArcy ✦✦✦✦✦
This LP (whose contents have been reissued many times) features the Miles Davis Sextet of 1959 without the leader. Altoist Cannonball Adderley and tenor saxophonist John Coltrane push each other on these six selections with this version of "Limehouse Blues" really burning. Coltrane's serious sound is a striking contrast to the jubilant Adderley alto; the latter is showcased on "Stars Fell on Alabama." With pianist Wynton Kelly, bassist Paul Chambers, and drummer Jimmy Cobb playing to their usual level, this gem is highly recommended. –*Scott Yanow*

● **Cannonball Adderley Quintet in San Francisco** / Oct. 18, 1959+Oct. 20, 1959 / Original Jazz Classics ✦✦✦✦
This live date with Bobby Timmons (p), Nat Adderley (cnt), Sam Jones (b), and Louis Hayes (d) contains the classic and soulful "This Here." This is an exciting session. –*Hank Davis*

Cannonball Adderley Collection, Vol. 1: Them Dirty Blues / Feb. 1, 1960 / ✦✦✦
The first of seven LPs that reissue recordings from his period with Riverside contains several notable selections. The first side (which has pianist Bobby Timmons well-featured with bassist Sam Jones, drummer Louis Hayes, cornetist Nat Adderley and the leader/altoist) includes the original versions of Timmons's "Dat Dere" (his follow-up to "This Here" which is heard here in two takes), Sam Jones's "Del Sasser" and Nat's "Work Songlo"; the latter was previously unissued. On the flip side (with Barry Harris in Timmons's place), the quintet performs the initial "official" version of "Work Song," a heated "Jeannine," "Easy Living," and "Them Dirty Blues." Lots of classic music comes from this influential soul jazz band. –*Scott Yanow*

Cannonball Adderley Collection, Vol. 5: The Quintet at The Lighthouse / Oct. 16, 1960 / Landmark ✦✦✦
This is a fine all-around set from the Cannonball Adderley Quintet of 1960 with the altoist/leader, cornetist Nat Adderley, pianist Victor Feldman, bassist Sam Jones, and drummer Louis Hayes. The fifth of seven LPs reissued by Orrin Keepnews and

315

taken from Adderley's Riverside years finds his band in top form on the original version of "Sack O' Woe," a previously unissued "Our Delight," Jimmy Heath's "Big 'P'" and "Blue Daniel" among others. It's a strong introduction to the music of this classic hard bop group. —*Scott Yanow*

The Quintet Plus / May 11, 1961 / Riverside ♦♦♦
This out-of-print LP, whose contents have reissued several times since, features the 1961 Cannonball Adderley Quintet (which includes cornetist Nat Adderley and pianist Victor Feldman) plus their guest Wynton Kelly on piano during four of the six tracks; Feldman switched to vibes for those songs. The music is quite enjoyable, high-quality funky jazz that could also be called hard bop. "Well You Needn't" and "Star Eyes" are highpoints. —*Scott Yanow*

Mercy, Mercy, Mercy / Oct. 20, 1966 / Blue Note ♦♦♦♦♦
This set (reissued on CD) is one of Cannonball Adderley's finest albums of his last decade. "Mercy, Mercy, Mercy," a soulful Joe Zawinul melody that is repeated several times without any real improvisation, became a surprise hit but the other selections on this live date ("Fun," "Games," "Sticks," "Hippodelphia," and "Sack O' Woe") all have plenty of fiery solos from the quintet (which is comprised of the leader on alto, cornetist Nat Adderley, pianist Joe Zawinul, bassist Victor Gaskin, and drummer Roy McCurdy). Cannonball sounds quite inspired (his expressive powers had expanded due to the unacknowledged influence of the avant-garde) and Nat shows just how exciting a player he was back in his prime. "Sack O' Woe" is particularly memorable. This CD, which is far superior to most of Cannonball's later Capitol recordings, is highly recommended. —*Scott Yanow*

Nat Adderley

b. Nov. 25, 1931, Tampa, FL
Cornet / Soul Jazz, Hard Bop
Nat Adderley's cornet (which in its early days was strongly influenced by Miles Davis) was always a complementary voice to his brother Cannonball in their popular quintet. His career ran parallel to his older brother for quite some time. Nat took up trumpet in 1946, switched to cornet in 1950 and spent time in the military, playing in an Army band during 1951–53. After a period with Lionel Hampton (1954–55), Nat made his recording debut in 1955, joined Cannonball's unsuccessful quintet of 1956–57 and then spent periods with the groups of J.J. Johnson and Woody Herman before hooking up with Cannonball again in Oct. 1959. This time the group became a major success and Nat remained in the quintet until Cannonball's death in 1975, contributing such originals as "Work Song," "Jive Samba" and "The Old Country" along with many exciting hard bop solos. Nat Adderley, who was at the peak of his powers in the early to mid-'60s and became adept at playing solos that dipped into the subtone register of his horn, has led his own quintets since Cannonball's death; his most notable sidemen were altoists Sonny Fortune (in the early '80s) and Vincent Herring. Although his own playing has declined somewhat (Adderley's chops no longer have the endurance of his earlier days), Nat has continued recording worthwhile sessions. Many of his recordings through the years (for such labels as Savoy, EmArcy, Riverside, Jazzland, Atlantic, Milestone, A&M, Capitol, Prestige, SteepleChase, Galaxy, Theresa, In & Out, and Landmark) are currently available. —*Scott Yanow*

Introducing Nat Adderley / Sep. 6, 1955 / EmArcy ♦♦♦

Branching Out / Sep. 1958 / Riverside ♦♦♦♦
This 1958 date had some of his hottest playing as a leader. Adderley concentrates on cornet, and there haven't been many on that instrument to take it into more abrupt and challenging harmonic contexts. Johnny Griffin's bluesy, taut tenor keeps things moving, while using pianist Gene Harris, bassist Andy Simpkins and drummer Bill Dowdy (better known as The Three Sounds) for a rhythm section was inspiring. —*Ron Wynn*

● **Work Songs** / Jan. 25, 1960–Sep. 15, 1960 / Riverside ♦♦♦♦♦
Guitarist Wes Montgomery was also aboard for *Work Song,* a Nat Adderley date with Bobby Timmons (piano), Louis Hayes (drums), Sam Jones, and Ketter Betts or Percy Heath (cello, bass). This was, of course, Nat Adderley's date and Montgomery's role was not so much that of guitarist extraordinaire, but as one of the plucked strings which give this date its particular ambience. A thoughtful and varied date with a multi-dimensional person-

ality, this has been previously issued as part of a two-fer. —*Bob Rusch, Cadence*

That's Right!: Nat Adderley & The Big Sax Section / Aug. 9, 1960+Sep. 15, 1960 / Riverside ♦♦♦♦
Nat Adderley has seldom played with more fire, verve, and distinction than he did on *That's Right!* It placed him in the company of an expanded sax section that included his brother Cannonball on alto, Yusef Lateef on tenor, flute and oboe, Jimmy Heath and Charlie Rouse on tenor, and baritone saxophonist Tate Houston. Solos crackled, the backing was tasty and stimulating, and the eight songs ranged from brisk standards to delightful originals. This CD reissue, despite lacking any new or alternate material, is most welcome due to the full, striking sound that the big reed section provided. —*Ron Wynn*

Natural Soul / Sep. 23, 1963 / Milestone ♦♦♦
With Kenny Burrell (g) and Junior Mance (p).   *AMG*

Gene Ammons

b. Apr. 14, 1925, Chicago, IL, **d.** Aug. 6, 1974, Chicago, IL
Sax (Tenor) / Bop, Soul Jazz, Hard Bop
Gene Ammons, who had a huge and immediately recognizable tone on tenor, was a very flexible player who could play bebop with the best (always battling his friend Sonny Stitt to a tie) yet was an influence on the R&B world. Some of his ballad renditions became hits and, despite two unfortunate interruptions in his career, Ammons remained a popular attraction for 25 years.

Son of the great boogie-woogie pianist Albert Ammons, Gene Ammons (who was nicknamed "Jug") left Chicago at age 18 to work with King Kolax's band. He originally came to fame as a key soloist with Billy Eckstine's orchestra during 1944–47, trading off with Dexter Gordon on the famous Eckstine record *Blowing the Blues Away*. Other than a notable stint with Woody Herman's Third Herd in 1949 and an attempt at co-leading a two-tenor group in the early '50s with Sonny Stitt, Ammons worked as a single throughout his career, recording frequently (most notably for Prestige) in settings ranging from quartets and organ combos to all-star jam sessions. Drug problems kept him in prison during much of 1958–60 and, due to a particularly stiff sentence, 1962–69. When Ammons returned to the scene in 1969 he opened up his style a bit, including some of the emotional cries of the avant-garde while utilizing funky rhythm sections, but he was still able to battle Sonny Stitt on his own terms. Ironically the last song that he ever recorded (just a short time before he was diagnosed with terminal cancer) was "Goodbye." —*Scott Yanow*
Groove: Ammon's big tone and bluesy sound was a huge influence on the jazz scene. The fact that he could play in many jazz styles made him even more seminal. I have tried to list some of his more soul jazz (organ combo) albums, but he recorded a lot and you may find you like a wide variety of his bluesy, soulful sessions. —*Michael Erlewine*

● **The Happy Blues** / Apr. 23, 1956 / Original Jazz Classics ♦♦♦♦♦
This is one of the great studio jam sessions. Tenor saxophonist Gene Ammons is teamed up with trumpeter Art Farmer, altoist Jackie McLean, pianst Duke Jordan, bassist Addison Farmer, drummer Art Taylor and the congas of Candido for four lengthy selections. Best is "The Happy Blues" which has memorable solos and spontaneous but perfectly fitting riffing by the horns behind each other's playing. The other numbers ("The Great Lie," "Can't We Be Friends" and "Madhouse") are also quite enjoyable, making this a highly recommended set. —*Scott Yanow*

Funky / Jan. 11, 1957 / Prestige ♦♦♦
A blues-oriented bop album that is funky jazz but not "funky" in the soul jazz sense of that word. An exception is the title cut, a bluesy tune with Kenny Burrell (g). With Jackie McLean (as), Art Farmer (tpt), and Mal Waldron (p). Recorded in NYC. —*Michael Erlewine*

Groove Blues / Jan. 3, 1958 / Original Jazz Classics ♦♦♦
On Jan. 3, 1958, Gene Ammons led one of his last all-star jam sessions for Prestige. The most notable aspect to this date (which resulted in two albums of material) is that it featured among its soloists John Coltrane, on alto. This CD, a straight reissue of one of the original LPs, includes baritonist Pepper Adams, the tenor of Paul Quinichette and Coltrane on two of the four selections, and Jerome Richardson's flute during three of the songs in addition to a fine rhythm section (pianist Mal Waldron, bassist

George Joyner and drummer Art Taylor). This set consists of three of Waldron's originals in addition to the standard ballad "It Might as Well Be Spring" and it (along with the CD *The Big Sound*) fully documents the productive day. —*Scott Yanow*

The Gene Ammons Story: Organ Combos / Jun. 17, 1960+Nov. 28, 1961 / Prestige ✦✦✦
Gene Ammons recorded frequently for Prestige during the 1950s and early '60s and virtually all of the tenor's dates were quite rewarding. This two-LP set reissues *Twistin' the Jug* plus part of *Angel Eyes* and *Velvet Soul*. Ammons, a bop-based but very versatile soloist, sounds quite comfortable playing a variety of standards and lesser-known material in groups featuring Jack McDuff or Johnny "Hammond" Smith on organ and either trumpeter Joe Newman or Frank Wess on tenor and flute. This version of "Angel Eyes" became a surprise hit. —*Scott Yanow*

Soul Summit / Jun. 13, 1961–Apr. 13, 1962 / Prestige ✦✦✦
This single CD reissues all of the music from two LPs titled *Soul Summit* and *Soul Summit, Vol. 2*. The latter session is one of the lesser known of the many collaborations of tenors Gene Ammons and Sonny Stitt, who are joined by organist Jack McDuff and drummer Charlie Persip. Their six performances are primarily riff tunes with "When You Wish upon a Star" taken at a medium pace and "Out in the Cold Again" the lone ballad. The second half of this CD features Ammons on two songs ("Love I've Found You" and a swinging "Too Marvelous for Words") with a big band arranged by Oliver Nelson, jamming "Ballad for Baby" with a quintet, sitting out of "Scram" (which stars McDuff and the tenor of Harold Vick) and backing singer Etta Jones on three numbers, of which "Cool, Cool Daddy" is the most memorable. Overall, this is an interesting and consistently swinging set that adds to the large quantity of recordings that the great Ammons did during the early '60s. —*Scott Yanow*

★ **Boss Tenors: Straight Ahead from Chicago 1961** / Aug. 27, 1961 / Verve ✦✦✦✦
There are perhaps no better tenors, no better jazz. This is definitive. With Sonny Stitt. —*Michael G. Nastos*

Brother Jack Meets the Boss / Jan. 23, 1962 / Prestige ✦✦✦
On *Brother Jack Meets the Boss*, one of the fathers of Chicago tenor, Gene Ammons, teamed with Jack McDuff in a quintet setting (Harold Vick, tenor sax; Eddie Diehl, guitar; Joe Dukes, drums) for the usual blues-based romp. Here McDuff was in particularly good form and Jug maneuvered with as much subtlety and changes as the genre and drummer allowed. —*Bob Rusch, Cadence*

Brother Jug / Nov 10, 1969–Nov. 11, 1969 / Prestige ✦✦✦
Stalwart soul jazz set from 1969, with Ammons blowing fiercely on tenor, backed by a group that included the swirling organ of Sonny Phillips and funky drumming by Bernard Purdie, plus a nice guest shot by guitarist Billy Butler on "Jungle Strut." —*Ron Wynn*

Sil Austin

b. Sep. 17, 1929, Dunnellon, Florida
Sax (Tenor) / R&B
R&B Tenor saxman and band leader Sil (Silvester) Austin was born September 17, 1929 in Dunnellon, FL. In 1946, Austin won a talent show at the Apollo theater in New York City for a version of "Danny Boy." In 1949, he worked with Roy Eldridge and then with Cootie Williams from 1949 to 1952. From 1953 to 1954 he was with Tiny Bradshaw. Ella Fitzgerald recorded Austin's compostion "Ping Pong" and then gave him the title as a nickname. He later signed with Mercury and recorded with his own band. His R&B hits include "Slow Walk." —*Michael Erlewine*

Slow Rock Rock / Wing ✦✦✦✦✦

Earl Bostic

b. Apr. 25, 1913, Tulsa, OK, d. Oct. 28, 1965, Rochester, NY
Sax (Alto) / R&B, Swing
Earl Bostic's roots and foundation were steeped in jazz and swing, but he later became one of the most prolific R&B bandleaders. His searing, sometimes bluesy, sometimes soft and moving, alto sax style influenced many players, including John Coltrane. His many King releases, which featured limited soloing and basic melodic and rhythmic movements, might have fooled novices into thinking Bostic possessed minimal skills; but Art

Blakey once said "Nobody knew more about the saxophone than Bostic, I mean technically, and that includes Bird." Bostic worked in several Midwest bands during the early '30s, then studied at Xavier University. He left school to tour with various groups, among them a band co-led by Charlie Creath and Fate Marable. He moved to New York in the late '30s, where he was a soloist in the bands of Don Redman, Edgar Hayes, and Lionel Hampton. Bostic also led his own combos, whose members included Jimmy Cobb, Al Casey, Blue Mitchell, Stanley Turrentine, Benny Golson and Coltrane. Bostic toured extensively through the '50s, while cutting numerous sessions for King. His recording of "Flamingo" in 1951 was a huge hit, as were the songs "Sleep," "You Go to My Head," "Cherokee," and "Temptation." Bostic recorded for Allegro, Gotham and King from the late '40s to the mid-'60s. He made more than 400 selections for King; the label would use stereo remakes of songs with different personnel, then use the same album numbers. After a heart attack, Bostic became a part-time player. His mid-'60s albums were more soul jazz than R&B. Several of his King LPs are available on CD. —*Ron Wynn and Michael Erlewine*

Groove: There are a ton of Bostic albums out there, at least in vinyl. Don't be put off by their hokey album titles, cover art, arrangements, and/or song lists. This guy rocks and was on just about all the time. Remeber that Stanley Turrentine and John Coltrane (and many other sax players) learned directly from Bostic. This is hard-rockin', raunchy R&B saxophone at its best. —*Michael Erlewine*

● **The Best of Earl Bostic** / 1956 / Deluxe ✦✦✦✦
A nice cross-section of this fiery alto-saxist's '50s output, it includes his hits "Sleep" and "Flamingo." —*Bill Dahl*

Dance Time / 1957 / King ✦✦✦✦✦
These are mostly uptempo instrumental R&B, pop, and dance/novelty tunes delivered with style and flair by the great Earl Bostic. He was among the finest honking saxophonists, and King kept pumping out collections of his singles throughout the '50s. —*Ron Wynn*

Bostic for You / 1957 / King ✦✦✦✦✦
Bostic's blistering renditions of old dance numbers transcend R&B and jazz barriers. —*Bill Dahl*

Showcase of Swinging Dance Hits / 1958 / King ✦✦✦
Perhaps his best rocking and uptempo instrumental pop and R&B material. This album was aimed at the jukebox market and weighted toward the hottest, most furiously played cuts in the Bostic repertoire. Bostic was as technically accomplished as any alto saxophonist in his era, but he wasn't able to show that while on King. This album was one of the few times that he was able to really show his skills on uptempo material. —*Ron Wynn*

Earl Bostic Plays Old Standards / King ✦✦✦
Some stirring renditions, furious solos, and alternately appealing and soothing alto statements by Earl Bostic. He's among the least recognized, yet important, members of the R&B sax class. His sidemen included Benny Golson, Mickey Baker, and John Coltrane. This collection was one of numerous albums Bostic issued on King during the '50s, and was briefly available on reissue in the Gusto series of the '70s. —*Ron Wynn*

25 Years of Rhythm and Blues Hits / 1960 / King ✦✦✦✦
One among a handful of really great Earl Bostic King albums. This wasn't merely a bunch of singles slapped together, but Bostic doing vintage R&B tunes that he loved. He also got ample space within the commercial restrictions to stretch out and really play rather than just quote the melody and add a few licks around it. —*Ron Wynn*

Jazz As I Feel It / Aug. 13, 1963–Aug. 14, 1963 / King ✦✦✦
Earl Bostic didn't have a chance to venture outside the honking R&B sphere often, and when he did he usually displayed the skills that were more evident in live performance. While this wasn't the kind of hard-edged playing many assume is the only way to play jazz, Bostic's fluid, relaxed, expressive alto solos show that he could play jazz as well as anything else. —*Ron Wynn*

Ray Bryant (Raphael Bryant)

b. Dec. 24, 1931, Philadelphia, PA
Piano / Bop, Swing, Soul Jazz
Although he could always play bop, Ray Bryant's playing combines older elements (including blues, boogie-woogie, gospel,

and even stride) into a distinctive, soulful and swinging style; no one plays "After Hours" quite like him.

The younger brother of bassist Tommy Bryant and the uncle of Kevin and Robin Eubanks (his sister is their mother), Bryant started his career playing with Tiny Grimes in the late '40s. He became the house pianist at the Blue Note in Philadelphia in 1953 where he backed classic jazz greats (including Charlie Parker, Miles Davis and Lester Young) and made important contacts. He accompanied Carmen McRae (1956–57), recorded with Coleman Hawkins and Roy Eldridge at the 1957 Newport Jazz Festival (taking a brilliant solo on an exciting version of "I Can't Believe That You're in Love with Me") and played with Jo Jones' trio (1958). Bryant settled in New York in 1959, played with Sonny Rollins, Charlie Shavers, and Curtis Fuller, and soon had his own trio. He had a few funky commercial hits (including "Little Susie" and Cubano Chant") which kept him working for decades. Bryant has recorded often throughout his career (most notably for Epic, Prestige, Columbia, Sue, Cadet, Atlantic, Pablo, and EmArcy) and even his dates on electric piano in the '70s are generally rewarding. However Ray Bryant is heard at his best when playing the blues on unaccompanied acoustic piano. —*Scott Yanow*

Groove: Ray Bryant puts out great blues piano for up-front evaluation or just easy, kick-back listening. This is bluesy jazz. —*Michael Erlewine*

Alone with the Blues / Dec. 19, 1958 / New Jazz ◆◆◆
A brilliant, frequently amazing session in which Ray Bryant demonstrates his command of the piano, facility with the blues, and superb solo technique. His version of "Lover Man" offers marvelous left-hand chords, while "Blues No. 3" is also a gem. —*Ron Wynn*

Groove House / May 22, 1963–Jun. 19, 1963 / Sue ◆◆◆

● **Montreux '77** / Jul. 13, 1977 / Pablo ◆◆◆◆

All Blues / Apr. 10, 1978 / Pablo ◆◆◆
Bryant has always had a wide repertoire but he sounds most at home when playing the blues. This trio date with bassist Sam Jones and drummer Grady Tate allows him to do just that with "Please Send Me Someone to Love" being the only nonblues on the program. Whether it be "All Blues," "Billie's Bounce" or "Jumpin' with Symphony Sid," Bryant explores an impressive variety of blues styles and grooves, leaving listeners with a happy feeling. —*Scott Yanow*

Blue Moods / Feb. 15, 1987 / EmArcy ◆◆◆◆
Outstanding trio date with Bryant offering teeming phrases, sweeping statements, and some wonderful ballads, backed by bassist Rufus Reid and drummer Freddie Waits. Not only great playing all around, but an excellent recording as well. —*Ron Wynn*

Rusty Bryant

b. Nov. 25, 1929, Huntington, WV, d. Mar. 25, 1991
Sax (Tenor) / Soul Jazz, Post-Bop
Among the finest funky and soul jazz tenors of the '70s, Bryant is noted for his thick tone, robust sound, and jam-session-style albums. Rusty Bryant is one of the original bar-walking sax players.

Royal G. "Rusty " Bryant was born on November 25, 1929 in Huntington, WV, but was raised in Columbus, OH. He credits Gene Ammons and Sonny Stitt as his main influences. He played with and learned from Tiny Grimes and Stomp Gordon, and was leading his own groups by 1951. Bryant toured with Hammond organist Mike Marr during the 1960s. He settled in Columbus, OH. —*Michael Erlewine & Ron Wynn*

Rusty Bryant Returns / Feb. 17, 1969 / Original Jazz Classics ◆◆◆
Rusty Bryant, a veteran R&B tenor player, was somewhat forgotten at the time of his debut Prestige album, but due to the commercial success of this former LP (reissued on CD in the OJC series), Bryant would record seven more sessions for Prestige during the next five years. Actually, this date is a bit surprising, with Bryant sticking exclusively to alto and sometimes using an electrified model similar to what Lou Donaldson was playing at the time. The music (mostly blues-oriented originals) is enjoyable, with plenty of boogaloos and soulful vamps. In addition to Bryant, the main soloists are guitarist Grant Green, in excellent form, and organist Sonny Phillips. —*Scott Yanow*

★ **Soul Liberation** / Aug. 1970 / Prestige ◆◆◆◆◆
soul jazz classic. His most popular composition. —*Ron Wynn*

Milt Buckner

b. Jul. 10, 1915, St. Louis, MO, d. Jul. 27, 1977, Chicago, IL
Organ, Piano / Swing
Milt Buckner had a dual career. As a pianist he largely invented the "locked hands" style (parallel chords) that was adopted by many other players including George Shearing and Oscar Peterson. And as an organist he was one of the top pre-Jimmy Smith stylists, helping to popularize the instrument.

The younger brother of altoist Ted Buckner (who played with Jimmie Lunceford), Milt Buckner grew up in Detroit and gigged locally in addition to arranging for McKinney's Cotton Pickers in 1934. He came to fame as pianist and arranger with Lionel Hampton (1941-48, 1950-52 and occasionally in later years) where he was a crowd pleaser. During 1948-50 Buckner led his own bands and after 1952 he generally played organ with trios or quartets. In later years he sometimes teamed up with Illinois Jacquet or Jo Jones. Buckner recorded many dates as a leader, particularly for Black & Blue in the 1970s. —*Scott Yanow*

Groove: There are some good Buckner solo albums and a few are listed here, but you will tend to find him as a sideman on albums by Illinois Jacquet, Arnett Cobb, and Clarence "Gatemouth" Brown. —*Michael Erlewine*

★ **Rockin' Hammond** / Feb. 22, 1956–Mar. 15, 1956 / Capitol ◆◆◆◆◆
Classic organ combo with a master. From blues to ballads. A fine representation of Buckner's brilliance. —*Michael G. Nastos*

Play Milt Play / Nov. 1966–Apr. 1971 / Esoldun ◆◆◆

● **Green Onions** / Feb. 21, 1975 / Inner City ◆◆◆◆
With French rhythm section, guitarist Roy Gaines, drummer Panama Francis. Funky and groove-laden. —*Michael G. Nastos*

Kenny Burrell (Kenneth Earl Burrell)

b. Jul. 31, 1931, Detroit, MI
Guitar / Bop
Kenny Burrell has been a very consistent guitarist throughout his career. Cool-toned and playing in an unchanging style based in bop, Burrell has always been the epitome of good taste and solid swing. Duke Ellington's favorite guitarist (though he never actually recorded with him), Burrell started playing guitar when he was 12 and debuted on records with Dizzy Gillespie in 1951. Part of the fertile Detroit jazz scene of the early '50s, Burrell moved to New York in 1956. Highly in-demand from the start, Burrell has appeared on a countless number of records during the past 40 years as a leader and as a sideman. Among his more notable associations have been dates with Stan Getz, Billie Holiday, Milt Jackson, John Coltrane, Gil Evans, Sonny Rollins, Quincy Jones, Stanley Turrentine, and Jimmy Smith. Starting in the early '70s Burrell began leading seminars and teaching, often focusing on Duke Ellington's music. He toured with the Phillip Morris Superband during 1985-86 and has led three-guitar quintets but generally Kenny Burrell plays at the head of a trio/quartet. —*Scott Yanow*

Groove: Burrell never stoops to playing needless riffs and other technical "noise"–virtuosity for its own sake. His melodic sense is strong and his playing elegant. Here is bluesy jazz that is easy to listen to, yet never boring or trite. As a sideman, Burrell has graced over 200 albums—J. Coltrane, Stan Getz, Billie Holiday, Milt Jackson, Hubert Laws, Sonny Rollins, Jimmy Smith, Stanley Turrentine, and more. You can always count on him for tasteful solos, and superb backup. The fact that his albums make great background music is no putdown. —*Michael Erlewine*

Blue Moods / Feb. 1, 1957 / Prestige ◆◆◆◆◆
Smooth, cool, yet musically impressive late '50s date that has both blowing session fervor and soulful undergirding. Burrell's fluid guitar voicings and Cecil Payne's robust baritone make nice partners, while Tommy Flanagan adds his usual sparkling piano riffs and solos, and bassist Doug Watkins teams with Elvin Jones, who shows he can drive a date without dominating things on drums. —*Ron Wynn*

Kenny Burrell / Feb. 1, 1957 / Prestige ◆◆◆
His first Prestige recording (in NYC) with an all-Detroit crew (plus baritone sax) in New York. Burrell as we love him—clear, bluesy, with a touch of funk. —*AMG*

K.B. Blues / Feb. 10, 1957 / Blue Note ✦✦✦
Worth searching for. Burrell with funky pianist Horace Silver and Hank Mobley on tenor sax. As you might guess, the tunes are mostly blues. —*AMG*

On View at the Five Spot Cafe / Aug. 26, 1959 / Blue Note ✦✦✦
This likable live set from guitarist Kenny Burrell has a strong supporting cast (Tina Brooks on tenor, either Bobby Timmons or Roland Hanna on piano, bassist Ben Tucker and drummer Art Blakey) and the original five-song program has been expanded on this CD to eight tunes. The swinging music, highlighted by "Lady Be Good," "Birks Works," the blues "36-23-36," and Burrell's feature on "Lover Man," is quite mainstream for the period and predictably excellent. —*Scott Yanow*

Bluesin' Around / Nov. 21, 1961–Apr. 30, 1962 / Columbia ✦✦
Released for the first time on this 1983 LP, the music on the set features guitarist Kenny Burrell in quartet/quintets with either tenor great Illinois Jacquet, trombonist Eddie Bert or altoist Leo Wright, and either pianist Hank Jones or organist Jack McDuff. It is odd that Columbia did not issue any of the straightahead music at the time, considering McDuff's popularity, for the results, even with a few dated numbers such as "Mambo Twist," are excellent. After a short while, this LP went out of print and the music has yet to resurface on CD. —*Scott Yanow*

● **Midnight Blue** / Jan. 6, 1963 / Blue Note ✦✦✦✦✦
This album was one of guitarist Kenny Burrell's best-known sessions for the Blue Note label, although it has yet to be reissued on CD. Burrell is matched with tenor saxophonist Stanley Turrentine, bassist Major Holley, drummer Bill English and Ray Barretto on conga for a blues-oriented date highlighted by "Chitlins Con Carne," "Midnight Blue," "Saturday Night Blues," and the lone standard "Gee Baby Ain't I Good to You." —*Scott Yanow*

Crash! / Feb. 26, 1963 / Prestige ✦✦✦
Burrell with Jack McDuff on the Hammond organ and Harold Vick on tenor sax. Includes the tune "Grease Monkey." —*AMG*

Freedom / Mar. 27, 1963 / Blue Note ✦✦✦✦
A date with the Kenny Burrell Sextet that includes Stanley Turrentine (sax), Herbie Hancock (p), Ben Tucker (b), Bill English (d), and Ray Barrett (cga). A funky blues set. —*AMG*

Blue Bash / Jul. 16, 1963 / Verve ✦✦✦
Groove great Kenny Burrell and Jimmy Smith (Hammond organ) together on the same album. Includes a rendition of "Fever." —*AMG*

Arnett Cobb

b. Aug. 10, 1918, Houston, TX, d. Mar. 24, 1989, Houston, TX
Sax (Tenor) / Swing, Early R&B
A stomping Texas tenor player in the tradition of Illinois Jacquet, Arnett Cobb's accessible playing was between swing and early rhythm & blues. After playing in Texas with Chester Boone (1934–36) and Milt Larkin (1936–42), Cobb emerged in the big leagues by succeeding Illinois Jacquet with Lionel Hampton's Orchestra (1942–47). His version of "Flying Home No. 2" became a hit and he was a very popular soloist with Hampton. After leaving the band, Cobb formed his own group but his initial success was interrupted in 1948 when he had to undergo an operation on his spine. After recovering, he resumed touring. But a major car accident in 1956 crushed Cobb's legs and he was reduced to using crutches for the rest of his life. However by 1959 he returned to active playing and recording. Cobb spent most of the 1960s leading bands back in Texas but starting in 1973 he toured and recorded more extensively including a tenor summit with Jimmy Heath and Joe Henderson in Europe as late as 1988. Arnett Cobb made many fine records through the years for such labels as Apollo, Columbia/Okeh, Prestige (many of the latter are available on the OJC series), Black & Blue, Progressive, Muse, and Bee Hive. —*Scott Yanow*

Groove: It is unfortunate that there is not a lot of Arnett Cobb available yet on CD. Your best bet may be to search the old vinyl bins for the odd survivor from another era. Worth finding. —*Michael Erlewine*

● **Blows for 1300** / May 1947–Aug. 1947 / Delmark ✦✦✦✦
This Delmark CD reissues all 15 of Arnett Cobb's recordings for Apollo. The spirited tenor (who straddled the boundaries between swing and early R&B) is in prime early form with his sextet on a variety of basic material, much of it blues-oriented.

Milt Larkins takes vocals on three of the tracks and there are short solos by either Booty Wood or Al King on trombone, but otherwise the main focus is on Cobb's tough tenor. This very accessible music is both danceable and full of exciting performances that were formerly rare. —*Scott Yanow*

Blow, Arnett, Blow / Jan. 9, 1959 / Prestige ✦✦✦✦
Seldom has there been any album that could more accurately be termed a blowing session than this 1959 date. It matched a pair of frenetic, furious tenor saxophonists in Arnett Cobb and Eddie "Lockjaw" Davis, and also boasted a propulsive organist in Strethen Davis, a resourceful bassist in George Duvivier, and an ideal drummer in Arthur Edgehill. Edgehill kept the rhythms tight and crashing, while Cobb and Davis exchanged blistering solos, honks, grunts and bluesy dialogues. Duvivier's heavy backbeat and lines, along with Davis' stomping riffs, added vital supporting ingredients and helped make this a soul jazz and jam session classic. The six cuts here are a delight for fans of steamy, joyous jazz with a soul/blues sensibility. —*Ron Wynn*

★ **Go Power!** / Jan. 9, 1959 / Prestige ✦✦✦✦✦
Madcap exchanges with Eddie "Lockjaw" Davis (ts). If you find it, savor the purchase. —*Ron Wynn*

Smooth Sailing / Feb. 27, 1959 / Original Jazz Classics ✦✦✦
Noteworthy appearance from undervalued Buster Cooper (tb). Textbook soul power; exemplary sax technique from Cobb. —*Ron Wynn*

The Best of Arnett Cobb / Feb. 27, 1959 / Prestige ✦✦✦
This is a compilation from five major Cobb albums: *Smooth Sailin', Party Time, More Party Time, Movin' Right Along,* and *Sizzlin'.* —*AMG*

Party Time / May 14, 1959 / Prestige ✦✦✦
Splendid soul, funk inflections, torrid Cobb at times; reflective and melancholy at other moments. Fine lineup, though Ray Barretto and Art Taylor sometimes seem to dash underneath. —*Ron Wynn*

Again with Milt Buckner / Jul. 23, 1973 / Black & Blue ✦✦✦
This tough, bluesy session with organist Milt Buckner appears only on import. —*Myles Boisen*

Funky Butt / Jan. 22, 1980 / Progressive ✦✦✦
Real funky jazz; not instrumental pop fodder. —*Ron Wynn*

John Coltrane

b. Sep. 23, 1926, Hamlet, NC, d. Jul. 17, 1967, New York, NY
Sax (Soprano), Sax (Tenor) / Avant-Garde, Hard Bop, Free Jazz
The most influential jazz musician of the past 35 years (only Miles Davis comes close), one of the greatest saxophonists of all time and a remarkable innovator, John Coltrane certainly made his impact on jazz!

Unlike most musicians, Coltrane's style changed gradually but steadily over time. His career can be divided into at least five periods: Early days (1947–54), searching stylist (1955–56), sheets of sound (1957–59), the classic quartet (1960–64), and avant-garde (1965–67). Originally an altoist, he played in a Navy band during his period in the military, recording four privately issued songs in 1946. He settled in Philadelphia and then toured with King Kolax (1946–47), switched to tenor when he played with Eddie "Cleanhead" Vinson (1947–48), joined the Dizzy Gillespie big band (1948–49), and was with Dizzy's sextet (1950–51). Radio broadcasts from the latter association find Coltrane sounding heavily influenced by Dexter Gordon and hinting slightly at his future sound. He followed that gig with periods spent with the groups of Gay Crosse (1952), Earl Bostic (1952), Johnny Hodges (1953–54), and in Philadelphia for a few weeks with Jimmy Smith (1955).

The John Coltrane story really starts with his joining the Miles Davis Quintet in 1955. At first some observers wondered what Miles saw in the 28-year-old tenor who had an unusual sound and whose ideas sometimes stretched beyond his technique. However Davis was a masterful talent scout who could always hear potential greatness. Coltrane improved month by month, and by 1956 was competing with Sonny Rollins as the top young tenor; he even battled him to a draw on their recording of "Tenor Madness." Coltrane (along with Red Garland, Paul Chambers, and Philly Joe Jones) formed an important part of the classic Miles Davis Quintet, recording with Miles for Prestige and Columbia during 1955–56. In addition, Trane was starting to be featured on many of Prestige's jam-session-oriented albums.

1957 was the key year in John Coltrane's career. Fired by Miles Davis due to his heroin addiction, Coltrane permanently kicked the habit. He spent several months playing with Thelonious Monk's Quartet, an mutually beneficial association that gave Monk long-overdue acclaim and greatly accelerated the tenor's growth. His playing became even more adventurous than it had been, he recorded *Blue Train* (his first great album as a leader) and, when he rejoined Miles Davis in early 1958, Coltrane was unquestionably the most important tenor in jazz. During his next two years with Davis, Trane (whose style had been accurately dubbed "sheets of sound" by critic Ira Gitler) really took the chordal improvisation of bop to the breaking point, playing groups of notes with extreme speed and really tearing into the music. In addition to being one of the stars of Davis' recordings (including *Milestones* and *Kind of Blue*), Coltrane signed a contract with Atlantic and began to record classics of his own; "Giant Steps" (with its very complex chord structure) and "Naima" were among the many highlights.

By 1960 John Coltrane was long overdue to be a leader, and Miles Davis reluctantly let him go. Trane's direction was changing from utilizing as many chords as possible (it would be difficult to get any more extreme in that direction) to playing passionately over one or two-chord vamps. He hired pianist McCoy Tyner, drummer Elvin Jones and went through several bassists (Steve Davis, Art Davis, Reggie Workman) before settling on Jimmy Garrison in late 1961. The first artist signed to the new Impulse label, Coltrane was given complete freedom to record what he wanted. He had recently begun doubling on soprano, bringing an entirely new sound and approach to an instrument previously associated with the Dixieland of Sidney Bechet (although Steve Lacy had already started specializing on it) and Coltrane's 1960 Atlantic recording of "My Favorite Things" became a sort of theme song that he revisited on a nightly basis.

John Coltrane continued to evolve during 1961–64. He added Eric Dolphy as part of his group for a period and recorded extensively at the Village Vanguard in late 1961; the lengthy explorations were branded by conservative critics as "anti-jazz." Partly to counter their stereotyping (and short memories), Trane recorded with Duke Ellington in a quartet, a ballad program and a collaboration with singer Johnny Hartman; his playing throughout was quite beautiful. But live in concert his solos (which could be 45 minutes in length) were always intense and continually searching. He utilized such songs as "Impressions" (which used the same two-chord framework as Miles Davis' "So What") and "Afro Blue" for long workouts and took stunning cadenzas on the ballad "I Want To Talk About You." In addition to the Impulse! recordings, European radio broadcasts have since been released that show Coltrane's progress and consistency. And in December 1964 he displayed his interest in Eastern religion by recording the very popular *A Love Supreme*.

In 1965 it all began to change. Influenced and inspired by the intense and atonal flights of Albert Ayler, Archie Shepp, and Pharoah Sanders, Coltrane's music dropped most of the melodies and essentially became passionate sound explorations. *Ascension* from mid-year featured six additional horns (plus a second bassist) added to the quartet for almost totally free improvisations. Fast themes (such as "One Down, One Up" and "Sun Ship") were quickly disposed of on the way to waves of sound. Coltrane began to use Pharoah Sanders in his group to raise the intensity level even more and when he hired Rashied Ali as second drummer, it eventually caused McCoy Tyner (who said he could no longer hear himself) and Elvin Jones to depart.

In 1966 Coltrane had a quintet consisting of his wife Alice on piano, Sanders, Ali, and the lone holdover Jimmy Garrison. After a triumphant visit to Japan, Coltrane's health began to fail. Although the cause of his death on July 17, 1967 was listed as liver cancer, in reality it was probably overwork. Coltrane used to practice ten to twelve hours a day and when he had a job (which featured marathon solos), he would often spend his breaks practicing in his dressing room! It was only through such singlemindedness that he could reach such a phenomenal technical level, but the net result was his premature death.

Virtually every recording that John Coltrane made throughout his career is currently available on CD, quite a few books about him have been written, and a video (*The Coltrane Legacy*) gives today's jazz followers an opportunity to see him performing on a pair of half-hour television shows. Since Coltrane's passing no other giant has dominated jazz on the same level. In fact many

other saxophonists have built their entire careers on exploring music from just one of John Coltrane's periods! —*Scott Yanow Groove:* Here is another jazz giant that is so seminal that he affected everyone who heard him. No, Coltrane is not a soul jazz groove artist. However, in tunes like "My Favorite Things," the groove is way deep and long. Blues and groove lovers will tend to go for earlier Coltrane, and some of them are listed below. If you have the bucks, the eight-disc set on Atlantic, *Heavyweight Champion: The Complete Atlantic Recordings of John Coltrane* is perhaps the most incredible music in one box I know of. —*Michael Erlewine*

★ **Blue Train** / Sep. 15, 1957 / Blue Note ✦✦✦✦✦
A landmark album—stunning. This is Coltrane's only Blue Note recording as a leader, and he never made a better album in this particular hard-bop style. A must-hear for all jazz fans, Blue Train includes Coltrane's most impressive early composition, "Moment's Notice." With outstanding performances from sidemen Lee Morgan (tpt), Curtis Fuller (tb), and Kenny Drew (p). —*Michael Erlewine*

★ **Heavyweight Champion: The Complete Atlantic Recordings** / Jan. 15, 1959–May 25, 1961 / Rhino/Atlantic ✦✦✦✦✦
John Coltrane's two years with Atlantic can be thought of as his "middle period" during which he evolved from his sheets of sound approach to intense explorations over two-chord vamps. It is difficult to see how Rhino could have done a better job with this reissue, for they have come out with every scrap that could be found from Coltrane's Atlantic period. On the seven-CD box set is reissued the complete contents of the albums *Bags & Trane, Giant Steps, Coltrane Jazz, My Favorite Things, Coltrane Plays the Blues, Olé Coltrane, The Avant-Garde,* and *Coltrane's Sound,* the selections originally issued on *Alternate Takes* and three "new" alternate takes, plus (for the final CD) many previously unheard versions of five numbers including nine takes of "Giant Steps"! With such supporting players as vibraphonist Milt Jackson (who was actually the co-leader of *Bags and Trane*), pianists Hank Jones, Cedar Walton, Tommy Flanagan, Wynton Kelly, and McCoy Tyner, bassists Paul Chambers, Charlie Haden, Percy Heath, Steve Davis, Art Davis and Reggie Workman, drummers Connie Kay, Lex Humphries, Art Taylor, Jimmy Cobb, Ed Blackwell and Elvin Jones, trumpeters Don Cherry and Freddie Hubbard and Eric Dolphy on alto and flute, it is not too surprising that the music is both innovative and classic. This perfectly-done box (which also has a fine booklet) is essential for all serious jazz collections. —*Scott Yanow*

★ **Giant Steps** / Apr. 1, 1959 / Atlantic ✦✦✦✦✦
This is one of John Coltrane's classic sets; in fact this CD reissue (which adds alternate takes to five of the seven original recordings) almost doubles one's pleasure. In "Giant Steps" Coltrane built a tongue-twister of chord changes (stretching bop to its logical breaking point) which he would soon abandon in favor of long drones on simpler patterns. Not only does this CD give one the two earliest versions of "Giant Steps" but also "Naima," "Cousin Mary," "Spiral," "Syeeda's Song Flute," the underrated but remarkable "Countdown" and "Mr. P.C." Recorded while Coltrane was still with Miles Davis' group, this CD (which mostly features pianist Tommy Flanagan, bassist Paul Chambers and drummer Art Taylor) made it obvious that Coltrane had something very important of his own to say and that he would need his own band in the future to fully express himself. —*Scott Yanow*

The Art of John Coltrane: The Atlantic Years / 1959–1961 / Atlantic ✦✦✦✦✦
Good anthology collecting several good tracks from Coltrane's Atlantic period, among them the earliest "My Favorite Things" and other standards and originals. Although these songs weren't as transcendent as the Impulse period, they were an important indicator of future directions. —*Ron Wynn*

Coltrane Plays the Blues / Oct. 24, 1960 / Atlantic ✦✦✦✦
Recorded during the same week as his original version of "My Favorite Things," this LP by John Coltrane features six blues-oriented originals (five by Trane) including "Blues to Bechet" and "Mr. Syms." The music is more melodic than usual with Coltrane playing soprano on two of the six tracks; "Blues to You" is the best showcase for his intense tenor. —*Scott Yanow*

Coltrane's Sound / Oct. 24, 1960 / Atlantic ✦✦✦✦
Although one may not think of *Coltrane's Sound* as being one

of John Coltrane's most famous recordings, when one looks at its contents it quickly becomes obvious that this set ranks near the top. This CD reissue contains such classic material as "Central Park West," "Equinox," a reharmonized (and influential) version of "Body and Soul," the underrated "Satellite," "Liberia" and an intense rendition of "The Night Has a Thousand Eyes." Also included on this reissue is an alternate version of "Body and Soul" and the lesser-known "262." Co-starring pianist McCoy Tyner, bassist Steve Davis and drummer Elvin Jones, this set is highly recommended. —Scott Yanow

★ **My Favorite Things** / Oct. 24, 1960–Oct. 26, 1960 / Atlantic ◆◆◆◆◆
This LP was very influential when it came out and remains a classic. The first full album by the classic John Coltrane Quartet (with pianist McCoy Tyner, drummer Elvin Jones and their bassist of the time Steve Davis) consists of a fiery "Summertime," the lyrical "But Not for Me," a nice ballad for 'Trane's soprano on "Everytime We Say Goodbye" and most importantly, the lengthy "My Favorite Things." On the latter Coltrane, who had used a seemingly endless number of chords on the prior year's "Giant Steps," reduces the chords to a minimum and plays passionately over a repetitious vamp, creating startlingly new music. This set has since been reissued on CD and in one form or another is essential. —Scott Yanow

Afro Blue Impressions / Oct. 22, 1963 / Pablo ◆◆◆◆
Taken from several European concerts (producer Norman Granz is vague about the exact dates but those listed are educated guesses), this double CD finds John Coltrane and his classic Quartet playing their standard repertoire of the period. The nine songs include "Chasin' the Trane," "My Favorite Things," "Afro Blue," "I Want to Talk About You," "Impressions," and "Naima." No new revelations occur but this is a strong all-around set of 'Trane near his peak. —Scott Yanow

Hank Crawford (Bennie Ross Crawford, Jr.)

b. Dec. 21, 1934, Memphis, TN
Piano, Sax (Alto) / R&B, Soul Jazz, Hard Bop
Hank Crawford's greatest contribution to music has been his soulful sound, one that is immediately idenitifiable and flexible enough to fit into several types of settings. Early on he played with B.B. King, Bobby Bland, and Ike Turner in Memphis before moving to Nashville to study at Tennessee State College. He gained fame with Ray Charles (1958–63), at first playing baritone before switching to alto and becoming the music director. During 1959–69 Crawford recorded a popular series of soul jazz albums for Atlantic that made his reputation. His 1970s sets for Kudu were more commercial and streakier but in 1982 Crawford started recording regularly for Milestone, often matched up with organist Jimmy McGriff or pianist Dr. John. An influence on David Sanborn, Crawford's very appealing sound can still be heard in prime form in the mid-'90s. —Scott Yanow
Groove: Hank Crawford has recorded a lot. He is another artist who can play it all. You may want to search for albums with a small group format or where he is working with known funky players like Jimmy McGriff, David Fathead Newman, Jimmy Ponder, or Dr. John. —Michael Erlewine

Soul Survivors / Jan. 29, 1986+Jan. 30, 1986 / Milestone ◆◆◆◆
With Jimmy McGriff (organ), George Benson (g), Mel Lewis (d). soul jazz the way they did it in the '60s (almost). —Ron Wynn

Mr. Chips / Nov. 1986 / Milestone ◆◆◆
The funk is more notable on this 1986 set. —Ron Wynn

Soul Brothers / Jun. 15, 1987+Jun. 16, 1987 / Milestone ◆◆◆
Hank Crawford with Jimmy McGriff on the Hammond B-3 and George Benson (or Jimmy Ponder) on guitar. Worth seeking out. —AMG

Steppin' Up / Jun. 15, 1987+Jun. 16, 1987 / Milestone ◆◆◆◆
W/ Jimmy McGriff (organ), Jimmy Ponder (g). Solid, exuberant soul jazz. —Ron Wynn

● **On the Blue Side** / Apr. 4, 1989+Aug. 9, 1989 / Milestone ◆◆◆◆◆
With Jimmy McGriff on Hammond organ and Jimmy Ponder on guitar. Funky, mellow, and gritty. —Ron Wynn

Portrait / Mar. 19, 1991–Mar. 20, 1991 / Milestone ◆◆◆
With David Fathead Newman on tenor sax, Jimmy Ponder on guitar, and Johnny Hammond on the organ. Here is Crawford's latest collection of funky cuts and mellow ballads. —Ron Wynn

King Curtis (Curtis Ousley)

b. Feb. 7, 1934, Fort Worth, TX, **d.** Aug. 14, 1971, New York, NY
Sax (Tenor) / R&B
King Curtis was the last of the great R&B tenor sax giants. He came to prominence in the mid-'50s as a session musician in New York, recording, at one time or another, for most East Coast R&B labels. A long association with Atlantic/Atco began in 1958, especially on recordings by The Coasters. He recorded singles for many small labels in the '50s own Atco sessions (1958–1959), then Prestige/New Jazz and Prestige/TruSound for jazz and R&B albums (1960–1961). Curtis also had a #1 R&B single with "Soul Twist" on Enjoy Records (1962). He was signed by Capitol (1963–1964), where he cut mostly singles, including "Soul Serenade." Returning to Atlantic in 1965, he remained there for the rest of his life. He had solid R&B single success with "Memphis Soul Stew" and "Ode to Billie Joe" (1967). Beginning in 1967, Curtis started to take a more active studio role at Atlantic—leading and contracting sessions for other artists, producing with Jerry Wexler and later on his own. He also became the leader of Aretha Franklin's backing unit, The Kingpins. He compiled several albums of singles during this period. All aspects of his career were in full swing at the time he was murdered in 1971. —Bob Porter

● **The New Scene of King Curtis** / 1960 / Original Jazz Classics ◆◆◆◆
Tenor and soprano saxophonist King Curtis made several R&B and pop recordings during his career, and also was a prolific session artist. What's not quite as well known was that he also made some jazz and blues recordings in the early '60s, among them this 1960 date that matched him with Wynton Kelly, Oliver Jackson, and Paul Chambers doing mostly hard bop, plus some blues backing Little Brother Montgomery. It was reissued on CD in 1985. —Ron Wynn

Soul Meeting / Sep. 18, 1960 / Prestige ◆◆◆◆◆
W/ Nat Adderley (tpt). Sparkling soul jazz with hot solos. —Ron Wynn

Old Gold / Sep. 19, 1961 / Tru ◆◆◆
King Curtis with Jack McDuff on the Hammond organ, Billy Butler and Eric Gale on guitar. Funky renditions of standards like "Honky Tonk" and "Fever." —AMG

Best of King Curtis / 1962–1967 / Prestige ◆◆◆◆◆
Authoritative soul jazz date. —Ron Wynn

Instant Groove / Apr. 1, 1968–Apr. 23, 1969 / Atco ◆◆◆

Soul Twist / Enjoy ◆◆◆◆◆
Here's a fabulous New York R&B collection with fellow tenor honkers Willis "Gatortail" Jackson and Noble Watts. There's 15 cuts, mostly instrumental. —Roots & Rhythm Newsletter

Soul Twist & Other Golden Classics / 196 / Collectables ◆◆◆◆◆
1960–1964 hits. The title cut was a 1962 smash, and this album is worthwhile for that alone. —Ron Wynn

Live at Fillmore / 1971 / Atco ◆◆◆◆◆

● **Instant Soul: The Legendary King Curtis** / 1994 / ◆◆◆◆◆
King Curtis has never been given a comprehensive collection until *Instant Soul,* which features the best instrumental singles the distinctive, soulful, and influential tenor saxophonist ever recorded. —Stephen Thomas Erlewine

Eddie "Lockjaw" Davis

b. Mar. 2, 1922, New York, NY, **d.** Nov. 3, 1986, Culver City, CA
Sax (Tenor) / Bop, Swing, Hard Bop
Possessor of a cutting and immediately identifiable tough tenor tone, Eddie "Lockjaw" Davis could hold his own in a saxophone battle with anyone. Early on he picked up experience playing with the bands of Cootie Williams (1942–44), Lucky Millinder, Andy Kirk (1945–46) and Louis Armstrong. He began heading his own groups from 1946. Davis' earliest recordings as a leader tended to be explosive R&B affairs with plenty of screaming from his horn; he matched wits successfully with Fats Navarro on one session. Davis was with Count Basie's Orchestra on several occasional (including 1952–53, 1957 and 1964–73) and teamed up with Shirley Scott's trio during 1955–60. During 1960–62 he collaborated in some exciting performances and recordings with Johnny Griffin, a fellow tenor who was just as combative as Davis. After temporarily retiring to become a

booking agent (1963–64), Davis rejoined Basie. In his later years Lockjaw often recorded with Harry "Sweets" Edison and he remained a busy soloist up until his death. Through the decades he recorded as a leader for many labels including Savoy, Apollo, Roost, King, Roulette, Prestige/Jazzland/Moodsville, RCA, Storyville, MPS, Black & Blue, Spotlite, SteepleChase, Pablo, Muse, and Enja. —*Scott Yanow*

Groove: Davis recorded a lot. so I have picked out a few albums where he is working with one of the B-3 masters. His work with Shirley Scott is consistent, and probably gives you the best entry point into this great bluesy tenor. —*Michael Erlewine*

Jaws / Sep. 12, 1958 / Prestige ✦✦✦
Tenorman Eddie "Lockjaw" Davis and organist Shirley Scott co-led a popular combo during 1956–60, recording many albums and helping to popularize the idiom. This particular CD reissue of an LP (which at 37 minutes is a bit brief) finds the quartet (with bassist George Duvivier and drummer Arthur Edgehill) interpreting eight swing standards, alternating ballads with romps. It's a fine all-around showcase for the accessible group. —*Scott Yanow*

Smokin' / Sep. 12, 1958+Dec. 5, 1958 / Original Jazz Classics ✦✦✦✦
Tenor saxophonist Eddie "Lockjaw" Davis recorded many albums with organist Shirley Scott during 1956–60, cutting enough material on two dates to fill up four records. The seven selections included on this brief 36-minute CD (a straight reissue of an LP recorded during the same period as Davis's better-known *Cookbook* albums) also include Jerome Richardson (switching between flute, tenor, and baritone) on three of the numbers, bassist George Duvivier and drummer Arthur Edgehill. Together the group swings hard on basic originals, blues and an occasional ballad, showing why this type of accessible band was so popular during the era. —*Scott Yanow*

The Best of Eddie Davis and Shirley Scott / Sep. 12, 1958–May 1, 1959 / Prestige ✦✦✦
Featuring Shirley Scott, it's taken from four sessions of Davis with Scott. —*AMG*

● **The Eddie Lockjaw Davis Cookbook, Vol. 3** / Dec. 15, 1958 / Prestige ✦✦✦✦
Tenorman Eddie "Lockjaw" Davis made quite a few records with organist Shirley Scott during the late '50s. The basic originals in their *Cookbook* series tended to have titles that dealt with cooking; in this case "Heat 'n Serve," "The Goose Hangs High" and "Simmerin'" apply as does the standard "My Old Flame." Jerome Richardson's flute, baritone and tenor gives this CD reissue some variety, bassist George Duvivier and drummer Arthur Edgehill are fine in support and Shirley Scott shows that she was one of the top organists to emerge after the rise of Jimmy Smith. But Davis is the main star and his instantly recognizable sound is the most memorable aspect to this swinging session. —*Scott Yanow*

● **The Eddie Lockjaw Davis Cookbook, Vol. 2** / Dec. 1958 / Original Jazz Classics ✦✦✦✦
Eddie "Lockjaw" Davis's "cookbook" series helped make the group that the tenorman had in the late '50s with organist Shirley Scott famous. The quintet (which also includes flutist Jerome Richardson, bassist George Duvivier, and drummer Arthur Edgehill) is heard on this CD reissue performing three Davis-Scott originals, "Stardust," "I Surrender Dear" and a version of "Willow Weep for Me" that was originally part of a sampler. The straightahead music is interpreted quite colorfully by Davis and his group, one of the first popular organ combos. —*Scott Yanow*

Very Saxy / Apr. 29, 1959 / Prestige ✦✦✦
W/ Buddy Tate, Coleman Hawkins, and Arnett Cobb. Red-hot jam session. Summit meeting of mainstream veterans. —*Ron Wynn*

Jaws in Orbit / May 1, 1959 / Original Jazz Classics ✦✦✦
Includes Shirley Scott on the Hammond organ. This is early Scott, not yet all that funky. Traditional swinging, uptempo music. —*AMG*

Eddie Lockjaw Davis with Shirley Scott / Jan. 31, 1960 / Moodsville ✦✦✦

Streetlights / Nov. 15, 1962 / Prestige ✦✦✦✦✦
This CD combines together the music from two complete LPs (*I Only Have Eyes for You* and *Trackin'*) that were recorded the

same day with the identical personnel. Eddie "Lockjaw" Davis's tough tenor is well featured with his regular group of the time, a combo consisting of the powerful organist Don Patterson (who dominates many of the ensembles), guitarist Paul Weeden (talented but quite obscure), drummer Billy James, and guest bassist George Duvivier. The emphasis is on standards and intense blowing (even on the ballads) with the set being a good example of a strong tenor organ band. —*Scott Yanow*

Jackie Davis

b. Dec. 13, 1920, Jacksonville, FL
Organ / Hard Bop, Soul Jazz
Organist Jackie Davis was born December 13, 1920 in Jacksonville, FL. He was playing around town since he was nine years old and became part of an orchestra at ten. At the age of eleven Davis had saved and bought his own piano for $45. He played for dances, one nighters, and wherever he could find a gig. He studied with Earl Hines.

Davis graduated from Florida A&M in 1942 with a degree in music. He was listening to players like Milt Herth and George Wright, but it was "Wild" Bill Davis who opened his eyes to the power of the organ.

He was a student of Louis Jordan and spent some 14 months in his band. He recorded with Capitol Records for 16 years.

Davis made several albums in the '50s and '60s for Pacific Jazz, Vic, Trend, Capitol, and Warner Bros. in the '50s and '60s, most of them done in a soul jazz vein, though he switched to gospel for his last recordings. These were mostly small trio or combo dates, though there was also one with a trombone group, another with a vocal choir. —*Michael Erlewine & Ron Wynn*

● **Easy Does It** / Jan. 15, 1963 / Warner Brothers ✦✦✦
Jumpin' Jackie / 1983 / Capitol

Miles Davis

b. May 25, 1926, Alton, IL, **d.** Sep. 28, 1991, Santa Monica, CA
Trumpet / Avant-Garde, Bop, Cool, Fusion, Hard Bop
Miles Davis had quite a career, one with so many innovations that his name is one of the few that can be spoken in the same sentence with Duke Ellington. As a trumpeter, Davis was never a virtuoso on the level of his idol Dizzy Gillespie but by 1947 he possessed a distinctive cool-toned sound of his own. His ballad renditions (utilizing a Harmon mute) were exquisite yet never predictable, he mastered and then stripped down the bebop vocabulary to its essentials and he generally made every note count; as with Thelonious Monk, less was more in Miles' music.

But Miles Davis was much more than just a trumpeter. As a bandleader he was a brilliant talent scout, able to recognize potential in its formative stage and bring out the best in his sidemen. Among the musicians who greatly benefitted from their association with Davis were Gerry Mulligan (virtually unknown when he played with Miles' Birth of the Cool Nonet), Gil Evans, John Coltrane, Red Garland, Paul Chambers, Philly Joe Jones, Cannonball Adderley, Bill Evans, Jimmy Cobb, Wynton Kelly, George Coleman, Wayne Shorter, Herbie Hancock, Ron Carter, Tony Williams, Chick Corea, Jack DeJohnette, Dave Holland, John McLaughlin, Joe Zawinul, Keith Jarrett, Steve Grossman, Gary Bartz, Dave Liebman, Al Foster, Sonny Fortune, Bill Evans (the saxophonist), Kenny Garrett, Marcus Miller, Mike Stern, and John Scofield. This partial list forms a who's who of modern jazz.

In addition to his playing and nurturing of young talent, Miles Davis was quite remarkable in his rare ability to continually evolve. Most jazz musicians (with the exceptions of John Coltrane and Duke Ellington) generally form their style early on and spend the rest of their careers refining their sound. In contrast Miles Davis every five years or so would forge ahead, and due to his restless nature he not only played bop but helped found cool jazz, hard bop, modal music, and his own unusual brand of the avant-garde and fusion. Jazz history would be much different if Davis had not existed.

Born in Alton, IL, Miles Davis grew up in a middle-class family in East St. Louis. He started on trumpet when he was nine or ten, played in his high-school band and picked up early experience gigging with Eddie Randall's Blue Devils. Miles Davis has said that the greatest musical experience of his life was hearing the Billy Eckstine Orchestra (with Dizzy Gillespie and Charlie Parker) when it passed through St. Louis.

In September 1944 Davis went to New York to study at

Juilliard but spent much more time hanging out on 52nd Street and eventually dropped out of school. He played with Coleman Hawkins, made his recording debut in early 1945 (an impressive and nervous session with Rubberlegs Williams), and by late 1945 was playing regularly with Charlie Parker. Davis made an impression with his playing on Bird's recordings of "Now's the Time" and "Billie's Bounce." Although influenced by Dizzy Gillespie, even at this early stage the 19-year-old had something of his own to contribute.

When Charlie Parker went with Gillespie out to California, Miles followed him a few months later by travelling cross-country with Benny Carter's Orchestra. He recorded with Parker in California and when Bird formed a quintet in New York the following year, Davis was a key member. By late 1948 when he went out on his own, Miles Davis had formed a nonet that with arrangements by Gerry Mulligan, Gil Evans and John Lewis, helped usher in "cool jazz." Although the group only had one paying job (two weeks in September 1948 as an intermission band for Count Basie at the Royal Roost), its dozen recordings for Capitol were highly influential in the West Coast jazz movement.

Typically, by the time his nonet dates were renamed "Birth of the Cool," Miles Davis had moved on. He played at the Paris Jazz Festival in 1949 with Tadd Dameron and during 1951–54 was recording music with such sidemen as J.J. Johnson, Jimmy Heath, Horace Silver, Art Blakey, and Sonny Rollins that directly led to hard bop. However this was very much an off period for Miles because he was a heroin addict who was only working on an irregular basis. In 1954 he used all of his will power to permanently kick heroin and his recording that year of "Walkin '," although overlooked at the time, is a classic.

1955 was Miles Davis' breakthrough year. His performance of "'Round Midnight" at the Newport Jazz Festival alerted the critics that he was "back." Davis formed his classic quintet with John Coltrane, Red Garland, Paul Chambers, and Philly Joe Jones and during 1955–56 they recorded four well-received albums for Prestige and 'Round Midnight for Columbia. Davis' muted ballads were very popular and he became a celebrity. Even the breakup of the quintet in early 1957 did not slow up the momentum. Miles recorded the first of his full-length collaborations with arranger Gil Evans (Miles Ahead) which would be followed by Porgy and Bess (1958) and Sketches of Spain (1960); on these recordings Davis became one of the first trumpeters to stretch out on flugelhorn. In 1957 he went to France to record the soundtrack for Lift to the Scaffold and then in 1958 he formed his greatest group, a super sextet with Coltrane, Cannonball Adderley, Bill Evans, Paul Chambers, and Philly Joe Jones. Although Evans and Jones were eventually succeeded by Wynton Kelly and Jimmy Cobb, all of the recordings by this remarkable group somehow live up to their potential with Milestones and Kind of Blue being all-time classics that helped to introduce modal (or scalar) improvising to jazz.

If Miles Davis had retired in 1960, he would still be famous in jazz history, but he had many accomplishments still to come. The sextet gradually changed with Adderley departing and Coltrane's spot being taken first by Sonny Stitt then Hank Mobley. Although 1960–63 is thought of as a sort-of resting period for Davis, his trumpet chops were in prime form and he was playing at the peak of his powers. With the departure of the rhythm section in 1963, it was time for Miles to form another group. By 1964 he had a brilliant young rhythm section (Herbie Hancock, Ron Carter and Tony Williams) who were open to the innovations of Ornette Coleman in addition to funky soul jazz. With George Coleman on tenor, the sidemen really inspired Davis and, although he was sticking to his standard repertoire, the renditions were full of surprises and adventurous playing. By late 1964 Coleman had departed and, after Sam Rivers filled in for a European tour, Wayne Shorter was the new tenor. During 1965–68 Miles Davis' second classic quintet bridged the gap between hard bop and free jazz, playing inside/outside music that was quite unique. Although at the time the quintet was overshadowed by the avant-garde players, in the 1980s the music of this group would finally become very influential, particularly on Wynton and Branford Marsalis.

During 1968–69 Miles Davis' music continued to change. He persuaded Hancock to use electric keyboards, Shorter started doubling on soprano, the influence of rock began to be felt and, after the rhythm section changed (to Chick Corea, Dave Holland

and Jack DeJohnette), Davis headed one of the earliest fusion bands. Rock and funk rhythms combined with jazz improvisations to form a new hybrid music and Miles' recordings of In a Silent Way and Bitches Brew (both of which used additional instruments) essentially launched the fusion era.

Many of Miles Davis' fans essentially write off his post-1968 music, not realizing that not all of the recordings sound the same and that some were more successful than others. If Miles Davis had sold out to gain a larger audience, then why did he record so many 20-minute jams that could not possibly be played on the radio? During 1970–75 the ensembles of his group (which sometimes utilized two or three guitars and a couple of keyboardists) became quite dense, the rhythms were often intense and Davis unfortunately often used electronics that distorted the sound of his horn. Actually, the only album from this era that is a complete failure is On the Corner (Davis is largely absent from that fiasco) and Live/Evil, Jack Johnson and 1975's Panagea all have memorable sections.

And then, suddenly, in 1975 Miles Davis retired. He was in bad health and, as he frankly discusses in his autobiography Miles, very much into recreational drugs. The jazz world speculated about what would happen if and when he returned. In 1981 Davis came back with a new band that was similar to his '70s group except that the ensembles were quite a bit sparser. The rock influence was soon replaced by funk and pop elements and, as he became stronger, Miles Davis' trumpet playing proved to still be in excellent form. He toured constantly during his last decade and his personality seemed to have mellowed a bit. Where once he had been quite forbidding and reluctant to be friendly to nonmusicians, Davis was at times eager to grant interviews and talk about his past. Although he had never looked back musically, in the summer of 1991 he shocked everyone by letting Quincy Jones talk him into performing Gil Evans arrangements from the past at the Montreux Jazz Festival. Even if he had Wallace Roney and Kenny Garrett take some of the solos, Davis was in stronger-than-expected form playing the old classics. And then two months later he passed away at the age of 65.

There are currently more than 120 valuable Miles Davis recordings in print including many live sets issued on European labels. Taken as a whole, these form quite a legacy. —Scott Yanow

Groove: Miles Davis is another great artist who helped to create and excell in so many different jazz styles that it can be confusing where to start listening. Kind of Blue is on every top-100 jazz-album list I have ever seen, and for good reason. Another fine place to begin is the Blue Note release called Ballads & Blues. I have listed some good albums below. Earlier Davis may be better. From the time of Bitches Brew on, blues lovers may have trouble getting into the sounds. But be sure to pay your respect to Miles Davis. He is the very heart of the blues and (like John Coltrane) has shaped the very core of jazz itself. —Michael Erlewine

★ **Ballads And Blues** / Apr. 20, 1953–Mar. 9, 1958 / Blue Note ✦✦✦✦✦

What a treat! An incredible compilation for those Davis fans who love his cooler bluesy/modal material. The brilliant producer Michael Cuscuna has combed through the early Davis "Birth of the Cool" sessions (1950), several Blue Note sessions in 1952 and 1954, plus one cut from the classic Adderley/Davis album Somethin' Else to create a cool blues compilation of Davis' stuff stripped of all the bop uptempo elements. The result is a precursor to Kind of Blue, an album that shows all of the bluesy cool Miles Davis that many of us are so very fond of. Don't miss it. —Michael Erlewine

★ **Bags Groove** / 1954 / Prestige ✦✦✦✦✦

Miles Davis & Modern Jazz Giants. Sterling sessions with Miles and Monk (p), Milt Jackson (vib), Sonny Rollins (ts), and Horace Silver (p). —Ron Wynn

Miles / 1955 / Prestige ✦✦✦

☆ **Cookin'** / Nov. 16, 1955–Oct. 26, 1956 / Prestige ✦✦✦✦

Trumpeter Davis (along with tenor saxophonist John Coltrane, pianist Red Garland, bassist Paul Chambers and drummer Philly Joe Jones) are heard on such tunes as "My Funnny Valentine" (Davis's earliest version of this standard), "Blues by Five," "Airegin" and a medley of "Tune Up" and "When Lights Are Low." This classic music has great sound. —Scott Yanow

★ **Workin'** / 1956 / Prestige ✦✦✦✦✦
Miles Davis' 1956 Quintet was one of his classic groups, featuring tenor saxophonist John Coltrane, pianist Red Garland, bassist Paul Chambers, and drummer Philly Joe Jones. They recorded four albums for Prestige in two marathon sessions. Among the highlights are "It Never Entered My Mind," "Four," "In Your Own Sweet Way," and two versions of "The Theme." The music is essential in one form or another. —*Scott Yanow*

☆ **Steamin'** / 1956 / Prestige ✦✦✦✦✦
This classic Prestige session (one of four) has been reissued many times. The release from the audiophile label DCC Jazz is a gold compact disc. Davis is heard with his classic quintet of 1956 (which featured tenor saxophonist John Coltrane, pianist Red Garland, bassist Paul Chambers, and drummer Philly Joe Jones) performing six numbers, all of which are somewhat memorable. Highpoints are "Surrey with the Fringe on Top," "Diane," and "When I Fall in Love;" Davis's muted tone rarely sounded more beautiful. —*Scott Yanow*

Relaxin' / 1956 / Original Jazz Classics ✦✦✦✦

Live in New York / 1957–1959 / Bandstand ✦✦✦

★ **Milestones** / Feb. 4, 1958–Mar. 4, 1958 / Columbia ✦✦✦✦✦
Kind of Blue might have received most of the acclaim but *Milestones*, the recorded debut of the Miles Davis Sextet, is in the same league. This remarkable supergroup (featuring Davis' trumpet, tenor saxophonist John Coltrane, altoist Cannonball Adderley, pianist Red Garland, bassist Paul Chambers, and drummer Philly Joe Jones) was arguably the greatest one Miles Davis ever led. "Two Bass Hit" features the two saxes trading off with fire and "Billy Boy" showcases the Red Garland trio (showing what they learned from Ahmad Jamal), but "Straight No Chaser" really demonstrates what a powerhouse band this was. —*Scott Yanow*

★ **Kind of Blue** / Mar. 2, 1959–Apr. 22, 1959 / Columbia ✦✦✦✦✦
Miles Davis' most famous recording remains his most influential. It is not just that this album helped popularize modal jazz (improvising based on modes or scales rather than running chord changes) or that it introduced two future standards ("So What" and "All Blues") and three other gems ("Freddie Freeloader," "Blue in Green," and "Flamenco Sketches"). Most impressive is how the solos of Miles Davis, John Coltrane, and Cannonball Adderley (what a lineup), despite their differing styles, fit the songs perfectly. —*Scott Yanow*

Live in Stockholm 1960 / Mar. 22, 1960 / Royal Jazz ✦✦✦✦✦
This remarkable two-CD set features John Coltrane with the Miles Davis Quintet just a short time before 'Trane went out on his own. Davis sounds inspired by his star tenor and although Coltrane was reportedly bored with the repertoire ("On Green Dolphin Street," "All Blues," "Fran-Dance," "Walkin'," and two versions of "So What," he is at his most explorative throughout this often-stunning music. In addition, the rhythm section (pianist Wynton Kelly, bassist Paul Chambers, and drummer Jimmy Cobb) had been together for two years and is really tight. This highly recommended set also includes a brief interview with Coltrane from this period. —*Scott Yanow*

Wild Bill Davis

b. Nov. 24, 1918, Glasgow, MO, d. 1995
Organ / Swing
Prior to the rise of Jimmy Smith in 1956, Wild Bill Davis was the pacesetter among organists. He actually played guitar and wrote arrangements for Milt Larkin's legendary band during 1939–42. Davis played piano with Louis Jordan's Tympany Five (1945–49) before switching to organ in 1950 and heading his own influential organ/guitar/drums trios. Davis was originally supposed to record "April in Paris" with Count Basie's Orchestra in 1955 but when he could not make the session, Basie used his arrangement for the full band and had a major hit. In addition to working with his own groups in the 1960s, Davis made several albums with his friend Johnny Hodges, leading to tours during 1969–71 with Duke Ellington. In the '70s he recorded for *Black & Blue* with a variety of swing all-stars and played with Lionel Hampton, appearing at festivals through the early '90s. —*Scott Yanow*
Groove: An early jazz-organ pioneer, Davis tends to be found in a large-group format. You can find him as a sideman if you look

for him. He played behind Illinois Jacquet, Lionel Hampton, Frank Foster, and Sonny Stitt on occasion. . —*Michael Erlewine*

Wild Bill Davis at Birdland / Mar. 21, 1955 / Epic ✦✦✦✦✦

The Music from Milk and Honey / Feb. 1962 / Prestige ✦✦

Con Soul and Sax / Jan. 7, 1965 / RCA ✦✦✦✦✦

★ **In Atlantic City** / Aug. 10, 1966+Aug. 11, 1966 / RCA ✦✦✦✦✦

Impulsions / May 9, 1972+May 10, 1972 / Black & Blue ✦✦✦

Joey De Francesco

b. 1971, Philadelphia, PA
Organ / Bop, Soul Jazz, Hard Bop
The comeback of the organ in jazz during the late '80s was partly due to the rise of Joey DeFrancesco, a brilliant and energetic player whose style is heavily influenced by Jimmy Smith.

Joey DeFrancesco was born April 10, 1971 in Springfield, PA and was raised in the Philadelphia area. The son of Papa John DeFrancisco, a fierce Hammond organ player himself, Joey got an early start on piano when he was five and within a year had switched to his father's instrument, the organ.

He won all kinds of major awards in high school including the Philadelphia Jazz Society's McCoy Tyner Scholarship. In the first Thelonious Monk International Jazz Piano Competition in 1987 he was a finalist at the age of 16. He is a decent player, too.

He had a record contract with Columbia, was playing with Miles Davis (1988) by the time he left high school and has led his own groups ever since. DeFrancesco is the most important new organist to emerge during the past decade. He has recorded for Columbia and Muse. —*Scott Yanow & Michael Erlewine*

● **Where Were You?** / 1991 / Columbia ✦✦✦✦✦
Nice mix-and-match quartet sessions. The lineup is split between esteemed veterans like Illinois Jacquet (sax) and Milt Hinton (b) and the younger Wallace Roney (tpt) and Kirk Whalum (ts). —*Ron Wynn*

Live at the 5 Spot / 1993 / Columbia ✦✦✦
Organist Joey DeFrancesco clearly had a good time during this jam session. His fine quintet (which has strong soloists in altoist Robert Landham, trumpeter Jim Henry and especially guitarist Paul Bollenback) starts things off with a runthrough of "rhythm changes" during "The Eternal One" and the hornless trio cuts loose on a swinging "I'll Remember April," but otherwise all of the other selections feature guests. Tenors Illinois Jacquet, Grover Washington, Jr., Houston Person, and Kirk Whalum all fare well on separate numbers (Jacquet steals the show on "All of Me") and on the closing blues DeFrancesco interacts with fellow organist Captain Jack McDuff. Few surprises occur overall (the tenors should have all played together) but the music is quite pleasing and easily recommended to DeFrancesco's fans. —*Scott Yanow*

Cornell Dupree

b. Dec. 1942, Fort Worth, TX
Guitar / Blues, Soul Jazz
Long a top R&B session player, Cornell Dupree led excellent jazz-oriented sets for Amazing and Kokopelli in the early '90s, showing that he was capable of also playing swinging jazz. Dupree was with King Curtis in 1962 before becoming a studio musician.

He has recorded with artists like Harry Belafonte, Joe Cocker, Michael Bolton, Lou Rawls, Roberta Flack, Robert Palmer, Lena Horn, and Mariah Carey—over 2500 albums as a sideman!

He toured with Aretha Franklin (1967–76) and a variety of top pop and R&B acts and in the early '70s worked with the group Stuff. His 1988 solo album *Coast to Coast* won a Grammy. Dupree's blues-oriented guitar style continues to be in demand. —*Michael Erlewine & Scott Yanow*

Shadow Dancing / May 1979 / MSG ✦✦✦
Dupree on guitar with Hank Crawford on alto sax and organist Jimmy Smith playing the electric piano. Includes a rendition of "The Creeper." —*AMG*

★ **Coast to Coast** / 1988 / Antilles ✦✦✦✦✦
& Who It Is. Some excellent session players sound hot on the R&B, tepid on the fusion. —*Ron Wynn*

● **Bop 'N' Blues** / Nov. 15, 1994–Feb. 13, 1995 / Kokopelli ✦✦✦✦
Guitarist Cornell Dupree has long been famous for his blues and R&B solos, so even he was surprised (and a bit apprehensive)

when label-head Herbie Mann suggested he record a variety of bop-oriented standards. As it turned out, several of the tunes were blues anyway (such as "Bags' Groove," "Now's the Time" and "Walkin'") and Dupree was free to adapt the other songs to his own style. "Freedom Jazz Dance" became a funky vamp while "My Little Suede Shoes" was drastically slowed down and stretched out. With backing from a versatile rhythm section and occasional contributions from altoist Bobby Watson, trumpeter Terell Stafford and baritonist Ronnie Cuber, Dupree sounds perfectly at home throughout this fine CD, even on "Manteca" and "'Round Midnight." —*Scott Yanow*

Charles Earland

b. May 24, 1941, Philadelphia, PA
Organ / Soul Jazz, Hard Bop
Charles Earland has played organ and other keyboards plus soprano sax. His style has been influenced by Jimmy Smith and Jimmy McGriff, and combines elements of soul jazz with blues, funk and pop. He doesn't have as heavy a sound as Groove Holmes or Jack McDuff, but has done some solid dates for Prestige, Muse and other labels. He became one of the most popular organists in the '70s using walking and rolling bass pedal lines in either soul jazz or jazz-rock and funk contexts. Earland actually began his career as a saxophonist working with McGriff. He began heading his own band in the '60s, and unable to either attract or keep organists in his bands, switched to the instrument in 1963. Earland played organ with Lou Donaldson in the late '60s, then issued his own albums on Choice and Prestige. His *Black Talk* album in 1969 featured his own compositions. The LP's success won Earland a long-term deal with Prestige. He started mixing soprano sax, synthesizer, electric piano and organ in his bands. During the '70s Earland appeared at the Montreux and Newport jazz festivals and played on the soundtrack for the film "The Dynamite Brothers." His '70s Prestige albums alternated between combos, large groups and some sessions with vocalists. His '73 date *Leaving This Planet* included guest appearances from Freddie Hubbard, Eddie Henderson and Joe Henderson. After a live session recorded in Montreaux in 1974, Earland switched labels to Mercury, cutting one studio date, then Muse for four albums. The first three reunited Earland with guitarist Jimmy Ponder, who'd played on his first album as a leader. He then recorded with Columbia on sessions ranging from large bands to dates with The Brecker Brothers and female vocalists. During the '80s and '90s, Earland returned to Muse for quartet/combo dates, including one co-led by George Coleman. —*Ron Wynn and Michael Erlewine*

Soul Crib / Nov. 1969 / Choice ✦✦

★ **Black Talk** / Dec. 15, 1969 / Original Jazz Classics ✦✦✦✦✦
This CD reissue of a Prestige date is one of the few successful examples of jazz musicians from the late '60s taking a few rock and pop songs and turning them into creative jazz. Organist Charles Earland and his sextet, which includes trumpeter Virgil Jones, Houston Person on tenor and guitarist Melvin Sparks, perform a variation of "Eleanor Rigby" titled "Black Talk," two originals, a surprisingly effective rendition of "Aquarius" and a classic rendition of "More Today than Yesterday." Fans of organ combos are advised to pick up this interesting set. —*Scott Yanow*

Soul Crib / 1969 / Choice ✦✦✦
Earland with George Coleman on tenor sax, Jimmy Ponder on guitar, and Walter Perkins on drums. —*Michael Erlewine*

Black Drops / Jun. 1, 1970 / Prestige ✦✦✦
Early soul jazz, occasional R&B and pop cuts from organist Charles Earland, just cutting his third album as a leader at that time. His organ solos were sometimes churning and impressive, but at other times bogged down in cliches and repetitive phrases. But the potential Earland showed on most cuts has since materialized. —*Ron Wynn*

Living Black / Sep. 17, 1970 / Prestige ✦✦✦
Funky taste of soul done at the Key Club in Newark. With Grover Washington, Jr. on tenor sax. —*Ron Wynn*

Soul Story / Apr. 3, 1971 / Prestige ✦✦✦
With Houston Person on tenor sax and Maynard Parker on guitar. —*AMG*

Leaving This Planet / Dec. 11, 1973–Dec. 13, 1973 / Prestige ✦✦✦✦✦
Great stints by Joe Henderson (sax), Eddie Henderson (tpt), and Freddie Hubbard (tpt). His most ambitious album. —*Ron Wynn*

Smokin' / 1977 / Muse ✦✦✦
Fine mid-'70s sextet set featuring Earland's customary soul jazz, blues, and funk, with uptempo and ballad originals. Tenor saxophonists David Schnitter and George Coleman excel, as does guitarist Jimmy Ponder. —*Ron Wynn*

Front Burner / Jun. 27, 1988–Jun. 28, 1988 / Milestone ✦✦✦
Comeback for veteran organist. "Mom & Dad" (in 10/4 time) is infectious. —*Michael G. Nastos*

Third Degree Burn / May 15, 1989–May 16, 1989 / Milestone ✦✦✦✦
Sparkling funky tenor from David "Fathead" Newman and solid organ from Earland. Also: Grover Washington, Jr. —*Ron Wynn*

Whip Appeal / May 23, 1990 / Muse ✦✦✦
Good, although sometimes lightweight, soul jazz and funk session from 1990. Fine solos by trumpeter Johnny Coles, tenor saxophonist Houston Person, and Earland, plus effective Latin backgrounds from Lawrence Killian on conga. —*Ron Wynn*

Mighty Burner / Prestige ✦✦

Jimmy Forrest

b. Jan. 24, 1920, St. Louis, MO, **d.** Aug. 26, 1980, Grand Rapids, MI
Sax (Tenor) / Swing, Early R&B
A fine all-around tenor player, Jimmy Forrest is best-known for recording "Night Train," a song that he "borrowed" from the last part of Duke Ellington's "Happy Go Lucky Local." While in high school in St. Louis, Forrest worked with pianist Eddie Johnson, the legendary Fate Marable and the Jeter-Pillars Orchestra. In 1938 he went on the road with Don Albert and then was with Jay McShann's Orchestra (1940–42). In New York Forrest played with Andy Kirk (1942–48) and Duke Ellington (1949) before returning to St. Louis. After recording "Night Train," Forrest became a popular attraction and recorded a series of jazz-oriented R&B singles. Among his most important later associations were with Harry "Sweets" Edison (1958–63), Count Basie's Orchestra (1972–77) and Al Grey with whom he co-led a quintet until his death. Forrest recorded for United (reissued by Delmark), Prestige/New Jazz (1960–62) and Palo Alto (1978) — *Scott Yanow*

★ **Night Train** / Nov. 27, 1951–Sep. 7, 1953 / Delmark ✦✦✦✦✦
This is tremendous early-'50s material from Forrest's days on the pioneering United label. The title cut was a huge jukebox and R&B hit. —*Ron Wynn*

All the Gin Is Gone / Dec. 10, 1959–Dec. 12, 1959 / Delmark ✦✦✦✦
Straight bop. Grant Green's (g) first recording session (in Chicago)—he was flown in from St. Louis by Forrest. W/ Harold Mabern (p), Elvin Jones (d). —*AMG*

Black Forrest / Dec. 10, 1959–Dec. 12, 1959 / Delmark ✦✦✦
Bop. From the same session as *All the Gin Is Gone*. Includes the lovely "But Beautiful," featuring Grant Green (g), with Forrest sitting this tune out. Recorded in Chicago. —*AMG*

Forrest Fire / Aug. 9, 1960 / New Jazz ✦✦✦✦
An exceptional date, with some instructive early Larry Young (organ) solos. —*Ron Wynn*

Out of the Forrest / Apr. 18, 1961 / Original Jazz Classics ✦✦✦✦
With Joe Zawinul (piano), Tommy Potter (bass), and Clarence Johnston (drums) backing Jimmy Forrest on eight tracks. An honest and rewarding big tenor date with a touch of Lester Young. This was excellent smokey soulful tenor playing which I think has probably been overlooked by many. —*Bob Rusch, Cadence*

Heart of the Forrest / Dec. 28, 1978 / Palo Alto ✦✦✦
A live date at the "Alibi Club" in Grand Rapids, MI, with Shirley Scott on Hammond organ. —*AMG*

Frank Foster

b. Sep. 23, 1928, Cincinnati, OH
Sax (Tenor) / Swing, Hard Bop
A very talented tenor saxophonist and arranger, Frank Foster has been associated with the Count Basie Orchestra off and on since 1953. Early on he played in Detroit with the many talented local players and, after a period in the Army (1951–53), he joined Basie's big band. Well-featured on tenor during his Basie years (1953–64), Foster also contributed plenty of arrangements and

such originals as "Down for the Count," "Blues Backstage" and the standard "Shiny Stockings." In the latter half of the 1960s Foster was a freelance writer. In addition to playing with Elvin Jones (1970–72) and occasionally with the Thad Jones-Mel Lewis Orchestra, he led his Loud Minority big band. In 1983 Foster co-led a quintet with Frank Wess and he toured Europe with Jimmy Smith in 1985. Although influenced by John Coltrane in his playing, Foster was able to modify his style when he took over the Count Basie ghost band in 1986, revitalizing it and staying at the helm until 1995. Outside of his Basie dates, Foster has led sessions for Vogue, Blue Note (1954 and 1968), Savoy, Argo, Prestige, Mainstream, Denon, Catalyst, Bee Hive, SteepleChase, Pablo, and Concord. —*Scott Yanow*

● **Soul Outing** / Jun. 27, 1966 / Prestige ✦✦✦
The House That Love Built / Sep. 1982 / Steeple Chase ✦✦✦✦
Two for the Blues / Oct. 11, 1983+Oct. 12, 1983 / Pablo ✦✦✦✦✦
Excellent duo set. —*Ron Wynn*

Grant Green

b. Jun. 6, 1931, St. Louis, MO, d. Jan. 31, 1979, New York, NY
Guitar / Soul Jazz, Hard Bop
Grant Green was born in St. Louis on July 6, 1931, learned his instrument in grade school from his guitar-playing father, and was playing professionally by the age of thirteen with a gospel group. He worked gigs in his home town and in East St. Louis, Illinois until he moved to New York in 1960 at the suggestion of Lou Donaldson. Green told Dan Morgenstern in a *Down Beat* interview, "The first thing I learned to play was boogie woogie. Then I had to do a lot of rock and roll. It's all blues, anyhow."

His extensive foundation in R&B combined with a mastery of bebop and simplicity that put expressiveness ahead of technical expertise. Green was a superb blues interpreter, and his later material was predominantly blues and R&B, though he was also a wondrous ballad and standards soloist. He was a particular admirer of Charlie Parker, and his phrasing often reflected it. Green played in the '50s with Jimmy Forrest, Harry Edison, and Lou Donaldson.

He also collaborated with many organists, among them Brother Jack McDuff, Sam Lazar, Baby Face Willette, Gloria Coleman, Big John Patton, and Larry Young. During the early '60s, both his fluid, tasteful playing in organ/guitar/drum combos and his other dates for Blue Note established Green as a star, though he seldom got the critical respect given other players. He was off the scene for a bit in the mid-'60s, but came back strong in the late '60s and '70s. Green played with Stanley Turrentine, Dave Bailey, Yusef Lateef, Joe Henderson, Hank Mobley, Herbie Hancock, McCoy Tyner, and Elvin Jones.

Sadly, drug problems interrupted his career in the '60s, and undoubtedly contributed to the illness he suffered in the late '70s. Green was hospitalized in 1978 and died a year later. Despite some rather uneven LPs near the end of his career, the great body of his work represents marvelous soul jazz, bebop, and blues.

A severely underrated player during his lifetime, Grant Green is one of the great unsung heroes of jazz guitar. Like Stanley Turrentine, he tends to be left out of the books. Although he mentions Charlie Christian and Jimmy Raney as influences, Green always claimed he listened to horn players (Charlie Parker and Miles Davis) and not other guitar players, and it shows. No other player has this kind of single-note linearity (he avoids chordal playing). There is very little of the intellectual element in Green's playing, and his technique is always at the service of his music. And it is music, plain and simple, that makes Green unique.

Green's playing is immediately recognizable—perhaps more than any other guitarist. Green has been almost systematically ignored by jazz buffs with a bent to the cool side, and he has only recently begun to be appreciated for his incredible musicality. Perhaps no guitarist has ever handled standards and ballads with the brilliance of Grant Green. Mosaic, the nation's premier jazz reissue label, issued a wonderful collection, *The Complete Blue Note Recordings with Sonny Clark,* featuring prime early '60s Green albums plus unissued tracks. Some of the finest examples of Green's work can be found there. —*Michael Erlewine and Ron Wynn*

Grant's First Stand / Jan. 28, 1961 / Blue Note ✦✦✦
His first album, with Baby Face Willette on Hammond organ and

Ben Dixon on drums. Hard to find. Some of this material was released in Japan. —*Michael Erlewine*

Green Blues / Mar. 15, 1961 / Muse ✦✦✦
With Frank Haynes on tenor sax, Billy Gardner on piano, Ben Tucker on bass, and Dave Bailer on drums. Originally issued on *Jazztime* under Dave Bailey's name, and now reissued in this format. This is early Green, his second session, and the music is straight-ahead mainstream jazz with a bluesy flavor. This material is available on *Reaching Out,* a release on the Black Lion label. —*Michael Erlewine*

Reaching Out / Mar. 15, 1961 / Black Lion ✦✦✦
Green is in fine form, as is pianist Gardner (better known as an organist), but the album is perhaps most valuable for the contributions of the obscure tenorman Frank Haynes who died in 1965; his sound will remind some a little of Stanley Turrentine. —*Scott Yanow, Cadence*

Green Street / Apr. 1, 1961 / Blue Note ✦✦✦✦
Most of guitarist Grant Green's recordings of the 1960s feature him in larger groups, making this trio outing with bassist Ben Tucker and drummer Dave Bailey (a CD reissue of the original LP plus two added alternate takes) a strong showcase for his playing. Green, whose main competitor on guitar at the time was Wes Montgomery, already had his own singing sound and a highly individual hornlike approach. He stretches out on a full set of attractive originals plus "'Round Midnight" and "Alone Together," so this reissue is an excellent introduction to his appealing and hard-swinging style. —*Scott Yanow*

Sunday Mornin' / Jun. 4, 1961 / Blue Note ✦✦✦
A Blue Note release that has not yet been reissued, this finds Green with Kenny Drew on piano, Ben Tucker on bass, and Ben Dixon on drums. Includes a rendition of "God Bless the Child," "Freedom March," and "Exodus." —*AMG*

Grantstand / Aug. 1, 1961 / Blue Note ✦✦✦✦
A quartet session with Yusef Lateef (ts, fl) and vintage Jack McDuff on the Hammond organ. Al Harewood on drums, the organ taking up the bass chores. The 15-minute "Blues in Maude's Flat" is very nice indeed, and "My Funny Valentine" (with Lateef on flute) is just plain lovely. No one does standards like Green. —*AMG*

Remembering / Aug. 29, 1961 / Blue Note ✦✦✦
Available perhaps in Japan, this early Green date includes Horace Parlan on piano, Wilber Ware on bass, and Al Harewood on drums. Mostly standards. —*AMG*

● **Born to Be Blue** / Dec. 11, 1961+Mar. 1, 1962 / Blue Note ✦✦✦✦✦
This is the one to get, a taste of what is in the (now out-of-print) Mosaic box set *The Complete Blue Note Recordings of Grant Green with Sonny Clark.* This is vintage Green with Sonny Clark on piano and Ike Quebec on tenor sax. The combination is mesmerizing. This is the stuff groove addicts dream of—a desert island classic pick. Green is the master of standards and the set includes "Someday My Prince Will Come," "Count Every Star," and "Back in Your Own Back Yard." Aside from being just the best jazz, it makes for great easy-listening music. Grandma will love it too. —*Michael Erlewine*

Gooden's Corner / Dec. 23, 1961 / Blue Note ✦✦✦✦✦
This is an album of real beauty and synergy between Green and pianist Sonny Clark, who, along with Sam Jones on bass and Louis Hayes on drums, rounds out the quartet. Green, an expert with standards, offers "Moon River," "On Green Dolphin Street," and "Count Every Star." This album was also released on *The Complete Blue Note Recordings of Grant Green and Sonny Clark.* —*Michael Erlewine*

★ **Complete Blue Note with Sonny Clark** / Dec. 23, 1961–Sep. 7, 1962 / Mosaic ✦✦✦✦✦
Guitarist Grant Green and pianist Sonny Clark recorded together on five separate occasions during the 1961–62 period but virtually none of the music was released domestically until decades later. These performances were clearly lost in the shuffle for the solos are of a consistent high quality and the programs were well-paced and swinging. Now on this Mosaic limited-edition four-CD boxed set, the long-lost music (much of which had been previously available only in Japan) is saved for posterity. Green and Clark blend together well, tenor saxophonist Ike Quebec joins their quartet for one session and the final two numbers add

Latin percussion. All of this music should be easily enjoyed by hard bop fans. Includes Blue Note albums *Gooden's Corner, Nigeria, Oleo, Born to Be Blue* (w/ Ike Quebec), plus unissued tracks. *—Scott Yanow*

Nigeria / Jan. 13, 1962 / Blue Note ♦♦♦♦♦
This is a great album with the classic synergy of Green and pianist Sonny Clark, who along with Sam Jones on bass and Art Blakey complete the quartet. This album was also released on *The Complete Blue Note Recordings of Grant Green and Sonny Clark.* Just classic Green. *—Michael Erlewine*

Oleo / Jan. 31, 1962 / Blue Note ♦♦♦♦♦
This is an another excellent album with Green and pianist Sonny Clark, who along with Sam Jones on bass and Louis Hayes on drums make the foursome. The entire album is fine with "My Favorite Things," an old favorite of Green. This album was also released on *The Complete Blue Note Recordings of Grant Green and Sonny Clark.* If you can find this album, or the Mosaic set anywhere, you will be very satisfied. The best. *—Michael Erlewine*

Feelin' the Spirit / Dec. 21, 1962 / Blue Note ♦♦♦♦
An entire album of spirituals—all jazz instrumentals. Green, already a bluesy guitarist, lets himself out in the gospel format. The result is an album that remains true to both the soul jazz and gospel genres. With Green on this date is Herbie Hancock on piano. Every Grant Green fan loves this unique gospel-toned album. It includes standards like "Just a Closer Walk with Thee," "Nobody Knows the Trouble I've Seen," and "Sometimes I Feel Like a Motherless Child." A Grant Green classic. *—Michael Erlewine*

Am I Blue? / May 16, 1963 / Blue Note ♦♦♦♦
A date for Blue Note with Joe Henderson (tenor sax), John Patton (Hammond organ), Johnny Coles (tpt), and Ben Dixon (d). *—AMG*

★ **Idle Moments** / Nov. 4, 1963+Nov. 11, 1963 / Blue Note ♦♦♦♦♦
Excellent mid-sized group album, with Green in good form. Bobby Hutcherson (vibes) in the group produces a somewhat different sound than the usual Green album, so make a note of that. Duke Pearson is there on piano along with Joe Henderson (ts), who is hot. All things considered, the groove is there and this is worth having. *—Michael Erlewine*

☆ **Matador** / May 20, 1964 / Blue Note ♦♦♦♦♦
This is an exceptional Grant Green album for several reasons. For one, it (along with *Solid*) is one of very few Green outings that is straight-ahead jazz, rather than out and out soul jazz. Second, this is one of Coltrane's finest bands with Green as the featured soloist rather than Coltrane-McCoy Tyner (p), Bob Cranshaw (b), and Elvin Jones (d). Coltrane had just finished recording his classic album *Crescent* and the band is hot. Green shows a lot of guts to lead this band, not to mention tackling the Coltrane hit "My Favorite Things," and he pulls it off. Green's soul jazz fans need not fear that this is too dry. This is a great album and classic Grant Green. *—Michael Erlewine*

Solid / Jun. 12, 1964 / Blue Note ♦♦♦♦♦
Not released until 1979, this set contains more challenging material than many of guitarist Grant Green's other Blue Note sessions. In a state-of-the-art sextet with tenor saxophonist Joe Henderson, altoist James Spaulding, pianist McCoy Tyner, bassist Bob Cranshaw, and drummer Elvin Jones, Green performs tunes by Duke Pearson, George Russell ("Ezz-thetic"), Sonny Rollins, Henderson ("The Kicker"), and his own "Grant's Tune." Perhaps this music was considered too uncommercial initially or maybe it was simply lost in the shuffle. In any case, this is one of Grant Green's finer recordings. *—Scott Yanow*

Talkin' About! / Sep. 11, 1964 / Blue Note ♦♦♦
A rare trio date for Grant Green with Larry Young (organ), and Elvin Jones (d). Although Green was the leader for this date, it is now available on the Mosaic label as part of *The Complete Blue Note Recordings of Larry Young.* One of the first albums by Larry Young. This is classic Green. *—AMG*

Street of Dreams / Nov. 16, 1964 / Blue Note ♦♦♦
Vibist Bobby Hutcherson joins Green, Larry Young (organ), and Elvin Jones (d) for this fine release, which is now available on the Mosaic label as part of *The Complete Blue Note Recordings of Larry Young.* This is great soul jazz. Larry Young and Green are, as usual, just excellent. Contains "Somewhere in the Night" and "Street of Dreams." *—Michael Erlewine*

I Want to Hold Your Hand / Mar. 31, 1965 / Blue Note ♦♦♦♦♦
Tenor saxophonist Hank Mobley joins Green, Larry Young (organ), and Elvin Jones (d) for this very excellent album, which is now available on the Mosaic label as part of *The Complete Blue Note Recordings of Larry Young* (worth getting while it is still available!) Unlike some of Young's later work, this music is in the soul jazz vein and under Green's lead. It has groove and great playing from Green and Young. *—Michael Erlewine*

His Majesty, King Funk / May 26, 1965 / Verve ♦♦♦
Don't be scared off by the title of this album; this is not Green's later commercial stuff. This is excellent Grant Green with Larry Young on organ, Harold Vick on sax, Ben Dixon on drums, and Candido Camero on conga—essentially a classic four-piece. And this is soul jazz with a deep groove. This is the last of five albums Green recorded with Larry Young. Produced by Creed Taylor, this is the only album Green did for Verve and perhaps his last real jazz album before several years of inactivity, after which he became somewhat more commercial in his approach. Includes the standard "That Lucky Old Sun." *—Michael Erlewine*

Iron City / 1967 / Muse ♦♦♦
Powerhouse trio recordings, with stomping organ from Big John Patton and Ben Dixon on drums. Includes the theme from "Black Orpheus" and "Work Song." *—Ron Wynn*

The Best of Grant Green, Vol. 1 / Oct. 19, 1993 / Blue Note ♦♦♦
While the "best-of" format often leaves quite a bit to be desired in a jazz setting, this set contains good Green material from his most productive period, the early and mid-'60s. There's a nice mix between uptempo and slower numbers, standards and his own compositions, as well as soul jazz and straight mainstream and bop material. Although this isn't as far-reaching or comprehensive as Green's Mosaic set, this set will satisfy the needs of those unfamiliar with his work or listeners who just want a good cross-section of his cuts. *—Ron Wynn*

Johnny Griffin

b. Apr. 24, 1928, Chicago, IL
Sax (Tenor) / Bop, Hard Bop
Once accurately billed as "the world's fastest saxophonist," Johnny Griffin (an influence tonewise on Rahsaan Roland Kirk) has been one of the top bop-oriented tenors since the mid-'50s. He gained early experience playing with the bands of Lionel Hampton (1945-47) and Joe Morris (1947-50), and also jammed regularly with Thelonious Monk and Bud Powell. After serving in the Army (1951-53), Griffin spent a few years in Chicago (recording his first full album for Argo) and then moved to New York in 1956. He held his own against fellow tenors John Coltrane and Hank Mobley in a classic Blue Note album, was with Art Blakey's Jazz Messengers in 1957 and proved to be perfect with the Thelonious Monk Quartet in 1958 where he really ripped through the complex chord changes with ease. During 1960-62 Griffin co-led a "tough tenor" group with Eddie "Lockjaw" Davis. He emigrated to Europe in 1963 and became a fixture on the Paris jazz scene both as a bandleader and a major soloist with the Kenny Clarke-Francy Boland Big Band. In 1973 Johnny Griffin moved to the Netherlands but has remained a constant world traveller, visiting the U.S. often and recording for many labels including Blue Note, Riverside, Atlantic, SteepleChase, Black Lion, Antilles, Verve, and some European companies. *—Scott Yanow*
Groove: Griffin plays a lot of bop and hard bop, and that may not be exactly what groove lovers are seeking. However, he is so good that you want at least to find one of those dates when he battles with Eddie "Lockjaw" Davis or some other tough tenor to take the measure of him. He plays a hard horn. *—Michael Erlewine*

Introducing Johnny Griffin / Apr. 17, 1956 / Blue Note ♦♦♦♦
A seminal date that shows Griffin's speed, technique, and power. *—Ron Wynn*

★ **A Blowing Session** / Apr. 6, 1957 / Blue Note ♦♦♦♦♦
More than just a mere "blowing session," these four jams (on a pair of standards and two Johnny Griffin compositions) match together three very different tenor stylists: Griffin, Hank Mobley, and John Coltrane. Although the solos and trade-offs are often quite combative, the result is a three-way dead heat, for each of these tenor greats has a different approach and a distinctive sound. Of all of the 1950s jam sessions, this is one of the most successful and exciting. *—Scott Yanow*

★ **The Congregation** / Oct. 13, 1957 / Blue Note ✦✦✦✦✦
The great tenor saxophonist Johnny Griffin is heard in top form on this near-classic quartet set. Assisted by pianist Sonny Clark, bassist Paul Chambers and drummer Kenny Dennis, Griffin is exuberant on "The Congregation" (which is reminiscent of Horace Silver's "The Preacher"), thoughtful on the ballads, and swinging throughout. It's recommended for bop collectors. —*Scott Yanow*

Griff and Lock / Nov. 4, 1960+Nov. 10, 1960 / Original Jazz Classics ✦✦✦✦
For a couple years in the early '60s, tenors Johnny Griffin and Eddie "Lockjaw" Davis co-led a popular quintet, jamming bop standards and occasional originals. Although their sounds were very different (one never had trouble telling them apart), their styles were quite complementary and their combative approaches constantly inspired each other to some heated playing. This former Jazzland LP finds the tough tenors at their best. —*Scott Yanow*

Toughest Tenors / Nov. 4, 1960–Feb. 5, 1962 / Milestone ✦✦✦
During the early '60s, Johnny Griffin and Eddie "Lockjaw" Davis matched forces and put together a consistently exciting quintet. The two tenors (both of whom had very distinctive sounds) brought out the best in each other in these frequently combative encounters. This two-LP set has 13 selections taken from five separate albums and gives one a well-rounded portrait of the legendary group. The music ranges from bop standards to a trio of Thelonious Monk tunes. —*Scott Yanow*

Soul Groove / May 14, 1963+May 16, 1963 / Atlantic ✦✦✦
A soul session with John Patton (or Hank Jones) on the Hammond organ and Matthew Gee on trombone. —*AMG*

Eddie Harris

b. Oct. 20, 1934, Chicago, IL
Sax (Tenor) / Soul Jazz, Hard Bop
Eddie Harris has had a diverse and erratic recording career, leading to many observers greatly underrating his jazz talents. Harris has had his own sound on tenor since at least 1960, his improvisations range from bop to free, he was a pioneer with utilizing the electric sax (and was much more creative on it than most who followed), he introduced the reed trumpet, is a fine pianist (one of his first professional jobs was playing piano with Gene Ammons), composed the standard "Freedom Jazz Dance" and, although his vocals are definitely an acquired taste, he is a skilled comedian.

After getting out of the military, Eddie Harris's very first recording resulted in a hit version of "Exodus." His high-note tenor playing (which managed to sound comfortable in the range of an alto or even soprano) was well-featured on a series of strong selling Vee Jay releases (1961–63). After two outings for Columbia (1964), he switched to Atlantic for a decade. In 1966 Harris started utilizing an electric sax and he debuted the popular "Listen Here" (although the 1967 recording is better-known). At the 1969 Montreux Jazz Festival Harris and Les McCann made for a very appealing combination, recording such songs as "Compared to What" and "Cold Duck Time." Harris's later output for Atlantic was streaky, sometimes rock-oriented and occasionally pure comedy. He has since generally recorded strong jazz sets for such labels as Impulse, Enja and SteepleChase and has remained a unique musical personality. —*Scott Yanow*

★ **Exodus to Jazz** / Jan. 17, 1961 / Vee-Jay ✦✦✦✦
Eddie Harris managed to have a hit ("Exodus") on his very first record. This CD reissue brings back the eight songs of the original LP (including "A.T.C.," "Little Girl Blue" and "Velocity") and adds the edited single versions of "Exodus" and "Alicia." From the start the young tenor had his own sound and he amazed some listeners by playing high notes (almost in the soprano range) with ease, always sounding quite relaxed. For this classic session, Harris is joined by an excellent Chicago-based quintet that includes pianist Willie Pickens and guitarist Joe Diorio. Highly recommended. —*Scott Yanow*

The Artist's Choice: the Eddie Harris Anthology / Jan. 1961–Feb. 20, 1977 / Rhino ✦✦✦
This two-CD sampler from Rhino Records jumps all over the place. Most of tenor saxophonist Eddie Harris's classics are here (including "Exodus," "Listen Here," and "Freedom Jazz Dance") but it is strange that the music was not programmed in strict chronological order since Harris (the master of the electronic sax) did evolve and go through different periods. Actually the

recordings from the 1960s tend to be far superior to Harris's later output and it is odd that none of his more successful comedy numbers from later years (or anything after 1977) were included. Although reasonable as an introduction to Eddie Harris's career, many aspects of this wide-ranging artist are missing and nearly all of this music is currently available on other CDs, making this twofer more of a frivolity than a necessity. —*Scott Yanow*

● **The Best of** / Sep. 1965–Dec. 1973 / Atlantic ✦✦✦✦
A skeletal anthology of some of Harris' Atlantic cuts. It leans toward hits, but does contain "Listen Here" and "Theme from Exodus." A good introductory album to his work. —*Ron Wynn*

☆ **Electrifying Eddie Harris** / Apr. 20, 1967 / Atlantic ✦✦✦✦
This is one of tenor saxophonist Eddie Harris's most famous and significant LPs. He displays his mastery of the electronic varitone saxophone (virtually the only player before John Klemmer to get his own sound on the electric sax) during the memorable "Theme in Search of a Movie" and particularly on his hit version of "Listen Here." A couple of tunes add a pair of percussionists and "Sham Time" features a horn section in back of Harris; the basic quartet is comprised of the leader, pianist Jodie Christian, bassist Melvin Jackson, and drummer Richard Smith. A classic date. —*Scott Yanow*

★ **Swiss Movement** / Jun. 1969 / Atlantic ✦✦✦✦
With Les McCann. Contains the monster hit "Compared to What." A must-buy. —*Michael G. Nastos*

Come on Down! / 1970 / Atlantic ✦✦✦
Eddie Harris, the master of the electrified tenor sax, ventured down to Miami, FL, for this studio LP, having a reunion with Ira Sullivan (who sticks to trumpet). Also in the supporting cast on the five Harris compositions and Sonny Phillips's "Fooltish" are guitarists Cornell Dupree and Jimmy O'Rourke, organist Billy Carter, and pianist Dave Crawford. The playing is excellent in a funky jazz idiom although not overly memorable. —*Scott Yanow*

The Electrifying Eddie Harris/Plug Me In / 1993 / Rhino ✦✦✦✦✦
This CD combines two fine Harris dates from 1967 and 1968. *The Electrifying Eddie Harris* had bluesy, soulful examples of Harris on baritone sax. "Listen Here" ranked second only to "Freedom Jazz Dance" among his most popular compositions, while he stretched out on "Spanish Bull." "Theme In Search Of A Movie," "Sham Time," and "Judie's Theme" were goodtime concessions to pop and jazz-soul audiences, yet still retained some fiber and spark. Once more, Harris found a good compromise between artistic and commercial concerns, although this date was more weighted toward funk and pop. —*Ron Wynn*

Gene Harris

b. Sep. 1, 1933, Benton Harbor, MI
Piano / Soul Jazz, Hard Bop
One of the most accessible of all jazz pianists, Gene Harris' soulful style (influenced by Oscar Peterson and containing the bluesiness of a Junior Mance) is immediately likable and predictably excellent. After playing in an Army band (1951–54) he formed a trio with bassist Andy Simpkins and drummer Bill Dowdy which was by 1956 known as the Three Sounds. The group was quite popular and recorded regularly during 1956–70 for Blue Note and Verve. Although the personnel changed and the music became more R&B-oriented in the early '70s, Harris retained the Three Sounds name for his later Blue Note sets. He retired to Boise, ID, in 1977 and was largely forgotten when Ray Brown persuaded him to return to the spotlight in the early '80s. Harris worked for a time with the Ray Brown Trio and has led his own quartets ever since, recording regularly for Concord and heading the Phillip Morris Superband on a few tours. —*Scott Yanow*
Groove: Gene Harris (The Three Sounds), along with Kenny Burrell, helped to write the book on bluesy jazz. The Stanley Turrentine album *Blue Hour* has Gene Harris and the Three Sounds on it. Worth looking for. Gene Harris is always very listenable either from a jazz perspective or as integral background music. —*Michael Erlewine*

● **Introducing the Three Sounds** / Sep. 16, 1958–Sep. 18, 1958 / Blue Note ✦✦✦✦✦

Feelin' Good / Jun. 28, 1960 / Blue Note ✦✦✦✦
Prototypical Three Sounds release. Elements of funk, soul jazz, and blues merge into a workable jazz concept. —*Ron Wynn*

Black and Blue / Jun. 29, 1991 / Concord Jazz ✦✦✦✦
Although there are few actual blues on this CD, pianist Gene
Harris gives all of the songs (whether complex standards, ballads
or near-blues) a bluesy feel, adding soul and a church feeling to
each of the melodies. With the assistance of guitarist Ron
Eschete, bassist Luther Hughes and drummer Harold Jones,
Harris is in typically fine form. —*Scott Yanow*

Red Holloway

b. 1927
Sax (Alto), Sax (Tenor) / Bop, Swing, Soul Jazz
An exuberant player with attractive tones on both tenor and alto,
Red Holloway is also a humorous blues singer. Whether it be
bop, blues, or R&B, Holloway can hold his own with anyone.
Holloway played in Chicago with Gene Wright's big band
(1943–46), served in the Army and then played with Roosevelt
Sykes (1948) and Nat Towles (1949–50) before leading his own
quartet (1952–61) during an era when he also recorded with
many blues and R&B acts. Holloway came to fame in 1963 while
touring with Jack McDuff, making his first dates as a leader for
Prestige (1963–65). Although he has cut many records in R&B
settings, Red Holloway is a strong bop soloist at heart as he
proved in the 1970s when he has battled Sonny Stitt on a tie on their
recorded collaboration. He has mostly worked as a leader since
then but has also guested with Juggernaut and the Cheathams
and played with Clark Terry on an occasional basis. —*Scott
Yanow*

Burner / Oct. 10, 1963 / Prestige ✦✦✦
Early date with Holloway and John Patton (or George Butcher)
on Hammond organ. —*AMG*

● **Cookin' Together** / Feb. 2, 1964 / Original Jazz Classics ✦✦✦✦✦
With the Jack McDuff Quartet (includes George Benson on guitar). A 1988 reissue of a textbook soul jazz date. —*Ron Wynn*

Brother Red / Feb. 6, 1964–Feb. 7, 1964 / Prestige ✦✦✦✦
The 11 selections included on this CD reissue include seven
songs from a session headed by tenor saxophonist Red Holloway
that used the members of the Jack McDuff Quintet (with the
organist, guitarist George Benson, bassist Wilfred Middlebrooks,
and drummer Joe Dukes), three pieces from a McDuff date in
which the lead voices are backed by an orchestra arranged by
Benny Golson, and a selection from a sampler. The material
varies a bit ("Wives and Lovers" and Holloway's soul ballad "No
Tears" are forgettable) but the blues and the uptempo pieces
(highlighted by "This Can't Be Love") are quite enjoyable and the
underrated saxophonist is in excellent form. —*Scott Yanow*

Red Soul / Dec. 1965 / Prestige ✦✦✦
Good to get, if you can find it. Holloway with Lonnie Smith on
organ and George Benson on guitar. Tunes like "Big Fat Lady"
and "Good and Groovy." —*AMG*

**The Late Show, Vol. 2: Live at Maria's Memory Lane Supper
Club** / May 1986 / Fantasy ✦✦✦

Richard "Groove" Holmes (Richard Arnold Holmes)

b. May 2, 1931, Camden, NJ, **d.** Jun. 29, 1991
Organ / Soul Jazz, Hard Bop
A great jazz organist, Groove Holmes taught himself organ and
developed a strongly swinging style with powerful bass lines and
a harmonic and melodic edge, something that reflects Holmes'
ability to play acoustic bass and the influence of saxophonists in
his approach. He worked in local New Jersey clubs for a number
of years. Holmes had successful albums with such guests as Les
McCann, Ben Webster, Gene Ammons, and Clifford Scott (using
the alias Joe Splink) in the early '60s. Though Holmes played
well, these sessions got more exposure due to their illustrious
guests. He did more trio settings in the mid-'60s, and also got better quality recordings. Holmes scored a huge pop hit with his version of "Misty." His late '60s releases yielded neither hits nor
memorable efforts, while his early '70s sessions, particularly those
with Jimmy McGriff in a pair of organ battles, were good. Holmes
turned in several fine efforts from the late '70s through the late
'80s, often working with Houston Person. But Holmes also experimented with various electronic keyboards during the '70s on
dates that are short of his best work. —*Ron Wynn and Bob Porter*
Groove: There are not a lot of bad Richard Groove Holmes
recordings and his vinyl stuff turns up here and there. Worth
snapping up. Many soul jazz listeners feel that Holmes is the

definitive organist when it comes to laying down a strong
groove. The recently reissued Holmes album *After Hours* on
Pacific Jazz might be a good place to start. —*Michael Erlewine*

Groovin' with Jug / Aug. 15, 1961 / Pacific Jazz ✦✦✦✦
Recorded live at The Black Orchid and at the Pacific Jazz Studio
earlier that afternoon. Ammons at his peak of popularity,
Holmes just about to become well-known—the only date they
ever played together. Both players are on. Holmes, also a bassist
and famous for his organ bass lines, can be heard to good advantage on "Morris the Minor." —*Michael Erlewine*

After Hours / 1961 / Pacific Jazz ✦✦✦✦✦
The original *After Hours* album had Joe Pass on guitar, and
Lawrence Marable on drums. This combines most of another
album, *Tell It Like It Is*, with Gene Edwards) on guitar. This is
early Groove Holmes, 13 tracks in all. This is fine soul jazz and
it is clear why many feel that Holmes is the man of the groove,
when it comes to the Hammond B-3. —*Michael Erlewine*

Soul Message / Aug. 3, 1965 / Original Jazz Classics ✦✦✦✦✦
Organist Richard "Groove" Holmes hit upon a successful formula on this Prestige session (reissued on CD in the OJC series),
mixing together boogaloo rhythms with emotional solos. His
doubletime version of "Misty" became a big hit, and the other
selections, including Horace Silver's "Song for My Father" and a
pair of soulful originals, are in a similar vein. The lone ballad of
the set ("The Things We Did Last Summer") is a fine change of
pace. With the assistance of guitarist Gene Edwards and drummer Jimmie Smith, Groove Holmes shows that it is possible to
create music that is both worthwhile and commercially successful. —*Scott Yanow*

Misty / Aug. 3, 1965–Aug. 12, 1966 / Original Jazz Classics
✦✦✦✦
Organist Richard "Groove" Holmes in the mid-'60s had a hit
with his medium-tempo rendition of "Misty." This CD reissue has
the original short version (which was cut as a 45) plus other
medium-tempo ballads performed in similar fashion. Holmes
and his trio (featuring guitarist Gene Edwards and drummer
George Randall) play enjoyable if not overly substantial versions
of such songs as "The More I See You," "The Shadow of Your
Smile," "What Now My Love," and "Strangers in the Night," trying unsuccessfully for another pop hit; the organist's sound is
more appealing than some of the tunes. —*Scott Yanow*

Best of Richard Groove Holmes / 1965–1967 / Prestige ✦✦

★ **Blue Groove** / Mar. 15, 1966 Mar. 29, 1967 / Prestige ✦✦✦✦✦
This CD, which reissues two former LPs by Richard "Groove"
Holmes (*Get Up & Get It* and *Soul Mist*), showcases the organist
in a quintet featuring the tenor of Teddy Edwards and guitarist
Pat Martino, with his trio, and (on two standards) with trumpeter
Blue Mitchell and tenor saxophonist Harold Vick. Overall, this
73-minute set has many fine solos, spirited ensembles and two
well-rounded programs. —*Scott Yanow*

★ **That Healin' Feelin'** / Aug. 26, 1968 / Prestige ✦✦✦✦✦
Rusty Bryant smokes on tenor, as does Richard "Groove" Holmes
on organ. —*Ron Wynn*

Comin' on Home / 1974 / Blue Note ✦✦✦
Funky and nice. —*Ron Wynn*

Shippin' Out / Jun. 1977 / Muse ✦✦✦✦
There is a lot of fine music here—all of it funky, spacious, clear.
This album feels good. It has some of that soul jazz magic. —
Michael Erlewine

Blues All Day Long / Feb. 24, 1988 / Muse ✦✦✦✦
With Houston Person (ts), Jimmy Ponder (g). Respectable, and
enjoyable later effort by Holmes. Slightly uptempo, but funky.
Very nice album. —*AMG*

Hot Tat / Sep. 5, 1989 / Muse ✦✦✦
One of the last recordings of "Groove" Holmes. W/ Houston
Person (ts), Cecil Bridgewater (tpt), and Jimmy Ponder (g). The
album is bit uneven, but it's good to know that someone is still
playing this old-style funk. There is some good guitar by Jimmy
Ponder. —*Michael Erlewine*

Joe Houston

b. Austin, TX
Guitar, Vocals / Rock & Roll, Blues
Joe Houston is a honking R&B saxman of wallpaper-peeling

potency who recorded for virtually every major independent R&B label in Los Angeles during the 1950s. When the jump blues tradition faded, he segued right into rock & roll, even cutting budget "twist" and "surf" albums for Crown that didn't sound very different from what he was doing a decade before.

Houston played around Houston (Texas, that is) with the bands of Amos Milburn and Joe Turner during the late '40s. It was Turner who got the young saxist his first deal with Freedom Records in 1949. Houston found his way to the West Coast in 1952 and commenced recording for labels big and small: Modern, RPM, Lucky, Imperial, Dootone, Recorded in Hollywood, Cash, and Money (as well as the considerably better-financed Mercury, where he scored his only national R&B hit, "Worry, Worry, Worry," in 1952).

Houston's formula was simple and savagely direct—he'd honk and wail as hard as he could, from any conceivable position: on his knees, lying on his back, walking the bar, etc. His output for the Bihari brothers' Crown label (where he was billed "Wild Man of the Tenor Sax") is positively exhilarating: "All Nite Long," "Blow Joe Blow," and "Joe's Gone" are herculean examples of single-minded sax blasting.

Houston remains active musically, emphasizing his blues vocal talent more than he used to. —*Bill Dahl*

● **Cornbread and Cabbage Greens** / Oct. 29, 1992 / Specialty ✦✦✦✦✦
Los Angeles was a mecca for honking, wailing R&B tenor saxmen during the 1950s, and Joe Houston was one of the wildest in town. Twenty-six blasting workouts from the early-to-mid-'50s mark this CD as the best digital indication of Houston's saxsational wailing now available (pretty much the only vintage one on the shelves, in fact). "All Night Long," "Celebrity Club Drag," and "Rockin' and Boppin'" are among the highlights, taken from the archives of John Dolphin's Recorded in Hollywood and Cash labels. —*Bill Dahl*

Rockin' at the Drive in / 1984 / Ace ✦✦✦✦✦
Fourteen characteristic sax-driven R&B tunes, most instrumental, from the '50s. There's no duplication with the Specialty *Cornbread and Cabbage Greens* CD, except for the well-known "All Night Long," so it's worth finding if you want more than one Houston collection. —*Richie Unterberger*

Willis "Gator" Jackson (Willis "Gator" Jackson)

b. Apr. 25, 1932, Miami, FL, **d.** Oct. 25, 1987, New York, NY
Sax (Tenor) / Soul Jazz, Hard Bop, Early R&B
An exciting tenor "saxophonist whose honking and squeals (although influenced by Illinois Jacquet) were quite distinctive, Willis Jackson was also a strong improviser who sounded perfectly at home with organ groups. He played locally in Florida early on until joining Cootie Williams (on and off during 1948–55). His two-sided honking feature "Gator Tail" with Cootie (which earned him a lifelong nickname) was a hit in 1948 and he started recording as a leader in 1950. Jackson was married to singer Ruth Brown for eight years and often appeared on her recordings during this era. His extensive series of Prestige recordings (1959–64) made him a big attraction on the organ circuit. Although generally overlooked by critics, Willis Jackson continued working steadily in the 1970s and '80s. In 1977 he recorded one of the finest albums of his career for Muse, *Bar Wars*. —*Scott Yanow*
Groove: Willis Jackson recorded a lot of soul jazz albums, many with Hammond B-3 masters like Charles Earland or Jack McDuff. It is unfortunate that not much of this material has been released on CD, so you may have to work over the vinyl bins. Whatever the case, you don't want to miss Willis "Gator" Jackson. —*Michael Erlewine*

★ **Call of the Gators** / Dec. 21, 1949–May 2, 1949 / Delmark ✦✦✦✦✦

On My Own / 1950 / Whiskey Women And.... ✦✦✦
1950–1955. Frenetic soul jazz; w/ torrid organ from Charles Earland. —*Ron Wynn*

Please Mr. Jackson / May 25, 1959 / Original Jazz Classics ✦✦✦✦
Quintet. 1988 reissue of fine soul jazz date. —*Ron Wynn*

Cool Gator / May 25, 1959–Aug. 16, 1960 / Original Jazz Classics ✦✦✦✦✦
Willis Jackson (tenor sax) was one of the prime exploiters of the

commercial funk exposure of the late '60s. *Cool Gator,* however, was a reasonably restrained LP made up of three dates. —*Bob Rusch, Cadence*

★ **Together Again** / May 25, 1959–Aug. 16, 1960 / Prestige ✦✦✦✦✦
Jackson with Jack McDuff on the Hammond B-3 and Bill Jennings on guitar. —*AMG*

The Best of Willis Jackson with Brother Jack McDuff / May 25, 1959–Aug. 16, 1960 / Prestige ✦✦✦

Together Again, Again / May 25, 1959–Dec. 31, 1961 / Prestige ✦✦✦
Jackson with Jack McDuff on the Hammond B-3 and Bill Jennings on guitar. Tunes like "Snake Crawl" and "Backtrack" should give you a clue as to the music on this album. —*AMG*

Thunderbird / Mar. 31, 1962 / Prestige ✦✦✦✦✦
Great Jackson, robust Freddy Roach organ. —*Ron Wynn*

Loose / Mar. 26, 1963 / Prestige ✦✦✦
Willis with Carl Wilson on Hammond organ. —*AMG*

More Gravy / Oct. 24, 1963 / Prestige ✦✦✦
Still more. Jackson with Carl Wilson on Hammond organ. —*AMG*

Star Bag / Mar. 22, 1968 / Prestige ✦✦✦
Willis Jackson with Trudy Pitts on the Hammond B-3. —*AMG*

Headed and Gutted / May 16, 1974 / Muse ✦✦✦✦
Brilliant soul jazz date. —*Ron Wynn*

In the Alley / 1976 / Muse ✦✦✦
Solid soul jazz from a tenor sax master of the style. Willis Jackson never tried to play intricate or elaborate solos; he relied on intensity, blues feeling, and simplicity to communicate his soulful messages. —*Ron Wynn*

★ **Bar Wars** / Dec. 21, 1977 / Muse ✦✦✦✦✦
Willis Jackson, a veteran of the jazz-oriented R&B music of the late '40s, was a powerful tenor in the tradition of Gene Ammons. This is a particularly exciting release with Charles Earland pumping away at the organ, guitarist Pat Martino offering a contrasting solo voice, and Jackson in top form, wailing away on the uptempo pieces. The CD reissue of the original LP adds two alternate takes to the program. The chord changes might be fairly basic but Willis Jackson plays with such enthusiasm and exuberance that it almost sounds as if he had discovered the joy of playing music. —*Scott Yanow*

Nothing Butt / Jun. 1980 / Muse ✦✦✦
Jackson with Charles Earland on the Hammond organ and Pat Martino on guitar. —*AMG*

Illinois Jacquet (Jean Baptiste Illinois Jacquet)

b. Oct. 31, 1922, Boussard, LA
Sax (Alto), Sax (Tenor) / Bop, Swing, Early R&B
One of the great tenors, Illinois Jacquet's 1942 "Flying Home" solo is considered the first R&B sax solo and spawned a full generation of younger tenors (including Joe Houston and Big Jay McNeely) who built their careers from his style and practically from that one song!

Jacquet, whose older brother Russell (1917–1990) was a trumpeter who sometimes played in his bands, grew up in Houston and his tough-toned and emotional sound defined the Texas tenor school. After playing locally, he moved to Los Angeles where in 1941 he played with Floyd Ray. He was the star of Lionel Hampton's 1942 big band ("Flying Home" became a signature song for Jacquet, Hampton, and even Illinois' successor Arnett Cobb), and also was with Cab Calloway (1943–44) and well-featured with Count Basie (1945–46). Jacquet's playing at the first Jazz at the Philharmonic concert (1944) included a screaming solo on "Blues" that found him biting on his reed to achieve high register effects; the crowd went wild. He repeated the idea during his appearance in the 1944 film short *Jammin' the Blues.* In 1945 Jacquet put together his own band and both his recordings and live performances were quite exciting. He appeared with JATP on several tours in the 1950's, recorded steadily and never really lost his popularity. In the 1960s he sometimes doubled on bassoon (usually for a slow number such as "'Round Midnight") and it was an effective contrast to his stomping tenor. In the late '80s Jacquet started leading an exciting part-time big band that thus far has only recorded one album, an Atlantic date from 1988. Through the years Illinois Jacquet (whose occasional features on alto are quite influenced by Charlie Parker) has recorded as a leader for such labels as Apollo, Savoy, Aladdin, RCA, Verve, Mercury, Roulette, Epic, Argo, Prestige, Black Lion, Black & Blue, JRC, and Atlantic. —*Scott Yanow*

Groove: This is where all that honkin', bar-walkin' sax came from—Mr. Illinois Jacquet. However, a lot of the more soul jazz flavored Jacquet is not available on CD. His work with organist Milt Buckner is worth seeking out. Jacquet wrote the book on the tough-tenor sound. —*Michael Erlewine*

The Message / May 7, 1963–May 8, 1963 / Argo ✦✦✦
With Kenny Burrell on guitar and Ralph Smith on organ. Booming, authoritative soul jazz, bop, and swing from tenor sax master Illinois Jacquet. He does stomping standards and screaming blues and drives a good combo through a program of routine but enjoyable tunes. —*Ron Wynn*

Go Power / Mar. 15, 1966–Mar. 17, 1966 / Cadet ✦✦✦
A rare trio date with Milt Buckner on organ and Alan Dawson on drums. —*AMG*

How High the Moon / Mar. 26, 1968–Sep. 16, 1969 / Prestige ✦✦✦
A worthy compilation of the best Prestige '60s cuts. —*Ron Wynn*

The Soul Explosion / Mar. 25, 1969 / Original Jazz Classics ✦✦✦✦✦
The great tenor Illinois Jacquet is joined by a ten-piece group that includes trumpeter Joe Newman and Milt Buckner on piano and organ for this 1969 Prestige studio session which has been reissued on CD by the OJC series. Jacquet is in prime form, particularly on "The Soul Explosion" (which benefits from a Jimmy Mundy arrangement), a definitive "After Hours" and a previously unissued version of "Still King." This blues-based set is full of soul but often swings quite hard with the focus on Jacquet's exciting tenor throughout. —*Scott Yanow*

★ **The Blues: That's Me!** / Sep. 16, 1969 / Original Jazz Classics ✦✦✦✦✦
Tenor saxophonist Illinois Jacquet is heard in top form throughout this quintet set with pianist Wynton Kelly, guitarist Tiny Grimes, bassist Buster Williams, and drummer Oliver Jackson. The music, which falls between swing, bop, and early rhythm & blues, is generally quite exciting, especially "Still King," "Everyday I Have the Blues" and the lengthy title cut. A particular surprise is a moody version of "'Round Midnight" which features some surprisingly effective Illinois Jacquet, on bassoon. This CD reissue is highly recommended. —*Scott Yanow*

Genius at Work / Apr. 13, 1971–Apr. 14, 1971 / JZM ✦✦✦
Trio with Milt Buckner on organ. Expert playing; smooth and cool—sometimes hot. —*Ron Wynn*

Illinois Jacquet with Wild Bill Davis / Jan. 15, 1973–Jan. 16, 1973 / Classic Jazz ✦✦✦
Powerhouse, rough-edged, and blistering on all counts. —*Ron Wynn*

★ **Blues from Louisiana** / Jul. 7, 1973 / Classic Jazz ✦✦✦✦✦
This was an odd record, taken either from different live sessions or as part of a bigger all star bash…"On A Clear Day" was open, loose and swingingly pushed by Jacquet's big throaty vibrato on tenor; "Marlow's L.A. Blues" was a slow, drawn-out funky teaser climactic and worried to death by organist Milt Buckner and Jacquet. —*Bob Rusch, Cadence*

Loot to Boot / LRC Jazz Classics ✦✦
Has duos with Jacquet and Wild Bill Davis on the Hammond B-3. —*AMG*

● **The Cool Rage** / Verve ✦✦✦✦✦
The Cool Rage reissued by tenor saxophonist Illinois Jacquet was culled from various Verve sessions. The two-record set included tracks from 4/21/58 with Wild Bill Davis (organ), Kenny Burrell (guitar) and Johnny Williams (drums). The music was a mixture of *Jazz At The Philharmonic* wailings, after-hour blues and relaxed Lestorian (Young) blowing. There were some nice tastes of Basie organ, an organist even for those who do not like organ. This was a nice look at '50s Jacquet. —*Bob Rusch, Cadence*

Illinois Jacquet & Wild Bill Davis / Black & Blue

Charles Kynard

b. 1933
Organ, Guitar (Bass), Guitar (Electric) / *Soul Jazz*
Kynard is an organist whose jazz-funk leanings rival his prede-

cessors and peers, though not eclipsing them. Solid, though never flashy. He also plays electric bass. Kynard's album *Reelin' with the Feelin'* has been sampled and appears on several acid-jazz releases. —*Michael G. Nastos & Michael Erlewine*

● **Charles Kynard** / 1962–1963 / World Pacific ✦✦✦✦✦
Kynard's best combo effort. Shows him in a more favorable light as a soul jazz proprietor. —*Michael G. Nastos*

Where It's at / 1962–1963 / Pacific Jazz ✦✦✦
Kynard with funky guitarist Howard Roberts, Clifford Scott (sax), and Milt Turner (d). This is Kynard's first album and it has not been reissued. —*AMG*

Professor Soul / Aug. 6, 1968 / Prestige
Charles Kynard with Cal Green on guitar and Johnny Kirkwood on drums. This 1968 gem, which has not been reissued, has a rendition of "Cristo Redentor." —*AMG*

The Soul Brotherhood / Mar. 10, 1969 / Prestige
They have got to reissue this one! Here is Kynard with Grant Green on guitar, Blue Mitchell on trumpet, and David "Fathead" Newman on sax. —*AMG*

★ **Reelin' with the Feelin'** / Aug. 11, 1969 / Prestige ✦✦✦✦
Kynard with Wilton Felder on sax, Joe Pass on guitar, Carol Kaye on bass, and Paul Humphrey on drums. This soul jazz date has been being sampled and used in recent acid-jazz albums. —*AMG*

Afro-Disiac / Apr. 6, 1970 / Prestige
Another Kynard gem that we are waiting for a reissue of. This album features Kynard with Grant Green on guitar and Houston Person on sax. I have not been able to find a copy, but those who know it say that this is the one to hear. I can't wait. —*Michael Erlewine*

Wa-Tu-Wa-Zui / Dec. 14, 1970 / Prestige
Kynard with Rusty Bryant on sax, Virgil Jones on trumpet, and Melvin Sparks on guitar. —*AMG*

Yusef Lateef (William Evans)

b. Oct. 9, 1920, Chatanooga, TN
Flute, Oboe, Sax (Tenor) / *Hard Bop*
Yusef Lateef has long had an inquisitive spirit and he was never just a bop or hard bop soloist. Lateef, who does not care much for the name "jazz," has consistently created music that stretched (and even broke through) boundaries. A superior tenor saxophonist with a soulful sound and impressive technique, Lateef by the 1950s was one of the top flutists around. He also developed into the best jazz soloist to date on oboe, an occasional bassoonist, and introduced such instruments as the argol (a double clarinet that resembles a bassoon), shanai (a type of oboe), and different types of flutes. Lateef played "world music" before it had a name and his output was more creative than much of the pop and folk music that passes under that label in the 1990s.

Yusef Lateef grew up in Detroit and began on tenor when he was 17. He played with Lucky Millinder (1946), Hot Lips Page, Roy Eldridge and Dizzy Gillespie's big band (1949–50). He was a fixture on the Detroit jazz scene of the 1950s where he studied flute at Wayne State University. Lateef began recording as a leader in 1955 for Savoy (and later Riverside and Prestige) although he did not move to New York until 1959. He had a reputation for versatility and for his willingness to use "miscellaneous instruments." Lateef played with Charles Mingus in 1960, gigged with Donald Byrd, and was well-featured with the Cannonball Adderley Sextet (1962–64). As a leader his string of Impulse recordings (1963–66) were among the finest of his career although Lateef's varied Atlantic sessions (1967–76) also had some strong moments. He spent time in the 1980s teaching in Nigeria. His Atlantic records of the late '80s were closer to mood music (or new age) than jazz but in the 1990s (for his own YAL label) Yusef Lateef has recorded a variety of music (all originals) including some strong improvised music with Ricky Ford, Archie Shepp, and Von Freeman. —*Scott Yanow*

Groove: Yusef Lateef is not a groove master. Lateef's fusion of blues and Eastern sounds was a pioneer effort and the sound he gets is unique—very lovely indeed. Blues lovers will know just where he is coming from. The Rhino/Atlantic 2-disc anthology *Every Village Has a Song* lays it all out for you. —*Michael Erlewine*

Every Village Has A Song / May 6, 1949–Mar. 1976 / Rhino/Atlantic ✦✦✦✦
This good two-disc set covers Lateef's tenure at Atlantic as well

as featuring formative material from early sessions for Transition, Prestige/Moodsville, Riverside, Impulse, Blue Note, and Savoy. The discs show Lateef honing a thick, bluesy, expressive tenor tone in the beginning, evolving into a superior or straight jazz player, then expanding his repertoire and choice of instruments and contexts. His flute playing became arguably superior to his tenor, while his solos on oboe, shenai, and other previously little-known instruments enabled Lateef to create arresting, fresh and ultimately significant music. While the sampler approach can't fully document his contributions, it's a solid introduction for those unfamiliar with his output. *—Ron Wynn*

Other Sounds / Oct. 11, 1957 / Original Jazz Classics ✦✦✦
These recordings are among his early African/Middle Eastern fusion efforts, with many exotic instruments. *—Myles Boisen*

Cry! / Tender / Oct. 11, 1957+Oct. 16, 1959 / Original Jazz Classics ✦✦✦✦
This well-rounded program, reissued on CD in the OJC program, features Yusef Lateef (tripling on tenor, flute, and oboe) heading a quintet also including trumpeter Lonnie Hillyer, pianist Hugh Lawson, bassist Herman Wright and drummer Frank Gant. The music alternates between straightahead pieces and more atmospheric and exotic works. An earlier track ("Ecaps") features Lateef with a different quintet that also includes flugelhornist Wilbur Harden. *—Scott Yanow*

Blues for the Orient / Oct. 11, 1957+Sep. 5, 1961 / Prestige ✦✦✦✦
This double LP from 1974 has the complete contents of two Yusef Lateef Prestige albums: *Eastern Sounds* and *The Sounds of Yusef*. The latter date (which has not yet been reissued on CD) is from 1957 and features Lateef, flugelhornist Wilbur Harden, pianist Hugh Lawson, bassist Ernie Farrow, and drummer Oliver Jackson all doubling on unusual instruments such as the argol, Turkish finger cymbals, a 7-Up bottle, balloons, a rabat, and an earthboard. They perform a romping version of "Take the 'A' Train," Harden's "Playful Flute," and three diverse Lateef originals. The later session, which has Lateef (on tenor, oboe and flute) playing with the Barry Harris trio, ranges from his famous version of "Love Theme from *Spartacus*," and "Blues for the Orient" to "The Plum Blossom" and several obscure but enjoyable originals. This music is highly recommended in one form or another. *—Scott Yanow*

Yusef Lateef / Oct. 11, 1957–Dec. 29, 1961 / Prestige ✦✦✦✦✦
This excellent two-LP set combines together material taken from three Yusef Lateef LPs; all of Lateef's Prestige and New Jazz recordings were very effectively reissued in Prestige's admirable two-fer series. Lateef, one of the first jazz musicians to integrate aspects of Middle Eastern music into his playing, not only performs on tenor and flute during these sessions but also oboe (he was probably jazz music's greatest oboeist ever) and the argol. These performances (with such sidemen as fluegelhornist Wilbur Hardin, trumpeter Lonnie Hillyer, and pianists Hugh Lawson and Barry Harris) range from atmospheric modal ballads to straightahead stomping. This two-fer is a fine example of Yusef Lateef at his best. *—Scott Yanow*

The Three Faces of Yusef Lateef / May 9, 1960 / Original Jazz Classics ✦✦✦✦✦
This is one of Yusef Lateef's most accessible sessions with such famous songs as "Goin' Home," "I'm Just a Lucky So and So," and the ancient standard "Ma He's Makin' Eyes at Me." Lateef (featured on tenor, flute, and oboe) is teamed up with pianist Hugh Lawson, cellist Ron Carter, bassist Herman Wright, and drummer Lex Humphries for a set of stimulating music which also includes a few of Lateef's thought-provoking originals. This CD reissue is recommended as are all of his recordings from the era. *—Scott Yanow*

The Centaur and the Phoenix / Oct. 4, 1960+Oct. 6, 1960 / Original Jazz Classics ✦✦✦✦
For this CD reissue of a Riverside date, the great multi-reedist Yusef Lateef (who switches between tenor, flute, oboe, and the argol) is joined on most selections by five other horns (including a bassoonist) and a rhythm section headed by pianist Joe Zawinul. The music has a lot of diversity, from stomps and ballads to Eastern-influenced explorations; two "bonus cuts" from the same date match Lateef with a four-piece rhythm section that includes pianist Barry Harris and two percussionists.

Highlights include "Everyday I Fall in Love," "Summer Song," "Jungle Fantasy," and "The Centaur and the Phoenix." Virtually everything that Yusef Lateef recorded during this era is well worth acquiring. *—Scott Yanow*

★ **Eastern Sounds** / Sep. 5, 1961 / Original Jazz Classics ✦✦✦✦✦
Although originally issued on the Moodsville label (a subsidiary of Prestige), this classic Yusef Lateef date is not all ballads. Accompanied by pianist Barry Harris, bassist Ernie Farrow and drummer Lex Humphries, Lateef (switching between tenor, oboe and flute) is quite memorable on such pieces as the "Love Theme from *Spartacus*," "Blues for the Orient," "Don't Blame Me," and "The Plum Blossom." He has long been a true original with an active musical curiosity and this set gives listeners a strong example of his work. *—Scott Yanow*

Jazz Around the World / Dec. 19, 1963–Dec. 20, 1963 / Impulse ✦✦✦✦
Yusef Lateef's Impulse recordings of 1963–66 were among the finest of his career. This out-of-print LP, his first effort for Impulse, features Lateef not only on tenor, flute and oboe but bassoon and shanas. Performing with a quintet that also includes trumpeter Richard Williams, pianist Hugh Lawson, bassist Ernie Farrow, and drummer Lex Humphries, Lateef plays a variety of folk melodies from other countries along with a few originals and a memorable version (on oboe) of "Trouble in Mind." *—Scott Yanow*

Re-Evaluations: The Impulse Years / Dec. 19, 1963–Jun. 16, 1966 / Impulse ✦✦✦✦
Multi-instrumentalist Yusef Lateef recorded eight albums for the Impulse label during the 1963–66 period. All are worth acquiring, but as a sampler this two-LP set (which draws its 18 selections from six of the albums) gives one a fine all-around picture of Lateef's many talents. He is heard on his highly appealing tenor, playing flute, jamming "Exactly like You" and an emotional "Trouble in Mind" on oboe, utilzing the exotic shannas and theremin (the latter being an early electronic instrument) and even having a few rare outings on alto. The music ranges from bop and ballads to some avant-garde explorations and mood pieces. *—Scott Yanow*

★ **Live at Pep's** / Jun. 29, 1964 / Impulse ✦✦✦✦✦
This mid-'60s concert was one of Lateef's finest, as it perfectly displayed his multiple influences and interests. There were hard bop originals, covers of jazz classics like Oscar Pettiford's "Oscarlypso" (a CD bonus track) and Leonard Feather's "Twelve Tone Blues," as well as an unorthodox but effective version of Ma Rainey's "C. C. Rider." On "Sister Mamie," "Number 7," and drummer James Black's "The Magnolia Triangle," Lateef moved away from strict jazz, although he retained his improvisational flair. Lateef played meaty tenor sax solos, entrancing flute and bamboo flute offerings, and also had impressive stints on oboe, shenai, and argol. This was a pivotal date in his career, and those unaware of it will get a treat with this disc. *—Ron Wynn*

A Flat, G Flat and C / May 8, 1966–May 9, 1966 / Impulse ✦✦✦✦
Yusef Lateef (heard on tenor, alto, flute, oboe, and the mysterious-sounding theremin) is in explorative and consistently colorful form on this out-of-print LP, one of many Impulse sessions that are long overdue to be reissued on CD. With the assistance of pianist Hugh Lawson, bassist Reggie Workman, and drummer Roy Brooks, Lateef performs ten songs (eight are his originals) that are all at least in abstract form related to the blues. Well worth several listens. *—Scott Yanow*

The Complete Yusef Lateef / May 31, 1967 / Atlantic ✦✦✦✦
Yusef Lateef's first Atlantic album was one of his better ones for the label. Performing on flute, tenor, alto, and oboe ("In the Evening"), Lateef is assisted by pianist Hugh Lawson, bassist Cecil McBee, and drummer Roy Brooks on a wide-ranging program that ranges from the feel of New Orleans and blues to boogaloo rhythms and the soulful spiritual "Rosalie." This LP is long overdue to be reissued on CD. *—Scott Yanow*

Harold Mabern

b. Mar. 20, 1936, Memphis, TN
Piano / Hard Bop
One of several excellent hard bop pianists from the Memphis

area, Harold Mabern has led relatively few dates through the years but he has always been respected by his contemporaries. He played in Chicago with MJT + 3 in the late '50s and then moved to New York in 1959. Mabern worked with Jimmy Forrest, Lionel Hampton, the Jazztet (1961–62), Donald Byrd, Miles Davis (1963), J.J. Johnson (1963–65), Sonny Rollins, Freddie Hubbard, Wes Montgomery, Joe Williams (1966–67), and Sarah Vaughan. During 1968–70 Mabern led four albums for Prestige. He was with Lee Morgan in the early '70s, and in 1972 he recorded with Stanley Cowell's Piano Choir. In more recent times Harold Mabern recorded as a a leader for DIW/Columbia and Sackville and toured with the Contemporary Piano Ensemble (1993–95). —*Scott Yanow*

Rakin' & Scrapin' / Dec. 23, 1968 / Prestige ✦✦✦✦
Any old Mabern album is great. The Memphis pianist is now in NYC. —*Michael G. Nastos*

Workin' and Wailin' / Jun. 30, 1969 / Prestige ✦✦✦
The date utilizes trumpeter Virgil Jones, tenor saxophonist George Coleman, bassist Buster Williams, and drummer Idris Muhammad on four challenging Mabern originals and Johnny Mandel's "A Time for Love." —*Scott Yanow*

● **Greasy Kid Stuff!** / Jan. 26, 1970 / Prestige ✦✦✦✦✦
This session is most memorable for, in addition to Mabern, Williams and Muhammad, it features trumpeter Lee Morgan and flutist Hubert Laws; the latter mostly plays some surprisingly passionate tenor that makes one wish he had performed on tenor more through the years. Excellent advanced hard bop music that hints at fusion. —*Scott Yanow*

Les McCann

b. Sep. 23, 1935, Lexington, KY
Piano, Vocals / Soul Jazz, Hard Bop
Les McCann reached the peak of his career at the 1968 Montreux Jazz Festival, recording "Compared to What" and "Cold Duck Time" for Atlantic *(Swiss Movement)* with Eddie Harris and Benny Bailey. Although he has done some worthwhile work since then, much of it has been anti-climatic.

Les McCann first gained some fame in 1956 when he won a talent contest in the Navy as a singer that resulted in an appearance on television on *The Ed Sullivan Show*. After being discharged, he formed a trio in Los Angeles. McCann turned down an invitation to join the Cannonball Adderley Quintet so he could work on his own music. He signed a contract with Pacific Jazz and in 1960 gained some fame with his albums *Les McCann Plays the Truth* and *The Shout*. His soulful funk style on piano was influential and McCann's singing was largely secondary until the mid-'60s. He recorded many albums for Pacific Jazz during 1960–64, mostly with his trio but also featuring Ben Webster, Richard "Groove" Holmes, Blue Mitchell, Stanley Turrentine, Joe Pass, the Jazz Crusaders, and the Gerald Wilson Orchestra. McCann switched to Limelight during 1965–67 and then signed with Atlantic in 1968. After the success of *Swiss Movement,* McCann emphasized his singing at the expense of his playing and he began to utilize electric keyboards. His recordings became less interesting from that point on and, after his Atlantic contract ran out in 1976, McCann appeared on records much less often. However he stayed popular and a 1994 reunion tour with Eddie Harris was quite successful. —*Scott Yanow*

● **Les McCann Anthology: Relationships** / Feb. 1960–Nov. 1972 / Rhino/Atlantic ✦✦✦✦✦
Keyboardist/vocalist Les McCann ranked among jazz's more successful populists, injecting healthy doses of blues, soul, and R&B vocals and feeling into his work without neglecting the improvisational end. McCann made hits, but didn't plug into any formula, moving back and forth between short, pop-centered arrangements and longer, looser funk jams. The 21 tracks on this twin-CD set range from trio works to complex, multi-artist suites, and include two songs from his tenure with Eddie Harris, plus collaborations with The Jazz Crusaders, Groove Holmes, Ben Webster, the Gerald Wilson orchestra, Stanley Turrentine, and Lou Rawls. —*Ron Wynn*

● **In New York** / Dec. 28, 1960 / Pacific Jazz ✦✦✦✦✦

Les McCann Sings / Aug. 1961 / Pacific Jazz ✦✦✦✦
A super set with Ben Webster (ts) and Groove Holmes on organ. soul jazz and blues at their best. —*Ron Wynn*

Les is More / 1967 / Night ✦✦
A tremendous soul jazz date composed of cuts previously in McCann's vaults. —*Ron Wynn*

★ **Swiss Movement** / Jun. 22, 1969 / Atlantic ✦✦✦✦✦

Jack McDuff (Eugene McDuffy)

b. Sep. 17, 1926, Champaign, IL
Organ / Soul Jazz, Hard Bop
A marvelous bandleader and organist as well as capable arranger, "Brother" Jack McDuff has one of the funkiest, most soulful styles of all time on the Hammond B-3. His rock-solid bass lines and blues-drenched solos are balanced by clever, almost pianistic melodies and interesting progressions and phrases. McDuff began as a bassist playing with Denny Zeitlin and Joe Farrell. He studied privately in Cinncinnati and worked with Johnny Griffin in Chicago. He taught himself organ and piano in the mid-'50s, and began gaining attention working with Willis Jackson in the late '50s and early '60s, cutting high caliber soul jazz dates for Prestige. McDuff made his recording debut as a leader for Prestige in 1960, playing in a studio pickup band with Jimmy Forrest. They made a pair of outstanding albums, *Tough Duff* and *The Honeydripper*. McDuff organized his own band the next year, featuring Harold Vick and drummer Joe Dukes. Things took off when McDuff hired a young guitarist named George Benson. They were among the most popular combos of the mid-'60s, and made several excellent albums. McDuff's later groups at Atlantic and Cadet didn't equal the level of the Benson band, while later dates for Verve and Cadet were uneven, though generally good. McDuff experimented with electronic keyboards and fusion during the '70s, then in the '80s got back in the groove with the Muse session *Cap'n Jack.* Other musicians McDuff played with in the '60s and '70s include Joe Henderson, Pat Martino, Jimmy Witherspoon, David "Fathead" Newman, Rahsaan Roland Kirk, Sonny Stitt, and Gene Ammons. There are only a few McDuff sessions available on CD, though they include the fine sessions with Forrest. His work with Benson has also been reissued on CD. —*Ron Wynn and Bob Porter*

McDuff's Greatest Hits / Jan. 25, 1960–Oct. 3, 1963 / Prestige ✦✦✦

The Honeydripper / Feb. 3, 1961 / Original Jazz Classics ✦✦✦✦✦
Pure soul jazz. This is first-rate jazz-funk, perhaps a little more bluesy than average—which is nice. His third album includes Grant Green on guitar and Jimmy Forrest on tenor sax. Just excellent. —*AMG*

Goodnight, It's Time to Go / Jul. 14, 1961 / Prestige ✦✦✦
McDuff on the Hammond B-3 along with Grant Green on guitar and Harold Vick on tenor sax. What more could you ask for? —*AMG*

On with It / Dec. 1, 1961 / Prestige ✦✦✦
McDuff on the Hammond B-3 with Grant Green on guitar and Harold Vick on tenor sax. Classic soul jazz grooves. —*AMG*

Mellow Gravy / Jan. 23, 1962 / Prestige ✦✦✦
Smoking Gene Ammons (ts) and the great Hammond B-3 from McDuff. —*Ron Wynn*

Best of Sonny Stitt with Jack Mc Duff / Feb. 16, 1962+Sep. 17, 1963 / Prestige ✦✦✦
Jack McDuff and Sonny Stitt? You bet. I'll buy that anytime. Some nasty stuff. —*AMG*

Screamin' / Oct. 23, 1962 / Original Jazz Classics ✦✦✦✦
Organist Jack McDuff teams up with his regular drummer Joe Dukes, altoist Leo Wright and guitarist Kenny Burrell for a spirited blues-oriented set which has been reissued on CD in the OJC series. "Soulful Drums," featuring Dukes's drum breaks, was a minor hit. Other selections on this generally fine organ date include spirited versions of "He's a Real Gone Guy," "After Hours," and "One O'Clock Jump" even if the title cut does not quite live up to its name! —*Scott Yanow*

Somethin' Slick / Jan. 8, 1963 / Prestige ✦✦✦
McDuff with Kenny Burrell on guitar and Harold Vick on tenor sax. —*AMG*

Crash! / Jan. 8, 1963+Feb. 26, 1963 / ✦✦✦✦✦
Organist Jack McDuff has long had a powerful style and the two former LPs that are combined on this single CD offer some

strong examples of his accessible playing. In both cases McDuff is joined by guitarist Kenny Burrell (in fact one of the two sets was originally under Burrell's name), drummer Joe Dukes and occasionally Ray Barretto on congas. In addition Harold Vick is on tenor for most selections and Eric Dixon guests on tenor and flute during three songs. Highlights include a driving "How High the Moon," "Love Walked In," and a pair of original blues: "Smut" and "Our Miss Brooks." McDuff and Burrell work together quite well. This 76-minute CD is easily recommended to fans of the jazz organ. —*Scott Yanow*

★ **Live!** / Jun. 5, 1963 / Prestige ✦✦✦✦✦
Good as organist Jack McDuff's studio recordings are from the early '60s, it is his live sets that are truly exciting. This single CD combines two former in-concert LPs and find McDuff leading a very strong group that features the young guitarist George Benson, tenorman Red Holloway, drummer Joe Dukes and on a few numbers the second tenor of Harold Vick. The material (cooking blues, standards, Latin numbers and originals) has plenty of variety and drive, McDuff really pushes Benson and Holloway, and the music is both accessible and creative. —*Scott Yanow*

Brother Jack McDuff Live! / Jun. 5, 1963 / Prestige ✦✦✦
With Red Holloway on tenor sax and George Benson on guitar. Quite strong commercially. Vintage soul jazz. —*Ron Wynn*

Best of Brother Jack McDuff / Jun. 5, 1963–Jul. 1964 / Prestige ✦✦✦
Textbook soul jazz from a founding father. Organist Brother Jack McDuff didn't invent the bluesy, riff- and backbeat-laden instrumental style called soul jazz, but he sure helped make it popular. This anthology contains some early '60s McDuff material, including some tracks with guitarist George Benson. You can get all this somewhere else, but as a sampler or introductory package, it's a good collection. —*Ron Wynn*

The Midnight Sun / Jun. 5, 1963–Feb. 1966 / Prestige ✦✦✦

Hallelujah Time! / Jun. 5, 1963–1966 / Prestige ✦✦✦

Live at the Jazz Workshop / Oct. 3, 1963 / Prestige ✦✦✦
Organist Jack McDuff enjoyed some pop recognition in 1963, when his combo recorded at The Jazz Workshop featured a young, blazing guitarist influenced by Wes Montgomery. George Benson's torrid licks and blues fills make this among his hottest albums, along with McDuff's always-smoking, relentless organ accompaniment, transitional lines, and solos. —*Ron Wynn*

Dynamic! / Feb. 6, 1964–Feb. 7, 1964 / Prestige ✦✦✦
With George Benson on guitar. —*AMG*

Live It Up / 1967 / Sugar Hill ✦✦✦
Steaming blues, jazz, funk, blues, and ballads keyed by the whirling, soulful solos, bass pedal work, and direction of organist Jack McDuff. This was one of four fine albums he did for Atlantic in 1966 and 1967. —*Ron Wynn*

★ **The Heating System** / 1971 / Cadet ✦✦✦✦✦
Plenty of funk, sax-wallop, and organ soul. —*Ron Wynn*

The Re-Entry / Mar. 1988 / Muse ✦✦✦✦
A late-'80s return to the sound of earlier recordings, it features Houston Person (ts). Not inspired, it's still a solid performance all around. —*Bob Porter*

Color Me Blue / May 1991+Mar. 1992 / Concord Jazz ✦✦✦✦✦
Recent cuts showing that organist Jack McDuff can still stomp through bluesy wailers, pound the bass pedals, and lead a hot combo through funky, exuberant numbers. He's heading a group with former band members like guitarist George Benson and drummer Joe Dukes, plus saxophonist Red Holloway, guitarist Ron Eschete, and Phil Upchurch, among others. —*Ron Wynn*

Jimmy McGriff

b. Apr. 3, 1936, Philadelphia, PA
Organ / Soul Jazz, Hard Bop
The finest blues soloist among organists, Jimmy McGriff can also play superb soul jazz, though he's turned in dreary performances on fusion and pop dates in the '70s. McGriff studied bass, drums, tenor sax, and vibes in his teens and attended Combe College of Music in Philadelphia and Juilliard. McGriff later studied electric organ with Jimmy Smith, Milt Buckner, and Groove Holmes. His debut record *I Got A Woman* for Sue was a Top 20 hit in 1962, and he followed it with *All About My Girl* and *Kiko* in 1963 and 1964. McGriff began a long relationship

with producer Sonny Lester in 1966, when he joined Solid State Records. The two later teamed at Blue Note, Capitol, Groove Merchant, and LRC. McGriff recorded many fine organ combo sides while also cutting R&B-tinged work during the '60s. He had a huge hit with "The Worm" in '68/'69, but also made the LP *The Big Band*, a stirring tribute to Count Basie. During the '70s McGriff made more solid small combo jazz dates, including some organ battles with Groove Holmes. But he also did trendy material utilizing multiple electronic keyboards. He didn't distinguish himself on several later LRC sessions. McGriff's earlier Groove Merchant recordings were his best in this period. McGriff, like Hank Crawford, got back to basics when he signed with Milestone in 1980. He's done several dates with Hank Crawford, and played with Al Grey. McGriff's early '90s Headfirst sessions mix electronic fusion material with organ jazz. —*Ron Wynn and Bob Porter*

McGriff has several distinct periods, and the quality of his recordings can depend upon which period you are listening to. For my money, his early stuff on the Sue label is his best, and unique in organ jazz in that it typifies what every soul jazz listener hopes to hear from early-'60s Hammond organ. Albums like "Got a Woman," "One of Mine," "At the Apollo," "Jimmy McGriff at the Organ," and "Blues for Mr. Jimmy" were all originally released on Sue and are now available on the Collectables label. The Collectables reissues have terrible sound quality; probably pulled from vinyl–who knows? In spite of the sound quality, the music is great and should be heard. These albums all have great cuts mixed in with mediocre or bad tracks. Even so, this is high-impact, driven McGriff that has little relation to much of his later work.

McGriff's work for Solid State and Groove Merchant under the production of Sonny Lester is, for the most part, well worth hearing. You can almost go by looking at how many players are on the session–the fewer the better. In particular, McGriff's larger band material in the late '70s should be avoided, since this is pop-oriented and has little jazz content.

Then comes McGriff's excellent work for Milestone; albums like *Countdown, Skywalk, State of the Art, The Starting Five, Blue to the Bone, Steppin Up,* and his collaboration with Hank Crawford, *Soul Survivors*. Produced by blues-funk expert Bob Porter, this series finds McGriff playing jazz and soul jazz and catering less to the pop market. Although never reaching the searing intensity of his early work on Sue, this is all very listenable.

In the early 1990s, McGriff on Headstart is more synthesizer-drenched pop pap. His Telarc material in the mid-1990s with alto saxist Hank Crawford is worth picking up. —*Michael Erlewine*

I Got A Woman / Sue-Collectables ✦✦✦✦
McGriff's first album is great. The title cut was in the top 20 in 1962. Also on the same album is "M.G. Blues" and "All About My Girl." This session features McGriff, Richard Easley on drums, and Walter Miller on guitar. High-impact early McGriff is the still the best, and this is the album that started it all. Three cuts available on the Collectable CD *A Toast to Jimmy McGriff's Golden Classics. –Michael Erlewine*

One of Mine / Sue-Collectables ✦✦✦
His second album, again on Sue. This has been reissued on Collectables. This session has McGriff with Morris Dow on lead guitar and harmonic, Larry Frazier on rhythm guitar, and Willie "Saint" Jenkins on drums. It features the title cut and "The Last Minute." Ten high-energy cuts. –*Michael Erlewine*

At the Apollo / Sue-Collectables ✦✦✦
The third album from McGriff on the Sue label was recorded live at New York's Apollo Theater in 1963. It features McGriff with Rudolph Johnson on tenor sax, Larry Frazier on guitar, and Willie Jenkins on drums. Contains a great version of "Red Sails in the Sunset" and "A Thing for Jug." –*Michael Erlewine*

Jimmy McGriff at the Organ / Sue-Collectables ✦✦✦✦
McGriff with Rudolph Johnson on soprano and tenor sax, Larry Frazier on guitar, and Jimmie Smith on drums. This album contains the classic McGriff cut "Kiko," "That's All," and "Hello Betty". This is drum/sax-driven McGriff at his best. –*Michael Erlewine*

Topkapi / Sue-Collectables ✦✦
This finds McGriff with pre-recorded tracks with a horn section, guitar, bass, drums, and a string section. The material was

arranged and directed by Fred Norman. The album consists of 12 movie and TV themes with McGriff and "orchestra." The orchestra sounds like Muzak, but McGriff sounds like McGriff. How the two got together beats me. –*Michael Erlewine*

Blues for Mr. Jimmy / Sue ✦✦✦
His last date for the Sue label is a trio, McGriff with Larry Frazier on guitar, and Jimmie Smith on drums. Nine bluesy tunes including "Turn Blue," a classic McGriff instrumental. –*Michael Erlewine*

Toast to Jimmy McGriff's Golden Classics / Collectables / ✦✦✦✦
This is a compilation of ten cuts taken from the six early Sue albums, one or two from each. The sound is bad, but it will give you a taste of the Sue material–all the best cuts. These early Sue albums are now all available on Collectables and worth hearing, despite the sound. –*Michael Erlewine*

Funkiest Little Band in the Land / LRC / ✦✦✦
This is a collection of McGriff with small bands during the years from 1968 to 1974, before he went to the large orchestra format. Produced by Sonny Lester, many of these appeared on the Groove Merchant label. Includes a lot of funky stuff with titles like "Super Funk," "Fat Cakes," "Groove Fly," and "Dig On It." There are 13 cuts and plenty of vintage Mcgriff. –*Michael Erlewine*

The Jazz Collector Edition Jimmy McGriff / ✦✦✦
This is a reissue of two 1970s McGriff albums, *Groove Grease* (1971) and *Main Squeeze* (1974) originally released on the Groove Merchant label. The first has McGriff with Jimmy Ponder (g) and Eddie Gladden (d). The second album has mixed personnel, including Everett Barksdale (g), Cliff Davis.(sax), Murray Wilson (tpt), and Johnny Board (baritone sax). In general, nice, laid-back playing. –*Michael Erlewine*

Georgia on My Mind / LRC / ✦✦✦
This is a compilation of sixteen selections from six sessions in the late 1960s and early 1970s, tunes from McGriff albums like *Let's Stay Together* (1966 and 1972 versions), *Fly Dude* (1972), and *Groove Grease* (1971). All small or smallish combos. Mostly standards; some few kickers. –Michael Erlewine

The Starting Five / Milestone / ✦✦✦✦
Here is McGriff with two terrific blues honkin' sax masters–Rusty Bryant and David "Fathead" Newman. Add Mel Brown and Wayne Boyd on guitar, plus Bernard Purdie on drums, and you have a recipe for funk. Produced by Bob Porter, this is perhaps the best of McGriff's Milestone output. –*Michael Erlewine*

Blue to the Bone / Milestone / ✦✦✦✦
McGriff with Bill Easley on sax, Melvin Sparks on guitar, Bernard Purdie on drums, and Al Grey on trombone. The trombone is not that often found in the small-organ combo format and may not appeal to everyone. Smooth, yet funky. –*Michael Erlewine & Ron Wynn*

Countdown / Milestone / ✦✦✦✦
His first for Milestone. Produced by Bob Porter, McGriff with two saxes, trombone, guitar, and drums for what the liner notes call a "big band sound" combo. Plenty of good funky organ. Some of the numbers are a little too smooth (too many horns) for my taste. –*Michael Erlewine*

Steppin' Up / Milestone / ✦✦✦
Jimmy McGriff with Hank Crawford on alto sax, Jimmy Ponder on guitar, Billy Preston on piano, and Vance James on drums–an excellent group. Produced by Bob Porter, this has tunes like "Something for Bubba," and Percy Mayfield's "River's Invitation" that are standouts. This combination of players is all that you need for some funky jazz. –*Michael Erlewine*

In a Blue Mood / Headfirst / ✦✦
One of his albums on Headfirst, after leaving Milestone and the great production work of Bob Porter. McGriff on organ and keyboards, plus a group with synthesizers, sax, guitar, drums, vocals, and what-not make this more pop-oriented fare than organ funk. Where's Bob Porter when you need him? –*Michael Erlewine*

Tribute to Basie / 1966 / ✦✦✦
Recorded in 1966 with the Jimmy McGriff Big Band, and it is a VERY large group. At the center of all these instruments is the one-man band organ sound of McGriff. This is a salute to Count Basie and includes 10 songs that he wrote or made a part of his repertoire. Actually, this works quite well. –*Michael Erlewine*

Soul Survivors / Milestone / ✦✦✦✦
Can't beat the lineup: McGriff with Hank Crawford on alto sax, George Benson (or Jim Pittsburgh) on guitar, and Bernard Purdie (or Mel Lewis) on drums. This is another of the fine Milestone recordings of McGriff produced by Bob Porter. No disappointments here. Includes version of "One Mint Julep," "Because of You," and the Crawford original "The Peeper." Very nice. –*Michael Erlewine*

Double Exposure / ✦✦✦
This album contains two albums, one by Groove Holmes and the other by Jimmy McGriff. They do not play together here. McGriff is with George Freeman on guitar, Eddie Gladden on drums, and James Peacock on conga. Six cuts by McGriff and five by Groove Holmes. The tunes "Catherine" and "Rainy Day" are very nice.–*Michael Erlewine*

Main Squeeze / 1976 / Groove Merchant ✦✦✦
McGriff with the funky guitar of Jimmy Ponder and Connie Lester on alto sax. –*Michael Erlewine*

● **Movin' Upside the Blues** / Dec. 19, 1980–Jan. 24, 1981 / Jazz America ✦✦✦✦✦
There are few better combinations for producing after hours funk than organist Jimmy McGriff and guitarist Jimmy Ponder. Irrepressably swinging McGriff is always in spitting distance of those down-home or South side blues. Ponder compliments with a lightness that brings an appealing optimism to the realities. If you haven't had a taste yet, start here; if you have had a taste and have room for more in your diet, this is a tasty dish. –*Bob Rusch, Cadence*

On the Blue Side / May 1990 / Milestone ✦✦✦✦
An updated version of the vintage McGriff formula: bluesy, soulful organ fare with a balance struck between jazz sensibility and a funk/R&B groove. –*Ron Wynn*

Oliver Nelson

b. Jun. 4, 1932, St. Louis, MO, d. Oct. 27, 1975, Los Angeles, CA
Sax (Alto), Sax (Tenor) / Post-Bop, Hard Bop
Oliver Nelson was a distinctive soloist on alto, tenor and even soprano but his writing eventually overshadowed his playing skills. He became a professional early on in 1947, playing with the Jeter-Pillars Orchestra and with St. Louis big bands headed by George Hudson and Nat Towles. In 1951 he arranged and played second alto for Louis Jordan's big band and followed with a period in the Navy and four years at a university. After moving to New York, Nelson worked briefly with Erskine Hawkins, Wild Bill Davis and Louie Bellson (the latter on the West Coast). In addition to playing with Quincy Jones' Orchestra (1960–61), between 1959–61 Nelson recorded six small-group albums and a big-band date; those gave him a lot of recognition and respect in the jazz world. *Blues and the Abstract Truth* (from 1961) is considered a classic and helped to popularize a song that Nelson had included on a slightly earlier Eddie "Lockjaw" Davis session, "Stolen Moments." He also fearlessly matched wits effectively with the explosive Eric Dolphy on a pair of quintet sessions. But good as his playing was, Nelson was in greater demand as an arranger, writing for big-band dates of Jimmy Smith, Wes Montgomery, and Billy Taylor, among others. By 1967, when he moved to Los Angeles, Nelson was working hard in the studios, writing for television and movies. He occasionally appeared with a big band, wrote a few ambitious works and recorded jazz on an infrequent basis, but Oliver Nelson was largely lost to jazz a few years before his unexpected death at age 43 from a heart attack. –*Scott Yanow*

● **Soul Battle** / Sep. 9, 1960 / Original Jazz Classics ✦✦✦✦✦
This intriguing session matches together three powerful tenor players: Oliver Nelson, King Curtis (a rare jazz outing) and Jimmy Forrest. With fine backup work by pianist Gene Casey, bassist George Duvivier and drummer Roy Haynes, the tenors battle to a draw on a set of blues and basic material (including a fine version of "Perdido"). This CD reissue adds one selection ("Soul Street") from the same date to the original LP program and is easily recommended to fans of big-toned tenors and straightahead swinging. –*Scott Yanow*

David "Fathead" Newman

b. Feb. 24, 1933, Dallas, TX
Flute, Sax (Alto), Sax (Tenor) / Soul Jazz, Hard Bop
A first-rate soul jazz, blues, R&B, and funk saxophonist and

flutist, David "Fathead" Newman has been a star in seminal bands, issued excellent recordings and been featured on several fine sessions. He can certainly play bebop and has shown surprising chops when so inclined, but that's not his strength. Hearing the gorgeous, huge Newman tenor sax tones filling the space left by a singer laying out, ripping through a 12-bar blues, interacting with an organist or guitarist, or just embellishing a melody, is one of jazz and popular music's great pleasures. His taste has sometimes deserted him, but when working in the right arena Newman's a wonderful player and bandleader. He got his "Fathead" nickname from a music teacher as a child. He began playing with local bands in Dallas, and later toured with Lowell Fulson and T-Bone Walker. Newman became a star while working with Ray Charles. He stayed with Charles a full decade in the '50s and '60s, and was a pivotal part of many landmark R&B dates. The sounds he made with Charles still guide Newman's music. He later worked with King Curtis in the mid-'60s. Newman began recording as a leader for Atlantic in the late '50s. He did several small combo sessions, then later worked with larger bands. Newman played with Blue Mitchell, Roy Ayers, Dr. John, and Ron Carter among others. Things began to go astray in the mid-'70s; there were some experiments with overdubbed strings and horns. But Newman returned to soul jazz and blues basics on Prestige, Muse, and Atlantic in the '80s. He's recorded for Milestone in the late '80s and '90s, still doing reliable blues and soul jazz, with an occasional bebop date. He's also recorded for Candid and Timeless, and worked with Cornell Dupree and Ellis Marsalis on a fine session for Amazing Records. Newman has a fair number of titles available on CD. Rhino issued a CD anthology of some earlier Atlantic dates in '93. —*Ron Wynn*

★ **House of David Newman: David "Fathead" Anthology** / 1952 / Rhino ✦✦✦✦✦
There have not been many saxophonists and flutists more naturally soulful than David "Fathead" Newman. This two-disc set captures Newman at his best. He never really was an album artist; each LP has had its nuggets, and that's what this captures. It has Newman wailing the blues, then stretching out in the Ray Charles band. He covers a Beatles tune, then an Aaron Neville number. He backs Aretha Franklin and pays homage to the great Buster Cooper. This is one anthology that can be recommended without hesitation, because there aren't going to be many complete Newman albums coming down the reissue pike. —*Ron Wynn*

Fathead: Ray Charles Presents David Newman / Nov. 5, 1958 / Atlantic ✦✦✦✦
The talented David Newman, who alternates on this album between tenor and alto, made his debut as a leader at this session. Since he was in Ray Charles' band at the time, Newman was able to use Charles on piano along with Hank Crawford (here called Bennie Crawford) on baritone, trumpeter Marcus Belgrave, bassist Edgar Willis, and drummer Milton Turner. The music is essentially soulful bebop with the highlights including "Hard Times," "Fathead," "Mean To Me," and "Tin Tin Deo." Everyone plays well and this was a fine start to David "Fathead" Newman's career. —*Scott Yanow*

Straight Ahead / Dec. 21, 1960 / Atlantic ✦✦✦✦
Newman with Wynton Kelly on piano, Paul Chambers on bass, and Charlie Persip on drums. —*AMG*

Lonely Avenue / Nov. 2, 1971–Nov. 4, 1971 / Atlantic ✦✦✦
Textbook soul jazz; fine vibes from Roy Ayers. —*Ron Wynn*

Back to Basics / May 1977–Nov. 1977 / Milestone ✦✦✦✦
A '91 CD reissue of a late '70s session by tenor saxophonist and flutist David Newman, which emphasized his patented soul jazz and blues while matching Newman with different players on various tracks, rather than having a fixed rhythm section. The top guest stars included keyboardists Hilton Ruiz and George Cables and guitarist Lee Ritenour. —*Ron Wynn*

Still Hard Times / Apr. 1982 / Muse ✦✦✦✦✦
Saxophonist in his prime. Tuneful and exuberant. —*Michael G. Nastos*

Fire! Live at the Village Vanguard / Dec. 22, 1988–Dec. 23, 1988 / Atlantic ✦✦✦✦
A nice outing that matches Newman with Stanley Turrentine (ts) and Hank Crawford (as). —*Ron Wynn*

Harold Ousley (Harold Lomax Ousley)
b. Jan. 33, 1929, Chicago, IL
Flute, Saxophone / Blues Jazz, Swing, Soul Jazz
A competent funk and soul jazz saxophonist and flutist, Harold Ousley's bluesy playing on organ combo dates, rock and roll tunes and backing vocalists was stronger than much of what he did when leading groups. His albums were often uneven, both in terms of compositional quality and playing. Ousley began his professional career in the '40s, and at one point backed Billie Holiday. During the '50s, he played with King Kolax and Gene Ammons and worked in circus bands. Ousley backed Dinah Washington at the 1958 Newport Jazz Festival, an engagement that led to him winning a recording deal. He traveled to Paris the next year with a song revue, then worked with Clark Terry, Howard McGhee, Machito and Joe Newman in the '60s. Ousley began leading his own groups and recording with organ combos, notably Brother Jack McDuff, in the mid-'60s. He worked with Lionel Hampton and Count Basie in the '70s. Ousley currently has no releases available on CD. —*Ron Wynn*

Tenor Sax / 1961 / Bethlehem ✦✦✦

★ **The People's Groove** / 1972 / Muse ✦✦✦✦✦
Saxophonist who worked with Dinah Washington. The all-star cast includes Ray McKinney (b), Bobby Rose (g), and Norman Simmons (p). —*Michael G. Nastos*

Don Patterson (Donald B. Patterson)
b. Jul. 22, 1936, Columbus, OH, d. Feb. 10, 1988
Organ / Soul Jazz, Hard Bop
Don Patterson began his musical career as a pianist, inspired by Erroll Garner. A solid soul jazz, blues, and hard bop organist with a pianistic background, Patterson didn't utilize the pedals or play with as much rhythmic drive as some other stylists, but developed a satisfactory alternative approach. Patterson's organ solos were smartly played, and more melodic than explosive. He switched from piano in 1956 after hearing Jimmy Smith. Patterson made his organ debut in 1959, and worked with Sonny Stitt, Eddie "Lockjaw" Davis, Gene Ammons, and Wes Montgomery in the early '60s. He recorded with Ammons, Stitt, and Eric Kloss in the early and mid-'60s. Patterson worked often in a duo with Billy James and made several recordings in the '60s and '70s as a leader. He and Al Grey worked together extensively in the '80s. Patterson recorded as a leader for Prestige and Muse. He has one session available on CD. —*Ron Wynn and Michael G. Nastos*
Groove: Unfortunately, like many of the great soul jazz players, not much Don Patterson has been released on CD. You will find him backing up any number of other players, however, like Sonny Stitt and Eddie "Lockjaw" Davis. —*Michael Erlewine*

Goin' Down Home / Jan. 22, 1963 / Cadet ✦✦✦
Trio with Patterson on the Hammond B-3, Paul Weeden on guitar, and Billy James on drums. Includes the Nat Adderley tune "Worksong." —*AMG*

The Best of Don Patterson / Mar. 19, 1964–Aug. 25, 1967 / Prestige ✦✦

The Exciting New Organ of Don Patterson / May 12, 1964 / Prestige ✦✦✦✦✦
Great album with Booker Ervin on tenor sax. —*AMG*

The Boss Men / Dec. 1965 / Prestige ✦✦✦
Don Patterson with Sonny Stitt on alto sax and Billy James on drums. —*AMG*

Mellow Soul / May 10, 1967 / Prestige ✦✦✦
A trio date with David Fathead Newman on sax and flute, plus Billy James on drums. —*AMG*

Four Dimensions / Aug. 25, 1967 / Prestige ✦✦✦
Patterson with Houston Person (sax), Pat Martino (g), and Billy James (d). —*Michael Erlewine*

● **Dem New York Blues** / Jun. 5, 1968+Jun. 2, 1969 / Prestige ✦✦✦✦✦
Despite claims to the contrary, organist Don Patterson was very much of the Jimmy Smith school, a hard-driving player with fine improvising skills but lacking a distinctive sound of his own. This CD (which reissues two complete LPs) features Patterson in prime form in a quintet with trumpeter Blue Mitchell, Junior Cook on tenor, and guitarist Pat Martino, and with a separate group that features trumpeter Virgil Jones and both George

Coleman and Houston Person on tenors. Although "Oh Happy Day" is a throwaway, Patterron's spirited renditions of the blues and standards make this a fairly definitive example of his talents. —*Scott Yanow*

Funk You / Sep. 24, 1968 / Prestige ✦✦✦
With Charles McPherson on alto sax, Sonny Stitt on alto/tenor, Pat Martino on guitar, and Billy James on drums. —*Michael Erlewine*

The Return Of . . . / Oct. 30, 1972 / Muse ✦✦✦✦
Quartet with Eddie Daniels (ts), Ted Dunbar (g), and Freddie Waits (d). Any Don Patterson album is worthwhile. —*Michael G. Nastos*

The Genius of the B-3 / Oct. 30, 1972 / Muse ✦✦✦✦✦
A fine album (fast and slow) with Patterson in excellent form. There is some very nice soul jazz here. CD clocks out at 43 minutes. —*Michael Erlewine*

These Are Soulful Days / Sep. 17, 1973 / Muse ✦✦✦✦✦
Quartet with this great Hammond B-3 organist, Jimmy Heath (sax), Pat Martino (g), and A. Heath (d). —*Michael G. Nastos*

Big John Patton

b. Jul. 12, 1935, Kansas City, MO
Organ / Soul Jazz, Hard Bop
A first-rate soul jazz and blues organist, Big John Patton's dates are among the most danceable, funky, and exuberant ever done at Blue Note. He wasn't as adventurous as Larry Young, but matched any organist for sheer energy and rousing fervor. Patton played piano in the late '40s, and toured with Lloyd Price in the mid and late '50s. He began playing organ in the '60s, and recorded with Lou Donaldson from 1962 to 1964. Patton also did sessions with Harold Vick, Johnny Griffin, Grant Green, and Clifford Jordan in the '60s, while doing his own dates with a trio. At various times Clifford Jarvis and James "Blood" Ulmer were members of Patton's trio. Bobby Hutcherson, Junior Cook, Blue Mitchell, and Richard Williams as well as Vick served as special guests on different sessions. Patton recorded with Johnny Lytle in 1977 and 1983. In obscurity during the 1970s when the Hammond organ was overshadowed by electric pianos and synthesizers, Patton's career was revived in the 1980s thanks in part to John Zorn singing his praises and using him on some recordings. Many of Patton's earlier recordings are now available on CD. —*Ron Wynn and Scott Yanow*

Blue John / Jul. 11, 1963–Aug. 2, 1963 / Blue Note ✦✦✦✦✦
This is a fairly bright bit of soul jazz, not quite as heavy as your normal soul jazz session. There is nice guitar by Grant Green. The trumpet of Tommy Turrentine and the stritch (two saxophones braced together) of George Braith are not your usual soul jazz instruments. The dual-horn sound of the stritch ends up sounding too much like honking car horns for my taste. It is hard to stay in the groove in the middle of the freeway. But any John Patton is worth having. —*Michael Erlewine*

Oh Baby / Mar. 8, 1965 / Blue Note ✦✦✦
Patton's fourth album for Blue Note. Big John Patton with Grant Green on guitar and Harold Vick on tenor sax. With tunes like "Fat Judy" and "Good Juice," there is no worry about there being a groove. The addition of a trumpet (Blue Mitchell) means you have a horn section, and this tends to be a little much now and again. Although a little on the light side, thanks to Patton and Green, the groove does go down. —*Michael Erlewine*

● **Let 'em Roll** / Dec. 11, 1965 / Blue Note ✦✦✦✦✦
Patton with Grant Green (guitar), Otis Finch (drums), and Bobby Hutcherson (vibes). Grant Green provides just superb assistance. While vibes is not a usual instrument for soul jazz sessions, this album works anyway and the groove is established. Grant Green and Patton are just a great combination. —*Michael Erlewine*

Boogaloo / Aug. 9, 1968 / Blue Note ✦✦✦
Big John Patton with a trumpet and sax, drums, and conga. Harold Alexander (sax) plays a little out for a standard soul jazz session and the combination of the horns amounts to what it should be—a horn section. For me, this never gets down to the business of being soul music. The groove is weak or not there. —*Michael Erlewine*

Understanding / Oct. 25, 1968 / Blue Note ✦✦
Patton with saxman Harold Alexander and drums. Alexander is playing sax that is just a tad too "out" for an organ combo than

is standard for soul jazz, thus turning the sound toward something other than a real groove. If you like progressive sax, you might be able to stay in the groove. Not me, the sound keeps popping me out. I like to get in the groove and ride. —*Michael Erlewine*

Accent on the Blues / Aug. 15, 1969 / Blue Note ✦✦✦

Soul Connection / Jun. 7, 1983 / Nilva ✦✦✦

Memphis To New York Spirit / Mar. 5, 1996 / Blue Note ✦✦
Although it was scheduled for release two times, *Memphis to New York Spirit* didn't appear until 1996, over 25 years after it was recorded. The album comprises the contents of two separate sessions—one recorded in 1970 with guitarist James "Blood" Ulmer, drummer Gene Ammons, and saxophonist/flautist Marvin Cabell; the other recorded in 1969 with Cabell, Williams, and saxophonist George Coleman—that were very similiar in concept and execution. Patton leads his combo through a selection of originals and covers that range from Wayne Shorter and McCoy Tyner to the Meters. Though the group is rooted in soul jazz, they stretch the limits of the genre on these sessions, showing a willingness to experiment, while still dipping into the more traditional blues and funk reserves. Consequently, *Memphis to New York Spirit* doesn't have a consistent groove like some other Patton records, but when it does click, the results are remarkable; it's a non-essential but worthy addition to a funky soul jazz collection. —*Stephen Thomas Erlewine*

Houston Person

b. Nov. 10, 1934, Florence, SC
Sax (Tenor) / Soul Jazz, Hard Bop
In the 1990s Houston Person has kept the soulful thick-toned tenor tradition of Gene Ammons alive, particularly in his work with organists. After learning piano as a youth, Person switched to tenor. While stationed in Germany with the army, he played in groups that also included Eddie Harris, Lanny Morgan, Leo Wright, and Cedar Walton. Person picked up valuable experience as a member of Johnny Hammond's group (1963–66) and has been a bandleader ever since, often working with his wife, singer Etta Jones. A duo recording with Ran Blake was a nice change of pace, but most of Houston Person's playing has been done in blues-oriented organ groups. He has recorded a consistently excellent series of albums for Muse. —*Scott Yanow*

Soul Dance / Nov. 18, 1968 / Prestige ✦✦✦
With Billy Gardner on organ. Although not as well produced or engineered as his '70s and '80s Muse recordings, this late '60s date is vintage Houston Person. He's doing the same mix of blues, ballads, and soul jazz cuts as always, although with a little less confidence, edge, and control than he displays on later albums. —*Ron Wynn*

● **Goodness!** / Aug. 25, 1969 / Original Jazz Classics ✦✦✦✦
Tenor saxophonist Houston Person was still a relatively new name at the time he recorded this set, his sixth session for Prestige. The funky music (which includes the hit title song) emphasizes boogaloos, danceable rhythms, and repetitious vamps set down by the rhythm section (organist Sonny Phillips, guitarist Billy Butler, electric bassist Bob Bushnell, drummer Frankie Jones, and Buddy Caldwell on congas), but it is primarily Person's passionate tenor solos that will come the closest to holding on to the attention of jazz listeners. The music is generally quite commercial and is certainly not recommended to bebop purists, although it has some strong moments. But overall these performances succeed more as background music than as creative jazz. —*Scott Yanow*

The Truth! / Feb. 23, 1970 / Prestige ✦✦✦
Another with Sonny Phillips on organ and Billy Butler on guitar. —*AMG*

Person to Person / Oct. 12, 1970 / Prestige ✦✦✦
Houston Person with Grant Green on guitar, Virgil Jones on trumpet, and Sonny Phillips on the Hammond B-3. —*AMG*

Stolen Sweets / Apr. 29, 1976 / Muse ✦✦✦✦✦
First-rate soul jazz, funk, blues, and ballads by tenor saxophonist Houston Person. Vocalist Etta Jones wasn't on this session, so things were mostly uptempo and cooking, with plenty of robust tenor from Person, tasty guitar by Jimmy Ponder, swirling organ riffs and support from Sonny Phillips, and percussion and rhythmic assistance from Frankie Jones and Buddy Caldwell. —*Ron Wynn*

The Nearness of Houston Person / Nov. 1977 / Muse ✦✦✦
Intimate, nicely played late '70s session by tenor saxophonist Houston Person that balances robust soul jazz and blues with stately ballads and standards featuring vocalist Etta Jones. When things heat up, organist Charles Earland helps punctuate Person's solos. Then, when Jones steps out front, it's Person who puts the accents behind her singing. —*Ron Wynn*

Suspicions / Apr. 24, 1980 / Muse ✦✦✦
Some robust funk and fine soul licks, plus solid mainstream fare. —*Ron Wynn*

The Party / Nov. 14, 1989 / Muse ✦✦✦✦✦
Good soul jazz and blues session, with young lion organist Joey DeFrancesco providing the funky undercurrent to tenor saxophonist Houston Person's thick, authoritative solos and Randy Johnston and Bertell Knox filling the spaces on bass and drums, plus Sammy Figueroa adding some Afro-Latin fiber for additional support. —*Ron Wynn*

● **Why Not!** / Oct. 5, 1990 / Muse ✦✦✦✦✦
Organ-tenor-trumpet session. Person's album includes hot contributions by young lions Harper Brothers plus Joey DeFrancisco on the Hammond Organ. —*Ron Wynn*

Ike Quebec

b. Aug. 17, 1918, Newark, NJ, **d.** Jan. 16, 1963, New York, NY
Sax (Tenor) / Swing, Early R&B
A magnificent "populist" saxophonist whose abilities were undervalued by many critics during his lifetime, Ike Quebec showed simple, compelling music need not be played in a simplistic manner. He had a pronounced swing bent in his style and tone, particularly the sound of Coleman Hawkins. But Quebec didn't simply parrot Hawkins; he displayed a huge, bluesy tone, swooping, jubilant phrases and played joyous uptempo tunes and evocative, slow blues and ballads. There were no false fingerings, or anything intricate; it was just direct, heartfelt solos. Quebec was once a pianist and part-time soft shoe artist, but switched to tenor in the '40s, playing the Barons of Rhythm. He worked with several New York bands, among them groups led by Kenny Clarke, Benny Carter, and Roy Eldridge. He co-wrote the song "Mop Mop" with Clarke, which was later recorded by Coleman Hawkins during one of the earliest bebop sessions. Quebec played from the mid-'40s into the early '50s with Cab Calloway's orchestra and also his spinoff unit, The Cab Jivers. Quebec cut one of Blue Note's rare 78 albums in the '40s, and also recorded for Savoy. His song "Blue Harlem" became a huge hit. Quebec also worked with Lucky Millinder and recorded with Calloway. Alfred Lion made Quebec Blue Note's A&R man in the late '40s, after Quebec repeatedly informed him about talented prospective signees. Quebec doubled for a while as a bandleader, but concentrated until the late '50s on recording and finding acts for the label. Some of the people he brought Lion included Thelonious Monk and Bud Powell. Quebec wrote "Suburban Eyes" for Monk's label debut. He began playing again in the late '50s, doing Blue Note sessions with Sonny Clark, Jimmy Smith, singer Dodo Green, and Stanley Turrentine, plus his own dates. Just as he was attracting renewed attention and some appreciation from critics who'd previously dismissed him as another honking R&B type, Quebec died of lung cancer in 1963. Mosaic has issued some superb Quebec boxed sets, *The Complete Blue Note Forties Recordings of Ike Quebec and John Hardee* and *The Complete Blue Note 45 Sessions*. —*Ron Wynn*
Groove: Ike Quebec is a direct hit with most blues fans. This guy plays from the heart in an understated yet warm manner that is endearing from the first listen. If you can obtain one of the albums with Quebec and Grant Green, then the magic gets even better. The Mosaic boxed set *The Complete Blue Note 45 Sessions* is worth an explanation. It was common practice to take the best cut from a popular album, put it on a 45, and release it to juke boxes all over the country. It meant extra income. A certain kind of soulful romantic bluesy sound was what did well on the Jukes—beer drinkin' music. Ike Quebec was asked to create such 45s just for juke-box release. There were no albums. People loved them and so will you. This is great bluesy music. You can order these by mail only from Mosaic Records, 35 Melrose Place, Stamford, CT 06904. Ask for their catalog—the best jazz reissues label on the planet. —*Michael Erlewine*

★ **Complete Blue Note Recordings** / Jul. 18, 1944–Sep. 23, 1946 / Mosaic ✦✦✦✦✦
This is an essential compilation of virtually all the early Quebec jazz dates. —*Ron Wynn*

☆ **Complete Blue Note 45 Sessions** / Jul. 1, 1959–Feb. 13, 1962 / Mosaic ✦✦✦✦✦
A wonderful three-disc collection of Quebec's 1959–1962 songs that packed jazz punch, had R&B appeal, and were originally recorded for and designed as singles for jukeboxes. —*Ron Wynn*

The Art of Ike Quebec / Nov. 13, 1961–Oct. 5, 1962 / Blue Note ✦✦✦
A '92 anthology featuring some super numbers by dynamic saxophonist Ike Quebec, a masterful blues, ballad, and honking R&B player. It's a good introductory set, although Mosaic has cornered the market on Ike Quebec sessions with its boxed sets featuring his full Blue Note dates. —*Ron Wynn*

Heavy Soul / Nov. 26, 1961 / Blue Note ✦✦✦✦
The thick-toned tenor Ike Quebec is in excellent form on this CD reissue of a 1961 Blue Note date. His ballad statements are quite warm and he swings nicely on a variety of medium-tempo material. Unfortunately organist Freddie Roach has a rather dated sound which weakens this session a bit; bassist Milt Hinton and drummer Al Harewood are typically fine in support. Originals alternate with standards with "Just One More Chance," "The Man I Love" and "Nature Boy" (the latter an emotional tenor-bass duet) being among the highlights. —*Scott Yanow*

● **Blue and Sentimental** / Dec. 16, 1961+Dec. 23, 1961 / Blue Note ✦✦✦✦✦
Hot, lusty, and wonderful. Quebec was a rare jazz musician who never lost his appeal in the R&B community. W/ Sonny Clark (p), Grant Green (g), Paul Chambers (b), Philly Joe Jones (d). —*Ron Wynn*

Congo Lament / Jan. 20, 1962 / Blue Note ✦✦✦
Africa meets Harlem with soul in a rousing Quebec date. —*Ron Wynn*

Easy Living / Jan. 20, 1962 / Blue Note ✦✦✦✦✦
This CD reissue (which adds three songs to the original LP) is really two sets in one. The first five selections are a blues-oriented jam session that matches together the contrasting tenors of Ike Quebec and Stanley Turrentine with trombonist Bennie Green, pianist Sonny Clark, bassist Milt Hinton, and drummer Art Blakey. However it is the last three numbers ("I've Got a Crush on You," "Nancy with the Laughing Face," and "Easy Living") that are most memorable; ballad features for Quebec's warm tenor. All in all this set gives one a definitive look at late-period Ike Quebec. —*Scott Yanow*

Soul Samba / Nov. 5, 1962 / Blue Note ✦✦✦

Mel Rhyne

b. Oct. 12, 1936, Indianapolis, IN
Organ / Hard Bop
Organist Mel Rhyne was born on October 12, 1936 in Indianapolis, where he grew up. Exposed to music from an early age by his family, he met Roland Kirk and Wilber Jackson as a teen. Rhyne was a major foil for Wes Montgomery from 1959 to 1964. He started out playing piano with Montgomery, but soon switched to a spinet organ and then on to the larger Hammond. Rhyne is featured on Montgomery's albums *Wes Montgomery Trio, Boss Guitar, Portrait of Wes*, and *Guitar On the Go*. His influences were Milt Buchner, Jackie Davis, and Wild Bill Davis. Although Rhyne has his own style, he admits to learning from Jimmy Smith. In the late 1960s, he teamed up with his brother Ron Rhyne (drums) and formed a group.
    In 1991, Rhyne made a comeback with guitarist Herb Ellis and his release of *Roll Call*. In 1992, Mel Rhyne released an album on Criss Cross Records, *The Legend*. Late in 1995, he recorded with Kenny Washington, Perter Bernstein, Ryan Kisor, and Eric Alexander.
    Rhyne has been characterised as the bridge between Jimmy Smith and Larry Young. He still plays in the Milwaukee area. —*Michael Erlewine & Michael G. Nastos*

Organizing / Mar. 31, 1960 / Jazzland ✦✦✦✦
With Johnny Griffin on tenor sax and Blue Mitchell on trumpet. —*Michael G. Nastos*

The Legend / Dec. 30, 1991 / Criss Cross ✦✦✦✦
● Boss Organ / Jan. 6, 1993 / Criss Cross ✦✦✦✦✦
Mel Rhyne, best known for his association in the 1960s with Wes
Montgomery, re-emerged with this Criss Cross CD as one of the
finest jazz organists around. He is matched with guitarist Peter
Bernstein, drummer Kenny Washington, and the young tenor
great Joshua Redman for a set of good-natured and often hard-
swinging performances. In addition to superior versions of "All
God's Chillun Got Rhythm" and "Jeannine," the quartet explores
lesser-known songs such as Hubert Laws's "Shades of Light,"
Stevie Wonder's "You and I," and Mel Torme's "Born to Be Blue."
The music is consistently stimulating and swinging. —Scott
Yanow

Shirley Scott

b. Mar. 14, 1934, Philadelphia, PA
Organ / Soul Jazz, Hard Bop
Shirley Scott surprised many people in 1992 when she appeared
on Bill Cosby's reprise of The Groucho Marx game and personality show "You Bet Your Life." Not that he'd picked her to be his
music director, but that she was playing piano. Her reputation
was cemented during the '60s on several superb, soulful
organ/soul jazz dates where she demonstrated an aggressive,
highly rhythmic attack blending intricate bebop harmonies with
bluesy melodies and a gospel influence, punctuating everything
with great use of the bass pedals. But Scott demonstrated an
equal flair and facility on piano, many days incorporating snatch-
es of anthemic jazz compositions while noodling in the background. The show was a bore, but it was great to see Scott back
in the spotlight. She began playing piano as a child, then trumpet in high school. Scott was working a club date in the mid-'50s
in Philadelphia when the owner rented her a Hammond B-3. She
learned quickly, and was soon leading both popular and artistically superior trios featuring either Eddie "Lockjaw" Davis or
then-husband Stanley Turrentine on tenor sax. The
Scott/Turrentine union lasted until the early '70s, and their musical collaborations in the '60s were among the finest in the field.
Scott continued recording in the '70s, working with Harold Vick
and Jimmy Forrest and then in the early '80s Dexter Gordon.
She also made a lot of appearances on television in New York
and Philadelphia. Scott recorded prolifically for Prestige in the
'50s and '60s, then for Impulse in the mid-'60s and Atlantic in
the late '60s. She moved to Chess/Cadet in the early '70s, and
also did sessions for Strata-East. In recent years, Scott has recorded for Muse and Candid. Her later material wasn't as consistent
as her best work for Prestige and Impulse. She only has a few
dates currently available on CD. —Ron Wynn and Bob Porter

Great Scott! / May 27, 1958 / Prestige ✦✦✦
Recorded live at the Front Room in Newark, NJ, the album
includes ten tracks with a quartet including Stanley Turrentine.
On a rare night for music, the band delivered on all counts. You
can't go wrong here. —Michael G. Nastos

Workin' / May 27, 1958–Mar. 24, 1960 / Prestige ✦✦✦
One of several trio and/or combo works that organist Shirley
Scott recorded for Prestige in the late '50s and early '60s. Her
swirling, driving lines, intense bass pedal support, and bluesy
fervor were ideal for the soul jazz format, and this is a typical
example. —Ron Wynn

Now's the Time / May 27, 1958–Mar. 31, 1964 / Prestige ✦✦✦
This is early Scott, several takes from different session for this
Prestige release. —Michael Erlewine

Soul Searching / Dec. 4, 1959 / Prestige ✦✦✦
Shirley Scott with Wendell Marshall on bass and Arthur Edgehill
on drums. Includes title tune and "Boss." —AMG

Stompin' / Apr. 8, 1960–Mar. 24, 1961 / Prestige ✦✦✦
Here is Scott with Ronnell Bring (p), Wally Richardson (g), Peck
Morrison (b), and Roy Haynes (d). Includes a rendition of Nat
Adderley's "Work Song." —Michael Erlewine

Soul Sisters / Jun. 23, 1960 / Prestige ✦✦✦
With Lem Winchester on vibes, George Duvivier on bass, and
Arthur Edgehill on drums. A dauntless, swinging affair. —Ron
Wynn

Like Cozy / Sep. 27, 1960 / Moodsville ✦✦
Her standard trio with George Duvivier on bass and Arthur
Edgehill on drums. —AMG

Satin Doll / Mar. 7, 1961 / Prestige ✦✦✦
With George Tucker on bass and Jack Simpkins on drums. A bit
more prim, though Scott still burns. —Ron Wynn

Hip Soul / Jun. 2, 1961 / Prestige ✦✦✦✦✦
Here is Stanley Turrentine recording under the name Stan
Turner. Slashing, aptly titled. —Ron Wynn

The Best of Shirley Scott and Stanley Turrentine / Jun. 2,
1961–Mar. 31, 1964 / Prestige ✦✦✦

Blue Seven / Aug. 22, 1961 / Prestige ✦✦✦
A quintet with Roy Brooks (d), Oliver Nelson (ts), and Joe
Newman (tpt) plays one Scott original, the title song by Sonny
Rollins, and an excellent "Wagon Wheels." —Michael G. Nastos

Hip Twist / Nov. 17, 1961 / Prestige ✦✦✦
Scott with Stanley Turrentine (sax), George Tucker (b), and Otis
Finch (d). Any Turrentine/Scott albums are worth hearing, even
with a title like this one. —Michael Erlewine

Shirley Scott Plays Horace Silver / Nov. 17, 1961 / Prestige
✦✦✦✦✦
Just what it says. The queen of the Hammond organ (along with
Henry Grimes (b) and Otis Finch (d)) plays compositions by the
funk-master himself, Horace Silver. Included are "Senor Blues"
and "The Preacher." —Michael Erlewine

Happy Talk / Dec. 5, 1962 / Prestige ✦✦✦
Trio with Scott with Earl May (b) and Roy Brooks (d). —AMG

★ Sweet Soul / Dec. 5, 1962 / Prestige ✦✦✦✦
Reissued from the "Happy Talk" session this features Earl May
on bass and Roy Brooks on drums. It includes a nice "Jitterbug
Waltz." All are standards. —Michael G. Nastos

Soul Is Willing / Jan. 10, 1963 / Prestige ✦✦✦✦✦
This is a good album that shows the husband and wife team of
Shirley Scott and Stanley Turrentine in their usual, excellent
form—a fine example of organ combo soul jazz. Now part of the
Prestige two-fer called Soul Shoutin'. —Michael Erlewine

★ Soul Shoutin' / Jan. 10, 1963+Oct. 15, 1963 / Prestige ✦✦✦✦✦
Organist Shirley Scott and her then-husband tenor great Stanley
Turrentine always made potent music together. This CD, which
combines the former Prestige LPs The Soul Is Willing and Soul
Shoutin', finds "Mr. T" at his early peak, playing some intense yet
always soulful solos on such pieces as Sy Oliver's "Yes Indeed,"
"Secret Love," and his memorable originals "The Soul Is Willing"
and "Deep Down Soul." Scott, who found her own niche within
the dominant Jimmy Smith style, swings hard throughout the set
and (together with drummer Grassella Oliphant and either
Major Holley or Earl May on bass) the lead voices play with such
consistent enthusiasm that one would think these were club performances. Highly recommended. —Scott Yanow

Drag 'Em Out / May 27, 1963 / Prestige ✦✦✦
Scott with Major Holley (b) and Roy Brooks (d). —AMG

For Members Only / Aug. 22, 1963 / Impulse ✦✦✦✦
An excellent date with Earl May on bass and Jimmy Cobb on
drums. —AMG

● For Members Only/Great Scott / Aug. 22, 1963–May 20, 1964
/ MCA/Impulse ✦✦✦✦✦
During the 1960s, Shirley Scott's Impulse albums were often split
between big band selections (with orchestras arranged by Oliver
Nelson) and trio features. This CD reissue from 1989 includes all
of the contents from two of Scott's better Impulse albums, Great
Scott and For Members Only. In general the eight trio numbers are
the most rewarding performances on the disc since the material is
fairly superior while the big band tracks emphasize then-current
show and movie tunes. Overall this generous CD gives one a good
overview of Shirley Scott's playing talents. —Scott Yanow

Travelin' Light / Feb. 6, 1964–Feb. 7, 1964 / Prestige ✦✦✦
Shirley Scott on the Hammond B-3 with Kenny Burrell on guitar. Released on Prestige. —AMG

● Blue Flames / Mar. 31, 1964 / Original Jazz Classics ✦✦✦✦✦
Recorded in Englewood Cliffs, NJ. With Turrentine and Stanley.
This is exactly the kind of straight-ahead funky music you would
expect from the Scott/Turrentine combination. No disappointments; just great music. Now available on CD (Prestige OJCCD-
328). —Michael Erlewine

Everybody Loves a Lover / Aug. 23, 1964 / Impulse ✦✦✦
Scott with Stanley Turrentine on tenor sax, Bob Cranshaw on
bass, and Otis Finch on drums. —AMG

The Great Live Sessions / Sep. 23, 1964 / ABC/Impulse ✦✦✦✦✦
Recorded live at the Front Room in Newark, NJ, the album
includes ten tracks with a quartet including Stanley Turrentine
(ts). On a rare night for music, the band delivered on all counts.
You can't go wrong here. —*Michael G. Nastos*

Queen of the Organ / Sep. 23, 1964 / Impulse ✦✦✦✦
A steamy, hot mid-'60s soul jazz session with soulful, bluesy
organist Shirley Scott providing some booming, funky solos.
This was one of several combo works she cut, usually with sax-
ophonist Stanley Turrentine, who was her husband at the time.
Anything Scott recorded from this period is worth hearing. —
Ron Wynn

Soul Song / Sep. 9, 1968 / Atlantic ✦✦✦
A date with Stanley Turrentine (sax) and some Eric Gale (guitar).
—*AMG*

Shirley Scott and the Soul Saxes / Jul. 9, 1969 / Atlantic ✦✦✦
Steamy workout with Scott, Hank Crawford (as), King Curtis (ts),
and David Neuman (ts). —*Ron Wynn*

One for Me / Nov. 1974 / Strata East ✦✦✦✦✦
The record is a beauty with Harold Vick, perhaps the most suited and sensitive horn player Ms. Scott has worked with…(a)
thoroughly enjoyable album of bop stream music, and while it
is nothing overly heavy or deep, it's thoughtfully and sensitively
produced and of its kind an almost perfect album. —*Bob Rusch,
Cadence*

Al Sears

b. Feb. 21, 1910, Macomb, IL, **d.** Mar. 23, 1990
Sax (Tenor) / Swing, Early R&B
It is ironic that tenor saxophonist Al Sears' one hit, "Castle Rock,"
was recorded under Johnny Hodges' name (the altoist is virtually absent on the record), denying Sears his one chance at fame.
Sears had actually had his first important job in 1928 replacing
Hodges with the Chick Webb band. However despite associations
with Elmer Snowden (1931–32), Andy Kirk (1941–42), Lionel
Hampton (1943–44) and with his own groups (most of 1933–41),
it was not until Sears joined Duke Ellington's Orchestra in 1944
that he began to get much attention. His distinctive tone, R&Bish
phrasing and abiltiy to build up exciting solos made him one of
Ellington's most colorful soloists during the next five years
although his period was overshadowed by both his predecessor
(Ben Webster) and his successor (Paul Gonsalves). Among Sears'
many recordings with Ellington are notable versions of "I Ain't
Got Nothing but the Blues" and a 1945 remake of "It Don't Mean
a Thing." Sears worked with Johnny Hodges' group during
1951–52, recorded a variety of R&B-oriented material in the
1950s and cut two excellent albums for Swingville in 1960
before going into semi-retirement. —*Scott Yanow*

● **Swing's the Thing** / Nov. 29, 1960 / Swingville ✦✦✦✦✦
Al Sears had the misfortune of having his one hit "Castle Rock"
released under the leadership of Johnny Hodges, cheating him of
his one chance at fame. A fine swing-based tenor who could
stomp and honk with the best of them (although he rarely
screamed), Sears had relatively few opportunities to record as a
leader and this CD (which reissues a 1960 LP) was one of his
last. Sears (along with pianist Don Abney, guitarist Wally
Richardson, bassist Wendell Marshall and drummer Joe
Marshall) sticks to basic originals, blues and standards and is in
top form on these swinging and generally accessible performances. —*Scott Yanow*

Sear-iously / Bear Family ✦✦✦

Horace Silver

b. Sep. 2, 1928, Norwalk, CT
Piano / Soul Jazz, Hard Bop
The leading composer and hard bop pioneer, Horace Silver's
piano solos have been a jazz force since the early '50s. He blended vintage R&B, bebop, gospel, blues, and Caribbean elements
into jazz in an inspired manner, writing and playing works that
were rhythmically and melodically simple, yet gripping and
compelling. His work has harmonic sophistication, but seldom
loses its earthiness and grit. He's been among the rare jazz musicians who've composed the bulk of their material. He's written
for combos and vocalists equally well, even on many occasions
providing lyrics to accompany his instrumental pieces. Silver
was a founding member of the original Jazz Messengers with

Art Blakey and his ensembles have helped introduce and/or nur-
ture quite a few careers including Blue Mitchell, Junior Cook,
Donald Byrd, Art Farmer, Joe Henderson, Woody Shaw, Tom
Harrell, Michael Brecker, and Randy Brecker. Silver began studying saxophone and piano in high school, listening heavily to the
blues and boogie woogie. He later mixed that with the Cape
Verdean folk music he'd heard as a child. Silver worked in 1950
on a date with Stan Getz, who'd come to make a guest appearance in Hartford. Getz tabbed Silver to work with him, and
Silver stayed for a year. Getz cut three of his compositions,
"Penny," "Potter's Luck," and "Split Kick." The next year Silver
moved to New York, where he worked with Coleman Hawkins,
Lester Young, Oscar Pettiford, and then Art Blakey. He recorded
with Lou Donaldson for Blue Note in 1954, and subsequently cut
his own trio sessions for the label shortly afterward, working
with bassists Gene Ramey, Percy Heath, or Curley Russell and
Blakey on drums. This began an association with Blue Note that
lasted nearly 30 years. Silver was co-leader from 1953 to 1955 of
a band with Blakey known as the Jazz Messengers. When Silver
departed in 1956, Blakey took over the leadership role. Silver's
groups became quite popular in the '50s and '60s. Such numbers
as "The Preacher," "Doodlin," "Sister Sadie," and "Song For My
Father" became jazz classics, and Silver's albums often crossed
over to R&B, soul and blues audiences. Ray Charles covered
"Doodlin" and Silver band members Mitchell, Joe Henderson,
Kenny Dorham, Clifford Jordan, and Hank Mobley went on to
lead their own bands. Silver's forays into hard bop, soul jazz and
funk made Blue Note both an artistic and commercial juggernaut. "Song For My Father" and "Cape Verdean Blues" both
charted in the mid-'60s. Silver began to experiment with concept
albums in the '70s, doing a trilogy he called "The United States
Of Mind." The jazz content of some of this was miminal, but he
experimented with strings, African and Indian percussion and
multiple vocalists. Silver left Blue Note at the end of the '70s,
forming his own label and issuing recordings he called "Holistic
Metaphysical Music." Much of Silver's late '70s and early '80s
material was in a quasi-religious bent, but he also established
Emerald, a subsidiary of Silveto, and issued vintage dates like
Horace Silver-Live 1964, which had unreleased versions of
"Senor Blues" and "Filthy McNasty." A new Silver album was
released in 1993 by Columbia, *It's Got To Be Funky*. There are
plenty of classic Silver sessions available on CD. —*Ron Wynn*
Groove: Horace Silver is another great jazz master and the pioneer of what we call funky jazz. Don't look for deep soul grooves
here, because that's not Silver's bag. We can thank him for reaching into blues and soul roots and showing jazz artists how to
give the music a little more substance at a time when bop was
just about played out. He wrote some lovely songs and has a
very special funky-jazz sound. —*Michael Erlewine*

★ **The Best of Horace Silver, Vol. 1** / 1953–1959 / Blue Note
✦✦✦✦✦
The Blue Note Years Vol 1 & 2. Excellent compilation on CD.
Two volumes. —*Michael G. Nastos*

★ **Horace Silver and the Jazz Messengers** / Nov. 13, 1954–Feb. 6,
1955 / Blue Note ✦✦✦✦✦
A true classic, this CD found pianist Horace Silver and drummer
Art Blakey co-leading the Jazz Messengers; Silver would leave a
year later to form his own group. Also featuring trumpeter
Kenny Dorham, Hank Mobley on tenor, and bassist Doug
Watkins, this set is most notable for the original versions of
Silver's "The Preacher" and "Doodlin," funky standards that
helped launch hard bop and both the Jazz Messengers and
Silver's quintet. Essential music. —*Scott Yanow*

Six Pieces of Silver / Nov. 10, 1956 / Blue Note ✦✦✦✦✦
The first classic album by the Horace Silver Quintet, this CD is
highlighted by "Senor Blues" (heard in three versions including
a later vocal rendition by Bill Henderson) and "Cool Eyes." The
early Silver quintet was essentially The Jazz Messengers of the
year before (with trumpeter Donald Byrd, tenor saxophonist
Hank Mobley, and bassist Doug Watkins while drummer Louis
Hayes was in Blakey's place) but already the band was starting
to develop a sound of its own. "Senor Blues" officially put Horace
Silver on the map. —*Scott Yanow*

☆ **Finger Poppin' with the Horace Silver Quintet** / Feb. 1, 1959 /
Blue Note ✦✦✦✦✦
The first recording by the most famous version of the Horace
Silver Quintet is also one of the highpoints of the pianist/com-

poser's career. Among the more memorable tracks of this classic set are "Juicy Lucy" (the epitome of funky jazz), "Cookin'" at the Continental" and "Come on Home" but all eight performances are superlative. With trumpeter Blue Mitchell, Junior Cook's tenor, bassist Eugene Taylor and drummer Louis Hayes, Horace Silver had found the perfect forum for his piano and his highly accessible songs. Essential music. — *Scott Yanow*

Blowin' the Blues Away / Aug. 10, 1959 / Blue Note ✦✦✦✦✦
The second recording by the classic version of the Horace Silver Quintet (with trumpeter Blue Mitchell, tenor saxophonist Junior Cook, bassist Eugene Taylor and drummer Louis Hayes) introduced Silver's compositions "Sister Sadie" and "Peace" (both of which became jazz standards) in addition to the title track. No jazz library is complete without at least three or four Horace Silver albums. — *Scott Yanow*

Senor Blues / Aug. 31, 1963 / Blue Note ✦✦✦

★ **Song for My Father** / Oct. 26, 1964 / Blue Note ✦✦✦✦✦
Horace Silver's most famous album includes the memorable title cut, four of his other recent compositions (including "Calcutta Cutie" and "Lonely Woman") and Joe Henderson's "The Kicker." Although trumpeter Blue Mitchell and tenor saxophonist Junior Cook reunited for "Calcutta Cutie," the remainder of this classic set features Henderson's tenor and trumpeter Carmell Jones. Funky hard bop at its best, this is essential music for any jazz collection. — *Scott Yanow*

Cape Verdean Blues / Oct. 1, 1965–Oct. 22, 1965 / Blue Note ✦✦✦✦✦
By late 1965 Horace Silver's Quintet featured trumpeter Woody Shaw and tenor saxophonist Joe Henderson and, on half of this set, the great trombonist J.J. Johnson sits in. "The Cape Verdean Blues," "Pretty Eyes," and Henderson's "Mo' Joe" are among the highlights of this high-quality set of funky hard bop by one of the pacesetting groups. — *Scott Yanow*

Serenade to a Soul Sister / Mar. 25, 1968–Mar. 25, 1968 / Blue Note ✦✦✦✦✦
One of the final classic albums by the Horace Silver Quintet, this set finds Silver using such sidemen as trumpeter Charles Tolliver, either Stanley Turrentine or Bennie Maupin on tenors and, on half of the tracks, the young drummer Billy Cobham. The six Silver compositions include "Psychedelic Sally" and "Serenade to a Soul Sister." This music is both timeless and very much of the period. — *Scott Yanow*

It's Got to Be Funky / Feb. 1993 / Columbia ✦✦✦✦
After a 13-year period in which he mostly recorded for his private Silveto label, pianist/composer Horace Silver was rediscovered by Columbia for this session. Rather than featuring a standard quintet as he did throughout his career, the funky pianist is heard with his trio, a six-piece brass ensemble and guest tenors Red Holloway, Eddie Harris, and Branford Marsalis; Andy Bey contributes four vocals. All of the music (except for a remake of "Song for My Father") was new and served as proof that the master of jazz-funk had not lost his stuff. — *Scott Yanow*

Jimmy Smith

b. Dec. 8, 1925, Norristown, PA
Organ / Soul Jazz, Hard Bop
Though he never received any exaggerated title like the king of soul jazz, Jimmy Smith certainly ruled the Hammond organ in the '50s and '60s. He revolutionized the instrument, showing it could be creatively used in a jazz context and popularized in the process. His Blue Note sessions from 1956 to 1963 were extremely influential and are highly recommended. Smith turned the organ into almost an ensemble itself. He provided walking bass lines with his feet, left hand chordal accompaniment, solo lines in the right, and a booming, funky presence that punctuated every song, particularly the uptempo cuts. Smith turned the fusion of R&B, blues and gospel influences with bebop references and devices into a jubilant, attractive sound that many others immediately absorbed before following in his footsteps. Smith initially learned piano, both from his parents and on his own. He attended the Hamilton School of Music in 1948, and Ornstein School of Music in 1949 and 1950 in Philadelphia. Smith began playing the Hammond in 1951, and soon earned a great reputation that followed him to New York, where he debuted at the Cafe Bohemia. A Birdland date and 1957 Newport Jazz Festival appearance launched Smith's career.

He toured extensively through the '60s and '70s. His Blue Note recordings included superb collaborations with Kenny Burrell, Lee Morgan, Lou Donaldson, Tina Brooks, Jackie McLean, Ike Quebec, and Stanley Turrentine, among others. He also did several trio recordings, some which were a little bogged down by the excess length of some selections. Smith scored more hit albums on Verve from 1963 to 1972, many of them featuring big bands and using fine arrangements from Oliver Nelson. These included the excellent *Walk On The Wild Side*. But Verve went to the well once too often seeking crossover dollars, loading down Smith's late '60s albums with hack rock covers. His '70s output was quite spotty, though Smith didn't stop touring, visiting Israel and Europe in 1974 and 1975. He and his wife opened a club in Los Angeles in the mid-'70s. Smith resumed touring in the early '80s, returning to New York in 1982 and 1983. He resigned with Blue Note in 1985, and has done more representative dates for them and Milestone in the '90s. — *Ron Wynn and Bob Porter*

Groove: Jimmy Smith is THE man on Hammond organ. At his best, he is the best there is. Which does not mean that all of his stuff is the best. It's not. He made a lot of albums and some of them are just average sounding. As a blues lover, I can't recommend his big band recordings, no matter how many awards they win. The fact to my ears is that the Hammond organ IS a big band-all by itself. Sticking Smith in the middle of a large group is just not helpful. You can't salt the salt, as they say. And you lose all of those crystal clear sax and guitar solos that come out in a trio or quartet. Stick with Smith's small combo stuff, and that means, until lately, his early stuff. — *Michael Erlewine*

A New Star–A New Sound: Jimmy Smith at the Organ, Vol. 1 / Feb. 13, 1956+Feb. 18, 1956 / Blue Note ✦✦✦✦✦
The debut of organist Jimmy Smith on records (he was already 30) was a major event, for he introduced a completely new and very influential style on the organ, one that virtually changed the way the instrument is played. This LP, which has not yet appeared on CD, features the already-recognizable organist in a trio with guitarist Thornel Schwartz and Bay Perry on drums. Highlights of this very impressive debut include "The Way You Look Tonight," "Lady Be Good," and Horace Silver's "The Preacher." — *Scott Yanow*

The Champ / Mar. 11, 1956 / Blue Note ✦✦✦✦✦
Recorded in NYC. When first issued, many thought there were two players here, or overdubs. Just early Smith cookin'. — *Michael Erlewine*

Greatest Hits, Vol. 1 / Mar. 27, 1956–Feb. 8, 1963 / Blue Note ✦✦✦✦✦
This double LP, even with its clichéd title, is a real gem. It contains eight of the greatest performances recorded by organist Jimmy Smith during his important period with Blue Note. "The Champ" from his second recording features Smith taking around 50 choruses on a blazing blues, and it set a standard that has still not been surpassed. Also included on this valuable two-fer (some of the material has since been reissued on CD) are "All Day Long," a 20-minute "The Sermon," "Midnight Special," "When Johnny Comes Marching Home," "Can Heat," "Flamingo," and "Prayer Meetin'." In the supporting cast are trumpeter Lee Morgan, altoist Lou Donaldson, Tina Brooks and Stanley Turrentine on tenors, guitarists Kenny Burrell, Thornel Schwartz and Quentin Warren, and drummers Art Blakey and Donald Bailey. This set serves as a perfect introduction to Jimmy Smith's early years and has lots of hard-swinging and soulful jams. — *Scott Yanow*

The Sounds of Jimmy Smith / Feb. 11, 1957 / Blue Note ✦✦✦
This LP, which has been included as part of a Mosaic Jimmy Smith three-CD box set, features the organist taking a pair of rare unaccompanied solos on "All the Things You Are" and a fairly free "The Fight" and jamming several songs ("Zing Went the Strings of My Heart," "Somebody Loves Me," and "Blue Moon") with his trio. Art Blakey fills in for drummer Donald Bailey on "Zing" while guitarist Eddie McFadden is heard throughout the three selections. Excellent straightahead jazz from the innovative organist. — *Scott Yanow*

A Date with Jimmy Smith, Vol. 1 / Feb. 11, 1957–Feb. 12, 1957 / Blue Note ✦✦✦
After cutting five albums with his trio, organist Jimmy Smith on Feb. 11, 1957, recorded with trumpeter Donald Byrd, altoist Lou

Donaldson and tenor saxophonist Hank Mobley in a sextet that also included guitarist Eddie McFadden and drummer Art Blakey. Among the five songs recorded that day, two (lengthy versions of "Falling in Love with Love" and "Funk's Oats") are included on this LP along with a shorter trio rendition of "How High the Moon" from two days later with McFadden and drummer Donald Bailey in a trio. All of this music has been reissued by Mosaic on a definitive CD box set. — *Scott Yanow*

A Date with Jimmy Smith, Vol. 2 / Feb. 11, 1957–Feb. 12, 1957 / Blue Note ✦✦✦
This LP is one of five that has been reissued by Mosaic in a three-CD box set. For the jam session date altoist Lou Donaldson has a duet with organist Jimmy Smith on "I'm Getting Sentimental over You," and together they match up forces in a sextet with trumpeter Donald Byrd, Hank Mobley on tenor, guitarist Eddie McFadden, and drummer Art Blakey, playing lengthy versions of Mobley's "Groovy Date" and Duke Ellington's "I Let a Song Go out of My Heart." All of the Jimmy Smith jam sessions are easily recommended to fans of straight-ahead jazz; get the Mosaic box! — *Scott Yanow*

The Best of Jimmy Smith / Feb. 12, 1957–Jan. 3, 1986 / Blue Note ✦✦✦✦✦
1958–1986. Small-group setting. Selections from some of Smith's best Blue Note albums, such as: *The Sermon, Go for Whatcha Know, Midnight Special, Back at the Chicken Shack, A New Sound*, and *At the Organ*. — *Michael Erlewine*

House Party / Aug. 25, 1957 / Blue Note ✦✦✦✦✦
Music from two different sessions are included on this enjoyable LP. All of organist Jimmy Smith's jam sessions are worth acquiring although several (such as this one) have been long out of print. Lengthy versions of "Au Privave" and "Just Friends" and more concise renditions of "Lover Man" and "Blues After All" match Smith with quite a variety of all-stars: trumpeter Lee Morgan, trombonist Curtis Fuller, Lou Donaldson or George Coleman on altos, Tina Brooks on tenor, guitarists Kenny Burrell or Eddie McFadden, and Art Blakey or Donald Bailey on drums. Everyone plays up to par and the passionate solos (and Smith's heated background riffing) keep the proceedings continually exciting. — *Scott Yanow*

Confirmation / Aug. 25, 1957+Feb. 25, 1958 / Blue Note ✦✦✦✦
Organist Jimmy Smith led a series of exciting jam sessions for Blue Note during 1957–60 including the three selections heard on this LP. These performances were not released for the first time until 1979, but their quality is as strong as Smith's other output from the era. "Confirmation" matches Smith with altoist Lou Donaldson, tenor saxophonist Tina Brooks, trumpeter Lee Morgan, guitarist Kenny Burrell, and drummer Art Blakey (talk about all-star groups) while a 15-minute rendition of "What Is This Thing Called Love" and a 20-minute "Cherokee" has Morgan, Burrell, Blakey, trombonist Curtis Fuller, and George Coleman on alto. The heated solos are quite enjoyable and the organist keeps the momentum constantly flowing throughout this happy set. — *Scott Yanow*

☆ **The Sermon** / Feb. 25, 1958 / Blue Note ✦✦✦✦✦
This CD reissue has two of the three selections (the 20-minute "The Sermon" and "Flamingo") from the original LP, adding five additional selections that are related. With such soloists as trumpeter Lee Morgan, trombonist Curtis Fuller, altoist Lou Donaldson, Tina Brooks on tenor, either Eddie McFadden or Kenny Burrell on guitar, and Art Blakey or Donald Bailey on drums. The straightahead music is as good as one would expect (with the lengthy title cut being the obvious highpoint), and the CD overall offers listeners a strong dose of Jimmy Smith's Blue Note period. — *Scott Yanow*

☆ **Cool Blues** / Apr. 7, 1958 / Blue Note ✦✦✦✦
This CD should greatly interest all Jimmy Smith collectors, including those who already have the original LP. In addition to four excellent selections (quintets with altoist Lou Donaldson, Tina Brooks on tenor, guitarist Eddie McFadden, either Art Blakey or Donald Bailey on drums, and the organist/leader), there are three previously unissued numbers from the same gig, featuring the quartet of Donaldson, Smith, McFadden, and Bailey. The repertoire is filled with blues and bop standards and the soloing is at a consistently high and hard-swinging level. Jimmy Smith fans will be pleased. — *Scott Yanow*

Home Cookin' / Jul. 14, 1958–Jun. 16, 1959 / Blue Note ✦✦✦✦
Organist Jimmy Smith and guitarist Kenny Burrell always had a

close musical relationship, making each of their joint recordings quite special. This LP features the pair along with drummer Donald Bailey and (on four of the seven songs) the obscure but talented tenor saxophonist Percy France. The emphasis is on blues and basic material including versions of "C. C. Rider," Ray Charles's "I Got a Woman," and several group originals, and as usual, the performances are swinging and soulful. — *Scott Yanow*

On the Sunny Side / Jul. 15, 1958 / Blue Note ✦✦✦✦
Organist Jimmy Smith recorded quite a bit of material for Blue Note during 1956-63. This 1981 LP released for the first time eight selections cut during four sessions in the late '50s. In all cases, Smith is joined by guitarist Kenny Burrell and drummer Donald Bailey; Stanley Turrentine makes the group a quartet on "The Sunny Side of the Street" while his fellow tenor Percy France does the same on his original "Apostrophe." All of the songs (other than the latter) are standards and the tunes generally clock in around a concise five minutes. The results are predictably swinging and highlights include "On the Sunny Side," "Since I Fell for You," "Bye Bye Blackbird," and "I'm Just a Lucky So and So." Excellent music. — *Scott Yanow*

☆ **Crazy! Baby** / Jan. 4, 1960 / Blue Note ✦✦✦✦✦
Unlike most of the Jimmy Smith recordings from the era, this CD reissue (which adds "If I Should Lose You" and "When Lights Are Low" to the original LP program) features organist Jimmy Smith's regular group (rather than an all-star band). With guitarist Quentin Warren and drummer Donald Bailey completing the trio, Smith is heard in peak form on swinging and soulful versions of such tunes as "When Johnny Comes Marching Home," "Makin' Whoopee," "Sonnymoon for Two," and "Mack the Knife." Despite claims and some strong challenges by others, there has never been a jazz organist on the level of Jimmy Smith. — *Scott Yanow*

Open House / Plain Talk / Mar. 22, 1960 / Blue Note ✦✦✦✦✦
A two-fer with two classic Smith albums, *Open House* and *Plain Talk* on one CD. Recorded in Hackensack, NJ. Studio session featuring Blue Mitchell (tpt), Ike Quebec (ts), and Jackie McClean (as). This is essentially a jam session without Smith's regular sidemen. More mainstream than most, but very nice tracks—fast and slow. This is an excellent album. — *Michael Erlewine*

★ **Back at the Chicken Shack** / Apr. 25, 1960 / Blue Note ✦✦✦✦✦
This may be the quintessential funky soul jazz album. Period. I know of no better single recording, and this is the one I would have to take to that desert island when I go. The term "all star" was coined for this group. Jimmy Smith is as hot as he gets and so is Stanley Turrentine on tenor sax. Just hot! Kenny Burrell is in top form, too, and Donald Bailey keeps the beat tight. Every jazz fan should hear it and every groove fan must own it. Also see the Smith album *Midnight Special*, which was recorded at the same session. — *Michael Erlewine*

☆ **Midnight Special** / Apr. 25, 1960 / Blue Note ✦✦✦✦✦
Recorded in Englewood Cliffs, NJ. Small Group. This was recorded at the same session as *Back at the Chicken Shack*, and it is also as fine—that is: magical! This is a must-have for jazz organ fans. With Stanley Turrentine (ts) and Kenny Burrell (g). Every collector of groove music should have a copy. — *Michael Erlewine*

Prayer Meetin' / Jun. 13, 1960+Feb. 8, 1963 / Blue Note ✦✦✦✦✦
Prayer Meeting was organist Jimmy Smith's final Blue Note recording until 1986. On this CD reissue two earlier selections featuring Smith, tenor saxophonist Stanley Turrentine, guitarist Quentin Warren, bassist Sam Jones (the only time on Blue Note that Smith used a bassist), and drummer Donald Bailey jam on versions of "Lonesome Road" and the original "Smith Walk"; both selections went unreleased until popping up on a 1984 Japanese CD. The bulk of this set is from February 8, 1963, featuring the same personnel without Jones. Highlights include the title cut, a soulful version of "When the Saints Go Marching In" and the Gene Ammons blues "Red Top." Excellent music. — *Scott Yanow*

I'm Movin on / Jan. 31, 1963 / Blue Note ✦✦✦
This CD reissue of a formerly rare date has a perfectly suitable title for it is the first of four albums that organist Jimmy Smith made within an eight-day period for Blue Note before permanently leaving the label for Verve. Although notable for matching Smith with guitarist Grant Green in what would be their

only joint recording (drummer Donald Bailey completes the trio), the music is fairly typical of a Jimmy Smith session with the repertoire including blues, a couple of standards and ballads. The solos are well-played but nothing too surprising occurs (except perhaps for the sappiness of "What Kind of Fool Am I"); the original LP program is expanded by the inclusion of two other selections from the same date. *—Scott Yanow*

Bucket! / Feb. 1, 1963 / Blue Note ✦✦✦
Recorded at Englewood Cliffs, NJ. Trio session. Typically resolute Smith cuts. *—Ron Wynn*

Rockin' the Boat / Feb. 2, 1963 / Blue Note ✦✦✦✦
Organist Jimmy Smith's next-to-last LP for Blue Note after a very extensive seven-year period is up to his usual level. With altoist Lou Donaldson joining Smith's regular group (which included guitarist Quentin Warren and drummer Donald Bailey), the quartet swings with soul on such fine numbers as "When My Dream Boat Comes Home," "Can Heat," "Please Send Me Someone to Love," and "Just a Closer Walk with Thee." With the exception of the closing ballad, "Trust in Me," all seven of the selections are closely related to the blues. This is fine music well deserving of being reissued on CD someday. *—Scott Yanow*

Live at the Village Gate / May 31, 1963 / Metro ✦✦✦✦
Recorded at the Villae Gate, NYC. Smith in a trio setting. Plenty of fine playing. *—Ron Wynn*

Blue Bash / Jul. 25, 1963–Jul. 26, 1963 / Verve ✦✦✦
Recorded in NYC. Good '60s sessions. *—Ron Wynn*

Organ Grinder Swing / Jun. 14, 1965–Jun. 15, 1965 / Verve ✦✦✦✦
Most of organist Jimmy Smith's recordings for Verve during the mid-to-late '60s were with big bands, making this trio outing with guitarist Kenny Burrell and drummer Grady Tate a special treat. This CD reissue is a throwback to Smith's Blue Note sets (which had concluded two years earlier) and gives the organists the opportunity to stretch out on three blues and three standards. This release shows that, even with all of his commercial success during the period, Jimmy Smith was always a masterful jazz player. *—Scott Yanow*

☆ **The Dynamic Duo** / Sep. 21, 1966+Sep. 28, 1966 / Verve ✦✦✦✦✦
This CD—a straight reissue of the original LP—is a classic. Organist Jimmy Smith and guitarist Wes Montgomery, both the main pacesetters on their instruments at the time, make for a perfect team on quartet renditions (with drummer Grady Tate and percussionist Ray Barretto) of "James and Wes" and "Baby, It's Cold Outside." However, it is the three numbers with a big band arranged by Oliver Nelson (particularly "Night Train" and a very memorable version of "Down by the Riverside") that really stick in one's mind. Although it is unfortunate that the Smith-Wes collaboration was short-lived (just one other album), it is miraculous that they did find each other and created this brilliant music. *—Scott Yanow*

Respect / Jun. 2, 1967+Jun. 14, 1967 / Verve ✦✦
Organist Jimmy Smith, joined by one of two guitar/bass/drums rhythm sections, mostly sticks to then-current R&B hits on this out-of-print LP. He does what he can with "Mercy, Mercy, Mercy," a brief "Respect," and "Funky Broadway" while contributing his own blues "T-Bone Steak." The 31-minute set has its moments but no real surprises, swinging funkily throughout. *—Scott Yanow*

The Boss / Nov. 20, 1968 / Verve ✦✦✦
Recorded at Paschal's La Carousel, Atlanta, GA. Lots of fine solos. George Benson (g) does best soul jazz work since McDuff days. *—Ron Wynn*

Root Down / Feb. 8, 1972 / Verve ✦✦
Recorded in Los Angeles. Typical soul jazz date. *—Ron Wynn*

Bluesmith / Sep. 11, 1972 / Verve ✦✦✦✦✦
It is ironic that one of Jimmy Smith's best Verve releases would be his next-to-last for the label. This surprisingly freewheeling but relaxed jam session also features Teddy Edwards on tenor, guitarist Ray Crawford, bassist Leroy Vinnegar, drummer Donald Dean, and the congas of Victor Pantoja. Together they perform five of Smith's fairly basic originals and Harvey Siders's "Mournin' Wes," a tribute for Wes Montgomery. Fine straightahead music that deserves to be reissued again. *—Scott Yanow*

Second Coming / 1980 / Mojo ✦✦✦
This undated impromptu session was unrehearsed, undubbed

and without alternate takes…it confirms where this great Jazz organist's heart is…it is especially good to see Mr. Smith return to the style he maintained during his salad days with Blue Note and Verve, when he was the Jazz-Bop organist. *—Bob Rusch, editor Cadence*

Off the Top / Jun. 7, 1982 / Elektra ✦✦✦✦
It had been nine years since organist Jimmy Smith recorded for a major label when Bruce Lundvall approached him to make an album for Elektra Musician. Smith plays some unusual material (including Lionel Richie's "Endless Love" and the "Theme from *M.A.S.H.*") on this LP but swings everything and has a particularly strong supporting cast—guitarist George Benson, Stanley Turrentine on tenor, bassist Ron Carter, and drummer Grady Tate. A fine comeback date. *—Scott Yanow*

Fourmost / Nov. 16, 1990–Nov. 17, 1990 / Milestone ✦✦✦✦✦
Organist Jimmy Smith has a reunion on this CD with his 30 plus-year associates tenor saxophonist Stanley Turrentine and guitarist Kenny Burrell along with drummer Grady Tate. Together they play spirited and creative versions of standards and blues. The highpoints include "Midnight Special," a swinging "Main Stem," Tate's warm vocal on "My Funny Valentine," and a lengthy rendition of "Quiet Nights." Suffice it to say that this all-star date reaches its potential and is easily recommended to fans of straightahead jazz. *—Scott Yanow*

Johnny "Hammond" Smith

b. Dec. 16, 1933, Louisville, KY.
Organ / Soul Jazz, Hard Bop
Johnny (Robert) "Hammond" Smith was born on December 16, 1933 in Louisville, KY. From a musical family, he learned piano early on. Bud Powell and Art Tatum were his idols. Originally a pianist based in Cleveland, after hearing Wild Bill Davis he switched to the organ. Also known as Johnny Hammond, Smith worked for a period in the late '50s as Nancy Wilson's accompanist but has spent most of his career as a leader, recording a series of enjoyable soul jazz albums for Prestige during 1959–1970. Although he also utilized synthesizers in the 1970s, Smith in more recent times has stuck exclusively to the organ in a style unchanged from three decades before. Johnny "Hammond" Smith is one of the many organists to come to prominence in the 1960s who was greatly influenced by Jimmy Smith. *—Michael Erlewine & Scott Yanow*

All Soul / Sep. 11, 1959 / New Jazz ✦✦✦
Smith with Thornell Schwart on guitar. *AMG*

That Good Feelin' / Nov. 4, 1959 / New Jazz ✦✦✦

Angel Eyes / Jun. 17, 1960 / Prestige ✦✦✦

The Best of Johnny Hammond Smith / May 12, 1961–Jan. 31, 1968 / Prestige ✦✦✦

The Stinger / May 7, 1965 / Prestige ✦✦✦✦
Organist Johnny "Hammond" Smith is a decent soul jazz player. He plays in short, swirling bursts and uses the bass pedals in a pounding, aggressive manner. These are primarily uptempo and funky jam numbers, particularly the title track. *—Ron Wynn*

● **Soul Talk** / May 19, 1969 / Prestige ✦✦✦✦
With Rusty Bryant on saxes, Wally Richardson on guitar, Bob Bushnell on bass, and Bernard Purdie on drums. *—Michael Erlewine*

Wild Horses Rock Steady / 1971 / Kudu ✦✦✦

Gambler's Life / 1974 / Salvation ✦✦✦

Forever Taurus / 1976 / Milestone ✦✦✦

Storm Warning / 1977 / Milestone ✦✦✦

Lonnie Smith (Lonnie Smith)

Organ / Blues Jazz, Soul Jazz
Not to be confused with Lonnie Liston Smith, organist Lonnie Smith has been on the soul jazz and jazz scene since the '60s.
Smith, who hails from Buffalo, NY, began his career as a trumpet player, forming a vocal group soon after high school. When he ran across the Hammon B-3, he was hooked. With his R&B background, he was soon attracting some real attention. He sat in with Jack McDuff's band in New York and there met George Benson. The two teamed up and were soon recording for Columbia as the George Benson Quartet, releasing the albums *It's Uptown* (1966) and *Cookbook* (1967).

Smith made his first solo album, *Finger Lickin' Good* later in 1967. During a recording session for Lou Donaldson, where Benson and Smith were called in to add some new sounds, he was heard by scout Frank Wolff. He was signed to the Blue Note label in 1968, and contracted for four albums: *Think, Turning Point, Move Your Hand,* and *Drives.* In 1971, Smith recorded *Live at Club Mozambique,* also released on Blue Note.

He's worked often with Lou Donaldson, and done sessions on his own. Smith can play the requisite bluesy licks, work the bass pedal, and offer good stomping numbers. Though he's recorded as a leader for Blue Note, CTI, and other labels, and done sessions with Donaldson, George Benson, Hank Crawford, and many other notables, Smith has just started to have a few sessions available on CD. —*Michael Erlewine & Ron Wynn*

Finger Lickin' Good / Nov. 1967 / Columbia ✦✦✦

● **Think** / Jul. 23, 1968 / Blue Note ✦✦✦✦✦
With Lee Morgan (tpt). This is an excellent 1986 reissue of a fine soul jazz Blue Note date by organist Lonnie Smith. —*Ron Wynn*

Move Your Hand / Sep. 9, 1969 / Blue Note ✦✦✦✦
Move Your Hand was recorded live at Club Harlem in Atlantic City on August 9, 1969. Organist Lonnie Smith led a small combo—featuring guitarist Larry McGee, tenor saxist Rudy Jones, bari saxist Ronnie Cuber, and drummer Sylvester Goshay—through a set that alternated originals with two pop covers, the Coasters' "Charlie Brown," and Donovan's "Sunshine Superman." Throughout, the band works a relaxed, bluesy and, above all, funky rhythm; they abandon improvisation and melody for a steady groove, so much that the hooks of the two pop hits aren't recognizable until a few minutes into the track. No one player stands out, but *Move Your Hand* is a thoroughly enjoyable, primarily because the group never lets their momentum sag throughout the session. Though the sound of the record might be somewhat dated, the essential funk of the album remains vital. —*Stephen Thomas Erlewine*

Drives / Dec. 1970 / Blue Note ✦✦✦
Lonnie Smith had the raw skills, imagination and versatility to play burning originals, bluesy covers of R&B and pop, or skillful adaptations of conventional jazz pieces and show tunes. Why he never established himself as a consistent performer remains a mystery, but this 1970 reissue shows why he excited so many people during his rise. Smith's solos on "Spinning Wheel" and his own composition, "Psychedelic PI," are fleet and furious, boosting the songs from interesting to arresting. He's also impressive on "Seven Steps To Heaven," while the array of phrases, rhythms and voicings on "Who's Afraid Of Virginia Woolf?" demonstrate a mastery of the organ's pedals and keys rivaling that of the instrument's king, Jimmy Smith. —*Ron Wynn*

Sonny Stitt (Edward Stitt)

b. Feb. 2, 1924, Boston, MA, **d.** Jul. 22, 1982, Washington, DC
Sax (Alto), Sax (Tenor) / Bop
Charlie Parker has had many admirers and his influence can be detected in numerous styles, but few have been as avid a disciple as Sonny Stitt. There was almost note-for-note imitation in several early Stitt solos, and the closeness remained until Stitt began de-emphasizing the alto in favor of the tenor, on which he artfully combined the influences of Parker and Lester Young. Stitt gradually developed his own sound and style, though he was never far from Parker on any alto solo. A wonderful blues and ballad player whose approach was one of the influences on John Coltrane, Stitt could rip through an uptempo bebop stanza, then turn around and play a shivering, captivating ballad. He was an alto saxophonist in Tiny Bradshaw's band during the early '40s, then joined Billy Eckstine's seminal big band in 1945, playing alongside other emerging bebop stars like Gene Ammons and Dexter Gordon. Later played in Dizzy Gillespie's big band and sextet. He began on tenor and baritone in 1949, and at times was in a two-tenor unit with Ammons. He recorded with Bud Powell and J.J. Johnson for Prestige in 1949, then did several albums on Prestige, Argo and Verve in the '50s and '60s. Stitt led many combos in the '50s, and rejoined Gillespie for a short period in the late '50s. After a brief stint with Miles Davis in 1960, he reunited with Ammons and for a while was in a three tenor lineup with James Moody. During the '60s, Stitt also recorded for Atlantic, cutting the transcendent *Stitt Plays Bird* that finally addressed the Parker question in epic fashion. He continued heading bands, though he joined The

Giants of Jazz in the early '70s. This group included Gillespie, Art Blakey, Kai Winding, Thelonious Monk and Al McKibbon. Stitt did more sessions in the '70s for Cobblestone, Muse and others, among them another definitive date, *Tune Up.* He continued playing and recording in the early '80s, recording for Muse, Sonet and Who's Who In Jazz. He suffered a heart attack and died in 1982. —*Ron Wynn and Bob Porter*

Groove: Here is another very prolific player that did all kinds of gigs, played all kinds of music. There are so many Sonny Stitt albums that it is hard to know where to begin. Take a look at some of the selections listed below, not all of which are available without a search. You will like Stitt, because he really kicks butt on the saxophone—one tough horn player. —*Michael Erlewine*

Sonny Stitt Blows the Blues / Dec. 21, 1959–Dec. 22, 1959 / Verve ✦✦✦

Stitt Meets Brother Jack / Feb. 16, 1962 / Prestige ✦✦✦✦
Sonny Stitt (who sticks on this CD reissue to tenor) meets up with organist Brother Jack McDuff (along with guitarist Eddie Diehl, drummer Art Taylor, and Ray Barretto on congas) for a spirited outing. Two standards ("All of Me" and "Time After Time") are performed with a variety of blues-based originals and the music always swings in a soulful boppish way. Worth picking up although not essential. —*Scott Yanow*

Soul Classics / Feb. 16, 1962–Feb. 15, 1972 / Prestige ✦✦
This CD is a sampler of Sonny Stitt's Prestige recordings. Stitt (mostly heard here on tenor) is accompanied by organists (Brother Jack McDuff, Don Patterson, or Gene Ludwig) on all but one selection but unfortunately half of the performances find him utilizing an electrified varitone sax that watered down his sound and buried his individuality. This set can be safely passed by. —*Scott Yanow*

Nuther Fu'ther / Feb. 19, 1962 / Prestige ✦✦✦
Fine soul jazz with Jack McDuff (organ). —*Ron Wynn*

● **Soul Summit** / Feb. 19, 1962 / Prestige ✦✦✦✦✦

Low Flame / Apr. 4, 1962 / Jazzland ✦✦✦
Stitt with Don Patterson on the Hammond B-3 and Paul Weedon on guitar. —*AMG*

My Mother's Eyes / May 1963 / Pacific Jazz ✦✦✦
This obscure LP finds Sonny Stitt sticking to tenor and playing a typical set filled with blues, standards and riff-filled originals. Organist Charles Kynard made his recording debut during this session, guitarist Ray Crawford and drummer Doug Sides are strong assets and the two versions of the emotional title cut are highpoints. It will take quite a search to locate the LP though. —*Scott Yanow*

Soul Shack / Sep. 17, 1963 / Prestige ✦✦✦
Sonny Stitt with Brother Jack McDuff on the Hammond B-3. —*AMG*

Primitivo Soul / Dec. 31, 1963 / Prestige ✦✦✦
Excellent soul jazz and blues numbers by alto and tenor saxophonist Sonny Stitt, who plays with almost unrelenting energy and drive throughout this session. This was a typical date, but Stitt's earthy playing moved it beyond cliche and convention. —*Ron Wynn*

● **Soul People** / Aug. 25, 1964 / Prestige ✦✦✦✦✦
There are dozens of Sonny Stitt records available at any particular time; this CD reissue is one of the better ones. Stitt (mostly sticking to tenor) battles fellow tenor Booker Ervin with assistance from the fine organist Don Patterson and drummer Billy James on five selections and a ballad medley from 1964. Because both Stitt and Ervin always had very individual sounds, their tradeoffs are quite exciting and end up a draw. Among the "bonus" cuts of this CD are a feature for Patterson with a trio in 1966 ("There Will Never Be Another You") and a collaboration between Stitt, Patterson, James, and guitarist Grant Green on a 1966 version of "Tune Up." Easily enjoyable and generally hard-swinging music. —*Scott Yanow*

Night Crawler / Sep. 21, 1965 / Prestige ✦✦✦
Good title. Here is Stitt with Don Patterson on the Hammond organ and drums. —*AMG*

Soul in the Night / Apr. 15, 1966 / Cadet ✦✦✦
Sonny Stitt with Odell Brown on the organ. —*AMG*

Deuces Wild / Sep. 11, 1966 / Atlantic ✦✦✦
With Don Patterson on the Hammond B-3. —*AMG*

Made for Each Other / Jul. 13, 1968 / Delmark ✦✦
Sonny Stitt's regular group of the period (which included organist Don Patterson and drummer Billy James) plays a wide variety of material on this LP, ranging from "The Very Thought of You" and two versions of "Funny" to "Blues for J.J." and some then-current pop tunes. Unfortunately the set is from the period when Stitt often used a Varitone electronic attachment on his alto and tenor which gave him a much more generic sound, lowering the quality of this music despite some strong improvisations. It is an okay set that could have been better. —*Scott Yanow*

Soul Electricity / Sep. 23, 1968 / Prestige ✦✦✦
Don Patterson on the Hammond organ and Billy Butler on guitar. —*AMG*

The Bubba's Sessions With Eddie "Lockjaw" Davis & Harry "Sweets" Edison / Nov. 11, 1981 / Who's Who ✦✦✦✦
The second of two Who's Who LPs recorded during a club appearance by Sonny Stitt (who doubles here on alto and tenor) has guest appearances by tenor saxophonist Eddie "Lockjaw" Davis and trumpeter Harry "Sweets" Edison in addition to fine backup work from pianist Eddie Higgins, bassist Donn Mast, and drummer Duffy Jackson. This may look like a budget album but the playing (particularly by Stitt) on the blues, standards, and ballads is top notch. Until the music is reissued on CD, this LP and the complementary set *Sonny, Sweets & Jaws* are collector's items. —*Scott Yanow*

Buddy Tate (George Holmes Tate)

b. Feb. 22, 1913, Sherman, TX
Clarinet, Sax (Tenor) / Swing
One of the more individual tenors to emerge from the swing era, the distinctive Buddy Tate came to fame as Herschel Evans' replacement with Count Basie's Orchestra. Earlier he had picked up valuable experience playing with Terrence Holder (1930-33), Count Basie's original Kansas City band (1934), Andy Kirk (1934-35) and Nat Towles (1935-39). With Basie a second time during 1939-48, Tate held his own with such major tenors as Lester Young, Don Byas, Illinois Jacquet, Lucky Thompson and Paul Gonsalves. After a period freelancing with the likes of Hot Lips Page, Lucky Millinder and Jimmy Rushing (1950-52), Tate led his own crowd-pleasing group for 21 years (1953-74) at Harlem's Celebrity Club. During this period Tate also took time out to record in a variety of settings (including with Buck Clayton and Milt Buckner) and he was the one of the stars of John Hammond's Spirituals to Swing concert of 1967. Tate has kept busy since the Celebrity Club association ended, recording frequently, co-leading a band with Paul Quinichette in 1975, playing and recording in Canada with Jay McShann and Jim Galloway, visiting Europe many times and performing at jazz parties; he was also a favorite sideman of Benny Goodman's in the late '70s. Although age had taken its toll, in the mid-'90s Buddy Tate played and recorded with both Lionel Hampton and the Statesmen of Jazz. —*Scott Yanow*

Broadway / May 9, 1972-May 10, 1972 / Black & Blue ✦✦✦
● **Midnight Slows, Vol. 4** / Jan. 1974 / Black & Blue ✦✦✦✦

Sam "The Man" Taylor (Samuel L. Taylor)

b. 1916
Clarinet, Saxophone, Sax (Baritone), Sax (Tenor) / R&B, Blues, Blues Jazz, Soul Jazz
A certified honking sax legend, Sam "The Man" Taylor's non-stop drive and power worked perfectly in swing, blues and R&B sessions. He had a huge tone, perfect timing and sense of drama, as well as relentless energy and spirit. An argument could be advanced that Teagarden was actually the greatest white blues singer, certainly among jazz musicians. Taylor began working with Scat Man Crothers and the Sunset Royal Orchestra in the late '30s. He played with Cootie Williams and Lucky Millinder in the early '40s, then worked six years with Cab Calloway. Taylor toured South America and the Caribbean during his tenure with Calloway. Then Taylor became the saxophonist of choice for many R&B dates through the '50s, recording with Ray Charles, Buddy Johnson, Louis Jordan, and Big Joe Turner among others. He also did sessions with Ella Fitzgerald and Sy Oliver. During the '60s, Taylor led his own bands and recorded in a quintet called The Blues Chasers. He currently has one session available

on CD recorded in the late '50s with Charlie Shavers and Urbie Green. —*Ron Wynn*

The Bad and the Beautiful / Sep. 2, 1962 / Prestige ✦✦✦

The Three Sounds (Three Sounds)

Ballads, Soul Jazz, Post-Bop
A group formed by pianist Gene Harris in the late '50s that evolved from original Four Sounds, a 1957 quartet. The trio was enormously popular in the late 50s, and the early- and mid-'60s, despite the fact much of its music was in light cocktail-lounge or soul jazz mode. Actually Harris was a fine bluesy stylist, and revisionist looks at Three Sounds material, especially a 1963 release with Anita O'Day, have resulted in some observers admitting they overlooked or undervalued this group. —*Ron Wynn*
Groove: Here is bluesy jazz at its best. That some jazz purists think it should be discounted because it makes as good background (read dinner) music as foreground listening is just silly. The fact that you can play this music for your Grandma is not a fault. It's a virtue. There is that great Three Sounds album under Stanley Turrentine's name, *Blue Hour.* —*Michael Erlewine*

★ **Introducing the Three Sounds** / Sep. 16, 1958+Sep. 18, 1958 / Blue Note ✦✦✦✦✦
With Gene Harris on both piano and celeste. This is their first album—easy to listen to, but excellent small-group jazz. The CD is 67 minutes. —*Michael Erlewine*

Bottoms Up / Feb. 11, 1959 / Blue Note ✦✦✦
Good Deal / May 20, 1959 / Blue Note ✦✦✦
Feelin' Good / Jun. 28, 1960 / Blue Note ✦✦✦
Moods / Jun. 28, 1960 / Blue Note ✦✦✦✦✦
Here We Come / Dec. 13, 1960-Dec. 14, 1960 / Blue Note ✦✦✦
It Just Got to Be / Dec. 13, 1960-Dec. 14, 1960 / Blue Note ✦✦✦
Hey! There / Aug. 13, 1961 / Blue Note ✦✦✦
● **Babe's Blues** / Aug. 31, 1961-Mar. 8, 1962 / Blue Note ✦✦✦✦✦
Underrated group. This is what many people look and hope for in an easy-listening album: a quality jazz recording that can be played in the foreground or background. 43 minutes on CD. —*Michael Erlewine*

Out of This World / Feb. 4, 1962-Feb. 8, 1962 / Blue Note ✦✦✦
Black Orchid / Mar. 7, 1962-Mar. 8, 1962 / Blue Note ✦✦✦
Blue Genes / Oct. 13, 1962 / Verve ✦✦✦
Live at the Living Room / 1964 / Mercury ✦✦✦
Vibrations / 1966 / Blue Note ✦✦✦
● **Live at the Lighthouse** / Jul. 1967 / Blue Note ✦✦✦✦✦
The Best of the Three Sounds / Oct. 19, 1993 / Blue Note

Bobby Timmons

b. Dec. 19, 1935, Philadelphia, PA, d. Mar. 1, 1974, NYC
Piano / Soul Jazz, Hard Bop
Bobby Timmons became so famous for the gospel and funky blues cliches in his solos and compositions that his skills as a Bud Powell-inspired bebop player have been long forgotten. After emerging from the Philadelphia jazz scene, Timmons worked with Kenny Dorham (1956), Chet Baker, Sonny Stitt and the Maynard Ferguson Big Band. He was partly responsible for the commercial success of both Art Blakey's Jazz Messengers and Cannonball Adderley's Quintet. For Blakey (who he was with during 1958-9), Timmons wrote the classic "Moanin'" and, after joining Adderley in 1959, his song "This Here" (followed later by "Dat Dere") became a big hit; it is little wonder that Adderley was distressed when Timmons in 1960 decided to return to the Jazz Messengers. "Dat Dere" particularly caught on when Oscar Brown, Jr. wrote and recorded lyrics that colorfully depicted his curious son. Timmons, who was already recording as a leader for Riverside, soon formed his own trio but was never able to gain the commercial success that his former bosses enjoyed. Stereotyped as a funky pianist (although an influence on many players including Les McCann, Ramsey Lewis, and, much later on, Benny Green), Timmons' career gradually declined. He continued working until his death at age 38 from cirrhosis of the liver. —*Scott Yanow*

★ **This Here Is Bobby Timmons** / Jan. 13, 1960–Jan. 14, 1960 / Original Jazz Classics ✦✦✦✦✦
Trio with Sam Jones (b) and Jimmy Cobb (d). This pianist's single best album. —*Michael G. Nastos*

★ **Moanin'** / Aug. 12, 1960–Sep. 10, 1963 / Milestone ✦✦✦✦✦
Compilation of five different albums 1960–1963. Great collection and collectable. —*Michael G. Nastos*

In Person / Oct. 1, 1961 / Original Jazz Classics ✦✦✦✦✦
Recorded with the Trio. —*AMG*

The Soul Man / Jan. 20, 1966 / Prestige ✦✦✦
With Wayne Shorter on tenor sax. Plenty of funk, blues, and soul jazz, plus great piano. —*Ron Wynn*

Soul Food / Sep. 30, 1966+Oct. 14, 1966 / Prestige ✦✦✦
Ron Carter on bass and Wayne Shorter on sax. —*AMG*

Stanley Turrentine

b. Apr. 5, 1934, Pittsburgh, PA
Sax (Tenor) / Soul Jazz, Hard Bop
While highly regarded in soul jazz circles, Stanley Turrentine is one of the finest tenor saxophonists in any style in modern times. He excels at uptempo compositions, in jam sessions, interpreting standards, playing the blues or on ballads. His rich, booming and huge tone, with its strong swing influence, is one of the most striking of any tenor stylist, and during the '70s and '80s made otherwise horrendous mood music worth enduring.

To give you an idea where Turrentine is coming from: Early on, he toured with the R&B band of Lowell Fulson (1950–1951), whose featured pianist at the time was a young Ray Charles. From 1953–1954 he worked with Earl Bostic (perhaps the greatest R&B sax player of all time), where he replaced John Coltrane. He also worked and cut his first albums with Max Roach (1959–1960). Turrentine started recording as a leader on Blue Note in 1959 and 1960, while also participating in some landmark Jimmy Smith sessions such as *Midnight Special, Back at the Chicken Shack* and *Prayer Meeting*.

His decade-plus association with Shirley Scott was both professional and personal, as they were married most of the time they were also playing together. They frequently recorded, with the featured leader's name often depending on the session's label affiliation. When they divorced and split musically in the early '70s, Turrentine became a crossover star on CTI. Several of his CTI, Fantasy, Elektra and Blue Note albums in the '70s and '80s made the charts. Though their jazz content became proportionally lower, Turrentine's playing remained consistently superb. He returned to straight ahead and soul jazz in the '80s, cutting more albums for Fantasy and Elektra, then returning to Blue Note. He's currently on the Musicmasters label. Almost anything Turrentine's recorded, even albums with Stevie Wonder cover songs, are worth hearing for his solos. Many of his classic dates, as well as recent material, is available on CD.

Turrentine is an original, a one-of-a-kind. He does not fit neatly into ordinary jazz categories. What makes Turrentine great is his deep love of the roots of jazz-blues and groove music. He never abandoned these roots to join the more cerebral set of jazz soloists. His recording partnership with Jimmy Smith has given us some of the finest funk groove music of all time, a high-water mark for both artists. This man likes to groove and play funky music! He won't be tamed.

"The Turrentine tenor displays none of the weak-kneed and frazzle-buttocked bleatings of many tenor sax deviates, but relies on the truly large tone of the big tenor sounds of the old masters." —Dudley Williams, reviewer for Blue Note
—*Bob Porter, Michael Erlewine, and Ron Wynn*

Look Out / Jun. 18, 1960 / Blue Note ✦✦✦✦✦
With Horace Parlan (p), George Tucker (b), and Al Harewood (d). Recorded at Englewood Cliffs, NJ. Small group. 1987 reissue of excellent soul jazz. —*Ron Wynn*

Blue Hour / Dec. 16, 1960 / Blue Note ✦✦✦✦✦
With the Three Sounds —Gene Harris (p), Andrew Simpkinds (b), and William Dowdy (d). Recorded in Englewood Cliffs, NJ. A small group setting. This is a beautiful album of relaxed, bluesy sound. —*Michael Erlewine*

The Best of Stanley Turrentine / 1960–1984 / Blue Note ✦✦

● **Up at Minton's** / 1961 / Blue Note ✦✦✦✦✦
This is a particularly solid double CD featuring tenor saxophonist Stanley Turrentine, guitarist Grant Green, pianist Horace Parlan, bassist George Tucker, and drummer Al Harewood during a frequently exciting live set. Although recorded early in the careers of Turrentine and Green, both lead voices are easily recognizable with Green actually taking solo honors on several of the pieces. Standards and a couple of blues make up the repertoire, giving listeners a definitive look at the soulful Mr. T. near the beginning of his productive musical life. —*Scott Yanow*

Comin' Your Way / Jan. 20, 1961 / Blue Note ✦✦✦✦
With Tommy Turrentine (tp), Horace Parlan (p), George Tucker (b), and Al Harewood (d). Recorded at Englewood Cliffs, NJ. Small group. 1988 reissue of a sumptuous '60s soul jazz date. Horace Parlan (p) at his bluesy best. —*Ron Wynn*

Up at Minton's, Vol. 1 / Feb. 23, 1961 / Blue Note ✦✦✦✦✦
Here is Turrentine with the groove master Grant Green on guitar together at New York's Minton's Playhouse for a live recording. This is very early Green, not long after he relocated to New York from St. Louis. The rhythm section is the trio known as Us Three—Horace Parlan (p), George Tucker (b), and Al Harewood (d). This is available as a two-CD set from Blue Note and should grace every Turrentine or Green fan's shelves. Although not as funky as he would get, this is wonderful easy-paced listening. Plenty of bluesy soulful music. —*Michael Erlewine*

Up at Minton's, Vol. 2 / Feb. 23, 1961 / Blue Note ✦✦✦✦✦

Dearly Beloved / Jun. 8, 1961 / Blue Note ✦✦✦✦
A trio recording from Blue Note has Turrentine with Shirley Scott on Hammond organ and Roy Brooks on drums. This is the first recording with Turrentine and Scott, who would work together for ten years, later getting married. —*Michael Erlewine*

Z.T.'s Blues / Sep. 13, 1961 / Blue Note ✦✦✦✦
An all-star lineup has Turrentine with Grant Green on guitar and Tommy Flanagan on piano. The rhythm section has Paul Chambers on bass and Art Taylor on drums. Green and Turrentine made few albums together, but the combination is a natural—the two greatest groove masters, bar none. Flanagan seldom appears in this type of setting and his playing is very tasteful. A studio recording by Rudy Van Gelder at Englewood Cliffs, NJ. If you can find a copy of this, it is a keeper. —*Michael Erlewine*

● **That's Where It's at** / Jan. 2, 1962 / Blue Note ✦✦✦✦✦
A Blue Note release with Les McCann on piano, Herbie Lewis on bass, and Otis Finch on drums. Small group format. Excellent (and exciting) soul jazz session with Turrentine blowing hot. —*Ron Wynn & Michael Erlewine*

Jubilee Shout / Oct. 18, 1962 / Blue Note ✦✦✦✦
Featuring Sonny Clark on piano and Kenny Burrell on guitar. Also including Tommy Turrentine (tp), Butch Warren (b), and Al Harewood (d). Recorded at Englewood Cliffs, NJ, by Rudy Van Gelder. Here is classic funky soul jazz groove, three uptempo, three slow. Sonny Clark (p) soars, Turrentine is red-hot. —*Ron Wynn & Michael Erlewine*

Never Let Me Go / Jan. 18, 1963+Feb. 13, 1963 / Blue Note ✦✦✦
An early Blue Note album with the Stanley Turrentine Quintet: Turrentine, Shirley Scott (organ), Major Bolley (b), Al Harewood (d), and Ray Barretto (cga). —*Michael Erlewine*

A Chip off the Old Block / Oct. 21, 1963 / Blue Note ✦✦✦✦
On Blue Note with Turrentine, Blue Mitchell (tp), Shirley Scott (organ), Earl May (b), and Al Harewood (d). This is a studio recording by Van Gelder. Bluesy with tunes like "Midnight Blue" and "Blues in Hoss' Flat." —*Michael Erlewine*

Hustlin' / Jan. 24, 1964 / Blue Note ✦✦✦
A classic small group with Turrentine on tenor sax, Shirley Scott on the Hammond organ, and Kenny Burrell on guitar. The rhythm section has Bob Cranshaw on bass and Otis Finch on drums. Includes a version of "Goin' Home." —*Michael Erlewine*

● **Let It Go** / Sep. 21, 1964+Apr. 15, 1966 / GRP/Impulse ✦✦✦✦✦
This is vital Turrentine with Shirley Scott on Hammond organ, Ron Carter on bass, and Mack Simpkins on drums. This album includes some additional tracks that were originally released on the Shirley Scott album *Everybody Loves a Lover*. Recorded in Englewood Cliffs, NJ. Husband and wife team Turrentine and Shirley Scott (organ) produce one classic soul jazz groove album. —*Michael Erlewine*

Rough 'n Tumble / Jul. 1, 1966 / Blue Note ✦✦✦✦
A somewhat larger group (eight pieces) with Grant Green (g),

Blue Mitchell (tp), James Spaulding (as), Pepper Adams (bar), and McCoy Tyner on piano. Recorded at NYC. One of his most popular, tightest soul jazz releases. —*Ron Wynn*

Easy Walker / Jul. 8, 1966 / Blue Note ✦✦✦✦
A small group with Turrentine, McCoy Tyner on piano, Bob Cranshaw on bass, and Mickey Roker on drums. This Blue Note album has yet to be released in the states. —*Michael Erlewine*

Ain't No Way / May 10, 1968 / Blue Note ✦✦✦
Turrentine in small-group format. The cast includes Shirley Scott on the Hammond organ, McCoy Tyner on piano, Jimmy Ponder on guitar, Bob Cranshaw on bass, and Ray Lucas on drums. Substitute Gene Taylor (b) and Billy Cobham (d) for some cuts. —*Michael Erlewine*

Common Touch! / Aug. 30, 1968 / Blue Note ✦✦✦
Turrentine with Shirley Scott on organ, Jimmy Ponder on guitar, Bob Cranshaw on bass, and Leo Morris on drums. Includes a rendition of "Lonely Avenue." Blue Note album, but not yet reissued. —*Michael Erlewine*

Look of Love / Sep. 29, 1968–Oct. 6, 1968 / Blue Note ✦✦✦✦
Larger group setting that was recorded at Englewood Cliffs, NJ. Both romantic and lusty, nice sessions. —*Ron Wynn*

Straight Ahead / Nov. 24, 1984 / Blue Note ✦✦✦
Recorded at Power Play Studios, Long Island City, NY. Smaller group. Turrentine with George Benson (g), Jimmy Smith (organ), Ron Carter (b), and Jimmy Madison (d). On two cuts, also Jimmy Ponder (g) and Les McCann (p). Great combination of musicians as on earlier cookers, but time has passed—it does not come off. Pleasant enough though, but lacks high spots. —*Michael Erlewine*

Ballads / Nov. 16, 1993 / Blue Note
Although he's a monster tenor soloist on funky, exuberant, bluesy soul jazz, Stanley Turrentine is even more awesome on ballads. His rich, steamy sound, full tone, and ability to pace and develop moods is ideal for show tunes and sentimental love songs. This nine-track set begins with Turrentine nicely caressing the melody and turning in a standout treatment on "Willow Weep For Me," continuing through tearjerkers ("Since I Fell For You") and blues anthems ("God Bless The Child"), and closing with Thad Jones' beautiful "A Child Is Born." Turrentine is matched with numerous premier players, and pianist McCoy Tyner, guitarist Jimmy Smith, and even Turrentine's brother Tommy (trumpet) gently support and complement the main soloist. One of the best Blue Note special discs, featuring moving, frequently hypnotic playing from a true tenor great. —*Ron Wynn*

Rudy VanGelder

Rudy Van Gelder is the legendary sound engineer whose technical ingenuity and love of music forever influenced the way we listen to recorded jazz. Van Gelder was a practicing optometrist in the late 1940s when he set up his first modest recording studio in the living room of his parents' home in Hackensack, NJ. In that room he would record most of the major East Coast jazz artists of the 1950s, including virtually every session for Blue Note and Prestige records, as well as many classical dates for Vox and other labels. In 1959, over a single weekend, Van Gelder moved his studio to his new home in the town of Englewoord Cliffs, NJ, where it has remained. Van Gelder has kept pace with the technical advances that have occurred since that time and remains as active as ever. (The above quoted with permission of Mosaic Records.)

Rudy Van Gelder is arguably modern jazz's greatest engineer. He began engineering Blue Note sessions in 1953 and was famous for clean, sonically impeccable and sharp recordings that were expertly balanced and ideal for jazz fans, critics and anyone anxious to hear accurate sound reproduction. Van Gelder was Blue Note's surrogate producer as well as engineering mainstay throughout its greatest days in jazz. He has recorded more hard-bop and original funk (soul jazz) than any other engineer. He pioneered techniques to properly record the Hammond B-3 and capture the subtle sounds of their Leslie speakers. No one has recorded the B-3 like Van Gelder.

He has remained active in jazz as a freelance engineer and continues recording at his Englewood Cliff home; among his most recent dates are a '93 session by trumpeter Wallace Roney.

Many of Van Gelder's vintage Blue Note sessions have been reissued on CD with little or no remastering other than conversion from analog to digital. Amazingly, many ostensibly comprehensive jazz reference guides carry little or no mention of his role in jazz history, an astonishing oversight. —*Michael Erlewine & Ron Wynn*

Harold Vick

b. Apr. 3, 1936, Rocky Mount, NC, **d.** Nov. 13, 1987, New York, NY
Sax (Tenor) / Soul Jazz, Hard Bop
An excellent thick-toned tenor, Harold Vick sounded quite at home in hard bop and soul jazz settings. His uncle Prince Robinson (a reed player from the 1920s) gave him a clarinet when he was 13 and three years later Vick switched to tenor. He rose to prominence playing with organ combos in the mid-'60s, recording and performing with Jack McDuff, Jimmy McGriff, and Big John Patton among others. He started recording as a leader in 1966 and among his other associations were Jack DeJohnette's unusual group Compost (1972), Shirley Scott in the mid-'70s and Abbey Lincoln with whom he recorded two Billie Holiday tributes for Enja just a short time before his death. —*Scott Yanow*

● **Steppin' Out** / May 21, 1963 / Blue Note ✦✦✦✦✦

Winston Walls

Soul Jazz, Hard Bop
Winston Walls was born in Charleston, WV, the son of well-known R&B pianist Harry Van Walls (with Joe Turner) . At 15 Walls already knew some piano and had been playing in church and school for several years. He then learned drums from Frank Thompson and got a job playing drums for Bill "Honky Tonk" Doggett's band. He soon switched to organ and filled in on breaks for Doggett.

He acknowledges Jimmy Smith and Jack McDuff as major influences and has toured the country, playing with the Pointer Sisters, Sonny Stitt, Dionne Warwick, Al Green, Charlie Pride, Ike & Tina Turner, and Lou Donaldson.

His jazz organ also includes elements of R&B, rock, country, and gospel. He once toured with Jimmy Smith, Groove Holmes, and Jack McDuff, but had never recorded a solo album.

Then, in 1993, he recorded a live session with fellow organist (and friend) Brother Jack McDuff, which has been released on Schoolkids' Records. —*Michael Erlewine & John Bush*

Boss Of The B-3 / Oct. 25, 1993–Oct. 26, 1993 / Schoolkids ✦✦✦✦

Grover Washington, Jr.

b. Dec. 12, 1943, Buffalo, NY
Sax (Alto), Sax (Soprano), Sax (Tenor) / Soul Jazz, Crossover
Washington is one of the most commercially successful saxophonists in jazz history. A versatile reed specialist, he is equally at home on soprano, alto, or tenor sax, and has recorded on flute and baritone sax. A much more creative improviser than his hit-making saxophone competitors, Washington has had hits with almost everything he has done, since his first album (*Inner City Blues*) for Kudu in 1971. His biggest albums, *Mr. Magic* (Kudu) and *Winelight* (Elektra), have also spawned hit singles. His recordings for Kudu, Motown, Elektra, and Columbia are mostly commercial in content but, given that, Washington's saxophone work is always first-rate and a good distance in front of his closest fusion rivals. —*Bob Porter*

Inner City Blues / Sep. 1971 / Motown ✦✦✦✦✦
Definitive early-'70s soul jazz date. Washington has seldom been more convincing. —*Ron Wynn*

★ **Mister Magic** / 1975 / Motown ✦✦✦✦✦

☆ **Winelight** / Jun. 1980 / Elektra ✦✦✦✦✦
Grover Washington, Jr., has long been one of the leaders in what could be called rhythm & jazz, essentially R&B-influenced jazz. *Winelight* is one of his finest albums, and not primarily because of the Bill Withers hit "Just the Two of Us." It is the five instrumentals that find Washington (on soprano, alto and tenor) really stretching out. If he had been only interested in sales, Washington's solos could have been half as long and he would have stuck closely to the melody. Instead he really pushes himself on some of these selections, particularly the title cut. A mem-

orable set of high-quality and danceable soul jazz. —*Scott Yanow*

Ernie Watts

b. Oct. 23, 1945, Norfolk, VA
Sax (Tenor) / Instrumental Pop, Post-Bop
Because he was involved in many commercial recording projects from the mid-'70s through the early '80s and on an occasional basis ever since, some observers wrote Ernie Watts off prematurely as a pop/R&B tenorman. Actually Watts' main hero has always been John Coltrane and his more recent work reveals him to be an intense and masterful jazz improviser who has developed his own sheets of sound approach along with a distinctive and soulful sound. After attending Berklee, he had an important stint with Buddy Rich's big band (1966–68) before moving to Los Angeles. Watts worked in the big bands of Oliver Nelson and Gerald Wilson, recorded with Jean-Luc Ponty in 1969 and became a staff musician for NBC, performing with the Tonight Show Band on a regular basis. His own records of the 1970s and early '80s were generally poppish (1982's *Chariots of Fire* was a big seller) and Watts played frequently with Lee Ritenour and Stanley Clarke in addition to recording with Cannonball Adderley (one of his idols) in 1972. However Ernie Watts' work became much more interesting from a jazz standpoint starting in the mid-'80s when he joined Charlie Haden's Quartet West and started recording no-nonsense quartet dates for JVC. —*Scott Yanow*

● **Ernie Watts Quartet** / Dec. 1987 / JVC ✦✦✦✦✦
After years of being heard primarily in commercial settings, Ernie Watts finally had an opportunity to record exactly what he wanted as a leader on this JVC CD. Watts, in a quartet with pianist Pat Coil, bassist Joel DiBartolo, and drummer Bob Leatherbarrow, features his Coltrane-influenced tenor and a bit of alto and soprano on some group originals and standards (including "My One and Only Love," "Skylark," and "Body and Soul"). One of his finest recordings to date. —*Scott Yanow*

Baby Face Willette

Vocals / Blues, Soul Jazz, Hard Bop
Originally on piano, Baby Face Willette switched to organ after being inspired by Chicago church organists Herman Stevens and Mayfield Woods. Not much available on CD. Willette recorded two fine albums with soul jazz giant Grant Green on guitar, *Face to Face* and *Stop and Listen*, both released in 1961. —*Michael Erlewine*

Face to Face / Jan. 30, 1961 / Blue Note ✦✦✦
● **Stop and Listen** / May 22, 1961 / Blue Note ✦✦✦

Larry Young (Larry [Aziz, Khalid Yasin Abdul] Young)

b. Oct. 7, 1940, Newark, NJ, **d.** Mar. 30, 1978, NYC
Organ / Fusion, Post-Bop, Hard Bop
Larry Young, also known as Khalid Yasin, offered as radical an approach on organ in the '60s as Jimmy Smith posed in the '50s. His free, swirling chords, surging lines and rock-influenced improvisations were an alternative to the groove-centered, blues and soul jazz sound that had become the organ's dominant direction. He brought John Coltrane's late '60s approach to the organ, generating waves of sound and greatly influencing any session he participated in during the '60s and '70s. Young studied piano rather than organ, though he later began playing organ in R&B bands in the '50s. He recorded in 1960 with Jimmy Forrest, and then did his first session for Blue Note as a leader. He worked and recorded with Grant Green in a hard bop vein in the mid-'60s, though he was beginning his experiments at that point. Young worked with Joe Henderson, Lee Morgan, Donald Byrd, and Tommy Turrentine and toured Europe in 1964. His album *Into Something* in 1965 alerted everyone Young was heading a different way. He played with Coltrane, recorded with Woody Shaw and Elvin Jones, then joined Miles Davis' band in 1969. Young worked with John McLaughlin in 1970 and was in Tony Williams' Lifetime with McLaughlin and Jack Bruce among others in the early '70s. He only made a couple of other records for Perception and Arista, both of them uneven but with some intriguing moments. Neither label had the vaguest idea what Young was trying to do, nor how they could sell it. Sadly, he died in 1978 at 38. He'd only made a handful of recordings, and his labels never knew what to make of his music. Mosaic issued a superb boxed set of Young's Blue Note recordings, a six-CD (nine-album) collection, *The Complete Blue Note Recordings Of Larry Young*. A very early session, *Testifying*, on New Jazz, was reissued by Fantasy in a limited edition in '92. Blue Note has an anthology package, *The Art of Larry Young*, available as well. —*Ron Wynn*

Groove: Larry Young has been called the jazz organist's "jazz organist." His first album, *Testifying*, sounds a little like Jimmy Smith when he's cookin', and the next few (with Grant Green on guitar) are just plain great soul jazz. From there on Larry Young takes the Hammond B-3 through soul jazz, beyond, and "out." Young's playing is different from other Hammond B-3 masters, quite unique, but very definitely worth hearing. Young manages to find a soft spot in every jazz organist's heart. —*Michael Erlewine*

Testifying / Aug. 2, 1960 / Original Jazz Classics ✦✦✦
Organist Larry Young was 19 when he made this, his debut recording. Although he would become innovative later on, Young at this early stage was still influenced by Jimmy Smith even if he had a lighter tone; the fact that he used Smith's former guitarist, Thornel Schwartz, and a drummer whose name was coincidentally Jimmie Smith kept the connection strong. R&Bish tenor Joe Holiday helps out on two songs and the music (standards, blues and ballads) always swings. Easily recommended to fans of the jazz organ. —*Scott Yanow*

Young Blues / Sep. 30, 1960 / Original Jazz Classics ✦✦✦✦✦
Organist Larry Young's second recording (cut shortly before he turned 20) is the best from his early period before he completely shook off the influence of Jimmy Smith. With guitarist Thornel Schwartz in top form, and bassist Wendell Marshall and drummer Jimmie Smith excellent in support, Young swings hard on a few recent jazz originals, some blues and two standards ("Little White Lies" and "Nica's Dream"). Recommended as a good example of his pre-Blue Note work. —*Scott Yanow*

Groove Street / Feb. 27, 1962 / Prestige ✦✦✦
Larry Young's third and final Prestige recording (reissued in the *OJC* series on CD) concludes his early period; he would next record as a leader two and a half years later on Blue Note, by which time his style would be much more original. For his 1962 outing, Young is joined by the obscure tenor Bill Leslie, guitarist Thornel Schwartz and drummer Jimmie Smith for some original blues and two standards ("I Found a New Baby" and "Sweet Lorraine"). Nothing all that substantial occurs but fans of Jimmy Smith will enjoy the similar style that Larry Young had at the time. —*Scott Yanow*

☆ **Complete Blue Note Recordings** / Sep. 11, 1964–Feb. 7, 1969 / Mosaic ✦✦✦✦✦
Larry Young, one of the most significant jazz organists to emerge after the rise of Jimmy Smith, is heard on this limited-edition six-CD set at the peak of his creativity. [The set comprises the following original albums: Grant Green *Talkin' About*, Larry Young *Into Somethin'*, Grant Green *Street of Dreams*, Grant Green *I Want to Hold Your Hand*, Larry Young *Unity*, Larry Young *Of Love and Peace*, Larry Young *Contrasts*, Larry Young *Heaven on Earth*, Larry Young *Mother Ship*, Larry Young *40 Years of Jazz, The History of Blue Note* (box 4 Dutch), Larry Young *The World of Jazz Organ* (Japanese), Larry Young *The Blue Note 50th Anniversary Collection Volune Two: The Jazz Message.*] Formerly available as nine LPs (three of which were actually under guitarist Grant Green's leadership), Young was still very much under Smith's influence on the first four sessions (which features a trio with Green and drummer Elvin Jones plus guests Sam Rivers or Hank Mobley on tenor and vibraphonist Bobby Hutcherson). However, starting with the monumental *Unity* session (a quartet outing with Joe Henderson on tenor, trumpeter Woody Shaw and Elvin Jones), Young emerged as a very advanced and original stylist in his own right. The final four dates are generally pretty explorative and feature such notable sidemen as altoist James Spaulding and Byard Lancaster, guitarist George Benson and trumpeter Lee Morgan along with some forgotten local players. This definitive Larry Young set is highly recommended. —*Scott Yanow*

Into Somethin' / Oct. 12, 1964 / Blue Note ✦✦✦✦✦
This album is available as part of the Mosaic box set *The Complete Blue Note Recordings of Larry Young*. With Sam

Rivers on tenor sax, Grant Green on guitar, and Elvin Jones on drums. First-rate set from dynamic organist. *—Ron Wynn*

★ **Unity** / Nov. 10, 1965 / Blue Note ✦✦✦✦✦
With Joe Henderson on tenor sax, Woody Shaw on trumpet, and Elvin Jones on drums. Recorded at Englewood Cliffs, NJ. Innovative, far-reaching organist. This album is available as part of the Mosaic box set *The Complete Blue Note Recordings of Larry Young. —Ron Wynn*

Of Love and Peace / Jun. 28, 1966 / Blue Note ✦✦✦✦✦
With Eddie Gale (tp), James Spaulding (as, fl), Herbert Morgan (ts), Wilson Moorman III, and Jerry Thomas (d).This album is available as part of the Mosaic box set *The Complete Blue Note Recordings of Larry Young. —AMG*

Contrasts / Sep. 18, 1967 / Blue Note ✦✦✦✦✦
Larger-group format with Tyrone Washington, Herbert Morgan (ts), Hank White (flg), Eddie Wright (g), Eddie Gladden (d) Stacey Edwards (cga), and Althea Young (vcl). This is more "out" than the earlier material and does not fit into the standard soul jazz

groove style. This album is available as part of the Mosaic box set *The Complete Blue Note Recordings of Larry Young. — Michael Erlewine*

Heaven on Earth / Feb. 9, 1968 / Blue Note ✦✦✦
Organist Larry Young, who really found his own sound back in 1965 with the classic *Unity* album, is deep in the funk on this later Blue Note album (which has been included in the Mosaic box set *The Conplete Blue Note Recordings of Larry Young*). With altoist Byard Lancaster, tenor saxophonist Herbert Morgan, guitarist George Benson and drummer Eddie Gladden completing the quintet, there are some explorative solos but the less imaginative funk rhythms lower the content of the music somewhat. Young's wife Althea Young has an effective vocal on "My Funny Valentine" but overall this is a lesser effort. *—Scott Yanow*

Mother Ship / Feb. 7, 1969 / Blue Note ✦✦✦
Larry Young with Lee Morgan (tp) and Herbert Morgan (ts). This is quite "out" compared to his soul jazz recordings. This album is available as part of the Mosaic box set *The Complete Blue Note Recordings of Larry Young. —AMG*

LANDMARK JAZZ ALBUMS

Putting aside the blues in jazz aspect, here is a list of landmark jazz albums that every jazz lover should hear. And this does not just represent my personal opinion. Any serious jazz listener would agree that these are classic albums that should be heard at least once. Whether you like them or not does not matter. It will show you the wide world of jazz and help you figure out what you do like, which directions to take, etc. One thing is certain: if you don't like these albums, it is not because they are lousy performances, but because it is not your kind of music. (This list is admittedly weak in traditional, swing, big-band jazz, and fusion.)

—Michael Erlewine

Air, *Air Lore*/Arista
Mose Allison, *I Don't Worry About a Thing*/Rhino/Atlantic
Louis Armstrong, *Hot Fives and Sevens Vol. 1–3*/JSP
Art Ensemble of Chicago, *Jackson in Your House*/
   Affinity 9
Count Basie, *The Original American Decca Record-ings*/
   MCA
Sidney Bechet, *The Bluebird Sessions*/Bluebird
Art Blakey, *Jazz Messengers with Thelonious Monk*/
   Atlantic
Anthony Braxton, *For Alto Saxophone*/Delmark
Clifford Brown, *Jazz Immortal*/Pacific Jazz
Dave Brubeck, *Take Five*/Columbia
Ornette Coleman, *The Shape of Jazz To Come*/Atlantic
John Coltrane, *A Love Supreme*/MCA
Chick Corea, *My Spanish Heart*/Polydor
Charlie Christian, *Solo Flight*/Columbia

Miles Davis, *Kind of Blue*/Columbia
Eric Dolphy, *Out to Lunch!*/Blue Note
Duke Ellington, *Blanton-Webster Band*/Bluebird
Bill Evans, *Sunday at the Village Vanguard*/OJC
Keith Jarrett, *The Koln Concert*/ECM
Erroll Garner, *Concert by the Sea*/Columbia
Stan Getz, *Getz/Gilberto*/Verve
Dizzy Gillespie, *In the Beginning*/Prestige
Herbie Hancock, *Maiden Voyage*/Blue Note
Billie Holiday, *The Quintessential Billie Holiday Vol. 1–9*/
   Columbia
Milt Jackson, *Bag's Groove*/Prestige
Roland Kirk, *Rahsaan*/Mercury
Shelly Manne, *At the Blackhawk*/OJC
Charles Mingus, *Mingus at Antibes*/Atlantic
Thelonious Monk, *Genius of Modern Music, Vol. 1–2*/
   Blue Note
Wes Montgomery, *Incredible Jazz Guitar of*
   Wes Montgomery/Riverside
Fats Navarro, *The Fabulous Fats Navarro, Vol. 1–2 /*
   Blue Note
Oliver Nelson, *Blues and the Abstract Truth*/Impulse
Herbie Nichols, *The Art of Herbie Nichols*/Blue Note
Oregon, *Out of the Woods*/Electra
Charlie Parker, *The Charlie Parker Story*/Savoy
Bud Powell, *The Amazing Bud Powell Vol. 1-2*/Blue Note
Sonny Rollins, *Saxophone Colossus*/OJC
Sun Ra, *The Heliocentric World of Sun Ra, Vol. 1*/ESP
Cecil Taylor, *Unit Structures*/Blue Note
McCoy Tyner, *The Real McCoy*/Blue Note

BLUES STYLES

THE ROOTS OF THE BLUES

The origins of the blues–a form which really didn't have a name until the early 20th century, although it had surely been around for some time before then–are impossible to pin down with any degree of certainty. There's the convenient thesis that the blues were imported to North America when African slaves were shipped to the continent in the centuries preceding the Civil War. Much of the blues is undeniably African in origin, but in fact there were many other influences that shaped the music as well. It's also reasonably certain that the blues did not take a recognizable shape until African-Americans were a large, established part of the population of the American South.

Formulating the origins of the blues is a much more difficult task than, say, describing the birth of rock 'n' roll. For one thing, there are no tapes or recordings available to trace and document the sounds as they coalesced prior to 1900. The standard historical record of written and oral accounts, too, is much sketchier than it is for comparitively recent genres. Offering postulations and generalizations in a short overview such as this, really, is just asking for trouble–there are plenty of blues and folklore scholars that will challenge whatever point of view is espoused, often armed with considerable evidence. This piece will simply identify some of the likely sources. Readers interested in investigating the topic in greater depth will find many book-length studies of the subject in libraries and bookstores with a large selection.

The African roots of the blues are undeniable, particularly in the griots of western Africa. The griots functioned as sorts of musical storytellers for their communities, no doubt singing about subjects like romance, family, famine, ruling governments, and struggle that are commonplace in blues music–and, indeed, folk/popular music as a whole. They often used stringed instruments that bore some resemblance to ones that became prevalent in blues. When Ali Farka Toure of Senegal reached an international audience in the 1980s and 1990s, he was frequently described as "the African John Lee Hooker"; it's possible that his work is also an illustration of the close ties between the blues and some strains of African music.

Blues music, however, most likely didn't approach anything resembling its 20th-century form until slavery was instituted in the American South. The mere fact that the slaves came from many different regions and spoke many different languages, for one thing, would have worked against the retention of the music of their homeland as they began working together. Subsequent generations lost the tongues of their mothers and fathers, by necessity adopting English, the language of their overlords.

The brutal and inhumane conditions of slavery, from some viewpoints, may have seemed to make it unlikely that any forms of artistic expression could develop and thrive. In some respects, however, slavery fostered such musical communication, simply as a means of making life bearable. Work songs and field hollers, some of the most oft-discussed precursors to the blues, were chanted and sung as the slaves worked or endured their punishment. They were also a means of telling stories, passing the endless hours of toil, or simply venting emotion that was impossible to express in more confined or closely supervised circumstances. The call-and-response quality of some blues music (and much gospel) may have derived in part from such singing; the blues' concentration upon earthy, day-to-day realities and struggles may have some of its roots in these styles as well.

The history of American popular music is often one of Black and White styles meeting and mixing. As wide as the racial divide was in slavery days, the music of American Blacks inevitably absorbed a lot of White flavor, from European, Southern folk, and Appalachian influences. In their limited contact with Whites, Blacks were also exposed to piano and string instruments that would figure strongly in their own music. By the time blues began to be recorded in the early 1920s, guitars and pianos were the most frequent instruments of choice among blues artists.

There was also the considerable influence of the church. Gospel music afforded the African-American community opportunities to sing with committed fervor. The harmonies and solo vocal styles associated with vocal music have left a strong imprint on Black music to this day, including the blues. Relatively recent releases like Mississippi Fred McDowell's recordings of spirituals in the 1960s demonstrate how strong the ties can be between down-home blues and gospel; Reverend Gary Davis was another acoustic bluesman known for performing a lot of gospel material.

The extraordinary power of the rural blues recorded in the 1920s and 1930s have sometimes left the impression that deep blues dominated the music of Southern Black communities. The repertoire of Black musicians from the Deep South was much more diverse than many people realize. Blues music was often only one element of their repertoire; some singers who only recorded blues music were likely able to play pop, country, and ragtime tunes as well in live performance, as the circumstances of the occasion demanded. Some of these musicians performed as part of traveling minstrel, vaudeville, and medicine shows; occasionally ones who toured with such concerns in the early 20th century would survive to make recordings in the early days of the LP, such as Pink Anderson. Ragtime styles also made their way onto blues records, not only via pianists but guitarists such as Reverend Gary Davis.

Jug bands and the all-around entertainers that have been dubbed "songsters" are sometimes also thought of as precursors to the blues, although many such musicians were actually contemporaries of the early blues artists, and recorded often in the 1920s and 1930s. Jug bands like the Mississippi Sheiks and those of Gus Cannon used instruments not associated with the blues these days, such as the washboard, kazoo, and fiddle. They also frequently espoused a good-time air, in contrast to the more melancholic tone of deep rural guitar blues. They were still a vital part of the African-American popular music of the South in the 1930s, although afterwards their styles were deemed hokey and passé, a relic of the minstrel tradition.

The wide repertoire of Southern Black music lived on in blues performers that have come to be called the "songsters," who are examined in greater depth in a separate piece. They could play blues, certainly, but also folk tunes, country songs, pop, ragtime, and spirituals. Some of the oldest bluesmen who made it onto record, such as pan quill pipe player Henry Thomas (famous for "Bull Doze Blues," which Canned Heat turned into "Going Up the Country'), were songsters. The eclecticism of the songsters lived on in some performers who became popular during the 1960s blues revival, such as Mance Lipscomb and Mississippi John Hurt. Leadbelly and Josh White could be called "songsters" of sort, although they were more commonly categorized as folk singers, or blues/folk singers.

The blues, or forms closely tied to the blues, had likely existed for some time, and in various blends of the previously described styles, before its famous "discovery," at least in terms of verified historical accounts, by W.C. Handy, who recalled hearing something resembling the blues as early as 1892. The incident that has been enshrined in popular legend, however, occurred in Tuwiler, Mississippi, in 1903, as Handy, a black bandleader of a minstrel orchestra, was waiting for a train. In his autobiography, Father of the Blues, he recalls listening to the guitarist that began to play:

"The singer repeated the line three times, accompanying him-

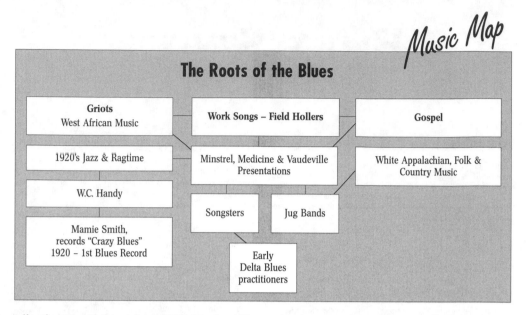

Music Map

The Roots of the Blues

Griots West African Music	**Work Songs – Field Hollers**	**Gospel**
1920's Jazz & Ragtime	Minstrel, Medicine & Vaudeville Presentations	White Appalachian, Folk & Country Music
W.C. Handy	Songsters · Jug Bands	
Mamie Smith, records "Crazy Blues" 1920 – 1st Blues Record	Early Delta Blues practitioners	

self on the guitar with the weirdest music I had ever heard. The tune stayed in my mind. When the singer paused, I leaned over and asked him what the words meant. He rolled his eyes, showing a trace of mild amusement. Perhaps I should have known, but he didn't mind explaining. At Morehead, the eastbound and westbound met and crossed the north and southbound trains four times a day...

"He was simply singing … as he waited. This was not unusual. Southern Negroes sang about everything. Trains, steamboats, steam whistles, sledge hammers, fast women, mean bosses, stubborn mules—all became subjects for their songs. They accompany themselves on anything from which they can extract a musical sound or rhythmical effect, anything from a harmonica to a washboard."

Despite his title "Father of the Blues," Handy did not invent the blues. He was responsible for popularizing them by copyrighting and publishing blues compositions. "Memphis Blues," published in 1912, was the first one; "St. Louis Blues," which followed in 1914, was his most successful, and indeed one of the most popular tunes of any kind in the 20th century, performed and recorded by numerous jazz, blues, and pop artists. Handy published/wrote other numbers in the same vein, such as "Yellow Dog Blues" and "Beale Street Blues" (named after the main thoroughfare of the Black community in Memphis).

"St. Louis Blues" can sound more like jazz than blues to contemporary listeners, perhaps reflecting the fact that Handy was steeped not the blues but in brass bands, which may have shaped his arrangements. The same can be said of the first popular blues recordings of the 1920s, mostly performed with jazz accompanists, who sang such pop- and jazz-influenced "blues" compositions as those devised by Handy. Arguably, these records reflected a more urban and pop-oriented sensibility than what you would have heard from the mouths of the proto-blues and early blues performers of the South.

Those early blues songs and singles, however, were responsible to some degree for codifying certain blues trademarks. The blues is too volatile a form to ever be standardized, but much of it is typified by a 12-bar structure and three-line verses that follow what is called an AAB rhyming scheme. These are the traits, more than any other, that have endured in much (perhaps most) acoustic and modern electric blues, live or recorded, to this day.

Modern mass communications—the phonograph record and radio—began to unify the blues stylistically, exposing listeners and musicians to sounds, similar and different, from other regions. The inherent demands of a two- or three-minute 78 RPM single also necessitated a brevity and conciseness, forcing musicians to cut down the length of their songs, and perhaps to adopt certain standard methods (like the 12-bar structure and AAB

scheme) to present their music commercially. The similar structure of many blues songs may have even been matters of convenience or imitation in many cases.

What's certain is that after the phenomenal success of Mamie Smith's "Crazy Blues" (the first blues record) in 1920, and many other women singers performing in a similar vein over the next few years, the record industry—then in its infancy—was eager to record blues artists of all kinds, with a particular eye toward what was then called the "race" (i.e. African-American) market. This led to labels scouring several regions for talent, particularly the South, where most blues performers were based. Here they encountered the guitarists who sang deep country blues, as well as songsters and jug bands. Blues was off and running as an established part of the music industry, with an ever-widening repertoire of songs and styles that has endured to this day as one of the most popular and important forms of American music.

–Richie Unterberger

6 Recommended Albums:

Various Artists, *Blues Masters, Vol. 10: Blues Roots* (Rhino)
Various Artists, *Afro-American Spirituals, Work Songs and Ballads* (Library of Congress)
Various Artists, *Negro Work Songs and Calls* (Library of Congress)
Various Artists, *The Sounds of the South* (Atlantic)
Eddie "One-String" Jones, *One String Blues* (Gazell)
Ali Farka Toure, *The Source* (Hannibal)

JUG BANDS

Jug bands may be only a footnote in the birth of the blues. Some may dispute whether they belong in the mainstream of blues history at all, finding it more convenient to categorize them as old-time folk music. The relatively few recordings that blues-influenced jug bands made in the 1920s and 1930s, at the very least, give us valuable insight into the roots of the blues, at a time when it had not solidified into guitar-based music that usually adhered to 12-bar structures. It also yields its share of high-spirited tunes in the bargain.

Some historians have speculated that at the turn of the century, jug band-type outfits were more common in the Southern African-American community than performers playing what we would now call the blues. The instrumentation and arrangements of the jug bands were often an outgrowth of the minstrel/vaudeville/traveling medicine shows that toured the South. String bands were a feature of many of these outfits, and the emphasis

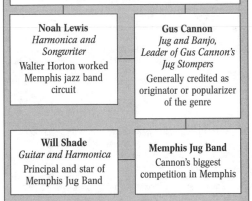

Jug Bands

Early Jazz Combos

Circa 1900 – 1920: Buddy Bolden, Kid Oliver,
Louis Armstrong, Original Dixieland Jazz Band

Noah Lewis	Gus Cannon
Harmonica and Songwriter	*Jug and Banjo, Leader of Gus Cannon's Jug Stompers*
Walter Horton worked Memphis jazz band circuit	Generally credited as originator or popularizer of the genre

Will Shade	Memphis Jug Band
Guitar and Harmonica	Cannon's biggest competition in Memphis
Principal and star of Memphis Jug Band	

was on good-time entertainment, not the hard times and weighty expression that many associate with the blues.

A great deal of the charm of the jug bands was due to the homemade, almost improvised nature of the instruments. There were kazoos, washboards, washtubs, spoons, and all manner of percussion produced by items more commonly associated with work tools or playthings; like jugs, but also pipes, pans, and more. Even the relatively conventional instruments, like fiddles and guitars, were sometimes made from scrap materials, like cigar boxes.

Elaborates Francis Davis in *The History of the Blues*, "Jug bands differed in size and instrumentation, though they invariably included either a harmonica or a kazoo as a lead melodic voice, a variety of string instruments, and at least one band member providing a bass line by blowing rhythmically across the top of a jug–a poor man's tuba, as it were. Like the rural fife-and-drum bands of which we have regrettably few recorded examples, jug bands can be heard as a missing link between the blues and the music of West Africa ...

"Along with the washboard bands in which a simple laundry device was transformed into a percussion instrument, the jug bands were a tribute to the ingenuity shown by impoverished rural Blacks in expressing themselves musically on whatever they found at hand. For that matter, [early jug band leader Gus] Cannon fashioned his first banjo out of a bread pan and a broom handle. And there are obvious parallels to be drawn between the use of such homemade or 'nonmusical' instruments then and similar practices in hip-hop, most notably 'scratching.'"

Many of the jug bands that were active in the early 1900s didn't have professional aspirations; the ones that did were doubtless undiscovered by record companies. Like the barrelhouse blues pianists of the early 1900s, their representation on record is fairly scant, and certainly not fully documented for listeners of future decades who wish to get a relatively complete picture of the style. And many of the ones that did get to record only issued a single or two before vanishing into oblivion, only accessible today via obscure compilations aimed at a very small and specialized collector market.

Of the jug bands that managed to record in the 1920s and 1930s, more noteworthy ones emerged from Memphis than anywhere else. The most influential were the ones led by Gus Cannon, much of whose repertoire was grounded in a definite blues base. The most celebrated of Cannon's local rivals were the Memphis

Jug Band; unlike many of the jug bands, they recorded prolifically, helping ensure that their reputation would outlive them. Individual stars within these bands were harmonica player Noah Lewis (an associate of Cannon's) and guitarist-harmonica player Will Shade, the most prominent member of the Memphis Jug Band.

Even at the time that Cannon and the Memphis Jug Band were recording, the jug band style was being threatened on several fronts. Country blues was evolving into a far more guitar-oriented form that put the emphasis on solo vocals; African-American bands were turning increasingly to swing and big band jazz. The jug bands may have reminded some African-Americans of a minstrel and blackface tradition that they were eager to evolve from, or even forget. The Depression meant a severe cutback on commercial blues recordings of all kinds, and the jug bands were hit especially hard; very few commercial jug band recordings were made after the 1930s, and by the subsequent decade, the genre had pretty much vanished as a commercial consideration anyway.

Long after the prime of the Memphis jug bands, however, the influence of the music would linger. The Rooftop Singers, one of the more commercial ensembles of the early '60s folk revival, took Gus Cannon's "Walk Right In" to the top of the pop charts in 1963. The folk revival also spun off a small jug band revival of its own, the most successful act being Jim Kweskin & His Jug Band, featuring Maria and Geoff Muldaur (although the group's repertoire was not limited to the blues). And the Grateful Dead, who dug very deep into the blues backlog for some of their covers, included Cannon's "Viola Lee Blues" on their first album.

—Richie Unterberger

5 Recommended Albums:

Gus Cannon's Jug Stompers, *The Complete Recordings* (Yazoo)
The Memphis Jug Band, *Memphis Jug Band* (Yazoo)
Various Artists, *The Jug & Washboard Bands, Vol. 1 (1924–31)* (RST Blues Documents)
Various Artists, *The Jug, Jook & Washboard Bands* (Blues Classics)
Jim Kweskin & His Jug Band, *Greatest Hits* (Vanguard)

DELTA BLUES

No other style of the blues has exerted such a grip on the popular imagination as the one associated with the Mississippi Delta. The image of the wracked bluesman hunched over his acoustic guitar, exorcising the demons from the depths of his soul, his rhythmic force often accentuated by thrilling slide guitar this is a caricature that originated from Delta blues. Like any caricature, it's prone to over-generalizations that tend to obscure the considerable stylistic range of the form, and the eccentricities to be found in the repertoire of its major exponents. But there's no doubt that Delta blues epitomizes the music at its most emotional and expressive.

The history of Delta blues is inseparable from the African-American culture of the region itself. The Delta refers to the northwestern part of the state, where the fertile soil gave rise to many plantations. These were owned by Whites and worked mostly by Blacks, who often harvested the land as sharecroppers. The conditions for sharecroppers may have been better than those they endured in slavery, but not by a great deal. Backbreaking labor and low wages were the norm, as well as racial intolerance and segregation.

No amount of romanticization can obscure the grinding poverty of the everyday lives of the plantation workers. But the conditions of the Delta were conducive to the development of a sort of indigenous music. Huge numbers of African-Americans were working and living together in close promixity, exchanging the music and folk traditions they had developed and experienced over generations. In many instances, they were too poor to travel even moderate distances (and in any case didn't have the spare time to do so), intensifying the ferment of musical elements that gave birth to a distinctive style.

As hard as the plantation work was, there was still time for entertainment, in both informal settings and weekend parties. Musicians were in demand for these events, and often they would circulate between different plantations. The solo guitarist was a natural fit for these situations; full bands would have found spontaneous ensemble traveling more difficult, both logistically and economically. In comparison to many other instruments, the gui-

Delta Blues

Charlie Patton
1st great star of the Delta Blues

Son House, Willie Brown, Tommy Johnson, Tommy McClennan, Ishmon Bracey, Robert Johnson, Skip James, Bukka White, Mississippi John Hurt	Johnny Shines, Eddie Taylor, Muddy Waters, Robert Nighthawk, John Lee Hooker, Howlin' Wolf, Elmore James, Mississippi Fred McDowell

tar was relatively inexpensive and more portable. These factors may have accounted for the predominance of the solo guitarist in Mississippi Delta blues (not to mention country blues as a whole). Delta blues was certainly one of the first forms of the music, if not the first, to emphasize the guitar, an association that characterizes much blues music to the present day.

Robert Palmer, a Delta blues authority as both a critic and a record producer (and author of a book-length study of the subject, *Deep Blues*), explains in his liner notes to *Blues Masters Vol. 8: Mississippi Delta Blues* that "Delta blues is a dialogue between the overt and the hidden. The music's apparent simplicity–basic verse forms, little or no harmonic content, melodies with as few as three principal pitches–is superficial. Apparently straightforward rhythmic drive often proves, on careful listening, to be the by-product of a mercurial interplay between polyrhythms, layered in complex relationships. The music's supreme rhythmic masters–Charley Patton, Robert Johnson–kept several rhythms going simultaneously, like a juggler with balls in the air or like the most gifted modern jazz drummers. Sometimes the music seems to lie behind the beat and rush just ahead of it at the same time....

"The simplest way to characterize the music's origin is as a turn-of-the-century innovation, accommodating the vocal traditions of work songs and field hollers to the expressive capabilities of a newly popular stringed instrument, the guitar. Older black ballads and dance songs, preaching and church singing, the rhythms of folk drumming, and the ring shout of 'holy dance' fed into the new music as well. But the richly ornamented, powerfully projected singing style associated with the field holler was dominant, which is hardly surprising; the Delta is more or less one big cotton field."

The man usually recognized as the first exponent of the Delta blues is Charlie Patton. Most blues scholars, and indeed many general fans, are now well aware that Patton didn't invent the Delta blues; he was simply one of the first to record it, and was adept at absorbing many of the regional elements that were in the air. As David Evans writes in *The Blackwell Guide to the Blues*, "In Patton's blues, and indeed in his spirituals, ballads, and ragtime tunes, may be found fully formed all the essential characteristics of the Deep South blues style–the gruff impassioned voice suggesting the influence of country preaching and gospel singing style (which he displayed on his religious recordings), the percussive guitar technique, the bending of strings and use of slide style, the driving rhythms and repeated riffs, the traditional lyric formulas, and the simple harmonic structures.

"Patton, however, also displays one highly individual characteristic: he sings about his own experiences and events he observed– frequently ones outside the realm of the usual man-woman relationships in the blues–always sharing his lyrics from a highly personal point of view." Indeed, the Delta blues as a whole were often more personal, earthy, and downcast than much popular music, reflecting the struggles and bitter realities of Southern Blacks in the early 1920s, as well as the basic details of rural life.

Other Mississippi bluesmen were already recording in the late 1920s. The most important of these was probably Tommy Johnson, a contemporary of Patton's who knew and learned much from the guitarist; Ishman Bracey, who was an associate of Johnson's for a long time, also did a good deal of recording in the era. Much of the activity in this scene centered around the plantation of Will Dockery, where Patton and Johnson would often play, influencing such Dockery residents as the young Howlin' Wolf. The success of Patton's recordings in the race market led labels to issue 78s by other Delta bluesmen, the most notable of which was Son House, another musician who knew Patton well.

The most individual and eccentric of the Delta bluesmen, Skip James, was in a sense not a Delta bluesman at all. James was based in the tiny Mississippi hill town of Bentonia, whose isolation may have contributed to the development of his musical idiosyncrasies. His minor guitar tunings and strange, often falsetto vocals are very unusual for the country blues genre. It's the dark, anguished power of his compositions, though, that may hold the most enduring appeal for listeners throughout the ages.

The devastating effects of the Depression on the music industry meant that Delta bluesmen were rarely afforded the opportunity to record after the 1930s. Hence the abrupt end of the recording careers of singers like James, House, and others in the early 1930s, not to be resumed until their rediscovery several decades later (if they were still alive, or could still be found). Many others, doubtlessly, never had the chance to record at all, due either to the lack of opportunity within the record business, or the simple luck of the draw when companies scouted for talent.

But the most legendary Delta bluesman of all, Robert Johnson, didn't do any of his recording until 1936. Several books and film productions have been based around his life, much of which is based on legend, as the basic facts of his life (many of which were garnered from acquaintances and traveling companions, such as guitarist Johnny Shines) are surrounded by considerable mystery and confusion. The apocryphal story of how he sold his soul to the devil at the crossroads (a prominent image in Southern Black music and culture) provided the basis for one of his most famous songs, and indeed for an entire Hollywood movie.

What we have for real, however, are the 29 songs he recorded in two sessions in 1936 and 1937. In addition to synthesizing much of what was best about the Delta blues, Johnson's songwriting, vocals, and instrumental skill also brought the music closer to a more modern sensibility, particularly in the haunted, agonized individuality of his songs. Famed talent scout and record producer John Hammond was trying to get in touch with Johnson to participate in the pivotal Spirituals To Swing concert at New York's Carnegie Hall in 1938, but the guitarist was impossible to locate. Shortly afterwards, it was discovered that he had died in August 1938, another incident that is shrouded in mystery, though many believe that he was poisoned.

Another Delta great who didn't make his best recordings until well after the early '30s was Bukka White. White, yet another guitarist who had met and been influenced by Charley Patton, actually made his recording debut in 1930 as a religious singer. His best music, however, dates from a 1940 session in Chicago. White's rhythmic guitar approach, tough lyrical attitude (he was fresh from a stint in Mississippi's notorious Parchman Farm), and accompaniment from Washboard Sam gave his music a hard-driving force. Combined with the fact that the fidelity on these sides is somewhat better than the more primitive recordings of the late '20s and '30s, this makes White's brand of Delta blues more accessible to many contemporary listeners than much of what was recorded a decade or so earlier.

The Delta blues, of course, didn't die just because it wasn't being recorded often. In the early 1940s, Muddy Waters was recorded for the Library of Congress by folklorist Alan Lomax, playing in an acoustic Delta style. Just a few years later, Waters would be bringing Delta blues into the electric age after moving to Chicago, using some of the same sources for songs, and playing guitar in a similar (but amplified) style. He was merely the most famous of the musicians who did so; others included Johnny Shines, Robert Nighthawk, John Lee Hooker, Howlin' Wolf, and Elmore James.

The Delta bluesmen that had never electrified, and never recorded after the 1930s, had seemingly vanished into the corridors of time. Until the early 1960s, that is, when young enthusiasts, fired by a revival of interest in the blues, determined to trace and track down survivors from the era. They found a lot more than they could have hoped for, both in the way of living embodiments of old blues traditions, and actual blues singers from the Delta who were known only as names on rare 78s.

Skip James, Son House, and Bukka White were all rediscovered in this fashion, and launched new recording and performing careers based around the folk circuit and the LP market. There were also discoveries of elderly guitarists who had never recorded in the first place, some of whom also began professional careers, Mississippi Fred McDowell being the most successful. All of them played to far greater audiences in their old age than they had in their prime, often touring internationally, providing one of the music industry's too-rare tales of cosmic justice.

Many listeners who have never heard bona fide Delta blues have been exposed to it indirectly via rock covers, particularly Cream's versions of Robert Johnson's "Cross Road Blues" (retitled "Crossroads") and Skip James' "I'm So Glad." The Rolling Stones did Robert Johnson's "Love In Vain" and Mississippi Fred McDowell's "I've Got to Move," and explored the Delta blues style with considerable success on albums like *Beggar's Banquet* and *Let It Bleed* in the late '60s. Bonnie Raitt toured with McDowell in his final years, and openly credited him as a major influence. Canned Heat and Captain Beefheart were two of the most prominent rock acts of the late '60s that delved into the Delta for much of their inspiration.

The surprise success of Robert Johnson's box set, which sold several hundred thousand copies in the early 1990s, supplied proof that the original article will continue to enthrall audiences. This in turn greased the wheels for the reissue of many other compilations of early Delta blues, helping to ensure that the sound–which can still be heard as a living music in pockets of the actual Delta–will not be forgotten by subsequent generations.

—Richie Unterberger

10 Recommended Albums:

Various Artists, *Blues Masters Vol. 8: Mississippi Delta Blues* (Rhino)
Robert Johnson, *The Complete Recordings* (CBS)
Skip James, *The Complete Early Recordings* (Yazoo)
Various Artists, *Roots of Robert Johnson* (Yazoo)
Charley Patton, *Founder of the Delta Blues* (Yazoo)
Tommy Johnson, *Complete Recorded Works* (Document)
Bukka White, *The Complete Bukka White* (Columbia)
Muddy Waters, *The Complete Plantation Recordings* (MCA)
Son House, *Delta Blues: The Original Library of Congress Sessions from Field Recordings 1941–42* (Biograph)
Mississippi Fred McDowell, *Mississippi Delta Blues* (Arhoolie)

PIEDMONT BLUES

Although Mississippi Delta blues may be the most renowned style of early acoustic blues, guitar-based forms of acoustic blues also thrived elsewhere. One of the most fertile regions was the Piedmont, the southeastern area of the United States stretching from Richmond, VA, to Atlanta, GA. It encompasses music made both in the Appalachian foothills and big cities. Atlanta, base of Blind Willie McTell, Barbecue Bob, and others, was the most active urban center of southeastern blues (early Atlanta blues, it should be noted, is sometimes associated by authorities with the Piedmont style, but sometimes not specifically affiliated with it, or simply grouped in with southeastern regional sounds as a whole).

Styles could vary considerably within this region, but they were often distinguished from other blues recorded in the 1920s and 1930s by a more rhythmic base, and an emphasis on finger-picking style of guitar playing. As Barry Lee Pearson explained in a previous edition of *The All Music Guide*, "The Piedmont guitar style employs a complex fingerpicking style in which a regular, alternating-thumb bass pattern supports a melody on treble strings. The guitar style is highly syncopated and connnects closely with an earlier string-band tradition integrating ragtime, blues, and country dance songs. It's excellent party music with a full, rock-solid sound."

The relatively large numbers of blind guitarists from this region that recorded–Blind Blake, Blind Boy Fuller, and Blind Willie McTell being the most famous–is less surprising when considering the daunting career prospects facing blind African-Americans of the era. Certainly they wouldn't be able to work at

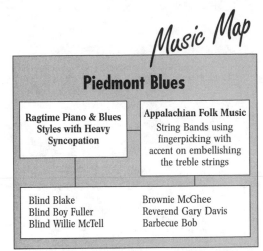

Music Map

Piedmont Blues

Ragtime Piano & Blues Styles with Heavy Syncopation	Appalachian Folk Music String Bands using fingerpicking with accent on embellishing the treble strings
Blind Blake Blind Boy Fuller Blind Willie McTell	Brownie McGhee Reverend Gary Davis Barbecue Bob

most of the jobs available to Southern Blacks at the time, most of which involved unskilled and unskilled manual labor. The limited social services available to Blacks made the prospect of useful education unlikely. Playing for money in urban neighborhoods, if one had the skills to entertain and the wherewithal to survive on the streets, was actually one of the better options.

Several of the Piedmont bluesmen were instrumental virtuosos whose versatility could encompass other styles as well; Blind Willie McTell proved himself a master of the 12-string guitar, a relatively uncommon instrument in country blues. Ragtime styles were a particularly significant influence, much more so than they were in the Delta. The tone tended to be lighter than Delta blues as well, though as songwriters the Piedmont players were certainly capable of serious reflection.

Ruminating further on the distinction between Delta and southeastern styles in *The History of the Blues*, Francis Davis speculates that the region's economy was "more diverse than that of Mississippi, and this contributed to a greater diversity of musical styles ... there were fewer restrictions on black mobility than in either Mississippi or Texas, and consequently, a greater degree of interplay between Black and White musicians. The songs of such Atlantic Seaboard fingerpickers as Blind Blake, Blind Willie McTell, and Blind Boy Fuller were more geniunely songlike than their contemporaries in the Delta and the Southwest. These guitarists were relative sophisticates, with an intuitive grasp of passing chords offsetting a rhythmic conception anchored in older ragtime and minstrel songs."

Plenty of Piedmont blues was recorded in the late 1920s and early 1930s. But as in other pockets of the blues market, the Depression–and then the onset of World War II–meant that recording activity of blues singers from the area came to a virtual halt. The style didn't die, but it was rarely documented on record from the mid-1930s onwards. Blind Boy Fuller died in 1941, and Blind Blake vanished; Willie McTell did some more recording for both the Library of Congress and commercial labels, though by the end of World War II, his style was appreciated more widely by folklorists than the commercial audience.

The blues revival of the '60s paid much more attention to Delta blues than southeastern styles, but the Piedmont influence was felt in the successful, lengthy careers of Reverend Gary Davis and the duo of Brownie McGhee and Sonny Terry, all of whom were extremely popular with folk audiences. Performers of subsequent eras have also continued to dip into the repertoire of the Piedmont school, the most prominent example being the Allman Brothers' blues-rock adaptation of McTell's "Statesboro Blues."

—Richie Unterberger

8 Recommended Albums:

Blind Willie McTell, *The Definitive Blind Willie McTell* (Columbia)
Blind Blake, *Ragtime Guitar's Foremost Fingerpicker* (Yazoo)
Blind Boy Fuller, *Blind Boy Fuller* (Document)
Barbecue Bob, *Chocolate to the Bone* (Yazoo)

Music Map

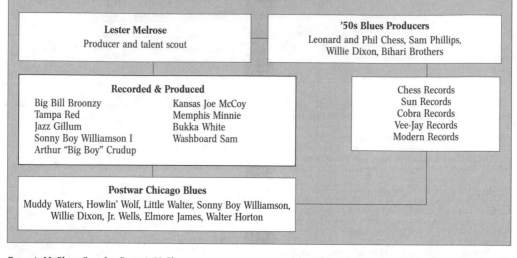

Lester Melrose & Early Chicago Blues

Lester Melrose
Producer and talent scout

'50s Blues Producers
Leonard and Phil Chess, Sam Phillips, Willie Dixon, Bihari Brothers

Recorded & Produced

Big Bill Broonzy
Tampa Red
Jazz Gillum
Sonny Boy Williamson I
Arthur "Big Boy" Crudup

Kansas Joe McCoy
Memphis Minnie
Bukka White
Washboard Sam

Chess Records
Sun Records
Cobra Records
Vee-Jay Records
Modern Records

Postwar Chicago Blues
Muddy Waters, Howlin' Wolf, Little Walter, Sonny Boy Williamson, Willie Dixon, Jr. Wells, Elmore James, Walter Horton

Brownie McGhee, *Complete Brownie McGhee* (Columbia/Legacy)
Reverend Gary Davis, *1935–49* (Yazoo)
Various Artists, *East Coast Blues, 1926–1935* (Yazoo)
Various Artists, *The Georgia Blues, 1927–33* (Yazoo)

LESTER MELROSE
& EARLY CHICAGO BLUES

Downhome Delta blues didn't mutate into Chicago electric blues overnight when Muddy Waters arrived on his train from Clarksdale, Mississippi in 1943. Even before Muddy had set foot in the city, Chicago had a thriving urban blues scene that did much to link country and urban styles. Much of the best blues to come out of the region in the 1930s and 1940s was recorded by one man, producer and A&R director Lester Melrose.

In the 1990s, with a record industry overstuffed with artists, producers, and corporate decision-makers from top to bottom, it's hard to imagine one person wielding as much influence as Melrose did at his peak. Two of the biggest labels in the world—Columbia and Victor—relied upon Melrose to develop much of the blues talent on its roster. (Victor placed these blues artists on a subsidiary, Bluebird.) The musicians that Melrose assembled read like a who's who of early blues, including Big Bill Broonzy, Tampa Red, Memphis Minnie, John Lee "Sonny Boy" Williamson, Big Joe Williams, Bukka White, Washboard Sam, and Arthur "Big Boy" Crudup.

Many of Melrose's artists came from rural backgrounds; you couldn't get much deeper into the Delta than Bukka White, whom Melrose recorded shortly after his release from a sentence at the notorious Parchman Farm. Melrose's chief contribution to modernizing the blues was to establish a sound with full band arrangements. With ensemble playing, a rhythm section, and even some electricity, these clearly prefigured the Chicago electric blues sound that would begin to explode in the late 1940s.

Comments Robert Palmer in *Deep Blues*, "Melrose's artists had downhome backgrounds: Tampa Red, a top-selling blues star since the late '20s, was from Georgia; John Lee 'Sonny Boy' Williamson, who was largely responsible for transforming the harmonica from an accompanying instrument into a major solo voice, was from Jackson, TN, just north of Memphis; Washboard Sam was from Arkansas; Big Bill Broonzy was a Mississippian by birth. But in the interests of holding onto their increasingly urbanized audience and pleasing Melrose, who was interested both in record sales and in lucrative publishing royalties, they recorded

several kinds of material, including jazz and novelty numbers, and began to favor band backing.

"During the mid-'30s the bands tended to be small–guitar and piano, sometimes a clarinet, a washboard, a string bass. But by the time Muddy arrived in Chicago, the 'Bluebird Beat,' as it has been called, was frequently carried by bass and drums. The music was a mixture of older black blues and vaudeville styles and material with the newer swing rhythms. Some of the records even featured popular Black jazzmen."

Melrose was the sort of all-around enterpreneur that was much more common in the early days of the music business. He was not just a producer in the sense of overseeing sessions, but also a talent scout and a song publisher. His involvement in the actual music, however, was substantial. He established a consistent sound for his productions by often using his artists to play on each other's records (often they would rehearse at Tampa Red's house). Washboard Sam, for instance, was often used to supply a percussive beat, even if (as on Bukka White's material) he was the sole accompanist. In this sense, too, Melrose helped establish prototypes for "house bands" that gave important labels like Chess an identifiable sound and led listeners to expect a certain artistic quality from a company's roster, rather than just a bunch of artists that all happened to play blues.

It didn't hurt, of course, that the musicians themselves were about as talented as any group that consistently worked for the same operation. For starters, there was the greatest early blues harmonica player in Sonny Boy Williamson I (not to be confused with the other great Sonny Boy Williamson, Rice Miller, who would later record for Chess); the best early woman blues singer/guitarist, Memphis Minnie; and Big Bill Broonzy, one of the most prolific songwriters of the pre-World War II era. He also did his part to push country blues into something approaching rock 'n' roll by recording Arthur "Big Boy" Crudup, whose "That's All Right Mama" was covered by Elvis Presley in 1954 for his first single.

Elvis would also turn in covers of Crudup's "My Baby Left Me" and "So Glad You're Mine" for two of his most exciting mid-'50s recordings. By that time, Melrose had been left in the dust by the rawer, louder, and far more electric Chicago blues sound that had been developed at Chess Records and elsewhere in the late 1940s and early 1950s. Ironically, Melrose had been the first to record Muddy Waters at a 1946 session, but Muddy really didn't find his voice in the studio until a couple of years later with Chess.

Melrose's assocation with Columbia and Victor had far-reaching consequences that ensured the preservation of his work for future generations, in ways that no one could have foreseen back in the 1930s and 1940s, when blues was recorded strictly for the "race" market. These powerful labels were still powerful players in the record industry 50 years later, when the compact disc began to take over from vinyl, and when the blues audience had expanded to include many Black and White collectors and enthusiasts. In the 1990s, much of the classic blues Melrose recorded has been reissued on CD. As a consequence it's far more widely available—and widely respected—than it's ever been before.

—*Richie Unterberger*

7 Recommended Albums:

Big Bill Broonzy, *Good Time Tonight* (CBS)
Memphis Minnie, *Hoodoo Lady (1933–37)* (CBS)
Tampa Red, *Guitar Wizard* (RCA)
Washboard Sam, *Rockin' My Blues Away* (RCA)
Bukka White, *The Complete Bukka White* (Columbia)
Sonny Boy Williamson I, *Throw a Boogie-Woogie (With Big Joe Williams)* (RCA)
Arthur "Big Boy" Crudup, *That's All Right Mama* (RCA)

CLASSIC WOMEN BLUES SINGERS

The image of the blues as a man hunched over his acoustic guitar in the Mississippi Delta–or, alternately, hunched over his electric axe or harmonica as he moans into a microphone at a sweaty club–is so ingrained in the collective consciousness that it comes as a shock to many to learn that the first blues stars were women. Indeed, women dominated the recorded blues field in the 1920s, the first decade in which a market for blues records existed. Except for the very most famous of these singers, these pioneers are largely forgotten today, having been retroactively surpassed in popularity by some Southern bluesmen who only recorded a precious handful of sides in the '20s and '30s. But these women were the performers who first took blues to a national audience.

The popularity of the early blueswomen was intimately tied to the birth of the recording industry itself. There were many kinds of nascent blues on the rise in the early 20th century–Delta guitarists, yes, but also songsters, jug bands, and dance bands that employed elements of jazz, blues, and pop. And there was the vaudeville stage circuit, which frequently featured women singers. Presenting productions that toured widely, the musicians involved couldn't help but be exposed to blues forms, if they hadn't been already.

It so happened that female-sung blues, with a prominent vaudeville-jazz-pop flavor, was the first kind of blues to be recorded for the popular audience. There are many possible reasons for this. Perhaps the record companies felt that other styles of blues were too raw to market. Or they may have been largely unaware of more rural and Southern blues styles. The female vaudevillian blues singers had a jazzier and more urban sound that commercial companies may have been more likely to encounter and stamp with approval.

What's far more certain is that "Crazy Blues," recorded by Mamie Smith in 1920, was the first commercial recording of what came to be recognized as the blues. By the standards of the day, the record was a phenomenal success, selling 75,000 copies within the first month–in an era, it must be remembered, when much of the U.S. population, and an even higher percentage of the U.S. African-American population, didn't own a record player. It set off an immediate storm of records in the same vein, by Smith and numerous other women.

But to today's listener, "Crazy Blues" hardly sounds like a blues at all. It sounds more like vaudeville, with a bit of the blues creeping into the edges of the vocal delivery and the song structure. The more judgmental might find that it resembles the music found in contemporary Broadway productions that offer a nostalgic facsimile of pre-Depression Black theater. The song has to be taken in the context of its era, however. It was the first time anything with some allegiance to the blues form had been recorded–and the industry quickly found that such productions were being bought not just by Blacks, but by all Americans.

Mamie Smith's success opened the floodgates for numerous blueswomen to record in the 1920s, often on the Okeh and Paramount labels. Ida Cox, Sippie Wallace, Victoria Spivey, Lucille Bogan, Ethel Waters, and Alberta Hunter are some of the most famous; there were many others. The best of them were Ma

Music Ma

Classic Women Blues Singers

Mamie Smith
"Crazy Blues" 1st Blues Record - 1920

Ida Cox, Sippie Wallace, Victoria Spivey, Lucille Bogan, Alberta Hunter	The Queens Bessie Smith Ma Rainey	Ethel Waters, Dinah Washington, Billie Holiday

Bonnie Raitt, Tracy Nelson, Janis Joplin

Rainey and Bessie Smith, both of whom had rawer, more emotional qualities that give their recordings a feel more akin to what later listeners expect of the blues.

Today, the early recordings by the "classic" female blues singers, as they have sometimes been labeled, sound as much or more like jazz as blues. The vocalists were usually accompanied by small jazz combos, often featuring piano, cornet, and other horn instruments. The guitar, the instrument associated with the blues more than any other, was frequently absent, and usually secondary when it was used. Lots of early jazz stars, in fact, can be heard on the early blueswomen's records, including Louis Armstrong, King Oliver, Duke Ellington, and Coleman Hawkins.

Yet the music *is* identifiable as blues, primarily via the vocal phrasing and the widespread use of the 12-bar song structures that are among the blues' most immediate trademarks. And it was not a form that thrived in isolation from the other styles of blues that were emerging throughout America. As top blues scholar Samuel Charters writes in his liner notes to *Blues Masters Volume 11: Classic Blues Women,* "Even the men living in the South and playing the blues for themselves and their neighbors learned many of their songs from the records that made their way down to local music stores or came through the post office from the mail-order blues companies in Chicago. If they didn't learn the songs themselves, they learned the form and the style of what the record companies thought of as the blues.

"So when the companies sent scouts to find new artists in the South, what they found were the same three or four ways of putting blues verses together. After the sweeping success of the first recordings by women blues artists, the 12-bar harmonic form on the records had become so ubiquitous that even the Delta players who only fingered a single chord on their guitars managed to suggest all the usual chord changes with their singing."

The blues could also be heard in the singers' frank discussions of topics like sex, infidelity, and money and drink problems, often with a palpable hurt. These were offered with a female perspective that has never been as widespread in the blues since, as the music came to be dominated by male performers after the Depression. Listeners from all eras can cut through the often scratchy recordings to find the seeds of the blues, and much modern pop music, in their depiction of hard times, and the struggle and endurance necessary to survive them. It's not all bleakness–the celebratory tunes could have a frank bawdiness, particularly when dealing with sexual double entendres, that would probably generate warning stickers if they were being purchased by today's teenagers.

The onset of the Depression meant hard times for the record business, as it did for every other industry. The craze for female blues singers, which may have already peaked in the mid-'20s, was over, and not just because of artistic trends. Record labels in general were recording less sides. And they weren't eager to devote a lot of resources to the "race" market, populated as it was the poorest Americans. These African-American listeners would have even less purchasing power in the 1930s, as the Depression lowered their already low standard of living.

But it wasn't just economic factors that heralded the demise of the classic women blues singers. Urban African-American music was becoming more uptempo and elaborate. The swing and big band sound came to fruition in the 1930s, making the staider accompaniment common to many '20s female blues recordings sound tame in comparison. And the vaudeville/theatrical circuit that supported the singers was crumbling, threatening their livelihood just years after they enjoyed positively unimaginable wealth (by the standards of African-Americans of the '20s). Many were unable to make records or, after a few years, even perform; the tale of Mamie Smith, who died penniless in 1946, is unfortunately not unique. Bessie Smith and Ma Rainey would themselves be dead by 1940.

It may be that many of the women who would have been blues singers had they started in the 1920s ended up as jazz ones. Jazz as a whole proved much more fruitful for women singers fronting a band than blues would in the ensuing decades. Billie Holiday, acclaimed by many as one of the finest singers of any kind in the 20th century, certainly owed a great deal to the female blues vocalists of the '20s. Several of her earlier sides in particular could just as well be classified as blues as jazz. The blues feel remained prominent in many if not most of the major female jazz singers, from Dinah Washington to Cassandra Wilson.

The original female blues stars of the '20s didn't always disappear entirely. Alberta Hunter, for instance, if anything became more popular after the 1920s, and made an unexpectedly successful comeback as a senior citizen in the 1970s and 1980s, after about 25 years of retirement. Ethel Waters expanded into jazz, and then into movies, getting an Academy Award nominiation for Best Supporting Actress for a 1949 film. Victoria Spivey, returning to active recording in the 1960s, started her own label; Bob Dylan made his first appearance on an official recording for the company, playing harmonica on a Big Joe Williams session.

The blues revival of the 1960s, however, largely passed the classic female blues singers by, though Sippie Wallace did record an album with the Jim Kweskin Jug Band. The vocalists were a considerable influence on pioneering '60s rock singers Janis Joplin and Tracy Nelson (who recorded an entire album of Ma Rainey and Bessie Smith songs in her folkie days), thereby influencing rock performers who had never heard the originals. In any case, the styles that the early women blues singers brought to record had by then infiltrated all of blues, rock, soul, and pop, to be heard in almost everyone from Aretha Franklin on down.

—*Richie Unterberger*

10 Recommended Albums:

Various Artists, *Blues Masters, Vol. 11: Classic Blues Women* (Rhino)
Bessie Smith, *The Collection* (CBS)
Ma Rainey, *Ma Rainey* (Milestone)
Sippie Wallace, *1923–29* (Alligator)
Victoria Spivey, *1926–31* (Document)
Mamie Smith, *In Chronological Order, Vol. 1* (Document)
Lucille Bogan, *1923–35* (Story of Blues)
Alberta Hunter, *Young Alberta Hunter* (Vintage Jazz)
Ethel Waters, *Jazzin' Babies' Blues, 1921–1927* (Biograph)
Various Artists, *Women's Railroad Blues: Sorry But I Can't Take You* (Rosetta)

JUMP BLUES

The currents of jazz and blues may have run closer together in the 1940s than they did in any other decade. One of the biggest offshoots of this cross-breeding was jump blues, a form that thrived in the late 1940s and early 1950s in particular. With its rhythmic swing, boisterous vocalists, and often lighthearted songs about partying, drinking, and jiving, it hasn't lent itself as extensively to critical analysis as styles like rural Delta guitarists or electric Chicago blues. During the decade or so when it thrived, however, it laid much of the groundwork for what became known as rhythm and blues, and thus by extension rock 'n' roll.

The roots of jump blues, like many popular styles that became widespread in the middle of the 20th century, can be traced to larger trends of social modernization. In the 1940s, the large big

bands of the 1930s scaled back into smaller combos, partially because of economic considerations (particularly during World War II) that made supporting a large ensemble difficult. There were still plenty of African-American patrons for dance halls, however, who wanted a sound that was both danceable and loud. This led many swing bands to place a greater emphasis on honking saxophones and hard-driving vocalists who could be heard over the din, often categorized after the event as "honkers and shouters."

There were many notable forerunners of the jump blues sound to be heard in the jazz community of the 1930s. Pianists like Meade Lux Lewis, Albert Ammons, and Jimmy Yancey devised boogie-woogie patterns; singers like Slim Gaillard and Cab Calloway sang hipster lyrics (sometimes dubbed "jive") with links to both blues and pop traditions. The midwestern cities of Kansas City and St. Louis acted as incubators for the jump blues scene, with their heritage of hot swing bands with vocalists that were open to the influence of the blues.

As Peter Grendysa writes in his liner notes to Rhino's *Blues Masters, Vol. 5: Jump Blues Classics*, "The antiphonal (call-and-response) characteristic of African music so evident in country blues and gospel was adapted by jump blues, often with the voice of the saxophone played against the vocalist, who shouted rather than sang the lyrics. The saxophone was played wth athletic power and exuberance; the saxman squeezing out honks, bleats, and squeals to the delight of the crowds and the dismay of traditional jazz fans. Strong backbeats were provided by the drummer's snares and rim shots on the second and fourth beats of every bar and reinforced by the bass player marking every beat."

Some of the first performers to sing in a readily identifiable jump blues style were very grounded in the jazz world. Big Joe Turner, one of the few performers to bridge the jazz, R&B, and rock 'n' roll eras, had been singing jazz since the late 1930s, even appearing at the famed Spirituals to Swing concert in 1938 at New York's Carnegie Hall. Turner may be more responsible than anyone else for founding the "shouting" school of R&B singing, emphasizing smooth but commanding vocal presence. Based (like Turner) in Kansas City, bandleader Jay McShann may be most famous for cultivating the talents of the young Charlie Parker, but he also did his part to create jump blues by employing Walter Brown, another of the earliest shouters.

The most influential architect of jump blues, however–indeed, one of the more significant figures in 20th century American music–was alto saxophonist and singer Louis Jordan. After serving in Chick Webb's band in the 1930s, he formed his own outfit, the Tympany Five. In the mid- and late-1940s, he ran off an astonishing series of R&B hits that set much of the tone for the jump blues genre, especially the fast, danceable rhythms and the joking, novelty-tinged lyrics–traits that did not pass unnoticed by Chuck Berry. Jordan was also a rock 'n' roll forefather in that he was one of the first R&B performers to make significant inroads into the pop and White audiences.

Jump blues really began exploding commercially after World War II, as America got set to relax and party after years of contributing to the war effort, as jazz headed off in directions less conducive to dancing, and as large numbers of African-Americans moved from the country to the city, taking some of the country blues tradition with them. The West Coast, particularly Los Angeles, was a hotbed of jump blues/proto-R&B. There was a large Black community (many recent arrivals), and large numbers of small combo bands looking to survive the transition from big bands to earthier small ones. And there were new independent labels cropping up–Specialty, Modern, Aladdin, Swingtime–that saw a niche for Black popular music that was being ignored by the majors.

Los Angeles in particular was a breeding ground for the saxophonists that would become known as the honkers–musicians who got a grainy, squealing tone and summon frenetic bursts of notes on the uptempo tunes. They were often great showmen in concert as well, playing on their backs sometimes to whip the crowds into more frenzy. Illinois Jacquet had set a model of sorts for the style on his classic soloing on Lionel Hampton's huge hit "Flying Home" and his work on the live Norman Granz Jazz At The Philharmonic recordings, which introduced a few elements that would become widespread in R&B and rock 'n' roll. Big Jay McNeely, Joe Houston, and Chuck Higgins were some of the most noteworthy saxophonists of the style, sometimes doing without

Music Map

Jump Blues

Small Jazz Combos '30s &'40s
Louis Armstrong Hot Five/Hot
Seven, Benny Goodman
Trio/Quartet/Sextet,
Count Basie's Kansas City Six

Big Bands with a Beat
Count Basie, Chick Webb,
Benny Goodman, Lionel Hampton,
Cab Calloway, Louis Prima

Boogie-Woogie Piano
Meade Lux Lewis,
Cow Cow Davenport,
Cripple Clarence Loston,
Albert Ammons, Jimmy Yancey

The Piano Players
Nat "King" Cole Trio,
Charles Brown, Amos Milburn,
Sammy Price

**Louis Jordan &
His Tympani Five**
*Most innovative and successful
jump blues combo of all time*

Jump Blues as Rock 'n' Roll
Louis Prima w/ Sam Butera,
Chuck Berry,
Bill Haley & the Comets

The Ladies
Wynona Carr, Camille Howard,
Big Mama Thornton, Ruth Brown,
Faye Adams, Lavern Baker,
Ann Cole, Big Maybelle

Honkers & Shouters
Big Jay McNeely, Big Joe Turner,
Joe Houston, Sam "the Man" Taylor,
Wynonie Harris, Roy Brown,
Red Prysock, Bullmoose Jackson,
Nappy Brown, Billy Wright

The Bands
Tiny Bradshaw, Roy Milton,
Joe Liggins, Jimmy Liggins,
Johnny Otis

vocals entirely, the sheer bravado of their solos being enough to build their studio tracks around.

The West Coast favored an urbane brand of jump blues that owed much to jazz. Electric guitar pioneer T-Bone Walker is usually thought of as a bluesman, but certainly his 1940s recordings–which are usually pegged as his best and most influential–incorporated a lot from jazz and jump blues. Though not a bluesman per se, Nat King Cole in his early days would approach a jump blues mood, and traces of his suave charm can be found in many 1940s jump blues sides.

Several West Coast bandleaders had a lot of success in the late 1940s with a sort of polished grit. On Specialty Records alone, there was Joe Liggins, his brother Jimmy, and Roy Milton. Milton, though only a hazily remembered figure, was a huge star in his day, landing well over a dozen singles in the R&B Top Ten in the late 1940s and early 1950s. His pianist, Camille Howard, was a notable recording artist in her own right, and a premier example of a jazz-boogie performer who seemed to have gotten dragged into the R&B world more by happenstance and the forces of historical change than anything else. Johnny Otis would organize a lot of L.A. talent as a bandleader, vocalist, talent scout, promoter, label owner, and general all-around champion of the scene.

The boogie-woogie-derived structure of much jump blues lent itself well to pianists, and several of the best jump blues singers also excelled at the keyboards. Prominent among them were Amos Milburn, who could handle both Charles Brown-ish ballads and rowdy songs about drinking, and Floyd Dixon, famous as the originator of "Hey Bartender," served to the masses decades later via the Blues Brothers. For those who liked their jump blues a bit rougher, there were the pre-eminent shouters, Roy Brown and Wynonie Harris. Both of them had big R&B hits with "Good Rockin' Tonight," and both were influences upon Elvis Presley, who would make the tune his second Sun single. Jump blues also had more room for female participation than many other blues sub-genres, with Camille Howard and Wynona Carr both scoring substantial successes for Specialty, and R&B-based singers like Big Maybelle and Big Mama Thornton recording singles heavily indebted to the style.

There were an enormous number of jump blues records cut between 1945 and 1955, and a brief survey of some of the most

famous pianists, bandleaders, saxophonists, shouters, and women singers still leaves out a great many names that are treasured by blues and R&B fans. Just to scratch the surface, you could mention shouter Nappy Brown, Tiny Bradshaw (who did the original version of "The Train Kept A-Rollin'"), Red Prysock, Bullmoose Jackson, the pre-Atlantic recordings of Ray Charles, and Billy Wright (the last of whom was Little Richard's chief early inspiration). The Savoy label alone recorded enough singers, briefly and extensively, to generate numerous various artist compilations.

Yet by the mid-'50s, the jump blues style was definitely on the wane. It was a story that has repeated itself numerous times throughout the history of pop–a whole school of stylists, seemingly at its peak, was swept aside by a horde of younger and rawer upstarts. It wasn't just a few Elvis Presleys and Little Richards, though–it was the whole tidal wave of rock 'n' roll.

Certainly the dividing line between jump blues and R&B is a very fine one. A transitional figure like Jackie Brenston, for instance, could fall into either camp. Early sides by Atlantic R&B artists like Ruth Brown and LaVerne Baker sometimes owed a lot to jump blues and the same could be said of early rock instrumentalists like Bill Doggett. And many early doo-wop sides have a lot of jump blues in them–listen to Drifters tracks like "Fools Fall In Love" or "Such a Night" for the evidence. But the hard fact was that R&B, and its close relation rock 'n' roll, had dropped much of the jazz and boogie-woogie so prominent in jump blues. The most raucous sounds of its saxophones were retained, but there was progressively more emphasis on electric guitars, group vocals, and younger performers with a greater appeal to teenagers.

By 1956, most of the jump blues stars were scuffling for survival. Some adapted to the rock 'n' roll era with some success, most notably Joe Turner and Johnny Otis; others tried to adapt to rock 'n' roll trends unsuccessfully, like Roy Brown and even Louis Jordan. There were a few, like Turner and Jimmy Witherspoon, who could slide back into the jazz world if they wished, having never strayed far from it in the first place. Sometimes an old star would surface unexpectedly like Amos Milburn, who had a surprise tenure with Motown in the early 1960s.

Unless you're a devoted collector or scholar, it can seem as though most jump blues greats have vanished into a black hole of history. Perhaps that's because the form bridged blues, jazz,

R&B, and pop, without quite fitting into any of the forms comfortably. Another factor is the general absence of hot guitar solos, a general touchstone for most modern fans connecting with older forms of blues.

Jump blues, however, is blues at its most fun–a call to arms not to bewail tribulations or reflect upon the abyss, but to let loose, wail, and party. In the bargain, it was probably *the* most important foundation for what became known in the 1950s as R&B, and gave us much of the rhythm and humor that we take for granted in contemporary rock, blues, and soul.

—*Richie Unterberger & Cub Koda*

12 Recommended Albums:

Various Artists, *Blues Masters Vol. 5: Jump Blues Classics* (Rhino)
Various Artists, *Blues Masters Vol. 14: More Jump Blues* (Rhino)
Big Joe Turner, *Big, Bad & Blue: The Joe Turner Anthology* (Rhino)
Louis Jordan, *The Best of Louis Jordan* (MCA)
Roy Milton, *Roy Milton & His Solid Senders* (Specialty)
T-Bone Walker, *The Complete Capitol Black & White Recordings* (Capitol)
Amos Milburn, *Down the Road Apiece: The Best of Amos Milburn* (EMI)
Joe Houston, *Cornbread and Cabbage Greens* (Specialty)
Floyd Dixon, *Marshall Texas is My Home* (Specialty)
Roy Brown, *Good Rocking Tonight: The Best of Roy Brown* (Rhino)
Wynonie Harris, *Bloodshot Eyes: The Best of Wynonie Harris* (Rhino)
Various Artists, *The Original Johnny Otis Show* (Savoy)

LOUISIANA BLUES

Long hailed as the birthplace of jazz, and a crucible of all kinds of roots sounds, New Orleans has influenced the course of American music as much as any other city. It does not, however, loom as large in the history of the blues as one might expect. Certainly regions like Chicago, Memphis, and the Mississippi Delta have produced many more performers of note; each of those areas also has a far more distinctive blues style. New Orleans is much more the champion of old-school jazz and funky rhythm and blues. But the city, and the state of Louisiana, have made some estimable contributions to the history of blues, even if these are somewhat harder to finger and pigeonhole than many others.

As Robert Palmer muses in *Deep Blues*, "It seems strange that New Orleans, the metropolis at the mouth of the Mississippi River, didn't attract more Delta bluesmen. Rice Miller and Elmore James performed there frequently during the '40s, playing in the streets before they graduated to club engagements, and other Mississippi bluesmen paid occasional visits. But New Orleans had its own indigenous brand of blues, a jazz-oriented style that had more to do with Texas and Kansas City music than with the Delta and often made use of the Afro-Caribbean rhythm patterns that have survived in the city's folklore since the celebrated slave gatherings that took place in Congo Square."

Not that deep blues was totally unknown in the region. Whatever vestiges of country blues may have remained in the area after World War II can be heard, at least in part, on *Bloodstains on the Wall: Country Blues From Specialty*, a compilation of performances recorded by the L.A.-based label in New Orleans. And some of the most traditional styles of Louisiana blues may have been preserved on sessions by Robert Pete Williams, who was recorded by folklorist Harry Oster in the Louisiana State Penitentiary in the late 1950s (Williams went on to make other records as well after his release from prison).

The most significant urban blues to originate from the city, however, was recorded in 1953 by Guitar Slim, who originally hailed from the Delta. "The Things That I Used To Do," one of the biggest R&B hits of 1954, was Slim's definitive statement, as much gospel/R&B as blues, with the spiritual, funky feel that characterizes much New Orleans music. It's been speculated that the bandleader on the session, a young Ray Charles, was inspired to try a similar fusion of the gospel and secular on his own records as a result of the record's enormous success. The blues factor of Guitar Slim's equation, though, was unmistakable in his electric guitar work, which by the standards of the time was unimaginably hard and fuzzy.

Most New Orleans R&B of the '50s could not be comfortably classified as blues, as Guitar Slim was. With its funky rhythms and pop/jazz influences, it looked forward to rock 'n' roll (or indeed *was* rock 'n' roll) and soul music much more than it looked to blues roots. The line between blues and R&B can get thin, of course, as it does with jump blues; many if not most of the great New Orleans R&B/rock performers had a bluesy feel. None of this should obscure the fact that whatever it's called, it's a mammoth body of great music, available on numerous reissues.

Some Crescent City artists were bluesier than others, though, one of the most famous being pianist Professor Longhair, a beloved figure who symbolizes New Orleans music to many listeners. A similar but more obscure figure is James Booker who, like Longhair, had a career renaissance in the '70s and '80s. For guitarists, you could check out Snooks Eaglin, who, in the songster tradition, led simultaneous careers as a commercial New

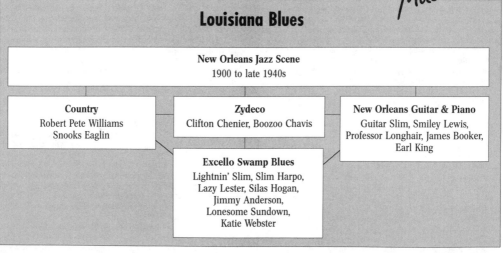

Louisiana Blues

Music Map

New Orleans Jazz Scene
1900 to late 1940s

Country
Robert Pete Williams
Snooks Eaglin

Zydeco
Clifton Chenier, Boozoo Chavis

New Orleans Guitar & Piano
Guitar Slim, Smiley Lewis,
Professor Longhair, James Booker,
Earl King

Excello Swamp Blues
Lightnin' Slim, Slim Harpo,
Lazy Lester, Silas Hogan,
Jimmy Anderson,
Lonesome Sundown,
Katie Webster

Orleans R&B artist (for Imperial) and an acoustic blues/folk singer (for Prestige, Arhoolie, and other labels). Imperial was also responsible for recording some West Coast blues artists in New Orleans with hopes of reviving their flagging careers, including Roy Brown and Pee Wee Crayton. New Orleans guitar blues was kept alive through the '60s by Earl King, who flavored his touch with rock and soul, a combination appreciated by Jimi Hendrix, who covered King's "Come On."

A more distinctive Louisiana blues sound, that of "swamp" blues, was produced elsewhere in the state by Baton Rouge artists Slim Harpo, Lightnin' Slim, Silas Hogan, Lonesome Sundown, and Lazy Lester. All of them recorded under the direction of Crowley, Louisiana producer Jay Miller, producing a unique blues sound and style characterized by lazy beats, relaxed vocals, doom-laden reverberant production, trebly guitar work, odd percussion effects, and wailing harmonica. Slim Harpo was the greatest of these figures, and his compelling combinations of snaky guitar riffs and raw harmonica blasts were a huge influence on several British Invasion bands. Indeed, he spun a virtual catalog of material that would be covered by U.K. groups, including "I'm a King Bee" and "Shake Your Hips" (the Rolling Stones), "Got Love If You Want It" (the Kinks and Yardbirds), "Don't Start Crying Now" (Them), and "Raining in My Heart" (the Pretty Things); Slim himself made a well-deserved entry into the Top Twenty in 1966 with "Baby Scratch My Back." Although not from Louisiana originally, pianist Katie Webster also made her mark on swamp blues, as a session musician for Jay Miller and a sporadic recording artist on her own.

New Orleans is a famed melting pot of sounds and cultures, and one of its most distinctive regional musics, zydeco, certainly owes a visible debt to the blues. Performers such as Clifton Chenier, Boozoo Chavis, and Rockin' Dopsie are in the main beyond the scope of this book, as they draw from cajun, pop, R&B, and folk sources more than blues to devise their rhythmic brew. The best of them are certainly worth checking out, however, as an interesting branch of the roots music tree with definite ties to the blues in the phrasing and some of the rhythms and songs.

Although blues does not have as extensive a tradition in New Orleans as it does in some other cities, it's better positioned to thrive in the area these days than in most other parts of the country, simply because the region has an extensive support system for locally performed roots music. That's true at both the club/juke-joint level and internationally renowned festivals; the annual New Orleans Jazz & Blues Festival features carloads of blues performers from all over (in addition to numerous other jazz, R&B, and rock acts). Family connections to the music seemed to have endured better in Louisiana than some other regions, and performers like Guitar Slim Jr., Kenny Neal (son of Raful), and Chris Thomas (son of Tabby) have all kept the blues flame burning with recent recordings.

—Richie Unterberger

14 Recommended Albums:

Various Artists, *Bloodstains on the Wall: Country Blues From Specialty* (Specialty)
Robert Pete Williams, *Those Prison Blues* (Arhoolie)
Guitar Slim, *Sufferin' Mind* (Specialty)
Professor Longhair, *Fess: Professor Longhair Anthology* (Rhino)
Slim Harpo, *Hip Shakin': The Excello Collection* (Rhino)
Snooks Eaglin, *The Complete Imperial Recordings* (Capitol)
Lightnin' Slim, *Rooster Blues* (Excello)
Lazy Lester, *I Hear You Knockin'* (Excello)
Lonesome Sundown, *I'm A Mojo Man* (Excello)
Silas Hogan, *Trouble* (Excello)
Katie Webster, *Katie Webster* (Paula)
Clifton Chenier, *Zydeco Dynamite: The Clifton Chenier Anthology* (Rhino)
Various Artists, *Alligator Stomp Vol. 1–3* (Rhino)
Various Artists, *Crescent City Soul: The Sound of New Orleans 1947–1974* (EMI)

HARMONICA BLUES

Perhaps there is something special about free reeds (harmonica, accordion, concertina) that appeals to the human ear and soul–the sounds made when air rushes over a metal reed. The blues

harp can have an intensity that reaches right past any personality barriers and grabs at the feelings like few instruments can. The plaintive wail of an acoustic harp (harmonica) and the powerful intensity of amplified harmonica are important sounds that are featured in the blues tradition.

Since the blues became amplified and electrified, the harmonica has been a staple for many bands–not as ubiquitous as the guitar, perhaps, but more the rule than the exception. The instrument has often served a horn-like function in the blues combo (giving rise to its nickname as the "Mississippi saxophone"), producing the sorts of full-bodied, grainy sounds that are nigh impossible to manufacture from string instruments.

Prior to World War II, the harmonica was not as prominent an instrument in live or recorded blues, and certainly very secondary in comparison to guitars and pianos. To get a facsimile of horn-like fullness, early blues recordings were apt to use other instruments; the kazoo was often employed on the records of jug bands (although Noah Lewis' work with Cannon's Jug Stompers are some of the earliest–and finest–recorded examples of blues harmonica on disc), and pan quill pipes were sometimes used, a famous example being Henry Thomas' "Bull Doze Blues" (which was remade into a pop hit by Canned Heat in the late '60s as "Going Up the Country"). The mysterious George "Bullet" Williams appears to be one of the first harmonica players to be recorded in the '20s before disappearing into the mists of time. DeFord Bailey was an extremely popular harmonica virtuoso in the 1920s and 1930s via his frequent appearances on the Grand Old Opry, though he was not solely a blues player, performing country and folk tunes as well. Sonny Terry may have been the most notable country blues harmonica man, later finding favor with the blues/folk crossover audience, both in his long-standing partnership with guitarist Brownie McGhee and his work as accompanist to artists like Leadbelly.

The man who did the most to popularize the instrument as well as linking country and urban blues together was undoubtedly John Lee "Sonny Boy" Williamson, now forever listed in the history books as Sonny Boy Williamson I. His use of "choked" notes and wah-wah hand effects, coupled with great songwriting and swinging vocals, made him the first great star of the instrument. His influence spread through the blues community like wildfire, spawning a raft of acolytes and making him literally one of the godfathers of the postwar Chicago scene. His recordings from the 1930s and 1940s popularized songs that would resurface in the repertoires of major Chicago blues stars like Junior Wells and Muddy Waters. His stabbing death in 1948 robbed the blues of one of its true original voices.

The reason for the numerical appendage to John Lee's name can be directly traced to a bit of chicanery involving a Mississippi blues harp genius named Rice Miller. Traversing the South in the '30s and '40s as Little Boy Blue, Miller worked with Robert Johnson, a young Howlin' Wolf and myriad others, living the hard life of an itinerant bluesman. When the Interstate Grocers Association decided to broadcast him live on the King Biscuit Time radio show on KFFA from Helena, Arkansas, they decided to change his name into something more recognizable to blues listeners. After the senseless death of Williamson (who never toured the South, but whose records were nonetheless enormously popular), Miller became "the original" Sonny Boy Williamson; blues reference works now differentiate between the two men by referring to Miller as Sonny Boy Williamson II. Sonny Boy II (actually older than John Lee by about 15 years) did a lot to popularize harmonica blues with his broadcasts in the 1940s and with his first recordings for the Trumpet label in the early '50s, the popularity of both eventually luring him north to Chicago where he became one of the shining jewels in the Chess Records blues crown.

But with the rise of the electric sound on the Chicago blues scene, the man who really changed it all was Little Walter, who is still acknowledged as the top virtuoso of blues harmonica. Walter Jacobs occupies a position in the history of the blues harmonica comparable to Charlie Parker's in the history of the jazz saxophone, or Jimi Hendrix's in the history of rock guitar. It was Walter, more than anyone else, who was responsible for establishing the basic vocabulary of the instrument, especially as it's used in electric blues bands.

A professional musician from about the time he entered his teenage years, Walter's arrival in Chicago in the late '40s found

Blues Harp (Harmonica): A Short History *Music Map*

Acoustic Beginnings (Chordal Harp)
Early acoustic harp included training whistle,
vaudeville, ragtime, jazz

Jug Memphis Bands
Will Shade, Gus Cannon,
Jug Stompers, with Noah Lewis

Grand Old Opry Radio with DeFord Bailey
Sonny Terry, foremost folk/blues acoustic players

John Lee Sonny Boy Williamson I
Major influence in the transition from chordal harp
to its use as a melodic-line-oriented, lead instrument

Down-Home Electric
Jimmy Reed, Dr. Isiah Ross

Sonny Boy Williamson II
(Rice Miller) An original blues giant with a unique
sound, and a touch of country never far away

Rhythm & Blues
Slim Harpo, Raful Neal, Lazy Lester

Urban Harps
Buster Brown, Mofo Buford, Frank Frost,
George Harmonica Smith.

Muddy Waters Blues Band
Muddy Waters was the Miles Davis of the blues. Almost every major harp player worked in his band–
even Junior Wells and Walter Horton. Yet is was Little Walter who set the tone for what became the
high-powered Chicago blues sound.

Big Walter Horton
Perhaps the most beautiful
of all harp players

Little Walter
High-intensity Chicago harp
at its best

Junior Wells
Outstanding funky blues

Great Younger Harp Players

James Cotton
The last of Muddy's great players

Paul Butterfield
The finest early White player

Phil Wiggins
Modern acoustic country harp

Charlie Musselwhite
Fine early White player

William Clarke
One of the best White players
today

Carey Bell
Good modern player

Jerry Portnoy
with Muddy Waters

Billy Branch
Aggressive young modern player

James Harman, Gary Primich,
Rod Piazza, King Biscuit Boy,
Paul deLay

---

him playing for tips on Maxwell Street in the then-popular style of Sonny Boy I. By the early '50s however, all of that changed, with Walter being one of the first to start amplifying his harp. Armed with a cheap microphone, cupping his hands over it to create incredible amounts of distortion through his amplifier, and taking rhythmic cues from jump blues and jazz, Little Walter popularized the sound most people associate with amplified blues harp. The volume and power increased when he began to record in the studio, first as a part of Muddy Waters' band on a brace of influential sides, and then (after his 1952 hit "Juke") as a solo artist. Walter also used several different kinds of harmonica to increase his sonic range, often alternating between a standard harp and a more complex chromatic one (sometimes in mid-song) that gave him a greater variety of tones and note choices.

In the original edition of *The Rolling Stone Record Guide*, John Swenson summed up Walter's mammoth significance well: "Every harmonica player after Little Walter has in some way been influenced by his style, especially rock players, from John Mayall to Magic Dick of the J. Geils Band. Jacobs was able to take hard bop melodic ideas from contemporary saxophonists and match them to a simpler but more forceful blues rhythm with heavily emphasized guitar parts, suggesting a further link between bop-era jazz players and rock 'n' roll. The Little Walter harmonica style thus transposed saxophone ideas into terms compatible with and influential on guitars." Not to be overlooked are his considerable talents as a songwriter, singer, and sideman, all of which helped make him one of the true greats of early electric Chicago blues.

Not as well-known as Little Walter was, no overview of blues harmonica greats could be considered complete without an equal nod to the "other Walter," the magnificent Big Walter Horton. Playing from the time he was a mere child, Horton was a fixture on the Memphis music scene, playing with everyone from semi-pro jug bands to the earliest electric combos. Several reports have Horton actually blowing amplified harp in the late '40s and the younger Jacobs learned much from the older musician when the two met up in Chicago in the early '50s. Capable of blowing with a sweet lyricism one moment and astonishing power the next, his style owed no stylistic debt to anyone and he could play both unamplified and electric styles with ease. The effect of Big Walter's harp is always soothing, slowing and opening up the time and the mind.

Most of the great Chicago electric blues harmonica players served at one time or another in the band of Muddy Waters. Little Walter, James Cotton, Junior Wells, the wonderful George "Harmonica" Smith, and Walter Horton all played and recorded with him in the '50s and early '60s. Cotton and Wells especially were successful in establishing careers as bandleaders in the 1960s, playing in styles which effectively drew from contemporary rock and soul influences. Each of them were only a little younger than Little Walter, but the king of the blues harmonica went into a sad decline in the 1960s that saw increasingly sporadic and unimpressive recordings before his death, at the age of 37, in 1968 in a street fight.

The harmonica was a more established presence in the blues of Chicago than anywhere else, and the city was home to several other notable players. Billy Boy Arnold cut some great singles for Vee-Jay records in the 1950s, and also made important contributions to rock 'n' roll as a sideman on some of Bo Diddley's early records. Some Chicago blues greats who were not really identified primarily as harmonica players could use the instrument effectively, like Jimmy Reed and Howlin' Wolf. Compilations like Sun Records Harmonica Classics, which features '50s blues recorded in Memphis, serve notice that not all harmonica blues of note originated from Chicago, and the country blues sounds of Joe Hill Louis and the one-man band of Doctor Ross offer a decided change of pace from the more pervasive Windy City sounds. Another stylistic strain also worth investigating is the swamp blues sound from Louisiana, with Slim Harpo and Lazy Lester being its two best-known exponents.

As Chicago blues was an enormous influence upon R&B-oriented British Invasion bands, it's no surprise that many U.K. rock groups of the '60s featured members (usually the lead vocalists) who were reasonably proficient on the instrument. It's not often noted, but singers like Mick Jagger, Keith Relf (of the Yardbirds), John Mayall, Van Morrison, and Paul Jones (of Manfred Mann) could blow with bluesy soul when appropriate. As the British Invasion turned into blues-rock and progressive rock, the instrument was used with less frequency, but could still be whipped out with impressive effect, as Mick Jagger demonstrated on "Midnight Rambler."

As further proof that good blues has no color, some of the best American harmonica blues players of recent years have been White. Paul Butterfield and Charlie Musselwhite–both of whom rose through the Chicago club scene in the 1960s and came by their blues honestly, learning first hand from their idols–certainly had technique and feeling to match the best of them, whether playing straight Chicago blues or (in Butterfield's case) blues rock. Notable White virtuosos of more recent years include Kim Wilson of the Fabulous Thunderbirds, Rod Piazza, Magic Dick, Paul deLay, and William Clarke–possibly the most inventive and original harmonica player currently out there.

Harmonica-playing bandleaders may not be as prominent as they were in the Chicago of the '50s and '60s, but harmonica is still very much part of the standard contemporary blues scene.

Many of the masters, like James Cotton, are still around and very active, for one thing; with his recent national album deals, Billy Boy Arnold may be more well known now (at least outside of Chicago) than he was when he was recording in the '50s. A recent blowout supersession of sorts (between Junior Wells, James Cotton, Carey Bell, and Billy Branch) demonstrated the enduring appeal of harmonica showcases. And two of the most noted modern acoustic blues acts, Satan & Adam and Cephas & Wiggins, prominently feature the instrument. And for every person who is inspired to take the instrument up to their lips and try and make a sound with it, there's always the chance that another blues master is a-borning. The history of blues harmonica is still being written.
—Richie Unterberger, Cub Koda and Michael Erlewine

16 Recommended Albums:

Various Artists, *Blues Masters Vol. 4: Harmonica Classics* (Rhino)
Sonny Terry, *The Folkways Years, 1944–63* (Smithsonian/Rounder)
Sonny Boy Williamson I, *Throw a Boogie-Woogie* (RCA)
Little Walter, *Essential* (Chess)
Little Walter, *Blues with a Feeling* (Chess)
Sonny Boy Williamson II, *King Bisuit Time* (Arhoolie)
Sonny Boy Williamson II, *Essential* (Chess)
Big Walter Horton, *Chicago–The Blues–Today! Volume 3* (Vanguard)
Big Walter Horton, *The Soul of Blues Harmonica* (Chess)
Junior Wells, *Hoodoo Man Blues* (Delmark)
William Clarke, *Blowin' Like Hell* (Alligator)
Various Artists, *Sun Records Harmonica Classics* (Rounder)
James Cotton, *Best of the Verve Years* (Verve)
The Paul Butterfield Blues Band, *Paul Butterfield Blues Band* (Elektra)
Charlie Musselwhite, *Ace of Harps* (Alligator)
Junior Wells, James Cotton, Carey Bell, and Billy Branch, *Harp Attack!* (Alligator)

MEMPHIS BLUES

A visit to Memphis' Beale Street these days is like walking through a museum or movie set. Clubs, stores, and even museums still do business, but more as an homage to the past than as a part of a vibrant present. For decades, however, Beale Street was known as "the Main Street of Negro America," a drag where Black business thrived during the day, and entertainment/nightlife during the night.

Music, naturally, was a big part of that scene, and although the blues weren't the only game in that part of town, it played a big part for several decades. As early as 1912, the community had an anthem, "Memphis Blues," penned by W.C. Handy. In the years prior to World War II, it was home to a diverse mixture of blues performers, from jugbands to Delta guitarists. In the early 1950s, it was the most important crucible of the electric blues bar Chicago. Memphis blues has also played a huge role in the evolution of American popular music via its influence on the early rockabilly music and '60s soul empire for which Memphis is also renowned.

As one of the major urban centers of the South, Memphis attracted a large African-American population for a long time before the blues became widely known. Though it wasn't far North enough for many Blacks, who went on to Northern cities (especially Chicago) for more racial tolerance and economic opportunity, Memphis was as far as many newcomers to the urban experience got. Even those who eventually went on to Chicago and other cities would frequently stop in Memphis on the way, whether to live for a few years or for only a bit.

W.C. Handy, one of the key forefathers of the blues, based himself and his band in Memphis in 1909. Handy's form of dance music was more blues-influenced than actual blues, and in the 20th century, Memphis was as well known or more for its jazz musicians (Jimmie Lunceford being one of the most famous) than its blues. To this day, Memphis harbors so many different types of roots music that its regional styles are difficult to categorize, and such was the case with Memphis blues prior to World War II. It was always around, but not nearly as identifiable as, for example, the Delta blues so abundant in Mississippi. The city was noted as the home of several blues jug bands (the Memphis Jug Band and Gus Cannon's group being some of the most famous), as well as

Music Map

Memphis Blues

W.C. Handy
Wrote "Memphis Blues" in 1912

Jug Bands & Street Musicians
Furry Lewis, Frank Stokes,
Gus Cannon, Robert Wilkins,
Memphis Willie Borum,
Noah Lewis, Will Shade,
Joe McCoy, Memphis Minnie,
Jack Kelly, Walter Horton

Memphis in the Late '40s/Early '50s
Joe Hill Louis, B.B. King,
Rufus Thomas, Walter Horton,
Hot Shot Love, Jimmy De Berry,
Howlin' Wolf, Bobby Blue Bland,
Junior Parker, Pat Hare,
Johnny Ace, Willie Johnson,
Sammy Lewis, Little Milton

Sun Rockabilly/Memphis R&B 1954-1968
Elvis Presley, Carl Perkins,
Jerry Lee Lewis, Albert King,
Stax Records

Memphis Soul Scene
Booker T. & the MGs,
Willie Mitchell, Bill Black Combo

a few fine blues guitarists, such as Furry Lewis and Robert Wilkins. Blues was often available at the park off Beale Street that now bears Handy's name, as local and itinerant musicians would often play for tips for anyone who was interested.

It was with the post-war amplification of the blues, however, that Memphis really began to leave its mark. Society itself was becoming more urban, higher-paced, and electrified, and two of the important figures in Memphis blues made much of their initial impact not as musicians, but as radio announcers on WDIA (the first radio station in the U.S. to employ an all-Black format, although it was White-owned). One was guitarist B.B. King, who used his experience at WDIA to perfect his diction and absorb the influence of gospel and early R&B music. With his 1951 #1 R&B hit "Three O'Clock Blues," King launched a hugely successful and influential career that was vital to the urbanization of the blues, and by extension blues' eventual entry into mainstream American culture.

The other important WDIA disc jockey was Rufus Thomas, all-around entertainment personality who, more than just about any other living legend, epitomizes Memphis music. Before working for WDIA, Thomas met King when he emceed amateur night shows at the Palace Theater on Beale Street. At that time Thomas may have been more of a general R&B scenester than a professional musician. But it was as a singer that he would play a vital role in Sun Records, the label that would do more to spread the influence of Memphis blues than any other.

Sun was run by Sam Phillips, a young man with a genuine feel and appreciation for the forms of Black popular music in the region. The company is most famous, of course, for launching the career of Elvis Presley, as well as several other rockabilly stars (Carl Perkins, Johnny Cash, Jerry Lee Lewis). When it began operations in the early '50s, however, it recorded mostly Black artists and the sounds were those of blues/R&B, rockabilly not having been invented yet. (The history of Sun is examined more fully in a separate essay.)

The Memphis Recording Service, as Sun was originally named, at first leased sides to other labels. Early records by B.B. King, Howlin' Wolf, Rosco Gordon, and others were handled by labels like Chess and RPM. Jackie Brenston's "Rocket 88" (actually Ike Turner's Kings Of Rhythm), from 1951, is often cited as one of the first rock 'n' roll records. With the Howlin' Wolf sides in particular, Phillips developed the harshly amplified, spare sound that would be characteristic of the Memphis blues he recorded during this period, which was somewhat rawer and more countrified than its Chicago cousin.

Phillips began putting his blues sides out on his label, Sun, rather than leasing them. Sun's first national R&B hit was Rufus Thomas' "Bear Cat," an answer record to Big Mama Thornton's

"Hound Dog." Thomas himself, ironically, only recorded one more single for the label (though he would become a soul star in the '60s and '70s at Stax). There was plenty of other talent around, and during the first half of the '50s Sun recorded seminal sides by Junior Parker, Walter Horton, James Cotton, Little Milton, and Rosco Gordon, as well as obscurities by the likes of Pat Hare, Joe Hill Louis, D.A. Hunt, and Doctor Ross that would attain legendary status among collectors and scholars decades later.

The rise and fall of Memphis electric blues in this period is heavily intertwined with developments at Sun Records. In 1954, Phillips began recording Elvis Presley, a 19-year-old who had done his share of hanging out on Beale Street, checking out the blues singers and buying his clothes at Lansky's, a Beale Street store that catered to many local Blacks. It's almost redundant to point this out now, but Elvis was the single most important figure in the birth of rockabilly, which blended country and western with blues, R&B, and elements of gospel and pop. Memphis blues singers had done much to foster this combination, especially given that Phillips developed much of his studio acumen by overseeing their sessions. Indeed, Elvis covered Junior Parker's biggest hit, "Mystery Train," for his last Sun single, and one of his greatest performances on record.

Phillips turned his focus to the White country and rockabilly artists on his roster, especially after selling Presley's contract to RCA in late 1955, which gave him the capital to properly promote Perkins, Cash, Lewis, et al.

The truth, of course, is more complicated than that. If he had made blues/R&B his only priority, Phillips would have been an admirable idealist, perhaps. He also would have been waging a futile fight against inevitable historical forces. The biggest of these was rock 'n' roll, of course, Black and White, which in 1956 overran the recording industry. Even within blues, though, there was the magnet of Chicago, with its monolithic blues scene and its most powerful label, Chess.

Even if rockabilly had not intervened, the Memphis community had already begun to lose its most promising musicians to other cities. Howlin' Wolf, perhaps the greatest of the blues talents to enter the Memphis Recording Service, was signed by Chess and moved to Chicago, well before Presley's advent. James Cotton (who joined Muddy Waters' band before becoming a star on his own) and guitarist Pat Hare (who also played with Waters for a while) also relocated to Chicago. Even Sonny Boy Williamson, a musician just across the Mississippi River (in Helena, AR) with some ties to the Memphis scene, would not truly make his mark until recording for Chess in Chicago. The city guaranteed blues performers more work, more musicians to choose from, and, should they be picked up by local labels, more effective national promotion.

It may also be that some of the blues artists in Memphis were in embryonic states of artistic development that could not be fully nurtured by the metropolis. Junior Parker and Little Milton, for instance, really hit their commercial stride as soul/blues artists in the '60s (and Little Milton would record for the Memphis-based Stax label, among others). B.B. King, another bluesman with prominent R&B and soul influences, became in the 1960s a national figure who recorded in various distant cities, cultivating a sound that was too broad in scope to be pigeonholed as part of a regional movement. Ike Turner (never really identified with the Memphis scene) would move his base of operations to St. Louis, and move into rock and soul with his wife Tina.

Memphis blues didn't die, of course; it was too deeply embedded in the city's music scene to do so. But the nature of the city's African-American popular music production in the '60s and '70s was very much soul, specifically at Stax and Hi Records. Stax usually had some blues/soul hybrids on its roster, achieving a good deal of success with Albert King, who worked with Booker T. & the MG's on many of his records. The demise of Stax in the mid-'70s, however, meant lean times for Black music as a whole in the city.

Blues is still heard and recorded in Memphis these days, even if it has a somewhat folkloric bent. Renowned blues scholar and author David Evans has marshalled some fine down-home blues for the High Water label in recent years, most notably by guitarist Jessie Mae Hemphill. B.B. King owns a club on Beale Street, although he hasn't lived in Memphis for ages. And though it's more of a tourist attraction than a happening area, Beale Street and vicinity offers several places of homage for the serious blues fan, including the Center for Southern Folklore; a good, if seriously undervisited, blues museum; the famous Schwab's variety store (serving the community since 1876); The Memphis Music Museum; Handy Park; and, a mile or two away, Sun Studios, which remains open for tours.

—*Richie Unterberger & Cub Koda*

10 Recommended Albums:

Memphis Jug Band, *Memphis Jug Band* (Yazoo)
Various Artists, *Ten Years in Memphis, 1927–1937* (Yazoo)
Various Artists, *A Sun Blues Collection* (Rhino)
Various Artists, *Blues Masters Vol. 12: Memphis Blues* (Rhino)
B.B. King, *The Best of B.B. King, Vol. 1* (Flair)
Howlin' Wolf, *Rides Again* (Flair)
Junior Parker, James Cotton, & Pat Hare, *Mystery Train* (Rounder)
Albert King, *Born under a Bad Sign* (Mobile Fidelity)
Various Artists, *Memphis Masters* (Yazoo)
Various Artists, *The Blues Came Down From Memphis* (Charly)

PIANO BLUES

The piano hasn't occupied as prominent a place in the blues as the guitar; in terms of blues virtuosos of recent decades, there may even be more harmonica players than keyboard specialists. The piano will certainly always have a place in the blues combo for both its rhythmic and melodic qualities, despite the hysterical predictions of some observers that the synthesizer will soon make it obsolete. Many of blues' finest singers and songwriters have been piano players; blues piano has also played a big part in influencing the directions of jazz, rock, and soul music.

Blues piano styles have much of their origins in the rough-and-tumble barrelhouses and railroad/lumber camps of the late 1800s and early 1900s. Here pianists had to develop a rhythmic, aggressive sound to be heard above the crowd, and to keep pace with the rowdy atmopshere. It's no accident that some of the early blues piano greats are noted for a "barrelhouse" style.

In some respects, early piano players may have been at a disadvantage when competing with guitarists and other instrumentalists. The acoustic guitar (or, say, the harmonica) is extremely portable, a big plus for musicians working the road in the days when private automobile travel was a lot less common. It might not have been as much as a drawback as one may think, though. Most settlements had entertainment establishments with house pianos; if residents or travelers could prove their skills, they were often welcome to have at it.

There's little question that considerably more blues guitarists were recorded than blues pianists in the early days of the phono-

graph. Blues scholars justifiably bewail the loss of important chapters in blues history because of the preferences of the companies responsible for recording blues in the 1920s and 1930s. Many pianists hardly recorded at all, and are now only represented on obscure import blues compilations. Many, no doubt, never had the opportunity to record at all.

Blues pianists, however, began to be recorded shortly after the first appearance of the blues itself on record. Some of the most significant early ones were Cow Cow Davenport, Roosevelt Sykes, and Clarence "Pine Top" Smith. Smith's "Pine Top's Boogie-Woogie," from 1929, is generally credited with introducing the term "boogie-woogie" into widespread use.

The boogie-woogie piano style is characterized by a 12-bar blues structure and constantly repeating rhythmic patterns of the left hand, while the right hand plays the melodies and improvisations. It quickly caught on, not just in blues, but in popular music as a whole; millions of people who couldn't tell you diddley squat about Robert Johnson know exactly what a boogie-woogie is. Boogie-woogie patterns would become a foundation of jazz in the 1930s and 1940s, jump blues in the 1940s and 1950s, and early R&B/rock 'n' roll in the 1950s.

Records by blues pianists in the 1930s, however, didn't necessarily showcase their instrumental skills. As Mike Rowe notes in *The Blackwell Guide to the Blues*, "There had been a subtle change in the market for piano blues. Those pianists, such as Leroy Carr, Walter Davis, and even Roosevelt Sykes, who had lasted out the Depression were popular for their songs and singing; that they played piano was incidental. While the sawmill pianists played for dancers and had to survive on pianistic prowess, the blues pianist of the urban 1930s had to achieve success as a singer or songwriter. Piano blues had been taken out of the lumber camps and whorehouses and into the homes of an increasingly sophisticated urban audience.

"This accent on the content of the song meant that pianists had little encouragement to stretch themselves, and Davis or Peetie Wheatstraw, for example, could make recording after recording using the same introduction and tempo, which tended to mask their abilities as pianists. Boogie-woogie had become integrated into blues accompaniments, and ragtime was all but eliminated. There was a smoother, more regular sound to the 1930s piano blues, and although a few field trips by Bluebird, Decca, and ARC preserved some regional styles, and the iconoclastic Texas piano in particular, it was the cities such as Chicago and St. Louis that provided the bulk of the artists."

Key figures in the urbanization of blues piano–really, in the urbanization of the blues as a whole–would include Big Maceo Merriweather, Champion Jack Dupree, Sunnyland Slim, and Jimmy Yancey. Boogie-woogie was certainly a big element in swing and big band jazz, and several blues-based boogie-woogie pianists, such as Meade Lux Lewis, Albert Ammons, and Pete Johnson, fed into the jazz tributary with work that straddled the line between the two genres. A Carnegie Hall appearance in 1938 featuring all three of the aforementioned boogie-woogie specialists did much to popularize and legitimize the style.

When the blues started to electrify in Chicago and elsewhere during the 1940s and 1950s, the guitar and harmonica assumed more prominence than the piano. This wasn't true on the West Coast, however, were jump blues reigned supreme between the mid-'40s and mid-'50s. Jump blues' blend of blues and jazz ingredients made it a natural for pianists, and some of jump blues' greatest performers were keyboardist/singers. Amos Milburn, Floyd Dixon, and Camille Howard were some of the best; their achievements are described in greater depth in the jump blues essay. Several other West Coast blues pianists made their mark with a more ballad-inclined, gospel-influenced R&B style, including Charles Brown, Percy Mayfield, Cecil Gant (a great boogie-woogie player as well), and–on his earliest sides–Ray Charles. The blues/jazz piano connection would be kept alive, to a much subtler degree, via the work of blues-and boogie-influenced soul/jazz organists/pianists of the '60s and '70s, such as Jimmy Smith, Big John Patton, and Jimmy McGriff.

There was still room for a piano in the classic-style Chicago electric blues lineup, as Otis Spann proved during his lengthy stint with Muddy Waters. It took a while for Spann to emerge from Waters' shadow, but recordings on his own established him as a worthy artist in his own right, and perhaps the finest of the post-World War II piano players. Other players of note on the

Music Map

Piano Blues Stylists by Region

St. Louis
Lee Green, Roosevelt Sykes,
Peetie Wheatstraw,
Henry Townsend, Walter Roland,
Walter Davis

Chicago
Willie Mabon, Otis Spann,
Detroit Jr., Henry Gray,
Eddie Boyd, Art Hodes

Texas
Alex Moore, Dr. Hepcat,
Rob Cooper, Dave Alexander,
Sammy Price

Indianapolis
Leroy Carr

Kansas City
Jay McShann, Count Basie,
Pete Johnson

New Orleans
Cousin Joe, Archibald,
Smiley Lewis, Jack Dupree,
Professor Longhair, Fats Domino

Memphis & The Delta
Little Brother Montgomery,
Sunnyland Slim, Booker T. Laury,
Memphis Slim, Jab Jones,
Piano Red, Mose Vinson

California
Charles Brown, Amos Milburn,
Percy Mayfield

Other Major Players
Speckled Red, Ray Charles

Chicago blues scene were Memphis Slim, Little Johnny Jones (whose two-fisted work as a member of Elmore James' Broomdusters made the absence of a rhythm guitar in that band totally unnoticeable), Roosevelt Sykes, Eddie Boyd, Willie Mabon, and Johnnie Johnson, who's probably more famous for his contributions to rock 'n' roll, as the pianist featured on many of Chuck Berry's classic sides.

Piano players as stars or singers, rather than side musicians, have been much thinner on the ground in the last few decades than they were 50–60 years ago. Louisiana was something of a pocket of blues and blues-influenced pianists; Professor Longhair, James Booker, and Katie Webster (all of whom have ties of varying strength to the region) developed some of the funkiest and most idiosyncratic styles to be found in the whole blues piano idiom. Memphis Slim and Pinetop Perkins, among others, kept old-school blues piano styles alive with frequent touring well past the 1960s. Keyboards are still a staple of many a blues band, and will probably remain so. But the day may have passed when piano players exerted as fundamental an influence on the direction of the blues as they did in the heyday of boogie-woogie and barrelhouse.
—*Richie Unterberger*

16 Recommended Albums:

Cow Cow Davenport, *Alabama Strut* (Magpie)
Roosevelt Sykes, *Roosevelt Sykes (1929–41)* (Story of Blues)
Leroy Carr, *Naptown Blues* (Yazoo)
Albert Ammons, *King of Boogie-Woogie (1939–1949)* (Blues Classics)
Meade Lux Lewis, *Complete Blue Note Recordings* (Mosaic)
Jimmy Yancey, *Vol. 1 (1939–40)* (Document)
Big Maceo, *King of Chicago Blues Piano, Vol. 1 & 2* (Arhoolie)
Amos Milburn, *Down the Road Apiece: The Best of Amos Milburn* (EMI)
Floyd Dixon, *Marshall Texas Is My Home* (Specialty)
Camille Howard, *Vol. 1: Rock Me Daddy* (Specialty)
Cecil Gant, *Rock the Boogie* (Krazy Kat)
Sunnyland Slim, *Sunnyland Slim* (Flyright)
Otis Spann, *Otis Spann Is the Blues* (Candid)
Professor Longhair, *Fess: Professor Longhair Anthology* (Rhino)
James Booker, *New Orleans Piano Wizard: Live!* (Rounder)
Memphis Slim, *Rockin' the Blues* (Charly)

SONGSTERS

The blues was such a young form when it first started to be recorded that not all of its early stars would have identified themselves as blues artists. Nor, indeed, were all of them blues artists all of the time. For many African-American singers and musicians, blues was just part of their repertoire. They were also able and willing to play country tunes, spirituals, popular standards, ragtime, jug band, folk songs, and more.

These are the artists labeled by researchers as "songsters." The songsters haven't fared nearly as well as, say, the acoustic guitarists of the Mississippi Delta in the annals of blues history. They often espouse a homey, sunny, good-timey air that is at odds with the serious, forceful image of the blues that many expect. To listeners accustomed to contemporary blues, rock, and pop, their arrangements and delivery can sound quaintly old-fashioned. Yet the best of the songsters made important contributions to blues history, worth recognizing even by those who much prefer their blues deep and down-home.

It's no accident that some of the most notable songsters were the very oldest blues singers to record; their material would naturally tend to be older in origin, and less shaped by the blues trends of the early 20th century. One of the most famous, and probably the oldest, was Henry Thomas (b. 1874). Only about a third of his two dozen sides were titled as blues; he also cut ballads, reels, and dance songs, often using the pan quill pipes, an unconventional instrument rarely heard today. He achieved a good deal of posthumous fame when his "Bull Doze Blues" was adapted by Canned Heat for their hit "Going Up the Country" in the late '60s. Bob Dylan included a song that Thomas had recorded, "Honey, Just Allow Me One More Chance," on his second LP (*Freewheelin' Bob Dylan*, 1963); the original liner notes explain that the tune "was first heard by Dylan from a recording by a now-dead Texas blues singer. Dylan can only remember that his first name was Henry."

One of the most frequently discussed songsters, Frank Stokes, betrayed the considerable influence of traveling medicine shows in which he participated. As a member of a cast that had to entertain lots of people in different regions, Stokes and similar songsters could have been expected to develop a wide range of material. Pink Anderson, another veteran of medicine shows, survived into the era of the long-playing record, and his '50s and '60s recordings offer better fidelity for those that find the primitive audio of the '20s too hard to handle.

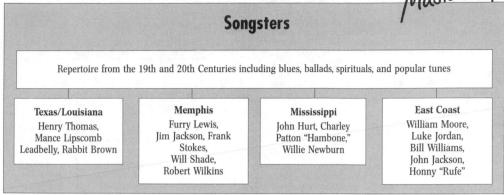

Music Map

Songsters

Repertoire from the 19th and 20th Centuries including blues, ballads, spirituals, and popular tunes

Texas/Louisiana	Memphis	Mississippi	East Coast
Henry Thomas, Mance Lipscomb Leadbelly, Rabbit Brown	Furry Lewis, Jim Jackson, Frank Stokes, Will Shade, Robert Wilkins	John Hurt, Charley Patton "Hambone," Willie Newburn	William Moore, Luke Jordan, Bill Williams, John Jackson, Honny "Rufe"

Mississipi John Hurt was another guitarist with songster leanings who survived into the folk revival. Hurt recorded some stellar material in the late 1920s, and then a number of LPs after his rediscovery in the early '60s. His early 78s are more esteemed by blues collectors than his latter efforts, but again you get the choice between better fidelity and performances that are closer to the source of the songster milieu, whatever your preference may be. Quite a few will want to hear Hurt in both contexts; his good-natured, gospel-influenced singing and accomplished fingerpicking makes his work more accessible to contemporary listeners than any of the original songsters.

The songster tradition lived on to a large degree in the work of subsequent singers who held strong appeal for both the blues and folk audiences. They've been usually classified as folk or folk/blues singers rather than songsters for this reason, and also because their work has less of an air of all-around entertainment than Stokes, Thomas, harmonica player DeFord Bailey (who was a regular on the Grand Ole Opry in the '20s and '30s), or '20s songsters like Peg Leg Howell.

The most famous of these blues/folk crossover artists was Leadbelly, discovered by John Lomax in a Louisiana prison in 1933. With his huge repertoire, stellar vocal and instrumental skills, and extremely colorful life, Leadbelly qualifies as one of the giants of 20th-century American music, worth learning about even by music fans who've never heard any of his records. The eclectic approach of Leadbelly enabled him to circulate easily in a New York-based community of folkies that also included Woody Guthrie and the duo of Brownie McGhee and Sonny Terry, two other performers who were also comfortable with both blues and folk.

Also treading the line between blues and folk was Josh White, who in his youth had recorded spirituals under his own name and blues under a pseudonym, along with the virtually forgotten Brother John Sellers. There was always a home for White on the folk circuit, and after the rediscovery of Hurt, Furry Lewis, and Mance Lipscomb (the latter of whom had never previously recorded) around 1960, acoustic blues legends also tapped into the folk constituency to get a second wind on their professional careers. Hurt, Lipscomb, and White were certainly not songsters in the classic sense, but their versatility owed quite a bit to the songster tradition, enabling them to bring the blues sensibility to many listeners who may have never been introduced to it otherwise.

—Richie Unterberger

11 Recommended Albums:

Henry Thomas, *Texas Worried Blues* (Yazoo)
Frank Stokes, *The Memphis Blues* (Yazoo)
Mississippi John Hurt, *1928 Sessions* (Yazoo)
Mississippi John Hurt, *The Immortal* (Vanguard)
Peg Leg Howell, *1928–29* (Matchbox)
Peg Leg Howell, *The Legendary Peg Leg Howell* (Testament)
Leadbelly, *King of the 12-String Guitar* (CBS)
Leadbelly, *Midnight Special* (Rounder)

Pink Anderson, *Ballad & Folksinger, Vol. 3* (Prestige/ Bluesville)
Josh White, *Legendary Josh White* (MCA)
Mance Lipscomb, *Texas Sharecropper & Songster* (Arhoolie)

WEST COAST BLUES

West Coast blues–it's undeniably a phrase with less instant hipster credibility than, say, Chicago blues or Delta blues. The cities of Los Angeles and San Francisco simply don't embody the hard times associated with the blues' origins in the South, or the hothouse conditions that gave rise to much classic electric blues in the North. As the stereotype would have it, life is mellower, the pace slower, the living easier, and the weather sunnier on the West Coast–not the kinds of conditions which have, in the minds of many listeners, been conducive to breeding the best kinds of blues music. The West Coast, however, has been home to many leading blues performers, although it may not have developed as identifiable a sound as some other regions.

When we talk about West Coast blues, we're really talking about California blues, most of which was centered around the Los Angeles and the San Francisco Bay areas. There's not much of a prewar Californian blues tradition, which must be at least partially attributable to the fact that the African-American communities there weren't nearly as large in the beginning of the 20th century. The Black population of the state, however, would swell in the 1940s, the westward migration enhanced by the need for immense manpower to work in the U.S. defense industry during World War II. These new arrivals needed entertainment, and the local jazz and blues club scene heated up quickly.

The towering figure of West Coast blues may be guitarist T-Bone Walker, a relocated Texan who had made his first recordings in the late 1920s. Walker was a crucial figure in the electrification and urbanization of the blues, probably doing more to popularize the use of electric guitar in the form than anyone else. Much of his material had a distinct jazzy jump blues feel, an influence that would characterize much of the most influential blues to emerge from California in the 1940s and 1950s.

Many of the most popular blues performers to base themselves in California during the 1940s and 1950s were originally from Texas, perhaps accounting from some of the earthiest qualities of West Coast blues. Besides Walker, there was Pee Wee Crayton (a guitarist who modeled his style after T-Bone's), Charles Brown, Lowell Fulson, Joe Houston, Amos Milburn, Johnny "Guitar" Watson, and (after the mid-'50s) Big Mama Thornton. At times it seemed as though Texas was the true breeding ground of West Coast blues–Los Angeles just happened to be where it was refined and recorded.

There was an obvious reason, however, why so much blues was recorded in Los Angeles, as it was the city where many of the independent labels specializing in blues and R&B originated in the 1940s. Specialty, Imperial, Aladdin, and the umbrella of labels run by the Bihari brothers (RPM, Modern, Kent, Flair, and Crown) were the most famous of these. Their importance cannot be overestimated, for the simple reason that they were determined to record and distribute blues music that the big major companies were uninterested in, or not even aware of in the first place.

The history of early West Coast blues is heavily intertwined with that of jump blues, the snappy, rhythmic hybrid of jazz and blues that reigned supreme over much of the R&B world in the late 1940s and early 1950s. That history is covered in greater depth in a separate essay. For now, it should be noted that many of the greatest jump blues musicians were based in California, be they acrobatic saxophonists (Big Jay McNeely, Joe Houston), pianist/vocalists (Amos Milburn, Floyd Dixon, Camille Howard, Little Willie Littlefield), guitarists (Walker, Crayton), or bandleaders like Roy Milton.

A flipside of the uptempo jump bluesters were the singers who specialized in piano ballads that also drew from gospel and the pop-jazz of Nat King Cole. Charles Brown and Percy Mayfield were the most prominent of these vocalists; Ray Charles, based in Seattle at the outset of his career but recording for the Los Angeles-based Swingtime label, also did quite a bit of recording in this vein before devising a more personal style. Today, these figures are all recognized as forefathers of soul music, making it a matter of good-natured debate as to whether they should be classified as blues or just plain R&B.

The R&B/blues line also gets thin when discussing the career of Johnny Otis, the bandleader who did as much as anyone to build the Los Angeles R&B community. Otis made plenty of blues/R&B hybrid recordings on his own, but he arguably made greater contributions as a promoter and organizer of live shows, DJ, producer, and general champion of talent. He did much to further the careers of Little Esther and Etta James, two singers who, again, are better classified as R&B singers than blues ones, though their allegiance to blues styles is certainly visible.

Urbane forms of blues may have dominated the early post-war Californian scene, but there was room for grittier performers as well, such as the aforementioned Pee Wee Crayton, and Johnny "Guitar" Watson, whose futuristic style has been rightly cited as an influence on Jimi Hendrix. Nor was it confined solely to Los Angeles. San Francisco and Oakland were home to a small but notable blues scene, the most prominent spokesman being Jimmy McCracklin, who had a crossover rock 'n' roll Top Ten hit in 1958 with "The Walk." Pee Wee Crayton was also based in San Francisco when he emerged, although he made his most important recordings in Los Angeles.

Blues, as it did throughout the rest of the country, fell on leaner times in California in the 1960s, as rock, surf, and soul dominated the industry. Los Angeles' increasingly central position within the recording industry may have, if anything, decreased the presence of the blues within the city itself. Rock and pop musicians of all kinds were flocking to L.A. studios, and the big and small companies–more of whom were based in L.A. now than anywhere else–wanted to come up with successes in these fields, not the blues, which were considered passé by many, and had certainly long passed its commercial peak.

Tireless keepers of the flame such as Johnny Otis and his son Shuggie, however, ensured that the blues community continued to function, even if at a somewhat subterranean level. As there has been everywhere since the 1960s, interest in the blues among the White audience on the West Coast has become much more commonplace. San Francisco and Los Angeles are each home to some of the biggest and most successful blues festivals in the world, and each have a decent number of venues for both local and visiting blues artists.

Some of the most notable blues performers of recent times have come from California, even if there's not much that can be pigeonholed as especially "regional" about their sound. Johnny Heartsman, who's been active since the 1950s, really made his true impact with nationwide audiences in the 1980s and 1990s. From San Francisco, Joe Louis Walker is one of the most successful bluesmen of recent times, noted for his effective incorporation of rock and gospel influences into his material. Walker established himself as a recording artist on the San Francisco Bay Area-based Hightone label, one of the top contemporary roots music companies in the United States.

Southern California has been home to many White blues bands as well, producing two noted harmonica virtuosos in William Clarke and Rod Piazza (and, way back in the 1960s, one of the most successful American blues-rock groups, Canned Heat).

West Coast Blues

T-Bone Walker
Texas Bluesman moves to California, popularized jazz style that becomes the West Coast Sound

| Pee Wee Crayton, Charles Brown, Lowell Fulson, Amos Milburn, Johnny Guitar Watson, Jimmy McCracklin | Roy Milton, Percy Mayfield, Nat "King" Cole, Johnny Otis, Ray Charles, Roy Brown, Big Jay McNeely, Joe Houston, Jimmy Liggins | Shuggie Otis, William Clarke, Johnny Heartsman, Canned Heat, Rod Piazza, Joe Louis Walker, Ted Hawkins |

And throughout the 1980s, you could walk down the tourist-congested boardwalk of Venice Beach in Los Angeles and find Ted Hawkins playing for change for passerby. A repository of acoustic folk/blues in the urban madness that now suffuses the L.A., Hawkins achieved recognition as one of the top practitioners of contemporary acoustic blues before his premature death in the mid-1990s–giving California, perhaps, the acoustic blues roots it never really had.

—*Richie Unterberger*

15 Recommended Albums:

T-Bone Walker, *The Complete Capitol/Black & White Recordings* (Capitol)
T-Bone Walker, *The Complete Imperial Recordings* (EMI)
Pee Wee Crayton, *Rocking Down on Central Avenue* (Ace)
Amos Milburn, *Down the Road Apiece: The Best of Amos Milburn* (EMI)
Floyd Dixon, *Marshall Texas Is My Home* (Specialty)
Roy Milton, *Roy Milton and His Solid Senders* (Specialty)
Percy Mayfield, *Poet of the Blues* (Specialty)
Charles Brown, *Driftin' Blues: The Best of Charles Brown* (EMI)
Johnny "Guitar" Watson, *Three Hours Past Midnight* (Flair)
Lowell Fulson, *San Francisco Blues* (Black Lion)
Johnny Otis, *The Johnny Otis Show* (Savoy)
Jimmy McCracklin, *Everybody Rock: Let's Do It! The Best of Jimmy McCracklin* (Domino)
Johnny Heartsman, *The Touch* (Alligator)
Joe Louis Walker, *The Gift* (Hightone)
Ted Hawkins, *Happy Hour* (Rounder)

CHICAGO BLUES

Probably no strain of blues has a more universally recognized form, feel, and sound than Chicago blues. Chicago is where the music became amplified and had the big beat put to it and like Muddy Waters said, the blues had a baby and they named it rock 'n' roll. As a simple point of reference, it's the music that most sounds like '50s rhythm and blues/rock 'n' roll, its first notable offspring; when you hear a TV commercial with blues in it, it's usually the Chicago style they're playing. It's the sound of amplified harmonicas, electric slide guitars, big boogie piano, and a rhythm section that just won't quit, with fierce, declamatory vocals booming over the top of it. It's the genius of Muddy Waters, Howlin' Wolf, Elmore James, and Little Walter knocking an urban audience on their collective ears at some smoky, noisy South side tavern, then transmitting that signal to the world. It's the infectious boogie of Hound Dog Taylor, John Brim, Jimmy Reed, and Joe Carter mining similar turf while Robert Nighthawk and Big John

Wrencher lay it down with rough and tumble combos Sunday mornings on the Maxwell Street open-air market. And it's the up-to-date, gospel-inspired vocals and B.B. King single-note style of Otis Rush, Magic Sam, and Buddy Guy meshing with it all. Though there's much primitive beauty to be found in this strain of the music, there's nothing subtle about it; its rough edge ambience is the sound of the Delta, coming to terms with the various elements of city life and plugging in and going electric to keep pace with a changing world. Chicago blues was the first style to reach a mass audience and, with the passage of time, the first to reach a worldwide audience as well. When average Joes think of the blues, one of two musical sounds pop into their brain pan; one is the sound of Delta blues–usually slide-played on an acoustic guitar. The other–if it's played through an amplifier–is almost always Chicago blues.

Although the Windy City had a burgeoning blues scene before World War II (see separate essay on Lester Melrose and Early Chicago Blues), a number of elements combined after the war to put the modern Chicago scene into motion.

First, there was the societal aftermath of World War II to deal with. Blacks–after serving their country and seeing how the rest of the world was–came back home, packed up their few belongings and headed north to greener pastures, better paying jobs and the promise of a better life. It was a simple case of "how ya keep 'em down on the farm"; once Blacks had left the oppression of Southern plantation life behind and "had seen the world," the prospect of toiling in a meat packing plant in Chicago looked a whole lot more upscale than standing behind a mule somewhere in Mississippi.

And so they headed north. This influx of new migrants all finding new jobs and housing also infused Chicago with a lot of capital to be had and spent in these flush post-War times. The rise of the independent recording label after shellac rationing (and the development of space-age plastics) also had a lot to do with the development of the sound as well. New record labels that dealt exclusively with blues for a Black market started to proliferate after 1950. Chess and its myriad subsidiaries and Vee-Jay had the lion's share of the market, but medium-to-tiny imprints like Ora-Nelle (an offshoot of the Maxwell Street Radio Repair Shop), JOB, Tempo Tone, Parkway, Cool, Atomic H, Cobra, Chance, Opera, United, States, Blue Lake, Parrot, C.J., and others all helped to bring the music to a wider audience.

Up to this point, John Lee "Sonny Boy" Williamson, Big Bill Broonzy, and Tampa Red were the three acknowledged kingpins of the local scene, but their hegemony was soon to be challenged and eventually relinquished to the new breed. The new migrants wanted to be citified and upscale, but still had strong down-home roots that needed to be tended to. The jazzier jump blues offerings in the city were fine, but newly arrived Southerners wanted something a little more gritty, packed with a little more realism and a lot more emotional wallop. One day a train dropped a young slide guitarist from Mississippi into the city and soon the new audience had the sound and the style that suited their needs, urban, rural, and emotional. Muddy Waters had come to Chicago and the sound of Chicago blues as we know it was about to be born.

Waters worked the house party circuit at first, driving a truck by day and playing his music wherever he had the chance. He fell in with a loose group of players which included guitarists Baby Face Leroy Foster, Blue Smitty, and Jimmy Rogers. Muddy tried to plug into the Melrose style recording scene three years after arriving, but a one-off recording session issued on Columbia under an assumed name did the singer little good. The sound was urban, but it wasn't *his* style, the sound that captivated his listeners at house rent parties along the South side.

Muddy noticed two things about playing in Chicago. One, he needed amplification if he was going to be heard over the noisy din in a neighborhood tavern. He needed an electric guitar and an amplifier to go with it and he needed to turn both of them full blast if he was going to make an impression. Secondly, he needed a band; not a band with trumpets and saxophones in it, but a modern version of the kind of string band he worked in around Clarksdale, MS. It stands as a testament to Muddy Waters' genius that he created the blueprint for the first modern electric blues band and honed that design into a modern, lustrous musical sheen. There had certainly been blues combos in the city previous to Waters' arrival, but none sounded like this.

Muddy's first band was called the Headhunters because of their habit of blowing any band they came in contact with off the stage, and usually taking their gig from them in the bargain. Although Muddy was having hits on Chess with just his guitar and a string bass in support, in a live situation it was a different matter entirely. Baby Face Leroy Foster was soon replaced by Elgar Edmonds (aka Elgin Evans) on drums, Jimmy Rogers wove complex second guitar patterns into the mix, and in due time, Otis Spann would bring his beautiful piano stylings to the combo, following Muddy's every move. But it was with the addition of harmonica genius Little Walter that the face of the Chicago blues sound began to change. If Muddy and Jimmy's guitars were amplified and cranked up, Walter got his own microphone and amplifier and responded in kind. Though others played electric before him (Walter Horton among them), it was Little Walter who virtually defined the role and sound of amplified harmonica as it sat in this new band context. His honking, defiant tone–full of distortion, hand-controlled compression wedded to swooping saxophone-styled licks–became *the* sound for every aspiring combo and harmonica player to go after. By the time Walter left Muddy to form his own band, the Jukes (named after his first instrumental), his sound was so pervasive that club owners would only hire combos that had a harmonica player working in that style. Bands would do without a drummer if need be, but the message was clear; one had to have that harp in order to work.

Soon there were newly amplified bands springing up everywhere and coming from everywhere, as the word was soon out that Chicago was quickly becoming the new promised land of the blues. The competition was fierce and tough, with lesser bands like Bo Diddley's Langley Avenue Jivecats or Earl Hooker working for tips on Maxwell Street, while others squeezed onto postage stamp-sized stages just trying to establish their reputations. Among these were future blues legends in the making Big Walter Horton, Johnny Shines, J.B. Lenoir, Snooky Pryor, Jimmy Reed, John Brim, Billy Boy Arnold, and J.B. Hutto. Muddy Waters' first challenge to his newly acquired crown as king of the circuit came from Memphis bluesman Howlin' Wolf. Wolf had just signed a contract with Chess Records and had a hit on the R&B charts to go with it. He came into town, looking for work and by all accounts, Muddy was most helpful in getting him started. But what started as professional courtesy soon blossomed into a bitter, intense rivalry between the two bandleaders that lasted until Wolf's death in 1976. They'd steal sidemen from each other, compete with each other over who would record Willie Dixon's best material and when booked on the same bill together, would pull every trick possible to try and outdo each other onstage.

The preponderance here on the club scene in Chicago is pivotal in understanding how the music developed. For all their business acumen and commercial expertise, Chess and every other Chicago label that was recording this music was doing it because it was *popular* music in the Black community. This was an untapped market that was tired of being spoon fed Billy Eckstine and Nat King Cole records and wanted to be sent back home, and a three-minute 78 of it just might hit the spot. Just like every other honest trend or development in American music, it simply happened; the people responded, and somebody was smart enough to record it and sell it.

But by the mid-'50s–as one bluesman put it–"the beat had changed." The blues *did* have a baby and they *did* name it rock 'n' roll. Suddenly everyone from Big Joe Turner to Bo Diddley were being lumped in with Elvis and Bill Haley and a hundred vocal groups named after birds or automobiles. The Black audience started to turn away from blues to the new music and suddenly the local scene needed a fresh transfusion of new blood. Over on the West side, younger musicians were totally enamored of the B.B. King style of playing and singing and began to incorporate both into a new Chicago blues hybrid. Working with a pair of saxes, a bass player and a drummer, most West Side combos were scaled down approximations of B.B.'s big band. When the group couldn't afford the sax section, the guitarists started throwing in heavy jazz chord-like fills to flesh out the sound. Suddenly Otis Rush, Buddy Guy, and Magic Sam were on equal footing with the established heavies, and even Howlin' Wolf and Elmore James started regularly recording and playing with saxophones. As rhythm and blues started getting a harder-edged sound as it moved into soul music territory by the mid-'60s, the blues started keeping its ear to the ground and its beat focused on the dance

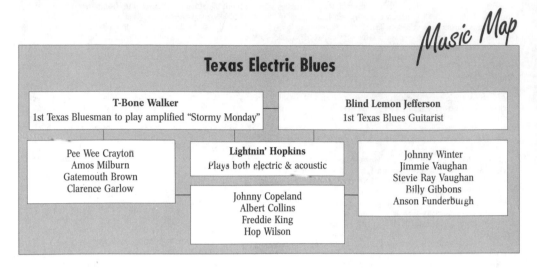

Music Map

Texas Electric Blues

T-Bone Walker
1st Texas Bluesman to play amplified "Stormy Monday"

Blind Lemon Jefferson
1st Texas Blues Guitarist

Pee Wee Crayton
Amos Milburn
Gatemouth Brown
Clarence Garlow

Lightnin' Hopkins
Plays both electric & acoustic

Johnny Copeland
Albert Collins
Freddie King
Hop Wilson

Johnny Winter
Jimmie Vaughan
Stevie Ray Vaughan
Billy Gibbons
Anson Funderburgh

floor. While the three primary grooves up til now had been a slow blues, a boogie shuffle and a "cut shuffle" (like Muddy's "Got My Mojo Working"), suddenly it was okay to put a blues to a rock groove, sometimes with quite satisfying results.

One of the first to mine this turf was harmonica ace Junior Wells. Wells' first hit, "Messing With The Kid," was blues with a driving beat and a great guitar riff, signaling that once again, the blues had reinvented itself to keep with the crowd. Working in tandem with Buddy Guy at Pepper's Lounge, the duo worked like a downscale miniature blues'n'soul show, combining funky beats with the most down in the alley blues imaginable. By the middle '60s, Chicago produced its first racially mixed combo with the birth of the highly influential Paul Butterfield Blues Band, featuring the high-voltage guitar work of Michael Bloomfield and members from Howlin' Wolf's rhythm section. And the permutations that have come since then and flourish in the current Chicago club scene echo those last two developments of the Chicago style. The beats and bass lines may get funkier in approach, the guitars might be playing in a more modern style, sometimes even approaching rock pyrotechnics, in some cases. But every time a harmonica player cups his instrument around a cheap microphone or a crowd calls out for a slow one, the structure may change, and every musician and patron doffs their symbolic hats in appreciation to Muddy Waters and the beginnings of the Chicago blues, still very much alive and well today.
—*Cub Koda*

14 Recommended Albums:

Muddy Waters, *The Best Of Muddy Waters* (MCA-Chess)
Little Walter, *The Best Of Little Walter* (MCA-Chess)
Jimmy Reed, *Speak The Lyrics To Me, Mama Reed* (Vee-Jay)
Howlin' Wolf, *Howlin' Wolf/Moanin' In The Moonlight* (MCA-Chess)
Various Artists, *Chicago/The Blues/Today!, Volumes 1–3* (Vanguard)
Junior Wells, *Hoodoo Man Blues* (Delmark)
Otis Rush, *1956–1958* (Paula)
Elmore James, *The Best Of Elmore James–The Early Years* (Ace)
Hound Dog Taylor, *Hound Dog Taylor & The HouseRockers* (Alligator)
Various Artists, *Blues Masters, Volume 2: Postwar Chicago* (Rhino)
Paul Butterfield, *Paul Butterfield Blues Band* (Elektra)
Magic Sam, *West Side Soul* (Delmark)

TEXAS ELECTRIC BLUES

The sound of Texas electric blues is difficult to define in general terms, not least because the sheer size of the state has given rise to several diverse sub-branches. Almost all blues fans can agree that they like the Texas sound; very few can actually agree

on what it *is*. What's more, it's a matter of some debate whether some major performers should be considered as Texas blues artists at all, since musicians like Freddie King, Bobby "Blue" Bland, T-Bone Walker, and Amos Milburn were only based there during part of their careers, often making their most influential recordings elsewhere. Saying that Texas blues has a distinctively earthy quotient won't do, either: What kind of blues worthy of the name *isn't* earthy?

In general terms, however, it can be said that Texas blues is a somewhat more variable animal than, say, Chicago blues or Memphis blues. A country feel is often detectable, and it's more open to outside R&B influences. Bold touches of brass are frequent, yet the guitar, usually played with dazzling single-string virtuosity, is king; the harmonica, in comparison to Chicago, is much more secondary. There's also a sense of joyous showmanship that often comes across on the records, which frequently have a small-club feel, even if they've been recorded in state-of-the-art studios.

Texas does have an estimable history of acoustic country blues talent. Blind Lemon Jefferson may be the most famous of the early Texas blues singers; Lightnin' Hopkins (who played in both acoustic and electric styles), aside from John Lee Hooker, may have made more records than any blues artist; Mance Lipscomb was a notable footnote to the early '60s blues revival, as one of the relatively few elderly bluesmen that emerged during that era who hadn't actually made any records before being "rediscovered." For the purposes of this piece, however, we'll focus on Texas blues after the advent of the electric guitar.

One Texan is the figure more responsible for electrifying the blues than any other. T-Bone Walker, born in 1910 in Texas, had in fact relocated to Los Angeles by the time he made his most influential sides in 1940s. Owing much to jazz as well as urban R&B, these were some of the first, if not the very first, blues sides that employed clean, horn-like single-string soloing in a style that came to be identified with much modern electric blues, from B.B. King on down. As John Morthland explains in the liner notes to *Texas Music Vol. 1: Postwar Blues Combos*, "After feeling out the possibilities created by electricity, he began phrasing saxlike lines that exploited the guitar's new tonal capabilities and hanged it from a rhythm to a lead instrument. Adapting rhythmic and harmonic ideas from jazz, T-Bone would hold his guitar sideways against his chest ... and drag his pick across the strings for a fat, clean sound that he'd break up with grinding downstrokes."

The Texas-L.A. connection was so well-traveled in the 1940s that it bore some resemblance to the railroad that shuttled seemingly nonstop between the Mississippi Delta and Chicago. Besides Walker, native Texans Amos Milburn, Pee Wee Crayton (a T-Bone Walker disciple), Charles Brown, Percy Mayfield, and Lowell Fulson all launched their careers after moving to California and hooking up with the independent R&B labels sprouting in Los Angeles.

Texas itself wasn't entirely bereft of recording opportunities. The most prominent R&B label, Duke/Peacock, was based in Houston. Duke/Peacock owner Don Robey was legendary for his iron hand, running his operation with a parsimonious, intimidating attitude that would result in hosts of anecdotes surfacing several decades later. Even today, some musicians are reluctant to discuss his rumored gangster-like tactics, and somewhat less so to note his practice of assigning songwriting credits and royalties to himself with reckless abandon.

Nevertheless, Duke/Peacock recorded some excellent blues in the '50s by artists like Big Mama Thornton, Junior Parker, and Bobby Bland. The latter two singers are not from Texas, but Bland in particular has come to represent the sort of blues/R&B/soul hybrids that are important facets of Texas blues, even if they were developed primarily in Texas studios, rather than within the Texas blues scene itself. Bland's extensive association with Duke/Peacock, which lasted throughout the '60s as well as the '50s, is usually rated as the finest blues/soul of all time, notable for its gospel vocal influence and blaring horn charts as well as its blues elements.

Bland's brassy soul blues may have been Texas' most successful blues export on record, but in practice, the guitar remained king. Clarence "Gatemouth" Brown, Johnny Copeland, and Albert Collins all began recording guitar-heavy material on Texas labels in the '50s, although Collins and Copeland wouldn't really achieve top-level national blues stardom for another two or three decades. Like most noted Texas electric blues guitarists, they were top showmen as well, the late Collins often using a guitar lead of 100 feet or so to enable him to wander around the audience while he played.

Freddie King is the most famous Texas blues guitarist to emerge during this era, though again it's almost arbitrary as to whether he should be classified as a Texas bluesman or not. He was born in Texas, but moved to Chicago as a teenager, and recorded his prime work for the Cincinnati-based King label. However you might classify his statehood, he was certainly one of the most important electric blues guitarists of his time, producing an authoritative, distorted tone that was a big influence on Eric Clapton in particular. He was also eager to incorporate R&B and soul influences into his repertoire, and was comfortable as both a vocal and instrumental artist, scoring his biggest hit with the instrumental "Hide Away" in 1961. Fans of Texas blues—indeed, blues fans of all kinds—should look for a video compilation of his mid-'60s performances on the Dallas-based R&B/soul television show, The Beat, which includes some guitar sparring with Clarence "Gatemouth" Brown (who led the house band). Although slide guitar wasn't heard much in Texas blues, Hop Wilson's idiosyncratic work on a non-pedal steel guitar in the '50s is a sound no lover of blues can afford to miss.

With its constant interchange between Black and White styles, it's not surprising that Texas developed a healthy White blues-rock scene in the late '60s and 1970s. Johnny Winter was the most well known of its early practitioners, playing in both traditional styles and more southern rock-influenced ones; his brother Edgar also had some national success, though with a far more rock-oriented sound. The late Texan Stevie Ray Vaughan is probably the most famous blues-rocker of recent times, and was the primary torch-bearer for the whole modern day blues-rock genre prior to his unexpected death in 1990.

Texas will likely continue to supply a stream of blues talent due to its oft-thriving club scene, particularly in Austin, Texas. The world is now well aware of the many talented White blues bands to emerge from the area, the best and most recognizable of those being the Fabulous Thunderbirds, which were founded by Stevie Ray Vaughan's brother Jimmie. The presence of one of the world's leading blues clubs, Antone's, in the city bodes well for ongoing development of regional blues talent.

—*Richie Unterberger*

10 Recommended Albums:

Various Artists, *Blues Masters Series, Vol. 3: Texas Blues* (Rhino)

Various Artist, *Texas Music, Vol. 1: Postwar Blues Combos* (Rhino)

T-Bone Walker, *The Complete Black & White Recordings* (Capitol)

Bobby "Blue" Bland, *I Pity the Fool* (MCA)

Clarence "Gatemouth" Brown, *The Original Peacock Recordings* (MCA)

Albert Collins, *Ice Pickin'* (Alligator)

Hop Wilson, *Steel Guitar Flash!* (Ace)

Freddie King, *Hide Away: The Best of Freddie King* (Rhino)

Johnny Winter, *Johnny Winter* (Columbia)

Stevie Ray Vaughan, *Greatest Hits* (Epic)

BLUES SLIDE GUITAR

The swooping, stinging sound of the slide guitar is one of the most striking and popular characteristics of the blues. It's also one of the sounds that most audibly links rural traditions with urban ones, and acoustic styles with the electric age. Some guitarists, like Elmore James and his acolytes Hound Dog Taylor and J.B. Hutto, have more or less built their entire style around it; many others brandish their command of the slide at least occasionally.

The origins of the use of the slide guitar in the blues—like many topics concerning the origins of the blues as a whole—are subject to varying historical interpretations. Some assert that the style didn't become widespread until it became popular in Hawaii in the 1890s, spreading to the mainland by the turn of the century. Joseph Kekuku has been credited with popularizing the concept of fretting guitar strings with objects rather than fingers, and the influence of the slide guitar as it was played in Hawaii became influential in pop music as a whole, not just within the blues.

On the other hand, in *Deep Blues*, Robert Palmer writes that "the slide technique was originally associated with an African instrument that has been reported from time to time in the American South, the single-stringed musical bow. One-stringed instruments played with sliders seem to have survived principally among Black children, who would nail a length of broom wire to a wall and play it with a rock or pill bottle slider.

"The appearance of Black slide guitarists in the early 1900s has often been linked to the popularization of a similar technique by Hawaiian guitarists, but slide guitar wasn't native to Hawaii; it was introduced there between 1893 and 1895, reputedly by a schoolboy, Joseph Kekuku. It did not spread from Hawaii to the mainland until 1900, when it was popularized by Frank Fererra, and by that time Black guitarists in Mississippi were already fretting their instruments with knives or the broken-off necks of bottles."

The instrument that Palmer refers to is sometimes called the diddley bow, and is perhaps more common than he infers in this passage. A lot of the children who played with the diddley bow as a household toy became guitar players who adapted the technique to a proper instrument. And some of those musicians became professional, taking the rudiments of the technique with them even when they moved from the barn to the city. One of the most fascinating blues albums of all time was recorded by Eddie "One-String" Jones in 1960, then a homeless man on Los Angeles' Skid Row, who played a piece of wire on a 2 x 4 board with a whiskey flask. His album, *One String Blues*, may be the closest modern listeners can get to hearing the square root of the blues. Another interesting variation to this homemade instrument can be heard on a handful of mid-'50s recordings on the Specialty label by Willie Joe Duncan playing a larger electric version of the diddley bow called the Unitar. Whatever the case, there can be no doubt that the slide guitar caught on quickly with blues musicians. Its keening wail emulated in some respects the moans and cries of the human voice, and was a great medium for conveying the intense emotions of the songs, whether joyful or sorrowful. It also did not demand a lot in the way of high-tech equipment: pocket knives and a thimble-shaped piece of metal were adaptable for the purpose. One of the most popular vehicles for playing slide was a bottleneck that was shaped over flame; hence the term for "bottleneck" guitar, which is slide guitar as produced by such a device.

In his liner notes to *Blues Masters, Vol. 15: Slide Guitar Classics*, Cub Koda further distinguishes the style from its possible Hawaiian origins: "The major difference came largely in how the instrument was held. Hawaiian guitar was played with the instrument lying flat on the player's lap; this style was adapted by Whites to form the steel-guitar sound in country music.

"But by and large…black blues musicians replaced the steel bar with a bottleneck or metal tube fitted to one finger and simply continued to play the guitar in the standard Spanish position. Although the slide produced the same whiny effects that the bar

Music Map

Blues Slide Guitar

African One -String "Diddley Bow"	Hawaiian Style Slide Guitar introduced by Joseph Kekuku, 1895. Slo Hoopi, Frank Ferarra

Eddie "One String" Jones, Willie Joe Duncan

Delta & Chicago Styles '30s & '40s	Chicago Electric – '50s to '60s
Son House, Charlie Patton, Bukka White, Robert Johnson, Furry Lewis, Kokomo Arnold, Casey Bill Weldon, Tampa Red, Big Joe Williams, Robert Nighthawk, Mississippi Fred McDowell	Muddy Waters, Robert Nighthawk, Elmore James, Hound Dog Taylor, J.B. Hutto, Johnny Littlejohn, Homesick James, Joe Carter, Earl Hooker

Blind Lemon Jefferson, Leadbelly, Black Ace, Texas Knives & Steel

Modern Slide Guitar

Bonnie Raitt, Ry Cooder, George Thorogood, Sonny Landreth, Johnny Winter, Billy Gibbons

did for Hawaiian guitarists, it was used more for lead fills, an extension of the singer's voice, allowing the instrument to be fretted for somewhat conventional chording when not in use. By the time examples of this type of playing started appearing on phonograph records in the late '20s, the banjo's days as a popular blues instrument were numbered; slide guitar was in."

The slide guitar is often associated with Delta blues, although its use was, in fact, widespread throughout the music. Delta bluesmen, however, may have been more responsible than any others for midwifing the style's transition from acoustic to electric music. Charlie Patton, the first great star of Mississippi blues, left several excellent recorded examples behind, utilizing the slide to answer his own vocal lines. His contemporaries Son House and Bukka White took the style and sound content one step further with their allegiance to the metal bodied National guitar, which produced a loud, astringent sound built more on sheer volume than subtlety. The Nationals and Dobro models were the true link between acoustic and electric guitars. They were called "ampliphonic" guitars in early catalogs and Delta players quickly adapted to them for two basic reasons: 1) they were loud enough to be heard over the din in a juke joint, and 2) they could be used to bash an adversary senseless with seemingly little damage to the instrument itself. Certainly Robert Johnson–an artist who had an absolute mastery of *all* guitar styles–is probably the best known Delta slide practioner, with his work on classics like "Crossroads Blues" and "Come On In My Kitchen" standing tall as the epitome of taste, tone and feeling that modern-day artists working in the genre still aspire to. There was Muddy Waters, influenced by both Son House and Robert Nighthawk, who electrified the blues in Chicago. His 1948 "I Can't Be Satified"/"Feel Like Going Home" single, repeatedly referred to as a defining moment of early electric blues, utilized prominent slide guitar. Robert Nighthawk, who started recording in the '30s on acoustic and later went electric, was also a prime mover and shaker on the instrument. Playing in standard guitar tuning (most slide players tune their instrument to an open chord, usually pitched to E or G), Nighthawk's touch and tone were the smoothest and creamiest. Though largely a forgotten figure today, Nighthawk taught his style to Waters and Chicago's most versatile blues guitarist, Earl Hooker, and his influence extended all the way to Southern rocker Duane Allman.

One guitarist went as far as to make the electric slide guitar his defining trademark. Even listeners who aren't blues fans can identify the classic riff that Elmore James used on "Dust My Broom,"

the song that probably embodies the electric slide guitar sound more than any other. James' strongest suit, his unsurpassed mastery of the electric slide idiom fused with extreme volume and a unrelenting attack which he put to use on numerous recordings in the 1950s and early 1960s, is still the most prevalent style of slide guitar playing being heard today. He spawned a raft of Chicago acolytes who adapted his raw sound and style to their own needs, among them Hound Dog Taylor, Joe Carter, and J.B. Hutto. Elmore James had a particularly strong influence on British guitarists of the 1960s. Brian Jones, whose slide work graced a handful of early Rolling Stones sides, worked on the British beat club circuit as Elmo(re) Lewis and Jeremy Spencer of Fleetwood Mac–the biggest band of the late-'60s British blues boom besides John Mayall's Bluesbreakers–worshiped James' approach, and his immersion in Elmore's style approached the level of recreated art. To the larger record-buying public, James was immortalized in a spoken aside on the Beatles' "For You Blue," a George Harrison composition that prominently featured slide in the Elmore style.

Many blues-rock guitarists picked up the slide style, like Jeff Beck and Mike Bloomfield; though it didn't dominate their playing, they could summon the technique when called for. The best American blues-rock slide guitarist was certainly Duane Allman, who put the sound in the spotlight on Allman Brothers staples like their update of Blind Willie McTell's "Statesboro Blues." Duane's style evolved from the combination of Elmore's distorted tone and Earl Hooker's elegant standard tuning flourishes wedded to the extreme volume from Marshall stack amplification. Another modern master of the slide idiom was Ry Cooder, who did not limit its application to the blues or blues-rock, using it for his diverse explorations of many kinds of roots music, as well as in his voluminous soundtrack work. And certainly no dissertation of modern slide styles could leave out George Thorogood and Bonnie Raitt, both of whom have gone on to great success in the rock field. Raitt, who toiled for years on the blues circuit before her breakthrough, is one of the finest slide players going, being prominently influenced (and personally instructed) by her mentors, Mississippi Fred McDowell and Son House. Thorogood's hamfisted approach took Hound Dog Taylor's bare-bones raucous style and reduced it even further, if such a notion was possible.

Today, the slide guitar continues to have a standard place in the repertoire of many blues performers, whether as an integral component or an occasional spotlight. Like the blues itself, its frequent use in mainstream settings like film soundtracks (by Cooder and

others) means that blues slide guitar is no longer thought of as something exotic, but as part of the vernacular of American music.
—*Richie Unterberger & Cub Koda*

8 Recommended Albums:

Various Artists, *Blues Masters, Vol. 15: Slide Guitar Classics* (Rhino)
Various Artists, *Slide Guitar–Bottle Knives & Steel, Vol. 1 & 2* (CBS)
Various Artists, *Bottleneck Guitar Masterpieces* (Yazoo)
Robert Johnson, *King of the Delta Blues Singers* (CBS)
Elmore James, *The Sky is Crying* (Rhino)
Hound Dog Taylor, *Hound Dog Taylor & The HouseRockers* (Alligator)
Eddie "One-String" Jones, *One-String Blues* (Gazell)
Robert Nighthawk, *Live on Maxwell Street* (Rounder)

JAZZ-BLUES CROSSOVER

Blues and jazz draw from a wellspring of similar roots in African-American popular music and culture. The paths of each genre have diverged widely since the beginning of the 1900s, but before 1950, the styles were often deeply intertwined with each other. It's a marriage that will endure to some degree as long as blues and jazz are around; even today, contemporary jazz acts throw in plenty of bluesy quotes, and many musicians boast service in both jazz bands and R&B/blues outfits. Many festivals spotlight both blues and jazz artists, the most famous of them being the annual New Orleans Jazz & Blues festival. Not many current artists, however, could be said to straddle the blues/jazz fence to such an extent that they could be classified as members of either camp.

The distinctions were much blurrier in the early 1900s, when both blues and jazz had yet to fully form their identities. The influence of ragtime music and barrelhouse piano styles were strong formative elements of each. W.C. Handy, the Father of the Blues, led brass bands whose instrumentation and arrangements were likely more akin to jazz. The first artists to record the blues

were women singers, but these were the blues more in song structure and vocal phrasing than in the jazz/pop arrangements, which employed jazz greats such as Louis Armstrong and Coleman Hawkins. (The significance of the classic female blues singers is detailed in a separate essay.) Much later, in the 1950s, traditional jazz bandleader Chris Barber would play a key role in exposing the blues in his native Britain by featuring bluesmen as part of his shows, often imported from the States.

The most active period of cross-fertilization between blues and jazz may have been the 1930s and 1940s, when swing and big band styles were at their peak, and when the blues was moving toward a fuller and more citified sound. Jazz was still often played in dance halls, and needed some singers and song structures to help maintain its accessibility. Blues was moving toward a more sophisticated sound that would soon encompass full bands and electricity. Each form had much to learn from the other.

Several of the early big bands featured vocalists that not only borrowed from the blues in their songs and phrasing, but in turn influenced the evolution of other bluesmen. Jimmy Rushing, in his work with Count Basie, may have been the first notable blues-based singer to front a big band with a precursor to the "shouting" style. This was developed to its fullest shortly afterwards by singers with Kansas City-based swing bands, including Big Joe Turner, Jimmy Witherspoon, and Walter Brown.

Brown and Witherspoon both sang with the band of pianist Jay McShann, the bandleader with whom Charlie Parker first recorded. McShann is one of the artists most likely to be found in either the blues or jazz section of fine record stores; Turner and Witherspoon, throughout their career, moved with ease between the jazz and R&B worlds, sometimes changing their focus to fit the requirements of the gig or the record date. Eddie "Cleanhead" Vinson, who doubled on vocals and saxophone, was another performer who would be hard to tie to either style; he could not only sing the blues, but could play bop jazz as well, and led a band including John Coltrane in the late '40s, long before Coltrane made his mark on the jazz world.

Besides the "shouters," the main tributary of blues feeding into jazz was found in the boogie-woogie pianists of the late '30s and early '40s. Taking some cues from blues styles that had been

Music Map

Jazz-Blues Crossover

| W.C. Handy | | Ragtime Piano |
| Father of the blues | | Barrelhouse Piano |

| | Jazz Combos early '20s | Boogie Woogie |
| | Louis Armstrong, King Oliver | Albert Ammons, Cow Cow Davenport, Pete Johnson, Cripple Clarence Lotton |

| Jimmy Rushing, Big Joe Turner, Jimmy Witherspoon | Mamie Smith & Classic Blues Singers | Jazz Combos late '30s |
| | Bessie Smith, Ma Rainey | Benny Goodman Sextet with Charlie Christian on guitar, Louis Prima |

| Jump Blues | T-Bone Walker | West Coast Blues |
| Illinois Jacquet, Lionel Hampton's "Flying Home" | | |

| | Organ/Piano Trios | |
| | Jimmy Smith, Jack McDuff, Jimmy McGriff, John Patton, Mose Allison, Sam Lazar | |

developed in barrelhouses, Albert Ammons, Pete Johnson, and Meade Lux Lewis were the most instrumental figures in introducing boogie-woogie to jazz. The famed Spirituals To Swing concerts in New York City's Carnegie Hall in the late 1930s found the marriage between the idioms at their peak, featuring pioneers like Ammons, Johnson, Lewis, and Turner on the same stage; Robert Johnson, interestingly, was also planned to be included in the events, but died before he could be contacted.

Jazz greats would often use bluesy riffs and signatures in their work; the Rhino collection *Blues Masters, Vol. 13: New York City Blues* contains some good illustrations. The wild sax solo of Illinois Jacquet in Lionel Hampton's "Flying Home" rates as a leading forerunner of R&B, particularly the "honking" style of sax associated with the form. The shouters, honkers, and boogie-woogie would coalesce in the 1940s into jump blues, which in some senses was the ultimate jazz-blues fusion. As pioneered by Louis Jordan, Roy Milton, and many others starting in the mid-'40s (again, detailed in a separate essay), jump blues took the above factors and added a raw power and playful pop elements (particularly in the vocals) to the equation, while maintaining a rhythmic base and instrumentation quite close to swing jazz in some ways.

Jump blues wasn't composed solely of the above elements. The introduction of the electric guitar had far-reaching effects on pop music that nobody could have guessed in 1940, when a jazzman, Charlie Christian, established himself as the first virtuoso of the instrument. Christian can't be considered a blues/jazz artist (though examples of bluesy playing can be heard in his scant body of recorded work), but there's no question that he was a huge influence on the jump blues guitarists, particularly T-Bone Walker, one of the key figures of both jump blues and West Coast blues. Walker's single-string solos owed so much to jazz, as played by Christian on guitar and other jazzers on other instruments, that a case can be made for classifying Walker as a blues/jazzman as well, though his songs and roots were very much in the blues camp.

On the whole, the end of the jump blues phenomenon spelled an end to the intense interchange between blues and jazz. Jazz was evolving into be-bop and beyond; jump blues fed into R&B and rock 'n' roll. Chuck Berry's "Maybellene" may owe a little to jazz, for example, but the distance between Chuck Berry and, say, a mid-'50s jazz artist like Clifford Brown is a lot further than the distance between Louis Jordan and Lionel Hampton. Jazz bands were less oriented toward the dance halls now, and less apt to employ singers for that purpose, although some (such as Joe Williams, not to be confused with Big Joe Williams the country blues singer) kept the flame of old-school Jimmy Rushing-type vocals alive.

It's interesting to note, though, that quite a few major jazzmen were schooled in blues/R&B bands, or recorded sessions with them to help pay the rent, from Coltrane and Coleman on down. There was some movement in the other direction as well; guitarist Mickey Baker originally had his heart set on being a jazz musician, but instead became one of the best blues influenced rock 'n' roll guitarists of all time–partly, again, as a result of being repeatedly called upon to play R&B sessions. Earl Bostic, who played in Lionel Hampton's band in the 1940s, found his true calling as an R&B saxophonist. Two respected jazz players, saxophonists David "Fathead" Newman and Hank Crawford, had bluesy leanings that would come in handy when they worked as sidemen on some of Ray Charles' bluesiest recordings. But even here, the relationship between blues and jazz grows increasingly tangential.

The blues-jazz link had another fling in the '60s, albeit in a somewhat distant form, in the work of several keyboardists. Organists Jack McDuff, Jimmy McGriff, Jimmy Smith, and John Patton, nowadays recognized as pioneers of "soul-jazz," often drew upon blues styles and material; one of Smith's biggest set pieces, for instance, was a cover of "I've Got My Mojo Working." Jazz pianist/vocalist Mose Allison (who began recording in the late 1950s) had a distinctive bluesy hipster style, both on originals like "Young Man's Blues" and "Parchman Farm," and covers of songs by Willie Dixon and Sonny Boy Williamson; he'd prove to be an unexpected influence on British groups like the Who, Yardbirds, and John Mayall, all of whom covered Allison songs. In Britain itself, Georgie Fame took up a blues/jazz style similar to Allison's, though with much more of a pop/R&B base.

—Richie Unterberger

15 Recommended Albums:

Various Artists, *Blues Masters, Vol. 11: Classic Blues Women* (Rhino)
Various Artists, *Blues Masters, Vol. 13: New York City Blues* (Rhino)
Jimmy Rushing, *The Essential Jimmy Rushing* (Vanguard)
Big Joe Turner, *Complete 1940–1944* (Official)
Jimmy Witherspoon & Jay McShann, *Jimmy Witherspoon & Jay McShann* (DA)
Albert Ammons, *King of Boogie (1939–1949)* (Blues Classics)
Meade Lux Lewis, *1939–1954* (Story of Blues)
Various Artists, *Blues Masters, Vol. 5: Jump Blues Classics* (Rhino)
Various Artists, *Blues Masters, Vol. 14: More Jump Blues* (Rhino)
Louis Jordan, *The Best of Louis Jordan* (MCA)
T-Bone Walker, *The Complete Capitol/Black & White Recordings* (Capitol)
Mose Allison, *Greatest Hits* (Prestige)
Ray Charles, *Blues & Jazz* (Rhino)
Various Artists, *Blue Funk: The History of the Hammond Organ* (Blue Note)
Eddie "Cleanhead" Vinson, *And Roomful of Blues* (Muse)

SOUL BLUES

The blues is sometimes stereotyped as a purist sort of music that strays little from its conventions. While it's true that it's more static than some other styles, it's never been immune from outside trends. The classic female blues singers of the '20s drew heavily from vaudevillian pop; blues electric guitar pioneer T-Bone Walker had a lot of jazz on his mind; the jump blues greats took from jazz and R&B in almost equal measures. And soul music has exerted a substantial influence upon the blues since the 1960s.

Some more skeptical blues fans may assert that many blues artists put some soul in their music as a matter of professional survival. The broader, more likely truth is that blues performers of the late 20th century cannot help but reflect some of the musical and social climate of their time. Soul music was one of the primary voices of African-American culture in the 1960s and 1970s. Much more often than not, performers schooled in the blues added soul flavor not just to adapt, but because they genuinely loved and were inspired by soul music.

Soul blues has been with us since soul music itself began to form as a distinct entity in the early '60s; precursors of soul music like Percy Mayfield and Charles Brown had already mixed R&B, gospel, and blues a good decade or more prior to that. The first, and maybe the best, of the soul/blues singers is Bobby "Blue" Bland. Bobby actually began recording in the early '50s, and always had a strong R&B flavor from the git-go. He truly reached his stride, however, in the 1960s, when he recorded an extraordinarily lengthy series of fine singles that incorporated horn charts and the sort of gospel-inflected vocals common to most great soul singers. Many of these weren't confined to the specialist blues markets, but were genuine big R&B hits, occasionally making the pop charts as well. Line up a few listeners against a wall, play them Bland's greatest hits, and ask them whether to classify the results as blues or soul; you'll probably end up with something close to a 50-50 split, or at the least with a lot of people who can't make up their minds.

Bland is an unusual textbook example of a virtually equal blues/soul hybrid. One of his chief inspirations, B.B. King, has never been thought of as a soul man, but has often had a prominent gospel and soul feel to his work. This was particularly true in the late '60s, when he frequently employed a large horn section, and for a while enlisted the services of arranger Johnny Pate, who had contributed to classic Chicago soul records by the likes of Major Lance and the Impressions. Two other Kings, Freddie and (especially) Albert, maintained some presence on the R&B charts with their blends of fierce blues guitar and contemporary soul-leaning material.

Horns were key ingredients in updating '50s blues, or '50s R&B/blues, for the '60s audiences. By extension, they also enabled some performers to maintain a foothold on the R&B charts, while the more guitar-harmonica-oriented "classic" combos were confined to more specialized audiences and a lower level of the club circuit. Junior Parker, Little Milton, and Lowell Fulson (famous for "Tramp")–all of whom had roots in pre-1960s blues and R&B–were some of the most successful of them. Some of the more purist-minded blues collectors much prefer these singers' earlier work, finding their later soul/blues too smooth and urbane, although in all cases these artists found their greatest popular success with their soul-conscious tunes.

Not all veterans in the '50s were as successful with this strategy. Amos Milburn, for instance, recorded an odd album for Motown in the early '60s that rounded off his jump blues with typical early '60s Motown production values. Although the results actually weren't that bad, it was an instant collector's item (and, predictably enough, reissued on CD with bonus cuts in the mid-1990s). It's not too well known that Motown occasionally tried to do similar things with a few other blues artists in the early '60s, as can be heard on the *Motown's Blue Evolution* compilation.

There were also a number of hard-core blues acts who simply added a dollop of soul to the proceedings without diminishing their basic power or substantially altering the focus of their guitar-bass-drums lineup. Major Chicago blues stars Junior Wells, Buddy Guy, and Magic Sam all made some of their best recordings in the 1960s; all of them added a bit of inventive soul sophistication in their songwriting and arrangements without sounding forced. Check out Wells' vocal mannerisms on much of his 1965 classic, *Hoodoo Man Blues* (also featuring Buddy Guy), which betrays a definite James Brown influence.

Speaking of JB, it wasn't unknown (although not very common either) for established soul singers to delve into the blues occasionally. Brown did this more often than most, though mostly limiting his blues excursions to album tracks. Nothing could hide the fact that he was far more talented and innovative as an R&B/soul/funk pioneer than a straight blues singer, but the double CD *Messin' with the Blues* compiles his most blues-oriented material; it's not so bad, and there's a lot more of it than you would guess.

In *The Blackwell Guide to Blues*, Jeff Hannusch defines soul blues as "singers that have a gospel background and who bring an urgent 'churchy' approach to their music." Such performers usually fall on the soul side of the soul/blues hybrid. Artists such as Otis Clay, Little Johnny Taylor, and O.V. Wright are apt to strike many listeners not so much as blues singers, but as soul singers with a bluesy feel. Whether you classify them within the rubric of the blues or not, there's no doubt that the aforementioned vocalists enjoy a lot of appeal among both blues and soul fans (who, of course, are often one and the same).

Soul/blues as an artistic force diminished, naturally, when soul music itself began to be superseded by disco in the mid-'70s, and then by rap and urban contemporary in the '80s and '90s, among the Black audience. The Malaco label was sort of a stronghold for "old-school" soul/blues, releasing efforts in the style by Z.Z. Hill, Denise LaSalle, and Latimore, as well as recording veterans who had fallen out of favor with mainstream audiences, such as Johnnie Taylor, Bobby "Blue" Bland, and Little Milton. Some of the Malaco titles proved surprisingly popular with a Black audience supposedly only concerned with less traditional styles. Hill's *Down Home* in particular was a popular success that exceeded all expectations.

More often than not, though, Malaco product was much more soul than blues. Many listeners who aren't concerned with critical distinctions would even be unlikely to classify it as soul/blues at all, but merely as rootsy soul. Popular blues and soul were so thin on the ground in the early half of the 1980s that one sometimes got the feeling that critics were championing the Malaco sound not on its merit, but because it was utilizing some of the proper approved ingredients, and there were so few other releases of the sort attracting any attention outside of the specialized/collector audiences.

Soul/blues as a label is applied to few current releases, but that may be because soul itself has been permanently absorbed into the fabric of contemporary blues. Many if not most of today's top electric blues performers–Robert Cray, Joe Louis Walker, Koko Taylor, and Jimmy Johnson (brother of soul singer Syl Johnson), to name a few–put a lot of soul flourishes into their songwriting, arrangements, and vocal delivery. The recently deceased Ted Hawkins also showed how soul could figure in contemporary acoustic blues. A rap-hip-hop/blues fusion, however, doesn't seem imminent, although White alternative rockers like Beck, G. Love, and Bobby Sichran have given it a try.

—Richie Unterberger

20 Recommended Recordings:

Bobby "Blue" Bland, *I Pity the Fool* (MCA)
Bobby "Blue" Bland, *Turn On Your Love Light* (MCA)
Various Artists, *Soul Shots, Vol. 7: Urban Blues* (Rhino)
B.B. King, *Blues on Top of Blues* (BGO)
Junior Parker, *Junior's Blues: The Duke Recordings, Vol. 1* (MCA)
Little Milton, *Chess Blues Master Series* (Chess)
Lowell Fulson, *Blue Days, Black Nights* (Ace)
Amos Milburn, *The Motown Sessions, 1962–1964* (Motown)
Various Artists, *Motown's Blue Evolution* (Motown)
James Brown, *Messing with the Blues* (Polydor)
Albert King, *Born under a Bad Sign* (Mobile Fidelity)
Various Artists, *The Stax Blues Brothers* (Stax)
Z.Z. Hill, *Down Home* (Malaco)
Junior Wells, *Hoodoo Man Blues* (Delmark)
Magic Sam, *West Side Soul* (Delmark)
Otis Clay, *Soul Man: Live in Japan* (Rooster Blues)
Johnnie Taylor, *Raw Blues* (Stax)
Robert Cray, *Strong Persuader* (Mercury)
Ted Hawkins, *Happy Hour* (Rounder)
Joe Louis Walker, *Blue Soul* (Hightone)

BLUES REDISCOVERIES

When blues enthusiasts pawed through their collection of rare 78s in the 1950s, performers like Robert Johnson, Bukka White, and Skip James were little more than names on a label. There was little, if any, historical information that documented how these singers lived, where they came from, how they came to be recorded (however briefly), or how they felt about their life and art. Looking at the records and imagining who the performers may have been seemed as futile as trying to touch a ghost; in many cases, it was uncertain whether these singers, few of whom had recorded after the early 1940s, were still alive or not.

A few of these collectors and enthusiasts became determined to tackle the challenge of chasing down these ghosts, dead or alive. Sam Charters' *The Country Blues* (published in 1959), and other scholarly studies that treated the blues as an art form worthy of serious respect, ignited a hunger for more information about its originators. Listening to the records (which, in the late 1950s, were themselves hard to come by) wasn't enough; surely these men and women had stories to tell, and, if they were still alive and healthy, more songs to sing. Folklorists and general enthusiasts such as Mack McCormick, David Evans, Chris Strachwitz, Alan Lomax, John Fahey, and Ed Denson, were dedicated enough to start to comb the American South for living embodiments of the blues tradition. What they found was more than they could have possibly hoped existed.

By the mid-'60s, Bukka White, Skip James, Son House, Mississippi John Hurt, and Furry Lewis had all been relocated. They had not willfully vanished into obscurity, or deliberately retired from music. Their recording careers had come to an end, often under premature circumstances. In most instances they continued to play music for live audiences, for their families, or simply for themselves. However, in the absence of opportunities to record in the studio, or to play for large audiences in an African-American community that was increasingly less interested in rural blues, they had turned to other sources of livelihood, unaware of the increasing appeal of their music to White audiences.

Finding these legends of the past often required efforts bordering on private detective work. Skip James and Son House, it has been reported, were rediscovered on the exact same day in 1964, though in widely differing circumstances; James was ill in Tunica County Hospital in Mississippi, while House wasn't in the South at all, having relocated to upstate New York about 20 years previously. John Fahey found Bukka White by writing a letter to "Bukka White, Old Blues Singer, c/o General Delivery, Aberdeen, MS" (a town that happened to be mentioned in one of White's songs); a relative of White's who worked for the post office chanced upon the correspondence, and helped direct Fahey to Memphis, where White had been living since the early 1940s.

No doubt a good film lies in the haphazard and semi-comic circumstances of these searches. In his novel *Nighthawk Blues*, Peter Guralnick tells of three obsessive blues collectors who, after years of passionate correspondence, decide to meet face-to-face and embark upon a search of the South for one of their heroes, only to find that they can't stand each other. Guralnick also tells the

Music Map

Blues Rediscoveries

Folklorists who searched and rediscovered or discovered the remaining greats and collected important information on the rest	The Greats that were found...
Alan Lomax, Mack McCormick, David Evans, Chris Strachwitz, Ed Denson, John Fahey, Al Wilson, Samuel Charters	Son House, Skip James, Mississippi John Hurt, Bukka White, Robert Pete Williams, Smoky Babe, Furry Lewis, Memphis Willie B., Drifting Slim, Mississippi Fred McDowell, Mance Lipscomb, Peg Leg Howell

true story, in his essay collection *Feel Like Going Home*, of the extreme difficulty in finding a bluesman who had already been rediscovered (Robert Pete Williams), as he navigates the Louisiana backroads with few clues or landmarks to guide him. Then there were the adjustments that some of the performers had to make as they readied themselves for new audiences. Dick Waterman, who located House in Buffalo and managed the guitarist, told the following story in Francis Davis' *History of the Blues*:

"A month or so later, we brought Son to Cambridge, Massachusetts, to get him ready for the Newport Folk Festival [and introduced him to] Al Wilson, who later moved to Los Angeles and was a founding member of the group Canned Heat. Al played open-tuning bottleneck and could play all the styles. He could play Bukka White, Son House, Charley Patton, and Blind Lemon Jefferson–he could really play. And he sat down with Son, knee to knee, guitar to guitar, and said, 'Okay, this is the figure that in 1930, you called "My Black Mama,"' and played it for him. And Son said, 'Yeah, *yeah*, that's me, that's me. I played that.'

"And then Al said, 'Now about a dozen years later, when Mr. Lomax came around, you changed the name to "My Black Woman," and you did it this way.' He showed him. And Son would say, 'Yeah, yeah. I got my recollection now, I got my recollection now.' And he would start to play, and the two of them played together. Then, Al reminded him of how he changed tunings, and played his own "Pony Blues" for him. There would not have been a rediscovery of Son House in the 1960s without Al Wilson. Really. Al Wilson taught Son House how to play Son House."

In many (but not all) cases, the actual skills of the performers were barely diminished, or undiminished. Since their "retirements," an LP market had developed for country blues, as well as a college/festival-oriented folk circuit that was eager to hear the music performed live. James, White, House, Hurt, and others resumed their careers with considerable success, with assistance from committed managers like Dick Waterman and sympathetic record labels like Vanguard.

Some purists held that the best work of these resuscitated legends were their original 78s, recorded in the artists' relative youth, in the 1920s and 1930s. Contemporary albums, they contended, were pale shadows of the glory of the vintage singles. For the most part, though, those who bought the LPs disagreed, finding them powerful statements on their own terms. There were also the considerations that in the '60s, before vintage blues reissue compilations were common, many listeners didn't have the patience to relocate the rare original singles; and even if they could hear the originals, non-fanatics often much preferred the clear sound of modern studios to the scratchy and hissy original 78s. Certainly James, Hurt, and White made some good records in the 1960s, and proved to be engaging and passionate live acts.

Another welcome result of the search for old blues legends was the discovery (as opposed to rediscovery) of elderly talents that had never recorded before. Folklorist Alan Lomax included Mississippi Fred McDowell on his landmark box set of the late 1950s, *The Sounds of the South*, which documented all sorts of American folk styles. McDowell went on to a lengthy and successful career that found him recording several albums, touring with Bonnie Raitt, and having one of songs, "You Got To Move,"

covered by the Rolling Stones on *Sticky Fingers*. Mance Lipscomb, a songster-type guitarist from Texas, released several well-received albums on Arhoolie. Robert Pete Williams was, like Leadbelly 25 years before him, discovered in the late '50s behind bars at a Louisiana penitentiary. Folklorist Harry Oster recorded him and helped arranged for his pardon, and Williams, one of the most idiosyncratic country bluesmen, went on to record more material and tour.

The 1960s, and in some cases the 1970s, found many of the rediscovered blues singers touring internationally, where they were sometimes filmed by organizations such as the BBC. Sometimes their compositions were covered by major rock groups, such as James' "I'm So Glad," giving those performers some measure of comfortable financial compensation for their work. In addition to generating some fine music, the blues revival enabled these originators to live out their later years with dignity, giving them the widespread acclaim they had often been denied in their younger years–an appropriate closure that any fan of the blues could appreciate.

—Richie Unterberger

9 Recommended Albums:

Various Artists, *Great Bluesmen at Newport* (Vanguard)
Skip James, *Skip James Today!* (Vanguard)
Mississippi John Hurt, *The Immortal* (Vanguard)
Son House, *Father of the Delta Blues: The Complete 1965 Sessions* (CBS)
Bukka White, *Big Daddy* (Biograph)
Robert Pete Williams, *Angola Prisoner's Blues* (Arhoolie)
Mississippi Fred McDowell, *Mississippi Delta Blues* (Arhoolie)
Mance Lipscomb, *Texas Sharecropper & Songster* (Arhoolie)
Peg Leg Howell, *The Legendary Peg Leg Howell* (Testament)

BRITISH BLUES

The term British blues is an anomaly. By rights, it shouldn't even exist. After all, Great Britain coming into the 20th century had no blues tradition, or any basis for it. Blues in Britain was an American import, much the same as rock 'n' roll, but predating it by a few years.

During the early 1950's, the first American blues artists had made brief sojourns to England and found the environment fertile. The bookings were good, the money better than they could get in America, and there was enthusiasm from a small but dedicated audience.

Big Bill Broonzy was the first American bluesman of any note to appear in England. He got to make his first of many recordings for France's Vogue label on that first visit to Europe, and was back a year later for another tour and more recording for Vogue.

Ironically, Broonzy did not play the material that he was most closely associated with in America on these tours. He was, of course, one of Chicago's top bluesmen, but the British weren't looking for authentic Chicago blues, but for something much more rudimentary. They perceived American blues as a brand of folk music, and for these appearances in England Broonzy adopted a deliberately archaic country blues persona, doing material that he had never really played before. He played acoustic guitar,

and performed folk songs on these tours, interspersing country blues with protest material that were perceived by British audiences as merely another strain of topical blues.

Broonzy returned again in 1955 and cut several sides for Pye Records; the producer for these sessions was future British pop recording impresario Joe Meek. Among those recordings, available on CD under the title *Big Bill Broonzy: The 1955 London Sessions*, are a handful of those topical songs, most notably the poignant "When Do I Get To Be Called A Man."

The man responsible for bringing Broonzy to England was Chris Barber, leader of a jazz band that included a small group dedicated to American blues. Guitarist Alexis Korner and blues harpist Cyril Davies formed the core of Barber's blues unit, performing a set during the band's shows that proved especially popular with a small but vocal part of Barber's audience.

Meanwhile, Barber continued to book American performers, who kept coming over and finding the atmosphere and the money very much to their liking. But it was Muddy Waters' visit to England in 1958 that provided the real flashpoint for British blues, as well as showing how far the English audiences had to go in their understanding of the genre.

Muddy went on stage in England for the first time backed by Otis Spann and members of Barber's band, playing an electric solid body Fender guitar. This was a shock to British audiences, especially the folk purists and jazz aficionados who made up most of the crowd that night–authentic American blues as the British understood it had nothing to do with electric guitar. More striking still, Muddy had his instrument turned up to his usual Chicago-scale decibel level. If the sight of the amplified guitar startled the audience, the slashing tone that it generated caused outrage and a near panic among the purists. Muddy's performances on the 1958 tour were greeted with ecstatic press coverage and unbridled enthusiasm by concertgoers, after the initial "shock" of his first performance wore off. His concerts had attracted thousands of fans from all over England who had only heard of him, including many younger blues enthusiasts who were only just beginning to discover the music that Korner and Davies had been playing all along.

By this time, Korner and Davies had split with Barber and after Muddy's tour, they chose to plug in themselves. From 1958 on, they began playing electric blues with a new, inspired urgency. The band was called Blues Incorporated, and featured, at various times, Art Wood (elder brother of Ron Wood) on vocals, Graham Bond, Long John Baldry, Charlie Watts, Jack Bruce and Ginger Baker. Basically anyone with talent and the right instrument could sit in, and those that did in the early period of the band's existence included Mick Jagger and Brian Jones.

By 1962, Blues Incorporated had been given a residency at the Marquee Club in London, and it was here that the band recorded their first album–and the first blues long-player ever made in England–for Britain's Decca Records. *R&B From the Marquee* was recorded live by producer/impresario Jack Good (best remembered for creating the American television series *Shindig*) after hours at the club.

But by the time it was released, Korner and Davies had split up over Korner's desire to add horns–which Davies abhorred–to the group's lineup. Davies formed the Cyril Davies All-Stars, a very promising group. The band got to record a handful of singles before Davies was stricken with leukemia and died early in 1964. Korner kept Blues Incorporated going in different incarnations through 1966, but by that time the main thrust of British blues had passed him by.

From the days of its residency at the Marquee, the original Blues Incorporated served as a catalyst for the formation of numerous bands that would lay claim to dominance of British blues. John Mayall's Bluesbreakers featuring Eric Clapton, the original Fleetwood Mac with Peter Green, and Cream, could all trace their roots back to Blues Incorporated.

But it was the Rolling Stones that dominated the pack. From 1963 onward the Rolling Stones were the definitive blues band, although after their chart-topping success with a cover of Willie Dixon's "Little Red Rooster," the blues would serve more as a source of inspiration than songs for the group's most visible work.

Meanwhile, American blues had become big business in England and throughout Europe. Beginning in 1962, with the first American Folk-Blues Festival organized by German blues enthusiast Horst Lippmann, dozens of American blues stars–including Muddy Waters, Howlin' Wolf, and Sonny Boy Williamson II–had begun making annual or semi-annual treks to Europe, appearing throughout Europe. These tours were extremely lucrative for the performers, and the fees were many times what these men and women could have expected to make in a week of working in American blues clubs. Some of the players, such as Eddie Boyd and Champion Jack Dupree, ultimately made their homes in Europe in the wake of their performing experience. The American and younger British blues enthusiasts also got to work together on occasion; Sonny Boy Williamson recorded with both the Yardbirds and the Animals, and also toured backed by both of those bands and the original R&B-based Moody Blues.

The Rolling Stones manifested their love of American blues in a slightly different fashion, covering songs by Willie Dixon and Muddy Waters on their singles and albums, and insisting that Howlin' Wolf be their featured guest for their debut appearance on *Shindig* in America. The sight of the Stones genuflecting before the 6' 4", 250-pound Howlin' Wolf (making his first appearance on American network television) revealed as much about the groups' origins and tastes as their own records of the era did, and more about the roots of British rock than any routinely vacuous interviews of the period.

Although there were a handful of British blues pianists and harpists, the dominant instrument was the guitar. Muddy Waters marveled at the array of axemen he encountered in England, many of whom impressed him with their technical skills, although he doubted that England could produce a truly effective blues singer. Eric Burdon and Mick Jagger came the closest in the vocal department, but among guitarists, the list was virtually endless, beginning with Eric Clapton, Keith Richards, Jeff Beck, and Brian Jones, and ending later in the decade with Jimmy Page, Mick Taylor, and Peter Green.

The Rolling Stones' success made it possible for their manager, Andrew "Loog" Oldham, to form his own independent label, Immediate Records, which became a vehicle for many lesser known blues-based outfits and performers, including Fleetwood Mac, Santa Barbara Machine Head (whose members later formed the core of the original Deep Purple), Savoy Brown, T.S. McPhee, Jo-Ann Kelly, and Dave Kelly. Jimmy Page, Jeff Beck, and Eric Clapton also recorded a large handful of instrumental tracks that later turned up on Immediate, to the distress and embarrassment of all concerned.

By 1966, the British blues boom had become an explosion as electric British blues began to dominate the entire field. Cream, Fleetwood Mac, the Yardbirds, Ten Years After, and, later on, Led Zeppelin–dominated by the sounds of guitarists Eric Clapton, Peter Green, Jeremy Spencer, Jeff Beck, Alvin Lee, and Jimmy Page–came to define British blues, and by the end of the 1960's, British blues had become a part of mainstream rock on both sides of the Atlantic. Absorbed by the British in the 1950s and very early 1960s, the blues as they played it was carried back across to America by bands like the Stones and the Animals, and reabsorbed by the Americans, in the guise of the Allman Brothers and other Southern rock bands of the era like ZZ Top.

—Bruce Eder

15 Recommended Albums:

Animals, *The Complete Animals* (EMI)
Blues Incorporated, *R&B From the Marquee* (Mobile Fidelity)
Duster Bennett, *Justa Duster* (Blue Horizon)
Cream, *Fresh Cream* (Polydor)
John Mayall's Bluesbreakers, *Featuring Eric Clapton* (Polygram)
John Mayall, *London Blues (1964–1969)* (Polygram)
Rolling Stones, *Rolling Stones (England's Newest Hitmakers)* (ABKCO)
Rolling Stones, *Rolling Stones Now!* (ABKCO)
Rolling Stones, *12 x 5* (ABKCO)
Yardbirds, *Five Live Yardbirds* (Rhino)
Yardbirds, *Smokestack Lightning* (Sony Music)
Fleetwood Mac, *Black Magic Woman* (Epic)
Various Artists, *Anthology of British Blues, Vols. 1 and 2* (Immediate)
Various Artists, *Dealing With the Devil* (Sony Music)
Various Artists, *Stroll On* (Sony Music)

BLUES ROCK

The blues and rock 'n' roll are often divided by the thinnest of margins. Blues, more than any other musical style, influenced the birth of rock 'n' roll, and the amplified electric blues of Chicago, Memphis, and other cities during the 1950s was separated from the new music only by its more traditional chord patterns, cruder production values, and narrower market. The term "blues rock" came into being only around the mid-'60s, when White musicians infused electric blues with somewhat louder guitars and flashy images that helped the music make inroads into the White rock audience.

Many of the early blues rockers were British musicians who had been schooled by Alexis Korner. Helping to organize the first overseas tours by many major American bluesmen, Korner–as well as his former boss Chris Barber, and his early collaborator Cyril Davies–was more responsible than any other musician for introducing the blues to Britain. More important, he acted as a

mentor to many younger musicians who would form the R&B-oriented wing of the British Invasion, including Jack Bruce, members of Manfred Mann, Eric Clapton, and, most significantly, the Rolling Stones, whose lead vocalist, Mick Jagger, sang with Korner before the Stones were firmly established. (The evolution of British blues is discussed in more depth in a separate piece.)

The Rolling Stones featured a wealth of blues in their early repertoire. They and other British groups like the Yardbirds and Animals brought a faster and brasher flavor to traditional numbers. They would quickly branch out from 12-bar blues to R&B, soul, and finally, original material of a much more rock-oriented nature, without ever losing sight of their blues roots. Several British acts, however, were more steadfast in their devotion to traditional blues, sacrificing commercial success for purism. These included the Graham Bond Organization (featuring future Cream members Jack Bruce and Ginger Baker) and, most significantly, John Mayall's Bluesbreakers. In early 1965, Mayall's group provided a refuge for Eric Clapton, who left the Yardbirds on the eve of international success in protest to their forays into pop-rock. His sole album with Mayall, *Bluesbreakers With Eric Clapton* (1966), was an unexpected Top Ten hit in the U.K. Clapton's lightning fast and fluid leads were vastly influential, both on fellow musicians and in introducing tough electric blues to a wider audience.

While Clapton would rapidly depart the Bluesbreakers to form Cream (who took blues rock to more amplified and psychedelic levels), Mayall continued to be Britain's foremost exponent of blues rock, as a bandleader of innumerable Bluesbreakers lineups. Many musicians of note were schooled by Mayall, the most prominent being Clapton's successors, Peter Green and future Rolling Stone Mick Taylor. Like Clapton, Green left Mayall after just one album, forming the first incarnation of Fleetwood Mac with a couple members of Mayall's rhythm section, John McVie and Mick Fleetwood.

Under Green's helm, Fleetwood Mac were the finest British blues-rock act of the late '60s. They invested electric Chicago blues with zest and humor, but their own material–featuring Green's icy guitar tone (praised by no less a master than B.B. King), rich vocals, and personal, often somber lyrics–was more impressive, and extremely successful in Britain, where they racked up several hit albums and singles. As a bandleader of rotating lineups featuring budding guitar geniuses, Chicago harmonica player Paul Butterfield was Mayall's American counterpart; the two even recorded a rare EP together in the late '60s. The Paul Butterfield Blues Band's first pair of albums featured the sterling guitar duo of Michael Bloomfield and Elvin Bishop, as well as members of Howlin' Wolf's band in the rhythm section. Willing to tackle soul, jazz, and even psychedelic jams in addition to Chicago blues, they were the first American blues-rock band, and the best.

While blues rock was less of a commercial or artistic force in the U.S. than the U.K., several other American blues rockers of note emerged in the '60s. Canned Heat were probably the most successful, reaching the Top 20 with "On The Road Again" and an electric update of an obscure rural blues number, "Going Up The Country." Steve Miller played mostly blues, with Barry Goldberg and as the leader of his own band, in his early days before tuning into the psychedelic ethos of his adopted base of San Francisco. The Electric Flag, featuring Michael Bloomfield, mixed blues-rock with psychedelic music and tentative outings into an early version of jazz-rock. Captain Beefheart was briefly a White counterpart to Howlin' Wolf before heading off on a furious avant-garde tangent, though his growling vocals always seemed to maintain an unfathomable link to the Delta.

In New York, Bob Dylan used Bloomfield on much of his *Highway 61 Revisited* album, and teamed with the Butterfield Band for his enormously controversial electric appearance at the 1965 Newport Folk Festival. John Hammond, Jr. recorded blues rock in the mid-'60s with future members of the Band, and Dion cut some overlooked blues-rock sides after being exposed to classic blues by the legendary Columbia A&R man John Hammond, Sr. The Blues Project–led by Al Kooper–often reworked blues songs with rock arrangements, although their musical vision was too eclectic to be pigeonholed as blues rock.

The influence of the first generation of blues rockers is evident in the early recordings of Jimi Hendrix, and indeed Jimi would always feature a strong element of the blues in his material. Albert King and B.B. King couldn't be called blues rockers by any stretch

Music Map

Blues Rock

Originators
Muddy Waters, Howlin' Wolf, Chuck Berry, Sonny Boy Williamson, Bo Diddley, Little Walter, Elmore James, Jimmy Reed, Robert Johnson, Willie Dixon, B.B. King, Albert King/Freddie King

The U.S.A.	The Present	The U.K.
Paul Butterfield Blues Band, Blues Project, Bob Dylan, John Hammond, Jr., Johnny Winter, Canned Heat, Steve Miller, Roy Buchanan	Stevie Ray Vaughan, The Fabulous Thunderbirds, Kenny Wayne Sheppard, Gary Moore, Chris Duarte, ZZ Top, George Thorogood, Robert Cray	Alexis Korner, Cyril Davies, Blues Incorporated, The Rolling Stones, John Mayall's Bluesbreakers, Cream, Ten Years After, Foghat, Savoy Brown, Rory Gallagher, Juicy Lucy, Chicken Shack, Climax Blues Band, Fleetwood Mac, The Yardbirds, The Animals

of the imagination, but their late '60s material betrays contemporary influences from the worlds of rock and soul that found them leaning more in that direction. Early hard rock bands like Led Zeppelin, Free, and the Jeff Beck Group played a great deal of blues, though not enough for purists to consider them actual blues acts.

The blues rock form became more pedestrian and boogie-oriented as the '60s came to a close. From Britain, Ten Years After, Savoy Brown, the Climax Blues Band, Rory Gallagher, Chicken Shack, Juicy Lucy, the Groundhogs, and Foghat all achieved some success. In the U.S., blues rock was the cornerstone of the Allman Brothers' innovative early '70s recordings (which in turned spawned the blues-influenced school of Southern rock), and Johnny Winter had success with a much more traditional approach.

Roy Buchanan, once billed (for a public television special) as "the best unknown guitarist in the world," had turned down an opportunity to join the Rolling Stones before concentrating on a solo career. Buchanan's vocals weren't strong enough to front a band, and thus his records were primarily instrumental showcases, although he did hire singers for his group. The same approach had been used by a couple of other brilliant guitarists with similar vocal liabilities, Jeff Beck and Harvey Mandel. Mandel, like Beck, was too eclectic to be categorized as a blues-rocker, but was often grounded in blues forms, and was a member of Canned Heat for a time.

Another guitarist who was more of an instrumentalist/composer than a singer, and who was associated with Captain Beefheart and the Rolling Stones, was Ry Cooder, whose palette is really way too diverse to fall within blues-rock. Some would classify another associate of Cooder's, Taj Mahal, as a blues-rocker, but an equal or greater number would simply see Mahal as a modern-day bluesman, albeit one with rock influences (especially in the mid-'60s, when he played with Cooder in an L.A. folk-rock-blues group, the Rising Sons).

While blues rock hasn't been a major commercial force since the late '60s, the style has spawned some hugely successful acts, like ZZ Top and Foghat, as well as influencing all hard rock since the late '60s to some degree. Those that kept the faith tended to concentrate on the more limited market of independent labels and small clubs, with the demand for party and boogie bands in small venues being a constant. Hence the appellation "bar band," one that serves as both a badge of honor and a putdown, depending upon the context and the tastes of the listener.

In general terms, second- and third-generation blues-rock bands have tended to prioritize instrumental virtuosity (unkinder souls would say instrumental flash) over vocal prowess. Guitarists Pat Travers and George Thorogood (noted for his crude, but effective, slide work) would fall in this category, as would Stevie Ray

Vaughan in the '80s, although his more tasteful excursions would find favor with both critics and popular audiences. Vaughan was based in Austin, Texas, a constant hotbed of blues-rock acts, due to its thriving roots music scene and small club circuit. The Fabulous Thunderbirds were easily the best–and most influential–of the blues-influenced outfits to emerge from that community. The success of '90s artists like Kenny Wayne Sheppard, Chris Duarte, and British guitarist Gary Moore shows that the audience for blues-rock is far from dead. Many guitarists, like Jeff Healey, Sonny Landreth, and Tinsley Ellis, enjoy a large and steady live following belied by their relatively modest record sales, as do original blues-rock vets like Johnny Winter. And, of course, some blues-influenced singer/guitarists are huge superstars, the biggest being Eric Clapton (who returned to pure blues on 1994's *From the Cradle*) and Bonnie Raitt (an accomplished slide blues guitarist who was more rooted in traditional blues styles when she began recording in the early '70s). Some Black blues bands have absorbed large influences from the rock world; the Robert Cray Band are the most well known of these, and there are others, such as Michael Hill's Blues Mob. And it is a cliche, but it is often true, that many white listeners would be unaware of black blues performers if they hadn't been led to them through the work of White blues-rock bands.

—Richie Unterberger

20 Recommended Albums:

John Mayall, *Bluesbreakers with Eric Clapton* (Deram)
John Mayall, *London Blues (1964–1969)* (PolyGram)
The Paul Butterfield Blues Band, *The Paul Butterfield Blues Band* (Elektra)
The Paul Butterfield Blues Band, *East-West* (Elektra)
Fleetwood Mac, *Black Magic Woman* (Epic)
Jimi Hendrix, *Blues* (MCA)
The Graham Bond Organization, *The Sound of '65* (Edsel)
Captain Beefheart, *Legendary A&M Sessions* (A&M)
Canned Heat, *Best of Canned Heat* (EMI)
Cream, *Fresh Cream* (Polydor)
John Hammond Jr., *So Many Roads* (Vanguard)
The Allman Brothers, *At Fillmore East* (Polydor)
Duffy Power, *Mary Open the Door* (Demon/Edsel)
Johnny Winter, *A Rock N' Roll Collection* (Columbia/Legacy)
Roy Buchanan, *Sweet Dreams: The Anthology* (Polydor)
Bonnie Raitt, *Bonnie Raitt* (Warner Bros.)
George Thorogood, *The Baddest of George Thorogood & the Destroyers* (EMI)

Music Map

Modern Acoustic Blues

Originators	The '60s and '70s	Today
Leadbelly, Blind Lemon Jefferson, Charlie Patton, Son House, Robert Johnson, Robert Pete Williams, John Lee Hooker, Jesse Fuller, Doctor Ross, Lightnin' Hopkins, J.B. Lenoir, Brownie McGhee, Sonny Terry, Mississippi Fred McDowell	Koerner, Ray & Glover, Dave Van Ronk, John Hammond, Jr., Taj Mahal, Ry Cooder, John Mayall, Duster Bennett, Jo Ann Kelly	Bonnie Raitt, John Cephas & Phil Wiggins, Ted Hawkins, Lonnie Pitchford, Rory Block, Corey Harris

Stevie Ray Vaughan, *Greatest Hits* (Epic)
The Fabulous Thunderbirds, *The Essential* (Chrysalis)
Eric Clapton, *From the Cradle* (Reprise)

MODERN ACOUSTIC BLUES

Modern acoustic blues isn't exactly a dying art, but it's certainly one that's bound to take a back seat to modern electric blues, perhaps forever. Electricity has been a staple of blues music for about 50 years. Emerging blues performers (and, for that matter, most middle-aged ones) have never known a world in which electric modern conveniences and electric instruments were not commonplace items. Being men and women of their time, most blues musicians are eager to make their mark with an electric sound, not an acoustic one. But there will always be a room for the intimate and stark qualities associated with acoustic instruments, and modern blues has had its share of interesting unplugged moments.

Electric bluesmen made conscious decisions to go unplugged for suitable occasions, especially when the folk circuit opened up to blues artists. John Lee Hooker, in particular, had simultaneous careers going for the electric R&B market and for the LP-oriented acoustic audience. To this day, he has an equal command of the electric and acoustic idioms. Snooks Eaglin and Lightnin' Hopkins were other important bluesmen who could alternate between the two worlds with grace. Labels like Arhoolie, Prestige, and Testament recorded plenty of acoustic blues in the 1960s, though these in the main reached back to a pre-World War II sensibility; one-man-band Dr. Isiah Ross' *Call the Doctor* outing on Testament is certainly worth hearing as an example of how full band arrangements can be emulated by one multi-instrumentalist.

One of the most overlooked and important pioneers of modern acoustic blues was J.B. Lenoir, who made his original mark as a second-tier electric Chicago blues guitarist in the 1950s. In the '60s, Lenoir found his greatest appreciation via European tours, and deliberately turned toward solo acoustic guitar arrangements. Lenoir recorded two acoustic albums, issued in Europe only, in the mid-'60s (with some minimal percussion from Fred Below and occasional backup vocal by Willie Dixon) that are notable not just for his full, rich guitar and vocals, but for their groundbreaking subject matter.

Lenoir had already revealed an unusually political bent in the 1950s on "Eisenhower Blues" and "Korea Blues." On the *Alabama Blues* and *Down in Mississippi* albums, he tackled the issues of civil rights, segregation, and Vietnam directly, as well as recording more celebratory songs that suggested African rhythmic and melodic roots. (The *Rolling Stone Record Guide* once called him the "Samuel Fuller of the blues," in acknowledgement of his social realism.) Lenoir, who died in 1967, is still an obscure figure, although he deeply impressed John Mayall, who recorded a song in his honor, and arranged for a posthumous compilation of some of his acoustic work.

Some of the most effective modern acoustic blues stylists had their roots in the blues/folk revival of the 1960s. Dave Van Ronk and Koerner, Ray, and Glover were among the earliest ones, but

the best blues guitarists to emerge from this scene were John Hammond and Rory Block. Hammond, inspired by the work of early bluesmen like Son House and Robert Johnson, has sometimes offered capable electric work as well; Block is a more acoustic-oriented performer, and also covers a great deal of material by the likes of Tommy Johnson and Charley Patton. It may that their principal contributions are as instrumentalists rather than singers/composers, but they've done a lot to preserve the traditions of deep acoustic blues.

The British blues boom of the late '60s gave rise to a few acoustic interpreters, most of whom are known, like Jo Ann Kelly, only as names on obscure import compilations. The most entertaining of the lot was probably Duster Bennett, who was once described as "England's answer to Jesse Fuller" for his remarkable one-man band performances. In the late 1960s John Mayall, never one to be satisfied with his personnel for too long, determined to explore an acoustic format while retaining a full band; *The Turning Point* (1969) was a very successful effort in this vein, both commercially and artistically.

For audiences with a rock orientation, the most accessible of the modern acoustic blues performers may be Taj Mahal, who's been making albums since the late '60s. Mahal is a master of Delta-ish acoustic blues, but is also eclectic, blending the blues sensibility with some rock and roots music influences, including calypso and reggae. That may make him too eclectic to be classified as a blues performer, at least in the eyes of some listeners, but it also ensures that his work holds greater interest for listeners who want something a little more ambitious than modern interpretations/updates of classic styles. An occasional associate of Taj's, Ry Cooder, could also be placed into this category. Cooder's plate is more diverse than Mahal's, and actually may be as diverse as anybody's, but often has a blues base. It's his soundtrack work, to the surprise of some, that often holds his bluesiest efforts.

Modern acoustic blues acts don't necessarily have to be solo performers. The duo act of John Cephas and Phil Wiggins have updated the Piedmont guitar-harmonica stylings of Brownie McGhee and Sonny Terry, occasionally nodding to gospel and R&B influences. Satan and Adam have had some success with a similar lineup, and Saffire, an all-woman trio, put a spin on things by mixing original material with covers of songs by classic women blues singers like Bessie Smith and Ma Rainey.

Some of the press championed Ted Hawkins as the great acoustic blues hope of the 1990s. Hawkins was "discovered" playing for tourists on the Venice Beach boardwalk in Los Angeles, and got much of his initial acclaim in England, rather than the United States. The acoustic guitarist owed a lot to soul music as well, his sweet vocals sometimes generating comparisons to Sam Cooke. After some albums for independent labels, Hawkins was discovered (again) by the major Geffen label, and may have been poised for a breakthrough to a wider audience before his unexpected death in the mid-1990s. His death, however, didn't mean the death of acoustic blues; younger performers are waiting in the wings, most notably Corey Harris, whose well-received acoustic

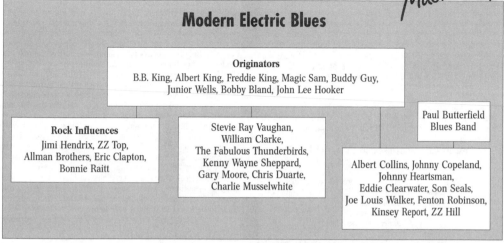

Music Map

Modern Electric Blues

Originators
B.B. King, Albert King, Freddie King, Magic Sam, Buddy Guy,
Junior Wells, Bobby Bland, John Lee Hooker

Rock Influences
Jimi Hendrix, ZZ Top,
Allman Brothers, Eric Clapton,
Bonnie Raitt

Stevie Ray Vaughan,
William Clarke,
The Fabulous Thunderbirds,
Kenny Wayne Sheppard,
Gary Moore, Chris Duarte,
Charlie Musselwhite

**Paul Butterfield
Blues Band**

Albert Collins, Johnny Copeland,
Johnny Heartsman,
Eddie Clearwater, Son Seals,
Joe Louis Walker, Fenton Robinson,
Kinsey Report, ZZ Hill

debut was noted for its African influence and its committed interpretation of Delta blues styles.

—*Richie Unterberger*

12 Recommended Albums:

John Lee Hooker, *The Country Blues of John Lee Hooker*
(Riverside)
Lightnin' Hopkins, *Lightnin' Hopkins* (Smithsonian/
Rounder)
Dr. Isiah Ross, *Call the Doctor* (Testament)
J.B. Lenoir, *Down in Mississippi* (L&R)
John Hammond, *Live* (Vanguard)
Rory Block, *High Heeled Blues* (Rounder)
Taj Mahal, *Taj Mahal* (CBS)
Ry Cooder, *Music By Ry Cooder* (Reprise)
John Mayall, *The Turning Point* (Deram)
John Cephas & Phil Wiggins, *Dog Days of August* (Flying Fish)
Ted Hawkins, *The Next Hundred Years* (DGC)
Corey Harris, *Between Night and Day* (Alligator)

MODERN ELECTRIC BLUES

Ask a room full of blues fans to appraise the state of contemporary electric blues, and you'll end up with almost as many opinions as there are people. In some senses, the blues has never been in better shape. Lots of major cities have clubs that feature the blues regularly, and the specialized market that attends to blues recordings is fairly healthy, though rarely cracking the pop charts. The blues has effectively penetrated the American mainstream via television specials, omnipresent use in films and commercials, and frequent representation at major music festivals.

Many blues fans, however, fret that the music isn't as good as it used to be, or at least isn't evolving in satisfactory directions. Every form of music will have its share of naysayers that bewail the passing of the good old days; it's human nature to find the grass greener on the other side of the fence. It's also hard to gain perspective on an era when you're right in the middle of it. But the blues, like everything else at the end of the 20th century, is in a state of post-modernism that can make it difficult to identify trends or major developments.

The period that "contemporary electric blues" refers to varies from analyst to analyst; more out of convenience than anything else, it can be defined as the decades following the "blues revival" of the 1960s. The survival of the blues itself, though often shaky, would never again be questioned. The challenge facing new and old artists alike would be to build upon the enormous body of classic work produced between 1920 and 1970 without sounding repetitious or abandoning the funda-

mental structures of the music. Looking back over the last couple of decades, we can at least zero in on a few widespread developments: the absorption of rock and soul influences, the proliferation of White blues or blues/rock bands, and the longevity/endurance of living legends who made their first recordings before the 1970s.

Rock and soul had already started to infiltrate hard-core electric blues in the 1960s, in the work of Junior Wells, Buddy Guy, Magic Sam, Albert King, Freddie King, Bobby Bland, and B.B. King, to name just a few. There was also the frequent blues influence to be found in the work of Jimi Hendrix, who could at some points have been considered something of an avant-garde bluesman. Electric blues combos of recent decades have continued to reflect the rock and soul scene, as heard in the fierce, lengthy guitar solos, the occasional funk-influenced rhythms, and the brass sections that are often used to punch things up on stage and in the studio. Some old-school Chicago electric blues players emerged into the spotlight in the 1970s, such as Fenton Robinson, Luther Allison, and Son Seals (who themselves were not ignorant of soul music). But much new talent boasted an increasing appetite for music that was somewhat less grounded in electric blues conventions, though retaining an urban polish.

Purists who dismiss the rock and soul-inflected blues artists of recent years as sell-outs are overlooking the fact that in order for the blues to survive as a living tradition, it cannot exist in a vacuum. From its inception, the blues has always responded to developments in popular music as a whole: the use of the guitar and piano in American folk and gospel, the percussive rhythms of jazz, the lyrics of Tin Pan Alley, and the widespread use of amplification and electric instruments all helped shape the evolution of the blues in the first half of the 20th century.

The blues artists that began to record in the 1970s and 1980s were also men and women of their time, listening not only to blues, but also to rock, pop, soul, and psychedelia. The result has been mixtures of the above elements, found in the funky, guitar-based sound of the Kinsey family, the soulish electric blues of Jimmy Johnson (brother of soul singer Syl Johnson), the African-leaning beats of some of Johnny Copeland's material, the soul-rock-blues fusion of Joe Louis Walker (who drew upon his extensive tenure on the gospel circuit), the horns that pepper some of Koko Taylor's records, or even the classical operatic training of the late Valerie Wellington. The most successful "crossover" efforts in these veins, by far, have been waxed by Robert Cray, whose modernized sound appeals to rock and pop audiences. His *Strong Persuader*, from 1986, became an unexpected pop hit, and he is one of the few blues performers of any era to dent the Top 40 of the pop album charts.

Those who like their soul-blues more downhome, and less oriented toward guitar showmanship, could look to offerings from the Malaco label, which gave a second lease on life to veterans like Z.Z. Hill, Bobby Bland, Denise LaSalle, and Johnnie Taylor. These records generally enjoyed a more predominantly Black audience than those by electric guitar-oriented bands, finding a niche among soul fans who felt disenfranchised by the move towards disco and rap music in R&B. For these listeners, Z.Z. Hill's *Down Home* album of the early '80s was just as pivotal a release as Robert Cray's *Strong Persuader*, demonstrating that earthy contemporary blues could achieve a measure of commercial success.

In recent years the torch for the limited contemporary soul-blues market has been picked up by the Atlanta-based Ichiban label. And zydeco, a whole strain of music with strong ties to the blues, whose exposure had primarily been limited to Louisiana, reached an all-time high of popularity in the 1980s and 1990s. Also providing a rawer alternative to slicker electric guitar sounds was the Fat Possum label, which gave deep South jukejoint veterans like Junior Kimbrough and R.L. Burnside their first national exposure.

The role of White musicians in the blues is a minefield of controversy in some quarters, as anyone who has read the letters section of *Living Blues* magazine over the last few years could tell you. The blues-rock explosion of the late '60s may have peaked with acts like Cream, Jimi Hendrix, and the Allman Brothers, but the number of bands performing and recording in the style has remained pretty high. They rarely scale the pop charts anymore (acts like Stevie Ray Vaughan and the Fabulous Thunderbirds being the exception), but work frequently in urban clubs, and record often for independent labels. And some rock stars, like Bonnie Raitt and Eric Clapton, keep elements of the blues at the top of the charts and throughout the airwaves, although they don't limit themselves to blues material exclusively.

By and large, the White blues bands of recent times place a greater emphasis on instrumental virtuosity than other factors. Many of them have also been called "bar bands," a designation that can carry positive or negative connotations, depending upon your taste. The most frequent criticism leveled at the performers is a lack of soul in the vocals, a lack of songwriting imagination, and a certain generic, shallow flashiness that sometimes gives way to overlong solos that play much better in a sweaty club than a compact disc.

The market is overcrowded with generic White blues band records (as it is with many other kinds of music, Black and White), but that shouldn't disguise the emergence of some genuine blues talents in recent decades. Texan Stevie Ray Vaughan was hailed as the Great White Hope in the blues field until his premature, accidental death in 1990, although he will most likely be remembered primarily as a guitarist rather than a singer. California was a breeding ground for modern harmonica virtuosos, including William Clarke, Rod Piazza, and Charlie Musselwhite (the last of whom had moved to the state after starting in Chicago in the 1960s). John Hammond, since the '60s, has been a living repository of sorts for most acoustic and electric blues guitar styles. The Fabulous Thunderbirds, featuring Jimmy Vaughan (brother of Stevie Ray) and Kim Wilson, were the best exponent of blues as you might experience it in a Texas club.

Blues, like jazz and folk, gives its performers a much longer lease on life than rock, rap, or pop. Blues acts do not so much reach a several-year peak and burn out, as they do reach that peak and maintain it, decade after decade. One of the pleasures of seeing B.B. King, Junior Wells, or Buddy Guy, is the knowledge that they'll sound about every bit as good now as they did 20 or 30 years ago. Such veterans have formed sturdy pillars of the modern electric blues scene simply by continuing to be themselves; Buddy Guy, for instance, seems to just get more and more popular, making inroads into the mainstream with his recent albums. And there's the case of John Lee Hooker, who reached his commercial peak as a senior citizen with his CD *The Healer*, and started to show up on the list of Grammy nominations after only about 40 years as a top bluesman.

In some cases the recent records of the blues vets don't match the best of their classic work, often due to a lack of good new material, or ill-conceived production, but the performers can usually be counted upon to deliver the goods live. To enhance the appeal of middle-aged and elderly blues artists, labels sometimes flavor their new releases with high-profile appearances by rock and pop stars. Hooker's '90s albums are prime examples of studio recordings that are jammed with celebrity cameos. It's an approach that doesn't wash well with many blues fans, but it does have the effect (as the Blues Brothers did in the late '70s) of leading lots of listeners with no blues schooling to the source, which can't be a bad thing.

The general ever-widening acceptance of the blues has also helped some performers break into a national audience after years or even decades of regional concentration and sporadic recording. Albert Collins, Johnny Copeland, and Johnny Heartsman are prominent examples of major bluesmen who began making records in the '50s and '60s, but are thought of as modern electric bluesmen that didn't make their true impact until the 1970s and 1980s. All of them proved extremely adaptable to the rock and soul influences that had infiltrated the music; fortunately the blues is willing to embrace artists who come into their musical prime in middle age, rather than dismiss them as non-contenders after a certain point in their youth.

If much contemporary blues has an easygoing, cheery air, that could be indicative of the whole form's emergence from the collector underground and African-American neighborhoods into the everyday fabric of life. Black America has changed a great deal since the early 1900s, as well, and this too is reflected in the lyrical and musical values of today's electric blues stars. For those who find the music's use at sporting events and television commercials gratuitously exploitative, there's plenty of the authentic thing to be found with just a little effort.

—Richie Unterberger

20 Recommended Albums:

Various Artists, *Blues Masters, Vol. 9: Postmodern Blues* (Rhino)
Various Artists, *Blues Fest: Modern Blues of the '70s* (Rhino)
Various Artists, *Blues Fest: Modern Blues of the '80s* (Rhino)
Various Artists, *Blues Fest: Modern Blues of the '90s* (Rhino)
Son Seals, *The Son Seals Blues Band* (Alligator)
Robert Cray, *Strong Persuader* (Mercury)
Z.Z. Hill, *Down Home* (Malaco)
The Kinsey Report, *Edge of the City* (Alligator)
Valerie Wellington, *Million Dollar Secret* (Flying Fish)
Joe Louis Walker, *The Gift* (Hightone)
Eric Clapton, *From the Cradle* (Reprise)
John Lee Hooker, *The Healer* (Chameleon)
Stevie Ray Vaughan, *Greatest Hits* (Epic)
The Fabulous Thunderbirds, *The Essential Fabulous Thunderbirds Collection* (Epic)
Albert Collins, *Ice Pickin'* (Alligator)
Johnny Copeland, *Bringin' It All Back Home* (Rounder)
Junior Kimbrough, *All Night Long* (Fat Possum)
R.L. Burnside, *Too Bad Jim* (Fat Possum)
Fenton Robinson, *I Hear Some Blues Downstairs* (Alligator)
Buddy Guy, *Damn Right, I've Got the Blues* (Silvertone)

BLUES LABELS

INDEPENDENT BLUES LABELS: THE 1940s AND 1950s

In many respects, 1945 was an incredibly scary time to be in America. World War II was finally over, and the country prepared to adjust from a wartime economy to a peacetime one that would need to reintegrate millions of returning veterans. The atomic bomb cast a cloud over the future of the planet; the rise of communism in the Soviet Union and Eastern Europe was sowing seeds of fear and paranoia. Many wanted to do nothing more than resume life as normal, but the fact was that changing geopolitics, new technology, and developing mass media meant that life could never be the same.

But at the same time, life had never been more exciting. The United States had finally recovered from the effects of the Depression, and those who had survived the war with their families and health intact were ready to relax and, to a degree, party. Music was needed, and with the end of wartime rationing of certain materials, the record industry could resume full-scale operations after years of manufacturing restrictions. It was in this uncertain, yet intoxicating, climate that a boomlet of independent labels helped lay the foundation for the recording and distribution of post-war blues music.

Historically, the music business has always been dominated by about a half-dozen "major" labels. Their names and initials change according to corporate transactions and mergers, but in the middle of the 1940s they were Columbia, Victor, Decca, Capitol, Mercury, and MGM. Ever since the blues began to be recorded, the major labels had paid some attention to the music, often placing the artists on subsidiary companies that were geared toward the "race" (i.e. Black) audience. Hence the appearance of so many CD reissues of ancient blues on huge labels like Sony and BMG.

An independent label formed in the 1940s faced enormous obstacles in competing against the majors, but also had enormous opportunities. Blues, R&B, and hillbilly artists were still recording for big companies in the 1940s, but not in great numbers; the labels focused their energies on pop music that was oriented towards White Americans. This, naturally, left a vacuum in the marketplace, and several million disenfranchised listeners. Blues, R&B, and country were exploding as live, regional phenomenons, but weren't adequately represented on record. Demand necessitated supply, and numerous independent labels emerged to fill the gap.

There were no rule books for the new upstarts to adhere to, and one imagines that day-to-day life for these fledgling operations was both nerve-wracking and tremendously exciting. They didn't have the funds, state-of-the-art studios, or massive distribution networks that gave the Columbias of the world such huge advantages. All of them had to do things the hard way, driving from town to town to push their latest singles from the trunks of their cars, collect payments from shaky distributors and retailers, and chat up the local DJs in hopes of getting their releases on the air. What they usually had, above all, were ears to the ground: a real feel for what the communities of minority audiences–Blacks, Southern Whites, and teenagers–were listening to, on the regional radio stations (itself an exploding phenomenon of the time), the jukeboxes, and in the dance halls. This was true whether the label owners were Black or, as they were in many cases, White, sometimes being minorities of sorts themselves with Jewish and/or immigrant backgrounds.

Out of this crazy-quilt milieu came the labels so near and dear to the hearts of millions of blues, rock, and R&B fans: Chess, Sun, Specialty, Aladdin, Modern, King, Atlantic, Imperial, Vee-Jay, Duke/Peacock, and others. None of them focused on the blues exclusively: indeed, few of them even focused on Black music exclusively. All of them, however, wanted in on the R&B market,

to varying degrees. And thus it was that most of the best blues artists of the 1940s and 1950s recorded for these labels.

As far as establishing a label or "house" sound, **Chess** and **Sun** were probably the most distinctive of these operations, and their histories are outlined in separate essays. While other prominent indies of the period may not have developed a production style as immediately distinctive, several made especially noteworthy contributions to blues and R&B history, and usually made a mark on rock 'n' roll as well. In the mid-1940s, several companies sprouted up in Los Angeles, where the record and entertainment industry (which was then centered in New York) was truly beginning to establish roots. These labels also did a great deal to develop styles of blues/R&B that became identified with the West Coast, particularly jump blues.

One of the most important L.A. operations was **Specialty**, founded in 1945 by Art Rupe; that same year, it had one of the first truly monster independent R&B hits, Roy Milton's "R.M. Blues." Milton was one of the label's biggest stars, scoring nearly 20 R&B hits in a jump blues style; Camille Howard (Milton's pianist), Jimmy Liggins, Joe Liggins, and Floyd Dixon also had hits for the label, employing the boogie-woogie pianos and honking saxes that were early R&B staples. Specialty was also one of the first companies to scout the burgeoning New Orleans R&B scene, recording hugely influential hits in the early half of the 1950s by Lloyd Price and Guitar Slim.

Specialty was not solely devoted to R&B; it had an extensive gospel line as well, the jewel in the crown being the Soul Stirrers, who featured the young Sam Cooke. They landed one of the biggest original rock 'n' roll stars, Little Richard, and also had some success in the rock field with Larry Williams and Don and Dewey. Yet by the late '50s, Specialty was winding down its activities, Art Rupe was finding lucrative economic opportunities outside of the record business. It's also been suggested that he was discouraged by the success of Sam Cooke, who became a huge pop star after Rupe, frightened of tampering with the gospel singer's track record, refused to release secular material by Cooke on Specialty, giving both Cooke and producer Bumps Blackwell their walking papers in the bargain. Numerous well-packaged Specialty reissues have appeared on the market since the label sold its catalog to Fantasy in 1990.

Aladdin, also formed in L.A. in 1945, was a virtual storehouse of West Coast jump blues/R&B pianists, recording Amos Milburn, Floyd Dixon, and Charles Brown. The "honking" element of West Coast jump blues was provided by saxophonist Big Jay McNeely. In the mid-'50s, like some other labels, they got a cut of the New Orleans R&B/rock scene with the vocal duo of Shirley & Lee.

Modern, yet another L.A. company formed in 1945 (by the Bihari brothers), also had some tentacles into the West Coast blues/R&B scene, with a roster including Floyd Dixon (who recorded for several labels during his prime), Etta James, and saxophonist Joe Houston. In comparison with Aladdin and Specialty, however, they had a greater taste for guitar-focused, grittier blues, releasing sides by Jimmy McCracklin, Johnny "Guitar" Watson, and Pee Wee Crayton. They were also aggressive in scouting talent outside of their region, distributing some of the first nationally popular recordings by blues legends John Lee Hooker, B.B. King, and Elmore James, all of whom were based east of the Mississippi. In the '50s, they formed active subsidiary labels, RPM and Flair; when times became leaner, however, they focused on budget LP compilations for another of their subsidiaries, the Crown label.

A final L.A. giant was **Imperial**, founded in the late 1940s. Although it made significant contributions to West Coast blues by recording guitarists T-Bone Walker and Jimmy McCracklin, it will be mainly remembered for its forays into New Orleans R&B. No other label based outside of New Orleans (and maybe none within in New Orleans) had as much success with Crescent City music,

Music Map

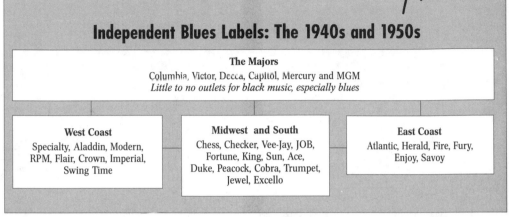

Independent Blues Labels: The 1940s and 1950s

The Majors
Columbia, Victor, Decca, Capitol, Mercury and MGM
Little to no outlets for black music, especially blues

West Coast	Midwest and South	East Coast
Specialty, Aladdin, Modern, RPM, Flair, Crown, Imperial, Swing Time	Chess, Checker, Vee-Jay, JOB, Fortune, King, Sun, Ace, Duke, Peacock, Cobra, Trumpet, Jewel, Excello	Atlantic, Herald, Fire, Fury, Enjoy, Savoy

principally with Fats Domino, who spun out a series of hits for about a decade. Dave Bartholomew was an instrumental factor in many of Imperial's New Orleans hits as a producer and arranger, for Domino and others; the label also recorded some blues-oriented singers in New Orleans, like Roy Brown, Pee Wee Crayton, and Snooks Eaglin, in attempts to give them a commercial direction more in line with rock 'n' roll's burgeoning popularity. The label's days as a major power came to end with its sale to Liberty in 1963, when Domino's chart success finally ceased, and the company's biggest star, Rick Nelson, had been lured away to a major label.

Chicago blues was considerably rawer and more guitar-based than the kind usually issued by the West Coast labels, and Chess, though the giant in the field, wasn't the only game in town. Vee-Jay, also based in the Windy City, had two of the most commercially successful bluesmen of the era, Jimmy Reed and John Lee Hooker (it should be noted that Hooker recorded for quite a few labels in his early career, often for several simultaneously, and occasionally under pseudonyms). Lesser-known but great sides were also recorded for Vee-Jay by harmonica player/singer Billy Boy Arnold and Eddie Taylor, who was Jimmy Reed's guitarist. In the early '60s, it had huge successes in the pop market with early recordings by the Four Seasons and the Beatles, but went belly-up in the mid-'60s.

A Chicago R&B label that flamed briefly and brightly was **Cobra**, who lured Chess bassist/arranger/songwriter Willie Dixon away for a brief time in the late '50s. If for nothing else, the label gained a niche in blues history for waxing classic early sides by Otis Rush that rate among the best and most chilling electric blues ever recorded. Magic Sam also recorded notable early sides for the label, although he wouldn't truly reach his peak until the '60s.

King, based in Cincinnati, was one of the most versatile independent labels of the time: R&B may have been its bread and butter, but it also made a great deal of key hillbilly records. But it certainly had an impressive roster of both blues shouters (Wynonie Harris, Bullmoose Jackson, Eddie "Cleanhead" Vinson) and instrumental-oriented honkers (Big Jay McNeely, organist Bill Doggett, Tiny Bradshaw, Earl Bostic, and others). In the 1960s it also had claim to one of the decade's most commercially successful blues guitarists, Freddie King. By that time, though, it was heavily reliant upon the empire of soul brother #1, James Brown. King was sold to Polydor in the early 1970s; in recent years compilations of important King R&B/blues artists have appeared on Rhino.

A major outpost of Southern blues was **Duke/Peacock**, founded by legendary micro-manager Don Robey in Houston. In addition to recording Big Mama Thornton and Texan guitarists like Clarence "Gatemouth" Brown, Duke did its part to point the way for soul by recording two of the leading soul-bluesmen, Bobby "Blue" Bland and Junior Parker. The label seemed comfortable with both guitar-focused material and sophisticated horn arrangements that played off the gospel-influenced vocals of Bland in particular.

Excello, though founded in Nashville, really made its mark on blues history through its Louisiana-based artists, including Slim Harpo, Lightnin' Slim, and Lazy Lester. These are the singers who, aided by producer Jay Miller, were the key exponents of "swamp blues." By lending the musicians sympathetic production and the freedom to be more or less themselves, Miller was one of several producers who cultivated a characteristic sound, Sam Phillips (at Sun) and Leonard Chess (at Chess) being two of the most notable others.

New York is not noted as a groundswell of down-home blues, and it may be that the key contribution of **Atlantic** was in tilling the field for R&B, rock 'n' roll, and soul, rather than developing straight blues. The company can't be overlooked, however, due to its crucial role in midwifing blues-derived R&B into more urbanized forms with a greater appeal to a younger audience. Joe Turner, Ray Charles, Sticks McGhee, Chuck Willis, Ruth Brown, and LaVern Baker were just some of the most prominent players with Atlantic contracts. And the label did record some straight-up blues, even if much of it tended to be with artists that made their most significant music for other operations.

A smaller notable independent based in New York City was Bobby Robinson's **Fire** label, with the active Fury and Enjoy subsidiaries. Robinson recorded some of the rawest guitar blues of the era, including some of Elmore James' best work. Buster Brown's "Fannie Mae" was one of the most undiluted blues records ever to make the Top Forty. And Fire was also responsible for Wilbert Harrison's #1 hit "Kansas City," which may be the ultimate example of shuffle blues transposed into rock 'n' roll, one of the key ingredients being Jimmy Spruill's scintillating guitar solo.

This roundup, it should be noted, has only encompassed some of the most active independent companies that recorded blues music between 1945 and 1960. Others made significant contributions, such as Savoy, which recorded a good deal of jump blues by Johnny Otis and others, and Trumpet, which released some primeval Southern blues in the early '50s by Sonny Boy Williamson and others. In the 1990s, Capricorn Records dedicated a series of box sets to such labels, including ones for Cobra, Fire/Fury, Jewel/Paula, and Swingtime. Charlie Gillett's *The Sound of the City*, a history of rock 'n' roll's first two decades, does an excellent job of detailing the many influential independent early rock and R&B labels, and is recommended further reading.

There were many tiny companies that released regional singles in small quantities; some lasted for only one or two 45s. Most of these can now only be enjoyed on small-run import reissues (if they even made it that far). But their deep obscurity, and the relatively raw production values employed on some of them, doesn't mean that they can't be just as enjoyable as sides produced on the "big" indies.

Independent rock and R&B labels, by and large, were reducing their blues rosters by the dawn of the 1960s. This was not necessarily, as some might charge, a reflection of lack of interest in the blues by the label owners, or ingratitude towards the artists that had helped put them on the map in the first place. The independents, it must be remembered, were not PBS; they were commercial enterprises that needed chart hits and cash flow. In focusing their energies elsewhere, they were usually responding to trends in the overall marketplace, most notably the increasing success of rock 'n' roll. And a lot of the biggest independents didn't even survive the competition of the era, going under or selling their catalog to other companies; Atlantic, which is still thriving today, is more the exception than the rule.

R&B itself was loosening its ties to the blues, and looking forward to soul music. Some artists, like Bobby Bland, Little Milton, Albert King, and Freddie King, were well-suited for adapting to the new era; unfortunately, most of the blues stars of the '40s and '50s were left out in the cold. It should be noted that a lot of indies didn't give up on the blues completely; Motown, the most successful of the whole lot, made little-noticed recordings with Amos Milburn and Earl King in the 1960s. But the commercial momentum of American pop had shifted away from blues and hardcore R&B, leaving the blues in the hands of a devoted but more specialized audience.

And the needs of that audience would be addressed from the 1960s onwards by independent companies. These, however, were independent companies that were not as concerned with commercial chart success as satisfying the tastes of a niche market that included increasingly younger, more affluent, and White listeners. The prime medium would not be the 45 single, but the long-playing record and, much later, the compact disc. The stories of those independents–Arhoolie, Delmark, Alligator, Fat Possum, and others–is told in a separate sidebar. The legacy of the earlier generation of independents is readily available for today's audience, however, on a plethora of CD reissues, several of which provide thematically linked (and sometimes, truth to tell, haphazard) overviews of the labels' valuable contributions to American music.

—*Richie Unterberger*

5 Recommended Albums:

Various Artists, *Chess Blues* (Chess)
Various Artists, *A Sun Blues Collection* (Rhino)
Various Artists, *The Specialty Story* (Specialty)
Various Artists, *Atlantic Blues Box* (Atlantic)
Various Artists, *The Cobra Records Story* (Capricorn)

SUN RECORDS— THE BLUES YEARS

In the late 1940s, Memphis, TN, was still very much a segregated city. The many boundaries that separated Black and White social life also separated the musical communities, despite the cracks starting to force open via radio stations like WDIA and WHBQ, which broadcast blues and R&B to young listeners in the region like Elvis Presley. Recognizing the genius of several blues performers in the Memphis area, there was one man, Sam Phillips, who became determined to record the music and bring it wider recognition.

As a radio engineer, Phillips had already gained technical expertise and appreciation for a wide variety of Black and White popular music. Recording and distributing it was a huge challenge, as it was for many other independent regional labels of the time that handled R&B or hillbilly records for minority audiences. Explained Phillips to Robert Palmer in *Deep Blues*, "I thought it was vital music ... and although my first love was radio, my second was the freedom we tried to give the people, Black and White, to express their very complex personalities, personalities these people didn't know existed in the '50s. I just hope I was a part of giving the influence to the people to be free in their expression."

How much of Phillips' operation was artistic altruism, and how much the hopes of a businessman seeing a gap in the existing market, continues to be a matter of some historical debate. There's no question, though, that Phillips was *the* man for recording blues in Memphis as the '50s dawned. Initially he focused not on pressing discs on his own label, but recording local sides at his Memphis Recording Service studio that would be leased to labels that were not in Memphis itself. Phillips was fortunate to be situated in a city that was a hotbed of blues talent, and he quickly arranged for recordings by B.B. King, Howlin' Wolf, Jackie

Brenston, Rosco Gordon, and others to be leased to the Modern and Chess labels.

"I opened the Memphis Recording Service," elaborated Phillips in *Good Rockin' Tonight* (by Colin Escott with Martin Hawkins), "with the intention of recording singers and musicians from Memphis and the locality who I felt had something that people should be able to hear. I'm talking about blues–both the country style and the rhythm style–and also about gospel or spiritual music and about White country music. I always felt that the people who played this type of music had not been given the opportunity to reach an audience. I feel strongly that a lot of the blues was a real true story. Unadulterated life as it was.

"My aim was to try and record the blues and other music I liked and to prove whether I was right or wrong about this music. I knew or I *felt* I knew, that there was a bigger audience for blues than just the Black man of the mid-South. There were city markets to be reached, and I knew that Whites listened to blues surreptitiously."

Any characteristic sound that could be attached to Phillips' blues productions resulted not so much from what he brought to the sessions, but what he *didn't* do. He was astute enough to realize that the singers and musicians had a power that would have been diminished by extraneous production or a conscious softening of rough edges. Thus, he concentrated on getting the best performances from his artists without coaxing them into changing their styles, and obtaining takes that were sufficiently commercial for release without losing their spontaneity.

He was also clever enough to capitalize upon accidents that could have been categorized as mistakes, as when Ike Turner's band (featuring vocalist-saxophonist Jackie Brenston) arrived at the studio with a damaged guitar speaker. Other producers might have cancelled the session until the speaker could be fixed, but Phillips and the musicians found they liked the distorted guitar sound it produced. It would end up featuring prominently on Brenston's big hit, "Rocket 88," which is repeatedly referred to by historians as one of the first rock 'n' roll records.

By 1952 Phillips, realizing that companies were going to start beating him to the punch by recording regional artists directly instead of leasing his masters, started the Sun label. (He had released a record by Joe Hill Louis in 1950 on the Phillips imprint.) The next few years found Sun releasing a few dozen blues/R&B sides that, although not nearly as great in quantity as those of Chess to the North, were nearly on the same level in terms of quality and historical influence. "Bear Cat," Rufus Thomas' answer record to Big Mama Thornton's "Hound Dog," was Sun's first big national R&B hit, although some of the sweetness went out of that triumph when a lawsuit from the "Hound Dog" publishers wiped out its profits.

Never releasing too much material by any one blues artist (although the vaults and subsequent reissues have yielded tons of unissued sides), Sun did have some further success in the R&B market with items like Junior Parker's "Feelin' Good." Parker's follow-up, "Mystery Train," didn't do as well, although it became one of the core classics of Memphis music, particularly after it was covered a couple of years later on the fifth and final single of a fellow Sun artist, Elvis Presley.

By that time, the focus of Sun Records had tilted almost entirely towards the White artists on its roster. Phillips had never stuck to recording Black musicians exclusively (although he issued almost nothing but blues records in the early days of the label), and the fortuitous discovery of Elvis in 1954 had resulted in the birth of rockabilly with Presley's first single, "That's All Right Mama." Elvis, of course, took much of his inspiration from the blues, both in vocal delivery and his choice of early cover material. By 1955, it became apparent that Elvis was Sun's ticket to much greater commercial success than anything they could achieve in blues/R&B, although the singles with Parker, Little Milton, James Cotton, and obscure artists like Doctor Ross, Frank Frost, Billy "The Kid" Emerson, and future Muddy Waters band guitarist Pat Hare seemed to bode well for continued success in the blues field.

Sun's subsequent move into rock 'n' roll has been criticized by some, including Rufus Thomas, but a quick look at the release schedule shows that Phillips was issuing blues singles alongside hillbilly records and the emerging rockabilly sound. Indeed, Phillips was recording Frank Frost for his Phillips International label in the '60s, after most of his big stars had left for greener pastures.

In *Good Rockin' Tonight*, Phillips himself rejoins, "Keep in

Music Map

Sun Records—The Blues Years

Sam Phillips
forms Memphis Recording Service, 1950, forms Sun Records, 1952

1950 – 1952 Records & Leases to Chess, 4 Star & Modern:	1952 – 1954/Sun Records Begins	1954 – 1959/Sun, Rockabilly, Country
Howlin' Wolf	Walter Horton	Elvis Presley
B.B. King	Jimmy De Berry	Johnny Cash
Joe Hill Louis	Little Milton	Jerry Lee Lewis
Walter Horton	Doctor Ross	Roy Orbison
Dr. Ross	Joe Hill Louis	Billy Riley
Jackie Brenston	James Cotton	Warren Smith
Rosco Gordon	Pat Hare	Sonny Burgess
Rufus Thomas	Frank Frost	Ray Harris
Harmonica Frank Floyd	Earl Hooker	Jack Earls
Ike Turner & The Kings of Rhythm	Charlie Booker	Charlie Feathers
	Billy the Kid Emerson	Carl Perkins
	Rosco Gordon	The Miller Sisters
	D.A. Hunt	Charlie Rich
	Mose Vinson	Ernie Chaffin
	Big Memphis Marainey	Barbara Pittman
	Rufus Thomas	

mind that there were a number of very good R&B labels. The base wasn't broad enough because of racial prejudice. It wasn't broad enough to get the amount of commercial play and general acceptance overall–not just in the South. So I knew what I had to do to broaden the base of acceptance."

Phillips achieved that by focusing on White country and–later–rockabilly artists, especially after he sold Presley's contract to RCA in late 1955 for $35,000, the bulk of which went back into his desperately cash-starved label. In retrospect, it seems he had little choice in the matter. Distributors were paying him on the sales of Presley singles with blues returns by the carload, and labels like Duke, RPM, and Chess were swiftly decimating his blues artist roster. The Bihari brothers (who owned the Crown, RPM, Modern, and Flair labels) actually started their Meteor label in Memphis with the express purpose of putting Phillips out of business. With the capital from the Presley sale, he was able to promote and distribute his remaining roster much more effectively. Carl Perkins, Johnny Cash, Jerry Lee Lewis, and Charlie Rich all became stars in the late '50s as Sun artists.

Whether Phillips could have done this with Black blues artists is doubtful. The sheer rawness of the Sun blues sides–both in the performances and the spartan production–still make them difficult to listen to today and made them even tougher to program on radio back then. As a businessman with a tiny two-person operation, Phillips was torn between the music he loved and what would sell and reach a wider audience. Also, by the time of the twin national breakthrough of Presley and Carl Perkins' "Blue Suede Shoes," blues was by and large a spent commercial force in the Black community, with doo-wop groups and R&B singers now dominating the charts. Thus it was that many of Phillips' blues artists had their greatest commercial success on other labels. One could reasonably argue that Presley, Perkins, Cash, and Lewis reached their artistic peak at Sun. But one could not say the same for B.B. King, Howlin' Wolf, Junior Parker, Little Milton, Walter Horton, and Rufus Thomas, all of whom truly found their calling with other concerns, often in much more of a blues/soul vein in the 1960s, or even (in Thomas' case) as a straight soul singer with few overt ties to the blues at all.

As such, the relatively slim oeuvre of Sun blues recordings is more of a vault for the embryonic talents of major blues performers than their very best work. Which is not to suggest that what was preserved wasn't very good, far from it. The Chess brothers, for all their business acumen and "feel" for the music, could never have produced sides with the stark, lonesome feel of Big Walter Horton's "Easy" or the violent agression contained in James Cotton's "Cotton Crop Blues." And in the broader sense, few labels have done as much to weave the blues into mainstream American culture as Sun, both by giving major bluesmen their first opportunity to record and reach audiences beyond the region, and by exposing it (albeit indirectly) to the American masses via its incorporation into the rockabilly of Presley, Perkins, et al.
—*Richie Unterberger & Cub Koda*

7 Recommended Sun Albums:

Various Artists, *A Sun Blues Collection* (Rhino)
Various Artists, *Sun Records: The Blues Years, 1950–1956* (Charly)
Junior Parker, James Cotton, & Pat Hare, *Mystery Train* (Rhino)
Howlin' Wolf, *Rides Again* (Flair/Virgin)
B.B. King, *The Memphis Masters* (Ace)
Various Artists, *Sun Records Harmonica Classics* (Rounder)
Joe Hill Louis, *The Be-Bop Boy* (Bear Family)

CHESS RECORDS

Some may argue that the history of blues is one of musicians, regions, and movements rather than something so business-oriented as a record label. Chess Records, however, is not just some record label. It's a sound in itself–a sound which, for many, epitomizes the best of Chicago blues, and maybe even the best electric blues has to offer. Through the recordings of Muddy Waters, Little Walter, Howlin' Wolf, and many other talents great and small, the Chicago-based label and its subsidiaries (Checker and Argo, later renamed Cadet) did an enormous amount to amplify

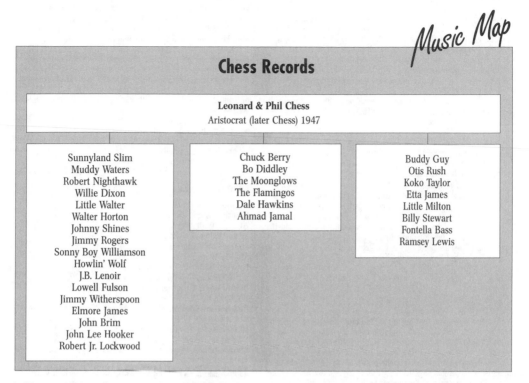

Music Map

Chess Records

Leonard & Phil Chess
Aristocrat (later Chess) 1947

Sunnyland Slim	Chuck Berry	Buddy Guy
Muddy Waters	Bo Diddley	Otis Rush
Robert Nighthawk	The Moonglows	Koko Taylor
Willie Dixon	The Flamingos	Etta James
Little Walter	Dale Hawkins	Little Milton
Walter Horton	Ahmad Jamal	Billy Stewart
Johnny Shines		Fontella Bass
Jimmy Rogers		Ramsey Lewis
Sonny Boy Williamson		
Howlin' Wolf		
J.B. Lenoir		
Lowell Fulson		
Jimmy Witherspoon		
Elmore James		
John Brim		
John Lee Hooker		
Robert Jr. Lockwood		

the blues, record some of its greatest talents, and bring the form into the modern era.

These are achievements that few could have foreseen when the label was founded by Leonard and Phil Chess in the 1940s. The brothers had come to the United States from Poland in the late 1920s. In 1947 Leonard Chess was a nightclub owner in Chicago, entering the record business by buying into the local Aristocrat label. Aristocrat was not a blues label at its outset, recording pop and jazz. Its Chicago base, however, was in close proximity to more blues talent than any other Northern city, with more musicians relocating from the South all the time.

In the late '40s, Chicago blues–in its raw, amplified state–had yet to be captured on record in all its primal immediacy. Aristocrat had skirted around the blues with jazz-blues sorts of outings by the likes of Andrew Tibbs, and employed guitarist Muddy Waters as a sideman on a 1947 single by pianist Sunnyland Slim. But it would be Muddy's own efforts, starting with 1948's "I Can't Be Satisfied"/"I Feel Like Going Home," that truly began to urbanize and electrify the sound of the Delta. The Chess brothers became progressively more active in the blues field, and by 1950 they had taken over the Aristocrat label entirely, changing its name to Chess.

Although Waters was already starting to use a full band in his club appearances, Chess at first went easy on all-out amplification in the recording studio, preferring not to tamper with the stripped accompaniment that had proved so succesful on Muddy's first big hit. Early classics were recorded with Waters accompanied by no one except Big Crawford on bass ("I Can't Be Satisfied") and sometimes just with Muddy and his electric guitar ("Rollin' Stone"). Other musicians like Little Walter (harmonica) and Jimmy Rogers (guitar) started to come in as well, not only on Muddy's singles, but on those of some other Chess artists. By the early '50s, the addition of drums made the switch to electric blues complete, providing in the process the prototype for the guitars-bass-drums-harmonica lineup that would serve as the "classic" model for both electric blues and rock 'n' roll.

Chess blues singles quickly developed an identifiable sound. A haunting and spacious echo was created by, according to Peter Guralnick's *Feel Like Going Home*, "rigging a loudspeaker and a microphone at both ends of a sewer pipe" and "a primitive system of tape delay." The voices and instruments often sounded slightly overamplified and recorded at levels that frequently intruded into the red zone. This resulted in recordings that preserved the focused punch of the small blues combo while maximizing its sonic power. Particularly in the early days, consistency was assured by using many of the same musicians (who often released records of their own as well) to play on Chess sessions, forming a sort of floating house band. "Session men" like Little Walter, Willie Dixon, and Jimmy Rogers are well known, of course; more obscure are performers like drummer Fred Below, whose swinging backbeat did much to establish the bedrock of both electric blues and rock 'n' roll.

While Phil Chess focused on the business end of the label, his brother Leonard concentrated on the studio. Historians have sometimes hinted that he was capturing magic more by accident than design. It's true that a Jewish Polish immigrant may not have been as attuned to the nuances of Delta-cum-Chicago blues as the musicians, but Chess deserves considerable credit for crafting the sound that appeared on the grooves. Leonard Chess apparently had a genuine knack for getting the best out of his performers in the studio and refining their material into a product that was both commercial and artistic. On more than one memorable occasion, dissatisfied with the drum sound he was getting, he played the bass drum himself.

Leonard Chess' principal aide de camp was house bassist Willie Dixon. Dixon worked countless sessions in the '50s and '60s, though he briefly left Chess in the late '50s to work for the Chicago-based rival Cobra label. It's as a songwriter, however, that Dixon will be most remembered, penning numerous classics for Waters, Little Walter, Howlin' Wolf, and many other artists in the Chess stable. Chess expanded its roster rapidly in the early half of the 1950s, as electric Chicago blues became a major presence on the R&B charts. On swings through other regions to distribute and promote their records, the Chess brothers would check out and sometimes sign talent. They would also lease material cut elsewhere, the most famous example being their distribution of several crucial sides cut by Sam Phillips in Sun Studios in Memphis. After a bitter rivalry with the Bihari brothers (to whom Phillips was also leasing material) Chess would place the most promising of the Sun recorded artists, Howlin' Wolf, on its own label.

There was plenty of home-grown talent in Chicago, of course. From within Muddy Waters' own band, Little Walter became a solo star, and Jimmy Rogers and pianist Otis Spann also had solid recording careers without nearly as much commercial success. The four W's–Waters, Walter, Wolf, and Sonny Boy Williamson– would become Chess' most durable blues artists. J.B. Lenoir, Lowell Fulson, and Willie Mabon, although not as iconic, also recorded a good deal of material for the label.

Chess' lengthy associations with Waters, Walter, Wolf, and Williamson were in fact more the exception than the rule. Throughout the '50s, it seemed like the label gave most major electric blues performers a trial at one time or another, although it wouldn't stick with them for very long. Thus it was that a who's who of modern blues passed through the Chess pipeline at one point or another. Elmore James, Otis Rush, John Lee Hooker, Johnny Shines, Robert Nighthawk, Billy Boy Arnold, Buddy Guy, and Memphis Minnie are not principally known for their Chess recordings, but all of them recorded or released products for the company, often in enough quantity to generate their own reissue LPs years later.

The wealth of Chess reissue LPs can give the understandable impression that the label was recording a bottomless well of classic blues throughout the '50s. However, Chess was never exclusively a blues concern, and in fact experienced its greatest commercial success with the rock 'n' roll artists Chuck Berry and Bo Diddley. The success of Berry in particular, and the diminished presence of electric blues on the R&B charts in the second half of the 1950s, meant that Chess began to put more effort into its non-blues product. That didn't just mean guitar rockers like Berry– Chess also recorded a good deal of R&B, doo-wop (Flamingos, Moonglows) and jazz (Ahmad Jamal), and even handled Dale Hawkins' great rockabilly recordings.

In the 1960s, blues occupied a less central position within the company. Blues was not the music of choice for many African-American listeners anymore, having been overtaken by rock 'n roll, R&B, and then modern soul music. Little Walter was in artistic decline, exacerbated by health and personal problems; Sonny Boy Williamson died in the mid-'60s; Muddy Waters, who had begun to tour England and Europe, was now broadening into the LP market, with albums such as *Muddy Waters: Folk Singer* being packaged for the White folk music crowd.

Chess' greatest commercial successes in the 1960s were not in the blues field, but in soul (with Etta James, Billy Stewart, and Fontella Bass) and soul-jazz (Ramsey Lewis). At this time the old guard rock 'n' rollers, Berry and Diddley, were finding their share of the marketplace shrinking. This sales decline, ironically, coincided with a period in which Chess Records were beginning to retroactively attain legendary status among some young White enthusiasts, particularly musicians in British Invasion bands. The Rolling Stones, who put a ton of Chess recordings into their early repertoire, paid homage to the label by recording at Chess Studios in 1964, in the midst of their first American tour.

Chess did not give up on their original stars, or the blues– Howlin' Wolf, for instance, recorded some of his greatest material in the '60s, and Koko Taylor established herself as one of the premier blueswomen. At times, however, it seemed to be making desperate attempts to make their blues artists sound more contemporary by adding rock and soul influences. Misbegotten albums–such as Waters' *Muddy, Brass & the Blues* (with overdubbed horns on some tracks), "supersession" albums pairing different bandleaders, psychedelic-influenced records with Waters (*Electric Mud*) and Howlin' Wolf (*This is Howlin' Wolf's New Album–He Doesn't Like It*)–all backfired artistically and commercially. Most of them have stayed mercifully unreissued in the digital age.

After Leonard Chess died in 1969, the company was sold to GRT, and control of the label passed to his son, Marshall. Chess in the '70s was a sad echo of its glory days, and Marshall and Phil Chess would soon leave the company (Marshall to head up the Rolling Stones' new label), which wound down its activities as an ongoing concern. That left a huge back catalog, coveted by collectors (and just plain fans) the world over.

Despite the almost inexhaustible supply of great blues material, the Chess reissue program of the past two decades has been erratic until quite recently. A couple of domestic series, ranging from thorough double-LP retrospectives to interesting packages of obscure performers like John Brim, were halted or went out of print as the Chess catalog changed ownership. For a time, it was owned by the Sugar Hill label (most famous for its early rap productions); the Sugar Hill series, too, soon came to a stop. For a while, Chess reissues were easier to acquire as imports than they

were in their land of origin, the United States. What's more, serious collectors, to their frustration, found many rare and unreleased tracks appearing on various European and Japanese compilations while remaining unavailable in the U.S.

Ownership of the catalog passed to MCA, with plans for comprehensive reissue programs remaining vague. Happily, this situation was remedied in the CD age, with Chess/MCA embarking upon a series of comprehensive reissues that restored almost all of the catalog to availability, including much of the rare and out-of-print material that had only surfaced on imports or bootlegs as well as material that had never surfaced.

The intentions and achievements of the Chess brothers have remained the subject of mixed scrutiny. They do, however, deserve an enormous amount of credit for recognizing the best in electric blues talent, distributing it, and translating it into recorded music that will endure for ages.

—*Richie Unterberger & Cub Koda*

15 Recommended Chess Albums

Various Artists, *Chess Blues Box*
Muddy Waters, *The Chess Box*
Howlin' Wolf, *The Chess Box*
Little Walter, *The Essential*
Sonny Boy Williamson, *The Essential*
Muddy Waters, *One More Mile*
Howlin' Wolf, *Ain't Gonna Be Your Dog*
Little Walter, *Blues with a Feeling*
Jimmy Rogers, *Chicago Bound*
J.B. Lenoir, *Natural Man*
Buddy Guy, *The Complete Chess Studio Sessions*
Koko Taylor, *What It Takes: The Chess Years*
Willie Dixon, *The Chess Box*
Otis Rush/Albert King, *Door to Door*
Elmore James, *Whose Muddy Shoes*

INDEPENDENT BLUES LABELS: THE 1960s TO THE PRESENT

While major labels continue to record a few major performers, such as Robert Cray and Buddy Guy, the overwhelming majority of contemporary blues music is to be found on independent companies–that is, labels that are not owned or distributed by the large corporations of Sony, BMG, CEMA, PGD, UNI, or WEA. Outfits such as Arhoolie, Delmark, Vanguard, Testament, Alligator, Hightone, and Fat Possum have played a huge role in both recording the best blues of the past few decades, and of preserving the best of past and living blues traditions. The relatively small commercial market for blues in recent times has virtually ensured that these operations are run by proprietors who are enthusiasts first, and their priorities are usually reflected of the music they release.

In the 1940s and 1950s, the blues enjoyed a much higher profile in the charts, carving out a sizable chunk of the R&B market. Independent labels like Chess, Sun, Vee-Jay, and Specialty were responsible for recording the greatest blues music of the era, often fostering production techniques that helped shape and advance the music itself. (The histories of these independents are detailed in other essays in this book.) But by the end of the 1950s, blues had lost much of its audience share to the onslaught of R&B and rock and roll; it would lose more in the '60s with the British Invasion, Motown, folk-rock, psychedelia, soul, and other tremors revolutionizing the world of popular music. Those independents that had recorded blues, if they survived into the 1960s, usually cut back or eliminated their blues rosters.

The decline of the blues as a commercial force, however, coincided with a couple of developments that would create an opening for entirely different kinds of independents. The late 1940s saw the introduction of the long-playing record, which in turn harvested more diverse sorts of productions than had been available on singles. The 1950s brought the stirrings of a folk/blues "revival" that widened the audience for blues music from its African-American base into an increasingly White and young listenership, often to be found in colleges and coffeehouses. Some of these fans were dedicated enough to write books on the subject, track down surviving blues legends, and make recordings of their own.

Some of the first modern blues independents took a folkloric approach to their releases, especially in the beginning. The

Prestige/Riverside/Bluesville family, in addition to recording first-generation country bluesmen like Pink Anderson, arranged for John Lee Hooker and Snooks Eaglin to record acoustic (or at least solo) material for albums, although Hooker and Eaglin maintained simultaneous electric, full-band recording careers for the R&B market. Once the blues revival was in gear in the 1960s, **Testament** produced recordings of obscure country blues singers like Jack Owens, and also arranged for overlooked electric Chicago bluesmen like Johnny Shines to get some quality studio time. It even released an album of topical songs about John Kennedy shortly after he was assassinated.

Arhoolie, founded by German immigrant Chris Strachwitz, took a sort of field recording approach to some of its best releases. Driving around Texas and the South, as several blues scholars of the time did in hopes of encountering legends past and present, Strachwitz also took time to record some of the more interesting musicians with whom he crossed paths. His first release, Mance Lipscomb's *Texas Songster* (1960), initially pressed in a quantity of only 250 copies, is still in print. Lipscomb, like some of Arhoolie's other finds–Robert Pete Williams (actually recorded by Harry Oster in 1959 and 1960) was the most famous–had never recorded before. But the label also cut sessions, under pretty basic conditions, with performers who already had something of a reputation, such as Lightnin' Hopkins.

Arhoolie didn't limit itself to newly recorded sessions, arranging (to this day) for reissues of vintage material by Hopkins, Sonny Boy Williamson, and far more obscure performers such as Black Ace. They also don't limit themselves to blues, covering roots/folk styles of all kinds–there are more cajun albums than blues ones in their catalog, which also includes quite a bit of world, country, and Tejano music. As we go to press in 1996, Arhoolie maintains a busy release schedule and large back catalog; they also founded the leading roots music mail-order service, Down Home Music, which was sold to different ownership a few years ago.

By traveling to the source and recording their artists without adornment, Arhoolie was in some senses following the path of folklorists like the Lomaxes, who had recorded legends like Leadbelly, Muddy Waters, and Son House for the Library of Congress. Arhoolie releases, as well as similar ones by some other labels, differed from the Library of Congress and Folkways catalogs, however, in crucial respects. Sure, they aimed to preserve important elements of the blues tradition that were overlooked, or maybe even in danger of extinction. However, their albums were not primarily produced for academic archives, but for general listening pleasure. Commercial considerations were not paramount, but if the releases could help the musicians make a living, and generate enough profit to keep the label owners above water (and able to record more blues/roots music), so much the better.

At the outset of the blues revival, the new blues independents usually focused on acoustic recordings. This might have reflected the influence of the folk crowd buying many of the records, and the precedents set by folkloric field recordings of previous times. The electric blues was somehow felt by some to be more authentic, less sullied by the dirty waters of mass production. Electric blues continued to thrive, though, and by the mid-'60s it was obvious that the same people buying Rolling Stones and Paul Butterfield albums would also be willing to take a crack at LPs by living Chicago blues legends.

The Chicago-based **Delmark** label was instrumental in translating the energy of contemporary electric blues onto LP for the '60s market. Delmark owner Bob Koester had been recording acoustic blues since the 1950s, when he worked with musicians like Sleepy John Estes and Big Joe Williams. In the late 1950s, he moved to Chicago, where he operated the Jazz Record Mart retail store. The store was a meeting ground for many key musicians and supporters of the blues scene; employees who worked at the Jazz Record Mart at one time include guitarist Mike Bloomfield, harmonica player Charlie Musselwhite, the founders of *Living Blues* magazine, and some future label owners, including Bruce Iglauer (who now runs Alligator Records).

"The Jazz Record Mart was like a bridge between the blues world on the South and West Sides and the growing world of White international blues fans who hung out at the Jazz Record Mart, who came here to find out about gigs, musicians," Iglauer told the *Chicago Tribune* in 1993. "There were little signs, pieces of paper taped to the walls about various gigs at ghetto taverns.

"It was an incredible flow of musicians through there because

Independent Blues Labels: The 1960s to the Present

Library of Congress Recordings	Chess Records *Biggest Commercial Blues Label*

Arhoolie, Testament, Delmark, Prestige Bluesville	Vanguard, Elektra *Folk labels record blues*

Alligator Records *Modern Era starts here*

Blind Pig, Blue Wave, Ichiban, Blacktop, Bullseye Blues, Hightone, Barrelhouse, Antone's, Flying Fish

Malaco, Rooster Blues, Fat Possum

it was one of the few ways that they could get a break. There weren't a lot of companies recording Chicago blues at that time, so musicians came to hang out at the Jazz Record Mart in hopes of attracting Bob's attention."

That's because Koester ran Delmark Records, which, like Arhoolie, did not limit itself to the blues, also releasing many fine and influential jazz albums by the likes of Sun Ra and the Art Ensemble of Chicago. He caught the lightning of Chicago electric club blues on record with his 1965 release by Junior Wells, *Hoodoo Man Blues*. As Koester claimed in the sleeve notes, "It is damn near the first LP by a Chicago blues band. Chess and a few other labels had reissued 45s by Muddy Waters, Sonny Boy Williamson, Howling Wolf, Jimmy Reed, Elmore James, etc. but virtually no one had tried to capture the Chicago blues sound free of the limitations of jukebox/airplay promotion."

Like some of the best blues producers, Koester realized that a less-is-more approach emphasizing spontaneity would make his artists comfortable and yield the best results in the studio. As Wells recalled in the same *Chicago Tribune* article, "When I did 'Hoodoo Man' for a guy a long time ago on a 78, he took it over to the radio station and asked them to play it. They threw it on the floor and broke it, stomped it. When I started recording for Bob, he wanted me to do the 'Hoodoo Man' and I really wasn't interested in doing it because of the disappointment from what happened to me when I was much younger. He kept talking to me about it, so I tried it and I'm proud of the record now ... Bob was the type of person, he just made everything so easy, you couldn't help but to get something good from it. He just let you go with it."

Hoodoo Man Blues also featured Buddy Guy on guitar (early pressings of the album credited the guitar work to the transparent pseudonym of "Friendly Chap"). *Hoodoo Man Blues* eventually passed the 50,000 mark in sales, an astronomical number for an independent blues album. It remains the best seller in the Delmark catalog, but the label would also record quite a few other important titles, most notably by Magic Sam,

J.B. Hutto, Jimmy Dawkins, and Luther Allison. Koester's label and store are still going strong today, though Koester himself is semi-retired.

Other labels made some important recordings of '60s electric blues for the LP market. **Vanguard**, which had already recorded significant acoustic '60s blues in the studio and at the Newport Folk Festivals, produced the excellent three-volume *The Blues Today!* series, featuring tracks by Wells, J.B. Hutto, Otis Spann, Otis Rush, Johnny Shines, James Cotton, and others. **Verve** (which was distributed by MGM) recorded LPs with Cotton that also crossed over to the rock audience to some extent. The label that would truly take electric Chicago blues to the end of the century, however, was the one founded by Bruce Iglauer, Alligator.

Iglauer was inspired to found Alligator, as he writes in the liner notes to the label's 25th anniversary collection, "by the music that I heard in the little clubs on the South and West Sides in the Black neighborhoods, where the city's (and the world's) greatest blues bands made music for their local fans. The blues clubs had been the heart of Chicago's Black music scene for over 30 years before I arrived there as a 'blues pilgrim' back in 1970. These weren't show lounges or theaters, but corner bars and taverns, often in grimly depressed neighborhoods, that put a chain across the doorway on weekends and charged 50 cents or a dollar to hear some of the most intense, fiery, and deeply emotional music you can imagine."

For a long time, Alligator was a one-man show, run by Iglauer out of his apartment. Releases by artists like Son Seals, Fenton Robinson, and Hound Dog Taylor put Alligator on the map, but the label didn't become a force until its *Living Chicago Blues* series of the late 1970s and early 1980s, exposing major overlooked talents such as Jimmy Johnson. Over five years later, the similar *New Bluebloods* anthology did the same for another generation of Chicago blues, including tracks by the Kinsey Report, Lil' Ed & the Blues Imperials, and Valerie Wellington.

Today Alligator's staff has swelled to over 20, and there are more than 150 albums in the catalog. Plenty of Chicago artists continue to record for the label, but Alligator has made a determined effort to seek talent from outside the region in recent years, including some Louisiana swamp blues performers. Uptempo Chicago-style blues is Alligator's most distinguishing trademark, but the roster has become fairly diverse, including White blues-rockers like Johnny Winter and Elvin Bishop, roots music gadfly Delbert McClinton, and acoustic artists Cephas & Wiggins, Saffire, and Corey Harris. It's also given several old-school veterans who were unable to pick up a contract for years a new lease on life, such as harmonica player Billy Boy Arnold. It also reissued long-unavailable recordings of primeval blues from the '50s from the Trumpet label.

Despite selling only about 10,000–25,000 copies of the average title, Alligator dominates the contemporary indie blues market; sometimes it seems that every other blues Grammy goes to the Alligator label. There are several other companies dedicated to the work of contemporary electric blues bands, Black and White, including Blind Pig, Black Top, and Antone's. There also continue to be roots/folk labels that issue occasional blues albums, such as Ichiban, Hightone, and Flying Fish.

Not every post-1960 blues label limited its aims to the collector audience. The most successful of these may have been **Malaco**, which in the minds of some fans is as much a soul/R&B label as a blues one. Its roster included soul stars fallen on leaner times, such as Johnnie Taylor and Bobby "Blue" Bland, as well as some younger acts. While much of their catalog appealed to the blues audience, it undoubtedly aimed for, and got, many listeners who hungered for some contemporary Southern soul-styled music in the absence of such recordings in the disco/dance/rap-dominated R&B charts. Z.Z. Hill's *Down Home Blues* (1982) was an unexpected commercial success, proving that not all independent blues albums had to be confined to a ghettoized listenership.

For those who found Malaco's brand of Southern blues/soul too slick, alternatives arose in the early 1990s that were rawer and more down-home than they probably could have imagined. The Mississippi-based **Fat Possum** label was founded in the early 1990s by two *Living Blues* contributors in their twenties, Matthew Johnson and Peter Lee. Dissatisfied with what they perceived as the unwarranted slickness of many contemporary blues recordings, they headed out to their own back yard for something different, cruising the juke joints and country stores of rural Mississippi, where a fierce and untamed brand of electric blues was played for the locals. The result was recordings by artists like R.L. Burnside and Junior Kimbrough that got some of the most positive critical attention of any 1990s blues releases.

Johnson told the *Boston Phoenix* that he and Lee decided to form Fat Possum "after hearing so many slick albums that sound nothing like what you hear on a Saturday night in Mississippi. We're trying to get a quality that's different from most of the other blues records you hear today. I find most of the blues records coming out just unlistenable. What is primitive to me people, we would consider slick. We prefer what [music critic and producer] Bob Palmer calls 'guerrilla recording,' just going out into the bars and juke joints and letting the tape roll."

It's tempting to think of Fat Possum's proprietors as updated variations of the blues revivalists of the 1960s, who searched the Southern back roads for living exponents of deep acoustic blues, overlooked and forgotten by the modern world. A difference, of course, is that these are electric musicians, playing not on their porches, but in centers of day-to-day community life. Their relative isolation from the urban world has resulted in a certain primitive quality–replete with odd tunings and unsteady time meters–that seems unaffected by the slicker qualities of contemporary music. Artists like CeDell Davis, who plays an irregularly tuned guitar with a table knife, are, if not representative of a dying breed, at the very least unique. The earthy quality of the Fat Possum releases is maintained by a pared-to-the-bone recording budget. Most albums are recorded in a day or two, in facilities like Jimmy's Auto Care in Oxford, Mississippi; the total budget for a full-length recording has never exceeded $4,000.

Despite the acclaim that's rung through higher echelons like the *New York Times*, Fat Possum's sales haven't torn the roof off the juke joint. After their first release (R.L. Burnside's *Bad Luck City*) moved 713 units, it considered folding. But the partners found an investor in John Herrmann, who plays keyboards for the Southern rock group Widespread Panic. Widespread Panic's label, Capricorn, is now distributing Fat Possum. The involvement of rock/blues scholar Robert Palmer in several releases as producer has also helped raise the label's profile.

Living Blues magazine founder Jim O'Neal's Mississippi-based **Rooster Blues** label makes similar albums. His activities, led him to a bona fide modern-day blues rediscovery of harmonica player Willie Cobb, who wrote the standard "You Don't Love Me." He refutes the notion that Rooster Blues and Fat Possum are comparable to archivists, bringing independent blues labels full circle to the folkloric activities of the late '50s and early '60s.

"The very little [recording] that was done over the past three decades or so was mostly folklorists or Europeans doing some kind of field recording," he told *Billboard.* "The contemporary blues here–the blues you were hearing in the juke joints–wasn't getting recorded. There's a void to be filled. There's still a lot of great talent. It's the birthplace of the blues, and it's still giving birth to a lot of great artists."

Concurred Fat Possum's Matthew Johnson in the *Boston Phoenix,* "We're not some kind of purists making field recordings. This is rockin' stuff; this music gets people moving. The stuff that purists go for is just garbage to me. Especially the acoustic records. Nobody plays acoustic guitar anymore except rich white people. Down here, a musician's got the juke box to compete with. The guys in Mississippi are the first to chuck their acoustic guitars when they bring back some good festival money."

—Richie Unterberger

10 Recommended Albums:

Mance Lipscomb, *Texas Songster* (Arhoolie)

Dr. Isiah Ross, *Call The Doctor* (Testament)

Various Artists, *Great Bluesmen at Newport* (Vanguard)

Junior Wells, *Hoodoo Man Blues* (Delmark)

Magic Sam, *West Side Soul* (Delmark)

Various Artists, *Chicago: The Blues Today! Vol. 1–3* (Vanguard)

Various Artists, *Living Chicago Blues, Vol. 1–4* (Alligator)

Various Artists, *New Bluebloods* (Alligator)

Various Artists, *25th Anniversary Collection* (Alligator)

R.L. Burnside, *Bad Luck City* (Fat Possum)

OTHER BLUES ESSAYS

THE BLUES AS FOLKLORE

The onslaught of the Depression in the 1930s spelled the end of the recording careers for many blues artists, as well as nipping many others in the bud before they had even had a chance to begin. Between the mid-1930s and mid-1950s, country blues was documented on record sporadically. The commercial record companies of the time had turned their attention elsewhere; wide interest in the blues' roots, from national and/or White audiences, wouldn't gain momentum until the seeds of the blues/folk revival were planted in the late 1950s.

Our archive of country blues style from this era–and indeed, our knowledge of traditional blues as a whole–would be much poorer if not for the pioneering efforts of a few dedicated folklorists. The institution most responsible for preserving this work was the Library of Congress, who arranged for important field recordings for use in their collection. While the tone and packaging of these performances could tend toward the scholarly and museum-like, more often they resulted in music that, unfettered by commercial considerations of sales and image, gave us a glimpse of authentic blues and folk.

By far, the most important of these archivists were John A. Lomax and his son Alan. The senior Lomax, a colorful figure worthy of a book of his own, had been collecting songs since his teenage years in the Southwest. After education at Harvard, he continued his field work on a more formal basis. As early as 1907, he made cylinder recordings of cowboy songs, which are the first folk songs in English to be recorded by an American. In 1910 he published a collection, *Cowboy Songs and Other Frontier Ballads*, one of the most famous works of its sort.

In the early 1930s, however, Lomax was struggling to make a living at his chosen profession. It was with great enthusiasm that he became curator of the Library of Congress' Archive of Folk Song. The Archive had been established in 1928, but under Lomax's efforts it would truly fulfill its mission of recording and preserving important American folk music. In these endeavors, he was greatly aided by his son, Alan, who was still a teenager when the Lomaxes set out to collect songs for John's *American Folk Songs and Ballads* project in 1933. The work would also involve a lot of recording, with what was then considered state-of-the-art portable equipment (which weighed a good 315 pounds).

The Lomaxes had only been on the road for a little over a month when they hit more paydirt than they could have ever expected. They did some of their recording in prison, figuring that long-time inmates were more apt to preserve traditional styles in the absence of contact with the outside world. July 1933 found them at Louisiana's Angola Penitentiary, where they discovered 12-string guitarist and singer Leadbelly, one of the major figures in 20th-century American music. In addition to being a galvanizing performer, Leadbelly was also a walking encyclopedia of American folk song, his repertoire encompassing blues, folk, spirituals, and more.

As Charles Wolfe & Kip Lornell observe in *The Life & Legend of Leadbelly*, "The recordings by Leadbelly made by the Lomaxes had historical significance beyond the fact that they were the first ones of a man who would become a major figure in American music. The whole idea of using a phonograph to preserve authentic folk music was still fairly new. Most of John Lomax's peers were involved in collecting songs the classic way: taking both words and melody down by hand, asking the singer to perform the song over and over until the collector had 'caught' it on paper...

"John Lomax sensed at once the limitations of this kind of method, especially when getting songs from African-American singers, whose quarter tones, blue notes, and complex timing often frustrated White musicians trying to transcribe them with European notation systems. The whole concept of field recording was, in 1933 and still today, radically different from the popular notion of recording. Field recordings are not intended as commercial products, but as attempts at cultural preservation. There is no profit motive, nor any desire to make the singer a 'star.' As have hundreds of folk song collectors after him, John Lomax had to persuade his singers to perform, to explain to them why their songs were important, and to convince the various authorities–the wardens, the trusties, the bureaucrats–that this was serious, worthwhile work. He faced the moral problem of how to safeguard the records and the rights of the singers–a problem he solved in this instance by donating the discs to the Library of Congress.

"He had to overcome the technical problems involved in recording outside a studio; one always hoped for quiet, with no doors slamming or alarms going off, but it was always a risk. His new state-of-the-art recording machine sported a new microphone designed by NBC, but there were no wind baffles to help reduce the noise when recording outside. Lomax learned how to balance sound, where to place microphones, how to work echoes and walls, and soon was a skilled recordist."

Leadbelly was released from prison shortly afterwards, becoming an assistant/chauffeur of sorts to Lomax. Their stormy relationship would dissolve with some acrimony within a few years, but not before Leadbelly had started a successful professional career, introducing many folk and blues classics to the public before his death in 1949. His Library of Congress recordings, eventually numbering over 200 songs, constitute much of his most important recorded work.

John and Alan Lomax didn't record only blues, or even focus on the blues. They recorded all sorts of folk music, from many different regions, including Cajun music, narratives of ex-slaves, and songs from California labor camps. By the late 1930s, John Lomax, already into his sixties, was less active in the field than Alan, who also recorded a dozen albums' worth of Jelly Roll Morton singing and talking. Alan also recorded pianists Albert Ammons, Meade Lux Lewis, and Pete Johnson for the Library of Congress around the time of the famous Spirituals to Swing concert (which took place in New York City's Carnegie Hall in 1938). All three of those pianists, though really part of jazz, made their imprint on blues history by helping to popularize the boogie-woogie style. The elder Lomax was not retired, and in 1940 made a significant contribution to the blues library by recording Blind Willie McTell.

Alan undertook his most important blues sessions on behalf of the Library of Congress in the early 1940s, as part of a project documenting Black music in Coahoma County, Mississippi. On these trips he found Muddy Waters and Son House, whose recordings were summaries of Delta blues styles past and present. House (who, apparently unbeknownst to Lomax, had already recorded a few commercial sides) would soon move to New York State, not to be rediscovered until the 1960s blues revival. Waters, who recorded for Lomax as an acoustic guitarist, would take Delta blues into the future after moving to Chicago in 1943. Lomax also made interesting deep blues recordings in 1946 with Big Bill Broonzy, Sonny Boy Williamson, and Memphis Slim that also included, as many of the Library of Congress recordings do, conversation with the participants; this was issued by Rykodisc in the 1990s as *Blues in the Mississippi Night*.

Alan Lomax, as stated previously, was not a blues specialist. He devoted the next five decades to championing folk music of all sorts. His late '50s recordings of styles associated with the

Music Map

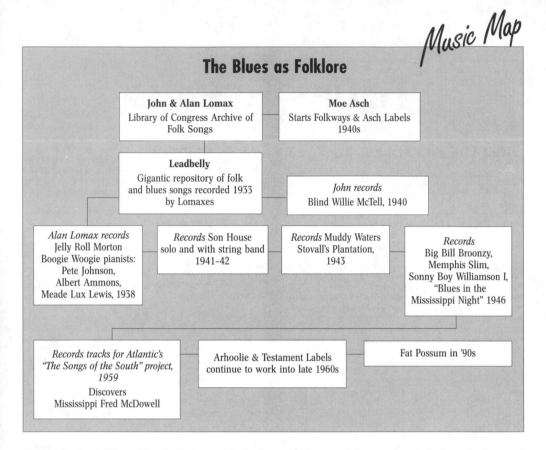

The Blues as Folklore

John & Alan Lomax
Library of Congress Archive of Folk Songs

Moe Asch
Starts Folkways & Asch Labels
1940s

Leadbelly
Gigantic repository of folk and blues songs recorded 1933 by Lomaxes

John records
Blind Willie McTell, 1940

Alan Lomax records
Jelly Roll Morton
Boogie Woogie pianists:
Pete Johnson,
Albert Ammons,
Meade Lux Lewis, 1938

Records Son House
solo and with string band
1941–42

Records Muddy Waters
Stovall's Plantation,
1943

Records
Big Bill Broonzy,
Memphis Slim,
Sonny Boy Williamson I,
"Blues in the
Mississippi Night" 1946

*Records tracks for Atlantic's
"The Songs of the South" project,
1959*
Discovers
Mississippi Fred McDowell

Arhoolie & Testament Labels
continue to work into late 1960s

Fat Possum in '90s

American South, available on Atlantic's *The Songs of the South* box set, resulted in the discovery of Mississippi Fred McDowell (who had never previously recorded), who became one of the most popular acoustic performers of the '60s blues revival. He was a director of the Newport Folk Festival, and his staunch love of traditional styles led to some notoriety when he expressed resistance to the introduction of electric instruments into festival events in the mid-'60s. Much of his life is recounted in his 1993 book, *The Land Where the Blues Began.*

The Library of Congress was not the sole organization dedicated to preserving traditional blues on record. Moe Asch's Folkways label, which began operations in the 1940s, recorded a mammoth body of folk music of all sorts, which naturally included some blues. Leadbelly, Brownie McGhee, and Sonny Terry were some of the most prominent blues artists who did some recordings for the Folkways label. Before his death, Asch sold the Folkways catalog to the Smithsonian, which is engaged in an ongoing series of CD reissues of important Folkways sessions.

Some of the early albums arising from the 1960s blues revival were folkloric in bent, inasmuch as they documented living exponents of rural traditions. There was Robert Pete Williams, for instance, discovered (like Leadbelly) at Angola Penitentiary in the late 1950s. The Arhoolie label presented many blues and folk artists *au naturel*, coming up with a major find in Texas songster Mance Lipscomb. Testament Records issued titles by Jack Owens, Mississippi Fred McDowell, and others. Yet these recordings differed from the Library of Congress and Folkways sessions in that they were less geared toward, well, the library, and more for the general listener. They were not just concerned with documenting obscure and threatened styles, but in presenting material that could be enjoyed on its own terms, and prove modestly profitable in a small commercial niche market.

That doesn't mean that the Library of Congress recordings need to remain stored in the library. The performers the Lomaxes

and others recorded may not have been playing for the general consumer, but they often gave their all. To an extent that the folklorists may not have realized, their work can serve purposes that are entertaining and inspirational, as well as educational.
—*Richie Unterberger*

11 Recommended Albums:

Leadbelly, *Midnight Special* (Rounder)
Leadbelly, *Leadbelly Sings Folk Songs* (Smithsonian/ Folkways)
Various Artists, *Afro-American Blues and Game Songs* (Library of Congress)
Various Artists, *Negro Blues and Hollers* (Library of Congress)
Various Artists, *Negro Work Songs and Calls* (Library of Congress)
Muddy Waters, *The Complete Plantation Recordings* (MCA)
Son House, *Delta Blues: The Original Library of Congress Sessions from Field Recordings 1941–42* (Biograph)
Blind Willie McTell, *Complete Library of Congress Recordings (1940)* (Document)
Various Artists, *Brownie McGhee & Sonny Terry Sing* (Smithsonian/Folkways)
Various Artists, *Blues in the Mississippi Night* (Rykodisc)
Robert Pete Williams, *Angola Prisoner's Blues* (Arhoolie)

THE BLUES REVIVAL

Any retrospective of the 1960s blues revival begs a rhetorical question: How could the blues be revived when it wasn't dead? Yes, in some respects, the blues scene was struggling in the late 1950s. The blues' presence on the R&B charts had been diminished by rock 'n' roll, doo-wop, and pure R&B recordings that were pointing the way for soul music. Country blues was rarely recorded; many of its greatest heroes had vanished into obscurity or died.

Music Map

Blues Revival

Oldtime	**Electric Originators**	**White guys plug in**
Bluesmen play for White audiences as part of Folk Music Revival, 1960s. Son House, Skip James, Mississippi John Hurt, Lightnin' Hopkins, John Lee Hooker	*(Who reach white audiences)* Muddy Waters, Howlin' Wolf, Sonny Boy Williamson, Albert King, B.B. King, Freddie King, Slim Harpo, Lightnin' Slim, Buddy Guy	*early-to-mid-'60s* Paul Butterfield Blues Band, John Mayall's Bluesbreakers, The Rolling Stones, The Animals, The Yardbirds

Yet the blues had never come close to dying. In urban centers, especially Chicago, electric blues legends continued to perform and record regularly, though they may have peaked in terms of vinyl sales. Hit blues singles on the R&B and even pop charts were not unknown; Jimmy Reed and John Lee Hooker had some of their biggest hits around 1960. Although the commercial market for acoustic blues was virtually nonexistent, many performers continued to play the music in Mississippi, Memphis, Texas, and elsewhere, either professionally, for their family or friends, or (in relatively rare cases) behind prison bars.

The "blues revival" really does not refer to the rebirth of the music, but an awakening of wider interest in the blues, particularly among younger White listeners. During its first few decades, blues recordings had been primarily marketed to Black consumers, and primarily played live to Black audiences. Blues performers that made a big impression with White listeners often had a good measure of crossover folk appeal, such as Leadbelly and Josh White. Names like Robert Johnson, Bukka White, and Charley Patton were virtually unknown; electric blues stars like Muddy Waters and Elmore James were not as totally obscure, but still little recognized within the White audience.

But in the late 1950s and early 1960s, young Whites were starting to trace American roots music backwards from rock 'n' roll, through to its sources in blues and folk. Often they were college-educated and relatively affluent, with affiliations in both the countercultural and academic communities. Some have taken a sociological perspective and mused that these listeners were rebelling against their comfortable, conformist upbringings, or hungering for an authenticity that they had been denied. The simpler explanation is that the blues was too good a thing to be kept a secret: larger and larger groups of Americans were responding to the power and magic of the music, especially after the blues revival made it easier to discover, hear, and see.

A small band of enthusiasts–their curiosity piqued by the great recordings they had been able to locate, and the little information that was available to them–began to undertake serious record collecting, documentation, and recording of the blues. Writers like Samuel Charters and Paul Oliver did a lot to get the ball rolling by publishing studies of the evolution of the blues that were both serious and accessible. Folklorists like Alan Lomax (who had been recording blues and folk for many years), and just plain fans like Chris Strachwitz and guitar virtuoso John Fahey, tracked down or discovered down-home blues singers for recording purposes. Often these champions of the blues would double as writers, record producers, promoters, and managers, fueled by their consuming love of the music.

Initially, the blues revival was acoustic in tone. This may have been the result of purists who felt that the authenticity of the music was smothered by electric amplification that pulled it from its populist roots (a theory that doesn't hold up well in light of the fact that millions of working-class African-Americans were listening to electric blues regularly). It could have also been a side effect of the coffeehouse/college circuit that promoted most blues shows for the White college audience in the early '60s, which emphasized acoustic performers, not electric ones. Many of the White

singers on the early '60s folk scene would include blues material in their sets, most notably Dave Van Ronk, Bob Dylan, and the trio of Koerner, Ray, & Glover.

The blues revival was aided and abetted by the development of the LP market. In 1960, those blues artists who recorded for an almost exclusively Black/R&B audience concentrated almost solely upon 45 RPM singles. To address the Whiter and more affluent market, they would focus upon long-playing records. In some cases, blues singers would maintain separate careers for the different markets, such as Snooks Eaglin, who recorded New Orleans R&B for Imperial, and as the blues/folk streetsinger Blind Snooks Eaglin for Prestige. John Lee Hooker had R&B hits with a full electric band, like "Boom Boom," at the same time he was recording acoustic LPs; the liner notes to some of his early albums seem almost apologetic about his electric recordings, as if to infer that his acoustic albums were more authentic.

Several labels addressed the widening White audience for blues, including Arhoolie, Testament, and the Prestige/Riverside/Bluesville family. Often they brought original bluesmen of the '20s and '30s back to the studio after several decades of professional retirement, or even found some elderly acoustic blues singers who had never received the opportunities to record in the first place (phenomenons which are examined in more depth in a separate essay). Large festivals booked these artists and made live recordings of the events, the most notable of which was the Newport Folk Festival. And blues performers began to cross the Atlantic in large numbers for European tours, which both exposed the music on a whole new international scale, and gave the performers themselves a sense of just how much they were treasured, by an audience they hadn't quite expected to reach.

The initial impetus of the blues revival largely ignored contemporary electric performers, but the purist ethic couldn't survive for long. In England at least, the die had been cast back in 1958, when Muddy Waters first toured Britain. American bluesmen had already been touring the country earlier in the 1950s, with assistance from British jazz and blues musicians like Chris Barber and Alexis Korner. Apparently British audiences conceived of the blues as a primarily acoustic medium as well, and were astounded when Waters showed up with an electric guitar. That proved too loud and brash for some British listeners and critics, who might have saved themselves the shock if they had just listened to a few of Muddy's records, virtually all of which were Chicago electric blues.

Recalled Waters in James Rooney's *Bossmen*, "When I first went to England in '58 I didn't have no idea what was going on. I was touring with Chris Barber–a Dixieland band. They thought I was a Big Bill Broonzy–which I wasn't. I had my amplifier and [pianist Otis] Spann and I was going to do a Chicago thing; we opened up in Leeds, England. I was definitely too loud for them then. The next morning we were in the headlines of the paper–'Screaming Guitar and Howling Piano.' That was when they were into the folk thing before the Rolling Stones."

When he made his next British tour in 1962, the tide had shifted. "I went back–took my acoustic with me–and everybody's hollering, 'Where's your amplifier?' I said, 'When I was here before they didn't like my stuff.' But those English groups had picked up on my stuff and went wild with it. I said, 'I never know what's going on.' A bunch of those young kids came around. They could play. They'd pick up my guitar and fool with it. Then the Rolling Stones came out named after my song, you know, and recorded 'Just Make Love to Me' and the next I knew they were out there. And that's how people in the States really got to know who Muddy Waters was."

Young musicians like the Rolling Stones were making their own brand of rhythm and blues, inspired by artists like Muddy Waters; Mick Jagger and Keith Richard had discovered their mutual interest in the music, in fact, when Keith spotted Mick carrying a Chess Records album in a train. They and other early British Invasion bands like the Yardbirds, Animals, Them, and the Kinks covered many blues and R&B songs on their early records, evolving a form of rock 'n' roll with heavy roots in the sources. Young British and American listeners were bound to be curious about the songs' original performers and writers, leading them back to the bluesmen and blueswomen themselves, many of whom were still in their prime.

Some purists have accused such bands of exploiting the music for their own ends, watering it down for a White teenage audience to achieve a commercial success that wouldn't have been possible with the real deal. It's an argument that doesn't wash for a lot of people. These groups were genuinely exciting and original, and quickly evolved from covering import records into writing their own material. Bands like the Beatles, Stones, and John Mayall's Bluesbreakers never made a secret of their influences, often taking time to publicly praise and acknowledge their inspirations, and refusing to pretend that they were the first to be playing such music; Jagger once commented in an interview, "What's the point in listening to us doing 'I'm a King Bee' when you can hear Slim Harpo do it?" The Rolling Stones went as far as to record at Chess Studios during their first tour, and to have Howlin' Wolf perform with them on television in the mid-'60s.

By the mid-'60s, America was beginning to develop its own White blues rockers, particularly in Chicago. Paul Butterfield led the best of these bands, which also included guitarists Michael Bloomfield and Elvin Bishop, as well as a Black rhythm section of veterans from the Chicago blues/R&B scene. Also gigging in Chicago were harmonica player Charlie Musselwhite, and (for a time) Steve Miller. In Southern California, one of the leading collectors of rare blues records, Bob Hite, helped form one of the most successful blues-rock bands of the late '60s, Canned Heat.

The blues-rock acts are discussed in a separate essay; their importance to the blues revival was helping to focus attention not just on acoustic bluesmen, but on Black electric blues bands and guitarists, many of whom had only been active for a decade or less, hardly qualifying for "revival." This also meant that such electric performers could now take a crack at the LP market, particularly if their 45 chart action wasn't so hot. Chess had already tried to sell Muddy Waters to the blues revival crowd with an album entitled *Muddy Waters, Folk Singer*, which actually wasn't much different from his prime electric material.

The Delmark label was one of the first to take the plunge into electric blues albums, with Junior Wells and Magic Sam. Wells' *Hoodoo Man Blues* (1965) is sometimes referred to as the first electric blues session conceived of as an *album* rather than a collection of tracks, and made no attempt to dilute the power or lower the volume for White listeners. Verve did the same with James Cotton, and Vanguard's excellent *The Blues Today!* series did much to present the blues as a living, thriving, often electric medium, not one that had to be presented as a sort of living museum piece in order to qualify for approval.

The albums in turn helped performers like Wells, Albert King, B.B. King, and Buddy Guy break into a whole new circuit that could find them sharing the bill with White rock bands, and playing to larger audiences that could include as many or more Whites as Blacks. Nor did their festival appearances have to be at folk events, which sometimes weren't eager to book electric acts; festivals devoted to blues, or giving equal weight to blues and jazz, began to appear, such as the Ann Arbor Blues Festival. Both enterprising small independents and large major labels belatedly became aware of the thousands of classic blues sides that were unavailable, leading to blues reissues programs that continue to expand to this day.

By the end of the 1960s, blues was not a dominant force on the commercial market, but nobody was checking for vital signs either–many of its greatest musicians were performing to bigger audiences, and making better livelihoods, than they ever had. Since then, there's more or less constant talk of the blues making a comeback, or surging in popularity–but never talk of the blues dying. The blues, it seems, will never die–and never need to be "revived" again.

—Richie Unterberger

10 Recommended Albums:

Various Artists, *Blues Masters, Vol. 7: Blues Revival* (Rhino)
Various Artists, *Blues at Newport: Newport Folk Festival 1959–64* (Vanguard)
Various Artists, *Chicago: The Blues Today! Vol. 1–3* (Vanguard)
Robert Pete Williams, *Angola Prisoner's Blues* (Arhoolie)
John Lee Hooker, *The Country Blues of John Lee Hooker* (Prestige)
Mance Lipscomb, *Texas Sharecropper & Songster* (Arhoolie)
Muddy Waters, *Folk Singer* (Chess)
The Rolling Stones, *The Rolling Stones (England's Newest Hitmakers)* (ABKCO)
The Paul Butterfield Blues Band, *The Paul Butterfield Blues Again* (Elektra)
John Mayall, *Bluesbreakers with Eric Clapton* (PolyGram)

THE BLUES BOX SET

Some would say that the blues was never meant to be an elite kind of thing, displayed on the mantelpiece like some kind of trophy. With the widespread popularity of the box set in the 1990s, though, that's what it sometimes becomes. The proliferation of box sets could be taken as an indication of the respect that classic rock, pop, and blues now generates in our culture (and marketplace). Not everyone, however, is certain that box sets are fulfilling their mission of offering the biggest bang for the buck.

Box sets have been a part of the music business for decades, although they were initially much more apt to be employed for classical recordings or special projects, like scholarly ethnomusicology documentaries. For the pop and rock audience, occasional box sets were produced (often in limited press runs) for artists with unusually devoted followings, like the Beatles, Elvis, and Brian Eno. This started to change in the mid-'80s, when a five-record live Bruce Springsteen box became a best seller. Around the same time, a Bob Dylan box set, *Biograph*, entered the Top Forty, which probably helped convince labels that there was a viable market for multi-disc archival retrospectives.

Biograph also set a model of sorts for box set packages: some classic hits, some key album cuts, some rarities, and some previously unreleased material, as well as a lavish booklet. It took a while for this new strategy to trickle down to the blues world. After all, a very small percentage of record owners of any kind ever buy box sets; an even smaller number buy them on anything approaching a regular basis. And, as we all know too well, the blues represents a very small share of the overall demographic that consumes music.

On the other hand, blues fans, at the risk of generalizing, take their music more seriously than the average Joe. Import companies such as Charly and Bear Family had realized this even before the mid-'80s, producing occasional box sets aimed squarely at the collector. And when they decided to go the box set route, they really went to town, often tracking down every item available, and raiding the vault for unreleased treasures and alternate takes.

When American companies began to issue blues boxes, they were considerably more selective, which is a mixed blessing. Many listeners, to be honest, lack the interest or patience to wade through every last B-side, or to hear successive alternate takes of the same song in a row. Box sets can be regarded as a selective weeding of an artist's oeuvre, in which only the very cream of the crop is bundled into a nifty package.

The Chess label, in particular, tapped into the market with enthusiasm, giving Muddy Waters, Howlin' Wolf, Willie Dixon, Chuck Berry, and Bo Diddley the box set treatment. There were also various artist box sets covering Chess material as a whole, an approach also employed by Specialty (which is now owned by Fantasy). Capricorn dug into the vaults of some somewhat obscure labels, such as Fire/Fury, Swingtime, Jewel/Paula, and Cobra. And the Robert Johnson box set (which was actually only two discs) was the surprise success story of the decade, selling several hundred thousand copies.

Not a great many blues heroes command a large enough following to make domestic box sets a viable proposition. Accordingly, plenty of two-disc packages are produced, sometimes in slip-cases, that fall just shy of bona fide "box" status. With the CD affording room for as much as 80 minutes a disc, however, such anthologies actually cram in as much music as would have fit on three or four average-length vinyl LPs. Chess, Legacy, and Rhino have been particularly active in establishing lines of double CDs; the recently established Capitol Blues series sometimes does this as well, and occasionally fits in *three* CDs to a standard-sized package, as they did with T-Bone Walker and John Lee Hooker.

Are there box sets out there that serve as introductions to the blues as a whole, or important blues styles? Not as many as you might think. Licensing hurdles, for one thing, are formidable obstacles to assembling material from many different labels in one place; even if they can be overcome, labels may find that complicated process not worth the bother or the expense. Thus it is that most various artist boxes tend to be material from the same label. The Smithsonian has put together a couple of all-purpose-type introductions to the blues, although listeners with a reasonably sizable blues collection may find little there that they don't already own. The 15-volume *Blues Masters* series on Rhino is really the best project of that sort ever attempted, but it isn't available in the box form, except for a package containing the first five volumes. A box that had all 15 might be a desirable thing, but would certainly cost in the neighborhood of $200 or more.

In any event, however, a lot of boxes don't exactly turn out to be the last word. Labels often can't resist adding some hard-to-find tracks: B-sides, unreleased outtakes, live cuts, and the like. The presence of such material is usually quite welcome. The problem is that the collectors who covet such morsels almost inevitably own the bulk of the famous material on the box set already, sometimes several times over. And the more general fan, who's buying the box mostly for the "hits," doesn't really care about the unreleased material, or finds it something of a distraction from the main menu.

All of which leads the collector to pose some pretty tough, but merited, questions. Who is the typical box set–with its mixture of hits, rarities, and album cuts–really satisfying? The casual fan will be more likely to pick up a greatest hits collection, or one or two albums, and leave it at that. The completist isn't satisfied either; it's rare that a box will doggedly cover everything that an artist has released during a certain time period, or for a certain label. For that, the big league collector will still favor those obscure import companies that do the job right.

Listeners who are serious fans of an artist, but not unduly concerned with fancy packaging or remastering, find themselves caught in the middle. Enticed by rare and unreleased cuts that appear on almost every one of these sets–but rarely make up the majority of the content–they often find themselves paying quite a few dollars for the five to 15 cuts from a multi-disc box that they really want, and repurchasing quite a bit of music that they already have in their collections, and had no intention of buying again. And it's rare that a record company will accomodate these discerning listeners by issuing a separate collection that only contains the sought-after rarities. You could say that box sets give you access to more blues music than ever before–but at a higher price.

—Richie Unterberger

BLUES REISSUES

Taxes, global warming, geopolitical strife, overpopulation, pollution, invasion of privacy by super-sophisticated technologies … ah, but living in the 1990s does have its small pleasures. One advantage that won't make as many headlines as the above calamities is the increasing ease of collecting vintage blues music. It is no exaggeration to say that, on the whole, it's much easier to collect blues recordings of the 1920s, or blues recordings of the 1950s, now than it was when the music was first released. Not everything's been reissued, of course, but today's blues collector is offered (some would say confronted) with a dazzling variety of options that would have been unimaginable even 20 years ago. Dozens of companies in the U.S. and abroad offer an extensive

line of blues reissues of all styles; some labels specialize in nothing but the blues.

Part of the reason that the blues needed to be "revived" in the 1960s was that the music itself was so hard to come by on record. There's a bit of romance attached to the old days, when being a blues collector was akin to being a member of a secret society. Finding original blues 78s by the likes of Son House and Blind Lemon Jefferson involved searching through thrift stores, garage sales, warehouses, old radio station libraries, or canvassing neighborhoods in which the residents were likely to own the singles (and part with them for a monetary sum). Finding old singles of just a few years back by electric Chicago bluesmen was no easy task either. Some of the most active blues collectors became celebrities themselves, such as Bob Hite (who helped form Canned Heat), acoustic guitarist John Fahey, and Barry Hansen, who gained fame as syndicated radio personality Dr. Demento.

Getting there is sometimes half the fun in record collecting, and no doubt there was an element of excitement involved in diving into a dumpster on the edge of town that's missing these days when we drive down to the local mini-mall. Most blues fans, though, cannot spare the time for such pursuits, chained to more mundane realities like jobs and families. Nor, frankly, do most of us want to spend weekends (or weeks) on end in search of the original recordings. For the most part, you can't beat blues reissues for convenience, in terms of both time and money saved.

Ever since the LP was introduced, there have been various artist and single artist blues compilations. Many (if not most) Chess Records albums of the 1950s and 1960s were essentially compilations of singles, offering handy primers for those born too late to get the original 45s, or those who simply wanted the best of them in one place. But overall, the reissue programs of big and small labels in the 1950s and 1960s were sporadic, perhaps because they didn't always have an idea of how large the potential audience was, or to whom it should be marketed. Robert Johnson's vastly influential *King of the Delta Blues Singers* LP, for instance, appeared in the early '60s on Columbia as a roots-of-jazz sort of title.

The true impetus for comprehensive blues reissues programs came from unexpected sources. British and European blues fans had long been remarkably enthusiastic collectors, dating back to the early '60s, when English kids like Mick Jagger would actually mail-order Chess albums direct from the company itself in Chicago. In the 1970s, British and European labels began to license and reissue vintage rock and blues in quantities that had been considered, for whatever reason, unrealistic in the land of the blues' origin, the United States.

Charly was the initial leader of the field, given a leg up on the competition with its pipeline to the vast Sun catalog. They were soon joined by companies like Ace, Bear Family, Beat Goes On, Flyright, Document, and others. Often the releases were packaged and thoroughly annotated with love and scholarship that had been conspicuously absent from many American productions of the type. There were even box sets, as well as previously unissued material that had never seen the light of day in the U.S.

This led to a frustrating situation for the many American consumers who wanted such albums. Most of the imports could be found with a little effort, in large stores or, failing that, specialty mail-order houses. The irony of needing to buy imports of such fundamentally American records was not lost on consumers or retailers, who shook their heads in half-disbelief at the necessity of needing to buy records from Europe or even Japan, usually at high prices, because U.S. labels wouldn't release the music. Due to some cumbersome legalities, at times American consumers found themselves unable to purchase material that was easily available to Japanese or European consumers, but could not be legally imported into the States.

The U.S., it should be noted, was not totally inactive in the blues reissue arena. Rhino, the leading American reissue company, produced occasional classy packages for artists like Slim Harpo; Arhoolie arranged for the re-release of some very obscure blues of all kinds. Yazoo was (and remains) incredibly active in the field of pre-World War II music, to the point where if any country or old-time blues packages were produced in the States, it seemed like a better-than-even bet that it would bear the Yazoo imprint.

Labels like Yazoo, Document, and Matchbox deserve a Red Badge of Courage of sorts for diving so deep into a field that will never yield big commercial returns. The companies are catering to the *very* specialized collector to offer music that is both out of fashion, and unable to compete with other reissues in terms of sound quality. Much of the material on their albums is remastered from existing copies of old 78s in dedicated archivists' collections, the source tapes (if there were any to begin with) having long vanished. This means that many modern-day listeners are simply unable to put up with the relatively primitive audio and the remaining scratches and hisses, although modern CD technology has paved the way for some surprisingly clear transfers.

Beginning in the late 1980s, the explosion of compact disc technology (which has rendered new vinyl releases all but obsolete) has led to a corresponding explosion in the reissue market. The logic behind this is quirky, but basically it seems as though many labels realized that many listeners were interesting in 'upgrading' their scratchy vinyl records with CDs of the same material. American labels in particular also realized that many consumers were interested in buying albums and compilations of artists whose work had lingered out of print for quite some time.

Thus they began reissuing their own back catalog in addition to licensing it, eventually creating entire subsidiaries like Legacy and Capitol Blues for that purpose. Relative to new artists, the production, royalty, and promotion costs on reissues were minimal. Many of these reissues added the further enticements of additional bonus tracks (sometimes unreleased, sometimes from rare non-LP singles), remastering and remixing, and scholarly liner notes. For artists with wide appeal, these factors were often combined into box sets (see separate essay).

The watershed event that led to the windfall of blues reissues is easy to pinpoint. In 1990, Columbia/Legacy released a double-CD box set of Robert Johnson recordings that, to the shock of everyone, sold over half a million copies. Here was undeniable proof that blues fans would support quality reissues in force, even old ones with relatively raunchy fidelity. Very few blues reissues could approach such sales figures–Robert Johnson, after all, has been mythologized to death, and praised to the heavens by numerous rock stars like Eric Clapton and Keith Richard. But it probably did serve as evidence that old blues reissues stood a very good chance of accumulating a modest profit, or at least breaking even. Columbia/Legacy itself embarked on a lengthy series of reissues that continues to the present, including some names that remain pretty obscure to pop audiences (Bukka White, Blind Willie Johnson, Blind Boy Fuller), and thematic anthologies devoted to the slide guitar and topical blues. The label also released no less than five Bessie Smith compilations as the kind of series that had historically only been undertaken by small foreign companies.

Another welcome development of the CD age has been the reactivation of most of the Chess catalog. MCA, indeed, produced several box sets for the greatest blues stars, as well as entire boxes showcasing the output of what was probably the greatest blues label of all time. Capricorn, which had experienced its greatest success as the home of the Allman Brothers, arranged for box sets spotlighting the contributions of smaller but significant labels to the blues, such as Fire/Fury, Jewel/Paula, Cobra, and Swingtime.

There's no question that CD technology has done much to increase the availability of vintage blues music. Whether it's the best format to hear the music, however, remains a hot matter of debate among fans and critics, despite the clarity of sound that can be achieved with state-of-the-art transfers from tape and vinyl.

Rock and R&B historian Charlie Gilliett, for instance, writes in *The Sound of the City* that "although compilations on CD provide a convenient way for the armchair listener to hear music from another ear, it's important to bear in mind that not all of them manage to recapture the true experience of how the music sounded at the time. The deep and wide grooves of 78 RPM singles generated a big, warm sound which progressively disappeared with each successive format–45 RPM singles, 33 RPM albums, and digitally-mastered CDs all tended to favor higher frequencies, at the expense of the 'bottom end.' Played through the huge speakers of jukeboxes, 78s delivered a massive sound which can only be vaguely approximated by CDs on a domestic hi-fi or portable system. Owners of Elvis' 78 RPM singles on Sun justifiably believe that no other format has come close to reproducing their impact. It may help to turn up the bass on your amp, but you'll never quite get there.

"When 45 RPM singles became the standard format for pop music, and the focus of mastering engineers shifted from jukeboxes to radio, it became common practice to vari-speed tapes to raise the tempo, add compression to make records seem louder, and boost treble frequencies to enable them to cut through on poor quality transistor radios. Sometimes records which sounded terrific on the radio could be hard to bear on a good home system, where their harsh, brittle power seemed inappropriate. So now, when mastering compilations of these old records, engineers have to strike a balance between acknowledging their original function while seeking to meet a new generation's expectations of a clean, clear sound from CDs. In general, there's a tendency for most recordings to sound more 'polite' on CD, and sometimes it can be hard to understand why some tracks were ever regarded as being exciting. There's no absolute rule–sometimes the CD version delivers a presence and warmth that had never been caught on vinyl–but often, CDs fail to recapture the hard-to-describe 'earthy' qualities present on the microgroove pressings."

Should you have a lot of money and time, a large network of collector-oriented stores, magazines, and swap meets still exists that caters to the vinyl collector, even if the market is small potatoes compared to the billions of units shifted at most retail outlets. But even recent CD blues reissues can be hard to find at the store, particularly if you don't live in a big metropolis. For that purpose, there are several mail-order companies that have large catalogs of blues and other roots music, two of the most prominent being Down Home Music and Midnight Records.

For those who want to dive into the world of blues reissues with gusto, but don't know quite where to start, one series can be recommended above all others. Rhino's 15-volume *Blues Masters* provides well-chosen and well-annotated overviews of the most important major blues styles, including Mississippi Delta blues, slide guitar, jump blues, Memphis blues, blues roots, classic blues women, Texas blues, harmonica blues, and Chicago blues. As the cliche goes, it's both informative and enjoyable, for the novice and the well-traveled blues fan alike. The series can serve both as a basic collection of classic blues, and as a port of entry that will help listeners discover their favorite styles and performers.

—Richie Unterberger

THE BLUES ON FILM

While there's a fair amount of blues on film from the past and present, blues fans have a less bountiful selection of goodies to choose from than rock and jazz lovers. The blues, usually lurking at the commercial margins, get less media exposure than some other forms of popular music. That means fewer cameras whirring at both television studios and live festivals; it also means fewer serious documentaries about the subject.

But the number of blues film clips may surprise you. In the early days of the music business, movie studios occasionally filmed musical shorts (called "soundies" for a time) that would run in theaters, as sort of Stone Age precursors to MTV. One of the first of these was a short film starring Bessie Smith that was built around her performance of the theme song, "St. Louis Blues." The blues revival of the 1960s found many of the rediscovered acoustic bluesmen being filmed for the first time, at folk festivals, by folklorists, or by television companies such as the BBC and PBS. As the blues assumes its rightful place as a pillar of American culture, there will no doubt be more and more historical documentaries of the music.

A trip to the video store (or, for that matter, a large music retail store) often yields a decent selection of blues videos to choose from, especially if you live in an urban area or university town. Those without access to these resources can still, for a larger cash outlay, order the videos themselves via roots music mail-order services such as Down Home Music. There are already so many blues videos that a comprehensive rundown is impossible to complete in a few paragraphs. Here we'll simply point readers to some of the best sources.

The two companies with the largest blues video catalogs are Vestapol and Yazoo. Vestapol's line is oriented toward the guitar player, with entire collections of clips for country blues guitar, Texas blues, and bottleneck guitar. Contrary to the impression you might get from a catalog listing, these are not instructional videos, but actual footage of the bluesmen and blueswomen themselves in performance. The appeal is not limited to guitar players (though they can certainly find much to admire); it's geared toward general blues fans, giving them a chance to watch their heroes in action.

There is an unavoidably inconsistent quality about the compilations, due to the varying nature of the sources. A sterling color clip from the BBC lies shoulder-to-shoulder, for instance, with grainy black-and-white footage in somebody's rundown kitchen (which can have an admitted charm all its own). The performances can vary as well; the elderly blues rediscoveries of the '60s can play as well as they did in their prime or, due to failing health, turn in performances that may have been best withheld from circulation, even given the rarity of clips in the field.

But this shouldn't dissuade blues enthusiasts from picking up Vestapol compilations, which are assembled with care. Each one is selected to ensure a diversity of content, and includes detailed liner notes about the musicians and the clips. Certainly the best of them are riveting; a trance-like John Lee Hooker playing solo, for instance, or a Swedish TV clip of Josh White suavely sticking a cigarette behind his ear as he plays. There are also entire compilations devoted to the work of major figures like Hooker, Albert King, and Freddie King. The Freddie King compilation *The Beat!!* is especially sweet, gathering about a dozen vintage color live film clips from a Texas-based R&B/soul TV show of the mid-'60s. (Vestapol also has several videos of jazz guitar players available.)

Yazoo is a name that most blues collectors associate with reissues of ancient country blues from the 1920s and 1930s. Their video line is more diverse than one might expect; indeed, it almost has to be, as there are few blues clips from the 1920s and 1930s of the kind of performers that Yazoo favors. The accent is still on country blues, with entire videos devoted to Furry Lewis, Son House, Big Joe Williams, and Mississippi Fred McDowell. More modern performers, however, are not ignored; there are also anthologies for Muddy Waters, John Lee Hooker, and Lightnin' Hopkins.

If you're still looking for more vintage film clips after exhausting the Vestapol and Yazoo catalog, you might want to try Rhino's two *Blues Masters* volumes. Companion pieces of sorts to the excellent 15-volume CD series of the same name, this unavoidably comes up short quantity-wise when stacked against the discs. But does offer footage of some of the greats, including Leadbelly, Muddy Waters, Buddy Guy, B.B. King, and less-expected figures like Mamie Smith, Roy Milton, and Jimmy Rushing. There is also BMG's similar *Bluesland*, affiliated with a blues history book of the same name.

Considering that only two photos of Robert Johnson have ever been circulated (and that was only after years of searching), it's ironic that there is now a video based around his work, *Search for Robert Johnson* (SMV). As the title implies, this is not so much a standard documentary (no footage, after all, exists) as a look into his environment, sources, and the few recollections we have been granted by his associates, narrated by John Hammond. Another video that delves into Mississippi deep blues is titled, logically enough, *Deep Blues*. Although critic Robert Palmer authored an excellent book by the name in the early 1980s, and is also involved in the video, this is not really a companion piece, but a look at Mississippi blues as it is played in the early 1990s. Accompanied by, of all people, ex-Eurhythmic Dave Stewart, Palmer spotlights the kind of contemporary, electric jukejoint Delta performers that have surfaced on the Fat Possum label, including Junior Kimbrough and R.L. Burnside.

For modern blues, there are occasional releases of concerts by big names such as B.B. King and Buddy Guy. A mid-1990s PBS history of the blues is also a good bet to make it to the video stores eventually, although the subject merits more than the three parts that the series allotted to it.

The milieu of the blues has yet to translate convincingly into fictional feature-length film treatments, despite the abundant fascinating source material. Maybe that's for the best; *Crossroads*, a mid-'80s Hollywood movie based around some aspects of the Robert Johnson legend, enraged purists even as it helped point some listeners that had been unaware of Mississippi Delta blues to the authentic thing. That film was scored by Ry Cooder, who has ensured that elements of traditional acoustic blues are conveyed to millions via his prolific soundtrack work. One movie worth keeping an eye out for that does not deal with the blues specifically, but does project aspects of the Southern Black experience that the blues details, is *Sounder*, with a soundtrack by Taj Mahal (who also has a small role in the film).

—Richie Unterberger

Focus on the Blues Harmonica

The harmonica has secured an enduring place in American music and a very special and central place in the blues.

Its history, as related in *A Brief History of the Harmonica*, distributed by the Hohner Company, and in *America's Harp*, an article by Michael Licht, is as follows. The harmonica, or mouth harp, is one of the family of free reed instruments–those which create a tone by the vibration of reeds which do not strike the frame to which they are attached. This free-reed concept led to the development of the Sheng (sublime voice), said to be invented in 3,000 BCE by the Chinese empress Nyn-Kwa, and brought by a traveler to Western Europe in the seventeenth century. The Sheng is the earliest expression of the principle later applied to such instruments as the concertina and harmonica.

The prototype of the instrument in its present state was invented in 1821 by Christian Friedrich Ludwig Buschmann, a 16-year-old German clockmaker who put 15 pitch pipes together, and called it a "mund-eaoline" (mouth-harp). Another clockmaker, Christian Messner, learned how to make the instruments and sold them on the side to other clockmakers.

In 1857, at 24 years of age, Matthias Hohner bought one and decided to produce it commercially, making 650 of them the first year.

He was made the mayor of his home town of Trossingen, which soon became the harmonica capital of the world. In 1932 his sons founded the State Music College of Trossingen, where harmonica, accordion, piano, and violin are still taught today. This school has graduated 3,000 harmonica players certified to teach the instrument.

Sometime before the outbreak of the Civil War, Hohner sent a few harmonicas to cousins who had emigrated to the United States, and they found the instrument to be extremely popular there. During the Civil War many soldiers on both sides had one and, along with peddlers and immigrants, helped spread the instrument throughout the country.

By the end of the century, America was purchasing more than half of the ten million instruments being manufactured in Germany every year. The Marine Band harmonica, still widely popular today, was introduced in 1896 when it sold for 50 cents. The harmonica was well on its way to becoming the most popular instrument in America's history.

The first steps towards blues stylings on the harmonica must have resulted from attempts at what the nineteenth century classical musician might have termed "programmatic music"–that is, music that attempted to paint a sound-picture. The unique sound potential of the harmonica enabled the more clever players to imitate many of the sounds that surrounded them every day.

Trains, for example, have inspired musicians of all eras. Arthur Honneger, the Swiss composer, created an orchestral train in his *Pacific 231*, while Duke Ellington created one for his orchestra in the "Happy Go Lucky Local." The "Orange Blossom Special" is a standard showcase tune for country fiddlers and banjo pickers, while "Honky Tonk Train Blues" by Meade Lux Lewis remains one of the most famous of all boogie-woogie piano compositions. Singer/guitarist Bukka White got on track with his famous "Panama Limited," which he performed in a bottleneck style.

In the hands of a master, however, the harmonica creates the most vivid portrait of all, due to its capacities for tone-bending and chordal rhythm. Some of the first recorded and best examples available on record are Palmer McAbee's "Railroad Piece," Freeman Stowers' "Railroad Blues," and DeFord Bailey's "Dixie Flyer Blues." Of the many Library of Congress field recordings of train tunes, examples by Ace Johnson and Richard Amerson are extraordinary. Countless numbers of harmonica players must have been expert at imitating trains, but the vast majority of them were never recorded either by folklorists or commercial record companies.

Trains were not the only subjects of these folk tone-poems, however. There were "mama blues," in which the harmonica imitated a baby calling out "mama" or "I want my mama"; "fox chases" that depicted these ritualistic events step-by-step, complete with vocal yelps and descriptive interjections; vignettes of escaped convicts being hunted down by the dogs, as well as pure barnyard scenes with animal sounds of all varieties, fill the harmonica repertory–some with uncanny realism.

The connection between this rural impressionism and the origin of what we recognize as blues-harp style lies in the way in the instrument is constructed and played. The ten-hole diatonic harmonica, the most common of the blues harmonicas, produces a major chord in the key of the harmonica when the holes are blown, and a dominant ninth chord in that same key when the holes are drawn. And, to put it simply, the lower part of the instrument is easier to manipulate when drawn, the upper when blown. That is, when each of the four lowest holes is drawn in a deflected manner, the tone bends and the pitch slides lower; and, when each of the highest four holes is blown in a deflected manner the pitch will also slide lower.

In addition to this, the players discovered that although each harmonica is pitched in a specific key, wherein the tonic or central pitch was located on the number one hole blow, it could be used effectively for other keys by using a different sound hole–blow or draw–as the tonic. Each key created a very different effect or mode that could be used for the purpose of varying the color. These alternative playing modes have become known as positions, of which there are four: straight harp or first position (C harp plays in the key of C); cross-harp or second position (C harp plays in key of G); third position (C Harp plays in key of D); and fourth position (C Harp plays in key of E). Other positions are used–but far less frequently.

Because the players found the lowest registers to be the most expressive, especially for the purposes of mimicry, they found themselves favoring the lowest holes drawn; especially #2, which became the central tone, or tonic. This meant that they were blowing their C Harp in the key of G–a perfect fifth higher than the actual key of the harp. This position produced cross-harp style, or second position.

First position, also known as straight-harp, consists of playing in the actual key of the harmonica, where the lowest hole (#1) when blown becomes tonic, and we play the C harp in the key of C. In this position the expressive high register is exploited. The most well-known master of this position is Jimmy Reed. Straight harp is also used by harmonica players to improvise over ragtime changes and for more folk-style melodies. That familiar, low, wailing sound, however, is an almost certain indication of cross-harp style.

Third position is achieved by making the lowest or first hole draw the tonic or central pitch; the C harp is played in the key of D. Little Walter is a master of third position and used it for a number of his instrumentals. The hallmark of third position is a very unusual and jazzy minor thirteenth chord with added eleventh that is produced when the holes are drawn. This sound is unforgettable.

Most rarely, a fourth position can be achieved by making the #2 hole blow the tonic; that is, playing our C harp in the key of E.

To the beginner this must be confusing, as it must have been for the first players who discovered these positions as well as for their guitar or piano-playing partners. There is a great example on record of a guitar and harmonica seemingly trying to get into the same key, as the guitar player was playing in the actual key of the harp while the harp player was playing in second position. Not until the very end of the tune were they finally in the same key. ("Just It," *Harmonicas Unlimited*, DLP 503/504.)

Harmonica players of classical and jazz music, however, obtain different keys and foreign tones to the key by using a chromatic harmonica rather than a diatonic one. A chromatic harp has a button on the side that when pushed raises the pitch of every blown or drawn tone one half-step. Larry Adler and John Sebastian, Sr., are two modern-day classic masters, while Toots Thielemans is probably the greatest jazz and pop player who is well known today. Blues players use the chromatic mostly in second or third position, in the same manner as the diatonic, to achieve a deep chordal timbre impossible to get on the smaller diatonic model. Bending is tougher, though, on the more sturdy chromatic type. Blues artists have been known to use two or more harps on the same tune–and, conversely, to use the same key harp for tunes pitched in different keys. Obviously, the players' talent, taste, and creativity are tested here.

The harmonica was for many reasons a very natural choice for the Southern African Americans in the developmental stages of the blues. It was small, inexpensive, durable, portable, and easy for the beginner to approach. Musically, it provided a modern and convenient substitute for the quills, an instrument made of three bound pieces of cane; and it was cheaper and easier to play than

the violin–whose place in blues the harmonica usurped. In addition, it had the ability to mimic everything from the human voice to trains, animals, and whistling, as well as the Cajun concertina, and the sophisticated stylings of the jazz-aged clarinet and cornet.

One could get a tremendous variety of tone color, attack, vibrato, tremelo, and glissando, not to mention effects made by manipulating the hand used to cup the harmonica. Moreover, it provided three definite registers, was equally expressive chordally and melodically, and covered the entire dynamic range from a whisper to a shout–quite an arsenal for the size and money.

There must have been an enormous number of African Americans playing the harmonica by the turn of the century, but not until 1924 do we get our first harmonica blues on record. Johnny Watson, known as Daddy Stovepipe, recorded "Sundown Blues" that year–demonstrating a sort of melodic/folky sound using straight or first position harp for fills and solos around his vocals. If various written accounts are true of this amazing performer, born in 1867, we find him touring with the Rabbit Foot Minstrels in the early 1900s, playing for tips in Mexico during the Depression, with zydeco bands in Texas by the end of the '30s, and on Chicago's Maxwell Street from the early '40s until his death in 1963.

Among the very finest players who recorded in or before 1930 were Robert Cooksey, Chuck Darling, and Blues Birdhead. Cooksey was a master of the vaudeville sound which he executed in a unique, virtuosic style. He recorded often with his partner Bobby Leecan through the '20s and '30s. Chuck Darling was a ragtime virtuoso whose complex lines wove effortlessly through all registers. James Simons, known also as Blues Birdhead or Harmonica Tim, is perhaps the best example of how the diatonic harp functioned as a jazz instrument in the early days of that music. His phrasing and timbre are a cross between those of Louis Armstrong and Johnny Dodds, vintage 1928. It is amazing to hear such an advanced jazz concept executed so perfectly on this instrument, and one wonders how it could be that this master recorded only once.

The very first wailing, cross-harp style player to record solo seems to have been the Alabaman, Jaybird Coleman, who made some 20 sides between 1927 and 1930. In his style we hear vestiges of the field holler and work song which were building blocks of the blues; and, through his music, we get an unadulterated and impassioned sense of the meaning of the blues in the South during the '20s. Jaybird entertained the troops during World War I, after which he toured the South with Big Joe Williams as part of the Rabbit Foot Minstrels show. He also toured with the Birmingham Jug Band, but seems to have spent a great deal of his time playing locally in the Birmingham/Bessemer, Alabama, region until he moved to West Memphis in 1949, the year before his death. Jaybird brought his unmistakable style to a large number of major Southern cities, inspiring and influencing many of the harp players of his era. It is perhaps one of blues' greatest ironies that he was managed in 1929 by the Ku Klux Klan.

The seeds of the modern-day blues harp that reached fruition in the golden era of mid-'50s Chicago were sown in the American musical mecca of Memphis, Tennessee. That city, which has played such a crucial role in almost every genre of indigenous American music, boasted the simultaneous presences of Noah Lewis, Jaybird Coleman, Will Shade, Jed Davenport, Hammie Nixon, John Lee Williamson, and Walter Horton, all–off and on–between the years of 1925 and 1930. It must have been a boiling pot of musical ideas as these musicians, not more than children at the time, played on the streets, in Handy Park, in clubs, with jug and jazz bands, and as solo attractions.

As reported in *Memphis Blues and Jug Bands*, by Bengt Olsson, jug bands probably started in Louisville and were active there from around 1915. By the early '30s there were at least six bands in Memphis. The two standout examples were the Memphis Jug Band with Will Shade on harp, and Gus Cannon's Jug Stompers with Noah Lewis on harp.

Noah Lewis was discovered in Ripley, Tennessee, by guitar and banjo player Gus Cannon; it is said that his harmonica playing was unparalleled at the time. As many masters of the day, he was able to play two harps at one time–one with his nose. His style is unique and could be said to represent a consummation of the early chordal-melodic technique being practiced in the South for many years. His playing displays a wealth of ideas, always executed to perfection. His recordings show him to be equally at home as part of a duo, a larger ensemble, or as a soloist. Unfortunately, no recordings seem to be available by the older musicians from whom he learned.

Will Shade, before founding the Memphis Jug Band in 1925, played with Furry Lewis and various medicine shows. After touring with the Memphis Jug Band, he joined the Ma Rainey show in Indiana in 1931, and later recorded under his own name in Chicago as well as with Little Buddy Doyle. Probably his most memorable tune is "Jug Band Waltz," which he recorded with the Memphis Jug Band in 1928. His unique style is in the same general mold as Noah Lewis, but his tone is darker and often he is more melodic.

Jed Davenport, on the other hand, had a distinctively wilder sound than his two contemporaries, often using a "flutter-tongue" technique that lent a metallic edge to his lines. Being flashy and dynamic, he was among the most exciting players of his time. He also recorded with Memphis Minnie, and with some local Memphis jazz bands in the early '30s, and played on the streets of Memphis off and on through the '60s. There can be no doubt that these three players represented the models of excellence for all aspiring bluesmen fortunate enough to have heard them.

If we were to search for one talent that linked this wonderful chordal-melodic style to the horn style pioneered in the 1930s, we might find Hammie Nixon, who actually learned from Noah Lewis and taught John Lee "Sonny Boy" Williamson.

Hammie Nixon was the perfect musical counterpart for the traditional blues guitarist/singer. He had a great talent for filling the sound while never covering it. Perhaps this expertise defeated a possible career as a leader, for he was always the sideman. He became known for his work with Little Buddy Doyle, Son Bonds, Yank Rachell, and especially with Sleepy John Estes, with whom he shared a partnership lasting over 50 years. It could be that Hammie recognized his niche, as did others, and that his career was perfectly suited to his talent. He had a unique sense of how to blow lines behind the singer's verses as sort of an obligato trumpet, spinning a fragile, contrapuntal web that surrounded and enhanced the overall sound.

Before Nixon joined Sleepy John Estes, Noah Lewis was Estes' partner, and Nixon learned much by hearing and watching the master at work. Through the '20s and '30s he practiced his trade on the streets and at parties and picnics, finding just the right riff or chordal touch to complement each song. According to David Evans (notes to High Water LP 1003), Nixon played often in Brownsville, Tennessee, a town that boasted a rich musical life for the blues musician throughout the '30s. There was much work available for a good player, and many travelled there to take advantage of the opportunities–among them Rice Miller (Sonny Boy Williamson II), Big Joe Williams, and John Lee Williamson (Sonny Boy Williamson I). It was perhaps in Brownsville that the next link of the chain was forged, as John Lee Williamson absorbed the style of Hammie Nixon, leaning more heavily on the melodic side, discarding much of the chordal work, and redoing this rural mix into a concept which he was to pioneer in Chicago in just a few years–a concept that was to shape the blues harp style into what it is a half century later.

It is necessary to digress at this point to consider the work of two very special and exceptional virtuosi: DeFord Bailey, and his disciple, Sonny Terry.

Although there were many fine harp players active between the wars, the most influential and widely known was unquestionably DeFord Bailey, the Harmonica Wizard. As told by Bengt Olsson in his May-June 1975 Living Blues article, "The Grand Ole Opry's DeFord Bailey," Bailey's story is as unique as any in all of music. In spite of his color, he was a featured performer in the Grand Ole Opry, playing in 48 out of 52 Opry broadcasts–twice as many as any other performer. Between 1925 and 1941, Bailey was heard every Saturday night playing virtuosic train tunes, blues, and all sorts of harmonica showcase instrumentals, inspiring players around the country–White and Black. Although there was more than just a touch of the backwoods influence in DeFord's playing (he was self-taught and learned as a child by imitating all of the animal and train sounds that he knew), his style was polished to the point of utter perfection–each original tune unique, each a gem. In addition to his astounding appearances on the Opry, Bailey was also the focus of the first major recording project in Nashville, Tennessee. During the years

1927-28 he recorded 11 tunes that were to set the standard for harmonica display pieces in recorded American blues.

Sonny Terry was 11 years younger than DeFord Bailey and was one of his innumerable admirers. Using the fox chases, train tunes, and original blues instrumentals as models, the younger player formed a basis for a personal style that would become world famous.

He began as a young child playing buck dances in his native Georgia, and then moved to the streets of North Carolina. He later toured as soloist with Doc Bizell's Medicine Show, before teaming with Blind Boy Fuller in 1934. His career breakthrough occurred when the great American producer John Hammond engaged him in New York City to participate in the From Spirituals to Swing concert in 1938 at Carnegie Hall.

In 1939 he met Brownie McGhee and there began one of the most famous musical partnerships in all of blues or, for that matter, all of American music. During the next 45 years, Sonny Terry and Brownie McGhee played concerts, clubs, and festivals. They appeared on radio, television, and motion pictures, making countless recordings together with other players, and as solo performers.

Sonny Terry was a tremendously influential player of brilliance whose career and talent could rival almost any other player in the history of blues. He was the finest exponent of the rural, chordal-rhythmic style characterized by whoops and hollers and driving chordal work. The vocal and harp work are so closely knit that one can hardly tell where one starts and the other takes over. He commands a wide variety of tone color and vibrato and an impeccable sense of timing–all of which combine to make his work instantly indentifiable and among the very best examples of this style of blues harp.

Prior to 1925, players were learning primarily by imitating the sounds of their surroundings, from older musicians who played in their area, by the instrumental styles heard on recordings, and from the music heard in the traveling shows such as the Rabbit Foot Minstrels.

However, when DeFord Bailey began his radio career in Nashville, he initiated an entirely new channel through which musicians would be influenced. James Cotton remembers, for example, that Rice Miller (Sonny Boy Williamson II) would talk of hearing DeFord Bailey on the radio. In the early '50s in Memphis, Cotton was able to hear blues on radio from noon until well into the night. And, in fact, he first became seriously interested in the harmonica after hearing Sonny Boy Williamson II on KFFA radio in the mid-'40s.

These beginnings of blues on radio, along with the dissemination of race records featuring contemporary harp styles, and the subsequent invention of the juke box–all in conjunction with the snowballing effects of the first great migration of African-Americans to the north (as detailed by Mike Rowe in his Chicago Blues: The City and the Music)–created an environment conducive to the assimilation of all existing styles of blues harp. The stage was set for the next plateau of growth for the instrument, as it soon would be participating in equal terms with the more urban piano and guitar stylings–and, later, with the full rhythm sections of the bands of the northern cities–especially Chicago.

Perhaps the finest Southern harp player to become an integral part of the modern professional Chicago blues scene was William "Jazz" Gillum, who traveled from Greenwood, Mississippi, to Chicago in 1923, beginning an active career that was to last until his death in 1966. He recorded more than 100 tunes on the Bluebird and Victor labels between 1934 and 1950, using some of the finest sidemen in Chicago including Big Bill Broonzy, Blind John Davis, and Ransom Knowling.

Gillum was at his best in a folksy or ragtime situation when he used the high end of the harmonica in first position (straight harp). Although he was not in the same class as Blues Birdhead or Chuck Darling, he was a respectable singer and player who, nonetheless, enjoyed great success.

Gillum's influence, or lack of it, on the younger players, must be evaluated against the backdrop of the Chicago blues world of the 1920s and 1930s. The Jazz Age placed blues in a collateral position; and, as a result, jazzmen playing in the contemporary ragtime vein were often engaged for blues sessions. The great Ma Rainey, for example, recorded with Tampa Red on some occasions and with jazz bands on others. As with many instrumentalists of the day, these classic blues singers can properly be regarded as belonging to either genre.

Players such as the legendary guitarist/singer Blind Blake found Chicago jazz to be a natural extension of their syncopated East Coast style. Blake often recorded with jazz horn players and singers; and, although it is brilliant work, it is not strictly blues. A real dichotomy of style exists in the work of guitarist/singer/pianist Lonnie Johnson, who was perhaps the only bluesman who could hold his own with the greatest jazzman of the day, Louis Armstrong, while still functioning as a bluesman on other occasions. Some other startling combinations were downhome Mississippi bluesmen Ishman Bracey and Tommy Johnson, both of whom were recorded with clarinetist Ernest "Kid" Michall of the Nehi Boys.

Because the vast marjoity of bluesmen lacked either the skill or inclination to play in the demanding contemporary jazz style, some resorted to a sort of comic-or "hokum"-style, replete with nonsense lyrics, kazoos (sometimes called jazzhorns), washboards, and catchy choruses occurring over the same repetitive set of rag-time chord changes. They sounded like jug bands minus jug and soul, and their function was simply to entertain. Although a few exceptionally talented artists such as Tampa Red was able to transcend this limited style, most, including Jazz Gillum, were not. His limitations were most obvious when he played in a "downhome" style using second position (cross-harp), and he seems to have had very little effect–if any–on the subsequent blues harp players in Chicago.

This entertainment-oriented strain of early urban blues in Chicago is documented excellently in Mike Rowe's aforementioned classic. He points out that "the urban blues were altogether more sophisticated–lighter in texture with the emotional power turned down and the beat turned up." And that, "It was probably a reaction to the trauma of the Depression years that the emphasis was more on entertainment." In addition, he describes a scene controlled almost entirely by Lester Melrose, a White businessman who recorded almost every bluesman of note in Chicago. Big Bill Broonzy, Tampa Red, Jazz Gillum, Big Joe Williams, Memphis Minnie, Lonnie Johnson, and John Lee "Sonny Boy" Williamson, among others, formed a remarkable reservoir of talent used over and over again in various combinations throughout the '30s and '40s on the Bluebird label as fodder for innumerable blues hits based on the proven "formula." Although this is a one-sided look at the entrepreneur, it paints a vivid portrait of the same old sound issuing from Chicago during these years.

In spite of the application of this assembly-line production technique, certain talents were of such magnitude that they seemed to jump out of their prescribed setting. One such talent was John Lee "Sonny Boy" Williamson from Jackson, Tennessee–the father of the modern blues harp style. John Lee Williamson's role in the evolution of the style can be compared to that of jazz pianist Earl Hines, who is credited with developing the "trumpet-style" right hand; or later, to pianist Bud Powell who expressed the bop style concepts of Charlie Parker and Dizzy Gillespie through his right-hand work. Like these two great pianists, Williamson created a strongly melodic potential for an instrument bound mostly to a chordal or subordinate role. He transformed the harp into a dynamic lead voice.

Williamson, the original Sonny Boy, played straight and cross-harp styles, ragtime-type tunes, and straight blues–all with enormous conviction and great style. His vocals were equally impressive, employing expressive vibrato and changing timbre. He used formula-like fills and cadence figures to frame his lines, and switched freely from a chordally dominated style to a predominantly single-note style–with all possible graduations between these two stylistic poles. He used sustained tones, short repeated notes and five-six note motives with great intelligence and care and might well have been the first harp player to construct solos consistently in this manner.

One truly amazing characteristic of Williamson's music is that in it, one hears not only the past (shades of Noah Lewis and Hammie Nixon are always present), but also the future. One hears some of the architecture of Little Walter, the vocal and instrumental phrasing of Sonny Boy II (Rice Miller), and the tone of Big Walter Horton–all virtually implied by the older musician's vocal and instrumental innovations. In addition, Williamson was the first of a long and distinguished modern line of accomplished singer/harp players who performed their own tunes.

He began his recording career in Chicago in 1937 with a series of records that featured him fronting his own group and per-

forming as a sideman with Big Joe Williams. He was enormously popular and successful but, tragically, was murdered one night in 1948 while walking home from a performance at the Plantation Club in Chicago. His career must be regarded as one of the most significant phases in the development of blues harp style.

Certain contemporary factors converged to exert a tremendous influence in blues music during the '40s. Perhaps the most significant of these was the so-called Petrillo Ban of 1942. Because James C. Petrillo, president of the Musicians Union, saw recordings and juke boxes as dire threats to the livelihood of musicians, he banned all union members from recording. "This and the strict rationing of shellac" (used for record production), recounts Paul Oliver in his *The Story of the Blues*, "effectively stopped the recording of blues." This two-year ban served to take blues out of the studio and into the clubs and streets where it was infused with new life.

In addition, another peak migration period of Blacks to the north was creating a bigger audience for blues; and a grassroots talent-search by the new independent label-owners in Chicago was providing encouragement and work for the younger players.

From the mid-'40s there collected in Chicago a nucleus of harp players whose work, based at least partially on that of John Lee Williamson, constituted a new style that gained more and more definition as the strictures of the Melrose empire loosened and independent record labels began to appear. Maxwell Street served as the perfect breeding ground for these avant-gardists who jammed there regularly, exchanging ideas and strutting their stuff. In addition, the South side was dotted with small clubs that seemed to unite the Black community, serving as both a sweet reminder of the good side of what many of them had left behind, as well as a musical signpost towards the future. Although the lines of development that these Chicago-based artists were pursuing were very different from the directions being taken by the players based in the South, Junior Wells refuses to think of it as a "city style." Wells is quoted as saying: "We had a country sound, but we also were getting into a different type thing. I wouldn't call it a city-type thing, I would just say we had learned some new riffs to put into the thing and it was more of an uptempo sound. We were listening to different type records."

It was in Chicago that the Brownsville, Helena, and Memphis styles coalesced into what is now regarded as the modern blues harp style and sound. So definitive are its markings, so powerful its effect, that almost one half-a-century later, it has changed hardly at all. Perhaps there is no reason for it to change. Of the many fine harp players practicing today it would be difficult to find many who did not get the basis of their style from players who were fully mature in the '50s.

Snooky Pryor, born in Lambert, Mississippi, moved permanently to Chicago in 1945, and was one of the first of these pioneers to record the new post-war Chicago sound. At his best, he is magnificent, displaying a perfect balance of chordal and melodic style. Using a tenor-range sound, he is capable of contrasting a beautifully smooth tone with a rough-edged compliment. From a stylistic/historical point of view, one hears in his work the infuence of all the major players of the day. He was greatly influenced by his favorite player Rice Miller (Sonny Boy Williamson II) whom he heard on KFFA radio, as well as by the original Sonny Boy, John Lee Williamson, with whom he sat in regularly. An astonishing track, "Boogie," recorded in 1947–48, reveals the note-for-note opening motif of "Juke," the masterpiece recorded by Little Walter in 1952. We will perhaps never know who first developed this classic line, or if, in fact, it was a cliche used by many harp players at the time. Snooky is in great form at the time of this writing–still playing in the style he helped create in the late '40s.

"I had admired the original Sonny Boy, Rice Miller, Big Walter…but when I met Little Walter, then it was an entirely different thing to me. Walter was the best–to me–that I had heard. The different things that he could do on the harmonica was an entirely different thing from what everyone else was doing. John Lee had the blues-type thing–Walter had the blues, but he had that uptempo stuff also…it was the execution that he was getting out of the harmonica." This Junior Wells quotation echoes that of Louis Myers, Walter's guitar player of many years: "All of them cats come along and try to play after John Lee died–but Little Walter was more important than all those cats. He was the best after John Lee…was none of them as good as Walter … and none of them that have come after [are as good]. He was the best in Chicago … the baddest." Lester Davenport, a veteran harp player on the Chicago scene since 1944 who recorded with Bo Diddley, says: "I would say that Little Walter was the greatest and most influential that ever played."

Marion "Little Walter" Jacobs was born in Louisiana in 1930. At 12 he was working the small clubs and streets of New Orleans, at 14 he played on Sonny Boy Williamson II's "King of Biscuit Time" of KFFA, at 15 he was in East St. Louis, Illinois, and St. Louis, Missouri–and, at 16 he was in Chicago on Maxwell Street. In 1947 he recorded for Ora-Nelle records and a year later was with Muddy Waters. During the next few years he toured and recorded with the Muddy Waters band and frequently recorded as a sideman with others. His breakthrough occurred with *Juke*, recorded for the Checker label in 1952. As soon as he realized that he had a hit, he left Waters' band to pursue a solo career, backed by the Aces, a band that was at the time fronted by Junior Wells. The band consisted of Louis Myers on guitar, his brother Dave Myers on bass, and Fred Below on drums–arguably the finest band that ever played. Walter's reputation grew throughout the country as well as England and Europe. He was recognized by some of the superstar rock groups of the '60s and recorded as late as 1968, the year he died a violent death.

Little Walter is considered by many peers, harp-playing disciples, blues scholars, and serious fans to be the greatest blues harp player who ever lived. A great musician, songwriter, harmonica player, bandleader–a genius. And, like many productive geniuses, his influences were many and varied. Honeyboy Edwards recalls Walter speaking of the profound effect on him by the musicians he heard in Louisiana as a child. Walter's third-position work, in fact, sounds sometimes like a Cajun concertina. Big Walter spoke of how he taught Walter in Memphis (Edwards introduced them in the '40s). Louis Myers remembers Walter hanging around John Lee Williamson–and how the older player took him under his wing. "John Lee liked Walter because he was young. He was a kid trying to learn," recalls Myers (who remembers this well because Robert Myers, Louis' brother, was playing gigs with John Lee Williamson at this time). On the other hand, Mike Rowe, in his *Chicago Blues: The City and the Music*, tells of Walter playing "all kinds of music" (probably waltzes, pop tunes, and polkas) "until he came under the influence of Big Bill Broonzy and Tampa Red." In addition, Willie Cobbs, Honeyboy Edwards, and Junior Wells all relate stories of Walter learning licks from the jazz horn players of the day–especially Louis Jordan and Bullmoose Jackson. Given the broad range of his style and the marked originality of his concept, it is entirely believable that Walter absorbed all of these influences–that he was learning from everything musical that appealed to him–and that he was capable of assimilating all of this into an original style.

In considering Walter's style, one must admire how masterfully he was able to use every existing technique of blues harp playing, and how easily he was able to shape each of them to his own expressive purpose. He used a rainbow of tone color and sometimes exploited that one facet for a solo ("Mean Old World"). His chordal work is fascinating, especially during his beautiful excursions into the dark choral regions of the chromatic harp or 12-hole diatonic, particulary in third position ("Lights Out"). His "bent" tones are extremely effective, because he was capable both of controlled glissandi (slidings) at any speed ("Blue Midnight") or of merely jumping to the bent tone with perfect intonation at any point in the phrase. His trills, bent or natural, were executed at varying speeds; his numerous types of vibrato; his shifts of tone color; his Monk-ish gift for playing slightly off the beat (introduction to "I Don't Play"); his jazz-oriented phrasing and overall concept (even Sonny Rollins would have been proud of inserting "A Tisket A Tasket," and then sequencing it in the very next phrase as Walter did in "Crazy Legs")–all of these techniques would have amounted to merely great virtuosity in the hands of a lesser artist. In addition, as a composer and soloist, perhaps Walter's greatest gift was his ability to perfectly balance his lines. He was always the master architect–creating original designs of consummate symmetry.

Walter was equally as creative and virtuosic in a supportive role, never disturbing the solo lines or integrity of the tune. Of the many songs he recorded as a sideman in the Muddy Waters band, "Forty Days and Forty Nights" and "I'm Ready" serve as fine examples of Walter's extraordinary talent in this capacity. In addi-

tion to making great tunes even greater, he was also able to make very ordinary ones such as Muddy's "Young Fashioned Ways" positively jump out of their grooves with his use of cross-rhythms and jazzy off-the-beat accents. Clearly, he was not challenged by Muddy's material then, and in fact, was not touring with him at the time–only recording with him at Chess' request.

Among Walter's many contributions to blues music in general, and to harmonica-playing specifically, one must acknowledge as paramount his elevating the amplified harp style to state-of-the-art status. One hears the gradual development in style from the acoustic work in "Louisiana Blues" to the modern amplified masterpiece, "Juke." There are various accounts of John Lee Williamson, Rice Miller, Snooky Pryor, Big Walter Horton, and Little Walter being the first to cup the harp against a microphone, thereby completely altering the timbral attack and overall playing style. One might conclude that this techinque was a natural and gradual result of trying to be heard over a rhythm section that grew bigger and louder from the late '40s on.

Like T-Bone Walker and Charlie Parker, Walter redefined for all time the role of his instrument and set standards of excellence that will perhaps never be surpassed.

While the blues was being revolutionized in the northern cities, a complimentary strain was being nurtured and developed by players who remained active in the South throughout the '40s and '50s. The central figure of this activity–Rice Miller or Sonny Boy Williamson II–was perhaps every bit as great and influential as Walter in his own way.

As enigmatic as any character in the blues pantheon, Rice Miller would not divulge his real name or date of birth, although Paul Oliver in his notes to Arhoolie CD 310 fixes his birthplace as Glendora, MS; and the year as either 1894 or 1899. [Reserach of government documents by *Living Blues* has revealed that Sonny Boy Williamson was born in 1910. This information was also confirmed by Williamson's surviving relatives.]

Sonny Boy II's musical achievement is sometimes overshadowed by the enormous humanity, sense of humor, and personality that pervades his work. One of the greatest blues lyricists that ever lived, he recorded relatively few instrumentals and gave equal time to both his highly expressive vocals and his harp-blowing, using both of these talents to underscore the humor, irony, and pathos that infuse his musical poems.

It is important to note that Sonny Boy Williamson was a born entertainer, and that his style was honed for the live, improvisational playing of the juke joints; and, starting regularly in 1941, the live radio broadcasts from KFFA in Helena, Arkansas. He was 40 years old when he made his first records for the Trumpet label in Jackson, Mississippi. Although there are some gems such as "Might Long Time," some of these early recordings are perhaps too loose to qualify as classics. When he began recording with Chess in Chicago, the change in both producers and sidemen helped to tighten the arrangements and make the tunes more memorable. Talents such as Robert Jr. Lockwood, Otis Spann, Lafayette Leake, and Fred Below helped Williamson turn out lasting works–Chicago classics such as "Help Me," "Trust My Baby," "Nine Below Zero," "Cross My Heart," and many others.

Although he may have lifted the basics of his style from his namesake at some time or another, Rice Miller represents a wholly original style that is the modern epitome of the "downhome blues." He lacks none of the technique that other more "modern" players had. His use of vibrato, sustained tones, trills, glissandi, varying timbral shades, sense of symmetry, along with his impeccable timing, were uniquely developed for his personal, expressive needs. If Walter was abstract perfection, Sonny Boy II was pure natural exuberance.

Rice Miller had many admirers who were greatly influenced by his style. In addition, though, he had a few who were his actual pupils, learning techniques directly from him. Among the first and most famous of these was Chester Burnett, known as the Howlin' Wolf. Williamson and Wolf teamed up and toured the jukes of Tennessee, Arkansas, and Mississippi. Wolf was in no way the virtuosic harp-blower that his teacher was, although he was truly a great bluesman. His playing–expressive and dynamic–was used to create fills and solos around his imposing vocals, and add even more punch and character to his now-classic original tunes.

While Little Walter was in Chicago presiding over the new urban developments, and Sonny Boy II was in Arkansas bringing the rural style into the '50s, there was a very important group of players ruling by committee in Memphis, Tennessee. Once again, this city was to serve as a focal point for the development of the blues in general and of the harp specifically. Howlin' Wolf, both Walters, both Sonny Boys, Jed Davenport, Jaybird Coleman, Sammy Lewis, Junior Parker, James Cotton–all of this talent was in and around Memphis at some time during the late '40s and early '50s. Appearing on radio, in clubs and on the streets and parks, some of these players were to begin their recording career there under the direction of Sam Phillips. Two very influential players who seemed to be always on the move between Chicago, Memphis, and points South were Big Walter Horton and Forrest City Joe Pugh.

"Big Walter was always in and out–a hard person to keep up with… always on the move," relates Junior Wells. Walter Horton was associated with almost all of the great blues scenes since he reputedly recorded as a child with the Memphis Jug Band in 1927. He claimed to have toured with the Ma Rainey Show in Indiana as well as with various bands in the South before settling for a brief time in Memphis in 1935. In 1940 he was on Chicago's Maxwell Street, and seemed to move between there and Memphis off and on from the 1940s to the '60s, playing and recording with many of the great bluesmen of the day including Muddy Waters, Jimmy Rogers, Robert Nighthawk, Howlin' Wolf, and Johnny Shines.

Although he never achieved much fame or fortune for his work, certain masterpieces such as "Easy," "Little Walter's Boogie," "Cotton Patch Hotfoot," and "Walkin' By Myself" (recorded as sideman with the Jimmy Rogers band) assure him a place among the very best players in history.

Sometimes called Mr. Tone, Big Walter played with as rich and deep a color as anyone. He also used various types and speeds of vibrato, trills, and glissandi that he employed with great imagination and flair. His playing bears the shades of Hammie Nixon, Will Shade, and even Jed Davenport; yet he delivers his sculptured lines with such swing that one finds believable his claim to have taught Little Walter.

If Walter Honton's output is uneven in quality it is because his career was interrupted by various bouts with sickness. In addition, he seemed to be teamed often with incompetent or unprepared sidemen and producers who ruined more than just a few of his best efforts. Big Walter, who represents a middle ground between the down-home and uptempo styles, was an exceptionally gifted and personal player, who had an enormous influence on postwar blues harp styles.

The enigmatic Forrest City Joe Pugh seems to have been a man of many parts. From his recordings, he seems little more than an expert imitator of John Lee Williamson; yet, Junior Wells remembers that he had a far deeper tone than Sonny Boy I: "I thought Forrest City Joe was great–but he didn't make it. I admired everything he did because he had such a deep, deep tone. He had a really, really deep tone…and notin' and shakin' the harp." James Cotton used to hear Forrest City play piano while playing harp on a rack, and added that "Forrest City was a boogie-woogie man. First time Big Walter ever heard boogie on the harp was from Forrest City Joe. He was his own man…independent. He had his own style and he influenced me quite a bit. During the late '40s and early '50s, I used to love to hear him play–he used to tell us about Chicago 'cause he'd been there and back. He was very, *very* good." Lester Davenport says: "He was great…I'd put him in the same category as Big Walter. He did a lot of things with the harmonica that other players didn't do. I only remember hearing him outside, playing by himself on the street–never in a club." It is very unfortunate that Joe Pugh died at age 34.

Jimmy Reed began his harp-playing career in the early '50s, recording as a sideman with John Brim, John Lee Hooker, and Eddie Taylor. Often these early recordings showcase his cross-harp style; however, he became a superstar due to his high-end playing in first position over the lay-back shuffle rhythms and fine second guitar work provided by his childhood friend and long-time partner, Eddie Taylor.

Although many of his harp-blowing peers in Chicago did not recognize him as a major talent at first, he was an enormous influence in Louisiana where he affected the work of an entire school of young players such as Silas Hogan, Lazy Lester, Louisiana Red, and the future star Slim Harpo. Reed continued to tour until his death in 1976.

James Cotton and Junior Wells, born within a year of each

other, are both brilliant musicians whose careers have intertwined for more than 50 years. Each of their styles, once extremely derivative, have become highly personal ones that are still evolving.

Cotton began imitating trains on the harmonica at age six. Three years later he ran away from home to learn from Rice Miller whom he heard on KFFA radio. A few years later he had taken over Williamson's band when the older master had gone to Jackson, Mississippi, to record. Cotton recorded with Howlin' Wolf in 1952, and two years later recorded the classic "Cotton Crop Blues" for Sun Records in Memphis. When he joined the Muddy Waters band after 1955, he was forced to play in a more urban style in order to fill the shoes of Walter, Junior, and George Smith–all of whom had preceded him. Since then he has toured and recorded with his own groups, being one of the few authentic bluesmen still working full time and one of the greatest harp players alive.

Junior Wells was influenced by all the major players of the day and, in fact, recorded tributes to Rice Miller and Little Walter. His debt to John Lee Williamson is obvious in his recording of a number of the original Sonny Boy tunes, including "Hoodoo Man Blues" and "Cut That Out."

Wells was influenced mostly, however, by Little Walter's "uptempo" sound and remembers being taken to meet him one day in the late '40s when Walter and Waters were playing the Ebony Lounge. Walter let Junior sit in and use his microphone and amplifier. Afterwards, Walter asked him if he played the saxophone. Junior said "Nah" and Walter said "Good, you'll be alright–you got the same ideas about doin' things that I have." About five years later, Wells was to replace Walter in the Muddy Waters band, before going out on his own. Wells' country feel is tempered a great deal by the swing style pioneered by Walter, leaving him with a very dynamic and individual approach to the instrument. He and Cotton are probably the two greatest authentic players alive and working.

–Larry Hoffman

Sources:

February, 1991: quotations from James Cotton, Lester Davenport, Honeyboy Edwards, Louis Myers, and Junior Wells taken from personal interviews with the author.

T.M.W. Dixon and J. Godrich, *Blues and Gospel Records* 1902–1943

David Evans, notes to *Tappin' That Thing*, High Water LP 1003

Sheldon Harris, *Blues Who's Who*

Mike Leadbitter and Neil Slaven, *Blues Records* 1943 to 1979, Volume One

Michael Licht, "Harmonica Magic: Virtuoso Display in American Folk Music," *Ethnomusicology*, Vol. XXIV, No. 2, May 1980

Paul Oliver, *The Story of the Blues*

Bengt Olsson, *Memphis Blues*

"The Grand Ole Opry's DeFord Bailey," *Living Blues*, May-June 1975, No. 21

Mike Rowe, *Chicago Blues: The City and the Music*

Focus on the Slide Guitar

"Then one night at Tutwiler, as I nodded in the railroad station while waiting for a train that had been delayed nine hours, life suddenly took me by the shoulder and wakened me with a start.

"A lean, loose-jointed Negro had commenced plunking a guitar beside me while I slept. His clothes were rags; his feet peeped out of his shoes. His face had on it some of the sadness of the ages. As he played, he pressed a knife on the strings of the guitar in a manner popularized by Hawaiian guitarists who used steel bars. The effect was unforgettable. His song, too, stuck me instantly.

'Goin' where the Southern cross the dog.'"

–W.C. Handy, Father of the Blues, 1903

This passage has often been quoted by blues writers who are stunned by the fact that the slide technique has lost none of its "unforgettable effect" despite the passage of nearly 100 years. Perhaps it is because the slide or bottleneck style of guitar playing provides an incomparably personalized approach to this most basic and personal musical idiom that is the blues.

For example, players have chosen from an array of slider materials that has included everything from polished bone; all sorts of knives; all shapes, portions, and sizes of bottles made of plastic or glass; to various types of metal or brass bars or tubes of any chosen diameter of length. A slider can be gripped in any manner desired or "worn" on whatever finger the player chooses. This decision has often been made according to whether the player laid the guitar across his knees, playing lap-style, or whether they held the instrument in the traditional manner. Lap-style players sacrifice the normal methods of chording, committing themselves to chords attacked by the slider.

In addition, the slide style has enlisted a great variety of guitar types over the years, such as the electric steel, played lap-style or on a stand; the National guitar ("bodies have been made of steel, brass, German silver, or wood," wrote Robert F. Gear in "The National Guitar," *Living Blues* 14, 1973); acoustic guitars of all shapes and sizes, with or without a chosen number of resonators (bulbous perforated additions to the front of the body). In fact, this consideration is so involved that is has become the subject of an upcoming book, *The History of National Resonator Instruments*, by Brozman, Centerstream Publications. Metal or steel guitars are particularly effective when played with a slider, of course, because they serve to heighten the sharp percussive effect of the slider on the strings. This was of great importance to the many blues artists who played for dancers in the loud country jukes, as well as for those who used pronounced rhythmic effects in their portrayal of trains.

It is well known that slide players have made extensive if not exclusive use of open tunings—that is, "scordatura" (retuning) of the guitar from "standard tuning" (E-A-D-G-B-E, low to high) to a full major chord. Many variations of open tunings appear on record, but the two most often used and cited are "Spanish" and "Vastopol." The former, often called "G-tuning," actually refers to any tuning with the chord factors 5-1-5-1-3-5 (D-G-D-G-B-D; sol-do-sol-do-mi-sol)—low to high, and often used as open A. The latter is often called "D-tuning," with the arrangement 1-5-1-3-5-1 (D-A-D-F#-A-D; do-sol-do-mi-sol-do)—low to high, and often used as open E. It is the intervallic arrangement of the strings that determines the type of tuning, regardless of concert key—which is often raised or lowered by retuning all of the strings by whole or half step, or by use of a capo. There are other tunings available; and, in fact, players freely invented their own specially-suited ones at will. Bruce Bastin, in *Red River Blues*, quotes Georgia bluesman Son Foster as saying: "I played with a slide too, played Spanish, C-Natural they call it. Vastopol. Tune the guitar in four or five different tunings for different kinds of music."

Analytically, these tunings had a great bearing on the musical qualities of a tune. Vastopol, for example, was the strongest arrangement, in that it presented the tonic as the lowest as well as the highest open string, making possible a dynamic presentation of the tonic chord at the twelfth fret—as heard in the familiar opening riff of "Dust My Broom." The open sixth string, of course, gave a great tonic "anchor" to the chord; and, the bottom pair of strings (five-six) gave easy access to the open fifth (do-sol) needed for the familiar blues shuffle background rhythm. Spanish, on the other hand, is somewhat weaker, perhaps a bit mystical, with its open fifth on the first and sixth open strings.

Open tunings in general were probably derived in the United States from the banjo, an instrument which is always tuned in this manner.

Standard tuning is also an option, especially for players who are primarily interested in using the slide for single-string melodies played on strings one, two, and three. Once the guitar has been tuned to an open chord, all the standard chord shapes and fingerings disappear, and the player either develops new ones or limits himself to the same open chord arrangement "transposed" to higher positions on the neck. That is, barred across the fifth fret the strings produce the IV (sub-dominant) chord; the seventh fret produces the V (dominant) chord; and, the twelfth produces the I (tonic) chord—one octave higher than open. All imaginable varieties of partial chording (triads, diads, etc.) are available in open tuning, as are techniques of slant-barring which provide simultaneous notes on different frets. Still, some of the finest melodic slide players have chosen to stick to standard tuning and chording—using the slider to coax exotic and melodic coloring from the treble strings.

Added to all of these choices, of course, are the usual options of all guitarists—choosing either a six or 12-string instrument, or one of the many number of doctored variants including those with seven or even nine strings. These mutant types were made from either 12-string guitars minus strings or six-string guitars plus any number of added strings. Each variation produced a subtle yet very definite and distinctive alteration of the overall timbral quality. Gus Cannon, in 1927, applied the slide technique to banjo on his recording of "Poor Boy"—achieving a haunting, infectious, and rare timbral quality.

The general concept of changing the sound of an instrument by "tampering" somehow with its make-up or by using a foreign second object to alter the attack or overall tone color is not at all uncommon in music. There is the bow used to stroke the orchestral string instruments which can also be plucked (pizzicato), the various mutes used to shade the timbre and reduce the volume of instruments—most commonly applied to brass but also to some winds and all strings as well. And, in addition, there are certain other techniques that have come about only recently such as the use of the bow to sound instruments such as the electric guitar, vibraphone, and even the timpani. Electric amplification, in fact, provides a dynamic example of the complete transformation of an instrument by an innovation designed originally only to make it somewhat louder.

The uncertain ancestry of the blues slide guitar technique has given rise to two main, divergent schools of thought. One believes the roots to be Hawaiian; the other, African. Although W.C. Handy cites the Hawaiian model in the opening quotation, and though Hawaiian music was recorded, distributed and made widely popular in early 20th-century America, one cannot help but to give the African theory more credence.

Historically, African music has always had a penchant for altering instruments to give them a more percussive edge. Attaching gourds (used as resonators), buzzers, and rattles to stringed instruments is very common there. In addition, one finds instruments with varying numbers of strings and tunings. Species of the harplute, for example, can be found with from five to 21 strings; and the kora, played in Guinea and Senegambia, has at least three different tunings used according to the piece. In addition, many of the African stringed instruments, like the two-stringed stopped lute, used a drone string to mark the pulse—not unlike the mesmerizing, open string tonic that sometimes pulses through every measure of Delta blues.

General Africanisms in blues and jazz have been studied and reported by such leading authorities as Samuel Charters, David Evans, Paul Oliver, and Gunther Schuller. The use of glissandi, "out-of-tune" blue notes, complex cross-rhythms, dropped ends of phrases, underlying drones, timbral contrasts, and call and response patterns all point to the African origin of the blues.

Slide guitar technique heightens the effect of many of these features, especially those dealing with glissandi, percussion, and overall vocal ambience. Evans theorizes, and in fact documents evidence of the slide style originating in the one-string "instruments" improvised by many Mississippi bluesmen out of broom-wire stretched across a wall and played with a small bottle used as a slider. He cites the African musical bow as a probable ancestor to this one-stringed phenomenon (David Evans, "Africa and the Blues," *Living Blues* 10, 1972; David Evans "Afro-American One-Stringed Instruments," *Western Folklore* 29). More modern, portable variations of these one-stringed instruments—called diddley bows—have been recorded in the '50s by One-String Sam (Blues Classics 12, *Detroit Blues*) and in the '80s by contemporary bluesman Lonnie Pitchford (L & R 42.309, *Mississippi Moan*).

Arguments for Hawaiian origin are based on the "slack-key" style of guitar playing that utilizes sliders and open tunings hallmarking the Hawaiian music craze that swept America during the first third of this century. "Even more heavily influenced by the steel guitar than the white country musicians were the black bottleneck guitar playing musicians and singers," writes Robert Armstrong in "The Impact of Hawaiian Music on American Music" (*Encyclopedia of Hawaiian Music and Musicians*; Ed. George Kanahele, University of Hawaii Press). And there is no doubt that it must have had some effect. For one thing, steel sliders were routinely sent by many companies to accompany every guitar purchased by mail order; and, for another, the lap-style technique employed by many bluesmen was undoubtedly of Hawaiian origin. Elmore James recorded a tune entitled "Hawaiian Boogie," and there is more than a taste of the Hawaiian influence in the playing of bluesman Casey Bill Weldon. Although Armstrong considers James' tune to be "a tribute to the origins of the blues slide guitar," it seems far more likely that the African-American banjos and diddley bows, in concert with the concept of a violin-inspired instrumental vocalese, conspired to bring about what is perhaps the most distinctive sound in all of blues.

There does not seem to be a linear development of slide guitar technique; rather, it seems to have burst on the scene–fully formed–somewhere around the turn of the century. It kept pace with developments in blues, adapting to electric amplification in the '40s, and the urban sophistication that was to follow as an inevitable consequence.

The main developmental lines seem to have been drawn regionally instead of chronologically. Schools of influence developed in Georgia, Texas, Louisiana, and Mississippi, and later in urban centers–especially Chicago and certain cities on the West Coast. One must approach such a course with care, however, because so many of the players were making records and traveling throughout the country, that the regional styles became disseminated and, hence, their geo-musical boundaries blurred.

It would be only fitting to begin tracing the slide style with somewhat of an anomaly: the Kentuckian, Sylvester Weaver–"the man who introduced the guitar to blues recording…the first country bluesman to record, and…the first black guitarist in any genre to record extensively." This quote is from an article by Jim O'Neal (_Living Blues_ 52, 1982: "Guitar Blues: Sylvester Weaver") that goes on to describe Weaver's accompaniments to classic blues singer Sara Martin's sides as "a radical departure from previous blues recording practice, as blues singers previously had recorded with piano, horns, and jazz bands." Weaver was an excellent musician, a professional conversant with the many forms and idioms of the day, singing and playing in jug bands as well as spiritual quartets. His voice was melodic yet reserved, sharing qualities of old-timey traditional music, minstrelsy, and vaudeville. One can pick out some runs later to be found in the playing of Reverend Gary Davis, earmarking Weaver as an early Piedmont model. Suffice it to say that Sylvester Weaver's "Guitar Blues," recorded in 1923, was the first blues slide guitar ever on record.

Three years later a very enigmatic and accomplished slide player and singer recorded 12 titles–six in Chicago for Paramount as Bo Weavil Jackson and six more in New York, one month later, as Sam Butler–and was never heard from again. Discussed by Paul Oliver in his _Blues Off the Record_, the assumption is that Jackson originally hailed from Alabama, and "was a synthesis of various sources who molded songs…blues…and spirituals … to his own individual way of singing and playing." He had an excellent, unique, and nervous style, using short, dry, staccato notes and chords in juxtaposition with expressive bass runs. He was surely among the most talented of the earliest recorded slide artists.

Atlanta, Georgia, the recording center of the Piedmont region, which can claim probably the greatest giant of the ragtime guitar–Blind Blake–can also claim some of the finest slide players including Blind Willie McTell and Kokomo Arnold, as well as a host of exceptional though now lesser-known talents such as Barbecue Bob, Fred McMullen, and Curley Weaver. Their playing is marked by a certain melodic sweetness, a lighter gait, and a particular elegance of style. Harmonically, there is a leaning toward ragtime changes characterized by chains of borrowed fifths (C-A-D-G-C). This style is further defined by the choice of 12-string guitar used to great effect with slider by McTell and Barbecue Bob. It is worth mentioning that many of the greatest voices in all of the blues have been attracted to the vocal qualities of the slide guitar. And, exceptional even in this select group, is the voice of Blind Willie McTell.

McTell traveled for a time with the slide guitarist/singer/evangelist Blind Willie Johnson, who hailed originally from south of Dallas, Texas. Steven Calt said it best in his notes to Yazoo 1058: "Perhaps no American folk musician ranks as high above his peers from an artistic standpoint as Blind Willie Johnson, whose playing is often so perfect that it cannot be improved upon, even in one's imagination." Indeed, the guitar lines are articulated so organically that he truly sounds in duet with himself–nowhere has the guitar been used as so real a second voice. And, when he is joined by a female singer, doubled by the slide a full two octaves above Johnson's false bass, there is created a mystical texture so profound and vivid that words become flatly inadequate.

Blind Willie Johnson was a huge popular success as well–a star

recording artist for Columbia Records' Race series, as David Evans points out in his notes to Yazoo 1078. His impact on slide guitarists–past and present–has been all-pervasive. Charlie Patton, a contemporary of Johnson, was recording gospel songs in a similar style, while Willie McTell was virtually imitating him, turning out religious slides under the name Blind Willie hoping to capitalize on the singer's popularity. Years later, Fred McDowell sang spirituals in the Johnson mold, while the steel player L.C. Robinson often named Blind Willie Johnson, who was a relative, as his first teacher. Given his genius and the extent of his popularity, few could have fallen outside the sphere of his influence, especially in the area of gospel music or of the slide guitar.

Musically, one can point to various techniques that made Johnson so great: his exceptional use of many notes to one stroke of the slide, his eerie sense of intonation when shading his or his partner's voice at the unison or octave, his mastery of many vibrato speeds, his driving sense of time punctuated by actually beating the body of the guitar or snapping the strings against the neck, his use of glissandi to finish or anticipate a sung line, his alternation of upper and lower strings in a kind of call-and-response pattern, his humming and moaning vocal style that together with the slide created a mesmerizing, hypnotic effect– the list could be longer.

If one endeavors to further define a Texas school of slide, you will come upon the undeservedly obscure singer/guitarist Willard "Ramblin'" Thomas, who might have been a kind of centerpiece to the evolving slide style in the "axis that connects Fort Worth and Dallas with Shreveport and other points east" ("Ramblin' Thomas," Ray Templeton: _Blues and Rhythm_, February 1988). It's difficult to believe that this artist would not have been influenced by Blind Willie Johnson, or that there was not some mutual influence between these two major talents recording and working in the same area during the same period. Thomas sculpted long musical lines on the guitar; he seems to be unique in conceiving of the guitar as an unbroken spectrum of potential three-octave melody. Thomas' penchant for monophonic slide lines coupled with his occasional alteration of treble and bass call-and-response patterns define a style very similar to that of Blind Willie Johnson. Thomas was very much influenced by Blind Lemon Jefferson and, especially, Lonnie Johnson, from whom he gleaned a harmonic sophistication to be found in his non-slide work which is actually far better than that of Blind Willie.

Two slide guitarist/singers associated with Ramblin' Thomas were Cryin' Sam Collins and King Solomon Hill (Chris Smith: notes to Yazoo 1079, _Cryin' Sam Collins_).

Collins, born the same year as Charlie Patton, tuned his third string terribly flat when playing slide in open tuning. On these occasions he was playing and recording on an out-of-tune instrument–a fact which was perhaps due to a lack of musicianship rather than to any Africanism. He did, however, have a distinctively high tenor voice which was well worth hearing. It bore evidence of minstrelsy; and, in fact, Collins' repertoire ranged widely–from spirituals to blues, minstrel songs, and contemporary popular tunes of the day. His slide work was executed very well, mostly on the treble strings, and with good vibrato–alternating sometimes with a plucked or "slide" bass. Lack of good musicianship was demonstrated also in amateurish attempts at more sophisticated harmonies (borrowed dominants and related changes in "Midnight Special") and by simply making a wrong chord change or by not making the appropriate chord changes to suite his vocal line.

King Solomon Hill recorded only six tunes but exhibited a fine guitar style–more sophisticated and musical than Collins. His voice was more similar to Collins' than to that of Willard Thomas, who sang in a lower register and with rather gruff timbre–more like the downhome, narrative sort of bluesman. Hill used short, strummed chords to mark time, and answered his vocals with vibrato-soaked slide lines on the treble strings; or, alternately, with plucked bass lines as a call-and-response pattern. Sometimes he would play interesting bass lines around or in counterpoint to his vocals.

In further tracing the slide lineage to this somewhat obscure and under-recorded area, one discovers two very talented prewar players who played lap-style: Oscar "Buddy" Woods, the Lone Wolf, and his student and partner, B.K. Turner, the Black Ace. Woods had a "good-timey" style and played some hokum numbers that he brought off in a wonderfully infectious style, sometimes as part of various groups such as the Wampus Cats and the Shreveport Home Wreckers. Black Ace, who recorded as late as 1960, adopted his mentor's style, which he executed in a somewhat more downhome manner.

A stunning harmonic twist consistently present in the music of both players is the use of the major flat VI chord (A flat major in the key of C), used often as a subdominant substitute–actually a borrowing from the parallel minor mode. This distinctive sound can also be heard in the work of Black Boy Shine (Harold Holiday), a Texas pianist of the period: and, perhaps the pianists were responsible for its introduction to the chordal vocabulary of these two fine players. Sam Charters reveals in *The Bluesmakers* that both men used "the heavy-necked steel guitar," and that Turner "learned the steel guitar technique from Woods holding the guitar across his lap using a glass medicine bottle as a slide."

Bruce Bastin, in *The Blackwell Guide to Blues Records*, states that "Oscar Woods' slide guitar technique in small-group playing was adapted by Harding 'Hop' Wilson to the flat, electric instument ... from the tradition of flat-picking Hawaiian-styled guitarists." Other very important influences on Wilson's playing are noted in Ray Topping's notes to *Hop Wilson and His Buddies* (Ace CHD 240): "... he absorbed the music of Blind Lemon Jefferson, and the steel players of hilbilly and western swing bands who played an important part in Texan music." Wilson, a fine and very expressive musician, used the steel guitar in small group settings and was a fixture in Houston's Third and Fifth Wards from about 1950 until his death in 1975.

Another blues electric steel player who began his career in Texas, eventually to become a part of the San Francisco/Oakland blues scene, starting from about 1940, was L.C. "Good Rockin'" Robinson. In Alan Govenar's *Meeting the Blues*, he states: "I picked up the steel mostly from seeing Leon McAuliffe. He was with Bob Wills [and the Texas Playboys, one of the greatest and most influential of the western swing bands]." Robinson was also influenced, as stated earlier, by his relative Blind Willie Johnson, who used to visit and play at young Robinson's home often. Robinson was recorded by both Chris Strachwitz and Steve LeVere.

There are at least two steel guitarists active in contemporary blues: Sonny Rhodes and Freddy Roulette. Rhodes makes his home near New York City but hails originally from Texas and was taught by L.C. Robinson, whom he met in California. His phrasing and timing on the instrument bear more than just a stylistic touch of Mississippians Elmore James and Albert King, and these influences both round off and sweeten some of those hard Texas edges.

Mike Rowe, in *Chicago: The City and its Music*, spoke of a particular Freddy Roulette solo as "the most exciting new sound to come out of Chicago in years"; and, indeed, this player–whose records are practically impossible to obtain–has displayed an enormously creative approach to the blues, and has recorded with such hidden giants as Earl Hooker. He also recorded some fascinating background work with the obscure Jackie and Tut and with Bo Diddley. He is perhaps the only guitarist in blues to incorporate the upper partials (9, 11, 13) of the chord by superimposing the appropriate triads in the manner of a modern jazz player, while not sacrificing blues essence in the process. He plays with an incomparable sense of swing and design and is a truly unique artist.

A very interesting electric steel player, Reverend Lonnie Farris, recorded one album in 1962, in Los Angeles, on which he demonstrated a modern, R&B-laden gospel style–dedicated to the service of the church. A performer at heart, the artist played guitar with his feet, behind his back, and in as many other unorthodox ways as he could devise. He began playing the lap steel in the late '40s. Although he refused to sell out to R&B or rock 'n' roll labels, he appeared often on television and even started his own record company in 1962.

One has to wonder what Oscar Woods and Ed Schaffer, the Shreveport Home Wreckers, thought of Memphis when they first recorded there in May 1930, for the Victor label. Did they hear Furry Lewis, Allen Shaw, or any other of the Memphis players who used slide? The stylistic differences would have made for very interesting jam sessions indeed. After all, slider K.C. Weldon had recorded with the Memphis Jug Band three years earlier, and Kokomo Arnold and Bukka White left their mark on the city right around the same time. Everything musical was possible there–and probably occurred on a regular basis.

Because the city of Memphis hosted so many different players and divergent styles of American folk music–especially the blues–since the turn of the twentieth century, it is not surprising that a truly indigenous Memphis style is not quite as apparent as are those of other regions. Charters aptly describes the Memphis vocal style as "rather straight and simple, without melismatic embellishment" and goes on to describe a "wider harmonic range, clear melody, and a sophisticated approach to older material...a softer, talkier blues" (*The Bluesmen*).

Furry Lewis was "almost an archetypal figure in the development of blues in the city," cited Charters, who "rediscovered" him in 1959, and "as a guitarist had few peers in Memphis in the '20s" (*The Bluesmen*). His slide guitar style often displayed an alternating thumb stroke between strings four and six, reminiscent of the Piedmont players or of Mississippi John Hurt, and this characteristic separated him from both the players of Mississippi and Texas. Lewis was not a slide specialist, and one gets the feeling that he made it his business to be able to play all styles well.

The player whose style points to a Hawaiian influence more than any other is Casey Weldon, who was billed as the Hawaiian Guitar Wizard. He is associated with Kansas City (hence his name–K.C.) as well as with Chicago, where he recorded in the mid-'30s. He made his first records, however, with the Memphis Jug Band in February 1927. He played lap-style, and his music is hallmarked by a Hawaiian, harp-like sliding tremolo on the treble strings, and a one-octave cadential arpeggio of the tonic chord from the fifth down (5-3-1-5).

A more obscure and impassioned player from the area was Allen Shaw, who recorded only two songs that were issued under his own name, and a very few more as accompanist. On "Moanin' the Blues," he plays an insistent drone bass with his thumb–a characteristic found often in the work of the Mississippi players. Yet his repetitive, fixed treble lines link him more with the songster style of Memphis.

An excellent example of how a "regional" theory of blues categorization can be misleading is demonstrated in the work and life of Kokomo Arnold who, although from Georgia, sounds more like a cross between the Mississippi Delta sliders and the Texas lap-style men. He was a profound influence on Robert Johnson. Paul Oliver traces the original basis for "Dust My Broom" to Arnold's "Sagefield Woman Blues"–adding to the well-known attributions of Johnson's "Sweet Home Chicago" to "Old Original Kokomo Blues," as well as Robert's borrowings from Kokomo's "Milk Cow Blues." Arnold was well-travelled and developed a unique, rhythmically-charged style that retained a sharp melodic emphasis. He was left-handed and often played his metal National guitar lap style, with a bottleneck on his little finger. He favored open-D tuning, sometimes with the use of a capo. He was one of the most popular bluesmen of the '30s–a fixture on the Chicago club scene along with stars such as Tampa Red, Memphis Minnie, and Big Bill Broonzy.

It is a great understatement to mention that there were undoubtedly many slide players of great brilliance and originality who were never recorded–either commercially or as part of any field research. The Library of Congress tapes of field recordings, for example, hold many examples of such nearly-anonymous players. If we were to elect one slide player to represent them, it could be Hambone Willie Newbern who, if not the originator, was indeed the first to record "Rollin' and Tumblin'," one of the greatest and most recorded slide anthems in blues literature. Charley Patton, Robert Johnson, Elmore James, Muddy Waters–these are only a few of the great bluesmen who have worked and reworked this tune during their careers.

Newbern was born in western Tennessee and, according to Paul Oliver, taught Sleepy John Estes in about 1913. He recorded his six titles in 1919 in Atlanta for Okeh, and worked for many years in Memphis. He was reportedly beaten to death in a Marvell, AR, prison sometime in the '40s (Oliver: *The Story of the Blues*).

As trite as it may sound, the blues probably *did* begin in Mississippi–later working its way north, to cities like Chicago where it readapted to its new audience. Whether the magic lay in the soil or the sun, it was potent enough to bring about the deepest and most intense strains of the blues–which still are dominant a century later. The Mississippi blues pantheon is well known to all who listen to the deep blues; and the deeper the understanding of the music, the more complex and fascinating become the relationships and influences that shaped the styles of the most influential players.

An unrecorded musician named Henry Sloan is reported to have been the teacher of Charley Patton, perhaps the first great bluesman of the Mississippi Delta. Patton's performances and recordings had an all-pervading influence throughout the South, and he became recognized as the greatest living bluesman of all time. Patton used the slide extremely effectively, as he did many other techniques, such as banging and slapping the guitar and snapping individual strings against the neck. Booker Miller, a contemporary and protégé of Patton, told Steven Calt and Gayle Wardlow that he had a Stella guitar at first, but had to change makes because "it took a Gibson to stand up to him…Charley was rough on boxes" (Calt, Wardlow: *King of the Delta Blues*).

He could play very delicately as well, though, and was adept at shading his vocal lines with the slider either an octave lower, higher, or at the unison over a rhythmic bass/chord pattern–getting a perfect balance between shades of melody and rhythmic drive. As in "Boll Weevil" he sets up an effective call-and-response pattern–sometimes finishing the lyric with sliding notes that function as phrases ("Spoonful"). He used single lines with great expression both on the bass and treble strings–even harmonizing them "organum-style" (in fourths or fifths) using the triads or diads made available by the particular type of open tuning he was using. He often played with Son Sims, a fiddle player whose microtonal shadings and rhythmic syncopations became echoed in Patton's solo slide work (*Devil Sent the Rain*).

Although known for his raucous singing and barrelhousing, some of his greatest slide work surfaced in his gospel songs–especially in "Prayer of Death." One can only imagine what a live performance of this must have been like on an inspired evening. According to Calt and Wardlow, he used the standard open tunings of A and E, tuning his guitar at least one full step above standard tuning in order to achieve a more penetrating sound. His slider was a pipe-like piece of brass, and at times–especially when performing spirituals–he would lay the guitar across his thighs and play lap style.

As with practically all artists of this rare caliber, Patton was the center of a wide constellation of players who emulated and imitated his work and life. Even Bukka White, who was never really influenced by Patton's style of playing, recalled that as a boy he wanted "to come to be a great man like Charley Patton" (Charters: *The Bluesmakers*). The two slide artists most directly influenced by Patton, who were later to become highly influential in their own right, were Eddie "Son" House and Chester Burnett, the Howlin' Wolf. The obvious disparity between these two artists displays the incredible breadth of Patton's influence, which had such deep significance to players of a wide stylistic range who were to be active almost a century after their mentor's style was fully formed.

Son House was a most intense and commanding blues presence. His preacher-like fervor rang out through both his live performances and his recordings. Although perhaps not in the very first rank of guitarists or singers, this artist transcended his limitations, leaving a recorded legacy that rivals any in blues history. In his case the whole was far greater than the sum of the parts; or, as Jim O'Neal put it, "The House was greater than all of the rooms."

House played a steel-bodied National with a brass slider which he wore on his third finger. He sang in the concert keys of D, A, B flat, and E using both Spanish and Sevastopol tunings. His most famous 1930 recordings were "My Black Mama" and "Preachin' Blues." Both of these tunes were learned from James McCoy and reworked later by Robert Johnson. "Preachin' Blues" was perhaps his most successful song artistically, employing a beautifully effective combination of percussive chord-slapping and treble slide work. "Pony Blues," recorded in Robinsonville, MS, by Alan Lomax for the Library of Congress in 1942, reveals the manner in which House reworked Patton's tunes, infusing them with his own musical personality. Of his 1965 recordings, *Sundown* is memorable for its full-chord octave glissandi, used as both fills and background. For all who saw him, what remains unforgettable is that stern presence, clothed in white shirt and black string tie–that crying, shouting, sliding blues preacher with a message for all time.

Another slider whose roots extended from Charley Patton through the blues revival of the '60s, '70s, and '80s was Big Joe Williams–the archetypal rambling bluesman who heard and played with practically everyone from the Mississippi Delta to St. Louis. His inimitable style, which remained consistently excellent through the years, is made even more personal by his "invention" and use of the nine-string guitar, which he made in the '40s by doubling the first, second, and fourth strings. He sometimes used a Dobro (the trademark name for an acoustic guitar with a metal resonator), as well as a standard six-string, and often capoed as far up the neck as the eleventh fret (From Steven Calt's notes to Mamlish 3810, *Big Joe Williams*). These traits, combined with his intense and very complex, whirlwind-like rhythmic style, punctuated by almost violent bass and treble string snappings in the Patton mold, made him very difficult to imitate (Mark Ryan's notes to Trumpet AA-702, *Delta Blues*). Probably among the first to use amplified slide guitar, Williams was a mentor to both Honeyboy Edwards and Muddy Waters.

Eddie Taylor was a musician who played with both Joe Williams and Howlin' Wolf. His roots stretch from Charley Patton and Son House to the more modern influences of Robert Nighthawk, Elmore James, and Muddy Waters. Although his career was tightly bound to backing Jimmy Reed, he was a very fine and expressive slide guitarist.

As House hung around Patton–learning and working to be accepted as a peer–so too did young Robert Johnson frequent the gigs of Patton, House, and Willie Brown (yearning to be one of these professional Delta bluesmen). Like many other superlative musicians, Johnson was involved in assimilating all of his many influences, a process that was interrupted by his untimely death. This was a time in blues history when the music was on the brink of transforming into an urban electric sound; and Johnson would inevitably have been a key figure in this process. However, as fate had it, his role was to absorb and perfect many of the extant blues styles–both vocal and instrumental–rendering him today the enduring symbol of the prewar blues.

It has been documented that Johnson had a teacher, Ike Zinnerman, who instructed him sometime in 1931–after his initial meetings with Son House, and before he became an accomplished player. Although it is unknown exactly what he taught Johnson (Robert Palmer in *Deep Blues* surmises it to be reflected in the artist's more melodic, non-slide numbers such as "From Four 'til Late"), we do know that Johnson's style closely resembled that of his original mentor Son House and, through him, Charley Patton. The exemplary collection, *The Roots of Robert Johnson* (Yazoo L-1073), with enlightening notes by Steven Calt, presents many of the performances on which Johnson based his style. Well-traveled slide expert Hambone Willie Newbern provided the basis for both "Travellin' Riverside Blues" and "If I Had Possession Over Judgment Day" in his "Rollin' and Tumblin'" (1929), while Son House's "My Black Mama" is the certain protoype of "Walkin' Blues" (Son House recorded a very different "Walkin' Blues" in 1930). Johnson reworked these materials to varying extents, and molded them into lasting monuments to the tradition, infusing them with great power, and delivering them with impeccable taste and flawless execution.

He used a slide on 11 of his 29 recorded titles. It controlled some ("Come On In My Kitchen," "Last Fair Deal Gone Down"), while spicing others ("Stones in My Passway," "Terraplane Blues"). He used it flawlessly, with other-worldly intonation as shading to his vocals ("Come On In My Kitchen"); and regularly as introductions, fills, and even as counterpoint to his vocals ("Crossroads Blues"). He used it chordally ("Last Fair Deal Gone Down"), creating a roaring rhythmic effect; and, even programmatically ("Come On In My Kitchen"), to portray the "howlin'" wind. Ironically, Johnson's most famous and enduring "slide" number, "I Believe I'll Dust My Broom," was performed naturally, without use of a slider.

It is an extraordinary coincidence that the three slide players who were closest to Robert Johnson were all born within months of each other, in 1915–also the year of Muddy Waters' birth. And, even greater fortune finds that two of them are still touring and recording at the time of this writing, over a half-century after Johnson made his records. In fact, the summer of 1991 found Johnny Shines, Robert Lockwood, Jr, and David "Honeyboy" Edwards at the Smithsonian Festival of American Folklife, reminiscing about their mentor along with pianist/guitarist Henry Townsend, who knew Johnson for a time in St. Louis.

Of the three first mentioned, Edwards was probably least

affected by Johnson's style. He plays in standard tuning when using a slide–Johnson always used open tunings–and had many other important influences, including non-sliders Tommy McClennan and Tommy Johnson. In addition, he has not recorded many of Johnson's tunes, with the exception of "Sweet Home Chicago," which has been an Edwards mainstay over the years. He is a fine guitarist who has used slide to great advantage.

Robert Jr. Lockwood, was Johnson's only hands-on student. Johnson taught the younger man–then a pianist–his tunes, note-for-note. In fact, Robert Palmer relates in *Deep Blues* that "at the time of Robert's death their repertoires were virtually identical." Lockwood returned the favor by being "the first artist to display Johnson's influence on recordings, and the first to carry his synthesis to Chicago" (Evans: *Blues Records*). These recordings, made in 1941 for the Bluebird label, are masterpieces. Especially on the slide number, "Little Boy Blue," we hear a more swing-oriented style than we associate with Robert Johnson–a style both funkier and jazzier than one might imagine. Although Lockwood has continued throughout his career to be a source of information about his stepfather–as well as a living tribute to his mentor's style, he long ago acquired a preference for the jazzy jump mode being played by Louis Jordan and other horn players of the day. A pioneer and uniquely gifted artist in his own right, Lockwood was one of the first single-string players in the Delta to play the more modern style, and was instrumental in initiating this in Chicago. An innovator at heart, he was soon to tire of the slide technique, preferring his explorations into jazz-oriented styles.

In Johnny Shines, however, we find an unabashed champion of Robert Johnson–perhaps his most staunch and true protege. Although Shines' first mentor was Howlin' Wolf (a Patton protégé), Shines met Johnson in 1933 and was his "running partner"–off and on–for the next five years. Shines' chilling vocal style made him an original, in spite of an almost religious adherence to Johnson's aesthetic. After an unheralded (although stylistically and historically significant) session with Columbia in 1946–on which he played no slide–and two non-slide numbers cut for Chess four years later, Shines finally came into his own in 1952 when he recorded for the JOB label. His first session produced "Fishtail Blues," a direct descendant of Johnson's "Terraplane Blues," and a cover of "Ramblin'" both using slide and played in the concert key of B flat in G tuning. Shines, a distinctive artist with his own musical personality, must always be remembered as one of Johnson's most significant disciples, who brought a very true sound image to Johnson's art to the post-war world.

There are certain rare players in the history of the blues whose enormous influence has been experienced mostly through reflection. Often it is because they were not able or chose not to explore larger avenues of exposure such as recordings, big-city performances, and other trappings of "road to success"–yet without their influence the music would have unfolded differently. Such an artist was Houston Stackhouse, the subject of a lengthy and informative *Living Blues* interview by Jim O'Neal (*Living Blues* 17).

Stackhouse was dubbed a "regional legend" by O'Neal–an artist who preferred the country jukes and houseparties in and around Helena, Arkansas, to the big-city opportunities that were offered to him by his peers and students. He was scheduled at one point to record with Robert Johnson, was part of the KFFA circle of musicians in Helena, and was associated with the greatest players of the day from Tommy Johnson to Little Walter. He played mostly in natural tuning and used a metal guitar until changing to an electric model in the '40s. In his work one hears the rough origins of the slide style later identified with mid-'50s Chicago. The quivers and shakes, the uncanny off-pitches that beg the tone–all of these characteristics make Stackhouse a seminal figure in the blues during its very vital mid-'40s transition.

CeDell "Big G" Davis, like his mentor Houston Stackhouse, has remained an obscure artist. Left with permanently crippled fingers from polio, contracted at age ten, he developed an upside-down and left-handed approach to the instrument, which he plays with a butter knife slider held in his right hand. This unique style, coupled with what sounds like standard tuning, creates a most individual "skewed" sound–distinctive and memorable. His pitches are off-center, as if he's playing the sliding trebel lead a microtone flat–the coloration is beautifully dark and fine. In addition, Davis has cultivated, perhaps more than any other player, the ability to maintain a steady shuffle rhythm on the bass strings while simultaneously ringing a contrapuntal slide line. At other times he buoys his slide lines with recurring bass riffs that are often boogie-oriented. His blues are deep, brooding, and forceful–played with a country finesse and Delta intensity.

Davis often played with Houston Stackhouse's cousin and most famous student, Robert Nighthawk. Born Robert McCollum, he later changed his name to McCoy because of some trouble with the law, and finally to Nighthawk after his popular record, "Prowling Night-Hawk." Nighthawk–who had met and heard Charlie Patton–was becoming a professional in the '30s when Elmore James and Robert Jr. Lockwood were just starting out, and Muddy Waters had just switched from harp to guitar. Nighthawk, too, was originally a harp player. He was taught the guitar and slide technique by his mentor, Houston Stackhouse. Robert Palmer describes Nighthawk's notes as "dripping slowly out of the amplifier like thick, oozing oil" (*Deep Blues*). And so they seemed–each one somehow leaving its own indelible design and coloring–simply unforgettable. Nighthawk recorded on Bluebird in the late '30s but achieved his individual style after switching to electric guitar in the mid-'40s. He was brought back into the studio some ten years later by Muddy Waters, who had received some musical pointers from him early in his career. It was at that time that Nighthawk recorded his masterpiece, "Sweet Black Angel," one of the most magnificent works of electric slide playing–and perhaps of all recorded blues.

Nighthawk's other main influence was the musical giant, Tampa Red, who had been in Chicago since the mid-'20s, and who was for two decades the most famous slide player of them all. In fact, Jim O'Neal reveals in his notes to Blues Classics 25, *Tampa Red, the Guitar Wizard*, that this guitarist released more 78s (over 150) than any other performer in blues history. In addition, his second release, "Tight Like That," was one of the biggest-selling Race records ever. Tampa Red is also credited with writing many blues standards that have been reworked by the most established artists in the field. Elmore James, Robert Nighthawk, Little Walter, B.B. King, Freddie King–all of these artists (and many others) have recorded such Tampa Red originals as "Sweet Little Angel," "Love Her with Feeling," and "It Hurts Me Too." Tampa Red teamed up with the greatest blues pianists in Chicago including "Georgia" Tom Dorsey, Maceo Merriweather, and Blind John Davis, on a series of records and club dates that made him one of the most popular bluesmen of all time. He was also an expressive and sensitive accompanist to such divas as Ma Rainey.

As a slide guitarist, Tampa Red's flawlessly precise style might be described as being melodically elegant; each note seems to follow with a sense of perfection and certainty–each note is delivered in an envelope of fine, mellow timbre. His lines are sculpted, laced with intricate detail, sure attacks, and gentle vibrato. He achieved a beauty of tone with a glass slider worn on his fourth finger, and often used a gold-colored National guitar, a triple-resonator National steel, and a hollow-body Gibson jazz model. Until about 1950, Tampa Red reigned as one of the most influential bluesmen in Chicago–and the most accomplished and famous player of the urban slide-style blues guitar.

Robert Nighthawk fused the homespun Delta intensity of Houston Stackhouse with the more deliberate artfulness of Tampa Red to achieve a most potent and narcotic synthesis–one that was to affect the work of many of the most talented players that were to follow. It should be noted that Nighthawk played in standard tuning, in the key of E (at least at the 1949 session), and relied on the treble strings for his slide lines. Don Kent, who knew Nighthawk in the 1960s, reports that he was using a steel or brass slider on his fourth finger. He is seen in pictures with a solid-body electric, a wooden acoustic, and a full-bodied Gretsch electric jazz model guitar. Nighthawk was surprisingly accomplished in his non-slide work as well, which was solidly in the tradition of Lonnie Johnson and Scrapper Blackwell.

Earl Hooker was a wonderfully gifted and innovative guitarist who learned directly from Robert Nighthawk. His wide-ranging musical palette incorporated genres as diverse as downhome blues (as practiced by his cousin John Lee Hooker), swing, hillbilly, and the bluesy psychedelia of Jimi Hendrix. He used everything he came across including two types of double-necked guitars–one with both six- and 12-string guitar necks, and another with a six-string neck and a (four-string) bass-guitar neck–as well as a variety of tone-altering pedals including a "wah-wah." Reportedly, Hooker was proficient on bass, organ, piano, banjo, harp, and mandolin, as well as guitar.

Praised by Houston Stackhouse, Albert King, B.B. King, Buddy Guy, and T-Bone Walker, Earl Hooker "achieved the reputation of being the finest guitarist in Chicago" before his death in 1975 (Mike Rowe, *Chicago Blues: The City and Its Music*). Not only a great slide player, but a fabulous and complete guitarist by any standard, Hooker's posthumous reputation has been tragically underplayed and overlooked. His influence can be heard in the styles of many of today's greatest players, including non-slide great Otis Rush, who once said, according to Jim O'Neal, that he fashioned the sound of his bends after Hooker's slide work. Veteran bluesman Jimmy Dawkins, who played with Hooker often in Chicago, said that what fascinated him most was the guitarist's ability to switch instantly from slide to natural mode; indeed, Hooker often sounds like two alternating players. Hooker's attraction to country music made him a natural to hook up with Fred Roulette, who was a sideman on many of Hooker's most exciting recordings. Earl Hooker's reputation is kept alive today by many of the greatest living blues musicians, who remember him as the best they ever heard.

Players such as Earl Hooker, and before him Son House and Furry Lewis, were able to feel their personal influence reflected in the work of other talented players. They were able to see their place in the music's history. There were at least two blues musicians, however, whose talents seemed to percolate in a time warp until the blues "revival" of the 1960s: Fred McDowell and Bukka White.

As Bruce Bastin relates in his notes to Flyright CD14, *Fred McDowell,* " [McDowell] was the perfect example of how much of the finest blues talent failed to be recorded in the 1920s and 1930s…When Alan Lomax discovered him in 1959, he had never recorded before…he was one of the first country bluesmen to carry his music to Europe." McDowell was a master of voice-shading, a device which he employed regularly an octave higher or lower than the sung line. Rhythmically, his playing was direct rather than crossed or contrapuntal. His blues were straightforward and melodic, often controlled by a single riff that dominated the entire musical context ("Kokomo Blues"). He could also be explosively percussive at times ("Shake 'Em on Down"). McDowell had a wonderful talent for making each of his tunes unique-unified in its own special way, like so many musical short stories.

Bukka White, on the other hand, was a continual victim of terribly bad luck. Fear of the worsening Depression caused ten of his 14 tunes recorded in 1930 to be unissued. His next session seven years later was shut down by a sheriff who arrested him for murder (a tale told to Sam Charters by Big Joe Williams, and related in *The Bluesmen*), a charge which eventually sent him to Parchman Prison–where he cut two sides for the Library of Congress. Influential in getting him released, the American Record Company recorded 12 sides which were issued and subsequently described as "folk music" by the *Amsterdam News*, one of the black New York newspapers (Charters: *The Bluesman*). Mostly, these records were simply ignored. It was 1940 and country blues was anachronistic at best; it would take another 23 years before White's time would come, as the taste for blues crossed over to the young, white audiences of the North.

White enjoyed a nice career after being "rediscovered" in 1963-playing concerts, festivals, and television shows, both at home and abroad. As a songwriter, he was known for his ability to create impromptu tunes based on his experiences-he called them "sky songs." As a player, he is remembered for his mosaic-like use of silence, and a thunderous, percussive-chordal style that he used to great advantage in the portrayal of trains (*The Panama Limited*). White sometimes played lap-style, with a knife or screwdriver, used a National steel guitar, a metal ring-like slider on his fourth finger, and preferred the open tunings of G and E.

Charlie Patton, unlike Bukka White, was recorded rather extensively early on, beginning in 1929. While Patton was unusually prolific in the studio, his career had actually started more than 20 years before his first recording session. One can only theorize about the evolutionary stages that might have occured.

The recordings of Muddy Waters provide a unique opportunity to trace the transition from early country blues to its Northern electric counterpart. Pete Welding, in his notes to *Muddy Waters Down on Stovall Plantation* (Testament T-2210) relates that: "… the singer stated (in 1941) that though his music had been patterned almost totally on that of Robert Johnson, he had never

heard him in person. Son House had shown him the essentials of Johnson's remarkable style." Clearly, the slide numbers "Country Blues (Numbers One and Two)," recorded by Alan Lomax for the Library of Congress, are remakes of Johnson's "Walkin' Blues," which Waters learned from Son House (as did Johnson). If not a giant of the country blues tradition, Waters was surely a major architect of the establishment and design of the amplified blues band. Tunes like "I Feel Like Goin' Home" (1948) show him translating his solo country bottleneck guitar style to electric guitar.

Muddy Waters' 1946 Columbia recordings, which were not released until 1971, show that he was already making electric music in an early Chicago ensemble style, with two guitars, piano, bass, and drums. As Robert Palmer points out in the brilliantly annotated *Muddy Waters: The Chess Box* (Chess CHD3-80002): "In the clubs, Muddy and his band were forging their own heavily amplified style. In the studio, Muddy was encouraged to emphasize his Delta roots." Nonetheless, such masterpieces as "Louisiana Blues" and "Long Distance Call" grace the blues repertoire with first-rank artistry. In addition, they brought the sound of slide guitar to a larger audience.

As Chess began to record Muddy Waters with more of a band sound, he played less guitar and concentrated more on his vocals. He always, however, reserved a spot for a solo slide number in his performances and recorded stinging, effective slide guitar on certain later tunes such as "Things That I Used to Do" (1963), "You Can't Lose What You Never Had" (1964), and "Who's Gonna Be Your Sweet Man" (1971).

To quote Mike Rowe: "In 1945 Waters was playing only bottleneck style … ('Blue') Smitty (Claude Smith) claimed to have taught Muddy how to use his fingers." (*Chicago Blues*). According to Smokey Smothers, early in his career Waters used a short, glass slider and played mostly in G-tuning, shifting later to a slider made of metal and a reliance on standard tuning, mostly in the key of E. Muddy Waters took slide guitar out of the black ghetto and into the larger American musical marketplace. His influence on subsequent slide players–directly and indirectly–as well as on the general language of blues is virtually inestimable.

Another giant of the blues pantheon, Howlin' Wolf, received his training from Charlie Patton and Robert Johnson. He used his slide guitar talent as part of a ferocious, all-imposing musical and physical presence. Beginning his recording career in Memphis for Sam Phillips and Sun Records in 1951, he soon became a fixture on Chicago's South Side. His occasional use of searing slide work on tunes like "Little Red Rooster"–like his effective harp-playing– was only a part of Wolf's magnificent coloration; but its inclusion helped to further embellish slide technique as a permanent characteristic of modern blues.

There is hardly a figure more identifiable with the electric bottleneck guitar sound than Elmore James. James was first inspired to play slide by Robert Johnson, who in 1937, along with Sonny Boy Williamson II (Rice Miller) and Robert Jr. Lockwood, was James' frequent companion. By adding Robert Nighthawk to this roster, we complete the list of ingredients that James needed to cook up his new style-one that still echoes proudly through the corridors of contemporary blues. While Muddy Waters' guitar gradually disappeared into the mix, giving rise to a kind of busy Chicago polyphony, James' became more and more prominent, becoming at last the undisputed lead voice in his tightly-knit groups. He transformed the role of electric slide-not unlike the part John Lee Williamson played in the development of blues harp-making it a dynamic lead instrument, capable of controlling the modern electric blues band. Although he invariably used open-D tuning, James always seemed fresh and exciting. He had a powerfully aggressive sound yet could be gentle when the mood turned subtle, solemn, or romantic. His unvarying excellence throughout most of his career can be attributed, in part, to his fine roster of sidemen–a list that included such luminaries as Johnny Jones, Wayne Bennett, Jimmy Spruill, J. T. Brown, Ike Turner, Maxwell Davis, Odie Payne, and Ransom Knowling. Add to these assets the fact that James' voice was one of the greatest in the history of the music and it becomes easily understandable that so many of his recordings rank among the highest order of blues classics. Although James did not record until 1951, he had been playing in an electric band (that included sax, trumpet, second guitar, and drums) since 1939. "Elmore's position in the Chicago scene is important; for, while Muddy updated Mississippi's blues for an early postwar audience, Elmore followed through the logical development and modernized them for all time" (Mike Rowe: *Chicago Blues: The City and Its Music*).

There are various stories regarding Homesick James Williamson, Elmore James' distant cousin. One finds him with his younger cousin Elmore, as kids, playing a one-string on the wall of a house. Another finds him touring the South with such players as Blind Boy Fuller, Big Walter Horton, Frank Stokes, Buddy Doyle, and, later, Rice Miller, Robert Jr. Lockwood, and Johnny Shines. According to a 1978 interview in *Blues Unlimited*, by Tim Schuller, Homesick James taught the "Dust My Broom" lick to Elmore James–who wasn't even playing at the time Homesick James originally learned it. In this interview he said,: "Elmore was a wonderful slide player for what he *did*. But if a man don't know but one or two runs, I don't call him that *much* of a slide player. But when a guy can play slide and play all the changes, like Earl Hooker, then you can say the man's a slide player. Elmore had a great voice..."

This might sound like jealousy were it not for the fact that Homesick James is an intelligent and superlative musician, secure in his own talents. He plays with an easy, graceful swing in a style more expansive and flexible than Elmore James. He played bass on many of Elmore's sides, and maintained a close personal and professional relationship with him for many years.

In the *Blues Unlimited* interview, Homesick James reports using Fender, Gretsch, and wood-bodied Dobro guitars, as well as every type of slider including a knife, thimble, bottleneck, and metal pipe. In addition, he favors D, C, and B-tunings along with open G. *Blues Unlimited* also quoted him as saying that "... the only worthwhile slide players were Hooker, Nighthawk, and Hound Dog–you can take the rest of these slide players, and put 'em in a paper bag, and throw them in the lake!"

The Hound Dog to whom Homesick referred was Hound Dog Taylor, a native of Natchez, Mississippi, and yet another slide player who claimed to have taught Elmore James the famed *Dust My Broom* lick (Jim O'Neal and R. T. Cuniff, *Living Blues* 4). Taylor claimed that James beat him to Chicago and "stole the stuff" that he heard "the Dog" play in Mississippi (Wesley Race, *Blues Unlimited* 73). Others contend that Taylor learned his style from James. What is important is that Hound Dog Taylor was instrumental in ushering the electric slide into the '70s, helping to rejuvenate its popularity in Chicago. His was a good-time boogie sound that translated to a variety of original instrumentals which found their way into the repertoires of other players, including those of non-sliders Freddie King and Magic Sam (O'Neal, *Living Blues* 4).

J. B. Hutto, however, told *Blues Unlimited* in 1970 that "out of all I've heard, Elmo [James] was the *best*...and would take time out and sit down and explain things to you." Hutto spoke of following James around "just about everywhere he went." Mike Rowe states that: "J. B. blew upon the Chicago scene with one of the noisiest and toughest bands ever...they sounded ready to devour everything in sight!" (Rowe: *Chicago Blues: The City and Its Music.*) Hutto's screaming treble strings strained, screeching

beyond the octave–testing the limits. This, coupled with the loose-knit arragements held together by his intense and very personal vocals, must have been a wake-up call to those listeners weaned on milkier stuff. Hutto was a powerful presence on the Chicago scene from the '40s through the '70s.

The natural heir to Hutto's style is his nephew, Li'l Ed Williams, who actually uses his late uncle's Gibson. He remembers listening as a child with his grandmother and aunts to Elmore James and Muddy Waters. In an interview (Donald Wilcox, *Living Blues* 95) Williams spoke of learning James' style through Hutto's influence. He is a very talented musician and a dynamic performer who perhaps has not yet found the key to his fullest artistic success.

The most recent link in the chain of Delta slide guitarists that originated with Charlie Patton is contemporary bluesman Lonnie Pitchford from Lexington, Mississippi. He coaxes complex and stirring rhythms from the one-string diddley bows that he both makes and plays. In addition, he uses a six-string to turn out convincing sets of Robert Johnson material learned directly from his mentor, Robert Jr. Lockwood Pitchford tends to modernize the style somewhat but maintains the character and integrity of his models.

At the time of this writing there are many fine artists who use slide guitar as an appreciable part of their repertoire. Instead of the hoboing, itinerant bluesmen of the past, they are distinguished American folk artists, many of whom tour worldwide, bringing the blues to audiences all over the globe. Adding to the players already mentioned are Big Jack Johnson, who will normally play four or five slide numbers a night, sometimes using a microphone stand; John Primer, who cut his teeth with Sammy Lawhorn in the great Junior Wells bands at Theresa's–and who has been touring with Magic Slim's band while launching a well-deserved and long overdue solo career (he has a CD on Wolf and one on Earwig soon to be released); talented veteran Smokey Smothers, who played and recorded with Howlin' Wolf, Freddie King, and Muddy Waters, and is still active on the club and festival circuits; the multi-talented Louis Myers, who plays everything and all styles so well that (ironically) he rarely receives any attention; Joe Louis Walker, who plays fine, down-home slide; Luther Allison, another multi-talented bluesman who has been living in France; Big Daddy Kinsey, whose silky slide work can be heard regularly in Chicago, along with that of his talented son, Donald Kinsey; the exciting, tough Johnny Littlejohn, one of the fine protégés of Wolf, Waters, and James; R. L. Burnside, whose mesmerizing drone bass and heartfelt vocalese evoke the deep solo tradition of the Delta; and James "Son" Thomas, whose music speaks to the hard life of the South. All of these players appear regularly, along with legions of the even lesser-known–continuing a living tradition that is truly not much changed since W.C. Handy first heard it that day in 1903, and wrote: "It'll take you by the shoulders and waken you with a start–the effect is unforgettable."

–Larry Hoffman

BOOKS

✦✦✦ **The Arrival of B.B. King,** *Charles Sawyer* (Da Capo, 1980) B.B King's authorized biography is a thoughtful and, for the most part, thorough document of his life through the late '70s. Drawing upon conversations with King, as well as early childhood mentors and past and present music/business associates, Sawyer details his rise from poverty in the Mississippi Delta through the chitlin circuit to the top level of American mainstream entertainment. He places a lot of emphasis upon context, which can be both an asset and a hindrance. The extensive passages about his sharecropping roots in the Delta yield an appreciation of the remarkable perseverance and talent King needed to overcome the barriers of prejudice and injustice. At other times Sawyer sets the table with unnecessary elaboration, devoting a bulk of one chapter, for instance, to the mid-'60s blues revival with analysis that will be redundant to many blues fans. He's best when he sticks to his subject, although some phases of King's career (like most of the '60s, prior to his breakthrough to the pop audience) are skimmed over with inappropriate haste. There are also extensive analyses (perhaps too extensive and analytical for general readers) of the unique properties of King's guitar style and compositions, including an appendix devoted solely to one B.B. King guitar solo. — *Richie Unterberger*

✦✦✦ **The Blackwell Guide to Blues Records,** *edited by Paul Oliver* (Blackwell, 1989) The most comprehensive reference book of its sort, not to say that it's even close to perfect, but that there's really not much competition. The Blackwell layout is daunting for the novice: lots of essays of varying quality on regional styles, wads of song listings, and many fine capsule reviews of albums, ranging from famous to very, very obscure. Divided into chapters covering both regions (such as postwar Chicago) and styles (piano blues, "downhome postwar blues"), it also covers subgenres like rhythm and blues and soul blues that some purists would have regarded as too diluted and commercial to include. It's not the kind of thing you can read in a few sittings, but if you have reasonable patience, there's a lot of valuable information here, and the authors are good at pinpointing the best anthologies and starting points. — *Richie Unterberger*

✦✦✦ **Bluesland,** *edited by Pete Welding & Toby Byron* (Dutton, 1991) A large, handsome, near-coffee-table-sized book with essays on twelve blues performers and some fine black-and-white pictures. Perhaps because the volume is well packaged (and a bit on the pricy side), it doesn't fully meet the high expectations readers might bring to the project. Some of the essays are very good, offering a mix of detail and insightful criticism (Robert Palmer on Professor Longhair, Pete Welding on B.B. King). Others are on the slim and perfunctory side, sometimes rehashing biographical material which is presented with greater depth and color elsewhere. The piece on Lonnie Johnson carries special interest, as the author, Chris Albertson, was responsible for rediscovering the guitarist on the eve of the blues/folk revival. Some purists would argue whether Etta James and Chuck Berry belong in a book about blues masters at all. There's some good stuff here, but these studies aren't definitive or, in some cases, even especially detailed. Which means that, considering the hefty ($26.95) price tag, you might want to check it out of the local library. — *Richie Unterberger*

✦✦✦ **The Blues Makers,** *Sam Charters* (Da Capo, 1991) This reprint combines two of Charters' previously published books, *The Bluesmen* (1967) and *Sweet as the Showers of Rain* (1977). In both of these, Charters focused upon profiles of pre-war country bluesmen, as well as devoting some space to overall analysis of regional styles (which includes paragraphs on some of the more obscure singers who didn't merit a chapter of their own). Much of the book is based upon research that Charters, one of the leading pioneers of the field, undertook in the late 1950s and 1960s. Thus, a lot of this is not as fascinating or useful as it once was, since subsequent research has filled out our knowledge of these men (almost every subject, incidentally, is male) and corrected some of Charters' inaccuracies and incomplete deductions. It's important to note, though, that Charters' efforts were among the key foundations of such subsequent research. Read today, it still has considerable value for blues fans, with portraits of Blind Blake, Sleepy John Estes, Furry Lewis, Frank Stokes, Son House, Charley Patton, Skip James, Blind Lemon Jefferson, Henry Thomas, Memphis Minnie, and several other giants of the music's early days. The more casual fan/reader, however, is better off with histories that are written in a more accessible tone. Charters describes numerous recordings in painstaking detail (remember, hardly anyone else had heard these items when he first wrote about them), and provides musical transcriptions that may bore those without the specialized knowledge to comprehend them. — *Richie Unterberger*

✦✦✦ **Blues: The British Connection,** *Bob Brunning* (Blanford Press, 1986) Brunning is not only an authority on British blues-rock, he was there–he played bass in the first lineup of Fleetwood Mac before John McVie joined, and went on to play with Savoy Brown and other blues-rock groups. This is a good survey of British blues-rock from the days of Alexis Korner through the 1980s, concentrating mostly on the 1960s, when the form was in its heyday. There are chapters devoted to all the major groups: the Yardbirds, John Mayall, Pretty Things, Spencer Davis, Manfred Mann, Graham Bond, Fleetwood Mac, the Groundhogs, Ten Years After, Chicken Shack, Rory Gallagher, and producer Mike Vernon. A lot of them are spiced by first-hand recollections from band members; the ones which aren't are considerably weaker. The sections on minor figures like Dave Kelly, Savoy Brown, and the Blues Band hold considerably less interest than the ones on the more important musicians, but the book does give a pretty complete picture of the scene. — *Richie Unterberger*

✦✦✦ **Bossmen: Bill Monroe & Muddy Waters,** *James Rooney* (Da Capo, 1971) What exactly, you might be wondering, does one have to do with the other? Well, both were responsible for fathering schools of music (bluegrass and electric blues, respectively) that influenced the course of rock and popular music. Both were outstanding bandleaders that schooled many musicians who went on to become innovators in their own right. Structured mostly as oral history, Rooney lets Monroe and Waters (the book is divided into two separate sections) talk at length about their collaborators, songwriting, recordings, and performances, as well as the many changes they witnessed in both music and society during their careers. Quotes by sidemen and other associates flesh out this interesting and very readable work, which should appeal to most readers interested in rock's roots, despite the very different styles that each man pioneered. — *Richie Unterberger*

✦✦✦ **Chicago Blues,** *Mike Rowe* (Da Capo, 1973) Originally published as *Chicago Breakdown*, this is an extremely thorough history of Chicago blues from its beginnings in the 1930s through about 1970, the heart of the volume devoted to the music's peak in the 15 years or so following World War II. Rowe not only accounts for all of the city's major blues artists (and probably all of its minor ones), but also gives detailed histories of all the city's blues labels, from Chess and Vee-Jay through J.O.B. and Cobra, down to outfits that hardly released anything. The text is enlivened by quotes from interviews with many of the major players on the scene, as well as many fine photographs, both of the musicians and the neighborhoods where they lived and played. It must be pointed out that this is too intensely detailed and scholarly for the general fan (though never condescending). Rowe goes on at considerable length about innumerable little-known singles, and even provides tables illustrating migration patterns from the South to Chicago; for those who are unfamiliar with many of the records and performers, some of the information will seem trivial (to the devotees, of course, much of it will be fascinating). Rowe does keep the big picture in mind at all times, though, writing passionately and keeping an eye on the larger trends that enabled the form to thrive, as well as the factors that precipitated its decline. He also reaches the intriguing conclusion, supported by some evidence, that Chicago electric blues did not arise as a result of displaced Southerners demanding the sounds they liked, but because Southern musicians reworked their music to meet the demands of the urban audience. —Richie Unterberger

♦♦♦ **The Country Blues**, *Samuel Charters* (Da Capo, 1959) This was one of the first book-length, serious studies of the blues, and perhaps the most influential of its time. Charters, as he admits in his introduction to a revised edition, "was trying to describe Black music and Black culture in a way that would immediately involve a certain kind of younger, middle-class White American." He did a good, straightforward, occasionally dry job of documenting important blues strains from the form's roots through the Delta to Chicago, including chapters devoted to both overall themes/styles and specific performers (such as Leroy Carr, Blind Lemon Jefferson, and Robert Johnson). It's not the first book you'd direct a beginner towards these days, both because it only goes up to the late 1950s, and because subsequent research has built upon Charters' more basic outlines considerably. Indeed, there are some factual errors and incomplete details in the text that Charters chose not to revise for subsequent editions. It also concentrates mostly upon rural guitar blues, largely bypassing developments such as jump blues, honkers and shouters, and West Coast blues. Its chief strengths are its utilization of Charters' own field research in the South (in which he spoke to several surviving bluesmen), and a detailed reconstruction of how major labels recorded the blues before World War II. —Richie Unterberger

♦♦♦♦♦ **Deep Blues**, *Robert Palmer* (Viking Press, 1981) Renowned critic and sometime musician Palmer traces the evolution of a major (perhaps *the* major) strain of blues, from rural Mississippi Delta acoustic forms through its move to the cities, particularly Chicago, where it became amplified and provided a bedrock foundation for rock & roll. There are more comprehensive, scholarly analyses of the blues available, but this is the most readable and accessible by a wide margin, with plenty of first-hand recollections from Muddy Waters, Robert Lockwood, Jr., Sam Phillips, and others. —Richie Unterberger

♦♦♦♦ **Elvis: The Illustrated Record**, *Roy Carr and Mick Farren* (Harmony, 1982) At the time this book appeared, there were no serious critical studies of Elvis' work. This remains the volume that, as the authors intended, "set the record straight." Features in-depth criticism, with enthusiastic but considered analysis, of every record Elvis made. Naturally–thankfully, actually–the early Sun and RCA sessions, as well as some isolated later critical triumphs like the late '60s albums, are covered in the most depth, with a scholarship that is both meticulous and compelling. Elvis' relatively brief eras of brilliance were punctuated by long ones of excruciating mediocrity, and the authors do not fail to point out the shortcomings of his many soundtracks and uninspired singles. Indeed, the stretch between 1961 and 1968 can make for pretty thin gruel, and these parts are inevitably much less interesting than the highlights, though the authors do a good job of dismissing, or lightly skipping over, his bad records with curt humor that doesn't waste words. Includes some good essays summarizing specific eras of his career, tons of sleeves and photos, and an exhaustive discography, including bootlegs. —Richie Unterberger

♦♦♦♦♦ **Encyclopedia of the Blues**, *Gerard Herzhaft* (The

University Of Arkansas Press, 1992) In spite of the fact that this was translated (very ably) from French, this is one of the best blues reference books–perhaps *the* best for someone who wants a comprehensive volume that doesn't become so specialized that novices get lost. Over 500 pages in length, the bulk is devoted to concise profiles of all major (and many minor) blues artists from the beginning of the 20th century to 1990. These are not only passionate and descriptive, but maintain a sense of critical perspective that identifies the performers' chief strengths and weaknesses, their most noteworthy recordings, and their importance within the blues as a whole. The profiles are supplemented by short rundowns of key blues genres such as Delta blues and female blues singers, a selected discography (with brief reviews) of the best blues albums, and a list of popular blues standards and their origins. There's also a list of specific recordings, which demonstrate some of the most characteristic and best uses of blues guitar, harmonica, and piano styles. —Richie Unterberger

♦♦♦♦ **Eric Clapton: Lost in the Blues**, *Harry Shapiro* (Da Capo, 1992) There are a few Clapton bios available, and while this one does not have a great deal of first-hand interview material, it does a very good straightforward job of following his musical progression through the Yardbirds and John Mayall to Cream, Blind Faith, Derek & the Dominos, and his lengthy solo career. Every album, as a soloist or group member, is discussed in considerable detail. The author draws upon dozens of previous interviews and press clippings, spanning the mid-'60s to the early '90s, and sheds some light on the several rather mysterious lulls and metamorphoses in the mercurial guitarist's career, especially the decisions to leave all of his groups just when they were peaking or about to launch to stardom, and his years as a secluded heroin addict in the early '70s. Includes meticulous discography, "groupography," and a review of the various guitars Clapton's used over the years. — *Richie Unterberger*

♦♦♦♦♦ **Feel Like Going Home**, *Peter Guralnick* (Vintage, 1971) Guralnick is one of America's premier writers and critics of roots music, and this collection of his early essays is an important work, offering sensitive and in-depth portraits of a gaggle of major early rock and blues stars: Jerry Lee Lewis, Howlin' Wolf, Charlie Rich, Muddy Waters, Skip James, Johnny Shines, Charlie Rich, and the owners of Sun and Chess Records. Guralnick spent a lot of time with each of his subjects, often observing them at home or on stage; in some cases, he was apparently the first journalist to treat the musician as a serious artist. Perhaps as a result, he landed some poignant and personal material, the kind that publicists have learned to shield from serious but inquisitive writers. Guralnick does tend to romanticize his heroes as artists who have never received their just due, but this is one of the best books of its kind. —Richie Unterberger

♦♦♦♦♦ **Good Rockin' Tonight: Sun Records and the Birth of Rock'n'roll**, *Colin Escott with Martin Hawkins* (St. Martin's Press, 1991) Excellent history of what was, in the final estimation, the label most responsible for launching rock & roll, although the contributions of other indies like Atlantic were also immensely important. Includes chapters on all the major Sun stars: Elvis, Johnny Cash, Carl Perkins, Jerry Lee Lewis, and Roy Orbison. Of equal interest, though, are the descriptions of owner/producer Sam Phillips' slap-echo studio sound and distinctive artistic vision, which also encompassed a wealth of blues and country music. Besides first- and second-hand interviews with the most famous characters in the Sun story, you also hear from more obscure performers and sidemen, and get profiles of relatively unheralded artists like Warren Smith and Junior Parker. Fascinating stuff, this is an updated version of a history first published around 1980, and includes a good deal of new information and many great photos. —Richie Unterberger

♦♦♦ **The Grove Press Guide to the Blues on CD**, *edited by Frank John Hadley* (Grove Press, 1993) The execution of this handbook was okay; where it really ran into problems was its overall conception. As the title says, it's a guide to blues on compact disc, not blues on record. What this means is that a great many important, essential blues recordings are not discussed because they were out-of-print or had not yet made the leap to the digital format when the book was issued. What's more, some major performers are not included, or, even worse, are represented by one or two of their worst efforts. The reviews and ratings are concise and astute, but simply don't afford reasonable overviews of the artists, or even the blues as a whole (there's a disproportionate amount of bad White blues or bar-band blues). The decision to limit the coverage to digital recordings guaranteed that the book would start to date quickly, as many landmark blues recordings did indeed make their belated way to CD in the years since the guide was printed. —*Richie Unterberger*

✦✦✦ The History of the Blues, *Francis Davis* (Hyperion, 1995) With this companion volume to the PBS series, Davis lays out the basic frameworks of the music's development, from its pre-20th century roots to Robert Cray. The major blues styles are covered in reasonable depth: acoustic Delta blues, female-sung vaudeville-blues hybrids of the 1920s, the amplified Chicago sound, the '60s blues revival, and modern soul-influenced blues by Cray, Ted Hawkins, and others. Blues histories tend toward the academic and scholarly more often than not, and Davis gets major points for crafting his text in an accessible, very readable fashion. He also, to his credit, is not content to mouth clichés, but to provide and occasionally champion interpretations that you won't often find elsewhere. His iconoclasm also gets to be a problem, though; he continually backtracks upon himself in a coy, hide-and-seek manner that becomes frustrating (typical sentence: "The blues is dead; the blues will never die. I don't know which it is, though I suspect it's both."). Also, considerable chunks of the story are untold, and some performers (such as Junior Wells, Jimmy Reed, and Son Seals) treated not so much disrespectfully as cursorily. It's not a bad overview, but Robert Palmer's *Deep Blues* still wins out as the best introductory overall study of the blues' evolution, although Palmer's book is not nearly as wide-ranging. —*Richie Unterberger*

✦✦✦✦✦ I Am the Blues, *Willie Dixon with Don Snowden* (Da Capo, 1989) If there was ever a man to give the inside story of Chicago blues, Dixon would seem to fit the bill; he wasn't a star, but as a producer, arranger, bass player, and especially songwriter, he did as much as anyone to shape modern electric blues. This autobiography lets Willie do much of the talking, with Snowden filling in other information and quoting from associates of Dixon, including artists and engineers at Chess Records. There are some pretty tasty recollections here, especially Dixon's memories of the groundbreaking '60s tours of Europe by leading blues stars, his disappointment with Chess' exploitative business practices (as a songwriter due many royalties, Dixon was as hurt by these as anyone), and first-hand memories of working out classics like "Hoochie Coochie Man" (with Muddy Waters) and "My Babe" (with Little Walter). There actually aren't as many fascinating stories as one might expect; Dixon doesn't go into great depth about the many legends he worked with (Chuck Berry, Bo Diddley, Howlin' Wolf, and others), doesn't discuss some of his most famous standards, and doesn't introspect heavily on the songwriting or creative processes in general. Worthwhile reading for the rock and blues fan, but not the goldmine of riches for which one might have hoped. —*Richie Unterberger*

✦✦✦ I Hear You Knockin', *Jeff Hannusch* (Swallow, 1983) Portraits of 31 major New Orleans R&B performers, ranging from the famous (Dave Bartholomew, Irma Thomas, Lee Dorsey, Allen Toussaint) to the semi-famous (Smiley Lewis, Guitar Slim, Chris Kenner, Frankie Ford) to the downright unknown (Tuts Washington, Bill Webb, Dorothy Labostrie). The level of detail is admirable: Hannusch gives the basic facts about the careers and records of his subjects, and usually provides plenty of first-hand quotes and memories as well. But it doesn't make for compelling reading, unless you're a Crescent City specialist. It's not so much that Hannusch is dry (although he's not the most colorful writer), but that he doesn't provide much critical insight into the music, or much of a context for appreciating his subjects' achievements. Peter Guralnick, for instance, manages to excel at describing the music of blues and country performers. Just as vitally, Guralnick lends his portraits a very human dimension by illustrating how environment and experiences help to shape his heroes' music, and assesses the significance of their achievements in the broad canvas of popular music. Hannusch is mostly content to detail who did what and when. Although the occasional colorful anecdote emerges, the tone is closer to a reference book than a volume that helps convey the incredibly rich, important, and colorful history of New Orleans rock and R&B. If you are very interested in the vivacious music of this equally vivacious city, it's still handy to have around, with an appendix/discography of important recordings and chart listings. —*Richie Unterberger*

✦✦✦✦ Jimi Hendrix: Electric Gypsy, *Harry Shapiro and Caesar Glebbeek* (St. Martin's, 1991) Hendrix's life story is such a difficult, elusive subject to tackle that a definitive biography may be an impossible goal. Although the memoirs by Mitch Mitchell, Noel Redding, and producer Eddie Kramer all have their value, for my money this is the best overall view of this extraordinarily complicated man's life and music. It's mammoth, weighing in at over 700 pages, but purposefully detailed. The authors examine every stage of his development, and every facet of his musicianship, from his R&B beginnings and his classic studio recordings to his charismatic live performances and innovations in studio technique, amplification equipment, and, of course, guitar playing. It draws upon a staggering mass of archival materials–interviews, letters, press accounts of the period, memories of his many musical colleagues and professional associates. The many rumors and contradictory anecdotes could lead to a quagmire, but the book takes care not to draw uninformed conclusions or pass judgement, presenting many points of view and cautiously offering interpretations to weigh. The large appendix is also quite valuable, offering a lengthy discography (a project in itself, given Hendrix's extraordinarily tangled recorded legacy), list of concerts performed, copious documentation of his equipment and many guitars, and family tree. —*Richie Unterberger*

✦✦✦ Jimi Hendrix: Inside the Experience, *Mitch Mitchell with John Platt* (Harmony, 1990) More than almost any other rock superstar, Hendrix has been subjected to different, at times downright wildly varying historical accounts, making it difficult to separate the likely from the unlikely. This book, not a biography but an oral history of sorts from the Experience drummer, is refreshingly straightforward. And, unlike some of the authors and associates who have written about Hendrix, Mitchell was very much there; in fact, he worked with Hendrix more closely than any other musician, although some accounts have painted the Experience (probably inaccurately) as a situation which constrained Hendrix creatively. Mitchell doesn't have axes to grind, or a big ego to inflate, so what you get are detailed, very interesting recollections of the tours, Hendrix's methods of working in the studio, key gigs such as Monterey and Woodstock, Jimi's influences, and the guitarist's innovative use of equipment. With lots of good photos, a good book for those more intereseted in the music than the mystique. —*Richie Unterberger*

✦✦✦✦ Last Train to Memphis: The Rise of Elvis Presley, *Peter Guralnick* (Little, Brown & Co., 1994). There are many biographies of Elvis, most of them cheap and shoddy productions that focus on the most sensational and morbid aspects of the King's life (though he did give them a lot to focus on). Guralnick is one of the top authorities on early rock & roll, and the natural candidate to write a biography that is both accurate and focused upon his art and music as much as his personal life. The first volume of a projected multi-part work, this covers what, for the majority of his fans, are his most interesting years, ending just after he leaves the United States in late 1958 to serve as a member of the army in Germany. The early years are thoroughly documented (there are almost 500 footnotes alone): the grinding poverty, the gospel influences, the months of pestering Sun Records to record him, the sculpting of his early rockabilly sound in the Sun Studios, the wild early tours, the early managers, the meteoric rise to fame after his contract was sold to RCA, the hangers-on he felt compelled to surround himself with from Memphis, the induction into the army. Lots of detail and balanced perspective between his personality and his music, only marred by some surprisingly perfunctory appraisals of some of his early sessions, particularly the ones at RCA. —*Richie Unterberger*

✦✦✦ The Legacy of the Blues, *Samuel Charters* (Da Capo, 1975) Twelve chapter-length portraits of major and minor bluesmen, including Lightnin' Hopkins, Bukka White, Robert Pete Williams, Juke Boy Booner, Sunnyland Slim, Champion Jack Dupree, Eddie Boyd, Memphis Slim, Big Joe Williams, and Snooks Eaglin. Charters is neither the best nor worst of interviewers/profilers, and the quality of the pieces is variable, usually according to how loquacious his subjects were. It's not the best project of its sort (Peter Guralnick and Stanley Booth, for instance, are more skilled at this sort of thing), but it will interest most blues fans with a particular curiosity in the featured artists. ––*Richie Unterberger*

✦✦✦✦✦ The Life & Legend of Leadbelly, *Charles Wolfe & Kip Lornell* (Harper Collins, 1992) Few 20th-century popular musicians had more fascinating lives than Leadbelly's. Even before he was discovered by folklorist John Lomax, he'd lived the typically tough life of a Black southern farmer, played for years with Blind Lemon Jefferson before either of them were well known, been jailed twice for murky murder/manslaughter charges, and sung his way to freedom by composing and delivering a pardon plea directly to the governor of Texas. Then things got even more interesting, as he worked for Lomax as an assistant, became a popular performer at New York high-society gatherings, and eventually fell in with a crowd that included Pete Seeger, the Weavers, Sonny Terry, and Brownie McGhee. To a large degree, many of the details of his life remain a mystery, particularly the years before his discovery at a Louisiana jail by Lomax. Wolfe and Lornell do a good, responsible job of piecing together the facts and the myths, offering speculation (particularly for the shadowy pre-Lomax years), but never unwarranted conclusions. They also provide a wealth of description and criticism of his recordings and songwriting, as well as a great deal of context for understanding both the origins of his music and the harsh social conditions by which they were framed. Leadbelly himself comes across as an extremely guarded, sometimes secretive man, hard to know and judge even for those who knew him best, right up until the end, when he was a renowned international figure. Extensively researched and accessibly written (though some familiarity with Leadbelly's work will enhance its appreciation), it's one of the best biographies of a major folk icon. —*Richie Unterberger*

✦✦✦✦✦ **Lost Highway**, *Peter Guralnick* (Vintage, 1979) Like his previous *Feel Like Going Home*, these are more first-rate, extremely human portrayals of major American roots musicians, going much heavier on the country & western this time around (though blues and early rock musicians are also included). Many musicians of the first echelon and a few more obscure noteworthies are included in this gallery of portraits, including Ernest Tubb, Hank Snow, Rufus Thomas, Bobby Bland, Scotty Moore, Charlie Feathers, Mickey Gilley, Waylon Jennings, Merle Haggard, James Talley, Joe Turner, Howlin' Wolf, and Otis Spann. —*Richie Unterberger*

✦✦✦ **Making Tracks**, *Charlie Gillett* (Souvenir Press, 1974) Gillett is the author of the first comprehensive (and still one of the most acclaimed) rock & roll histories, *The Sound of the City*. This is his history of Atlantic Records, the most successful independent to survive from rock & roll's earliest days. More a history of the music than the business, anyone who's interested in early R&B and rock will find a lot of absorbing reading here. Gillett interviewed Atlantic principals Ahmet Ertegun and (to a significantly greater degree) Jerry Wexler extensively, yielding a lot of first-hand recollections about the early careers of such important artists as Ruth Brown, Clyde McPhatter, Joe Turner, Ray Charles, Solomon Burke, Otis Redding, and Aretha Franklin. Important ancillary figures like Jesse Stone, songwriters Jerry Leiber and Mike Stoller, and Rick Hall of Fame Studios in Muscle Shoals, AL, also get a chance to speak. Gillett is principally an R&B and soul man, so Atlantic's ventures into pop, British rock, and British rock are covered in considerably less depth, although they aren't neglected. —*Richie Unterberger*

✦✦✦ **Peter Green: Founder of Fleetwood Mac**, *Martin Celmins* (Castle Communications, 1995) Like Syd Barrett and Brian Wilson, Peter Green is a figure of such musical talent and personal eccentricity that he holds an ongoing fascination for fans and rock historians. One of the premier late '60s British blues-rockers as the leader of the original incarnation of Fleetwood Mac, and one of the few blues-rockers to expand beyond rocked-up derivations to a more eclectic and personal vision, he turned his back on the music business in 1970. This wasn't a mere temperamental fit; he *really* turned his back, holding a series of low-paying jobs, working on a kibbutz in Israel, giving his money away to charity, and only occasionally playing professionally. This fine, compact bio both documents his musical talents and probes the myths surrounding his mysterious behavior, both at the peak of his stardom and his subsequent departure from the music scene. Most of Green's chief musical associates offer lengthy recollections, including John Mayall (with whom Green first became known, when he filled Eric Clapton's position in the Bluesbreakers), Mick Fleetwood, John McVie, and lesser-knowns such as Bob Brunning (who briefly played bass in Mac's first line-up). Although Green is often thought of as an acid casualty in the manner of Syd Barrett, that judgement is pretty much laid to rest by the fact that Green himself, interviewed in the mid-1990s, offered Celmins quite a few lucid first-hand recollections and

comments of his own for this volume. This doesn't negate the tragic dimensions of Green's post-Mac career, which found him at times incarcerated and drugged for psychological problems, and fitfully returning to music with subpar bunches of (by and large) hacks. Those who consider Green one of the finest British rock musicians of his time will find this an even-handed, non-sensationalistic portrait of one of the few stars to refuse to play the music business game, and demonstrate his philosophy via deeds, not just words. Includes a lengthy discography of official and unofficial recordings. —*Richie Unterberger*

✦✦✦ **The Rolling Stones: An Illustrated Record**, *Roy Carr* (Harmony, 1976) Though flawed, this is the best critical survey of the Stones' work, reviewing every release through *Black and Blue*. That leaves nearly 20 years uncovered, but it could be argued that it nonetheless encompasses just about everything worthwhile. The inconsistency of depth is frustrating; some albums are discussed rather cursorily, and *Between the Buttons* is, unbelievably, dismissed as a trivial affair in the course of several sentences. On the other hand, there are a lot of critical insights and details about the recording and production of masterpieces from "I Wanna Be Your Man" on through "Paint it Black," "Beggar's Banquet," and the rest of their classic material. A running diary of notable incidents and quotes from the band is interspersed throughout, along with photos, a lengthy interview with Mick Jagger, and the most comprehensive discography and tour itineraries (complete with bootlegs and session appearances) of their prime years ever assembled. —*Richie Unterberger*

✦✦✦ **The Roots of the Blues**, *Samuel Charters* (Da Capo, 1981) No one will be able to pinpoint the origins of the blues with total accuracy. But most can agree that a key root was the indigenous music of Western Africa, from where many of the slaves that were shipped to America came. In 1974, blues scholar Samuel Charters traveled to Gambia, Senegal, and Mali to try to document existing vestiges of African music that may have influenced the development of the blues. This is his narrative of the journey, in which, as he readily admits, he found at least as many questions as answers. While he did get close to the source in some elements of the village griots that he met and recorded, as well as the songs he heard in a Senegalese Creole village, he didn't find a great deal that made explicit connections to blues as it is heard and performed in the United States. It doesn't mean that this isn't interesting reading, not just for the musical analysis (which gets a bit wordy at times), but for Charters' well-related impressions of contemporary African society, and his bracing tale of tracking down traces of present-day slavery in Gambia, generations after the practice had supposedly started to die. —*Richie Unterberger*

✦✦✦ **Rhythm Oil**, *Stanley Booth*, (Pantheon, 1991) He hasn't written prolifically, and he hasn't written much about music that was performed after the early '70s, but Memphis writer Booth is one of the best chroniclers of blues, soul, and rock that draws upon those influences. This collection of essays, often drawn from first-person experiences with the musicians at recording sessions, concerts, and their homes, includes good pieces on Otis Redding, Furry Lewis, B.B. King, Elvis, Janis Joplin, Al Green, James Brown, and little-known but widely respected Memphis jazz pianist Phineas Newborn. An adept critic, Booth's special skill is drawing upon the cultural ambience of the music–often Memphis, almost always the American South–to give a deeper understanding of how their environment, professional and personal, informs their art. —*Richie Unterberger*

✦✦✦ **Searching for Robert Johnson**, *Peter Guralnick* (E.P. Dutton, 1989) The life of the most famous Delta bluesman is shrouded in mystery–there's little that can be documented, and although several other blues performers of the time have first-hand memories of Johnson, they can be vague and contradictory. This slim (83-page) volume, in which Guralnick pieces together what is known and critiques Johnson's recordings, is more like a long essay than a book. It's not flimsy, though. The author talked extensively with Johnny Shines and Robert Lockwood, the two musicians who knew Johnson the best, to relate some first-hand perspectives about what the man was like. He also refers often to the research of blues scholar Mack McCormick for details of Johnson's volatile family and personal life, describes Robert's recording sessions thoroughly, and makes intelligent, cautious speculations about the forces that drove the guitarist. Also includes a comprehensive discography (with descriptive reviews) of Johnson's meager body of work, as well as of records by performers that influenced Johnson, and which Johnson influenced. Useful, but ridiculously overpriced (at $14.95) for such a thin book; time to raid the local library again. *—Richie Unterberger*

✦✦✦✦✦ **The Sound of the City**, *Charlie Gillett* (Da Capo, 1970) Originating as a university thesis, this was the first attempt to write a comprehensive history of rock & roll, dealing with the form primarily in musical terms, not celebrity or popular culture ones. It's still one of the best, although the coverage only extends into the early '70s. Gillett's scholarship, though quite readable, is intensely detailed, accurately describing the cross-fertilization of vocal, instrumental, and production styles from the mid-'40s through the next several decades. He views the struggle of independent labels, as well as the struggle of major labels to come to terms with rock's popularity, as one of the most important undercurrents of rock; hence the performers are often discussed in terms of their labels and producers, as well as their regions or styles. Gillett's tastes run towards R&B and roots rock, and singles rather than album-length statements; some readers may be taken aback by his bluntly clinical, not-wholly-enthusiastic assessments of the Beatles, Jimi Hendrix, Elvis Presley, and other major rock deities. And the focus, concerned with what's in the grooves rather than personality and attitude, may strike some as too detached and analytical. Gillett covered an enormous amount of ground with this volume, though, intelligently and objectively, and this remains an important foundation of rock scholarship. The Da Capo revised edition adds a little material to the 1970 printing, basically just extending the coverage a year or two into the 1970s. *—Richie Unterberger*

✦✦✦✦ **The True Adventures of the Rolling Stones**, *Stanley Booth* (Vintage, 1984) The Rolling Stones' story is a diffuse and murky one that doesn't lend itself nearly as well to retelling as the Beatles'. This book, originally titled *Dance with the Devil*, is not the most linear of those efforts, but it is the best. Memphis journalist Booth, a friend of the band (particularly Keith Richards), traveled with them through much of their famous late 1969 tour of America. In the account that he finally published 15 years later, he alternates between first-hand reportage of the tour and a history of the band, from their scuffling boues beginnings in the early '60s through their rise to fame and the death of Brian Jones. Not much is spared in either part of the tale; the fierce infighting that resulted in the ouster (which, to a large degree, was self-imposed) of Jones, the backstage groupies and drugs, the violence at Altamont, the pushy businessmen and promoters, the decadent ennui of a megastar touring band are all here, documented entertainingly without undue moralizing. Especially interesting are the sections on Altamont, of course, and the recording of several tracks at Muscle Shoals for Sticky Fingers, to which Booth was an eyewitness. *—Richie Unterberger*

✦✦✦ **Unsung Heroes Of Rock'n'roll**, *Nick Tosches* (Charles Scribner's Sons, 1984) Brief profiles of 25 pioneers of rock & roll, mostly from the decade before rock & roll was widely known (1945–55). Some are extremely famous (Nat King Cole, Louis Jordan, Big Joe Turner, Bill Haley), but most are known these days to collectors (Stick McGhee, Cecil Gant, Skeets McDonald, Hardrock Gunter); most are early R&B performers, a few are hillbilly C&W singers. Tosches' style is not for everybody, emphasizing lewd and suggestive angles that some may find offensive. He is also of the unequivocal conviction that rock & roll peaked, in essence, before it really started, and his biases can be irritating. Still, this is a handy primer that illustrates how deep rock & roll's roots lie in the most energetic R&B and C&W of the late 40s and early '50s, although the mid-'50s are commonly thought of as the music's true starting point. The lengthy final section includes a chronology of the development of rock & roll from 1945 to 1955, and discographies for all of the performers profiled. *—Richie Unterberger*

✦✦✦✦✦ **What Was the First Rock'n'roll Record?** , *Jim Dawson & Steve Propers* (Faber & Faber, 1992) Everyone can agree that rock & roll came into being sometime in the decade after World War II, but its exact origins can be hard to pinpoint. This is an absolutely fascinating study of 50 key records which pointed the way for rock & roll, or popularized it, between 1944 and 1956. It doesn't so much answer the question posed by the title as illustrate how many divergent strands of music were involved in rock's conception, and what a fascinating and exciting process it was. Major singles by Louis Jordan, John Lee Hooker, Fats Domino, Muddy Waters, Bill Haley, and Elvis are discussed in depth; as are ones by much more obscure artists such as Hardrock Gunter, Big Boy Crudup, Stick McGhee, Jackie Brenston, and Arkie Shibley. Besides explaining the significance of each record with detailed musical analysis, the authors tracked down key artists, session musicians, and producers for their comments, unearthing a wealth of compelling anecdotes. Essential for anyone interested in rock's birth. *—Richie Unterberger*

✦✦✦ **Wild Animals**, *Andy Blackford* (Sidgwick & Jackson, UK, 1986) The Animals' peak as a truly important group in the mid-'60s was brief, and accordingly, this biography is on the slim side. Appropriately, it focuses almost entirely on the original lineup, before Eric Burdon took the Animals name in 1966 and fronted a variety of psychedelic and hard rock bands for the next few years. For Animals and British Invasion fans, there are a fair number of interesting stories here, including the conception of their classic "House of the Rising Sun," the group's dislike of their more pop-oriented (though excellent) hit singles, and the conflicts between them and producer Mickey Most, and manager Mike Jeffries. There are lots of quotes from members of the band, but in some important respects, it's disappointing. Some of their great singles are barely discussed, and Blackford isn't a top-notch writer, occasionally wandering from the subject into tangents about the era's pop culture. *—Richie Unterberger*

MAGAZINES

Blues Access

The brainchild of radio show host Cary Wolfson (who won a W.C. Handy Award in 1987 and 1991), Blues Access Magazine was inspired by the Whole Earth Catalog's byline "Access to Tools"–thus, access to blues. It was first published in February of 1990 at 16 pages (all newsprint), but today is almost 100 pages with four-color glossy covers. What you find between these covers is a lot of eye and mind candy for the blues lover.

It contains everything from full-length feature articles to some twenty columns–filled with info (departments). Lots of pictures too. Issues include many well-written reviews, hundreds of new releases (with descriptions), guitar patterns, societies, resources–the works. There is enough information in one issue to seriously tie up your spare time for days. And the ads are just as interesting–major labels, releases, tours, and festivals. When you are done looking at the ads alone, you have a pretty fair idea of what's happening out there in blues world. If you have never seen a copy, go out and get one. You'll not regret it. You can reach them at (303) 443-7245 or write to Blues Access, 1455 Chestnut Place, Boulder, CO 80304-3153. Internet fans can reach them at their web address of http://www.he.net/~blues–*Michael Erlewine*

Blue Suede News

This doesn't deal with the blues exclusively or primarily, concentrating on roots musics of various sorts (blues, R&B, rockabilly, rock & roll, country) past and present (more past than present). The writing and production standards are also closer to fanzine territory than the blues glossies, although they've come a long way over the years. Blues specialists may find it worth picking up for the occasional blues feature and its huge review section, which always covers lots of contemporary blues albums and reissues. (Box 25, Duvall, WA 98019-0025)–*Richie Unterberger*

Blues & Rhythm

Britain's top blues periodical is less comprehensive than its U.S. counterparts, and more devoted to retrospectives and reissue reviews than the contemporary scene. It's a high-quality operation, though, with lively and informed writing, combining interviews/features with an extensive review section. Doesn't limit itself to blues exclusively, also covering some R&B and a little bit of soul. There are also columns for news, live reports, obits, and in-depth examinations of rare recordings. (Byron Foulger, 1 Cliffe Lane, Thornton, Bradford BD13 3DX, UK)–*Richie Unterberger*

Blues Review

Bimonthly glossy is a bit slicker in the production department than the two other major blues mags (*Living Blues* and *Blues Access*). There's a similar concentration of features and new release/reissue reviews, as well as some special-interest columns for live reviews, product surveys, "Cyberblues" (blues on the Internet), and guitar transcriptions. The coverage is perhaps more inclusive of White acts than its peers, and less devoted to historical pieces. That shouldn't be taken as implied criticism–there's room for all three major U.S. blues magazines, which basically cover much of the same thematic ground without duplicating each other too often. (916 Douglas Dr., #101, Endwell, NY 13760)–*Richie Unterberger*

Living Blues

With the establishment of *Blues Access* and *Blues Revue* as class productions in the 1990s, *Living Blues* is no longer as dominant in its field as it once was. But the bimonthly probably remains the best blues publication available, and in fact one of the best specialized music magazines of any kind. Features huge (if occasionally rambling) interviews with major and minor blues performers, a big review section that covers a high percentage of available blues releases and reissues (lots of imports included), news, obituaries, and miscellaneous other features. It's upgraded its production values recently without sacrificing the depth and integrity of the content. Well-written and accessible to the general reader, not just a scholarly publication for blues fanatics. (Hill Hall, Room 301, University, MS 38677-9836)–*Richie Unterberger*

INDEX

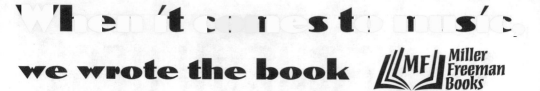